have the same inheritance rights as other children. The ruling was believed to be the first on the controversial issue by any state supreme court.

Also in January 2002, Marshall addressed the Massachusetts Bar Association Conference, where she called for "a revolution in the administration of justice" stating that the court system needed to improve its management system as well as its staffing and budget controls. In March
6 2002, her discussion of the court system's problems were amplified in a 52-page report that was published by a blue-ribbon panel appointed by Marshall.

THE GOVERNMENT [THAT THE FRAMERS OF THE CONSTITUTION] DEVISED REQUIRED SEVERAL AMENDMENTS, A CIVIL WAR, AND MOMENTOUS SOCIAL TRANSFORMATION TO ATTAIN THE SYSTEM OF CONSTITUTIONAL GOVERNMENT, AND ITS RESPECT FOR THE INDIVIDUAL FREEDOMS AND HUMAN RIGHTS, THAT WE HOLD AS FUNDAMENTAL TODAY.
THURGOOD MARSHALL

FURTHER READINGS

Teicher, Stacy A. 2000." A Subtle Revolution as Women Lead the Bench." *Christian Science Monitor* (January 5).

Lavoie, Denise. 2002. "Court Rules on Posthumous Conception." *Associated Press* (January 2)

MARSHALL PLAN

After WORLD WAR II, Europe was devastated and urgently needed an organized plan for reconstruction and economic and technical aid. The Marshall Plan was initiated in 1947 to meet this need.

The originator of the plan, U.S. Secretary of State George C. Marshall, introduced it in a speech at Harvard University on June 5, 1947. He pointed out two basic reasons for providing aid to Europe: the United States sought the reestablishment of the European countries as independent nations capable of conducting valuable trade with the United States; and the threat of a Communist takeover was more prevalent in countries that were suffering economic depression.

In 1947 a preliminary conference to discuss the terms of the program convened in Paris. The Soviet Union was invited to attend but subsequently withdrew from the program, as did other Soviet countries.

Sixteen European countries eventually participated, and, in July 1947, the Committee for European Economic Cooperation was established to allow representatives from member countries to draft a report that listed their requirements for food, supplies, and technical assistance for a four-year period.

The Committee for European Economic Cooperation subsequently became the Organization of European Economic Cooperation, an expanded and permanent organization that was responsible for submitting petitions for aid. In 1948, Congress passed the Economic Cooperation Act (62 Stat. 137), establishing funds for the Marshall Plan to be administered under the Economic Cooperation Administration, which was directed by Paul G. Hoffman.

Between 1948 and 1952, the sixteen-member countries received more than $13 billion dollars in aid under the Marshall Plan. The plan was generally regarded as a success that led to industrial and agricultural production, while stifling the Communist movement. The plan was not without its critics, however, and many Europeans believed the COLD WAR hostilities between the Soviet nations and the free world were aggravated by it.

◊ MARSHALL, THURGOOD 7

Thurgood Marshall, the first African American to serve on the U.S. Supreme Court, saw law as a catalyst for social change. For nearly 60 years, as both a lawyer and a jurist, Marshall worked to dismantle the system of SEGREGATION and improve the legal and social position of minorities.

Marshall was born July 2, 1908, in Baltimore, the son of a Pullman porter and a schoolteacher. He was a graduate of Lincoln University, a small, all-black college in Pennsylvania, and Howard University Law School in Washington, D.C. At Howard, Marshall excelled under the guidance of Vice Dean CHARLES HAMILTON HOUSTON, the first African American to win a case before the U.S. Supreme Court. Houston encouraged his students to become not just lawyers but "social engineers" who could use the legal system to improve society. Marshall graduated first in his law class in 1933.

Marshall's attendance at predominantly black Howard University illustrates the barriers faced by African Americans during the early twentieth century. Although Marshall wished to attend law school at the University of Maryland (a public institution in his home town of Baltimore), he was prohibited by law from doing so because of his race. This injustice helped set Marshall on a course of opposing all forms of official segregation that denied equal opportunities to African Americans.

After law school, Marshall set up a practice in Baltimore, representing indigent clients in civil rights cases. In 1936, his mentor Houston offered him a position with the National Association for the Advancement of Colored People (NAACP),

and in 1940, Marshall became director of the NAACP LEGAL DEFENSE AND EDUCATIONAL FUND, a position he held until 1961. Determined to eliminate segregation, Marshall coordinated a nationwide campaign to integrate higher education. He filed several successful lawsuits against public graduate and professional schools that refused to accept African-American students. These suits paved the way for similar cases at the high school and elementary school levels. Marshall also journeyed throughout the deep South, traveling fifty thousand miles a year to fight JIM CROW LAWS (a series of laws that provided for racial segregation in the South) and to represent criminal defendants.

Thurgood Marshall.
LIBRARY OF CONGRESS

Marshall argued 32 cases before the U.S. Supreme Court and won 29 of them. No doubt his most famous and far-reaching triumph before the High Court was BROWN V. BOARD OF EDUCATION OF TOPEKA, KANSAS, 347 U.S. 483, 74 S. Ct. 686, 98 L. Ed. 873 (1954). In that case, the father of African-American student Linda Brown sued the school board of Topeka, Kansas, over its segregation policy. Brown was required by law to attend an all African-American school several blocks from her home even though an all white public school was located in her own neighborhood. Under Kansas law, cities of more than 15,000 people, such as Topeka, could choose to operate segregated schools. Marshall argued that these segregated schools, defended by officials as "separate but equal," were unconstitutional.

8 The SEPARATE-BUT-EQUAL doctrine originated in PLESSY V. FERGUSON, 163 U.S. 537, 16 S. Ct. 1138, 41 L. Ed. 256 (1896), a case allowing segregated public accommodations for whites and blacks. In a plainspoken argument, Marshall dismissed as fallacy the notion that segregated schools offered the same educational experiences to black and white students. Sociological and psychological studies demonstrated that black children were in fact harmed by the policy of school segregation. The students' self-esteem was damaged and their future diminished when they were forced to accept inadequate facilities, equipment, and educational opportunities. Marshall argued that the only purpose segregation served was to perpetuate the myth of African-Americans' inferiority. A unanimous Court agreed and struck down the separate-but-equal doctrine, a

THURGOOD MARSHALL 1908–1993

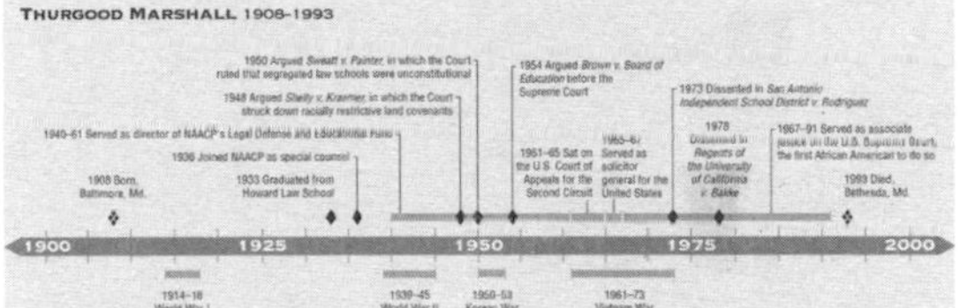

THE FUTURE OF SOCIAL SECURITY

The payment of OLD-AGE, SURVIVORS, AND DISABILITY INSURANCE (OASDI) benefits has been a
9 cornerstone of U.S. social welfare policy since the establishment of the SOCIAL SECURITY ADMINISTRATION in 1935. At the same time, the long-term financial stability of OASDI has been a constant worry. In the early years of the twenty-first century, concerns about Social Security mounted as policy makers assessed the impact of the retirement of the "Baby Boom" generation. Many younger people raised the issue of "generation equity." They express doubt that Social Security benefits will be available when they retire, and anger that they will be forced to pay, through payroll taxes, for the baby boomers' retirement benefits.

IN FOCUS

Reform of the Social Security system has always been a political hot potato. Retirees and those approaching retirement form a strong LOBBYING force, and they zealously protect their benefits. Employers and employees are equally vocal in their opposition to higher payroll taxes to fund OASDI. Thus, changes in Social Security required bipartisan support, which materialized in the face of an impending Social Security crisis. The 1982–83 National Commission on Social Security Reform successfully secured from Congress the short-term financing of OASDI. As a result, Congress passed a series of laws meant to accumulate surpluses as a hedge against future burdens. The Social Security surplus is the amount by which revenue from the federal payroll tax exceeds the amount of Social Security benefits paid out.

Shortly after these new laws went into effect, Social Security began running a surplus. Surplus Social Security revenue can be used to fund other government programs and to help retire the national debt. During the favorable economic climate of the late 1990s, Congress began to use the surplus to pay down the federal debt, hoping to better position the government to meet its obligations to future retirees. And, in 2000, the federal government generated enough revenue so that the entire Social Security surplus was available for paying off debt.

The state of Social Security became a major campaign issue in the 2000 elections, with both Republicans and Democrats attempting to appear as though they were guardians of Social Security assets. Candidates from both parties promised to create a "lockbox," meaning that the Social Security surplus would be spent entirely on debt retirement. With the advent of fiscally lean years in the early 2000s, the lockbox approach was largely disregarded by politicians who advanced other ideas about what to do with Social Security surpluses. These ideas included using the surplus to help offset decreases in revenues brought about by tax cuts and using the surplus to fund new or expanded spending initiatives.

Analysts argue that the real issue often is clouded. It is not how to spend the surplus now, but how to maintain the long-term solvency of the Social Security trust fund. Planners estimate that the income from the trust fund will exceed expenses each year until 2020. The trust fund balances will then start to decline as investments are redeemed to meet the increased expenses from a swelling retired workforce. Although it is estimated that 75 percent of the costs would continue to be met from current payroll and income taxes, in the absence of any changes, full benefits could not be paid beginning in 2030.

In its 1996 report, the Social Security Administration's Advisory Council looked at various long-term financing options for OASDI. The council could not reach consensus on a specific long-term plan, but it did suggest several types of financing that represent a marked departure from previous efforts to fund Social Security. The council noted that past efforts have generally featured cutting benefits and raising tax rates on a "pay-as-you-go" basis. The council agreed that this approach must be changed and offered three ways of restoring financial solvency.

One approach, called Maintenance of Benefits (MB), calls for an increase in income taxes on OASDI benefits, a redirection of some revenue from other trust funds, and, most importantly, the adoption of a plan allowing the federal government to invest a portion of the trust fund assets directly in common stocks. Rates of returns on stocks have historically exceeded those on federal government bonds, where all Social Security

A person who continues to work past the retirement age may lose some benefits because Social Security is designed to replace lost earnings. If earnings from employment do not exceed the amount specified by law, the person receives the full benefits. If earnings are greater than that amount, one dollar of benefit is withheld for every two dollars in wages earned above the exempt amount. Once a person reaches age 70, however, he does not have to report earnings to the SSA, and the benefit is not reduced.

Survivors' Benefits Survivors' benefits are paid to family members when a worker dies. Survivors can receive benefits if the deceased worker was employed and contributed to Social

momentous victory for Marshall, affecting public schools in twenty-one states.

Marshall was appointed to the U.S. Court of Appeals for the Second Circuit in 1961, and served there until 1965 when he was named SOLICITOR GENERAL for the United States. He was appointed to the U.S. Supreme Court in 1967 by President LYNDON B. JOHNSON and served as an associate justice for 24 years.

While on the Court, Marshall was known more for his impassioned dissents than for his majority opinions. In particular, as a staunch opponent of CAPITAL PUNISHMENT, he regularly voiced his disagreement with the majority in death penalty cases. He was also a firm backer of AFFIRMATIVE ACTION and contributed one of his most famous dissents in REGENTS OF THE UNIVERSITY OF CALIFORNIA V. BAKKE, 438 U.S. 265, 98 S. Ct. 2733, 57 L. Ed. 2d 750 (1978). In that case, Marshall criticized the high court's ruling that a public medical school's policy of reserving 16 of 100 spots for minority students was unconstitutional. Marshall also dissented in *San Antonio Independent School District v. Rodriguez,* 411 U.S. 1, 93 S. Ct. 1278, 36 L. Ed. 2d 16 (1973), disagreeing with the majority view that a Texas property tax system used to fund public education was acceptable, even though it allowed wealthier districts to provide a better school system for students in those districts than less wealthy districts could provide. Marshall objected strongly to the property tax arrangement, claiming that it deprived poor children of an equal education.

Marshall wrote the majority opinion in *Amalgamated Food Employees Union v. Logan Valley Plaza,* 391 U.S. 308, 88 S. Ct. 1601, 20 L. Ed. 2d 603 (1968), in which the Court declared that a shopping center was a public forum from which picketers could not be barred by private owners.

Marshall retired from the Court in 1991, but continued his criticism of government policies that were detrimental to African Americans or other disenfranchised groups.

Marshall died on January 24, 1993, in Bethesda, Maryland. Upon Marshall's death, nearly 20,000 mourners filed by his casket during the 12 hours it lay in state in the Great Hall of the U.S. Supreme Court.

FURTHER READINGS

Bland, Randall Walton. 2001. *Justice Thurgood Marshall: Crusader for Liberalism: His Judicial Biography (1908–1993).* Bethesda, Md.: Academica Press.

Clemon, U.W., and Bryan K. Fair. 2003. "Lawyers, Civil Disobedience, and Equality in the Twenty-First Century: Lessons from Two American Heroes. *Alabama Law Review,* 54 (spring): 959–83.

Kennedy, Randall. 1999. "Thurgood's Coming": Long Before He Became the Nation's First Black Supreme Court Justice, Thurgood Marshall Was a Lawyer on the Razor's Edge of American Social Struggle. *American Lawyer* 21 (December): 94

Maloy, Richard H.W. 1999. "Thurgood Marshall and the Holy Grail—the Due Process Jurisprudence of a Consummate Jurist." *Pepperdine Law Review* 26 (January): 289–352.

Tushnet, Mark V. 1997. *Making Constitutional Law: Thurgood Marshall and the Supreme Court, 1961–1991.* New York: Oxford Univ. Press.

Williams, Juan. *Thurgood Marshall: American Revolutionary.* 2000. New York: Times Books.

CROSS-REFERENCES 10

Civil Rights Movement; Integration; School Desegregation.

MARTIAL LAW

The exercise of government and control by military authorities over the civilian population of a designated territory.

Martial law is an extreme and rare measure used to control society during war or periods of civil unrest or chaos. According to the Supreme Court, the term *martial law* carries no precise
meaning (*Duncan v. Kahanamoku,* 327 U.S. 304, 11
66 S. Ct. 606, 90 L. Ed. 688 [1946]). However, most declarations of martial law have some common features. Generally, the institution of martial law contemplates some use of military force. To a varying extent, depending on the martial law order, government military personnel have the authority to make and enforce civil and criminal laws. Certain civil liberties may be suspended, such as the right to be free from unreasonable SEARCHES AND SEIZURES, FREEDOM OF ASSOCIATION, and freedom of movement. And the writ of HABEAS CORPUS may be suspended (this writ allows persons who are unlawfully imprisoned to gain freedom through a court proceeding).

In the United States, martial law has been instituted on the national level only once, during the Civil War, and on a regional level only once, during WORLD WAR II. Otherwise, it has been limited to the states. Uprisings, political protests, labor strikes, and riots have, at various times, caused several state governors to declare some measure of martial law.

Martial law on the national level may be declared by Congress or the president. Under

WEST'S ENCYCLOPEDIA *of* AMERICAN LAW

2ND EDITION

For Reference

Not to be taken from this room

WEST'S ENCYCLOPEDIA *of* AMERICAN LAW

2ND EDITION

VOLUME 7

MC TO PL

THOMSON

GALE

Detroit • San Diego • San Francisco • New Haven, Conn. • Waterville, Maine • London • Munich

West's Encyclopedia of American Law, 2nd Edition

Project Editors
Jeffrey Lehman
Shirelle Phelps

Editorial
Andrew C. Claps, Pamela A. Dear, Jason M. Everett, Lynn U. Koch, John F. McCoy, Jeffrey Wilson, Jennifer M. York, Ralph Zerbonia

Research
Barbara McNeil

Editorial Support Services
Ryan Cartmill, Mark Hefner, Sue Petrus

Data Capture
Katrina Coach, Nikita Greene, Beverly Jendrowski, Elizabeth Pilette, Beth Richardson

Indexing Services
Lynne Maday

Permissions
Margaret A. Chamberlain

Imaging and Multimedia
Dean Dauphinais, Leitha Etheridge-Sims, Mary Grimes, Lezlie Light, Dan Newell, David G. Oblender, Chris O'Bryan

Product Design
Cynthia Baldwin, Kate Scheible

Composition and Electronic Capture
Evi Seoud, Mary Beth Trimper

Manufacturing
Rhonda Williams

This publication is a creative work fully protected by all applicable copyright laws, as well as by misappropriation, trade secret, unfair condition, and other applicable laws. The authors and editors of this work have added value to the underlying factual material herein through one or more of the following: coordination, expression, arrangement, and classification of the information.

For permission to use material from this product, submit your request via Web at http://www.gale-edit.com/permission or you may download our Permissions Request form and submit your request by fax of mail to:

Permissions Department
The Gale Group, Inc.
27500 Drake Rd.
Farmington Hills, MI 48331-3535
Permissions Hotline:
248-699-8006 or 800-877-4253, ext. 8006
Fax: 248-699-8074 or 800-762-4058

Inside cover photograph reproduced by permission of the Library of Congress (Thurgood Marshall).

Since this page cannot legibly accommodate all copyright notices, the acknowledgments constitute an extension of the copyright notice.

While every effort has been made to ensure the reliability of the information presented in this publication, The Gale Group, Inc. does not guarantee the accuracy of the data contained herein. The Gale Group, Inc. accepts no payment for listing; and inclusion in the publication of any organization, agency, institution, publication service, or individual does not imply endorsement of the editors or publisher. Errors brought to the attention of the publisher and verified to the satisfaction of the publisher will be corrected in future editions.

Library of Congress Cataloging-in-Publication Data
West's encyclopedia of American law / Jeffrey Lehman, editor, Shirelle Phelps, editor.— 2nd ed.
  p. cm.
  Includes bibliographical references and index.
  ISBN 0-7876-6367-0 (hardcover set : alk. paper)
  1. Law—United States—Encyclopedias. 2. Law—United States—Popular works. I. Lehman, Jeffrey. II. Phelps, Shirelle.
  KF154.W47 2004
  349.73'03—dc22   2004004918

ISBN 0-7876-6367-0 (set), ISBN 0-7876-6368-9 (vol. 1), ISBN 0-7876-6369-7 (vol. 2), ISBN 0-7876-6370-0 (vol. 3), ISBN 0-7876-6371-9 (vol. 4), ISBN 0-7876-6372-7 (vol. 5), ISBN 0-7876-6373-5 (vol. 6), ISBN 0-7876-6374-3 (vol. 7), ISBN 0-7876-6375-1 (vol. 8), ISBN 0-7876-6376-X (vol. 9), ISBN 0-7876-6377-8 (vol. 10), ISBN 0-7876-6378-6 (vol. 11), ISBN 0-7876-6379-4 (vol. 12), ISBN 0-7876-9420-7 (vol. 13)

This title is also available as an e-book. ISBN 0-7876-9373-1 (set)
Contact your Gale sales representative for ordering information.

Printed in the United States of America
10 9 8 7 6 5 4 3 2 1

DEDICATION

West's Encyclopedia of American Law (WEAL) is dedicated to librarians and library patrons throughout the United States and beyond. Your interest in the American legal system helps to expand and fuel the framework of our Republic.

CONTENTS

The U.S. legal system is admired around the world for the freedoms it allows the individual and the fairness with which it attempts to treat all persons. On the surface, it may seem simple, yet those who have delved into it know that this system of federal and state constitutions, statutes, regulations, and common-law decisions is elaborate and complex. It derives from the English common law, but includes principles older than England, along with some principles from other lands. The U.S. legal system, like many others, has a language all its own, but too often it is an unfamiliar language: many concepts are still phrased in Latin. The second edition of *West's Encyclopedia of American Law (WEAL)* explains legal terms and concepts in everyday language, however. It covers a wide variety of persons, entities, and events that have shaped the U.S. legal system and influenced public perceptions of it.

MAIN FEATURES OF THIS SET

Entries

This encyclopedia contains nearly 5,000 entries devoted to terms, concepts, events, movements, cases, and persons significant to U.S. law. Entries on legal terms contain a definition of the term, followed by explanatory text if necessary. Entries are arranged alphabetically in standard encyclopedia format for ease of use. A wide variety of additional features, listed later in this preface, provide interesting background and supplemental information.

Definitions Every entry on a legal term is followed by a definition, which appears at the beginning of the entry and is italicized. The Dictionary and Indexes volume includes a glossary containing all the definitions from *WEAL*.

Further Readings To facilitate further research, a list of Further Readings is included at the end of a majority of the main entries.

Cross-References *WEAL* provides two types of cross-references, within and following entries. Within the entries, terms are set in small capital letters—for example, LIEN—to indicate that they have their own entry in the encyclopedia. At the end of the entries, related entries the reader may wish to explore are listed alphabetically by title.

Blind cross-reference entries are also included to direct the user to other entries throughout the set.

In Focus Essays

In Focus essays accompany related entries and provide additional facts, details, and arguments on particularly interesting, important, or controversial issues raised by those entries. The subjects covered include hotly contested issues, such as abortion, capital punishment, and gay rights; detailed processes, such as the Food and Drug Administration's approval process for new drugs; and important historical or social issues, such as debates over the formation of the U.S. Constitution.

Sidebars

Sidebars provide brief highlights of some interesting facet of accompanying entries. They complement regular entries and In Focus essays by adding informative details. Sidebar topics include the Million Man March and the branches of the U.S. armed services. Sidebars appear at the top of a text page and are set in a box.

Biographies

WEAL profiles a wide variety of interesting and influential people—including lawyers, judges, government and civic leaders, and historical and modern figures—who have played a part in creating or shaping U.S. law. Each biography includes a timeline, which shows important moments in the subject's life as well as important historical events of the period. Biographies appear alphabetically by the subject's last name.

ADDITIONAL FEATURES OF THIS SET

Enhancements Throughout *WEAL*, readers will find a broad array of photographs, charts, graphs, manuscripts, legal forms, and other visual aids enhancing the ideas presented in the text.

Indexes *WEAL* features a cases index and a cumulative index in a separate volume.

Appendixes

Three appendix volumes are included with *WEAL*, containing hundreds of pages of docu-ments, laws, manuscripts, and forms fundamental to and characteristic of U.S. law.

Milestone Cases in the Law

A special Appendix volume entitled Milestones in the Law, allows readers to take a close look at landmark cases in U.S. law. Readers can explore the reasoning of the judges and the arguments of the attorneys that produced major decisions on important legal and social issues. Included in each Milestone are the opinions of the lower courts; the briefs presented by the parties to the U.S. Supreme Court; and the decision of the Supreme Court, including the majority opinion and all concurring and dissenting opinions for each case.

Primary Documents

There is also an Appendix volume containing more than 60 primary documents, such as the English Bill of Rights, Martin Luther King Jr.'s Letter from Brimingham Jail, and several presidential speeches.

Citations

Wherever possible, *WEAL* entries include citations for cases and statutes mentioned in the text. These allow readers wishing to do additional research to find the opinions and statutes cited. Two sample citations, with explanations of common citation terms, can be seen below and opposite.

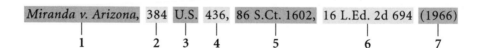

1. *Case title.* The title of the case is set in i and indicates the names of the parties. The suit in this sample citation was between Ernesto A. Miranda and the state of Arizona.
2. *Reporter volume number.* The number preceding the reporter name indicates the reporter volume containing the case. (The volume number appears on the spine of the reporter, along with the reporter name).
3. *Reporter name.* The reporter name is abbreviated. The suit in the sample citation is from the reporter, or series of books, called *U.S. Reports,* which contains cases from the U.S. Supreme Court. (Numerous reporters publish cases from the federal and state courts.)
4. *Reporter page.* The number following the reporter name indicates the reporter page on which the case begins.
5. *Additional reporter page.* Many cases may be found in more than one reporter. The suit in the sample citation also appears in volume 86 of the *Supreme Court Reporter,* beginning on page 1602.
6. *Additional reporter citation.* The suit in the sample citation is also reported in volume 16 of the *Lawyer's Edition,* second series, beginning on page 694.
7. *Year of decision.* The year the court issued its decision in the case appears in parentheses at the end of the cite.

Brady Handgun Violence Prevention Act, Pub. L. No. 103–159, 107 Stat. 1536 (18 U.S.C.A. §§ 921–925A)

| 1 | 2 | 3 | 4 | 5 | 6 | 7 | 8 |

1. *Statute title.*
2. *Public law number.* In the sample citation, the number 103 indicates this law was passed by the 103d Congress, and the number 159 indicates it was the 159th law passed by that Congress.
3. *Reporter volume number.* The number preceding the reporter abbreviation indicates the reporter volume containing the statute.
4. *Reporter name.* The reporter name is abbreviated. The statute in the sample citation is from *Statutes at Large.*
5. *Reporter page.* The number following the reporter abbreviation indicates the reporter page on which the statute begins.

6. *Title number.* Federal laws are divided into major sections with specific titles. The number preceding a reference to the U.S. Code stands for the section called Crimes and Criminal Procedure.
7. *Additional reporter.* The statute in the sample citation may also be found in the *U.S. Code Annotated.*
8. *Section numbers.* The section numbers following a reference to the *U.S. Code Annotated* indicate where the statute appears in that reporter.

CONTRIBUTORS

Editorial Reviewers
Matthew C. Cordon
Frederick K. Grittner
Stephanie Schmitt
Linda Tashbook
M. Uri Toch

Contributing Authors
James Cahoy
Matthew C. Cordon
Richard J. Cretan
Mark Engsberg
Frederick K. Grittner
Lauri R. Harding
David R. Johnstone
Theresa J. Lippert
Frances T. Lynch
George A. Milite
Melodie Monahan
Kelle Sisung
Scott D. Slick

**Contributors to
Previous Edition**
Richard Abowitz
Paul Bard
Joanne Bergum
Michael Bernard
Gregory A. Borchard
Susan Buie

Terry Carter
Sally Chatelaine
Joanne Smestad Claussen
Richard Cretan
Lynne Crist
Paul D. Daggett
Susan L. Dalhed
Lisa M. DelFiacco
Suzanne Paul Dell'Oro
Dan DeVoe
Joanne Engelking
Sharon Fischlowitz
Jonathan Flanders
Lisa Florey
Robert A. Frame
John E. Gisselquist
Russell L. Gray III
Frederick K. Grittner
Victoria L. Handler
Heidi L. Headlee
James Heidberg
Clifford P. Hooker
Marianne Ashley Jerpbak
Andrew Kass
Margaret Anderson Kelliher
Christopher J. Kennedy
Anne E. Kevlin
Ann T. Laughlin
Laura Ledsworth-Wang
Linda Lincoln

Gregory Luce
David Luiken
Jennifer Marsh
Sandra M. Olson
Anne Larsen Olstad
William Ostrem
Lauren Pacelli
Randolph C. Park
Gary Peter
Michele A. Potts
Reinhard Priester
Christy Rain
Brian Roberts
Debra J. Rosenthal
Mary Lahr Schier
Mary Scarbrough
Theresa L. Schulz
John Scobey
James Slavicek
Scott D. Slick
David Strom
Wendy Tien
Douglas Tueting
Richard F. Tyson
Christine Ver Ploeg
George E. Warner
Anne Welsbacher
Eric P. Wind
Lindy T. Yokanovich

❖ MCCAIN, JOHN SIDNEY

Senator John McCain spent 22 years in the U.S. Navy before becoming a Republican congressman, and then a senator, from Arizona. He did not have a typical military career, however. McCain endured five-and-a-half years as a prisoner of war in Vietnam. He, nevertheless, prefers to be known for what he has accomplished as an elected official. In 1998, he won credit as an antitobacco crusader. McCain's name became synonymous with a drive to sharply decrease smoking in America by raising taxes and halting tobacco companies' ability to shield themselves from lawsuits. That bill eventually lost support, and the senator redirected his energy into other issues, such as campaign-finance reform and TELECOMMUNICATIONS legislation.

John Sidney McCain was born on August 29, 1936, in the Panama Canal Zone, to John Sidney McCain Jr. and Roberta (Wright) McCain. He grew up on naval bases in the United States and overseas. The elder McCain was an admiral who served as commander of American forces in the Pacific during the VIETNAM WAR. In fact, the family has a long lineage in the U.S. military. McCain's paternal grandfather, John S. McCain Sr. was also an admiral, as well as commander of all aircraft carriers in the Pacific during WORLD WAR II. He and McCain's father were the first father-and-son admirals in the history of the U.S. Navy.

McCain graduated from Episcopal High School in Alexandria, Virginia, in 1954 and then attended the U.S. Naval Academy in Annapolis, Maryland, where he took courses in electrical engineering. There, he was known as a rowdy and insubordinate student, whose demerits for his antics detracted from his otherwise respectable grades. He graduated in 1958, toward the bottom of his class (790 out of 795), but nevertheless was accepted to train as a naval aviator.

On October 26, 1967, the lieutenant commander lifted off from the carrier Oriskany in an A-4E Skyhawk on a mission over the Vietnamese capital, Hanoi. Above the city, an anti-aircraft missile sliced off the plane's right wing, forcing McCain to eject. With both arms broken, a shattered knee, and a broken shoulder, he landed in a lake where a Vietnamese man extracted him. Subsequently, a crowd beat him, stabbed him with a bayonet, and took him into custody. He did not receive care for his wounds for nine days. When officials learned of his father's high rank, they admitted him to a hospital and later placed him with an American cellmate, who helped to nurse him back to health. Because of his father's status, McCain was offered an early release after just seven months. He denied it, insisting on following the U.S. prisoner-of-war code of conduct, which holds that prisoners should only accept release in the order in which they were captured.

After five-and-a-half years as a prisoner of war in Vietnam, McCain and the rest of the men in Hanoi were released on March 17, 1973. McCain was given a hero's welcome upon his

"GLORY IS NOT A CONCEIT. IT IS NOT A DECORATION FOR VALOR. GLORY BELONGS TO THE ACT OF BEING CONSTANT TO SOMETHING GREATER THAN YOURSELF, TO A CAUSE, TO YOUR PRINCIPLES, TO THE PEOPLE ON WHOM YOU RELY AND WHO RELY ON YOU IN RETURN."
—JOHN MCCAIN

John McCain.
AP/WIDE WORLD
PHOTOS

return to the United States, meeting President RICHARD NIXON and California Governor RONALD REAGAN and receiving the Silver Star, Bronze Star, Legion of Merit, Purple Heart, and Distinguished Flying Cross. He went to the National War College in Washington, D.C., in 1973 and 1974, but he missed flying. After returning to the skies as a training-squadron commander, he was promoted to the rank of captain in 1977.

In 1977, the Navy named McCain its liaison to the U.S. Senate, marking the beginning of his political aspirations. He retired from the Navy in 1981 and moved to Phoenix to work for his wife's father, a beer distributor. In 1982, despite his newcomer status in the state, he ran for the House of Representatives from Arizona's First Congressional District—a Republican-

dominated area taking up much of Phoenix— and won. Unopposed in the 1984 primary, he was re-elected by a large majority over his Democratic opponent. His conservative voting record followed the party line rather faithfully during the Reagan years. He supported prayer in public schools, the Gramm-Rudman deficit-reduction bill, the use of lie-detector tests in certain forms of employment, and the reintroduction of certain handgun sales. He voted against the EQUAL RIGHTS AMENDMENT and against budgeting extra funds for the Clean Air Act. Understandably hawkish in his views on the military, he opposed the 1983 nuclear-freeze resolution and supported more funding for MX missile development and other programs.

McCain showed in many ways that he was not afraid to voice his own opinion. He approved of sanctions in the apartheid-era South Africa, voting to override President Reagan's VETO, and also spoke out against a maneuver to cut millions of dollars from a program that provided food to poor persons in order to give raises to administrators. He also stood against direct U.S. intervention in Central America.

In 1986, McCain ran unopposed in the primary for the U.S. Senate seat that was to be vacated when Arizona's political icon BARRY GOLDWATER retired. He won the general election and was appointed to the Armed Services Committee and its subcommittees on readiness, personnel, and seapower; the Indian Affairs Committee; and the Senate Commerce, Science, and Transportation Committee. He also lobbied for the rights of veterans and pushed to normalize relations with Vietnam, a goal that he realized on July 11, 1995. His early record was punctuated by the passage of the line-item veto, a power that was given to the president in order to erase certain elements of a bill, usually

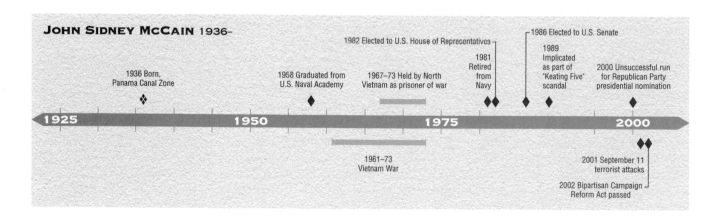

JOHN SIDNEY McCAIN 1936–

1936 Born, Panama Canal Zone

1958 Graduated from U.S. Naval Academy

1967–73 Held by North Vietnam as prisoner of war

1982 Elected to U.S. House of Representatives

1981 Retired from Navy

1986 Elected to U.S. Senate

1989 Implicated as part of "Keating Five" scandal

2000 Unsuccessful run for Republican Party presidential nomination

1925   1950   1975   2000

1961–73 Vietnam War

2001 September 11 terrorist attacks

2002 Bipartisan Campaign Reform Act passed

inserted by representatives who were trying to add special-interest or narrow-constituent issues on to a larger, unrelated bill. Although the federal courts eventually struck down the line-item veto in 1997, McCain became known as the champion fighting against "pork-barrel politics," even hiring a staff member to sit in the Senate Gallery and to spot any instances of such dealings at all hours.

McCain also rankled fellow Republicans when he took up the issue of campaign-finance reform. Wanting to make sweeping changes to the way fund raising is handled, he joined forces with Democrat Russell Feingold around 1995. They sought to draft a bill that would limit private donations to campaigns for public office, as well as to even the balance between lavishly funded incumbents and their opponents. The unpopular measure was not taken seriously at first. "We were like the guys who introduced the metric system," McCain told Michael Lewis in the *New York Times Magazine*. Although Democrats have come out heavily in support of the idea, Lewis observed, "Their enthusiasm derives from their certainty that Republicans will find a way to kill it." The bill's most lofty intention was to close the loophole that allows parties to accept general donations and then re-route them to specific candidates; these funds are called "soft money." The House of Representatives passed a version of the bill in August 1998, but the Senate blocked it.

The lowest point in McCain's career was in 1989. He was counted as one of the notorious "Keating Five," along with Senators John Glenn, Donald Riegle, Dennis DeConcini, and Alan Cranston. They were implicated in a scandal to protect Charles Keating, the owner of Lincoln Savings and Loan. Keating gave generously to the senators and, in return, he expected them to shelter him from federal bank regulators after his dealings had ruined his financial institution and cost taxpayers more than $3 billion to bail out. The Senate Ethics Committee investigated the matter and found that although McCain had exercised "poor judgment," he was not guilty of any wrongdoing. The affair hurt his reputation in the short term, but not fatally, and he was re-elected in 1992. McCain's later efforts, in addition to campaign-finance reform, included an attention-getting $516 billion proposed bill that made tobacco companies more vulnerable to lawsuits filed by smokers and their families. He further proposed to sharply increase taxes on the sub-stance. The measure made headlines for much of the first half of 1998, until it was voted down, generally due to its emphasis on raising taxes for those who buy tobacco products. In addition, McCain was involved in a telecommunications-reform measure, pushing to install INTERNET connections in schools, to cut satellite- and cable-television costs, and to introduce local telephone competition.

In 1999, McCain published his memoir *Faith of My Fathers*; the book hit the best-seller list and was in its 12th printing one year later. In 2000, McCain ran for president but lost the Republican nomination to GEORGE W. BUSH. That year, McCain underwent surgery to remove a cancerous lesion after a recurrence of the melanoma that he had experienced in 1993. McCain returned to the Senate, where he continued his maverick ways to the point where some analysts began to speculate that he might switch parties. McCain made it clear that he had no intention of leaving the REPUBLICAN PARTY, taking as his model the "trust-busting" president THEODORE ROOSEVELT who campaigned vigorously against corporate financial FRAUD and misfeasance.

In the new millennium, McCain continued to take stands that left him at odds with his own party. He continued to fight for campaign-finance reform. He also voted against President Bush's tax cuts, and sponsored legislation to raise automobile-emissions standards. McCain also joined with Democrats to propose background checks for persons buying firearms at gun shows, a ban on college-sports gambling, and financial-statement disclosure for corporations that deduct executives' stock options.

FURTHER READINGS

Birnbaum, Jeffery H. 2003. "McCain's Mutiny." *Fortune* (February 17).

Drew, Elizabeth. 2002. *Citizen McCain*. New York: Simon & Schuster.

John McCain Senate site. Available online at <mccain.senate.gov> (accessed April 12, 2003).

Karaagac, John. 2000. *John McCain*. Lanham, Md.: Lexington Books.

MCCARRAN-FERGUSON ACT OF 1945

The McCarran-Ferguson Act of 1945 (15 U.S.C.A. § 1011 et seq.) gives states the authority to regulate the "business of insurance" without interference from federal regulation, unless federal law specifically provides otherwise.

The act provides that the "business of insurance, and every person engaged therein, shall be subject to the laws of the several States which relate to the regulation or taxation of such business." Congress passed the McCarran-Ferguson Act primarily in response to the Supreme Court case of *United States v. South-Eastern Underwriters Ass'n,* 322 U.S. 533, 64 S. Ct. 1162, 88 L. Ed. 1440 (1944). Before the *South-Eastern Underwriters* case, the issuing of an insurance policy was not thought to be a transaction in commerce, which would subject the insurance industry to federal regulation under the COMMERCE CLAUSE. In *South-Eastern Underwriters,* the Court held that an insurance company that conducted substantial business across state lines was engaged in interstate commerce and thus was subject to federal antitrust regulations. Within a year of *South-Eastern Underwriters,* Congress enacted the McCarran-Ferguson Act in response to states' concerns that they no longer had broad authority to regulate the insurance industry in their boundaries.

The McCarran-Ferguson Act provides that state law shall govern the regulation of insurance and that no act of Congress shall invalidate any state law unless the federal law specifically relates to insurance. The act thus mandates that a federal law that does not specifically regulate the business of insurance will not PREEMPT a state law enacted for that purpose. A state law has the purpose of regulating the insurance industry if it has the "end, intention or aim of adjusting, managing, or controlling the business of insurance" (*U.S. Dept. of Treasury v. Fabe,* 508 U.S. 491, 113 S. Ct. 2202, 124 L. Ed. 2d 449 [1993]).

The act does not define the key phrase "business of insurance." Courts, however, analyze three factors when determining whether a particular commercial practice constitutes the business of insurance: whether the practice has the effect of transferring or spreading a policyholder's risk, whether the practice is an integral part of the policy relationship between the insurer and the insured, and whether the practice is limited to entities within the insurance industry (*Union Labor Life Insurance Co. v. Pireno,* 458 U.S. 119, 102 S. Ct. 3002, 73 L. Ed. 2d 647 [1982]).

The McCarran-Ferguson Act does not prevent the federal government from regulating the insurance industry. It provides only that states have broad authority to regulate the insurance industry unless the federal government enacts

legislation specifically intended to regulate insurance and to displace state law. The McCarran-Ferguson Act also provides that the SHERMAN ANTI-TRUST ACT OF 1890, 15 U.S.C.A. § 1 et seq., the CLAYTON ACT OF 1914, 15 U.S.C.A. § 12 et seq., and the Federal Trade Commission Act of 1914, 15 U.S.C.A. §§ 41–51, apply to the business of insurance to the extent that such business is not regulated by state law.

Courts have distinguished between the general regulatory exemption of the McCarran-Ferguson Act and the separate exemption provided for the Sherman Act, which is the federal ANTITRUST LAW. Cases involving the applicability of the Sherman Act to state-regulated insurance practices take a narrower approach to the phrase "business of insurance" and apply the three criteria set forth in the *Pireno* case. In other cases that do not involve the federal antitrust exemption of the McCarran-Ferguson Act, the Supreme Court takes a broader approach. It has thus defined laws enacted for the purpose of regulating the business of insurance to include laws "aimed at protecting or regulating the performance of an insurance contract" (*Fabe*). Insurance activities that fall within this broader definition of the business of insurance include those that involve the relationship between insurer and insured, the type of policies issued, and the policies' reliability, interpretation, and enforcement (*Securities & Exchange Commission v. National Securities,* 393 U.S. 453, 89 S. Ct. 564, 21 L. Ed. 2d 668 [1969]).

FURTHER READINGS

Macey, Jonathan R., and Geoffrey P. Miller. 1993. "The McCarran-Ferguson Act of 1945: Reconceiving the Federal Role in Insurance Regulation." *New York University Law Review* 68 (April).

Russ, Lee R., and Thomas F. Segalla. 1995. *Couch on Insurance.* 3d ed. Rochester, N.Y.: Clark Boardman Callaghan.

MCCARRAN INTERNAL SECURITY ACT

Legislation proposed by Senator PATRICK ANTHONY MCCARRAN *and enacted by Congress in 1950 that subjected alleged members of designated Communist-action organizations to regulation by the federal government.*

The McCarran Internal Security Act, also known as the Subversive Activities Control Act of 1950 (50 U.S.C.A. § 781 et seq.), was part of a legislative package that was designated as the

Internal Security Act of 1950. Congress passed such statutes in response to the post-World War II COLD WAR during which many public officials perceived a threat of violent and forcible overthrow of the U.S. government by U.S. Communist groups that advocated this objective. Among other things, the legislation required members of the Communist party to register with the attorney general, and the named organizations had to provide certain information, such as lists of their members. It established the Subversive Activities Control Board to determine which individuals and organizations had to comply with the law and the procedures to be followed. Failure to satisfy the statutory requirements subjected the individual or organization to criminal prosecution and stiff fines.

Congress repealed the registration requirements of the law in 1968 as a result of a number of decisions by the U.S. Supreme Court that declared certain aspects of the law unconstitutional.

CROSS-REFERENCES

Communism.

❖ MCCARRAN, PATRICK ANTHONY

Patrick Anthony McCarran was born August 8, 1876, in Reno, Nevada. He graduated from the University of Nevada in 1901 and took up farming for a few years before his admission to the Nevada bar in 1905.

McCarran's career as a jurist was centered in Nevada. He practiced law from 1905 to 1907 in Tonopah and Goldfield, two areas that experienced prosperity due to mining successes. He served as district attorney of Nye County for the

Patrick A. McCarran.
AP/WIDE WORLD
PHOTOS

next two years before establishing a law practice in Reno. He entered the judiciary in 1912, presiding as associate justice of the Nevada Supreme Court; he rendered decisions as chief justice during 1917 and 1918. He subsequently practiced law until 1926, when he was defeated in an attempt to win election to the U.S. Senate.

In 1932, McCarran again sought a Senate seat and was successful. He represented Nevada until 1954, serving as chairman of the Judiciary Committee, from 1943 to 1946 and from 1949 to 1953, and of the Subcommittee on Foreign Economic Cooperation from 1950 to 1952.

During his lengthy participation in the Senate, McCarran was known for his outspoken

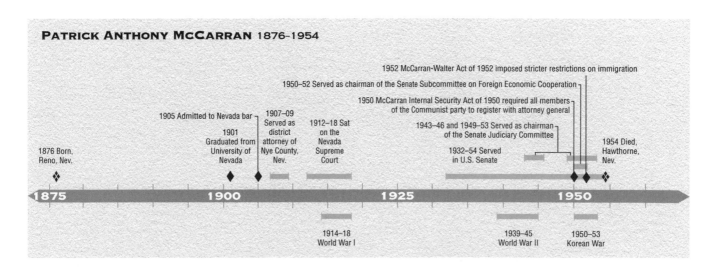

PATRICK ANTHONY MCCARRAN 1876–1954

1952 McCarran-Walter Act of 1952 imposed stricter restrictions on immigration

1950–52 Served as chairman of the Senate Subcommittee on Foreign Economic Cooperation

1950 McCarran Internal Security Act of 1950 required all members of the Communist party to register with attorney general

1905 Admitted to Nevada bar

1907–09 Served as district attorney of Nye County, Nev.

1901 Graduated from University of Nevada

1912–18 Sat on the Nevada Supreme Court

1943–46 and 1949–53 Served as chairman of the Senate Judiciary Committee

1876 Born, Reno, Nev.

1932–54 Served in U.S. Senate

1954 Died, Hawthorne, Nev.

1875   1900   1925   1950

1914–18 World War I

1939–45 World War II

1950–53 Korean War

beliefs. Most notable was his support of two pieces of controversial legislation that were passed despite the opposition of President HARRY S. TRUMAN. The MCCARRAN INTERNAL SECURITY ACT of 1950 (50 U.S.C.A. § 781 et seq.) declared that all members of the Communist party must register with the attorney general; it also prohibited anyone with Communist connections to become involved in the government. The McCarran-Walter Act of 1952 (8 U.S.C.A. § 1101 et seq.) imposed stricter restrictions on immigration.

McCarran died September 28, 1954, in Hawthorne, Nevada.

CROSS-REFERENCES

Communism.

❖ MCCARTHY, EUGENE JOSEPH

Eugene Joseph McCarthy served as a member of the U.S. House of Representatives from 1949 to 1959 and as a U.S. senator from 1959 to 1971. He was a liberal Democrat who served in the shadow of his fellow Minnesota senator, HUBERT H. HUMPHREY. His opposition to the VIETNAM WAR led to his candidacy for the Democratic presidential nomination in 1968. Although ultimately unsuccessful, his candidacy galvanized the antiwar constituency and helped persuade President LYNDON B. JOHNSON not to seek re-election.

McCarthy was born March 29, 1916, in Watkins, Minnesota, the son of a livestock buyer. He graduated from Saint John's University, in Collegeville, Minnesota, in 1935, and worked on a master's degree at the University of Minnesota during the late 1930s while he was a high-school teacher in Mandan, North Dakota. McCarthy

returned to Saint John's in 1940 to teach economics. After deciding not to join the priesthood, he left Saint John's in 1943 and served in the War Department's Intelligence Division until the close of WORLD WAR II in 1945.

After the war, McCarthy joined the faculty at the College of St. Thomas, in St. Paul, where he taught sociology. In 1948, he was elected to the U.S. House of Representatives, beginning a 22-year political career in Washington, D.C. During the 1950s McCarthy worked on labor and agricultural issues and maintained a liberal Democratic voting record. In 1957, he established an informal coalition of members of Congress, later formally organized as the House Democratic Study Group, to counter anti–civil rights actions of southern Democrats.

McCarthy was elected to the U.S. Senate in 1958 and became a respected member of the body. His wit and scholarly, understated manner became recognized nationally, but his demeanor was no match for that of Humphrey, his energetic and voluble colleague. In 1964, President Johnson generated publicity during the Democratic National Convention by floating both senators' names for the vice presidential slot on his re-election ticket. In the end, he chose Humphrey.

In 1965, McCarthy joined the Senate Foreign Relations Committee, which was to become the center of congressional opposition to the Vietnam War. Although in 1964 McCarthy had voted for the TONKIN GULF RESOLUTION (78 Stat. 384), which had given President Johnson the power to wage war in Vietnam, he soon had doubts about the wisdom of U.S. involvement. In January 1966, McCarthy and 14 other senators signed a public letter urging Johnson not to

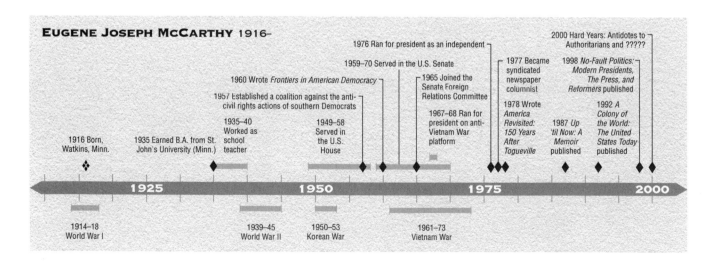

resume bombing of North Vietnam after a brief holiday truce. From that first public criticism of the Vietnam War, McCarthy became a consistent, vocal opponent, making speeches against the war in 1966 and 1967.

In November 1967, McCarthy announced his candidacy for president, based specifically on Johnson's Vietnam policies. Although McCarthy's campaign was not taken seriously at first, an outpouring of support by largely unpaid, politically inexperienced student volunteers on college campuses across the country captured national attention and gave his candidacy political momentum. This momentum was demonstrated when McCarthy won 20 of the 24 New Hampshire delegates in the state's March 1968 primary. President Johnson narrowly won the popular vote in New Hampshire, but the delegates' response was a devastating blow for an incumbent president.

Encouraged by McCarthy's success, Senator ROBERT F. KENNEDY, of New York, joined the race. McCarthy was embittered by Kennedy's decision because McCarthy had wanted Kennedy to run all along, but because Kennedy had refused, McCarthy ran instead. Kennedy had refused to contest Johnson's re-election when the odds appeared in the president's favor. Johnson, sensing the difficulty of his re-election, dropped out of the race in March 1968. Vice President Humphrey entered the race after Johnson's withdrawal.

From April to June 1968, McCarthy and Kennedy waged a series of primary battles. McCarthy won the first three, then lost four of the next five to Kennedy. Humphrey refused to run in the primaries, collecting his delegates through state political conventions and the cooperation of local party leaders.

Kennedy was assassinated in June 1968, and the race then centered on McCarthy and Humphrey. Humphrey won the nomination, but unprecedented violence at the Democratic National Convention in Chicago helped to doom his candidacy against RICHARD M. NIXON. McCarthy refused to campaign for Humphrey, largely because Humphrey was reluctant to articulate a proposal to end the Vietnam War. Humphrey lost the November election to Nixon by a smaller margin than had been predicted, leading some Democratic leaders to complain that McCarthy's unwillingness to campaign for the ticket had cost Humphrey the election.

McCarthy declined to run for re-election to the Senate in 1970. Humphrey ran successfully

Eugene J. McCarthy.
LIBRARY OF CONGRESS

in his place. McCarthy ran a lackluster presidential campaign in 1972 and a better-organized independent presidential campaign in 1976. He lost both races and subsequently retired from the political arena.

McCarthy endorsed RONALD REAGAN in 1980 over incumbent president JIMMY CARTER and his running mate, Minnesotan Walter Mondale. In 1982, McCarthy ran for senator in Minnesota but was defeated in the Democratic primary by Mark Dayton.

After leaving active politics, McCarthy concentrated on teaching, political commentary, and poetry writing. In 1998, he published *No-Fault Politics: Modern Presidents, the Press, and Reformers*. In 2001, a documentary film titled, *I'm Sorry I Was Right: Eugene McCarthy* was released. In the film, McCarthy discusses his past experiences, extrapolates on lessons learned from the Vietnam War, warns against the growing power of the military-industrial complex, and recites some of his poetry. In 2003, McCarthy continued to write, to travel the country, and to speak out against the war in Iraq.

FURTHER READINGS

Callahan, John. 2003. "As War Looms." *Commonweal* (March 14).

Colford, Paul D. 1998. "Eugene McCarthy, Revisited." *Newsday* (August 26).

Eisele, Albert. 1972. *Almost to the Presidency: A Biography of Two American Politicians.* Blue Earth, Minn.: Piper.

"THE WAR IN VIETNAM IS OF QUESTIONABLE LOYALTY AND CONSTITUTIONALITY DIPLOMATICALLY INDEFENSIBLE . . . EVEN IN MILITARY TERMS [AND] MORALLY WRONG."
—EUGENE MCCARTHY

McCarthy, Abigail. 1972. *Private Faces, Public Places.* New York: Doubleday.

McCarthy, Eugene. 1969. *The Year of the People.* New York: Doubleday.

❖ MCCARTHY, JOSEPH RAYMOND

Joseph Raymond McCarthy was a U.S. senator who during the early 1950s conducted a highly controversial campaign against supposed Communist infiltration of the U.S. government. His accusations and methods of interrogation of witnesses came to be called "McCarthyism," a term that remains a part of the U.S. political vocabulary. Though he was ultimately censured for his activities by the Senate, McCarthy was, between 1950 and 1954, the most powerful voice of anti-COMMUNISM in the United States.

McCarthy was born November 14, 1908, in Grand Chute, Wisconsin. He graduated from Marquette University in 1935 with a bachelor of laws degree. He practiced law in Wisconsin until 1939, when he was elected a circuit court judge. During WORLD WAR II, McCarthy served in the Marine Corps as a tailgunner. He progressed to the rank of captain and was awarded several commendations for his military achievements.

McCarthy used his wartime record as "Tailgunner Joe" to help upset Republican Senator ROBERT M. LAFOLLETTE Jr., in the 1946 Wisconsin primary election. McCarthy was elected to the Senate in 1946 and reelected in 1952.

During his first three years in office, McCarthy was an undistinguished and relatively unknown senator. He catapulted to public attention, however, after giving a speech in Wheeling, West Virginia, in February 1950. In the speech, McCarthy charged that 205 Communists had

Joe McCarthy. ARCHIVE PHOTOS, INC.

infiltrated the STATE DEPARTMENT. He claimed that Communist subversion had led to the fall of China to the Communists in October 1949. A Senate investigating committee ordered McCarthy to produce evidence of his accusations, but he was unable to produce the names of any Communists.

Despite this failure to produce evidence, McCarthy escalated his anti-Communist crusade. He accused Democratic President HARRY S. TRUMAN's administration of harboring Communists and of failing to stop Communist aggression. His accusations struck a chord with many U.S. citi-

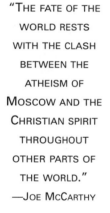

"THE FATE OF THE WORLD RESTS WITH THE CLASH BETWEEN THE ATHEISM OF MOSCOW AND THE CHRISTIAN SPIRIT THROUGHOUT OTHER PARTS OF THE WORLD."
—JOE MCCARTHY

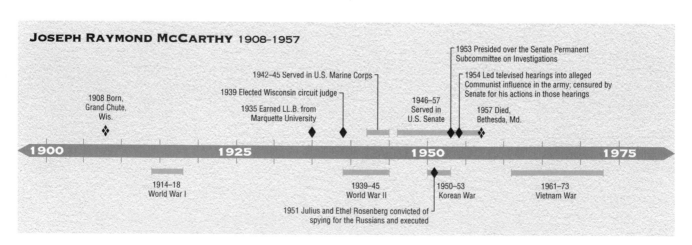

JOSEPH RAYMOND MCCARTHY 1908–1957

1908 Born, Grand Chute, Wis.

1935 Earned LL.B. from Marquette University

1939 Elected Wisconsin circuit judge

1942–45 Served in U.S. Marine Corps

1946–57 Served in U.S. Senate

1953 Presided over the Senate Permanent Subcommittee on Investigations

1954 Led televised hearings into alleged Communist influence in the army; censured by Senate for his actions in those hearings

1957 Died, Bethesda, Md.

1900   1925   1950   1975

1914–18 World War I

1939–45 World War II

1950–53 Korean War

1961–73 Vietnam War

1951 Julius and Ethel Rosenberg convicted of spying for the Russians and executed

zens, who were fearful of the growth of Communism and the menace of the Soviet Union as well as angry at the U.S. government's apparent inability to prevent the spread of Communism.

In 1953 McCarthy became the chair of the Senate's Government Committee on Operations and head of its permanent subcommittee on investigations. Though DWIGHT D. EISENHOWER, a Republican, became president in 1953, McCarthy used the investigations subcommittee to continue his campaign against Communist subversion in the federal government. McCarthy brought persons before his committee who he claimed were "card-carrying" Communists. He made colorful and clever accusations against these witnesses, who, as a result, often lost their jobs and were labeled as subversive. Evidence that a person had briefly joined a left-wing political group during the 1930s was used by McCarthy to suggest that the person was a Communist or a Communist sympathizer.

McCarthy attacked some of the policies of President Eisenhower, yet the president was reluctant to criticize the popular senator. In April 1954 McCarthy leveled charges against the U.S. Army, claiming the secretary of the army had concealed foreign ESPIONAGE activities. Thirty-six days of televised hearings ensued, known as the "Army-McCarthy hearings." McCarthy was unable to substantiate any of his allegations. During the course of the hearings, McCarthy's aggressive and intimidating tactics backfired, turning public opinion against him.

After the Democrats regained control of the Senate in the November 1954 elections, McCarthy was replaced as chair of the investigating committee by Senator JOHN L. MCCLELLAN of Arkansas. McClellan, who had been critical of McCarthy's approach, helped lead an effort to censure McCarthy for his methods and for his abuse of other senators. In 1955, the Senate, on a vote of 67 to 22, moved to censure McCarthy.

The censure vote marked the decline of McCarthy's political influence. He died on May 2, 1957 in Bethesda, Maryland.

FURTHER READINGS

Cunningham, Jesse G., ed. 2003. *The McCarthy Hearings.* San Diego, Calif.: Greenhaven Press.

Herman, Arthur. 2000. *Joseph McCarthy: Reexamining the Life and Legacy of America's Most Hated Senator.* New York: Free Press.

Kinsler, Joseph. 2001. "Joseph McCarthy, the Law Student." *Marquette Law Review* 85 (winter): 467–79.

John L. McClellan.
LIBRARY OF CONGRESS

CROSS-REFERENCES

Cohn, Roy Marcus; Cold War; Red Scare; Welch, Joseph Nye.

❖ MCCLELLAN, JOHN LITTLE

John Little McClellan served as a U.S. senator from 1942 to 1977. During the 1950s, McClellan rose to national prominence for his opposition to the methods used by Senator JOSEPH R. MCCARTHY in investigating alleged Communist subversion. McClellan succeeded McCarthy as chair of the investigating subcommittee and conducted probes of union corruption, graft, and ORGANIZED CRIME between 1955 and 1973.

McClellan was born on February 25, 1896, in Sheridan, Arkansas. He was admitted to the Arkansas bar in 1913 and served a tour of military duty in WORLD WAR I. He maintained a private law practice in Arkansas before becoming a prosecuting attorney in 1927. McClellan left the post in 1930 to resume private practice, but abandoned law for DEMOCRATIC PARTY politics in 1935, when he was elected to the U.S. House of Representatives. In 1942 he began a career in the U.S. Senate that would span thirty-five years.

McClellan was largely unknown outside of Arkansas until the 1950s. In 1953, he was named to the special investigating subcommittee headed by Republican Senator Joseph R. McCarthy of Wisconsin. McCarthy had become a national figure for his controversial charges of Communist subversion in the STATE DEPARTMENT and other

"MOUNTING CRIME AND CORRUPTION ARE INSIDIOUSLY GNAWING AT THE VITALITY AND STRENGTH OF OUR REPUBLIC."
—JOHN MCCLELLAN

divisions of the federal government. McCarthy was a master of the media, attracting front-page coverage for his allegations. However, his use of the investigating committee angered McClellan, who objected to McCarthy's unsubstantiated accusations and to his brow-beating of witnesses.

In 1954, following a contentious, thirty-six day televised hearing dealing with the Army's alleged concealment of foreign ESPIONAGE, McCarthy's popularity declined. McClellan served on a committee that investigated McCarthy's actions during these hearings. The committee concluded McCarthy should be censured by the Senate for his abusive methods and for his "contemptuous" conduct toward a subcommittee that had investigated his finances in 1952. McClellan and an overwhelming majority of his colleagues censured McCarthy on these charges.

After the Democrats regained control of the Senate in the November 1954 elections, McClellan replaced McCarthy as chair of the investigating committee. In 1957 he drew national attention as chair of the Senate Select Committee on Improper Activities in the Labor or Management Field. As presiding officer, he directed investigations of several powerful LABOR UNIONS. He forcefully questioned the leadership of the Teamsters Union, including Dave Beck and James (Jimmy) Hoffa. The McClellan Committee's investigation revealed that the Teamsters Union and other groups had taken union funds for private use and that there were clear links between the Teamsters and organized crime. One result of the probe was the expulsion of the Teamsters and two other unions from the AMERICAN FEDERATION OF LABOR AND CONGRESS OF INDUSTRIAL ORGANIZATIONS (AFL-CIO).

The corruption uncovered by McClellan's committee also led to the passage of the Labor-Management Reporting and Disclosure Act of 1959, commonly known as the LANDRUM-GRIFFIN ACT (29 U.S.C.A. § 401 et seq.). This act sought to prevent union corruption and to guarantee union members that unions would be run democratically.

In 1961 McClellan investigated the fraudulent agricultural dealings of Texas businessman Billy Sol Estes. In 1963 McClellan was involved with the investigation of organized crime. During the hearings, Joseph Valachi, a member of an organized crime family, gave graphic testimony of its inner workings. McClellan continued to organize investigations as part of the Permanent Investigations Subcommittee until 1973, when he became head of the Senate Appropriations Committee.

McClellan died on November 27, 1977 in Little Rock, Arkansas.

MCCULLOCH V. MARYLAND

McCulloch v. Maryland is a keynote case, 17 U.S. (4 Wheat.) 316, 4 L.Ed. 579 (1819), decided by the U.S. Supreme Court that established the principles that the federal government possesses broad powers to pass a number of types of laws, and that the states cannot interfere with any federal agency by imposing a direct tax upon it.

This case represents another illustrative example of the ongoing debate among the founders of the U.S. constitutional government regarding the balance of powers between the states and the federal government. The Federalists were in favor of a strong central government, whereas the Republicans wanted the states to retain most powers. Those who wrote and ratified the U.S. Constitution ultimately agreed to grant the federal government certain specific powers known as the enumerated powers—listed in the Constitution—and concluded with

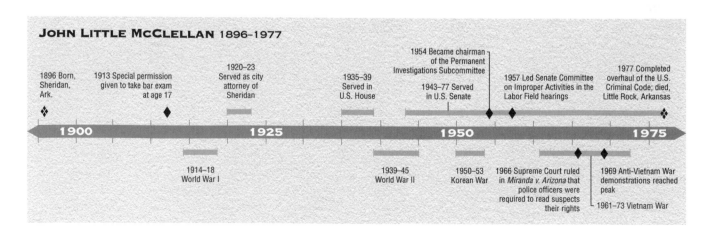

JOHN LITTLE MCCLELLAN 1896–1977

1896 Born, Sheridan, Ark.

1913 Special permission given to take bar exam at age 17

1920–23 Served as city attorney of Sheridan

1935–39 Served in U.S. House

1954 Became chairman of the Permanent Investigations Subcommittee

1943–77 Served in U.S. Senate

1957 Led Senate Committee on Improper Activities in the Labor Field hearings

1977 Completed overhaul of the U.S. Criminal Code; died, Little Rock, Arkansas

1914–18 World War I

1939–45 World War II

1950–53 Korean War

1966 Supreme Court ruled in *Miranda v. Arizona* that police officers were required to read suspects their rights

1969 Anti-Vietnam War demonstrations reached peak

1961–73 Vietnam War

a general provision that permitted Congress to make all laws that are necessary and proper for the carrying out of the foregoing powers, as well as all other powers vested in the U.S. government by the Constitution. Some people were fearful that such a provision, which is called the NECESSARY AND PROPER CLAUSE of the Constitution, was a blanket authorization for the federal government to regulate the states.

Subsequently, a series of articles—which came to be called the *Federalist Papers*—were published in New York newspapers. These articles defended the clause on the basis that any power only constitutes that ability to do something, and that the power to do something is the power to utilize a means of doing it. It is necessary for a legislature to have the power to make laws; therefore, the proper means of exercising that power is by making "necessary and proper" laws. The Constitution was, therefore, ratified in 1789 with the Necessary and Proper Clause.

In exercise of the power conferred by that clause, the first Congress enacted a law in 1791 that incorporated a national bank called the BANK OF THE UNITED STATES, which operated as a private bank, took deposits of private funds, made private loans, and issued bank notes that could be used like money. In addition, wherever branches were established, it operated as a place for the federal government to deposit its funds. The legislation that incorporated the bank stated in its preamble that it would be extremely conducive to the successful operation of the national finances, would aid in the obtaining of loans for the use of the government in sudden emergencies, and would produce considerable advantages to trade and industry in general.

That bank charter was allowed to expire in 1811; however, a second Bank of the United States was incorporated in 1816 with one-fifth of its stock owned by the United States, and it became extremely unpopular. This was particularly true in the South and West, where it first overexpanded credits and then drastically limited them, thereby contributing to the failure of many state-chartered banks. A number of states attempted to keep branches of the national bank out of their states by passing laws proscribing any banks not chartered by the state or by imposing heavy taxes on them. The only bank affected by these laws was the Bank of the United States. The tremendous dispute that subsequently arose between the federal and state governments required resolution by the Supreme Court.

Maryland had one of the least stringent rules against the bank, which required that any bank or branch that was not established subject to the authority of the state must use special stamped paper for its bank notes and, in effect, pay 2 percent of the value of the notes as a tax or pay a general tax of $15,000 a year. Maryland brought suit against McCulloch, cashier of the Bank of the United States, for not paying the tax and won a judgment for the amount of the penalties. An appeal was brought to the Supreme Court by McCulloch.

Chief Justice JOHN MARSHALL wrote the majority opinion of the Court, which reversed the Maryland judgment. The Court held that the federal government has the power to do what is necessary and proper, which included the grant of authority to establish a national bank. Maryland, therefore, had no right to tax the bank, a conclusion which was based upon the theory that "the power to tax is the power to destroy." A state cannot have authority under the Constitution to destroy or tax any agency that has been properly set up by the federal government. On that basis, the law that was passed by the legislature of Maryland that imposed a tax on the Bank of the United States was unconstitutional and void.

FURTHER READINGS

Killenbeck, Mark R. 2003. "Madison, M'Culloch, and Matters of Judicial Cognizance: Some Thoughts on the Nature and Scope of Judicial Review." *Arkansas Law Review* 55 (winter): 901–32.

Newmyer, R. Kent. 2000. "John Marshall, *McCulloch v. Maryland,* and the Southern States' Rights Tradition." *John Marshall Law Review* 33 (summer): 875–934.

Pettifor, Bonnie, and Charles E. Petit. 2003. *McCulloch v. Maryland: When State and Federal Powers Conflict.* Berkeley Heights, N.J.: Enslow.

Rakove, Jack N. 1997. "The Origins of Judicial Review: A Plea for New Contexts. *Stanford Law Review* 49 (May): 1031–64.

CROSS-REFERENCES

Constitution of the United States; Federalism; *Federalist Papers.*

MCGRAIN V. DAUGHERTY

A landmark decision of the Supreme Court, *McGrain v. Daugherty,* 273 U.S. 135, 47 S.Ct. 319, 71 L.Ed. 580 (1927), recognized the implicit power of either House of Congress to hold a witness in a congressional investigation in CONTEMPT for a refusal to honor its summons or to respond to its questions.

During the mid-1920s, there were numerous allegations that the U.S. JUSTICE DEPARTMENT was being mismanaged by its administrator, HARRY DAUGHERTY, the attorney general of the United States. In response to the charges, the Senate passed a resolution that empowered an investigatory committee to hear evidence as to whether Daugherty failed to prosecute various violations of the ANTITRUST LAWS. Mally S. Daugherty, who was a bank president as well as the brother of the attorney general, refused to respond to a subpoena that was issued by the committee on two occasions, ordering him to appear and to bring designated bank ledgers. The president pro tempore of the Senate issued a warrant to his sergeant at arms that Mally Daugherty be taken into custody. A deputy of the sergeant at arms took Daugherty into custody in Cincinnati, Ohio. Daugherty brought a HABEAS CORPUS action for his release in federal district court in Ohio. The court declared that the attachment and detention of the witness was void on the ground that the Senate exceeded its powers in directing the investigation and in ordering the seizure of Daugherty. The deputy made a direct appeal to the Supreme Court, which accepted the case for review.

The Court defined two issues: whether the Senate or House of Representatives has authority to use its own process to compel a private person to appear as a witness and to testify before it or one of its committees in order that Congress can perform a legislative function that it has under the Constitution; and whether the process that was used in this case was directed toward that purpose. Before addressing those questions, however, the Court reviewed some of Daugherty's assertions. Daugherty argued that there was no statutory provision for a deputy and that even if there were, the deputy had no power to execute the warrant, since it was addressed to the sergeant at arms. The Court disagreed. It explained that deputies were authorized to act for the sergeant at arms by virtue of a standing order adopted by the Senate and that Congress recognized their status by establishing and making appropriations for their compensation.

Daugherty also used the FOURTH AMENDMENT provision that "no warrants shall issue, but upon PROBABLE CAUSE, supported by oath or affirmation," to assert that the warrant was void because its basis was an unsworn committee report. The Court rejected this argument on the ground that the committee members were acting pursuant to their oath as Senators when they issued the warrant. When committee members act on matters within their knowledge, probable cause exists for the action of the committee. The warrant withstood constitutional muster.

Daugherty also claimed that the warrant was deficient because it stated that he be "brought before the bar of the Senate then and there" to testify. It was not a subpoena to appear before the Senate, nor did he refuse to do so. The Court dismissed this assertion, because it considered the warrant an auxiliary process used by the committee that was acting for the Senate to compel the witness to provide testimony sought by the subpoena.

The Court finally addressed the central issues of the case: the constitutional authority of the Senate to act in such a manner; and whether the warrant in this case was appropriate. It reasoned that while the power to investigate was not explicitly given to Congress by the Constitution, it was traditionally recognized as implicit in the legislative function since it is a means to obtain necessary information. The Court also referred to various federal laws that demonstrated that either house of Congress has the power to commence investigations and gather evidence concerning activities within its jurisdiction; that committees may conduct such investigations; that in order to fully implement the power to investigate, either house may punish uncooperative witnesses; and witnesses may be given IMMUNITY from criminal prosecutions that derive from their testimonies before the committees. Based upon tradition and statutes, the Court concluded that each house of Congress has auxiliary powers that are essential in order to effectuate its express powers, but neither house has unlimited "general" power to investigate private matters and force testimony. The Senate acted within its powers when it authorized a committee to investigate Daugherty. When the committee sought Daugherty's testimony, it was as a means to perform a legislative function since the purpose of the inquiry was to determine whether the attorney general and the Department of Justice—subjects of congressional regulations and appropriations—were properly performing their duties. The Court deemed that Daugherty's seizure and detention were appropriate because of his wrongful refusal to appear and testify before a lawful congressional committee. It reversed the order of the district court that released Daugherty from custody.

CROSS-REFERENCES

Congress of the United States.

✧ MCGRANERY, JAMES PATRICK

James Patrick McGranery was a U.S. representative and a federal judge prior to his appointment as attorney general of the United States. He served as attorney general under President HARRY S. TRUMAN from April 1952 to January 1953.

McGranery was born July 8, 1895, in Philadelphia. His Irish Catholic parents, Patrick McGranery and Bridget Gallagher McGranery, were devout, hardworking, and practical. They sent McGranery to local parochial schools, and they did not discourage their son when he chose to quit school and enter the workforce. McGranery was a high-school student when he landed his first full-time job at a Philadelphia printing plant. He remained a card-carrying member of a Philadelphia printer's union for most of his life.

When the United States entered WORLD WAR I, McGranery left his job to enlist in the Army. He served as a balloon observation pilot and as adjutant with the 111th Infantry. At the end of the war, he returned home with a broader view of the world and a strong determination to resume his education. He entered Philadelphia's Maher Preparatory School in 1919 to complete the entrance requirements for Temple University.

The war experience also sparked McGranery's interest in law and government. While at Temple, and later at Temple Law School, he became active in local ward politics. Soon after graduat-

James P. McGranery.
LIBRARY OF CONGRESS

ing and passing the bar examination in 1928, he was tapped by Philadelphia ward bosses to manage the local campaign of Democratic presidential candidate Alfred E. Smith, of New York. Smith ultimately lost his presidential bid, but McGranery was exhilarated by the political process and eager to attempt his own run for office. He hastily made a bid for a vacant clerk-of-court seat, and was defeated.

McGranery's introduction to the political process showed him the need for a solid political base, and it convinced him that a base of supporters could be cultivated through the PRACTICE OF LAW. To that end, he established the firm of Masterson and McGranery. He started to represent clients with known political influence, including police officers and firefighters, and leaders of their unions. While building his practice, McGranery made two more failed attempts

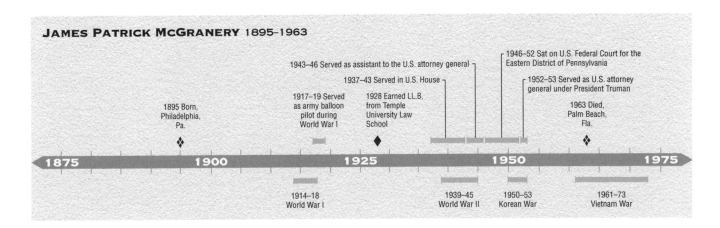

JAMES PATRICK McGRANERY 1895–1963

1946–52 Sat on U.S. Federal Court for the Eastern District of Pennsylvania

1943–46 Served as assistant to the U.S. attorney general

1937–43 Served in U.S. House

1952–53 Served as U.S. attorney general under President Truman

1917–19 Served as army balloon pilot during World War I

1928 Earned LL.B. from Temple University Law School

1895 Born, Philadelphia, Pa.

1963 Died, Palm Beach, Fla.

| 1875 | 1900 | 1925 | 1950 | 1975 |

1914–18 World War I

1939–45 World War II

1950–53 Korean War

1961–73 Vietnam War

at elected office—as a candidate for district attorney in 1931, and as a candidate for the U.S. Congress in 1934.

Finally, in 1936, McGranery had paid his dues and curried the favor he needed. He was elected as a Democrat to represent Pennsylvania's Second Congressional District, by a margin of almost 25,000 votes over his Republican opponent. He was reelected in 1938, 1940, and 1942. Just before his second term in Congress, McGranery married Attorney Regina T. Clark, of Philadelphia, with whom he had three children: James Patrick, Jr., Clark, and Regina.

During his years in Congress, McGranery served on the House Banking and Currency, Interstate, Foreign Commerce, and Ways and Means Committees. His voting record was consistent with his allegiance to President FRANKLIN D. ROOSEVELT and the DEMOCRATIC PARTY.

McGranery resigned his seat in the fall of 1943 when his congressional district was eliminated by reapportionment. Roosevelt was reluctant to lose McGranery's longtime support, so he offered to create a position for McGranery in the JUSTICE DEPARTMENT as assistant to Attorney General FRANCIS BIDDLE. McGranery accepted. He served as the department's chief administrative officer and chief liaison with Congress and other federal departments and agencies during the WORLD WAR II years. He also reviewed board-of-appeals findings under the Selective Service Act (50 U.S.C.A. App. 451-471a).

After the war, McGranery remained in the Department of Justice to serve as chief assistant to Truman's first attorney general, TOM C. CLARK. Though McGranery held a position of prominence, he was not as involved or influential under Clark as he had been under Biddle. History suggests that Clark shut McGranery out of high-profile or sensitive cases, including one involving a vote-fraud allegation in the president's home district; a mail-fraud case against a bond dealer who raised funds for Truman, which was dismissed; and an investigation of *Amerasia*, a left-wing magazine devoted to Asian affairs. McGranery resigned his post in October 1946 to accept an appointment from Truman to the federal bench in the Eastern District of Pennsylvania.

Judge McGranery quickly established a reputation as a tough jurist. Critics described him as high-handed, autocratic, and inclined to favor the government's position on any given issue.

Even former attorney general Biddle acknowledged that McGranery was essentially an advocate rather than a judge.

In one celebrated pronouncement, McGranery ruled in 1949 that Representative Earl Chudoff (D-Pa.) could not appear as a defense attorney in McGranery's court because, as a government employee, the congressman had an inherent conflict in representing a client in a federal proceeding (*Chudoff v. McGranery*, 179 F.2d 869).

During his years on the federal bench, McGranery's name was often mentioned in connection with nominations to Democratic Party and government posts including chairman of the Democratic National Committee, postmaster general, and attorney general. It was just as often discounted because of McGranery's personal reputation. McGranery was well-known to be given to emotional outbursts; he had a history of erratic behavior dating back to his early days in the Department of Justice.

Despite warnings from a number of quarters, Truman asked McGranery to fill the attorney general post in the spring of 1952, following the departure of J. HOWARD MCGRATH. Truman had reluctantly asked for McGrath's resignation after McGrath had failed to cooperate with, and later fired, a special assistant who had been named to investigate corrupt practices inside the Department of Justice and the Bureau of Internal Revenue. A confirmation committee in Congress briefly raised the issue of McGranery's participation in the *Amerasia* incident and speculated that he might try to block the ongoing Department of Justice investigation just as McGrath had. Nevertheless, after some discussion, McGranery was confirmed as attorney general. To the surprise of many of his longtime critics, he oversaw a thorough inquiry that led to numerous dismissals and prosecutions in both the Department of Justice and the Bureau of Internal Revenue.

McGranery made a number of other contributions as attorney general, including the initiation of antitrust cases in the oil and steel industries, the diamond trade, and magazine wholesaling; the prosecution of American Communist Party leaders; the deportation of organized-crime figures; and the instigation of Department of Justice support for the cause of school INTEGRATION in BROWN V. BOARD OF EDUCATION OF TOPEKA, KANSAS (347 U.S. 483, 74 S. Ct. 686, 98 L. Ed. 873 [1954]). His office

"NO SPECIFIC INTENT TO MONOPOLIZE IS NECESSARY; THE ONLY RELEVANT INTENT IS THE INTENT TO ENTER INTO THE BUSINESS ARRANGEMENTS WHICH GIVE RISE TO THE POWER."
—JAMES MCGRANERY

helped to provide the basis for that decision overruling the "separate-but-equal" doctrine.

At the close of the Truman administration, McGranery practiced law in Washington, D.C., and Philadelphia. He died on December 23, 1962, in Palm Beach, Florida.

❖ MCGRATH, JAMES HOWARD

James Howard McGrath, a three-term governor and U.S. senator from Rhode Island, served as SOLICITOR GENERAL and attorney general of the United States under President HARRY S. TRUMAN.

McGrath was born November 28, 1903, in Woonsocket, Rhode Island, and reared in nearby Providence. His father, James J. McGrath, worked as a knitter in a woolen mill before venturing into real estate and insurance. He rose to prominence through his association with the Independent Order of Foresters (a fraternal insurance organization), handling the company's affairs in the New England states. His mother, Ida E. May McGrath, used her training as a bookkeeper to manage the family's financial affairs while her husband was on the road.

As a young boy, McGrath set out to win a subscription contest at a Providence newspaper by targeting his father's business colleagues as potential subscribers. He sold a record number of new subscriptions and, in the process, captured the attention of the newspaper's owner, Rhode Island senator Peter G. Gerry.

When he was not selling newspapers, McGrath attended Providence's La Salle Academy. He completed his undergraduate studies in 1922 and enrolled at Providence College. During his college years, McGrath was a founding member and the first president of the Young Men's Democratic League of Rhode Island.

By graduation day in 1926, McGrath knew he wanted a career in politics. While waiting to attend law school, McGrath approached Senator Gerry and asked for a summer job. Gerry remembered the young man and put him to work in his senate office. McGrath worked for Gerry until his graduation from Boston University Law School in 1929. Following his ADMISSION TO THE BAR, McGrath joined a Providence law firm and decided to marry. He and his wife, Estelle A. Cadorette McGrath, had one son, James David McGrath, in 1930.

Though 1929 and 1930 were years of change and new beginnings for McGrath, his interest in politics remained constant. He had been named vice chairman of the Rhode Island Democratic State Committee in 1928; by 1930, he was chairman of the committee and ready to make his own place in the political arena. McGrath's first political appointment came in late 1930 when he was named city solicitor of Central Falls, Rhode Island. He served in that post for four years before resigning to accept a second appointment as U.S. district attorney for Rhode Island in 1934.

With McGrath's growing prominence in legal and business circles came growing influence in Rhode Island's DEMOCRATIC PARTY. From his position as chairman of the Rhode Island Democratic State Committee, he rose to chairman of the Rhode Island delegation at the Democratic National Convention in 1932. Age twenty-eight at the time, he was the youngest man ever to hold the job.

By 1940, he had laid the foundation for a successful bid for the state's highest office. He

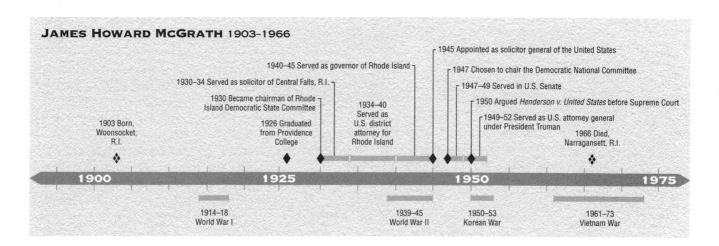

JAMES HOWARD MCGRATH 1903–1966

1945 Appointed as solicitor general of the United States

1940–45 Served as governor of Rhode Island

1947 Chosen to chair the Democratic National Committee

1930–34 Served as solicitor of Central Falls, R.I.

1947–49 Served in U.S. Senate

1930 Became chairman of Rhode Island Democratic State Committee

1950 Argued *Henderson v. United States* before Supreme Court

1934–40 Served as U.S. district attorney for Rhode Island

1949–52 Served as U.S. attorney general under President Truman

1903 Born, Woonsocket, R.I.

1926 Graduated from Providence College

1966 Died, Narragansett, R.I.

1900   1925   1950   1975

1914–18 World War I

1939–45 World War II

1950–53 Korean War

1961–73 Vietnam War

sought and received the gubernatorial nomination from the Democratic party, and he defeated Republican incumbent William H. Vanderbilt by a large margin.

McGrath served as governor of Rhode Island for three consecutive terms. In that office, he revised the state tax structure, reorganized the juvenile court system, established a labor relations board, and started a WORKERS' COMPENSATION fund. During WORLD WAR II, he continued to serve as governor while chairing the Rhode Island State Council of Defense and assisting the U.S. TREASURY DEPARTMENT with war financing activities.

McGrath's work was noticed by national Democratic leaders including President FRANKLIN D. ROOSEVELT. It was not long before he was asked to serve on a committee to organize the 1944 Democratic National Convention and to help secure the presidential nomination for Roosevelt's vice president, Truman. McGrath, who had seconded Truman's vice presidential nomination at the previous convention, was an eager and hardworking member of the committee. He liked Truman—and the feeling was mutual.

After Truman's election, in October 1945, McGrath was rewarded with an appointment to the post of solicitor general of the United States. As solicitor general, he successfully defended the constitutionality of the Public Holding Company Act (15 U.S.C.A. § 79 et seq.) and fully supported an international military tribunal's conviction of Japan's General Tomoyuki Yamashita for WAR CRIMES.

In 1946 McGrath was elected to the U.S. Senate. While in office, McGrath fought the removal of wartime economic controls and the reduction of income taxes instituted during the war years. He thought the additional money should be used to broaden SOCIAL SECURITY initiatives, underwrite national HEALTH INSURANCE, and fund education. He also encouraged his colleagues to speak out on HUMAN RIGHTS issues, charging that in the years before World War II, the United States almost encouraged the Nazis by not speaking out against them.

In September 1947, McGrath became Truman's handpicked candidate to chair the Democratic National Committee and to orchestrate the president's reelection bid. McGrath was formally elected to the post a month later.

Under McGrath's leadership, the party in 1948 waged a tough, and sometimes divisive,

"[COMMUNISTS] ARE EVERYWHERE—IN FACTORIES, OFFICES, BUTCHER SHOPS, ON STREET CORNERS, IN PRIVATE BUSINESS—AND EACH CARRIES IN HIMSELF THE GERMS OF DEATH FOR SOCIETY."
—JAMES MCGRATH

national effort that carried many state and local Democratic candidates into office and resulted in Truman's narrow victory over THOMAS E. DEWEY.

After the election, McGrath returned to the Senate. Almost immediately, the Rhode Island Charities Trust came under investigation by a Senate subcommittee. As a trustee, McGrath was called to explain the organization's financial practices. The investigation ran its course without result, but a cloud remained over McGrath's personal finances.

McGrath's declining sphere of influence was most evident when he tried to find support for his legislative initiatives. He continued to sponsor unpopular measures addressing social issues, including a CIVIL RIGHTS bill supported by the administration in late 1949. His efforts to push the bill through the Senate further angered powerful southern Democrats he had offended during the presidential campaign by ending a policy of racially segregating the staff at Democratic national headquarters. (Though this change in policy had caused tremendous turmoil within the party and precipitated a loss of support in many southern states, it had also helped to deliver the crucial black vote needed in 1948 to carry Illinois, New York, and Ohio.)

It was in this climate that McGrath was appointed to replace TOM C. CLARK as U.S. attorney general after Truman named Clark to the U.S. Supreme Court. The press blasted McGrath's appointment, saying it demonstrated a terrible lack of judgment on Truman's part. McGrath resigned his Senate seat in December 1949 to accept the appointment.

With Truman's blessing, McGrath continued to be a strong advocate for civil rights. During his term as attorney general, the JUSTICE DEPARTMENT first challenged the constitutionality of racial SEGREGATION. McGrath argued a number of important cases before the U.S. Supreme Court in the spring of 1950, including a landmark case in which the High Court outlawed discriminatory dining arrangements in railroad cars (*Henderson v. United States*, 339 U.S. 816, 70 S. Ct. 843, 94 L. Ed. 1302).

Though he had a few bright moments, McGrath's subordinates and colleagues did not consider him a particularly effective attorney general. His most egregious error occurred when a House Ways and Means subcommittee uncovered evidence of corruption in the Bureau of

Internal Revenue and in the Tax Division of the Justice Department. Truman's initial response, in January 1952, was to announce that the Justice Department would investigate and clean up any corruption in the government. When critics objected to the Justice Department's investigating itself, the president appointed New York Republican Newbold Morris to conduct an independent investigation of the charges.

Initially, McGrath promised full cooperation, but he had second thoughts when Morris asked him and other top Justice Department officials to complete a detailed financial questionnaire. Calling the questionnaire a violation of individual rights and an invasion of privacy, McGrath refused to complete or submit the document— or to order his subordinates to do so. Three days later, McGrath forced Truman's hand by firing the special investigator and resuming charge of the investigation. In the political uproar that followed, the president had no choice but to ask for McGrath's resignation.

After leaving office, McGrath continued to be active in Democratic politics. In 1956 he managed Senator Estes Kefauver's vice presidential campaign, and in 1960, he made an unsuccessful attempt to regain his old Senate seat. After retiring from politics, he practiced law and managed his many business interests. McGrath died on September 2, 1966, in Narragansett, Rhode Island.

M.C.J.

An abbreviation for master of comparative JURISPRUDENCE, *a degree awarded to foreign lawyers trained in* CIVIL LAW *countries who have successfully completed a year of full-time study of the Anglo-American legal system.*

The M.C.J. degree is ordinarily offered by universities and law schools that have comparative law departments. It is awarded to highly qualified foreign lawyers who intend to return to the legal profession in a foreign country after completion of their studies in the United States.

❖ MCKENNA, JOSEPH

Joseph McKenna rose from humble immigrant roots as a baker's son to a position of prominence in California Republican politics. McKenna served as county district attorney (1866–1870), U.S. Congressman, justice of the Ninth U.S. Circuit court (1892–1897), and, briefly, U.S. attorney general (1897). His controversial nomination to the Supreme Court in 1897 led to a twenty-seven-year tenure.

McKenna was born in Philadelphia on August 10, 1843, to Irish immigrant parents. He became head of the family at age fifteen when his father died shortly after moving the eight-member household to California. By age twenty-two, and while working several jobs, McKenna had studied enough law on his own to pass the California bar. One year later, despite little experience, he was elected district attorney for Solano County. He owed his rapid success to help from railroad baron LELAND STANFORD, the state's governor. In time, his loyalty to Stanford earned him three straight Republican nominations for Congress. He finally won in 1885. In Washington, D.C., McKenna opposed business regulations, supported federal land grants to the railroads, and sponsored legislation that would have made Chinese immigrants carry identification cards.

In 1892, on the urging of Stanford, who had become a U.S. senator, President BENJAMIN

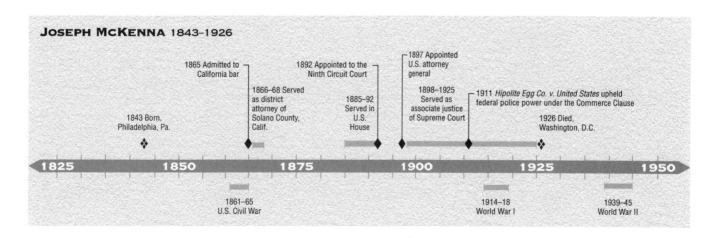

JOSEPH McKENNA 1843–1926

1843 Born, Philadelphia, Pa.

1865 Admitted to California bar

1866–68 Served as district attorney of Solano County, Calif.

1885–92 Served in U.S. House

1892 Appointed to the Ninth Circuit Court

1897 Appointed U.S. attorney general

1898–1925 Served as associate justice of Supreme Court

1911 *Hipolite Egg Co. v. United States* upheld federal police power under the Commerce Clause

1926 Died, Washington, D.C.

1825　1850　1875　1900　1925　1950

1861–65 U.S. Civil War

1914–18 World War I

1939–45 World War II

HARRISON appointed McKenna to the Ninth Circuit Court of Appeals. Opponents protested that McKenna was unqualified and, moreover, beholden to railroad interests, but the nomination succeeded. He held the seat for four years, largely without incident or note; yet occasionally he proved his critics right about his allegiances. In *Southern Pacific Co. v. Board of Railroad Commissioners,* 78 F. 236 (C.C.N.D. Cal. 1896), for example, he blocked the California legislature's attempt to set railroad fares, arguing that the proposed rates were unfair to the railroads.

While serving on the Ways and Means Committee in Congress, McKenna had befriended fellow Republican WILLIAM MCKINLEY. McKinley became president in 1896 and in 1897 made McKenna U.S. attorney general. Only a few months later, McKinley nominated McKenna to fill a vacancy on the U.S. Supreme Court created by the departure of Justice STEPHEN FIELD. Again, there was opposition, with newspapers and lawmakers calling him unfit for the responsibility. However, the nomination succeeded.

Of McKenna's 633 opinions, only a handful were majority opinions. These came in important cases, however, such as *Hipolite Egg Co. v. United States,* 220 U.S. 45, 31 S. Ct. 364, 55 L. Ed. 364 (1911), one of the decisions during the era that upheld federal POLICE POWER under the Constitution's COMMERCE CLAUSE. Generally regarded as a hard-working justice, his body of

opinions shows that he developed a pragmatism and clarity of expression in his twenty-seven years on the bench. Slowed by age, he resigned in 1925 under the advice of Chief Justice WILLIAM HOWARD TAFT. He died several months later on November 21, 1926, in Washington, D.C.

FURTHER READINGS

Friedman, Leon, and Fred L. Israel, eds. 1969. *The Justices of the United States Supreme Court, 1789–1969: Their Lives and Major Opinions.* New York: Chelsea House.

❖ MCKINLEY, JOHN

John McKinley served on the U.S. Supreme Court as an associate justice from 1837 to 1852. During the 1820s, McKinley built his career in the Alabama legislature. He later served in both the U.S. Senate and the House of Representatives. At a time when westward expansion brought federal and state governments into conflict over the use of land, McKinley was a strong advocate of STATES' RIGHTS and affordable land for settlers. In 1837, President MARTIN VAN BUREN appointed McKinley to the Court, where McKinley sat for 15 years. McKinley complained endlessly about the great deal of travel required by Supreme Court justices at that time. He produced only 20 opinions and two concurrences during his tenure, and he is largely remembered for his dissent on behalf of states' rights in *Bank of Augusta v. Earle,* 38 U.S. (13 Pet.) 519, 10 L. Ed. 274 (1839).

Born in Culpeper County, Virginia, on May 1, 1780, McKinley studied law in Kentucky and passed the bar examination in 1800. While practicing law in Kentucky and later Alabama over the next 20 years, McKinley developed an interest in politics. He won the first of his several elections to the state legislature in 1820. Later, by shrewdly changing political allegiances from presidential candidate HENRY CLAY to the more popular ANDREW JACKSON, he was elected to the U.S. Senate in 1826. His chief concern in office was land legislation. As settlers pushed westward, McKinley favored the interests of small land buyers over those of big speculators. He also argued for the primacy of state control over land within state borders, taking the traditional states'-rights view that denied the validity of federal authority. As his political fortunes rose and fell, McKinley lost a bid for re-election to the Senate in 1830 and then alternated between serving terms in the Alabama legislature and the U.S. House of Representatives.

In 1837, McKinley had returned to the Alabama legislature as a representative when Congress increased the number of seats on the U.S. Supreme Court from seven to nine. President Van Buren first offered one of the seats to another Alabama lawmaker, WILLIAM SMITH, who declined. McKinley accepted, but not without reservation. He was chiefly bothered by the need to travel upwards of 5,000 miles every year.

During McKinley's time, justices had responsibility not only over the Court itself, but also over the federal circuit courts, which required them to travel in a practice known as *circuit riding*. In charge of the largest circuit, the Ninth, McKinley loathed this obligation. Twice, in 1838 and 1842, McKinley asked Congress to absolve him of the responsibility, which he claimed exposed him to undue personal expense and the risk of yellow fever. Embittered by lack of sympathy for his complaints, he sometimes neglected to visit all of the courts in his circuit, a failure that brought him criticism.

In 1839, McKinley wrote his most notable opinion, in the case of *Bank of Augusta v. Earle*. Rooted in a state banking dispute, the case concerned the constitutional limitations of state power to regulate business—specifically, how far a state could go in excluding a corporation from doing business within its borders. On the circuit court, McKinley ruled that states have broad powers, and the opinion provoked outrage from corporations, attorneys, and even McKinley's colleague, U.S. Supreme Court Justice JOSEPH STORY. When the case reached the high court, the 8-to-1 majority took a far more moderate view. In dissent, McKinley adhered to his position: A state could properly limit business activity to corporations that were chartered in it, and it should be free to reject the business of any outside corporation.

John McKinley.
ETCHING BY ALBERT ROSENTHAL. ARCHIVE PHOTOS, INC.

As his health deteriorated in his later years, McKinley did less circuit riding, and after 1845 he played a very limited role in the Court's affairs. He remained on the Court until his death in Louisville, Kentucky, on July 19, 1852.

FURTHER READINGS

Friedman, Leon, and Fred L. Israel, eds. 1969. *The Justices of the United States Supreme Court, 1789–1969: Their Lives and Major Opinions.* New York: Chelsea House.

❖ MCKINLEY, WILLIAM

William McKinley served as the twenty-fifth president of the United States, from 1897 until his death from an assassin's bullet in 1901. A conservative Republican who advocated high tariffs to protect U.S. industry, McKinley waged the SPANISH-AMERICAN WAR and at the end of it gained overseas territories for the United States.

"THE NATURAL SOCIETY OF NATIONS CANNOT SUBSIST, IF THE RIGHTS WHICH EACH HAS RECEIVED FROM NATURE ARE NOT RESPECTED."
—JOHN MCKINLEY

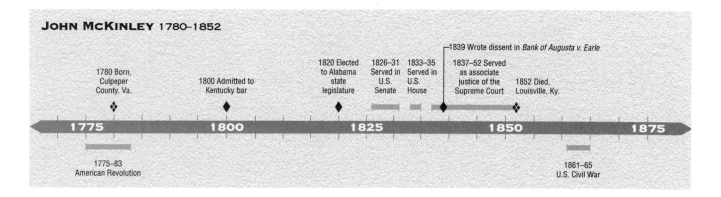

JOHN MCKINLEY 1780–1852

1780 Born, Culpeper County, Va.

1800 Admitted to Kentucky bar

1820 Elected to Alabama state legislature

1826–31 Served in U.S. Senate

1833–35 Served in U.S. House

1837–52 Served as associate justice of the Supreme Court

1839 Wrote dissent in *Bank of Augusta v. Earle*

1852 Died, Louisville, Ky.

1775   1800   1825   1850   1875

1775–83 American Revolution

1861–65 U.S. Civil War

William McKinley.
LIBRARY OF CONGRESS

McKinley was born January 29, 1843, in Niles, Ohio. As a young man, he briefly attended Allegheny College, in Meadville, Pennsylvania; taught school; and fought in the Union army during the Civil War, attaining the rank of major. McKinley was aide-de-camp to the regimental commander, RUTHERFORD B. HAYES, who was later governor of Ohio and the nineteenth U.S. president. After the war McKinley studied law with an attorney and attended Albany Law School, in New York. He was admitted to the Ohio bar in 1867, and established a law practice in Canton, Ohio, which remained his official residence for the rest of his life. From 1869 to 1871, he served as county attorney.

McKinley's political ambitions were nurtured by Hayes. McKinley became active in Ohio

Republican politics and was elected to the U.S. House of Representatives in 1876. McKinley was an outspoken advocate of higher tariffs, believing that U.S. industry and U.S. workers were protected by the taxation of imported foreign goods. His stand on tariffs culminated in the McKinley Tariff Act of 1890, which raised duties on many imports to the highest levels up to that time. The act was an unpopular measure, and McKinley was voted out of office in the election of 1890.

McKinley returned to Ohio, where he was elected governor in 1891 and reelected governor in 1893. Mark Hanna, a wealthy Ohio industrialist and a leader in national Republican politics, became McKinley's benefactor and helped him secure the 1896 Republican presidential nomination. The Democratic candidate was WILLIAM JENNINGS BRYAN, who supported free coinage of silver, arguing that it would increase the money supply and thus help farmers and small-business owners. McKinley, who advocated retaining the gold standard, defeated Bryan, with Hanna raising large sums of money from big business to support the campaign. The money was used to help fund more than three hundred delegations and more than 750,000 people who traveled to McKinley's front porch in Canton to hear him campaign.

As president, McKinley signed the Currency Act of 1900 (31 Stat. 45), institutionalizing the gold standard until the 1930s. However, his first term was dominated by foreign affairs and overseas territorial expansion. When McKinley took office, a national independence movement had arisen in Cuba, seeking freedom from Spain. The United States tried to remain neutral while negotiating a solution acceptable to both sides. On February 15, 1898, the U.S. warship *Maine* blew up in the Havana harbor. Though later

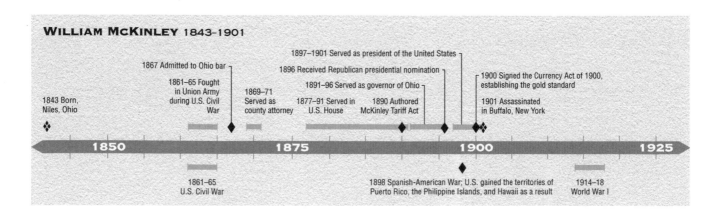

WILLIAM MCKINLEY 1843–1901

1897–1901 Served as president of the United States

1867 Admitted to Ohio bar

1896 Received Republican presidential nomination

1861–65 Fought
in Union Army
during U.S. Civil
War

1869–71
Served as
county attorney

1891–96 Served as governor of Ohio

1900 Signed the Currency Act of 1900,
establishing the gold standard

1843 Born,
Niles, Ohio

1877–91 Served in
U.S. House

1890 Authored
McKinley Tariff Act

1901 Assassinated
in Buffalo, New York

1850   1875   1900   1925

1861–65
U.S. Civil War

1898 Spanish-American War; U.S. gained the territories of
Puerto Rico, the Philippine Islands, and Hawaii as a result

1914–18
World War I

investigation suggested that a boiler explosion sank the *Maine* and killed its crew, immediate public reaction, inflamed by the newspapers owned by William Randolph Hearst, blamed Spain for the attack. At McKinley's request Congress approved a declaration of war.

The Spanish-American War was brief, with Spain agreeing to terms in August 1898. Cuba gained its independence, though the United States reserved the right to intervene to ensure stability. Under the peace treaty, Spain transferred to the United States its claims to Puerto Rico and the Philippine Islands. In addition, the U.S. Congress voted in July 1898 to take possession of the Hawaiian Islands. This territorial expansion increased the United States' international prestige as a imperialist power, but some citizens questioned its constitutionality and whether it fit with the U.S. national character. The U.S. Supreme Court decided the legal question in 1901 in a set of decisions known as the *Insular* cases. The Court held that these new possessions were domestic territory of the United States, under the full control of Congress, and the residents of these new dependencies did not have the rights of citizens (*De Lima v. Bidwell*, 182 U.S. 1, 21 S. Ct. 743, 45 L. Ed. 1041; *Downes v. Bidwell*, 182 U.S. 244, 21 S. Ct. 770, 45 L. Ed. 1088).

In the 1900 presidential election, McKinley easily again defeated Bryan, who continued to campaign for free silver and against U.S. imperialism.

On September 6, 1901, McKinley was shot by Leon F. Czolgosz, an anarchist who had dreamed of killing a prominent person, at the Pan-American Exposition, in Buffalo, New York. An infection set into McKinley's wound, and he died September 14, in Buffalo. Vice President THEODORE ROOSEVELT succeeded McKinley as president.

FURTHER READINGS

Morgan, H. Wayne. 2003. *William McKinley and His America*. rev. ed. Kent, Ohio: Kent State Univ. Press.

MCKINNEY ACT

The Stewart B. McKinney Homeless Assistance Act, 42 U.S.C.A. 11301 et seq. (1989 Supp.), was named after the Republican congressman from Connecticut. It authorizes the HOUSING AND URBAN DEVELOPMENT DEPARTMENT to coordinate the disbursement of unused federal property to community groups interested in providing shelter to HOMELESS PERSONS, especially elderly persons, handicapped persons, families with children, Native Americans, and veterans. The Interagency Council on the Homeless (Pub. L. No. 100-77, 101 Stat. 484, 42 U.S.C.A. 11301 (b) (1) [1989]) distributes information on how to use benefits under the act.

Initially, priority to receive excess properties was given to homeless providers rather than local communities. However, the Base Closure and Community Redevelopment Act of 1994 (Pub. L. No. 103-421, Oct. 25, 1994, 108 Stat. 4346) amended the McKinney Act by eliminating homeless providers' priority. The result is that homeless providers' needs are considered simultaneously in a community's reuse planning.

Funding and support for the McKinney Act has been reduced, especially with the 1996 WELFARE reform, because the act functions in connection with other related legislation. In one recent funding cycle, nearly three thousand requests for transitional housing were submitted, but only 818 proposals could be funded under the act.

In 1996, to assist homeless individuals, the 104th Congress appropriated $823 million for the emergency shelter grants program (as authorized under subtitle B of title IV of the McKinney Act), the supportive housing program (as authorized under subtitle C of title IV of the McKinney Act), the section 8 moderate rehabilitation single room occupancy program (as authorized under the United States Housing Act of 1937 [Sept. 1, 1937, ch. 896, 50 Stat. 888], as amended, pursuant to section 441 of the McKinney Act), and the shelter plus care program (as authorized under subtitle F of the title IV of the McKinney Act) (110 Stat 2874).

FURTHER READINGS

Foscarinis, Maria. 1996. "Downward Spiral: Homelessness and Its Criminalization." *Yale Law and Policy Review* 14.

❖ MCLEAN, JOHN

John McLean served as associate justice on the U.S. Supreme Court for thirty-two years, one of the longest tenures in the history of the Court.

McLean was born on March 11, 1785, in New Jersey but was raised primarily near Lebanon, Ohio, where his father staked out land that later became the family farm. McLean attended a county school and later was tutored by two schoolmasters, Presbyterian ministers,

"IN THE [DRED SCOTT V. SANDFORD] ARGUMENT, IT WAS SAID THAT A COLORED CITIZEN WOULD NOT BE AN AGREEABLE MEMBER OF SOCIETY. THIS IS MORE A MATTER OF TASTE THAN LAW . . . [FOR] UNDER THE LATE TREATY WITH MEXICO WE MADE CITIZENS OF ALL GRADES, COMBINATIONS, AND COLORS."
—JOHN MCLEAN

John McLean.
LIBRARY OF CONGRESS

and paid them with money he earned working as a farm hand. In 1804, at the age of nineteen, he began working as an apprentice to the clerk of the Hamilton County Court of Common Pleas in Cincinnati and also studied law with Arthur St. Clair and John S. Gano, two distinguished Cincinnati lawyers.

In 1807 McLean was admitted to the bar, married, and returned to Lebanon to open a printing office. He began publishing the Lebanon *Western Star,* a partisan journal supporting the Jeffersonian party. Three years later McLean gave his newspaper and printing business to his brother to concentrate full-time on the PRACTICE OF LAW. At the same time, McLean, who had been raised Presbyterian, con-

verted to Methodism, an experience that would have a strong impact throughout his life. He was active in church affairs and wrote articles about the Bible, and in 1849 he was named honorary president of the American Sunday School Union.

In 1812, after a year serving as examiner in the U.S. Land Office in Cincinnati, McLean was elected to the U.S. House of Representatives at the age of twenty-seven and was reelected two years later. During his two terms in the House, McLean was a staunch supporter of President JAMES MADISON and his efforts to wage the WAR OF 1812. McLean, unhappy with the salary paid to members of Congress and wanting to be closer to his wife and children, chose not to run again in 1816 and returned home. Back in Ohio, McLean easily won election to one of four judgeships on the Ohio Supreme Court, a demanding position that required him to "ride the circuit," or hear cases throughout the state.

In 1822 McLean was again drawn to politics and made an unsuccessful bid for the U.S. Senate. Shortly after McLean lost the election, President JAMES MONROE appointed him commissioner of the General Land Office in Washington, a direct result of McLean's earlier hard work to secure Monroe's nomination for the presidency. The position meant a large increase in salary and led to McLean's appointment the next year to the position of postmaster general. During his six years as postmaster general, McLean expanded the number of routes and deliveries, established thousands of new post offices, and increased the size of the U.S. POSTAL SERVICE to almost 27,000 employees.

Though he served as postmaster under JOHN QUINCY ADAMS, McLean used his considerable political skills to establish ties with ANDREW JACKSON, who defeated Adams for the presi-

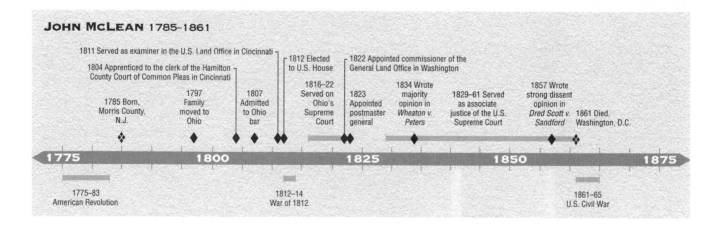

JOHN MCLEAN 1785–1861

1811 Served as examiner in the U.S. Land Office in Cincinnati

1804 Apprenticed to the clerk of the Hamilton County Court of Common Pleas in Cincinnati

1812 Elected to U.S. House

1822 Appointed commissioner of the General Land Office in Washington

1785 Born, Morris County, N.J.

1797 Family moved to Ohio

1807 Admitted to Ohio bar

1816–22 Served on Ohio's Supreme Court

1823 Appointed postmaster general

1834 Wrote majority opinion in *Wheaton v. Peters*

1829–61 Served as associate justice of the U.S. Supreme Court

1857 Wrote strong dissent opinion in *Dred Scott v. Sandford*

1861 Died, Washington, D.C.

1775   1800   1825   1850   1875

1775–83 American Revolution

1812–14 War of 1812

1861–65 U.S. Civil War

dency in 1828. As a result, McLean was appointed to the U.S. Supreme Court, winning confirmation easily.

McLean remained interested in politics during his tenure on the Supreme Court and was even seriously considered as a nominee for the presidency at several national conventions, though his name was withdrawn from consideration each time. His last bid came in 1860, a year before his death, when he was one of the Republican party's candidates. The nomination instead went to ABRAHAM LINCOLN.

While an associate justice on the High Court, McLean wrote a number of significant opinions, including a strong dissent in the *Dred Scott* case of 1857 (DRED SCOTT V. SANDFORD, 60 U.S. 393 (Mem), 19 How. 393, 15 L. Ed. 691). In *Dred Scott*, a slave sued his master for freedom after he had been taken to live on free soil for several years. The Supreme Court held that African Americans could not be U.S. citizens and that Congress could not pass legislation preventing SLAVERY. McLean, however, who had long opposed slavery, argued that Congress could exclude slavery from the territories and could also liberate slaves living in "free" states. McLean's most significant majority opinion came in 1834 in WHEATON V. PETERS, a dispute between two of the Court's reporters of decisions (33 U.S. 591, 8 Pet. 591, 8 L. Ed. 1055 (Mem.) (U.S. Pa., Jan. Term 1834)). Richard Peters sought to republish decisions that had previously been published by HENRY WHEATON, his predecessor. Wheaton, worried that he would sell fewer opinions and thus lose profits, sued Peters, alleging COPYRIGHT infringement. McLean, writing for the Court, held that the opinions were in the public domain and thus no copyright had been violated.

Though McLean enjoyed a long and distinguished career as a jurist, his personal life was less happy. Three of his four daughters died young, as did a brother, and he also lost his first wife in 1840. He and his second wife had one son who died only a few weeks after birth. Though McLean's own health began to fail as early as 1859, he continued to serve on the Court until his death from pneumonia April 4, 1861.

FURTHER READINGS

Cushman, Clare. 1995. *The Supreme Court Justices: Illustrated Biographies 1789–1995*. Washington, D.C.: Congressional Quarterly.

Witt, Elder, ed. 1990. *Guide to the U.S. Supreme Court*. 2d ed. Washington D.C.: Congressional Quarterly.

MCNABB-MALLORY RULE

A federal judicial doctrine that operates to exclude from evidence a confession that is obtained from a person who was not brought before a judicial officer promptly after the person's arrest.

The McNabb-Mallory rule, which is applicable only in federal prosecutions, derives from the U.S. Supreme Court cases of *McNabb v. United States*, 318 U.S. 332, 63 S. Ct. 608, 87 L. Ed. 819 (1943), and *Mallory v. United States*, 354 U.S. 449, 77 S. Ct. 1356, 1 L. Ed. 2d 1479 (1957). The McNabb-Mallory rule is not a constitutional rule but is based on federal law and on the federal judiciary's authority to oversee the administration of criminal justice within the federal courts. The purpose of the rule is to provide protection against an arresting officer's "secret interrogation" of a suspect prior to the suspect's appearance before a judicial officer. Before *McNabb*, authorities could effectively and without penalty delay a suspect's presentment before a judicial officer in order to obtain a confession. *McNabb* held that the penalty for obtaining confessions as a result of such a delay is the exclusion of the confession at trial.

In *McNabb*, a federal revenue agent was killed when agents attempted to arrest members of the McNabb family, a clan of Tennessee mountaineers. The agents subsequently arrested three of the McNabbs and placed them in a detention cell for more than fourteen hours. Over the course of the next two days, federal agents interrogated the McNabbs and finally obtained confessions from them. Based primarily on these confessions, which were admitted into evidence at trial, a jury convicted the McNabbs of second-degree murder. On appeal, however, the U.S. Supreme Court held that the McNabbs' confessions should have been excluded from trial because the federal agents had improperly obtained the confessions by delaying their appearance before a judicial officer. A federal law at the time required federal law officers to take a person charged with any crime before the nearest U.S. commissioner or judicial officer. Relying on this law and on the Court's supervisory authority to oversee justice in the federal court system, the Court held that the confessions should have been excluded from evidence at trial. The Court noted in its decision that the arresting officers had "subjected the accused to the pressures of a procedure which is wholly incompatible with the vital but very restricted duties of the investigating and arresting officers of the Government and which tends to undermine the integrity of the criminal proceeding."

Federal courts questioned whether the *McNabb* EXCLUSIONARY RULE applied only in determining whether a confession was voluntary or whether it applied only when the presentation of the arrested person before a federal magistrate was unnecessarily delayed. Subsequently, the Supreme Court in *Upshaw v. United States,* 335 U.S. 410, 69 S. Ct. 170, 93 L. Ed. 100 (1948), clarified that a confession was "inadmissible if made during the illegal detention due to failure promptly to carry a prisoner before a committing magistrate."

The *McNabb* case preceded the adoption of the Federal Rules of Criminal Procedure in 1944. Rule 5(a) provided that an arresting officer must bring an arrested person "without unnecessary delay" before the nearest available federal magistrate. In *Mallory,* the Court held that the *McNabb* ruling concerning exclusion of improperly obtained confessions applied equally to rule 5(a). Justice FELIX FRANKFURTER, writing for the Court, stated:

> The scheme for initiating a federal prosecution is plainly defined. The police may not arrest upon mere suspicion but only on "probable cause." The next step in the proceeding is to arraign the arrested person before a judicial officer as quickly as possible so that he may be advised of his rights and so that the issue of PROBABLE CAUSE may be promptly determined. The arrested person may, of course, be "booked" by the police. But he is not to be taken to police headquarters in order to carry out a process of inquiry that lends itself, even if not so designed, to eliciting damaging statements to support the arrest and ultimately his guilt.

Because the defendant in *Mallory* had been interrogated for more than seven hours, during which time a judicial officer was readily available for ARRAIGNMENT, the Court held that the defendant's confession should have been excluded from evidence at trial.

The McNabb-Mallory rule is not mandated by the Constitution. As a result, Congress frequently attempted to repeal the McNabb-Mallory rule by legislative act. Finally, in 1968, Congress passed the Omnibus Crime Control and Safe Streets Act (42 U.S.C.A. § 3701 et seq.), which allowed the admission of a confession at trial as long as the confession was "voluntary." The act made the delay in an arrested person's

appearance before a judicial officer one of several factors for the courts to consider in determining whether the person's confession was voluntary and therefore admissible. Nevertheless, Supreme Court cases since *McNabb* and *Mallory* have mandated the McNabb-Mallory rule in certain cases, such as requiring that a person be brought before a federal magistrate promptly after arrest in a case of an arrest without a warrant. The McNabb-Mallory rule stands for the proposition that the federal judiciary may supervise the administration of justice in the federal courts and, in the exercise of that function, exclude evidence obtained in violation of federal law.

Although the McNabb-Mallory rule is not applicable to prosecutions of individuals in state court proceedings, some states have a similar rule. Other states exclude confessions of a defendant only if the confession was involuntarily made during the period of pre-arraignment detention.

FURTHER READINGS

LaFave, Wayne R., and Jerold H. Israel. 1984. *Criminal Procedure.* Vol. 1. St. Paul, Minn.: West.

Rhodes, Mark S. 1985. *Orfield's Criminal Procedure under the Federal Rules.* 2d ed. Rochester, N.Y.: Lawyer's Cooperative.

CROSS-REFERENCES

Criminal Law; Criminal Procedure.

❖ MCREYNOLDS, JAMES CLARK

James Clark McReynolds served as an associate justice of the U.S. Supreme Court from 1914 to 1941. McReynolds was a very conservative justice who gained prominence for his opposition to the NEW DEAL legislation of the 1930s and for his unprecedented number of opinions declaring acts of Congress unconstitutional.

McReynolds was born on February 3, 1862, in Elkton, Kentucky, the son of a prominent surgeon. McReynolds graduated from Vanderbilt University in 1882 and then attended the University of Virginia law school, graduating in 1884. He established a law practice in Nashville and became a successful business attorney. In 1900 he was appointed a professor of law at Vanderbilt.

During the period 1886 to 1900, McReynolds established himself as a conservative Democrat, running unsuccessfully in 1886 for Congress despite substantial Republican support. Although a Democrat, he found favor with Republican president THEODORE ROOSEVELT, who appointed McReynolds assistant U.S. attorney general in 1903. He remained in the JUSTICE DEPARTMENT until 1907.

In that year he moved to New York and joined a large law firm. In 1913 Democratic president WOODROW WILSON appointed McReynolds attorney general. He gained prominence for his prosecution of antitrust cases but left the post in 1914 when Wilson appointed him to the Supreme Court.

McReynolds's conservatism was consistent and unbending. He believed in a restricted role for the federal government, which meant that he opposed federal social and economic regulation. His views matched those of most of his fellow justices during the 1920s and 1930s, but the Great Depression and the New Deal legislation of President FRANKLIN D. ROOSEVELT soon put McReynolds in the spotlight. McReynolds, along with Justices GEORGE SUTHERLAND, WILLIS VAN DEVANTER, and PIERCE BUTLER, a group known as the "Four Horsemen," became the core of opposition to federal efforts to revitalize the economy and create a social safety net. McReynolds voted with the majority to strike down as unconstitutional the NATIONAL INDUSTRIAL RECOVERY ACT, 48 Stat. 195 (1933), in *Schechter Poultry Corporation v. United States,* 295 U.S. 495, 55 S. Ct. 837, 79 L. Ed. 1570 (1935), and the Agricultural Adjustment Act, 7 U.S.C.A. § 601 et seq., in *United States v. Butler,* 297 U.S. 1, 56 S. Ct. 312, 80 L. Ed. 477 (1936).

As McReynolds and the Court struck down each new piece of New Deal legislation, Roosevelt became frustrated. He proposed a "court-packing" plan that would have added additional justices to the Court, in hope of gaining a more

James C. McReynolds.
LIBRARY OF CONGRESS

sympathetic majority. Although Congress rejected Roosevelt's plan, the national debate over the role of the federal government and the recalcitrance of the Supreme Court led more moderate members of the Court to change their positions and vote in favor of New Deal proposals.

McReynolds was outraged at this switch and the resulting expansion of the federal government. Now in the minority, he issued stinging dissents against what he believed were unconstitutional acts by the national government. In *Steward Machine Co. v. Davis,* 301 U.S. 548, 57 S. Ct. 883, 81 L. Ed. 1279 (1937), he dissented from a decision that upheld the SOCIAL SECURITY ACT OF 1935, 42 U.S.C.A. § 301 et seq., castigating the idea that the Constitution gave the federal

"LOGIC AND TAXATION ARE NOT ALWAYS THE BEST FRIENDS."
—JAMES MCREYNOLDS

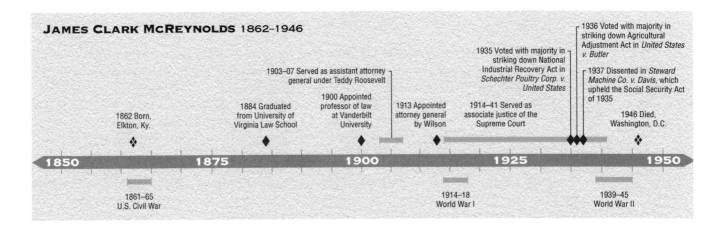

JAMES CLARK MCREYNOLDS 1862–1946

1903–07 Served as assistant attorney general under Teddy Roosevelt

1935 Voted with majority in striking down National Industrial Recovery Act in *Schechter Poultry Corp. v. United States*

1936 Voted with majority in striking down Agricultural Adjustment Act in *United States v. Butler*

1900 Appointed professor of law at Vanderbilt University

1937 Dissented in *Steward Machine Co. v. Davis,* which upheld the Social Security Act of 1935

1862 Born, Elkton, Ky.

1884 Graduated from University of Virginia Law School

1913 Appointed attorney general by Wilson

1914–41 Served as associate justice of the Supreme Court

1946 Died, Washington, D.C.

1850   1875   1900   1925   1950

1861–65 U.S. Civil War

1914–18 World War I

1939–45 World War II

government the right to provide "public charity throughout the United States."

On a personal level, McReynolds ranks as one of the most troubling figures ever to sit on the Court. A virulent anti-Semite, McReynolds treated Justices LOUIS D. BRANDEIS and BENJAMIN N. CARDOZO, both Jews, with undisguised contempt. He refused to sign joint opinions with Brandeis or sit next to Brandeis at official Court ceremonies.

Increasingly isolated, McReynolds retired in 1941. He died on August 24, 1946, in Washington, D.C.

MECHANIC'S LIEN

A charge or claim upon the property of another individual as security for a debt that is created in order to obtain priority of payment of the price or value of work that is performed and materials that are provided in the erection or repair of a building or other structure.

CROSS-REFERENCES

Lien.

MEDIATION

A settlement of a dispute or controversy by setting up an independent person between two contending parties in order to aid them in the settlement of their disagreement.

In INTERNATIONAL LAW, mediation is the friendly interference of one state in the controversies of nations. It is recognized as a proper action to promote peace among nations.

The individual who intervenes in order to help the other parties settle their dispute is called a *mediator*.

CROSS-REFERENCES

Alternative Dispute Resolution.

MEDIATION, INTERNATIONAL LAW

One of the procedures for the peaceful settlement of international disputes is mediation, which is the direct participation by a third country, individual, or organization in resolving a controversy between states. The mediating state may become involved at the request of the parties to the dispute or on its own initiative. In its role as mediator the intervening state will take part in the discussions between the other states and may propose possible solutions. A related procedure is the offer of good offices, where a state will take various actions to bring the conflicting states into negotiations, without necessarily taking part in the discussions leading to settlement.

MEDICAID

A joint federal-state program that provides HEALTH CARE *insurance to low-income persons.*

Medicaid was enacted in 1965 as an amendment to the Social Security Act of 1935 (title XIX, 42 U.S.C.A. § 1396), entitling low-income persons to medical care. The program is a joint federal-state endeavor, with the federal government providing money to the states, which provide additional financing and administer medical programs for the poor that satisfy federal standards. Medicaid has become a major social WELFARE program. By 1995, 34 million people were covered by Medicaid, including 17 million children.

Before 1965, a patchwork of programs financed by state and local governments, along with charities and community hospitals, provided indigent persons with limited health care. Most of these programs provided emergency health care services. President LYNDON B. JOHNSON supported Medicaid as well as MEDICARE legislation for retired persons in 1965. The enactment of Medicaid meant that persons who met federal financial eligibility requirements were entitled to health care.

Medicaid furnishes at least five general categories of treatment: inpatient hospital services, outpatient hospital services, laboratory and X-ray services, skilled nursing home services, and physicians' services. Generally, each of these services is available to treat conditions that cause acute suffering, endanger life, result in illness or infirmity, interfere with the capacity for normal activity, or present a significant handicap. In addition, all states provide eye and dental care and prescription drugs. Almost all states provide physical therapy, hospice care, and rehabilitative services.

Medicaid is a "vendor" plan because payment is made directly to the vendor (the person or entity that provides the services) rather than to the patient. Only approved nursing homes, physicians, and other providers of medical care are entitled to receive Medicaid payments for their services. Since the early 1970s, rising medical costs have placed financial pressures on the

A sample mechanic's lien

Mechanics Lien

NOTICE OF CLAIM OF MECHANICS LIEN

The undersigned claimant hereby claims a mechanic's lien under section

_____

of the Civil Code of the State of _____ and hereby declares the following:

1. That a statement of claimant's demand, after deducting all just credits and offsets, in the sum of

   $_____.

2. That the name of the owner[s], or reputed owner[s] of the property is [are]:

   _____

   _____

3. A general statement of the kind of work done or materials furnished by claimant, or both is:

   _____

   _____

   _____

   _____

4. That the name[s] of the person[s] by whom claimant was employed or to whom claimant furnished the materials is [are]

   _____

   _____

5. A description of the property sought to be charged with the lien is:

   [legal description of property].

DATED: _____   _____
                                          [Signature of Claimant]

Medicaid program. Consequently, health care providers are not fully reimbursed for the services they provide to Medicaid patients. Because of lower reimbursement payments, one-third of physicians limit the number of Medicaid patients they see, and one-quarter of them refuse to accept any Medicaid patients.

The federal government, through statutes and regulations, has enacted an increasing number of criteria for the states to follow in administering the Medicaid program. For example, from 1987 to 1992, the federal government imposed 30 mandates on states that related to eligibility, reimbursement, and services. The intent of these mandates was to reduce variations among the states and to create more consistency in the coverage to low-income persons.

Under federal law, states cannot reduce other welfare benefits that people receive when they become eligible for Medicaid. State plans cannot impose a citizenship or residency requirement other than requiring that an applicant be a resident of the state. No age requirement exists, and everyone receiving welfare may apply for Medicaid. People who are "medically needy" because they are unable to cover costs for their medical care are also eligible, even if their incomes or resources exceed the level that would qualify them for welfare. Beginning in 1988, Medicaid was extended to the "working poor"— low-income persons who have jobs with no health coverage.

When Medicaid began, persons who were eligible had the right to select their own doctors, hospitals, or other medical facilities. Because of skyrocketing medical expenditures, almost all states have received waivers from the federal government concerning the choice of physician. These states now direct most of their Medicaid clients to private, MANAGED CARE programs. *Managed care* is a general term that refers to health plans that attempt to control the cost and quality of care by coordinating medical and other health-related services.

The federal government has also granted waivers to states that prefer to pay for home and community care for elderly beneficiaries who otherwise would end up in nursing homes. This type of care is less expensive than nursing home care and allows state funds to be stretched further.

The federal government reimburses states based mainly on their per capita income. States with high per capita incomes, such as New York and Illinois, receive 50 cents from the federal government for every dollar they spend on Medicaid. Poorer states receive more, with Mississippi receiving reimbursement of 79 percent. The average reimbursement level is 57 percent.

Medicaid FRAUD has plagued the program. The size and complexity of the system, with each state administering Medicaid differently, create opportunity for health care providers and state employees to engage in abuse. It is estimated that ten percent of Medicaid expenditures are paid on fraudulent claims by vendors. Relatively little fraud is attributable to individuals who provide false information to receive Medicaid benefits.

Another problem for Medicaid has been the growing number of middle-class, elderly persons who divest their assets, usually to their children, to meet the Medicaid financial guidelines and qualify for state-paid nursing home care. This practice results in cases where the truly needy cannot find a bed in a nursing home. In addition, the divestiture of assets imposes additional financial pressures on a program that already has difficulty meeting the demands of the truly needy. If an individual or couple gives away or sells a resource at less than fair market value, the SOCIAL SECURITY ADMINISTRATION must report such a transfer to the state Medicaid agency. A TRANSFER OF ASSETS may result in a period of ineligibility for certain Medicaid-covered nursing home services.

The U.S. Supreme Court, in *Wisconsin Department of Health and Family Service v. Blumer,* 534 U.S. 473, 122 S. Ct. 962, 151 L. Ed. 2d 935 (2002), upheld a Medicaid formula for determining Medicaid eligibility for a person needing nursing home care. More than 30 states developed Medicaid rules that used an "income-first" formula, while the remainder of the states used a "resource-first" formula to help determine eligibility for Medicaid assistance and the proper amount of income for the community spouse. The "income-first" rule generally calls upon the community spouse to count more of his or her assets toward his spouse's nursing home care. The "resource-first" rule allows the spouse to keep more assets, in the belief that income from these assets will help to support the community spouse.

The state of Wisconsin used the income-first formula. A married coupled challenged this formula, and the U.S. Supreme Court determined that either formula could be used by a state without violating the Medicare Catastrophic Coverage Act of 1988 (MCCA). The Court placed great emphasis on the fact that the HEALTH AND HUMAN SERVICES DEPARTMENT (HHS) had issued several statements in support of the income-first rule and noted that in late 2001 HHS had proposed a rule that would formalize this support.

The seriousness of these fraudulent transfers led Congress in 1996 to make a person criminally liable who "knowingly and willfully disposes of assets (including by any transfer in trust) in order for an individual to become eligible for medical assistance" (42 U.S.C.A. § 1320a–7b(a)). A person convicted of this offense may be fined $25,000 and imprisoned for five years.

The Balanced Budget Act of 1997 provided a new opportunity for states to further expand HEALTH INSURANCE coverage for children under Medicaid. The legislation created a new State Children's Health Insurance Program under Title XXI of the SOCIAL SECURITY ACT. Funding is available to states for this voluntary program.

A state's allotment may be used to expand Medicaid, to develop a new program or to expand an existing program to provide health insurance to uninsured children, or to implement a combination of the two approaches. Up to ten percent of a state's allotment may be used for administrative costs, outreach, or other health care services for children. The new funds must be used to serve children below age 19 living in families with incomes at or below 200 percent of the federal poverty level.

The increase in state and federal expenditures on Medicaid ($240 billion in 2003) and in federal mandates to states on administration of the program have led to calls for reform. Reform efforts, which have been based on the payment to the states of block grants for medical assistance, have been unsuccessful. President GEORGE W. BUSH asked Congress to consider a block grant program for Medicaid in his 2003 legislative proposals. His proposal would give more authority to the states to set eligibility requirements. By 2003, 45 million people qualified for Medicaid assistance.

FURTHER READINGS

Bove, Alexander A., Jr. 1996. *The Medicaid Planning Handbook: A Guide to Protecting Your Family's Assets from Catastrophic Nursing Home Costs.* 2d ed. Boston: Little Brown.

Bremner, Faith. 2002 "Kempthorne Pleased with Bush Medicaid Reform Plan." *Gannett News Service* (February 24).

CROSS-REFERENCES

Health Care Law; Health Insurance.

MEDICAL EXAMINER

A public official charged with investigating all sudden, suspicious, unexplained, or unnatural deaths within the area of his or her appointed jurisdiction. A medical examiner differs from a CORONER *in that a medical examiner is a physician. Medical examiners have replaced coroners in most states and jurisdictions.*

Medical examiners determine such things as the positive identification of a corpse, the time of death, whether death occurred at the location where the corpse was found, and the manner and cause of death. They conduct autopsies and other medical tests to determine any or all of the details of death. They often work in conjunction with a legal team, such as a state prosecutor's office, and will testify at trial as to their findings and determinations. In that regard, a medical examiner's testimony is that of an expert witness, subject to cross-examination by counsel or refutation by the testimony of other expert witnesses.

MEDICAL MALPRACTICE

Improper, unskilled, or negligent treatment of a patient by a physician, dentist, nurse, pharmacist, or other HEALTH CARE *professional.*

NEGLIGENCE is the predominant theory of liability concerning allegations of medical malpractice, making this type of litigation part of TORT LAW. Since the 1970s, medical malpractice has been a controversial social issue. Physicians have complained about the large number of malpractice suits and have urged legal reforms to curb large damage awards, whereas tort attorneys have argued that negligence suits are an effective way of compensating victims of negligence and of policing the medical profession.

A person who alleges negligent medical malpractice must prove four elements: (1) a duty of care was owed by the physician; (2) the physician violated the applicable standard of care; (3) the person suffered a compensable injury; and (4) the injury was caused in fact and proximately caused by the substandard conduct. The burden of proving these elements is on the plaintiff in a malpractice lawsuit.

Physicians, as professionals, owe a duty of care to those who seek their treatment. This element is rarely an issue in malpractice litigation, because once a doctor agrees to treat a patient, he or she has a professional duty to provide competent care. More important is that the plaintiff must show some actual, compensable injury that is the result of the alleged negligent care. Proof of injury can include the physical effects of the treatment performed by the physician, but it can also include emotional effects. The amount of compensation at issue is usually a highly contested part of the litigation.

Causation may also be a vigorously litigated issue because a physician may allege that the injuries were caused by physical factors unrelated to the allegedly negligent medical treatment. For example, assume that a physician is sued for the negligent prescription of a drug to a patient with coronary artery disease and that the patient died of a heart attack. The plaintiff's estate cannot recover damages for the heart attack unless there is sufficient proof to show that the medication was a contributing cause.

The critical element is standard of care, which is concerned with the type of medical care that a physician is expected to provide. Until the 1960s the standard of care was traditionally regarded as the customary or usual practice of members of the profession. This standard was referred to as the "locality rule," because it recognized the custom within a particular geographic area. This rule was criticized for its potential to protect a low standard of care as long as the local medical community embraced it. The locality rule also was seen as a disincentive for the medical community to adopt better practices.

Most states have modified the locality rule to include both an evaluation of the customary practices of local physicians and an examination of national medical standards. Physicians are called to testify as expert witnesses by both sides in medical malpractice trials because the jury is not familiar with the intricacies of medicine. Standards established by medical specialty organizations, such as the American College of Obstetricians and Gynecologists, are often used by these expert witnesses to address the alleged negligent actions of a physician who practices in that specialty. Nonconformance to these standards is evidence of negligence, whereas conformance supports a finding of due care.

Other rules govern the standard of care evaluation. A few states apply the "respectable minority rule" in evaluating a physician's conduct. This rule holds that a physician is not negligent merely by electing to pursue one of several recognized courses of treatment. Some states use the "error in judgment rule." This principle exempts a physician from liability if the malpractice is based on the physician's error in judgment in choosing among different methods of treatment or in diagnosing a condition.

Medical malpractice litigation began to increase in the 1960s. Tort lawyers were able to break the traditional "conspiracy of silence" that discouraged physicians from testifying about the negligence of colleagues or serving as expert witnesses. By the 1970s physicians alleged that malpractice claims were interfering with their medical practices, with insurance companies either refusing to write malpractice policies for them or charging inflated premiums.

Over the years, physicians and health care providers argued that malpractice claims were also driving up the cost of health care. They contended that jury verdicts in the millions of dollars had to be passed on to the consumer in the form of higher insurance premiums and physician fees. In addition, many physicians were forced to practice "defensive medicine" to guard against malpractice claims. Defensive medicine refers to the conducting of additional tests and procedures that are not medically necessary but that would assist in defeating a negligence claim.

In response to rising malpractice suits, many states pushed for "tort reform" measures. Such measures limit the amount of damages a patient can recover for noneconomic losses, such as pain and suffering, and PUNITIVE DAMAGES. For example, in 1975, California enacted the Medical Injury Compensation Reform Act, which limits recovery of noneconomic damages at $250,000 and restricts the amount of fees that may be recovered by lawyers. Several other states adopted similar measures based on the California model.

The medical community, however, continued to fight for widespread tort reform among the states, and at the national level. They cited insurance increases in the late 1990s and early 2000s, which put further pressure on doctors' and hospitals' earnings—earnings that had been shrinking under MANAGED CARE. Some areas of medicine were particularly hard hit. In New York and Florida, for example, obstetricians, gynecologists, and surgeons—the doctors who are sued the most frequently—pay more than $100,000 a year for $1 million in coverage.

In 2003, President GEORGE W. BUSH addressed the medical community's concerns by endorsing legislation that would place a $250,000 cap on noneconomic damages at the national level. According to Bush, who spoke before an AMERICAN MEDICAL ASSOCIATION (AMA) advocacy conference, "There are too many frivolous lawsuits against good doctors, and the patients are paying the price." The president cited the fact that the federal government suffers losses of $28 million per year as a result of liability insurance and defensive medicine practices.

Critics who contest tort-reform laws argue that medical malpractice awards account for only one percent of the total yearly NATIONAL HEALTH CARE expenditures. They also claim that such reforms protect insurance companies and physicians, and not the patients. Trial attorneys point the finger at the insurance companies. They claim that insurers keep prices artificially low while competing for market share and new revenue. When the economy is sluggish and the market is slow, they increase premiums because they are no longer able to use STOCK MARKET gains to subsidize low rates. Proponents of reform continue to maintain, however, that a federal cap will ultimately result in lower medical costs and greater medical access for the general population.

FURTHER READINGS

Finkelstein, Joel B. March 17, 2003. "Bush to AMA: Tort Reform a Must." *American Medical News.* Available online at <www.ama-assn.org/sci-pubs/amnews/pick_03/gvl10317.htm> (accessed September 9, 2003).

Loiacono, Kristin. 2003. "A Good Fight in the House Over Medical Malpractice 'Reform'." *Trial* 11.

CROSS-REFERENCES

Health Care Law; Managed Care; Patients' Rights; Physicians and Surgeons.

MEDICARE

A federally funded system of health and hospital insurance for persons aged 65 and older and for DISABLED PERSONS.

The Medicare program provides basic HEALTH CARE benefits to recipients of SOCIAL SECURITY and is funded through the Social Security Trust Fund. President HARRY S. TRUMAN first proposed a medical care program for the aged during the late 1940s, but Medicare was not enacted until 1965, as one of President Lyndon B. Johnson's GREAT SOCIETY programs (42 U.S.C.A. §§ 1395 et seq.).

Medicare went into effect in 1966 and was first administered by the SOCIAL SECURITY ADMINISTRATION. In 1977, the Medicare program was transferred to the newly created Health Care Financing Administration (HCFA). The HCFA is concerned with the development of policies, programs, procedures, and guidance regarding Medicare recipients, the providers of services—such as hospitals, nursing homes, and physicians—and other organizations that are closely related to the Medicare program.

Unlike other federal programs, Medicare is not supported by a large, federal organizational hierarchy. The federal government enters into contracts with private insurance companies for the processing of Medicare claims. Health care providers must meet state and local licensing laws and standards set by the HCFA in order to qualify for Medicare payments for their services.

Eligibility for Medicare does not depend on income. Almost everyone aged 65 and older is entitled to Medicare coverage. Disabled persons under age 65 may receive Medicare benefits after they have been collecting Social Security or railroad disability payments for at least two years. Workers do not have to retire at age 65 in order to be protected by Medicare. People who have not worked long enough under Social Security to receive retirement benefits may enroll in the plan by paying a monthly premium. For those individuals who are not covered under Social Security and who are too poor to pay the monthly premium, MEDICAID, the state and federal program for low-income persons, is available.

Medicare is divided into a hospital insurance program and a supplementary medical insurance program. The Medicare hospital insurance plan is funded through Social Security payroll taxes. It covers reasonable and medically necessary treatment in a hospital or skilled nursing home, meals, regular nursing-care services, and the cost of necessary special care. Medicare also pays for home health services and hospice care for terminally ill patients.

The hospital insurance program extends coverage based on "benefit periods." An episode of illness is termed a benefit period and starts when the patient enters the hospital or nursing home facility and ends 60 days after the patient has been discharged from the facility. A new benefit period starts with the next hospital stay, and there is no limit to the number of benefit periods that a person can have. In any benefit period, Medicare will pay the cost of hospitalization for up to 90 days. The patient must pay a one-time deductible fee for the first 60 days in a benefit period and an additional daily fee called a co-payment for hospital care for the following 30 days. Apart from these payments, Medicare covers the full cost of hospital care.

Medicare also pays for the first 20 days of care in a skilled nursing home and for expenses exceeding a daily minimum amount for the next 80 days when certain conditions show that such care is necessary. Payment also may be made for up to 100 home-health visits provided by a home-health agency for up to 12 months after the patient's discharge from a hospital or nursing home, provided that certain conditions apply.

Medicare's supplementary medical insurance program is financed by monthly insurance premiums paid by people who sign up for coverage, combined with money contributed by the federal government. The government contributes the major portion of the cost of the program, which is funded out of general tax revenues. Persons who enroll pay small, annual, deductible fees for any medical costs incurred above that amount during the year, and also a regular monthly premium. Once the deductible has been paid, Medicare pays 80 percent for any bills incurred for physicians' and surgeons' services, diagnostic and laboratory tests, and other services. Doctors are not required to accept Medicare patients, but almost all do. Payments may not be made for routine physical checkups, drugs and medicines, eyeglasses, hearing aids, dentures, or orthopedic shoes.

Medicare bases its 80 percent payment for medical expenses on what is considered to be a reasonable charge for each kind of service. The reasonable charge is an amount that is determined by the insurance organizations that process Medicare claims for the federal government, based on the customary charge for that service in that part of the country.

Medicare payments may be sent directly to the doctor or provider of the service or to the patient. In 1994, 93 percent of all charges to Medicare patients for covered physician services were billed directly to the insurance systems rather than to the patients themselves. Thus, few patients need to be reimbursed for payments that they had made directly to the physician or another provider of services. Under either method, the patient receives a notice after the doctor or provider files a medical insurance claim. The notice details the medical service and explains the expenses that are covered by Medicare and are approved; how much of the charge is credited toward the annual deductible amount; and how much Medicare has paid. A person who disagrees with the decision on the claim may ask the insurance company to review the decision. A formal hearing may be held on claims that, if paid, would total at least $100. Cases that involve $1,000 or more can eventually be appealed to a federal court.

The financial future of Medicare has been a hotly debated issue since the 1980s. In 1995, Medicare covered 37 million people. The number of people eligible for Medicare will continue to rise as the post–World War II baby boom generation begins to retire.

Other factors have had an impact on the financial future of Medicare. The quality of medical care has increased life expectancies.

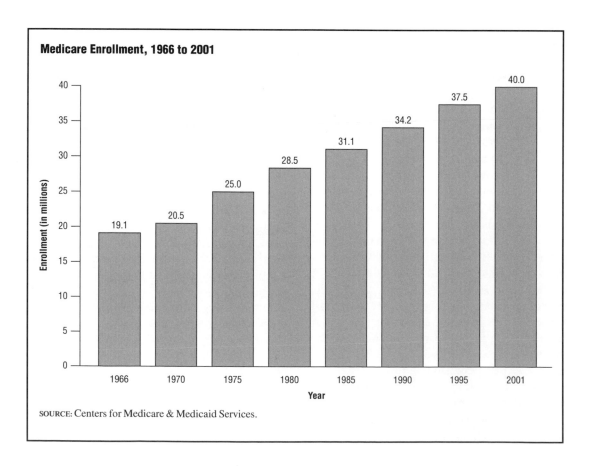

Medicare Enrollment, 1966 to 2001

SOURCE: Centers for Medicare & Medicaid Services.

Nearly three years have been added to life expectancies since Medicare was created. Modern medicine is likely to continue this trend, which means that Medicare will be taking care of people for longer. Another factor is the increased cost of medical care itself, which takes more resources out of the system.

Medicare's hospital insurance is financed by a payroll tax of 2.9 percent, divided equally between employers and workers. The money is placed in a trust fund and is invested in U.S. Treasury SECURITIES. A surplus accumulated during the 1980s and early 1990s, but the program's outlays are projected to rise more rapidly than the future payroll-tax revenues.

Changing the financing of Medicare has proved difficult. In 1988, Congress passed legislation to expand Medicare to cover the health care costs associated with catastrophic illnesses. The new coverage was to be financed by a surtax on the incomes of taxpayers over the age of 65. Elderly citizens and organizations such as the AMERICAN ASSOCIATION OF RETIRED PERSONS vigorously protested the tax. In the face of this opposition, Congress repealed the law in 1989.

In *Fischer v. United States,* 529 U.S. 667 S. Ct. 1780, 146 L. Ed. 2d 707 (2000), the U.S. Supreme Court addressed the issue of criminal aspects with respect to payment of Medicare benefits to an institution. Fischer, while president and part owner of Quality Medical Consultants, Inc. (QMC), negotiated a $1.2 million loan to QMC from West Volusia Hospital Authority (WVHA), a municipal agency that is responsible for operating two Florida hospitals, both of which participate in the federal Medicare program. In 1993 WHVA received between $10 and $15 million in Medicare funds. After a 1994 audit of WHVA raised questions about the QMC loan, the petitioner was indicted for violations of the federal BRIBERY statute, including defrauding an organization that receives benefits under a federal assistance program. A jury convicted him on all counts, and the district court sentenced him to prison, imposed a term of supervised release, and ordered the payment of restitution. On appeal, the petitioner argued that the government had failed to prove WHVA, as the organization affected by his wrongdoing. The U.S. Court of Appeals for the Eleventh Circuit rejected his argument and affirmed his conviction.

In 2003, President George W. Bush and Congress worked together to pass a new law to bring people with Medicare more choices in health care coverage and better health care benefits. The new Medicare Prescription Drug Improvement and Modernization Act of 2003 was passed. This new law preserved and strengthened the Medicare program by adding important new prescription drug and preventive benefits and provides extra help to people with low incomes. Seniors are still able to choose doctors, hospitals, and pharmacies.

If seniors are happy with the Medicare coverage they have, they can keep it exactly the same. Or, if they choose, may enroll in new options. One of the major changes is the Drug Discount Cards which began in 2004. Medicare-Approved Drug Discount Cards will help seniors save on prescription drugs. Medicare will contract with private companies to offer new drug discount cards until a Medicare prescription drug benefit starts in 2006. The cards will save seniors 10–25% on prescription drugs. The enrollment period for the cards is May 2004 through December 31, 2005.

Other highlights of the new law include a Medicare Advantage Plan, new and improved preventive benefits for 2005, prescription drug plans for 2006, and Health Savings Accounts for all Americans, which will work just like an Individual Retirement Account (IRA), whereby Americans will be able to set aside money each year, tax free, in Health Savings Accounts.

For the latest information on Medicare visit the Medicare web site at <www.medicare.gov>

FURTHER READINGS

Channick, Susan Adler. 2003. "The Ongoing Debate Over Medicare: Understanding the Philosophical and Policy Divides." *Journal of Health Law* 36 (winter): 59-106.

CROSS-REFERENCES

Elder Law; Health Care Law; Health Insurance; Managed Care; Physicians and Surgeons; Senior Citizens.

❖ MEESE, EDWIN, III

Edwin Meese III served as U.S. attorney general from 1985 to 1988. A close and trusted advisor to President RONALD REAGAN, Meese sought to advance the president's conservative agenda. His tenure, however, was clouded by allegations of ethical violations that eventually led to his resignation.

Meese was born on December 2, 1931, in Oakland, California. He graduated from Yale

Ed Meese.
BETTMANN/CORBIS

University in 1953 and received his law degree from the University of California School of Law at Berkeley in 1958. From 1958 to 1967, Meese worked as a deputy district attorney for Alameda County, California.

From 1967 to 1969, Meese served then-California governor Ronald Reagan as secretary of legal affairs. In 1969, Meese became executive assistant to the governor, and in the following year he was made chief of staff. After Reagan left

office, Meese worked in business and law, becoming the director of the Center for Criminal Justice and a professor of law at the University of California at San Diego in 1977.

When President Reagan took office in 1981, he appointed Meese as counselor to the president. In that role, Meese became an important advisor on domestic policy. Meese and Reagan shared a common agenda on legal topics. They sought to make ABORTION illegal and to restrict criminal defendants' rights, and were also in agreement on the issues of AFFIRMATIVE ACTION, and judicial activism. Meese helped to reshape the federal judiciary by advising the president on the appointments for more than half the federal judgeships.

In 1984, Reagan nominated Meese to be U.S. attorney general. Meese encountered fierce opposition from Senate Democrats, who questioned his commitment to CIVIL RIGHTS and his personal ethics. Meese admitted that he had paid no interest over 20 months on a $60,000 unsecured loan from a trust headed by John McKean, a California accountant whom he barely knew. McKean was later appointed, with the help of Meese, to the U.S. POSTAL SERVICE board of governors, a part-time position that paid $10,000 a year. This and other charges concerning Meese's personal finances contributed to a 13-month delay in his confirmation. The Senate eventually confirmed Meese, who became attorney general in March 1985.

As attorney general, Meese served as Chairman of the Domestic Policy Council and the National Drug Policy Board and was a member of the NATIONAL SECURITY COUNCIL. Meese

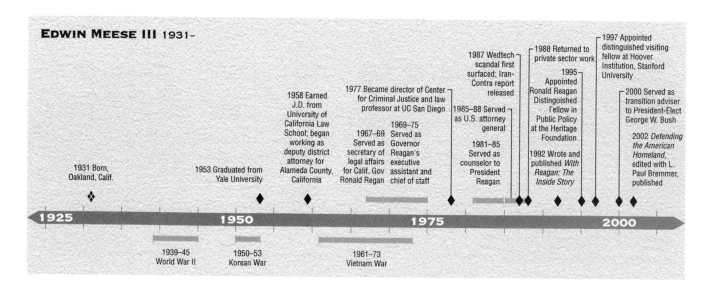

EDWIN MEESE III 1931–

1931 Born, Oakland, Calif.

1953 Graduated from Yale University

1958 Earned J.D. from University of California Law School; began working as deputy district attorney for Alameda County, California

1967–69 Served as secretary of legal affairs for Calif. Gov Ronald Regan

1969–75 Served as Governor Reagan's executive assistant and chief of staff

1977 Became director of Center for Criminal Justice and law professor at UC San Diego

1981–85 Served as counselor to President Reagan

1985–88 Served as U.S. attorney general

1987 Wedtech scandal first surfaced; Iran-Contra report released

1992 Wrote and published *With Reagan: The Inside Story*

1995 Appointed Ronald Reagan Distinguished Fellow in Public Policy at the Heritage Foundation

1988 Returned to private sector work

1997 Appointed distinguished visiting fellow at Hoover Institution, Stanford University

2000 Served as transition adviser to President-Elect George W. Bush

2002 *Defending the American Homeland*, edited with L. Paul Bremmer, published

1925   1950   1975   2000

1939–45 World War II

1950–53 Korean War

1961–73 Vietnam War

sought to establish tough policies against PORNOGRAPHY. He appointed a Commission on Pornography, which issued a controversial two-volume report in 1986 that stated that there was a causal link between violent pornography and aggressive behavior toward women. The report also claimed that nonviolent, sexually explicit material contributed to sexual violence, a conclusion that many social scientists challenged. The report broke new ground in its exploration of the problem of CHILD PORNOGRAPHY.

In 1987, Meese came under scrutiny for his role in the IRAN-CONTRA scandal, which involved a 1985 arms-for-hostages deal with Iran. The key issue in that scandal, which involved presidential aides Oliver L. North and John M. Poindexter, as well as other administration officials, was whether President Reagan had been aware of these activities in 1985. Meese announced on November 24, 1986, that the president had not known about the deal.

A congressional Iran-Contra committee issued its report in November 1987. It stated that Meese had failed to give the president sound legal advice. The report suggested that Meese had not fully investigated the scandal and that he might have participated in a cover-up. In addition, the committee determined that he had failed to take appropriate steps to prevent North and Poindexter from destroying critical evidence. INDEPENDENT COUNSEL Lawrence Walsh, who investigated Iran-Contra, issued a report in 1993 that stated Meese that had made a false statement in 1986 when he said that Reagan had not known about the 1985 deal. Walsh did not seek a criminal charge against Meese because he did not have a key piece of evidence, the notes of former defense secretary Caspar W. Weinberger, until 1991.

While Iran-Contra plagued Meese, a more serious problem arose, known as the Wedtech scandal. The scandal began in February 1987 and grew to involve other highly placed members of the Reagan administration, as well as government officials in New York, where the Wedtech Corporation was located. The Wedtech Corporation sought DEFENSE DEPARTMENT contracts in the early 1980s. The company hired E. Robert Wallach, Meese's former law school classmate and personal attorney, to lobby the government on its behalf. In 1982, Meese helped Wedtech, at Wallach's urging, to get a special hearing on a $32 million Army engine contract, which the Army considered Wedtech unqualified to perform.

Soon after the meeting, the contract was awarded to Wedtech, and one of Meese's top deputies went to work for the corporation. A federal criminal investigation unraveled a string of illegal conduct that led to the conviction of Wallach and other public officials.

Independent Counsel James C. McKay investigated the Wedtech contract and other allegations of misconduct by Meese. In July 1988, he issued his report, which did not call for the filing of any criminal charges against Meese for his actions in Wedtech or his failure to file an income tax return on capital gains. McKay did conclude, however, that Meese may have been "insensitive to the appearance of impropriety."

Following the filing of McKay's 830-page report, Meese announced his resignation, effective at the end of August 1988. Meese claimed that the report vindicated his actions.

In 1992, Meese published his memoirs, *With Reagan: The Inside Story*. In the new millennium, Meese held the Ronald Reagan Chair in Public Policy at the HERITAGE FOUNDATION, a conservative "think tank" based in Washington, D.C. He continued to work as a consultant, writer, and lecturer on a variety of topics including public policy and the American legal system.

FURTHER READINGS

Barrett, John Q. 1998. *All or Nothing, or Maybe Cooperation: Attorney General Power, Conduct, and Judgment in Relation to the Work of an Independent Counsel. Mercer Law Review.* 49 (Winter).

Powell, H. Jefferson. 1999. *The Constitution and the Attorneys General.* Durham, N.C: Carolina Academy Press.

MEETING OF CREDITORS

One of the first steps in federal BANKRUPTCY *proceedings whereby the creditors of a debtor meet in court to present their claims against him or her and a trustee is named to handle the application of the debtor's assets to pay his or her debts.*

MEETING OF MINDS

The mutual agreement and assent of the parties to a contract to its substance and terms.

The "meeting of the minds" that is required to make a contract is not predicated on the subjective purpose or intention of one of the parties that is not brought to the attention of the other party, but it is based on the purpose and intention that has been made known or that, from all the circumstances, should be known.

"CONSTITUTIONAL INTERPRETATION IS NOT THE BUSINESS OF THE COURT ONLY, BUT ALSO PROPERLY THE BUSINESS OF ALL BRANCHES OF GOVERNMENT."
—ED MEESE

MEGAN'S LAW

Megan's Laws are named for Megan Kanka, a seven-year-old girl from New Jersey who was sexually assaulted and murdered in 1994 by a neighbor who, unknown to the victim's family, had been previously convicted for SEX OFFENSES against children. Megan's Laws are state and federal statutes that require convicted sex offenders to register with local police. Sex offenders are required to register with local police and to notify law enforcement authorities whenever they move to a new location. The statutes establish a notification process to provide information about sex offenders to law enforcement agencies and, when appropriate, to the public. The type of notification is based on an evaluation of the risk to the community from a particular offender.

The brutality of the crimes in the Megan Kanka case provided the impetus for laws that mandate registration of sex offenders and corresponding community notification. In 1994, Congress passed the Jacob Wetterling Crimes Against Children and Sexually Violent Offender Registration Act, Title 17, 108 Stat.2038, as amended, 42 U.S.C. § 14071. This precursor to a federal Megan's Law conditioned certain federal law enforcement funds on state adoption of sex-offender registration laws and set minimum standards for state programs. By 1996, every State, the District of Columbia, and the Federal Government had enacted some variation of Megan's Law.

Under the federal Megan's Law statute, states have discretion to establish criteria for disclosure, but they must make private and personal information on registered sex offenders available to the public. The premise of Megan's Law is that communities will be better able to protect their children if they are informed of the descriptions and whereabouts of high-risk sex offenders. Notification of sex-offender information to the community assists law enforcement in investigations, provides legal grounds to detain known sex offenders, may deter sex offenders from committing new offenses, and offers citizens information that they can use to protect their children.

Megan's Laws were not created without controversy. Opponents argue that the statutes encourage acts of VIGILANTISM and do not give offenders who have paid their dues the chance to merge back into society. But actions taken against the convicted sex offender, including VANDALISM of property, verbal or written threats, or actual physical violence against the offender, their family, or employer, could lead to arrest and prosecution for criminal acts. Despite these concerns, however, federal and state legislatures have continued to reinforce and broaden the scope of these statutes.

On May 17, 1996, federal efforts to strengthen the Jacob Wetterling Act got a boost when President BILL CLINTON signed an amendment to the VIOLENT CRIME CONTROL AND LAW ENFORCEMENT ACT OF 1994 (42 U.S.C. 14071); the amendment is known as Megan's Law. This legislation directs all state legislatures to adopt laws requiring convicted sex offenders to register with their local law enforcement agency after release. Additionally, the federal Megan's Law mandates states to grant access to sex-offender registries to the public. Although sex-offender registration for law enforcement purposes had been required previously, the idea of community notification was relatively new.

The legislation has undergone many adaptations in the states. While the details of state Megan's Laws differ from jurisdiction to jurisdiction, conviction of any one or more of the following offenses will require convicts to register pursuant to Megan's Laws:

- aggravated sexual assault,
- sexual assault,
- aggravated criminal sexual contact,
- endangering the welfare of a child by engaging in sexual conduct that would impair or debauch the morals of the child,
- luring or enticing,
- kidnapping (if the victim is a minor and the offender not a parent),
- criminal restraint, and
- false imprisonment.

Megan's Laws have guidelines that list factors law that enforcement agencies are to consider when weighing the risk of re-offense. These include some or all of the following:

- post-incarceration supervision,
- the status of therapy or counseling,
- criminal background,
- degree of remorse for criminal acts,
- substance abuse,
- employment or schooling status,
- psychological or psychiatric profile, and
- any history of threats or of STALKING locations where children congregate.

State sex offender registries include sex offenders' names, descriptions and photographs, addresses, places of employment or school (if applicable), descriptions of the offenders' vehicles and license plate numbers, and brief descriptions of the offenses for which the sex offender was convicted. Prosecutors and courts are responsible for determining who should receive direct notice of the presence of a particular individual in a community.

In 2003, 39 states provided access to sex-offender information in searchable databases on the INTERNET. Arkansas, California, Colorado, Hawaii, Idaho, Maine, Maryland, Massachusetts, Nevada, Rhode Island, and Vermont either did not provide Internet access or restricted access. Various law enforcement agencies and some private citizens or civic groups also publish listings that are specific to counties or communities. Most, if not all, of these sites are freely available regardless of the residence of the individual who is searching for information.

As with the state laws themselves, state sex-offender databases have little or no uniformity. Some, like those for Alaska, Connecticut, and Florida, include photographs, physical descriptions, dates of birth, and details concerning the offenses for which offenders were convicted. The Virginia sex-offender list stores home and work addresses, while Indiana's contains only the city where the sex offender resides.

Most of the databases permit searching by zip code or name. Kansas allows searching by partial zip codes, while Alaska and Delaware allow searching by street name or by partial address, and Indiana permits searching by SOCIAL SECURITY number.

While Megan's Laws do provide some measure of increased security for some parents and individuals who are concerned about the likelihood of convicted sex offenders in their midst, they cannot guarantee the public's protection from offenders who are determined to re-offend. The statutes cannot even guarantee absolute accuracy of the information contained on their registries. While offenders must register with the local police upon release from prison, many give incomplete or even false details. Others have given their details, but have traveled to areas where no one has been warned about them for the purposes of committing additional sex offenses. Critics of the measures point out that only 80 percent of pedophiles comply with registration requirements in the US, as compared

with 97 percent in the United Kingdom. They also note that most cases of CHILD ABUSE occur within the family, and suggest that victims might stay silent if they know that a family member will be prosecuted. But in spite of these arguments, Megan's Laws receive widespread support in communities and legislatures.

In addition to compliance and enforcement problems with Megan's Laws, privacy advocates have challenged existing public-records laws that allow the availability of personal data via websites. In 2003, the U.S. Supreme Court handed down major decisions upholding the constitutionality of Megan's Laws. The Court upheld Connecticut's Megan's Law by a vote of 9 to 0 and upheld Alaska's legislation in a 6-to-3 decision.

In *Connecticut Dept. of Public Safety v. Doe*, 123 S. Ct. 1160, 155 L. Ed. 2d 98, 71 USLW 4125, 71 USLW 4158, 3 Cal. Daily Op. Serv. 1957, 2003 Daily Journal D.A.R. 2471, 16 Fla. L. Weekly Fed. S 140 (2003). Connecticut's Megan's Law was challenged by a convicted sex offender, JOHN DOE. Doe protested that the Internet listing violated his DUE PROCESS rights because he was never given a hearing to disprove the suggestion that he might represent a continuing danger to the community. A federal judge and a three-judge federal appeals court panel agreed with Doe, striking down the law. But the Supreme Court overturned those decisions, stating that the key factor causing sex offenders to be listed in Connecticut's Internet registry is a prior conviction for a sex offense, not whether an individual might present a continued danger to the community.

A California Justice Department exhibit at the 1997 L.A. County Fair provides opportunity to search a database of registered sex offenders. Under the federal Megan's Law statute, states can establish criteria for disclosure but must make information on registered sex offenders available to the public.

AP/WIDE WORLD PHOTOS

The court said that statutes such as Connecticut's Megan's Law provide an important service that helps to protect society from those who would prey on its weakest members. Even though Megan's Laws create certain burdens for sex offenders, the court wrote that such laws do not amount to a form of EX POST FACTO punishment, nor do they violate the Constitution's due process requirements.

In the Alaska case, *Smith v. Doe*, 123 S. Ct. 1140, 155 L. Ed. 2d 164, 71 USLW 4125, 71 USLW 4182, 3 Cal. Daily Op. Serv. 1974, 2003 Daily Journal D.A.R. 2474, 16 Fla. L. Weekly Fed. S. 142 (2003) (No. 01-729). Alaska's Megan's Law was challenged by two convicted sex offenders who already had served their prison sentences prior to passage of that state's version of the law. The two men, John Doe I and John Doe II, argued that the law was another form of punishment imposed after they already had completed their punishment. They claimed that the law failed to recognize the possibility that they might be rehabilitated and that they might no longer pose a danger to others. In previous litigation, a federal judge found no ex post facto violation, but an appeals court panel reversed, striking down the law.

The high court wrote that Alaska's Megan's Law is a civil, non-punitive regulatory effort to account for the whereabouts of convicted sex offenders. Writing for the majority, Justice Kennedy stated that there was nothing in the statute to suggest that the legislature intended to create anything other than a civil scheme designed to protect the public from harm. And even though the law applied to sex offenders who already had been released from prison, it was not an extra form of punishment.

In these two cases, the U.S. Supreme Court effectively disposed of the principal legal arguments against Megan's Laws. In short, the Court found that state laws that are designed to use the Internet to notify parents of the presence of convicted rapists and child molesters in their own neighborhoods do not violate the constitutional rights of the listed sex offenders.

FURTHER READINGS

Ahearn, Laura A. 2001. *Megan's Law Nationwide and. . .The Apple of My Eye: Childhood Sexual Abuse Prevention Program.* N.Y.: Prevention Press USA.

Cohen, Fred, and Elizabeth Rahmberg-Walsh. 2001. *Sex Offender Registration and Community Notification: A 'Megan's Law' SourceBook.* Kingston, N.J.: Civic Research Institute.

Hodgson, James F., and Debra S. Kelley, eds. 2002. *Sexual Violence: Policies, Practices, and Challenges in the United States and Canada.* Westport, Conn: Praeger.

MEMBERSHIP CORPORATION

A company or organization that is formed for purposes other than generating a profit.

Common examples of membership corporations are religious societies and trade unions.

CROSS-REFERENCES

Beneficial Association.

MEMORANDUM

An informal record, in the form of a brief written note or outline, of a particular legal transaction or document for the purpose of aiding the parties in remembering particular points or for future reference.

A memorandum may be used in court to prove that a particular contract was made. For instance, in a real estate transaction, a memorandum can be used to show that the parties to a sale have entered into an agreement to sell a particular parcel at an indicated price, in addition to other details of the agreement. This type of memorandum is also referred to as a binder.

An attorney might use a memorandum to explain and summarize a specific point of law for a judge or for another attorney.

A memorandum decision is a written decision, issued by a court, which reports the ruling, and the decisions and orders of the court. It does not, however, contain an opinion, which is an explanation of the rationale upon which the decision was based.

MEMORANDUM DECISION

A court's decision that gives the ruling (what it decides and orders done), but no opinion (reasons for the decision).

A memorandum decision is not subject to appeal by the dissatisfied party.

MENS REA

As an element of criminal responsibility, a guilty mind; a guilty or wrongful purpose; a criminal intent. Guilty knowledge and wilfulness.

A fundamental principle of CRIMINAL LAW is that a crime consists of both a mental and a physical element. Mens rea, a person's awareness of the fact that his or her conduct is criminal, is the mental element, and *actus reus*, the act itself, is the physical element.

The concept of mens rea developed in England during the latter part of the common-law era (about the year 1600) when judges began to hold that an act alone could not create criminal liability unless it was accompanied by a guilty state of mind. The degree of mens rea required for a particular common-law crime varied. Murder, for example, required a malicious state of mind, whereas LARCENY required a felonious state of mind.

Today most crimes, including common-law crimes, are defined by statutes that usually contain a word or phrase indicating the mens rea requirement. A typical statute, for example, may require that a person act knowingly, purposely, or recklessly.

Sometimes a statute creates criminal liability for the commission or omission of a particular act without designating a mens rea. These are called STRICT LIABILITY statutes. If such a statute is construed to purposely omit criminal intent, a person who commits the crime may be guilty even though he or she had no knowledge that his or her act was criminal and had no thought of committing a crime. All that is required under such statutes is that the act itself is voluntary, since involuntary acts are not criminal.

Occasionally mens rea is used synonymously with the words *general intent*, although general intent is more commonly used to describe criminal liability when a defendant does not intend to bring about a particular result. SPECIFIC INTENT, another term related to mens rea, describes a particular state of mind above and beyond what is generally required.

MENSA ET THORO

[Latin, From bed and board.] A type of DIVORCE *that is a partial termination of the duties of a marital relationship.*

A divorce *mensa et thoro* is one that does not provide a HUSBAND AND WIFE with the right to remarry but that permits them to live separately. Such a divorce does not dissolve the marriage but amounts to a *legal separation.*

MENTAL ANGUISH

When connected with a physical injury, includes both the resultant mental sensation of pain and also the accompanying feelings of distress, fright, and anxiety. As an element of damages implies a relatively high degree of mental pain and distress; it is more than mere disappointment, anger, worry, resentment, or embarrassment, although it may include all of these, and it includes mental sensation of pain resulting from such painful emotions as grief, severe disappointment, indignation, wounded pride, shame, despair, and/or public humiliation. In other connections, and as a ground for DIVORCE *or for compensable damages or an element of damages, it includes the mental suffering resulting from the excitation of the more poignant and painful emotions, such as grief, severe disappointment, indignation, wounded pride, shame, public humiliation, despair, etc.*

MENTAL CRUELTY

A course of conduct on the part of one spouse toward the other spouse that can endanger the mental and physical health and efficiency of the other spouse to such an extent as to render CONTINUANCE *of the marital relation intolerable. As a ground for* DIVORCE, *it is conduct that causes embarrassment, humiliation, and anguish so as to render life miserable and unendurable or to cause a spouse's life, person, or health to become endangered.*

❖ MENTSCHIKOFF, SOIA

Soia Mentschikoff was a distinguished legal scholar and educator whose career encompassed several "firsts" for women in the legal profession.

Mentschikoff was born April 2, 1915, in Russia where her father, a resident of New York City, was working. In 1918 her family returned to New York where Mentschikoff graduated from Hunter College in 1934 and from Columbia Law School in 1937.

At Columbia Mentschikoff met KARL LLEWELLYN, a professor of law and the chief reporter, or drafter, of the UNIFORM COMMERCIAL CODE (UCC) for the American Law Institute (the Uniform Commercial Code is a model for laws dealing with business and commercial transactions that has been adopted, at least in part, by all the states, except Louisiana, and the District of Columbia). Initially, Mentschikoff worked with Llewellyn on the UCC as his research assistant; from 1949 through 1954 she was the associate chief reporter of the code. Subsequently, she became a consultant to the Permanent Editorial Board for the UCC.

After the UCC was completed, Mentschikoff became increasingly interested in the interna-

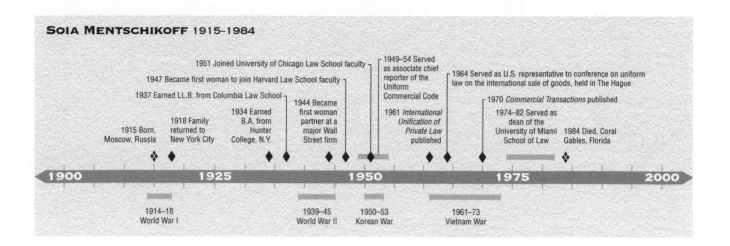

SOIA MENTSCHIKOFF 1915–1984

1951 Joined University of Chicago Law School faculty

1947 Became first woman to join Harvard Law School faculty

1937 Earned LL.B. from Columbia Law School

1949–54 Served as associate chief reporter of the Uniform Commercial Code

1964 Served as U.S. representative to conference on uniform law on the international sale of goods, held in The Hague

1934 Earned B.A. from Hunter College, N.Y.

1944 Became first woman partner at a major Wall Street firm

1970 *Commercial Transactions* published

1915 Born, Moscow, Russia

1918 Family returned to New York City

1961 *International Unification of Private Law* published

1974–82 Served as dean of the University of Miami School of Law

1984 Died, Coral Gables, Florida

1900   1925   1950   1975   2000

1914–18 World War I

1939–45 World War II

1950–53 Korean War

1961–73 Vietnam War

tional aspects of COMMERCIAL LAW. In 1964 she was one of the U.S. representatives at a diplomatic conference held at The Hague to consider a uniform law on the international sale of goods. She later became an adviser to the STATE DEPARTMENT on matters involving international sales and international ARBITRATION.

In 1947 Mentschikoff joined the faculty at the Harvard Law School, the first time a woman had taught at that school. Three years earlier in 1944, she had achieved another first by becoming the first woman partner at a major Wall Street firm. In 1951 Mentschikoff and Llewellyn, whom she had married in 1947, joined the faculty at the University of Chicago Law School. To satisfy the school's anti-nepotism rule, Llewellyn was named a "professor" while Mentschikoff was a "professorial lecturer" until his death in 1962 when she became a professor. In 1974 Mentschikoff became the dean of the University of Miami School of Law, a position that she held until 1982.

Mentschikoff died June 18, 1984, in Coral Gables, Florida.

MERCANTILE

Relating to trade or commerce; commercial; having to do with the business of buying and selling; relating to merchants.

A *mercantile agency* is an individual or company in the business of collecting data about the financial status, ability, and credit of individuals who are engaged in business. Once this information is compiled, it is sold by the agency to its customers, who are known as subscribers. Mercantile agencies are known as credit bureaus in current usage.

MERCHANTABLE

Salable; of quality and type ordinarily acceptable among vendors and buyers.

An item is deemed merchantable if it is reasonably fit for the ordinary purposes for which such products are manufactured and sold. For example, soap is merchantable if it cleans. In general, a seller or manufacturer is required by law to make products of merchantable quality. In the event that the items do not meet with the proper standards, a suit can be brought against the seller or manufacturer by anyone who is injured as a result.

CROSS-REFERENCES

Product Liability; Sales Law.

MERCIAN LAW

A major body of Anglo-Saxon customs that, along with the Dane law and the West Saxon law, continued to constitute the law in England in the days immediately following the Norman Conquest.

MERCY KILLING

See EUTHANASIA.

❖ MEREDITH, JAMES HOWARD

CIVIL RIGHTS pioneer and activist James Howard Meredith put his life at risk by being the first African American to attend the University of Mississippi in 1962. After the state repeatedly blocked his attempts to register at the university, a legal battle waged by Meredith and the National Association for the Advancement of Colored People (NAACP) achieved a landmark victory for INTEGRATION. When violence erupted on the day that Meredith enrolled, President JOHN F. KENNEDY sent several thousand U.S. Army troops to the campus to quell bloody rioting. Armed federal marshals protected Meredith in every classroom until he graduated in 1963. In 1966, the James Meredith March against Fear united traditional and radical civil rights leaders in a voter-registration march across Mississippi. Meredith was shot, but he recovered and joined MARTIN LUTHER KING, JR., and others in a month-long demonstration that marked a turning point in the civil rights struggle. In later years, Meredith, who had always maintained independence from the inheritors of the CIVIL RIGHTS MOVEMENT, became one of their sharpest critics.

Meredith was born June 25, 1933, in Kosciusko, Mississippi. He was one of ten children of Roxy Patterson Meredith and Moses Cap, a poor farmer in Kosciusko. As a young child, Meredith became aware of racism. He would refuse the nickels and dimes that a local white man regularly gave to black children, calling the gifts degrading. More painful was the realization he made as a young man on a trip to visit relatives in Detroit, where he saw blacks and whites sharing the same public facilities. He rode the train home from this brush with integration, and when he arrived in Memphis, the conductor told him to leave the whites-only car. "I cried all the way home," Meredith later recalled, "and vowed to devote myself to changing the degrading conditions of black people." He also had other ambitions and goals. Ever since a childhood visit to a white doctor's office, he had harbored a dream of attending the University of Mississippi, the physician's alma mater.

After high school, in 1951, Meredith joined the U.S. Air Force. He rose to the rank of staff sergeant, earned credits toward a college degree,

James Meredith.
AP/WIDE WORLD PHOTOS

and served in the KOREAN WAR. Following his discharge in 1960, he attended the all-black Jackson State College, but the courses he wanted to take were offered only at the state university. As a 28-year-old, he followed with hopefulness the speeches of President John F. Kennedy, which promised greater enjoyment of opportunity for all U.S. citizens. Change was in the air, and many African Americans were heartened by the portents in Kennedy's 1961 inaugural address. On the same day that Kennedy became president, Meredith applied for admission to the University of Mississippi.

The school turned down his application. Mississippi still practiced SEGREGATION, and

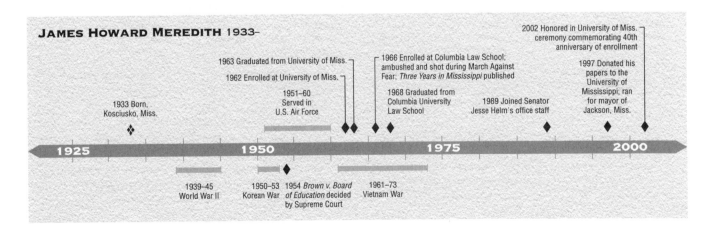

JAMES HOWARD MEREDITH 1933–

2002 Honored in University of Miss. ceremony commemorating 40th anniversary of enrollment

1963 Graduated from University of Miss.

1966 Enrolled at Columbia Law School; ambushed and shot during March Against Fear; *Three Years in Mississippi* published

1997 Donated his papers to the University of Mississippi; ran for mayor of Jackson, Miss.

1962 Enrolled at University of Miss.

1951–60 Served in U.S. Air Force

1968 Graduated from Columbia University Law School

1989 Joined Senator Jesse Helm's office staff

1933 Born, Kosciusko, Miss.

1925   1950   1975   2000

1939–45 World War II

1950–53 Korean War

1954 *Brown v. Board of Education* decided by Supreme Court

1961–73 Vietnam War

that meant that no African Americans could attend the all-white university. Even seven years after BROWN V. BOARD OF EDUCATION 347 U.S. 483, 74 S. Ct. 686, 98 L. Ed. 873 (1954), southern states resisted complying with the U.S. Supreme Court's decision that compulsory segregation was unconstitutional. Knowing that he had a constitutional right that the state refused to recognize, Meredith turned to the NAACP Legal Defense and Education Fund. This arm of the civil rights organization, accustomed to fighting segregation cases, extended help to him. Meredith and his attorneys fought some 30 court actions against the state.

At last, a federal court ruled that a qualified student could not be denied admission on the ground of race. Meredith had won, but the court order infuriated segregationists. Playing to popular sentiment, Mississippi Governor Ross Barnett promised to stop Meredith. Barnett pressured the state legislature to give him authority over university admissions, a power that usually was exercised by the state college board.

As Meredith's enrollment date, September 20, 1962, approached, Meredith received death threats; Barnett continued to promise to prevent his enrollment; and segregationists spread the word to be at "Ole Miss" to save it from integration. On the day that Meredith arrived to register, white students massed around a Confederate flag chanting anti-integration slogans. Barnett stood blocking the door to the admissions office. A university official read a proclamation naming Barnett as acting registrar, by order of the university's board of trustees, and a satisfied Barnett told Meredith that his application was denied.

The governor's action was purportedly good politics in his home state. Across the South, leaders such as Alabama Governor GEORGE WALLACE were prospering politically by staging similar acts of defiance. However, Barnett's refusal to let Meredith in was a serious problem for Washington, D.C. It represented a challenge to the authority of the federal courts, and in a short time, the JUSTICE DEPARTMENT entered the dispute. Attorney General ROBERT F. KENNEDY confronted Barnett, demanding assurances that Meredith's next attempt to register would be successful and that the student would be protected. Barnett gave none. He replied that the situation was beyond his control. Where civil rights were concerned, the young attorney general was quickly learning that only federal intervention could bring the southern states under

the mandate of the courts. He sent 500 federal marshals to the University of Mississippi campus with strict orders: They were to protect Meredith, but not to shoot anyone. Only tear gas and clubs were to be used for their own defense.

On September 30, Meredith arrived at Ole Miss to try to enroll for a second time. Protected by the marshals, he finally registered, and then took refuge in his dormitory. Students and outsiders gathered in front of the school's administration building, known as the Lyceum. The angry mob began throwing rocks at the outnumbered marshals, who were soon besieged by thousands of new protesters streaming onto the campus. A vicious riot erupted, with the armed agitators firing shots and hurling rocks, bricks, bottles, flaming gas, and acid. By late evening on the day Meredith registered, a French journalist and an onlooker were dead. More than 160 marshals were wounded; the rest were exhausted, and their tear gas supply was running out. Reluctantly, Kennedy dispatched 5,000 Army troops to Ole Miss; their numbers were finally enough to disperse the mob and to regain control of the battered campus.

Meredith attended classes under armed guard, but persevered, graduating in August 1963. By the summer of 1966, Meredith was enrolled at Columbia University School of Law, but he interrupted his studies to launch a bold personal demonstration for civil rights. Meredith announced plans to march across the state of Mississippi, covering the 220 miles from Memphis to Jackson in 16 days. The James Meredith March against Fear would show African Americans that they could safely assert their right to vote, despite years of legal obstruction, harassment, and murder. As he had done at Ole Miss, Meredith ignored several death threats, proclaiming that he would survive his long march along the state's back roads.

On June 5, 1966, Meredith set out from Memphis with an ebony walking stick that an African chieftain had given him. When he crossed into Mississippi the following morning, he was ambushed and shot; remarkably, he survived. His assailant, an unemployed member of the KU KLUX KLAN, pleaded guilty and received a five-year prison sentence (of which three years were suspended). While Meredith recovered in his hospital bed, he was visited by the leaders of major civil rights organizations. A group including STOKELY CARMICHAEL, of the STUDENT NON-VIOLENT COORDINATING COMMITTEE

(SNCC), and Dr. King wanted to stage a protest. Meredith wanted to go on. He continued the march joined by other civil rights workers.

The marchers completed their journey by late June against often-violent opposition. It was a great symbolic victory for civil rights, but the movement itself had begun to factionalize. King and his supporters, who advocated peaceful resistance, were at odds with Carmichael's BLACK POWER MOVEMENT, which advocated violence if necessary to secure equal rights for African Americans.

Meredith returned to Columbia, completing his law degree in 1968. In the years that followed, Meredith embarked on a series of pursuits. He studied economics at a Nigerian university, established the African Development and Reunification Association, and worked as a consultant, financial planner, tree farmer, and educator.

In the 1980s, Meredith returned to the public eye, this time as a critic of integration, WELFARE, and AFFIRMATIVE ACTION, programs that he believed did more to hurt black people than to help them. He joined the staff of conservative senator JESSE HELMS and later supported former Ku Klux Klan member David Duke, whose welfare views he praised, in Duke's campaign for governor of Louisiana. He also took a series of walks that were reminiscent of his 1966 march, to promote his conservative vision. Meredith is the author of *Three Years in Mississippi* (1966).

Meredith published an historical work entitled *Mississippi: A Volume of Eleven Books* in 1995. In March 1997, the University of Mississippi's J.D. Williams Library accepted Meredith's donation of his personal papers, which are now housed in the library's Special Collections branch. In September 2002, Meredith was a participant in a forum sponsored by the Kennedy Library to commemorate the 40th anniversary of his admission to the University of Mississippi.

FURTHER READINGS

Doyle, William. 2001. *An American Insurrection: The Battle of Oxford, Mississippi, 1962.* New York: Doubleday.

Harris, Janet. 1967. *The Long Freedom Road: The Civil Rights Story.* Blue Ridge Summit, Pa.: McGrawHill.

Levy, Peter B. 1992. *Let Freedom Ring: A Documentary History of the Modern Civil Rights Movement.* New York: Praeger.

Motley, Constance Baker. 1999. *Equal Justice Under Law: An Autobiography.* New York: Farrar Straus and Giroux.

Weisbrot, Robert. 1990. *Freedom Bound: A History of America's Civil Rights Movement.* New York: Norton.

MERGER

The combination or fusion of one thing or right into another thing or right of greater or larger importance so that the lesser thing or right loses its individuality and becomes identified with the greater whole.

In contract law, agreements are merged when one contract is absorbed into another. The merger of contracts is generally based on the language of the agreement and the intent of the parties. The merger of contracts is not the same as a merger clause, which is a provision in a contract stating that the written terms cannot be varied by prior or oral agreements.

Estates affecting ownership of land are merged where a greater estate and a lesser estate coincide and are held by the same individual. For example, merger occurs when a person who leases land from another subsequently is given ownership of it upon the death of the lessor who has so provided in his will.

In CRIMINAL LAW, the commission of a major crime that includes a lesser offense results in the latter being merged in the former. For example, the crime of rape includes the lesser offense of SEXUAL ABUSE which is merged into one prosecution for rape.

CROSS-REFERENCES

Lesser Included Offense; Mergers and Acquisitions.

MERGERS AND ACQUISITIONS

Methods by which corporations legally unify ownership of assets formerly subject to separate controls.

A merger or acquisition is a combination of two companies where one corporation is completely absorbed by another corporation. The less important company loses its identity and becomes part of the more important corporation, which retains its identity. A merger extinguishes the merged corporation, and the surviving corporation assumes all the rights, privileges, and liabilities of the merged corporation. A merger is not the same as a consolidation, in which two corporations lose their separate identities and unite to form a completely new corporation.

Federal and state laws regulate mergers and acquisitions. Regulation is based on the concern that mergers inevitably eliminate competition between the merging firms. This concern is most acute where the participants are direct rivals, because courts often presume that such arrangements are more prone to restrict output and to increase prices. The fear that mergers and acquisitions reduce competition has meant that the government carefully scrutinizes proposed mergers. On the other hand, since the 1980s, the federal government has become less aggressive in seeking the prevention of mergers.

Despite concerns about a lessening of competition, U.S. law has left firms relatively free to buy or sell entire companies or specific parts of a company. Mergers and acquisitions often result in a number of social benefits. Mergers can bring better management or technical skill to bear on underused assets. They also can produce economies of scale and scope that reduce costs, improve quality, and increase output. The possibility of a takeover can discourage company managers from behaving in ways that fail to maximize profits. A merger can enable a business owner to sell the firm to someone who is already familiar with the industry and who would be in a better position to pay the highest price. The prospect of a lucrative sale induces entrepreneurs to form new firms. Finally, many mergers pose few risks to competition.

Antitrust merger law seeks to prohibit transactions whose probable anticompetitive consequences outweigh their likely benefits. The critical time for review usually is when the merger is first proposed. This requires enforcement agencies and courts to forecast market trends and future effects. Merger cases examine past events or periods to understand each merging party's position in its market and to predict the merger's competitive impact.

Types of Mergers

Mergers appear in three forms, based on the competitive relationships between the merging parties. In a horizontal merger, one firm acquires another firm that produces and sells an identical or similar product in the same geographic area and thereby eliminates competition between the two firms. In a VERTICAL MERGER, one firm acquires either a customer or a supplier. Conglomerate mergers encompass all other acquisitions, including pure conglomerate transactions where the merging parties have no evident relationship (e.g., when a shoe producer buys an appliance manufacturer), geographic extension mergers, where the buyer makes the same product as the target firm but does so in a different geographic market (e.g., when a

baker in Chicago buys a bakery in Miami), and product-extension mergers, where a firm that produces one product buys a firm that makes a different product that requires the application of similar manufacturing or marketing techniques (e.g., when a producer of household detergents buys a producer of liquid bleach).

Corporate Merger Procedures

State statutes establish procedures to accomplish corporate mergers. Generally, the board of directors for each corporation must initially pass a resolution adopting a plan of merger that specifies the names of the corporations that are involved, the name of the proposed merged company, the manner of converting shares of both corporations, and any other legal provision to which the corporations agree. Each corporation notifies all of its shareholders that a meeting will be held to approve the merger. If the proper number of shareholders approves the plan, the directors sign the papers and file them with the state. The SECRETARY OF STATE issues a certificate of merger to authorize the new corporation.

Some statutes permit the directors to abandon the plan at any point up to the filing of the final papers. States with the most liberal corporation laws permit a surviving corporation to absorb another company by merger without submitting the plan to its shareholders for approval unless otherwise required in its certificate of incorporation.

Statutes often provide that corporations that are formed in two different states must follow the rules in their respective states for a merger to be effective. Some corporation statutes require the surviving corporation to purchase the shares of stockholders who voted against the merger.

Competitive Concerns

Horizontal, vertical, and conglomerate mergers each raise distinctive competitive concerns.

Horizontal Mergers Horizontal mergers raise three basic competitive problems. The first is the elimination of competition between the merging firms, which, depending on their size, could be significant. The second is that the unification of the merging firms' operations might create substantial market power and might enable the merged entity to raise prices by reducing output unilaterally. The third problem is that, by increasing concentration in the relevant market, the transaction might strengthen the ability of the market's remaining participants to coordinate their pricing and output decisions. The fear is not that the entities will engage in secret collaboration but that the reduction in the number of industry members will enhance tacit coordination of behavior.

Vertical Mergers Vertical mergers take two basic forms: forward INTEGRATION, by which a firm buys a customer, and backward integration, by which a firm acquires a supplier. Replacing market exchanges with internal transfers can offer at least two major benefits. First, the vertical merger internalizes all transactions between a manufacturer and its supplier or dealer, thus converting a potentially adversarial relationship into something more like a partnership. Second, internalization can give management more effective ways to monitor and improve performance.

Vertical integration by merger does not reduce the total number of economic entities operating at one level of the market, but it might change patterns of industry behavior. Whether a forward or backward integration, the newly acquired firm may decide to deal only with the acquiring firm, thereby altering competition among the acquiring firm's suppliers, customers, or competitors. Suppliers may lose a market for their goods; retail outlets may be deprived of supplies; or competitors may find that both supplies and outlets are blocked. These possibilities raise the concern that vertical integration will foreclose competitors by limiting their access to sources of supply or to customers. Vertical mergers also may be anticompetitive because their entrenched market power may impede new businesses from entering the market.

Conglomerate Mergers Conglomerate transactions take many forms, ranging from short-term joint ventures to complete mergers. Whether a conglomerate merger is pure, geographical, or a product-line extension, it involves firms that operate in separate markets. Therefore, a conglomerate transaction ordinarily has no direct effect on competition. There is no reduction or other change in the number of firms in either the acquiring or acquired firm's market.

Conglomerate mergers can supply a market or "demand" for firms, thus giving entrepreneurs liquidity at an open market price and with a key inducement to form new enterprises. The threat of takeover might force existing managers to increase efficiency in competitive markets.

Conglomerate mergers also provide opportunities for firms to reduce capital costs and overhead and to achieve other efficiencies.

Conglomerate mergers, however, may lessen future competition by eliminating the possibility that the acquiring firm would have entered the acquired firm's market independently. A conglomerate merger also may convert a large firm into a dominant one with a decisive competitive advantage, or otherwise make it difficult for other companies to enter the market. This type of merger also may reduce the number of smaller firms and may increase the merged firm's political power, thereby impairing the social and political goals of retaining independent decision-making centers, guaranteeing small business opportunities, and preserving democratic processes.

Federal Antitrust Regulation

Since the late nineteenth century, the federal government has challenged business practices and mergers that create, or may create, a MONOPOLY in a particular market. Federal legislation has varied in effectiveness in preventing anticompetitive mergers.

Sherman Anti-Trust Act of 1890 The SHERMAN ANTI-TRUST ACT (15 U.S.C.A. §§ 1 et seq.) was the first federal antitrust statute. Its application to mergers and acquisitions has varied, depending on its interpretation by the U.S. Supreme Court. In *Northern Securities Co. v. United States,* 193 U.S. 197, 24 S. Ct. 436, 48 L. Ed. 679 (1904), the Court ruled that all mergers between directly competing firms constituted a combination in restraint of trade and that they therefore violated Section 1 of the Sherman Act. This decision hindered the creation of new monopolies through horizontal mergers.

In *Standard Oil Co. of New Jersey v. United States,* 221 U.S. 1, 31 S. Ct. 502, 55 L. Ed. 619 (1911), however, the Court adopted a less stringent "rule of reason test" to evaluate mergers. This rule meant that the courts must examine whether the merger would yield monopoly control to the merged entity. In practice, this resulted in the approval of many mergers that approached, but did not achieve, monopoly power.

Clayton Anti-Trust Act of 1914 Congress passed the CLAYTON ACT (15 U.S.C.A. §§ 12 et seq.) in response to the *Standard Oil Co. of New Jersey* decision, which it feared would undermine the Sherman Act's ban against trade restraints and monopolization. Among the provisions of the Clayton Act was Section 7, which barred anticompetitive stock acquisitions.

The original Section 7 was a weak anti-merger safeguard because it banned only purchases of stock. Businesses soon realized that they could evade this measure simply by buying the target firm's assets. The U.S. Supreme Court, in *Thatcher Manufacturing Co. v. Federal Trade Commission,* 272 U.S. 554, 47 S. Ct. 175, 71 L. Ed. 405 (1926), further undermined Section 7 by allowing a firm to escape liability if it bought a controlling interest in a rival firm's stock and used this control to transfer to itself the target's assets before the government filed a complaint. Thus, a firm could circumvent Section 7 by quickly converting a stock acquisition into a purchase of assets.

By the 1930s, Section 7 was eviscerated. Between the passage of the Clayton Act in 1914 and 1950, only 15 mergers were overturned under the ANTITRUST LAWS, and ten of these dissolutions were based on the Sherman Act. In 1950, Congress responded to post–World War II concerns that a wave of corporate acquisitions was threatening to undermine U.S. society, by passing the Celler-Kefauver Antimerger Act, which amended Section 7 of the Clayton Act to close the assets loophole. Section 7 then prohibited a business from purchasing the stock or assets of another entity if "the effect of such acquisition may be substantially to lessen competition, or to tend to create a monopoly."

Congress intended the amended section to reach vertical and conglomerate mergers, as well as horizontal mergers. The U.S. Supreme Court, in *Brown Shoe Co. v. United States,* 370 U.S. 294, 82 S. Ct. 1502, 8 L. Ed. 2d 510 (1962), interpreted the amended law as a congressional attempt to retain local control over industry and to protect small business. The Court concluded that it must look at the merger's actual and likely effect on competition. In general, however, it relied almost entirely on market share and concentration figures in evaluating whether a merger was likely to be anticompetitive. Nevertheless, the general presumption was that mergers were suspect.

In *United States v. General Dynamics,* 415 U.S. 486, 94 S. Ct. 1186, 39 L. Ed. 2d 530 (1974), the Court changed direction. It rejected any antitrust analysis that focused exclusively on market-share statistics, cautioning that although statistical data can be of great significance, they are "not conclusive indicators of anticompetitive effects." A merger must be viewed in the context of its particular industry. Therefore, the Court held that "only a further examination of the particular market—its structure, history, and probable future—can provide the appropriate setting for judging the probable anticompetitive effect of the merger." This totality-of-the-circumstances approach has remained the standard for conducting an antitrust analysis of a proposed merger.

Federal Trade Commission Act of 1975 Section 5 of the FEDERAL TRADE COMMISSION Act (15 U.S.C.A. § 45), prohibits "unfair method[s] of competition" and gives the Federal Trade Commission (FTC) independent jurisdiction to enforce the antitrust laws. The law provides no criminal penalties, and it limits the FTC to issuing prospective decrees. The JUSTICE DEPARTMENT and the FTC share enforcement of the Clayton Act. Congress gave this authority to the FTC because it thought that an administrative body would be more responsive to congressional goals than would the courts.

Hart-Scott-Rodino Antitrust Improvements Act of 1976 The Hart-Scott-Rodino Antitrust Improvements Act (HSR) (15 U.S.C.A. § 18a) established a mandatory premerger notification procedure for firms that are parties to certain mergers. The HSR process requires the merging parties to notify the FTC and the Department of Justice before completing certain transactions. In general, an HSR premerger filing is required when (a) one of the parties to the transaction has annual net sales (or revenues) or total assets exceeding $100 million and the other party has annual net sales (or revenues) or total assets exceeding $10 million; and (b) the acquisition price or value of the acquired assets or entity exceeds $15 million. Failure to comply with these requirements may result in the RESCISSION of completed transactions and may be punished by a civil penalty of up to $10,000 per day.

HSR also established mandatory waiting periods during which the parties may not "close" the proposed transaction and begin joint operations. In transactions other than cash tender offers, the initial waiting period is 30 days after the merging parties have made the requisite premerger notification filings with the federal agencies. For cash tender offers, the waiting period is 15 days after the premerger filings. Before the initial waiting periods expire, the federal agency that is responsible for reviewing the transaction may request the parties to supply additional information relating to the proposed merger. These "second requests" often include extensive interrogatories (lists of questions to be answered) and broad demands for the production of documents. A request for further information may be made once, and the issuance of a second request extends the waiting period for ten days for cash tender offers and 20 days for all other transactions. These extensions of the waiting period do not begin until the merging parties are in "substantial compliance" with the government agency's request for additional information.

If the federal government decides not to challenge a merger before the HSR waiting period expires, a federal agency is highly unlikely to sue at a late date to dissolve the transaction under Section 7 of the Clayton Act. The federal government is not legally barred from bringing such a lawsuit, but the desire of the federal agencies to increase predictability for business planners has made the HSR process the critical period for federal review. However, the decision of a federal agency not to attack a merger during the HSR waiting period does not preclude a lawsuit by a state government or a private entity. To facilitate analysis by the state attorneys general, the National Association of Attorneys General (NAAG) has issued a Voluntary Pre-Merger Disclosure Compact under which the merging parties can submit copies of their federal HSR filings and the responses to second requests with NAAG for circulation among states that have adopted the compact.

Merger Guidelines

In the vast majority of antitrust challenges to mergers and acquisitions, the matters have been resolved by consent order or decree. The Department of Justice and the FTC have sought to clarify they way they analyze mergers through merger guidelines issued May 5, 1992 (4 Trade Reg. Rep. [CCH] ¶ 13,104). These guidelines are not "law" but enforcement-policy statements. Nevertheless, the antitrust enforcement agencies will use them to analyze proposed transactions.

The 1992 merger guidelines state that most horizontal mergers and acquisitions aid competition and that they are beneficial to consumers. The intent of issuing the guidelines is to "avoid unnecessary interference with the larger universe of mergers that are either competitively beneficial or neutral."

The guidelines prescribe five questions for identifying hazards in proposed horizontal mergers: Does the merger cause a significant increase in concentration and produce a concentrated market? Does the merger appear likely to cause adverse competitive effects? Would entry sufficient to frustrate anticompetitive conduct be timely and likely to occur? Will the merger generate efficiencies that the parties could not reasonably achieve through other means? Is either party likely to fail, and will its assets leave the market if the merger does not occur?

The guidelines essentially ask which products or firms are now available to buyers, and where could buyers turn for supplies if relative prices increased by five percent (the measure for assessing a merger-generated price increase). The guidelines redraw market boundaries to cover more products and a greater area, which tends to yield lower concentration increases than U.S. Supreme Court merger decisions of the 1960s.

Mergers in the Telecommunications Industry

Beginning in 1980, with President Ronald Reagan's administration, the federal government has adjusted its policies to allow more horizontal mergers and acquisitions. The states have responded by invoking their antitrust laws to scrutinize these types of transactions. Nevertheless, mergers and acquisitions have increased throughout the U.S. economy, and this has been especially true in the TELECOMMUNICATIONS industry.

Beginning in the mid 1980s and extending to the mid 1990s, each of the three major television networks, ABC, CBS, and NBC, was purchased by another corporation. In 1985, Capital Cities purchased ABC for $3.5 billion. The same year, General Electric (G.E.) purchased RCA, and in 1985, G.E. purchased NBC. Westinghouse purchased CBS in 1994 for $5.4 billion, and the Walt Disney Co. purchased Capital Cities/ABC for $19 billion in 1995. Other mergers also had a major impact on the industry. In 1989, Time, Inc. merged with Warner Corporation to form the largest media conglomerate in the world, and in 1993, Viacom, Inc. purchased Paramount Corporation in an $8.2 billion deal.

These mergers were major news at the time, and they still have an impact on the industry. Congress deregulated much of the industry with the passage of the Telecommunications Act of 1996, Pub. L. No. 104-104, 110 Stat. 56 (codified in scattered sections of 47 U.S.C.A.). It was the most significant legislative change in the industry since the passage of the Communications Act of 1934, 48 Stat. 1064. The act called for more open competition among companies within the industry, designed for the purpose of improving services to consumers. The result of the legislation was a wide number of mergers among smaller and larger companies within the industry.

Almost immediately after the passage of the Telecommunications Act, four of the seven Bell telephone regional holding companies announced proposed mergers. More mergers occurred among Bell companies and other local carriers. At least 13 significant mergers in the industry occurred in 1996 alone. Time Warner merged with Turner Broadcasting in 1996 in a $6.7 billion deal, creating the largest media corporation in the world. Worldcom, Inc. purchased MFS Communications for $12.4 billion to become the first local and long-distance telephone company since 1984. Westinghouse/CBS purchased Infinity Broadcasting for $4.9 billion, allowing Westinghouse/CBS to become the dominant power in the radio market.

These mergers continued throughout the 1990s and beyond. For instance, Time Warner merged with America Online, Inc. in 2000 in a $166 billion deal to form the largest convergence of INTERNET access and content in the world. Although some companies and consumer groups complained that the formation of these conglomerate companies could stifle competition and control prices, these mergers have become commonplace.

The Future of Mergers and Acquisitions

Although a number of factors influence mergers and acquisitions, the market is the primary force that drives them. The late 1990s saw an unprecedented influx in mergers. In 1999, companies filed a record 4,700 Hart-Scott-Rodino filings, about three times the number received in 1995. The total dollar value of the mergers announced in 1998—$11 trillion—was ten times the amount since 1992. The rash of mergers in the telecommunications industry accounted for many of these mergers, but companies in other industries were involved as well.

Another factor in the rise in mergers during the late 1990s was a booming economy, which grew at unprecedented levels. As the country faced recession in the following decade, many companies were forced to downsize, and the number of major mergers decreased accordingly. Improvements in the economy, as well as potential legislative changes, could very well spark another wave of mergers.

FURTHER READINGS

Ginsburg, Martin D. and Jack S. Levin. 1989. *Mergers, Acquisitions and Leveraged Buyouts.* Chicago: Commerce Clearing House.

Marks, Mitchell Lee. 2003. *Charging Back up the Hill: Workplace Recovery after Mergers, Acquisitions, and Downsizings.* San Francisco: Jossey-Bass.

CROSS-REFERENCES

Antitrust Law; Bonds "Michael R. Milken: Genius, Villain, or Scapegoat?" (Sidebar); Golden Parachute; Junk Bond; Restraint of Trade; Scorched-Earth Plan; Unfair Competition.

MERIT SYSTEM

System used by federal and state governments for hiring and promoting governmental employees to civil service positions on the basis of competence.

The merit system uses educational and occupational qualifications, testing, and job performance as criteria for selecting, hiring, and promoting civil servants. It began in the federal government circa 1883. The merit system was established to improve parts of the governmental work force previously staffed by the political patronage or spoils system, which allowed the political party in power the opportunity to reward party regulars with government positions. The merit system has been adopted by state and local governments as well.

MERIT SYSTEMS PROTECTION BOARD

The Merit Systems Protection Board (MSPB) ensures that federal civil servants are hired and retained based on merit. In overseeing the personnel practices of the federal government, the board conducts special studies of the merit systems; hears and decides charges of wrongdoing and employment appeals of adverse agency actions; and orders corrective disciplinary actions against an executive agency or employee when appropriate. The board's independent special counsel investigates, among other things, prohibited personnel practices and allegations of activities proscribed by civil service laws, rules, and regulations, and prosecutes officials who violate civil service rules and regulations.

The MSPB is a successor agency to the U.S. Civil Service Commission, which had been established by act of Congress on January 16, 1883. The duties and authority of the board are specified in 5 U.S.C.A. §§ 1201–1206 (1978).

The board has responsibility for hearing and adjudicating appeals by federal employees of adverse personnel actions, such as removals, suspensions, and demotions. It also resolves cases involving re-employment rights, the denial of periodic step increases in pay, actions against ADMINISTRATIVE LAW judges, charges of merit-system violations, and prohibited personnel practices, including charges in connection with WHISTLE-BLOWING (i.e., the reporting of illegal acts). When President BILL CLINTON reauthorized the MSPB and the Office of Special Counsel in 1994, he directed that federal employee whistle-blowers and other victims of prohibited personnel practices receive additional protections. Clinton instructed the agencies to follow appropriate procedures to protect the constitutional rights of such federal employees.

The board has the authority to enforce its decisions and to order corrective and disciplinary actions. An employee or applicant for employment who is involved in an appealable action that also involves an allegation of discrimination may ask the EQUAL EMPLOYMENT OPPORTUNITY COMMISSION to review a board decision. Final decisions and orders of the board are appealable to the U.S. Court of Appeals for the Federal Circuit.

The board reviews regulations issued by the Office of Personnel Management (OPM) and has the authority to require agencies to cease compliance with any regulation that could constitute a prohibited personnel practice. It also conducts special studies on the civil service and other EXECUTIVE BRANCH merit systems and reports to the president and the Congress on whether the federal workforce is being adequately protected against political abuses and prohibited personnel practices.

The Office of the Special Counsel is responsible for investigating allegations and other information concerning prohibited personnel practices; prohibited political activities by federal and certain state and local employees; ARBITRARY or capricious withholding of information in violation of the FREEDOM OF INFORMATION ACT (5 U.S.C.A. § 552 et seq.) (1986); prohibited discrimination when found by appropriate authority; and other activities that are prohibited by any civil service law, rule, or regulation. The special counsel initiates disciplinary and corrective actions before the board when warranted.

The special counsel is also responsible for receiving and referring to the appropriate agency information that evidences a violation of any law, rule, or regulation; mismanagement; gross waste of funds; abuse of authority; or substantial and specific danger to public health or safety.

Since the late 1990s, the board has expanded the amount of information on its web site. Federal employees who wish to file an appeal may download forms and rules. In addition, the decisions of the board are now posted on its web site, <www.mspb.gov>.

FURTHER READINGS

Merit Systems Protection Board Web site. Available online at <www.mspb.gov> (accessed November 11, 2003).

U.S. Government Manual Web site. Available online at <www.gpoaccess.gov/gmanual> (accessed November 10, 2003).

CROSS-REFERENCES

Administrative Agency; Administrative Law and Procedure; Bureaucracy; Merit System.

MERITS

The strict legal rights of the parties to a lawsuit.

The word *merits* refers to the substance of a legal dispute and not the technicalities that can affect a lawsuit. A judgment on the merits is the final resolution of a particular dispute.

MESNE

Intermediate; intervening; the middle between two extremes, especially of rank or time. In feudal law, an intermediate lord; a lord who stood between a tenant and the chief lord; a lord who was also a tenant.

CROSS-REFERENCES

Feudalism.

METES AND BOUNDS

The boundary lines of land, with their terminal points and angles. A way of describing land by listing the compass directions and distances of the boundaries. It is often used in connection with the Government Survey System.

MEXICO AND THE UNITED STATES

Relations between the United States and Mexico are among the most important and complex that each nation maintains. They are shaped by a mixture of mutual interests, shared problems, and growing interdependence. The United States is particularly concerned with illegal immigration, narcotics trafficking, environmental POLLUTION, and economic stability.

The scope of U.S.-Mexican relations goes far beyond diplomatic and official contacts, entailing extensive commercial, cultural, and educational ties. More than one million legal crossings are made from Mexico to the United States every day. Along the 2,000-mile shared border, state and local governments interact closely. The two countries seek to resolve many issues, ranging from combating narcotics trafficking to improving and protecting the shared environment.

The U.S. government has long recognized that a stable and economically prosperous Mexico is fundamental to U.S. interests. Since 1981, the United States-Mexico Binational Commission, composed of numerous U.S. cabinet members and their Mexican counterparts, has met annually to discuss an array of topics, including trade and investment opportunities, financial cooperation, anti-narcotics cooperation, and migration.

Mexico is a major trading partner with the United States. Mexican exports in 2001 totaled $159 billion, with 88.4 percent of its exports going to the United States. Of Mexico's 2001 imports totaling $168 billion, 68.4 percent of the imports were from the United States. In January 1994, Mexico joined CANADA AND THE UNITED STATES in the NORTH AMERICAN FREE TRADE AGREEMENT (NAFTA), which will phase out all tariffs among the nations over a 15-year period. U.S. LABOR UNIONS and some businesses were concerned that the lower tariffs would induce more U.S. companies to relocate factories to Mexico because of lower labor costs there.

The United States played a major role in stabilizing the Mexican economy in 1995. The Mexican government, unable to meet its foreign debt obligations, devalued its peso in December 1994. The resulting financial crisis threatened the stability of other emerging-market economies in Latin America. The United States led a group of international lenders that made available to Mexico more than $40 billion in international financial assistance, including $20 billion from the United States. Although Mexico suffered a severe recession in 1995, the Mexican government's implementation of tough stabilization measures averted an even more serious collapse. The economy began to recover in 1996, and by 1997 Mexico was able to repay the United States the $12.5 billion in loans that it actually had used.

A major concern of the United States has been illegal immigration from Mexico. The desire of Mexicans to leave their country is fueled by a large population (more than 103 million in 2002) and a shortage of well-paying jobs. The U.S. Border Patrol has grown in response to the large number of Mexicans crossing the border illegally. More than 4,000 agents police the border, an increase of 50 percent from 1993, and the number is expected to grow. Parts of the 2,000-mile border have become militarized zones. Steel fences run through deserts and up over hillsides. Border Patrol agents use high-technology surveillance equipment to track the movement of illegal ALIENS. In some sectors, the NATIONAL GUARD and Army personnel assist the Border Patrol.

The Mexican-U.S. border is also the leading entry point into the United States for illegal narcotics. It is estimated that drug traffickers smuggle about $10 billion worth of narcotics into the United States each year, making marijuana, heroin, cocaine, and methamphetamine some of Mexico's most lucrative exports. U.S. and Mexican officials offer differing explanations for the trafficking. U.S. officials blame the alleged cor-

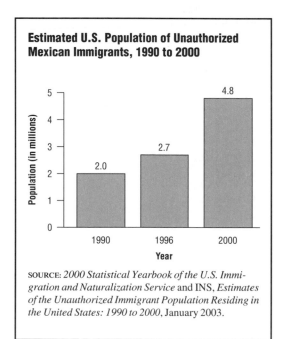

Estimated U.S. Population of Unauthorized Mexican Immigrants, 1990 to 2000

SOURCE: *2000 Statistical Yearbook of the U.S. Immigration and Naturalization Service* and INS, *Estimates of the Unauthorized Immigrant Population Residing in the United States: 1990 to 2000*, January 2003.

ruption of Mexican law enforcement officials for allowing large-scale traffickers to continue their operations. Mexican officials argue that the problem lies on the other side of the border, where the appetite of U.S. drug users drives the trafficking.

The United States has steadily restricted the Mexican drug trade through aggressive patrol of the borders and searches at border checkpoints. Nevertheless, NAFTA has increased legitimate border traffic, overwhelming U.S. customs officers at the checkpoints. It is estimated that officers can only search about seven percent of all vehicles crossing the border.

In response, the U.S. DRUG ENFORCEMENT ADMINISTRATION has sought to develop closer ties with Mexican drug enforcement officials. However, concern about the corruption of government officials has hurt relations between the countries. Mexico has failed to arrest several drug lords whom the United States has long sought and has failed to implement anti-narcotics legislation passed in 1996. In February 1997, the official in charge of Mexico's antidrug war, General Jesus Gutierrez Rebollo, was arrested for allegedly being on the payroll of the leader of the Juárez, Mexico, drug cartel. Although the United States stood by the Mexican government, it made clear that Mexico must make progress in arresting major drug lords, extraditing drug criminals to the United States, prosecuting MONEY LAUNDERING, and fighting internal corruption. With some experts claiming that Mexico is responsible for 70 percent of the illegal drugs in the United States, the war on drugs remains a source of friction between the two countries.

The United States and Mexico have sought to resolve common environmental issues, particularly in border areas where rapid population growth, urbanization, and industrialization have caused serious problems. In 1992, the United States and Mexico developed the Integrated Border Environment Plan, under which the two countries have worked to construct wastewater treatment plants; strengthen cooperative planning and enforcement efforts; reduce pollution, develop planning, training, and education; and improve understanding of the border environment.

The second phase of the 1992 border plan, called Border XXI, will promote environmental and sustainable development in the U.S.-Mexican border region through increased public participation and improved coordination among local, state, and federal agencies to maximize cooperative and effective use of limited resources. In addition, the plan will encompass environmental health issues and natural-resource protection.

As part of NAFTA's environmental agreement, the United States, Mexico, and Canada have created a North American Commission on Environmental Cooperation. This commission is charged with strengthening environmental laws and addressing common environmental concerns.

In 1993, the United States and Mexico established two institutions to address the environmental infrastructure needs of the border region. The Border Environmental Cooperation Commission (BECC) works with local communities to develop plans for better meeting their need for environmental facilities, including wastewater treatment plants, drinking-water systems, and solid-waste-disposal facilities. In addition, the two countries created the North American Development Bank to obtain private-sector capital to finance the construction of border environmental facilities certified by the BECC.

The International Boundary Commission, which was established as a permanent, joint commission by treaty in 1889, is responsible for solving U.S.-Mexican water and boundary problems. These issues include distribution between the two countries of the waters of the Colorado and Rio Grande Rivers, and joint operation of international dams on the Rio Grande to control floods, conserve water, and generate electricity. Since the early 1980s, the commission has focused on border sanitation problems and has studied groundwater resources along the boundary.

When President GEORGE W. BUSH took office in 2001, he immediately entered into discussions with Mexican President Vicente Fox. One of the items on his agenda was the creation of a guest-worker program, which would allow thousands of Mexican nationals to work in the United States as guests, mostly in agriculture. A number of groups opposed the proposal. A United States-Mexico Migration Panel, a binational group consisting of 30 members from both nations, agreed that the two countries should collaborate to meet several objectives, including making visas more available to Mexican citizens, improving cooperation between Mexican and

U.S. law enforcement to counter human SMUGGLING, and improving Mexico's economy. The negotiations were part of Fox's efforts toward economic development and social reform.

The SEPTEMBER 11TH ATTACKS of 2001 largely put a halt to these negotiations. The United States immediately shifted its attention to protecting its lands against terrorist attacks, including enhancing and improving border patrol. In 2002, Congress abolished the Immigration and Naturalization Service, creating from the agency the Bureau of Citizenship and Immigration Services and the Directorate of Border and Transportation Security. Both agencies are part of the HOMELAND SECURITY DEPARTMENT.

The slowdown in the U.S. economy and the change of focus on the part of the United States from Latin America concerns to those related to TERRORISM caused a minor strain on U.S.-Mexico relations. Fox was criticized when he unsuccessfully sought to win concessions from the United States over immigration issues. Nevertheless, these strains have not eroded the economic relationship between the two countries, as trade between the United States and Mexico is expected to rise during the first decade of the twenty-first century.

FURTHER READINGS

Bosworth, Barry, et al. eds. 1997. *Coming Together? Mexico-United States Relations*. Washington, D.C.: Brookings Institution Press.

U.S.-Mexico Binational Commission site. 1997. Available online at www.fas.usda.gov/itp/bnc/us-mexico/us mexico.html> (accessed March 19, 2003).

CROSS-REFERENCES

Aliens; Drugs and Narcotics; Environmental Law; Water Rights.

MICHIGAN V. TUCKER

Michigan v. Tucker, 417 U.S. 433, 94 S. Ct. 2357, 41 L. Ed. 2d 182, was a critical 1974 Supreme Court decision that limited the constitutional authority of the *Miranda* rights that the Court had developed in the landmark decision in MIRANDA V. ARIZONA, 384 U.S. 436, 86 S. Ct. 1602, 16 L. Ed. 2d 694 (1966). In *Michigan v. Tucker,* the Court concluded that the *Miranda* rights were procedural safeguards and not rights protected by the Constitution.

The FIFTH AMENDMENT to the Constitution contains the Self-Incrimination Clause, which guarantees a person the right to refuse to answer questions that might implicate the person in a crime. The Court in *Miranda* announced a set of warnings that law enforcement officers must give a suspect before an interrogation. These well-known warnings direct that a suspect be advised of the right to remain silent, be warned that any statement the suspect makes may be used as evidence against the person, be told of the right to have a lawyer present during interrogation, and if the suspect cannot afford an attorney, the right to have a lawyer appointed to represent the suspect. The Court believed that this set of warnings would create a uniform policy for all law enforcement officers to follow. The penalty for ignoring the *Miranda* warning was the exclusion at trial of any statements or confessions made by the defendant.

In *Michigan v. Tucker,* the Court was confronted with a suspect in a brutal rape whose interrogation had occurred prior to the Court's ruling in *Miranda*. Nevertheless, the police officers who interrogated Thomas W. Tucker advised him of his right to remain silent and his right to an attorney. They did not advise him, however, that he had a right to a free lawyer. Tucker waived his rights and proceeded to name a person who he claimed could provide an alibi. That person, however, provided incriminating evidence against Tucker. Tucker objected to the admission of his statements and sought the protection of the *Miranda* rights that the Court had announced after his arrest but prior to his trial. Tucker also asked that the alibi witness not be allowed to testify because Tucker had provided that information during his interrogation.

The trial judge excluded all of Tucker's statements but allowed the alibi witness to testify. A jury convicted Tucker, and his appeals were denied by the Michigan courts. He then filed a HABEAS CORPUS action in federal court, alleging that the admission of the alibi witness's testimony was tainted by the failure of the police to give him his full *Miranda* rights. Both the federal district court and the court of appeals agreed with Tucker, reversing the conviction.

The U.S. Supreme Court disagreed with the lower courts. Justice WILLIAM H. REHNQUIST, writing for the majority, articulated in general terms the difference between a *Miranda* violation and a constitutional violation of a defendant's Fifth Amendment right against self-incrimination. The Court found that there was a difference between incriminating statements that are actually "coerced" or "compelled" and those obtained merely in violation of the *Miranda* warning. The former are violations of the Fifth Amendment, whereas the latter are violations of a set of procedural safeguards. Violations of the procedural safeguards, by themselves, will not result in the suppression of the defendant's statements. In this case Tucker's statements had not been coerced; therefore, the testimony of the alibi witness was permissible.

Rehnquist noted that *Miranda*:

> recognized that these procedural safeguards [the warnings] were not themselves rights protected by the Constitution but were instead measures to insure that the right against compulsory self-incrimination was protected.... The suggested safeguards were not intended to "create a constitutional straitjacket," but rather to provide practical reinforcement for the right against compulsory self-incrimination.

This meant that the failure of police to provide a complete set of warnings, by itself, would not taint the interrogation and force the suppression of the statements. A court had to then look at the conduct of the police to determine if the suspect had been coerced into making incriminating statements.

In this case Rehnquist found that Tucker's interrogation did not bear "any resemblance to the historical practices at which the right against compulsory self-incrimination was aimed.... [H]is statements could hardly be termed involuntary as that term has been defined in the decisions of this Court." Rehnquist emphasized that the Court's determination that the case did not involve compulsion sufficient to breach the right of self-incrimination did not mean that police could disregard the *Miranda* warning. The question was "how sweeping [were] the judicially imposed consequences of this disregard." Absent evidence that a defendant's statement was coerced, the Court was not willing to exclude evidence because the police failed to follow the procedures set out in *Miranda*.

The distinction in *Tucker* between what Rehnquist called "prophylactic rules" and constitutional rights reappeared in *New York v. Quarles*, 467 U.S. 649, 104 S. Ct. 2626, 81 L. Ed. 2d 550 (1984), and *Oregon v. Elstad*, 470 U.S. 298, 105 S. Ct. 1285, 84 L. Ed. 2d 222 (1985). In *Quarles* the Court recognized a "public safety" exception to the requirement that the *Miranda* warning be given, reasoning that "the need for answers to questions in a situation posing a threat to the public safety outweighs the need for the prophylactic rule protecting the Fifth Amendment's privilege against self-incrimination."

In *Elstad* the Court held that a second confession, immediately preceded by the *Miranda* warning, was admissible, although an earlier statement from the defendant had been obtained in violation of *Miranda*. The Court noted that suppression of a defendant's statements assumes a "constitutional violation" but that unwarned questioning in itself violated only prophylactic standards laid down to safeguard against such a violation. Using the reasoning in *Tucker* the Court ruled that a noncoercive *Miranda* violation will not result in the suppression of the "accused's own voluntary testimony." The implication of *Tucker* and the two later decisions is that all types of evidence will not be suppressed because of *Miranda* violations.

FURTHER READINGS

Brandt, Charles. 1988. *The Right to Remain Silent.* New York: St. Martin's.

Graham, Fred P. 1970. *The Self-Inflicted Wound: The Warren Court's Revolutionary Ruling in Criminal Law.* New York: Macmillan.

White, Welsh S. 2003. *Miranda's Warning Protections: Police Interrogation Practices after Dickerson.* Ann Arbor, Mich.: Univ. of Michigan.

CROSS-REFERENCES

Criminal Law; Criminal Procedure; Custodial Interrogation; Due Process of Law; Right to Counsel.

MIDNIGHT JUDGES

Presidents throughout history have sought to influence law through their judicial appointments. However, the skirmish involving the midnight judges had a much broader significance: it belonged to a fight that had begun shortly after the WAR OF INDEPENDENCE between the leaders of the new nation. The argument pitted the Federalists (led by JOHN ADAMS) against the Republicans (led by THOMAS JEFFERSON) over a fundamental problem: how much power should be given to the federal government and, in particular, the federal judiciary? The answer would influence the course of U.S. law for generations to come.

When Adams lost the 1800 election, the nation was only twenty-four years old. The Constitution, ratified in 1789, was even younger. For more than two decades, the Federalists and the Republicans had argued over their competing visions of strong federal government versus

STATES' RIGHTS. The 1800 election crystallized these opposing philosophies. Adams and the Federalists accused the Republicans of intending to plunder property and undermine civilized society. On the other side, Jefferson and the Republicans attacked the Federalists for trying to subvert the guarantees of the BILL OF RIGHTS. The election tipped the balance of power. With the Republicans capturing the White House and Congress, it appeared that Jefferson's party would at last have the upper hand.

But the Federalists intended to preserve their power. Just before time ran out on the Adams administration, they enacted the Judiciary Act of 1801. This sweeping law struck at a key point of contention: the jurisdiction of the federal courts. The Republicans wanted the federal courts to be constrained, but the new law gave these courts increased jurisdiction over land and BANKRUPTCY cases. The federal courts now had greater authority at the expense of the states. The act added six new federal circuits with sixteen new judges. As a final measure, they also added dozens of new justices of the peace to the District of Columbia. Between December 12 and March 4, President Adams, with the approval of the Senate, busily stacked the courts with his own people. If the Federalists could not control Washington through elected office, they would at least dictate the composition of the judiciary.

The Republicans could not tolerate this bold maneuver. Enraged, Jefferson declared that "the Federalists have retired into the judiciary as a stronghold" where his own party's efforts would be "beaten down and erased." Once in power the Republicans quickly repealed the 1801 act, thus restoring the original jurisdictional authority of the federal courts. But removing the midnight judges presented a difficult constitutional question. The Constitution provided that federal judges were to hold office as long as they demonstrated good behavior—in effect, for life. The Republicans' plan was therefore to abolish the new circuit courts. The Federalists called this an unconstitutional attack on the independence of the judiciary and predicted that the Supreme Court—which was dominated by Federalists—would not allow it. The Republican-controlled Congress stalled a decision on their actions by eliminating the 1802 term of the Court.

The action only delayed an inevitable ruling. Fortunately for the Republicans, Adams had to leave office before he could secure commitments from his appointees, and several declined to serve. Those who accepted did not manage to challenge their removal. But one appointment of a midnight judge had gone largely unnoticed, and it proved to be one of the most important appointments in U.S. history. This was the nomination of JOHN MARSHALL as chief justice of the Supreme Court. Marshall, who was an ardent Federalist, viewed President Jefferson as nothing less than an "absolute terrorist."

In 1803, when the Court reconvened, it ruled on a case that arose from Adams's District of Columbia appointments. Prevented from receiving his commission as a JUSTICE OF THE PEACE, William Marbury asked the Court to order that his commission be honored.

The Court's landmark opinion in MARBURY V. MADISON, 5 U.S. (1 Cranch) 137, 2 L. Ed. 60 (1803), settled the immediate dispute and partially answered the constitutional question at stake. Writing for the unanimous Court, Chief Justice Marshall dismissed Marbury's suit on the grounds that the Supreme Court lacked jurisdiction. Marshall wanted to avoid an impasse between the judiciary and the White House. However, Marshall's opinion also greatly expanded the power of the Court by holding that the judiciary has the power to say what the law is, and, if necessary, to overturn acts of Congress that it finds unconstitutional. The Court did this in *Marbury* for the first time in history, striking down a section of the JUDICIARY ACT OF 1789.

The problem of the midnight judges was settled, but with unexpected results. The judges appointed by Adams could not take office, and in this way the Federalists were thwarted. Yet in an indirect way, they triumphed. Marshall would serve on the Supreme Court for the next thirty-four years and in the process become perhaps the greatest chief justice in history. Moreover, with his opinion in *Marbury v. Madison*, the Court established its power of JUDICIAL REVIEW, a principal goal of the Federalists.

FURTHER READINGS

Lukens, Robert J. 1997. "Jared Ingersoll's Rejection of Appointment as One of the "Midnight Judges" of 1801: Foolhardy or Farsighted?" *Temple Law Review* 70 (spring): 189–231.

CROSS-REFERENCES

Constitution of the United States; Supreme Court of the United States.

MIGRATORY BIRD TREATY OF 1918

The Migratory Bird Treaty of 1918 between the United States and Great Britain prohibited the killing of many species of birds that traversed certain parts of the United States and Canada. Such species were of great value both as a source of food and because they destroyed insects injurious to vegetation, but they were in danger of extermination through lack of protection.

The state of Missouri sought to have the treaty declared an unconstitutional interference with the rights that are reserved to the states by the TENTH AMENDMENT to the Constitution. In *Missouri v. Holland,* 252 U.S. 416, 40 S.Ct. 382, 64 L.Ed. 641 (1920), the Supreme Court held that a valid treaty must prevail over state law, even if a federal statute on the subject would be unconstitutional. Acts of Congress are the supreme law of the land only when made pursuant to the Constitution, and treaties are accorded the same status when made under the authority of the United States.

MILITARY GOVERNMENT

A government that is established during or after military occupation by the victorious country in an armed conflict. According to INTERNATIONAL LAW, *the territory that has been placed under the authority of a hostile army continues to belong to the state that has been ousted. However, it may be ruled by the occupiers under a special regime.*

When a country's army achieves decisive victory over an enemy, the victor may supplement military presence in the enemy territory with some type of government. If the victor is a signatory to certain international agreements, it must follow international RULES OF WAR that outline the rights and responsibilities when governing a territory under belligerent occupation. This military government is not the same as MARTIAL LAW, although the occupiers may impose martial law as part of maintaining order.

The rules of military government are established in various international agreements, primarily the Hague Conference of 1907 and the Geneva Conference of 1949. These documents provide guidelines on such topics as rights and duties of the occupying power, protection of civilians, treatment of prisoners of war, coordination of relief efforts, property rights of the ousted state, and other wartime and postwar concerns. A country that establishes a military government and steps beyond its allotted rights

runs the risk of international censure or criticism. Countries sometimes try to deny that they have imposed a military government. For example, in the Persian Gulf War, Iraq claimed that Kuwait is an Iraqi province and therefore not eligible for the protections given by the law of belligerent occupation.

The U.S. CIVIL WAR (1861–1865) contributed to the development of rules for military behavior and belligerent occupation. The *Lieber Instructions* is considered a first attempt to codify the laws of war as they existed during the Civil War era. Columbia College Professor Francis Lieber prepared this list of laws in 1863 at the request of President ABRAHAM LINCOLN. They led in part to the Brussels Conference of 1887 and the Hague Conferences of 1899 and 1907 on land warfare. The *Lieber Instructions* included sections on military jurisdiction, protection of persons, and public and private property of the enemy.

The U.S. Civil War pitted the Confederacy— a group of southern states that wanted to secede from the United States—against Union forces, made up of primarily northern and newly formed states. After the victory of Union forces, the U.S. government had to decide how to treat the defeated South. Some vocal members of Congress insisted that because the Confederate states had violated the Constitution by seceding, they had committed "state suicide" and should be treated like conquered provinces.

These politicians finally got their way in 1867, two years after the war ended. State governments were abolished in the rebel states, and the territory was split into five districts, each commanded by a major general of the Union army. Gradually public opinion in the North pushed for home rule for the South, and by 1870 all southern states were restored to the Union. President RUTHERFORD B. HAYES took office in 1877 and removed the army from the last three occupied southern states.

Certain species of birds that traverse the U.S. and Canada, including these snow geese, are protected by the Migratory Bird Act of 1918. The Supreme Court held that this treaty, and others like it, must prevail over state law, even if a federal statute concerning the same matter would be held unconstitutional.

AP/WIDE WORLD PHOTOS

By means of the Hague and Geneva Conferences, and organizations such as the International Committee of the Red Cross, the rules of war have evolved beyond those in the *Lieber Instructions*. When following these general rules, victorious countries continue to have broad discretion in how they govern conquered zones. The United States has used various approaches to establish postwar governments. For example, after WORLD WAR II, the United States established very different types of governments to oversee the reconstruction of Germany and Japan, which were defeated by Allied forces.

After Germany surrendered in World War II, the country and its capital were each divided into four zones. Government of the zones was assigned to four different countries: the United States, Great Britain, France, and the Soviet Union. The occupiers differed in their opinions about what type of permanent government should follow military occupation, and the zones occupied by the Soviet Union became communist East Germany. The other zones became democratic West Germany. The two Germanys were reunited in October 1990.

Unlike the military government in Germany, the U.S. occupation of Japan did not involve a large military presence. After Japan surrendered, its existing civilian governing structure was left mostly intact, directed by General Douglas MacArthur and the Supreme Command of the Allied Powers (SCAP). During occupation, Japan—a nation of seventy million people—was supervised by 600,000 troops, whose number was soon reduced to 200,000.

During more than six years of U.S. occupation, the Japanese Diet (legislature) met and passed laws that were subject to VETO by SCAP. The Japanese army and navy were abolished, weapons were destroyed, 4,200 Japanese were found guilty of WAR CRIMES, Shinto was disestablished as the state religion, and a new constitution—the "MacArthur Constitution"—was adopted. SCAP accomplished land reform, strengthened trade unions, and placed limits on Japan's powerful monopolistic corporations.

After World War II the international community agreed that more safeguards were necessary to protect civilians and their property in occupied territories. As a result the Fourth Geneva Conference was established in 1949 to tackle these issues.

In more recent times, the United States, after invading Grenada and Panama, established a military government in each country during a brief belligerent occupation.

FURTHER READINGS

Chapman, William. 1991. *Inventing Japan: An Unconventional Account of the Post-War Years.* New York: Prentice-Hall Parkside.

Craven, Avery. 1969. *Reconstruction: The Ending of the Civil War.* New York: Holt, Rinehart.

de Mulinen, Frederic. 1987. *Handbook on the Law of War for the Armed Forces.* Geneva: International Committee of the Red Cross.

Dolan, Ronald E., and Robert L. Worden. 1992. *Japan: A Country Study.* Federal Research Division, Library of Congress. Headquarters, Department of the Army. Washington, D.C.: U.S. Government Printing Office.

Lawson, Gary, and Guy Seidman. 2001. "The Hobbesian Constitution: Governing Without Authority." *Northwestern University Law Review* 95 (winter): 581–628.

Thomas, David Yancey. 2001. *A History of Military Government in Newly Acquired Territory of the United States.* Buffalo, N.Y.: William S. Hein.

CROSS-REFERENCES

Military Law.

MILITARY LAW

The body of laws, rules, and regulations that have been developed to meet the needs of the military. It encompasses service in the military, the constitutional rights of service members, the military criminal justice system, and the INTERNATIONAL LAW *of armed conflict.*

The Framers of the Constitution vigorously debated the necessity and advisability of a standing army. Federalists such as ALEXANDER HAMILTON and JAMES MADISON argued that a standing army was needed for the maintenance of a unified defense. Others, like THOMAS JEFFERSON and GEORGE MASON, were fearful of instituting a military establishment that could be an instrument of governmental abuse. They argued that the Constitution should prohibit, or at least limit, the size of the armed forces. The opposing sides compromised by approving a standing army but limiting appropriations for its support to two-year terms, thereby imposing a continual check on the military's activities.

The authority of the government to maintain a military and to develop rules and regulations governing it is found in Article I, Section 8, of the Constitution, which grants Congress the power to provide for the common defense and to raise and support armed forces.

The U.S. Supreme Court confirmed the legality of the standing army in EX PARTE MILLI-

GAN, 71 U.S.(4 Wall.) 2, 18 L. Ed. 281 (1866). It held that the Constitution allows Congress to enact rules and regulations to punish any member of the military when he or she commits a crime, in times of war or peace and in any location. The Court further confirmed the constitutionality of MARTIAL LAW in situations where ordinary law is insufficient to secure public safety and private rights.

Service in the Military

Congress's duty to provide for the national defense is carried out through four basic routes into military service: enlistment, activation of reservists, CONSCRIPTION, and appointment as an officer.

Typically, military enlistment entails a six-year service obligation, usually divided between active and reserve duty. Enlistees agree to abide by the provisions of the UNIFORM CODE OF MILITARY JUSTICE, (UCMJ) obey lawful orders, serve in combat as required, and accept any changes in status or benefits brought about by war or statutory amendments. In return, the military branch agrees to provide the enlistee with compensation and to honor promises concerning assignment, education, compensation, and support of dependents.

Enlistment is open to persons who are at least 17 years old and who enter into the enlistment agreement voluntarily. It is not available to declared homosexuals (although the military may not inquire as to sexual orientation) or to unmarried parents of children under 18 years of age. Enlistees are required to sign the enlistment agreement and, in most cases, to take the oath of allegiance.

Enlistment in the armed forces creates both a contractual obligation and a change in the recruit's legal status. (See *United States v. Grimley,* 137 U.S. 147, 11 S. Ct. 54, 34 L. Ed. 636 [1890].) Although personal service contracts are generally not enforceable, the courts recognize the special legal status of military enlistees and have required those who breach the enlistment contract to remain in the service or serve a prison term. However, after the institution of the all-volunteer military during the 1970s and 1980s, the courts relied more on traditional contract law when ruling on breach-of-enlistment suits. (See *Woodrick v. Hungerford,* 800 F.2d 1413 [5th Cir. 1986], *cert. denied,* 481 U.S. 1036, 107 S. Ct. 1972, 95 L. Ed. 2d 812 [1987], and *Cinciarelli v. Carter,* 662 F.2d 73, 213 U.S. App. D.C. 228 [D.C. Cir. 1981], where the courts applied contract law principles and found that the enlistments in question were void or voidable.)

Reservists or NATIONAL GUARD members are civilians who are subject to active service to execute laws, suppress insurrections, and repel invasions. Several suits by state governors have challenged congressional power to call up reservists. In *Perpich v. Department of Defense,* 496 U.S. 334, 110 S. Ct. 2418, 110 L. Ed. 2d 312 (1990), a suit by Minnesota's governor challenging Congress's authority to call reservists to active duty, the U.S. Supreme Court confirmed that the reserve system, under which members serve in both the state National Guard and the federal National Guard, is a necessary and proper exercise of Congress's power to raise and support armies.

Conscription, also known as the draft, is another route by which individuals are inducted into military service. The draft was the primary means of filling the ranks of the military from WORLD WAR I through WORLD WAR II, the KOREAN WAR, and the VIETNAM WAR. Although many cases challenged the constitutionality of conscription, the U.S. Supreme Court has consistently held that Congress's power to conscript Americans for military service is "beyond question." (See *United States v. O'Brien,* 391 U.S. 367, 88 S. Ct. 1673, 20 L. Ed. 2d 672 [1968].) Deferments and exemptions from the draft were granted for certain physical, mental, and religious reasons, or where induction would cause an undue hardship on the draftee or the draftee's family. The draft was abolished in 1972.

The final method of entry into the military is through appointment as an officer. Officer appointments are governed by the Appointments Clause of the Constitution (Art. II, Sec. 2, Cl. 2). Officers are appointed to a rank within a specific branch of the service.

Most military personnel serve their entire tour of duty and are discharged without any complications. An honorable discharge must be issued when a service member's record reflects acceptable military conduct and performance of duty (32 C.F.R. pt. 41, app. A). An honorable discharge cannot be denied without DUE PROCESS OF LAW. (See *United States ex rel. Roberson v. Keating,* 121 F. Supp. 477 [N.D. Ill. 1949].) A general discharge under honorable conditions may be issued when the service member's record does not warrant an honorable discharge because of ineptitude, defective attitude, or apathy (32 C.F.R. pt. 41, app. A).

A discharge under other than honorable conditions may be issued under certain circumstances indicating that a service member's behavior is inconsistent with conduct expected of military personnel (32 C.F.R. pt. 41, app. A, pt. 2). In most cases, the service member must be notified and given an opportunity to request review of the discharge by an administrative review board.

Bad-conduct and dishonorable discharges are punitive discharges that may be issued only after a full COURT-MARTIAL. Each results in loss of veterans' benefits and, in some cases, loss of CIVIL RIGHTS.

In addition to discharges, separations from military service may be accomplished through administrative proceedings (10 U.S.C.A. § 1169). The Department of Defense outlines the reasons, guidelines, and procedures for administrative separation (32 C.F.R. pt. 41, app. A). Administrative separation may be allowed to permit a service member to pursue educational opportunities or to accept public office; to alleviate hardship or dependency; to accommodate the demands of pregnancy or parenthood; to address religious concerns or conscientious objections; or to address physical and mental conditions that interfere with an assignment or the performance of duty.

Administrative separation may be initiated when a service member is found to have engaged in homosexual conduct. The National Defense Authorization Act for Fiscal Year 1994, Pub. L. No. 103-160, Nov. 30, 1993, 107 Stat. 1547, states, "The presence in the armed forces of persons who demonstrate a propensity or intent to engage in homosexual acts would create an unacceptable risk to the high standards of morale, good order and discipline, and unit cohesion that are the essence of military capability." The courts have consistently upheld the congressional prerogative to discharge homosexuals from the military.

During the 1980s, the military discharged service members for homosexual orientation as well as homosexual conduct. In 1993, President BILL CLINTON attempted to change the military's policy of discharging gays and lesbians because of their sexual orientation. He struck a compromise with those who were opposed to changing the policy in the National Defense Authorization Act of 1994, which requires separation from service of individuals who voluntarily declare their homosexuality, but bars military personnel from inquiring into a service member's sexual orientation. This has become known as the "don't-ask-don't-tell" policy.

Two administrative bodies review military discharges: the Discharge Review Board and the Board for Correction of Military Records. Service members also may seek JUDICIAL REVIEW of a discharge, but the courts generally require exhaustion of administrative remedies before they will accept jurisdiction over a discharge review. (See *Seepe v. Department of Navy*, 518 F.2d 760 [6th Cir. 1975], and *Woodrick v. Hungerford*, 800 F.2d 1413 [5th Cir. 1986], *cert. denied*, 481 U.S. 1036, 107 S. Ct. 1972, 95 L. Ed. 2d 812 [1987].)

Rights of Service Members

In the past, some legal analysts contended that those in the military receive a level of constitutional protection that is inferior to that afforded to civilians. However, in *United States v. Stuckey*, 10 M.J. 347 (1981), the Court of Military Appeals (now called the U.S. Court of Appeals for the Armed Services) held that "the BILL OF RIGHTS applies with full force to men and women in the military service...."

Congress, under its authority to regulate the armed forces, generally determines the due process and EQUAL PROTECTION rights of service personnel, and most courts defer to congressional authority in this area. However, the U.S. Supreme Court has made it clear that Congress must heed the Constitution when it enacts legislation that concerns the military.

Because both the FIRST AMENDMENT and the authority to regulate the military are found in the Constitution, a balance must be struck between First Amendment freedoms and the needs of the military. For example, Article 88 of the UCMJ makes it a crime for a commissioned officer to use contemptuous words against the president, vice president, Congress, and other government officials. Although this probably would be a violation of First Amendment FREEDOM OF SPEECH outside the military context, constitutional challenges to Article 88 have consistently failed. In *United States v. Howe*, 37 C.M.R. 555 (A.B.R. 1966), *reconsideration denied*, 37 C.M.R. 429 (C.M.A. 1967), a second lieutenant was convicted of violating Article 88 when he participated in an antiwar demonstration in which he carried a sign derogating President LYNDON B. JOHNSON. The court allowed his conviction to stand, even though he was off duty and wearing civilian clothes at the time of the demonstration. Similar limitations on the speech of enlisted personnel have been upheld, as well.

Military personnel are entitled to certain rights and benefits by virtue of their service. They retain the right to vote and participate in the election of the government. For income and property tax purposes, they retain the domicile in which they reside at the time of enlistment and cannot be taxed by other states where they may be stationed. The Soldiers and Sailors Civil Relief Act Amendments of 1942 (SSCRA) (50 U.S.C.A. app. §§ 514–591) protects military personnel from legal or financial disadvantage that results from their being ordered to active duty. A variety of remedies to alleviate hardship are available under the SSCRA, including stays of civil proceedings; stays of execution of judgments, attachments, or garnishments; protection against foreclosures on real or PERSONAL PROPERTY; a cap on interest rates charged on obligations incurred before active duty; and protection against evictions.

The Uniformed Services Employment and Reemployment Rights Act of 1994 (38 U.S.C.A. §§ 4301 et seq.) requires employers to rehire former employees who serve in the military for five years or less, with certain exceptions. The act also protects insurance, PENSION, and fringe benefits. The Veterans' Preference Act (1944) (5 U.S.C.A. §§ 2108 and 3309–3320) grants an employment preference to certain veterans and their survivors and enhances their job security.

Veterans also receive education benefits under the Post-Vietnam Era Veterans' Educational Assistance Program (1976) (38 U.S.C.A. ch. 32) and the New GI Bill (1987) (38 U.S.C.A. ch. 30). Education benefits are granted to spouses and dependent children of certain veterans in the Survivors' and Dependents' Educational Assistance Act (38 U.S.C.A. § 3501). Finally, most veterans are eligible for assistance in purchasing a home under a federal lender-guarantee program that lowers the mortgage interest rate and down payment that a veteran must pay (38 U.S.C.A. § 3710).

Under some circumstances, military personnel may seek compensation from the federal government for injury or death that occurs during service under the FEDERAL TORT CLAIMS ACT (28 U.S.C.A. §§ 2675). The most notable exceptions under the act are claims that arise out of combat during time of war and claims that arise while the service member is in a country outside the United States. In addition, the Military Claims Act (10 U.S.C.A. § 2733) provides an administrative remedy for those who incur damage to, or loss of, property, personal injury, or death caused by a civilian employee or a member of the ARMED SERVICES. The Military Claims Act addresses injuries that are not covered by the Federal Tort Claims Act.

Military Criminal Justice System

The military justice system is the primary legal enforcement tool of the armed services. It is similar to, but separate from, the civilian criminal justice system. The Uniform Code of Military Justice, first enacted in 1950, is the principal body of laws that apply to members of the military. Military tribunals interpret and enforce it.

There are several rationales for a separate military justice system. The system's procedures are efficient and ensure swift and certain decisions and punishments, which are essential to troop discipline. By comparison, the civilian criminal justice system can be cumbersome and slow and may yield unanticipated or inconsistent results. Speedy trials and predictable decisions aid the military in its effort to maintain order and uniformity. This, in turn, contributes to national security. In addition, the court-martial system fulfills the civilian public's expectation of a disciplined and efficient military.

In addition to enhancing discipline, order, uniformity, efficiency, and obedience, the UCMJ addresses certain offenses that are unique to the military, such as desertion, insubordination, or absence without leave. Finally, the military requires a uniform system that can be administered at the location of the crime to adjudicate offenses committed by service members outside U.S. jurisdiction.

The jurisdiction of the military courts is established when the court is properly convened, the membership of the court satisfies the requirements of the UCMJ, the court has the power to try the accused, and the offense is addressed in the UCMJ. The UCMJ provides that military courts have jurisdiction over all members of the armed services and certain civilians who meet limited, well-defined criteria.

The three tiers of military courts are courts-martial, Courts of Criminal Appeals, and the United States Court of Appeals for the Armed Services.

Courts-Martial The three types of courts-martial—summary, general, and special—comprise the trial level of the military justice system.

Courts-martial were originally authorized by an amendment to the Articles of War (Act of March 3, 1863, ch. 75, sec. 30, 12 Stat. 736). The amendment gave courts-martial jurisdiction over military personnel in times of war, insurrection, or rebellion to prosecute such crimes as murder, ROBBERY, ARSON, BURGLARY, rape, and other common crimes. The UCMJ authorizes military commanders to convene courts-martial on an ad hoc basis to try a single case or several cases of service members who are suspected of having violated the code.

Summary Courts-Martial Summary courts-martial adjudicate minor offenses. Their jurisdiction is limited to enlisted personnel. Summary courts-martial may impose a sentence of confinement for not more than one month, hard labor without confinement for not more than 45 days, restriction to specified limits for not more than two months, or FORFEITURE of not more than two-thirds of one month's pay (UCMJ art. 20, 10 U.S.C.A. § 820). Although the summary court-martial is intended to dispose of petty criminal cases promptly, it must fully and fairly investigate both sides of the case. Nevertheless, the protections guaranteed in special or general courts-martial are diminished in a summary hearing. Therefore, a summary court-martial may be conducted only with the consent of the accused.

The defendant in a summary court-martial may consult with military counsel before trial but is not entitled to military defense counsel at the hearing. A summary court-martial is presided over by a single commissioned officer who conducts the trial with minimal input from adversarial counsel and acts as judge, fact finder, and counsel. Thus, a summary court-martial is more similar to the inquisitorial courts of the civil-law system than to the Anglo-American adversarial model. Summary courts-martial are employed less frequently than are other types of courts-martial. With increased recognition of the constitutional rights of the accused during the last part of the twentieth century, their use has greatly diminished.

Special Courts-Martial A special court-martial generally consists of a military judge and at least three armed-service members. However, under Article 16(2) of the UCMJ (10 U.S.C.A. § 816(2)), the members may sit without a judge, or the accused may choose to be tried by a judge alone.

The military-judge position was authorized by the Military Justice Act of 1968 (UCMJ art. 26, 10 U.S.C.A. § 826). The military judge's role is similar to that of a civilian trial judge. Military judges do not determine penalties and may only instruct the members of the court, who act as a jury, as to the kind and degree of punishment that the court may legally impose, unless the accused elects to have the judge sit as both judge and jury. This dual role is permissible only in non-capital cases. In any case, the judge rules on all legal questions.

The UCMJ requires that service members who are selected for the special court-martial be the best qualified to serve, as measured by their age, education, training, experience, length of service, and judicial temperament.

Special courts-martial have jurisdiction over most offenses under the UCMJ and may impose a range of sentences, including confinement for no longer than six months; three months of hard labor without confinement; a bad-conduct discharge; forfeiture of pay not to exceed two-thirds of monthly pay; withholding of pay for no more than six months; or a reduction in rank (UCMJ art. 19, 10 U.S.C.A. § 819).

General Courts-Martial The general court-martial is the most powerful trial court in the military justice system. A general court-martial is presided over by either a military judge and at least five service members, or a judge alone if the accused so requests and the case involves a non-capital offense (UCMJ art. 16(1), 10 U.S.C.A. § 816(1)). General courts-martial may try all offenses under the UCMJ and may impose any lawful sentence, including the death penalty, dishonorable discharge, total forfeiture of all pay and allowances, and confinement. General courts-martial have jurisdiction over all persons who are subject to the UCMJ.

A general court-martial may be convened only by a high-ranking official, such as the president, the secretary of a military branch, a general, or a commander of a large unit or major installation. The commander of a smaller unit may only convene a special court-martial. Trial attorneys who are appointed to represent the accused in a general court-martial must be certified military lawyers. Verbatim recordings of general courts-martial are required by the Rules for Court-Martial.

The constitutionality of the court-martial system has been upheld in a number of cases under the theory that the military constitutes a separate society that requires its own criminal justice system. The U.S. Supreme Court has consistently deferred to the authority of the military, as conferred by Congress, to govern its members. In *Solorio v. United States,* 483 U.S. 435, 107 S. Ct. 2924, 97 L. Ed. 2d 364 (1987), the Court held that "Congress has primary responsibility for the delicate task of BALANCING the rights of servicemen against the needs of the military.... [W]e have adhered to this principle of deference in a variety of contexts where, as here, the constitutional rights of servicemen were implicated."

Courts of Criminal Appeals The intermediate appellate courts in the military justice system are the four Courts of Criminal Appeals (CCA), one for each branch of the armed services (i.e., the Army, Navy, Air Force, and Marines). Before 1995, these courts were called the Courts of Military Review (CMR).

The Military Justice Act of 1968 (10 U.S.C.A. § 866) established the CMR to review court-martial convictions. They generally have three-judge panels that review all cases in which the sentence exceeds one year of confinement, involves the dismissal of a commissioned officer, or involves the punitive discharge of an enlisted person (UCMJ art. 66, 10 U.S.C.A. § 866). Courts of Criminal Appeals may review findings of fact and findings of law and may reduce the sentence, dismiss the charges, or order a new trial.

Review by the CCA is mandatory and automatic in cases where the sentence is death, dismissal, dishonorable or bad-conduct discharge, or imprisonment for one year or more, and the right to appellate review has not been waived or an appeal has not been withdrawn. CCA judges may be commissioned officers or civilians, but all must be members of a bar of a federal court or of a state's highest court. The judges are selected by the JUDGE ADVOCATE general of the appropriate service branch. CCA judges do not have tenure or fixed terms. They serve at the pleasure of the judge advocate general. Decisions of the CCA are subject to review by the United States Court of Appeals for the Armed Forces.

U.S. Court of Appeals for the Armed Forces Congress established the U.S. Court of Appeals for the Armed Forces (USCAAF), formerly known as the Court of Military Appeals (CMA), in 1950 (10 U.S.C.A. § 867). It is the highest civilian court that is responsible for reviewing decisions of military tribunals. It is exclusively an appellate criminal court. The court consists of three civilian judges appointed by the president, with the advice and consent of the Senate, to serve 15-year terms.

The USCAAF has jurisdiction over all cases in which the death penalty is imposed, all cases sent by the judge advocate general for review after CCA review, and certain appeals petitioned by the accused that the court agrees to review. The court may only review QUESTIONS OF LAW. Decisions of the USCAAF may be appealed to the U.S. Supreme Court, which may grant or deny review.

Jurisdictional Questions Involving Military Courts On a number of occasions in U.S. history, the jurisdiction of military courts has come into question. Congress resolved many of these disputes through legislation, the most significant of which was the Uniform Code of Military Justice. Although military courts generally have powers that are analogous to those of their counterparts in the civilian system, they are subject to limitations in the federal laws creating them.

The U.S. Supreme Court resolved a major jurisdictional question involving the military courts in *Clinton v. Goldsmith,* 526 U.S. 529, 119 S. Ct. 1538, 143 L. Ed. 2d 720 (1999). The Court ruled that the USCAAF did not have the authority to issue an INJUNCTION preventing the U.S. Air Force from dropping a convicted officer from its rolls. The decision made clear that the president has the power to fire military personnel for the same offenses that resulted in their courts-martial and convictions.

In 1996, Congress passed legislation that expanded the president's authority over the military. The president was empowered to drop from the rolls of the armed forces any officer who had been sentenced by a court-martial to more than six months' confinement and who had served at least six months. The case in *Goldsmith* arose when an Air Force major, who was HIV-positive, continued to have unprotected sex after a superior had ordered him to inform his sexual partners of his disease. When the officer had sex with two partners, including a fellow officer and a civilian, he was convicted by a court-martial of willful disobedience of an order from a superior officer and two other related charges.

The officer appealed his conviction to the Court of Criminal Appeals and, later, the

USCAAF, seeking an injunction to prevent the president and the Air Force from dropping the officer from the Air Force rolls. Although the CCA refused, indicating that it lacked jurisdiction, the USCAAF issued the injunction. A unanimous U.S. Supreme Court, per Justice DAVID H. SOUTER, ruled that the USCAAF lacked this form of injunctive power. According to the Court, the USCAAF's authority is limited to the review of sentences imposed by courts-martial and appellate decisions by the Court of Criminal Appeals.

Law of Armed Conflict

The international law of armed conflict applies to situations involving an armed, hostile conflict that is not a civil or internal matter.

An armed conflict may begin by declaration of war, by the announcement of one governmental entity that it considers itself at war with another, or through the commission of hostile acts by the military forces of one entity against another. In the past, a formal declaration of hostilities was required before a conflict was legally interpreted as a war. Thus, in *Savage v. Sun Life Assurance Co.,* 57 F. Supp. 620 (W.D. La. 1944), the court found that the insured, who died in the Japanese attack on Pearl Harbor, had not died as a result of war because the United States had not yet formally declared itself at war with Japan. Rather, the court found that the insured's death was accidental and that his beneficiary could collect double indemnity under an accidental death policy. In modern times, the outbreak of hostilities even without a formal declaration or ultimatum is regarded as war in a legal sense, unless both parties deny the existence of a state of war.

Armed conflict may be terminated by a peace treaty, a cessation of hostilities and establishment of peaceful relations, unconditional surrender, or subjugation.

The United States, as a member of the UNITED NATIONS, is bound by the U.N. Charter, which requires that its members refrain from the threat or use of force in any manner that is not consistent with U.N. policies. In addition, the United States is a signatory to most major treaties relating to warfare, including the Hague Conference of 1907, the Geneva conferences of 1929 and 1949, and the Genocide Convention of 1948. All of these treaties set forth basic principles that govern the conduct of war: Force should be directed only at targets that are directly related to the enemy's ability to wage war (military necessity); the degree of force used should be directly related to the importance of the target and should be no more than is necessary to achieve the military objective (proportionality); and the force used should cause no unnecessary suffering, destruction of civilian property, loss of civilian life, or loss of natural resources (humanitarian principle). In addition, the Hague Conference provided that captured prisoners may not be killed; captured towns may not be pillaged; and the property, rights, and lives of civilians in armed conflict areas must be respected.

In addition to written treaties relating to war, international armed conflict is governed by customary international law, or the COMMON LAW of armed conflict. Under this constantly evolving body of law, certain conduct is proscribed because world opinion forbids it. In *Ex parte Quirin,* 317 U.S. 1, 63 S. Ct. 2, 87 L. Ed. 3 (1942), *order modified by* 63 S. Ct. 22, the Court upheld jurisdiction of a military tribunal over German saboteurs who used civilian disguises, even though no written law or treaty justified their trial. The Court based its decision on the ground that infiltration by disguise violated the customary law of armed conflict. (See also *The Paquete Habana,* 175 U.S. 677, 20 S. Ct. 290, 44 L. Ed. 320 [1900].) The customary law of war is based on the same principles embodied in the Hague Conference and subsequent treaties and reflects international agreement that actions that are inconsistent with those principles should not go unpunished even in the absence of express prohibitions. Many nations, including the United States, have codified significant portions of the common law of armed conflict. (See U.S. Department of the Army, *The Law of Land Warfare* [Field Manual 27-10, 1956].)

In response to the SEPTEMBER 11TH ATTACKS in 2001, when terrorists hijacked four U.S. planes and used them to destroy the World Trade Center in New York and seriously damage the Pentagon, President GEORGE W. BUSH led the country into a WAR ON TERRORISM. As part of this war, Bush signed a military order on November 13, 2001 that, among other provisions, allows the United States to try suspected terrorists in a military tribunal, rather than the federal court system.

According to the order, "To protect the United States and its citizens, and for the effective conduct of military operations and prevention of terrorist attacks, it is necessary for individuals subject to this order . . . to be detained, and, when tried, to be tried for violations of the laws of war and other applicable laws by military tribunals." The order authorizes the secretary of defense to issue regulations establishing military commissions to try any and all offenses subject to the order. These regulations must ensure a full and fair trial and must provide rules pertaining to procedures, evidence, issuance of process, qualifications of attorneys, and other similar matters.

The DEFENSE DEPARTMENT issued regulations on March 21, 2002. Many of the provisions in the regulations are similar or analogous to rules that apply in the civilian courts. These regulations provide that an accused must be provided with a defense counsel, or may choose his or her own attorney. The accused is presumed innocent until proven guilty, and the prosecution must prove its case BEYOND A REASONABLE DOUBT. The rules also ensure the rights against SELF-INCRIMINATION and DOUBLE JEOPARDY.

As the United States engaged in military action in Afghanistan, suspected members of the Taliban regime and the al-Qaeda organization were held at U.S. military bases, and could have been subjected to the military tribunals. Supporters of this plan indicate that military tribunals are necessary because the United States is at war with terrorists, and alien enemies are generally not afforded the protection of the U.S. Constitution at times of war. Moreover, supporters note that during critical wars in the nation's history, leaders often have used military tribunals. These leaders include GEORGE WASHINGTON, during the Revolutionary War; ABRAHAM LINCOLN, during the Civil War; and FRANKLIN DELANO ROOSEVELT, during World War II.

Critics note that the use of military tribunals has serious constitutional implications. Certain constitutional rights might not apply in a military tribunal as they do in the regular court system. Whereas a conviction in a regular court requires a unanimous vote, a military tribunal, which makes all determinations of the law and the facts, must agree by a two-thirds majority. Moreover, a trial in a military court need not be held in public, and the right to an appeal is limited. No ruling by a military tribunal is final until approved by the president or the secretary of defense.

Bush's order generally has not been popular overseas, as the use of these tribunals has been seen as a means by which the U.S. can avoid fair trials in its civilian system. Nevertheless, the Bush administration has defended the development of the system. According to Bush, "We are an open society, but we are at war. We must not let foreign terrorists use the forums of liberty to destroy freedom itself."

FURTHER READINGS

Bishop, Joseph W., Jr. 1974. *Justice Under Fire: A Study of Military Law.* New York: Charterhouse.

Duignan, Kathleen A. 1996. "Military Justice." *Federal Lawyer* 43.

Falvey, Joseph L. 1995. "United Nations Justice or Military Justice." *Fordham International Law Journal* 19.

Fuger, Stanley J. 1992. "Military Justice." *Connecticut Bar Journal* 66.

Gilligan, Francis A. 1990. "Civilian Justice v. Military Justice." *Criminal Justice* 5 (summer).

Kohlmann, Ralph H. 1996. "Saving the Best Laid Plans." *Army Lawyer* 3 (August).

U.S. Department of Defense. 2002. *Manual for Courts-Martial.* Washington, D.C.: Department of Defense.

Wiener, Frederick B. 1989. "American Military Law in the Light of the First Mutiny Act's Tricentennial." *Military Law Review* 126 (fall).

Winthrop, William. 2000. *Military Law and Precedents.* Buffalo, N.Y.: William S. Hein & Co., Inc.

CROSS-REFERENCES

Arms Control and Disarmament; Conscientious Objector; Gay and Lesbian Rights; Geneva Conventions, 1949; Genocide; GI Bill; Just War; Military Government; Military Occupation; Militia; Nuremberg Trials; Rules of War; Selective Service System; Solomon Amendment; Veterans Affairs Department; War; War Crimes.

MILITARY OCCUPATION

Military occupation occurs when a belligerent state invades the territory of another state with the intention of holding the territory at least temporarily. While hostilities continue, the occupying state is prohibited by INTERNATIONAL LAW from annexing the territory or creating another state out of it, but the occupying state may establish some form of military administration over the territory and the population. Under the MARTIAL LAW imposed by this regime, residents are required to obey the occupying authorities and may be punished for not doing so. Civilians may also be compelled to perform a variety of nonmilitary tasks for the occupying authorities, such as the repair of roads and buildings, provided such work does not contribute directly to the enemy war effort.

Although the power of the occupying army is broad, the military authorities are obligated under international law to maintain public order, respect private property, and honor individual liberties. Civilians may not be deported to the occupant's territory to perform forced labor nor impressed into military service on behalf of the occupying army. Although measures may be imposed to protect and maintain the occupying forces, existing laws and administrative rules are not to be changed. Regulations of the Hague Conventions of 1907 and, more importantly, the 1949 GENEVA CONVENTION for the Protection of Civilian Persons in Time of War have attempted to codify and expand the protection afforded the local population during periods of military occupation.

CROSS-REFERENCES

War.

MILITIA

A group of private citizens who train for military duty in order to be ready to defend their state or country in times of emergency. A militia is distinct from regular military forces, which are units of professional soldiers maintained both in war and peace by the federal government.

In the United States, as of the early 2000s, the NATIONAL GUARD serves as the nation's militia. Made up of volunteers, the National Guard acts under the dual authority of both the federal and state governments. According to the Constitution, Congress can call the National Guard into federal service for three purposes: to enforce federal laws, to suppress insurrections, and to defend against invasions. State governors can call upon the National Guard for emergencies that are prescribed by state law.

The American militia system has its roots in ancient English tradition, dating back to the Anglo-Saxon militia that existed centuries before the Norman Conquest in 1066. This militia, known as the *fyrd*, consisted of every able-bodied male of military age. It was traditionally used for defense only, and the sovereign could call upon the fyrd to fight if the men would be able to return to their homes by nightfall. Fyrd members were required to supply their own weapons, which they could use only in the service of the king.

After 1066 the victorious Normans retained this militia system, and successive English monarchs continued to rely on citizen soldiers for national defense. During the reign of the Tudors (1485–1603), professional forces began to be used in England, but their main task was to train the local militias, which were much less expensive to use than their professional counterparts. The major element of training was the muster, which was a mandatory gathering of all able-bodied free males, age 16 to 60, for the purpose of appraising the participants, their weapons, and their horses. Mustering was an ancient ritual, but during her reign Queen Elizabeth I systematized the practice, requiring musters four times a year and authorizing payment for those attending. Even with this enhanced level of organization, however, musters were as much social occasions as they were military drills. Participants looked forward to musters as an opportunity to eat and drink heavily before engaging in fights and mock battles.

When the English began to establish colonies in North America in the seventeenth century, the colonial governments continued to require all able-bodied free men to possess arms and to participate in the colonial militias. Each colony formed its own militia unit, appointing officers, providing training, and building its own fortifications. The function of each colonial militia was principally to defend the settlers' homes and villages against Indian raids, and at this they were largely successful.

Colonial militias were much less effective when used for offensive purposes on extended campaigns far from the militia members' homes. GEORGE WASHINGTON discovered this when, as a colonel in the Virginia militia, he had great difficulty recruiting enough men to fight the French and Indian War, which lasted from 1754 to 1763. Few men were willing to report for duty. Of those who did, few were well armed, and many quickly deserted the troops and returned home. Some militia officers instituted drafts to recruit more men, but even then, many of the draftees simply paid less-qualified men to report in their places. The British were finally able to win the war when Prime Minister William Pitt made changes in recruiting policies and the military bureaucracy, which made serving in the militia more palatable for the American colonists.

After Great Britain defeated France in the French and Indian War, it was left with a greatly enlarged North American empire to manage and finance. Large numbers of British troops were stationed in America, and the colonists were expected to quarter them and to pay various taxes and fees, including the well-known Stamp Tax, to finance the troops. These additional taxes were one of the principal grievances that motivated the American colonists to prepare for revolution and to form the select militia units that became known as the "Minutemen"; this name reflected the fact that the men were trained to respond instantly when called. The Minutemen first saw action when the Massachusetts unit was called to defend the colonists' military stores at Lexington and Concord on April 19, 1775.

During the Revolutionary War, American military forces consisted of a combination of state militias, specially trained militia units (such as the Minutemen), and the Continental Army, a small professional force created by Congress. The militia was much more effective than it had been during the French and Indian War because its members were fighting for a cause in which they fervently believed. In addition, the militia system had been reorganized and strengthened: there were more training days, the punishment was more severe for missing musters, and fewer men were exempted from military duty. Even so, militia forces were much less reliable than the professional army, and commanders found it difficult to plan their moves, never knowing exactly how many men would show up and how long they might stay. Ultimately, however, the militias played a critical role in helping the colonists to defeat the British, supplying enough men to keep the Continental Army going and providing, on very short notice, large numbers of armed men for brief periods of emergency service.

When state delegates met in 1787 to create the Constitution for the new United States of America, the principal division was between those delegates who favored a strong central government and those who preferred to leave more power to the states. The former wanted a strong standing military, and the latter argued for greater reliance on the state militias. The issue of a standing military was particularly controversial because many Americans were suspicious of the very concept of a standing army, associating it with the tyranny they had experienced under Great Britain. Nevertheless, because most of the delegates were more concerned about invasion than domestic tyranny, Congress was given the power to create a standing army if it so chose. Advocates of state power did achieve a partial victory, however, in that authority over the state militias was divided between the federal government and the state governments. Congress was given the authority to organize, arm, and discipline the militia, but states were given the power to appoint officers and provide training. Congress, not the president, was given the power to summon state militias into federal service for just three specific tasks: "to execute the laws of the Union, suppress insurrections, and repel invasions" (Art. I, Sec. 8, Cls. 15, 16).

During his first term as president, George Washington worked with Secretary of War Henry Knox to reorganize and strengthen the militia. They sent their plan to Congress, and after heated debate Congress, on May 9, 1792, passed what became known as the Uniform Militia Act (1 Stat. 264). This law, which remained the basic militia law until the twentieth century, stated that all free, able-bodied white men, age 18 to 45, were required to serve in their state militias and that they were obligated to supply themselves with the appropriate firearms and equipment. The law provided certain specifications for how militia units were to be organized, but Congress left many details to the states and declined to include sanctions for states or individuals who failed to comply with the law. As a result, the act had little legal weight and served mostly as a recommendation to the states.

All 15 states passed laws in response to the Uniform Militia Act. These laws had some provisions in common, such as the right of the people to keep and bear arms and the exemption of conscientious objectors from military duty; the laws varied in other areas, such as in the frequency of training and the methods for selecting officers. In general, the Uniform Militia Act and the laws passed in response to it created many strong and effective state militias; in addition to being an indispensable part of ceremonies and parades, state militia units manned coastal forts, guarded criminals, enforced quarantines, and assisted the police. However, the many state laws prevented the integration of the various state militias into a reliable force for federal purposes. The federal government often lacked even basic information about the strength and organization of the state militias, making it difficult to make full use of them for military purposes.

Despite the many weaknesses of the militia system, it continued to receive widespread support in the nineteenth century from politicians and the public, who were eager to avoid the expense of a standing army and who viewed the idea of the citizen-soldier as crucial for the maintenance of U.S. freedom and independence. In reality, however, the militia system was often ineffective and unreliable, as during the WAR OF 1812 when militia units were chronically undermanned and poorly prepared. Despite calls for reforms, the militia system declined steadily during the nineteenth century. Less training was required, fewer men attended, and fewer still had firearms, instead showing up for training with cornstalks and broomsticks.

By the 1830s and 1840s, several states had weakened or abolished their systems of compulsory service, relying instead on volunteers. As a result, the militia units became more ceremonial and elitist in nature, as members donned expensive uniforms and equipment to march in parades and other festivals. These volunteer units were useful to state and local authorities because they often assisted the local police in maintaining law and order, which were frequently disrupted by riots and protests, particularly in larger cities.

After the Civil War, in which militia units played a crucial role by supplementing the regular armies of both the Union and the Confederacy, the militia system again went into a decline. A shortage of funds required cutbacks in militia programs, and military service became more unattractive as the rapid growth of industrialism led to frequent labor strikes, which the Army was required to police. According to Russell F. Weigley, a prominent military historian, "The main effect of industrialism seems to have been to reduce inclination and time for amateur soldiering, and thus to weaken the militia institutions inherited from the rural past."

The National Guard, a volunteer militia distinct from professional military forces, can be pressed into service by state governors in response to emergencies prescribed by state law. Here a National Guard member keeps watch during the 1992 Los Angeles riots.

BETTMANN

One rejuvenating factor for the militia during this time, however, was the formation of the National Guard Association (NGA) in 1879. This organization was formed to represent the militia's interests before federal and state governments and the public. The name "National Guard," borrowed from the French, was chosen because most states at the time were already using that term to designate their organized volunteer companies. The leaders of the National Guard Association insisted that their units were an integral part of the U.S. military establishment but also maintained the importance of the guard's connection to individual states. In 1887 the NGA achieved its first victory by persuading Congress to raise the federal annual appropriation to arm the guard to $400,000.

At the beginning of the twentieth century, Congress and President WILLIAM MCKINLEY began work to reform the nation's military structure and operations. Secretary of War Elihu Root saw that the United States needed a workable reserve system, rather than the militia, which still operated under the Uniform Militia Act of 1792. Root worked with leaders from the NGA to create a REORGANIZATION PLAN, and the result was the passage in 1903 of the Dick Act (32 Stat. 775), so named for Major General Charles Dick, who had played a large role in creating and supporting the bill. This act formally repealed the Uniform Militia Act of 1792 and extended federal involvement with the National Guard in peacetime. More federal funds were made available to state National Guard units, and in return the state units were required to drill their troops 24 times a year, train reservists in summer encampments, and submit to annual inspections by federal officers.

In the years leading up to WORLD WAR I, professional officers in the regular army and leaders of the National Guard consistently opposed each other on the issue of establishing a national reserve free from all ties to the states. The NGA contended that National Guard units were the proper national reserve, but military professionals argued that national security could not depend on reserves that had two commanders-in-chief and two chains of command—federal and state. In congressional hearings held in 1916, then ex-Secretary of War Root argued against the guard as a reliable reserve: "The idea … that forty-eight different governors can be the basis for developing an efficient, mobile national army is quite absurd."

Proponents of a national reserve won the debate, and on June 3, 1916, President WOODROW WILSON signed the National Defense Act (39 Stat. 166), which for the first time created reserve components of the regular services under exclusive federal control. The act also conferred federal status on the National Guard, with the federal government providing more funding and exerting more control over it. National Guard units still reported to the state governors and served on a statewide basis, but guardsmen could now be drafted directly into federal service for the duration of an emergency. Guard members now had to take LOYALTY OATHS to the United States as well as to their home states, and the War Department could cut federal aid to the guard unit of any state that failed to comply with the mandates of the act.

This basic system established in 1916 has continued to be maintained with few changes over the course of the twentieth century. The state National Guard units report to both the state and federal governments, but when they are called into federal service, state governors lose their authority over them. This state and federal authority conflicted several times in the 1950s and 1960s, when guard units from southern states were called into federal service to enforce federal desegregation mandates over the objections of the state governors.

Another type of militia, not recognized by the federal or state governments, is the private militia. Private militias are composed of private citizens who train for armed combat. The formation of private militias became more common in the United States in the early 1990s as some political groups armed themselves to demonstrate their opposition to certain policies and practices of the federal government. One of the most publicized private militia groups was the Montana Freemen, who were involved in a lengthy standoff with agents of the FEDERAL BUREAU OF INVESTIGATION in 1996.

One of the most horrifying events of the 1990s, the Oklahoma City bombing in 1995, had a significant impact on private militias in the United States during that decade. Although the bombings, which killed 169 people, were not carried out by an identified private militia, a number of individuals reportedly were drawn to join these private groups after witnessing the attack. The total number of private militia groups climbed to an estimated 370 in 1996, according to the Southern Poverty Center, which is well-known for tracking hate groups in the United States.

Militia groups faded quickly in the latter half of the 1990s, however. Law enforcement officials began cracking down on the groups, and many members reportedly became impatient in training for the causes of the various militia. By 1999, the total number of private militias in the U.S. had shrunk to an estimated total of 68. Law enforcement officials continue to track militia, citing their extremist beliefs and their propensity for conspiring to commit acts of violence.

FURTHER READINGS

Fields, William S., and David T. Hardy. 1992. "The Militia and the Constitution: A Legal History." *Military Law Review* 136 (spring).

Freilich, Joshua D. 2003. *American Militias: State-Level Variations in Militia Activities.* New York: LFB Scholarly Pub. LLC.

Hardaway, Robert, Elizabeth Gormley, and Bryan Taylor. 2002. "The Inconvenient Militia Clause of the Second Amendment: Why the Supreme Court Declines to Resolve the Debate over the Right to Bear Arms." *St. John's Journal of Legal Commentary* 16 (winter): 41–146.

Huhn, Wilson. 1999. "Political Alienation in America and the Legal Premises of the Patriot Movement." *Gonzaga Law Review* 34 (spring): 417–43.

Mahon, John K. 1983. *History of the Militia and the National Guard.* New York: Macmillan.

Maslowski, Peter, and Allan R. Millett. 1994. *For the Common Defense: A Military History of the United States.* New York: Free Press.

Mulloy, D. J. 2004. *American Extremism: History, Politics and the Militia Movement.* London, New York: Routledge.

Uviller, H. Richard, and William G. Merkel. 2002. *The Militia and the Right to Arms, or How the Second Amendment Fell Silent.* Durham, NC: Duke Univ. Press.

Weigley, Russell F. 2000. *A Great Civil War: A Military and Political History.* Bloomington, IN: Indiana Univ. Press.

———. 1975. *New Dimensions in Military History.* Novato, Calif.: Presidio.

———. 1967. *History of the United States Army.* New York: Macmillan.

Wolfson, Andrew. 2001. "Militias Dwindle Since Oklahoma City Bombing." *USA Today.* Available online at <www.usatoday.com/news/nation/2001-04-23-mcveigh-militias1.htm> (accessed October 4, 2003).

CROSS-REFERENCES

Armed Services; Gun Control; Military Law; Second Amendment; Second Amendment "Private Militias" (In Focus).

MILL

One-tenth of one cent: $0.001. A mill rate is used by many localities to compute property taxes. For example, some states levy a one-time nonrecurring *tax of two mills per dollar (0.2%) on the fair market value of all notes, bonds, and other obligations for payment of money that are secured by mortgage, deed of trust, or other lien on real property in lieu of all other taxes on such property.*

❖ MILL, JOHN STUART

John Stuart Mill was the leading English political philosopher of the middle and late nineteenth century. Mill's writings on individual freedom, most notably the essay "On Liberty" (1859), have had a profound influence on U.S. CONSTITUTIONAL LAW. His "libertarian theory" continues to attract those opposed to government interference in the lives of individuals.

Mill was born on May 20, 1806, in London. His father, James Mill, was a leading proponent of UTILITARIANISM, a political theory that claimed that the greatest happiness of the greatest number should be the sole purpose of all public action. James Mill provided his son with an unorthodox but extensive education. John Mill began studying Greek at the age of three, and by the age of 17 he had completed advanced courses in science, philosophy, psychology, and law.

In 1822 Mill began working as a clerk for his father at India House, the large East Indian trading company. He rose to the position of chief of the examiner's office and stayed with the company until his retirement in 1858.

Mill's real passion, however, was political and social philosophy. In 1826 he had a serious mental crisis that caused him to reevaluate the tenets of utilitarianism and to reconsider his own purpose and aim in life. At the same time, he became acquainted with Harriet Taylor, a gifted thinker who would become Mill's collaborator and later his wife. Largely ignored by historians, Taylor is now credited as a major contributor to Mill's published works.

Mill's essay "On Liberty" remains his major contribution to political thought. He proposed that self-protection is the only reason an individual or the government can interfere with a person's liberty of action. Outside of preventing harm to others, the state has no legitimate reason to compel a person to act in the way the government wishes. This principle has proved complex in application, because it is difficult to determine which aspects of behavior concern only individuals and which concern other members of society.

In chapter two of "On Liberty," Mill considered the benefits that come from FREEDOM OF SPEECH. He concluded that, except for speech that is immediately physically harmful to others (like the classic example of the false cry of "fire" in a crowded theater, cited by OLIVER WENDELL HOLMES JR.), no expression of opinion, written or oral, ought to be prohibited. Truth can only emerge from the clash of contrary opinions; therefore, robust debate must be permitted. This "adversarial" theory of the necessary nature of the search for truth and this insistence on the free marketplace of ideas have become central elements of U.S. free speech theory.

Mill also applied his principle of liberty to action as well as speech. Mill believed that "experiments of living" maximize the development of human individuality. Restraints on action should be discouraged, even if the actions are inherently harmful to the individuals who engage in them. Mill claimed that society should not be allowed to prohibit fornication, the consumption of alcohol, or even POLYGAMY.

Mill asserted the importance of personal development and the negative impact of conditioning and conformity which he believed tended to stunt or stifle individual development. The liberty he proclaimed was one in which all individuals are equally free to develop innate tal-

"THE WORTH OF A STATE, IN THE LONG RUN, IS THE WORTH OF THE INDIVIDUALS COMPOSING IT."
—JOHN STUART MILL

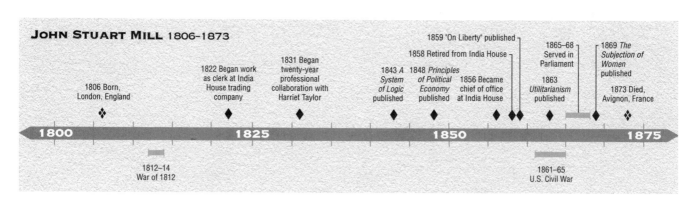

JOHN STUART MILL 1806–1873

1806 Born, London, England

1822 Began work as clerk at India House trading company

1831 Began twenty-year professional collaboration with Harriet Taylor

1843 *A System of Logic* published

1848 *Principles of Political Economy* published

1856 Became chief of office at India House

1858 Retired from India House

1859 "On Liberty" published

1863 *Utilitarianism* published

1865–68 Served in Parliament

1869 *The Subjection of Women* published

1873 Died, Avignon, France

1800   1825   1850   1875

1812–14 War of 1812

1861–65 U.S. Civil War

ents and abilities. He assumed that individuals will naturally tend to be drawn toward what they are good at doing and this natural ability, freely allowed to develop, enhances and contributes to all society.

Mill's other works include *A System of Logic* (1843), *Principles of Political Economy* (1848), *The Subjection of Women* (1869), and *Autobiography* (1873).

Mill served in Parliament from 1865 to 1868. He was considered a radical because he supported the public ownership of natural resources, compulsory education, BIRTH CONTROL, and social and legal equality for women. His advocacy of women's suffrage contributed to the creation of the suffrage movement.

Mill died on May 7, 1873, in Avignon, France.

FURTHER READINGS

Capaldi, Nicholas. 2003. *John Stuart Mill: A Biography.* New York: Cambridge Univ. Press.

Mill, John Stuart. 1960. *The Autobiography of John Stuart Mill.* New York: Columbia Univ. Press.

Ofseyer, Jeremy J. 1999. "Taking Liberties with John Stuart Mill. *Annual Survey of American Law* 1999 (fall): 395–433.

Packe, Michael St. John. 1954. *The Life of John Stuart Mill.* New York: Macmillan.

Passavant, Paul A. 1996. "A Moral Geography of Liberty: John Stuart Mill and American Free Speech Discourse." *Social & Legal Studies* 5 (September): 301–20.

Rose, Phyllis. 1984. *Parallel Lives: Five Victorian Marriages.* New York: Vintage.

Ten, C.L., ed. 1999. *Mill's Moral, Political, and Legal Philosophy.* Aldershot, Hants, England; Brookfield, Vt.: Ashgate: Dartmouth.

CROSS-REFERENCES

Bentham, Jeremy; Libertarianism; Utilitarianism.

◆ MILLER, LOREN

Loren Miller was a municipal court judge and housing discrimination specialist whose involvement in the early stages of the CIVIL RIGHTS MOVEMENT earned him a reputation as a tenacious fighter for equal housing opportunities for minorities.

Miller was born January 20, 1903, in Pender, Nebraska, the son of a post–Civil War migrant from the South. His family moved to Kansas when he was a boy, and he graduated from high school in Highland, Kansas. Later, he attended the University of Kansas; Howard University; and Washburn University, in Topeka, Kansas, where he earned his bachelor of laws degree in 1928. He was admitted to the Kansas bar the same year, and practiced law there for one year before moving to California to pursue his first interest, journalism. He worked for the *California News,* a Los Angeles newspaper, from 1929 to 1933.

Miller returned to the field of law when he married and was admitted to the California bar in 1933. By the 1940s, he was raising his voice in protest over policies and practices that discriminated against African Americans. In the wake of WORLD WAR II, many blacks had left their rural and southern homes to seek economic opportunity in California, only to face discrimination and bias, particularly in housing. By 1947, Miller had represented more than one hundred plaintiffs seeking to invalidate housing covenants that prevented blacks from purchasing or renting housing in certain areas. As a board member of the AMERICAN CIVIL LIBERTIES UNION (ACLU), he became a well-known spokesman for the rights of minorities to enjoy equal access to housing and education. He was openly critical of

"THE NEGRO HAS BEEN THE WARD OF THE SUPREME COURT OF THE UNITED STATES FOR MORE THAN A HUNDRED YEARS."
—LOREN MILLER

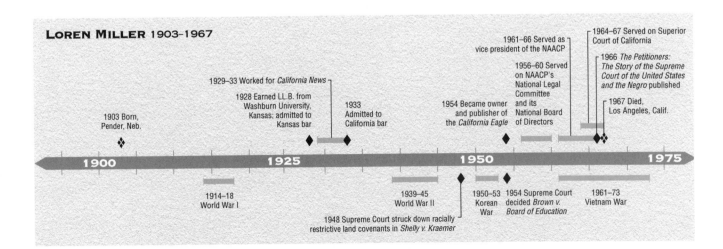

LOREN MILLER 1903–1967

1903 Born, Pender, Neb.

1928 Earned LL.B. from Washburn University, Kansas; admitted to Kansas bar

1929–33 Worked for *California News*

1933 Admitted to California bar

1954 Became owner and publisher of the *California Eagle*

1956–60 Served on NAACP's National Legal Committee and its National Board of Directors

1961–66 Served as vice president of the NAACP

1964–67 Served on Superior Court of California

1966 *The Petitioners: The Story of the Supreme Court of the United States and the Negro* published

1967 Died, Los Angeles, Calif.

1900   1925   1950   1975

1914–18 World War I

1939–45 World War II

1948 Supreme Court struck down racially restrictive land covenants in *Shelly v. Kraemer*

1950–53 Korean War

1954 Supreme Court decided *Brown v. Board of Education*

1961–73 Vietnam War

the Federal Housing Authority (FHA), declaring that FHA policies fostered a Jim Crow policy that kept blacks confined to "tight ghettos" and provoked racial tension. Commenting on the effect of racially restrictive covenants, he noted that contrary to the claims of those who supported the covenants, residential SEGREGATION did not preserve public peace and GENERAL WELFARE but rather resulted in "nothing but bitterness and strife."

In 1954 Miller's love of journalism prompted his return to the newspaper business. He became the owner and publisher of the *California Eagle*, a weekly newspaper with wide circulation in the African American community. He also contributed numerous articles to such journals as the *Crisis*, the *Nation*, and *Law in Transition*. Later, Miller was named cochair of the West Coast legal committee of the National Association for the Advancement of Colored People (NAACP). In that capacity, he became the first U.S. lawyer to win an unqualified verdict outlawing residential restrictive covenants in real estate sales that involved FHA or VETERANS ADMINISTRATION (VA) financing. Perhaps the most celebrated case Miller was involved in was *Shelley v. Kraemer,* 334 U.S. 1, 68 S. Ct. 836, 92 L. Ed. 1161 (1948), in which the U.S. Supreme Court declared that racial covenants on property cannot be enforced by the courts.

Miller was one of the first to recognize that bias in housing would be an explosive social issue in the United States. The greatest tension, he predicted, would exist where an all-white area adjoined an all-black area, because "there white Americans stand eternal guard to keep their Negro fellow Americans out." He denounced as "money lenders" and "hucksters of prejudice" the owners of slum properties where many members of minorities are forced to live under substandard conditions because of the "artificial housing shortages . . . in the Negro community."

In 1964, Governor Edmund G. Brown of California appointed Miller to the Superior Court of California, where he served until his death. He was vice president of the NAACP (1961–66); a member of the NAACP's National Legal Committee and of its National Board of Directors (1956–60); a member of the national committee of the ACLU; and vice president of the National Bar Association, an organization of African American attorneys. Miller was also a member of the California Advisory Commission on Civil Rights, vice president of the National Committee against Discrimination in Housing, and a member of the NAACP LEGAL DEFENSE AND EDUCATIONAL FUND.

In 1966, Miller wrote *The Petitioners: The Story of the Supreme Court of the United States and the Negro,* a book that recounts the vital role of the U.S. Supreme Court in shaping the lives of African Americans in the U.S. He and his wife, Juanita Ellsworth Miller, had two sons, Loren Jr., and Edward. Miller died in Los Angeles on July 14, 1967.

❖ MILLER, SAMUEL FREEMAN

Samuel Freeman Miller served as an associate justice of the U.S. Supreme Court from 1862 to 1890. During his long tenure on the Court, Miller played a major role in restricting the reach of the FOURTEENTH AMENDMENT into areas of the law reserved to the states. He is most famous for writing the majority opinion in the SLAUGHTER-HOUSE CASES, 83 U.S. (16 Wall.) 36, 21 L. Ed. 394 (1873).

Miller was born on April 5, 1816, in Richmond, Kentucky, and grew up on a farm. He attended Transylvania University, where he earned a medical degree in 1838. Miller practiced medicine for ten years, and during that time he taught himself law. In 1847, he was admitted to the Kentucky bar, and soon afterward he abandoned his medical practice for a law practice in Knox County, Kentucky.

Miller became more interested in politics after he became an attorney. A member of the WHIG PARTY, Miller was opposed to SLAVERY, a position that caused him difficulty in Kentucky as pro-slavery sentiment began to rise. In 1850, he moved to Iowa, which was more tolerant of his antislavery views. He established a law practice in Keokuk, Iowa, and became a prominent member of the REPUBLICAN PARTY and a supporter of Abraham Lincoln's presidential campaign in 1860.

Lincoln appointed Miller to the U.S. Supreme Court in 1862, during the most difficult period for the Union during the Civil War. Miller voted to sustain Lincoln's suspension of HABEAS CORPUS and to try civilians by military courts-martial. Following the war, Miller voted to uphold the constitutionality of LOYALTY OATHS that were required of former Confederates who wished to hold public office.

Miller is best known for his majority opinion in the *Slaughter-House Cases* in 1873. At issue was the scope of the authority in the Fourteenth Amendment, which had been passed in 1868 to guarantee that states could not restrict the constitutional rights of citizens and businesses. The case involved a Louisiana state law that allowed one meat company the exclusive right to slaughter livestock in New Orleans. Other packing companies were required to pay a fee for using the slaughterhouses. Those companies filed suit, claiming that the law violated the PRIVILEGES AND IMMUNITIES CLAUSE of the Fourteenth Amendment, which stated that "no state shall make or enforce any law which shall abridge the privileges or immunities of citizens of the United States."

Miller upheld the Louisiana MONOPOLY law, ruling that the Privileges and Immunities Clause had a limited effect because it only reached privileges and immunities guaranteed by U.S. citizenship, not state citizenship. The law in question concerned state rights; therefore, the Fourteenth Amendment had no effect. In Miller's view, the Fourteenth Amendment was designed to grant former slaves legal equality, and not to grant expanded rights to the general population. In addition, Miller was concerned that a broad interpretation of the Fourteenth Amendment would give too much power to the federal government and that it could distort the concept of FEDERALISM, which grants the states a large measure of power and autonomy.

Having set the standard for interpreting the Fourteenth Amendment, Miller and most members of the Court followed it during the 1870s and 1880s. Miller and the Court struck down state-sponsored RACIAL DISCRIMINATION under the amendment but refused to do the same to private discrimination, most notably in the CIVIL RIGHTS CASES, 109 U.S. 3, 3 S. Ct. 18, 27 L. Ed. 835 (1883). In these cases, the Court held that federal laws that banned private discrimina-

Samuel F. Miller.
LIBRARY OF CONGRESS

tion in public transportation and public accommodation were unconstitutional because the Fourteenth Amendment only reaches state-enacted discrimination.

In a nonjudicial role, Miller served on the electoral commission that counted the electoral votes in the deadlocked and disputed presidential election of 1876 between RUTHERFORD B. HAYES and SAMUEL J. TILDEN. During the 1880s, some Republican leaders promoted Miller as a presidential candidate, but nothing came of it.

Miller died on October 13, 1890, in Washington, D.C.

FURTHER READINGS

Fairman, Charles. 2002. *Mr. Justice Miller and the Supreme Court, 1862-1890.* Union, N.J.: Lawbook Exchange.

Hall, Kermit L., ed. 1992. *The Oxford Companion to the Supreme Court of the United States.* New York: Oxford Univ. Press.

"IT DOES NOT . . . FOLLOW, THAT WHEN A WORD WAS USED IN A STATUTE . . . SEVENTY YEARS SINCE, THAT IT MUST BE HELD TO INCLUDE EVERYTHING TO WHICH THE SAME WORD IS APPLIED AT THE PRESENT DAY."
—SAMUEL MILLER

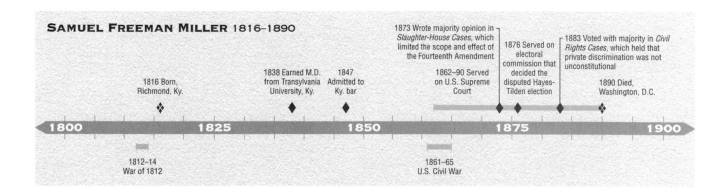

SAMUEL FREEMAN MILLER 1816–1890

1816 Born, Richmond, Ky.

1838 Earned M.D. from Transylvania University, Ky.

1847 Admitted to Ky. bar

1862–90 Served on U.S. Supreme Court

1873 Wrote majority opinion in *Slaughter-House Cases*, which limited the scope and effect of the Fourteenth Amendment

1876 Served on electoral commission that decided the disputed Hayes-Tilden election

1883 Voted with majority in *Civil Rights Cases*, which held that private discrimination was not unconstitutional

1890 Died, Washington, D.C.

1800   1825   1850   1875   1900

1812–14 War of 1812

1861–65 U.S. Civil War

Ross, Michael A. 2003. *Justice of Shattered Dreams: Samuel Freeman Miller and the Supreme Court During the Civil War Era.* Baton Rouge: Louisiana State Univ. Press.

CROSS-REFERENCES

States' Rights.

MILLER V. CALIFORNIA

Arguably the most important in a series of late-twentieth-century Supreme Court cases laying down the definition of OBSCENITY and setting down the boundaries as to how and when communities could regulate obscene materials. *Miller v. California,* 413 U.S. 15, 93 S. Ct. 2607, 37 L. Ed. 2d 419 (1973) remained the Supreme Court's final word on most types of PORNOGRAPHY into the twenty-first century. While the test set down for defining obscenity in *Miller v. California* has been modified and expanded by subsequent court cases since the original decision was handed down in 1973, it has never been overturned and forms the starting point for nearly all U.S. court cases dealing with obscenity prosecutions.

Pre-Miller Obscenity Cases

Miller v. California and its companion case, *Paris Adult Theatre I v. Slaton,* 413 U.S. 49, 93 S. Ct. 2628, 37 L. Ed. 2d 446, (1973), marked the culmination of a period when the Supreme Court laid down several tests for obscenity, the most famous and succinct of which was Justice Potter Stewart's comment in his concurrence in *Jacobellis v. State of Ohio* 378 U.S. 184, 84 S. Ct. 1676, 12 L. Ed. 2d 793 (1964), "I know it when I see it." For years, U.S. courts had generally followed the definition of obscenity contained in the 1868 British case, *Regina v. 3 L.R.-Q.B. 360 (1868).* That case said the definition of obscenity was "whether the tendency of the matter charged is to deprave and corrupt those whose minds are open to such immoral influences and into whose hands a publication of this sort may fall." Courts differed as to whether just one passage of the material was sufficient to prove this tendency or whether the work had to be examined as a whole.

But in 1957, the Supreme Court explicitly rejected *Regina v. Hicklin* in ROTH V. UNITED STATES 354 U.S. 476, 77 S. Ct. 1304, 1 L. Ed. 2d 1498,(1957). In that case, a divided Supreme Court first ruled for the first time that obscenity was beyond constitutional protection. The Court went on to rule that the new standard for judging obscenity was whether to an average person, applying contemporary community standards, the dominant theme of material taken as a whole appealed to prurient interest. In imposing an average person standard, the Court departed from *Hicklin*'s more broad definition to allow a finding of obscenity wherever there were "minds open to ... immoral influences."

Unfortunately, the Supreme Court's obscenity test in *Roth* seemed to create more problems than it solved, for both lower courts and the high court itself, partially because it proved difficult to determine who the average person in a community was and whether local, state, or national standards were to be applied in trying to divine this person. Also, measuring the dominance of obscenity within a piece of material was not an easy task for most courts. In *A Book Named 'John Cleland's Memoirs of a Woman of Pleasure' v. Attorney General of Massachusetts,* 383 U.S. 413, 86 S. Ct. 975, 16 L. Ed. 2d 1, (1966), the high court further added that the material in question had to be utterly without redeeming social value, a standard that many prosecutors complained was almost impossible to meet.

With all the confusion, the stage was set for the court to make a definitive statement on obscenity. This is what the court tried to do in *Miller v. California.* But for years after the decision was handed down, commentators debated whether the court had succeeded.

Miller v. California

Under a California obscenity statute, Marvin Miller was convicted for mailing illustrated brochures advertising "adult" books. The California appeals court used the tests previously enunciated by the court to uphold Miller's conviction. The Supreme Court took up the case as an opportunity to reconsider its previous holdings.

The resulting 5–4 decision imposed a new test for determining obscenity. In a decision written by Chief Justice WARREN BURGER, the Court imposed a new three-part test for determining whether a work was obscene. Burger wrote: "The basic guidelines for the trier of fact must be: (a) whether 'the average person, applying contemporary community standards' would find that the work, taken as a whole, appeals to the prurient interest, (b) whether the work depicts or describes, in a patently offensive way, sexual conduct specifically defined by the applicable state law; and (c) whether the work, taken as a whole, lacks serious literary, artistic, political, or scientific value."

In handing down this decision, Burger reaffirmed that obscenity and pornography are not protected by the FIRST AMENDMENT. He explicitly rejected the "utterly without redeeming social value" test in favor of the third prong of his formula, which was viewed as an easier standard for prosecutors to meet. He also stated that no one could be subjected to prosecution "for the sale or exposure of obscene materials unless these materials depict or describe patently offensive 'hardcore' sexual conduct specifically defined by the regulating state law, as written or construed."

Burger went further than past Supreme Court decisions in attempting to define what would constitute hardcore pornography. While emphasizing that "it is not our function to propose regulatory schemes for the States" he said that "It is possible . . . to give a few plain examples of what a state statute could define for regulation: (a) patently offensive representations or descriptions of ultimate sexual acts, normal or perverted, actual or simulated; and (b) patently offensive representation or descriptions of masturbation, excretory functions, and lewd exhibition of the genitals."

The companion case of *Paris Adult Theatre I v. Slaton*, handed down on the same day, ruled that as long as state laws met the *Miller* test, they could regulate hardcore pornography even if the showing of such pornography was limited to consenting adults. Chief Justice Burger, who wrote the majority opinion in *Paris Adult Theatre*, stated that "States have a legitimate interest in regulating commerce in obscene material and in regulating exhibition of obscene material in places of public accommodation, including so-called 'adult' theaters from which minors are excluded." Such regulations can be likened to when "legislatures and administrators act to protect the physical environment from POLLUTION and to preserve our resources of forests, streams, and parks, they must act on such imponderables as the impact of a new highway near or through an existing park or wilderness area," according to Burger.

The *Miller* and *Paris Adult Theatre* rulings did not meet with unanimous acclaim even when they were being handed down. In a dissent in *Miller*, Justice WILLIAM O. DOUGLAS wrote: "I do not think we, the judges, were ever given the constitutional power to make definitions of obscenity. If it is to be defined, let the people debate and decide by a constitutional amendment what they want to ban as obscene and what standards they want the legislatures and the courts to apply." Despite such criticisms, both rulings remained the law of the land in regards to obscenity prosecutions. Subsequent Supreme Court rulings imposed a "reasonable person" standard on the third prong "serious value" test and allowed states to impose a more stringent criterion for CHILD PORNOGRAPHY. But as of 2003, *Miller* was undisturbed as the test for pornography and obscenity in U.S. courts.

FURTHER READINGS

Brockwell, P. Heath. 1993–1994. "Grappling with *Miller v. California*: The Search for an Alternative Approach to Regulating Obscenity." *Cumberland Law Review* 24.

Carter, T. Barton, Juliet Lushbough Dee, and Harvey L. Zuckman. 2000. *Mass Communication Law.* St. Paul, Minn.: West Group.

Cohen, Daniel Mark. 2003. "Unhappy Anniversary—Thirty Years Since *Miller v. California*: The Legacy of the Supreme Court's Misjudgment on Obscenity." *St. Thomas Law Review* 15 (spring).

CROSS-REFERENCES

Obscenity; Pornography.

❖ MILLER, WILLIAM HENRY HARRISON

William Henry Harrison Miller served as U.S. attorney general from 1889 to 1893, in the administration of President BENJAMIN HARRISON. Miller, Harrison's law partner and political adviser, was recognized for his incorruptibility.

Miller was born on September 6, 1840, in Augusta, New York. His connection with Benjamin Harrison appeared preordained, because Miller was named after the ninth president, William Henry Harrison, the grandfather of Benjamin. Miller attended country schools and Whitestown Seminary before enrolling at Hamilton College, from which he graduated in 1861.

He studied law in the office of future U.S. Supreme Court Chief Justice MORRISON R. WAITE and was admitted to the Indiana bar in 1865. He started a law practice in Peru, Indiana, and also held the office of county school examiner. In 1866 he moved his law practice to Fort Wayne, Indiana. He remained there until 1874, when he moved to Indianapolis and became the law partner of General Benjamin Harrison.

Harrison had achieved fame as a Civil War commander. For his heroism in leading the Seventieth Indiana Regiment, President ABRAHAM

William Henry Harrison Miller.
LIBRARY OF CONGRESS

LINCOLN promoted him to brigadier general. Upon his return to Indianapolis, Harrison began to build a political career. Miller entered Harrison's law firm and the political arena. He soon became a trusted adviser to Harrison, who ran unsuccessfully for the Indiana governorship in 1876. Harrison later served in the U.S. Senate from 1881 to 1887, and in 1888 he was the Republican nominee for president. It was during the 1888 campaign that Miller served as a confidential adviser to Harrison, who defeated President GROVER CLEVELAND.

Harrison, who had promised the country a Legal Deal, appointed six lawyers and two businessmen to his cabinet. Miller was named attorney general, a position he held for the four years of the Harrison administration. In 1890 Congress passed the SHERMAN ANTI-TRUST ACT (15 U.S.C.A. § 1 et seq.), which outlawed trusts and monopolies that restrained trade. Miller did not make any effort, however, to use the new legislation.

The Harrison administration was untouched by scandal, but an economic depression in the West severely hurt the REPUBLICAN PARTY. Democrat Grover Cleveland defeated Harrison in the 1892 election. Miller returned to Indianapolis in March 1893 and resumed his law practice.

He died on May 25, 1917, in Indianapolis.

FURTHER READINGS

Justice Department. 1985. *Attorneys General of the United States, 1789–1985.* Washington, D.C.: U.S. Government Printing Office.

❖ MILLETT, KATHERINE MURRAY

Katherine Murray Millett is a writer and sculptor who is best known for her groundbreaking work of feminist literary criticism, *Sexual Politics* (1969). Although she abandoned criticism after writing that book, turning to works of fiction and autobiography, *Sexual Politics* became a starting point for scholars working in FEMINIST JURISPRUDENCE.

Millett was born on September 14, 1934, in St. Paul, Minnesota. She was educated at the University of Minnesota, Oxford University, and Columbia University. As a graduate student and part-time instructor in English at Columbia during the 1960s, she became active in the CIVIL RIGHTS MOVEMENT. Millett soon focused her attention on sexual discrimination against women. Her dissertation shifted from traditional literary criticism to an analysis of the sexual subordination of women in the works of novelists D.H. Lawrence, Henry Miller, and Norman Mailer. She was granted a Ph.D. degree in

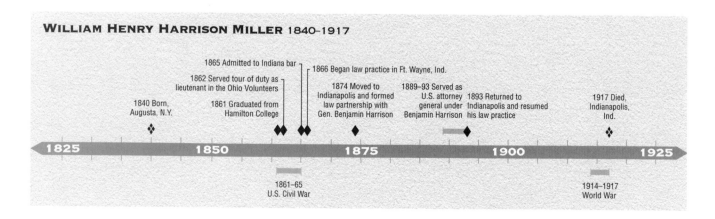

WILLIAM HENRY HARRISON MILLER 1840–1917

1865 Admitted to Indiana bar
1866 Began law practice in Ft. Wayne, Ind.
1862 Served tour of duty as lieutenant in the Ohio Volunteers
1874 Moved to Indianapolis and formed law partnership with Gen. Benjamin Harrison
1889–93 Served as U.S. attorney general under Benjamin Harrison
1893 Returned to Indianapolis and resumed his law practice
1840 Born, Augusta, N.Y.
1861 Graduated from Hamilton College
1917 Died, Indianapolis, Ind.

1825   1850   1875   1900   1925

1861–65 U.S. Civil War
1914–1917 World War

1970, on the heels of the publication of *Sexual Politics,* a revised version of her dissertation.

The book became a national best-seller overnight, attracting both strong support and vitriolic opposition. Millett argued that in the twentieth century, social and technological change had helped women in the United States to begin redefining gender roles. In the face of change, the male-dominated society had sought to preserve a patriarchal social structure and the patriarchal family through an ideology of sexual domination and violence. This ideology was most fully expressed in novels written by men and acclaimed by male intellectuals and critics.

Millett charged D.H. Lawrence with glorifying masculinity, Henry Miller with exalting the sexual degradation of women, and Norman Mailer with promoting a cult of virility. She believed that writers served as a mirror on U.S. culture and helped to explain why women have been sexually subordinated. Sexual subordination, in Millett's view, is tied to the economic and political subordination of women.

Sexual Politics was published before the field of feminist JURISPRUDENCE had been started. Millett's analysis of sexual subordination in literature inspired feminist legal scholars to examine U.S. law for patriarchal influences. In their attacks on PORNOGRAPHY, law professor CATHARINE A. MACKINNON and writer ANDREA DWORKIN derived many of their ideas from Millett's work.

After writing *Sexual Politics* Millett wrote *Flying,* an autobiography (1974), and a novel, *Sita* (1976). Her personal life has been marked by periods of mental illness and institutionalization. She wrote about this part of her life in *The Loony Bin Trip* (1990). She published *The Politics of Cruelty* in 1994, which explored the use of torture in the modern world, and another memoir, *A.D.,* in 1995.

In the later 1990s, Millett had difficulty finding work, and most of her books went out of print. In the new millennium, the University of Illinois has republished *Sexual Politics* and several other of her works. In 2000, Millett became an adjunct professor at New York University. In 2001, she published *Mother Millett,* her story of caring for her dying mother.

FURTHER READINGS

Bullock, Alan, and R.B. Woodings, eds. 1983. *20th Century Culture: A Biographical Companion.* New York: Harper & Row.

Davis, Flora. 1999. *Moving the Mountain: The Women's Movement in America Since 1960.* Champaign: Univ. of Illinois Press.

Evans, Sara. 1980. *Personal Politics: The Roots of Women's Liberation in the Civil Rights Movement and the New Left.* New York: Random House.

Rose, Phyllis, ed. 1993. *Women's Lives.* New York: Norton.

CROSS-REFERENCES

Sex Discrimination; Women's Rights.

MILLIGAN, EX PARTE

An 1866 Supreme Court decision, *Milligan ex parte,* 71 U.S. (4 Wall.) 2, 18 L.Ed. 281, recognized that a civilian and citizen of a state that is not invaded by hostile forces during wartime is not subject to the jurisdiction of a COURT-MARTIAL.

In 1864, Lambdin P. Milligan, a civilian, was arrested in Indiana for conspiracy, insurrection, and other crimes arising from his alleged involvement in organizing a secret military unit

"IT IS INTERESTING THAT MANY WOMEN DO NOT RECOGNIZE THEMSELVES AS DISCRIMINATED AGAINST; NO BETTER PROOF COULD BE FOUND OF THE TOTALITY OF THEIR CONDITIONING."
—KATHERINE MURRAY MILLETT

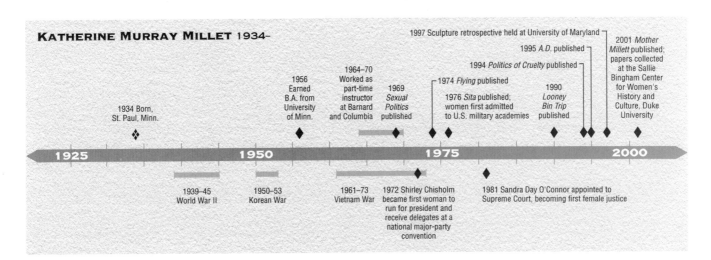

KATHERINE MURRAY MILLET 1934–

1934 Born, St. Paul, Minn.

1956 Earned B.A. from University of Minn.

1964–70 Worked as part-time instructor at Barnard and Columbia

1969 *Sexual Politics* published

1974 *Flying* published

1976 *Sita* published; women first admitted to U.S. military academies

1990 *Looney Bin Trip* published

1994 *Politics of Cruelty* published

1995 *A.D.* published

1997 Sculpture retrospective held at University of Maryland

2001 *Mother Millett* published; papers collected at the Sallie Bingham Center for Women's History and Culture, Duke University

1925   1950   1975   2000

1939–45 World War II

1950–53 Korean War

1961–73 Vietnam War

1972 Shirley Chisholm became first woman to run for president and receive delegates at a national major-party convention

1981 Sandra Day O'Connor appointed to Supreme Court, becoming first female justice

in the state to assist the Confederacy. His arrest and detention were made pursuant to the orders of General Alvin P. Hovey, commander of the military district of Indiana. He was brought to trial before a military commission in Indianapolis, convicted, and sentenced to death. Milligan applied for a writ of HABEAS CORPUS to the Supreme Court, challenging the jurisdiction of the military commission to try and sentence him.

The Court acknowledged that Article III, Section 2, Clause 3 of the Constitution—which provides "that the trial of all crimes, except in cases of IMPEACHMENT, shall be by jury"—and other constitutional provisions safeguarded this right. It recognized, however, that in times of war, various civil liberties and the right to challenge illegal detention by a writ of habeas corpus may be suspended. MARTIAL LAW might be imposed, however, only where an actual invasion of enemy forces effectively stopped the operation of the civil government.

The military argued that the designation of Indiana as a military district with a commander because of the constant threat of invasion by Confederate troops justified the imposition of martial law. The military commission, therefore, had lawful jurisdiction under the "laws and usages of war." The Court rejected this argument. The state of Indiana had not opposed federal authority, its civil and criminal courts continued to operate during the war, and Milligan was a civilian who was not connected to the military. Although civil liberties and habeas corpus could be suspended in wartime, to permit the military commission to determine the fate of Milligan, a civilian, in a state which was loyal to the Union, and where there was only a mere threat of invasion and the courts were open, would usurp the powers of the courts in violation of the Constitution. The Court decided that the military commission had no jurisdiction over Milligan and therefore ordered Milligan's release.

MINE AND MINERAL LAW

The law governing the ownership, sale, and operation of mines, quarries, and wells, and the rights to natural resources found in the earth.

The extraction of natural resources from the earth is governed by specific laws dealing with mines and minerals. Federal and state governments have mine and mineral laws to protect the health and safety of miners, encourage the efficient use of natural resources, protect the environment, and raise tax revenues.

A mine is an excavation in the soil and subsoil from which ores, coal, or other mineral substances are removed. A mineral is valuable, inert matter created by forces of nature and found either on or in the earth. A mineral right is the possessory interest in minerals in the ground. The owner of the mineral rights has the right to enter the land and occupy it for the purpose of removing the minerals. It is possible for someone to own the mineral rights and mine the minerals without owning the land itself.

The federal government has played a large role in the exploitation of mineral resources by granting mineral rights, called PATENTS, to persons and companies that wish to mine on land owned by the federal government. The Mining Act of 1872 has remained unchanged since its enactment during the presidential administration of ULYSSES S. GRANT. The law tried to help small prospectors by making land more affordable. It set the price of mineral rights to federal property at between $2.50 and $5.00 an acre and gave prospectors the right to mine without paying ROYALTIES. A royalty is the payment by the lessor to the owner of the property of a percentage of the value of the minerals that are mined.

The Mining Act of 1872 has drawn increased criticism since the 1980s because of the small amount of money companies pay to obtain mineral rights valued at millions and even billions of dollars and because the companies do not have to pay a royalty to the federal government. Most of the federal land is located in the West. Western legislators have been unwilling to amend the law, out of fear that changes would reduce employment and depress the mining industry. Attempts to amend the act to raise the price of mineral rights and to impose a royalty have met fierce resistance by western lawmakers and the mining industry, which is dominated by companies located outside the United States.

Mining operations are considered one of the main sources of environmental POLLUTION. Under the Mining Act of 1872, mining companies are not required to clean up mining sites that are on federal property. The ENVIRONMENTAL PROTECTION AGENCY estimates that cleaning up fifty-five of the United States' most dangerous mines will cost taxpayers $32 billion. On lands that are not owned by the federal government, state and federal environmental regulations require mining companies to clean up and restore their mining sites.

Mining is a dangerous occupation. Since the late 1960s, state and federal legislation has set numerous operating standards regarding dust and gas concentrations in the mines, as well as general rules regarding roof support. These provisions attempt to prevent explosions, mine collapses, and the breathing of tainted air. The Federal Mine Safety and Health Act of 1977 (30 U.S.C.A. § 801) is a comprehensive safety and health act that applies to all metal and nonmetal mines, including coal mines.

CROSS-REFERENCES

Environmental Law; Land-Use Control "The West Wrestles with D.C." (In Focus); Law of the Sea; Miner's Codes; Solid Wastes, Hazardous Substances, and Toxic Pollutants.

MINERAL RIGHT

An interest in minerals in land, with or without ownership of the surface of the land. A right to take minerals or a right to receive a royalty.

Mineral right is a term encompassing all the ways a person can have a possessory interest in minerals in the ground. It includes the right to enter the land and occupy it in order to remove the minerals. Mineral rights can be retained when land is sold or conveyed, thus making it possible for someone to own the right to mine the minerals without owning the land. A right of entry onto the land can be held by the grantor who retains the mineral rights, or other arrangements can be made to gain access to the minerals. Mineral rights can be leased or sold. A landowner who leases mineral rights often receives a royalty, or a percentage of the value of the minerals which are mined by the leaseholder.

CROSS-REFERENCES

Mine and Mineral Law.

MINER'S CODES

During the era of Western settlement in the middle of the nineteenth century, various forms of primitive legal practices were instituted to bring order to the frontier; many formal legal codes evolved from these early precepts, including the Miner's Codes.

Originally the codes were various traditional laws that were respected throughout mining camps in the West. The codes were recorded, and their purpose was to establish guidelines for fil-

ing and determining claims and arbitrating disagreements among miners. The miner's "courts" rendered decisions in disputes, and the tenets of the codes guaranteed their enforcement.

The Gregory Diggings Code of Colorado was the best example of a functioning system based on the laws of the Miner's Code. The Gregory Code successfully produced a harmonious political and judicial system that was imitated by other mining towns. Between 1861 and 1862, the legislature of the Colorado territory formally adopted the canons of the Gregory Code.

CROSS-REFERENCES

Mine and Mineral Law.

MINIMUM CONTACTS

See PERSONAL JURISDICTION.

MINIMUM WAGE

The minimum hourly rate of compensation for labor, as established by federal statute and required of employers engaged in businesses that affect interstate commerce. Most states also have similar statutes governing minimum wages.

Along with a requirement for overtime pay and restrictions on child labor, the minimum-wage law is one of the most significant, substantive obligations created more than 50 years ago by the FAIR LABOR STANDARDS ACT of 1938 (FLSA) (29 U.S.C.A. §§ 201 et seq.). The FLSA culminated a long struggle for state and federal protective legislation for workers that had begun during the nineteenth century.

The original campaign for minimum-wage legislation in the United States began at the state

Traditionally respected regulations that governed mining camps in the frontier West were known as the Miner's Codes. Such seemingly primitive laws can prove effective and evolve into formally adopted legislation.
LIBRARY OF CONGRESS

level and resulted from growing public concern about the prevalence of sweatshops—workhouses where recent immigrants, women, and young children were paid substandard wages. Proponents of minimum-wage legislation appealed to society's sense of obligation to act through its elected officials to ensure an adequate standard of living for all working citizens.

In 1912, Massachusetts, an industrial state, was the first state to enact minimum-wage legislation. The momentum continued, and by 1920 13 states, Puerto Rico, and the District of Columbia had enacted minimum-wage programs. The Great Depression moved even more states to enact protective minimum-wage legislation, and by 1938 25 states had some form of minimum-wage law. In creating minimum wage legislation, the states generally used three minimum wage models. The Massachusetts model established a wage commission that recommended voluntary minimum-wage rates based on what commission members determined was the best combination of a "living wage" for employees and the "financial condition" of the employer's business. The next model established a similar wage commission but disregarded the financial conditions of the employer, made the minimum wage compulsory, and established sanctions for non-compliance. The third law, the Utah model, established a flat rate of minimum compensation for all covered workers.

Despite the success of state legislatures in creating minimum-wage laws, state supreme courts and, ultimately, the U.S. Supreme Court rejected as unconstitutional any legislation that interfered with an employer's freedom to contract with employees over wages.

Under the leadership of President FRANKLIN D. ROOSEVELT, Congress passed the NATIONAL INDUSTRIAL RECOVERY ACT OF 1933 (NIRA) (June 16, 1933, ch. 90, 48 Stat. 195). NIRA granted the president authority to establish minimum-wage and maximum-hour standards for all private-industry workers. Its legal basis was the federal government's power to regulate interstate commerce. The U.S. Supreme Court, however, rejected the NIRA's legal basis as unconstitutional in *ALA Schechter Poultry v. United States,* 295 U.S. 495, 55 S. Ct. 837, 79 L. Ed. 1570 (1935). In fact, from 1923 in *Adkins v. Children's Hospital,* 261 U.S. 525, 43 S. Ct. 394, 67 L. Ed. 785, to 1937 in *Morehead v. New York ex rel. Tipaldo,* 298 U.S. 587, 56 S. Ct. 918, 80 L. Ed. 1347, the Court consistently ruled against the constitutionality of all minimum-wage legislation.

During his second administration, President Roosevelt worked with members of Congress to create a modified version of the labor provisions of the NIRA, and in 1937 the FLSA was introduced. Although national business lobbies and agricultural interests vigorously fought the proposed legislation—even organized labor did not support it—Congress passed the FLSA, and it was signed into law on June 25, 1938. Referring to the FLSA the night before signing the bill into law, President Roosevelt declared, "Except perhaps for the SOCIAL SECURITY ACT, it is the most far-reaching, the most far-sighted program for the benefit of workers ever adopted." In a landmark decision in 1941 (*United States v. Darby,* 312 U.S. 100, 61 S. Ct. 451, 85 L. Ed. 609), the U.S. Supreme Court found the FLSA constitutional:

> [I]t is no longer open to question that the fixing of a minimum wage is within the legislative power and the bare fact of its exercise is not a denial of DUE PROCESS under the Fifth more than under the Fourteenth Amendment.

The minimum-wage law has evolved significantly since the Court declared it constitutionally sound in *United States v. Darby.* The federal minimum wage remains the same until Congress passes a bill to raise it and the president signs the bill into law. The minimum wage started at 25¢ per hour, and Congress has increased it 18 times. Since the law was enacted, increases to the minimum wage have been signed into law by Presidents HARRY S. TRUMAN, DWIGHT D. EISENHOWER, JOHN F. KENNEDY, LYNDON B. JOHNSON, RICHARD M. NIXON, JIMMY CARTER, GEORGE H. W. BUSH, and BILL CLINTON. The increases in the minimum wage have been sporadic. For example, the wage rose five times in the inflationary 1970s but was unchanged for the last nine years of the 1980s. In 1989, the FLSA was amended to raise the minimum wage in two steps: from $3.35 to $3.80 per hour on April 1, 1990, and from $3.80 to $4.25 per hour on April 1, 1991.

Every time Congress considers legislation to increase the minimum wage, it must ponder what constitutes a living wage—a wage that is sufficient to provide a worker with food, clothing, and shelter. Along those lines, the CONGRESSIONAL RESEARCH SERVICE estimated that the minimum wage would have to rise to $6.75 per hour in 1996 to equal the purchasing power that it represented in 1978.

Congress most recently amended the minimum-wage law with the Minimum Wage Increase Act of 1996 (Pub. L. No. 104-188, sec. 2104(a), 110 Stat. 1228 [amends sec. 206]). Congress increased the minimum wage to $4.75 per hour effective October 1, 1996 and increased it to $5.15 per hour effective September 1, 1997.

The minimum wage is the most direct and definitive measure to guarantee workers a living wage, but the FLSA (and thus its minimum-wage provisions) does not protect all employees. In 1988, of the approximately 110 million wage and salary earners in the United States, the FLSA did not cover about eight million workers because of coverage limits, nor another 28 million workers because of exemptions.

The minimum-wage law can be enforced by employees themselves, by the secretary of labor, or by the attorney general. Under section 216(b) of the FLSA, employees can file suit in federal or state court to enforce their rights to minimum wages and overtime compensation. Employees also can seek redress if employers retaliate against them for trying to enforce their rights under the FLSA. The secretary of labor can enforce the act on behalf of employees under sections 216(c) and 217 by either filing a wage suit on behalf of the employees or by seeking an INJUNCTION.

If a suit by either the employees or the secretary of labor is successful, the FLSA authorizes recovery of any unpaid minimum wages and/or overtime compensation; with some exceptions, the injured party may be able to recover an equal amount in LIQUIDATED DAMAGES, as well. In addition, employees who win FLSA suits may be awarded attorneys' fees. For repeated or willful violations of the minimum-wage provisions, the secretary is authorized to assess civil penalties, subject to administrative review, of up to $1,000 per violation (29 U.S.C.A. § 217(e)).

Finally, the attorney general has the authority to file criminal actions for FLSA violations, although this authority has rarely been used.

Although the FLSA is the most significant federal wage statute, a number of other laws impose minimum-wage obligations on entities that perform work for the federal government. For example, the DAVIS-BACON ACT (40 U.S.C.A. §§ 276a–276a–5) applies to contracts in excess of $2,000 to work on federal buildings or other

Minimum Hourly Wage, by State, in 2003

State	Basic Minimum Rate (per hour)
Alabama	No state minimum wage law
Alaska	$7.15
Arizona	No state minimum wage law
Arkansas	$5.15
California	$6.75
Colorado	$5.15
Connecticut	$6.90[a]
Delaware	$6.15
District of Columbia	$6.15
Florida	No state minimum wage law
Georgia	$5.15
Hawaii	$6.25
Idaho	$5.15
Illinois	$5.15
Indiana	$5.15
Iowa	$5.15
Kansas	$2.65
Kentucky	$5.15
Louisiana	No state minimum wage law
Maine	$6.25
Maryland	$5.15
Massachusetts	$6.75
Michigan	$5.15
Minnesota	$5.15 (large employer) $4.90 (small employer)
Mississippi	No state minimum wage law
Missouri	$5.15 (large employer) $4.00 (small employer)
Montana	$5.15
Nebraska	$5.15
Nevada	$5.15
New Hampshire	$5.15
New Jersey	$5.15
New Mexico	$4.25
New York	$5.15
North Carolina	$5.15
North Dakota	$5.15
Ohio	$4.25 (large employer) $3.25 (medium employer) $2.80 (small employer)
Oklahoma	$5.15 (large employer) $2.00 (other employer)
Oregon	$6.90
Pennsylvania	$5.15
Rhode Island	$6.15
South Carolina	No state minimum wage law
South Dakota	$5.15
Tennessee	No state minimum wage law
Texas	$5.15
Utah	$5.15
Vermont	$6.25
Virginia	$5.15
Washington	$7.01
West Virginia	$5.15
Wisconsin	$5.15
Wyoming	$5.15

[a]Increased by statue in 2004.

SOURCE: U.S. Department of Labor, Employment Standards Administration Wage and Hour Division.

public works; the Walsh-Healey Act (41 U.S.C.A. §§ 35–45) applies to employers that provide materials, supplies, and equipment to the United States under contracts exceeding $10,000; and the Service Contract Act (41 U.S.C.A. §§ 351–358) applies to contracts in excess of $2,500 to provide services to the federal government. These statutes all require contracting entities to pay workers the prevailing wage in the locality.

As of 2003, the federal minimum wage has remained at $5.15 per hour for non-exempt employees. However, in 11 states, particularly those in northwestern and northeastern parts of the United States, the state minimum wage is higher than that of the federal government. Under the FLSA, if a state's minimum wage is higher, then that rate applies to employees working in that state.

The following 11 states provide a higher minimum wage than the federal standard (with the applicable hourly rate in parentheses), according to information from the U.S. LABOR DEPARTMENT: California ($6.75); Oregon ($6.90); Washington ($7.01); Maine ($6.25); Vermont ($6.25); Massachusetts ($6.75); Delaware ($6.15); Connecticut ($7.10); Rhode Island ($6.15); Alaska ($7.15); and Hawaii ($6.25).

The law in a few states still provides a minimum wage that is lower than the federal rate, although the latter continues to apply. Rates in American Samoa are established by a special industry committee, which determines rates for particular industries, rather than all covered employees. Like the states, an employer in American Samoa may choose to set rates at a higher level than the standard set by the committee.

FURTHER READINGS

Levitan, Sar A., and Richard A. Belous. 1979. *More Than Subsistence: Minimum Wages for the Working Poor*. Baltimore: Johns Hopkins Univ. Press.

Linder, Marc. 1990. "The Minimum Wage as Industrial Policy: A Forgotten Role." *Journal of Legislation* 16.

Norlund, Willis J. 1988. "A Brief History of the Fair Labor Standards Act." *Labor Law Journal* 39.

Quigley, William P. 1996. "'A Fair Day's Pay for a Fair Day's Work': Time to Raise and Index the Minimum Wage." *St. Mary's Law Journal.* 27.

Waltman, Jerold L. 2000. *The Politics of the Minimum Wage*. Urbana: University of Illinois Press.

Wright, Russell O. 2003. *Chronology of Labor in the United States*. Jefferson, N.C.: McFarland & Company, Inc.

CROSS-REFERENCES

Child Labor Laws; Employment Law; Labor Law; National Recovery Administration; New Deal.

MINISTER

See AMBASSADORS AND CONSULS; DIPLOMATIC AGENTS.

MINISTERIAL

Done under the direction of a supervisor; not involving discretion or policymaking.

Ministerial describes an act or a function that conforms to an instruction or a prescribed procedure. It connotes obedience. A *ministerial act* or *duty* is a function performed without the use of judgment by the person performing the act or duty.

MINITRIAL

A private, voluntary, and informal type of ALTERNATIVE DISPUTE RESOLUTION.

The minitrial is an alternative dispute resolution (ADR) procedure that is used by businesses and the federal government to resolve legal issues without incurring the expense and delay associated with court litigation. The minitrial does not result in a formal adjudication but is a vehicle for the parties to arrive at a solution through a structured settlement process. It is used most effectively when complex issues are at stake and the parties need or wish to maintain an amicable relationship.

Though minitrials can be arranged under rules negotiated by the parties, they usually conform to procedures used by facilitators of ADR. The parties sign an agreement consenting to a minitrial and then each chooses a management representative to sit on the panel. These representatives have the authority to negotiate a settlement. The parties also select a "neutral adviser" to sit on the panel. The adviser must be independent and impartial, as this person will moderate the minitrial. If the parties cannot agree on a neutral adviser, the ADR facilitating agency may make the selection. The parties pay an equal share of the adviser's fees and bear their own minitrial costs.

Prior to the minitrial the parties select and then provide the neutral adviser with background materials. The parties also file legal briefs and exhibits with the adviser that contain information they intend to present at what is termed the "information exchange." This exchange is, in effect, the minitrial. The parties must agree on the length of briefs and the due dates for documents.

At the information exchange each party makes presentation, and each party is entitled to make a rebuttal. As with all other procedures, the parties must either agree on the lengths of their presentations and rebuttals or let the neutral adviser set the time limits. During this information exchange the neutral adviser acts as a moderator rather than a judge. Factual witnesses and expert witnesses may also make presentations. The members of the panel may ask questions of the presenters. In addition to the lawyers representing the parties, each management representative may have advisers in attendance.

After the conclusion of the information exchange, the management representatives meet by themselves to see if they can resolve the dispute. The information exchange should have revealed the strengths and weaknesses of each party's case and motivated the representatives to settle the dispute. If they cannot resolve the dispute on their own, they may ask the neutral adviser to meet with them separately, or jointly, and give an oral opinion on the issues and the likely outcome at trial of each issue. The representatives may also ask the neutral adviser to issue a written opinion and to mediate the negotiations and settlement terms.

If an agreement is reached it is set out in writing and signed by the representatives. The agreement is legally binding on the parties. If the parties cannot settle, the proceedings will terminate 30 days after the date of the information exchange.

An important difference between a court trial and a minitrial is that the RULES OF EVIDENCE do not apply at the minitrial except for the rules governing PRIVILEGED COMMUNICATIONS and attorney work product. Another difference is that minitrials are not recorded, so no transcript can be produced. Finally, the proceedings are totally confidential and any offers or statements made in the process are inadmissible at a court trial.

FURTHER READINGS

Mayer, Bernard. 2000. *The Dynamics of Conflict Resolution.* New York: Jossey-Bass.

Moore, Christopher W. 2003. *The Mediation Process: Practical Strategies for Resolving Conflict.* 3d ed. New York: Jossey-Bass.

Nolan-Haley, Jacqueline. 2001. *Alternative Dispute Resolution in a Nutshell.* 2d ed. St. Paul, Minn.: West.

MINOR

An infant or person who is under the age of legal competence. A term derived from the CIVIL LAW, *which described a person under a certain age as less than* so many years. *In most states, a person is no longer a minor after reaching the age of 18 (though state laws might still prohibit certain acts until reaching a greater age; e.g., purchase of liquor). Also, less; of less consideration; lower; a person of inferior condition.*

MINORITY

The state or condition of a minor; infancy. Opposite of majority. The smaller number of votes of a deliberative assembly; opposed to majority. In context of the Constitution's guarantee of EQUAL PROTECTION, *minority does not have merely numerical denotation but refers to identifiable and specially disadvantaged groups such as those based on race, religion, ethnicity, or national origin.*

❖ MINTON, SHERMAN

Sherman Minton served as an associate justice of the U.S. Supreme Court from 1949 to 1956. A strong supporter of President FRANKLIN D. ROOSEVELT's NEW DEAL policies when he served as a U.S. senator from Indiana, Minton maintained a consistent judicial philosophy that allowed the legislative and executive branches wide discretion without judicial interference.

Minton was born on October 20, 1890, in Georgetown, Indiana. He graduated from Indiana University in 1915 and earned a law degree from Yale Law School in 1916. He entered the private PRACTICE OF LAW in Indiana but also devoted himself to DEMOCRATIC PARTY politics. In 1934 he was elected to the U.S. Senate, where he served one term. While in the Senate, Minton was a staunch supporter of Roosevelt's legislative efforts, including the president's plan to "pack" the Court with extra justices to break the conservative majority that had ruled many pieces of New Deal law unconstitutional. Minton lost his seat in the 1940 election.

In 1941 President Roosevelt first appointed Minton to advise him on military agencies and planning and then nominated him to the U.S. Court of Appeals for the Seventh Circuit. President HARRY S. TRUMAN, who got to know Minton when they served in the Senate together, elevated him to the Supreme Court in 1949. During his confirmation process, Minton refused to testify before the SENATE JUDICIARY

"ONE'S ASSOCIATES, PAST AND PRESENT, . . . MAY PROPERLY BE CONSIDERED IN DETERMINING FITNESS AND LOYALTY [FOR A JOB]."
—SHERMAN MINTON

Sherman Minton.
U.S. SUPREME COURT

COMMITTEE, claiming it would be improper to testify. Surprisingly, the committee did not object.

During his seven years on the Court, Minton maintained his belief that the judiciary should not intrude on the actions of the other branches unless absolutely required. His conservative view led him to support decisions that upheld anticommunist policies such as LOYALTY OATHS and restrictions on the civil liberties of subversives. Minton, writing for the majority in *Adler v. Board of Education,* 342 U.S. 485, 72 S. Ct. 380, 96 L. Ed. 517 (1952), ruled that a New York statute that prohibited members of politically subversive groups from teaching in public schools was permissible.

As a result of his deference to the other branches of government, Minton was the only dissenter in YOUNGSTOWN SHEET AND TUBE CO. V. SAWYER, 343 U.S. 579, 72 S. Ct. 863, 96 L. Ed. 1153 (1952). In this case President Truman had claimed executive authority when he seized U.S. steel mills in 1952 as the steel workers union went on strike. This occurred during the second year of the KOREAN WAR. Truman needed steel for war production and wanted to make sure that a pay hike would not cause higher steel prices, which would increase inflation in the national economy. The majority rejected Truman's claim to inherent executive power in the Constitution to protect the public interest in times of crisis. Minton sided with the president's position.

Minton suffered serious health problems for several years and resigned from the Court for health reasons in 1956. He died on April 9, 1965, in New Albany, Indiana.

FURTHER READINGS

Gugin, Linda C., and James E. St. Clair. 1997. *Sherman Minton: New Deal Senator, Cold War Justice.* Indianapolis: Indiana Historical Society.

Radcliff, William F. 1997. "A Lawyer's Biography of Sherman Minton." *Res Gestae* 40 (June).

———. 1996. *Sherman Minton: Indiana's Supreme Court Justice.* Indianapolis: Guild Press of Indiana

MINUTE BOOK

An account where official proceedings are recorded.

A minute book refers to a book kept by the clerk of a court for recording a summary of all the judicial orders in a proceeding. The records are identified by case numbers.

It also refers to a record of official actions taken at a meeting of a board of directors or of the stockholders of a corporation.

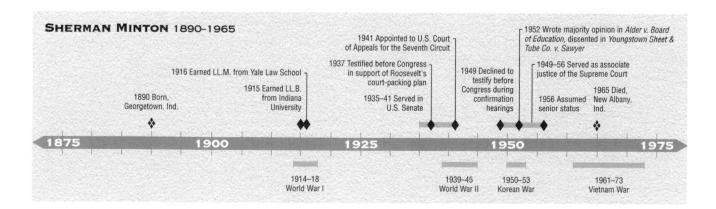

SHERMAN MINTON 1890–1965

1890 Born, Georgetown, Ind.

1916 Earned LL.M. from Yale Law School

1915 Earned LL.B. from Indiana University

1937 Testified before Congress in support of Roosevelt's court-packing plan

1935–41 Served in U.S. Senate

1941 Appointed to U.S. Court of Appeals for the Seventh Circuit

1949 Declined to testify before Congress during confirmation hearings

1952 Wrote majority opinion in *Alder v. Board of Education,* dissented in *Youngstown Sheet & Tube Co. v. Sawyer*

1949–56 Served as associate justice of the Supreme Court

1956 Assumed senior status

1965 Died, New Albany, Ind.

1875   1900   1925   1950   1975

1914–18 World War I

1939–45 World War II

1950–53 Korean War

1961–73 Vietnam War

MINUTES

The written record of an official proceeding. The notes recounting the transactions occurring at a meeting or official proceeding; a record kept by courts and corporations for future reference.

MIRANDA V. ARIZONA

Miranda v. Arizona was a landmark decision, 384 U.S. 436, 86 S. Ct. 1602, 16 L. Ed. 2d 694 (1966), in the field of CRIMINAL PROCEDURE. In *Miranda*, the U.S. Supreme Court declared a set of specific rights for criminal defendants. The *Miranda* warning, named after Ernesto Miranda, one of the petitioners in the case, is a list of rights that a law enforcement officer must read to anyone arrested for a criminal act.

Before the High Court's decision in *Miranda*, the law governing CUSTODIAL INTERROGATION of criminal suspects varied from state to state. In many states statements made by criminal defendants who were in custody and under interrogation by law enforcement officials were admissible at trial, even though the defendants had not been advised of their legal rights. If the totality of the circumstances surrounding the statements indicated that the suspect made the statements voluntarily, it did not matter that officers had not apprised the suspect of his legal rights.

The totality of the circumstances rule was effective even if a defendant was in custody. Generally a defendant was considered in custody if the person was not free to leave the presence of law enforcement officers. The basic legal rights for criminal defendants subjected to custodial interrogation included the FIFTH AMENDMENT right against SELF-INCRIMINATION and the RIGHT TO COUNSEL, this latter right established by the Court two years earlier in ESCOBEDO V. ILLINOIS, 378 U.S. 478, 84 S. Ct. 1758, 12 L. Ed. 2d 977 (1964).

The *Miranda* case involved four criminal defendants. Each of the defendants was appealing a conviction based in part on the failure of law enforcement officers to advise him, prior to custodial interrogation, of his right to an attorney or his right to remain silent.

Ernesto Miranda, the first defendant listed in the case, was arrested on March 18, 1963, at his home in Arizona and taken to a Phoenix police station. At the station witnesses identified Miranda as a rapist. Police then brought Miranda to an interrogation room where he was questioned by two police officers.

The officers did not tell Miranda that he had a right to an attorney, and Miranda confessed to the crime in two hours. Miranda wrote a confession on a piece of paper and signed the paper. At the top of the paper was a typed statement saying that Miranda had made the confession voluntarily and with full knowledge of his legal rights. Miranda was convicted of rape and KIDNAPPING in an Arizona state court. The circumstances involving the other three defendants were similar, all three confessing after a period of custodial interrogation without the assistance of legal counsel.

The U.S. Supreme Court agreed to hear appeals from all four defendants, joining the appeals into a single review. A divided Court affirmed the California Supreme Court's decision against one of the defendants and reversed the guilty verdicts against Miranda and the other two.

The majority opinion, written by Chief Justice EARL WARREN, began with a review of POLICE INTERROGATION activities and a detailed formulation of new rules for law enforcement personnel.

The opening of the *Miranda* majority opinion set a grave tone:

> The cases before us raise questions which go to the roots of American criminal JURISPRUDENCE: the restraints society must observe consistent with the Federal Constitution in prosecuting individuals for crime. More specifically, we deal with the admissibility of statements obtained from an individual who is subjected to custodial police interrogation and the necessity for procedures which assure that the individual is accorded his privilege under the Fifth Amendment to the Constitution not to be compelled to incriminate himself.

The 1966 decision of the Supreme Court in Miranda v. Arizona *set forth specific rights for criminal defendants. Ernesto Miranda (right), one of the petitioners, with his attorney, John J. Flynn.*

BETTMANN/CORBIS

The Court described in detail the unfairness and coercion used by some law enforcement officers engaged in interrogation. The majority also took note of deceptive practices in interrogation. For example, officers would put a suspect in a lineup and tell the person that he or she had been identified as a suspect in the instant crime as well as other crimes even though no such identifications had taken place. The suspect would confess to the instant crime to avoid being prosecuted for the fictitious crimes. The majority noted that these examples were exceptions, but it also stated that they were sufficiently widespread to warrant concern.

The Court then outlined the now-familiar procedures that law enforcement officers would have to follow thereafter. They would have to tell persons in custody that they have the right to remain silent, that they have the right to an attorney, that if they cannot afford an attorney the court will appoint an attorney, and that anything they say can be used in a criminal prosecution.

Ultimately, the Court held that statements made by a criminal suspect in custody would not be admissible at trial unless the suspect had made a knowing and intelligent waiver of his legal rights after being apprised of the various legal rights and after being given an opportunity to exercise those rights. The majority assured the law enforcement community that it did not intend to hamper criminal investigations and prosecutions. The Court pointed out that interrogations were still a perfectly legitimate investigative tool, that questioning a suspect without advising the suspect of legal rights before taking the suspect into custody was still legitimate, and that volunteered statements were likewise legitimate.

Justice TOM CLARK dissented to the decisions with respect to all defendants except the one whose conviction was upheld. According to Clark, the Court should have continued to accept the totality of the circumstances test for determining whether a defendant's statements or confession were made voluntarily. Clark concluded that only the defendant whose conviction was upheld gave a confession that was not voluntary.

Justices JOHN M. HARLAN, POTTER STEWART, and BYRON R. WHITE dissented in all the cases. In an opinion authored by Harlan, the dissent argued that the majority had exaggerated the evils of normal police questioning. According to Harlan, "Society has always paid a stiff price for

law and order, and peaceful interrogation is not one of the dark moments of the law."

Another dissent by White argued that the majority had gone too far in imposing such procedural requirements on the law enforcement community. White predicted that the new procedures would prevent the early release of the truly innocent because they discourage statements that would quickly explain a situation. According to White, the procedures were "a deliberate calculus to prevent interrogations, to reduce the incidence of confessions and pleas of guilty and to increase the number of trials." "I have no desire whatsoever," wrote White, "to share the responsibility for any such impact on the present criminal process."

The *Miranda* case was remarkable in at least two ways. The opinion mandated important procedural changes that had to be followed by every law enforcement official across the country. In addition, the majority opinion's survey of interrogation tactics sent a rare notice to the law enforcement community that the Court was aware of, and would not tolerate, abuse in interrogation.

Two years after the decision in *Miranda*, congressional anger at the decision led to the passage of 18 U.S.C.A. § 3501 (1996), which restored voluntariness as a test for admitting confessions in federal court. The U.S. JUSTICE DEPARTMENT, however, under attorneys general of both major political parties, refused to enforce the provision, believing the law to be unconstitutional. The law lay dormant for several decades until the Fourth Circuit Court of Appeals in 1999 ruled that Congress had the constitutional authority to pass the law. *United States v. Dickerson*, 166 F.3d 667 (4th Cir. 1999).

The Supreme Court disagreed with the Fourth Circuit. In a 7–2 decision, the Court ruled that because *Miranda* had been based on the Fifth and Fourteenth Amendments, Congress did not have the constitutional authority to overrule the decision through legislation. *Dickerson v. United States*, 530 U.S. 428, 120 S. Ct. 2326, 147 L. Ed. 2d 405 (2000). In addition, the Court refused to overrule *Miranda*. Chief Justice WILLIAM H. REHNQUIST, who has been a frequent critic of the decision, wrote the majority opinion that upheld the decision. According to Rehnquist, the ruling had become "part of our national culture" with respect to law enforcement.

However, the *Miranda* holding has been pared down by the High Court. In 1985 the

Court held that if a defendant makes an incriminating statement without the *Miranda* warning and then later receives the *Miranda* warning and confesses, the confession should not be excluded from trial (*Oregon v. Elstad*, 470 U.S. 298, 105 S. Ct. 1285, 84 L. Ed. 2d 222 [1985]).

In *Illinois v. Perkins*, 496 U.S. 292, 110 S. Ct. 2394, 110 L. Ed. 2d 243 (1990), the Court held that the *Miranda* warning is not required when a suspect who is unaware that he or she is speaking to a law enforcement officer gives a voluntary statement. In *Withrow v. Williams*, 507 U.S. 680, 113 S. Ct. 1745, 123 L. Ed. 2d 407 (1993), the Court held that a prisoner can not base a HABEAS CORPUS petition on the failure of law enforcement to give *Miranda* rights before interrogation.

In *Moran v. Burbine*, 475 U.S. 412, 106 S. Ct. 1135, 89 L. Ed. 2d 410 (1986), however, the Court appeared to return to the totality of the circumstances test. In *Moran,* a lawyer representing a criminal suspect, Brian Burbine, called the police station while Burbine was in custody. The lawyer was told that Burbine would not be questioned until the next day. In fact, Burbine was questioned that day, and he confessed, without requesting the lawyer and after being told his *Miranda* rights. According to the Court, the conduct of the police fell "short of the kind of misbehavior that so shocks the sensibilities of civilized society as to warrant a federal intrusion into the criminal processes of the States." Although law enforcement had not given Burbine a full opportunity to exercise his right to an attorney, a 6–3 majority of the Court concluded that, on the facts of the case, the incriminating statements were made voluntarily and that excluding them was therefore not required.

In 2002, the Supreme Court granted certiorari to consider a case involving the question of whether police officers are required to give criminal suspects their *Miranda* rights even if the suspects are never brought to trial. In 1997, Oliverio Martinez, a farm worker, was shot and injured by police officers during a struggle. A police sergeant, Ben Chavez, questioned Martinez for 45 minutes while the latter lay in a hospital bed. Chavez never gave Martinez his *Miranda* warnings, and Martinez insisted that he did not want to answer the questions.

The Ninth Circuit Court of Appeals determined that this questioning violated Martinez's constitutional rights, thus allowing him to recover under 42 U.S.C.A. SECTION 1983 (Supp. 2003). *Martinez v. City of Oxford*, 270 F.3d 852 (9th Cir. 2001). However, a sharply divided Supreme Court reversed the Ninth Circuit's decision on appeal. CHAVEZ V. MARTINEZ, 123 S. Ct. 1994, 155 L. Ed. 2d 984 (2003). Although the Court in *Chavez* did not overrule *Miranda*, the Court further limited the scope of the decision by holding that the failure by the officer to read Martinez's *Miranda* warnings did not violate Martinez's constitutional rights and could not be used as a basis for recovery under 42 U.S.C.A. § 1983. According to the Court, per Justice CLARENCE THOMAS, *Miranda* warnings merely offer protection against violations of constitutional rights, but the failure to provide these warnings is not itself a constitutional violation. Moreover, because Martinez was never required to be a witness against himself in a criminal trial, the fact that the officer asked coercive questions did not violate Martinez's Fifth Amendment right against self-incrimination, according to the Court.

FURTHER READINGS

Einesman, Floralynn. 1999. "Confessions and Culture: the Interaction of *Miranda* and Diversity." *Journal of Criminal Law and Criminology* 90 (fall).

Klein, Susan R. 2001. "*Miranda's* Exceptions in a Post-*Dickerson* World." *Journal of Criminal Law and Criminology* (spring): 567–96.

Lane, Charles. 2002. "Justices Ponder the Reach of Miranda Rights Ruling." *Washington Post.*

Thomas, George C., III. 2000. "The End of the Road for *Miranda v. Arizona*? On the History and Future of Rules for Police Interrogation." *American Criminal Law Review* 37 (winter).

"Will Miranda Survive? *Dickerson v. United States:* the Right to Remain Silent, the Supreme Court, and Congress." 2000. *American Criminal Law Review* 37 (summer).

CROSS-REFERENCES

Coercion; Criminal Procedure; Criminal Law; Due Process of Law; Exclusionary Rule; Fruit of the Poisonous Tree.

MISCARRIAGE OF JUSTICE

A legal proceeding resulting in a prejudicial outcome.

A miscarriage of justice arises when the decision of a court is inconsistent with the substantive rights of a party.

MISCEGENATION

Mixture of races. A term formerly applied to marriage between persons of different races. Statutes prohibiting marriage between persons of different races have been held to be invalid as contrary to the EQUAL PROTECTION CLAUSE *of the Constitution.*

MISCHIEF

A specific injury or damage caused by another person's action or inaction. In CIVIL LAW, *a person who suffered physical injury due to the* NEGLIGENCE *of another person could allege mischief in a lawsuit in* TORT. *For example, if a baseball is hit through a person's window by accident, and the resident within is injured, mischief can be claimed. It is distinct from malicious mischief, which is a criminal act usually involving reckless or intentional behavior such as* VANDALISM.

MISDEMEANOR

Offenses lower than felonies and generally those punishable by fine, penalty, FORFEITURE, *or imprisonment other than in a penitentiary. Under federal law, and most state laws, any offense other than a felony is classified as a misdemeanor. Certain states also have various classes of misdemeanors (e.g., Class A, B, etc.).*

MISFEASANCE

A term used in TORT LAW *to describe an act that is legal but performed improperly.*

Generally, a civil defendant will be liable for misfeasance if the defendant owed a duty of care toward the plaintiff, the defendant breached that duty of care by improperly performing a legal act, and the improper performance resulted in harm to the plaintiff.

For example, assume that a janitor is cleaning a restroom in a restaurant. If he leaves the floor wet, he or his employer could be liable for any injuries resulting from the wet floor. This is because the janitor owed a duty of care toward users of the restroom, and he breached that duty by leaving the floor wet.

In theory, misfeasance is distinct from NONFEASANCE. *Nonfeasance* is a term that describes a failure to act that results in harm to another party. Misfeasance, by contrast, describes some affirmative act that, though legal, causes harm. In practice, the distinction is confusing and uninstructive. Courts often have difficulty determining whether harm resulted from a failure to act or from an act that was improperly performed.

To illustrate, consider the example of the wet bathroom floor. One court could call a resulting injury the product of misfeasance by focusing on the wetness of the floor. The washing of the floor was legal, but the act of leaving the floor wet was improper. Another court could call a resulting injury the product of nonfeasance by focusing on the janitor's failure to post a warning sign.

FURTHER READINGS

Kionka, Edward J. 1988. *Torts.* St. Paul, Minn.: West.

CROSS-REFERENCES

Malfeasance.

MISPRISION

The failure to perform a public duty.

Misprision is a versatile word that can denote a number of offenses. It can refer to the improper performance of an official duty. In Arkansas, for example, rule 60 of the Arkansas Rules of Civil Procedure provides that a judgment, decree, or order may be vacated or modified "for misprisions of the clerk." In this sense *misprision* refers to neglect, mistake, or subterfuge on the part of the court clerk who performed the paperwork for the judgment, decree, or order.

Misprision also can refer to seditious or rebellious conduct against the government or the courts. This is an archaic usage of the word. Organized rebellion against the government is now uniformly referred to as SEDITION or insurrection.

The most familiar and popular use of the term *misprision* describes the failure to report a crime. In England, beginning in the thirteenth century, the failure to report a crime became itself a crime. According to tradition, it was a citizen's duty to "raise the hue and cry" by reporting crimes, especially felonies, to law enforcement authorities (*Branzburg v. Hayes*, 408 U.S. 665, 92 S. Ct. 2646, 33 L. Ed. 2d 626 [1972], quoting WILLIAM BLACKSTONE).

The crime of misprision still exists in England, but it has never been fully embraced in the United States. The first Congress passed a misprision of felony statute in 1789. The statute holds, "Whoever, having knowledge of the actual commission of a felony ... conceals and does not as soon as possible make known the same to some judge or other person in civil or military authority under the United States" is guilty of misprision of felony and can be punished with up to three years in prison.

Under the federal statute, the prosecution must prove the following elements to obtain a misprision of felony conviction: (1) another person actually committed a felony; (2) the defendant knew that the felony was committed; (3) the defendant did not notify any law enforcement or judicial officer; and (4) the defendant took affirmative steps to conceal the felony. Precisely what constitutes active concealment is a QUESTION OF FACT that depends on the circumstances of the case. Lying to a police officer satisfies the requirement, but beyond that generally accepted rule, little is certain about the definition of active concealment.

Almost every state has rejected the crime of misprision of felony. Thus, persons are under no duty to report a crime. One policy reason for rejecting misprision is that the crime is vague and difficult to apply to real situations. Another reason is that the crime is seen as an unacceptable encroachment on civil freedom. In 1822 the U.S. Supreme Court cautioned against misuse of the misprision of felony statute, stating, "It may be the duty of a citizen to . . . proclaim every offense which comes to his knowledge; but the law which would punish him in every case, for not performing this duty, is too harsh" (*Marbury v. Brooks*, 20 U.S. [7 Wheat.] 556, 5 L. Ed. 522).

The Supreme Court has not completely abandoned the duty to report criminal activity. In *Roberts v. United States*, 445 U.S. 552, 100 S. Ct. 1358, 63 L. Ed. 2d 622 (1980), the High Court held that a court can increase a criminal defendant's sentence if the defendant refuses to cooperate with government officials investigating a related crime. Also, a journalist who has knowledge of a crime may be compelled to reveal the source of that knowledge (*Branzburg v. Hayes*).

The federal misprision of felony statute remains on the books, but the crime rarely has been prosecuted. On the state level, most states have either abolished or refused to enact misprision of felony laws. South Carolina is the only state that has prosecuted the misprision of a felony.

In *State v. Carson*, 262 S.E.2d 918, 274 S.C. 316 (1980), Isaac E. Carson, the EYEWITNESS to a murder, refused to give law enforcement authorities information regarding the murder because he feared for his life if he cooperated with authorities. Carson was prosecuted and convicted of misprision of felony and sentenced to three years in prison.

The prosecution of Carson was based on the COMMON LAW. South Carolina did not have a misprision of felony statute. Instead the prosecution relied on title 14, chapter 1, section 50, of the Code of Laws of South Carolina. Under this statute the common law of England continues in effect in South Carolina. On appeal by Carson, the Supreme Court of South Carolina affirmed the conviction. According to the court, the prosecution was valid because misprision of felony was a crime at common law in England and because the South Carolina legislature had not taken steps to repeal the common-law crime of misprision of felony.

The crime of misprision of felony is similar to the crime of acting as an ACCESSORY after the fact because both crimes involve some affirmative act to conceal a crime. Two basic differences are that the crime of misprision is committed even if the defendant does not give aid to the criminal and misprision is committed only if the underlying crime is completed.

FURTHER READINGS

Gould, Keri A. 1993. "Turning Rat and Doing Time for Uncharged, Dismissed, or Acquitted Crimes: Do the Federal Sentencing Guidelines Promote Respect for the Law?" *New York Law School Journal of Human Rights* 10.

Guerra, Sandra. 1996. "Family Values?: The Family as an Innocent Victim of Civil Drug Asset Forfeiture." *Cornell Law Review* 81.

Mosteller, Robert P. 1992. "Child Abuse Reporting Laws and Attorney-Client Confidences: The Reality and the Specter of Lawyer as Informant." *Duke Law Journal* 42.

MISREPRESENTATION

An assertion or manifestation by words or conduct that is not in accord with the facts.

Misrepresentation is a TORT, or a civil wrong. This means that a misrepresentation can create civil liability if it results in a pecuniary loss. For example, assume that a real estate speculator owns swampland but advertises it as valuable commercially zoned land. This is a misrepresentation. If someone buys the land relying on the speculator's statement that it is commercially valuable, the buyer may sue the speculator for monetary losses resulting from the purchase.

To create liability for the maker of the statement, a misrepresentation must be relied on by the listener or reader. Also, the speaker must know that the listener is relying on the factual correctness of the statement. Finally, the listener's reliance on the statement must have been reasonable and justified, and the misrepresentation must have resulted in a pecuniary loss to the listener.

A misrepresentation need not be intentionally false to create liability. A statement made with conscious ignorance or a reckless disregard for the truth can create liability. Nondisclosure of material or important facts by a fiduciary or an expert, such as a doctor, lawyer, or accountant, can result in liability. If the speaker is engaged in the business of selling products, any statement, no matter how innocent, may create liability if the statement concerns the character or quality of a product and the statement is not true. In such a case, the statement must be one of fact. This does not include so-called puffing, or the glowing opinions of a seller in the course of a sales pitch (such statements as "you'll love this car," or "it's a great deal").

A misrepresentation in a contract can give a party the right to rescind the contract. A RESCISSION of a contract returns the parties to the positions they held before the contract was made. A party can rescind a contract for misrepresentation only if the statement was material, or critical, to the agreement.

A misrepresentation on the part of the insured in an insurance policy can give the insurer the right to cancel the policy or refuse a claim. An insurer may do this only if the misrepresentation was material to the risk insured against and would have influenced the insurer in determining whether to issue a policy. For example, if a person seeking auto insurance states that she has no major chronic illnesses, the insurer's subsequent discovery that the applicant had an incurable disease at the time she completed the insurance form probably will not give the insurer the right to cancel the auto policy. However, if the person was seeking HEALTH INSURANCE, such a misrepresentation may justify cancellation of the policy or a denial of coverage. Generally, cancellation or denial of insurance coverage for a misrepresentation can occur only if the insurance applicant was aware of the inaccuracy of the statement.

FURTHER READINGS

Kionka, Edward J. 1988. *Torts*. St. Paul, Minn.: West.

CROSS-REFERENCES

Consumer Protection; Product Liability; Sales Law; Tort Law.

MISSOURI COMPROMISE OF 1820

The Missouri Compromise of 1820 was a congressional agreement that regulated the extension of SLAVERY in the United States for the next 30 years. Under the agreement the territory of Missouri was admitted as a slave state, the territory of Maine was admitted as a free state, and the boundaries of slavery were limited to the same latitude as the southern boundary of Missouri: 36° 30' north latitude.

The issue of slavery had been troublesome since the drafting of the Constitution. Slaveholding states, concerned that they would be outvoted in Congress because their white population was much smaller than that of the free states, extracted concessions. Under the Constitution, representation of the U.S. House of Representatives was based on the total white population and three-fifths of the black population. The Constitution apportioned two senators for each state.

By 1820, however, the rapid growth in population in the North left Southern states, for the first time, with less than 45 percent of the seats in the House. The Senate was evenly balanced between eleven slave and eleven free states. Therefore, Missouri's 1818 application for statehood, if approved, would give slave-holding seats a majority in the Senate and reduce the Northern majority in the House.

After a bill was introduced in the House in 1818 to approve Missouri's application for statehood, Representative James Tallmadge of New York introduced an amendment that prohibited the further introduction of slavery in Missouri and required that any slave born there be emancipated at age 25. The bill passed the House but was defeated in the Senate, where Southern strength was greater.

In 1819 the free territory of Maine applied for statehood. Speaker of the House HENRY CLAY of Kentucky saw this event as an opportunity to maintain the balance of free and slave states. He made it clear to Northern congressmen that Maine would not be admitted without an agreement to admit Missouri. Clay was successful, getting the Northern congressmen to drop their amendment restricting slavery while winning Southern congressmen over to the idea of limiting slavery to the 36° 30' north latitude. This provision, in effect, left unsettled portions of the LOUISIANA PURCHASE north and west of Missouri free from slavery. The only area remaining for further expansion of slavery was the future territory of Arkansas and Oklahoma. Clay managed to pass the compromise in the House by a three-vote margin. Missouri and Maine were to be admitted to the Union simultaneously to preserve the sectional equality in the Senate.

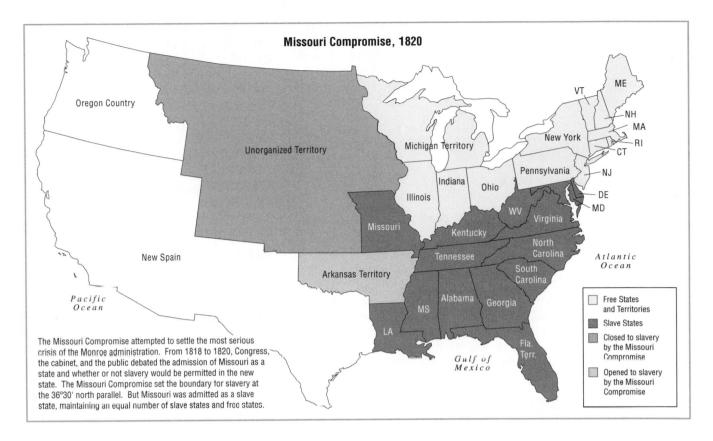

Missouri Compromise, 1820

Oregon Country

Unorganized Territory

Michigan Territory

New York

VT

ME

NH

MA

RI

CT

NJ

DE

MD

Pennsylvania

Indiana

Ohio

Illinois

WV

Virginia

Missouri

Kentucky

New Spain

Tennessee

North Carolina

Atlantic Ocean

Arkansas Territory

South Carolina

Alabama

Georgia

MS

LA

Fla. Terr.

Pacific Ocean

Gulf of Mexico

Free States and Territories

Slave States

Closed to slavery by the Missouri Compromise

Opened to slavery by the Missouri Compromise

The Missouri Compromise attempted to settle the most serious crisis of the Monroe administration. From 1818 to 1820, Congress, the cabinet, and the public debated the admission of Missouri as a state and whether or not slavery would be permitted in the new state. The Missouri Compromise set the boundary for slavery at the 36°30' north parallel. But Missouri was admitted as a slave state, maintaining an equal number of slave states and free states.

In 1821 Missouri complicated matters, however, by inserting a provision into its state constitution that forbade any free blacks or mulattoes (people of mixed Caucasian and African-American heritage) to enter the state. Northern congressmen objected to this language and refused to give final approval for statehood until it was removed. Clay then negotiated a second compromise, removing the contested language and substituting a provision that prohibited Missouri from discriminating against citizens from other states. It left unsettled the question of who was a citizen. With this change Missouri and Maine were admitted to the Union.

The Missouri Compromise of 1820 merely postponed the conflict over slavery. As new territories were annexed to the Union, new compromises with slavery became necessary. The COMPROMISE OF 1850 redrew the territorial map of slavery and altered the 36° 30' north latitude prescription of the Missouri Compromise. California was admitted as a free state, and the Utah and New Mexico territories were open to slavery. The KANSAS-NEBRASKA ACT of 1854 repealed the Missouri Compromise. This new law provided for the organization of two new territories that allowed slavery, Kansas and Nebraska, both north of the 1820 Missouri Compromise line of 36° 30' north latitude. The land open to slavery drove deep into the north and west.

The constitutionality of the Missouri Compromise itself was challenged in the landmark U.S. Supreme Court case of DRED SCOTT V. SANDFORD, 60 U.S. (19 How.) 393, 15 L. Ed. 69 (1857). Scott, a slave, had lived with his master in the free state of Illinois and also in part of the Wisconsin territory, where slavery had been federally prohibited under the Missouri Compromise. After his master died, Scott sued in the Missouri courts for his freedom, on the grounds that he had lived in a free territory. The Supreme Court ruled against Scott, with Chief Justice ROGER B. TANEY holding that the FIFTH AMENDMENT denies Congress the right to deprive persons of their property without DUE PROCESS OF LAW. Therefore, the Missouri Compromise prohibiting slavery north of 36° 30' was unconstitutional. The decision wiped away the Missouri Compromise but also raised the issue of whether slavery could be regulated by any government anywhere in the Union.

FURTHER READINGS

Benton, Thomas Hart. 2003. *Historical and Legal Examination of that Part of the Decision of the Supreme Court of*

Missouri Compromise (map showing boundaries of free and slave states).

ILLUSTRATION BY ERIC WISNIEWSKI. GALE GROUP

the United States in the Dred Scott Case.... Buffalo, N.Y.: W.S. Hein.

Finkelman, Paul. 1997. *Dred Scott v. Sandford: A Brief History with Documents.* Boston: Bedford Books.

O'Fallon, James M. 1998. "Under Construction: The Constitution and the Missouri Controversy." *Oregon Law Review* 77 (summer): 381–403.

Whitman, Sylvia. 2002. "Henry Clay & Daniel Webster: Two Pillars of the Union." *Cobblestone* 23 (January): 34–39.

MISTAKE

An unintentional act, omission, or error.

Mistakes are categorized as a MISTAKE OF FACT, MISTAKE OF LAW, or mutual mistake. A mistake of fact occurs when a person believes that a condition or event exists when it does not. A mistake of law is made by a person who has knowledge of the correct facts but is wrong about the legal consequences of an act or event. A mutual mistake arises when two or more parties have a shared intention that has been induced by a common misbelief.

MISTAKE OF FACT

An error that is not caused by the neglect of a legal duty on the part of the person committing the error but rather consists of an unconscious ignorance of a past or present material event or circumstance or a belief in the present existence of a material event that does not exist or a belief in the past existence of a material event that did not exist.

Mistake of fact can be a factor in reducing or eliminating civil liability or criminal culpability. A mistake of fact is of little consequence unless it is born of unconscious ignorance or forgetfulness. A person cannot escape civil or criminal liability for intentional mistakes.

In contract law a mistake of fact may be raised as a defense by a party seeking to avoid liability under the contract. Also, a mistake of fact can be used affirmatively to cancel, rescind, or reform a contract. A mistake of fact can affect a contract only if the mistaken fact was material, or important, to the agreement.

For example, assume that a bookseller has agreed to sell a copy of a Virginia Woolf novel that was signed by the late author. Assume further that the buyer is only interested in buying the book because it contains Woolf's signature. The seller knows this, and with an authentic signature the book fetches a very high price. If it is later discovered that the signature was actually forged decades earlier and neither the seller nor the buyer knew of the forgery, this would be a mistake of fact material to the deal, and the buyer would have the right to return the book and get her money back. This example illustrates a mutual mistake, or a material fact that is mistaken by both parties. In such a case, the party who is adversely affected by the mistake has the right to cancel or rescind the contract.

In the event of a unilateral mistake, only one party to the agreement is mistaken about a material fact. In such a case, the party adversely affected by the mistake will not be able to void the contract unless the other party knew or should have known of the mistake, or unless the other party had a duty to disclose the mistaken fact. For example, assume that a person owns an expensive sports car that is in perfect condition. Assume further that a neighbor asks the owner if he will sell the car, and the owner responds, "I will sell this car for thirty bills." If the neighbor returns with $30, no contract is formed because the neighbor mistakenly thought that the owner meant $30 when actually the owner was using slang for $30,000. Further, the neighbor should have known that an expensive sports car would not be sold for $30.

If a party to a contract assumes the risk that a material fact may be different than expected, that party will not be able to recover any losses when the fact turns out to be different. For example, assume that a farmer sells a horse to a buyer who wants to use the horse for polo games. Neither the farmer nor the buyer knows whether the horse will be suitable for polo, and the farmer makes no guarantees. If the horse proves unsuitable, the buyer will not be able to rescind the deal because the farmer made no warranties as to the horse's suitability for polo. To avoid such a result, parties to a contract may agree, as part of the deal, to cancel or rescind the contract if a certain fact related to the contract later proves unacceptable to one of the parties.

If a contract can be reformed, a court may not allow a party to rescind a contract on account of mistake of fact. The court reforms a contract to reflect the true intent of the parties. For example, assume that a footwear retailer offers to buy 100 mukluks from a mukluk manufacturer for $10 a pair. Assume further that the retailer mistakenly orders 100 mukluks for $100 a pair. If the mukluk manufacturer delivers 100 mukluks and later demands $100 for each pair, the retailer can ask a court to reform the contract to reflect a price of $10 a pair. This action generally occurs when the mistake makes the agreement UNCONSCIONABLE. If, for example, the retailer had offered to pay $101 a pair and the retailer later discovered that the standard price was $100, the retailer would likely be stuck with the contract.

A mistake involving the use of force in the defense of property can give rise to civil liability. Generally, if a person has a privilege to enter onto property, a landowner or tenant has no right to use force to keep the intruder off the property. If, however, the intruder causes a reasonable, mistaken belief that the property must be defended, a landowner or tenant may have the right to use force to repel the intruder. For example, if an electricity meter reader arrives to read a meter at night wearing dark clothing and a ski mask, a resident on the property may not be liable for a reasonable use of force necessary to expel the intruder. The meter reader can be considered to have caused the mistaken belief on the part of the resident that the property was being invaded by someone with no privilege to enter.

In CRIMINAL LAW an honest and reasonable mistake of fact can eliminate the mens rea element of criminal responsibility. *Mens rea* is Latin for "guilty mind," and, along with an act, a guilty mind, or a criminal intent, is required before a person can be held criminally responsible for most crimes. For example, assume that a person who buys stolen goods honestly and reasonably believed that the goods actually belonged to the seller. This would negate the criminal intent necessary to be convicted of receiving stolen goods, and the buyer would not be held criminally liable.

If a mistake of fact in a criminal case does not negate mens rea, it may reduce it. For example, if a person honestly and reasonably, but mistakenly, believes that DEADLY FORCE is necessary to preserve her own life, she may not be found guilty of murder if a death results from the deadly force. The mistake reduced the mens rea necessary to be convicted of murder. That is, the person did not have the SPECIFIC INTENT to kill without justification or excuse. She may be found guilty of MANSLAUGHTER, a HOMICIDE less serious than murder, if her actions were unreasonable. She may even be found not guilty of any homicide if the judge or jury finds that she was not reckless or negligent in the killing. This is a QUESTION OF FACT to be determined by the judge or jury sitting on the case.

In some criminal and civil cases, no mens rea is required for liability. Such cases involve STRICT LIABILITY crimes. STATUTORY RAPE is an example of a strict liability crime. It does not matter whether the defendant knew that the victim was too young to have sexual relations or whether the defendant intended to have sex with a minor. In such a case, a mistake of fact is no defense. Strict liability crimes are generally those that endanger the public WELFARE, such as toxic waste dumping and the sale of alcohol to minors.

FURTHER READINGS

"Contracts." 1994. *SMH Bar Review.*

Cox, Archibald S. 1988. *The Court and the Constitution.* Boston: Houghton Mifflin.

"Criminal Law and Procedure." 1994. *SMH Bar Review.*

Hedges, Andrew. 1999. "Defendant Entitled to Mistake-of-Fact Instruction." *Res Gestae* 43 (November): 19.

Kionka, Edward J. 1988. *Torts.* St. Paul, Minn.: West.

O'Neill, Patricia A. 2001. "Criminal Law: Jury Instructions—Mistake of Fact in Rape Cases." *Massachusetts Law Review* 86 (fall): 67.

Porsdam, Helle. 1999. *Legally Speaking: Contemporary American Culture and the Law.* Amherst, Mass.: Univ. of Massachusetts.

CROSS-REFERENCES

Mens Rea.

MISTAKE OF LAW

A misconception that occurs when a person with complete knowledge of the facts reaches an erroneous conclusion as to their legal effect; an incorrect opinion or inference, arising from a flawed evaluation of the facts.

Generally, a mistaken belief about a law is no defense to a violation of that law. All persons are presumed to know and understand the law, except minors, persons who lack mental capacity to contract with others, and, in criminal cases, persons who are insane. There are, however, a few other rare exceptions to this general rule.

A mistake of law may be helpful to criminal defendants facing prosecution for a specific-intent crime. A specific-intent crime requires that a defendant act with a criminal intent beyond the general intent required to commit the act. Murder, for example, is a specific-intent crime. The prosecution must show that the defendant specifically intended to kill the victim without justification. MANSLAUGHTER, conversely, requires only a showing that the defendant intended to do those actions that caused the death. If a defendant is charged with a specific-intent crime, the defendant's reasonable mistaken belief about the law may reduce the defendant's criminal liability.

For example, assume that a defendant is accused of robbing another person. Assume further that the defendant was actually trying to retrieve money that the alleged victim owed to the defendant. A court may hold that the defendant mistakenly believed that the law allows SELF-HELP in such situations and that the mistaken belief about the law negated the SPECIFIC INTENT required for the crime. That is, the defendant did not have the specific intent to gain control over the property of another person. Generally, a mistake of law is helpful to criminal defendants only in specific-intent cases. For general-intent and STRICT LIABILITY crimes, a mistake of law is no defense.

There are other exceptions to the general rule that ignorance of the law is no excuse. If a defendant relied on a statute that permitted a certain act and the act is later made illegal, the defendant cannot be prosecuted. This applies to general-intent and strict liability crimes as well as specific-intent crimes. If a defendant reasonably relies on a judicial decision, an opinion, or a judgment that is later reversed, the reversal does not retroactively make a related act illegal. Similarly, if a defendant acts with reasonable reliance on an official statement of law in an administrative order or from an official interpretation by a public officer or government agency, the defendant may use the mistake-of-law defense. Mistaken advice from an attorney, however, does not create a mistake-of-law defense.

FURTHER READINGS

"Criminal Law and Procedure." 1994. *SMH Bar Review.*

Kionka, Edward J. 1988. *Torts.* St. Paul, Minn.: West.

MISTRIAL

A courtroom trial that has been terminated prior to its normal conclusion. A mistrial has no legal effect and is considered an invalid or nugatory trial. It differs from a "new trial," which recognizes that a trial was completed but was set aside so that the issues could be tried again.

A judge may declare a mistrial for several reasons, including lack of jurisdiction, incorrect jury selection, or a deadlocked, or hung, jury. A deadlocked jury—where the jurors cannot agree over the defendant's guilt or innocence—is a common

reason for declaring a mistrial. Extraordinary circumstances, such as death or illness of a necessary juror or an attorney, may also result in a mistrial. A mistrial may also result from a fundamental error so prejudicial to the defendant that it cannot be cured by appropriate instructions to the jury, such as improper remarks made during the prosecution's summation.

In determining whether to declare a mistrial, the court must decide whether the error is so prejudicial and fundamental that expenditure of further time and expense would be wasteful, if not futile. Although the judge has the power to declare a mistrial and discharge a jury, this power should be "exercised with great care and only in cases of absolute necessity" (*Salvatore v. State of Florida,* 366 So. 2d 745 [Fla. 1978], *cert. denied,* 444 U.S. 885, 100 S. Ct. 177, 62 L. Ed. 2d 115 [1979]).

For example, in *Ferguson v. State,* 417 So. 2d 639 (Fla. 1982), the defendant moved for a mistrial because of an allegedly improper comment made by the prosecution during closing argument. The prosecution stated that not only was defense counsel asking the jury to find a scapegoat for the defendant's guilt, he was also putting the blame on someone who had already been found guilty. The appellate court found that the lower court had properly denied the motion for a mistrial because the prosecutor's comment fell within the bounds of "fair reply."

A mistrial in a criminal prosecution may prevent retrial under the DOUBLE JEOPARDY provision of the FIFTH AMENDMENT, which prohibits an individual from being tried twice for the same offense, unless required by the interests of justice and depending on which party moved for the mistrial. Typically, there is no bar to a retrial if the defendant requests or consents to a mistrial. A retrial may be barred if the court grants a mistrial without the defendant's consent, or over his objection. If the mistrial results from judicial or prosecutorial misconduct, a retrial will be barred. In *United States v. Jorn,* 400 U.S. 470, 91 S. Ct. 547, 27 L. Ed. 2d 543 (1971), the Supreme Court held that reprosecuting the defendant would constitute double jeopardy because the judge had abused his discretion in declaring a mistrial. On his own motion, the judge had declared a mistrial to enable government witnesses to consult with their own attorneys.

CROSS-REFERENCES

Criminal Procedure; Harmless Error; Hung Jury.

❖ MITCHELL, JOHN NEWTON

John Newton Mitchell served as U.S. attorney general from 1969 to 1972. A key political adviser to President RICHARD M. NIXON, Mitchell was later convicted of crimes associated with the WATERGATE scandal, becoming the first attorney general to serve time in a federal prison.

Mitchell was born September 5, 1913, in Detroit. He worked his way through Fordham University and Fordham Law School playing semiprofessional hockey. After graduating from law school in 1938, he was admitted to the New York bar and began work in a New York City law firm. He was made a partner in 1942. During WORLD WAR II, he served as a torpedo boat commander in the U.S. Navy.

Mitchell became rich and prominent as a municipal bond lawyer, devising new ways for states and municipalities to finance construction projects. He met Richard M. Nixon in 1962, when Nixon joined a prominent New York law firm. At that time Nixon appeared to have no political future; he had lost the 1960 presidential election and the 1962 California gubernatorial election. In 1967 Mitchell's firm merged with Nixon's and the pair became confidants.

Mitchell served as Nixon's campaign manager for the presidency in 1968. He forged a conservative coalition of southern and western states that helped carry Nixon to victory over Vice President HUBERT H. HUMPHREY. During the campaign Mitchell claimed he would never accept a cabinet position if Nixon was elected. Despite these statements Mitchell accepted the post of attorney general in 1969.

As attorney general, Mitchell led the JUSTICE DEPARTMENT in a sweeping law-and-order drive that many critics believed went too far. He

John N. Mitchell.
CONSOLIDATED/
ARCHIVE PHOTOS

increased the number of telephone wiretaps on private citizens and generally clamped down on political dissenters, especially those who opposed U.S. involvement in the VIETNAM WAR. A number of these Justice Department initiatives were later ruled illegal by the courts. For example, in *Ellsberg v. Mitchell*, 353 F. Supp. 515 (D.D.C. 1973), the department sought to prosecute Daniel Ellsberg for leaking secret documents to the press regarding military involvement in Vietnam. The release of the Pentagon Papers infuriated the Nixon White House. The case was dismissed after Ellsberg's attorneys informed the court that a secret White House security group (the "plumbers") had illegally

"YOU WILL BE BETTER ADVISED TO WATCH WHAT WE DO INSTEAD OF WHAT WE SAY."
—JOHN MITCHELL

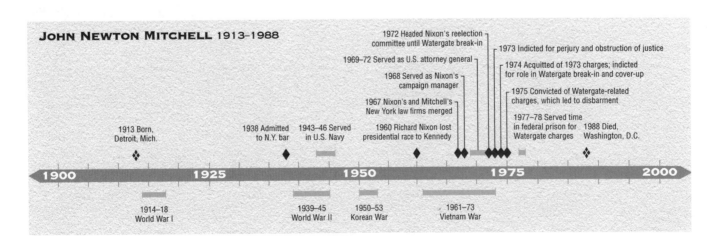

JOHN NEWTON MITCHELL 1913–1988

1972 Headed Nixon's reelection committee until Watergate break-in

1973 Indicted for perjury and obstruction of justice

1969–72 Served as U.S. attorney general

1974 Acquitted of 1973 charges; indicted for role in Watergate break-in and cover-up

1968 Served as Nixon's campaign manager

1967 Nixon's and Mitchell's New York law firms merged

1975 Convicted of Watergate-related charges, which led to disbarment

1913 Born, Detroit, Mich.

1938 Admitted to N.Y. bar

1943–46 Served in U.S. Navy

1960 Richard Nixon lost presidential race to Kennedy

1977–78 Served time in federal prison for Watergate charges

1988 Died, Washington, D.C.

1900   1925   1950   1975   2000

1914–18 World War I

1939–45 World War II

1950–53 Korean War

1961–73 Vietnam War

broken into the office of Ellsberg's psychiatrist in search of damaging evidence. The dismissal was also based on the Justice Department's refusal to produce wiretap records pertaining to Ellsberg.

Mitchell resigned as attorney general in February 1972 to head President Nixon's reelection committee. On June 17, 1972, five men were arrested after breaking into Democratic National Committee headquarters at the Watergate building complex in Washington, D.C. They and two other men associated with the White House and the reelection committee were charged with BURGLARY and WIRETAPPING. Mitchell denied playing any part in the Watergate incident but resigned from the reelection committee post in July.

In May 1973 he was indicted in New York City for perjury and OBSTRUCTION OF JUSTICE in an alleged scheme to secretly contribute cash to the Nixon reelection campaign. He was acquitted of the charge in 1974. In that same year, however, he was indicted for conspiracy, obstruction of justice, giving false testimony to a GRAND JURY, and perjury, for his role in the Watergate break-in and cover-up. He was convicted of these charges in 1975 and sentenced to two-and-a-half to eight years in prison. After exhausting his criminal appeals, he entered federal prison in June 1977. His sentence was later reduced to one to four years after he made a statement of contrition. He was paroled in January 1978.

His criminal convictions led to his disbarment in 1975. Following his release he served as an international business consultant. He died on November 9, 1988, in Washington, D.C.

FURTHER READINGS

Justice Department. 1985. *Attorneys General of the United States, 1789–1985.* Washington, D.C.: U.S. Government Printing Office.

"WE ARE GOING TO HAVE AN OUTBURST AGAINST THIS DISCOVERY BUSINESS UNLESS WE CAN HEDGE IT WITH SOME APPEARANCE OF SAFETY AGAINST FISHING EXPEDITIONS."
—WILLIAM MITCHELL

◈ MITCHELL, WILLIAM DE WITT

William de Witt Mitchell was a distinguished lawyer who became the fifty-fourth attorney general of the United States.

Mitchell was born on September 9, 1874, in Winona, Minnesota. He was the son of William Mitchell, a distinguished justice of the Minnesota Supreme Court for whom the William Mitchell College of Law in St. Paul is named. The younger Mitchell left Minnesota at the age of fourteen to attend preparatory school in New Jersey. He then entered Yale University to study electrical engineering, but during vacations back in Minnesota, he pursued his interest in the law, spending time discussing legal issues with his father and with other judges and attorneys who were family friends. As a result, after two years at Yale, he transferred to the University of Minnesota for pre-law studies. After receiving his bachelor of arts degree in 1895 and his bachelor of laws degree in 1896, he was admitted to the bar and took a position as a law clerk with Stringer and Seymour, a St. Paul law firm.

When the SPANISH-AMERICAN WAR broke out in 1898, Mitchell enlisted in the Fifteenth Minnesota Volunteer Infantry, where he became a second lieutenant and served as a JUDGE ADVOCATE for the Second U.S. Army Corp. When the war ended, he returned to St. Paul and Stringer and Seymour. After his father lost his seat on the state supreme court in an election, Mitchell and the elder Mitchell established a law partnership with two other lawyers. Though his father died in 1900, Mitchell continued to practice law until another war—World War I—intervened. Mitchell again returned to military service as an infantry officer until 1919, when he rejoined his law firm, becoming a senior partner in 1922.

In 1925, through an influential friend in Washington, Mitchell's name was brought to the

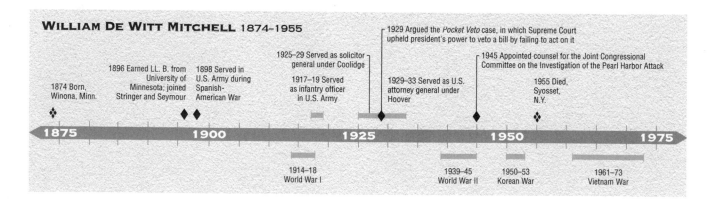

WILLIAM DE WITT MITCHELL 1874–1955

1874 Born, Winona, Minn.

1896 Earned LL. B. from University of Minnesota; joined Stringer and Seymour

1898 Served in U.S. Army during Spanish-American War

1925–29 Served as solicitor general under Coolidge

1917–19 Served as infantry officer in U.S. Army

1929 Argued the *Pocket Veto* case, in which Supreme Court upheld president's power to veto a bill by failing to act on it

1929–33 Served as U.S. attorney general under Hoover

1945 Appointed counsel for the Joint Congressional Committee on the Investigation of the Pearl Harbor Attack

1955 Died, Syosset, N.Y.

1875   1900   1925   1950   1975

1914–18 World War I

1939–45 World War II

1950–53 Korean War

1961–73 Vietnam War

attention of President CALVIN COOLIDGE, who was seeking to fill the position of SOLICITOR GENERAL. Coolidge, a Republican, offered Mitchell, a Democrat, the job, passing over several better-known Republican candidates. As solicitor general, under the direction of the U.S. attorney general, Mitchell was primarily responsible for representing the government of the United States before the U.S. Supreme Court in cases in which the United States had an interest. Mitchell, though he had intended to hold the position for only two years and then return to private practice, was solicitor general until 1929, appearing before the Court in thirty-four cases.

That year, upon the recommendation of several justices on the Supreme Court, newly elected President HERBERT HOOVER appointed Mitchell to be U.S. attorney general. Though his new role involved a wide and daunting range of responsibilities (including acting as a member of the president's cabinet), Mitchell continued to occasionally argue important cases himself before the High Court. One significant case was *Okanogan, Methow, San Poelis, Nespelem, Colville, and Lake Indian Tribes or Bands of State of Washington v. United States,* 279 U.S. 655, 49 S. Ct. 463, 73 L. Ed. 894 (1929), better known as the *Pocket Veto* case. In that decision the Supreme Court upheld the president's power to VETO a bill by failing to return it to Congress when Congress was in recess.

At the end of the Hoover administration, Mitchell returned to private practice, joining a New York law firm. Twelve years later, in 1945, Mitchell was appointed counsel for the Joint Congressional Committee on the Investigation of the Pearl Harbor Attack. Though he was selected unanimously and had virtually unfettered access to all departments, records, and personnel involved in the incident, Mitchell was unhappy with the slow pace of the committee's inquiry and left the position after less than three months to again return to private practice in New York. While practicing he served on several important commissions and was chairman of the Committee on Federal Rules of Civil Procedure, which was charged with redrafting rules governing practice in the federal courts. He died on August 24, 1955, in Syosset, New York, at the age of eighty-one.

MITIGATING CIRCUMSTANCES

Circumstances that may be considered by a court in determining culpability of a defendant or the extent of damages to be awarded to a plaintiff. Mitigating circumstances do not justify or excuse an offense but may reduce the severity of a charge. Similarly, a recognition of mitigating circumstances to reduce a damage award does not imply that the damages were not suffered but that they have been partially ameliorated.

In criminal cases where the death penalty may be imposed, the Supreme Court has held that, under the Eighth and Fourteenth Amendments, juries must be instructed that they may consider mitigating circumstances such as the defendant's youth, mental capacity, or childhood abuse so that they may reach a reasoned and moral sentencing decision. (See *Penry v. Lynaugh,* 492 U.S. 302, 109 S. Ct. 2934, 106 L. Ed. 2d 256 [1989].) Mitigating circumstances may be used to reduce a charge against a defendant. In *People v. Morrin,* 31 Mich. App. 301, 187 N.W.2d 434 (1971), the Michigan Court of Appeals reversed and remanded Morrin's conviction on first-degree murder charges because he committed the murder in the heat of passion caused by adequate legal provocation. The court found that because of these mitigating circumstances, the evidence was insufficient to support a first-degree murder conviction, which requires malice aforethought.

In civil actions mitigating circumstances may be considered to reduce damage awards or the extent of the defendant's liability. In *Cerretti v. Flint Hills Rural Electric Cooperative Ass'n,* 251 Kan. 347, 837 P.2d 330 (1992), the Supreme Court of Kansas held that a court, in reviewing a damage award, may consider any mitigating circumstances that affected the intent of the defendant, the financial worth of the defendant, or the plaintiff's expenses.

Many states allow defendants in DEFAMATION actions to prove mitigating circumstances by showing that they acted in GOOD FAITH, with honesty of purpose, and without malice in speaking or publishing the defamatory words. If the court is convinced that legitimate mitigating circumstances existed, it may reduce the amount of damages the defendant is required to pay. In *Roemer v. Retail Credit Co.,* 44 Cal. App. 3d 926, 119 Cal. Rptr. 82 (1975), the defendant claimed that the plaintiff defaced the wall of his office, thereby mitigating the defendant's liability for defamatory statements. However, the court did not allow the defendant to introduce this evidence because he could not prove that the plaintiff was responsible for the defacement.

CROSS-REFERENCES

Capital Punishment; Criminal Law.

MITIGATION OF DAMAGES

The use of reasonable care and diligence in an effort to minimize or avoid injury.

Under the mitigation of damages doctrine, a person who has suffered an injury or loss should take reasonable action, where possible, to avoid additional injury or loss. The failure of a plaintiff to take protective steps after suffering an injury or loss can reduce the amount of the plaintiff's recovery. The mitigation of damages doctrine is sometimes called minimization of damages or the doctrine of AVOIDABLE CONSEQUENCES.

In contract law the non-breaching party should mitigate damages or risk a reduction in recovery for the breach. For example, assume that a property owner and home builder contract for the construction of a home in exchange for payment of $50,000. Assume further that the builder begins constructing the home but that the owner wrongfully cancels the contract before the builder has finished construction. If the builder must sue the owner to recover the unpaid portion of the contract price, a court may reduce the amount of money that the builder recovers if the builder does not try to avoid additional loss. For example, the builder could sell the materials already purchased for the job or use the materials in another job. The savings that the builder realizes will be deducted from the loss incurred on the contract in computing the builder's net recovery in court.

In TORT LAW mitigation of damages refers to conduct by the plaintiff that, although not constituting a civil wrong itself, may reduce the plaintiff's recovery. For example, if the victim of an assault used provocative words prior to the assault, the words may mitigate the plaintiff's damages. Most states limit mitigation of damages for provocative words to a possible reduction in PUNITIVE DAMAGES, as opposed to COMPENSATORY DAMAGES.

A tort victim also should act to mitigate damages subsequent to the wrongful acts of another. For instance, assume that the victim in the assault example suffers a broken leg. If the victim refuses to get medical treatment and the leg eventually must be amputated, the defendant may be liable only for the reasonable medical expenses to repair a broken leg. Because a reasonable person would seek medical attention after suffering a broken leg, a court could find it unreasonable to make the defendant pay for additional damage that the victim could have prevented with minimal effort.

If it is unreasonable to expect the victim to mitigate damages following the injury, the defendant may be held liable for subsequent injury to the victim that stems from the wrongful act. For example, if the assault victim lives alone in a rural area without a source of transportation, and if the leg requires amputation because the victim could not get to a hospital, the defendant may be held liable not only for a broken leg but for the medical expenses, pain and suffering, and lost wages associated with the amputation.

FURTHER READINGS

Kionka, Edward J. 1988. *Torts,* St. Paul, Minn.: West.

Knapp, Charles L., and Nathan M. Crystal. 1987. *Problems in Contract Law: Cases and Materials.* 2d ed. Boston: Little, Brown.

"Torts." 1994. *SMH Bar Review.*

MITTIMUS

A court order directing a sheriff or other police officer to escort a convict to a prison.

A mittimus is a written document. It can command a jailer to safely keep a felon until he or she can be transferred to a prison. A mittimus also refers to the transcript of the conviction and sentencing stages, which is duly certified by a clerk of court.

MIXED ACTIONS

Lawsuits having two purposes: to recover real property and to obtain monetary damages.

Mixed actions take their character from real actions and personal actions. Originally the common-law courts in England concentrated on rights involving the possession of land. The relief granted was an order to give over possession of the real property in dispute. These were the real actions. Only later were FORMS OF ACTION developed to permit a lawsuit for monetary damages in a personal or mixed action. Then the sheriff might be ordered to collect a fine and later damages, out of the loser's profits, which were the rents and income from land, and out of any PERSONAL PROPERTY. Special procedures existed for mixed actions that concerned the sort of relief sought in both real and personal actions.

M'NAGHTEN RULE

A test applied to determine whether a person accused of a crime was sane at the time of its commission and, therefore, criminally responsible for the wrongdoing.

The M'Naghten rule is a test for criminal insanity. Under the M'Naghten rule, a criminal defendant is not guilty by reason of insanity if, at the time of the alleged criminal act, the defendant was so deranged that she did not know the nature or quality of her actions or, if she knew the nature and quality of her actions, she was so deranged that she did not know that what she was doing was wrong.

The M'Naghten rule on criminal insanity is named for Daniel M'Naghten, who, in 1843, tried to kill England's prime minister Sir Robert Peel. M'Naghten thought Peel wanted to kill him, so he tried to shoot Peel but instead shot and killed Peel's secretary, Edward Drummond. Medical experts testified that M'Naghten was psychotic, and M'Naghten was found not guilty by reason of insanity.

The public chafed at the verdict, and the House of Lords in Parliament ordered the Lords of Justice of the Queen's Bench to fashion a strict definition of criminal insanity. The Lords of Justice complied and declared that insanity was a defense to criminal charges only if

> at the time of the committing of the act, the party accused was labouring under such a defect of reason, from a disease of the mind, as not to know the nature and quality of the act he was doing; or, if he did know it, that he did not know he was doing what was wrong. (*Queen v. M'Naghten*, 8 Eng. Rep. 718 [1843])

The aim of the M'Naghten rule was to limit the INSANITY DEFENSE to cognitive insanity, a basic inability to distinguish right from wrong. Other tests formulated by legislatures and courts since *M'Naghten* have supplemented the M'Naghten rule with another form of insanity called volitional insanity. Volitional insanity is experienced by mentally healthy persons who, although they know what they are doing is wrong, are so mentally unbalanced at the time of the criminal act that they are unable to conform their actions to the law.

In 1843 Daniel M'Naghten tried to kill England's prime minister Sir Robert Peel. At trial, M'Naghten was found not guilty by reason of insanity.
HULTON DEUTSCH COLLECTION

The M'Naghten rule was adopted in most jurisdictions in the United States, but legislatures and courts eventually modified and expanded the definition. The definition of criminal insanity now varies from jurisdiction to jurisdiction, but most of them have been influenced by the M'Naghten rule.

Many jurisdictions reject volitional insanity but retain cognitive insanity with a minor variation on the M'Naghten definition. Under the M'Naghten rule, a person was legally insane if she was so deranged that she did not know what she was doing. Under many current statutes, a person is legally insane if she is so deranged that she lacks substantial capacity to appreciate the criminality of her conduct.

The difference between the two definitions is largely theoretical. In theory, the latter definition is more lenient because it requires only that a person lack substantial capacity to appreciate her conduct.

FURTHER READINGS

Kaplan, John, and Robert Weisberg. 1991. *Criminal Law: Cases and Materials.* 2d ed. Boston: Little, Brown.

CROSS-REFERENCES

Durham Rule; Insanity Defense.

MOCK TRIAL

A simulated trial-level proceeding conducted by students to understand trial rules and processes. Usually tried before a mock jury, these proceedings are different from MOOT COURT proceedings, which simulate appellate arguments.

Mock trials are sometimes used as an ALTERNATIVE DISPUTE RESOLUTION tool, in which parties that are not inclined to negotiate may see how the merits of their respective cases stand when argued before neutral evaluators.

MODEL ACTS

Statutes and court rules drafted by the American Law Institute (ALI), the AMERICAN BAR ASSOCI-ATION *(ABA), the* COMMISSIONERS ON UNI-FORM LAWS, *and other organizations. State legislatures may adopt model acts in whole or in part, or they may modify them to fit their needs. Model acts differ from* UNIFORM ACTS, *which are usually adopted by the states in virtually the same form proposed by the American Law Institute and other organizations.*

The ALI was founded in 1923 by a group of American judges, lawyers, and law professors. Its goal was to resolve uncertainty and complexity in American law by promoting clarification and simplicity in the law. Since its founding, the organization has worked with other scholarly organizations to draft model and uniform statutes that may be adopted by the various state legislatures.

One of the most successful of ALI's model acts is the MODEL PENAL CODE. First adopted in 1962, it has had a major influence on the way that states draft penal codes. In fact, the major-ity of states revised their penal codes based upon the provisions of the Model Penal Code. The code attempts to, among other things, create uniformity in such controversial areas as the authority of the courts in sentencing and how to define specific crimes, including criminal HOMI-CIDE and KIDNAPPING. In 2002, the ALI announced that it was launching a reexamina-tion and revision of the sentencing provision of the code.

The ABA also approves drafts of model laws and rules. The Model Business Corporation Act (MBCA) is an example of a model act approved by the ABA that was implemented successfully. The MBCA was first adopted in 1950 and revised substantially in 1969, 1971, and 1983. It addresses all aspects of corporate legal structure, from bylaws to shareholder rights to fiduciary responsibilities. At least 18 states have adopted the act in its entirety. Many other states have adopted significant portions of the act.

Other model acts adopted in whole or in part by the states include the Model Rules of Profes-sional Conduct, the Model Probate Code, the Model Class Actions Act, the Model Juvenile Court Act, and the Model Survival and Death Act.

FURTHER READINGS

Goldstein, Elliott. 1985. "Revision of the Model Business Corporation Act." *Texas Law Review* 1471.

MODEL PENAL CODE

The Model Penal Code (MPC) is one of the most important developments in American law, and perhaps the most important influence on American CRIMINAL LAW since it was completed in 1962. Conceived as a way to stan-dardize and organize the often-fragmentary criminal codes enacted by the states, the MPC has influenced a large majority of states to change their laws. Although some provisions of the MPC are now considered outdated, and the code fails to address many important recent criminal law issues, its impact could still be felt as the country entered the twenty-first century.

Members of the American Law Institute (ALI), a group of judges, lawyers, and legal scholars whose purpose is to clarify and improve the law, began working on the Model Penal Code in 1952. The group had abandoned two previous attempts to create a model criminal code. The third attempt took ten years, and the ALI produced numerous drafts, reports, and revisions.

Herbert Wechsler, a Columbia Law School professor, served as the chief reporter, or princi-pal drafter. From 1953 to 1962, ALI council members examined, considered, and debated the work of Wechsler, his staff, and his advisors in a total of 31 drafts. Finally, in 1962, the MPC was completed and published.

The impact of the MPC was immediate. For many states, the notion of codifying their crim-inal code was a foreign one—their criminal statutes were often poorly organized and did not define their crimes. The MPC arranged matters differently, organizing itself into four parts: (1) general provisions containing definitional func-tions and presumptive rules; (2) definitions of specific offenses; (3) provisions governing treat-ment and correction; and (4) provisions govern-ing the organization of corrections departments and divisions such as the divisions responsible for PAROLE or PROBATION.

Several elements of the MPC have changed the way criminal law is administered in the United States. A good example of this is in the issue of *mens rea,* meaning state of mind or guilty mind. Previous state criminal statutes took a scattershot approach to mens rea, requiring it for some crimes and not for others, and using multiple terms to measure culpability. The MPC stated simply that a person is not guilty of an offense unless he or she acted purposely, knowingly, recklessly, or negligently, as the law may require, with respect to each material element of the offense. It then proceeded to define what these terms meant in a criminal law context, and what types of conduct would satisfy these terms. The clarity and simplicity of this approach made it desirable for many states to replace their codes with MPC-influenced codes. Following the introduction of the MPC, 36 states adopted new criminal codes, all of them influenced by the MPC and some of them using the exact language of the MPC for their statutes. Even if they did not adopt the language, some states used the MPC's model of organization as a starting point.

In addition, the MPC's influence is felt in the courts, where judges often rely on the code when handling substantive criminal law decisions. It has also become an important teaching tool in law schools, where the commentaries accompanying the code are read, as well as the code itself, in an attempt to gain insight into criminal law. Although the MPC has come under some criticism in recent years, with some critics suggesting that it may be time for revision, it remains firmly ensconced as an influence in the criminal laws of more than two-thirds of the states.

FURTHER READINGS

Dubber, Markus Dirk. 2000. "Penal Panopticon: The Idea of a Modern Model Penal Code." *Buffalo Criminal Law Review* 4.

Lynch, Gerard E. 2000. "Towards a Model Penal Code, Second (Federal?): The Challenge of the Special Part." *Buffalo Criminal Law Review* 4.

Robinson, Paul H., and Jane A. Grall. 1983. "Element Analysis in Defining Criminal Liability: The Model Penal Code and Beyond." *Stanford Law Review* 35 (April).

MODEL RULES OF PROFESSIONAL CONDUCT

See PROFESSIONAL RESPONSIBILITY.

MODIFICATION

A change or alteration in existing materials.

Modification generally has the same meaning in the law as it does in common parlance. The term has special significance in the law of contracts and the law of sales.

The parties to a completed and binding contract are free to change the terms of the contract. Changes to a preexisting contract are called *contract modifications*. If the parties agree to modify the contract, the modification will be enforceable in a court of law.

A contract modification may be either written or oral, with some exceptions. An oral modification is unenforceable if the contract specifies that modifications must be in writing (*United States ex rel. Crane Co. v. Progressive Enterprises, Inc.,* 418 F. Supp. 662 [E.D. Va. 1976]). As a general rule, a modification should be in writing if it increases or decreases the value of the contract by $500 or more.

In contracts between parties who are not merchants, a modification should be supported by some consideration, which is the exchange of value, or something to solidify an agreement. Courts impose this requirement to prevent FRAUD and deception in the modification of contracts. Consideration operates as evidence that the parties have agreed to the modification. Without the requirement of consideration, a party to a contract could declare that the contract should be modified or canceled whenever such a demand was advantageous.

In contracts between merchants, a modification need not be supported by consideration. Derived from article 2, section 209, of the UNIFORM COMMERCIAL CODE, this rule is designed to honor the intent of commercial parties without requiring the time-consuming technicalities of consideration.

Like any non-merchant, a merchant is free to reject a proposed modification, but a merchant may waive the right to reject a modification by failing to object to the modification. For example, if an electrician doing work as a subcontractor notifies the general contractor that the electrical work will be more expensive than anticipated, the general contractor may be obliged to pay for the extra expenses if she fails to object before the electrician begins the work. There must be a legitimate commercial reason for such a contract modification, and the modification must be reasonable in light of the standards within the particular industry. Courts are free to strike down contract modifications that are brought about by duress or bad faith.

CROSS-REFERENCES

Sales Law.

MODUS OPERANDI

[Latin, Method of working.] A term used by law enforcement authorities to describe the particular manner in which a crime is committed.

The term *modus operandi* is most commonly used in criminal cases. It is sometimes referred to by its initials, M.O. The prosecution in a criminal case does not have to prove modus operandi in any crime. However, identifying and proving the modus operandi of a crime can help the prosecution prove that it was the defendant who committed the crime charged.

Modus operandi evidence is helpful to the prosecution if the prosecution has evidence of crimes committed by the defendant that are similar to the crime charged. The crimes need not be identical, but the prosecution must make a strong and persuasive showing of similarity between the crime charged and the other crimes. The prosecution may introduce evidence from prior or subsequent crimes to prove modus operandi only if the other crimes share peculiar and distinctive features with the crime charged. The features must be uncommon and rarely seen in other crimes, and they must be so distinct that they can be recognized as the handiwork of the same person.

For example, assume that a defendant is on trial for armed ROBBERY. In the robbery the defendant is alleged to have brandished a pistol and ordered the victim to relinquish cash and valuables. Assume further that the defendant has committed armed robbery in the past by brandishing a pistol and demanding cash and valuables. A prosecutor might be able to introduce the evidence into trial to show the defendant's motive, intent, or state of mind, or to identify the weapon used in the crime. However, the prosecutor could not argue to the judge or jury that the robberies were so similar as to demonstrate that it was the defendant who committed that particular robbery, because it is not unusual for a robber to brandish a pistol and demand cash and valuables in the course of an armed robbery.

Now assume that a defendant is charged with robbing a movie theater that was showing the movie *Showgirls* and that the defendant was wearing a glittering, flamboyant Las Vegas-style cabaret costume during the robbery. Assume

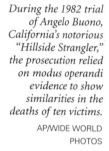

During the 1982 trial of Angelo Buono, California's notorious "Hillside Strangler," the prosecution relied on modus operandi evidence to show similarities in the deaths of ten victims.

AP/WIDE WORLD PHOTOS

further that the prosecution has evidence that the defendant, while dressed as a Las Vegas dancer, has robbed other movie theaters showing the movie *Showgirls*. The prosecution could introduce this evidence into trial to prove modus operandi and show that it was the defendant who committed the crime, because the method of armed robbery used in the crimes was both similar and distinctive.

When offering evidence to prove modus operandi, the prosecution does not have to prove BEYOND A REASONABLE DOUBT that the other crimes occurred. Rather, the prosecution simply must present sufficient evidence to show that the act took place and was committed by the defendant.

CROSS-REFERENCES

Criminal Law; Criminal Procedure.

MOIETY

One-half.

Joint tenants own their estate by the moiety.

CROSS-REFERENCES

Joint Tenancy.

MONEY LAUNDERING

The process of taking the proceeds of criminal activity and making them appear legal.

Laundering allows criminals to transform illegally obtained gain into seemingly legitimate funds. It is a worldwide problem, with approximately $300 billion going through the process annually in the United States. The sale of illegal narcotics accounts for much of this money. Those who commit the underlying criminal activity may attempt to launder the money themselves, but increasingly a new class of criminals provides laundering services to ORGANIZED CRIME. This new class consists of lawyers, bankers, and accountants.

Criminals want their illegal funds laundered because they can then move their money through society freely, without fear that the funds will be traced to their criminal deeds. In addition, laundering prevents the funds from being confiscated by the police.

Money laundering usually consists of three steps: placement, layering, and integration. Placement is the depositing of funds in financial institutions or the conversion of cash into negotiable instruments. Placement is the most diffi-

cult step. The easiest way to begin laundering large amounts of cash is to deposit them into a financial institution. However, under the federal Bank Secrecy Act of 1970 (BSA), 31 U.S.C.A. §§ 5311 et seq., financial institutions are required to report deposits of more than $10,000 in cash made by an individual in a single day. To disguise criminal activity, launderers route cash through a "front" operation; that is, a business such as a check-cashing service or a jewelry store. Another option is to convert the cash into negotiable instruments, such as cashier's checks, money orders, or traveler's checks.

Layering involves the wire transfer of funds through a series of accounts in an attempt to hide the funds' true origins. This often means transferring funds to countries outside the United States that have strict bank-secrecy laws. Such countries include the Cayman Islands, the Bahamas, and Panama. Once deposited in a foreign bank, the funds can be moved through accounts of "shell" corporations, which exist solely for laundering purposes. The high daily volume of wire transfers makes it difficult for law enforcement agencies to trace these transactions.

Integration involves the movement of layered funds, which are no longer traceable to their criminal origin, into the financial world, where they are mixed with funds of legitimate origin.

Many banks did not comply with the BSA during the 1970s and early 1980s. Following several federal investigations where it was revealed that banks had failed to report billions of dollars of cash transactions, reporting requirements were strengthened. Congress also enacted the Money Laundering Control Act of 1986 (MLCA), 18 U.S.C.A. §§ 1956 et seq. This statute criminalizes money laundering itself. It centers its attention on the criminals and conspirators who seek to launder the proceeds of illegal activity, including merchants, bankers, and members of the professions who assist criminals with money laundering. Another provision of the MLCA authorizes the government to confiscate all property that is traceable to violations of laws against money laundering.

After the SEPTEMBER 11TH ATTACKS on the United States in 2001, the federal government began to investigate more closely the connection between TERRORISM and the sale of illegal drugs. According to President GEORGE W. BUSH, "[T]errorists use drug profits to fund their cells to commit acts of murder. If you quit drugs, you join the fight against terror in America." Terrorists have laundered money through such foreign countries as Colombia and Afghanistan. In September 2002, the DRUG ENFORCEMENT ADMINISTRATION opened a museum exhibit in New York entitled "Target America: Traffickers, Terrorists and You" in an effort to educate the American public about the connection between drug sales and terrorism.

FURTHER READINGS

Lilley, Peter. 2003. *Dirty Dealing: The Untold Truth about Global Money Laundering.* 2d ed. Sterling, Va.: Kogan Page.

Sulltzer, Scott. 1995. "Money Laundering: The Scope of the Problem and Attempts to Combat It." *Tennessee Law Review* 63.

U.S. Department of the Treasury. 2000. *The National Money Laundering Strategy for 2000.* Washington, D.C.: Department of the Treasury.

Vukson, William B.Z., ed. 2003. *Organized Crime & Money Laundering.* Toronto, Ont.: G.7 Report Inc.

Woods, Brett F. 1998. *The Art & Science of Money Laundering: Inside the Commerce of the International Narcotics Traffickers.* Boulder, Colo.: Paladin Press.

CROSS-REFERENCES

Banks and Banking.

MONEY PAID

The technical name given a declaration in ASSUMPSIT *in which the plaintiff declares that the defendant had and received certain money. A* COMMON-LAW PLEADING, *stating that the defendant received money that, in* EQUITY *and good conscience, should be paid to the plaintiff.*

MONOPOLY

An economic advantage held by one or more persons or companies deriving from the exclusive power to carry on a particular business or trade or to manufacture and sell a particular item, thereby suppressing competition and allowing such persons or companies to raise the price of a product or service substantially above the price that would be established by a free market.

In a monopoly, one or more persons or companies totally dominates an economic market. Monopolies may exist in a particular industry if a company controls a major natural resource, produces (even at a reasonable price) all of the output of a product or service because of technological superiority (called a natural monopoly), holds a patent on a product or process of production, or is otherwise granted government permission to be the sole producer of a product or service in a given area.

U.S. law generally views monopolies as harmful because they obstruct the channels of free competition that determine the price and quality of products and services that are offered to the public. The owners of a monopoly have the power, as a group, to set prices, to exclude competitors, and to control the market in the relevant geographic area. U.S. ANTITRUST LAWS prohibit monopolies and any other practices that unduly restrain competitive trade. These laws are based on the belief that equality of opportunity in the marketplace and the free interactions of competitive forces result in the best allocation of the economic resources of the nation. Moreover, it is assumed that competition enhances material progress in production and technology while preserving democratic, political, and social institutions.

History

Economic monopolies have existed throughout much of human history. In England, a monopoly originally was an exclusive right that was expressly granted by the king or Parliament to one person or class of persons to provide some service or goods. The holders of such rights, usually the English guilds or inventors, dominated the market. By the early seventeenth century, the English courts began to void monopolies as interfering with free of trade. In 1623, Parliament enacted the Statute of Monopolies, which prohibited all but specifically excepted monopolies. With the Industrial Revolution of the early nineteenth century, economic production and markets exploded. The growth of capitalism and its emphasis on the free play of competition reinforced the idea that monopolies were unlawful.

In the United States, during most of the nineteenth century, monopolies were prosecuted under COMMON LAW and by statute as market-interference offenses in attempts to stop dealers from raising prices through techniques such as buying up all available supplies of a material, which is called "cornering the market." Courts also refused to enforce contracts with harsh provisions that were clearly unreasonable restraints of trade. These measures were largely ineffective.

Government Regulation

Congress intervened after abuses became widespread. In 1887, Congress, pursuant to its constitutional power to regulate interstate commerce, passed the INTERSTATE COMMERCE ACT (49 U.S.C.A. § 1 et seq.) in response to the monopolistic practices of railroad companies. Although competition among railroad companies for long-haul routes was great, it was minimal for short-haul runs. Railroad companies discriminated in the prices they charged to passengers and shippers in different localities by providing rebates to large shippers or buyers, in order to retain their long-haul business. These practices were especially harmful to farmers because they lacked the volume of traffic necessary to obtain more favorable rates. Although states attempted to regulate the railroads, they were powerless to act where interstate commerce was involved. The Interstate Commerce Act was intended to regulate shipping rates. It mandated that charges be set fairly, and it outlawed unreasonable discrimination among customers through the use of rebates or other preferential devices.

Congress soon moved ahead on another front, enacting the SHERMAN ANTI-TRUST ACT OF 1890 (15 U.S.C.A. §§ 31 et seq.). A trust was an arrangement by which stockholders in several companies transferred their shares to a set of trustees in exchange for a certificate that entitled them to a specified share of the consolidated earnings of the jointly managed companies. The trusts came to dominate a number of major industries, destroying their competitors. The Sherman Act prohibited such trusts and their anticompetitive practices. From the 1890s through 1920, the federal government used the act to break up these trusts.

The Sherman Act provides for criminal prosecution by the federal government against corporations and individuals who restrain trade, but criminal sanctions are rarely sought. The act also provides for civil remedies for private persons who start an action under it for injuries caused by monopolistic acts. The award of treble damages (the tripling of the amount of damages awarded) is authorized under the act in order to promote the interest of private persons in safeguarding a free and competitive society and to deter violators and others from future illegal acts.

The Clayton Anti-Trust Act of 1914 (15 U.S.C.A. §§ 12 et seq.) was passed as an amendment to the Sherman Act. The CLAYTON ACT specifically defined which monopolistic acts were illegal but not criminal. The act proscribed price discrimination (the sale of the same product at different prices to similarly situated buy-

ers), exclusive-dealing contracts (sales on condition that the buyer stop dealing with the seller's competitors), corporate mergers, and interlocking directorates (the same people serving on the boards of directors of competing companies). Such practices were illegal only if, as a result, they materially reduced competition or tended to create a monopoly in trade.

The Federal Trade Commission Act of 1914 (15 U.S.C.A. §§ 41 et seq.) established the FEDERAL TRADE COMMISSION, the regulatory body that promotes free and fair competitive trade in interstate commerce through the prohibition of price-fixing arrangements, FALSE ADVERTISING, boycotts, illegal combinations of competitors, and other methods of UNFAIR COMPETITION.

Congress passed the ROBINSON-PATMAN ACT of 1936 (15 U.S.C.A. §§ 13 et seq.) to amend the Clayton Act. The act makes it unlawful for any seller engaged in commerce to directly or indirectly discriminate in the sale price charged on commodities of comparable grade and quality where the effect might injure, destroy, or prevent competition unless the seller discriminated in order to dispose of perishable or obsolete goods or to meet the equally low price of a competitor.

Exemptions

Despite these legal prohibitions, not all industries and activities are subject to them. LABOR UNIONS monopolize the labor force and take concerted action to improve the wages, hours, and working conditions of their members. The Clayton Act and the NORRIS-LAGUARDIA ACT of 1932 (29 U.S.C.A. §§ 101 et seq.) recognized that unions would be powerless without this monopolistic behavior and therefore made unions immune from antitrust laws.

A government-awarded monopoly, such as the right to provide electricity or natural gas to a region of the country, is exempt from antitrust laws. Government agencies regulate these industries and set reasonable rates that the company may charge.

Sometimes an industry is a natural monopoly. This type of monopoly is created as a result of circumstances over which the monopolist has no power. A natural monopoly may exist where a market for a particular product or service is so limited that its profitable production is impossible except when done by a single plant that is large enough to supply the entire demand. Natural monopolies are beyond the reach of antitrust laws.

Special-interest industries, such as agricultural and fishery marketing associations, banking and insurance industries, and export trade associations, are also immune from antitrust laws. Major league BASEBALL has been exempted from antitrust laws as well.

The phenomenal popularity of the personal computer (PC) in the 1980s and 1990s catapulted Microsoft Corporation past manufacturing corporations as a preeminent business organization in the United States and the world. With the explosion of interest in the INTERNET in the mid-1990s, Microsoft moved aggressively to market its Internet Explorer (IE) web browser and to crush its competitor, Netscape. Having already secured a monopoly with its Windows Operating System, Microsoft seemed poised to dominate Internet software. However, in 1998, 19 state attorneys general joined the U.S. JUSTICE DEPARTMENT in filing an antitrust lawsuit against Microsoft. The suit alleged that the software company forced computer manufacturers (known as original equipment manufacturers or OEMs) to license and distribute Microsoft's IE in exchange for the right to pre-install Microsoft's Windows 95 operating system on new PCs. Microsoft contended that IE was an integral part of Windows 95 and that it could not be separated without causing the operating system as a whole to malfunction. The plaintiffs argued that Microsoft was engaged in an illegal TYING ARRANGEMENT, by conditioning the purchase of a popular product (Windows 95) on the purchase of an additional, unrelated product (IE.)

The case came to trial in October 1998 before U.S. District Court Judge Thomas Penfield Jackson, sitting without a jury. Jackson ruled for the plaintiffs in November 1999, finding that the facts fully justified the conclusion that Microsoft had sought monopoly power through illegal means. He appointed Chief Judge RICHARD A. POSNER of the U.S. Court of Appeals for the Seventh Circuit to mediate the case, in hopes of bringing the bitter conflict to a quick conclusion. However, Posner could not broker a settlement, and Jackson issued his final order in April 2000. He ordered that Microsoft be split into two companies and that the companies desist from monopolistic conduct. A federal appeals court overturned this decision in June 2001. Although the panel agreed that Microsoft had engaged in monopolistic practices, it found that Judge Jackson had committed misconduct by making derogatory comments about Microsoft. The case was sent back to another district court judge, who encouraged new settlement talks. In August 2002, the U.S. Department of Justice and the states agreed to a settlement in which Microsoft did not have to split apart. Instead, Microsoft agreed to allow OEMs and consumers to add and remove access to certain Windows features and to set defaults for competing software. Microsoft also made available to software developers a host of software interfaces and tools at no charge, to allow the developers to write Windows applications.

FURTHER READINGS

Lucarelli, Bill. 2004. *Monopoly Capitalism in Crisis.* New York: Palgrave Macmillan.

Ottosen, Garry K. 1990. *Monopoly Power: How It Is Measured and How It Has Changed.* Salt Lake City, Utah: Crossroads Research Institute.

Scherer, F.M. 1993. *Monopoly and Competition Policy.* Brookfield, Vt.: Edward Elgar.

Zoninsein, Jonas. 1990. *Monopoly Capital Theory: Hilferding and Twentieth-Century Capitalism.* New York: Greenwood Press.

CROSS-REFERENCES

Antitrust Law; Combination in Restraint of Trade; Interstate Commerce Commission; Mergers and Acquisitions; Public Utilities; Restraint of Trade.

MONROE DOCTRINE

The Founding Fathers of the United States of America sought to establish a foreign policy that was compatible with the surge of nationalism that engulfed the new country during its first century of independence. The Monroe Doctrine, proposed by President JAMES MONROE in 1823, contributed to the formation of such a policy.

Certain events in 1821 prompted the creation of the doctrine. An insurrection in the colonies under Spanish rule in Latin America resulted in freedom for the colonies, but several European nations threatened to intervene on Spain's behalf and restore the former colonies to Spanish domination. Both the United States and Great Britain saw the advantages of trade with the new Latin American nations and feared further European interference in future disputes. As a result, British Foreign Secretary George Canning approached the U.S. emissary in London, RICHARD RUSH, with a proposal for the formation of a dual alliance to protect the interests of the two countries. According to Canning's plan, the United States and Great Britain would oppose any intervention in the Spanish colonies by any European country except Spain.

President Monroe was agreeable to the terms of Canning's proposition, as were Secretary of War JOHN C. CALHOUN and former Presidents THOMAS JEFFERSON and JAMES MADISON. Secretary of State JOHN QUINCY ADAMS, however, presented an alternative view. Adams believed that Britain's interests in Latin America were sufficiently strong to encourage Britain's defense of those nations whether or not the United States agreed to Canning's proposal. Adams favored the development of a U.S. policy without alliance with Britain.

On December 2, 1823, Monroe presented the terms of the Monroe Doctrine, which Adams had helped to develop. The doctrine contained four significant elements: the American continents were to be regarded as independent, with no further settlement by European nations; the nations of the Western Hemisphere were deemed republics, as opposed to the European system of monarchies; European intervention in the affairs of nations of the Western Hemisphere was prohibited and would be viewed as a threat to the security of the United States; and, conversely the United States promised to refrain from involvement in European affairs.

CROSS-REFERENCES

"Monroe Doctrine" (Appendix, Primary Document).

❖ MONROE, JAMES

James Monroe was the fifth president of the United States and a distinguished diplomat. His administration was marked by several foreign-policy accomplishments, including the MONROE DOCTRINE, and a period of domestic tranquility that has been called the Era of Good Feelings.

Monroe was born in Westmoreland County, Virginia, on April 28, 1758. He attended the College of William and Mary at the age of 16 but left in 1776 to fight in the Revolutionary War. He was wounded at the Battle of Trenton but served until the end of the war.

During this period he became acquainted with THOMAS JEFFERSON, then governor of Virginia. Monroe soon adopted Jefferson as his teacher and mentor, a relationship that would endure throughout Monroe's life. In 1780 Monroe began studying law with Jefferson, and in 1786 he established a law practice in Fredericks-

This undated cartoon from the New York Herald *depicts European potentates observing U.S. naval might*
CORBIS

burg, Virginia. Politics, however, proved a more powerful attraction than a legal career.

Monroe became a member of the Virginia House of Delegates in 1782, and from 1783 to 1786 he participated in the CONTINENTAL CONGRESS. Monroe, like Jefferson, did not favor a highly centralized federal government. He preferred a government system under the ARTICLES OF CONFEDERATION, which allocated greater powers to the states, as opposed to the Constitution, which gave the federal government more authority. He did believe in the development of the West and worked with Jefferson to enact laws to further this purpose.

In 1786 he retired from Congress. In 1788 Monroe participated in the Virginia convention that ratified the new federal Constitution. He was elected to the U.S. Senate in 1790 and served until 1794. After the expiration of his senatorial term, Monroe served as minister to France. President GEORGE WASHINGTON appointed Monroe to this position despite Monroe's opposition to the Washington administration's policies. When Monroe did not follow his diplomatic instructions and made intemperate remarks about policies with which he disagreed, Washington recalled him in 1796.

Monroe quickly reentered Virginia politics. He was elected governor in 1799 and served a three-year term. In 1802 President Jefferson sent Monroe back to France as a special envoy. He and ROBERT R. LIVINGSTON negotiated the LOUISIANA PURCHASE from France in 1803. Following this success, Jefferson named Monroe minister to England, where he served until 1806.

"LET US BY ALL WISE AND CONSTITUTIONAL MEASURES PROMOTE INTELLIGENCE AMONG THE PEOPLE AS THE BEST MEANS OF PRESERVING OUR LIBERTIES."
—JAMES MONROE

James Monroe.
LIBRARY OF CONGRESS

Again Virginia politics beckoned. Monroe served briefly as governor but left in 1811 to join the cabinet of President JAMES MADISON. He was SECRETARY OF STATE from 1811 to 1817 and secretary of war, during the WAR OF 1812 and from 1814 to 1815. The successful conclusion of the war and the military triumphs of General ANDREW JACKSON helped boost Monroe's popularity.

In 1816 he was elected president of the United States as a member of the DEMOCRATIC-REPUBLICAN PARTY. The FEDERALIST PARTY disappeared after the election, and most politicians belonged to the Democratic-Republican party. With an end to the political feuding of the early years of the Republic, Monroe was able to promote what has been called the Era of Good Feelings. His popularity was so great that he was unopposed for reelection in 1820.

Monroe's presidency produced important domestic legislation, including the MISSOURI COMPROMISE OF 1820, which limited the extension of SLAVERY into new territories. His main efforts, however, were directed at foreign affairs. The Rush-Bagot Treaty, drafted in 1817, restricted the increase of armaments in the Great Lakes area. In 1818 Great Britain agreed to the forty-ninth parallel as the boundary between the United States and Canada from Lake of the Woods on the Minnesota-Ontario border as far west as the Rocky Mountains. In 1819 U.S. diplomats convinced Spain to cede Florida to the United States in return for the cancellation of $5 million in U.S. claims against Spain.

In 1823 Monroe presented the most significant measure of his administration, the Monroe Doctrine. During the Napoleonic Wars, Spain had lost interest in its American colonies. Most of the colonies declared their independence, but the United States was concerned that Spain might try to reassert control. The Monroe Doctrine declared that the Western Hemisphere was closed to further European colonization and that any European intervention would be regarded as a threat to the security of the United States. Conversely, the United States agreed not to intervene in European matters. The Monroe Doctrine would be invoked several times by future presidential administrations.

After leaving the presidency in 1824, Monroe retired to Oak Hill, his estate in Virginia that was near Jefferson's Monticello. He served as a regent of the University of Virginia and in 1829 presided over the Virginia Constitutional Convention.

Monroe's last years were difficult. He left public service a poor man and was too old to rebuild his law practice. He was forced to sell his home and move to New York City to live with his daughter. He died there on July 4, 1831.

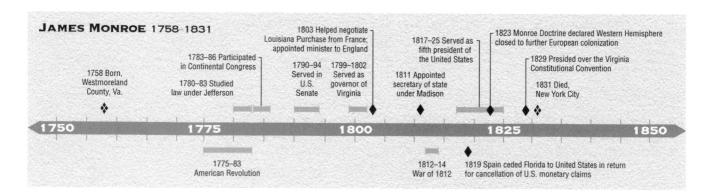

JAMES MONROE 1758–1831

1758 Born, Westmoreland County, Va.

1780–83 Studied law under Jefferson

1783–86 Participated in Continental Congress

1790–94 Served in U.S. Senate

1799–1802 Served as governor of Virginia

1803 Helped negotiate Louisiana Purchase from France; appointed minister to England

1811 Appointed secretary of state under Madison

1817–25 Served as fifth president of the United States

1823 Monroe Doctrine declared Western Hemisphere closed to further European colonization

1829 Presided over the Virginia Constitutional Convention

1831 Died, New York City

1750   1775   1800   1825   1850

1775–83 American Revolution

1812–14 War of 1812

1819 Spain ceded Florida to United States in return for cancellation of U.S. monetary claims

FURTHER READINGS

Ammon, Harry. 1971. *James Monroe: The Quest for National Identity.* New York: McGraw-Hill.

Wilmerding, Lucius. 1960. *James Monroe: Public Claimant.* New Brunswick, NJ: Rutgers Univ. Press.

CROSS-REFERENCES

Missouri Compromise of 1820; Monroe Doctrine; "Monroe Doctrine" (Appendix, Primary Document).

Charles-Louis de Secondat, Baron de la Brède et de Montesquieu.
LIBRARY OF CONGRESS

❖ MONTESQUIEU, CHARLES-LOUIS DE SECONDAT, BARON DE LA BRÈDE ET DE

Charles-Louis de Secondat, Baron de la Brède et de Montesquieu, was a French social and political philosopher whose ideas about laws and government had great influence on the leaders of the American Revolution and the Framers of the U.S. Constitution.

Montesquieu was born January 18, 1689, in La Brède, France, just outside of Bordeaux, to an aristocratic family with considerable landholdings. As a young man, he studied Latin, French, history, and the law before graduating from the University of Bordeaux in 1708. In 1715 he married Jeanne Lartigue, whose family brought him substantial wealth, and a year later his uncle died and left him his title and his property, making Montesquieu extremely rich. While his wife remained in La Brède managing his estate, Montesquieu traveled and enjoyed the social and intellectual life of Paris, attending fashionable salons and meeting with leading thinkers in the areas of politics and literature. He also served as *president á mortier,* or justice, of the Bordeaux *parlement,* an office he inherited from his uncle.

In 1728 Montesquieu left Paris for a three-year trip through Europe. Montesquieu closely examined the people and cultures of the countries he visited, paying particular attention to England, where he was intrigued by the level of political and religious freedom the people there enjoyed, as well as the country's bustling mercantile economy. He remained in England for eighteen months. During this time he was introduced into the most prestigious intellectual and social circles, was admitted to court, was made a fellow of the Royal Society, and attended several sessions of Parliament. Montesquieu's experience in England was critical in shaping his political philosophies because it proved to him that a society could combine the RULE OF LAW with political freedom.

After returning home in May 1731, Montesquieu spent the next fifteen years working on

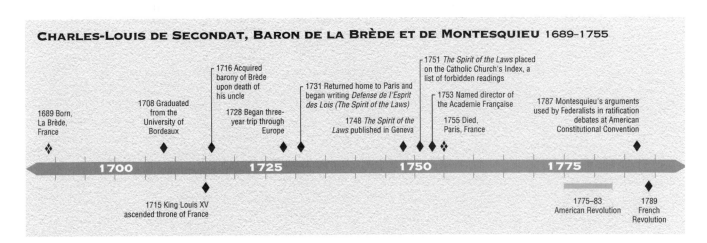

CHARLES-LOUIS DE SECONDAT, BARON DE LA BRÈDE ET DE MONTESQUIEU 1689–1755

1689 Born, La Brède, France

1708 Graduated from the University of Bordeaux

1716 Acquired barony of Brède upon death of his uncle

1728 Began three-year trip through Europe

1731 Returned home to Paris and began writing *Defense de l'Esprit des Lois (The Spirit of the Laws)*

1748 *The Spirit of the Laws* published in Geneva

1751 *The Spirit of the Laws* placed on the Catholic Church's Index, a list of forbidden readings

1753 Named director of the Academie Française

1755 Died, Paris, France

1787 Montesquieu's arguments used by Federalists in ratification debates at American Constitutional Convention

1700   1725   1750   1775

1715 King Louis XV ascended throne of France

1775–83 American Revolution

1789 French Revolution

his masterpiece, *De l'Esprit des lois* (literally *On the Spirit of the Laws,* but usually translated as *The Spirit of the Laws*). In this immense and loosely connected work, containing more than six hundred chapters grouped into thirty-one books, Montesquieu combined a lifetime of thoughts and personal observations concerning governments, laws, and human nature. His topics ranged from detailed analyses of ancient history to the effects of climate on national character. By closely examining a wide variety of societies through time and across cultures, Montesquieu sought to identify the basic principles underlying how laws work, how they evolve, and how they differ from country to country and culture to culture.

The Spirit of the Laws was published in 1748 in Geneva. It was a huge and immediate success; by the end of 1749, twenty-two other editions, including many translations, had reached all over Europe and across the ocean to the North American colonies. The work also generated considerable controversy, particularly with church authorities. They objected to Montesquieu's intellectual approach, which was grounded in the then radical notion that laws were not divinely inspired or handed down by ancient lawgivers such as Moses but evolved naturally out of everything that influences life in a country, including traditions, habits, history, religion, economics, and climate. Laws, Montesquieu believed, could be rationally studied and then adjusted to increase liberty for all. He responded to criticisms of his work in 1750 with *Defense de l'Esprit des lois,* but the Catholic Church nevertheless put *The Spirit of the Laws* on the church's Index in 1751, which meant that Catholics were forbidden to read it. Despite this official censure, Montesquieu was named director of the Academie Française in 1753.

On January 29, 1755, Montesquieu became ill with what appears to have been influenza, and his health quickly deteriorated. His sickness generated much attention; many people viewed it as symbolic of the great conflict between established religion and the forces of reason and enlightenment that marked the eighteenth century. During his illness Montesquieu's house was filled with friends monitoring his condition, including messengers from the king. Montesquieu died on February 10, 1755, and was buried in the parish church of Saint-Sulpice.

As was the case in Europe, Montesquieu was a leading intellectual figure in the American

colonies, and *The Spirit of the Laws* was a standard subject of close study for young American scholars. Figures show that Montesquieu's works, particularly *The Spirit of the Laws,* were widely disseminated through American booksellers and libraries, and Montesquieu's ideas were frequently discussed in newspapers and journals. Montesquieu's works were found in the personal libraries of nearly all of the country's founding fathers, including BENJAMIN FRANKLIN, JOHN ADAMS, THOMAS JEFFERSON, and JAMES MADISON.

Different elements of the theories Montesquieu outlined in *The Spirit of the Laws* were popular in America at different times, varying with political conditions and developments. In general, however, the most influential portions of the work were chapters 3 and 6 of book XI, in which Montesquieu analyzed the English constitution, a discussion that heavily influenced the SEPARATION OF POWERS later enshrined in the U.S. Constitution. In his analysis Montesquieu outlined the basic principle of the English constitution, which was—and still is—not an actual document but an unwritten consensus regarding the proper rules of governing based on such historical documents as the MAGNA CHARTA, the body of COMMON LAW, court decisions, precedents, and tradition.

According to Montesquieu, although England did not have the perfect system of government, it was the best system to be found in modern Europe because it allowed for the greatest degree of liberty, which Montesquieu defined as the right "to do what one should want to do, and not being forced to do what one should not want to do." For Montesquieu, liberty was, essentially, the right to be left alone.

This type of liberty, Montesquieu argued, was only possible under a government specifically constituted to protect citizens from the oppression of their rulers and the aggressions of each other, while allowing for the representation of a wide range of popular interests. For citizens to maintain their liberty against the encroachment of oppressive rulers, a government had to be composed of separate and balanced powers that would check and moderate each other, thus leaving the people a maximum degree of freedom under the laws.

To Montesquieu, England most closely approximated this model because its government divided the three main functions of government—the legislative, the executive, and the

"USELESS LAWS WEAKEN THE NECESSARY LAWS."
—BARON CHARLES-LOUIS DE MONTESQUIEU

judicial—into three separate branches: the Parliament, the monarch, and the courts. The powers of these branches were so intertwined that the branches needed each other to operate and also served to moderate each other's actions. For example, the king or queen could VETO parliamentary legislation, but the monarch's actions were limited by Parliament's power of the purse. Because no single branch was able to dominate the other branches or the populace at large, the people were left with a large degree of political freedom. Because the branches had to operate together, their forces counterbalanced each other and resulted in a guarantee of freedom and a bulwark against political tyranny. Although Montesquieu did not present the English system as the perfect model for democratic government, he did praise it for being the only government in modern Europe constituted for the specific purpose of maximizing political liberty.

Montesquieu's description of the basic principles of the English constitution and his emphasis on political liberty held great appeal for the English colonists in North America, particularly beginning in the 1760s when those colonists were chafing under taxes and restrictions imposed by Parliament that they thought undermined their constitutional rights. Montesquieu was frequently quoted in newspapers, pamphlets, and speeches as colonists protested the oppressive powers of Parliament and defended their right to political liberty. His description of the English constitution became a model against which the colonists contrasted what they saw as the injustice and corruption of the actual English government.

After the Revolutionary War ended, Montesquieu again became a principal authority as political leaders set about to create a constitution for the new United States of America. Most of the architects of the Constitution were thoroughly acquainted with Montesquieu's ideas, and at the Constitutional Convention of 1787, *The Spirit of the Laws* was frequently cited as delegates attempted to lay down the principles for a government that would maximize political liberty while also maintaining the rule of law. The Framers followed many of Montesquieu's maxims, including his insistence upon a separation of powers and his belief that a country's laws must not be imposed from above but conform to the genius, or nature, of the citizens of that country.

Montesquieu's arguments were also used in the debates over the ratification of the Constitution that followed the Constitutional Convention. He was cited with particular frequency in *The Federalist Papers,* which were written by James Madison, ALEXANDER HAMILTON, and JOHN JAY to argue in favor of the new Constitution. The writers cited Montesquieu at length in defense of the wisdom of confederating the states into a single republic and of creating a government based upon a separation of powers. Although other scholars had also written on the separation of powers principle, Montesquieu was most closely associated with it, as James Madison noted in *The Federalist,* no. 47: "The oracle who is always consulted and cited on this subject, is the celebrated Montesquieu. If he be not the author of this invaluable precept in the science of politics, he has the merit at least of displaying and recommending it most effectually to the attention of mankind." Montesquieu's arguments were also frequently used in the debates over the Constitution at the individual state conventions. Both proponents and opponents of the new Constitution respected him as a political authority, and both used his writings to bolster their arguments.

After the ratification of the Constitution in 1789, Montesquieu continued to remain an authority on the creation of laws and the rule of government. *The Spirit of the Laws* continued to be taught at COLLEGES AND UNIVERSITIES, and leaders of both political parties, the Republicans and the Federalists, used his arguments to advance their own. Montesquieu's only significant detractor was Thomas Jefferson, who believed, along with friends involved in the impending revolution in France, that Montesquieu was too enamored with England and its constitution. After the French Revolution and the radical changes it wrought, Montesquieu's writings came to seem dated and less relevant, and they gradually faded from the political debates. Even so, his work continued to exert a lasting influence on the laws of the United States through the Constitution that was so significantly shaped by his ideas.

FURTHER READINGS

Bergman, Matthew P. 1990. "Montesquieu's Theory of Government and the Framing of the American Constitution." *Pepperdine Law Review* 19 (December).

Carrese, Paul O. 2003. *The Cloaking of Power: Montesquieu, Blackstone, and the Rise of Judicial Activism.* Chicago: Univ. of Chicago Press.

Rodgers, Joseph P. 1997. "Suspending the Rule of Law? Temporary Immunity as Violative of Montesquieu's

Republican Virtue as Embodied in George Washington. *Cleveland State Law Review* 45 (spring): 301–27.

CROSS-REFERENCES

Constitution of the United States; Federalist Papers.

MONTGOMERY BUS BOYCOTT

The Montgomery bus boycott was a mass protest by African American citizens in the city of Montgomery, Alabama, against SEGREGATION policies on the city's public buses. It was nine years before the CIVIL RIGHTS ACT OF 1964 would change the nation forever. But in 1955, when ROSA PARKS refused to give up her seat on a public bus to a white man, she was arrested and jailed for violating state segregation laws. She did not realize at the time that her actions would have an immediate effect on other members of the African American community and a lasting effect on the national history of CIVIL RIGHTS. The resultant massive boycott lasted for 11 months. It ended in late 1956 when the U.S. Supreme Court ruled that public bus segregation (the case involved the City of Montgomery) was unconstitutional. *Browder v. Gayle*, 352 U.S. 903.

Several of Rosa Parks' friends were members of the Women's Political Council (WPC), an organization of black professionals founded in 1946. As early as 1953, WPC members had been actively pursuing changes in bus segregation law through communications with Mayor W.A.

Gayle. They requested that black persons be allowed to sit from back toward front and whites from front toward back until a bus was filled. They also demanded more bus stops located in black residential communities. When the talks produced little result, WPC president Jo Ann Robinson sent a final letter to the mayor in May 1954, advising that plans were being made to ride less, if at all, on the buses.

Notwithstanding waning use of the public bus system by Montgomery's black citizens, it was Rosa Parks's actions on December 1, 1955, that ignited a more organized boycott. Following her arrest, WPC members prepared a leaflet and made thousands of copies to distribute through local churches the following Sunday. They asked for a show of support for Rosa Parks in a one-day boycott of the city's buses. On December 5, 1955, 90 percent of Montgomery's black citizens avoided use of the public buses.

Wanting to capitalize on the momentum, church ministers in the area quickly mobilized and organized the Montgomery Improvement Association as the flagship entity to lead a formal boycott. The ministers elected 27-year-old newcomer, MARTIN LUTHER KING JR., as the spokesperson for the new organization. Formal demands were made to the city and the bus company. African Americans wanted more courteous service, black bus drivers hired for the black routes, and a first-come, first-served (but still segregated) rider policy.

To punctuate the seriousness of the protests, Montgomery citizens (black and white) formed what was locally referred to as a "taxicab army." They refused to ride the public buses and instead walked to their destinations or hailed taxicabs driven by African Americans. As part of the boycott, the taxi drivers had agreed to charge a reduced rate of ten cents per person, equal to the public bus fare. When riders began sharing taxicab fares and riding together in the same direction, city officials declared it illegal. In response, people began donating their own vehicles to transport riders. Others began volunteering their services as drivers for those who needed to travel farther than they could walk. By the end of the first week, more than 20,000 black citizens of Montgomery were getting rides to work through the Montgomery Improvement Association.

In February 1956, city officials obtained an INJUNCTION against the boycott and used a

Rosa Parks's refusal to give up her bus seat to a white man on December 1, 1955, sparked the 11-month long Montgomery Bus Boycott.

AP/WIDE WORLD PHOTOS

1921 law prohibiting the hindrance of a bus as grounds to arrest 156 protesters. Martin Luther King Jr. was also arrested, convicted, and ordered to pay fines. Ultimately, Fred Gray, a young black Montgomery attorney, filed an action on behalf of a group of black citizens. He sought a DECLARATORY JUDGMENT finding Alabama's state statutes and Montgomery city ordinances unenforceable and unconstitutional under the FOURTEENTH AMENDMENT to the U.S. Constitution. The laws and ordinances required separate accommodations on any commercial vehicle operated by any motor transportation company within the state of Alabama and the city of Montgomery. The bus company, in response, had alleged that segregation on privately owned buses was valid under the laws.

A three-member federal panel struck down the laws, finding the 1954 Supreme Court ruling in BROWN V. BOARD OF EDUCATION (repudiating a "separate but equal" principle) applicable to city buses. The U.S. Supreme Court upheld the decision, and the successful boycott ended in major victory.

FURTHER READINGS

Bermanzohn, Sally Avery. 2000. "Violence, Nonviolence, and the Civil Rights Movement." *New Political Science.* 22.

"Montgomery Bus Boycott." Excerpted from *Dr. Martin Luther King Jr. Papers Project: Encyclopedia.* Undated. Available online at <www.stanford.edu/group/King/about_king/encyclopedia/bus_boycott.html>; website home page at <www.stanford.edu> (accessed August 5, 2003.)

Swann-Wright, Dianne. 2000. "The Montgomery Bus Boycott." *Footsteps* 2.

CROSS-REFERENCES

Civil Rights Acts; Discrimination.

MONUMENT

Anything by which the memory of a person, thing, idea, art, science or event is preserved or perpetuated. A tomb where a dead body has been deposited.

In REAL-PROPERTY *law and surveying, visible marks or indications left on natural or other objects indicating the lines and boundaries of a survey. Any physical object on the ground that helps to establish the location of a boundary line called for; it may be either natural (e.g., trees, rivers, and other land features) or artificial (e.g., fences, stones, stakes, or the like placed by human hands).*

❖ MOODY, WILLIAM HENRY

William Henry Moody, Supreme Court appointee of THEODORE ROOSEVELT, served the Court from 1906 to 1910. The Massachusetts Republican, representative, and two-time cabinet member supported the progressive policies of his era. He was especially respected by his colleagues for his skill in the area of ANTITRUST LAW. Moody's service on the Court was ended prematurely due to health problems.

Moody was born on December 23, 1853, in Newbury, Massachusetts from a long line of New England, Puritan ancestry. He was educated at Phillips Academy and found his first real success in life as an athlete on the Harvard baseball team. He graduated from Harvard in 1876 with honors in history, ranking third in his class. After Harvard, he worked in the law office of RICHARD DANA. He was admitted to the bar in 1878.

Moody established a private practice in Haverhill, Massachusetts, and served as the city solicitor for two years (1888–1890). In 1890 he

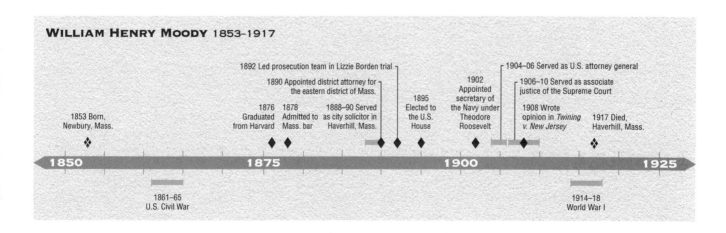

WILLIAM HENRY MOODY 1853–1917

1853 Born, Newbury, Mass.

1876 Graduated from Harvard

1878 Admitted to Mass. bar

1888–90 Served as city solicitor in Haverhill, Mass.

1890 Appointed district attorney for the eastern district of Mass.

1892 Led prosecution team in Lizzie Borden trial

1895 Elected to the U.S. House

1902 Appointed secretary of the Navy under Theodore Roosevelt

1904–06 Served as U.S. attorney general

1906–10 Served as associate justice of the Supreme Court

1908 Wrote opinion in *Twining v. New Jersey*

1917 Died, Haverhill, Mass.

1850   1875   1900   1925

1861–65 U.S. Civil War

1914–18 World War I

William H. Moody.
LIBRARY OF CONGRESS

and Company, the Supreme Court first formulated the "stream of commerce" doctrine, which held corporations responsible for all of their interstate commercial activities.

After the resignation of Associate Justice HENRY B. BROWN, Roosevelt appointed Moody to the Supreme Court in 1906. Moody's most important opinion with the Court was probably that in *Twining v. New Jersey,* 211 U.S. 78, 29 S. Ct. 14, 53 L. Ed. 97 (1908), which held that the Fourteenth Amendment's DUE PROCESS CLAUSE did not incorporate the FIFTH AMENDMENT right against SELF-INCRIMINATION and apply it to the states. *Twining* was overruled in 1964 by *Malloy v. Hogan,* 378 U.S. 1, 84 S. Ct. 1489, 12 L. Ed. 2d 653.

Moody continued to serve the Court until 1910, at which time acute rheumatism forced his retirement. He died July 2, 1917, in Haverhill, Massachusetts.

FURTHER READINGS

Friedman, Leon, and Fred L. Israel, eds. 1969. *The Justices of the United States Supreme Court, 1789–1969: Their Lives and Major Opinions.* Vol. III. New York: Chelsea House.

Witt, Elder, ed. 1990. *Guide to the U.S. Supreme Court.* 2d ed. Washington, D.C.: Congressional Quarterly.

❖ MOORE, ALFRED

As an associate justice, Alfred Moore served on the U.S. Supreme Court for five years. The ardent federalist, whose life and political career involved danger, controversy, and principled stands, left little mark on the Court's business during his service from 1799 to 1804. Although he fought in the Revolutionary War and later held high office in North Carolina, Moore's fire had mostly left him by the time President JOHN ADAMS appointed him to the Supreme Court. Even at a time when the Court decided major cases, he either acquiesced to the majority or did not participate in certain decisions because of poor health. He wrote just one opinion, *Bas v. Tingy,* 4 U.S. (4 Dall.) 37, 1 L. Ed 731 (1800), important only in its historical relevance to the United States' undeclared naval war with France in the last years of the eighteenth century.

Moore was a youth during the country's difficult transition from British colony to independent nation. Born on May 21, 1755, in New Hanover County, North Carolina, he was the son of Maurice Moore, a colonial judge. Moore studied in Boston before being educated in law by his father, and he was admitted to the North

was appointed district attorney for the eastern district of Massachusetts. He was one of the state's two prosecutors in the trial of LIZZIE BORDEN, who was charged with murdering her father and stepmother with an ax in 1892. Although Borden was acquitted, Moody won respect for his performance in the trial.

Shortly after the Borden case, the Republicans nominated Moody to a seat in Congress. He was elected to the House of Representatives in November 1895 and became one of its most influential members. On April 30, 1902, he resigned from the House to become Theodore Roosevelt's secretary of the Navy.

Two years later he was appointed attorney general. He successfully argued the landmark antitrust case of *Swift and Company v. United States,* 196 U.S. 375, 25 S. Ct. 276, 49 L. Ed. 518 (1905), before the Supreme Court. The government had obtained an INJUNCTION against the trust by arguing that a combination of corporations and individuals, after purchasing livestock and converting it to fresh meat, sold products in interstate commerce in such a manner as to suppress competition both in livestock and fresh meats. The trust appealed the injunction. Moody won a perpetual injunction, but the trust ignored it. Moody was infuriated and instigated a GRAND JURY investigation in Chicago, which led to indictment of all the major packers. Through Moody's success in prosecuting Swift

Carolina bar at the age of twenty in 1775. Soon after, he fought against the British, first as a soldier and then as a saboteur. During the war, Moore's brother, father, and uncle were killed, the family plantation was ransacked, and their home was destroyed.

Moore was a member of the North Carolina legislature in 1782 and 1792. From 1782 to 1791, he served as the state's attorney general, arguing one particularly important case, *Bayard v. Singleton*, 1 N.C. (Mart.) 5 (1787), which marked one of the first complete discussions of the doctrine of JUDICIAL REVIEW (the authority of courts to determine the validity of legislation under the Constitution). A federalist who firmly believed in central government, he spearheaded North Carolina's ratification of the U.S. Constitution in 1788. In 1791 Moore took the strongest personal stand of his career when he resigned from the office of attorney general; he stepped down over the state legislature's creation of the office of SOLICITOR GENERAL with powers equivalent to his, an action he saw as unconstitutional. He won reelection to the legislature but failed in a 1795 bid for the U.S. Senate by one vote.

In 1799 President John Adams nominated Moore to fill a vacancy on the U.S. Supreme Court created by the death of Associate Justice JAMES IREDELL. The next five years were pivotal ones for the Supreme Court, which expanded its powers of judicial review under the highly influential Chief Justice JOHN MARSHALL. However, failing health minimized Moore's role. He did not participate in the most important decision of his day, MARBURY V. MADISON, 5 U.S. (1 Cranch) 137, 2 L. Ed. 60 (1803).

Moore's only recorded Supreme Court opinion is a five-paragraph statement on the undeclared naval war between France and the United

Alfred Moore.
ETCHING BY ALBERT ROSENTHAL. SUPREME COURT OF THE UNITED STATES

States. This war reached its height in 1798 and 1799 and was fought chiefly over French claims to seize all cargo of British origin from both British and U.S. ships. Although Congress passed many acts in relation to the conflict, problems arose over the ownership of goods that were recaptured, and in one instance the issue was resolved by determining whether France and the United States were enemy nations. When *Bas v. Tingy* reached the Supreme Court in 1800, each of the four justices hearing the case agreed that the two nations were indeed foes. Moore's opinion declared, "It is for the honor and dignity of both nations . . . that they should be called enemies."

In 1804 Moore resigned from the Court. He died on October 15, 1810, in Bladen County, North Carolina, leaving as part of his legacy

"IF WORDS ARE BUT THE REPRESENTATIVE OF IDEAS, . . . BY WHAT OTHER WORD [CAN] THE IDEA OF THE RELATIVE SITUATION OF AMERICA AND FRANCE BE COMMUNICATED, THAN BY THAT OF HOSTILITY OR WAR?"
—ALFRED MOORE

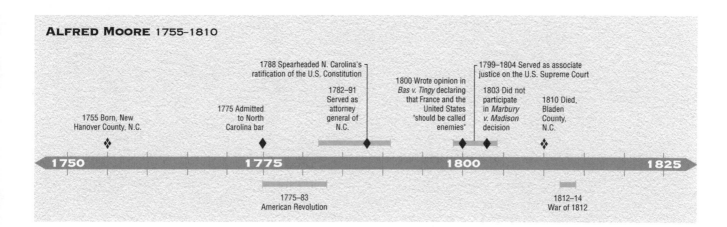

ALFRED MOORE 1755–1810

1788 Spearheaded N. Carolina's ratification of the U.S. Constitution

1782–91 Served as attorney general of N.C.

1800 Wrote opinion in *Bas v. Tingy* declaring that France and the United States "should be called enemies"

1799–1804 Served as associate justice on the U.S. Supreme Court

1803 Did not participate in *Marbury v. Madison* decision

1755 Born, New Hanover County, N.C.

1775 Admitted to North Carolina bar

1810 Died, Bladen County, N.C.

1750   1775   1800   1825

1775–83 American Revolution

1812–14 War of 1812

the establishment of the University of North Carolina.

FURTHER READINGS

Friedman, Leon, and Fred L. Israel, eds. 1969. *The Justices of the United States Supreme Court, 1789–1969: Their Lives and Major Opinions.* New York: Chelsea House.

Witt, Elder, ed. 1990. *Guide to the U.S. Supreme Court.* 2d ed. Washington, D.C.: Congressional Quarterly.

MOOT

An issue presenting no real controversy.

Moot refers to a subject for academic argument. It is an abstract question that does not arise from existing facts or rights.

Moot court is a cocurricular or extracurricular activity in law school where students have the opportunity to write briefs and present oral arguments on hypothetical cases.

MOOT COURT

A method of teaching law and legal skills that requires students to analyze and argue both sides of a hypothetical legal issue using procedures modeled after those employed in state and federal appellate courts.

In the mid-1700s moot courts in the United States had a tradition of debate and oratory revered in undergraduate institutions such as Yale College. Moot court exercises have changed in the United States since that time. Law instructors present hypothetical cases and students argue them before professors or other lawyers, who serve as judges. Hypothetical cases often address matters of current political and constitutional import.

Moot court requirements vary from law school to law school, with most schools mandating that students participate at least once in a moot court argument before receiving their law degree. Many law schools offer a series of moot court opportunities for students of differing skill levels and legal interests. The activity is competitive by nature, and students vie for honors within their school and in regional and national moot court competitions featuring teams of students from several law schools.

Moot court helps students learn to analyze legal issues; its larger purpose is to teach students the practical side of practicing law. Typically, law students are given a detailed hypothetical fact scenario that raises one or more legal issues. Often these fact patterns are based on real cases on appeal to a state's highest court or the U.S. Supreme Court. Students choose or are assigned the position on the issue to be argued. They then conduct legal research, finding statutes, regulations, and case law that both support their position and detract from it. An important part of the moot court process is to teach students to overcome legal authority (statutes, regulations, and cases) that cuts against their position.

Students then draft appellate briefs, which are formal legal papers combining a recital of the facts of the case with analysis and argument of the legal issues raised. As with real appellate courts, moot courts generally dictate many specific requirements for a brief, including the size of the paper, the width of the margins, and the maximum number of pages. Citations to legal authority must also be listed in a uniform style.

Once the briefs are written, students prepare for the second phase of moot court advocacy: oral argument. Oral argument demands preparation, organization, and the ability to think quickly and respond convincingly when questioned. The student appears before a panel of judges (typically law professors, actual judges, or other students) and presents her or his position on the legal issue. Each student has a time limit, normally five to ten minutes, to convince the panel. As with real appellate courts, judges on the panel are free to interrupt the student advocate frequently and at any time to ask questions about the facts of the case, legal authority for or against the student's position, or the student's thoughts and opinions about the case's outcome. Students learn to anticipate difficult questions about their legal position and respond intelligently and persuasively. Following oral argument, the moot court panel often will review the student's performance.

Moot court is modeled after the appellate procedure employed in state and federal courts. Moot court is sometimes confused with mock trials, a similar learning method by which students conduct a jury trial based on a hypothetical fact pattern. Where moot court emphasizes legal research, analysis, writing, and oratory, mock trials emphasize jury persuasion techniques and a thorough familiarity with the RULES OF EVIDENCE.

Top moot court advocates from law schools throughout the country compete each year at a variety of national moot court competitions, many having a focus on a specific area of the law.

The National Moot Court Competition is held annually in New York City and focuses on issues of CONSTITUTIONAL LAW. The Philip C. Jessup INTERNATIONAL LAW Moot Court Competition, held each spring in Washington, D.C., is sponsored by the American Society of International Law and the International Law Students Association. The Chief Judge Conrad B. Duberstein National BANKRUPTCY Moot Court is an annual competition focusing on bankruptcy issues.

FURTHER READINGS

Bucholtz, Barbara K., Martin A. Frey, and Melissa L. Tatum. 2002. *The Little Black Book: A Do-It-Yourself Guide for Law Student Competitions.* Durham, N.C.: Carolina Academic Press.

Davis, Tracy Hamrick. 1995. "The Holderness Moot Court Bench." *North Carolina Law Review* 73 (January).

Mellhorn, Donald F., Jr. 1995. "A Moot Court Exercise: Debating Judicial Review Prior to *Marbury v. Madison.*" *Constitutional Comment* 12 (winter).

Teply, Larry L. 2003. *Law School Competitions in a Nutshell.* St. Paul, Minn.: Thomson/West.

CROSS-REFERENCES

Legal Education.

MORAL LAW

The rules of behavior an individual or a group may follow out of personal conscience and that are not necessarily part of legislated law in the United States.

Moral law is a system of guidelines for behavior. These guidelines may or may not be part of a religion, codified in written form, or legally enforceable. For some people moral law is synonymous with the commands of a divine being. For others, moral law is a set of universal rules that should apply to everyone.

Ethical principles held primarily by the followers of Christianity have influenced the development of U.S. secular law. As a result, Christian moral law and secular law overlap in many situations. For example, murder, theft, prostitution, and other behaviors labeled immoral are also illegal. Moral turpitude is a legal term used to describe a crime that demonstrates depravity in one's public and private life, contrary to what is accepted and customary. People convicted of this crime can be disqualified from government office, lose their license to practice law, or be deported (in the case of immigrants).

Passing laws is relatively easy when public policy makers can unanimously identify behavior that is socially unacceptable. Policy makers can then attempt to enforce socially correct behavior through legal channels. However, in many other situations, it is far more difficult to determine what behavior the government should promote, if any. When a government seeks to implement a code of conduct that may conflict with the U.S. Constitution, the courts are generally called upon to determine the law's validity.

ABORTION is an area where legal and moral principles converge and often conflict. In 1973 the U.S. Supreme Court ruled in ROE V. WADE, 410 U.S. 113, 93 S. Ct. 705, 35 L. Ed. 2d 147, that a woman's decision to have an abortion is a private choice that is protected by the Constitution, at least until the end of the first trimester of pregnancy. After a fetus is viable (able to survive outside the womb), the state may regulate the woman's pregnancy and prohibit abortion except if the woman's life is in danger.

Some advocates of legalized abortion as well as some critics believe that the current legal situation is inadequate. To protect either the rights of the pregnant woman or the rights of the fetus is a moral question that individuals decide for themselves. Yet the extent to which people should be allowed to act on their beliefs and exercise their rights is debated in the arena of legislative and judiciary decision making.

Medical science is a field where evolving technology can create moral crises that have legal consequences. The AMERICAN MEDICAL ASSOCIATION sponsors a Council on Ethical and Judicial Affairs, which debates such problems as assisted suicide, harvesting organs over the objections of family, and whether to include HIV status on autopsy reports.

Many public policy issues form a crossroad of legal and moral law, including EUTHANASIA, assisted suicide, same-sex marriages, and CAPITAL PUNISHMENT.

FURTHER READINGS

McWilliams, Peter. 1993. *Ain't Nobody's Business If You Do.* Los Angeles: Prelude Press.

Tivnan, Edward. 1995. *The Moral Imagination: Confronting the Ethical Issues of Our Day.* New York: Simon & Schuster.

CROSS-REFERENCES

Acquired Immune Deficiency Syndrome; Animal Rights; Death and Dying; Ethics, Legal; Fetal Rights; Fetal Tissue Research; Gay and Lesbian Rights; Genetic Engineering; Genetic Screening; Health Care Law; Health Insurance; Jurisprudence; Natural Law; Organ Donation Law; Organ Transplantation; Patients' Rights; Slavery; Surrogate Motherhood.

MORAL RELATIVISM

The philosophized notion that right and wrong are not absolute values, but are personalized according to the individual and his or her circumstances or cultural orientation. It can be used positively to effect change in the law (e.g., promoting tolerance for other customs or lifestyles) or negatively as a means to attempt justification for wrongdoing or lawbreaking. The opposite of moral relativism is moral absolutism, which espouses a fundamental, NATURAL LAW of constant values and rules, and which judges all persons equally, irrespective of individual circumstances or cultural differences.

Within the U.S. justice system, constant values or rules (represented by constitutional, statutory, or case law) are intended to be structurally tempered to accommodate moral relativity. For example, OLIVER WENDELL HOLMES, who served on the U.S. Supreme Court from 1902 to 1932, is credited with being the first Supreme Court justice to state that the U.S. Constitution was an organic document—a living constitution subject to changing interpretation. Many times since, Supreme Court justices, in their opinions, have referred to the notion of "evolving" law when modifying, refining, or, in rare circumstances, overruling earlier precedent. Likewise, statutory laws are enacted or repealed by Congress or state legislators in an effort to best reflect the principles and mores of their constituency.

Notwithstanding this flexible approach to law, moral relativism often plays a significant role in the shaping of law and the punishment of criminals. In 2002, *U.S. News & World Report* cited a Zogby International poll of 401 randomly selected college seniors, which was commissioned by the National Association of Scholars. According to the results, 73 percent of the students interviewed indicated that they were taught by professors that uniform standards of right and wrong do not exist, but were instead dependent upon individual values and cultural diversity. Such attitudes and perceptions affect not only the thinking of subsequent generations of politicians and lawmakers, but also the courtroom adjudication of existing laws.

In many jury trials, defense attorneys attempt to persuade jurors that the law should be applied differently to a particular defendant. Examples of persuasive arguments may include such operative language as requesting that jurors be "more fair" or "more just" to a particular defendant, or that in order for "justice to be served," jurors must excuse the defendant's conduct as justifiable under the circumstances.

FURTHER READINGS

Cauthen, Kenneth. 2001. *The Ethics of Belief: A Bio-Historical Approach.* Lima, Ohio: CSS Publishing.

CROSS-REFERENCES

Jury Nullification; Moral Law.

MORAL TURPITUDE

A phrase used in CRIMINAL LAW to describe conduct that is considered contrary to community standards of justice, honesty, or good morals.

Crimes involving moral turpitude have an inherent quality of baseness, vileness, or depravity with respect to a person's duty to another or to society in general. Examples include rape, forgery, ROBBERY, and solicitation by prostitutes.

Many jurisdictions impose penalties, such as deportation of ALIENS and disbarment of attorneys, following convictions of crimes involving moral turpitude.

MORATORIUM

A suspension of activity or an authorized period of delay or waiting. A moratorium is sometimes agreed upon by the interested parties, or it may be authorized or imposed by operation of law. The term also is used to denote a period of time during which the law authorizes a delay in payment of debts or performance of some other legal obligation. This type of moratorium is most often invoked during times of distress, such as war or natural disaster.

Government bodies may declare moratoria for a broad range of reasons. For example, a local government may attempt to regulate property development by imposing a moratorium on the issuance of building permits. The legality of such a moratorium is generally determined by measuring its impact on the affected parties. In 1987 the U.S. Supreme Court held that certain moratoria on property development may be unconstitutional takings, thus making it more difficult for local governments to slow development in their communities (*First English Evangelical Lutheran Church v. Los Angeles County,* 482 U.S. 304, 107 S. Ct. 2378, 96 L. Ed. 2d 250). On the other hand, in 1995 the Court upheld a thirty-day moratorium on lawyer advertising that was challenged as an infringement of FIRST AMENDMENT rights

(*Florida Bar v. Went For It, Inc.,* 515 U.S. 618, 115 S. Ct. 2371, 132 L. Ed. 2d 541).

Many state legislatures have passed moratorium legislation in response to popular demand for debt relief during emergencies. The constitutionality of these statutes is determined using a two-pronged analysis. First, the courts consider the effect of the moratorium on the rights of the parties to the impaired contract. If the moratorium changes only the remedy for breach and not the terms of the contract, it is generally upheld (see *Sturges v. Crowninshield,* 17 U.S. [4 Wheat.] 122, 4 L. Ed. 529 [1819]). Second, if the moratorium is a response to a bona fide emergency, it is upheld (see *Johnson v. Duncan,* 3 Mart. 530 [La. 1815], upholding a moratorium passed when the British invaded Louisiana in 1814).

As a function of its POLICE POWER, a state may suspend contractual rights when public welfare, health, or safety are threatened. However, this police power is limited by standards of reasonableness. During the WORLD WAR I housing shortage, some New York landlords raised rents to exorbitant levels and evicted tenants who failed to pay. In response to what it perceived as a public health and safety emergency, the state legislature passed a law that limited rentals to reasonable amounts, gave courts authority to determine reasonableness, and prohibited landlords from evicting tenants willing to pay reasonable rents. The law was sustained by the U.S. Supreme Court in *Marcus Brown Holding Co. v. Feldman,* 256 U.S. 170, 41 S. Ct. 465, 65 L. Ed. 877 (1921).

An example of a contemporary debt moratorium is the Minnesota Mortgage Moratorium Act (1933 Minn. Laws 514), passed by the Minnesota legislature in response to a sharp rise in foreclosures on mortgaged farm property. The constitutionality of the act was challenged in *Home Building & Loan Association v. Blaisdell,* 290 U.S. 398, 54 S. Ct. 231, 78 L. Ed. 413 (1934), in which the Supreme Court upheld the legislation based on five criteria: a bona fide emergency existed; the statute addressed a legitimate societal interest; debt relief was granted only under limited conditions; contractual rights were reasonably protected; and the legislation was of limited duration. This act was extended until 1942. Fifty years later the Minnesota legislature responded again to public pressure to relieve farm debts by passing another Mortgage Moratorium Act (Minn. Stat. § 583.03 [Supp. 1983]).

FURTHER READINGS

Amundson, Roland C., and Lewis J. Rotman. 1984. "Depression Jurisprudence Revisited: Minnesota's Moratorium on Mortgage Foreclosure." *William Mitchell Law Review* 10.

MORMON CHURCH

The Mormon Church is a religious body founded in 1830 in Fayette, New York, by Joseph Smith. It is also known as the Church of Jesus Christ of Latter-day Saints, or LDS Church. There are 7.7 million Mormons worldwide. Approximately two-thirds reside in the United States, with the highest concentration in the western states, especially Utah. The church, which is headquartered in Salt Lake City, Utah, encountered legal difficulties during its early years because of its practice of POLYGAMY and its opposition to the use of COMMON LAW as legal precedent. The church's differences with the U.S. government led to armed conflict in the late 1800s.

Joseph Smith based his teachings on his translation of hieroglyphic messages revealed to him on several golden plates. Smith's translation of these divine messages is known as the Book of Mormon. The Book of Mormon and the Bible form the basis of Mormon belief.

During the early 1800s, Smith and his followers settled in Kirtland, Ohio, and Jackson County, Missouri, where they were persecuted because of their beliefs. They moved to Illinois and helped establish the town of Nauvoo, where the church prospered. However, local residents became inflamed over rumors that Smith and his followers were practicing polygamy, or plural marriage. Smith and his brother Hyrum were arrested and taken to Carthage, the county seat. On June 27, 1844, they were both shot and killed by a group of townspeople.

Smith was succeeded by Brigham Young, the head of the church's Council of the Twelve Apostles. In 1846 Young organized and directed church members to follow him from Nauvoo to the Great Salt Basin in the Utah Territory. They settled there and established the headquarters of the church in Salt Lake City.

In Utah the Mormon Church prospered and grew. In addition to leading the church, Young became provisional governor of the Utah Territory in 1849. In that capacity he and the other members of the government, most of whom were Mormons, defied the U.S. government by

Brigham Young was
the second president
of the Mormon
Church and colonizer
of Utah. The church's
resistance to the
application of
common law resulted
in conflict with the
federal government
during the 1800s.
UNDERWOOD &
UNDERWOOD/CORBIS

Church had acknowledged polygamy as one of its tenets. Mormon teaching of the time held that men were obligated to have multiple wives. Common law provides that marriage to more than one living husband or wife is a felony and that any marriages other than the first are void.

When President MILLARD FILLMORE assigned three federal judges to the Utah Territory in the 1850s, Young became concerned that the new judges would impose common-law precedent. He attempted to blunt their impact by urging the legislature to prohibit judges from using common-law precedent in Utah. On January 14, 1854, the legislature passed a bill that prohibited any law from being read, cited, or adopted in Utah unless it had been enacted by the legislature or the governor. This bill directly contravened the Organic Act of Utah of 1850 (9 Stat. 453) by which the U.S. Congress created the Utah Territory. The act gave the U.S. Supreme Court and the federal district courts of the territory both common-law and EQUITY jurisdiction and established that the laws of the United States applied in the territory. In 1856 the Territorial Supreme Court held that the Organic Act extended common law over the Territory of Utah and that the legislature violated the Organic Act when it forbade the use of common law in Utah (*People v. Moroni Green*, 1 Utah 11 [1856]).

Tensions continued to mount between Mormons and the federal government. In May 1857 President JAMES BUCHANAN dispatched 2,500 U.S. Army troops to Utah to remove Young from office and enforce federal authority. Anticipating the federal troops' arrival, a group of angry Mormons joined forces with a group of Paiute Indians who attacked and killed 120 settlers traveling through the territory in September 1857. Mormon leaders feared that the attack, known as the Mountain Meadows Massacre, would lead to further reprisals by the federal government. They sent sympathetic church members to destroy the Army's supplies, thereby delaying the troops' arrival. The Mormons' resistance came to be known as the Utah War. By the time the troops arrived in the summer of 1858, tensions had eased considerably, and under a negotiated settlement, troops were stationed outside Salt Lake City without incident.

The Mormon Church's resistance to the application of common law continued through the late 1800s. A number of cases reached the Territorial Supreme Court, which repeatedly

rejecting common law as valid legal precedent in Utah. Common law, as distinct from statutory law, is English precedent adopted by U.S. courts. Over time, common law became part of U.S. JURISPRUDENCE except where it was expressly abrogated. Although Young patterned the structure of Utah's territorial government after the other state governments, with executive, legislative, and judicial branches, he believed that the United States should abandon all vestiges of English tradition. According to Young, the application of common law allowed judges too much latitude to impose standards that did not comport with public will.

Young's opposition to the application of common law reached its nadir over the issue of polygamy. By the mid-1800s, the Mormon

affirmed that common law is valid in the territory. (See *Murphy v. Carter*, 1 Utah 17 [1868], and *Godebe v. Salt Lake City*, 1 Utah 68 [1870]). In *First National Bank of Utah v. Kinner*, 1 Utah 100 (1873), the court held that the people of the Utah territory had tacitly agreed to the application of common law. In 1878 the U.S. Supreme Court settled the question of whether the common-law prohibition of polygamy applied in the territory. In *Reynolds v. United States*, 98 U.S. (8 Otto) 145, 25 L. Ed. 244, the plaintiff argued that the common-law prohibition of polygamy was unconstitutional because it violated the FIRST AMENDMENT guarantee of freedom of religion. The Court disagreed and held that religious freedom does not encompass the practice of polygamy and that laws prohibiting the practice are constitutional. The Court stated that to allow Mormons to practice plural marriage "would be to make the professed doctrines of religious belief superior to the law of the land, and in effect permit every citizen to become a law unto himself. Government could exist only in name under such circumstances."

By the 1890s the Mormon Church had officially abandoned the practice of plural marriage. In 1896 Utah became a state, and in 1898 the legislature passed a measure that declared that the common law "shall be the rule of decision in all courts of this state" (The Revised Statutes of the State of Utah, § 2488). The common law continues to carry the force of precedent in Utah, except for the common law of crimes, which the legislature abolished in 1973 (Utah Code Ann. § 76-1-105; repealed, Utah Code Ann. § 68-2-3; replaced by Utah Code Ann. § 68-3-1).

FURTHER READINGS

Acts, Resolutions and Memorials Passed at the Several Annual Sessions of the Legislative Assembly of the Territory of Utah. 1855. Salt Lake City: Caine.

Eliason, Eric A., ed. 2001. *Mormons and Mormonism: An Introduction to an American World Religion.* Urbana: Univ. of Illinois Press.

Flor, Victoria Slind. 1998. "Mormons' Impact on the Law is Singular; a Coherent World View Informs Approach to Lawmaking, Lawsuits, the Constitution and Lawyers." *The National Law Journal* 21 (October 26): A1.

Homer, Michael. 1996. "The Judiciary and the Common Law in Utah." *Utah Bar Journal* 9 (September).

Mauro, Tony. 2003. "Mormon Land Dispute Tests First Amendment." *Legal Times* 26 (April 28): 11.

Ostling, Richard, and Joan K. Ostling. 2000. *Mormon America: The Power and the Promise.* San Francisco: HarperSanFrancisco.

MORTALITY TABLES

A means of ascertaining the probable number of years any man or woman of a given age and of ordinary health will live. A mortality table expresses on the basis of the group studied the probability that, of a number of persons of equal expectations of life who are living at the beginning of any year, a certain number of deaths will occur within that year.

Such tables are used by insurance companies to determine the premium to be charged for those in the respective age groups.

MORTGAGE

A legal document by which the owner (i.e., the buyer) transfers to the lender an interest in real estate to secure the repayment of a debt, evidenced by a mortgage note. When the debt is repaid, the mortgage is discharged, and a satisfaction of mortgage is recorded with the register or recorder of deeds in the county where the mortgage was recorded. Because most people cannot afford to buy real estate with cash, nearly every real estate transaction involves a mortgage.

The party who borrows the money and gives the mortgage (the debtor) is the mortgagor; the party who pays the money and receives the mortgage (the lender) is the mortgagee. Under early English and U.S. law, the mortgage was treated as a complete transfer of title from the borrower to the lender. The lender was entitled not only to payments of interest on the debt but also to the rents and profits of the real estate. This meant that as far as the borrower was concerned, the real estate was of no value, that is, "dead," until the debt was paid in full—hence the Norman-English name "mort" (dead), "gage" (pledge).

The mortgage must be executed according to the formalities required by the laws of the state where the property is located. It must describe the real estate and must be signed by all owners, including non-owner spouses if the property is a homestead. Some states require witnesses as well as acknowledgement before a NOTARY PUBLIC.

The mortgage note, in which the borrower promises to repay the debt, sets out the terms of the transaction: the amount of the debt, the mortgage due date, the rate of interest, the amount of monthly payments, whether the lender requires monthly payments to build a tax and insurance reserve, whether the loan may be repaid with larger or more frequent payments without a pre-payment penalty, and whether failing to make a payment or selling the property will entitle the lender to call the entire debt due.

State courts have devised varying theories of the legal effect of mortgages: Some treat the mortgage as a conveyance of the title, which can be defeated on payment of the debt; others regard it as a lien, entitling the borrower to all of the rights of ownership, as long as the terms of the mortgage are observed. In California a deed of trust to a trustee who holds title for the lender is the preferred security instrument.

At COMMON LAW, if the borrower failed to pay the debt in full at the appointed time, the borrower suffered a complete loss of title, how-ever long and faithfully the payments had been made.

Courts of EQUITY, which were originally ecclesiastical courts, had the authority to decide cases on the basis of moral obligation, fairness, or justice, as distinguished from the law courts, which were bound to decide strictly according to the common law. Equity courts softened the harshness of the common law by ruling that the debtor could regain title even after default, but before it was declared forfeited, by paying the debt with interest and costs. This form of relief is known as the equity of redemption.

Nowadays, nearly all states have enacted statutes incorporating the equity of redemption, and many also have enacted periods of redemp-tion, specifying lengths of time within which the borrower may redeem. Although some debtors, or mortgagors, are able to avoid foreclosure through the equity of redemption, many are not, because redeeming means coming up with the balance of the mortgage plus interest and costs, something that a financially troubled debtor might not be able to accomplish. However, because foreclosure upends the agreement between mortgagor and mortgagee and creates burdens for both parties, lenders are often will-ing to work with debtors to help them through a period of temporary difficulty. Debtors who run into problems meeting their mortgage obliga-tions should speak to their lender about devel-oping a plan to avert foreclosure.

Failure to redeem results in foreclosure of the borrower's rights in the real estate, which is then sold by the county sheriff at a public fore-closure sale. At a foreclosure sale, the lender is the most frequent purchaser of the property.

If the bid at the sale is less than the debt, even if it is for fair market value, the lender may be granted a deficiency judgment for the balance of the debt against the debtor, with the right to resort to other assets or income for its collection.

Often other creditors bid at the sale to pro-tect their interest as judgment creditors, second mortgagees, or mechanic's lien claimants. All such persons must be notified of the foreclosure suit and must be given a right to bid at the sale to protect their claims. Similar protections are afforded transactions involving deeds of trust.

A fixed-rate mortgage carries an interest rate that will be set at the inception of the loan and will remain constant for the length of the mort-gage. A 30-year mortgage will have a rate that is fixed for all 30 years. At the end of the 30th year, if payments have been made on time, the loan is fully paid off. To a borrower, the advantage is that the rate will remain constant, and the monthly payment will remain the same throughout the life of the loan. The lender is taking the risk that interest rates will rise and that it will carry a loan at below-market interest rates for some or part of the 30 years. Because of this risk, there is usually a higher interest rate on a fixed-rate loan than the initial rate and payments on adjustable rate or balloon mortgages. If the rates fall, homeown-ers may pay off the loan by refinancing the house at the then-lower interest rate.

An adjustable-rate mortgage (ARM) pro-vides a fixed initial interest rate and a fixed ini-tial monthly payment for a short period of time. With an ARM, after the initial fixed period, which can be anywhere from six months to six years, both the interest rate and the monthly payments adjust on a regular basis to reflect the then-current market interest. Some ARMs may be subject to adjustment every three months, while others may be adjusted once per year. Moreover, some ARMs limit the amount that the rates may change. While an ARM usually carries a lower initial interest rate and a lower initial monthly payment, the purchaser is taking the risk that rates may rise in the future.

An alternative form of financing, usually a last resort for those who do not qualify for other mortgages, is called owner financing or owner carryback. The owner finances or "carries" all or part of the mortgage. Owner financing often involves balloon mortgage payments, as the monthly payments are frequently interest-only. A balloon mortgage has a fixed interest rate and a fixed monthly payment, but after a fixed

A sample plain-language mortgage note

Plain-Language Mortgage Note

Multistate

NOTE

FHA Case No. _____

December 6, 2000
    (Date)

101 MAIN STREET, ATLANTA, GEORGIA 30341
(Property Address)

1. PARTIES

"Borrower" means each person signing at the end of this Note, and the person's successors and assigns. "Lender" means ABC **MORTGAGE COMPANY** and its successors and assigns.

2. BORROWER'S PROMISE TO PAY; INTEREST

In return for a loan received from Lender, Borrower promises to pay the principal sum of **One Hundred Twenty-Five Thousand Six Hundred Fifty and 00/100 dollars (U.S. $125,650.00)**, plus interest, to the order of Lender. Interest will be charged on unpaid principal, from the date of disbursement of the loan proceeds by Lender, at the rate of **Eight and 00/100 percent (8%)** per year until the full amount of principal has been paid

3. PROMISE TO PAY SECURED

Borrower's promise to pay is secured by a mortgage, deed of trust or similar security instrument that is dated the same date as this Note and called the "Security Instrument". That Security Instrument protects the Lender from losses which might result if Borrower defaults under this Note.

4. MANNER OF PAYMENT

(A) Time

Borrower shall make a payment of principal and interest to Lender on the first day of each month beginning on **February 1st, 2001**. Any principal and interest remaining on the first day of **January, 2031**, will be due on that date, which is called the "Maturity Date".

(B) Place

Payment shall be made at **1000 South Street, Atlanta, GA 30342** or at such other place as Lender may designate in writing by notice to Borrower.

(C) Amount

Each monthly payment of principal and interest will be in the amount of **$921.97**. This amount will be part of a larger monthly payment required by the Security Instrument, that shall be applied to principal, interest and other items in the order described in the Security Instrument.

(D) Allonge to this note for payment adjustments

If an allonge providing for payment adjustments is executed by Borrower together with this Note, the covenants of the allonge shall be incorporated into and shall amend and supplement the covenants of this Note as if the allonge were a part of this Note. [Check applicable box]

☐ Graduated Payment Allonge   ☐ Growing Equity Allonge   ☐ Other [Specify]

5. BORROWER'S RIGHT TO PREPAY

Borrower has the right to pay the debt evidenced by this Note, in whole or in part, without charge or penalty, on the first day of any month.

6. BORROWER'S FAILURE TO PAY

(A) Late Charge for Overdue Payments

If Lender has not received the full monthly payment required by the Security Instrument as described in Paragraph 4(C) of this Note by the end of fifteen calendar days after the payment is due, Lender may collect a late charge in the amount of **Four and 00/100 percent (4%)** of the overdue amount of each payment.

(B) Default

If Borrower defaults by failing to pay in full any monthly payment, then Lender may, except as limited by regulations of the Secretary in the case of payment defaults, require immediate payment in full of the principal balance remaining due and all accrued interest. Lender may choose not to exercise this option without waiving its rights in the event of any subsequent default. In many circumstances regulations issued by the Secretary will limit Lender's rights to require immediate payment in full in the case of payment defaults. This Note does not authorize acceleration when not permitted by HUD regulations. As used in this Note, "Secretary" means the Secretary of Housing and Urban Development of his or her designee.

(C) Payment of Costs and Expenses

If Lender has required immediate payment in full, as described above, Lender may require Borrower to pay costs and expenses including reasonable and customary attorneys' fees for enforcing this Note. Such fees and costs shall bear interest from the date of disbursement at the same rate as the principal of this Note.

[continued]

A sample plain-language mortgage note (continued)

Plain-Language Mortgage Note

7. WAIVERS

Borrower and any other person who has obligations under this Note waive the rights of presentment and notice of dishonor. "Presentment" means the right to require Lender to demand payment of amounts due. "Notice of dishonor" means the right to require Lender to give notice to other persons that amounts due have not been paid.

8. GIVING OF NOTICES

Unless applicable law requires a different method, any notice that must be given to Borrower under this Note will be given by delivering it or by mailing it by first class mail to Borrower at the property address above or at a different address if Borrower has given Lender notice of Borrower's different address.

Any notice that must be given to Lender under this Note will be given by first class mail to Lender at the address stated in Paragraph 4(B) or at a different address if Borrower is given a notice of that different address.

9. OBLIGATIONS OF PERSONS UNDER THIS NOTE

If more than one person signs this Note, each person is fully and personally obligated to keep all of the promises made in this Note, including the promise to pay the full amount owed. Any person who is a guarantor, surety or endorser of this Note is also obligated to do these things. Any person who takes over these obligations, including the obligations of a guarantor, surety or endorser of this Note, is also obligated to keep all of the promises made in this Note. Lender may enforce its rights under this Note against each person individually or against all signatories together. Any one person signing this Note may be required to pay all of the amounts owed under this Note.

BY SIGNING BELOW, Borrower accepts and agrees to the terms and covenants contained in this Note.

_____ (Seal)
Borrower - **SAM F. MAGUIRE, JR.**

_____ (Seal)
Borrower -

_____ (Seal)
Borrower -

_____ (Seal)
Borrower -

FHA Multistate Fixed Rate Note - 2/91

---

period of time, such as five or ten years, the whole balance of the loan becomes due at once, meaning that the buyer must either pay the balloon loan off in cash or refinance the loan at current market rates.

A home-equity loan is usually used by homeowners to borrow some of the equity in the home. This may raise the monthly housing payment considerably. More and more lenders are offering home-equity lines of credit. The interest might be tax-deductible because the debt is secured by a home. A home-equity line of credit is a form of revolving credit secured by a home. Many lenders set the credit limit on a home-equity line by taking a percentage of the home's appraised value and subtracting from that the balance owed on the existing mortgage. In determining the credit limit, the lender will also consider other factors to determine the homeowner's ability to repay the loan. Many home-equity plans set a fixed period during which money may be borrowed. Some lenders require payment in full of any outstanding balance at the end of the period.

Home-equity lines of credit usually have variable, rather than fixed, interest rates. The variable rate must be based on a publicly available index such as the prime rate published in major daily newspapers or a U.S. Treasury bill rate. The interest rate for borrowing under the home-equity line will change in accordance with the index. Most lenders set the interest rate at the value of the index at a particular time plus a margin, such as 3 percentage points. The cost of borrowing is tied directly to the value of the index. Lenders sometimes offer a temporarily discounted interest rate for a home-equity line. This is a rate that is unusually low and that may last for a short introductory period of merely a few months.

The costs of setting up a home-equity line of credit typically include a fee for a property appraisal, an application fee, fees for attorneys, title search, mortgage preparation and filing fees, property and title insurance fees, and taxes. There also might be recurring maintenance fees for the account, or a transaction fee every time there is a draw on the credit line. It might cost a significant amount of money to establish the home-equity line of credit, although interest savings often justify the cost of establishing and maintaining the line.

The federal TRUTH IN LENDING ACT, 15 U.S.C.A. §§ 1601 set. seq., requires lenders to disclose the important terms and costs of their home-equity plans, including the APR, miscellaneous charges, the payment terms, and information about any variable-rate feature. If the home involved is a principal dwelling, the Truth in Lending Act allows three days from the day the account was opened to cancel the credit line. This right allows the borrower to cancel for any reason by informing the lender in writing within the three-day period. The lender then must cancel its security interest in the property and return all fees.

A second mortgage provides a fixed amount of money that is repayable over a fixed period. In most cases, the payment schedule calls for equal payments that will pay off the entire loan within the loan period. A second mortgage differs from a home-equity loan in that it is not a line of credit, but rather a more traditional type of loan. The traditional second-mortgage loan takes into account the interest rate charged plus points and other finance charges. The annual percentage rate for a home-equity line of credit is based on the periodic interest rate alone. It does not include points or other charges.

A reverse mortgage works much like a traditional mortgage, only in reverse. It allows homeowners to convert the equity in a home into cash. A reverse mortgage permits retired homeowners who own their home and have paid all of their mortgage to borrow against the value of their home. The lender pays the equity to the homeowner in either payments or a lump sum. Unlike a standard home-equity loan, no repayment is due until the home is no longer used as a principal residence, a sale of the home, or the death of the homeowner.

A deed of trust is similar to a mortgage, with one important exception: If the borrower breaches the agreement to pay off the loan, the foreclosure process is typically much quicker and less complicated than the formal mortgage-foreclosure process. While a mortgage involves a relationship between the borrower/homeowner and the bank/lender, a deed of trust involves the homeowner, the lender, and a title insurance company. The title insurance company holds legal title to the real estate until the loan is paid in full, at which time the company transfers the property title to the homeowner.

Subdivision or condominium-development mortgages that cover a large tract of land are blanket mortgages. A blanket mortgage makes possible the sale of individual lots or units, with the proceeds applied to the mortgage, and partial release of the mortgage recorded to clear the title for that lot or unit.

Construction mortgages need special treatment depending on state construction-lien law. Often the loan proceeds are placed in escrow with title insurance companies to make certain that the mortgage remains a first lien, with priority over contractors' construction liens.

Open-end mortgages make possible additional advances of money from the lender without the necessity of a new mortgage.

The time of repayment may be extended by a recorded extension of mortgage. Other real estate may be added to the mortgage by a spreading agreement. Mortgaged real estate may be sold, with the buyer taking either "subject to" or by "assuming" the mortgage. In the former case, the buyer acknowledges the existence of the mortgage and, upon default, may lose the title. By assuming the mortgage, the buyer promises to repay the debt and may be personally liable for a deficiency judgment if the sale brings less than the debt.

Lenders regularly assign mortgages to other investors. Assignments with recourse are guarantees by the one who assigns the mortgage that that party will collect the debt; those WITHOUT RECOURSE do not contain such guarantees. Assignments with recourse usually involve lower-risk properties or those of relatively stable or rising value. Assignments without recourse tend to involve riskier properties. Mortgages assigned without recourse are often sold at a price discounted well below their market value.

Before the Great Depression of the 1930s, most mortgages were "straight" short-term mortgages, requiring payments of interest and lump-sum principal, with the result that when incomes dropped, many borrowers lost their properties. That risk is minimized today because commercial lenders take fully amortized mortgages, in which part of the periodic payment

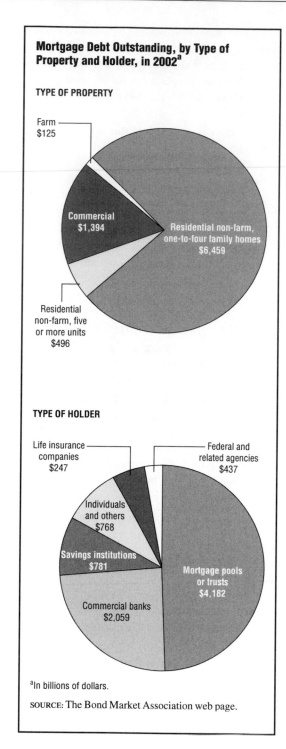

Mortgage Debt Outstanding, by Type of Property and Holder, in 2002[a]

TYPE OF PROPERTY

Farm
$125

Commercial
$1,394

Residential non-farm, one-to-four family homes
$6,459

Residential non-farm, five or more units
$496

TYPE OF HOLDER

Life insurance companies
$247

Federal and related agencies
$437

Individuals and others
$768

Savings institutions
$781

Mortgage pools or trusts
$4,182

Commercial banks
$2,059

[a]In billions of dollars.

SOURCE: The Bond Market Association web page.

applies first to interest and then to principal, with the balance reduced to zero at the end of the term.

Several agencies of the federal government have assisted the mortgage market by infusion of capital and by guarantees of repayment of mortgages. The Federal Housing Administration made possible purchases of real estate at low interest rates and with low down payments. The VETERANS AFFAIRS DEPARTMENT (VA) also guarantees home loans to certain veterans on favorable terms. Both agencies contributed greatly to the growth of the housing market after WORLD WAR II. During the late 1950s, private corporations began insuring repayment of conventional mortgages.

The GOVERNMENT NATIONAL MORTGAGE ASSOCIATION (Ginnie Mae), created by the U.S. government in 1968, makes possible trading in mortgages by investors by guaranteeing mortgage-backed SECURITIES.

The FEDERAL NATIONAL MORTGAGE ASSOCIATION (Fannie Mae) is a private corporation, chartered by the U.S. government, that bolsters the supply of funds for home mortgages by buying mortgages from banks, insurance companies, and savings and loans.

Inflation in the 1970s made long-term fixed-rate mortgages less attractive to lenders. In response, lenders devised three types of mortgage loans that enable the rate of interest to vary in case of rises in rates: the variable-rate mortgage, graduated-payment mortgage, and the adjustable-rate mortgage. These mortgages are offered at initial interest rates that are somewhat lower than those for 20- to 30-year fixed-rate mortgages.

Home-equity loans are typically second mortgages to the holder of the first mortgage, advancing funds based on a percentage of the owner's equity; that is, the amount by which the value of the real estate exceeds the first mortgage balance.

CROSS-REFERENCES

Amortization.

MORTMAIN

[French, Dead hand.] A term to denote the conveyance of ownership of land or tenements to any corporation, religious or secular.

Traditionally, such transfers were made to religious corporations. Like any corporation, the religious society had unlimited, perpetual duration under the law. It could, therefore, hold land permanently unlike a natural person, whose property is redistributed upon his or her death. The holdings of religious corporations grew as contributions were received from their members. Because such holdings were immune from responsibilities for taxes and payment of feudal dues, greater burdens were placed on noncorporate secular property. Therefore, land in mortmain was said to be held in perpetuity in one dead hand, that of the corporation.

MORTMAIN ACTS

Statutes designed to prevent lands from being perpetually possessed or controlled by religious corporations.

The first mortmain act in England was enacted during the reign of King Edward I. A later statute passed during the reign of King George II was the model for subsequent mortmain acts in that it prevented the transfer of lands to charities unless the gift complied with certain requirements. Mortmain acts have been abolished by statute.

In the law governing wills, statutes based upon the original mortmain acts have been passed in some states to restrict the power of a testator to make gifts to charities. These modern statutes, also called mortmain acts, protect only the immediate family of a decedent from disinheritance by death-bed gifts to charities when the will is executed within the statutory period.

❖ MOSELEY-BRAUN, CAROL ELIZABETH

Carol Moseley-Braun was the first woman and first African-American to serve as assistant majority leader of the Illinois House of Representatives; later, she became the first woman and first African-American to hold executive office in Cook County (Chicago), Illinois. In 1992, she became the first African-American woman from

Carol Moseley-Braun.
AP/WIDE WORLD PHOTOS

the state of Illinois to be elected to the U.S. Senate, where she served until 1998.

Carol Elizabeth Moseley was born on August 16, 1947 in Chicago, the daughter of a police officer and a medical technician. She earned her Bachelor of Arts degree from the University of Illinois at Chicago in 1969. She then went to the University of Chicago Law School, where she was awarded her juris doctor degree in 1972. After earning her law degree, she spent one year as an associate with the firm of Davis, Miner, and Barnhill.

In 1973, Moseley-Braun was appointed assistant U.S. attorney for the Northern District

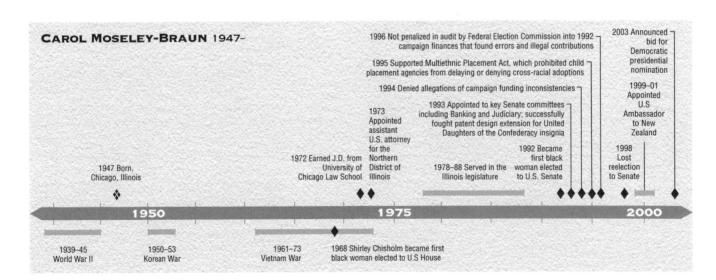

CAROL MOSELEY-BRAUN 1947–

1996 Not penalized in audit by Federal Election Commission into 1992 campaign finances that found errors and illegal contributions

1995 Supported Multiethnic Placement Act, which prohibited child placement agencies from delaying or denying cross-racial adoptions

1994 Denied allegations of campaign funding inconsistencies

1993 Appointed to key Senate committees including Banking and Judiciary; successfully fought patent design extension for United Daughters of the Confederacy insignia

1973 Appointed assistant U.S. attorney for the Northern District of Illinois

1972 Earned J.D. from University of Chicago Law School

1978–88 Served in the Illinois legislature

1992 Became first black woman elected to U.S. Senate

2003 Announced bid for Democratic presidential nomination

1999–01 Appointed U.S Ambassador to New Zealand

1998 Lost reelection to Senate

1947 Born, Chicago, Illinois

1950   1975   2000

1939–45 World War II

1950–53 Korean War

1961–73 Vietnam War

1968 Shirley Chisholm became first black woman elected to U.S House

of Illinois, a position she held until 1977. Her election to the Illinois state legislature in 1978 started her on the road that would eventually lead to the U.S. Senate. While a member of the Illinois House, Moseley-Braun rose to the position of assistant majority leader, becoming the first African-American and the first woman to do so.

Moseley-Braun's last position before being elected to the U.S. Senate was Cook County recorder of deeds and registrar of titles. She was also the first woman and first African-American to hold this, or any, executive office in Cook County.

Moseley-Braun entered the Illinois primary and upset two-term Democratic incumbent Alan J. Dixon. She then played upon voters' unhappiness with the sagging U.S. economy to clinch her victory over Republican Richard S. Williamson and to become the first African-American woman elected to the U.S. Senate.

Moseley-Braun's rise to national office was not without controversy. During her campaign against Williamson, it was reported that she had received over $28,000 in royalty payments from the sale of timber on land owned by her mother, a nursing home resident whose care was being paid for by MEDICAID. Moseley-Braun did not report the income to either the INTERNAL REVENUE SERVICE or Medicaid, as required by law. She later repaid the state $15,239 for her mother's nursing home expenses.

During her term in the Senate, Moseley-Braun was appointed to some of the most powerful and influential Senate committees: Banking, Housing and Urban Affairs; Small Business; and Judiciary. She also became a member of the Congressional Black Caucus.

In May 1993, just a few months after her induction into the Senate, she challenged Senator STROM THURMOND (R-S.C.), the Senate's most senior member at the time. The two debated a bill that would have extended the design patent on the insignia of the United Daughters of the Confederacy (UDC), which featured the Confederate flag. Arguing that the flag was a symbol of a time in U.S. history when African-Americans were held as human chattel under the flag of the Confederacy, Moseley-Braun persuaded her colleagues on the Judiciary Committee not to extend the UDC patent.

The issue was not dead, however. In July 1993, Senator JESSE HELMS (R-N.C.) included the patent extension as an amendment to another bill. The Senate voted 52–48 to approve the amendment. Undaunted, Moseley-Braun vowed to filibuster to reverse the vote. She lobbied her fellow Senators to reconsider the vote on the Helms amendment. She argued that the Confederate flag had no place in our modern times, no place in the Senate, and no place in our society. The Senate reconsidered its vote and finally tabled the Helms amendment, effectively killing it, by a vote of 75–25.

Moseley-Braun was narrowly defeated for re-election in 1998, losing to wealthy Republican Peter Fitzgerald in a heated race in Illinois. Immediately following her defeat, she served from 1998 to 1999 as a consultant on school construction to the EDUCATION DEPARTMENT. In 1999, with the support of President BILL CLINTON, she was nominated to be the U.S. ambassador to New Zealand and Samoa. Her appointment was approved by a 96–2 vote in the Senate. She served for two years in that position.

In 2003, Moseley-Braun served as executive vice president at Good Works International, a global policy and strategy consulting company. Although some expected her to run again for the Senate in 2004, she decided to enter the presidential race instead, announcing the decision in 2003. In the early stages of her campaign, she received support and endorsements from several feminist and minority political-action groups.

FURTHER READINGS

Moseley-Braun, Carol. 1995. "Interracial Adoption." *A.B.A. Journal* 45.

Page, Clarence. 2003. "Dems' Dilemma: Moseley-Braun vs. Sharpton." *Daily Press* K3.

MOST-FAVORED-NATION STATUS

A method of establishing equality of trading opportunity among states by guaranteeing that if one country is given better trade terms by another, then all other states must get the same terms.

In the twentieth century, the history of world trade is dominated by the move from protective tariffs to free trade. International agreements have permitted most of the world's nations to export their products without facing discriminatory duties. A key concept in the liberalization of trade is most-favored-nation (MFN) status.

MFN status is a method of preventing discriminatory treatment among members of an international trading organization. MFN status provides trade equality among partners by

> "HOW WE CHARACTERIZE THE DEBATE WILL HAVE A CRITICAL IMPACT ON HOW WE CHARACTERIZE THE OUTCOME."
> —CAROL MOSELEY-BRAUN

ensuring that an importing country will not discriminate against another country's goods in favor of those from a third. Once the importing country grants any type of concession to the third-party country, this concession must be given to all other countries.

For example, assume that the United States government negotiates a bilateral trade agreement with Indonesia that provides, among other things, that a duty of $1 will be charged for imported Indonesian television sets. All countries that have MFN status will pay no more than a $1 duty to export televisions to the United States. If the United States later negotiates a duty of 75¢ with Japan for imported televisions, Indonesia and all other MFN countries will pay 75¢, despite Indonesia's original agreement to pay more duty.

The number of countries with MFN status increased after WORLD WAR II with the GENERAL AGREEMENT ON TARIFFS AND TRADE (GATT) treaty, which was signed by many nations in 1948. Article I of the GATT requires that exports of all contracting parties to the treaty should be treated alike by other contracting parties, immediately and without condition. Thus, each member's exports are treated on the best terms (or "most favored" terms) available to any GATT member.

The MFN status proclaimed in the GATT has been granted to about 180 countries. Only a handful of communist countries have been denied MFN status.

The United States is forbidden by law to grant MFN status to communist countries that do not have free-market economies. The practical effect is that imports from these countries are subject to much higher tariffs. An amendment to the Trade Act of 1974, however, created a loophole. The president may waive the MFN restriction on an annual basis if the communist country permits free emigration or if MFN status would lead to increased emigration. By law, the president must tell Congress each year of the administration's intention to renew or deny MFN status benefits to a communist country. Congress has sixty days to overturn the decision and would then need a two-thirds majority to override a presidential VETO.

China has been the main beneficiary of this loophole. Since 1979 China has been granted MFN status. After China suppressed its democracy movement and the Tiananmen Square protest in 1989, Congress opposed continuation of the country's MFN status, yet both President GEORGE H. W. BUSH and President BILL CLINTON renewed China's MFN benefits.

MOTHERS AGAINST DRUNK DRIVING

Mothers Against Drunk Driving (MADD) is a nonprofit organization with more than 600 chapters nationwide. MADD seeks to find effective solutions to the problems of drunk driving and underage drinking, while also supporting those persons whose relatives and friends have been killed by drunk drivers. MADD has proven to be an effective organization, successfully LOBBYING for tougher laws against drunk drivers.

MADD was founded by a small group of California women in 1980 after 13-year-old Cari Lightner was killed by a hit-and-run driver who had previous drunk driving convictions. Although the offender was sentenced to two years in prison, the judge allowed him to serve time instead in a work camp and a halfway house. Candy Lightner, the victim's mother, worked to call attention to the need for more appropriate, vigorous, and equitable actions on the part of law enforcement and the courts in response to alcohol-related traffic deaths and injuries. Lightner and a handful of volunteers campaigned for tougher laws against impaired driving, stiffer penalties for committing crimes, and greater awareness about the seriousness of driving drunk.

As the California group drew public attention, other individuals who had lost relatives or who had been injured by drunk drivers formed local chapters. Beginning in 1995, MADD embarked on a five-year plan to reduce the proportion of alcohol-related traffic fatalities by 20 percent by the year 2000. This "20 by 2000" campaign was a comprehensive approach that embraced both previous positions and goals and new objectives. Five main areas are addressed: youth issues, enforcement of laws, sanctions, self-sufficiency, and responsible marketing and service.

By 1997 MADD membership had grown to three million people, making it the largest victim-advocate and anti-drunk-driving organization in the United States and the world. In addition to local chapters, MADD has state offices in 29 states. Coordination of the organization is handled by a national headquarters staff of approximately 60 individuals located in

Irving, Texas, who direct training, seasonal and ongoing education and awareness programs, national fund-raising, media campaigns, and federal and state legislative activities.

Also in 1997, MADD sponsored the first National Youth Summit to Prevent Underage Drinking. The summit was attended by 435 teens representing each of the U.S. congressional districts. In 1998, with support from MADD members, "Zero Tolerance" legislation was passed in all 50 states.

Youth issues include enforcement of the 21-year age requirement for purchasing and consuming alcohol, ZERO TOLERANCE for underage drivers who drink, and limits on advertising and marketing of alcoholic beverages to young people.

MADD also endorses the use of sobriety checkpoints by law enforcement and lowering the blood alcohol count for drunk driving to .08 percent. As for sanctions, MADD advocates administrative revocation of the licenses of drunk drivers, the confiscation of license plates and vehicles, progressive sanctions for repeat offenders, and mandatory confinement for repeat offenders. The organization wants drunk drivers to pay for the cost of the system that arrests, convicts, and punishes them. Funding for enforcement through fines, fees, and other assessments will make this system self-sufficient. Finally, MADD wants businesses that serve alcohol to be more vigorous in preventing customers from becoming intoxicated. MADD seeks the end of "happy hours" and other promotions that encourage irresponsible drinking.

In 2000, MADD observed its twentieth anniversary with the slogan "Twenty years of making a difference!" The organization noted that annual deaths from drinking and driving have decreased from approximately 28,000 in 1980 to 16,068 in 2000. MADD also pointed out that preliminary statistics showed that the percentage of alcohol-related fatal traffic crashes had declined from 57 percent in 1982 to 38 percent in 2000. In 2002 MADD reported that 34 states and the District of Columbia had passed laws making it illegal to drive with a blood alcohol count of more than 0.08.

FURTHER READINGS

MADD. Available online at <www.madd.org> (accessed July 28, 2003).

CROSS-REFERENCES

Driving Under the Influence (DUI); Drunkard; Drunkenness.

MOTION

A written or oral application made to a court or judge to obtain a ruling or order directing that some act be done in favor of the applicant. The applicant is known as the moving party, or the MOVANT.

In the U.S. judicial system, procedural rules require most motions to be made in writing and can require that written notice be given in advance of a motion being made. Written motions specify what action the movant is requesting and the reasons, or grounds, for the request. A written motion may contain citations to case law or statutes that support the motion. A motion almost always contains a recitation of the facts of the case or the situation prompting the movant to make the request.

For example, suppose that a plaintiff in a lawsuit has refused to submit to a deposition—questioning under oath—by the defendant. The defendant therefore files a motion with the court to compel in an effort to compel the plaintiff to attend the deposition. The written motion briefly explains the nature of the lawsuit, describes the efforts made by the defendant to get the plaintiff to submit to a deposition, addresses any known reasons for the plaintiff's failure to cooperate, and recites the statute that permits the taking of depositions in civil litigation. The motion may also request that the issue be addressed at a hearing before the judge with all parties present.

Once the judge receives the motion, he or she may grant or deny the motion based solely on its contents. In the alternative, the judge may schedule a hearing. At a motion hearing, each party has an opportunity to argue its position orally, and the judge can ask specific questions about the facts or the law. The judge's decision on the motion is called an order.

Under some circumstances motions can be made orally. Oral motions frequently occur during trials, when it is impractical to draft a written motion. A common oral motion occurs during witness testimony. Witnesses sometimes give inadmissible testimony before an attorney can object. When that happens, the attorney must object and move the court to strike the inadmissible testimony from the record. Motions for mistrial—made when courtroom proceedings are fraught with errors, inadmissible evidence, or disruptions so prejudicial to a party's case that justice cannot be served—often are made orally. Sometimes judges themselves take action on

A sample motion to dismiss form

Motion to Dismiss Form

Motion To Dismiss, Presenting Defenses Of Failure To State A Claim, Of Lack Of Service Of Process, Of Improper Venue, And Of Lack Of Jurisdiction Under Rule 12(B)

The defendant moves the court as follows:

1. To dismiss the action because the complaint fails to state a claim against defendant upon which relief can be granted.

2. To dismiss the action or in lieu thereof to quash the return of service of summons on the grounds (a) that the defendant is a corporation organized under the laws of Delaware and was not and is not subject to service of process within the Southern District of New York, and (b) that the defendant has not been properly served with process in this action, all of which more clearly appears in the affidavits of M. N. and X. Y. hereto annexed as Exhibit A and Exhibit B respectively.

3. To dismiss the action on the ground that it is in the wrong district because (a) the jurisdiction of this court is invoked solely on the ground that the action arises under the Constitution and laws of the United States and (b) the defendant is a corporation incorporated under the laws of the State of Delaware and is not licensed to do or doing business in the Southern District of New York, all of which more clearly appears in the affidavits of K. L. and V. W. hereto annexed as Exhibits C and D, respectively.

4. To dismiss the action on the ground that the court lacks jurisdiction because the amount actually in controversy is less than ten thousand dollars exclusive of interest and costs.

Signed: _____
         Attorney for Defendant.

Address: _____

Notice of Motion

To: _____
    Attorney for Plaintiff.

_____

Please take notice, that the undersigned will bring the above motion on for hearing before this Court at Room XX, United States Court House, Foley Square, City of New York, on the XXX day of XXXX, 20XX, at 10 o'clock in the forenoon of that day or as soon thereafter as counsel can be heard.

Signed: _____
         Attorney for Defendant.

Address: _____

behalf of a party, such as changing or adding necessary language to a PLEADING without a motion from a party. This is known as making an amendment on the court's own motion.

A motion to dismiss asks the court to dismiss an action because the initial pleading, or complaint, fails to state a CAUSE OF ACTION or claim for which the law provides a remedy. For example, a complaint alleges that an employer unfairly fired an employee but does not allege illegal discrimination or labor practices. Merely firing an employee for unfair reasons is not illegal; thus a court may dismiss this complaint.

A motion to strike asks the court to remove from the record inadmissible evidence or language in pleadings that is redundant, immaterial, impertinent, or scandalous. A party can file a motion for a more definite statement when the language in a pleading is so vague or ambiguous that the party cannot reasonably be expected to draft a responsive pleading.

A motion for SUMMARY JUDGMENT, also known as a motion for judgment on the pleadings, asks the court to make a judgment solely on the facts set forth in the pleadings, without the necessity of trial. A court will grant a summary judgment motion when the material facts of the case are not in dispute and all that remains to be determined are QUESTIONS OF LAW. For example, in *Stieber v. Journal Publishing Co.*, 120 N. M. 270, 901 P.2d 201 (App. 1995), the court found that the issue of whether a newspaper company's treatment of a reporter was extreme and outrageous was a legal question, not a factual question. In that case the reporter, Tamar Stieber, sued her employer for, among other things, intentional infliction of emotional distress. Stieber charged that the newspaper asked her to write so many daily stories that she could not perform her duties as a special projects reporter. To recover for the TORT of intentional infliction of emotional distress, the court noted, Stieber had to prove that the newspaper's conduct was so extreme and outrageous as to go "beyond all possible boundaries of decency, and to be regarded as atrocious, and utterly intolerable in civilized community." The court ruled that as a MATTER OF LAW, Stieber failed to prove this allegation, and the lower court's summary judgment was affirmed.

A motion in limine, also made before trial, asks the court to prohibit an opposing party from offering evidence or referring to matters that would be highly prejudicial to the movant during a trial. A motion to suppress is similar to a motion in limine but asks the court to keep out of a criminal trial evidence that was obtained illegally, usually in violation of the Fourth, Fifth, or Sixth Amendments to the U.S. Constitution. For example, a defendant in a murder trial may move the court to suppress her confession because she was questioned without being told of her right to have an attorney present.

Following a trial but before a jury verdict, a party may move for a directed verdict, asking the judge to make a judgment without letting the jury reach a verdict. Following a jury verdict, a party may move for JUDGMENT NOTWITH-STANDING THE VERDICT, or JNOV. This motion requests that the court enter a judgment contrary to the jury verdict, and is granted when no reasonable jury could have reached that verdict. A motion for a new trial asks the judge to order a new trial, setting aside the judgment or verdict, because the trial was improper or unfair. This motion is sometimes brought as the result of newly discovered evidence.

FURTHER READINGS

Dessem, R. Lawrence. 2001. *Pretrial Litigation in a Nutshell.* 3d ed. St. Paul, Minn.: West Group.

CROSS-REFERENCES

Civil Procedure; Criminal Procedure.

MOTIVE

An idea, belief, or emotion that impels a person to act in accordance with that state of mind.

Motive is usually used in connection with CRIMINAL LAW to explain why a person acted or refused to act in a certain way—for example, to

support the prosecution's assertion that the accused committed the crime. If a person accused of murder was the beneficiary of a life insurance policy on the deceased, the prosecution might argue that greed was the motive for the killing.

Proof of motive is not required in a criminal prosecution. In determining the guilt of a criminal defendant, courts are generally not concerned with *why* the defendant committed the alleged crime, but *whether* the defendant committed the crime. However, a defendant's motive is important in other stages of a criminal case, such as police investigation and sentencing. Law enforcement personnel often consider potential motives in detecting perpetrators. Judges may consider the motives of a convicted defendant at sentencing and either increase a sentence based on avaricious motives or decrease the sentence if the defendant's motives were honorable—for example, if the accused acted in defense of a family member.

In criminal law, motive is distinct from intent. Criminal intent refers to the mental state of mind possessed by a defendant in committing a crime. With few exceptions the prosecution in a criminal case must prove that the defendant intended to commit the illegal act. The prosecution need not prove the defendant's motive. Nevertheless, prosecutors and defense attorneys alike may make an issue of motive in connection with the case.

For example, if a defendant denies commission of the crime, he may produce evidence showing that he had no motive to commit the crime and argue that the lack of motive supports the proposition that he did not commit the crime. By the same token, the prosecution may produce evidence that the defendant did have the motive to commit the crime and argue that the motive supports the proposition that the defendant committed the crime. Proof of motive, without more evidence tying a defendant to the alleged crime, is insufficient to support a conviction.

A HATE CRIME is one crime that requires proof of a certain motive. Generally, a hate crime is motivated by the defendant's belief regarding a protected status of the victim, such as the victim's religion, sex, disability, customs, or national origin. In states that prosecute hate crimes, the prosecution must prove that the defendant was motivated by animosity toward a protected status of the victim. Hate-crime laws are exceptions to the general rule that proof of motive is not required in a criminal prosecution.

In CIVIL LAW a plaintiff generally need not prove the respondent's motive in acting or failing to act. One notable exception to this general rule is the TORT of MALICIOUS PROSECUTION. In a suit for malicious prosecution, the plaintiff must prove, in part, that the respondent was motivated by malice in subjecting the plaintiff to a civil suit. The same applies for a malicious criminal prosecution.

FURTHER READINGS

Binder, Guyora. 2002. "The Rhetoric of Motive and Intent." *Buffalo Criminal Law Review* 6 (fall).

Candeub, Adam. 1994. "Motive Crimes and Other Minds." *University of Pennsylvania Law Review* 142 (June).

Pillsbury, Samuel H. 1990. "Evil and the Law of Murder." *University of California at Davis Law Review* 24.

Constance Baker Motley.
THE BETTMANN ARCHIVE

❖ MOTLEY, CONSTANCE BAKER

Constance Baker Motley played an integral role in defending legislation that was created to protect the rights of all Americans. Her work on landmark civil rights cases in the 1940s, 1950s, and 1960s helped to abolish SEGREGATION in schools and changed the way in which the U.S. Constitution is interpreted. Motley was the first African-American woman to be elected to the New York State Senate; the first African-American and the first woman to be elected as Manhattan borough president; and the first female African American federal judge.

Motley was born in New Haven, Connecticut, on September 14, 1921, one of nine children. The America in which Motley grew up was segregated. As a child going to a beach in Mil-

ford, Connecticut, Motley was turned away because of the color of her skin. When she returned home, she asked her parents, both West Indian immigrants, why the color of her skin meant that she could not go swimming. Her parents were unfamiliar with U.S. segregation and had no answer.

As a teenager, Motley became fascinated with U.S. history, particularly the Civil War, ABRAHAM LINCOLN, and the EMANCIPATION PROCLAMATION. She sought out role models in her community to help her focus her interests and began attending meetings at a local adult

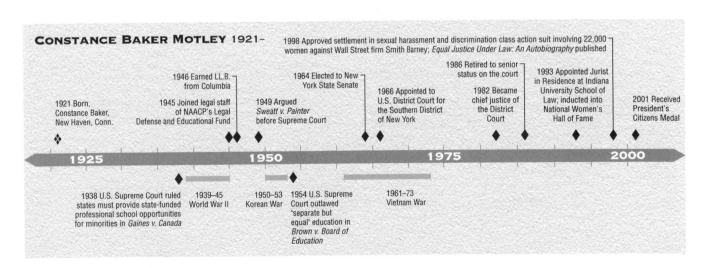

CONSTANCE BAKER MOTLEY 1921–

1998 Approved settlement in sexual harassment and discrimination class action suit involving 22,000 women against Wall Street firm Smith Barney; *Equal Justice Under Law: An Autobiography* published

1946 Earned LL.B. from Columbia

1964 Elected to New York State Senate

1986 Retired to senior status on the court

1993 Appointed Jurist in Residence at Indiana University School of Law; inducted into National Women's Hall of Fame

1921 Born, Constance Baker, New Haven, Conn.

1945 Joined legal staff of NAACP's Legal Defense and Educational Fund

1949 Argued *Sweatt v. Painter* before Supreme Court

1966 Appointed to U.S. District Court for the Southern District of New York

1982 Became chief justice of the District Court

2001 Received President's Citizens Medal

1925   1950   1975   2000

1938 U.S. Supreme Court ruled states must provide state-funded professional school opportunities for minorities in *Gaines v. Canada*

1939–45 World War II

1950–53 Korean War

1954 U.S. Supreme Court outlawed "separate but equal" education in *Brown v. Board of Education*

1961–73 Vietnam War

community center. At that center, she came in contact with George W. Crawford, a prominent black lawyer in New Haven, who told her about the case of *Missouri ex rel. Gaines v. Canada*, 305 U.S. 337, 59 S. Ct. 232, 83 L. Ed. 208 (1938).

At the time of *Gaines*, Missouri was like many southern states that maintained all-white professional schools, sending qualified minority law school applicants to schools in other states. The U.S. Supreme Court ruled in *Gaines* that Missouri's admissions practice did not offer an equal educational opportunity to minority students and that it therefore violated the EQUAL PROTECTION CLAUSE of the FOURTEENTH AMENDMENT. That verdict meant that many states had to re-evaluate their school systems and either create new schools specifically for black students or desegregate existing white graduate schools. Crawford told Motley that he believed that the *Gaines* case would prompt states to create separate schools to avoid desegregation.

The *Gaines* case inspired Motley to attend law school. She wanted to be a lawyer in order to fight for CIVIL RIGHTS, as Abraham Lincoln had done. However, when she approached her father about following her dream, he told her that college was a financial impossibility on his wages as a chef at a Yale fraternity house.

After graduating from high school as an honor student in 1939, Baker spent 18 months working for the National Youth Administration in New Haven. Disturbed by blacks' lack of interest in the community center, she decided to address her peers at a meeting at the center. As president of the New Haven Youth Council, Motley spoke about the apparent apathy of blacks toward the center, which she suggested stemmed from the lack of black involvement in setting policy and designing projects for the center. Clarence Blakeslee, the successful, white businessman who had been the primary donor for the community center, heard Motley speak and was very impressed. He offered to pay for Motley's education.

Accepting the offer, Motley attended New York University, where she received a bachelor of arts degree in economics. She then went to Columbia University School of Law, where she received her law degree in 1946. While still at Columbia, Motley got a job with the National Association for the Advancement of Colored People (NAACP) Legal Defense and Educational Fund, clerking for chief counsel THURGOOD

MARSHALL, who would later sit on the U.S. Supreme Court.

Motley joined the NAACP during WORLD WAR II and worked on many cases involving black servicemen. These soldiers told of segregation in the armed forces and protested that punishments given to black soldiers were outrageous compared with those given to white soldiers for similar infractions. Motley worked on hundreds of COURT-MARTIAL cases that earned the NAACP much notoriety. Her work with the NAACP enabled her to try cases in federal courts and even to try ten cases before the U.S. Supreme Court. Motley often was the first African-American attorney, and usually the first female African-American attorney, to be seen in many of those courtrooms.

In the late 1940s, the NAACP decided to focus on eliminating segregation in education. Motley's first case after she had completed law school took the *Gaines* case a step further. It involved Herman Marion Sweatt (*Sweatt v. Painter*, 339 U.S. 629, 70 S. Ct. 848, 94 L. Ed. 1114 [1949]) who was denied admission to the law school at the University of Texas solely because he was black. Under pressure from the NAACP, the school set up a makeshift classroom for Sweatt in the basement of a building, obtained books for him, and assigned him four professors from the faculty. However, the U.S. Supreme Court held that the state had violated the Equal Protection Clause because Sweatt's inability to interact with fellow classmates made his education inferior. Motley tried other cases involving segregation in professional schools and was a driving force in reforming their admission practices, thus paving the way for minority professionals in this country.

In 1954, Motley helped to write legal briefs for the landmark case BROWN V. BOARD OF EDUCATION OF TOPEKA, KANSAS, 347 U.S. 483, 74 S. Ct. 686, 98 L. Ed. 873 (1954). In *Brown,* the Court ruled that segregated schools were unconstitutional as a violation of the Equal Protection Clause of the U.S. Constitution. The case was a major victory for civil rights advocates and fueled Motley's hope for real change in U.S. attitudes toward minority groups.

In the 1960s, Motley turned her attention toward minority children. She was concerned about the inadequate schooling for black children, the slum conditions in which many were forced to live, and the high rates of unemployment in black communities. She wanted new

"THE STRUGGLE FOR RACIAL EQUALITY IS LIKE A PRAIRIE FIRE. YOU MAY SUCCEED IN STAMPING OUT THE STRUGGLE FOR EQUALITY IN ONE CORNER AND, LO AND BEHOLD, IT APPEARS SOON THEREAFTER SOMEWHERE ELSE."
—CONSTANCE BAKER MOTLEY

legislation to address these problems. In 1964, Motley became the first African-American woman to be elected to the New York State Senate. In 1965, she relinquished her Senate seat when she was elected president of the borough of Manhattan. From that post, she worked to revitalize Harlem and to advance urban renewal.

In 1966, when President LYNDON B. JOHNSON appointed Motley to the U.S. District Court for the Southern District of New York, protest from southerners held up her appointment from January to August. Later, when President Johnson nominated Motley to the U.S. Court of Appeals, male opposition pressured him into withdrawing her name.

Since she became a federal judge, Motley has ruled on more than 2,500 cases. In 1982, Motley became chief judge of the court. She assumed senior status in 1986.

In 1993, Motley was inducted into the National Women's Hall of Fame, and in 1998 she published *Equal Justice Under Law: An Autobiography*. In the new millennium, Motley continued to hear cases as a senior U.S. district court judge. She has been the recipient of numerous honorary degrees and awards, including the NAACP Legal Defense Fund's Equal Justice Award. In 2001, President BILL CLINTON awarded her the Presidential Citizens Medal.

FURTHER READINGS

Berry, Dawn Bradley. 1996. *The 50 Most Influential Women in American Law*. Los Angeles: Contemporary Books.

Gilbert, Lynn, and Gaylen Moore. 1981. *Particular Passions: Talks with Women Who Have Shaped Our Times*. New York: Potter.

Orfield, Gary, Susan E. Eaton, and Elaine R. Jones. 1997. *Dismantling Desegregation: The Quiet Reversal of Brown v. Board of Education*. New York: New Press.

Plowden, Martha Ward. 1993. *Famous Firsts of Black Women*. Gretna, La.: Pelican.

Stoddard, Hope. 1970. *Famous American Women*. New York: Cromwell.

CROSS-REFERENCES

Civil Rights Movement; Integration; School Desegregation.

MOVANT

One who makes a motion before a court. The applicant for a judicial rule or order.

Generally, it is the job of the movant to convince a judge to rule, or grant an order, in favor of the motion. Rules and legal precedent within particular jurisdictions, as well as the type of motion sought, dictate the burdens of proof and persuasion each party must meet when a court considers a motion.

For example, one common type of motion is a motion for SUMMARY JUDGMENT. This motion is made shortly before a trial commences and is granted if the pleadings, depositions, answers to interrogatories, and affidavits indicate that no genuine dispute as to any material fact exists and that the movant is entitled to a favorable judgment as a MATTER OF LAW. In other words, if the facts of the case are not disputed, it is easier, faster, and less expensive for a judge to simply rule on the legal issues that apply to those facts, avoiding a trial altogether.

A summary judgment movant in most jurisdictions has the burden of showing that no genuine issue of material fact exists and that, by law, the undisputed facts support a judgment in the movant's favor. But once the movant meets this burden, the opposing party is given a chance to refute the movant's argument. The opposing party will try to establish that there is a genuine dispute about a material fact in the case and that the law does not support a judgment in the movant's favor.

For example, assume a case in which a fashion model is suing a newspaper for publishing her picture without her knowledge or permission in an advertisement for a nightclub. Shortly before trial the newspaper makes a motion for summary judgment. The movant newspaper admits that the photograph of the model ran in the newspaper and that the newspaper did not have the model's permission to publish it. The newspaper argues, however, that the model has no right under current law to sue the newspaper, which merely sells space for advertisements, and that her only legal recourse is in suing the advertiser that placed the advertisement in the newspaper. Thus, the newspaper has argued that no material facts are in dispute. The movant has also shown that, given the incontestable material facts, the law would support a judgment in favor of the newspaper.

Now the burden shifts to the model, who must demonstrate the existence of a disputed fact that, if proven, would make the newspaper legally liable. She may do this by producing an affidavit—a sworn written statement—by a former newspaper employee alleging that the newspaper did not merely print the advertisement but actually created the advertisement with the model's picture for the nightclub. Because this material fact, if proven, could make the newspaper legally liable, the court would deny the movant's summary judgment motion.

In most jurisdictions the burden of producing evidence supporting the granting or denial of a summary judgment motion shifts between the movant and the opposing party, but the ultimate burden of persuading the court remains with the movant. A movant's burdens of proof and persuasion differ depending on the jurisdiction and the type of motion. In Hawaii, a movant in a criminal case seeking to have the trial continued or postponed because a witness is unavailable must show that the movant has exercised due diligence in finding the witness; the witness would provide substantial favorable evidence; the witness is otherwise available and willing to testify; and the movant would be materially prejudiced by a denial of the CONTIN-UANCE (*State v. Lee*, 9 Hawai'i App. 600, 856 P.2d 1279 [1993]). In Utah a movant requesting that the court set aside its CHILD SUPPORT award because of a judicial mistake in failing to use a required joint custody worksheet in computing the amount of child support need only demonstrate the existence of a judicial mistake. A denial of the motion by the trial court, without an explanation as to why it deviated from the joint custody worksheet requirement, was an ABUSE OF DISCRETION and was reversed and remanded by an appellate court (*Udy v. Udy*, 893 P.2d 1097 [Utah App. 1995]).

FURTHER READINGS

Foremaster, Gary T. 1987. "The Movant's Burden in a Motion for Summary Judgment." *Utah Law Review* 1987.

MOVE

To make an application to a court for a rule or order, or to take action in any matter. The term comprehends all things necessary to be done by a litigant to obtain an order of the court directing the relief sought. To propose a resolution, or recommend action in a deliberative body. To pass over; to be transferred, as when the consideration of a contract is said to move *from one party to the other. To occasion; to contribute to; to tend or lead to.*

MOVIE RATING

A classification given to a commercially released motion picture that indicates to consumers whether the film contains sex, profanity, violence, or other subject matter that may be inappropriate for persons in certain age groups.

The idea for a nationwide movie rating system took root in the late 1960s. In 1966 Jack Valenti, a former aide to President LYNDON B. JOHNSON, became president of the Motion Picture Association of America (MPAA). That same year the film *Who's Afraid of Virginia Woolf* was completed. The film used terms such as *screw* and *hump* to refer to sexual intercourse. Because these terms were considered controversial language, Valenti met with officials at Warner Brothers before the film's release, and the group decided which terms could be deleted and which ones were necessary to the film's content.

The experience led Valenti in 1968 to implement a voluntary film ratings system, which has remained in effect, in varying forms, since that time. The MPAA that year created the Classification and Ratings Administration (CARA) to designate films with one of four ratings: G (general audiences), M (mature audiences), R (children under 16 years of age not admitted without parent or guardian), and X (children under 17 years of age not admitted). Three years later M became PG (parental guidance suggested). In 1984, in response to violence in the movie *Indiana Jones and the Temple of Doom,* the film review board instituted the PG-13 rating, which cautions parents that the film's contents may be inappropriate for children under age 13. In 1990 the board responded to criticism that the X rating unfairly categorized artistic adult films, such as *Midnight Cowboy,* with hard-core PORNOGRAPHY. In that year the board replaced X with NC-17.

In the movie business, a better rating is generally a lower rating. Movies typically make more money when they appeal to the widest possible audience. This rule holds true particularly with motion picture video sales. Many video outlets limit their inventory to movies with ratings no higher than PG-13 or R. Some theaters refuse to show movies with the NC-17 rating, and some newspapers refuse to carry advertisements for movies with the NC-17 rating. A movie studio therefore wants its film to earn the least restrictive rating possible.

One exception to this general rule is the marketing of pornographic films. Because studies have suggested that sexually explicit films become more desirable when they are restricted, the pornographic film industry voluntarily labels its films X or XXX in an effort to increase sales. XXX is a marketing tool, not an actual MPAA rating.

Although the MPAA publicizes the meaning of each rating, most moviegoers do not know how the ratings are assigned. A ratings board, consisting of 11 members, views approximately 600 films a year, discusses each film's content, and chooses a rating for each film. Valenti and the board's chair choose all the board members and keep their identities secret to prevent film producers and studios from attempting to influence them. The members work full-time, serving terms of varying length. Members must be parents and cannot be involved with the motion picture industry, but they must meet no other requirements. Members base their ratings on a set of MPAA guidelines, some of which are precise whereas others call for individual taste and judgment. According to one MPAA guideline, a certain word used merely as an expletive in a film may garner a PG rating whereas the same word used to convey a sexual meaning may result in an R rating.

Directors who are unhappy with the board's rating may cut or edit objectionable film footage and resubmit the movie, or they may appeal the rating. Movie producers have the right to know the reason behind the rating their film receives. However, directors and producers have complained that the board's reasons are often unclear or too general, requiring them to edit a film several times before it receives the target rating. Some directors have added especially gory scenes to the first version of a film with the idea that they will cut the gore during the ratings process, leaving the film in its intended state with the desired rating.

Because the movie ratings system is a voluntary process not under government control, FIRST AMENDMENT protections do not apply to ratings. If filmmakers believe that the rating for their film is too restrictive, they may appeal to a special board, which is composed of movie industry professionals rather than laypersons. The board screens the film, consults with the original ratings board, and listens to the complaints of the producer or director before voting. A two-thirds majority will overturn the original rating, and the decision of the appeals board is final.

No law requires filmmakers to undergo the ratings process; it is strictly voluntary. Yet, with very few exceptions, filmmakers comply. The system has the support of major film studios, theater owners, and video rental chains that rely on customer satisfaction for a healthy business.

It is the movie industry that pays for the privilege of having a film rated; the producer of a film pays a fee for this service that is based on the cost of film production.

The ratings system has critics. Filmmakers complain that the system is ARBITRARY and point to instances in which films with similar content have different ratings. Producers and directors have also alleged racism, arguing that films depicting sexual encounters between African Americans receive more restrictive ratings than films involving sex between white characters. Critics also allege sex bias in that movies with frontal nude shots of women commonly receive R ratings, whereas movies with similar nude shots of men commonly receive X or NC-17 ratings. And major studios, say some critics, receive better treatment from the ratings board than do smaller, independent studios, which also have less money to spend on reediting and resubmitting movies in an effort to achieve a better rating.

FURTHER READINGS

Brown, Jay. 1993. *Rating the Movies*. Lincolnwood, IL: Publications International.

Cole, David. 1994. "Playing by Pornography's Rules: The Regulation of Sexual Expression." *University of Pennsylvania Law Review* 143 (November).

Katz, Michael. 1996. "The Precursor: Movie Ratings." *Broadcasting and Cable* 8 (May 19).

Margulies, Edward, and Stephen Rebello. 1993. *Bad Movies We Love*. New York: Plume Books.

Mosk, Richard M. 1997. "Motion Picture Ratings in the United States." *Cardozo Arts & Entertainment Law Journal* 15 (spring): 135–45.

"The Ratings Game: Movies' Ratings Can Have Strong Effect on Box Office's Rental Performances." 1994. *Video Store* 16 (May 1).

CROSS-REFERENCES

First Amendment; Pornography; X Rating.

❖ MUELLER, ROBERT SWANN, III

Robert Swann Mueller III became the sixth director of the FEDERAL BUREAU OF INVESTIGATION (FBI) on September 4, 2001. In that position, Mueller has faced conflict and controversy stemming from a host of problems concerning spy scandals, terrorist activities, and accusations that the Bureau had developed a "culture of arrogance" that impeded its ability to function.

Mueller was born in New York City on August 7, 1944. He graduated from Princeton University in 1966. He also received a master's degree in International Studies from New York University. In 1973, he received his Juris Doctor from the University of Virginia School of Law, where he also served on the Law Review.

Mueller served for three years as an officer in the U.S. Marine Corps. He spent one year in the Third Marine Division in Vietnam. He was awarded the Bronze Star, the Purple Heart, two Navy commendation medals, and the Vietnamese Cross of Gallantry.

After his military service, Mueller embarked on a multifaceted career that saw him moving between private practice and government positions while building a record of support from Republicans as well as Democrats. From 1973 to 1976, Mueller worked as a litigation associate at the law firm of Pillsbury, Madison & Sutro in San Francisco. Between 1976 and 1981, he served in a number of positions in the Civil and Criminal Divisions of the Office of the U.S. Attorney, Northern District of California in San Francisco.

From 1986 to 1987, Mueller served as U.S. Attorney for the District of Massachusetts, where he had been Chief of the Criminal Division from 1982 to 1985. While he served in these offices, Mueller gained experience prosecuting a wide variety of cases, including RACKETEERING cases, complex tax and financial FRAUD cases, drug conspiracies, government corruption, and cases involving terrorists.

Mueller was a partner in the Boston firm of Hill & Barlow from 1988 to 1989. From 1989 to 1990, he worked in the JUSTICE DEPARTMENT as the assistant to Attorney General Richard L. Thornburgh. In June 1990, he was nominated by President GEORGE H.W. BUSH to be Assistant Attorney General in charge of the department's

Criminal Division. While in that position, Mueller oversaw a number of high-profile cases including the prosecutions of former Panamanian president Manuel Noriega and New York organized-crime boss John Gotti and the investigation into the 1988 bombing of Pan Am flight 103.

From 1993 to 1995, Mueller practiced law as a partner in Hale & Dorr, a Boston firm where he centered his work on sophisticated transactions, including complex litigation, WHITE-COLLAR CRIME, and internal corporate reviews. From 1995 to 1998, Mueller worked in the HOMICIDE Section of the office of U.S. Attorney for the District of Columbia, becoming Section Chief in 1997. Some former colleagues viewed this as a step down for a man who had supervised an entire division of the Department of Justice, but Mueller explained that he felt obligated to do what he could to stop the horrendously high murder rate of young people in the nation's capital.

In August 1998, Mueller became interim U.S. Attorney for the Northern District of California. He was nominated by President BILL CLINTON on the recommendation of Democratic Senator Barbara Boxer and confirmed by the Senate to the permanent position in October, 1999. Mueller held that position until August 2001. Between January and May of 2001, he also served as Acting Deputy General of the U.S. Department of Justice.

In May 2001, FBI Director Louis Freeh announced his resignation. His eight-year tenure had been marked by criticism of several high-profile cases, including that of Oklahoma City bomber Timothy McVeigh and turncoat FBI agent Robert Hanssen. Two months later,

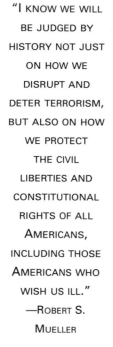

"I KNOW WE WILL BE JUDGED BY HISTORY NOT JUST ON HOW WE DISRUPT AND DETER TERRORISM, BUT ALSO ON HOW WE PROTECT THE CIVIL LIBERTIES AND CONSTITUTIONAL RIGHTS OF ALL AMERICANS, INCLUDING THOSE AMERICANS WHO WISH US ILL."
—ROBERT S. MUELLER

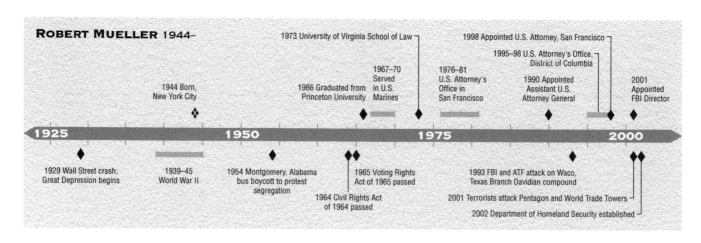

ROBERT MUELLER 1944–

1973 University of Virginia School of Law

1998 Appointed U.S. Attorney, San Francisco

1995–98 U.S. Attorney's Office, District of Columbia

1944 Born, New York City

1966 Graduated from Princeton University

1967–70 Served in U.S. Marines

1976–81 U.S. Attorney's Office in San Francisco

1990 Appointed Assistant U.S. Attorney General

2001 Appointed FBI Director

1925   1950   1975   2000

1929 Wall Street crash; Great Depression begins

1939–45 World War II

1954 Montgomery, Alabama bus boycott to protest segregation

1965 Voting Rights Act of 1965 passed

1964 Civil Rights Act of 1964 passed

1993 FBI and ATF attack on Waco, Texas Branch Davidian compound

2001 Terrorists attack Pentagon and World Trade Towers

2002 Department of Homeland Security established

Mueller was nominated by President GEORGE W. BUSH to fill a ten-year term as director of the FBI. Mueller was confirmed to the position in August 1, 2001, by a Senate vote of 98–0.

Despite enjoying broad bipartisan support, Mueller faced a number of difficult challenges involving interdepartmental communications, the continuing investigations into alleged terrorist activities, and the restructuring of the department's bureaucracy. Controversies continued to arise, including criticism regarding the FBI's failure to act on information that preceded the SEPTEMBER 11TH TERRORIST ATTACKS and the FBI's announcement in April 2003 that a former FBI agent might have caused serious losses of classified information during his affair with a prominent Chinese businesswoman who was accused of being a double agent working for China.

FURTHER READINGS

Mueller, Robert S. 2003. "Congressional Statement, 2003: War on Terrorism" (statement) Available online at <www.fbi.gov/congress/congress03/mueller021103.htm> (accessed July 25, 2003).

"Profile: FBI Chief Robert Mueller." 2003. Available online at <news.bbc.co.uk/2/hi/americas/1424760.stm> (accessed July 25, 2003).

"Robert S. Mueller, III." 2003. Available online at <www.fbi.gov/libref/directors/mueller.htm> (accessed April 21, 2003).

MULTIDISTRICT LITIGATION

A procedure provided by federal statute (28 U.S.C.A. § 1407) that permits civil lawsuits with at least one common (and often intricate) QUESTION OF FACT *that have been pending in different federal district courts to be transferred and consolidated for pretrial proceedings before one judge.*

Congress has given the federal judicial system a mechanism to help manage complex and protracted civil lawsuits that are related to each other. Under 28 U.S.C.A. § 1407, the Judicial Panel on Multidistrict Litigation has the authority to transfer related cases to one federal judge for "coordinated and consolidated pretrial discovery" in advance of trial. The panel is composed of seven federal judges based throughout the United States, who have been appointed by the chief justice of the U.S. Supreme Court. The panel's clerk's office is located in Washington, D.C.

Certain types of litigation are good candidates for transfer and consolidation to a single judge. TORTS involving a disaster (usually airplane crashes), PRODUCT LIABILITY, TRADE-MARK and patent infringement, SECURITIES violations, and antitrust issues have typically used multidistrict transfer.

Section 1407 transfers are initiated either by motion of a party or by the panel itself. The panel's decision whether to make a transfer is guided by a number of criteria: the existence of one or more common questions of fact within the group of cases being considered; whether transfer would be "for the convenience of parties and witnesses [and would] promote the just and efficient conduct of such actions" (section 1407(a)); the residence of the principal witnesses; the locations where the actions were initially filed; and the likelihood that transfer will avoid conflicting rulings. In general, economy and convenience become the determining factors.

Once the panel decides that a transfer is appropriate, it must select the appropriate judicial district to handle the litigation. There are no statutory guidelines governing the assignment of the consolidated case, but the panel considers the location of the judicial district in relation to the residences of the parties, the scene of the disaster (if the case involves such a situation), the business headquarters of the parties, the location with the highest concentration of relevant documents, and how easily the location of a judicial district can be reached. Apart from these factors, the panel seeks to place transferred cases in courts that have the time to oversee the complexities of the litigation.

After a district is chosen and a federal district judge is selected to manage the group of cases, the judge exercises full judicial powers over the case. The judge will enter a "practice and procedure order" that governs all matters leading to trial. During the pretrial stage, the parties use the discovery process to find out as much as they can about each other's case.

Under the statute, once all pretrial proceedings have been concluded, the judge remands the case to the panel, along with a recommendation as to how the panel should proceed in setting the cases for trial. Though the statute implies that the cases be remanded to their districts of inception for trial, the panel usually transfers a case back to the judge who handled the pretrial proceedings.

Federal multidistrict litigation is governed by the Rules of Procedure of the Judicial Panel on Multidistrict Litigation and the *Manual for*

Complex Litigation. The panel's *In re Concrete Pipe,* 302 F. Supp. 244 (J.P.M.L. 1969), contains many additional factors that it may consider in deciding whether to transfer a case.

At the state level, similar transfer and consolidation methods have been employed to deal with complex litigation. States have appointed judges to oversee product liability cases involving products such as asbestos, breast implants, and tobacco.

FURTHER READINGS

Whitman, M. Hamilton, and Diane Festino Schmitt. 1996. "Multidistrict Litigation: A Primer on Practice before the Panel." *The Business Line*—Newsletter of Ober and Kaler. Available online at <www.business-line.com> (acccessed November 10, 2003).

CROSS-REFERENCES

Civil Procedure; Federal Courts.

MULTILEVEL DISTRIBUTORSHIP

A type of referral sales scheme by which an individual who purchases a particular item from a company agrees to solicit and provide additional buyers for the product in exchange for a commission or rebate from the company.

This type of plan is also known as a pyramid sales scheme and is against the law in many jurisdictions.

CROSS-REFERENCES

Consumer Protection.

MULTIPLICITY OF ACTIONS

Several unnecessary attempts to litigate the same claim or issue.

The law strongly disfavors multiplicity of actions because of the public policy to promote judicial efficiency and to furnish speedy relief to an injured party. The rule against splitting a claim provides that if a plaintiff sets forth only certain aspects of the CAUSE OF ACTION in a complaint, he or she will be barred from raising the remaining aspects in a subsequent suit. If the plaintiff sues upon any portion of a particular claim, all other aspects of the claim are merged in this judgment if the plaintiff wins and are barred if the plaintiff does not win. For example, a plaintiff who claims $10,000 due under a single, indivisible contract and files two separate suits, for $5,000 each, will be permitted to litigate only the first suit, since the contract claim is a single cause of action.

MUNICIPAL

In its narrower and more common sense, pertaining to a local governmental unit, commonly a city or town. In its broader sense, pertaining to the public or governmental affairs of a state, nation, or of a people. Relating to a state or nation, particularly when considered as an entity independent of other states or nations.

MUNICIPAL CORPORATION

An incorporated political subdivision of a state that is composed of the citizens of a designated geographic area and which performs certain state functions on a local level and possesses such powers as are conferred upon it by the state.

A municipal corporation is a city, town, village, or borough that has governmental powers. A municipality is a city, town, village, or, in some states, a borough. A corporation is an entity capable of conducting business. Cities, towns, villages, and some boroughs are called municipal corporations because they have the power to conduct business with the private sector.

Generally, the authority to govern the affairs within a state rests with the state legislature, the governor, and the state judicial system. However, states give localities limited powers to govern their own areas. The origin of the municipal corporation varies from state to state. Municipal corporations are given the power to govern through either the state constitution or state statutes, or through the legislative grant of a charter.

States give municipalities the power to create an official governmental body, such as a board or council. Members of this body are elected by voters who live within the voting boundaries of the municipality. The local body has the power to pass ordinances, or local laws. These laws may not conflict with state or federal laws.

Most states grant so-called home rule powers to municipalities in the state constitution and state statutes. Home rule is a flexible grant of power from the state to the voters of a municipality. The first grant of home rule was given to the city of St. Louis in 1875 when the state of Missouri created a new state constitution that gave the city the power to create its own government.

Home rule gives municipalities the power to determine their own goals without interference from the state legislature or state agencies. It gives municipalities room to experiment with new approaches to government without first seeking approval from the state. It also allows municipalities to act more quickly on issues of local concern because they do not have to seek approval for their actions from the state legislature. Although home rule powers are broad, in no event may a municipality enact a law that is specifically precluded by state law or that is contrary to state law. For example, a municipality may not vote to decriminalize narcotics that are illegal under state law. It may, however, strengthen existing state laws. For instance, a municipality may act to restrict the sale of alcohol to a greater degree than is done in other municipalities.

The alternative to home rule is Dillon's Rule, a set of principles related to municipal power formulated by the influential jurist John Forest Dillon in 1872. Under Dillon's Rule, municipalities exercise only the limited powers specifically granted by the state, the powers necessary to carry out the specifically granted powers, and the powers indispensable to the declared purposes of the municipality. Few states rely on Dillon's Rule, and the trend among states is to give municipalities more power in deciding local issues.

The governmental authority most commonly exercised by municipalities is the POLICE POWER. The term *police power* does not refer to the authority to create police departments, although it does include that power. Police power is the power of state and local governments to enact laws governing health, safety, morals, and general public welfare. On the local level, such ordinances range from the provision of local police to ZONING laws to laws on domestic partnerships. The authority of states to exercise police power can be found in the TENTH AMENDMENT to the U.S. Constitution. States, in turn, grant police power to municipalities, and the municipalities exercise that power within their respective borders. The grant of police power from the state to municipalities can be found in state constitutions or state statutes.

States also commonly give their municipalities the power to enter into contracts. This power can be exercised only by action of the local governing body. The body must give notice of its intent to hire a private party for local government work. For example, if a municipality seeks a contractor to construct a building, the municipality must publish a notice of its intentions in a local newspaper and post other notices in public places. A municipality should not hire a private company if a member of the governing body has a financial interest in the company.

A municipality must exercise ordinary and reasonable care in providing safe public places and safe public services. If a municipality fails to exercise reasonable care, it may be held liable for resulting injuries. For example, if a person falls through a manhole and into the sewer, the city may be liable for any injuries resulting from the fall if the manhole cover was not secure. In this respect, a municipality may be liable for its NEGLIGENCE just like an individual. The most common TORT cases against municipalities are based on personal injuries caused by defects or obstructions in public streets, sidewalks, drains, and sewers.

Since the 1960s, cities across the United States have begun to decay because of lack of resources. To increase municipal resources, cities have imposed a variety of fees on private developers. Such fees include charges for building permit approvals, plat approvals, and water or sewer connection; impact fees that take into account future costs of a development; and special assessments for benefits given to a developer by the city. For example, a city may impose a transportation exaction fee on the developer of a residential subdivision to pay for the laying and maintenance of new roads that must be built to serve the subdivision. Developers have argued that such fees force private parties to pay for public functions, and they have attacked the fees as being beyond the power of the city government. In some cases their challenges have been upheld.

Municipal corporations are an important feature of the political structure of the United States. Incorporating a municipality gives it the freedom to form a society that is distinct from other localities in the state and around the country. This idea of local control is the same concept that animates the constitutional division of the country into a collection of smaller states. By giving municipalities some autonomy, individuals are more capable of participating in politics and gaining a measure of control over their lives than if political activity occurred only on the federal and state levels.

FURTHER READINGS

Goodnow, Frank J. 1997. *Municipal Home Rule: A Study in Administration*. Buffalo, N.Y.: W.S. Hein.

Howard, Linda G., and Chere Calloway, co-chairs, 2002. *Second Annual Municipal Law Institute*. New York: Practising Law Institute.

Mulcahy, Charles C., and Michelle J. Zimet. 1996. "Impact Fees for a Developing Wisconsin." *Marquette Law Review* 79.

Powell, Frona M. 1990. "Challenging Authority for Municipal Subdivision Exactions: The Ultra Vires Attack." *DePaul Law Review* 39.

CROSS-REFERENCES

Land-Use Control.

MUNIMENTS OF TITLE

Documents that serve as evidence of ownership of real or PERSONAL PROPERTY. Written instruments, such as stock certificates or deeds to land, by which an owner is enabled to defend his or her ownership rights.

The *muniment of title* doctrine provides that when ownership of property has been litigated between two parties and title has been adjudicated to be held by one of the two, the loser is not able to relitigate the matter with anyone who relies upon the title of the winner.

MUNN V. ILLINOIS

See GRANGER MOVEMENT.

MURDER

The unlawful killing of another human being without justification or excuse.

Murder is perhaps the single most serious criminal offense. Depending on the circumstances surrounding the killing, a person who is convicted of murder may be sentenced to many years in prison, a prison sentence with no possibility of PAROLE, or death.

The precise definition of murder varies from jurisdiction to jurisdiction. Under the COMMON LAW, or law made by courts, murder was the unlawful killing of a human being with malice aforethought. The term *malice aforethought* did not necessarily mean that the killer planned or premeditated on the killing, or that he or she felt malice toward the victim. Generally, *malice aforethought* referred to a level of intent or recklessness that separated murder from other killings and warranted stiffer punishment.

The definition of murder has evolved over several centuries. Under most modern statutes in the United States, murder comes in four varieties: (1) intentional murder; (2) a killing that resulted from the intent to do serious bodily injury; (3) a killing that resulted from a depraved heart or extreme recklessness; and (4) murder committed by an ACCOMPLICE during the commission of, attempt of, or flight from certain felonies.

Some jurisdictions still use the term *malice aforethought* to define intentional murder, but many have changed or elaborated on the term in order to describe more clearly a murderous state of mind. California has retained the malice aforethought definition of murder (Cal. Penal Code § 187 [West 1996]). It also maintains a statute that defines the term *malice*. Under section 188 of the California Penal Code, malice is divided into two types: express and implied. Express malice exists "when there is manifested a deliberate intention unlawfully to take away the life of a fellow creature." Malice may be implied by a judge or jury "when no considerable provocation appears, or when the circumstances attending the killing show an abandoned and malignant heart."

In *Commonwealth v. LaCava*, 783 N.E.2d 812 (Mass. 2003), the defendant, Thomas N. LaCava, was convicted of the deliberate, premeditated murder of his wife. LaCava admitted to the shooting and the killing, but he claimed that due to his diminished mental capacity, he could not form the requisite malice when he committed the killing, so as to be convicted of first degree murder. The Supreme Judicial Court of Massachusetts found that Massachusetts law permits psychiatric evidence to attack the premeditation aspect of murder. However, the judge's instructions to the jury regarding the definition of murder was sufficient to render the error harmless, according to the court.

Many states use the California definition of implied malice to describe an unintentional killing that is charged as murder because the defendant intended to do serious bodily injury, or acted with extreme recklessness. For example, if an aggressor punches a victim in the nose, intending only to injure the victim's face, the aggressor may be charged with murder if the victim dies from the blow. The infliction of serious bodily injury becomes the equivalent of an intent to kill when the victim dies. Although the aggressor in such a case did not have the express desire to kill the victim, he or she would not be charged with assault, but with murder. To understand why, it is helpful to consider the alternative: When a person dies at the hands of an aggressor, it does not sit well with the public conscience to preclude a murder charge simply because the aggressor intended only to do serious bodily injury.

Some murders involving extreme recklessness on the part of the defendant cause extreme public outrage. In *People v. Dellinger*, 783 P.2d 200 (Cal. 1989), the defendant, Leland Dellinger, was found guilty of the murder of his two-year-old stepdaughter. The primary cause of the child's death was a fractured skull caused by trauma to the head. However, other evidence showed that the child had large quantities of cocaine in her system when she died. Moreover, her mother discovered that the defendant had fed the child wine through a baby bottle. Due to the defendant's "wanton disregard for life," the verdict of murder was proper, according to the California Supreme Court.

A person who unintentionally causes the death of another person also may be charged with murder under the depraved-heart theory. Depraved-heart murder refers to a killing that results from gross negligence. For example, suppose that a man is practicing shooting his gun in his backyard, located in a suburban area. If the man accidentally shoots and kills someone, he can be charged with murder under the depraved-heart theory, if gross NEGLIGENCE is proven.

In *Turner v. State*, 796 So. 2d 998 (Miss. 2001), the defendant, Jimmy Ray Turner, was convicted of the murder of his wife. The couple had contemplated DIVORCE, but had apparently reconciled. After their reconciliation, they went together to the defendant's parents' house to return a borrowed shotgun. As they walked to the parents' house, the defendant, who testified that he did not think the shotgun was loaded, demonstrated to his wife how he carried the gun with his fingers on the trigger and walked with his arms swinging. His wife stopped suddenly, bumping into the defendant. The shotgun fired, killing the wife. Although the defendant was not charged with premeditated murder, he was indicted and convicted of depraved-heart murder due to his gross negligence in handling the shotgun.

Most states also have a felony murder statute. Under the felony murder doctrine, a person who attempts or commits a specified felony may be held responsible for a death caused by an accomplice in the commission of the felony; an attempt to commit the felony; or flight from the felony or attempted felony. For example, if two persons rob a bank and during the ROBBERY one of them shoots and kills a security guard, the perpetrator who did not pull

the trigger nevertheless may be charged with murder.

The felonies that most commonly give rise to a felony murder charge are murder, rape, robbery, BURGLARY, KIDNAPPING, and ARSON. Many states add to this list. Maine, for example, adds gross sexual assault and escape from lawful custody (Me. Rev. Stat. Ann. tit. 17-A, § 202 [West 1996]). Generally, felony murder liability lies only if the death was a reasonably foreseeable consequence of the felony, a felony attempt, or flight from the crime. For example, courts have held that death is a reasonably foreseeable consequence of armed robbery.

Most states divide the crime of murder into first and second degrees. In such states, any intentional, unlawful killing done without justification or excuse is considered second-degree murder. The offense usually is punished with a long prison term or a prison term for life without the possibility of parole. Second-degree murder can be upgraded to first-degree murder, a more serious offense than second-degree murder, if the murder was accomplished with an aggravating or special circumstance. An aggravating or special circumstance is something that makes the crime especially heinous or somehow worthy of extra punishment.

California lists some 20 different special circumstances that can boost a murder from second to first degree, including murder carried out for financial gain; murder committed with an explosive; murder committed to avoid or prevent a lawful arrest; murder to perfect or attempt an escape from lawful custody; murder of a law enforcement officer, prosecutor, judge, or elected, appointed, or former government official; murder committed in an especially heinous, atrocious, or cruel fashion where the killer lay in wait for, or hid from, the victim; murder where the victim was tortured by the killer; murder where the killer used poison; or murder where the killing occurred during the commission of, aid of, or flight from certain felonies. These felonies include rape, robbery, kidnapping, burglary, arson, train wrecking, sodomy, the performance of a lewd or lascivious act upon a child under age 14, and oral copulation with a child under age 14 (Cal. Penal Code § 190.2 [West 1996]).

If a murder does not qualify by statute for first-degree murder, it is charged as second-degree murder. A second-degree murder may be downgraded to MANSLAUGHTER if mitigating factors were involved in the killing, such as

Women Murdered on the Job

The workplace can be a dangerous environment, exposing workers to hazards that can cause accidents, disease, and sometimes death. But the workplace also is a place where murders are committed. Statistics indicate that there is a large difference between the number of men and the number of women killed on the job. Fifteen percent of men who die at work are murdered, whereas 35 percent of female workplace deaths are the result of homicides.

It is believed that the high number of female workplace murders is based in part on the kinds of jobs women take in the economy. Many work in retail jobs, clerking at late-night convenience stores where robberies often occur and where security is often lacking. Analysts also believe that male perpetrators select retail stores where they believe that they can easily overpower a female employee.

Other workplace murders of women are committed by former boyfriends and husbands who are upset over a separation. Some psychologists believe that these men associate the woman's job with independence and the breakup of their relationship. Murdering a former wife or lover is a way for a man to reassert his dominance.

Finally, some murders of women appear to be committed out of resentment over the loss of a job at the workplace and the perception that women are to blame for the job loss. Roughly five percent of all the murders committed in the workplace, male and female, are committed by former or current employees.

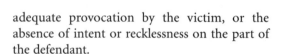

adequate provocation by the victim, or the absence of intent or recklessness on the part of the defendant.

Maine has simplified the law of murder. In Maine, a person is guilty of murder if he or she intentionally or knowingly causes the death of another human being, engages in conduct that manifests a depraved indifference to the value of human life and causes death, or intentionally or knowingly causes another human being to commit suicide by the use of force, duress, or deception (Me. Stat. tit. 17-A § 201 [1996]). Maine also has a felony murder statute. It does not divide murder into degrees.

Sentencing for murder varies from state to state, and according to degrees in the states that have them. Second-degree murder usually is punished with more than 20 years in prison. A person convicted of second-degree murder in Minnesota, for example, may be sentenced to prison for not more than 40 years. Some states, such as California, allow a sentence up to life in prison for second-degree murder.

In some states that have a first-degree murder charge, the crime is punished with a life term in prison without the possibility of parole. In other states, first-degree murder is punishable by death. A defendant's criminal history may affect sentencing for a murder conviction. The greater the criminal history, the more time the defendant is likely to serve. The criminal history of a murder defendant may even cause a murder charge to be upgraded from second degree to first degree. In California, for example, a murder defendant who has a prior conviction for murder faces an automatic first-degree murder charge.

The strongest defenses to a murder charge are provocation and SELF-DEFENSE. If the defendant acted completely in self-defense, this fact may relieve the defendant of all criminal liability. If it does not relieve the defendant of all liability, self-defense at least may reduce the charge from murder to manslaughter. Provocation rarely results in complete absolution, but it may reduce the defendant's criminal liability. For example, suppose that a family is being tormented by a neighbor for no apparent reason. The neighbor has damaged the family's property, assaulted the children, and killed the family dog. If the father kills the neighbor and is charged with murder, the father may argue that the provocation by the victim was so great that if he is to be found criminally liable at all, he should be found liable for manslaughter, not murder.

A defendant's subjective belief that he or she was under attack by a victim at the time of a killing may be a basis for a claim of self-defense. In *Henderson v. Texas*, 906 S.W.2d 589 (Tex. App. 1995), the defendant, Sherri Henderson, was convicted of the murder of a victim whom she shot outside of a nightclub. The victim had engaged in a fight with the defendant's sister inside the club, and the fight later moved outside. The defendant carried a gun that she had purchased a few days before, apparently for protection from her estranged husband. The facts in the case were in dispute, but the defendant found her sister bleeding from the head when she went to the parking lot. She claimed that she saw someone reach for a weapon, and she fired into a crowd, hitting and fatally wounding the woman who had fought her sister. The jury apparently believed the prosecution's claim that the defendant had intentionally shot at the victim after seeing her sister on the ground, and Henderson was convicted of murder. However, the Texas appellate court reversed the trial court's conviction, holding that evidence of the defendant's subjective beliefs regarding her attacker's identity and evidence of prior attacks on the defendant by her husband were relevant to her claim for self-defense.

Insanity is another defense to a murder charge. If a defendant was suffering from such a defect of the mind that he or she did not know what he or she was doing, or the defendent did not know that what he or she was doing was wrong, the defendant may be found not guilty by reason of insanity. In some states, the defendant may be found guilty but mentally ill. In either case, the result is the same: The defendant is confined to a mental institution instead of a prison.

The INSANITY DEFENSE has many critics, and it especially comes under fire when a defendant commits an atrocious killing. In 2001, the nation was shocked by the story about Andrea Yates, who drowned each of her five young children in a bathtub. The children's ages ranged from six months to seven years old at the time of the killings. Yates was estranged from her husband and contacted him shortly after the killings. She subsequently confessed to the crime but claimed the defense of insanity. Her counsel argued that because she suffered from schizophrenia, which had first surfaced several years earlier, she did not know the difference between right and wrong at the time of the killings. According to testimony, she had considered stabbing her first child shortly after his birth.

The insanity defense failed, however, and Yates was convicted and sentenced to life in prison.

The modern law of murder is relatively static, but minor changes are occasionally proposed or implemented. Some legislatures have debated the idea of striking assisted suicide from murder statutes. Some have considered proposals making doctors liable for murder if they perform a third-trimester ABORTION. Many have made changes with respect to juveniles. Juveniles accused of murder used to be tried in juvenile courts, but in the 1980s and 1990s, legislatures passed laws to make juvenile murder defendants over the ages of 14 or 15 stand trial as adults. This change is significant because a juvenile defendant convicted in the juvenile justice system might go free upon reaching a certain age, such as 21. A juvenile defendant who is tried in adult court does not have such an opportunity and may be sentenced to prison for many years, or for life without parole. A juvenile may be put to death upon conviction for murder but only if he or she was age 16 or older at the time of the offense (*Thompson v. Oklahoma*, 487 U.S. 815, 108 S. Ct. 2687, 101 L. Ed. 2d 702 [1988]).

Mass Murders and Serial Killings

The public is often fascinated, although also horrified, by stories of mass murders and serial killings. This fascination is evidenced by the popularity of such films as *Natural Born Killers* and *Silence of the Lambs*. When a mass murder or serial killing occurs, it often receives considerable media attention. Stories are revisited for years following the incidents, as experts and novices alike try to determine the causes of why these tragedies occur and how they can be prevented. Although statistics show that mass murders and serial killings are more common now than they have been in the past, this type of killings is still rather rare.

Criminologists and other experts distinguish between a serial killer and a mass murderer, although the profiles of these perpetrators are often similar. A serial killer is most often a younger, white male, who targets specific strangers near his work or home. This type of killer is typically a sociopath who kills to satisfy delusional personal needs and desires through killing by physical force. Serial killers such as Jack the Ripper, David Berkowitz, Ted Bundy, and John Wayne Gacy are household names. A mass murderer is likewise often a young, white male, who acts deliberately and methodically in carrying out his killings. One of the most celebrated mass murderers was Charles Joseph Whitman, who in 1966 climbed a tower at the University of Texas at Austin and engaged in a 90-minute shooting spree. He shot 44 people, killing 14, before being fatally shot by a police officer. The motivation of either a serial killer or a mass murderer obviously varies by the killer, but experts note that it is often terror, power, revenge, or profit.

The United States and several other countries have been especially horrified by a number of school shootings in the past decade. One of the most horrific of these shootings occurred at Columbine High School in Littleton, Colorado on April 20, 1999. Two teenagers, Dylan Klebold and Eric Harris, went on a shooting rampage throughout the school, killing 12 students and injuring more than 20, before finally killing themselves. Since 1996, more than 25 schools in the United States have suffered from school shootings, as have schools in such countries as Canada, Sweden, Scotland, and Germany. Because the perpetrators of these murders are usually teenagers, experts have investigated these shootings closely, in order to identify potential signs that an unbalanced student might consider resorting to violence.

FURTHER READINGS

Fox, James Alan, and Jack Levin. 1998. "Multiple Homicide: Patterns of Serial and Mass Murder." *Crime and Justice.*.

Hobson, Charles L. 1996. "Reforming California's Homicide Law." *Pepperdine Law Review* 23.

LaFave, Wayne R. 2000. *Criminal Law* 3d ed. St. Paul, Minn.: West Group.

CROSS-REFERENCES

Capital Punishment; Criminal Law; Death and Dying; Felony-Murder Rule; Homicide; Insanity Defense; Juvenile Law.

❖ MURPHY, FRANCIS WILLIAM

As a champion of civil liberties in the WORLD WAR II era, Francis ("Frank") William Murphy had an extraordinary political and legal career. An associate justice of the U.S. Supreme Court from 1940 to 1949, he previously had served in local, state, and federal government. He was appointed U.S. governor general of the Philippine Islands in 1935, elected governor of Michigan in 1936, and appointed U.S. attorney general in 1939. Murphy's support for workers, women, and members of religious and racial minority groups, as well as his broad reading of the First

> "OFFICIAL COMPULSION TO AFFIRM WHAT IS CONTRARY TO ONE'S RELIGIOUS BELIEFS IS THE ANTITHESIS OF FREEDOM OF WORSHIP."
> —FRANCIS MURPHY

and Fourth Amendments, distinguished him at a time when both the federal government and the Court moved slowly in upholding CIVIL RIGHTS.

Born in Sand Beach (later Harbor Beach), Michigan, April 13, 1890, Murphy was the son of an Irish Catholic country lawyer and a devoutly religious mother. He studied at the University of Michigan before being admitted to the state bar in 1914. He then went off to fight in France and Germany in WORLD WAR I. On returning to Michigan, he acquired legal experience by working in the state attorney general's office and in private practice. He next became judge for the principal criminal court in Detroit, which in turn led to a political career. A pro-labor Democrat, Murphy was mayor of Detroit from 1930 to 1933.

In the midst of the Great Depression, Murphy supported FRANKLIN D. ROOSEVELT for president in 1932. President Roosevelt rewarded him with appointment as the governor general of the Philippine Islands. Murphy enacted MINIMUM WAGE laws and supported women's suffrage while helping to effect the country's transition to independence. Returning to Michigan, he campaigned and won election as governor in 1936. That year the historic sit-down strike by 135,000 automobile workers proved to be the turning point in Murphy's career. He refused to deploy state police against the unpopular strikers and as a consequence lost his reelection bid in 1938.

President Roosevelt named him to his administration. Although Murphy wanted to be secretary of war—and, indeed, would spend several years trying to find ways to join the war effort—Roosevelt had other plans. The president made him U.S. attorney general. Murphy established the first civil liberties unit in the JUSTICE DEPARTMENT and brought suit against trust companies and a powerful DEMOCRATIC PARTY boss, Thomas J. Pendergast of Kansas City. In 1939 the death of Associate Justice PIERCE BUTLER opened the so-called Catholic seat on the Supreme Court, and Roosevelt gave it to a reluctant Murphy, who thought himself less qualified than others.

Murphy served for nine years as an associate justice. He wrote 199 opinions. Inherently suspicious of government power and passionately devoted to the rights of the weak, Murphy supported civil rights in nearly every case. He scorned the federal government's treatment of Japanese Americans during World War II, for example, and at other times sided with the claims of workers and religious minority groups.

This philosophy found its best expression in 1944. "The law knows no finer hour," Murphy wrote in one of his many dissents, "than when it cuts through formal concepts and transitory emotions to protect unpopular citizens against discrimination and persecution" (*Falbo v. United States,* 320 U.S. 549, 64 S. Ct. 346, 88 L. Ed. 305). That case was one of several in the 1940s involving church-state issues that concerned the rights of the Jehovah's Witnesses, in this case a CON-SCIENTIOUS OBJECTOR. Murphy often voted in favor of upholding FIRST AMENDMENT claims; for example, he joined the majority in ending compulsory flag-saluting for children in public schools (*West Virginia State Board of Education v. Barnette,* 319 U.S. 624, 63 S. Ct. 1178, 87 L. Ed. 1628 [1943]). In another important speech case, Murphy wrote the majority opinion protecting LABOR UNION picketing (*Thornhill v. Alabama,* 310 U.S. 88, 60 S. Ct. 736, 84 L. Ed. 1093 [1940]). Yet more often than not, his broader reading of individual rights led him into dissent against the majority.

On and off the Court, Murphy faced criticism for his idealism. He was seen as too emotional at the expense of strict legal thinking. He was the target of the popular barb, "justice tempered with Murphy." His personal life only fed his somewhat prim reputation, because he was a hypochondriac who never drank, smoked, or married. Chief Justice HARLAN F. STONE disliked him for another reason: he thought Murphy was too reliant on his law clerks.

Although Murphy occasionally seemed out of step with both the Court and his times, his broad vision of civil liberties was later vindi-

Frank Murphy.
LIBRARY OF CONGRESS

cated. In particular, he believed in vigorous application of the Fourth Amendment's prohibition of unreasonable SEARCHES AND SEIZURES by the police. Murphy dissented in *Wolf v. Colorado,* 338 U.S. 25, 69 S. Ct. 1359, 93 L. Ed. 1782 (1949), where the Court refused to apply to the states what already existed for federal courts: the ban on admitting improperly seized evidence in a trial. He wrote that the majority, by leaving state courts out of the equation, was allowing "lawlessness by officers of the law." Twelve years later, in 1961, a different Supreme Court agreed with him and overruled *Wolf* in the landmark case MAPP V. OHIO, 367 U.S. 643, 81 S. Ct. 1684, 6 L. Ed. 2d 1081 (1961).

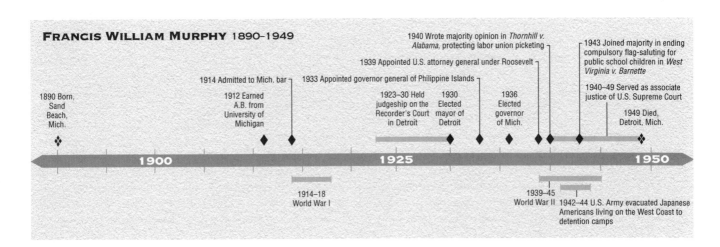

FRANCIS WILLIAM MURPHY 1890–1949

1890 Born, Sand Beach, Mich.

1912 Earned A.B. from University of Michigan

1914 Admitted to Mich. bar

1923–30 Held judgeship on the Recorder's Court in Detroit

1930 Elected mayor of Detroit

1933 Appointed governor general of Philippine Islands

1936 Elected governor of Mich.

1939 Appointed U.S. attorney general under Roosevelt

1940 Wrote majority opinion in *Thornhill v. Alabama,* protecting labor union picketing

1943 Joined majority in ending compulsory flag-saluting for public school children in *West Virginia v. Barnette*

1940–49 Served as associate justice of U.S. Supreme Court

1949 Died, Detroit, Mich.

1900   1925   1950

1914–18 World War I

1939–45 World War II

1942–44 U.S. Army evacuated Japanese Americans living on the West Coast to detention camps

Murphy died on July 19, 1949 in Detroit, Michigan.

FURTHER READINGS

Friedman, Leon, and Fred L. Israel, eds. 1969. *The Justices of the United States Supreme Court, 1789–1969: Their Lives and Major Opinions.* New York: Chelsea House.

Witt, Elder, ed. 1990. *Guide to the U.S. Supreme Court.* 2d ed. Washington, D.C.: Congressional Quarterly.

CROSS-REFERENCES

Flag; Japanese American Evacuation Cases.

MUSIC PUBLISHING

The contractual relationship between a songwriter or music composer and a music publisher, whereby the writer assigns part or all of his or her music copyrights to the publisher in exchange for the publisher's commercial exploitation of the music.

Music publishing has been an important part of the U.S. entertainment industry since the early twentieth century. Songwriters contract with music publishing companies to exploit their songs, with both parties sharing the income generated from the songs. Before the introduction of musical recordings, songwriters and publishers earned their income primarily from the sale of sheet music. In the modern era, songs can be commercially exploited in many types of media, including recordings, radio, television, film, and video. Music publishing is governed by U.S. COPYRIGHT law, but much of the law of music publishing is negotiated through private contractual agreements.

Music publishers are powerful intermediaries between songwriters and recording companies. Typically, a music publisher demands copyright ownership from the songwriter, along with half of the ROYALTIES. A publisher may make a large cash advance to a popular or promising songwriter, but often the advance is minimal. In return, the publisher seeks to place the songwriter's compositions with performers who will make a recording. In addition, a publisher will try to place songs in films, television shows, and advertisements. If the songwriter is also a performer, the publisher will assist the artist in obtaining a recording contract. The publisher also assumes the responsibility of collecting royalties and giving the songwriter his share.

Publishing income comes from various sources, but it is separate from income derived from retail sales of recordings. Income from recording sales flows to the owner of the record-

ing (usually the record company), which then pays a contractually negotiated recording royalty to the performer. The owner of the recording separately pays the publisher of the recorded compositions a mechanical royalty for the right to record, copy, and distribute copies of the composition. These royalties are called mechanical royalties because the license is for mechanical recording and reproduction of the composition.

Under U.S. copyright law, a publisher is required to grant a mechanical license to anyone wishing to record a composition that has previously been recorded and released commercially. This is called a compulsory license, and the minimum rate that must be paid to the publisher for such a license is set by Congress at a few cents for each copy made of a recording of the composition. Normally, however, a record label that wishes to record a publisher's composition will negotiate a private license with the publisher rather than follow the strict accounting and reporting rules that accompany recording under a compulsory license. Because of this situation, the statutory compulsory license rate has become the effective ceiling rate for recording a composition, because no one need pay more than the rate set by law.

A lucrative part of music publishing involves performance royalties. Performance royalties are paid when a song is played on the radio or television, used by businesses for background music, or used by clubs for dance music or by bands performing at a club. A popular song can earn thousands and sometimes millions of dollars through the collection of performance royalties. However, it would be too demanding for a publisher to sign performance licenses with every club, radio station, and business office that might use a particular song. Instead publishers and songwriters register with a performing rights organization (PRO) to collect fees on their behalf.

The three PROs in the United States are the American Society of Composers, Authors, and Publishers (ASCAP), Broadcast Music Inc. (BMI), and the Society of European State Authors and Composers (SESAC). The PROs negotiate blanket licenses with all who use music for profit. Such fees can range from less than one hundred dollars for a small business using music to enhance its business environment, to hundreds of thousands of dollars or millions of dollars for large-scale broadcasting entities. The PROs then monitor radio and television broadcasts, and then using a complex statistical model, they pay publishers and songwriters based on projected actual uses of a song. When a composition is registered with a PRO, the registrant informs the PRO what percentages of royalties are to be paid to the publisher and songwriter. The PRO issues separate payments to the publisher and to the songwriter (or songwriters). A particular songwriter may only be registered with one PRO at a given time to avoid confusion as to which PRO is responsible for collecting performance royalties on the songwriter's behalf. The use of blanket licenses allows an artist to perform compositions written by another songwriter without first requesting the songwriter's permission.

As opposed to mechanical licenses, there is no statutory rate for the use of a song in films and television advertisements (synchronization licenses), in radio advertisements (transcription licenses), or for sale as sheet music (print licenses). These fees are negotiated separately between the user and the music publisher. The licensee pays the entire fee to the publisher, who then pays the songwriter's share to the songwriter.

Recording artists who feel that the publishers have cheated them out of part of their royalties often take the publishers to court. High-profile artists have sued, claiming that their celebrity and marketability has not given them leverage against the music industry. The pop star Michael Jackson, who was wildly successful in the 1980s, launched a lawsuit against Universal Music Group (UMG) in 2003 claiming that UMG owed him millions of dollars in royalties from music he recorded (alone and with his brothers) that was released after 1980. In September a judge in Los Angeles threw out part of Jackson's lawsuit. Jackson had given up his rights to all songs released before 1979 in a deal with the music publisher Motown (which was later bought by UMG). Jackson attempted to cancel the 1980 agreement with Motown as part of his suit, but the judge ruled that there was no justification to cancel the agreement; consequently, all pre-1980 tunes were removed from the suit.

Musicians also sue each other for copyright infringement. In the case of *Three Boys Music Corporation v. Bolton*, 212 F.3d 477 (9th Cir. 2000), a jury awarded rhythm-and-blues group the Isley Brothers $5.4 million in a lawsuit against the singer-songwriter Michael Bolton and his co-writer. The Isley Brothers maintained that Bolton and Goldmark's 1991 song *Love is a Wonderful Thing* was substantially similar to their song of the same name, released in 1966. While Bolton and Goldmark contended that they had not deliberately copied the song, the jury felt they were similar enough to prove the Isleys' case. The Ninth Circuit Court of Appeals upheld the verdict.

Since the 1960s, many popular musical performers have written their own musical compositions. Some of these artists choose to "self-publish," forgoing relationships with publishers and thus retaining full ownership and control of their copyrights. These artists are more often songwriters whose compositions are so unique that they are not likely to be recorded by other performers. Therefore, this type of artist will receive little benefit from an outside publisher's marketing efforts. However, because the music industry's royalty structure assumes that publishing income will be paid to a publisher, a self-published artist often will set up her own publishing company under an assumed name to receive publishing income. A self-published artist will frequently hire an accounting firm to handle specific administrative functions such as royalty collection, for a much smaller fee than a full-service music publisher would demand.

In the early 2000s, the advent of music-sharing over the INTERNET has begun to change the face of the recording industry. With file-sharing software such as Napster and KaZaA, individuals can trade favorite songs and download them to their computers. The recording industry began retaliating with a series of lawsuits, as did individual artists such as the rapper Dr. Dre and the heavy metal band Metallica. Although the creators of file-sharing software have made efforts to comply with copyright laws and work with music publishers, the computer has made music PIRACY a significant issue. The Recording Industry Association of America (RIAA) went on the offensive in the summer of 2003 with a series of legal actions. It filed 261 lawsuits against individuals who allegedly downloaded and shared music illegally. Since some of those named were children and others were adults who claimed their grandchildren had downloaded the music, it was widely believed that the move was more to make a point than to go after ordinary citizens. The RIAA also went after COLLEGES AND UNIVERSITIES, a huge market for file-sharing, and a number of colleges have begun to crack down on illegal music sharing. This situation has raised issues of privacy (should a college be required to report a student caught downloading pirated music, or does the student have the right to anonymity, for example), and as technology continues to become more sophisticated the issue will undoubtedly need to be explored carefully and continuously.

FURTHER READINGS

"Judge Rejects Part of Michael Jackson's Lawsuit Against Music Giant." September 20, 2003. *Reuters.*

Krasilovsky, M. William, and Sidney Shemel. 1995. *This Business of Music: A Practical Guide to the Music Industry for Publishers, Writers, Record Companies, Producers, Artists, Agents.* New York: Watson-Guptill.

Liggett, Mark, and Cathy Liggett. 1993. *The Complete Handbook of Songwriting: An Insider's Guide to Making It in the Music Industry.* New York: Dutton/Plume.

Lubell, Sam. 2003. "Campuses Move to Block Music Sharing." *New York Times.* (Oct. 2)

Sanders, Rob. 2000. "The Second Circuit Denies Music Publishers the Benefits of the Derivative Works Exception." *Southwestern University Law Review* 29 (spring): 655–79.

Satorius, Daniel M., ed. 1993. *The Practical Musician.* St. Paul, Minn.: Minnesota Continuing Legal Education.

Sobel, Lionel S. 2000. "The Nuts, Bolts, and Politics of the Evolution of Music Law." *Sedona Conference Journal* 1 (July): 235–43.

Veiga, Alex. 2003. "Recording Industry Suing Hundreds of Music Swappers." *Charlotte Observer.* (Sept 8)

Whitsett, Tim. 2000. *Music Publishing: The Real Road to Music Business Success.* 5th ed. Vallejo, Calif.: MixBooks.

CROSS-REFERENCES

Broadcasting; Entertainment Law; Intellectual Property; License; Royalty.

❖ MUSSEY, ELLEN SPENCER

At a time when women in the United States were often excluded from higher education, Ellen Spencer Mussey helped found a coeducational law school to promote the social and economic advancement of women.

In 1896, Mussey and colleague EMMA M. GILLETT sponsored a series of lectures in Washington, D.C., aimed at attracting and training female lawyers. The lectures were primarily for local women whose professional goals were frustrated by the men-only admission policies of most law schools in the District. After two years of well-received lectures, Mussey and Gillett expanded their curriculum and formally established Washington College of Law, a coeducational institution that later became part of American University. Mussey was the law school's first dean; she was succeeded by Gillett in 1913.

Mussey was born May 13, 1850, in Geneva, Ohio, to Platt Rogers Spencer and Persis Duty Spencer. After attending Lake Erie Seminary, in Painesville, Ohio, and Rockford Seminary, in Rockford, Illinois, Mussey moved to Washington, D.C., where she worked as a principal for the Spencerian Business College. She married lawyer Reuben Delavan Mussey in 1871 and had two children, Spencer Mussey and William Hitz Mussey. Under her husband's tutelage, Mussey read law and eventually attended the Law School of Cornell University in the summer of 1896.

When Mussey's husband became seriously ill, she took over the daily operation of his law office. After his death in 1892, Mussey was admitted to the D.C. bar. (At that time, a law degree was not required for bar admission.) She became one of very few women from her generation to be admitted to practice before the U.S. Supreme Court and the U.S. Court of Claims. In private practice, Mussey specialized in international and real estate law. At the request of

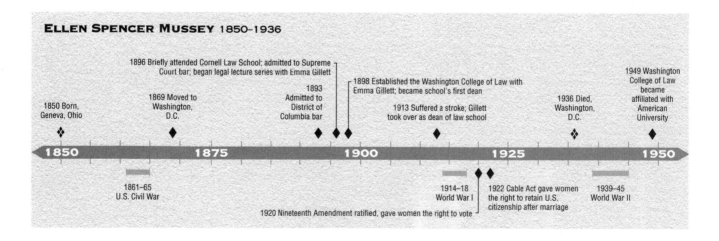

ELLEN SPENCER MUSSEY 1850–1936

1850 Born, Geneva, Ohio

1869 Moved to Washington, D.C.

1893 Admitted to District of Columbia bar

1896 Briefly attended Cornell Law School; admitted to Supreme Court bar; began legal lecture series with Emma Gillett

1898 Established the Washington College of Law with Emma Gillett; became school's first dean

1913 Suffered a stroke; Gillett took over as dean of law school

1936 Died, Washington, D.C.

1949 Washington College of Law became affiliated with American University

1861–65 U.S. Civil War

1914–18 World War I

1920 Nineteenth Amendment ratified, gave women the right to vote

1922 Cable Act gave women the right to retain U.S. citizenship after marriage

1939–45 World War II

American Red Cross founder Clara Barton, she became the Red Cross's first staff attorney.

A social reformer, Mussey was a major force behind new legislation giving women the same rights as men over children, property, and earnings. She also pushed for laws allowing women to keep their U.S. citizenship after marrying foreign citizens.

Mussey served as editor of *American Monthly* magazine, committee chair for the National Council of Women, and delegate to the 1911 International Council of Women held in Stockholm. She also helped organize the National Association of Women Lawyers and the Women's Bar Association of the District of Columbia.

Mussey died April 21, 1936, in Washington, D.C., at the age of eighty-five. She had overcome long-standing societal barriers to pursue her professional interests and social agenda. Washington College of Law was the crowning achievement of her illustrious career.

MUSSOLINI, BENITO

Benito Mussolini ruled as dictator of Italy from 1922 to 1943. His political philosophy, which he called fascism, was based on the total domination of the government in all spheres of political, social, economic, and cultural life. Initially seen by the Italian people as a hero, Mussolini was driven from government before the end of WORLD WAR II.

Mussolini was born in Dovia di Predappio, Italy, on July 29, 1883, the son of a socialist blacksmith. He embraced SOCIALISM as a teenager and as a young man became a schoolteacher and socialist journalist in northern Italy. In 1902 he moved to Switzerland and earned a living as a laborer. He returned to Italy in 1904 to perform his required military service and then resumed his teaching.

His wanderlust, however, resumed. He went to Trent, Austria, in 1909 and worked for a socialist newspaper. He was expelled from Austria after he publicly urged the return of Trent to Italy. In 1912 he became editor of *Avanti!*, the most important Italian socialist newspaper, with headquarters in Milan. When WORLD WAR I broke out in August 1914, Mussolini proved unwilling to toe the socialist line. Socialists argued that disputes between nations were not their concern and that Italy should stay out of the conflict. Mussolini disagreed, whereupon the socialists expelled him from the party.

Benito Mussolini.
GALE

This expulsion radically changed Mussolini's political outlook. He founded *Il Popol d'Italia* (The People of Italy), a strident newspaper that argued that Italy should enter the war against Germany. When Italy did join the war, Mussolini enlisted in the army and served from 1915 to 1917, when he was wounded.

After the war Mussolini started his own political movement. In 1919 he formed the Fascist party, called the Fasci di Combattimento. The name *fascism* is derived from the Latin *fascis*, meaning *bundle*. The fasces is a bundle of rods strapped together around an axe. A symbol of authority in ancient Rome, it represented absolute, unbreakable power. Mussolini promised to recreate the glories of the Roman Empire in a movement that was nationalistic, antiliberal, and antisocialist.

Mussolini's movement struck a chord with lower-middle-class people. Supporters wore black shirts and formed private militias. In 1922 Mussolini threatened a march on Rome to take over the government. King Victor Emmanuel capitulated to this threat and asked Mussolini to form a government. Once in power Mussolini abolished all other political parties and set out to transform Italy into a fascist state.

Initially Italians and foreign observers saw Mussolini as a strong leader who brought needed discipline to the economy and social structure of Italy. He poured money into building the infrastructure of a modern country. In a country known for disorganization, it was said that Mussolini made the trains run on time. He also, however, abolished trade unions and closed newspapers that did not follow the party line. He used the police to enforce his rule and imprisoned thousands of people for their political views.

In the 1930s Mussolini sought to make Italy an international power. In 1935 Italy invaded the East African country of Ethiopia. Mussolini ignored the League of Nations' demand that he withdraw and proceeded to conquer the country. In 1936 he sent Italian troops to support General Francisco Franco's Loyalist Army in the Spanish Civil War. By the end of the 1930s, Mussolini also moved closer to ADOLF HITLER and Nazi Germany. In 1939 he invaded nearby Albania.

Mussolini did not enter World War II until June 1940, when he invaded the south of France. At first his alliance with Hitler appeared propitious. However, the Italian army suffered defeat in North Africa, and the Allies invaded Sicily in 1943. Mussolini's regime crumbled. King Victor Emmanuel dismissed Mussolini as the head of state on July 25, 1943. Mussolini was briefly imprisoned, but German troops rescued him. Hitler directed Mussolini to head an Italian puppet state in northern Italy, then under the control of German forces. As the Allies moved north in 1945, Mussolini tried to escape to Switzerland. He was captured by Italian partisans and shot on April 28, 1945. The bodies of Mussolini and his mistress, Clara Petacci, were displayed to jeering crowds on the streets of Milan.

FURTHER READINGS

Axelrod, Alan. 2001. *The Life and Work of Benito Mussolini.* Indianapolis, Ind.: Alpha.

Bosworth, R.J.B. 2002. *Mussolini.* London: Arnold; New York: Oxford Univ. Press.

"MUST CARRY" LAW

See MASS COMMUNICATIONS LAW (sidebar).

MUTILATION

Cutting, tearing, erasing, or otherwise changing a document in a way that changes or destroys its legal effect. It is a federal crime to mutilate public records, coins, or passports.

In CRIMINAL LAW, *the crime of violently, maliciously, and intentionally giving someone a serious permanent wound.*

MUTINY

A rising against lawful or constituted authority, particularly in the naval or ARMED SERVICES.

In the context of CRIMINAL LAW, mutiny refers to an insurrection of soldiers or crew members against the authority of their commanders. The offense is similar to the crime of SEDITION, which is a revolt or an incitement to revolt against established authority, punishable by both state and federal laws.

MUTUAL COMPANY

A corporation in which members are the exclusive shareholders and the recipients of profits distributed as dividends in proportion to the business that such members did with the company.

The most common kind of mutual company is a mutual insurance company. In this type of organization, which is a cooperative association, the members are both the insurers and the insured. Such companies exist for the purpose of satisfying the insurance needs of their members at a minimal cost. The members contribute through a system of premiums or assessments, forming a fund from which all losses and liabilities are paid. Any profits are divided among the members of the company in amounts proportionate to their individual interests.

The members of a mutual company choose the management. Professional associations that offer their members insurance coverage often form mutual insurance companies.

MUTUAL FUND

A fund, in the form of an investment company, in which shareholders combine their money to invest in a variety of stocks, bonds, and money-market investments such as U.S. Treasury bills and bank certificates of deposit.

Mutual funds provide a form of investment that is both relatively safe and relatively lucrative. Mutual funds offer investors the advantages of professional management of invested money and diversification of that investment. Mutual fund managers assume the responsibility of investigating and researching financial markets and selecting the combination of stocks, bonds, and other investment vehicles to be bought and sold. Thus, consumers purchase shares in a mutual fund and rely on the expertise of the mutual fund manager, whose job is to provide them with the highest possible return on their investments.

Investing in a mutual fund is not as safe as investing in a bank or a SAVINGS AND LOAN ASSOCIATION. The federal government normally insures money deposited in banks or savings and loan associations; if one of those institutions fails, each of its deposits of up to $100,000 generally is guaranteed. This is not true of other investment vehicles such as stocks and bonds, which by their nature rise and fall in value and offer no guarantees. But investing in a mutual fund usually is considered to be safer than investing in individual stocks and bonds. Mutual fund managers observe the financial markets and take advantage of trends that affect the fund by buying and selling various components of the fund. And because a mutual fund is diverse—comprised perhaps of a hundred or more different kinds of stocks, bonds, or other investments—even the complete failure of one stock will make a relatively small impact on the fund's overall success.

There are two general types of mutual funds. An investor in an open-end fund may request at any time that the fund buy back, or redeem, that investor's shares. The price of shares in an open-end fund is based on the market value of the fund's portfolio of investments. Investors in open-end funds may be charged additional fees known as loads. Front-end loads are charged when the investor purchases shares in a mutual fund; back-end loads are subtracted from the redemption price. Open-end funds are sold by SECURITIES dealers and brokers and financial planners, or they are sold directly to the investor by the fund's sales staff.

Closed-end funds are traded on stock exchanges or the over-the-counter market. Unlike open-end funds, closed-end funds usually have a fixed number of shares, which are purchased and redeemed at their market price plus a commission.

Mutual funds are broadly classified according to three types of investment objectives: growth of capital, stability of capital, or current income. Most funds are geared toward one or two of these objectives. For example, money-market funds invest in instruments like U.S. Treasury bills, which are relatively safe and generally stable. Therefore many investors view money-market funds as a good alternative to a bank account. Other funds seek stability of capital by investing in blue-chip stocks and high-quality bonds. Some funds are potentially more lucrative, but far riskier. Growth funds are somewhat aggressive, investing in speculative securities that show promise over time for slow but steady long-term return. Income funds also tend to be speculative, often investing in high-risk, high-yield securities with the goal of greater short-term return.

Within the three broad categories of mutual funds are numerous subcategories. Funds that seek both growth and income are known as balanced funds. Sector funds invest in certain types of businesses, such as the computer industry. Some funds strive to fulfill a political agenda, such as investing in environmentally responsible companies or companies that actively promote women and minorities. Precious metals funds, municipal bond funds, and international stock funds are other examples of mutual fund categories. Other funds are far less specialized and allow the fund manager free reign to compile and alter the fund's portfolio.

Mutual fund shareholders receive periodic investment income, or dividends, which comes from dividends and interest earned by the various securities that make up the fund's portfolio. Shareholders often elect to have these dividends reinvested into the mutual fund. Investors in mutual funds may choose to make monthly payments into the fund or have a specified amount automatically withdrawn from a bank account or savings and loan association account each month. Some companies offer a variety of open-end mutual funds with different investment objectives and allow investors a simple way to switch their money from one fund to another as their savings goals change.

Securities laws, both state and federal, govern mutual funds. Some statutes regulate the organization of investment companies and the sale of securities by brokers and dealers. Federal securities laws that regulate mutual funds include the Securities Act of 1933 (15 U.S.C.A. § 77a et seq.), the Securities Exchange Act of 1934 (15 U.S.C.A. § 78a et seq.), and the Investment Company Act of 1940 (15 U.S.C.A. § 80a–1 et seq.).

FURTHER READINGS

Baer, Gregory, and Gary Gensler. 2002. *The Great Mutual Fund Trap: An Investment Recovery Plan.* New York: Broadway Books.

Blake, Erica. 2000. "A Review and Analysis of the Monitoring of Personal Investment Transactions and the Implementation of Codes of Ethics." *Annual Review of Banking Law* 19 (annual): 637–53.

United States General Accounting Office. 2003. *Mutual Funds: Greater Transparency Needed in Disclosures to*

Investors: Report to Congressional Requesters. Washington, D.C.: General Accounting Office.

MUTUAL MISTAKE

An error of both parties to a contract, whereby each operates under the identical misconception concerning a past or existing material fact.

For example, a customer goes to the sample room of an interior decorator to select a carpet and asks the clerk to show him a navy carpet, which he subsequently purchases and takes with him. The sales slip notes that the carpet purchased is navy. When, upon examining the carpet in daylight, the customer discovers that it is black, not navy as he thought when he bought it, a mutual mistake would have occurred, since both the seller and buyer were in error concerning the correct color of the carpet sold. Since there had never been a true and complete meeting of the minds, no mutual assent was actually arrived at, and the buyer would be entitled to return the carpet and obtain a full refund.

MUTUALITY OF OBLIGATION

The legal principle that provides that unless both parties to a contract are bound to perform, neither party is bound.

MY LAI MASSACRE

The event known as the "My Lai Massacre" was one of the darkest moments of the VIETNAM WAR, and further fueled the already growing anti-war movement in the United States. On March 16, 1968, U.S. Army troops murdered more than 300 unarmed Vietnamese women, children, and elderly persons. When the facts of the massacre became known, war crime charges were brought against 30 soldiers, and there was a marked increase in both domestic and foreign pressure to end the war.

The Vietnam War began in the 1940s as a war of liberation between Vietnamese nationalists called the Viet Minh and the French who controlled Vietnam. The Viet Minh sought help from Communist China in the mid-1950s, bringing the conflict to the attention of the United States. In 1954 the French were decisively defeated, and the country was temporarily divided into North Vietnam and South Vietnam. Most of the Viet Minh and their supporters relocated to North Vietnam. When the provisional head of South Vietnam refused to hold reunification elections, hostilities resumed.

Fearing a communist takeover if the North Vietnamese won, the United States provided economic and military aid, and by 1967 the United States had almost 400,000 troops in the country. Viet Cong, Vietnamese soldiers who had trained in the North and moved back to the South to conduct guerilla warfare, were especially feared. Dressed to blend in with the peasants who populated South Vietnamese villages, the Viet Cong carried on a stealthy campaign of sabotage and murder. American soldiers, who did not speak Vietnamese and were unable to distinguish between Viet Cong combatants and the general population, were anxious and wary whenever they traveled into the rural countryside. Knowing that many villagers were sympathetic to the Viet Cong added to their stress.

My Lai was part of the Song My village located in South Vietnam's Quang Ngai Province. The area had been heavily mined by the Viet Cong, and in the weeks preceding the massacre, numerous members of "Charlie Company," a unit of the U.S. Army's American Division, had been injured or killed by the mines. Under the direction of Captain Ernest Medina, a group of about 120 anxious and angry soldiers from Charlie Company entered My Lai on a mission to "search [out] and destroy" enemy soldiers.

According to later EYEWITNESS reports, the soldiers, under orders from their platoon leader Lieutenant William L. Calley, used rifles, machine guns, bayonets, and grenades to kill the villagers. Old men, women who begged and prayed for mercy, children, and babies were murdered by the soldiers. Several young girls were raped and killed. Estimates of the number of villagers massacred at My Lai ranged from 300 to 500; the final army estimate was 347. Of the 100 soldiers who entered My Lai about 30 participated in the killing. Most of the other soldiers did not participate, but they did not try to stop the killing. Some testified later that they thought their lives would be in danger if they tried to stop their fellow soldiers.

Informed of the incident by Captain Hugh C. Thompson, an army helicopter pilot who had managed to save a few of the villagers, the U.S. Army did nothing. Ron Ridenhour, an army helicopter gunner, was told about the massacre shortly after it took place. After leaving the service, Ridenhour wrote detailed letters to the Pentagon, Congress, and the White House asking for an investigation. In November 1969 the army appointed General William R. Peers to look into Ridenhour's charges.

After a four-month army investigation that included listening to 398 witnesses and collecting thousands of pages of testimony, charges were initially brought against 30 of the participants; that number was subsequently reduced to 13. Nine enlisted men and four officers faced charges ranging from murder to dereliction of duty for covering up the incident.

In November 1969 Seymour Hersh's newspaper story about the events of My Lai and subsequent follow-up reports shocked and horrified people around the world. The stories ignited waves of controversy over U.S. presence in Vietnam and increased pressure to bring an end to the war.

In 1971 five members of Charlie Company including Captain Medina and Lt. Calley were subjected to courts-martial. Captain Medina was represented by prominent defense attorney F. LEE BAILEY and was acquitted of all charges. Lt. Calley was the only soldier convicted. He was found guilty of the premeditated murder of more than 20 Vietnamese civilians and sentenced to life imprisonment. His sentence was later reduced to 10 years and he was paroled in September 1975.

In May 1998 three former U.S. soldiers who had placed themselves at risk to save some of the civilians at My Lai were awarded (one posthumously) the army's prestigious Soldier's Medal.

FURTHER READINGS

Bilton, Michael, and Kevin Sim. 1993. *Four Hours in My Lai.* New York: Penguin Books.

Karnow, Stanley. 1984. *Vietnam: A History.* New York: Penguin Books.

Sheehan, Neil. 1989. *A Bright and Shining Lie.* New York: Vintage Books.

CROSS-REFERENCES

Vietnam War.

NAACP

Founded in 1909, the organization formerly known as the National Association for the Advancement of Colored People and now called simply NAACP is the oldest and largest CIVIL RIGHTS organization in the United States. Headquartered in Baltimore, Maryland, with a staff of more than 220 persons, the interracial NAACP works for the elimination of RACIAL DISCRIMINATION through LOBBYING, legal action, and education. With its victories in landmark Supreme Court cases such as BROWN V. BOARD OF EDUCATION, 347 U.S. 483, 74 S. Ct. 686, 98 L. Ed. 873 (1954), as well as its sponsorship of grassroots social programs, the NAACP has been a leader in the effort to guarantee that African Americans and members of other racial minorities receive EQUAL PROTECTION under the law.

The NAACP grew out of race riots that occurred in Springfield, Illinois, in August 1908. Shocked at the violence directed against African Americans by white mobs in Abraham Lincoln's hometown, William English Walling, a white socialist, wrote a magazine article that called for the formation of a group to come to the aid of African Americans. The following year, Walling met with two young white social workers, Mary White Ovington and Henry Moskowitz, and began planning a course of action. They enlisted the aid of Oswald Garrison Villard, grandson of the abolitionist WILLIAM LLOYD GARRISON, to publicize the Conference on the Status of the Negro, to be held that May. The conference drew several hundred people, many of whom would unite a year later as the NAACP.

Although originally the NAACP leadership was largely white, since the 1920s, it has been primarily African American. The organization drew many of its original white members from progressive and socialist ranks, and most of its first African American members through the leadership of the historian and sociologist W. E. B. DU BOIS. Du Bois and BOOKER T. WASHINGTON were the two principal African American leaders of the day. Du Bois had led the Niagara Movement, an African American protest organization, since 1905, and he brought the membership of that organization into the NAACP. He was named director of publicity and research for the NAACP in 1910, and he edited the organization's highly respected journal, *The Crisis*, until 1934.

From the beginning, the NAACP made legal action on behalf of African Americans a top priority. It won early Supreme Court victories in *Guinn v. United States*, 238 U.S. 347, 35 S. Ct. 926, 59 L. Ed. 1340 (1915), which overturned the GRANDFATHER CLAUSE as a means of disfranchising black voters, and in *Buchanan v. Warley*, 245 U.S. 60, 38 S. Ct. 16, 62 L. Ed. 149 (1917), which barred municipal ordinances requiring racial SEGREGATION in housing. The *grandfather clause* imposed a literacy test on persons who were not entitled to vote prior to 1866. This meant that all slaves and their descendants had to pass a rigorous literacy test based on knowledge of the state constitution and other highly technical documents. Few, if any, African Americans passed the test.

The NAACP appointed its first African American executive director, JAMES WELDON JOHNSON, in 1920. Under Johnson and his successor, Walter White, who led the organization from 1931 to 1955, the NAACP worked for the passage of a federal antilynching law. Although unsuccessful in its efforts to pass a federal law, the NAACP brought public attention to the brutality of LYNCHING and helped to significantly reduce its occurrence. As a result, lynching—which is the infliction of punishment, usually hanging, by a mob without trial—is now illegal in every state.

In 1941 the NAACP established its Washington, D.C., bureau as the legislative advocacy and lobbying arm of the organization. The bureau does the strategic planning and coordination of NAACP political action and legislation program. It acts as the liaison between NAACP units and government agencies, and it coordinates the work of other organizations that support NAACP programs and proposals.

The bureau sponsors the annual Legislative Mobilization which informs participants of the NAACP legislative agenda, monitors and advocates for NAACP civil rights and related legislation, and prepares an annual "Report Card" showing how each member of Congress voted on key civil rights issues.

For its early litigation efforts, the NAACP relied on lawyers who volunteered their services. In 1934, the group hired CHARLES HAMILTON HOUSTON, an African American and dean of Howard Law School, as its first full-time attorney. The following year, Houston started a legal campaign to end school segregation. Houston was assisted by THURGOOD MARSHALL, a young lawyer who would go on to argue many cases before the Supreme Court and in 1967 would become the first African American appointed to the Court. In 1940, the NAACP appointed Marshall director-counsel of its new legal branch, the NAACP LEGAL DEFENSE AND EDUCATIONAL FUND (LDF). In 1957, the LDF became a separate entity.

After succeeding in Supreme Court cases concerning unequal salary scales for black teachers and segregation in graduate and professional schools, the NAACP achieved its most celebrated triumph before the Court in *Brown*, a

decision that declared racial segregation in public schools to be unconstitutional.

The *Brown* decision sparked another civil rights initiative, the Montgomery, Alabama, bus boycott of 1955. The boycott catapulted MARTIN LUTHER KING JR. to national recognition and spurred the creation of the SOUTHERN CHRISTIAN LEADERSHIP CONFERENCE (SCLC). By the early 1960s, the SCLC, the STUDENT NONVIOLENT COORDINATING COMMITTEE (SNCC), the CONGRESS OF RACIAL EQUALITY (CORE), and the NATIONAL URBAN LEAGUE all promoted civil rights for African Americans. These groups adopted a direct-action approach to promoting African American interests by conducting highly publicized sit-ins and demonstrations.

The NAACP, meanwhile, drew criticism for its devotion to traditional legal and political means for seeking social change. ROY WILKINS, executive director of the NAACP from 1955 to 1975, voiced his preference for traditional tactics over "the kind that picks a fight with the sheriff and gets somebody's head beaten" (Spear 1984, 7:402). Although many viewed it as overly conservative in its civil rights approach, the NAACP helped pass important civil rights legislation such as the CIVIL RIGHTS ACT OF 1964 (42 U.S.C.A. § 2000a et seq.), the VOTING RIGHTS ACT OF 1965 (42 U.S.C.A. § 1973 et seq.), and the FAIR HOUSING ACT OF 1968 (42 U.S.C.A. § 3601 et seq.). The NAACP remained an interracial group and spurned the call for black nationalism and separatism voiced by SNCC, the BLACK PANTHERS, and other groups that turned to blacks-only membership later in the 1960s.

Unlike many of the more radical civil rights groups, the NAACP outlasted the turbulent 1960s. However, it experienced setbacks during the 1970s in Supreme Court cases such as *Bradley v. Millikin*, 418 U.S. 717, 94 S. Ct. 3112, 41 L. Ed. 2d 1069 (1974), which overturned efforts to integrate largely white suburban public school districts and largely black urban districts, and REGENTS OF UNIVERSITY OF CALIFORNIA V. BAKKE, 438 U.S. 265, 98 S. Ct. 2733, 57 L. Ed. 2d 750 (1978), which placed limits on AFFIRMATIVE ACTION programs.

BENJAMIN L. HOOKS succeeded Wilkins as NAACP director in 1977. He held that office until 1993, when he was replaced by Benjamin F. Chavis Jr. Leadership and funding problems plagued the NAACP during the mid-1990s. After a SEXUAL HARASSMENT suit was filed against Chavis in 1994, the NAACP board of

National Association for the Advancement of Colored People

1905	W. E. B. Du Bois and others founded the Niagara Movement
1908	Race riots erupted in Springfield, Illinois, Abraham Lincoln's hometown
1909	On 100th anniversary of Lincoln's birthday, more than sixty citizens issued a "call" for a national conference to renew the struggle for civil and political liberty; the group and conference formed the foundation of the NAACP
1910	National Association for the Advancement of Colored People (NAACP) chosen as group's name at second annual conference; William Walling chosen as executive director; W. E. B. Du Bois chosen as director of publicity and research and editor of the *Crisis*
1911	NAACP incorporated
1915	In *Guinn v. United States*, the Supreme Court struck down grandfather clauses in state constitutions as unconstitutional barriers to voting rights granted under the Fifteenth Amendment
1917	Supreme Court barred municipal ordinances requiring racial segregation in housing in *Buchanan v. Warley*
1920	NAACP appointed its first African American executive director, James Weldon Johnson
1923	Supreme Court ruled in *Moore v. Dempsey* that exclusion of African Americans from a jury was inconsistent with the right to a fair trial
1931	Walter White appointed to succeed Johnson as director of NAACP
1934	Charles Hamilton Houston hired as NAACP's first full-time attorney
1936	Thurgood Marshall joined NAACP as special counsel
1940	NAACP created separate legal arm, the NAACP Legal Defense and Educational Fund, and appointed Marshall as its director-counsel
1941	Secretary of Army authorized first segregated airman unit, the 99th Squadron, better known as the Tuskegee Airmen
1948	Marshall's team argued *Shelley v. Kraemer*, which struck down racially restrictive (land) covenants; President Truman abolished racial segregation in armed services by executive order
1950	In *Sweatt v. Painter*, Supreme Court ruled racially segregated professional schools inherently unequal and therefore unconstitutional; first integrated combat units saw action in Korea
1954	Marshall's team argued *Brown v. Board of Education of Topeka, Kansas*, which ruled racial segregation in public schools unconstitutional
1955	Roy Wilkins appointed to succeed White as NAACP's executive director
1961	Marshall appointed to U.S. Court of Appeals for the Second Circuit; Jack Greenberg succeeded Marshall as director of LDF
1964	NAACP lobbying led to passage of the Civil Rights Act of 1964
1965	NAACP lobbying led to passage of the Voting Rights Act of 1965
1967	Thurgood Marshall became first African American associate justice of the Supreme Court
1968	NAACP lobbying led to passage of the Fair Housing Act of 1968
1972	U.S. Supreme Court declared existing capital punishment laws unconstitutional in *Furman v. Georgia*
1974	NAACP experienced a setback when Supreme Court overturned efforts to integrate largely white suburban school districts with largely black urban districts in *Milliken v. Bradley*
1976	Georgia, Florida, and Texas drafted new death penalty laws; Supreme Court upheld these new laws
1977	Benjamin Hooks succeeded Wilkins as NAACP's executive director
1978	Supreme Court placed limits on affirmative action programs in *Regents of University of California v. Bakke*
1993	Benjamin F. Chavis Jr. appointed to succeed Hooks as NAACP's executive director
1994	NAACP board of directors voted to oust Chavis after sexual harassment suit was filed against him
1995	Myrlie Evers-Williams replaced William F. Gibson as chairman of the NAACP board of directors
1996	NAACP board appointed Kweisi Mfume, a U.S. representative from Maryland, as president and chief financial officer; Mfume cut national staff by third as first step in returning NAACP to financial health
1997	NAACP launched the Economic Reciprocity Program
2000	TV diversity agreements; retirement of the debt and first six years of a budget surplus; largest black voter turnout in 20 years
2001	Cincinnati riots; development of five year strategic plan

SOURCE: NAACP web page; *Simple Justice* by Richard Kluger (1975).

directors voted to oust him as executive director. The following year, it dismissed board chairman William F. Gibson and replaced him with MYRLIE EVERS-WILLIAMS, the widow of civil rights activist MEDGAR EVERS. Seeking to put aside its troubles, on February 20, 1996, the NAACP board appointed Kweisi Mfume, a U.S. representative from Maryland and head of the Congressional Black Caucus, as the organization's new president and chief executive officer. To restore the organization's financial stability, Mfume cut back the national staff by one-third.

Among its many tasks, the NAACP works on the local level to handle cases of racial discrimination; offers referral services, tutorials, and day care; sponsors the NAACP National Housing Corporation to help develop low- and moderate-income housing for families; offers programs to youths and prison inmates; and maintains a law library. It also lobbies Congress regarding the appointment of Supreme Court justices.

The NAACP accepts people of all races and religions as members. In the early 2000s it had a membership of over 500,000, with 2,200 units (including more than 600 youth councils and college chapters) in the United States and around the world. The organization continues to struggle with the need to increase membership and retain relevancy while advocating for various civil rights issues. In 2000 the board instituted mandatory training for NAACP local leadership. More than 10,000 branch officers and executive committee members attended the training, and the organization removed 800 officers and committee members who did not attend.

The NAACP has also taken steps to build coalitions with black youth. NAACP president Kweisi Mfume sits on the board of Summit Action Network, a coalition of hip hop music stars as well as record company executives and community organizations that seek to educate and mobilize fans of rap music to register and vote in local and national elections. In addition, the NAACP has sought to overcome political differences and gain the support of the country's major Latino civil right organizations including the LEAGUE OF UNITED LATIN AMERICAN CITIZENS (LULAC) and the NATIONAL COUNCIL OF LA RAZA. In January 2003 the NAACP announced that the UNITED NATIONS had designated it as a non-governmental organization (NGO). The NGO designation meant that the NAACP could advise and consult with foreign governments and with the U.N. secretariat on issues relating to HUMAN RIGHTS.

In 2001 the NAACP signed a new three-year contract with Mfume to continue as the organization's president and CEO. Mfume continued to move ahead with his action agenda that emphasizes civil rights, political empowerment, educational excellence, economic development, and health and youth outreach. The NAACP Board of Directors continued to implement its plan to streamline and strengthen the governing procedures of the organization. For the first time since its inception in 1909, the board began revising and updating its constitution and bylaws. Up to this point each NAACP unit including state conferences, youth councils, college chapters, and local chapters had its own constitution and bylaws. The goal of the board is to have a uniform set of governing documents that are understandable and "user-friendly."

FURTHER READINGS

NAACP. Available online at <www.naacp.org> (accessed July 28, 2003).

Rhym, Darren. 2002. *The NAACP.* Philadelphia: Chelsea House.

Schneider, Mark R. 2002. *We Return Fighting: The Civil Rights Movement in the Jazz Age.* Boston: Northeastern Univ. Press.

CROSS-REFERENCES

Discrimination.

NAACP LEGAL DEFENSE AND EDUCATIONAL FUND

In 1940 the organization formerly known as the National Association for the Advancement of Colored People and now called the NAACP launched the Legal Defense and Educational Fund (LDF). Since its founding, the organization has been involved in more cases before the U.S. Supreme Court than any other nongovernmental organization.

The NAACP, which had been founded in 1909 to support CIVIL RIGHTS, soon found itself needing direction and aid as it sought to help people find their way through the criminal justice system. Under the leadership of future Supreme Court Justice THURGOOD MARSHALL, the LDF was created to provide information about the criminal justice system and legal assistance to indigent African Americans.

In 1957, three years after the Supreme Court's landmark decision in BROWN V. BOARD OF EDUCATION OF TOPEKA, KANSAS, 347 U.S. 483, 47 S.Ct. 686, 98 L.Ed. 873, which held that SEGREGATION in public schools was unconstitutional, the LDF was established as an entirely separate organization from the NAACP. The LDF is headquartered in New York City and has regional offices in Washington, D.C., and Los Angeles. The LDF has close to two dozen attorneys on staff whose work is supplemented by assistance from hundreds of attorneys around the United States.

The LDF primarily works with issues involving education, AFFIRMATIVE ACTION, fair employment and economic access, issues related to voting and other forms of civic and political participation, and criminal justice issues including the death penalty and prison reform. With more than 100 active cases, the LDF has one of the largest legal caseloads of any public service organization in the country.

While the primary focus of the LDF is on court cases, the fund also monitors legislation, provides advocacy, education research, and builds coalitions with related organizations. The scope of LDF activity has also widened to include advocacy for other minorities in this country as well as for global HUMAN RIGHTS. To this end, the LDF has aided in the establishment of similar organizations that advocate for other minority groups in the United States. Additionally, the fund has used its experience and legal expertise to help form public interest legal organizations in Brazil, Canada, and South Africa.

In addition to the *Brown* case which resulted in a flood of legal cases around the country relating to SCHOOL DESEGREGATION, the LDF won a number of significant cases in the 1950s that concerned housing discrimination, voting access, jury selection, the use of forced confessions, and access to counsel by indigent persons.

In the 1960s the LDF provided counsel for MARTIN LUTHER KING JR., and other civil rights activists. The LDF also began its drive to abolish CAPITAL PUNISHMENT. LDF provided counsel in numerous death penalty cases and was able to stop executions in the United States between 1966 and 1978. Since 1965 the LDF has published *Death Row USA*, a list of death-row inmates.

In the 1980s and 1990s, the LDF undertook hundreds of CLASS ACTION suits against employers, unions, and governmental units that have helped secure and safeguard the employment rights of thousands of workers.

The LDF also continued to support major VOTING RIGHTS legislation and to be involved in numerous cases aimed at securing voting rights for minorities. In the early 2000s the LDF continued to be involved in cases stemming from the redistricting of congressional districts after the 2000 census. After the 2000 presidential election, the LDF and five other civil rights organizations filed a class action lawsuit against Florida's SECRETARY OF STATE and other elected officials alleging that a significant number of minority citizens were unable to vote or faced severe obstacles in trying to register and vote.

In the early 2000s the Fund continued its fight in support of equal education and affirmative action. In February 2003 the LDF filed briefs in two major suits that challenged the use of race-conscious criteria in the admissions programs of the University of Michigan law school and its undergraduate School of Literature, Science, and the Arts. In June the Supreme Court decided in favor of the University of Michigan race-conscious criteria for admissions (*Grutter v. Bollinger*, 539 U.S., _____, 123 S.Ct. 2235, 156 L.Ed.2d 304 [U.S., Jun. 23, 2003]).

FURTHER READINGS

Greenberg, Jack. 1994. *Crusaders in the Courts: How a Dedicated Band of Lawyers Fought for the Civil Rights Revolution.* New York: BasicBooks.

Kluger, Richard. 2004. *Simple Justice: The History of Brown v. Board of Education and Black America's Struggle for Equality.* Rev. ed. New York: Knopf.

Orfield, Gary, Susan E. Eaton, and Elaine R. Jones. 1997. *Dismantling Desegregation: The Quiet Reversal of Brown v. Board of Education.* New York: New Press.

NAACP Legal Defense and Educational Fund. Available online at <www.naacpldf.org> (accessed July 28, 2003).

Schwartz, Bernard. 1986. *Swann's Way: The School Busing Case and the Supreme Court.* New York: Oxford Univ. Press.

CROSS-REFERENCES

Civil Rights Acts; Equal Protection; NAACP.

❖ NADER, RALPH

Considered the father of the CONSUMER PROTECTION movement, Ralph Nader has had a great effect on U.S. law and public policy of the late twentieth century. Nader's advocacy on behalf of consumers and workers hastened into reality many features of the contemporary political landscape. The work of this lawyer and irrepressible gadfly of the powers that be, which began in the mid-1960s, has led to the passage of numerous consumer-protection laws in such areas as automobiles, mining, insurance, gas pipelines, and meatpacking, as well as the creation of government agencies such as the National Highway Traffic Safety Administration, the Occupational Safety and Health Administration, the ENVIRONMENTAL PROTECTION AGENCY, and the CONSUMER PRODUCT SAFETY COMMISSION. Nader himself has founded many well-known consumer advocacy groups, including the Public Interest Research Group, the Clean Water Action Project, the Center for Auto Safety, and the Project on Corporate Responsibility. His goal in these efforts, he has said, is "nothing less than the qualitative reform of the industrial revolution."

Nader was born February 27, 1934, in Winsted, Connecticut, to Nadra Nader and Rose Bouziane Nader, Lebanese immigrants who owned and operated a restaurant and bakery. He is the youngest of five children. He attended the Gilbert School and Princeton University on scholarships. At Princeton, he entered the WOODROW WILSON School of Public and International Affairs, and he graduated magna cum laude and Phi Beta Kappa in 1955. During an era of conformity, his challenges to school authorities and procedures at Princeton made him stand out. At one point, he protested the use of the poisonous insecticide dichlorodipehnyltrichloroethane (DDT) on campus trees.

After Princeton, Nader attended Harvard Law School, where he edited the *Harvard Law Record,* and graduated with distinction in 1958.

"THE MOST IMPORTANT OFFICE IN AMERICA FOR ANYONE TO ACHIEVE IS FULL-TIME CITIZEN."
—RALPH NADER

Ralph Nader.

It was at Harvard that he first became interested in auto safety. After studying auto-injury cases, in 1958 he published his first article on the subject, "American Cars: Designed for Death," in the *Harvard Law Record*. It contained a thesis that he would bring to national attention in the mid-1960s: Auto fatalities result not just from driver error, as the auto industry had maintained, but also from poor vehicle design. Nader followed his law degree with six months of service in the Army and then a period of personal travel through Latin America, Europe, and Africa. Upon his return, he established a private law practice in Hartford, Connecticut created an informal legal aid society, and lectured from 1961 to 1963 at the University of Hartford.

Having worked at the local level for auto-safety regulations in the years subsequent to his graduation from Harvard, Nader decided to go to Washington, D.C., in 1964, where he hoped to have more influence. Through his friendship with Daniel P. Moynihan, who then was serving as assistant secretary of labor, Nader worked as a consultant at the DEPARTMENT OF LABOR and wrote a study that called for federal responsibility over auto safety.

Nader left the Department of Labor in May 1965 and devoted himself to completing what would become his most celebrated book, *Unsafe at Any Speed: The Designed-in Dangers of the American Automobile*. The book was published later that year and quickly became a best-seller. In it, Nader painted a grim picture of motor vehicle injuries and fatalities, noting that 47,700 people were killed in auto accidents in 1964. He made an eloquent appeal for federal car-safety standards that would both prevent accidents from occurring and better protect passengers in the event of an accident. The book also communicated a philosophy regarding public regulation of technology that would cause him to do battle on many other issues. "A great problem of contemporary life," he wrote, "is how to control the power of economic interests which ignore the harmful effects of their applied science and technology." Nader has devoted his life to solving this problem.

Taking some of his inspiration from the CIVIL RIGHTS MOVEMENT, Nader stood up to the

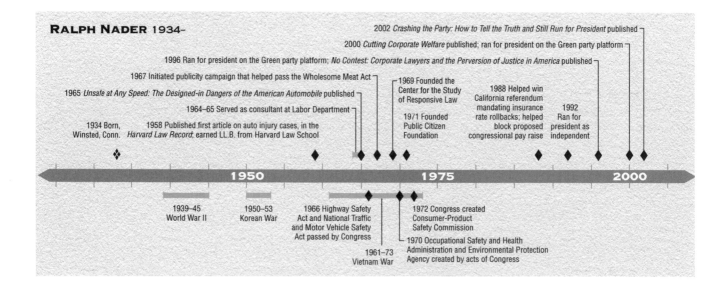

RALPH NADER 1934–

2002 *Crashing the Party: How to Tell the Truth and Still Run for President* published

2000 *Cutting Corporate Welfare* published; ran for president on the Green party platform

1996 Ran for president on the Green party platform; *No Contest: Corporate Lawyers and the Perversion of Justice in America* published

1967 Initiated publicity campaign that helped pass the Wholesome Meat Act

1969 Founded the Center for the Study of Responsive Law

1965 *Unsafe at Any Speed: The Designed-in Dangers of the American Automobile* published

1964–65 Served as consultant at Labor Department

1988 Helped win California referendum mandating insurance rate rollbacks; helped block proposed congressional pay raise

1992 Ran for president as independent

1971 Founded Public Citizen Foundation

1934 Born, Winsted, Conn.

1958 Published first article on auto injury cases, in the *Harvard Law Record*; earned LL.B. from Harvard Law School

1950   1975   2000

1939–45 World War II

1950–53 Korean War

1966 Highway Safety Act and National Traffic and Motor Vehicle Safety Act passed by Congress

1972 Congress created Consumer-Product Safety Commission

1970 Occupational Safety and Health Administration and Environmental Protection Agency created by acts of Congress

1961–73 Vietnam War

most powerful companies in the world. His book targeted the safety problems of the Chevrolet Corvair, a product of the world's largest company, General Motors (GM). He convincingly marshaled evidence that the driver could lose control of the Corvair even when it was moving slowly, thus making it "unsafe at any speed." The Goliath GM did not take kindly to the stones thrown by this David, and the company began a campaign of harassment and intimidation that was intended to abort Nader's efforts. Subsequent congressional committee hearings in 1966 revealed that GM's campaign against Nader had involved harassing phone calls and attempts to lure Nader into compromising situations with women. The company formally apologized before Congress for these tactics.

Many politicians in Washington, D.C., and many Americans were receptive to Nader's ideas. In 1966, in his State of the Union address, President LYNDON B. JOHNSON called for a national highway safety act. Later that year, Congress passed the Highway Safety Act (80 Stat. 731 [23 U.S.C.A. § 401 note]) and the National Traffic and Motor Vehicle Safety Act (80 Stat. 718 [15 U.S.C.A. § 1381 note]). The latter created a new government body, later named the National Highway Traffic Safety Administration, that oversaw the creation of federal safety standards for automobiles and was also empowered to authorize recalls of unsafe vehicles. In subsequent years, these laws and others for which Nader had advocated helped to bring about a marked decrease in traffic fatalities per vehicle mile. As the *Washington Post* exclaimed, on August 30, 1966, "[A] one-man lobby for the public prevailed over the nation's most powerful industry."

Nader's first work in the area of auto safety remains his most famous consumer advocacy. However, he has remained a tireless proponent of consumers' and workers' rights on many different fronts. Shortly after his triumph with auto regulation, Nader initiated a publicity campaign that helped to pass the Wholesome Meat Act, 81 Stat. 584, 19 U.S.C.A. 1306 (1967), which established stricter federal guidelines for meatpacking plants. By the late 1960s, he began to mobilize college students who joined him in his investigations of public policy and the effectiveness of government regulations. These young forces came to be called "Nader's Raiders," and many of them eventually rose to positions of influence in the government and in public pol-

icy organizations. By the mid-1970s, the various groups that Nader had created, including Public Interest Research Groups in many states, were doing research and financing legal action in relation to myriad public policy issues, including tax reform, consumer-product safety, and corporate responsibility.

During Ronald Reagan's presidency in the 1980s, Nader's influence in Washington, D.C., declined, particularly as the Reagan administration dismantled much of the government regulation that Nader had helped to establish. He did not give up his cause, however. In the late 1980s, he was again in the media spotlight, this time through his attempts to lower car-insurance rates in California and to block a proposed congressional pay increase. During the 1980s and 1990s, he also addressed the savings-and-loan bailout problem, well before it became high on the nation's agenda; opposed the use of chlorofluorocarbons (CFCs), which damage the ozone layer; and worked to prevent limitations on damages that consumers may receive from corporations through civil lawsuits.

Nader has run for president three times, including the 1992, 1996, and 2000 elections. In 1992, he entered the race as a write-in candidate. Four years later, he was nominated as a candidate by the GREEN PARTY, which has its strongest support in California. With political activist Winona LaDuke as his running mate, he ran a no-frills campaign, accepting no taxpayer money, eschewing advertising, and often traveling alone. He earned 684,902 votes that year, including two percent of the votes in California.

Nader ran again in the 2000 election. He raised more than $8 million for the campaign, some $30 million less than REFORM PARTY candidate PAT BUCHANAN. Running again with LaDuke, Nader finished third in the election, with 2,882,955 votes, while Buchanan finished with 448,895. Several supporters have urged Nader to run again in the 2004 election.

Nader has written and edited dozens of books during his career, including *Crashing the Party*, which details his run during the 2000 presidential election. Other books include *The Consumer and Corporate Accountability* (1973), *Corporate Power in America* (1973), *Working on the System: A Comprehensive Manual for Citizen Access to Federal Agencies* (1974), *Government Regulation: What Kind of Reform?* (1976), *The Big Boys: Power and Position in American Business* (1986), and *Collision Course: The Truth about Airline Safety* (1994). He also has founded or helped to found a number of consumer and other advocacy organizations.

FURTHER READINGS

Herrnson, Paul S., and John C. Green, eds. 1998. *Multiparty Politics in America*. Lanham, Md.: Rowman & Littlefield.

Martin, Justin. 2002. *Nader: Crusader, Spoiler, Icon*. Cambridge, Mass.: Perseus.

Nader, Ralph. 2002. *Crashing the Party: Taking on the Corporate Government in an Age of Surrender*. New York: Thomas Dunne Books/St. Martin's Press.

———. 2000. *The Ralph Nader Reader*. New York: Seven Stories Press.

———. 1972. *Unsafe at Any Speed: The Designed-in Dangers of the American Automobile*. Rev. ed. New York: Grossman.

Nader, Ralph, and Wesley J. Smith. 1996. *No Contest: Corporate Lawyers and the Perversion of Justice in America*. New York: Random House.

CROSS-REFERENCES

Green Party.

NAKED CONTRACT

From the Latin term nudum pactum, *or "bare promise" An agreement between two parties that is without any legal effect because no consideration has been exchanged between the parties. A naked contract is unenforceable.*

In ROMAN LAW, a nudum pactum was an informal agreement that was not legally enforceable, because it did not fall within the specific classes of agreements that could support a legal action. A pactum could, however, create an exception to or modification of an existing obligation.

NAME

The designation of an individual person or of a firm or corporation. A word or combination of words used to distinguish a person, thing, or class from others.

An individual's name is comprised of a name given at birth, known as the *given name* or *first name*, selected by the parents, and the surname or last name, which identifies the family to which he or she belongs. Ordinarily an individual is not properly identified unless he or she is called or described by this given name in addition to the surname. This rule has significance, among other times, when students are designated in school records and when parties are called or referred to in legal proceedings, including CHILD CUSTODY actions. The general rule is that when identity is certain, a small variance in name, such as that caused by typographical errors, is unimportant.

The method by which an individual can change his or her name is usually prescribed by state statutes and involves filing a certificate in, or making an application to, a court. Whether or not a name change will be granted is ordinarily a matter of judicial discretion.

In recent years, some married women have begun to depart from the traditional practice of taking their husband's surname upon marriage. Instead they retain their birth names, the surnames possessed before marriage. While some states subscribe to the rule that a woman's legal name is her husband's surname, others hold that an individual can be known by whatever name he or she desires as long as such designation is used consistently and in the absence of a fraudulent purpose. A number of states have specifically provided that a wife is not required to use her husband's surname, or that she can use it in her personal life while continuing to use her birth name in her profession.

NAPOLEONIC CODE

The first modern organized body of law governing France, also known as the Code Napoleon or Code Civil, enacted by Napoléon I in 1804.

In 1800, Napoléon I appointed a commission of four persons to undertake the task of compiling the Napoleonic Code. Their efforts, along with those of J. J. Cambacérès, were instrumental in the preparation of the final draft. The Napoleonic Code assimilated the private law of France, which was the law governing transactions and relationships between individuals. The Code, which is regarded by some commentators as the first modern counterpart to ROMAN LAW, is currently in effect in France in an amended form.

The Napoleonic Code is a revised version of the Roman law or CIVIL LAW, which predominated in Europe, with numerous French modifications, some of which were based on the Germanic law that had been in effect in northern France. The code draws upon the Institutes of the Roman Corpus Juris Civilis for its categories of the civil law: property rights, such as licenses; the acquisition of property, such as trusts; and personal status, such as legitimacy of birth.

Napoléon applied the code to the territories he governed—namely, some of the German states, the low countries, and northern Italy. It was extremely influential in Spain and, eventually, in Latin America as well as in all other European nations except England, where the COMMON LAW prevailed. It was the harbinger, in France and abroad, of codifications of other areas of law, such as CRIMINAL LAW, CIVIL PROCEDURE, and COMMERCIAL LAW. The Napoleonic Code served as the prototype for subsequent codes during the nineteenth century in twenty-four countries; the province of Québec and the state of Louisiana have derived a substantial portion of their laws from it. Napoléon also promulgated four other codes: the Code of Civil Procedure (1807), the COMMERCIAL CODE (1808), the Code of Criminal Procedure (1811), and the Penal Code (1811).

NARAL PRO-CHOICE AMERICA

NARAL Pro-Choice America, founded in 1969 as the National Abortion and Reproductive Rights Action League, is a nonprofit organization that was formed primarily to maintain a woman's legal right to have an abortion. The mission of NARAL, however, has broadened to include supporting policies that enable women and men to make responsible decisions about sexuality, contraception, pregnancy, childbirth, and abortion. NARAL is comprised of a network of 35 state affiliates and has 500,000 members. It has proven to be an effective organization, promoting pro-choice candidates for state and federal offices and LOBBYING for pro-choice legislation.

Since the U.S. Supreme Court legalized abortion in ROE V. WADE, 410 U.S. 113, 93 S. Ct. 705, 35 L. Ed. 2d 147 (1973), opponents of abortion have sought to overturn or limit this decision. NARAL has vigorously defended *Roe* but has also encouraged better sex education and the use of BIRTH CONTROL to make abortion less often necessary. Through NARAL Pro-Choice America PAC, its POLITICAL ACTION COMMITTEE, NARAL has been a driving force behind the election of many pro-choice candidates. NARAL Pro-Choice America PAC mounts campaigns to elect pro-choice candidates and defeat candidates opposed to legalized abortion, using paid advertising and get-out-the-vote efforts.

The NARAL Pro-Choice America Foundation, a charitable organization founded in 1977, supports research and legal work, publishes substantive policy reports, mounts public education campaigns and other communications projects, and provides leadership training for grassroots activists. The NARAL Foundation and NARAL employ a computerized state-by-state database, NARAL*STAR (State Tracking of Abortion Rights), which provides up-to-the-minute information for NARAL staff, affiliates, policy makers, media, and coalition partners on state laws related to reproductive rights, pending legislation, state constitutions, and state executive branches.

NARAL and the NARAL Foundation regularly publish *Who Decides? A State-by-State Review of Abortion Rights,* a compilation of abortion-related information in each state, including the position on choice of elected officials, summaries of selected statutes and regulations, and recent legislative activity.

NARAL worked with the President BILL CLINTON administration to reverse policies of the RONALD REAGAN and GEORGE H.W. BUSH presidential administrations dealing with abortion. It helped remove bans on the testing of RU-486 (a nonsurgical abortion method), the use of fetal tissue in scientific research, and the provision of abortion services at military hospitals. NARAL also played a major role in the passage of the Freedom of Access to Clinic Entrances Act, which places certain restrictions on protestors' ability to obstruct or hinder persons seeking access to abortion services. Since 1996, when Congress enacted a bill banning the practice of partial-birth ABORTIONS, NARAL has been on the defensive. Though President Bill Clinton vetoed the bill, many states have since passed laws banning the procedure, and Congress continues to debate the issue.

The election of GEORGE W. BUSH as president in 2000 and the gain of Republican seats in both the House and Senate in 2002 strengthened the position of abortion opponents and gave increased urgency to the NARAL pro-choice mission. The organization continues to fight for increased access to federal funding of abortions for poor women, federal employees, and women in the military. It has mounted vigorous campaigns opposing President Bush's judicial nominees who are opposed to abortion. The organization also launched "Generation Pro-Choice," a Web site aimed at educating college students and younger women about their reproductive rights and encouraging them to become pro-choice advocates.

FURTHER READINGS

NARAL. Available online at <www.naral.org> (accessed July 28, 2003).

CROSS-REFERENCES
Abortion; Fetal Rights; Women's Rights.

NARCOTICS ACTS

Background

Control over, and prevention of, the distribution and usage of narcotic drugs has been a major priority of the federal government and the various state governments since the early part of the twentieth century. Notwithstanding these efforts, statistics on the use of narcotics in the United States remain startling. According to statistics from the U.S. DRUG ENFORCEMENT ADMINISTRATION, between 10,000 and 24,000 metric tons of marijuana were available on American streets. This is in addition to large quantities of other forms of narcotics, including: 260–270 metric tons of cocaine, 110–140 metric tons of methamphetamine, and 13–18 metric tons of heroin.

According to the National Household Drug Survey on Drug Abuse, conducted by the SUBSTANCE ABUSE AND MENTAL HEALTH SERVICES ADMINISTRATION, 55.6 percent of respondents between the ages of 18 and 25 said that they had used illicit drugs. This compares to 53.3 percent of respondents between the ages of 26 and 34, and 28.4 percent of respondents between the ages of 12 and 17. The National Institute on Drug Abuse's 2002 Monitoring the Future Study found that 53 percent of high-school seniors claimed to have used narcotics, including 41 percent who said that they had used drugs in the past year, and 25.4 percent who said that they had used drugs in the past month.

The efforts of law enforcement officers have had some effect on the use and transfer of narcotics in the past, although these efforts have been costly. In 2001, federal agents seized approximately 1,215 metric tons of marijuana, 106 metric tons of cocaine, 3.6 metric tons of methamphetamine, and 2.5 metric tons of heroin. The costs to society in enforcing narcotics laws have continued to increase. In 1992, the total estimated costs to society of narcotics use was $102 billion. By 2000, this number had grown to $160 billion, including almost $15 billion in HEALTH CARE costs.

Development of Federal Narcotics Laws

During the Civil War, forms of opiates were considered "miracle" drugs that could be used as anesthetics when a doctor performed surgery. Without opiates, surgeries during that period, which often consisted of amputations, involved a group of men holding down a patient while a doctor sawed off the limb of a patient. By the 1870s, opiates, cocaine and other drugs were used in a variety of medical concoctions, leading to increases in addictions.

The use of opium, cocaine, and other drugs continued through most of the nineteenth century. The type of addiction during that time that caused the most concern was alcoholism, and because the causes of addiction and the dangers of narcotics were both unknown, doctors recommended morphine and heroin as remedies for addiction to alcohol. Cocaine was also used in tonics, such as the mixture that became known as Coca-Cola. Moreover, patients, including those of Sigmund Freud, were treated for depression with cocaine.

Congress enacted the PURE FOOD AND DRUG ACT OF 1906, ch. 3915, 34 Stat. 768, which formed the FOOD AND DRUG ADMINISTRATION (FDA) and gave it the power to regulate food and drugs. Drug addiction began to drop as a result of early FDA regulations. Eight years later, Congress enacted the Harrison Tax Act, ch. 1, 38 Stat. 789, which prohibited the dispensation and distribution of narcotic drugs. In 1922, Congress enacted the Narcotics Drug Import and Export Act, ch. 202, 42 Stat. 596, which prohibited importation and use of opium and other narcotics except for medical purposes.

Between 1922 and 1970, Congress enacted several additional laws that were designed to curb narcotics importation, trade, and use. Drugs such as marijuana and heroin were prohibited, as was the cultivation of opium poppies. The Narcotic Control Act of 1956, ch. 629, 70 Stat. 567 criminalized the transport of narcotics, including marijuana. Some legislation began to focus upon rehabilitation of narcotics addicts. For example, the Narcotic Addict Rehabilitation Act of 1966, Pub. L. No. 89-793, 80 Stat. 1438, provided for treatment of addicts as an alternative to incarceration.

Comprehensive Drug Abuse and Control Act

By the late 1960s, illicit drug use in the United States had become widespread. Moreover, use of narcotics became more open, causing concerns among many communities, law enforcement personnel, and legislators. Existing narcotics laws were failing to curb the usage of narcotics drugs. For example, about half of the amphetamines and barbiturates produced legally in the United States were being distributed through illegal means.

In response to these problems, Congress in 1970 enacted the Controlled Substances Act (CSA) as Title II of the Comprehensive Drug Abuse Prevention and Control Act, Pub. L. No. 91-513, 84 Stat. 1242. The CSA developed a complex regulatory system designed to control the distribution of drugs. It established five schedules of drugs, with each schedule representing the degree with which the drug is likely to be abused and the level of accepted medical use. Most narcotics, such as marijuana, cocaine, and heroin, fall within Schedule I, which includes drugs with high potential for abuse and with no accepted medical use.

The CSA has been amended dozens of times since is original enactment. In 1974, Congress enacted the Narcotic Addict Treatment Act of 1974, Pub. L. No. 93-281, 88 Stat. 124, which allows practitioners to dispense narcotics for detoxification and similar purposes. Other amendments to the CSA have established federally funded prevention and treatment programs, including drug-awareness education programs.

Anti-Drug Acts and National Drug Control Policy

Despite Congress' efforts to strengthen narcotics laws through the CSA, use and abuse of narcotics remained a major national problem in the 1980s. By 1984, narcotics were a part of an $80 million industry in the United States, and use of illicit drugs had reached epidemic proportions according to findings by Congress. Law enforcement officers were able to interdict only five to 15 percent of the drugs entering into the country. Moreover, statistics showed a high correlation between drug use and criminal activities. For example, about 90 percent of heroin users relied upon crime to fund their habit.

The National Narcotics Act of 1984, Pub. L. No. 98-473, 98 Stat. 2168 established the National Drug Enforcement Policy Board to coordinate efforts among federal agencies to combat narcotics trade and for other programs. Four years later, Congress enacted the National Narcotics Leadership Act of 1988 as Subtitle A of the Anti-Drug Abuse Act of 1988, Pub. L. No. 100-690, 102 Stat. 4181, which replaced the board with the OFFICE OF NATIONAL DRUG CONTROL POLICY. This office continues to imple-

ment the country's policies regarding education about the dangers of drug abuse as well as efforts to stifle the drug trade. The Office of National Drug Control Policy and the U.S. Drug Enforcement Administration are the two main federal agencies that are responsible for addressing narcotics issues in the United States.

State Narcotics Acts

Many states have enacted statutes to address narcotics trade and usage within their borders. The vast majority of states adopted the Uniform Narcotics Drug Act, which was first approved by the COMMISSIONERS ON UNIFORM LAWS and other organizations in 1930. That act and other state laws limited the production of marijuana and generally prohibited more dangerous drugs, including cocaine and heroin. In 1970, the same year that Congress approved the federal Controlled Substances Act, the Commissioners approved the Uniform Controlled Substances Act. This uniform law was eventually approved by 46 states. Although it was updated in 1990 and 1994, few states adopted the amended version.

FURTHER READINGS

Jonas, Stephen. 1990. "Solving the Drug Problem: A Public Health Approach to the Reduction of the Use and Abuse of Both Legal and Illegal Recreational Drugs." *Hofstra Law Review* 751.

U.S. Department of Justice, Drug Enforcement Administration. 2003. *Drugs of Abuse.* Washington, D.C.: U.S. Government Printing Office.

CROSS-REFERENCES

Drugs and Narcotics; Office of National Drug Control Policy.

NATION OF ISLAM

The Nation of Islam (NOI) is a religious and political organization whose origins are somewhat mysterious. Wallace D. Fard, later known as Master Wallace Fard Muhammad, established the NOI in Detroit during the 1930s. Fard Muhammad, a traveling salesman who sold African silks and advocated self-sufficiency and independence for African Americans, taught Elijah Poole the history of what Fard Muhammad called the Lost-Found Nation of Islam—descendants of the tribe of Shabazz from the Lost Nation in Asia. Fard Muhammad taught Poole in part that Mr. Yacub, a black mad scientist, created what was called the devil race—the white race—approximately six thousand years ago, and that the devil race would rule the world for the next six thousand years.

Elijah Poole was born in Sandersville, Georgia in 1897. His father, who was a Baptist preacher, had been a slave. At the age of twenty-six, Poole moved to Detroit with his family. In 1930 in Detroit, he met W. D. Fard, the founder of the Lost-Found Nation of Islam. When Fard disappeared in 1934, Poole—then known as Elijah Muhammad—moved to Chicago, where he organized his own following and established the headquarters of the Nation of Islam. Elijah Muhammad remained the spiritual and organizational leader of the NOI from 1934 until his death in 1975. During that time, the NOI became recognized as a black nationalist religious organization that advocated racial separatism and self-sufficiency for African Americans. Often called Black Muslims, the NOI's members are required to adhere to a strict moral and disciplinary code. Men members typically wear suits and ties, and women members are required to wear modest clothing, typically white gowns or saris. The NOI's teachings forbid the eating of pork and the consumption of alcohol or tobacco.

In the early 1950s and 1960s, the NOI called for racial separatism in the United States, and at times protested against police brutality and filed suit against various police departments in response to alleged police brutality. It also frequently recruited members in large cities and prisons. In 1947, Malcolm Little—who later became Malcolm X—converted to Islam and joined the NOI while incarcerated in a Massachusetts prison. As a national minister and spokesman for the NOI, MALCOLM X was a fiery speaker and proponent of the organization's concerns. However, during the early 1960s, ideological differences developed between Malcolm X and Elijah Muhammad, and in 1964, Malcolm X formally left the NOI.

Shortly after Elijah Muhammad's death in 1975, his son Warith Deen Muhammad renounced black separatism and the origins of Black Muslims and established the World Community of Al-Islam in the West, later called the American Muslim Mission. NOI minister Louis X, who later became Louis Farrakhan, initially supported Warith Muhammad but soon reestablished the NOI. Other organizations and factions also split off from the original NOI, including the more militant Lost-Found Nation of Islam, which publishes the weekly newspaper *Muhammad Speaks*. In the mid-1990s, Farrakhan's organization was generally known as the NOI.

Like Malcolm X, Farrakhan is a fiery orator and skilled leader. Yet, he and the NOI have been criticized for anti-Semitic and antiwhite statements as well as conspiracy theories concerning Jewish American business leaders. Khalid Muhammad, a former NOI spokesman, was especially known for the excoriating statements and speeches he gave at many U.S. colleges in the late 1980s and early 1990s. Although the NOI later expelled Khalid Muhammad, his speeches contributed to a continuing debate as to whether so-called hate speech should be punished or regulated by U.S. universities.

During the early and mid-1990s, Farrakhan and the NOI appeared to be shifting their political focus away from black separatism and toward a more universalist or mainstream approach. The NOI also has begun to develop various major business ventures, including the operation of a restaurant in a poor neighborhood on Chicago's South Side. Its security arm—the Fruit of Islam—has been involved in providing security for housing projects in Baltimore, Chicago, and Washington, D.C., under contracts with public agencies such as the Chicago Housing Authority. In October 1995, the NOI and Farrakhan were instrumental in organizing the Million Man March, bringing together hundreds of thousands of African American men in Washington, D.C.

FURTHER READINGS

Carson, Clayborne. 1991. *Malcolm X: The FBI File*. New York: Carroll & Graf.

Karim, Benjamin, with Peter Skutches, and David Gallen. 1992. *Remembering Malcolm: The Story of Malcolm X from Inside the Muslim Mosque*. New York: Carroll & Graf.

Lee, Martha F. 1996. *The Nation of Islam: An American Millenarian Movement*. Syracuse, N.Y.: Syracuse Univ. Press.

Tsoukalas, Steven. 2001. *The Nation of Islam: Understanding the "Black Muslims."* Phillipsburg, N.J.: P & R.

CROSS-REFERENCES

Hate Crime; Civil Rights Movement.

NATIONAL ASSOCIATION OF BROADCASTERS

The National Association of Broadcasters (NAB) is comprised of representatives of radio and television stations and networks. The NAB, which has a membership of 7,500, seeks to ensure the viability, strength, and success of free over-the-air broadcasters (companies that do not charge customers for service, as do cable and satellite television operators). It serves as an information resource to the industry, and it also lobbies the FEDERAL COMMUNICATIONS COMMISSION (FCC) for regulations favorable to the radio and television industry. The NAB is headquartered in Washington, D.C., with a staff of approximately 165 employees.

The organization was founded in 1922, when radio broadcasting was in its infancy. Founded as the National Association of Radio Broadcasters, it changed its name to the National Association of Radio and Television Broadcasters in 1951, when it absorbed the Television Broadcasters Association. In 1958 it changed its name to the National Association of Broadcasters. In 1985 it absorbed the Daytime Broadcasters Association, and in 1986 it absorbed the National Radio Broadcasters Association.

The NAB seeks to maintain a favorable legal, governmental, and technological climate for free over-the-air broadcasting. Its legal and regulatory department represents broadcasters before the FCC and other federal agencies, as well as before courts and other regulatory bodies. This department provides legal guidance to NAB members through "counsel memos," legal memoranda that identify and explain current legal issues for broadcasters.

The NAB opposes legislation that would require broadcasters to provide free air time to political candidates. In addition, it is opposed to discounting the commercial rates stations charge to candidates, contending that broadcasters now provide candidates with heavily discounted air time.

Because the NAB represents the interests of free over-the-air broadcasters, it has sought to protect the industry from the inroads made by cable and satellite television. For example, as TV viewers in rural areas began to buy home satellite equipment, Congress passed laws in 1988 and 1994, with the encouragement of the NAB, that restrict access to network programming sent by satellite only to those viewers who live outside the local market of over-the-air network affiliates. By 1997 satellite operators and the NAB were in court, because the NAB sought to end the practice of some operators who flout the law and provide network signals to satellite subscribers who are already served by their local network affiliates.

Aside from LOBBYING and bringing legal actions, the NAB provides members with other benefits. Its research library contains ten thousand volumes, and its staff includes experts in science and technology and research and planning. For its members, the NAB publishes a monthly newsletter, *NAB World*, as well as the weekly publications *RadioWeek* and *TV Today*. The NAB annual spring convention is the world's largest showcase for broadcast, postproduction multimedia and TELECOMMUNICATIONS hardware, software, and services. The convention draws more than 100,000 attendees.

In order to educate citizens in the United States about the principles of free speech and other topics concerning the industry, the NAB started the NAB Education Foundation. The foundation conducts research and education activities on issues such as FIRST AMENDMENT rights relating to program content, editorial opinions, and commercial speech. The foundation also provides economic data regarding advertiser-supported broadcasting, examines the impact of new technologies on the industry and the public, and seeks to train, with an emphasis on diversity, new leaders in the broadcasting field.

FURTHER READINGS

National Association of Broadcasters. Available online at <www.nab.org> (accessed July 28, 2003).

CROSS-REFERENCES

Broadcasting; Telecommunications; Television.

NATIONAL ASSOCIATION OF MANUFACTURERS

The National Association of Manufacturers (NAM) is the oldest and largest broad-based industrial trade association in the United States. NAM seeks to enhance the competitiveness of manufacturers by LOBBYING for legislation and regulations conducive to U.S. economic growth and to increase understanding among policy makers, the media, and the general public about the importance of manufacturing to U.S. economic strength. NAM is comprised of more than 14,000 member companies and subsidiaries of which more than 80 percent are small manufactures, plus 350 member associations in all 50 states. NAM member companies and affiliated associations produce about 85 percent of U.S. manufactured goods and employ more than 18 million persons. NAM, which has 175 professional and support staff, is headquartered in Washington, D.C., with ten regional offices located across the United States.

NAM was founded in Cincinnati, Ohio, in 1895, in the midst of a economic recession. Many major manufacturers saw a need to find new markets for their products in other countries. At its organizing convention, NAM adopted a number of objectives, including the retention and supply of home markets with U.S. products, extension of foreign trade, development of reciprocal trade relations between the United States and foreign governments, rehabilitation of the U.S. Merchant Marine, construction of a canal in Central America, and improvement and extension of U.S. waterways.

NAM soon became a dominant influence in U.S. economic and political affairs. It lobbied for higher tariffs on imported goods and for the creation of the U.S. DEPARTMENT OF COMMERCE in 1903, and it called for states to enact workers' compensation laws. During the 1930s, NAM vigorously opposed many of President FRANKLIN D. ROOSEVELT'S NEW DEAL proposals. In the 1940s and 1950s, it lobbied for the passage of federal laws restricting the power and internal governance of LABOR UNIONS.

In the 1990s, NAM undertook new initiatives. The Manufacturing Institute was established to provide information on modern industry. This organization distributes monthly mailings to Congress, conducts research on technology and exports, produces research reports, commissions public opinion polls, and disperses books and educational CD-ROMs to schools.

NAM and the Manufacturing Institute joined forces in the 1990s with key partners in the Partnership for a Smarter Workforce and other efforts to identify the best ways to train employees. In 1997 the institute established the Center for Workforce Success and an awards program for outstanding manufacturing workers. In addition, NAM has lobbied for increased accountability and results in taxpayer-funded training programs.

NAM has increased its lobbying on international economic issues. The association played a key role in a number of trade policy victories during the 1990s, including the NORTH AMERICAN FREE TRADE AGREEMENT (NAFTA) and the certification of China as a most favored nation. NAM also lobbied vigorously for a national campaign to facilitate exports.

In response to a decline in jobs and a decrease in the number of small manufacturing companies brought on by a weakening economy in the early 2000s, NAM established its "Strategy for Growth and Manufacturing Renewal" to focus attention on the issues affecting manufacturing. These issues include changes to tax and trade policies, energy-related concerns, asbestos litigation, innovations to technology, and development of worker skills.

FURTHER READINGS

National Association of Manufacturers. Available online at <www.nam.org> (accessed July 28, 2003).

CROSS-REFERENCES

Manufactures.

NATIONAL ASSOCIATION OF REALTORS

The National Association of Realtors (NAR) is made up of residential and commercial realtors who are brokers, salespeople, property managers, appraisers, and counselors, and others working in the real estate industry. NAR began as the National Association of Real Estate Exchanges in 1908 with a membership of 120. In 2003 its membership numbered over 840,000, making it the world's largest professional association. Members belong to one or more of 1,700 local real estate associations and boards and 54 state and territory associations. NAR headquarters are in Washington, D.C.

NAR provides a national facility for professional development, research, and exchange of information among its members, the public, and government. More importantly, it plays an influential role in shaping public policies at the local, state, and national level that affect real property. Through its legislative and LOBBYING efforts, NAR seeks to protect the real estate industry from what it considers burdensome legislative and regulatory changes and to advocate for legislative and regulatory changes that enhance the conduct of real estate business. At the national level, NAR analyzes federal issues and lobbies Congress and regulatory agencies.

The 1998 NAR legislative agenda included rewriting federal law that governs the disclosure of closing costs at the time a real estate purchase is completed. In addition, NAR supports federal legislation that would give persons more rights to contest a government "taking" their property through the power of EMINENT DOMAIN.

NAR also participates in the political process through its Realtor Political Action Committee (RPAC). This committee, currently one of the largest trade association PACs, contributes campaign funds to federal political candidates and encourages members to volunteer for candidates. The committee also educates voters on issues that affect home ownership and real estate.

Apart from political involvement, NAR seeks to make its viewpoint known through legal advocacy. The NAR Legal Action Committee provides financial support to legal cases that seek establish a favorable precedent for real estate brokerage or that seek to preserve the rights to own, use, and transfer real property. The NAR also participates in lawsuits involving real estate by filing AMICUS CURIAE (friend of the court) briefs in cases that will set legal precedent.

The NAR has established a code of ethics to enhance the professionalism of its members. In addition, it has created NAR sections, professional institutes, societies, and counsels that allow members to communicate with others in their particular real estate specialty. These specialty groups include Counselors of Real Estate, the Commercial Investment Real Estate Institute, the Institute of Real Estate Management, the Real Estate Brokerage Managers Council, the Residential Sales Council, the Real Estate Buyers Agent Council, and the Appraisal Section. Education and certification in these specializations enable members to receive professional designations, identifying them as highly qualified specialists to business associates and the public.

In 1998 NAR launched a national consumer education initiative called the "Public Awareness Campaign" to inform the public about the significant role played by realtors in real estate transactions. Also, in 1998 NAR created the National Realtors Database System (NRDS), an INTERNET database that gave members the opportunity to update their own records online. In 1997 the NAR established REALTOR.com, its official Internet site. In 2003 REALTOR.com featured more than 1.5 million property listings that were viewed by millions of consumers.

FURTHER READINGS

National Association of Realtors. Available online at <www.realtor.org> (accessed July 28, 2003).

CROSS-REFERENCES

Real Estate; Real Property.

NATIONAL CHARACTER OF AIRCRAFT

The nationality of an aircraft is determined by the state in which the aircraft is registered. This principle was recognized by state practice soon after air flight proved feasible and was incorporated into the Convention on International Civil Aviation of December 7, 1944 (Chicago Convention). Applying the same concept of nationality to aircraft as is applied to maritime vessels provides a basis for a state to maintain jurisdiction over an aircraft while it is flying through international airspace and establishes the power of the state to regulate what happens on board the aircraft regardless of its location. Under the Chicago Convention, contracting states register aircraft according to their domestic laws. When it registers an aircraft, the state must also certify that the craft is airworthy and has appropriate markings identifying the nationality and registration of the aircraft.

CROSS-REFERENCES

Airlines.

NATIONAL COOPERATIVE BANK

The National Consumer Cooperative Bank (NCCB) was created and chartered by the National Consumer Cooperative Bank Act (92 Stat. 499, 12 U.S.C.A. 3001), enacted on August 20, 1978. The bank is directed by the act to encourage the development of new and existing cooperatives. The bank provides specialized credit and technical assistance to eligible cooperatives that provide goods, services, housing, and other facilities to their members as ultimate consumers. The bank is itself structured as a cooperative financial institution. Under its congressional charter, the bank is directed to make loans and offer its services throughout the United States, its territories and possessions, and the Commonwealth of Puerto Rico.

The act provided that the federal government would contribute the initial capitalization of the bank through the purchase of the bank's Class A stock. All 15 members of the bank's board of directors are appointed by the president of the United States. The act contemplated that the number of president-appointed directors was to decrease gradually as borrowers and cooperatives eligible to borrow purchased Class B and Class C stock in the bank.

In 1981 the act was amended by Title III, subtitle C, of the Omnibus Budget Reconciliation Act of 1981 (95 Stat. 433). The 1981 act converted the federal government's initial capitalization of the bank, formerly represented by Class A stock, into Class A capital notes, held by the secretary of the treasury. The act further mandated that after the Final Government Equity Redemption Date (FGERD), as defined by the National Consumer Cooperative Bank Act, the bank's Class B and C stockholders would elect 12 of the bank's 15 directors. The remaining three were to be appointed by the president with the advice and the consent of the Senate. The president is directed by the act, as amended, to select one member from among proprietors of small business concerns, one member from among the officers of the agencies and departments of the United States, and one member from among persons having extensive experience in the cooperative field representing low-income eligible cooperatives.

The bank is operated by a board of directors under bylaws and policies it prescribes consistent with the National Consumer Cooperative Bank Act.

The bank's credit and technical assistance to cooperatives is intended to improve the quality and availability of goods and services to consumers. The bank makes loans to eligible cooperatives at prevailing market interest rates.

The bank encourages broad-based ownership, control, and active participation by members in eligible cooperatives. The bank also seeks to maintain broad-based control of the bank by its voting stockholders.

The National Consumer Cooperative Bank Act established the Office of Self-Help Development and Technical Assistance within the bank. Cooperatives that are eligible to receive assistance from the bank may be eligible to qualify for financial and technical assistance from the office. The office may provide financial assistance to newly developed or established cooperatives that cannot qualify for a bank loan, or when the membership of the cooperative consists substantially of low-income persons or it provides services to low-income persons.

The Omnibus Budget Reconciliation Act of 1981 directed that as soon as practical after the FGERD, the board of directors of the bank would establish a nonprofit corporation under the laws of the District of Columbia to succeed the office and to carry out the functions of the office. That nonprofit corporation, the Consumer Cooperative Development Corporation, was incorporated on December 30, 1982.

In 1985, the NCCB became a private financial institution and changed its name to National Cooperative Bank (NCB). At the same time, the Consumer Cooperative Development Corporation became the NCB Development Corporation (NCBDC). In 1986 the NCB registered with the SECURITIES AND EXCHANGE COMMISSION and performed its first private placement. The NCB, in 1995, launched the Community Association Loan Program that provided financing for condominium, townhouse, and other owner associations. By 2000, the NCB had provided more than $6 billion in financing to homes, school facilities, assisted living units, and other community developments.

FURTHER READINGS

National Cooperative Bank. Available online at <www.ncb.coop> (accessed July 28, 2003).

U.S. Government Manual Website. Available online at <www.gpoaccess.gov/gmanual> (accessed November 10, 2003).

CROSS-REFERENCES

Housing and Urban Development Department.

NATIONAL COUNCIL OF LA RAZA

The National Council of La Raza (NCLR) is the largest Hispanic advocacy organization in the United States. The NCLR was founded in 1968 as a nonpartisan nonprofit organization dedicated to reducing discrimination and poverty and to improving the lives and economic opportunities of Hispanic Americans. The NCLR has over 270 formal affiliates serving 40 states, the District of Columbia, and Puerto Rico. These affiliates, along with a nationwide network of more than 30,000 groups and individuals, provides information and services to more than 3.5 million Hispanics annually.

Headquartered in Washington, D.C., the NCLR has field offices in Chicago, Los Angeles, Phoenix, San Antonio, and San Juan, Puerto Rico. These offices focus on program operations, management, and governance, as well as resource development. The NCLR Washington, D.C.-based Policy Analysis Center is a major Hispanic "think tank" that is known for its political independence, its advocacy expertise, and its extensive analysis of issues affecting Hispanics nationwide. The NCLR has given public testimony and commentary on topics concerning CIVIL RIGHTS, tax policy, free trade, affordable housing, employment and training, and HEALTH CARE. The organization's Census Information Center (CIC) functions as a national clearinghouse for census data and other information regarding Hispanics in the United States.

In addition to implementing "big picture" strategies such as policy research and analysis, the NCLR also concentrates its efforts on detailed "capacity-building" tactics aimed at working with local community-based Hispanic groups in both urban and rural areas throughout the United States and its territories. The NCLR has long espoused a philosophy of self-help and collaboration. Unlike many advocacy organizations that provide help only to their own local chapters, the NCLR gives resources and assistance to other local Hispanic organizations, especially those that aid low-income and disadvantaged Hispanics. The organization also sponsors "issue networks" that provide information and assistance on such issues as HIV/AIDS, health, education and leadership.

In order to more closely relate the national policy aspects of its work with the grassroots views of its constituents, the NCLR has also established "local policy centers" at six of its community-based affiliates. In addition, the NCLR works with other major groups such as the LEAGUE OF UNITED LATIN AMERICAN CITIZENS (LULAC), the oldest Hispanic advocacy organization in the United States, and the Mexican American Legal Defense and Education Fund (MALDEF), which was founded in 1968 as the legal arm of LULAC.

The NCLR works closely with the private sector and has established a Corporate Board of Advisors consisting of senior executives and staff from 25 major corporations. The advisory board provides information and assistance to the NCLR on numerous programs and projects, from education and health initiatives to public relations and fund-raising. The NCLR has broad-based financial support. The organization receives more than two-thirds of its funding from corporations and foundations; the rest comes from government sources.

In all of its efforts, the NCLR focuses on cooperation and collaboration. NCLR staff work with various issue-based coalitions and associations on topics ranging from energy conservation to WELFARE reform. The NCLR also undertakes joint projects with other major national organizations such as the NATIONAL URBAN LEAGUE and the NAACP.

The NCLR authors major reports, for example, the 1995 report that analyzed the effect of computer verification procedures, the use of identification cards, and immigration policies on Hispanic Americans; a 1996 report on the impact of federal tax policy on Hispanic working families; and a 1998 statistical report on the educational status of Hispanics. It also authors numerous publications and publishes a quarterly newsletter, *Agenda*.

Because the Hispanic American population consists of a diverse number of groups including Mexican Americans, Chicanos, and Latin Americans, the need for an organization that can recognize the diversity and also still provide unity of purpose is paramount. NCLR President Raul Yzaguirre, who joined the NCLR in 1974, had in 2003 led the organization for more than 25 years. The NCLR has a 33-member board of directors and its bylaws require that board members be geographically diverse and that they represent various nationality groups. According to the information published in the 2000 U.S. Census, Hispanics have surpassed African Americans as the largest ethnic group in the United States. Between immigration and native births, the Hispanic population increased 58 percent in the 1990s to 35.3 million in 2000. In light of these demographic changes, the NCLR constituency plays a larger role in U.S. politics and economics.

FURTHER READINGS

National Council of La Raza. Available online at <www.nclr.org> (accessed July 28, 2003).

Olmos, Edward James, ed. 1999. *Americanos: Latino Life in the United States.* Boston: Little Brown.

Portes, Alejandro. 2001. *Legacies: The Story of the Immigrant Second Generation.* Berkeley: Univ. of California Press.

Suro, Roberto. 1998. *Strangers Among Us: How Latino Immigration is Transforming America.* New York: Knopf.

CROSS-REFERENCES

Civil Rights Acts; Discrimination; Equal Protection; Mexico and the United States.

NATIONAL CREDIT UNION ADMINISTRATION

The National Credit Union Administration (NCUA) is responsible for chartering, insuring, supervising, and examining federal credit unions (FCUs) and for administering the National Credit Union Share Insurance Fund. The NCUA also manages the Central Liquidity Facility, a mixed-ownership government corporation, the purpose of which is to supply emergency loans to member credit unions.

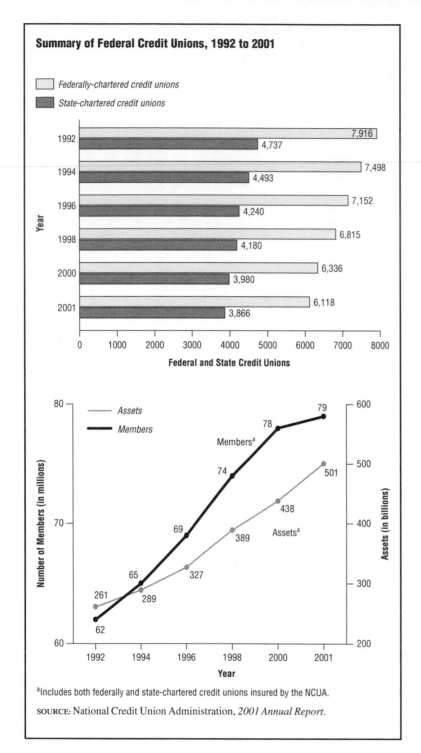

Summary of Federal Credit Unions, 1992 to 2001

☐ Federally-chartered credit unions
■ State-chartered credit unions

Year	Federally-chartered	State-chartered
1992	7,916	4,737
1994	7,498	4,493
1996	7,152	4,240
1998	6,815	4,180
2000	6,336	3,980
2001	6,118	3,866

Federal and State Credit Unions

— Assets
— Members

Members[a]
Number of Members (in millions): 62, 65, 69, 74, 78, 79
Assets[a] (in billions): 261, 289, 327, 389, 438, 501

Year: 1992, 1994, 1996, 1998, 2000, 2001

[a]Includes both federally and state-chartered credit unions insured by the NCUA.

SOURCE: National Credit Union Administration, *2001 Annual Report*.

A credit union (CU) is a financial cooperative that aids its members by improving their economic situation through encouraging thrift among its members and providing them with a source of credit for provident purposes at reasonable rates of interest. Federal CUs serve occupational, associational, and residential groups, thus benefiting a broad range of citizens throughout the country.

The NCUA was established by an act of March 10, 1970 (84 Stat. 49, 12 U.S.C.A. 1752) and reorganized by an act of November 10, 1978 (92 Stat. 3641, 12 U.S.C.A. 226 note), as an independent agency in the EXECUTIVE BRANCH of the federal government. The NCUA regulates and insures all FCUs and insures state-chartered CUs that apply for and qualify for share insurance. As of 2003, total assets of federally chartered CUs exceeded $172 billion, and the assets of all federally insured state-chartered CUs exceeded $104 billion.

Programs and Activities

The NCUA grants FCU charters to groups sharing a common bond of occupation or association or to groups within a well-defined neighborhood, community, or rural district. A preliminary investigation is made to determine if certain minimum standards are met before granting a federal charter.

Supervisory activities are carried out through examiner contacts and through periodic policy and regulatory releases from the administration. The administration also maintains an early warning system designed to identify emerging problems as well as to monitor operations between examinations.

The administration conducts periodic examinations of federal credit unions to determine their solvency and compliance with laws and regulations and to assist credit union management in improving operations.

The act of October 19, 1970 (84 Stat. 994, 12 U.S.C.A. 1781 et seq.) provides for a program of share insurance. The insurance is mandatory for federal credit unions and optional for state-chartered credit unions that meet NCUA standards. Credit union members' accounts are insured up to $100,000. The National Credit Union Share Insurance Fund charges each insured credit union a premium of one-twelfth of 1 percent of the total member accounts (shares) outstanding at the end of the preceding calendar year.

High interest rates and insurance losses in the 1980s brought the insurance fund close to insolvency. In 1985, Congress approved a plan that enabled the credit unions to recapitalize the fund. The 1990s were marked by major changes including deregulation, expanded eligibility for membership, mergers, and an increase in member services. In 2001 the NCUA chartered, regulated, and/or insured more than 10,000 credit unions across the United States.

FURTHER READINGS

National Credit Union Administration. Available online at <www.ncua.gov> (accessed July 28, 2003).

U.S. Government Manual Website. Available online at <www.gpoaccess.gov/gmanual> (accessed November 10, 2003).

CROSS-REFERENCES

Credit; Credit Union.

NATIONAL DRUG CONTROL POLICY, OFFICE OF

See OFFICE OF NATIONAL DRUG CONTROL POLICY.

NATIONAL EDUCATION ASSOCIATION

The National Education Association (NEA) is a nonprofit and nonpartisan professional organization made up of elementary and secondary school teachers, higher education faculty, education support professionals, school administrators, and others interested in public education. The NEA, which was founded in 1857, is the oldest and largest U.S. organization dealing with public education. The organization has more than 2.7 million members and is headquartered in Washington, D.C. The organization has approximately 565 staff members in its headquarters and regional offices. The association's budget for fiscal year 2002–03 was more than $267 million.

The NEA has 51 state-level affiliates that include 50 state associations and the Federal Education Association. The more than 14,000 local NEA affiliates include approximately 800 higher education affiliates. Anyone who works for a public school district, a college or university, or any other public institution devoted primarily to education is eligible to join the NEA. It also has special membership categories for retired educators and college students studying to become teachers.

The NEA is a volunteer-based organization supported by a network of staff at the local, state, and national levels. At the local level, NEA affiliates are active in various capacities, such as conducting professional workshops on discipline and bargaining contracts for school district employees. At the state level, NEA affiliates

regularly lobby legislators for the funds for public education, campaign for higher professional standards for the teaching profession, and file legal actions to protect ACADEMIC FREEDOM. At the national level, the NEA coordinates innovative projects to restructure how learning takes place and lobbies Congress on behalf of public education.

NEA members nationwide set association policy by meeting at their annual representative assembly every July. NEA members at the state and local levels elect the more than 9,000 assembly delegates, who, in turn, elect the top NEA officers, debate issues, and set NEA policy.

The NEA has been a vigorous opponent of efforts to privatize education through the use of tuition VOUCHERS. It rejects the arguments of voucher advocates that vouchers improve student learning, provide meaningful parental choice, and increase educational opportunities for low-income students. Instead, the NEA contends that vouchers are costly and that they are not the panacea for the problems in public education.

The NEA has also expressed concerns about laws that allow the creation of charter schools, which are deregulated, autonomous public schools. Advocates of charter schools believe that freeing some public schools from many state and local mandates will encourage educational innovation, create greater parental involvement, and promote improvement of public education in general. The NEA, while not opposing the concept of charter schools, has lobbied for sufficient oversight of these new schools, believing that public accountability is necessary.

The election of GEORGE W. BUSH as president in 2000 and the gain of Republican seats in both the House and Senate in 2002 strengthened the position of voucher supporters and gave increased urgency to continuing NEA opposition. In 2003, faced with a weakening economy and the consequent tightening of state and local budgets, NEA continued to oppose the privatization of work traditionally performed by school district employees and pressed for reduced class sizes and the need to train more teachers as millions of veteran teachers neared retirement.

FURTHER READINGS

Berube, Maurice R. 1988. *Teacher Politics: The Influence of Unions.* New York: Greenwood Press.

Lieberman, Myron. 2000. *The Teacher Unions: How They Sabotage Educational Reform and Why.* San Francisco: Encounter Books.

National Education Association. Available online at <www.nea.org> (accessed July 28, 2003).

CROSS-REFERENCES

Education Law; Public.

NATIONAL ENVIRONMENTAL POLICY ACT OF 1969

The National Environmental Policy Act of 1969 (NEPA) (42 U.S.C.A. § 4331 et seq.) was a revolutionary piece of legislation. NEPA established for the first time national policies and goals for the protection of the environment. NEPA aims to encourage harmony between people and the environment, promote efforts to prevent or eliminate damage to the environment and the biosphere, and enrich the understanding of ecological systems and natural resources important to the country.

NEPA is divided into two titles. Title I contains a basic national charter for protection of the environment. Section 101 is entitled "Declaration of the National Environmental Policy." Title II establishes the Council on Environmental Quality (CEQ), an EXECUTIVE BRANCH watchdog organization that monitors the progress toward the goals set forth in Section 101 of NEPA. The CEQ advises the president on environmental issues and provides guidance to all federal agencies, which are required by NEPA to cooperate with the CEQ. The CEQ prepares an ANNUAL REPORT on environmental quality, evaluates federal programs and activities affecting the environment, and gathers and provides statistical information.

NEPA requires that every federal agency submit an environmental impact statement (EIS) with every legislative recommendation or program proposing major federal projects that will most likely affect the quality of the surrounding environment. An EIS may be required for such projects as rerouting an interstate highway, building a new dam, or expanding a ski resort on federally owned land. The first question NEPA asks is whether the proposed action merits a "categorical exclusion." If an action has been studied in the past and does not have significant impact, or if it can be compared with different activities that the law defines as not having significant impact, then no further NEPA studies are necessary.

The agency can then implement its proposed action.

If the proposed action is not excluded from further study, the next question asked is whether the action will have a significant impact on the environment. If the answer is yes, NEPA outlines a detailed process for an EIS. If the answer is unknown, a less detailed study or an environmental assessment (EA) is prepared.

An EA is an overview of potential impacts. Enough analysis is done to determine either that the more detailed EIS is necessary or that the action will not have a significant impact on the environment.

Preparing the EIS is a well-defined process. A notice of intent is published in the *Federal Register* informing the public that a study will be done. The general public, federal and state agencies, and Native American tribes are given the opportunity to comment on the proposal. Next, a draft EIS is written, and a forty-five-day period for public comment is set. At the end of the comment period, the federal agency drafts a final EIS that responds to oral and written comments received during the public review of the draft. The agency, after a thirty-day waiting period, issues its record of decision, which discusses the decision, identifies the alternatives, and indicates whether all practicable means to avoid or minimize environmental harm from the selected alternative were adopted. The federal agency may then begin to implement its decision.

The EIS is a tool to assist in decision making, providing information about the positive and negative environmental effects of the proposed undertaking and its alternatives. The EIS must also examine the impact of not implementing the proposed action. In this no-action alternative, the agency may continue to use existing approaches. Although NEPA requires agencies to consider the environmental consequences of their actions, it does not force them to take the most environmentally sound alternative nor does it dictate the least expensive alternative.

FURTHER READINGS

Matthews, Joan Leary. 2003. "Restrictive Standing in State NEPA and Land Use Cases: Have Some States Gone Too Far?" *Zoning and Planning Law Report* 26 (May): 1–8.

Snowden, Suzanne O. 2003. "Judicial Review and Environmental Analysis Under NEPA: 'Timing is Everything.'" *Environmental Law Reporter* 33 (January): 10050–61.

CROSS-REFERENCES

Air Pollution; Environmental Law; Environmental Protection Agency; Land-Use Control; Pollution; Solid Wastes, Hazardous Substances, and Toxic Pollutants; Water Pollution.

NATIONAL FEDERATION OF INDEPENDENT BUSINESSES

The National Federation of Independent Businesses (NFIB) is the largest U.S. advocacy organization representing small and independent businesses. The NFIB has a membership of 600,000 business owners, including commercial enterprises, manufacturers, family farmers, neighborhood retailers, and service companies. The total membership employs more than 7 million people and reports annual gross sales of approximately $747 billion.

Founded in 1943, the NFIB was created to give small and independent business a voice in government decision making. The NFIB is recognized as one the most influential LOBBYING organizations in the United States, working with state and federal legislators and regulators. Its administrative headquarters are located in Nashville, Tennessee, but its public policy headquarters are in Washington, D.C. The NFIB also has state legislative offices in all 50 state capitals.

The governance of the NFIB differs from that of more traditional lobbying organizations. The NFIB uses the balloting of its membership, rather than a steering committee or a board of directors, to determine NFIB policies. In addition, it seeks to prevent UNDUE INFLUENCE by one member or group of members by setting a maximum contribution of dues. Minimum dues are $100, and the maximum dues contribution is $1,000. The NFIB follows these procedures so that the policies it advances will reflect the consensus of the business community rather than the narrow interests of any particular trade group. Once the ballots are counted—five times a year on federal issues and at least once a year on state issues—NFIB lobbyists carry the message to Congress and the state legislatures.

The NFIB opposes higher taxes on business and government regulation. At the state level, it works to lower the rates businesses are required to pay for workers' compensation insurance. At the federal level, it has campaigned for cutting the federal deficit, stopped an effort to raise employment taxes, and fought to increase the deductibility of HEALTH INSURANCE premiums for the self-employed.

The NFIB has been a critic of the ENVIRONMENTAL PROTECTION AGENCY, the Occupational Safety and Health Administration, and the INTERNAL REVENUE SERVICE, believing that these federal agencies stifle the productivity and profitability of business through over-regulation. It emphasizes the need for a free-market economy, noting that small business produces 38 percent of the gross domestic product.

In the late 1990s, the NFIB broadened its scope and began to support pro-small business candidates for state and national office. In 2000, the organization established the NFIB Legal Foundation, which advocates for small business in the courts and strives to educate its members on legal issues. In addition, the NFIB POLITICAL ACTION COMMITTEE "NFIB SAFE Trust PAC" uses member contributions to support candidates who are pro-small business. Issues concerning NFIB in 2003 included tax relief, including permanent repeal of the inheritance tax, affordable HEALTH CARE, MEDICAL MALPRACTICE law reform, caps on civil suit damages, and affordable high-speed access to the INTERNET.

FURTHER READINGS

National Federation of Independent Businesses. Available online at <www.nfib.org> (accessed July 28, 2003).

CROSS-REFERENCES

Business Affected with a Public Interest.

NATIONAL FIREARMS ACT OF 1934

The first attempt at federal gun-control legislation, the National Firearms Act (NFA) only covered two specific types of guns: machine guns and short-barrel firearms, including sawed-off shotguns. It did not attempt to ban either weapon, but merely to impose a tax on any transfers of such weapons. Despite these limitations, it led to a precedent-setting U.S. Supreme Court decision.

In the 1930s, the United States faced a run of much-publicized gangster violence, led by such well-known criminals as John Dillinger, AL CAPONE, Baby Face Nelson, and Bonnie and Clyde. The sensationalistic aspect of their crimes convinced the administration of President FRANKLIN D. ROOSEVELT that something needed to be done to control the spread of weapons into the general population. U.S. Attorney General HOMER CUMMINGS and his staff began the process of drafting recommended legislation that would achieve this goal.

Cummings and his staff quickly determined that, rather than ban weapons and run afoul of the SECOND AMENDMENT, they would try to tax such weapons out of circulation. As originally proposed, the NFA covered a fairly broad range of weapons, but as passed by Congress, it's scope was narrowed to cover only "A shotgun or rifle having a barrel of less than eighteen inches in length, or any other weapon, except a pistol or revolver, from which a shot is discharged by an explosive if such weapon is capable of being concealed on the person, or a machine gun."

The statute levied a $200 tax on each firearm defined as above, for any transfer involving the firearm. The tax was to be paid by the transferor, and to be represented by appropriate stamps to be provided by the commissioner. It was declared unlawful for anyone to sell or receive a firearm in violation of this section, and they could be fined $2,000 and imprisoned for up to five years for violating it.

While the $200 tax does not seem like much in current dollars, it represented a very large amount in 1934—in many cases the tax was more than the cost of the firearm itself. The act also required dealers of the listed firearms to register with the federal government, and also required for firearms sold before the effective date of the act, that "every person possessing a firearm shall register, with the collector of the district in which he resides, the number or other mark identifying such firearm, together with his name, address, place where such firearm is usually kept, and place of business or employment, and, if such person is other than a natural person, the name and home address of an executive officer thereof."

The NFA did not inspire as much controversy in 1934 as gun-control acts do today, in part because of the general public perception that crime was out of control and in part because anti-gun-control groups such as the NATIONAL RIFLE ASSOCIATION (NRA) did not have nearly the strength or LOBBYING power they would later have. In fact, the NRA formed its legislative affairs division, a precursor to its powerful lobbying arm, in 1934 in belated response to the NFA. Nevertheless, the NFA did result in several lawsuits claiming the law was unconstitutional, one of which reached the Supreme Court.

In *Miller v. United States*, 307 U.S. 174, 59 S.Ct. 816, 83 L.Ed. 1206 (U.S.Ark. 1939), two men were charged with transferring a double barrel 12-gauge shotgun in violation of the NFA. A federal district court quashed the indictment, ruling that the NFA did indeed violate the Second Amendment. But the Supreme Court, in a unanimous decision, disagreed.

Writing for the court, Justice JAMES MCREYNOLDS famously dismissed the defendants case with this statement: "the absence of any evidence tending to show that possession or use of a 'shotgun having a barrel of less than eighteen inches in length' at this time has some reasonable relationship to the preservation or efficiency of a well regulated militia, we cannot say that the Second Amendment guarantees the right to keep and bear such an instrument." McReynolds added that "certainly it is not within JUDICIAL NOTICE that this weapon is any part of the ordinary military equipment or that its use could contribute to the common defense." He also noted that many states had adopted gun-control laws over the years.

The NFA is still in force, codified in amended form at 26 USCA § 5801 et. seq. As the first federal gun-control legislation, it set the stage for all other federal GUN CONTROL laws, and its legacy overshadows the scope of the law and the limited number of weapons to which it actually applied.

FURTHER READINGS

Blodgett-Ford, Sayoko. "The Changing Meaning of the Right to Bear Arms." *Seton Hall Constitutional Law Journal* 6.

Heskin, Keersten. 1994. "Easier than Obtaining a Driver's License: The Federal Licensing of Gun Dealers." *Florida Law Review* 46 (December).

Nosanchuk, Mathew S. 2002. "The Embarrassing Interpretation of the Second Amendment." *Northern Kentucky Law Review* 29.

CROSS-REFERENCES

Second Amendment; Gun Control.

NATIONAL GAY AND LESBIAN TASK FORCE

The National Gay and Lesbian Task Force (NGLTF) is a nonprofit organization that supports grassroots organizing and advocacy for lesbian, gay, bisexual, and transgender rights. Founded in 1973, NGLTF works to strengthen the gay and lesbian movement at the state and local levels while connecting these activities to a national agenda. It is recognized as the leading activist organization in the national gay and lesbian movement, and serves as a national resource center for state and local organizations. Its headquarters are in Washington, D.C.

NGLTF works to combat antigay violence and antigay legislative and ballot measures. It also lobbies state and federal governments to end job discrimination and repeal SODOMY laws. With the arrival of HIV and AIDS in the 1980s, NGLTF sought government funding of medical research, and has campaigned for reform of the HEALTH CARE system.

In 1997 NGLTF played a major role in the creation of a new national political organization, the Federation of Statewide Lesbian, Gay, Bisexual, and Transgender Political Organizations. The purpose of the federation, which draws its membership from 32 state groups, is to strengthen the efforts of these statewide groups through a network that will foster strategizing across state lines, building stronger state organizations, and developing good working relationships between state and national groups. The need for the federation grew out of meetings of statewide activists at the NGLTF annual Creating Change Conference, held each November in a major U.S. city.

The federation consists of 16 executive committee members, selected from each region of the country, who will develop the federation's mission. NGLTF serves as coordinator of the federation, supporting its work through the creation and dissemination of information and materials and the making of regular conference calls.

At the federal level, NGLTF was unsuccessful in its opposition to the 1996 Defense of Marriage Act (DOMA), which permits states to bar legal recognition of same-sex marriages performed in other states. In 1988 NGLTF renewed its efforts to have Congress expand the federal mandate for prosecution of HATE CRIMES including crimes that are committed against people because of their sexual orientation. The Hate Crimes Prevention Act (S. 1529 and H.R. 3081) would add hate crimes based on an individual's real or perceived sexual orientation to the list of bias crimes that the federal government can prosecute.

In 2002, the NGLTF Policy Institute released the first and largest-ever study of gay, lesbian, bisexual and transgender African Americans. This study documented among these groups significant numbers of individuals with children, high levels of political participation, and widespread experiences of racism and homophobia.

NGLTF, through its policy institute, conducts research and publishes studies on many topics, including CIVIL RIGHTS, workplace discrimination, violence, health, campus activities, and families.

FURTHER READINGS

National Gay and Lesbian Task Force. Available online at <www.ngltf.org> (accessed July 28, 2003).

CROSS-REFERENCES

Civil Rights; Discrimination; Equal Protection; Gay and Lesbian Rights: Same-Sex Marriage.

NATIONAL GUARD

The National Guard is the term for the state-organized units of the U.S. Army and Air Force, composed of citizens who undergo training and are available for service in national or local emergencies. National Guard units are organized in each of the 50 states, the District of Columbia, and Puerto Rico. The National Guard units are subject to the call of the governor of their state or territory, except when ordered into federal service by the president of the United States. Entry into the National Guard is by voluntary enlistment. The National Guard is trained to work in conjunction with the active forces of the Army and Air Force. Much of its value comes from its service in times of peace, when the Guard provides emergency aid to victims of national disasters and assists law enforcement authorities during civil emergencies.

"Citizen-soldiers" have come a long way since the American Revolution. The Army National Guard has fought in every major war in which the United States has been involved, from the American Revolution to the VIETNAM WAR and the 2003 war in Iraq. Since the end of the Vietnam War, the Guard has been engaged in all U.S. national defense missions. Not only is the National Guard devoted to the defense of the United States and its allies, it is also involved in a number of other activities, such as dealing with emergencies like civil disturbances, riots, and natural disasters, and helping law enforcement agencies to keep illegal drugs off the streets.

After the American Revolution, the First CONGRESS OF THE UNITED STATES did not consider the formation of a militia a top priority, and it disbanded the Continental Army. Congress did not officially debate the notion of a militia until the Constitutional Convention in 1787. The Constitution authorized a standing army in its Army Clause (art. I, § 8, cl. 12) and provided for a militia under the Militia Clauses (U.S. Const. art. I, § 8, cls. 15–16). Under the Constitution, the militia is to be available for federal service for three distinct purposes: "to execute the Laws of the Union, suppress Insurrections and repel Invasions." Congress is to organize and discipline the militia, and the states are to appoint officers and train the soldiers.

The National Guard, whose main responsibility since its inception had been the protection of colonial settlements, faced its first significant challenge when it tried to defend the settlements from Native American domination. In 1789, the federal government formed a War Department of approximately 700 men for the purpose of defending U.S. soil and its settlements from Native American attack. These small armies failed, and Congress responded to the failure of its small armies to fight off Native Americans in the West by enacting the Militia Act of 1792 (May 8, 1792, ch. 33, I Stat. 271 [repealed 1903]); this act was the militia's only permanent organizing legislation for more than 100 years. While the act governed the militia, the United States endured three wars—the WAR OF 1812, the Civil War, and the Spanish-American War—and the militia was ineffective in all three. Congress replaced the act with the Dick Act of 1903 (32 Stat. 775) to transform "a frontier police force into a respected and modern fighting machine."

The Dick Act provided for an organized militia—to be named the National Guard—that would conform to the organization of the Army, be equipped through federal funds, and be trained by Army instructors. The act consisted of 26 sections and set forth new provisions that had previously only applied to the Army, but now also applied to the newly formed National Guard, including a nine-month limit for reservists' service on active duty, a provision that when on active duty, the reservists would be guided by Army rules and regulations and would receive the same pay as that given to Army soldiers, and a new requirement for the performance of 24 drills per year and a five-day summer camp. The act also gave states' governors certain powers over their Guard units, such as the power to excuse their troops from any of the drills or summer camp.

Congress amended and strengthened the Dick Act when it passed the National Defense Act of 1908, on May 27, 1908, ch. 204, 35 Stat. 399 (amending Dick Act of Jan. 21, 1903, ch. 196, 32 Stat. 775), which provided that the Guard could not only be called into services within or outside of United States territory but could also be called into service for as long as the president deemed necessary, no longer subject to a nine-month limitation. The National Defense Act of 1916 (June 3, 1916, ch. 134, 39 Stat. 166) separated the Army, the reserves, and the militia and "federalized" the National Guard.

Several years later Congress declared the National Guard a part of the Army, and the National Guard became solely authorized by the Army Clause of the Constitution when Congress passed the Act of 1933 (48 Stat. 149, 155). This act provided that reserve soldiers would no longer be drafted into federal service and that they would be ordered to active duty only if "Congress declared a national emergency and authorized the use of troops in excess of those of the Regular Army."

Since 1933 federal law has provided that persons who enlist in a state National Guard unit simultaneously enlist in the National Guard of the United States, a part of the Army. The enlistees retain their status as state National Guard members unless and until ordered to active federal duty and revert to state status upon being relieved from federal service.

The authority to order the Guard to federal duty was limited to periods of national emergency until Congress passed the Armed Forces Reserve Act of 1952 (66 Stat. 481), which authorized orders "to active duty or active duty for training" without any emergency requirement but provided that such orders could not be issued without the consent of the governor of the state concerned. The act also set forth the mission of the reserve components and defined some important terms. For example, the act clarified that the U.S. armed forces are the Army, Navy, Air Force, the Marine Corps, and the Coast Guard, and that the seven reserve components are the National Guard, the Army Reserve, the Navy Reserve, the Marine Corps Reserve, the Air National Guard, the Air Force Reserve, and the Coast Guard Reserve. According to the act, the purpose of the reserve components is to provide "trained units and qualified individuals to be available for active duty in the Armed Forces of the United States in time of war or national emergency, and at such other times as the national security may require."

Further, the act declares that "the National Guard . . . [is] an integral part of the first line defenses of this Nation [and must be maintained at all times].... [W]henever ... units and organizations are needed for the national security in excess of those of the Regular components ..., the National Guard ... shall be ordered into the active military service of the United States and continued therein so long as such necessity exists."

The legal basis of the National Guard is founded not only in federal constitutional and statutory law but in state constitutions and statutes as well. The original "militia," which eventually became known as the Army National Guard, began as a domestic force made up of untrained men led by political generals. The Army Clause of the Constitution gives Congress the power to provide and maintain a Navy and make rules for the government and regulation of the land and naval forces. The Militia Clauses of the Constitution authorize the states to organize the National Guard but give Congress the power to employ the Guard in the service of the country.

Article II, Section 2, of the Constitution states that the president of the United States is the "Commander in Chief of the Army and Navy of the United States, and of the Militia of the several States, when called into the actual Service of the United States."

The Framers of the Constitution authorized Congress to recognize a militia that was largely controlled by the states. The states generally have maintained control over the militia during times of peace but not during war or national emergency. However, after two state governors refused to consent to federal training missions abroad for their Guard units, the gubernatorial consent requirement was partially repealed in 1986 by the Montgomery Amendment, which provides that a governor cannot withhold consent for reservists to be on active duty outside the United States because of any objection to the location, purpose, type, or schedule of such duty. The Supreme Court affirmed the constitutionality of the Montgomery Amendment in *Perpich v. Department of Defense,* 496 U.S. 334, 110 S. Ct. 2418, 110 L. Ed. 2d 312 (1990). According to the Court, the Militia Clause of the Constitution granted independent rights to both the states and the federal government to train the militia. Congress is free to train the militia as it sees fit, provided it does not prevent the states from also conducting training.

Ultimately, the National Guard enjoys a dual status as both a state militia and as an integral part of the federal armed forces. Although the

National Guard units help with sandbagging efforts during the March 1997 flooding of the Ohio and Cumberland rivers in Smithland, Kentucky. National Guard units are a part of the federal armed forces but are called to service primarily by state authorities.

AP/WIDE WORLD PHOTOS

Guard continues to perform important domestic functions, the federal government has ultimate power when it requires the National Guard for national defense.

In the 1990s and early 2000s, the significance of the National Guard as a major part of the country's national defense system increased. In 1991 more than 75,000 reservists participated in the first Gulf War ("Desert Storm"). Since that time, components of the National Guard have completed missions in Haiti, Bosnia, and Kosovo. After the SEPTEMBER 11TH TERRORIST ATTACKS, more than 50,000 National Guard members were called upon to provide security at home and abroad. In 2003, National Guard members and reservists played a crucial role in the war against Iraq.

FURTHER READINGS

Bovarnick, Jeff. 1991. "*Perpich v. United States Department of Defense:* Who's in Charge of the National Guard?" *New England Law Review* 26.

Breitenbach, Roy W. 1989. "*Perpich v. United States Department of Defense:* Who Controls the Weekend Soldier?" *St. John's Law Review* 64.

Derthick, Martha. 1965. *The National Guard in Politics.* Cambridge, Mass.: Harvard Univ. Press.

National Guard. Available online at <www.ngb.army.mil> (accessed July 28, 2003).

Rich, Steven B. 1994. "The National Guard, Drug Interdiction and Counterdrug Activities, Posse Comitatus: The Meaning and Implications of 'In Federal Service.'" *Army Law* 35.

Theurer, Kenneth M. 1994. "Low-Level Conflicts and the Reserves: Presidential Authority Under 10 U.S.C. sec. 673b." *University of Cincinnati Law Review* 62.

CROSS-REFERENCES
Militia.

NATIONAL HEALTH CARE

The development of a national system of HEALTH CARE in the United States has remained a major topic of debate throughout the United States, especially since the 1980s. Healthcare costs in the United States have risen dramatically during the past 40 years, due in part to longer average life spans, which give rise to greater costs because older citizens require greater care, and the employment of technologies that extend the life of patients, which generally results in greater spending. Insurance costs have likewise increased dramatically, and a relatively large percentage of U.S. citizens and other residents are uninsured or underinsured. According to information from the CENSUS BUREAU in 2001, 41.2 million Americans, constituting 14.2 percent of the population, did not have HEALTH INSURANCE.

The healthcare system is largely controlled by the free market, which is believed to provide limitations on how much physicians and other specialists can charge to their patients. However, many critics of the current system, including organizations composed of physicians, note that the system has become largely bureaucratic and that cost-cutting measures and pressures caused by competition and the need for profit have reduced the effectiveness of medical practice. Despite these problems, many commentators have not been able to agree as to the proper level of control that state or federal governments should have over health care.

Following WORLD WAR II, the number of Americans that had private insurance policies grew dramatically. In 1965, Congress approved the development of MEDICARE and MEDICAID to assist the elderly and the poor in being able to afford medical care. The vast majority of U.S. citizens were covered by either private or public insurance at that time. However, healthcare costs experienced a dramatic growth during the 1970s, and employers were forced to pay for the bulk of this increase as they paid their employees' premiums. Many companies in the early 1980s began to require employees to pay deductibles on their insurance policies, and some small companies began to refuse to provide insurance at all.

Beginning in the 1980s, scholars and other commentators began to propose a variety of major reforms to the healthcare system to create a truly national system. In 1989, an article in the *New England Journal of Medicine* by David Himmelstein and Steffe Woolhander maintained that the system of health care in the United States was failing. A considerable amount of concern by those authors and others was directed towards the overhead costs and other administrative expenses incurred by insurance companies and healthcare providers. According to one study in 1987, the total cost of healthcare administration was an estimated $96.8 billion to $120.4 billion, accounting for 19.3 to 24.1 percent of the total spending on health care in the United States. In 1989, the more than 1,500 private health insurers in the United States consumed an estimated eight percent of their total revenues through overhead costs.

A number of commentators compared the healthcare system in the United States with the national system in Canada. Administrative healthcare costs in the United States were estimated in 1983 to be 60 percent higher than those in Canada, and Canada's system provides healthcare coverage for all of its citizens. Canada employs a so-called *single-payer* form of national health insurance in which the federal government administers and finances the plan. All Canadians are covered under the plan, which provides for a basic benefit package. Citizens are not required to pay a deductible or co-payment, and the government forbids private insurance companies from duplicating the services provided under the government plan. The single-payer approach reduces overhead expenses dramatically because the government pays the medical costs directly to the provider.

Although many in the medical community supported proposals to adopt a form of the single-payer model, critics noted the population of the United States is roughly ten times the population of Canada. These critics also noted that the costs of such a system would be paid for with taxes, so citizens are required to pay for this system indirectly. Moreover, adoption of such a system would involve a high level of governmental involvement, which conservative commentators dislike.

Other proposals for national health care have been introduced and have likewise been advocated unsuccessfully. Some proposals include mandates that all employers provide insurance coverage to all employees. Other proposals focus on market-based solutions, including the development of medical savings accounts holding funds, which individuals could use to spend for healthcare costs. The competing sides to the debate are generally unable or unwilling to compromise their positions, and the reform effort remains largely a matter of rhetoric.

The issue of healthcare reform was a major debate during the 1992 presidential campaign. Most of the Democratic candidates, including eventual nominee BILL CLINTON, advocated their own strategies for this reform, as did the incumbent president GEORGE H.W. BUSH. Clinton's proposal, which was a compromise between several reform alternatives, purported to guarantee practically universal coverage by requiring employers to provide health insurance to all full-time employees. The plan would have also established a national health board and an ADMINISTRATIVE AGENCY that would have been responsible for determining the maximum allowable growth rate of insurance premiums of private insurers.

After Clinton was elected, the healthcare reform initiative was a top priority in the first two years of his first term. However, Clinton encountered many roadblocks. He was criticized for having his wife, HILLARY RODHAM CLINTON, take the lead in promoting the proposal. The plan was also very complex, and the administration was criticized for failing to articulate it properly to the public. Several bills that would have given rise to major healthcare reform were introduced before Congress in 1993 and 1994, but Congress refused to take action with respect to most of them. The most significant of these bills was the National Health Security Act, S. 1757, 103d Cong., in 1994, but its consideration was stalled at the committee level.

Republicans won a sweeping victory in the 1994 congressional elections, and the enthusiasm for providing a national healthcare system declined. Evidence also suggested that increases in healthcare costs had begun to stabilize. From 1993 to 1997, U.S. spending on health care remained at 13.5 percent of the country's gross national product (GNP). In 1997, the United States experienced only a 4.8 percent increase in healthcare spending, which was an all-time low. Moreover, by 1997, private companies and individuals paid about 53.6 percent of the overall health expenditures, which was considerably less than the percentage paid 20 years prior.

Although major healthcare reform in the United States appears less likely than it did dur-

ing the early 1990s, commentators note that the poor still suffer from the market-based system. Many lower-class workers suffer more than non-workers, primarily due to the current public insurance systems, especially Medicaid. These workers are often paid too much to qualify for Medicaid, yet their employers do not provide insurance and the workers cannot afford to pay insurance premiums from private companies. Even more disconcerting to many observers is the number of children who are uninsured and whose families do not qualify for Medicaid. As many as 8.5 million children under the age of 18 are uninsured, according to the 2001 census.

Beyond the political and economic considerations in the debate regarding national health care are questions of whether citizens in the United States possess the right to such care. Few people question that Congress has the power, both under the COMMERCE CLAUSE and Spending Clause of the Constitution, to enact national healthcare legislation, but some maintain that health is one of the basic HUMAN RIGHTS that the Constitution impliedly protects. Other commentators disagree strongly, noting that no citizen has the inherent right to health care and that health care providers deserve to be paid the market value for their services. Other critics add that the intervention required of the government in a national healthcare system would make citizens too dependent upon the state, which could lead the government to take excessive control over its citizens' lives.

FURTHER READINGS

Hacker, Jacob S. 1996. "National Health Care Reform: An Idea Whose Time Came and Went." *Journal of Health Politics, Policy, and Law* 21 (winter).

"National Power and Health Care" (panel discussion). 1995. *Cornell Journal of Law and Public Policy* 7 (spring).

CROSS-REFERENCES

Medicaid; Medicare.

NATIONAL INDUSTRIAL RECOVERY ACT OF 1933

The National Industrial Recovery Act of 1933 (NIRA) was one of the most important and daring measures of President FRANKLIN D. ROOSEVELT'S NEW DEAL. It was enacted during the famous First Hundred Days of Roosevelt's first term in office and was the centerpiece of his initial efforts to reverse the economic collapse of the Great Depression. NIRA was signed into law on June 16, 1933, and was to remain in effect for two years. It attempted to make structural changes in the industrial sector of the economy and to alleviate unemployment with a public works program. It succeeded only partially in accomplishing its goals, and on May 27, 1935, less than three weeks before the act would have expired, the U.S. Supreme Court ruled it unconstitutional.

Economists, scholars, politicians, and the public at large were deeply divided as to the underlying causes of the Great Depression and the best means to bring it to an end. In the months following Roosevelt's inauguration, his advisers, along with members of Congress and representatives from business and labor, drafted the legislation that was introduced in Congress on May 15, 1933, as the National Industrial Recovery Act. The division of opinions about the Depression was reflected in those who drafted NIRA, and the act drew both praise and criticism from across the political spectrum. Nevertheless, the urgency of the economic situation (with unemployment exceeding 30 percent in many parts of the country) pressured Congress to act.

The House of Representatives passed the NIRA by a vote of 325 to 76. When it reached the Senate, however, several powerful senators opposed the bill. Some progressives favored alternative legislation authored by Alabama Senator HUGO L. BLACK, which promoted a 30-hour workweek. Some senators were concerned that the act suspended the enforcement of ANTITRUST LAWS at the same time that it called on businesses to play a major role in drafting "codes of fair competition." The Senate eventually approved the bill by a margin of seven votes.

NIRA was divided into three sections, or titles. Title I promoted centralized economic planning by instituting codes of fair competition for industry. Title II provided $3.3 billion for public works projects. Title III contained minor amendments to the Emergency Relief and Construction Act of 1932 (47 Stat. 709).

Title I of the act declared a "national emergency productive of widespread unemployment and disorganization of industry, which burdens interstate and foreign commerce, affects the public WELFARE, and undermines the standards of living of the American people." To correct this situation, NIRA proposed to "remove obstructions to the free flow of interstate and foreign commerce, . . . to eliminate unfair competitive practices, . . . to increase the consumption of industrial and agricultural products by increasing purchasing power, to reduce and relieve

unemployment [and] to improve standards of labor." NIRA was designed to accomplish these goals through the codes of fair competition, which were essentially sets of rules created on an industry-by-industry basis governing wages, prices, and business practices. The codes were intended to arrest the downward spiral of the economy in which high unemployment depressed wages, which decreased public purchasing power, leading to lower prices and profits (as desperate businesses tried to undersell one another), putting further downward pressure on wages. It was hoped that organized cooperation between business and government would correct what was perceived by some to be waste and inefficiency in the free-market economy.

NIRA created the NATIONAL RECOVERY ADMINISTRATION (NRA) to oversee the drafting and implementation of the codes of fair competition. The agency was modeled, in part, after the War Industries Board, which had operated during WORLD WAR I. To lead NRA, Roosevelt chose former General Hugh S. Johnson, who had served as a liaison between the U.S. Army and the War Industries Board during World War I.

NRA began its work with great fanfare and initially received enthusiastic public support. A massive public relations campaign included the largest parade in the history of New York City. Businesses that adopted the codes were encouraged to advertise the fact by displaying the NRA blue eagle logo with its motto, "We do our part."

The NRA worked with businesses to establish the mandated codes for fair competition. Industrial groups then submitted proposed codes to the president for his approval. The president approved the codes only if the submitting organization did not restrict membership and was representative of the industry, and if the codes themselves promoted the policy of the act. Although the codes were exempt from antitrust laws, they were to neither foster monopolies nor discriminate against small businesses. Once approved, the codes became legally enforceable standards for that trade or industry.

Under Section 3(c) of the act, federal district courts had jurisdiction over code violations, and U.S. district attorneys were given authority to seek court orders to compel violators to comply with the codes. Section 3(f) provided that any violation affecting interstate or foreign commerce was to be treated as a misdemeanor for which an offender could be fined not more than $500 for each offense.

Under Section 7(a), industry codes were required to include provisions for the protection of labor. For example, provisions for minimum wages and the right to COLLECTIVE BARGAINING were to increase workers' deflated purchasing power, and limits on the number of work hours were to increase employment by spreading the available hours of work among more employees. Section 7(a) also provided that an employee must not be required to join a company union or be prevented from joining a union as a condition of employment.

Section 7(a) had such far-reaching consequences that some labor historians have called it the MAGNA CHARTA of the labor movement. Nationwide, union membership grew dramatically. The Amalgamated Clothing Workers, for example, doubled its membership from 60,000 to 120,000 between early 1933 and mid-1934. The United Mine Workers of America quadrupled its membership, from 100,000 to 400,000, less than a year after passage of NIRA.

Under the supervision of the NRA, several hundred industry codes were rapidly enacted, but public support soon diminished. The codes tended to increase efficiency and employment, improve wages and hours, prevent price cutting and UNFAIR COMPETITION, and encourage collective bargaining. However, they also tended to raise prices and limit production. Businesses found the codes burdensome. More than 540 codes were promulgated, and it was not unusual for one business to be governed by several, or even several dozen, codes. The codes sometimes conflicted with each other, and businesses occasionally had to pay their workers different rates of pay at different times of the day.

Laborers were also unhappy with NIRA. In spite of some NRA successes, such as the end of child labor in the textile industry, many in the labor community alleged that the NRA's interpretation of the labor provisions favored employers. In addition, labor was dissatisfied with the activities of the NRA regarding unions. It appeared that Congress had intended Section 7(a) of NIRA to assist employees in self-organizing and to discourage company unions. However, the NRA did not actively seek to prohibit the creation of company unions, nor were NRA representatives available to protect individuals from being coerced into joining company unions.

Title II of NIRA created the Public Works Administration (PWA) to award $3.3 billion in

The NIRA created the National Recovery Administration (NRA) to oversee the drafting and implementation of the codes of fair competition. Businesses adopting the codes were encouraged to advertise the fact by displaying the NRA blue eagle logo and motto, "We do our part."

AP/WIDE WORLD PHOTOS

contracts for the construction of public works. (The government did not directly employ workers on PWA projects, as it did in a later New Deal program with a similar name, the Works Progress Administration [WPA].) Secretary of the Interior Harold L. Ickes ran the PWA. Ickes was scrupulously honest in choosing projects and awarding contracts, and he insisted that funds not be wasted. He was successful in that respect. However, the result was that the benefits of the public works provisions of NIRA were realized too slowly to have much immediate effect on national recovery.

Nevertheless, the PWA did oversee an enormous number and variety of public works projects, including schools, hospitals, post offices, courthouses, roads, bridges, water systems, and waste treatment plants. Its two most prominent projects were the construction of the Triborough Bridge in New York City and the completion of the Boulder (now called the Hoover) Dam on the Colorado River in Arizona. Ultimately the PWA completed more than 34,000 projects around the country.

In spite of the gradual success of the Public Works Administration, the NRA continued to lose the support of the public and its government sponsors. Three weeks before NIRA's two-year expiration date, the Supreme Court unanimously declared it unconstitutional in *Schechter Poultry Corp. v. United States,* 295 U.S. 495, 55 S. Ct. 837, 79 L. Ed. 1570 (1935). The Court held that the act impermissibly delegated legislative power to the NRA and that the application of the act to commerce within the state of New York exceeded the powers granted to the federal government under the COMMERCE CLAUSE of the U.S. Constitution. The Commerce Clause gives Congress the power to regulate commerce between states, but not within an individual state.

In response to *Schechter* and to other decisions invalidating New Deal legislation, Roosevelt delivered a famous speech on May 31, 1935, in which he criticized the Supreme Court for employing "the horse and buggy definition of interstate commerce." Subsequent New Deal legislation incorporated some elements of NIRA, most notably the labor provisions of Section 7(a), and ultimately survived the scrutiny of the Supreme Court.

FURTHER READINGS

Badger, Anthony J. 2002. *The New Deal: The Depression Years, 1933–40*. Chicago: Ivan R. Dee.

Boardman, Fon W. 1967. *The Thirties: America and the Great Depression*. New York: Walck.

Leuchtenburg, William E. 1963. *Franklin D. Roosevelt and the New Deal, 1932–1940*. New York: Harper & Row.

Powell, Jim. 2003. *FDR's Folly: How Roosevelt and His New Deal Prolonged the Great Depression*. New York: Crown Forum.

Watkins, T.H. 1993. *The Great Depression: America in the 1930s*. Boston: Little, Brown.

CROSS-REFERENCES

Labor Law; Labor Union.

NATIONAL LABOR RELATIONS ACT
See WAGNER ACT.

NATIONAL MEDIATION BOARD
The National Mediation Board is a three-person board created in 1934 by an act amending the Railway Labor Act (45 U.S.C.A. §§ 151–158, 160–162, 1181–1188) to resolve disputes in the railroad and airline industries that could disrupt travel or imperil the economy. The board also handles railroad and airline employee representation disputes and provides administrative and financial support in adjusting minor grievances in the railroad industry. At the time the board was created, railroads were the dominant carriers of passengers and commercial goods. Railroad strikes were common, which disrupted travel and the national economy. In addition, friction between railroad companies and the

railroad LABOR UNIONS made negotiation of employment issues difficult.

The National Mediation Board was created to address these issues, first for railroads and later for commercial airlines. The board's major responsibility is the mediation of disputes over wages, hours, and working conditions that arise between rail and air carriers and organizations representing their employees. The board also investigates representation disputes and certifies employee organizations as representatives of crafts or classes of carrier employees.

The board may become involved in mediation when the parties fail to reach accord in direct bargaining. Either party may request the board's services, or the board may become involved on its own. Once the board has entered the process, negotiations continue until the board determines that its efforts to mediate have been unsuccessful, at which time it seeks to induce the parties to submit the dispute to ARBITRATION. If either party refuses arbitration, the board issues a notice stating that the parties have failed to resolve the dispute through mediation. The notice triggers a thirty-day cooling-off period, after which either side may avail itself of SELF-HELP, which may include an employee strike.

The board must notify the president when the parties have failed to reach agreement through the board's mediation efforts and when the labor dispute, in the judgment of the board, threatens substantially to interrupt interstate commerce to a degree that would deprive any section of the country of essential transportation service. In these cases the president has the discretion to appoint an emergency board to investigate and report on the dispute. In these situations self-help is barred for sixty days after the appointment of the emergency board.

If a carrier's employees cannot agree on who will represent them, the board must investigate the dispute and determine by a secret ballot election or other appropriate means to whom a representation certificate should be issued. In the course of this process, the board must determine the craft or class in which the employees seeking representation properly belong.

Disputes in the railroad industry concerning rates of pay, rules, or working conditions are referred to the National Railroad Adjustment Board. This board has four divisions, each one consisting of an equal number of representatives of the carriers and of national organizations of employees. In deadlocked cases the National Mediation Board is authorized to appoint a referee to sit with the members of the division for the purpose of making an award.

No national adjustment board has been established in the airline industry. Air carriers and employees have established bargaining relationships that create a grievance procedure with a board to resolve the conflicts. The National Mediation Board is frequently called on to name a neutral referee to serve on these kinds of boards when the parties cannot agree on such an appointment themselves.

The board consists of a chair and two other members. Its headquarters are in Washington, D.C.

FURTHER READINGS

Knibb, Shaunta M. 1997. "The Jurisdictional Shadowland between the NLRB and the National Mediation Board: Who's in Charge?" *Washington Law Review* 72 (January).

National Mediation Board Website. Available online at <www.nmb.gov> (accessed January 20, 2004).

Newman, Todd A. 2000. "A Suggested Approach to Applying the National Mediation Board's Railroad Merger Procedures." *Labor Lawyer* 15 (winter-spring).

U.S. Government Manual Website. Available online at <www.gpoaccess.gov/gmanual> (accessed November 10, 2003).

CROSS-REFERENCES

Labor Law.

NATIONAL ORGANIZATION FOR THE REFORM OF MARIJUANA LAWS

The National Organization for the Reform of Marijuana Laws (NORML) is a nonprofit organization dedicated to the legalization of marijuana. Founded in 1970, NORML remains the leading national advocate for legalization. NORML, which believes adult private use of marijuana should be legal, seeks the repeal of federal anti-marijuana laws. Repeal would allow states to experiment with different models of legalization. During the 1970s, NORML led the successful efforts to decriminalize minor marijuana offenses in 11 states and significantly lower penalties in all others. During the 1980s, however, the decriminalization movement lost political appeal when presidents RONALD REAGAN and GEORGE H.W. BUSH committed their administrations to the "war on drugs."

NORML has a five-person staff at its national headquarters in Washington, D.C. It is governed by a board of directors that includes prominent attorneys, scientists, and researchers. NORML provides information to the national news media for marijuana-related stories and lobbies state and federal legislators to permit the medical use of marijuana and to reject attempts to treat minor marijuana offenses more harshly. NORML also functions as the umbrella group for a national network of activists committed to ending marijuana prohibition.

NORML also assists those who are arrested on marijuana charges through a legal committee (NLC) comprised of 350 criminal defense attorneys. The NLC also sponsors NORML legal seminars, notifies NORML of important judicial decisions and law enforcement trends, and provides NORML with copies of briefs and other legal documents. These lawyers regularly defend victims of marijuana prohibition and sometimes set important legal precedents.

The NORML AMICUS CURIAE committee files amicus curiae (friend of the court) briefs in important or novel marijuana-related legal actions at the appellate court level. This committee, which is comprised of experienced NORML criminal defense attorneys from around the country, gives NORML the opportunity to contribute its point of view in cases that may have national importance.

In 1997, NORML established the NORML Foundation, a nonprofit organization that sponsors public advertising campaigns to educate the public about the costs of marijuana prohibition and the benefits of alternative policies. In 1999, the organization adopted a mission statement that advocated the repeal of the prohibition of responsible marijuana use by adults.

NORML has actively supported efforts to legalize the medical use of marijuana for those patients suffering from serious illnesses and medical conditions, including glaucoma, AIDS, multiple sclerosis, quadriplegia and paraplegia, and the side effects of chemotherapy, despite the fact that federal law still prohibits such use. As of 2003, nine states (Alaska, Arizona, California, Colorado, Hawaii, Maine, Nevada, Oregon, and Washington) still had laws in effect that legalized the medical use of marijuana.

FURTHER READINGS

National Organization for the Reform of Marijuana Laws. Available online at <www.norml.org> (accessed July 28, 2003).

CROSS-REFERENCES

Drugs and Narcotics; Drug Enforcement Administration.

NATIONAL ORGANIZATION FOR WOMEN

The National Organization for Women (NOW) is the largest organization of feminist activists in the United States, numbering more than 500,000 members. A nonpartisan organization, it has more than 550 chapters in all 50 states and the District of Columbia. It receives its funding from membership dues and private donations. NOW has used both traditional and nontraditional means to push for social change. Traditional activities have included extensive electoral and LOBBYING work, and the filing of lawsuits. NOW also has organized mass marches, rallies, pickets, counter-demonstrations, and nonviolent civil disobedience. Its headquarters are located in Washington, D.C.

NOW was established in 1966 in Washington, D.C., by people attending the Third National Conference of the Commission on the Status of Women. Among the 28 NOW founders was its first president, BETTY FRIEDAN, author of *The Feminine Mystique* (1963). In its original statement of purpose, NOW declared to "take action to bring women into full participation in the mainstream of American society now, exercising all privileges and responsibilities thereof in truly equal partnership with men."

As part of its efforts to pursue economic equality and other rights for women, NOW launched a nationwide campaign in the 1970s to pass the EQUAL RIGHTS AMENDMENT (ERA) to the U.S. Constitution. Though the ERA ultimately failed to be ratified, NOW efforts helped the organization. NOW became a huge network of more than 200,000 activists and began operating with multimillion-dollar annual budgets. Leaders organized POLITICAL ACTION COMMITTEES, NOW/PAC and NOW Equality PAC, that raised hundreds of thousands of dollars for pro-ERA candidates.

NOW priorities are promoting economic equality, including an amendment to the U.S. Constitution that will guarantee equal rights for women; championing ABORTION rights, reproductive freedom, and other women's health issues; opposing racism and opposing bigotry against lesbians and gays; and ending violence against women. The organization has proved effective in many of these areas. NOW points to sweeping changes that put more women in political posts; increased educational, employment, and business opportunities for women; and the enactment of tougher laws against violence, SEXUAL HARASSMENT, and discrimination.

Its 1992 "Elect Women for a Change" campaign sent an unprecedented number of feminist women and men to the U.S. Congress. NOW has combated harassment and violence by organizing the first "Take Back the Night" marches and establishing hot lines and shelters for battered women. NOW has also successfully prosecuted lawsuits against antiabortion groups that bombed and blocked clinics and laws that deprived lesbian women of custody of their children. NOW has also consistently sought economic equality for women in the workplace, exposing both the "glass ceiling" that professional women face in advancing in the workplace and the difficult circumstances that poor women face in the United States.

FURTHER READINGS

Friedan, Betty. 1963. *The Feminine Mystique.* New York: Dell.

Haney, Eleanor Humes. 1985. *A Feminist Legacy: The Ethics of Wilma Scott Heide and Company.* Buffalo: Margaretdaughters.

National Organization for Women. Available online at <www.now.org> (accessed July 29, 2003).

CROSS-REFERENCES

Equal Rights; "National Organization for Women Statement of Purpose" (Appendix, Primary Document); Women's Rights.

NATIONAL RECOVERY ADMINISTRATION

In 1933, the United States was in the throes of a severe economic depression. Unemployment was widespread, and the economic system was in chaos. An emergency measure was needed to alleviate the situation, and the members of President FRANKLIN DELANO ROOSEVELT'S NEW DEAL administration attempted to ease the problem with the passage of the NATIONAL INDUSTRIAL RECOVERY ACT (NIRA) (48 Stat. 195).

The chief provision of the act was the establishment of business codes to be enforced nationally. The codes included rules regarding fair competition, discontinuance of antitrust regulations for a two-year period, voluntary participation in unions, and establishment of shorter hours and better wages.

In June 1933, the National Recovery Administration (NRA) was created to supervise the execution of the NIRA under the direction of Hugh S. Johnson. During its first year, the NRA worked on the industrial codes; all participating businesses displayed a blue eagle, a sign of patriotism as well as acceptance of the program.

Many people regarded the NRA as too powerful, and in 1935 the U.S. Supreme Court declared the CODIFICATION system of the NRA unconstitutional in SCHECHTER POULTRY CORP. V. UNITED STATES, 295 U.S. 495, 55 S. Ct. 837, 79 L. Ed. 1570, due to the incorrect granting of legislative authority to the EXECUTIVE BRANCH.

In 1936 the controversial NRA came to an end. During its brief existence, employment was stimulated, child labor was prohibited, and labor organization was encouraged.

FURTHER READINGS

Bellush, Bernard. 1975. *The Failure of the NRA.* New York: Norton.

Himmelberg, Robert F. 1976. *The Origins of the National Recovery Administration: Business, Government, and the Trade Association Issue, 1921–1933.* New York: Fordham Univ. Press.

NATIONAL REPORTER SYSTEM

See CENTURY DIGEST®; DECENNIAL DIGEST®; FEDERAL REPORTER®.

NATIONAL RIFLE ASSOCIATION

The National Rifle Association (NRA) is an organization that promotes the sport of shooting rifles and pistols in the United States. In 2001, the NRA had replaced the AMERICAN ASSOCIATION OF RETIRED PERSONS as Washington's most powerful LOBBYING group, according to *Fortune* magazine's top 25 list. The organization reports a membership of more than 4 million, which included 1 million new members alone in 2000. The membership includes hunters, target shooters, gun collectors, firearms manufacturers, and police personnel. From its headquarters in Washington, D.C., the NRA has been a dominant voice in the debate over GUN CONTROL.

With a budget of more than $200 million, the NRA maintains its own $35 million state-of-the-art lobbying machine, which includes as its major branch the NRA Institute for Legislative Action. The lobbying component is complete with an in-house telemarketing department, its own newscast, and 1 million political organizers at the precinct level. The NRA considers itself America's foremost defender of the SECOND AMENDMENT of the U.S. Constitution, which preserves the right of the people to bear arms.

The NRA platform prefers gun safety programs and the intensified enforcement of existing federal gun laws to an increase in the number of restrictions on gun owners.

Formed by New York charter in 1871, the NRA defined its original goal to "promote and encourage rifle shooting on a scientific basis," according to co-founder Colonel William C. Church. He and fellow co-founder, fellow Union veteran George Wingate, were dismayed by the lack of sportsmanship shown by Union troops and wanted to set up a rifle range for practice. With contributions from New York State, the new organization purchased the Creed Farm on Long Island in 1872 and opened it to members in 1873 under the name of "Creedmoor," the first official NRA shooting range. When political opposition to the promotion of marksmanship arose in New York, Creedmoor was deeded back to the state. A new range was established in Sea Girt, New Jersey.

The NRA targeted America's youth from the onset, and by 1903 was promoting shooting sports and competition matches through the establishment of rifle clubs at all major colleges, universities, and military academies. In addition to training and education in marksmanship, the association published *The American Rifleman*, which helped keep its members abreast of new bills and laws affecting firearms. In 1934, the NRA formed its Legislative Affairs Division, which engaged in direct mail efforts to apprise members of legislative facts regarding and analyses of pending bills. Although it was not involved in direct lobbying efforts at that time, the NRA later formed the Institute for Legislative Action in 1975, organized for the "the political defense of the Second Amendment."

During WORLD WAR II, the association offered its shooting ranges to the U.S. government and helped develop training materials for personnel and industrial security. NRA members also volunteered to reload ammunition for those guarding war plants. Through a series of gun control laws enacted between the WORLD WAR I and II, Britain found itself virtually disarmed and vulnerable when Germany began its European invasions. The NRA's efforts to encourage assistance for Britain in 1940 resulted in the collection of more than 7,000 firearms for Britain's defense against German invasion.

Following the war, the NRA concentrated on the hunting community and in 1949, in conjunction with the state of New York, set up the first hunter education program. In 1973, it launched its second magazine, *The American Hunter*. Although hunter education courses eventually became the assumed responsibility of state fish and game departments, the NRA continued to manage its Youth Hunter Education Challenge (YHEC), a program that as of 2003 was active in 43 states and three Canadian provinces, with youth enrollment of more than 40,000.

Since 1956, the association has been instrumental in law enforcement training as well. With the introduction of its Police Firearms Instructor Certification Program in 1960, the NRA became the only national trainer of law enforcement officers, and by 2000, more than 10,000 individuals had become NRA-certified graduates. The association's certified instructors train about 750,000 civilian gun owners each year, conducting gun safety programs for children in addition to personal security and protection seminars, as well as marksmanship training, for adults.

The NRA in the 1990s, in addition to fighting gun control, worked to pass state laws that made it easier for gun owners to carry their weapons in public. The "right-to-carry" movement is based on the idea that any trained, law-abiding citizen has a right to get a permit from the government to carry a firearm. As a result of the NRA's lobbying efforts, 14 states have passed right-to-carry laws and 24 other states have liberalized their statutes.

The NRA has also fought efforts by city and county governments to regulate firearms. It has lobbied for state PREEMPTION statutes, which declare that only the state government may pass firearms laws. Through its efforts, Wisconsin, Pennsylvania, and several other states passed preemption laws in 1995. Despite its longtime success in fighting gun control, the increasingly belligerent NRA rhetoric became a problem for the organization in the mid-1990s. Former President GEORGE H.W. BUSH, a lifetime member, resigned from the NRA to protest a fund-raising letter that contained anti-government statements.

The association announced the publication of its third periodical, *The American Guardian*, which proved to be less esoteric in content and catered more to topics such as recreational use of firearms and SELF-DEFENSE. Concomitant with the new publication was an internal effort to purge the organization of radical, right-wing gun

enthusiasts and develop a more general appeal. From 1997 to 2003, actor Charleton Heston served as the organization's president. Kayne Robinson, a former police officer and Marine, took over as president after Heston announced that he was suffering from a neurological disorder

Politically and historically, supporters for both the NRA and the gun-control movement have split along party lines. The NRA essentially backed so-called conservative candidates and views, such as those typically held by the REPUBLICAN PARTY or the LIBERTARIAN PARTY; those who sought stricter limitations on gun ownership tended to support Democratic candidates. At the end of the twentieth century, the delineation became more nebulous, not only among politicians but also between lobbying groups. While the organization generally opposes all forms of gun control as abridgements upon individuals' constitutional rights, many NRA members had aligned with what they refer to as "common-sense" gun control efforts. The militant gun control movement, however, splintered into extremist and middle-ground factions within their own ranks. The NRA generally holds that the criminals create gun violence, not the 48 percent of the electorate who constitute law-abiding gun owners.

FURTHER READINGS

Davidson, Osha Gray. 1998. *Under Fire: The NRA and the Battle for Gun Control.* Expanded ed. Iowa City: Univ. of Iowa Press.

LaPierre, Wayne R. 2002. *Shooting Straight: Telling the Truth About Guns in America.* Washington, D.C.: Regnery.

Rodengen, Jeffrey L. 2002. *NRA: An American Legend.* Fort Lauderdale, Fla.: Write Stuff Enterprises.

National Rifle Association. Available online at <www.nra .org> (accessed July 29, 2003).

Patrick, Brian Anse. 2002. *The National Rifle Association and the Media: The Motivating Force of Negative Coverage.* New York: Peter Lang.

CROSS-REFERENCES

Gun Control; Libertarian Party.

NATIONAL RIGHT TO LIFE COMMITTEE

The National Right to Life Committee (NRLC) is a nonprofit organization that seeks to end legalized ABORTION in the United States. Founded in 1973, following the U.S. Supreme Court's decision in ROE V. WADE, 410 U.S. 113, 93 S. Ct. 705, 35 L. Ed. 2d 147 (1973), which held that women had a constitutional right to abortion, the NRLC has become the leading antiabortion organization in the United States. It has more than 7 million members, with 3,000 local chapters and 50 state affiliates. It is headquartered in Washington, D.C., and has an annual budget of more than $9 million. The *National Right to Life News*, a biweekly newsletter, has a circulation of 135,000.

From its inception, the NRLC has sought the passage of a constitutional amendment banning abortion. Though this effort has not been successful, the NRLC has played an important role in state and federal legislation regulating and restricting abortion, and has been instrumental in restricting government funding of abortions to poor women. The NRLC has a POLITICAL ACTION COMMITTEE that endorses and campaigns for candidates who support its agenda, which includes opposition to some forms of BIRTH CONTROL as well as physician-assisted suicide. The committee states that it does not take a position on issues such as contraception, sex education, CAPITAL PUNISHMENT, and national defense.

The NRLC has lobbied for federal legislation banning partial-birth abortions. Though Congress passed the Partial-Birth Abortion Ban Act in 1996 and 1997, President BILL CLINTON vetoed the measure both times. The act remained the highest priority of the NRLC, which has helped secure state legislation banning the abortion procedure in 17 states. It also supports legislation that would make it a federal offense to transport an individual age 17 or under across a state line for an abortion if this action circumvents the application of a state law requiring parental involvement in a minor's abortion.

The NRLC operates four outreach programs: National Teens for Life, American Victims of Abortion, National Pro-Life Religious Council, and Black Americans for Life. National Teens for Life organizes various activities for its teenage members, including speaking in schools and to youth groups, volunteering in crisis pregnancy centers, peer counseling, debating, and helping adult groups work to pass legislation. American Victims of Abortion is comprised of women who have had an abortion. This group lobbies legislators and seeks to educate the media about the physical and emotional risks associated with abortion. The National Pro-Life Religious Council seeks "to articulate the historic Judeo-Christian perspective concerning

human life issues," and "to support efforts that discourage and prevent acts that dehumanize and harm women, the unborn, DISABLED PERSONS, the elderly, and those who are medically dependent." Black Americans for Life attempts to discourage African American women from having abortions.

The NRLC political action committee spent over $2 million during the 1996 elections. In 1999, NLRC opposition to campaign finance reform caused a divisive split between the NLRC and pro-life Democrats who accused the organization of becoming increasingly identified with the REPUBLICAN PARTY. The election of GEORGE W. BUSH as president in 2000 and the gain of Republican seats in both the House and Senate in 2002 strengthened the position of abortion opponents including the NRLC. As a number of state legislatures with anti-abortion majorities began to pass restrictive legislation, many analysts waited to see if Supreme Court retirements would lead President Bush to appoint a judge or judges who might vote to reverse *Roe v. Wade*, given the opportunity.

FURTHER READINGS

Grunwald, Michael. "Campaign Finance Issue Divides Abortion Foes." 1999. *Washington Post* (September 14).

National Right to Life Committee. Available online at <www.nrlc.org> (accessed July 30, 2003).

CROSS-REFERENCES

Abortion; Fetal Rights; Women's Rights.

NATIONAL SECURITY COUNCIL

The National Security Council (NSC) is the U.S. president's principal forum for considering national security and foreign policy matters; the council consists of senior national security advisors and cabinet officials. Since its inception under President HARRY TRUMAN, the function of the NSC has been to advise and assist the president on national security and foreign policies. The council also serves as the president's principal arm for coordinating these policies among various government agencies.

The NSC was established by the National Security Act of 1947, as amended (50 U.S.C.A. § 402), and was placed in the Executive Office of the President by REORGANIZATION PLAN No. 4 of 1949 (5 U.S.C.A. app.). The NSC was designed to provide the president with a foreign-policy instrument independent of the STATE DEPARTMENT.

President George W. Bush meets with the National Security Council in October 2001.

REUTERS NEWMEDIA INC./CORBIS

The NSC is chaired by the president. Its statutory members, in addition to the president, include the vice president and the secretaries of state and defense. The chair of the Joint Chiefs of Staff is the statutory military advisor to the council, and the director of the CENTRAL INTELLIGENCE AGENCY is the statutory intelligence advisor. The secretary of the treasury, the U.S. representative to the UNITED NATIONS, the assistant to the president for national security affairs, the assistant to the president for economic policy, and the chief of staff to the president are invited to all meetings. The attorney general and the director of the OFFICE OF NATIONAL DRUG CONTROL POLICY attend meetings pertaining to their jurisdiction. Other officials are invited, as appropriate.

The NSC began as a small office supporting the president, but its staff has grown over the years. It is headed by the assistant to the president for national security affairs, who is also referred to as the national security advisor. The NSC staff performs a variety of activities for the president and the national security advisor. The staff participates in presidential briefings, assists the president in responding to congressional inquiries, and prepares public remarks. The NSC staff serves as an initial point of contact for departments and agencies that want to bring a national security issue to the president's attention. The staff also participates in interagency working groups organized to assess policy issues in coordinated fashion.

The issues concerning national security are wide ranging. Foreign and military relations with other countries have generally taken center stage, but international TERRORISM, narcotics control, and world economic issues have been brought before the NSC. In most administrations, the national security advisor has played a key role in formulating foreign policy. For example, as national security advisor during the Nixon administration, HENRY KISSINGER was the *de facto* SECRETARY OF STATE, developing policy on the VIETNAM WAR, the opening of relations with communist China, and negotiating with Israel and the Arab nations for a peaceful solution to problems in the Middle East.

The image of the NSC was tarnished in the 1980s during the Reagan administration. Two successive national security advisors, Robert C. McFarlane and Rear Admiral John M. Poindexter, and NSC staffer Lieutenant Colonel Oliver L. North participated in the IRAN-CONTRA AFFAIR. They violated a congressional ban on U.S. military aid to the Nicaraguan anticommunist Contra rebels by providing the rebels with funds obtained by the secret sale of military weapons to Iran.

Under the administration of President GEORGE H.W. BUSH in the early 1990s, the NSC was reorganized to include a Principals Committee, Deputies Committee, and eight Policy Coordinating Committees. Under President BILL CLINTON, NSC membership was expanded to include the secretary of the Treasury, the U.S representative to the United Nations, and the assistant to the president for Economic Policy as well as the president's chief of staff and his national security advisor. In 2001 President GEORGE W. BUSH appointed Dr. Condoleezza Rice to be his national security advisor. She was the first woman appointed to that position. The NSC has been involved in American foreign policy decisions that have ranged from sending troops to Panama in 1989 and to Iraq in 1991 and 2003, as well as dealing with such issues as international trafficking in illegal drugs, U.N. peacekeeping missions, strategic ARMS CONTROL policy, and global environmental affairs.

FURTHER READINGS

National Security Council at the White House. Available online at <www.whitehouse.gov/nsc> (accessed July 30, 2003).

U.S. Government Manual Website. Available online at <www.gpoaccess.gov/gmanual> (accessed November 10, 2003).

CROSS-REFERENCES

Executive Branch; Presidential Powers; State Department.

NATIONAL TRANSPORTATION SAFETY BOARD

The National Transportation Safety Board (NTSB) is a federal investigatory board headquartered in Washington, D.C., whose mandate is to ensure safe public transportation. Established in 1966 as part of the DEPARTMENT OF TRANSPORTATION, the NTSB investigates accidents, conducts studies, and makes recommendations to federal agencies and the transportation industry. It is chiefly known for its highly visible role in civil aviation accidents, which it has sole authority under federal law to investigate. Additionally, the NTSB probes certain marine accidents and accidents that occur in the use of railroads, highways, and pipelines. The five members of the board are appointed by the president.

The NTSB grew out of the long history of federal oversight of aviation. As early as 1926, Congress required the investigation of civil aviation crashes under the Air Commerce Act (Pub. L. No. 69-254, 44 Stat. 568). Over the next three decades, lawmakers created a maze of regulatory agencies, including the Civil Aeronautics Authority and the FEDERAL AVIATION ADMINISTRATION (FAA). The Federal Aviation Act of 1958 (Pub. L. No. 85-726, 72 Stat. 731) gave duties for investigating accidents to the Civil Aeronautics Board (CAB), intending for the board to study aircraft and the actions of their pilots in the hopes of preventing future disasters.

As the airline industry grew, Congress reorganized its regulatory scheme. With passage of the Department of Transportation Act of 1966 (Pub. L. No. 89-670, 80 Stat. 935), lawmakers created the NTSB within the Department of Transportation and gave it the responsibilities formerly held by the CAB. However, the NTSB often ended up conducting investigations of the FAA. In 1974, in an attempt to avoid conflicts between agencies, Congress made the NTSB an independent board by passing the Independent Safety Board Act of 1974 (49 U.S.C.A. app. § 1901 [1982]). The act gave the NTSB sole responsibility for investigating airline crashes.

The investigatory powers of the NTSB are quite broad. Once its teams are dispatched to the site of an accident, they maintain exclusive control over the scene. Their authority includes seizing all evidence for examination, including an airline's flight recorder (the so-called "black box"). They can also bar other parties from their proceedings—an important element of autonomy given the inevitable litigation that follows airline accidents. In subsequent stages of an investigation, the NTSB is empowered to demand records, testimony, and other information from airline officials. The purpose of its work is to prepare public reports of two types: factual reports and interpretive analyses of accidents to determine their PROBABLE CAUSE.

The use of NTSB reports in court is controversial. Under federal law they are intended to be used to prevent future accidents from occurring, and therefore they are released to the public. But to a certain extent, they are forbidden by law from being used in civil lawsuits. Some form of this rule has been in effect since the creation of the CAB in 1958. Section 1441(e) of the Independent Safety Board Act of 1974 stated, "No part of any report or reports of the National Transportation Safety Board relating to any accident or the investigation thereof, shall be admitted as evidence or used in any suit or action for damages growing out of any matter mentioned in such report or reports." However, courts have permitted civil litigants to use some NTSB report material, and the regulations have changed in response. Only the so-called probable cause reports are strictly impermissible in civil lawsuits, and NTSB employees are permitted only to testify as to factual matters surrounding their investigations. These limitations have upset some attorneys who argue that civil litigants should have full access to all NTSB data, but defenders have argued that the standard is necessary to protect the board's autonomy.

Since its creation in 1967, the NTSB has investigated over 114,000 aviation accidents and more than 10,000 surface transportation accidents. The organization has issued more than 11,600 recommendations regarding transportation safety to over 2,200 recipients. Many of these recommendations became the basis for safety features incorporated into surface, air, and water vehicles. Since 1990, the NTSB has highlighted various issues such as protecting child passengers, use of SEAT BELTS, and recreational boating safety in its "Most Wanted" list of transportation safety improvements. NTSB investigators are on call 24 hours a day, 365 days a year,

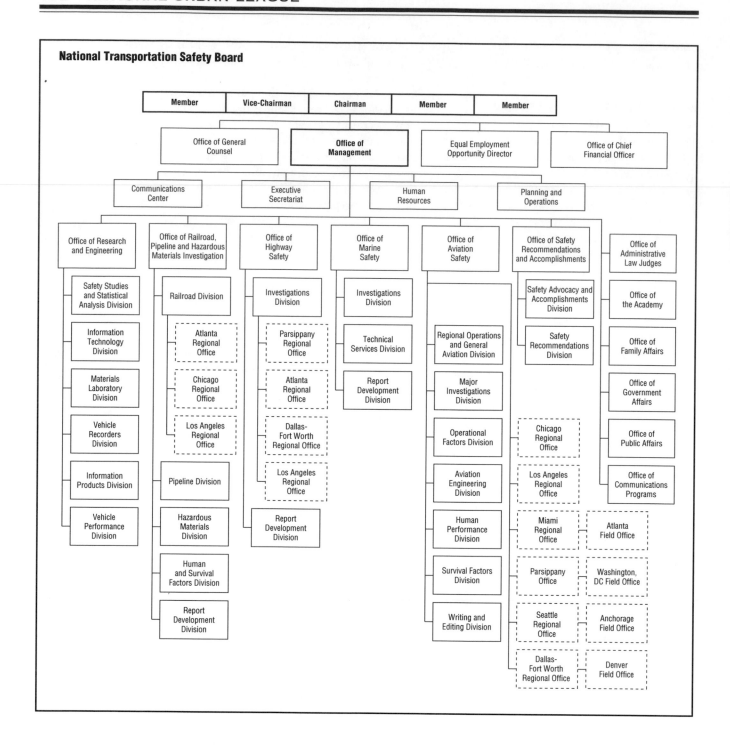

National Transportation Safety Board

traveling throughout the United States and all over the world to investigate major accidents.

FURTHER READINGS

Atwood, Roy Tress. 1987. "Admissibility of National Transportation Safety Board Reports in Civil Air Crash Litigation." *Journal of Air Law and Commerce* 53 (winter).

Cook, Joseph T. 1992. "Let Safety Board Give the Facts." *National Law Journal* (October 26).

National Transportation Safety Board. Available online at <www.ntsb.gov> (accessed July 30, 2003).

U.S. Government Manual Website. Available online at <www.gpoaccess.gov/gmanual> (accessed November 10, 2003).

CROSS-REFERENCES

Airlines; Federal Aviation Administration.

NATIONAL URBAN LEAGUE

The National Urban League, more commonly known as the Urban League, is a nonprofit, multiracial organization that is dedicated to the elimination of racial SEGREGATION and discrimination and to the enhancement of economic and educational opportunities for African Americans throughout the United States. The Urban League, which was founded in 1910 and is headquartered in New York City, has more than 100 affiliates in 34 states and the District of Columbia.

In 1896, the U.S. Supreme Court's decision in PLESSY V. FERGUSON 163 U.S. 537, 16 S.Ct. 1138, 41 L.Ed. 256 (1896), which held that "separate but equal" accommodations for blacks and whites was constitutional, led to a severe system of segregation in the South in which so-called JIM CROW LAWS barred blacks from schools, jobs, and many public places including hotels, bars, and restaurants. The early 1900s saw the beginnings of a migration of blacks from the rural South moving North to find better jobs and economic stability for their families.

Upon arriving in the Northern states, however, many blacks found themselves still excluded from decent housing, jobs, and education. Mostly rural in background, many were bewildered by the customs and mores of urban living. Realizing that these newcomers desperately needed help, the Committee on Urban Conditions among Negroes was established in New York City on September 29, 1910.

In 1911, the committee merged with two other organizations to form the National League on Urban Conditions among Negroes. The organization began by counseling black migrants and training black social workers but soon expanded its activities into such areas as housing, employment, education, recreation, and health and sanitation. By the end of WORLD WAR I, the organization had 81 staff members working in New York and in affiliates that had been established in 30 other cities. In 1919 the organization became known as the National Urban League.

Throughout the Great Depression the Urban League crusaded for the INTEGRATION of blacks into segregated LABOR UNIONS and for inclusion in President FRANKLIN D. ROOSEVELT's NEW DEAL programs that were aimed at fostering economic recovery. During WORLD WAR II, the League continued to fight for integration of the trade unions, particularly those involved in defense work and in the ARMED SERVICES. After the war, the league worked with businesses to train black workers for various trades and to

encourage Fortune 500 companies to participate in job fairs held on black college campuses.

In 1942 Mrs. Mollie L. Moon started the first Urban League Guild in New York City. Guild members were volunteers who helped League efforts and its programs. The guild placed particular emphasis on information, fund-raising, and leadership development. The activities of the New York Guild were so productive that many others were started by Urban League affiliates. In 1952 the National Council of Guilds was established. In 2003 the National Council oversaw the work of guilds in more than 85 cities.

In 1961 Whitney M. Young Jr. became the league's executive director. Under his leadership the organization grew from 60 chapters to 98, and numerous large American corporations and foundations made contributions that supported job and housing programs as well as other social WELFARE programs. Young's ten-point program calling for federal funding to help reduce poverty among blacks became the basis for President Lyndon Johnson's "War on Poverty" that was aimed at reducing poverty for all Americans.

In 1972 Vernon E. Jordan Jr. became the league's fifth executive director. Jordan oversaw a number of new initiatives in the areas of business development, housing, and education. He established the league as a major channel for passing federal funds to urban community programs and services. He also emphasized voter registration, and programs dealing with energy conservation, protection of the environment, and new job roles for women.

John Jacob, who expanded the league's mission and established the Permanent Development Fund, succeeded Jordan in 1982. Jacob advocated for programs to fight crime in black neighborhoods, to reduce teenage pregnancies, and to help single parents. In 1994 Jacob was succeeded by Hugh B. Price, an attorney who emphasized AFFIRMATIVE ACTION, economic empowerment, and the importance of diversity in an increasingly multi-ethnic society.

In 2000 the league recast its Washington Operations Office as the Institute for Opportunity and Equality. The Institute conducts research, analyzes policy, and advocates for significant issues including employment, criminal justice, community development, and economic policy.

In April 2003, the Urban League named Milton Little as interim president and CEO to replace Price who resigned in November 2002. The new president will oversee the operations of the league, which in 2003 had a budget of more than $40 million and was the oldest and largest community-based U.S. organization dedicated to helping blacks achieve racial and economic parity.

FURTHER READINGS

Moore, Jesse Thomas. 1981. *A Search for Equality: The National Urban League, 1910–1961*. University Park: Pennsylvania State Univ. Press.

National Urban League. Available online at <www.nul.org> (accessed July 30, 2003).

CROSS-REFERENCES

Civil Rights Acts; Civil Rights Movement; Discrimination; Equal Rights; NAACP.

NATIONALITY

See ALIENS.

NATIVE AMERICAN GRAVES PROTECTION AND REPATRIATION ACT OF 1990

Years of the U.S. government granting a free hand to those who wished to examine Native American remains came to an end with the passage of the Native American Graves Protection and Repatriation Act of 1990 (NAGPRA) (25 U.S.C. § 3001 et. seq.). This act marks a reversal of previous U.S. government policies, not only providing protection for Native American burial sites but also helping Native Americans take possession of the remains of their ancestors currently in the hands of museums and other scientific institutions. The law supports the idea that Native Americans have the right to determine the proper disposal of the remains of their ancestors, although it has come under some criticism by the scientific community for its potential to stifle research into ancient American tribes.

Among the many contentious issues that have afflicted the relationship between Native Americans and the U.S. government, none has been more difficult than the issue of the remains of Native American tribes. The U.S. Government has traditionally seen these remains as worthy of archeological and scientific study and has awarded wide latitude to those who want to examine them. In contrast, Native Americans tend to see the archeologists and museums who have dug up and taken possession of these remains over the years as little more than "grave robbers" and have demanded that the burial places of their ancestors be respected.

The law's origin lies in the CIVIL RIGHTS MOVEMENT of the 1960s and its affect on Native Americans, who began advocating changes in American laws that they saw as promoting a disrespect for their culture. Among the most egregious examples of this was the Antiquities Preservation Act of 1906, which made almost all Native American burial sites into "objects of antiquity" or "archaeological resources" and in effect gave the federal government the right to determine their fate. This became unacceptable to Native Americans, and in response to their complaints, the federal government passed the 1979 Archaeological Resource Protection Act, (16 U.S.C. § 470aa-470ii), which made it more difficult to excavate on Native American lands, and the 1989 National Museum of the American Indian Act (20 U.S.C.A. § 80q), which required the Smithsonian Institute to repatriate remains to tribes that could show that they were related to the remains.

But Native American groups saw these laws as inadequate, so in 1990, Congress passed the sweeping Native American Graves Protection and Repatriation Act. NAGPRA for the first time establishes that the ownership or control of Native American cultural items, including remains that are excavated or discovered on federal or tribal lands, shall rest with the Native American tribes themselves. Priority is given first to the lineal descendants of the Native American whose remains were discovered, or in any case in which such lineal descendants cannot be ascertained, in the Native American tribe on whose tribal land such objects or remains were discovered; and then to the Native American tribe that has the closest cultural affiliation with such remains or objects and which, upon notice, states a claim for such remains or objects.

If the cultural affiliation of the objects cannot be reasonably ascertained, and if the objects were discovered on federal land that is recognized by a final judgment of the Indian Claims Commission or the U.S. Court of Claims as the aboriginal land of some Indian tribe, the ownership title will go to the Native American tribe that is recognized as occupying the area in which the objects were discovered, if the tribe states a claim for such remains or objects. However, if it can be shown by a PREPONDERANCE OF THE EVIDENCE that a different tribe has a stronger cultural relationship with the remains or objects than the tribe or organization that currently occupies the area, then ownership of the remains will go to the Indian tribe that has the strongest demonstrated relationship.

In addition, NAGPRA requires federal agencies and each museum that has possession or control over holdings or collections of Native American human remains to compile an inventory of such items and, to the extent possible based on information possessed by such museum or federal agency, identify the geographical and cultural affiliation of such item. The agency or museum must supply notice to any tribe that it finds was affiliated with the remains. The agency and museum must repatriate any items where a claim has been established by known lineal descendant of the Native American or of the tribe; or where a cultural affiliation is shown by a preponderance of the evidence based upon geographical, kinship, biological, archaeological, anthropological, linguistic, folkloric, oral traditional, historical, or other relevant information or expert opinion. For unassociated funerary objects, sacred objects, or objects of cultural patrimony, the museum or agency must return such objects where the requesting party is the direct lineal descendant of an individual who owned the sacred object, where the requesting Indian tribe or Native Hawaiian organization can show that the object was owned or controlled by the tribe or organization, or where the requesting Native American tribe can show that the sacred object was owned or controlled by a member thereof, provided that in the case where a sacred object was owned by a member thereof, there are no identifiable lineal descendants of said member, or the lineal descendants have failed to make a claim for the object.

The only exception is that repatriation is not required of such items that are indispensable for completion of a specific scientific study, the outcome of which would be of major benefit to the United States. Such items shall be returned by no later than 90 days after the date on which the scientific study is completed. Museums may also retain material until competing claims are resolved, and they are protected against claims by aggrieved parties if objects are returned in GOOD FAITH. Finally, the law establishes a seven-member commission, three of whom must be from Native-American tribes, three of whom represent the scientific community, and one of

whom is appointed by the secretary from a list approved by the other six members, for the purpose of resolving certain disputes under the legislation. Two of the three Native Americans appointed to this commission must be traditional religious leaders.

NAGPRA for the first time gives Native Americans control over their ancestors burial remains, and ensures repatriation for remains and other sacred objects that currently reside in museums and with other federal agencies. It is an important milestone in the relationship between the United States and its Native American inhabitants

FURTHER READINGS

Afrasiabi, Peter R. 1997. "Property Rights in Ancient Human Skeletal Remains." *Southern California Law Review* 70.

Hibbert, Michelle. 1998/1999. "Galileos or Grave Robbers? Science, the Native American Graves Protection and Repatriation Act, and the First Amendment." *American Indian Law Review* 23.

Platzman, Steven Winter. 1992. "Objects of Controversy: The Native American Right to Repatriation." *American University Law Review* 41.

NATIVE AMERICAN RIGHTS

In the United States, persons of Native American descent occupy a unique legal position. On the one hand, they are U.S. citizens and are entitled to the same legal rights and protections under the Constitution that all other U.S. citizens enjoy. On the other hand, they are members of self-governing tribes whose existence far predates the arrival of Europeans on American shores. They are the descendants of peoples who had their own inherent rights—rights that required no validation or legitimation from the newcomers who found their way onto their soil.

These combined, and in many ways conflicting, legal positions have resulted in a complex relationship between Native American tribes and the federal government. Although the historic events and specific details of each tribe's situation vary considerably, the legal rights and status maintained by Native Americans are the result of their shared history of wrestling with the U.S. government over such issues as tribal sovereignty, shifting government policies, treaties that were made and often broken, and conflicting latter-day interpretations of those treaties. The result today is that although Native Americans enjoy the same legal rights as every other U.S. citizen, they also retain unique rights in such areas as hunting and fishing, water use, and GAMING operations. In general, these rights are based on the legal foundations of tribal sovereignty, treaty provisions, and the "reserved rights" doctrine, which holds that Native Americans retain all rights not explicitly abrogated in treaties or other legislation.

Tribal Sovereignty

Tribal sovereignty refers to the fact that each tribe has the inherent right to govern itself. Before Europeans came to North America, Native American tribes conducted their own affairs and needed no outside source to legitimate their powers or actions. When the various European powers did arrive, however, they claimed dominion over the lands that they found, thus violating the sovereignty of the tribes who already were living there.

The issue of the extent and limits of tribal sovereignty came before the U.S. Supreme Court in *Johnson v. McIntosh,* 21 U.S. (8 Wheat.) 543, 5 L. Ed. 681 (1823). Writing for the majority, Chief Justice JOHN MARSHALL described the effects of European incursion on native tribes, writing that although the Indians were "admitted to be the rightful occupants of the soil . . . their rights to complete sovereignty, as independent nations, were necessarily diminished, and their power to dispose of the soil, at their own will, to whomsoever they pleased, was denied by the original fundamental principle, that discovery gave exclusive title to those who made it." The European nations that had "discovered" North America, Marshall ruled, had "the sole right of acquiring the soil from the natives."

Having acknowledged this limitation to tribal sovereignty in *Johnson,* however, Marshall's opinions in subsequent cases reinforced the principle of tribal sovereignty. In *Cherokee Nation v. Georgia,* 30 U.S. (5 Pet.) 1, 8 L. Ed. 25 (1831), Marshall elaborated on the legal status of the Cherokees, describing the tribe as a "distinct political society that was separated from others, capable of managing its own affairs, and governing itself." In *Worcester v. Georgia,* 31 U.S. (6 Pet.) 515, 8 L. Ed. 483 (1832), Marshall returned to the issue, this time in an opinion denying the state of Georgia's right to impose its laws on a Cherokee reservation within the state's borders. He rejected the state's argument, writing "The Cherokee nation . . . is a distinct community, occupying its own territory, with boundaries accurately described, in which the laws of Georgia can have no force." Reviewing the history of relations between native tribes and the colonizing European powers, Marshall cited the Indians' "original natural rights," which he said were limited only by "the single exception of that imposed by irresistible power, which excluded them from intercourse with any other European potentate than the first discoverer of the coast of the particular region claimed."

The cumulative effect of Marshall's opinions was to position Native American tribes as nations whose independence had been limited in just two specific areas: the right to transfer land and the right to deal with foreign powers. In regard to their own internal functions, the tribes were considered to be sovereign and to be free from state intrusion on that sovereignty. This position formulated by Marshall has been modified over the years, but it continues to serve as the foundation for determining the extents and limits of Native American tribal sovereignty. Although Congress has the ultimate power to limit or abolish tribal governments, until it does so each tribe retains the right to self-government, and no state may impose its laws on the reservation. This position was reiterated in a 1978 U.S. Supreme Court case, *United States v. Wheeler,* 435 U.S. 313, 98 S. Ct. 1079, 55 L. Ed. 2d 303, in which Justice POTTER STEWART concluded that "Indian tribes still possess those aspects of sovereignty not withdrawn by treaty or statute, or by implication as a necessary result of their dependent status."

The ways that individual tribes exercise their sovereignty vary widely, but, in general, tribal authority is used in the following areas: to form tribal governments; to determine tribal membership; to regulate individual property; to levy and collect taxes; to maintain law and order; to exclude non-members from tribal territory; to regulate domestic relations; and to regulate commerce and trade.

Treaty Rights

From the time Europeans first arrived in North America, they needed goods and services from Native Americans in order to survive. Often, the terms of such exchanges were codified in treaties, which are contracts between sovereign nations. After the American Revolution, the federal government used treaties as its principal method for acquiring land from the Indians. From the first treaty with the Delawares in 1787 to the end of treaty making in 1871, the federal

government signed more than 650 treaties with various Native American tribes. Although specific treaty elements varied, treaties commonly included such provisions as a guarantee of peace; a cession of certain delineated lands; a promise by the United States to create a reservation for the Indians under federal protection; a guarantee of Indian hunting and fishing rights; and a statement that the tribe recognized the authority or placed itself under the protection of the United States. Treaty making ended in 1871, when Congress passed a rider to an Indian appropriations act providing, "No Indian nation or tribe . . . shall be acknowledged or recognized as an independent nation, tribe, or power with whom the United States may contract by treaty . . ." (25 U.S.C.A. § 71). This rider was passed largely in response to the House of Representatives' frustration that it was excluded from Indian affairs because the constitutional power to make treaties rests exclusively with the Senate. Since 1871, the federal government has regulated Native American affairs through legislation, which does not require the consent of the Indians involved, as treaties do.

Indian treaties may seem like historical documents, but the courts have consistently ruled that they retain the same legal force that they had when they were negotiated. Despite frequent challenges and intense opposition, courts have upheld guaranteed specific tribal rights, such as hunting and fishing rights. Often, disputes over treaty rights arise from conflicting interpretations of the specific language of treaty provisions. In general, there are three basic principles for interpreting treaty language. First, uncertainties in Indian treaties should be resolved in favor of the Indians. Second, Indian treaties should be interpreted as the Indians signing the treaty would have understood them. Third, Indian treaties are to be liberally construed in favor of the Indians involved. Courts have consistently upheld these principles of treaty interpretation, which clearly favor the Indians, on the basis that Indian tribes were the much weaker party in treaty negotiations, signing documents written in a foreign language and often with little choice. Liberal interpretation rules are designed to address the great inequality of the parties' original bargaining positions.

The route taken by Cherokees from southern Appalachia to Oklahoma in 1838 is called the Trail of Tears. Supreme Court decisions of that time called the native tribes "the rightful occupants of the soil" but also held that Europeans had "discovered" North America and had the right to "acquir[e] the soil from the natives."

PAINTING BY ROBERT LINDNEUX. THE GRANGER COLLECTION, NEW YORK

Reserved Rights Doctrine

Another crucial factor in the interpretation of Native American treaties is what is known as the reserved rights doctrine, which holds that any rights that are not specifically addressed in a treaty are reserved to the tribe. In other words, treaties outline the specific rights that the tribes gave up, not those that they retained. The courts have consistently interpreted treaties in this fashion, beginning with *United States v. Winans,* 198 U.S. 371, 25 S. Ct. 662, 49 L. Ed. 1089 (1905), in which the U.S. Supreme Court ruled that a treaty is "not a grant of rights to the Indians, but a grant of rights from them." Any right not explicitly extinguished by a treaty or a federal statute is considered to be "reserved" to the tribe. Even when a tribe is officially "terminated" by Congress, it retains any and all rights that are not specifically mentioned in the termination statute.

Federal Power over Native American Rights

Although Native Americans have been held to have both inherent rights and rights guaranteed, either explicitly or implicitly, by treaties with the federal government, the government retains the ultimate power and authority to either abrogate or protect Native American rights. This power stems from several legal sources. One is the power that the Constitution gives to Congress to make regulations governing the territory belonging to the United States (Art. IV, Sec. 3, Cl. 2), and another is the president's constitutional power to make treaties (Art. II, Sec. 2, Cl. 2). A more commonly cited source of federal power over Native American affairs is the COMMERCE CLAUSE of the U.S. Constitution, which provides that "Congress shall have the Power . . . to regulate Commerce with foreign Nations, and among the several States, and with the Indian Tribes" (Art. I, Sec. 8, Cl. 3). This clause has resulted in what is known as Congress's "plenary power" over Indian affairs, which means that Congress has the ultimate right to pass legislation governing Native Americans, even when that legislation conflicts with or abrogates Indian treaties. The most well-known case supporting this congressional right is *Lone Wolf v. Hitchcock,* 187 U.S. 553, 23 S. Ct. 216, 47 L. Ed. 299 (1903), in which Congress broke a treaty provision that had guaranteed that no more cessions of land would be made without the consent of three-fourths of the adult males from the Kiowa and Comanche tribes. In justifying this abrogation, Justice EDWARD D. WHITE declared that when "treaties were entered into between the United States and a tribe of Indians it was never doubted that the *power* to abrogate existed in Congress, and that in a contingency such power might be availed of from considerations of governmental policy."

Another source for the federal government's power over Native American affairs is what is called the "trust relationship" between the government and Native American tribes. This "trust relationship" or "trust responsibility" refers to the federal government's consistent promise, in the treaties that it signed, to protect the safety and well-being of the tribal members in return for their willingness to give up their lands. This notion of a trust relationship between Native Americans and the federal government was developed by U.S. Supreme Court Justice John Marshall in the opinions that he wrote for the three cases on tribal sovereignty described above, which became known as the Marshall Trilogy. In the second of these cases, *Cherokee Nation v. Georgia,* Marshall specifically described the tribes as "domestic dependant nations" whose relation to the United States was like "that of a ward to his guardian." Similarly, in *Worcester v. Georgia,* Marshall declared that the federal government had entered into a special relationship with the Cherokees through the treaties they had signed, a relationship involving certain moral obligations. "The Cherokees," he wrote, "acknowledge themselves to be under the protection of the United States, and of no other power. Protection does not imply the destruction of the protected."

The federal government has often used this trust relationship to justify its actions on behalf of Native American tribes, such as its defense of Indian fishing and hunting rights and the establishment of the Bureau of Indian Affairs. Perhaps more often, however, the federal government has used the claim of a trust relationship to stretch its protective duty toward tribes into an almost unbridled power over them. The United States, for example, is the legal title-holder to most Indian lands, giving it the power to dispose of and manage those lands, as well as to derive income from them. The federal government has also used its powers in ways that seem inconsistent with a moral duty to protect Indian interests, such as terminating dozens of Indian tribes and consistently breaking treaty provisions. Because the trust responsibility is moral rather than legal, Native American tribes have had very little power or ability to enforce the promises and obligations of the federal government.

Several disputes have erupted over the relationship between the federal government and Native Americans. Beginning in 1998, beneficiaries of Individual Indian Money (IIM), which is held in trust by the federal government, brought a CLASS ACTION against the secretary of the interior and others, alleging mismanagement and breach of fiduciary duties against trustee-delegates of the funds. The case has spawned dozens of orders and rulings by the U.S. District Court for the District of Columbia.

In 1999, the district court in *Cobell v. Babbitt*, 91 F. Supp. 2d 1 (D.D.C. 1999), found that the secretary of the interior and others had violated their fiduciary duties and ordered the secretary to file quarterly reports detailing progress in fulfilling these orders. The U.S Court of Appeals for the District of Columbia Circuit affirmed this ruling in *Cobell v. Norton*, 240 F.3d 1081 (D.C. Cir. 2001). Since the appeals court ruling, the district court has considered numerous motions and has issued several orders, including a holding that the secretary of the interior and the secretary of the Treasury were guilty of civil CONTEMPT for refusing to comply with a court order to produce certain documents.

Other issues involving the federal government's power over Native Americans have likewise resulted in litigation. The struggle to define the jurisdictional boundaries between Native American tribal courts and state courts has occupied the federal courts for many years. Although Indian reservations are deemed sovereign states, both Congress and the U.S. Supreme Court have placed limitations on their sovereignty. Therefore, as specific issues arise about tribal court jurisdiction, the federal courts must intervene to decide these cases.

Such was the case in *Nevada v. Hicks*, 533 U.S. 353, 121 S. Ct. 2304, 150 L. Ed. 2d 398 (2001), in which the U.S. Supreme Court ruled that tribal courts do not have jurisdiction to hear federal CIVIL RIGHTS lawsuits concerning allegedly unconstitutional actions by a state government officer on tribal land. The case arose when the home of a member of the Fallon Paiute-Shoshone Tribes of western Nevada was searched under suspicion that the tribe member had killed a bighorn sheep in violation of Nevada law. The tribe member brought a federal civil rights lawsuit against the game warden who had searched his house. The suit was brought in tribal court, which ruled that it had jurisdiction to hear the claim against the warden.

The district court and the U.S. Court of Appeals for the Ninth Circuit both found that the warden was required to exhaust his remedies in the tribal court before proceeding to federal court. The U.S. Supreme Court, per Justice ANTONIN SCALIA disagreed, finding that Congress had not extended the jurisdiction of tribal court to hear federal civil rights claims. The case severely limits the scope of tribal jurisdiction.

Hunting and Fishing Rights

Hunting and fishing rights are some of the special rights that Native Americans enjoy as a result of the treaties signed between their tribes and the federal government. Historically, hunting and fishing were critically important to Native American tribes. Fish and wildlife were a primary source of food and trade goods, and tribes based their own seasonal movements on fish migrations. In addition, fish and wildlife played a central role in the spiritual and cultural framework of Native American life. As the Court noted, access to fish and wildlife was "not much less necessary to the existence of the Indians than the atmosphere they breathed" (*United States v. Winans*, 198 U.S. 371, S. Ct. 662, 49 L. Ed. 2d 1089 [1905]).

When Native American tribes signed treaties consenting to give up their lands, the treaties often explicitly guaranteed hunting and fishing rights. When the treaties created reservations, they usually gave tribe members the right to hunt and fish on reservation lands. In many cases, treaties guaranteed Native Americans the continued freedom to hunt and fish in their traditional hunting and fishing locations, even if those areas were outside the reservations. Even when hunting and fishing rights were not specifically mentioned in treaties, the reserved-rights doctrine holds that tribes retain any rights, including the right to hunt and fish, that are not explicitly abrogated by treaty or statute.

Controversy and protest have surrounded Native American hunting and fishing rights, as state governments and non-Indian hunters and fishers have fought to make Native Americans subject to state hunting and fishing regulations. The rights of tribal members to hunt and fish on their own reservations have rarely been questioned, because states generally lack the power to regulate activities on Indian reservations. Tribes themselves have the right to regulate hunting and fishing on their reservations, whether or not they choose to do so. Protests have arisen, however, over the rights of Native Americans to hunt and fish off of their reservations. Such rights can be acquired in one of two ways. In some instances, Congress has reduced the size of a tribe's reservation, or terminated it completely, without removing the tribe's hunting and fishing rights on that land. In other cases, treaties have specifically guaranteed tribes the right to hunt and fish in locations off the reservations. In the Pacific Northwest, for example, treaty provisions commonly guaranteed the right of tribes to fish "at all usual and accustomed grounds and stations," both on and off their reservations. Tribes in the Great Lakes area also reserved their off-reservation fishing rights in the treaties they signed.

These off-reservation rights have led to intense opposition and protests from non-Indian hunters and fishermen and state wildlife agencies. Non-Indian hunters and fishermen resent the fact that Indians are not subject to the same state regulations and limits imposed on them. State agencies have protested the fact that legitimate conservation goals are compromised when Indians can hunt and fish without having to follow state wildlife regulations. The U.S. Supreme Court, however, has consistently upheld the off-reservation hunting and fishing rights of Native Americans. In the 1905 case *United States v. Winans,* it ruled that treaty language guaranteeing a tribe the right to "tak[e] fish at all usual and accustomed places" indeed guaranteed access to those usual and accustomed places, even if they were on privately owned land.

The most intense opposition to Native American off-reservation hunting and fishing rights has occurred in the Pacific Northwest, where tribal members have fought to defend their right to fish in their traditional locations, unhindered by state regulations. In a series of cases involving the state of Washington and local Native American tribes, the federal courts ruled on aspects of the extent and limits of tribal fishing rights. In a 1942 case, *Tulee v. Washington,* 315 U.S. 681, 62 S. Ct. 862, 86 L. Ed. 1115, the Court ruled that tribal members could not be forced to purchase fishing licenses because the treaties that their ancestors had signed already

reserved the right to fish in the "usual and accustomed places."

That case was followed by a series of cases involving the Puyallup Indian tribe that became known as *Puyallup I, Puyallup II,* and *Puyallup III.* In the first of those cases, the Court ruled that the state of Washington has the right, in the interest of conservation, to regulate tribal fishing activities, as long as "the regulation meets appropriate standards and does not discriminate against the Indians" (*Puyallup Tribe v. Department of Game,* 391 U.S. 392, 88 S. Ct. 1725, 20 L. Ed. 2d 689 [1968]). In the second case, the Court ruled that the state's prohibition on net fishing for steelhead trout was discriminatory because its effect was to reserve the entire harvestable run of steelhead to non-Indian sports fishermen (*Department of Game v. Puyallup Tribe,* 414 U.S. 44, 94 S. Ct. 330, 38 L. Ed. 2d 254 [1973]). In its ruling, the Court declared that the steelhead "must in some manner be fairly apportioned between Indian net fishing and non-Indian sports fishing." Finally, in *Puyallup III,* the Court ruled that the fish caught by tribal members on their reservation could be counted against the Indian share of the fish (*Puyallup Tribe v. Department of Game,* 429 U.S. 976, 97 S. Ct. 483, 50 L. Ed. 2d 583 [1976]).

This notion of a fair APPORTIONMENT of fish was clarified by *United States v. Washington,* 384 F. Supp. 312 (W.D. Wash. 1974), in which the court determined that treaty language guaranteeing tribes the right to take fish "in common with all citizens of the Territory" guaranteed the Indians not just the right to fish but also the right to a certain percentage of the harvestable run, up to 50 percent. This decision set off a firestorm of controversy throughout the Pacific Northwest. Hundreds of legal disputes erupted over the allocation of individual runs of salmon and steelhead, and state and non-Indian fishing interests attacked the decision. The U.S. Supreme Court ultimately upheld the decision in a collateral case, *Washington v. Washington State Commercial Passenger Fishing Vessel Ass'n* 443 U.S. 658, 99 S. Ct. 3055, 61 L. Ed. 2d 823 (1979). In that case, the Court upheld the district court's ruling and went on to clarify the details of the way the fish should be apportioned. Writing for the majority, Justice JOHN PAUL STEVENS stated that the treaties guaranteed the tribes "so much as, but no more than, is necessary to provide the Indians with a livelihood— that is to say a moderate living." A "fair apportionment," he said, would be 50 percent of the fish, emphasizing that 50 percent was the maximum, but not the minimum, amount of fish to which the Indians were entitled.

The Court resolved a decade-old legal dispute in 1999 involving Indian fishing and hunting rights with the decision in *Minnesota v. Mille Lacs Band of Chippewa Indians*, 526 U.S. 172, 119 S. Ct. 1187, 143 L. Ed. 2d 270 (1999). It ruled in favor of the Chippewa Indians' right to fish and hunt in northern Minnesota without state regulation. By a 5-4 vote, the Court upheld an appeals court decision finding that the tribe's rights under an 1837 treaty were still valid. The ruling marked a final victory for the tribe in its long fight to assert its treaty rights and to defend its cultural traditions.

Brought by the tribe in 1990, the lawsuit proved highly controversial in Minnesota, which regarded it as a threat to the $54 million in tourism revenue generated by the Mille Lacs Lake resort industry. But two lower federal courts and the U.S. Supreme Court rejected the state's arguments that the 162-year old treaty had been invalidated by presidential order, later treaties, and even by Minnesota's gaining of statehood. The U.S. Supreme Court's majority opinion, written by Justice SANDRA DAY O'CONNOR, detailed the history of the treaty and subsequent actions that the state, nine counties, and landowners claimed had rendered the treaty invalid. She found nothing in this historical information that had bearing on the continued validity of the treaty.

Water Rights

Access to water is another area in which Native Americans enjoy special rights. The issue of WATER RIGHTS has been most pertinent in the western part of the United States, where most Indian reservations are located and where water is the scarcest. In the West, rights to water are determined by the "appropriative" system, which holds that water rights are not connected to the land itself. Rather, the right to water belongs to the first user who appropriates it for a beneficial use. That appropriator is guaranteed the right to continue to take water from that source, unhindered by future appropriators, as long as the water continues to be put to a beneficial use. When the appropriator ceases to use the water, he or she loses the right to it. In contrast to this appropriative system, states in the East, where water is plentiful, follow the "riparian" system, which gives the owner of land bordering a body of water the right to the reasonable use of that water. All riparian owners are guaranteed the right to a continued flow of water, whether or not they use it continuously.

Native American water rights combine the features of the appropriative and riparian systems. The legal foundation for Indian water rights is the 1908 U.S. Supreme Court case *Winters v. United States*, 207 U.S. 564, 28 S. Ct. 207, 52 L. Ed. 340. That case involved a Montana Indian reservation that had a river as one of its borders. After the reservation was established, non-Indian settlers diverted the river's water, claiming that they had appropriated the water after the reservation was created but before the Indians had begun to use the water themselves. The U.S. Supreme Court ruled against the settlers, finding that when the reservation was created, reserved water rights for the Indians were necessarily implied. It was unreasonable, the Court argued, to assume that Indians would accept lands for farming and grazing purposes without also reserving the water that would make those activities possible.

A second important case involving Native American water rights is *Arizona v. California*, 373 U.S. 546, 83 S. Ct. 1468, 10 L. Ed. 2d 542 (1963). In that case, as in *Winters*, the U.S. Supreme Court held that the establishment of a reservation necessarily implied the rights to the water necessary to make the land habitable and productive. *Arizona* went beyond *Winters*, however, in also ruling on the quantity of water to which the reservation had a right. Although competing water users argued that the amount of water reserved to the reservation should be limited to the amount that was likely to be needed by the relatively small Indian population, the Court ruled that the Indians were entitled to enough water "to irrigate all the practicably irrigable acreage on the reservation," a much more generous allotment.

Based on *Winters* and *Arizona*, Native American water rights today are determined by a set of principles called "*Winters* rights." First, Congress has the right to reserve water for federal lands, including Indian reservations. Second, when Congress establishes a reservation, it is implied that the reservation has the right to water sources within or bordering the reservation. Third, reservation water rights are reserved as of the date of the reservation's creation. Competing users with earlier appropriation dates take precedence, but those with later dates are

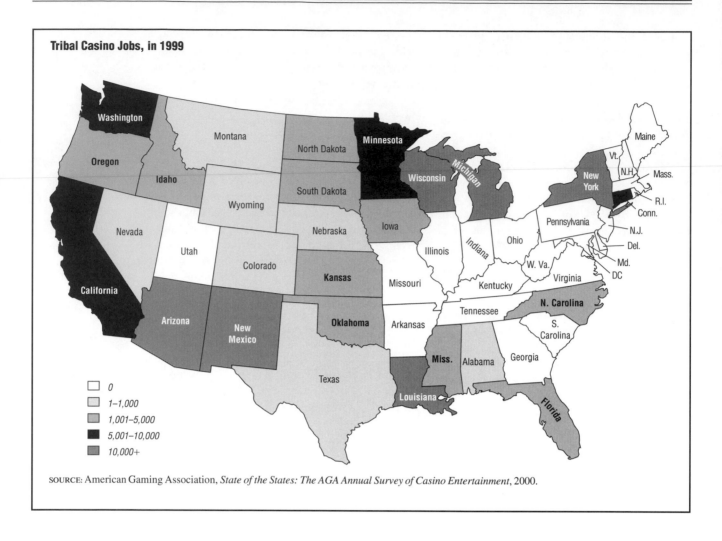

Tribal Casino Jobs, in 1999

Legend:
- ☐ 0
- 1–1,000
- 1,001–5,000
- 5,001–10,000
- 10,000+

SOURCE: American Gaming Association, *State of the States: The AGA Annual Survey of Casino Entertainment*, 2000.

subordinate. Fourth, the amount of water reserved for Indian use is the amount necessary to irrigate all of the practically irrigable land on the reservation. Finally, *Winters* rights to water are not lost through non-use of the water. All of these rights apply to both surface water and groundwater.

Even with the acknowledgement of Native Americans' *Winters* rights, water use in the West continues to be highly contested, as reservations fight to maintain their rights against the competing demands of state governments and non-Indian users. Several issues are yet to be resolved, such as the precise quantity of water that is needed to irrigate all "practically irrigable acreage" and the question of whether states can regulate non-Indian water users on Indian reservations. Because of the high costs and other difficulties involved in litigation, many tribes and states are choosing to try to negotiate water rights and then ask to Congress or the courts to approve their agreements.

Gaming Rights

In recent years, gaming has become one of the most important areas of economic development for Native American tribes. Since 1979, when the federal courts ruled that tribal-sponsored gaming activities were exempt from state regulatory law, the Indian gaming industry has grown tremendously, with more than 200 tribes operating gaming establishments. These operations have been extremely lucrative for the tribes running them; in 1993 the gross gambling revenues from class II and class III tribal gaming operations amounted to approximately $2.6 billion. By comparison, Atlantic City had revenues of $3.3 billion the same year. Tribe members benefit from the creation of jobs on the reservation and from the cash generated, which some tribal governments choose to distribute through direct payments to tribe members and others choose to reinvest in improving reservation infrastructure, educational facilities, and other programs and services designed to benefit tribe members.

The impetus for the growth of Native American gaming began in the late 1970s, when the Oneida tribe in Wisconsin and the Seminole tribe in Florida sought to open high-stakes bingo operations on their reservations. The applicable laws in those states imposed limitations on the size of jackpots and the frequency of bingo games. The tribes asserted, however, that as sovereign nations, they were not bound by such limitations; they claimed that they could operate bingo games and regulate them under tribal law, deciding for themselves how large prizes could be and how often games could be played. Both suits ended up in federal court, and both tribes won (*Seminole Tribe of Florida v. Butterworth*, 658 F. 2d 310 [5th Cir. 1981]; *Oneida Tribe of Indians v. Wisconsin*, 518 F. Supp. 712 [W.D. Wis. 1981]). The rulings in both cases hinged on whether the states' laws concerning gaming were criminal laws that prohibited gaming, or civil laws that regulated gaming. If the laws were criminal-prohibitory, they could be applied to activities on Indian reservations, but if they were civil-regulatory, they could not. The courts ruled that because the states allowed bingo games in some form, the laws were civil-regulatory and thus did not apply to gaming operations on Indian reservations.

Other tribes subsequently sued in federal court on the same issue and also won. The issue finally reached the U.S. Supreme Court in *California v. Cabazon Band of Mission Indians,* 480 U.S. 202, 107 S. Ct. 1083, 94 L. Ed. 2d 244 (1987). In that case, the Court accepted the criminal-prohibitory/civil-regulatory distinction of the lower courts, ruling that the Cabazon Band of Mission Indians in California had the right to operate high-stakes bingo and poker games on its reservation because the state's gaming laws were civil-regulatory and thus could not be applied to on-reservation gaming activities.

Concern over Indian gaming had been building in Congress during the 1980s, and Congress responded to *California v. Cabazon* by passing the Indian Gaming Regulatory Act (IGRA), (25 U.S.C.A. §§ 2701 et seq.) in 1988. The IGRA specifically provides that Indian tribes "have the exclusive right to regulate gaming activity on Indian lands if the gaming activity is not specifically prohibited by Federal law and is conducted within a State which does not, as a matter of CRIMINAL LAW and public policy, prohibit such gaming activity." The sponsors of the IGRA claimed that one of the bill's main goals was to use gaming as a means of "promoting tribal economic development, self-sufficiency, and strong tribal governments." Nevertheless, many tribal leaders were opposed to the provisions of IGRA, regarding them as infringements on tribal sovereignty.

The IGRA provides the general framework for regulating Indian gaming. Its principal provision is the classification of Indian gaming, with each category of games being subject to the different regulatory powers of the tribes, the states, and federal agencies, including the National Indian Gaming Commission (NIGC), which was created by the IGRA. The IGRA classifies games into three types. Class I games are traditional Indian games, such as those played in connection with tribal ceremonies or celebrations; those games are regulated exclusively by the tribes. Class II games include bingo and related games; those games are regulated by the tribes, with oversight from the NIGC. Class III games include all games that do not fall into classes I and II, including casino-style games, parimutuel wagering, slots, and dog and horse racing. Class III games, according to the IGRA, may be conducted if three conditions are met: if the state in which the tribe is located permits any such games for any purposes; if the tribe and the state have negotiated a compact that has been approved by the secretary of the interior; and if the tribe has adopted an ordinance that has been approved by the chair of the NIGC.

Indian gaming and the IGRA continue to face opposition from various quarters. Tribal leaders view state regulation as a violation of their tribal sovereignty. The proprietors of non-Indian gaming establishments have attempted to slow or to stop the growth of Indian gaming, viewing it as a threat to their own enterprises. In some cases, tribal and state governments have had great difficulties negotiating the details of tribal-state compacts. These areas of difficulty and dissatisfaction suggest that Indian gaming may be subject to further legislation in the future.

Gaming has led to unprecedented growth for tribal economies, providing thousands of jobs for Indians and non-Indians and drastically improving the financial well-being of the tribes that have operated successful gaming establishments. Although some legislators have expressed concern over the expansion of gaming activities and the problems associated with increased gambling, Indian gaming generally enjoys broad public support. Native Americans have described it as "the return of the white buffalo," a traditional Native American symbol of good fortune.

The U.S. Supreme Court has stepped in to resolve several controversies regarding gaming rights. In *Chickasaw Nation v. United States*, 534 U.S. 84, 122 S. Ct. 528, 151 L. Ed. 2d 474 (2001), the Court held that revenues from pull-tab games, similar to lottery tickets, at Chickasaw Nation gaming operations could be taxed under Chapter 35 of the INTERNAL REVENUE CODE. The ruling also applied to the Choctaw Nation, which offered a similar type of pull-tab game. The U.S. Court of Appeals for the Tenth Circuit, in reviewing the Chickasaw Nation's gaming activities, ruled that revenue from these games amounted to gambling revenues, rather than lottery revenues. The Federal Circuit, however, reached an opposite conclusion with respect to the Choctaw Nation in *Little Six, Inc. v. United States*, 210 F.3d 1361 (Fed. Cir. 2000).

The U.S. Supreme Court, per Justice STEPHEN BREYER, found that the INTERNAL REVENUE SERVICE had properly levied a tax on these gaming activities. Although states are not required to pay these taxes, the applicable provisions in the tax laws applied specifically to the Indian tribes. Although Court precedent suggested that statutes regarding Indian tribes should be construed liberally in favor of the Indian tribes, Breyer found the statute to be unambiguous by its terms.

FURTHER READINGS

Cox, Michael D. 1995. "The Indian Gaming Regulatory Act: An Overview." *St. Thomas Law Review* 7.

Getches, David H., et al. 1998. *Cases and Materials on Federal Indian Law.* 4th ed. St. Paul, Minn.: West Group.

Hutchins, Francis G. 2000. *Tribes and the American Constitution.* Brookline, Mass.: Amarta Press.

Johnson, Dana. 1995. "Native American Treaty Rights to Scarce Natural Resources." *UCLA Law Review* 43.

Kelly, Joseph M. 1995. "Indian Gaming Law." *Drake Law Review* 43.

McNeil, Heidi L. 1994. *Indian Gaming—Prosperity, Controversy.* PLI order no. B4-7077. New York: Practising Law Institute.

Pevar, Stephen L. 2002. *The Rights of Indians and Tribes: The Authoritative ACLU Guide to Indian and Tribal Rights.* 3d ed. Carbondale: Southern Illinois Univ. Press.

CROSS-REFERENCES

Cherokee Cases; Fish and Fishing; Indian Child Welfare Act; Interior Department. See also primary documents in "Native American Rights" section of Appendix.

NATURAL AND PROBABLE CONSEQUENCES

Those ramifications of a particular course of conduct that are reasonably foreseeable by a person of average intelligence and generally occur in the normal course of events.

The individual who is guilty of misconduct in contract or TORT is responsible for the natural and probable consequences of the act or omission that proximately causes loss or injury to the plaintiff. Based on the usual experience of human beings, if the consequences were to be expected, a plaintiff can recover damages from a defendant who caused the injuries.

Breach of Contract

Damages for breach of contractual agreement are those that result naturally from the violation of contract provisions and that are reasonably contemplated by the parties when the contract is made. Factors to be considered in determining what damages might have reasonably been considered include the nature and purpose of the contract as well as the accompanying conditions of which the parties were aware when the contract was executed. Damages that do not stem naturally from a breach of contract are not recoverable, nor are damages that are not within the reasonable contemplation of the parties. There is no requirement that the promisor compensate the injured party for harm that the promisor or any reasonable person upon making the contract would not have reason to foresee as the predictable outcome of a breach.

Torts

An individual who is guilty of committing a tort is liable for loss or injury that is the natural and probable result of his or her act or omission. It is sufficient that consequences are merely possible, since they must be reasonably foreseeable in order to serve as an adequate basis for the recovery of damages.

Prospective and Anticipated Consequences

In a situation where a CAUSE OF ACTION is complete, prospective damages reasonably certain to ACCRUE may be recovered as part of the natural and probable consequences of the defendant's action.

Breach of Contract Prospective damages are recoverable in cases involving an ANTICIPATORY REPUDIATION of contract. If the breach does not serve to discharge the entire contract but rather gives rise to subsequent actions, future damages must be recovered in successive actions. This type of situation might arise in an action for breach of a lease for the rental of an apartment in which the breach occurs during the fourth month of a twelve-month lease. Successive actions will have to be brought for the breach occurring from the fifth to twelfth months.

Torts Damages in tort actions are not limited to the period that ends with the institution of the lawsuit. In an action for personal injury, for example, the jury can properly consider the potential consequences of an injury that might require a major operation at some time in the future in assessing the present value of an injury as opposed to future damages. Damages can be awarded to a plaintiff who has adequately established that there will be future effects from an injury precipitated by the defendant's misconduct. The amount of certainty required in the assessment of future damages varies from one jurisdiction to another; however, no recovery can be permitted for the mere possibility of future consequences of harm inflicted by the defendant.

Damage to Property All types of damages, including past, current, and prospective, can be recovered in a singleaction for permanent damage to or TRESPASS on real estate. If the cause of the injury can be abated through an expenditure of labor or money, future damages will not be recovered.

NATURAL LAW

The unwritten body of universal moral principles that underlie the ethical and legal norms by which human conduct is sometimes evaluated and governed. Natural law is often contrasted with positive law, which consists of the written rules and regulations enacted by government. The term natural law *is derived from the Roman term* jus naturale. *Adherents to natural law philosophy are known as naturalists.*

Naturalists believe that natural law principles are an inherent part of nature and exist regardless of whether government recognizes or enforces them. Naturalists further believe that governments must incorporate natural law principles into their legal systems before justice can be achieved. There are three schools of natural law theory: divine natural law, secular natural law, and historical natural law.

Divine natural law represents the system of principles believed to have been revealed or inspired by God or some other supreme and supernatural being. These divine principles are typically reflected by authoritative religious writings such as Scripture. Secular natural law represents the system of principles derived from the physical, biological, and behavioral laws of nature as perceived by the human intellect and elaborated through reason. Historical natural law represents the system of principles that has evolved over time through the slow accretion of custom, tradition, and experience. Each school of natural law influenced the Founding Fathers during the nascent years of U.S. law in the eighteenth century and continue to influence the decision-making process of state and federal courts today.

Divine Natural Law

Proponents of divine natural law contend that law must be made to conform to the commands they believe were laid down or inspired by God, or some other deity, who governs according to principles of compassion, truth, and justice. These naturalists assert that the legitimacy of any enacted human law must be measured by its consonance with divine principles of right and wrong. Such principles can be found in various Scriptures, church doctrine, papal decrees, and the decisions of ecclesiastical courts and councils. Human laws that are inconsistent with divine principles of morality, naturalists maintain, are invalid and should neither be enforced nor obeyed. St. Thomas Aquinas, a theologian and philosopher from the thirteenth century, was a leading exponent of divine natural law.

According to Judeo-Christian belief and the Old Testament, the Ten Commandments, were delivered to Moses by God on Mount Sinai. These ten laws represent one example of divine natural law. The Bible and Torah are thought by many to be other sources of divine natural law because their authors are said to have been inspired by a divine spirit. Some Christians point to the CANON LAW of the Catholic Church, which was applied by the ecclesiastical courts of Europe during the Middle Ages, as another source of divine natural law.

Before the Protestant Reformation of the sixteenth century, Europe was divided into two competing jurisdictions—secular and religious. The emperors, kings, and queens of Europe governed the secular jurisdiction, and the pope presided over the religious jurisdiction. The idea that monarchs ruled by "divine right" allowed the secular jurisdiction to acquire some of the authority of religious jurisdiction. Moreover, the notion that a "higher law" transcends the rules enacted by human institutions and that government is bound by this law, also known as the RULE OF LAW, fermented during the struggle between the secular and religious powers in Europe before the American Revolution. For example, HENRY DE BRACTON, an English judge and scholar from the thirteenth century, wrote that a court's allegiance to the law and to God is above its allegiance to any ruler or lawmaker.

The influence of divine natural law pervaded the colonial period of U.S. law. In 1690 English philosopher JOHN LOCKE wrote that all people are born with the inherent rights to life, liberty, and estate. These rights are not unlimited, Locke said, and may only be appropriated according to the fair share earned by the labor of each person. Gluttony and waste of individual liberty are not permitted, Locke argued, because "[n]othing is made by God for man to spoil or destroy."

In the Declaration of Independence, THOMAS JEFFERSON, borrowing from Locke, wrote that "all men are created equal . . . and are endowed by their creator with certain inalienable rights . . . [including] life, liberty and the pursuit of happiness." Jefferson identified the freedom of thought as one of the inalienable rights when he said, "Almighty God has created the mind free, and manifested his supreme will that free it shall remain by making it altogether insusceptible of restraint." In *Powell v. Pennsylvania,* 127 U.S. 678, 8 S. Ct. 1257, 32 L. Ed. 253 (1888), the Supreme Court recognized the importance of the divine influence in early U.S. law, stating that the "right to pursue happiness is placed by the Declaration of Independence among the inalienable rights of man, not by the grace of emperors or kings, or by the force of legislative or constitutional enactments, but by the Creator."

The U.S. Constitution altered the relationship between law and religion. Article VI establishes the Constitution as the supreme law of the land. The FIRST AMENDMENT prohibits the government from establishing a religion, which means that a law may not advance one religion at the expense of another or prefer a general belief in religion to irreligion, atheism, or agnosticism. Although the Supremacy and Establishment Clauses seemingly preclude the judiciary

from grounding a decision on Scripture or religious doctrine, state and federal courts have occasionally referred to various sources of divine natural law.

For example, in *Edwards v. Aguillard,* 482 U.S. 578, 107 S. Ct. 2573, 96 L. Ed. 2d 510 (1987), the Supreme Court said that "the Founding Fathers believed devotedly that there was a God and that the inalienable rights of man were rooted in Him." In *McIlvaine v. Coxe's Lessee,* 6 U.S. 280, 2 Cranch 280, 2 L. Ed. 279 (1805), the Supreme Court relied on the Bible as "ancient and venerable" proof that expatriation had long been "practiced, approved, and never restrained."

Confronted with the question as to whether the conveyance of a particular piece of land was legally enforceable, the Supreme Court stated that it would consider "those principles of abstract justice, which the Creator of all things has impressed on the mind of his creature man, and which are admitted to regulate, in a great degree, the rights of civilized nations" (*Johnson v. M'Intosh,* 21 U.S. 543, 8 Wheat. 543, 5 L. Ed. 681 [1823]). In DRED SCOTT V. SANDFORD, 60 U.S. 393, 19 How. 393, 15 L. Ed. 691 (1856), the Supreme Court held that slaves were the property of their owners and were not entitled to any constitutional protection. In a dissenting opinion, however, Justice JOHN MCLEAN wrote that a "slave is not mere chattel. He bears the impress of his Maker, and is amenable to the laws of God and man."

In the later twentieth century (in a judgment overturned in LAWRENCE V. TEXAS, 539 U.S. ___, 123 S.Ct. 2472, 156 L.Ed.2d 508 [2003]), the Supreme Court relied on Judeo-Christian standards as evidence that homosexual SODOMY is a practice not worthy of constitutional protection because it has been condemned throughout the history of western civilization (*Bowers v. Hardwick,* 478 U.S. 186, 106 S. Ct. 2841, 92 L. Ed. 2d 140 [1986] [Burger, J., concurring]). State and federal courts also have considered Judeo-Christian standards when evaluating the constitutionality of statutes prohibiting bigamy and INCEST. For example, *Benton v. State,* 265 Ga. 648, 461 S.E.2d 202 (1995), upheld the constitutionality of a Georgia statute prohibiting incest.

Despite the sprinkling of cases that have referred to Scripture, religious doctrine, and Judeo-Christian heritage, such sources of divine natural law do not ordinarily form the express basis of judicial decisions. At the same time, it cannot be said that state and federal courts have completely eliminated any reliance on natural-law principles. To the contrary, many controversial legal disputes are still decided in accordance with unwritten legal principles that are derived not from religion, but from secular political philosophy.

Secular Natural Law

The school of natural law known as secular natural law replaces the divine laws of God with the physical, biological, and behavioral laws of nature as understood by human reason. This school theorizes about the uniform and fixed rules of nature, particularly human nature, to identify moral and ethical norms. Influenced by the rational empiricism of the seventeenth- and eighteenth-century Enlightenment thinkers who stressed the importance of observation and experiment in arriving at reliable and demonstrable truths, secular natural law elevates the capacity of the human intellect over the spiritual authority of religion.

Many secular natural law theorists base their philosophy upon hypotheses about human behavior in the state of nature, a primitive stage in human evolution before the creation of governmental institutions and other complex societal organizations. In the state of nature, John Locke wrote, human beings live according to three principles—liberty, equality, and self-preservation. Because no government exists in the state of nature to offer police protection or regulate the distribution of goods and benefits, each individual has a right to self-preservation that he or she may exercise on equal footing with everyone else.

This right includes the liberties to enjoy a peaceful life, accumulate wealth and property, and otherwise satisfy personal needs and desires consistent with the coterminous liberties of others. Anyone who deprives another person of his or her rights in the state of nature, Locke argued, violates the principle of equality. Ultimately, Locke wrote, the state of nature proves unsatisfying. Human liberty is neither equally fulfilled nor protected. Because individuals possess the liberty to delineate the limits of their own personal needs and desires in the state of nature, greed, narcissism, and self-interest eventually rise to the surface, causing irrational and excessive behavior and placing human safety at risk. Thus, Locke concluded, the law of nature leads people to establish a government that is empowered to protect life, liberty, and property.

Lockean JURISPRUDENCE has manifested itself in the decisions of the Supreme Court. In *Powell v. Pennsylvania,* 127 U.S. 678, 8 S. Ct. 1257, 32 L. Ed. 253 (1888), Justice STEPHEN J. FIELD wrote that he had "always supposed that the gift of life was accompanied by the right to seek and produce food, by which life can be preserved and enjoyed, in all ways not encroaching upon the equal rights of others." In another case the Supreme Court said that the "rights of life and personal liberty are the natural rights of man. To secure these rights . . . governments are instituted among men" (*U.S. v. Cruikshank,* 92 U.S. 542, 2 Otto 542, 23 L. Ed. 588 [1875]).

In the spirit of Lockean natural law, the Fifth and Fourteenth Amendments to the Constitution prohibit the government from taking "life, liberty, or property without due process of law." The concept of "due process" has been a continuing source of natural law in constitutional jurisprudence. If Lockean natural law involves theorizing about the scope of human liberty in the state of nature, constitutional natural law involves theorizing about the scope of liberty protected by the Due Process Clauses of the Fifth and Fourteenth Amendments.

On their face the Due Process Clauses appear to offer only procedural protection, guaranteeing litigants the right to be informed of any legal action being taken against them and the opportunity to be heard during an impartial hearing where relevant claims and defenses may be asserted. In the 200 years following the writing of the Constitution, however, federal courts interpreted the Due Process Clauses to provide substantive protection against ARBITRARY and discriminatory governmental encroachment of fundamental liberties. Similar to the rational empiricism by which Enlightenment thinkers identified HUMAN RIGHTS in the state of nature, federal judges have identified the liberties protected by the Due Process Clauses through a reasoned elaboration of the Fifth and Fourteenth Amendments.

The federal judiciary has described the liberty interest protected by the Due Process Clauses as an interest guaranteeing a number of individual freedoms, including the right to personal autonomy, bodily integrity, self-dignity, and self-determination (*Gray v. Romeo,* 697 F. Supp. 580 [1988]). The word *liberty,* the Supreme Court stated, means something more than freedom from physical restraint. "It means freedom to go where one may choose, and to act in such manner ... as his judgment may dictate for the promotion of his happiness ... [while pursuing] such callings and avocations as may be most suitable to develop his capacities, and give to them their highest enjoyment" (MUNN V. ILLINOIS, 94 U.S. 113, 4 Otto 113, 24 L. Ed. 77 [1876] [Field, J., dissenting]).

The full breadth of constitutional liberty, the Supreme Court has said, is best explained as a rational continuum safeguarding every facet of human freedom from arbitrary impositions and purposeless restraints (*Poe v. Ullman*, 367 U.S. 497, 81 S. Ct. 1752, 6 L. Ed. 2d 989 [1961]). The government may not intrude upon this liberty unless it can demonstrate a persuasive countervailing interest. However, the more that the U.S. legal system cherishes a particular freedom, the less likely a court is to enforce a law that infringes upon it.

In this regard the Supreme Court has identified certain fundamental rights that qualify for heightened judicial protection against laws threatening to restrict them. This list of fundamental rights includes most of the specific freedoms enumerated in the BILL OF RIGHTS, as well as the FREEDOM OF ASSOCIATION; the right to vote and participate in the electoral process; the right to marry, procreate, and rear children; and the right to privacy. The right to privacy, which is not expressly enumerated anywhere in the Constitution, guarantees the freedom of adults to use BIRTH CONTROL (GRISWOLD V. CONNECTICUT, 381 U.S. 479, 85 S. Ct. 1678, 14 L. Ed. 2d 510 [1965]) and the right of women to terminate their pregnancy before the fetus becomes viable (ROE V. WADE, 410 U.S. 113, 93 S. Ct. 705, 35 L. Ed. 2d 147 [1973]).

During the 1990s the right to privacy was enlarged to recognize the right of certain terminally ill or mentally incompetent persons to refuse medical treatment. In *Cruzan v. Missouri Department of Health*, 497 U.S. 261, 110 S. Ct. 2841, 111 L. Ed. 2d 224 (1990), the Supreme Court ruled that a person who is in a persistent vegetative state, marked by the absence of any significant cognitive abilities, may seek to terminate life-sustaining measures, including artificial nutrition and hydration equipment, through a parent, spouse, or other appropriate guardian who demonstrates that the incompetent person previously expressed a clear desire to discontinue medical treatment under such circumstances.

The Court of Appeals for the Ninth Circuit later cited *Cruzan* in support of its decision establishing the right of competent but terminally ill patients to hasten their death by refusing medical treatment when the final stages of life are wrought with pain and indignity (*Compassion in Dying v. Washington*, 79 F.3d 790 [9th Cir. 1996]). However, the Court of Appeals for the Second Circuit ruled that physicians possess no due process right to assist terminally ill patients in accelerating their death by prescribing a lethal dose of narcotics (*Quill v. Vacco*, 80 F.3d 716 [2d Cir. 1996]). Similarly, in a notorious case involving Dr. JACK KEVORKIAN, the Michigan Supreme Court ruled that patients have no due process right to physician-assisted suicide (*People v. Kevorkian*, 447 Mich. 436, 527 N. W. 2d 714 [1994]).

In the *Cruzan* decision, the manner in which the Supreme Court recognized a qualified right to die reflects the Enlightenment tradition of secular natural law. Where Locke inferred the inalienable rights of life, liberty, and property from observing human behavior, the Supreme Court said in *Cruzan* that "a Constitutionally protected liberty interest in refusing unwanted medical treatment may be inferred from our prior decisions."

For example, in *Jacobson v. Massachusetts*, 197 U.S. 11, 25 S. Ct. 358, 49 L. Ed. 643 (1905), the Supreme Court protected the constitutional right of a person to decline a smallpox vaccination that was required by state law. In *Washington v. Harper*, 494 U.S. 210, 110 S. Ct. 1028, 108 L. Ed. 2d 178 (1990), the Court ruled that the liberty interest guaranteed by the Due Process Clauses prohibits the government from compelling prisoners to take antipsychotic drugs. These cases, as well as others, the Supreme Court reasoned in *Cruzan*, establish that all U.S. citizens have a general right to refuse unwanted medical treatment, which includes the specific right of certain mentally incompetent and terminally ill persons to hasten their death.

Historical Natural Law

Another school of natural law is known as historical natural law. According to this school, law must be made to conform with the well-established, but unwritten, customs, traditions, and experiences that have evolved over the course of history. Historical natural law has played an integral role in the development of the Anglo-American system of justice. When King James I attempted to assert the absolute power of the British monarchy during the seventeenth century, for example, English jurist SIR EDWARD COKE argued that the sovereignty of the crown was limited by the ancient liberties of the English people, immemorial custom, and the rights prescribed by MAGNA CHARTA in 1215.

Magna Charta also laid the cornerstone for many U.S. constitutional liberties. The Supreme Court has traced the origins of grand juries, petit juries, and the writ of HABEAS CORPUS to Magna Charta. The EIGHTH AMENDMENT proportionality analysis, which requires that criminal sanctions bear some reasonable relationship to the seriousness of the offense, was foreshadowed by the Magna Charta prohibition of excessive fines (*Solem v. Helm*, 463 U.S. 277, 103 S. Ct. 3001, 77 L. Ed. 2d 637 [1983]). The concept of due process was inherited from the requirement in Magna Charta that all legal proceedings comport with the "law of the land" (IN RE WINSHIP, 397 U.S. 358, 90 S. Ct. 1068, 25 L. Ed. 2d 368 [1970]).

DUE PROCESS OF LAW, the Supreme Court has observed, contains both procedural and historical aspects that tend to converge in criminal cases (ROCHIN V. CALIFORNIA, 342 U.S. 165, 72 S. Ct. 205, 96 L. Ed. 183 [1952]). Procedurally, due process guarantees criminal defendants a fair trial. Historically, due process guarantees that no defendant may be convicted of a crime unless the government can prove his or her guilt BEYOND A REASONABLE DOUBT. Although the REASONABLE DOUBT STANDARD can be found nowhere in the express language of the Constitution, the Supreme Court has said that the demand for a higher degree of persuasion in criminal cases has been repeatedly expressed since "ancient times" through the common-law tradition and is now "embodied in the Constitution" (*In re Winship*).

The legacy of the trial of JOHN PETER ZENGER, 17 Howell's State Trials 675, further illustrates the symbiotic relationship between history and the law. In 1735, Zenger, the publisher of the *New York Weekly Journal*, was charged with libeling the governor of New York. At trial Zenger admitted that he had published the allegedly harmful article but argued that the article was not libelous because it contained no inaccurate statements. However, in the American colonies, truth was not considered a defense to LIBEL actions. Nonetheless, despite Zenger's admission of harmful publication and lack of a cognizable legal defense, the jury acquitted him.

The Zenger acquittal spawned two ideas that have become entrenched in U.S. jurisprudence. First, the acquittal gave birth to the idea that truth is indeed a defense to accusations of libel. This defense received constitutional protection under the First Amendment in NEW YORK TIMES V. SULLIVAN, 376 U.S. 254, 84 S. Ct. 710, 11 L. Ed. 2d 686 (1964). Looking back, the Supreme Court came to describe the Zenger trial as "the earliest and most famous American experience with freedom of the press" (*McIntyre v. Ohio Elections Commission*, 514 U.S. 334, 115 S. Ct. 1511, 131 L. Ed. 2d 426, [1995]).

The Zenger trial is also the progenitor of JURY NULLIFICATION, which is the power of a jury, as the conscience of the community, to acquit defendants against whom there is overwhelming evidence of guilt in order to challenge a specific law, prevent oppression, or otherwise achieve justice. For example, the Zenger jurors issued an acquittal despite what amounted to a confession by the defendant in open court. Some observers have compared the Zenger trial to the trial of O. J. SIMPSON, in which the former football star was acquitted of a double HOMICIDE notwithstanding DNA EVIDENCE linking him to the crimes. According to these observers, JOHNNIE COCHRAN, defense attorney for Simpson, implored the jurors to ignore the evidence against his client and render a verdict that would send a message denouncing POLICE CORRUPTION, perjury, and racism.

All three schools of natural law have influenced the development of U.S. law from colonial to modern times. In many ways the creation and ratification of the Constitution replaced Scripture and religion as the ultimate source of law in the United States. The federal Constitution makes the people the fundamental foundation of authority in the U.S. system of government. Many of the Framers characterized the Constitution as containing "sacred and inviolate" truths. In the same vein, THOMAS PAINE described the Constitution as a "political Bible."

In 1728 many Americans understood that the COMMON LAW encompassed the Law of Nature, the Law of Reason, and the Revealed Law of God, which are equally binding at all times, in all places, and to all persons. The law of history could have been added to this list. Between 1776 and 1784, 11 of the original 13 states made some allowance for the adoption of the English common law. One federal court said that the Constitution "did not create any new rights to life, liberty or due process. These rights had existed for Englishmen since Magna Charta. The Declaration of Independence . . . merely declared and established these rights for the American colonies" (*Screven County v. Brier Creek Hunting & Fishing Club*, 202 F. 2d 369 [5th Cir. 1953]). Thus, natural law in the United States may be best understood as the integration of history, secular reason, and divine inspiration.

FURTHER READINGS

Berman, Harold J. 1983. *Law and Revolution: The Formation of the Western Legal Tradition.* Cambridge: Harvard Univ. Press.

George, Robert P., ed. 2003 *Natural Law.* Burlington, Vt.: Ashgate/Dartmouth.

Harris, Philip Anthony. 2002. *The Distinction Between Law and Ethics in Natural Law Theory.* Lewiston, N.Y.: Edwin Mellen Press.

Horwitz, Morton J. 1992. *The Transformation of American Law, 1780–1860.* New York: Oxford Univ. Press.

Levy, Leonard W. 1963. *Jefferson and Civil Liberties: The Darker Side.* Chicago: Elephant Paperback.

Locke, John. 1980. (First printed in 1690.) *Second Treatise on Government.* Indianapolis: Hacket Publishing.

Norberto, Bobbio. 1993. *Thomas Hobbes and the Natural Law Tradition.* Chicago: Univ. of Chicago Press.

Pierce, Christine. 2001. *Immovable Laws, Irresistible Rights: Natural Law, Moral Rights, and Feminist Ethics.* Lawrence: Univ. Press of Kansas.

Pojman, Louis P. 1995. *Ethics: Discovering Right and Wrong.* Belmont, Calif.: Wadsworth.

Weinreb, Lloyd. 1987. *Natural Law and Justice.* Cambridge, Mass.: Harvard Univ. Press.

Wood, Gordon S. 1972. *The Creation of the American Republic: 1776–1787.* New York: Norton.

Zuckert, Michael P. 1994. *Natural Rights and the New Republicanism.* Princeton, N.J.: Princeton Univ. Press.

CROSS-REFERENCES

Abortion; Constitution of the United States; Death and Dying; Hobbes, Thomas; Jurisprudence; Libel and Slander; "Second Treatise on Government" (Appendix, Primary Document).

NATURAL LAW PARTY

Citizens of Fairfield, Iowa, formed the Natural Law Party in April 1992. In a few short months, the party had succeeded in placing its presidential ticket on the ballot in 28 states for the 1992 election. By 1996 the party was offering candidates for elective office in all 50 states.

Fairfield, Iowa, is the site of Maharishi International University, a school that teaches students to use transcendental meditation (TM) to achieve good health and a heightened awareness and understanding of the self and the world. The school, founded by Maharishi Mahesh Yogi, has provided the Natural Law Party with the inspiration and resources to enter the field of electoral politics.

The Natural Law Party has fashioned an unusual and ambitious political platform. The party endorses the practice of TM as a humane and cost-effective way to rehabilitate convicted and accused criminals. The party offers a proactive alternative to the current HEALTH CARE system, a system that party candidates call "disease care." Instead of pouring millions of dollars each year into the creation of drugs to manage disease, the Natural Law Party would promote health education and stress management, along with TM, as ways to avoid disease.

Dr. John S. Hagelin has been the standardbearer for the Natural Law Party. Hagelin, a renowned physicist, was the party's nominee for president in 1992 and 1996. Although he is a professor at the Maharishi International University and a staunch proponent of the benefits of TM, Hagelin has worked to expand the party's scope beyond the TM message. The party emphasizes the importance of social equality for all persons, and party candidates talk of world peace as a reachable goal. The party platform also stresses environmental protection. For example, the party endorses alternative methods of energy production, such as a redirection of resources away from fossil fuels and toward renewable energy.

Although party membership has grown rapidly, and may be over 100,000 members, the party's goals in the political process have proved elusive. In 1996 Hagelin was one of only five presidential candidates who was on enough ballots to conceivably win the election in the ELECTORAL COLLEGE and from a party that had held primaries. Hagelin, along with REFORM PARTY candidate H. Ross Perot and LIBERTARIAN PARTY candidate Harry Browne, sought to par-

John S. Hagelin (far right) was the Natural Law Party's presidential candidate in 1992, 1996, and 2000.

AP/WIDE WORLD PHOTOS

ticipate in the nationally televised presidential debates based on these accomplishments. However, the Commission on Presidential Debates, a private nonprofit organization formed by the Democratic and Republican National Committees, concluded that Hagelin, Perot, and Browne had no realistic chance of winning the election and thus excluded all three from the debates. Hagelin won 113,667 votes in the national election, or about 0.12 percent of the vote.

In 1999 Hagelin announced his candidacy for both the Natural Law Party and the Reform Party presidential nominations. When the Reform Party split over the candidacy of PATRICK BUCHANAN, supporters of Hagelin took the name Independence Party. In the 2000 elections, Natural Law-Independence Party coalition candidates received more than 1.4 million votes. In March 2003 the Natural Law Party condemned the invasion of Iraq by the United States. In April 2003, the Natural Law Party announced that Representative Dennis Kucinich (D-Oh.) had reintroduced his legislation to establish a U.S. Department of Peace, legislation that Hagelin had helped to draft.

FURTHER READINGS

Carlson, Peter. 2000. "A Two-System Party Results in Dual (and Dueling) Nominees." *Washington Post* (August 14).

Natural Law Party. Available online at <www.natural-law.org>.

Roth, Robert. 1999. *A Reason to Vote: Breaking the Two-Party Stranglehold.* New York: St. Martin's Griffin.

CROSS-REFERENCES

Libertarian Party; Third Party.

NATURALIZATION

The process under federal law whereby a foreign-born person may be granted citizenship. In order to qualify for naturalization, an applicant must meet a number of statutory requirements, including those related to residency, literacy, and education, as well as an exhibition of "good moral character" and a demonstration of an attachment to constitutional principles upon which the United States is based.

CROSS-REFERENCES

Aliens; Citizens.

NAVIGABLE RIVERS

See INTERNATIONAL WATERWAYS.

NAVIGABLE WATERS

Waters that provide a channel for commerce and transportation of people and goods.

Under U.S. law, bodies of water are distinguished according to their use. The distinction is particularly important in the case of so-called navigable waters, which are used for business or transportation. Jurisdiction over navigable waters belongs to the federal government rather than states or municipalities. The federal government can determine how the waters are used, by whom, and under what conditions. It also has the power to alter the waters, such as by dredging or building dams. Generally a state or private property owner who is inconvenienced by such work has no remedy against the federal government unless state or private property itself is taken; if such property is taken, the laws of EMINENT DOMAIN would apply, which may lead to compensation for the landowner.

The basis for federal jurisdiction over navigable waters lies in the U.S. Constitution. Since the early nineteenth century, the U.S. Supreme Court has held that the COMMERCE CLAUSE (Article 1, Section 8) gives the federal government extensive authority to regulate interstate commerce. This view originated in 1824 in the landmark case of GIBBONS V. OGDEN, 22 U.S. (9 Wheat.) 1, 6 L. Ed. 23. In *Gibbons,* the Court was faced with deciding whether to give precedence to a state or federal law for the licensing of vessels. It ruled that navigation of vessels in and out of the ports of the nation is a form of interstate commerce and thus federal law must take precedence. This decision led to the contemporary exercise of broad federal power over navigable waters, and in countless other areas of interstate commerce.

In practical terms federal regulation of navigable waters takes many forms. One area of this regulation covers matters of transportation and commerce: for example, rules governing the licensing of ships and the dumping of waste. A second area applies to the alteration of the navigable waters, which is strictly controlled by federal law. The Rivers and Harbors Appropriation Act of 1899 forbids building any unauthorized obstruction to the nation's navigable waters and gives enforcement powers to the U.S. Army Corps of Engineers. A third area of regulation involves WORKERS' COMPENSATION claims. The concept of navigable waters is important in claims made under the Longshore and Harbor Workers' Compensation Act of 1988

(33 U.S.C.A. §§ 901–950). The act provides that employers are liable for injuries to sailors that occur upon navigable waters of the United States.

The vast body of federal regulation concerning navigable waters frequently gives rise to litigation, and in many cases the courts have the difficult job of determining whether particular bodies of water are navigable (and thus subject to the law or regulation in question). Lakes and rivers are generally considered navigable waters, but smaller bodies of water may also be navigable. Attempting to address years of problematic litigation, the U.S. Supreme Court in 1979 created four tests for determining what constitutes navigable waters. Established in *Kaiser Aetna v. United States*, 444 U.S. 164, 100 S. Ct. 383, 62 L. Ed. 2d 332, the tests ask whether the body of water (1) is subject to the ebb and flow of the tide, (2) connects with a continuous interstate waterway, (3) has navigable capacity, and (4) is actually navigable. Using these tests, courts have held that bodies of water much smaller than lakes and rivers also constitute navigable waters. Even shallow streams that are traversable only by canoe have met the test.

FURTHER READINGS

"Annotated Federal Statutes of Limitation: Title 33—Navigation and Navigable Waters." 1995. *Southwestern University Law Review* 24 (winter).

Arnold, Alvin L. 1993. "Navigable Waters: Four Tests to Determine Navigability." *Real Estate Law Report* 22 (January).

Kullman, Aimee P. 1994. "Expanding the Scope of 'Navigable Waters' under the LHWCA." *Tulane Maritime Law Journal* 19 (winter).

CROSS-REFERENCES

Admiralty and Maritime Law; Pilot; Riparian Rights; Water Rights.

NAVY DEPARTMENT

The navy is one of three primary components of the U.S. military. Incorporating the Marine Corps, it serves along with the army and the air force as part of the nation's defense. The navy's mission is to protect the United States as directed by the president or the secretary of defense by the effective prosecution of war at sea. With its Marine Corps component, the navy's objectives are to seize or defend advanced naval bases; support, as required, the forces of all military departments of the United States; and maintain freedom of the seas. The Department

of the Navy includes the U.S. Coast Guard when it is operating as a service in the navy.

The U.S. Navy was founded on October 13, 1775, when Congress enacted the first legislation creating the Continental Navy of the American Revolution. The Department of the Navy and the Office of Secretary of the Navy were established by the act of April 30, 1798 (10 U.S.C.A. §§ 5011, 5031). For nine years before that date, by act of August 7, 1789 (1 Stat. 49), the conduct of naval affairs was under the secretary of war. The National Security Act Amendments of 1949 provided that the Department of the Navy be a military department within the DEPARTMENT OF DEFENSE (63 Stat. 578).

Office of the Secretary of the Navy

The secretary of the Navy is the head of the Department of the Navy. Appointed by the president of the United States, the secretary serves under the direction, authority, and control of the cabinet-level secretary of defense (10 U.S.C.A. § 5031). The secretary is responsible for the policies and control of the navy, including its organization, administration, functioning, and efficiency. Next in succession for the position is the under secretary of the navy, who functions as deputy and principal assistant to the secretary and has full authority in the general management of the department.

Civilian Executive Assistants The civilian executive assistants are the principal advisers and assistants to the secretary of the navy. They include the under secretary of the navy, the assistant secretaries of the navy, and the general counsel of the navy. With department-wide responsibilities for administration, the civilian executive assistants carry out their duties in harmony with the statutory positions of the chief of naval operations, who is the principal military adviser and executive to the secretary regarding naval matters, and the commandant of the Marine Corps, who is the principal military adviser and executive regarding Marine Corps matters. Each is authorized and directed to act for the secretary within his or her assigned area of responsibility.

Staff Assistants The staff assistants to the secretary of the navy are the naval inspector general, the comptroller of the navy, the auditor general of the navy, and the chief of information. The secretary or the law has established the following positions and boards for administrative purposes.

Judge Advocate General The JUDGE ADVO-CATE general is the senior officer and head of the Judge Advocate General's Corps and the Office of the Judge Advocate General. The officer's primary responsibilities are to administer military justice throughout the Department of the Navy, perform functions required or authorized by the UNIFORM CODE OF MILITARY JUSTICE, and provide technical supervision for the Naval Justice School at Newport, Rhode Island. In cooperation with the general counsel to the navy, the judge advocate general also has broad responsibility for providing legal advice and related services to the secretary of the navy on military justice, ethics, ADMINISTRATIVE LAW, ENVIRONMENTAL LAW, operational and INTERNATIONAL LAW and treaty interpretation, and litigation involving these issues. Officers of the Judge Advocate General's Corps and judge advocates of the Marine Corps provide a variety of legal services to both individual service members and naval commands, ranging from personal representation for individual service members for courts-martial to legal services for naval commands on matters such as investigations and claims.

Naval Criminal Investigative Service The director of the Naval Criminal Investigative Service commands a worldwide organization with representation in more than 160 geographic locations to provide criminal investigation, counterintelligence, law enforcement, information, and personnel security support to the U.S. Navy and Marine Corps, both ashore and afloat.

Office of Naval Research Established by act of Congress on August 1, 1946 (10 U.S.C.A. §§ 5150–5153), the Office of Naval Research is the integrated headquarters of the navy for science and technology investment. It manages funding for basic research, exploratory development, advanced technology development, manufacturing technologies, and small business support.

Personnel Boards The Naval Council of Personnel Boards has four components:

1. The Naval Discharge Review Board reviews, pursuant to 10 U.S.C.A. § 1553, the discharge or dismissal of former members of the U.S. Navy and Marine Corps, except in cases of COURT-MARTIAL. It determines whether, under reasonable standards of naval law and discipline, a discharge or dismissal should be changed and, if so, what change should be made.

2. The Naval Complaints Review Board reviews, upon request, decisional documents and index entries created by the Naval Discharge Review Board after April 1, 1977, to determine whether they conform to applicable regulations of the Department of Defense and the Department of the Navy.

3. The Naval Clemency and Parole Board reviews, pursuant to 10 U.S.C.A. §§ 953–954, U.S. Navy and Marine Corps court-martial cases referred to it and grants or denies clemency and, pursuant to 10 U.S.C.A. § 952, reviews and directs that parole be granted or denied.

4. The Physical Evaluation Board organizes and administers disability evaluations within the Department of the Navy, pursuant to 10 U.S.C.A., ch. 61, and other applicable provisions of law and regulation.

Naval Records The Board for Correction of Naval Records is the highest echelon of review of administrative errors and injustices suffered by members and former members of the U.S. Navy and Marine Corps. Established under 10 U.S.C.A. § 1552 to give the secretary of the navy direction on taking actions that otherwise would require congressional decision, the board relieves Congress of the need for additional legislation. This statutory civilian board reviews service members' complaints about actions taken by various boards and officials in the department. The secretary of the navy, acting through this board of civilians of the executive part of the department, is authorized to change naval or military records to correct an error or to remove an injustice.

United States Navy

Chief of Naval Operations The chief of naval operations is the highest-ranking officer of the naval service. The chief is the U.S. Navy member of the Joint Chiefs of Staff, the group of senior military officers who advise the president. Under the secretary of the navy, the chief of naval operations exercises command over certain central executive organizations, assigned shore activities, and the Operating Forces of the Navy.

In the broadest terms, the chief of naval operations is responsible for the navy's readiness and for executing military orders. The chief plans for and provides the personnel, material, weapons, facilities, and services to support the needs of the navy, with the exception of the Fleet

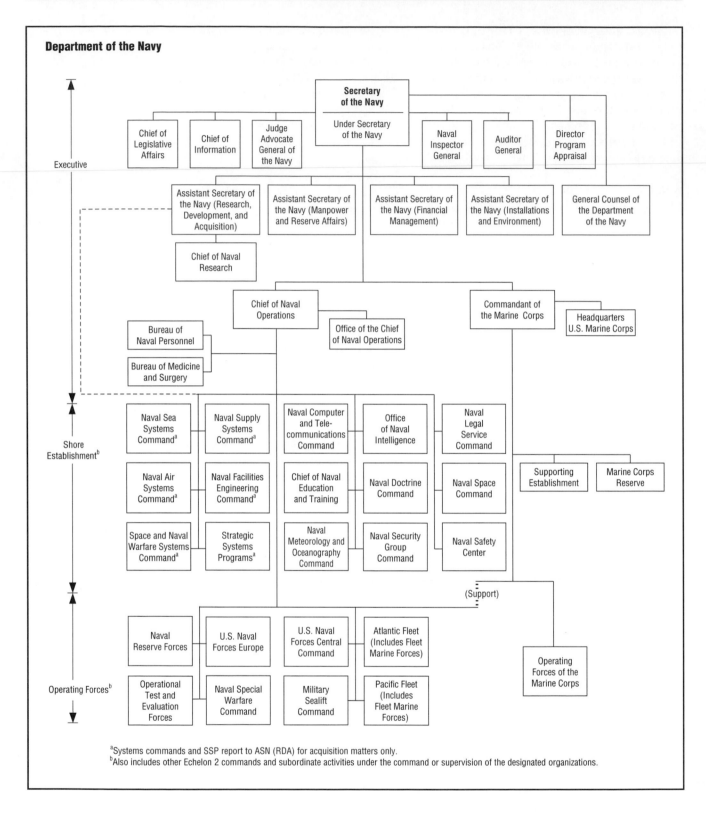

Department of the Navy

[a] Systems commands and SSP report to ASN (RDA) for acquisition matters only.
[b] Also includes other Echelon 2 commands and subordinate activities under the command or supervision of the designated organizations.

Marine Forces; maintains water transportation services, including sea transportation services for the Department of Defense; directs the Naval Reserve; and exercises authority for matters of naval administration, including matters related to customs and traditions of the naval service, security, intelligence, discipline, communications, and operations.

Operating Forces of the Navy The Operating Forces of the Navy are responsible for naval operations necessary to carry out the Department of the Navy's role in upholding and advancing the national policies and interests of the United States. The Operating Forces of the Navy include the several fleets, seagoing forces, Fleet Marine Forces, and other assigned Marine Corps forces, the Military Sealift Command, and other forces and activities as may be assigned by the president or the secretary of the navy.

The U.S. Navy's two fleets are composed of ships, submarines, and aircraft. The Pacific Fleet operates throughout the Pacific and Indian Oceans, and the Atlantic Fleet operates throughout the Atlantic Ocean and Mediterranean Sea. Additionally, the Naval Forces, Europe, is composed of forces from both fleets.

Navy Command Structure The chief of naval operations manages and supports the Operating Forces of the navy through an organizational structure that is composed of sea systems, air systems, space and naval warfare systems, supply systems, naval facilities, strategic systems, naval personnel, naval medicine, oceanography, space command, legal services, computers and TELECOMMUNICATIONS, cryptology, intelligence, education and training, and naval doctrine command.

United States Marine Corps

The United States Marine Corps was established on November 10, 1775, by resolution of the CONTINENTAL CONGRESS. The Marine Corps's composition and functions are detailed in 10 U.S.C.A. § 5063. Within the Department of the Navy, it is organized to include not less than three combat divisions and three aircraft wings, along with additional land combat, aviation, and other services. Its purpose is to provide forces necessary to seize or defend advanced naval bases and to conduct land operations essential to a naval campaign. In coordination with the U.S. Army and the U.S. Air Force, the Marine Corps develops the tactics, techniques, and equipment used by landing forces in amphibious (involving both sea and land) operations.

The Marine Corps also provides detachments and organizations for service on armed vessels of the navy, provides security detachments for the protection of naval property at naval stations and bases, and performs such other duties as the president may direct.

The Marine Corps is composed of the Marine Corps headquarters, the Operating Forces, and the supporting establishment. The Operating Forces consist of Fleet Marine Force Atlantic, Fleet Marine Force Pacific, Marine Corps Reserve, Marine Security Forces, and Marine Detachments Afloat. The supporting establishment includes recruiting activities, training installations, reserve support activities, ground and aviation installations, and logistics bases.

Basic combat units of the marines are deployed as Marine Air Ground Task Forces (MAGTFs). There are four types of MAGTFs: the Marine Expeditionary Force, the Marine Expeditionary Brigade, the Marine Expeditionary Unit, and the Special Purpose MAGTF. Each group has a command element, a ground combat element, an aviation combat element, and a combat service support element. Marine Expeditionary Forces are routinely deployed on amphibious ships to the Mediterranean Sea, Persian Gulf, and Pacific Ocean. Larger MAGTFs can rapidly deploy by air, sea, or any combination of means from both coasts of the United States and bases in the western Pacific to respond to emergencies worldwide.

United States Naval Academy

The United States Naval Academy is the undergraduate college of the naval service. Located in Annapolis, Maryland, the academy offers a comprehensive four-year program that stresses excellence in academics, physical education, professional training, conduct, and honor. It prepares young men and women to be professional officers in the U.S. Navy and Marine Corps. All graduates receive a bachelor of science degree in one of 18 majors.

FURTHER READINGS

Navy Website. Available online at <www.navy.mil> (accessed July 30, 2003).

U.S. Government Manual Website. Available online at <www.gpoaccess.gov/gmanual> (accessed November 10, 2003).

CROSS-REFERENCES

Armed Services; Defense Department; Military Law.

NEAR V. MINNESOTA

FREEDOM OF THE PRESS is a bedrock constitutional principle. However, the presumption that the press cannot be restrained from publishing stories was not established until 1931, when the U.S. Supreme Court issued its landmark ruling in *Near v. Minnesota*, 283 U.S. 697, 51 S. Ct. 625, 75 L. Ed. 1357. This FIRST AMENDMENT decision has become a core constitutional precedent that protects the press from unwarranted government interference in the newsroom.

The case grew out of the state of Minnesota's disgust at the rise of yellow journalism. Sensationalistic newspapers peddled the alleged financial and sexual misdeeds of prominent politicians and community leaders. These papers angered the subjects of the lurid stories, who demanded that something be done. In response the Minnesota legislature enacted a law in 1925 that provided for the abatement (prevention of publishing), as a public NUISANCE, of a "malicious, scandalous and defamatory newspaper, magazine or other periodical." Under the law, which was dubbed the Minnesota Gag Law, a judge could also stop the publication of a newspaper if the judge concluded it was "obscene, lewd, and lascivious." The judge determined these facts without a jury and was empowered to enter an INJUNCTION ordering no future publication. A person who violated the injunction and continued to publish could be charged with CONTEMPT, fined $1000, and sentenced up to 12 months in jail. A publisher could defend the periodical using truth as a defense, but the publisher had to demonstrate "good motives" and "justifiable ends."

The city of Minneapolis used the law to prosecute J.M. Near, the publisher of the *Saturday Press*. The paper reported stories about POLICE CORRUPTION and RACKETEERING and did so in a lively but reasonably accurate manner. Near's stories angered the mayor and police chief, who were alleged to have connections with ORGANIZED CRIME and may have been guilty of dereliction of their duties. Near's newspaper was tinged with anti-Semitism, anti-labor, and anti-Catholic sentiments, so he drew little sympathy. In November 1927 the court issued an injunction ordering Near to destroy the last three months of the *Press* and forbidding him to publish any future editions of the newspaper or any publication that contained the same type of material. The judge had effectively prevented Near from publishing anything that did not conform to the good taste of Minnesota judges. The Minnesota Supreme Court upheld the law and the order against Near, paving the way for the U.S. Supreme Court to hear the case.

The U.S. Supreme Court, in a 5–4 decision, overturned the injunction and ruled the Minnesota statute unconstitutional as a PRIOR RESTRAINT on the press. Chief Justice CHARLES EVANS HUGHES, in his majority opinion, noted

that the law was "unusual, if not unique," yet it raised important issues concerning freedom of the press and FREEDOM OF SPEECH. In prior decisions the Court had begun to read some of the provisions of the BILL OF RIGHTS into the FOURTEENTH AMENDMENT, thereby making these rights applicable to the actions of state governments as well as the federal government. Hughes stated that there was "no doubt" that freedom of the press and freedom of speech were protected by the Fourteenth Amendment's DUE PROCESS CLAUSE against actions by state and local governments. However, these freedoms were not absolute, and the state could punish those who abuse these freedoms.

Chief Justice Hughes dismissed "mere errors" by the trial court and went to the constitutional issues. He pointed out that the gag law did not seek to redress individual wrongs, such as LIBEL against the police chief or mayor. These officials remained free to sue Near for libel and extract damages from him for his defamatory statements. Instead, the gag law was meant to protect the "public morals" and "general welfare" of the community. The law was in part troubling because the prosecutor did not have to prove the falsity of the charges in the newspaper. Moreover, the defense of truth was limited by a showing of good motives and justifiable ends. The Minnesota court made these points clear when it stated that there is "no constitutional right to publish a fact merely because it is true."

The Minnesota statute also troubled the majority because it protected public as well as private citizens. Charges against public officials "by their very nature, create a scandal." Another concern was that the object of the statute was not punishment "in the ordinary sense of the word" but the suppression of the newspaper. Therefore, a publisher who ignored the law and the court order in order to continue to expose official corruption will be shut down by the state. A publisher who seeks to continue publication must bow to official CENSORSHIP and produce a newspaper that is not "malicious, scandalous, or defamatory."

Having laid out the features of the law and the Court's initial concerns, Hughes reviewed the history of freedom of the press in England and quoted approvingly from Blackstone that liberty of the press consists in laying no previous restraints upon publication and not in freedom from censure for criminal matter when published. Hughes concluded that this principle had been honored since the birth of the Republic and that there had been "almost an entire absence of attempts to impose previous restraints upon publications." Public officials must have their actions subject to public investigation and criticism. If the charges are false they may sue under libel laws. Only in exceptional circumstances should the government be granted a prior restraint.

Justice PIERCE BUTLER, in a dissenting opinion joined by Justices GEORGE SUTHERLAND, William Van Devanter, and JAMES MCREYNOLDS, criticized the Court for broadening the scope of freedom of the press. Moreover, the Court's decision had violated principles of FEDERALISM by using the Fourteenth Amendment to overturn a state law. Butler also contended that the action of the law did not constitute a prior restraint. Once the court concluded that writings were malicious, the state's POLICE POWER could be used to prohibit many types of questionable expression.

Near was a landmark case because it applied the First Amendment's freedom of the press and freedom of speech provisions to state government actions through the Fourteenth Amendment. In addition, the case announced a principle that has defined freedom of the press. Absent exceptional circumstances, editors and publishers know they are free to print their stories about public officials without fear of retribution through state censorship.

FURTHER READINGS

Friendly, Fred. 1981. *Minnesota Rag: The Scandal Sheet that Shaped the Constitution.* New York: Random House.

Meyerson, Michael I. 2001. "Rewriting *Near v. Minnesota:* Creating a Complete Definition of Prior Restraint." *Mercer Law Review* 52 (spring).

Pilgrim, Tim A. 1991. "Dictum Recasts the First Amendment: A Revisionist Examination of *Near v. Minnesota.*" *Communications and the Law* 13 (June).

"Symposium: *Near v. Minnesota,* 50th Anniversary." 1981. *Minnesota Law Review* 66 (November).

CROSS-REFERENCES

Censorship; Freedom of Speech; Freedom of the Press.

NECESSARIES

Things indispensable, or things proper and useful, for the sustenance of human life.

Traditional law required a husband to support his wife during their marriage irrespective of the wife's own means, her own ability to support herself, or even her own earnings, which, according to the Married Women's Property Acts passed in the mid-nineteenth century, she could do with as she pleased. The wife had no corresponding duty to support her husband. A husband owed the same support to the couple's children. He had the legal obligation to provide "necessaries" for his wife and children, which encompass food, clothing, lodging, HEALTH CARE, education, and comfort. Modern FAMILY LAW is now gender neutral: husbands and wives have an equal and mutual obligation to provide necessaries.

Courts rarely let themselves be involved in family disputes concerning necessaries while the marriage is ongoing. Depending on a couple's income, what is deemed "necessary" will vary widely. Although the level at which a spouse is to be maintained during marriage should correspond to the couple's station in life, successful litigation defining support obligations during marriage is rare. When a couple separates or divorces, maintenance and support become issues for the courts.

The law has recognized the wife's traditional authority to purchase necessaries. If a husband fails to fulfill his duty of support, his wife is authorized to purchase what necessaries she or their child needs, on the husband's credit and even against his express wishes. Beyond the basic necessities, courts look to the couple's circumstances. In some cases fur coats, gold watches, jewelry, and expensive furniture have been deemed necessaries. It is up to the merchant to show that the unauthorized purchases were in fact necessaries, and the merchant will not collect from the husband if the husband actually furnished appropriate necessaries to his wife and family.

The future of the necessaries rule is unclear. It may become gender neutral by evolving to protect purchases by the nonearning spouse in role-divided marriages, or it may disappear altogether because of the increasing financial independence of marriage partners and the attendant blurring of role division.

CROSS-REFERENCES

Alimony; Child Support; Divorce; Husband and Wife.

NECESSARY AND PROPER CLAUSE

The specific powers and duties of the U.S. Congress are enumerated in several places in the Constitution. The most important listing of these powers is in Article I, Section 8, which identifies in 17 paragraphs the many important powers of Congress. The last paragraph grants to Congress the flexibility to create laws or otherwise to act where the Constitution does not give it the explicit authority to act. This clause is known as the Necessary and Proper Clause, although it is not a federal power, in itself.

The Necessary and Proper Clause allows Congress "To make all Laws which shall be necessary and proper for carrying into Execution the [enumerated] Powers, and all other Powers vested by this Constitution in the Government of the United States, or in any Department or Officer thereof." (Article I, Section 8, Clause 18). It is also sometimes called the "elastic clause." It grants Congress the powers that are *implied* in the Constitution, but that are not explicitly stated. That is why the powers derived from the Necessary and Proper Clause are referred to as implied powers.

The correct way to interpret the Necessary and Proper Clause was the subject of a debate between Secretary of the Treasury ALEXANDER HAMILTON and Secretary of State THOMAS JEFFERSON. Hamilton argued for an expansive interpretation of the clause. His view would have authorized Congress to exercise a broad range of implied powers. On the other hand, Jefferson was concerned about vesting too much power in any one branch of government. He argued that "necessary" was a restrictive adjective meaning *essential*. Jefferson's interpretation would have strengthened STATES' RIGHTS. GEORGE WASHINGTON and JAMES MADISON favored Hamilton's more flexible interpretation, and subsequent events helped to foster the growth of a strong central government. Their debate over the Necessary and Proper Clause between Hamilton and Jefferson came to a head in a landmark U.S. Supreme Court case, MCCULLOCH V. MARYLAND, 17 U.S. 316 (1819).

McCulloch v. Maryland was the first case in which the U.S. Supreme Court applied the Necessary and Proper Clause. Some constitutional historians believe that the opinion in *McCulloch v. Maryland* represents an important act in the ultimate creation of the U.S. federal government. The case involved the question of whether Congress had the power to charter a bank. At first, this question might seem inconsequential, but underlying it are larger questions that go to the foundations of constitutional interpretation. To some extent, they are still debated.

The First Bank of the United States was established in 1791, but it had failed in 1811 due to a lack of support from Congress. Inflation in the years following the WAR OF 1812 compelled President James Madison and Congress to establish a new national bank, which was chartered in 1816. The new bank established branches throughout the states. Many state-chartered banks resented the cautious policies of the BANK OF THE UNITED STATES. Their directors sought assistance from their state legislatures to restrict the operations of the Bank of the United States. Accordingly, Maryland imposed a tax on the bank's operations, and when James McCulloch, a cashier of the Baltimore branch of the Bank of the United States, refused to pay the Maryland tax, the issue went to court.

The questions before the U.S. Supreme Court involved whether the state or national government held more power. Central to this issue was the Court's interpretation of the Necessary and Proper Clause. The Court held that the state of Maryland could not undermine an act of Congress. The states were subordinate to the federal government. This ruling established that Congress could use the Necessary and Proper Clause to create a bank even though the Constitution does not explicitly grant that power to Congress. Chief Justice JOHN MARSHALL's opinion not only endorsed the constitutionality of the bank, but went on to uphold a broad interpretation of the federal government's powers under the Constitution. The case quickly became the legal cornerstone of subsequent expansions of federal power.

FURTHER READINGS

Newmyer, R. Kent. 2001. *John Marshall and the Heroic Age of the Supreme Court.* Baton Rouge: Louisiana State Univ. Press.

Simon, James F. 2002. *What Kind of Nation: Thomas Jefferson, John Marshall, and the Epic Struggle to Create a United States.* New York: Simon & Schuster.

Wilson, Bradford P., and Ken Masugi, eds. 1998. *The Supreme Court and American Constitutionalism.* Lanham, Md.: Rowman & Littlefield.

NECESSITY

A defense asserted by a criminal or civil defendant that he or she had no choice but to break the law.

The necessity defense has long been recognized as COMMON LAW and has also been made part of most states' statutory law. Although no federal statute acknowledges the defense, the Supreme Court has recognized it as part of the common law. The rationale behind the necessity defense is that sometimes, in a particular situation, a technical breach of the law is more advantageous to society than the consequence of strict adherence to the law. The defense is often used successfully in cases that involve a TRESPASS on property to save a person's life or property. It also has been used, with varying degrees of success, in cases involving more complex questions.

Almost all common-law and statutory definitions of the necessity defense include the following elements: (1) the defendant acted to avoid a significant risk of harm; (2) no adequate lawful means could have been used to escape the harm; and (3) the harm avoided was greater than that caused by breaking the law. Some jurisdictions require in addition that the harm must have been imminent and that the action taken must have been reasonably expected to avoid the imminent danger. All these elements mirror the principles on which the defense of necessity was founded: first, that the highest social value is not always achieved by blind adherence to the law; second, that it is unjust to punish those who technically violate the letter of the law when they are acting to promote or achieve a higher social value than would be served by strict adherence to the law; and third, that it is in society's best interest to promote the greatest good and to encourage people to seek to achieve the greatest good, even if doing so necessitates a technical breach of the law.

The defense of necessity is considered a justification defense, as compared with an excuse defense such as duress. An action that is harmful but praiseworthy is justified, whereas an action that is harmful but ought to be forgiven may be excused. Rather than focusing on the actor's state of mind, as would be done with an excuse defense, the court with a necessity defense focuses on the value of the act. No court has ever accepted a defense of necessity to justify killing a person to protect property.

Most states that have codified the necessity defense make it available only if the defendant's value choice has not been specifically contradicted by the state legislature. For example, in 1993 the Massachusetts Supreme Judicial Court rejected the necessity defense of two people who were prosecuted for operating a needle-exchange program that was intended to reduce the transmission of AIDS through the sharing of contaminated hypodermic needles (*Massachu-*setts v. Leno, 415 Mass. 835, 616 N.E.2d 453). Their actions violated a state law prohibiting the distribution of hypodermic needles without a physician's prescription. In rejecting the defense, the court held that the situation posed no clear and imminent danger. The court reasoned that citizens who disagree with the legislature's policy are not without remedy, as they can seek to have the law changed through popular initiative.

The necessity defense has been used with sporadic and very limited success in the area of civil disobedience since the 1970s. The most common circumstances involve public protests against ABORTION, NUCLEAR POWER, and NUCLEAR WEAPONS. Virtually all abortion protesters who have tried to avail themselves of the defense have lost. The courts have reasoned that because the right to an abortion is constitutionally protected, it cannot simultaneously be a legally recognized harm justifying illegal action. In these cases the courts have also denied the defense on the basis that the criminal act of protest would not stop abortions from occurring; that the harm caused by the act was greater than the harm of abortion; and that legal means of protest, such as demonstrating outside of the clinic rather than entering the clinic or trespassing on its property, were available. Consequently, according to the courts, there was no necessity for the protesters to break the law. In the vast majority of cases in which protesters, trespassing on property, blocked the entrance to nuclear plants, the courts have denied the necessity defense on the grounds that there was no imminent danger and that the trespassing protesters could not reasonably have believed that their actions would halt the manufacture of nuclear materials (see, e.g., *State v. Marley*, 54 Haw. 450, 509 P.2d 1095 [Haw. 1973]). The defense has also been denied in civil disobedience cases involving protests against U.S. policy abroad, the homeless problem, lack of funding for AIDS research, harmful logging practices, prison conditions, and human and ANIMAL RIGHTS violations.

Necessity has been used successfully by inmates who escape from prison under certain circumstances. In *Spakes v. State*, 913 S.W.2d 597 (Tex. Crim. App. 1996), the highest criminal court in Texas allowed the jury to be instructed on the necessity defense before deliberating the verdict for an inmate whose three cellmates had planned an escape and threatened to slit his throat if he did not accompany them. The defendant inmate argued that because of the terribly violent crimes of which his cellmates had been convicted (one had bragged about chopping his girlfriend up with an ax), he accompanied them and escaped. Even though he made no attempt to return himself to custody when he was separated from his cellmates, the court still allowed the defense. In contrast, most jurisdictions have held that an escapee must make an attempt to surrender or report to authorities as a condition for asserting the necessity defense. These courts have reasoned that once the immediate threat is no longer present, the action of escape is no longer necessary, and consequently it should end.

FURTHER READINGS

Fleishman, Michael. 2003. "Under the Influence of Necessity." *Arizona Law Review* 45 (spring).

Goldberg, Stephanie B. 1993. "Necessity Defense Fails in Massachusetts." *American Bar Association Journal* 79 (October).

Levenson, Laurie L. 1999. "Criminal Law: The Necessity Defense." *National Law Journal* (October 11).

Pearson, James O., Jr. 1992. "'Choice of Evils': Necessity, Duress, or Similar Defense to State or Local Criminal Charges Based on Acts of Public Protest." *American Law Reports.* 5th ed. Vol. 3.

Ripstein, Arthur. 1999. *Equality, Responsibility, and the Law.* New York: Cambridge Univ. Press.

Schulkind, Laura J. 1989. "Applying the Necessity Defense to Civil Disobedience Cases." *New York Law Review* 64 (April).

Stone, Stephanie. 1996. "No Surrender Requirement for Escapees Claiming Necessity Defense, Rules Texas." *West's Legal News* (January 12).

NEGATIVE COVENANT

A provision found in an employment agreement or a contract of sale of a business that prohibits an employee or seller from competing in the same area or market.

A negative covenant is commonly used by businesses, particularly those that depend upon trade secrets for their success. An employer wants to ensure that a former employee will not parlay information, skills, customer lists, and personal relationships with clients acquired on the job to gain a better position with a competitor or to start his or her own business. An employer also wants to protect his or her business in the competitive marketplace against the use of the unique personal skills of a former employee. An employer can achieve these objectives by including a negative COVENANT in the employment contract. Such a provision specifies that the employee will not work for a competitor or start a competing business for a period of time after leaving the employer. The covenant must be reasonable in its scope and duration. It cannot bar the employee from working at all, anywhere, or for an unreasonable length of time.

A court enforces a negative covenant by granting an INJUNCTION prohibiting the employee from working in a competitive enterprise as described in the covenant. It will do so only when necessary to protect the former employer's legitimate interests.

A contract for the sale of a business often includes a negative covenant at the insistence of the buyer. A buyer wants to protect and capitalize on the good will of the business he or she buys. He or she must have an opportunity to get to know and serve the customers if the business is to continue to be successful. The value of the business is undermined if the seller can open a competing enterprise next door, thereby keeping some of the good will that was sold to the buyer. A negative covenant under which the seller agrees not to open a competing enterprise for a reasonable period of time within a reasonable distance from the original business is a frequent provision in a sales contract.

NEGLECT

An omission to do or perform some work, duty, or act.

As used by U.S. courts, the term *neglect* denotes the failure of responsibility on the part of defendants or attorneys. Neglect is related to the concept of NEGLIGENCE, but its rather limited use in the law sets it apart from that much broader doctrine. Generally speaking, neglect means omitting or failing to do something that is required. Neglect is often related to timeliness: examples include the failure of a taxpayer to file a timely income tax return and the failure of an attorney to meet a deadline for filing an appeal. In determining whether to rule against a party, courts consider the reason for the neglect, which can range from unavoidable accidents and hindrances to the less acceptable extreme of carelessness and indifference to duty.

Special terminology applies to some forms of neglect. Culpable neglect exists where a loss arises from an individual's carelessness, improvidence, or folly. Willful neglect applies to marital cases; it refers to the neglect of one spouse, historically the husband, to provide such essentials as food, shelter, and clothing to the other spouse, either because of refusal or indifference.

Excusable neglect is used to grant exceptions in cases where neglect was the consequence of accident, unavoidable hindrance, reliance on legal counsel, or reliance on promises made by the adverse party. Excusable neglect can serve as the basis for a motion to vacate a judgment, as in the case of explaining why a deadline for filing an appeal could not be met. Under the Federal Rules of Civil Procedure, excusable neglect authorizes a court to permit an act to be done after the official deadline has expired (Fed. R. Civ. P. 6(b)).

CROSS-REFERENCES

Child Abuse; Necessaries.

NEGLIGENCE

Conduct that falls below the standards of behavior established by law for the protection of others against unreasonable risk of harm. A person has acted negligently if he or she has departed from the conduct expected of a reasonably prudent person acting under similar circumstances.

In order to establish negligence as a CAUSE OF ACTION *under the law of* TORTS, *a plaintiff must prove that the defendant had a duty to the plaintiff, the defendant breached that duty by failing to conform to the required standard of conduct, the defendant's negligent conduct was the cause of the harm to the plaintiff, and the plaintiff was, in fact, harmed or damaged.*

The concept of negligence developed under ENGLISH LAW. Although English COMMON LAW had long imposed liability for the wrongful acts of others, negligence did not emerge as an independent cause of action until the eighteenth century. Another important concept emerged at that time: legal liability for a failure to act. Originally liability for failing to act was imposed on those who undertook to perform some service and breached a promise to exercise care or skill in performing that service. Gradually the law began to imply a promise to exercise care or skill in the performance of certain services. This promise to exercise care, whether express or implied, formed the origins of the modern concept of "duty." For example, innkeepers were said to have a duty to protect the safety and security of their guests.

The concept of negligence passed from Great Britain to the United States as each state (except Louisiana) adopted the common law of Great Britain (Louisiana adopted the CIVIL LAW of France). Although there have been important developments in negligence law, the basic concepts have remained the same since the eighteenth century. Today negligence is by far the widest-ranging tort, encompassing virtually all unintentional, wrongful conduct that injures others. One of the most important concepts in negligence law is the "reasonable person," which provides the standard by which a person's conduct is judged.

The Reasonable Person

A person has acted negligently if she has departed from the conduct expected of a reasonably prudent person acting under similar circumstances. The hypothetical reasonable person provides an objective by which the conduct of others is judged. In law, the reasonable person is not an average person or a typical person but a composite of the community's judgment as to how the typical community member should behave in situations that might pose a threat of harm to the public. Even though the majority of people in the community may behave in a certain way, that does not establish the standard of conduct of the reasonable person. For example, a majority of people in a community may jaywalk, but jaywalking might still fall below the community's standards of safe conduct.

The concept of the reasonable person distinguishes negligence from intentional torts such as ASSAULT AND BATTERY. To prove an intentional tort, the plaintiff seeks to establish that the defendant deliberately acted to injure the plaintiff. In a negligence suit, however, the plaintiff seeks to establish that the failure of the defendant to act as a reasonable person caused the plaintiff's injury. An intoxicated driver who accidentally injures a pedestrian may not have intended to cause the pedestrian's injury. But because a reasonable person would not drive while intoxicated because it creates an unreasonable risk of harm to pedestrians and other drivers, an intoxicated driver may be held liable to an injured plaintiff for negligence despite his lack of intent to injure the plaintiff.

The law considers a variety of factors in determining whether a person has acted as the hypothetical reasonable person would have acted in a similar situation. These factors include the knowledge, experience, and perception of the person, the activity the person is engaging in, the physical characteristics of the person, and the circumstances surrounding the person's actions.

Knowledge, Experience, and Perception
The law takes into account a person's knowledge, experience, and perceptions in determining whether the individual has acted as a reasonable person would have acted in the same circumstances. Conduct must be judged in light of a person's actual knowledge and observations, because the reasonable person always takes this into account. Thus, if a driver sees another car approaching at night without lights, the driver must act reasonably to avoid an accident, even though the driver would not have been negligent in failing to see the other car.

In addition to actual knowledge, the law also considers most people to have the same knowledge, experience, and ability to perceive as the hypothetical reasonable person. In the absence of unusual circumstances, a person must see what is clearly visible and hear what is clearly audible. Therefore, a driver of a car hit by a train at an unobstructed railroad crossing cannot claim that she was not negligent because she did not see or hear the train, because a reasonable person would have seen or heard the train.

Also, a person cannot deny personal knowledge of basic facts commonly known in the community. The reasonable person knows that ice is slippery, that live wires are dangerous, that alcohol impairs driving ability, and that children might run into the street when they are playing. To act as a reasonable person, an individual must even take into account her lack of knowledge of some situations, such as when walking down a dark, unfamiliar corridor.

Finally, a person who undertakes a particular activity is ordinarily considered to have the knowledge common to others who engage in that activity. A motorist must know the rules of the road and a product manufacturer must know the characteristics and dangers of its product, at least to the extent they are generally known in the industry.

Special Skills If a person engages in an activity requiring special skills, education, training, or experience, such as piloting an airplane, the standard by which his conduct is measured is the conduct of a reasonably skilled, competent, and experienced person who is a qualified member of the group authorized to engage in that activity. In other words, the hypothetical reasonable person is a skilled, competent, and experienced person who engages in the same activity. Often persons practicing these special

skills must be licensed, such as physicians, lawyers, architects, barbers, pilots, and drivers. Anyone who performs these special skills, whether qualified or not, is held to the standards of conduct of those properly qualified to do so, because the public relies on the special expertise of those who engage in such activities. Thus, an unlicensed driver who takes his friends for a joyride is held to the standard of conduct of an experienced, licensed driver.

The law does not make a special allowance for beginners with regard to special skills. The learner, beginner, or trainee in a special skill is held to the standard of conduct of persons who are reasonably skilled and experienced in the activity. Sometimes the beginner is held to a standard he cannot meet. For example, a first-time driver clearly does not possess the experience and skill of an experienced driver. Although it may seem unfair to hold the beginner to the standards of the more experienced person, this standard protects the general public from the risk of a beginner's lack of competence, because the community is usually defenseless to guard against such risks.

Physical Characteristics The law takes a person's physical characteristics into account in determining whether that person's conduct is negligent. Whether a person's conduct is reasonable, and therefore not negligent, is measured against a reasonably prudent person with the same physical characteristics. There are two reasons for taking physical characteristics into account. A physically impaired individual cannot be expected to conform to a standard of conduct that would be physically impossible for her to meet. On the other hand, a physically challenged person must act reasonably in light of her handicap, and she may be negligent in taking a risk that is unreasonable in light of her known physical limitations. Thus, it would be negligent for a blind person to drive an automobile.

Mental Capacity Although a person's physical characteristics are taken into account in determining negligence, the person's mental capacity is generally ignored and does not excuse the person from acting according to the reasonable person standard. The fact that an individual is lacking in intelligence, judgment, memory, or emotional stability does not excuse the person's failure to act as a reasonably prudent person would have acted under the same circumstances. For example, a person who causes a forest fire by failing to extinguish his campfire cannot claim that he was not negligent because he lacked the intelligence, judgment, or experience to appreciate the risk of an untended campfire.

Similarly, evidence of voluntary intoxication will not excuse conduct that is otherwise negligent. Although intoxication affects a person's judgment, voluntary intoxication will not excuse negligent conduct, because it is the person's conduct, not his or her mental condition, that determines negligence. In some cases a person's intoxication is relevant to determining whether his conduct is negligent, however, because undertaking certain activities, such as driving, while intoxicated poses a danger to others.

Children Children may be negligent, but they are not held to the same standard of conduct as adults. A child's conduct is measured against the conduct expected of a child of similar age, intelligence, and experience. Unlike the standard for adults, the standard of reasonable conduct for children takes into account subjective factors such as intelligence and experience. In this sense the standard is less strict than for adults, because children normally do not engage in the high-risk activities of adults and adults dealing with children are expected to anticipate their "childish" behavior.

In many states children are presumed incapable of negligence below a certain age, usually seven years. In some states children between the ages of seven and fourteen years are presumed to be incapable of negligence, although this presumption can be rebutted. Once a person reaches the age of majority, usually eighteen years, she is held to adult standards of conduct.

One major exception to the rules of negligence exists with regard to children. If a child is engaging in what is considered an "adult activity," such as driving an automobile or flying an airplane, the child will be held to an adult standard of care. The higher standard of care imposed for these types of activities is justified by the special skills required to engage in them and the danger they pose to the public.

Emergencies The law recognizes that even a reasonable person can make errors in judgment in emergency situations. Therefore, a person's conduct in an emergency is evaluated in light of whether it was a reasonable response under the circumstances, even though, in hindsight, another course of action might have avoided the injury.

In some circumstances failure to anticipate an emergency may constitute negligence. The reasonable person anticipates, and takes precautions against, foreseeable emergencies. For example, the owner of a theater must consider the possibility of a fire, and the owner of a swimming pool must consider the possibility of a swimmer drowning. Failure to guard against such emergencies can constitute negligence.

Also, a person can be negligent in causing an emergency, even if he acts reasonably during the emergency. A theater owner whose negligence causes a fire, for instance, would be liable for the injuries to the patrons, even if he saved lives during the fire.

Conduct of Others Finally, the reasonable person takes into account the conduct of others and regulates his own conduct accordingly. A reasonable person must even foresee the unlawful or negligent conduct of others if the situation warrants. Thus, a person may be found negligent for leaving a car unlocked with the keys in the ignition because of the foreseeable risk of theft, or for failing to slow down in the vicinity of a school yard where children might negligently run into the street.

Proof of Negligence

In a negligence suit, the plaintiff has the burden of proving that the defendant did not act as a reasonable person would have acted under the circumstances. The court will instruct the jury as to the standard of conduct required of the defendant. For example, a defendant sued for negligent driving is judged according to how a reasonable person would have driven in the same circumstances. A plaintiff has a variety of means of proving that a defendant did not act as the hypothetical reasonable person would have acted. The plaintiff can show that the defendant violated a statute designed to protect against the type of injury that occurred to the plaintiff. Also, a plaintiff might introduce expert witnesses, evidence of a customary practice, or CIRCUMSTANTIAL EVIDENCE.

Statutes Federal and state statutes, municipal ordinances, and administrative regulations govern all kinds of conduct and frequently impose standards of conduct to be observed. For example, the law prohibits driving through a red traffic light at an intersection. A plaintiff injured by a defendant who ignored a red light can introduce the defendant's violation of the statute as evidence that the defendant acted negligently.

However, a plaintiff's evidence that the defendant violated a statute does not always establish that the defendant acted unreasonably. The statute that was violated must have been intended to protect against the particular hazard or type of harm that caused injury to the plaintiff.

Sometimes physical circumstances beyond a person's control can excuse the violation of a statute, such as when the headlights of a vehicle suddenly fail, or when a driver swerves into oncoming traffic to avoid a child who darted into the street. To excuse the violation, the defendant must establish that, in failing to comply with the statute, she acted as a reasonable person would have acted.

In many jurisdictions the violation of a statute, regulation, or ordinance enacted to protect against the harm that resulted to the plaintiff is considered negligence *per se*. Unless the defendant presents evidence excusing the violation of the statute, the defendant's negligence is conclusively established. In some jurisdictions a defendant's violation of a statute is merely evidence that the defendant acted negligently.

Experts Often a plaintiff will need an expert witness to establish that the defendant did not adhere to the conduct expected of a reasonably prudent person in the defendant's circumstances. A juror may be unable to determine from his own experience, for example, if the medicine prescribed by a physician was reasonably appropriate for a patient's illness. Experts may provide the jury with information beyond the common knowledge of jurors, such as scientific theories, data, tests, and experiments. Also, in cases involving professionals such as physicians, experts establish the standard of care expected of the professional. In the above example, the patient might have a physician offer EXPERT TESTIMONY regarding the medication that a reasonably prudent physician would have prescribed for the patient's illness.

Custom Evidence of the usual and customary conduct or practice of others under similar circumstances can be admitted to establish the proper standard of reasonable conduct. Like the evidence provided by expert witnesses, evidence of custom and habit is usually used in cases where the nature of the alleged negligence is beyond the common knowledge of the jurors. Often such evidence is presented in cases alleging negligence in some business activity. For example, a plaintiff suing the manufacturer of a punch press that injured her might present evidence that all other manufacturers of punch presses incorporate a certain safety device that would have prevented the injury.

A plaintiff's evidence of conformity or non-conformity with a customary practice does not establish whether the defendant was negligent; the jury decides whether a reasonably prudent person would have done more or less than is customary.

Circumstantial Evidence Sometimes a plaintiff has no direct evidence of how the defendant acted and must attempt to prove his case through circumstantial evidence. Of course, any fact in a lawsuit may be proved by circumstantial evidence. Skid marks can establish the speed a car was traveling prior to a collision, a person's appearance can circumstantially prove his or her age, etc. Sometimes a plaintiff in a negligence lawsuit must prove his entire case by circumstantial evidence. Suppose a plaintiff's shoulder is severely injured during an operation to remove his tonsils. The plaintiff, who was unconscious during the operation, sues the doctor in charge of the operation for negligence, even though he has no idea how the injury actually occurred. The doctor refuses to say how the injury occurred, so the plaintiff will have to prove his case by circumstantial evidence.

In cases such as this, the doctrine of RES IPSA LOQUITUR (the thing speaks for itself) is invoked. *Res ipsa loquitor* allows a plaintiff to prove negligence on the theory that his injury could not have occurred in the absence of the defendant's negligence. The plaintiff must establish that the injury was caused by an instrumentality or condition that was under the defendant's exclusive management or control and that the plaintiff's injury would not have occurred if the defendant had acted with reasonable care. Thus, in the above example, the plaintiff can use *res ipsa loquitor* to prove that the doctor negligently injured his shoulder.

Duty

A defendant is not liable in negligence, even if she did not act with reasonable care, if she did not owe a duty to the plaintiff. In general, a person is under a duty to all persons at all times to exercise reasonable care for their physical safety and the safety of their property. This general standard of duty may lead to seemingly unjust results. For example, if a property owner leaves a deep hole in her backyard with no warnings or barriers around the hole, she should be liable if her guest falls into the hole. But what if a trespasser enters the backyard at night and falls into the hole? Although the property owner was negligent in failing to guard against someone falling into the hole, it would be unfair to require the property owner to compensate the trespasser for his injury. Therefore, the law states that a property owner does not have a duty to protect a trespasser from harm.

The law uses the concept of duty to limit the situations where a defendant is liable for a plaintiff's injury. Whether a defendant has a duty to protect the plaintiff from harm is a question decided by the court, not the jury. Over time, courts have developed numerous rules creating and limiting a person's duty to others, and sometimes duties are established or limited by statute. Whether the defendant owes the plaintiff a duty depends upon the relationship between the defendant and the plaintiff.

A preexisting relationship can create an affirmative duty to exercise reasonable care to protect another person from harm. For example, an inn has an affirmative duty to protect its guests, a school has a duty to its pupils, a store has a duty to its customers, and a lifeguard has a duty to swimmers.

One always has a duty to refrain from taking actions that endanger the safety of others, but usually one does not have a duty to render aid or prevent harm to a person from an independent cause. A common example of this limitation on duty is the lack of a duty to go to the aid of a person in peril. An expert swimmer with a boat and a rope has no duty to attempt to rescue a person who is drowning (although a hired lifeguard would). A physician who witnesses an automobile accident has no duty to offer emergency medical assistance to the accident victims.

Sometimes a person can voluntarily assume a duty where it would not otherwise exist. If the doctor who encounters an automobile accident decides to render aid to the victims, she is under a duty to exercise reasonable care in rendering that aid. As a result, doctors who have stopped along the highway to render medical assistance to accident victims have been sued for negligence. Many states have adopted "good samaritan" statutes to relieve individuals who render emergency assistance from negligence liability.

Even if a plaintiff establishes that the defendant had a duty to protect the plaintiff from

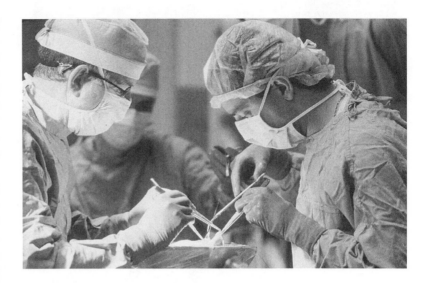

The law of negligence imposes higher standards on individuals who engage in activities that require special skills and training. For example, someone who engages in the practice of medicine must act as a reasonably skilled, competent, and experienced physician would.

NATHAN BENN/CORBIS

harm and breached that duty by failing to use reasonable care, the plaintiff must still prove that the defendant's negligence was the proximate cause of her injury.

Proximate Cause

Perhaps no issue in negligence law has caused more confusion than the issue of proximate cause. The concept of proximate cause limits a defendant's liability for his negligence to consequences reasonably related to the negligent conduct. Although it might seem obvious whether a defendant's negligence has caused injury to the plaintiff, issues of causation are often very difficult. Suppose, for example, that a defendant negligently causes an automobile accident, injuring another driver. The colliding cars also knock down a utility pole, resulting in a power outage. Clearly the defendant's negligence has in fact caused both the accident and power outage. Most people would agree that the negligent defendant should be liable for the other driver's injuries, but should he also be liable to an employee who, due to the failure of her electric alarm clock, arrives late for work and is fired? This question raises the issue of proximate cause.

Actually, the term *proximate cause* is somewhat misleading because as a legal concept it has little to do with proximity (in time or space) or causation. Rather, proximate cause is related to fairness and justice, in the sense that at some point it becomes unfair to hold a defendant responsible for the results of his negligence. For example, Mrs. O'Leary's negligent placement of her lantern may have started the Great Chicago

Fire, but it would be unjust to hold her responsible for all the damage done by the fire.

In determining whether a defendant's negligence is the proximate cause of a plaintiff's injury, most courts focus on the foreseeability of the harm that resulted from the defendant's negligence. For example, if a driver negligently drives his automobile, it is foreseeable that he might cause an accident with another vehicle, hit a pedestrian, or crash into a storefront. Thus, the driver would be liable for those damages. But suppose the negligent driver collides with a truck carrying dynamite, causing an explosion that injures a person two blocks away. Assuming that the driver had no idea that the truck was carrying dynamite, it is not foreseeable that his negligent driving could injure a person two blocks away. Therefore the driver would not be liable for that person's injury under this approach. When applying this approach, courts frequently instruct juries to consider whether the harm or injury was the "natural or probable" consequence of the defendant's negligence.

A minority of courts hold the view that the defendant's negligence is the proximate cause of the plaintiff's injury if the injury is the "direct result" of the negligence. Usually a plaintiff's injury is considered to be the direct result of the defendant's negligence if it follows an unbroken, natural sequence from the defendant's act and no intervening, external force acts to cause the injury.

Intervening Cause

Sometimes a plaintiff's injury results from more than one cause. For instance, suppose a defendant negligently injures a pedestrian in an automobile accident. An emergency room doctor negligently treats the plaintiff, aggravating her injury. The doctor's negligence is an "intervening cause" of the plaintiff's injury. A cause of injury is an INTERVENING CAUSE only if it occurs subsequent to the defendant's negligent conduct.

Just because an intervening cause exists, however, does not mean that the defendant's negligent conduct is not the proximate cause of the plaintiff's injury. The defendant remains liable if he should have foreseen the intervening cause and taken it into account in his conduct. If a defendant negligently spills a large quantity of gasoline and doesn't clean it up, he will not be relieved of liability for a resulting fire merely because another person causes the gasoline to ignite, because it is foreseeable that the gasoline might be accidentally ignited. Also, it is foreseeable that a sudden gust of wind might cause the fire to spread quickly.

Even if an intervening cause is foreseeable, however, in some situations the defendant will still be excused from liability. If the intervening cause is the intentional or criminal conduct of a third person, the defendant is not liable for this person's negligent conduct. In the example where the defendant spilled gasoline and did not clean it up, he is not responsible for the resulting fire if someone intentionally ignites the gas. Also, sometimes a third person will discover the danger that the defendant created by his negligence under circumstances where the third person has some duty to act. If the third person fails to act, the defendant is not liable. In the gasoline example, suppose the defendant, a customer at a gas station, negligently spills a large quantity of gas near the pumps. The owner of the gas station sees the spilled gasoline but does nothing. The owner of the gas station, not the defendant, would be liable if another customer accidentally ignites the gasoline.

Sometimes, however, a completely unforeseeable event or result occurs after a defendant's negligence, resulting in harm to the plaintiff. An abnormal, unpredictable, or highly improbable event that occurs after the defendant's negligence is known as a "superseding cause" and relieves the defendant of liability. For example, suppose a defendant negligently blocks a road causing the plaintiff to make a detour in her automobile. While on the detour, an airplane hits the plaintiff's car, killing the plaintiff. The airplane was completely unforeseeable to the defendant, and thus he cannot be held liable for the plaintiff's death. The airplane was a superseding cause of the plaintiff's death.

Even great jurists have had difficulty articulating exactly what constitutes proximate cause. Although the law provides tests such as "foreseeability" and "natural, direct consequences," ultimately the issue of proximate cause is decided by people's sense of right and wrong. In the example where the defendant spills gasoline and does not clean it up, most people would agree that the defendant should be liable if a careless smoker accidentally ignites the gasoline, even if they could not articulate that the smoker was a foreseeable, intervening cause of the fire.

Defenses to Negligence Liability

Even if a plaintiff has established that the defendant owed a duty to the plaintiff, breached that duty, and proximately caused the defendant's injury, the defendant can still raise defenses that reduce or eliminate his liability. These defenses include contributory negligence, comparative negligence, and ASSUMPTION OF RISK.

Contributory Negligence Frequently, more than one person has acted negligently to create an injury. Under the common-law rule of contributory negligence, a plaintiff whose own negligence was a contributing cause of her injury was barred from recovering from a negligent defendant. For example, a driver negligently enters an intersection in the path of an oncoming car, resulting in a collision. The other driver was driving at an excessive speed and might have avoided the collision if she had been driving more slowly. Thus, both drivers' negligence contributed to the accident. Under the doctrine of contributory negligence, neither driver would be able to recover from the other, due to her own negligence in causing the accident.

The doctrine of contributory negligence seeks to keep a plaintiff from recovering from the defendant where the plaintiff is also at fault. However, this doctrine often leads to unfair results. For example, even if a defendant's negligence is the overwhelming cause of the plaintiff's injury, even slight negligence on the part of the plaintiff completely bars his recovery. Also, the negligence of many defendants such as corporations, manufacturers, and landowners creates no corresponding risk of injury to themselves. In such cases the doctrine of contributory negligence, which can completely eliminate the liability for their negligence, reduces their incentive to act safely. As a result, courts and statutes have considerably weakened the doctrine of contributory negligence.

Comparative Negligence Most states, either by court decision or statute, have now adopted some form of comparative negligence in place of pure, contributory negligence. Under comparative negligence, or comparative fault as it is sometimes known, a plaintiff's negligence is not a complete bar to her recovery. Instead the plaintiff's damages are reduced by whatever percentage her own fault contributed to the injury. This requires the jury to determine, by percentage, the fault of the plaintiff and defendant in causing the plaintiff's injury. For example, suppose a plaintiff is injured in an automobile accident and sustains $100,000 in damages. The jury determines that the plaintiff was 25 percent

responsible for the accident and that the defendant was 75 percent responsible. The plaintiff will then be allowed to recover 75 percent of her damages, or $75,000.

Most states have adopted the "50 percent rule" of comparative negligence. Under this rule the plaintiff cannot recover any damages if her negligence was as great as, or greater than, the negligence of the defendant. This rule partially retains the doctrine of contributory negligence, reflecting the view that a plaintiff who is largely responsible for her own injury is unworthy of compensation. A minority of states have adopted "pure comparative fault." Under that rule even a plaintiff who is 80 percent at fault in causing her injury may still recover 20 percent of damages, reflecting the defendant's percentage of fault.

Assumption of Risk Under the assumption of risk defense, a defendant can avoid liability for his negligence by establishing that the plaintiff voluntarily consented to encounter a known danger created by the defendant's negligence. Assumption of risk may be express or implied. Under express assumption of risk, persons agree in advance that one person consents to assume the risk of the other's negligence. For example, a skier who purchases a lift ticket at a ski resort usually expressly agrees to assume the risk of any injury that might occur while skiing. Thus, even if the ski resort negligently fails to mark a hazard on a trail resulting in an injury to a skier, the ski resort may invoke the assumption of risk defense in the skier's subsequent lawsuit.

Assumption of risk may also be implied from a plaintiff's conduct. For example, the defendant gives the plaintiff, a painter, a scaffold with a badly frayed rope. The plaintiff, fully aware of the rope's condition, proceeds to use the scaffold and is injured. The defendant can raise the implied assumption of risk defense. This defense is similar to the contributory negligence defense; in the above example, the defendant might also argue that the plaintiff was contributorily negligent for using the scaffold when he knew the rope was frayed.

The implied assumption of risk defense has caused a great deal of confusion in the courts because of its similarity to contributory negligence, and with the rise of comparative fault, the defense has diminished in importance and is viable today only in a minority of jurisdictions.

FURTHER READINGS

Bar-Gill, Oren, and Omri Ben-Shahar. 2003. "The Uneasy Case for Comparative Negligence." *American Law and Economics Review* 5 (spring).

Buswell, Henry F. 1997. *The Civil Liability for Personal Injuries Arising out of Negligence.* Littleton, Colo.: F.B. Rothman.

Cupp, Richard L., Jr., and Danielle Polage. 2002. "The Rhetoric of Strict Products Liability Versus Negligence: An Empirical Analysis." *New York University Law Review* 77 (October).

Henderson, James A., Jr. 2002. "Why Negligence Dominates Tort." *UCLA Law Review* 50 (December).

CROSS-REFERENCES

Alcohol; Automobiles; Good Samaritan Doctrine; Guest Statutes; Last Clear Chance; *MacPherson v. Buick Motor Co.*; Natural and Probable Consequences; *Palsgraf v. Long Island Railroad Company*; Product Liability; Rescue; *Rylands v. Fletcher*; Strict Liability.

NEGLIGENT ENTRUSTMENT

The act of leaving an object, such as an automobile or firearm, with another whom the lender knows or should know could use the object to harm others due to such factors as youth or inexperience.

Negligent entrustment claims arise when an unlicensed, incompetent, or reckless driver causes damages while driving a motor vehicle owned by someone else. A party injured by such a driver must generally prove five components of this TORT: (1) that the owner entrusted the vehicle to the driver; (2) that the driver was unlicensed, incompetent, or reckless; (3) that the owner knew or should have known that the driver was unlicensed, incompetent, or reckless; (4) that the driver was negligent in the operation of the vehicle; and (5) that the driver's NEGLIGENCE resulted in damages (*Amaya v. Potter*, 94 S.W.3d 856 [Tex. App. 2002]).

If a plaintiff proves these elements, an owner may be liable for the full amount of damages caused by the driver. In some instances, the plaintiff may also recover PUNITIVE DAMAGES from the owner, particularly if the owner himself acted recklessly in entrusting the vehicle to the driver (*Allstate Ins. Co. v. Wade*, 579 S.E.2d 180 [Va. 2003]).

FURTHER READINGS

Kionka, Edward J. 1999. *Torts in a Nutshell.* 3d ed. St. Paul, Minn.: West Group.

NEGOTIABLE INSTRUMENT

A COMMERCIAL PAPER, *such as a check or promissory note, that contains the signature of the maker or drawer; an unconditional promise or order to pay a certain sum in cash that is payable either upon demand or at a specifically designated time to the order of a designated person or to its bearer.*

NEGOTIATE

To conduct business transactions; to deal with another individual in regard to a purchase and sale; to bargain or trade. To conclude by way of agreement, bargain, or compact. To transfer a negotiable instrument, such as a promissory note, or other COMMERCIAL PAPER.

❖ NELSON, JOHN

John Nelson was a prominent U.S. lawyer, congressman, and diplomat who served as attorney general of the United States under President JOHN TYLER.

Nelson was born on June 1, 1791 (some sources say 1794), in Frederick County, Maryland. As a young boy, he was educated by private tutors; subsequently, he entered the College of William and Mary at Williamsburg, Virginia. He graduated in 1811 and went on to study law with attorneys in both Virginia and Maryland. He was admitted to the bar in 1813 and established a practice in his hometown.

In 1820 Nelson was elected to the U.S. House of Representatives as a Democrat. He

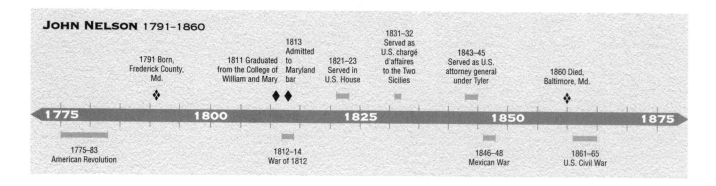

JOHN NELSON 1791–1860

1791 Born, Frederick County, Md.

1811 Graduated from the College of William and Mary

1813 Admitted to Maryland bar

1821–23 Served in U.S. House

1831–32 Served as U.S. chargé d'affaires to the Two Sicilies

1843–45 Served as U.S. attorney general under Tyler

1860 Died, Baltimore, Md.

1775 1800 1825 1850 1875

1775–83 American Revolution

1812–14 War of 1812

1846–48 Mexican War

1861–65 U.S. Civil War

took the oath of office on March 4, 1821, and served until March 3, 1823. He did not run for reelection but did support Andrew Jackson's presidential bid in 1828.

Over the next two decades, Nelson served the U.S. government in a number of unofficial capacities. He received the first of his official appointments from President Jackson in 1831, when he was named to a diplomatic post in Naples. He served as U.S. charge d'affaires (*charge d'affaires* is a title accorded lower-level diplomats) to Two Sicilies from October 24, 1831, to October 15, 1832. (The Two Sicilies was an independent Bourbon/Spanish-ruled kingdom located in southern Italy prior to that country's unification in the mid-1860s. The kingdom's capital was Naples.)

When Tyler assumed the presidency following the death of President WILLIAM H. HARRISON, he named Nelson attorney general of the United States. Nelson held a cabinet post as SECRETARY OF STATE ad interim at the same time. (The position of attorney general was not a cabinet-level post at the time.) Nelson served in both capacities from 1843 to 1845.

In his later years, Nelson resumed the PRACTICE OF LAW in Baltimore, Maryland. He died there on January 8, 1860 and is buried at Baltimore's Greenmount Cemetery.

FURTHER READINGS

Monroe, Dan. 2002. *The Republican Vision of John Tyler.* San Antonio: Texas A&M Univ. Press.

Peterson, Normal. 1989. *The Presidencies of William Henry Harrison and John Tyler.* Lawrence: Univ. Press of Kansas.

❖ NELSON, SAMUEL

Samuel Nelson served as an associate justice of the U.S. Supreme Court from 1845 to 1872. He brought with him experience as a politician,

Samuel Nelson.
U.S. SUPREME COURT

lawyer, and judge, which had included service as chief justice of the New York Supreme Court. His nomination to the U.S. Supreme Court by a desperate President JOHN TYLER came only after several prior nominees had declined or had been rejected by the U.S. Senate.

Nelson was born in Hebron, New York, on November 10, 1792. He entered Middlebury College, in Vermont, at the age of 15 and graduated in 1813. Nelson chose a career in law, and during his twenties he managed a successful private practice in real estate and COMMERCIAL LAW that brought him political recognition. In 1821, he was the youngest delegate to serve in the New York state constitutional convention. His judicial career began in 1823 with his appointment as a judge to the U.S. Court of Appeals for the Sixth Circuit. In 1831, he began a 14-year tenure on the New York Supreme

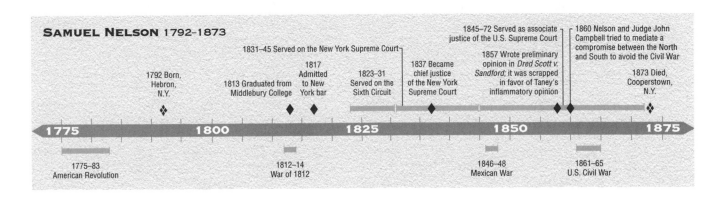

SAMUEL NELSON 1792–1873

1831–45 Served on the New York Supreme Court

1845–72 Served as associate justice of the U.S. Supreme Court

1860 Nelson and Judge John Campbell tried to mediate a compromise between the North and South to avoid the Civil War

1857 Wrote preliminary opinion in *Dred Scott v. Sandford;* it was scrapped in favor of Taney's inflammatory opinion

1792 Born, Hebron, N.Y.

1813 Graduated from Middlebury College

1817 Admitted to New York bar

1823–31 Served on the Sixth Circuit

1837 Became chief justice of the New York Supreme Court

1873 Died, Cooperstown, N.Y.

1775 — 1800 — 1825 — 1850 — 1875

1775–83 American Revolution

1812–14 War of 1812

1846–48 Mexican War

1861–65 U.S. Civil War

Court, during the last four years of which he served as its chief justice. (Since 1847, New York's highest court has been called the New York Court of Appeals.) There, Nelson developed a reputation for common sense and a belief in the limits of judicial power.

In 1845, President Tyler turned to Nelson in desperation. The president's attempts to fill a vacant seat on the U.S. Supreme Court had produced more than half a dozen nominees, all of whom had refused the nomination or had failed to win Senate approval. Nelson, a last-minute substitution, sailed through the nomination process.

Nelson believed that the Court should move cautiously in matters pertaining to the expressed will of Congress. He wrote the original majority opinion in the *Dred Scott* decision that upheld the institution of SLAVERY (DRED SCOTT V. SANDFORD, 60 U.S. [19 How.] 393, 15 L. Ed. 691 [1857]). Nelson's opinion sought to avoid answering the highly controversial question of slavery. But under political pressure from Southern justices on the Court, his opinion was scrapped, and Chief Justice Roger B. Taney's inflammatory opinion was substituted. Taney's decision led to violent protest and deepened hostilities that ultimately led to the Civil War. Nelson died December 13, 1873.

FURTHER READINGS

Friedman, Leon, and Fred L. Israel, eds. 1969. *The Justices of the United States Supreme Court, 1789–1969: Their Lives and Major Opinions.* New York: Chelsea House.

NET

The sum that remains following all permissible deductions, including charges, expenses, discounts, commissions, or taxes.

Net assets, for example, are what remain after an individual subtracts the amount owed to creditors from his or her assets. *Net pay* is the salary an individual actually receives after deductions such as INCOME TAX and SOCIAL SECURITY payments.

NET WORTH

The difference between total assets and liabilities; the sum total of the assets of an individual or business minus the total amount owed to creditors.

The net worth of a corporation is ordinarily determined by subtracting the liabilities from the assets, or by adding the capital account to the surplus account, as shown in the balance sheet of the company.

NEUTRALITY

The state of a nation that takes no part in a war between two or more other powers.

Since the nineteenth century, INTERNATIONAL LAW has recognized the right of a nation to abstain from participation in a war between other states. In an international war, those taking no part are called neutrals. This means that a neutral state cannot provide assistance to the belligerents, the principal hostile powers, or to their allies, who cooperate and assist them.

The law of neutrality that emerged from the nineteenth century was codified in several of the Hague Conferences of 1907, including No. 3, Convention Relative to the Opening of Hostilities (requiring notice to neutrals of a state of war); No. 5, Convention Respecting Rights and Duties of Neutral Powers and Persons in Case of War on Land; and No. 11, Convention Relative to Certain Restrictions with Regard to the Exercise of the Right of Capture in Naval War.

Once a state decides on a position of neutrality, it must take steps to prevent its territory from becoming a base for military operations of a belligerent. It must prevent the recruiting of military personnel, the organizing of military expeditions, and the constructing, outfitting, commissioning, and arming of warships for belligerent use. A neutral state is under no obligation to prevent private persons or companies from advancing credits or selling commodities to belligerents. Such sales are not illegal under the international law of neutrality. A neutral state may, if it chooses, go beyond the requirements of international law by placing an embargo upon some or all sales or credits to belligerents by its nationals. If it does so, it has the obligation to see that legislation, commonly referred to as neutrality laws, is applied impartially to all belligerents. Once enacted, neutrality laws are not to be modified in ways that would advantage one party in the war.

For most of its history, the United States tried to remain neutral during the wars among European states. President GEORGE WASHINGTON issued a neutrality proclamation in 1793 after the outbreak of war between France and the European allies. Congress enacted its first neutrality law in 1794 (1 Stat. 381), which prohibited private individuals from accepting a foreign military commission, outfitting military vessels for a foreign state, or enlisting or hiring persons for the service of a foreign state.

This legislation proved generally effective in accomplishing its objectives, but it did not deter citizens who wished to support revolutionary belligerent or insurgent movements in South and Central America during the nineteenth century. The Mexican Revolution of 1910 and the counterrevolution that followed led to the trafficking in arms and ammunition across the border. In response, Congress enacted, in 1912, its first arms embargo (37 Stat. 630), a prohibition not required by international law. It authorized the president, upon finding that conditions of violence in an American country were promoted by procurement of arms or munitions of war in the United States, to prohibit further export of them.

With the rise of international conflicts around the world in the 1930s, Congress passed the Neutrality Acts of 1935, 1936, and 1937 (49 Stat. 1081, 49 Stat. 1152, 50 Stat. 121). These laws required registration and licensing by a National Munitions Control Board of all persons trading in munitions and a mandatory embargo on the export of arms, ammunition, and implements of war, and on loans and credits to all belligerents or to neutrals for transshipment to belligerents. An embargo would take effect when the president found a state of war to exist.

The desire of the United States to remain neutral has been called isolationism. During the 1930s the U.S. public did not want the United States entangled with the international strife perpetrated by Italy, Germany, and Japan. In 1935, President FRANKLIN D. ROOSEVELT invoked the arms embargo provision after the Italian invasion of Ethiopia and the consequent war. With the outbreak of the European war in 1939, limiting the conflict by an arms embargo was no longer possible. Although isolationist sentiment was strong, there was also a growing feeling that the Allies needed support against Nazi aggression. The Roosevelt administration, with some difficulty, secured the repeal of the arms embargo in the Neutrality Act of 1939 (22 U.S.C.A. § 441). Because this repeal could work to the advantage only of Great Britain and France, it was a deliberately non-neutral act.

The United States remained a neutral state before its entry into WORLD WAR II in December 1941, yet it took actions that undermined its status. In 1940, the United States entered into an agreement for the transfer of 50 old destroyers to Great Britain in exchange for leased naval and air bases in British islands off the Atlantic coast of the United States. Congress took a further step in the LEND-LEASE ACT of 1941 (55 Stat. 31) by agreeing to provide munitions, food, machinery, and services to Great Britain and the other Allies without immediate cost, thus eliminating their difficulty in finding dollar credits for purchases. Later repayment could be made in kind or property or other acceptable benefits. Under the Lend-Lease Act, the United States made huge shipments before and after entering the war.

Following the passage of the Lend-Lease Act, the United States became increasingly involved in direct military assistance, permitting U.S. merchant ships to transport war materials to the Allies, using U.S. pilots to deliver bombers to Canada and Britain, and using naval vessels for a "neutrality patrol" in the Atlantic that assisted in protecting belligerent convoys against submarines.

Much of the 1939 act remains in force (22 U.S.C.A. §§ 441–457), including the president's authority to find and proclaim a state of war, prohibition of travel by citizens in belligerent ships, and prohibition of financial transactions by persons in the United States with belligerents or solicitation or collection of contributions for a belligerent except for humanitarian purposes. The authority for an arms embargo, which was revoked in 1941, has not been reinstated. Sales by U.S. individuals and companies are governed by the international law of neutrality, unless Congress enacts a specific embargo provision.

In the post–World War II era, the U.S. government has committed several neutrality violations. Its conduct was less than disinterested and neutral in the overthrow of the Guatemalan government in 1954, in its sponsorship of the Bay of Pigs military expedition against Cuba in 1961, in its intervention in the civil war in the Dominican Republic in 1965, and in its aid to those who overthrew the Salvador Allende government in Chile in 1973.

Congress did enact the Arms Export Control Act of 1976 (22 U.S.C.A. §§ 2751–2796c [1989 Supp.]), which was designed to restrict the transfer of arms to nations that support international TERRORISM. The IRAN-CONTRA AFFAIR that emerged as a political scandal in President Ronald Reagan's administration involved violations of this act. The transfer of arms to Iran, a nation that supported terrorism, and the financial and military support of a right-wing revolutionary group in Nicaragua violated congressional legislation and, in the case of Nicaragua, thwarted the desire of Congress to remain neutral in the conflict.

FURTHER READINGS

Chadwick, Elizabeth. 2002. *Traditional Neutrality Revisited: Law, Theory, and Case Studies.* New York: Kluwer Law International.

Gabriel, Jurg Martin. 2002. *The American Conception of Neutrality After 1941.* New York: Palgrave Macmillan.

Havel, Brian F. 2000. "An International Law Institution in Crisis: Rethinking Permanent Neutrality." *Ohio State Law Journal* 6 (February).

Politakis, George. 1998. *Modern Aspects of the Laws of Naval Warfare and Maritime Neutrality.* London, New York: Kegan Paul International.

Vagts, Detlev F. 1999. "The Traditional Legal Concept of Neutrality in a Changing Environment." *American University International Law Review* 14 (January-February).

NEW DEAL

"I pledge you, I pledge myself, to a new deal for the American people." In July 1932, FRANKLIN DELANO ROOSEVELT said these words to the delegates at the Democratic National Convention, who had just elected him the party's candidate for president of the United States.

Roosevelt's New Deal was a response to the tumultuous events of the years leading to his nomination. After WORLD WAR I, the people of the United States experienced unprecedented prosperity. Consumers of all income levels were buying goods "on time" by putting a few dollars down and paying a few dollars a month. Record numbers of people were also using the installment-buying concept to purchase stocks. The number of stockbrokers grew from fewer than 30,000 in 1920 to more than 70,000 in 1929. Stockbrokers allowed their clients to "buy on margin," meaning that a customer only had to pay 10–15 percent down on a stock, with the BROKER lending the client the rest and being repaid when the stock went up in value. By 1929, the skyrocketing prices in the STOCK MARKET indicated continued prosperity to some economists, but to others it signaled impending doom. So much investment had been done on margin that stockbrokers had borrowed money from banks that by then were also heavily in debt. Stock prices began rapidly dropping in September 1929, and on "Black Thursday," October 24, 1929, they plummeted beyond all belief, devastating thousands of brokerage houses. By the following Tuesday, October 29, virtually all stocks were worthless. Millionaires became paupers overnight. People who had invested their savings woke up to find themselves penniless. This was the start of the Great Depression.

HERBERT HOOVER was the president at the time of the great stock market crash. He initially refused to believe that there was a problem, and even in April 1930, when more than three million people had lost their jobs, he continued in vain to reassure people that everything was fine. Because people were afraid of losing their jobs and running out of money, they refused to engage in the free-spending ways of the past and chose to save rather than to spend their money. This behavior, in turn, created a new cycle of problems. Because many banks had failed during the crash, people no longer trusted them, and kept their money at home, which depleted the supply of capital that banks needed. People also refused to buy new products and instead repaired old ones. Because few people were buying new products, companies were forced to close and to lay off employees. Many people were evicted from their homes for failing to make payments, and often several members of extended families lived together. The number of HOMELESS PERSONS soared, as did cases of malnutrition. President Hoover still remained firm in his stance that government aid was not an option. He believed that private charity could take care of those individuals who could not take care of themselves and that the ingenuity of private business would cure the ills of the country, not government intrusion. The American people resented President Hoover's attitude. The camps of makeshift shacks in which many people lived after being evicted were called Hoovervilles, and slogans such as Hard Times Are Hoover-ing over Us were heard everywhere. By December 1931, the unemployment rate was more than 13.6 million, a third of the labor force. When President Hoover sent military troops with bayonets and tear gas to disband the Bonus Army—a group of World War I veterans who had come to Washington, D.C., to seek early payment of a promised bonus for fighting in the war—his approval among U.S. voters plunged irrevocably.

Although the Republicans knew that the Democratic presidential candidate would more than likely win, they nominated Hoover again in 1932. The Democratic nominee, Franklin D. Roosevelt, won all but six states and received 22 million votes, as compared to Hoover's 15 million. Roosevelt came from a wealthy family, had served as assistant secretary of the navy and as governor of New York, and had battled polio courageously. His promised "new deal" was anxiously awaited.

The day after he was inaugurated, Roosevelt requested a special session of Congress to convene and declared a week-long bank holiday. He guaranteed that at the end of one week's time, banks that the government found to be sound and secure would reopen. Roosevelt also announced a MORATORIUM on the export of gold. Because foreign investors required trading to be done in gold (paper money was believed to be too risky) the combination of the moratorium and the bank holiday effectively put the economy of the United States on hold. After the week had passed, Roosevelt held the first of his famous "fireside chats" via the radio to reassure the American people. As promised, the majority of the banks reopened. Many people followed Roosevelt's advice and again placed their money in the banks. During those same first weeks, Roosevelt and Congress worked together to repeal PROHIBITION, allowing the sale and consumption of alcohol to resume.

These moves were only the beginning of what is referred to as the Hundred Days. More legislation was passed during the first hundred days of Roosevelt's presidency than had been passed in any similar period of any previous presidency. Roosevelt worked with young lawyers, professors, and social workers to create legislation that was meant to get people working and spending once again. To relieve the immediate need for food and shelter, Roosevelt ushered through Congress the Federal Emergency Relief Administration, which granted $500 million in aid to the states for distribution to people in need.

Next came congressional approval of Roosevelt's Civilian Conservation Corps Act (ch. 383, 50 Stat. 319). The government paid young men between the ages of 18 and 25 for six months to one year to do construction or conservation work. The men built bridges, dams, and roads and planted more than 17 million acres of new forests. They were paid $30 per month and were required to send most of their money home to their families.

The Agricultural Adjustment Act of 1933 (AAA), 7 U.S.C.A. §§ 601 et seq., also was passed during these first hundred days. Farmers were growing large surpluses of crops such as wheat and corn, and these surpluses drove prices down

even though the farmers' expenses were rising. The AAA sought to reduce the surplus of crops by paying farmers not to grow them. Although some Americans questioned this practice because so many people were starving, the theory of the plan bore out, and by 1936 farmers were receiving $1.02 per bushel of wheat, as compared to the 38 cents per bushel that they had received in 1932.

Toward the end of the hundred days, Congress enacted the NATIONAL INDUSTRIAL RECOVERY ACT OF 1933 (NIRA), (ch. 90, 48 Stat. 195) and created the National Industrial Recovery Administration to implement the act's goals. The legislation's main goal was to stimulate dormant factories and industries and to get people back to work. The National Industrial Recovery Administration believed that the best way to do this was to create a series of codes (746 in all) that companies had to follow in the marketplace. These codes regulated everything from a minimum hourly wage to the maximum number of hours per week that an employee could work. They controlled advertising and business production and output. Fearing a return of the high unemployment rate, one code forbade industry from developing technological advances that would lead to employee layoffs.

NIRA represents the first direct government involvement in business operations. It allowed industries and business to engage in previously prohibited monopolistic price-fixing so that one manufacturer could not underprice its goods to drive a competitor out of business. The legislation allowed workers to unionize and to bargain

Unemployed men gather at a Chicago soup kitchen in February 1931. Roosevelt's New Deal was a response to the severe economic decline that engulfed the nation in the first years of the Great Depression. Two years after the September 1929 crash of the stock market 33 percent of the labor force was unemployed.
NATIONAL ARCHIVES AND RECORDS ADMINISTRATION

One of the most popular programs of the New Deal was the Works Progress Administration, which created more than 250,000 projects, putting millions of people to work.

AP/WIDE WORLD PHOTOS

collectively for better pay and working conditions. This was all done with the goal of increasing business profits, which, in turn, would create more jobs and more spending. However, NIRA posed difficulties for many business owners, who were forced to restructure their business operations.

One of the most popular programs of the New Deal was the Works Progress Administration (WPA), which created more than 250,000 projects, putting millions of people to work. Most of the money and effort went to public construction of bridges, roads, and government buildings such as post offices. Writers were employed to interview town residents and to compile local histories. Actors and musicians were hired to bring theater and live music to residents of rural towns, who otherwise had little opportunity to see live performances.

After the first 18 months of the New Deal, five million previously unemployed people had found work. However, Roosevelt and his New Deal were not without their critics. When wealthy people realized that Roosevelt was intending not to return the country to the precrash status quo but rather to reform the entire national economic structure, they soon turned

on him, calling him a traitor to his class. They disliked Roosevelt for the new taxes imposed on them, and some believed rumors that Roosevelt wanted to make the United States a socialist state under his dictatorship. The leaders of big business, once beholden to Roosevelt for getting their businesses back on track, were now among his most forceful critics.

Wealthy people were not Roosevelt's only critics. People to the political left of Roosevelt thought that he had let the common man down. Socialists such as UPTON SINCLAIR and some Democrats such as Huey Long, the senator from Louisiana, complained that Roosevelt and his New Deal did not do enough for the lower and middle classes of society. Despite criticism from many angles, the majority of U.S. citizens loved Roosevelt, re-electing him by a landslide in 1936 over the Republican nominee, Alfred M. Landon.

One significant reason for Roosevelt's considerable popularity was the passage of the SOCIAL SECURITY ACT OF 1935 (42 U.S.C.A. § 301 et seq.)—the first piece of legislation in the history of the United States to address social welfare. The legislation provided people over the age of 65 with a monthly PENSION from the federal government. It also contained provisions for unemployment insurance and for aid to children. Although this form of government charity also had its critics, Roosevelt was pleased with it because it was proof that he had not forgotten the common man.

The early successes of the New Deal created a boldness that eventually led to its demise. By the mid 1930s, the U.S. Supreme Court began to strike down New Deal legislation as unconstitutional exercises of congressional power. In *Schechter Poultry Corp. v. United States,* 295 U.S. 495, 55 S. Ct. 837, 79 L. Ed. 1570 (1935), for example, the Court struck down the heart of Roosevelt's New Deal legislation, the NIRA. The Schechter brothers were wholesale kosher poultry distributors who did business within the state of New York. They were convicted of violating the Live Poultry Code, including wage-and-hour violations. The Court unanimously held that the federal government could only control trade between states, not trade within one state. Even liberal justices on the Court who had supported previous New Deal legislation found the challenged provisions unconstitutional. The following year, the Court struck down the Bituminous Coal Conservation Act of 1935, ch. 824, 49 Stat. 991, because its enactment was not based upon a power that Congress possessed under the Constitution. *Carter v. Carter Coal Co.*, 298 U.S. 238, 56 S. Ct. 855, 80 L. Ed. 1160 (1936).

Many legal actions against other New Deal legislation were piling up, and in a fast and furious move in 1937, Roosevelt proposed a restructuring of the high court through the addition of a new justice to the Court for each justice over the age of 70. At the time of this proposal, six of the nine justices were over the age of 70, including Chief Justice CHARLES EVANS HUGHES and associate justices WILLIS VAN DEVANTER, JAMES MCREYNOLDS, LOUIS BRANDEIS, GEORGE SUTHERLAND, and PIERCE BUTLER. Roosevelt tried to place a nonpolitical spin on his proposal, citing instances where changes to the composition of the Court had been made before, as well as the heavy workload for nine justices, but he could not disguise his blatant attempt to pack the Court with liberal justices who saw things his way. Roosevelt refused to concede, which resulted in months of Senate debates that cost him many supporters.

Rather than exploding, the controversy retreated as the Court began supporting many pieces of New Deal legislation. In NLRB V. JONES & LAUGHLIN STEEL CORP., 301 U.S. 1, 57 S. Ct. 615, 81 L. Ed. 893 (1937), the Court upheld the constitutionality of the National Labor Relations Act, which was purportedly based upon the COMMERCE CLAUSE of the Constitution. Prior to *Jones & Laughlin Steel Corp.*, Van Devanter resigned from the Court and was replaced by HUGO BLACK. The Court's structure changed dramatically over the eight years following the decision, as the majority of justices retired or resigned from the court, including the following: Sutherland (1938); BENJAMIN CARDOZO (1938); Brandeis (1939); Butler (1939); Hughes (1941); McReynolds (1941); HARLAN STONE (1941); and Roberts (1945).

Although, in the end, the makeup of the Court was just as Roosevelt wanted, he suffered losses in support and confidence that he never regained. Many people felt that the New Deal legislation had granted labor too much power, and they were resentful of the unionization efforts, which led to strikes that were often violent. Finally, the unemployment rate in late 1937 to mid 1938 soared from five million to eleven million. Roosevelt and his vision for a New Deal lost congressional support. No further reform legislation was passed during Roosevelt's time in the White House. Although the country was much better off than it had been when he took office in 1932, the Great Depression continued. It ended not by legislation, but by the coming of WORLD WAR II.

The political machine of the New Deal and its dominant social policy continued for decades after the last piece of its legislation was passed. Although its demise can not be traced to one single event, by the time RONALD REAGAN was elected president in 1980, the era of the New Deal was effectively over.

FURTHER READINGS

Fraser, Steve, and Gary Gerstle. 1989. *The Rise and Fall of the New Deal Order*. Princeton, N.J.: Princeton Univ. Press.

Freedman, Russell. 1990. *Franklin Delano Roosevelt*. New York: Clarion Books.

Schraff, Anne E. 1990. *The Great Depression and the New Deal*. New York: Watts.

Stewart, Gail B. 1993. *The New Deal*. New York: New Discovery Books.

CROSS-REFERENCES

Banks and Banking; Labor Law; Labor Union; National Recovery Administration; *Schechter Poultry Corp. v. United States*; Social Security; Welfare.

NEW PARTY

The New Party is a grassroots progressive political organization that focuses on local elections and uses the concept of multiple-party nomination or "fusion" to build coalitions with other like-minded organizations and political parties. Despite a major setback from a 1997 U.S. Supreme Court decision which held that states are not required to permit fusion, the New Party, which uses the slogan "Building a New Majority from the Ground Up," won 300 of the first 400 races it entered between 1992 and 2002.

Fed up with what they saw as only minor distinctions between the Democratic and Republican parties as well as a lack of commitment by the majority parties to the concepts of democracy and corporate accountability, a group of TRADE UNION members, low-income community activists, environmentalists, minority voters, and other supporters started the New Party in New York in 1992. Fueled by a vision based on recognition of the moral equality of each person, the New Party sought to build a multi-ethnic party of activists dedicated to taking back the reins of democracy from an increasingly powerful alliance of corporations and corporate media that has come to dominate the U.S. political system.

The organization has established a series of "New Party Principles" that include full public financing of elections and universal voter registration; establishment of the right to democratic self-organization for workers, consumers and others; a children's BILL OF RIGHTS; community control and equitable funding for schools; a safe and secure community environment; a prohibition of discrimination based on race, gender, age, country of origin, and sexual orientation; and the safeguarding of civil liberties, reproductive rights, and the right to privacy.

Economic principles include a progressive tax system, creation of a sustainable economy that includes protection of the environment, full employment and a guaranteed minimum income for all adults, a reduction in defense spending, and progressive international trade practices.

The organization started in 1992 with a strategy of selecting local contests and building alliances with other small progressive parties. In the view of New Party organizers, the current winner-take-all system for political elections has stifled debate that would otherwise include minor party candidates. This system has also restrained the development of alternative political parties because many voters are afraid to "waste" their vote on a candidate who has little or no chance of winning.

The New Party espouses the concept of fusion in order to grow its political base. In politics fusion means the practice of permitting political parties to allow the name of another party's candidate to be placed on the ballot line. In fusion races the votes a candidate receives on all ballot lines are totaled and the candidate with the most votes would be declared the winner.

Fusion was popular in the 1800s, the best-known example being when presidential candidate WILLIAM JENNINGS BRYAN was nominated by both the Democrats and the Populist "People's Party" in 1896. The increasing popularity of fusion came to be viewed as a threat by the major parties, and many state legislatures began to pass statutes that prohibited it. Between 1896 and 1907 fusion was banned in 18 states. In 2001 fusion was legal in eight states: Connecticut, Delaware, Mississippi, New York, South Carolina, South Dakota, Utah, and Vermont.

In 1994 the Twin Cities chapter of the New Party gave its nomination to Andy Dawkins, a Democratic incumbent legislator who was running for reelection. Dawkins agreed to the fusion nomination and there was no objection from the state DEMOCRATIC PARTY. However, the state of Minnesota objected and the New Party sued. The district court dismissed the case, but it was reversed on appeal by the Eighth Circuit Court of Appeals, which held that the state ban on fusion imposed a severe burden on the New Party's FREEDOM OF ASSOCIATION by not allowing it to nominate the candidate it had selected. The Eighth Circuit's decision was reversed by the U.S. Supreme Court in *Timmons v. Twin Cities Area New Party*, 520 U.S. 351, 117 S.Ct. 1364, 137 L.Ed.2d 589 (1997), which held, in a 6–3 vote, that the FIRST AMENDMENT does not require states to permit fusion voting.

This decision was disappointing to the New Party and other minor parties who had hoped to use fusion throughout the country to leverage the voting power of their supporters. Members of the New Party vowed to move forward with their agenda of running candidates for local level elections including school boards and city councils, mayoral races, and state assemblies. The organization is also pursuing a long-term strategy for changing state election laws to permit fusion voting.

FURTHER READINGS

New Party Website. Available online at <www.newparty .org> (accessed July 30, 2003).

CROSS-REFERENCES

Third Party.

NEW YORK CONSTITUTION OF 1777

The first constitution of the state of New York was adopted on Sunday, April 20, 1777, at Kingston, New York, by a convention of delegates empowered by the people of the colony to establish a state government. It marks the birth of the state of New York. The constitution was not submitted to the people for ratification, but it became effective immediately upon its adoption by the convention.

The New York Constitution of 1777 was framed amidst the chaos of the Revolutionary War. Three men were instrumental in drafting the constitution: JOHN JAY, ROBERT R. LIVINGSTON, and Gouverneur Morris. All three were affluent young men (ages 30, 29, 24, respectively, at the time of their appointments) with little experience in public affairs. John Jay is generally credited as being the primary author of the constitution.

The first constitution faithfully adhered in many respects to the English constitutional system of government. Some delegates, however, were incensed upon discerning minor deviations from ENGLISH LAW in the proposed constitution. The patterning of the New York Constitution of 1777 after the English governmental prototype was not actually inconsistent with the objectives of the Revolutionary War. Even though there were structural similarities between the system of government set forth in the New York Constitution of 1777 and the English system, the impact of the laws upon the lives of the people of New York and their British counterparts was different, due to the abandonment by America of the class system of government that prevailed in England. The oppressiveness of English rule was eradicated, but the valid fundamental legal principles were retained. The English constitutional system of government was applied to the extent that its principles conformed to the concept of a republican form of government. The reliance upon the English system was also attributable to the inexperience of the draftsmen, who felt comfortable with the basic precepts and established traditions of English law. Even they realized, however, that some changes were essential. The people of New York were permitted to choose the chief executive instead of having sovereign authority do so on their behalf. It also was deemed necessary to alter the parliamentary system, and as a result, the House of Lords and the Colonial Council were transformed into the state senate.

On April 20, the entire proposed constitution was presented, and, after several inconsequential revisions and some major ones, it was read and adopted by a vote of 32–1. John Jay was not present for the adoption of the constitution, since he had been called away as a result of his mother's death on April 17. He had wanted to include certain amendments to the constitution, and he expressed dismay over what he perceived to be its rather hasty adoption. The fact that less than one-third of the entire convention attended the discussions of the constitution was attributable to compelling personal reasons and the exigencies of the Revolutionary War. The turmoil created by the latter factor explains why the constitution was adopted on a Sunday; the delegates convened whenever possible, irrespective of weekend dates.

The New York Constitution of 1777 was a relatively brief document that covered only a few topics. Some significant provisions, particularly those pertaining to the Council of Revision and the Council of Appointment, were added while the constitution was being evaluated by the convention.

The resolutions adopted by the Third Provincial Congress, providing for the election of the convention, and the Declaration of Independence, which has been set out in its entirety, comprise the preliminary segment. The body of the constitution contains forty-five brief sections, which were labeled "articles" at that time. The powers granted to the new government are expressed in rather austere language. The framers retained the essential nature of the colonial government but removed its royal features. The judicial system of the colony and the local governments generally remained unaltered.

The constitution delineates new executive and legislative branches, administrative authority, and abstract rights, which are few in number and concise, including, but not limited to, VOTING RIGHTS, freedom of religion, and the right of trial by jury. Although the constitution created the legislative, executive, and judicial branches of government, the framers combined their functions due to their ignorance of the concept, significance, and ramifications of the SEPARATION OF POWERS. In addition to lawmaking power, they vested the legislature with executive authority through the Council of Appointment, which consisted of four senators selected annually by the assembly. The higher courts were granted authority over legislation through the Council of Revision, comprised by the judges of the supreme court, the chancellor, and the governor. As a result, the governor's power was severely circumscribed. Since he was under the control of the Council of Appointment, the governor was divested of the responsibility for official appointments. He also was deprived of unabridged VETO power, because the judges of the Council of Revision could overrule him.

The constitution has a few provisions pertaining to the separate powers of the senate and assembly, including the power of the assembly to issue ARTICLES OF IMPEACHMENT and to choose the members of the Council of Appointment. The legislature was authorized to elect the state treasurer, administer contracts with Indians, and to naturalize ALIENS. The U.S. Constitution, however, eventually preempted this right of naturalization. The legislature was proscribed from enacting bills of attainder, and from creating any courts, except common law courts. The constitution fixed the terms of judicial officers and provided for the election of state and local officials. Article 35 continued the English statutory and COMMON LAW, and colonial legislation, to the extent they were applicable under the new form of government. Miscellaneous provisions established a state militia, ratified English grants, and barred the clergy from holding office.

The state made tremendous progress as a result of this constitution, in spite of its inherent limitations. Its system of JURISPRUDENCE evolved and expanded. The constitution established the university and the common school, and colleges, academies, and libraries were nurtured. It provided for the administration of assistance to the indigent. A system of taxation was formulated, political subdivisions were created, and the statutory law was frequently revised. The constitution also prompted the drafting of a plan for the construction of the canals. The New York Constitution of 1777 was an extremely valuable document, and its fundamental principles became prompted in subsequent constitutions. It remained in effect until it was superseded by the Constitution of 1821.

NEW YORK TIMES CO. V. SULLIVAN

A landmark U.S. Supreme Court case, *New York Times Co. v. Sullivan*, 376 U.S. 254, 84 S. Ct. 710, 11 L. Ed. 2d 686 (1964), extended the FIRST AMENDMENT's guarantee of free speech to LIBEL cases brought by public officials. The Supreme Court sought to encourage public debate by changing the rules involving libel that had previously been the province of state law and state courts.

New York Times v. Sullivan grew out of events occurring during the 1960s CIVIL RIGHTS MOVEMENT in Alabama. In 1960, MARTIN LUTHER KING JR., and other CIVIL RIGHTS leaders conducted protests against SEGREGATION in Montgomery, Alabama. Their efforts met fierce resistance from Montgomery public officials. Civil rights leaders placed a full-page advertisement in the *New York Times* seeking contributions for civil rights causes in the South. Signed by sixty-four prominent leaders in public affairs, religion, trade unions, and the performing arts, the advertisement, entitled "Heed Their Rising Voices," stated that thousands of southern African American students were engaging in

nonviolent demonstrations in positive affirmation of the right to live in human dignity. The ad went on to charge that these demonstrations had been met with a "wave of terror" by state and local governments. Alleged events that backed up this charge were described, but no particular public official was named.

L.B. Sullivan, the Montgomery city commissioner responsible for supervising the city police department, filed a libel suit against four African American clergyman and the *New York Times* in Alabama state court. Sullivan alleged that the advertisement implicitly libeled him. Libel is a civil TORT and consists of injuring someone's reputation by reporting falsehoods about that person.

At trial Sullivan proved that the advertisement contained a number of minor inaccuracies about described incidents. The jury had to determine whether the statements in the advertisement were "of and concerning" Commissioner Sullivan. The judge instructed the jury that under Alabama law, if the statements were found libelous, falsity and malice were presumed, and damages could be awarded without direct proof of financial loss. The jury concluded that the statements did concern Sullivan and awarded him $500,000 for injuries to his reputation and profession.

The U.S. Supreme Court reversed, holding that the RULE OF LAW applied by Alabama violated the First Amendment. Justice WILLIAM J. BRENNAN JR., in his majority opinion, placed the legal issues in the context of "a profound national commitment to the principle that debate on public issues should be uninhibited, robust, and wide-open, and that it may well include vehement, caustic, and sometimes unpleasantly sharp attacks on government and public officials." Brennan maintained that erroneous statements are inevitable in free debate and must be protected if freedom of expression is to have the "breathing space" it needs to survive.

The advertisement was squarely a public expression and protest, and fell within constitutional protection. Neither the allegedly defamatory content of the ad, nor the falsity of some of its factual statements, nor the NEGLIGENCE of anyone in preparing or publishing it forfeited this protection. Brennan dismissed the idea that courts were free to conclude that libelous statements were made "of and concerning" a particular person when the statements on their face did not make even an oblique reference to the individual. Brennan stated that there is "no legal alchemy" by which a court constitutionally can establish that "an otherwise impersonal attack on governmental operations was a libel of an official responsible for those operations."

Brennan then set out the rule that reshaped libel law. A public official could recover in a libel action only if and when a court found that the libelous statement about the official was made with " 'actual malice'—that is, with knowledge that it was false or with reckless disregard of whether it was false or not." As long as the press has an "absence of malice," public officials are barred from recovering damages for the publication of false statements about them.

In separate concurring opinions, Justices HUGO L. BLACK and WILLIAM O. DOUGLAS differed with Justice Brennan over whether the press should ever be held liable in DEFAMATION of public officials. They concluded that the First Amendment provided an absolute IMMUNITY for criticism of the way public officials do their public duty. Anything less than absolute immunity encourages "deadly danger" to a free press by state libel laws that harass, punish, and ultimately destroy critics.

In the years since New York Times, some critics have argued that Black and Douglas were right. The "reckless disregard" requirement has allowed highly intrusive inquiries into the reportorial and editorial processes of the mass media. In addition, the "chilling effect" of libel suits has not been diminished because of the case. If a jury finds reckless disregard, it can award enormous damage awards against the press.

Other critics of the decision believe it affords too much protection to the press. Public officials unfairly libeled by the press rarely file libel suits because of the difficulty of proving actual malice. This prevents them from establishing in a court of law the falsity of the statements at issue.

FURTHER READINGS

Fireside, Harvey. 1999. New York Times v. Sullivan: Affirming Freedom of the Press. Springfield, N.J.: Enslow.

Kane, Thomas. 1999. "Malice, Lies, and Videotape: Revisiting New York Times v. Sullivan in the Modern Age of Political Campaigns." Rutgers Law Journal 30 (spring).

Whitten, Kristian D. 2002. "The Economics of Actual Malice: A Proposal for Legislative Change to the Rule of New York Times v. Sullivan." Cumberland Law Review 32 (spring).

CROSS-REFERENCES

Freedom of Speech; Freedom of the Press; Libel and Slander; New York Times Co. v. Sullivan (Appendix, Milestone Case).

NEW YORK TIMES CO. V. UNITED STATES

New York Times Co. v. United States, (per curiam) 403 U.S. 713, 91 S. Ct. 2140, 29 L. Ed. 2d 822 (1971), often referred to as the Pentagon Papers case, concerned the government's attempt to prohibit the New York Times and the Washington Post from publishing portions of a secret government study on the VIETNAM WAR. The documents in the study became known as the Pentagon Papers. The United States contended that publication of the Pentagon Papers could prolong the Vietnam War and hinder efforts to return U.S. prisoners held in Vietnam. The Times and the Post claimed that the government was engaging in CENSORSHIP. Thus, the case pitted the rights of the newspapers under the FIRST AMENDMENT against the duty of the EXECUTIVE BRANCH to protect the nation. The case drew significant national attention as it went through the judicial system and the public wondered what the Pentagon Papers contained.

The Pentagon Papers case addressed whether a PRIOR RESTRAINT on the press can be justified under the First Amendment. A "prior restraint" is the imposition of a restraint on the publication of information before the information is published. There are two basic types of prior restraints. One consists of a government order or court INJUNCTION that prohibits a person from communicating certain information. The other basic type of prior restraint occurs when a license or permit is required before a particular type of expression may be used. New York Times v. United States involved the first type of prior restraint, since the government sought a court injunction prohibiting the newspapers from publishing portions of the Pentagon Papers. Other than the Pentagon Papers case, the most important Supreme Court case discussing prior restraints is NEAR V. MINNESOTA, 283 U.S. 697, 51 S. Ct. 625, 75 L. Ed. 1357 (1931), which held that under the First Amendment, prior restraints on free speech are justified only in "exceptional cases," such as when the information to be published would include "the sailing dates of transports or the number and location of troops."

In the Pentagon Papers case a divided Supreme Court, in a decision that contains a separate opinion from each of the nine justices, refused to enjoin publication of the Pentagon Papers, emphasizing the First Amendment's strong presumption against any prior restraint on free speech. The justices' reasons for their decisions varied widely. Two justices believed that *any* prior restraint on the press amounts to censorship in clear violation of the First Amendment, whereas three justices believed that publication of the Pentagon Papers should have been delayed until the courts had more time to evaluate the impact of publication on national security. Because the case sped through the judicial system and the justices' opinions varied widely, it does not provide a clear statement of First Amendment law on prior restraint. For example, the Court failed to specify when, if ever, a prior restraint on the press might be allowed. The case is of great significance, however, as a statement that a prior restraint on the FREEDOM OF SPEECH is almost never justified.

From June 12 to 14, 1971, the *New York Times* published a series of articles about the origins of the Vietnam War. The articles were based on a 47-volume DEFENSE DEPARTMENT study covering the years 1945 to 1968, which had been leaked to the *Times* by Daniel Ellsberg, a former Defense Department analyst. Although the study contained only information regarding events that occurred before 1968, the government contended that the study contained "secret" and "top secret" information. Further, the government alleged that publication of the information could prolong the Vietnam War and threaten the safe return of U.S. prisoners of war. On June 15, 1971, the government sued in New York federal district court, seeking an injunction prohibiting the *Times* from continuing to publish information from the Pentagon Papers. Soon after, the *Washington Post* began publishing material from the study; accordingly, the government sought a similar injunction against the *Post* in the District of Columbia.

The actions against the *Times* and the *Post* were rushed through the courts because of the unique national importance of the issues and the widespread national public attention the cases were receiving. Although the federal district courts both refused to issue a permanent injunction against publication of the Pentagon Papers, publication was temporarily enjoined pending appeals by the United States. Less than two weeks after the *Times* published its first articles, the Supreme Court heard arguments on the cases, and five days later, on June 30, 1971, issued its decision.

The Supreme Court decided on a 6–3 vote that a prior restraint could not be imposed on publication of the Pentagon Papers. In a brief opinion the whole Court noted that the government "carries a heavy burden of showing justification for the imposition of such a restraint" and stated that the government had failed to meet that burden. The brief opinion reflected the widely varying views of the nine justices. The Court could not agree on a precise standard for determining when the government may impose a prior restraint on free speech or even whether the government could *ever* impose a prior restraint.

In concurring opinions Justices HUGO L. BLACK and WILLIAM O. DOUGLAS both stated, in very strong language, that prior restraints on the freedom of expression are never justified, no matter what the circumstances. Black, commenting on the government's argument that prior restraints might be justified in certain circumstances, stated, "I can imagine no greater perversion of history. . . . Both the history and language of the First Amendment support the view that the press must be left free to publish news, whatever the source, without censorship, injunctions or prior restraints." Black and Douglas both believed that "every moment's CONTINUANCE of the injunctions . . . amounts to a flagrant, indefensible, and continuing violation of the First Amendment."

The other four justices who concurred in the judgment, Justices WILLIAM J. BRENNAN JR., POTTER STEWART, BYRON R. WHITE, and THURGOOD MARSHALL, each believed that the government could impose a prior restraint in certain extraordinary circumstances, such as where the publication of information could endanger U.S. soldiers, but that those circumstances were not present in the *Pentagon Papers* case. Stewart was the only justice who offered a standard for determining when a prior restraint could be imposed, stating that a prior restraint would be appropriate only where publication "will surely result in direct, immediate, and irreparable damage to our Nation or its people." White, while agreeing that the circumstances did not warrant a prior restraint on the publication of the Pentagon Papers, opined that the newspapers might be criminally liable under ESPIONAGE laws if they published sensitive national secrets. Marshall based his argument on the separate powers of the three branches of the government. He believed that, because Congress had declined to pass a statute authorizing the courts to enjoin publication of sensitive national secrets, the Supreme Court lacked authority to enjoin publication of the Pentagon Papers.

Chief Justice WARREN E. BURGER, Justices JOHN MARSHALL HARLAN, and HARRY A. BLACKMUN dissented, all strongly objecting to the "unseemly haste" with which the courts heard and decided the case. Harlan stated, "With all respect, I consider that the Court has been almost irresponsibly feverish in dealing with these cases." Blackmun commented:

[T]his, in my opinion, is not the way to try a lawsuit of this magnitude and asserted importance. It is not the way for federal courts to adjudicate, and be required to adjudicate, issues that allegedly concern the Nation's vital welfare. The country would be none the worse off were the cases tried quickly to be sure, but in the customary and properly deliberative manner.

The dissenting justices thus believed that the publication of the Pentagon Papers should have been enjoined until the courts had adequate time to evaluate carefully the legal issues and the impact of publication of the documents on the interests of the United States.

The decision was hailed as a great victory for advocates of FREEDOM OF THE PRESS. For the first time in the nation's history, the government had succeeded, if only during the appeals of the case, in precluding the press from publishing news in its possession. At least in the circumstances presented by the case, however, the Supreme Court held that such a prior restraint on freedom of speech violates the First Amendment. The practical effect of the decision, which carefully avoided any mention of the contents of the Pentagon Papers, was far less dramatic than suggested by the attention it received. The newspapers never did publish the portions of the Pentagon Papers that the government claimed were the most sensitive. In addition, further publication of the Pentagon Papers by newspapers around the country did not attract a great deal of attention or significantly affect the United States' policy on Vietnam. The *Pentagon Papers* case remains, however, an important precedent in support of freedom of the press under the First Amendment.

FURTHER READINGS

Glendon, William R. 1993. "Fifteen Days in June That Shook the First Amendment: A First Person Account of the Pentagon Papers Case." *New York State Bar Journal* 65 (November).

Godofsky, Stanley, and Howard M. Rogatnick. 1988. "Prior Restraints: The Pentagon Papers Case Revisited." *Cumberland Law Review* 18 (spring).

Gora, Joel M. 1998. "The Pentagon Papers Case and the Path Not Taken: A Personal Memoir on the First Amendment and the Separation of Powers." *Cardozo Law Review* 19 (March).

Practicing Law Institute (PLI). 1996. *The Pentagon Papers: Excerpts from the Record,* by William R. Glendon. Patents, Copyrights, Trademarks, and Literary Property Course Handbook series, PLI order no. G4-3963.

Rudenstine, David. 1998. *The Day the Presses Stopped: A History of the Pentagon Papers Case.* Berkeley: Univ. of California Press.

Salisbury, Harrison E. 1980. *Without Fear or Favor: The New York Times and Its Times.* New York: Times Books.

Seymour, Whitney North, Jr. 1994. "Press Paranoia—Delusions of Persecution in the Pentagon Papers Case." *New York State Bar Journal* 66 (February).

CROSS-REFERENCES

Executive Branch; First Amendment; Precedent; Prior Restraint.

NEWS REPORTER'S PRIVILEGE

See EVIDENCE.

❖ NEWTON, HUEY PERCY

Huey Percy Newton was a cofounder and leader of the BLACK PANTHER PARTY FOR SELF-DEFENSE, a group formed in 1966 in Oakland to organize African Americans against police brutality and racism. Convicted or charged with several murders and assaults during his life, Newton was shot and killed in 1989 in the same poor Oakland neighborhood where he had begun mobilizing African Americans to arm themselves in SELF-DEFENSE more than twenty years earlier.

Newton was born on February 17, 1942, in New Orleans, the son of a sharecropper who was once nearly lynched for talking back to his white bosses. When Newton was one year old, his family moved to Oakland. By the time he was fourteen, Newton had been arrested for gun possession. He was illiterate when he graduated from high school, but he taught himself to read before attending Merritt College in Oakland and the San Francisco School of Law. In 1966 while at Merritt he met BOBBY SEALE, with whom he formed the Black Panther Party for Self-Defense in response to Malcolm X's call to African Americans to take up arms to defend themselves against the police. The armed and uniformed Panthers patrolled Oakland streets, interrupting arrests and other police activities when they believed that African Americans were being mistreated.

"I SUGGESTED THAT WE USE THE PANTHER AS OUR SYMBOL . . . [BECAUSE] THE PANTHER IS A FIERCE ANIMAL, BUT HE WILL NOT ATTACK UNTIL HE IS BACKED INTO A CORNER; THEN HE WILL STRIKE OUT."
—HUEY NEWTON

Huey Newton.
AP/WIDE WORLD
PHOTOS

Newton was designated minister of defense and was a spokesperson for the party. The party drew national attention in May 1967, when six armed Panthers and about twenty supporters burst into the California Assembly at Sacramento to protest its plan to ban possession of loaded firearms within city limits. Though Newton did not participate in that event, the Oakland police increased their surveillance on him and his fellow Panthers.

On October 28, 1967, a scuffle during a routine traffic check escalated into a gun battle that left Newton with a bullet wound in his stomach, one police officer dead, and another wounded. Newton was convicted in 1968 of voluntary MANSLAUGHTER, but the California Court of Appeals overturned the conviction in 1970 because of the omission of key jury instructions.

Newton's second and third trials ended in hung juries, and the charges were dismissed in 1972.

Newton's political agenda for the Black Panthers had moved beyond issues of police brutality to a Marxist revolutionary call for change in U.S. society. Newton called for the release of all African Americans from jail and for the payment of compensation to African Americans for centuries of economic exploitation by white America.

When Newton was released from prison in 1972 following his successful appeal of the manslaughter charge, Black Panther Party membership in forty-five cities had fallen to fewer than one thousand people. J. EDGAR HOOVER, head of the FEDERAL BUREAU OF INVESTIGATION (FBI), had targeted the Panthers as a dangerous, politically subversive group. The FBI used informants and fake documents and letters to undermine the party. Panthers in many cities were subjected to local police harassment as well. In addition, Newton became embroiled in a dispute over the direction of the party with ELDRIDGE CLEAVER, the party's minister of information.

By the mid-1970s, the Black Panthers had abandoned their violent image and had begun community service programs, including free health clinics, a children's breakfast program, and drug abuse counseling. By the early 1980s, however, the Black Panthers had effectively disbanded.

Newton's role in the Black Panthers gradually diminished in the 1970s, as he had to contend with new criminal charges. In 1974 he was charged with murdering a seventeen-year-old girl and later with pistol-whipping a tailor. He

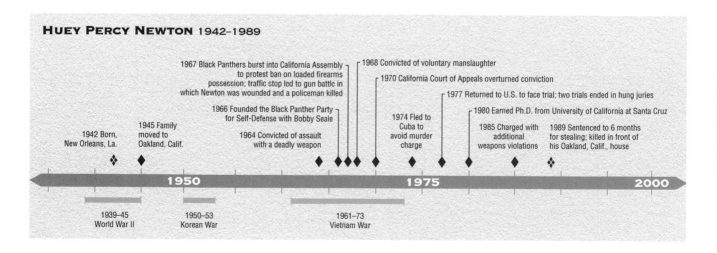

HUEY PERCY NEWTON 1942–1989

1967 Black Panthers burst into California Assembly to protest ban on loaded firearms possession; traffic stop led to gun battle in which Newton was wounded and a policeman killed

1968 Convicted of voluntary manslaughter

1970 California Court of Appeals overturned conviction

1977 Returned to U.S. to face trial; two trials ended in hung juries

1966 Founded the Black Panther Party for Self-Defense with Bobby Seale

1980 Earned Ph.D. from University of California at Santa Cruz

1974 Fled to Cuba to avoid murder charge

1964 Convicted of assault with a deadly weapon

1985 Charged with additional weapons violations

1989 Sentenced to 6 months for stealing; killed in front of his Oakland, Calif., house

1942 Born, New Orleans, La.

1945 Family moved to Oakland, Calif.

1950   1975   2000

1939–45 World War II

1950–53 Korean War

1961–73 Vietnam War

fled to Cuba to avoid prosecution but returned in 1977. His two murder trials ended in hung juries, and the assault case was dropped when the tailor refused to testify.

Newton was found guilty in 1978 of being an ex-felon in possession of a handgun and was found guilty of a second count of the same charge in 1979. During this period he worked on the completion of his doctoral dissertation at the University of California at Santa Cruz. He was awarded a Ph.D. degree in 1980 for his work, "War Against the Panthers: A Study of Repression in America." After lengthy appeals Newton was sentenced in 1981. He was charged with additional weapons violations in 1985 but was acquitted by a jury in 1986. After being paroled on the earlier weapons charges, he was returned to prison twice for violation of PAROLE following arrests for possession of narcotics paraphernalia and failure to submit to required drug testing.

Newton's downward spiral continued. In March 1989 he was sentenced to six months in jail after PLEADING no contest to a charge of cashing for his own use a $15,000 state aid check earmarked for the Oakland Community School, which the Black Panther party operated. The school had been closed in 1982 in the face of allegations that federal and state funds had been misused.

Newton was found shot dead on an Oakland street on August 22, 1989.

FURTHER READINGS

Jeffries, Judson L. 2002. *Huey P. Newton: The Radical Theorist.* Jackson: Univ. Press of Mississippi.

Newton, Huey P. 1996. *War Against the Panthers: A Study of Repression in America.* New York: Writers and Readers.

PBS. 2002. "A Huey P. Newton Story." Available online at <www.pbs.org/hueypnewton> (accessed January 20, 2004).

Pearson, Hugh. 1994. *The Shadow of the Panther: Huey Newton and the Price of Black Power in America.* Reading, Mass.: Addison-Wesley.

NEXT FRIEND

An individual who acts on behalf of another individual who does not have the legal capacity to act on his or her own behalf.

The individual in whose name a minor's lawsuit is brought, or who appears in court to represent such minor's interest. The French term *prochein ami* has been used to designate such an individual, but the term GUARDIAN AD LITEM *is more commonly used.*

At COMMON LAW, when an individual was unable to look after his or her own interests or manage his or her lawsuit, the court would appoint a person to represent that individual's legal interests. In court terminology this person was called a next friend, which is derived from the French term *prochein ami*. Individuals requiring a next friend included minors, persons who were mentally ill or mentally retarded, infirm or senile persons, and others whose disabilities prevented them from managing their affairs.

State statutes now set the qualifications and duties of a person who acts as a next friend, but these laws more commonly designate this person a *guardian ad litem*, or a court-appointed special advocate. Regardless of the designation, this person's responsibilities are now confined to representing a minor or incompetent person in a lawsuit or court proceeding. At common law, a next friend represented a plaintiff, whereas a *guardian ad litem* represented a defendant. This distinction has been removed in modern law.

A next friend is not a party to a lawsuit but an officer of the court. When the lawsuit is concluded, the next friend's duty ends. The next friend has no right to control the property of the person she or he represents or to assume custody of that person. These rights may be given to a person designated by a court as a minor's or incompetent person's guardian.

Guardians ad litem are commonly used in family and juvenile courts, where the best interests of the child require an independent, neutral person to safeguard the child's rights. The increased number of these representatives has led states to develop training and certification programs for individuals wishing to serve as next friends or *guardians ad litem*. Though attorneys also may represent juveniles, next friends provide valuable assistance to the courts.

CROSS-REFERENCES

Infants.

NEXT OF KIN

The blood relatives entitled by law to inherit the property of a person who dies without leaving a valid will, although the term is sometimes interpreted to include a relationship existing by reason of marriage.

CROSS-REFERENCES

Descent and Distribution.

NIHIL

[Latin, Nothing.] *The abbreviated designation of a statement filed by a sheriff or constable with a court describing his or her unsuccessful attempts to serve a writ, notice, or process upon the designated person.*

The complete phrase *nihil est* refers to a failure to serve any writ while the term *nihil habet* describes the failure to serve a writ SCIRE FACIAS or another writ.

The term *nil* is a contracted form of *nihil.*

❖ NIMMER, MELVILLE BERNARD

Melville B. Nimmer was a leading authority on COPYRIGHT law.

Nimmer was born June 6, 1923. He graduated from the University of California at Berkeley in 1947 and from Harvard Law School in 1950. After law school he obtained a position in the legal department at Paramount Pictures where he remained until 1957 when he entered private practice. Nimmer continued to be involved with the motion picture industry, however, and served as general counsel to the Writers Guild of America, which represents film and television writers. He was the chief negotiator for the guild during a five-month strike in 1960 where the right to receive residuals for the showing of theatrical films on television was established.

Although Nimmer's work in the film industry involved questions of copyright law, he had to learn the subject largely by reading cases on his own. At that time copyright law was a relatively unimportant discipline. Few lawyers specialized in it, and no law school offered courses in the subject as part of its regular curriculum. In the last decades, however, copyright questions have become a major concern for many industries, including the computer industry.

Nimmer became a leading authority in the growing field. His treatise *Nimmer on Copyright* (first published in 1963 with frequent revisions thereafter) became the standard work on the subject. A companion volume *Nimmer on Freedom of Speech* appeared in 1984. When he died, Nimmer was working on a book entitled *World Copyright,* which was to contain chapters on all significant copyright laws in the world.

In 1962 Nimmer joined the faculty at the University of California at Los Angeles School of Law and continued to teach there until his death. At the university Nimmer came into contact with the student protests and antiwar demonstrations and became increasingly interested in the FREEDOM OF SPEECH issues that the demonstrations raised. In *Cohen v. California,* 403 U.S. 15, 91 S. Ct. 1780, 29 L. Ed. 2d 284 (1971), Nimmer represented a protestor who was charged with disturbing the peace because he entered a courthouse wearing a jacket inscribed with a vulgar protest against the draft. The U.S. Supreme Court ruled in favor of the protester on the ground that the words presented no danger of violence and that the state therefore had no compelling reason to suppress them.

Nimmer died November 23, 1985, in Los Angeles, California.

FURTHER READINGS

Low, Charlotte. 1982. "Profile." *Los Angeles Daily Journal* (April 19).

"Melville B. Nimmer Symposium." 1987. *UCLA Law Review* 34 (June-August).

Van Alstyne, William W. 1996. "Remembering Melville Nimmer: Some Cautionary Notes on Commercial Speech." *UCLA Law Review* 43 (June).

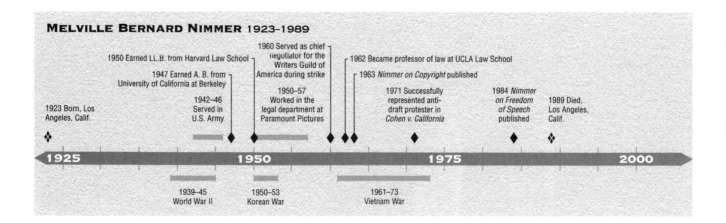

MELVILLE BERNARD NIMMER 1923–1989

1923 Born, Los Angeles, Calif.

1942–46 Served in U.S. Army

1947 Earned A. B. from University of California at Berkeley

1950 Earned LL.B. from Harvard Law School

1950–57 Worked in the legal department at Paramount Pictures

1960 Served as chief negotiator for the Writers Guild of America during strike

1962 Became professor of law at UCLA Law School

1963 *Nimmer on Copyright* published

1971 Successfully represented anti-draft protester in *Cohen v. California*

1984 *Nimmer on Freedom of Speech* published

1989 Died, Los Angeles, Calif.

1925   1950   1975   2000

1939–45 World War II

1950–53 Korean War

1961–73 Vietnam War

NINETEENTH AMENDMENT

The Nineteenth Amendment to the U.S. Constitution reads:

> The right of citizens of the United States to vote shall not be denied or abridged by the United States or by any State on account of sex. Congress shall have power to enforce this article by appropriate legislation.

The Nineteenth Amendment was enacted in 1920, after a 70-year struggle led by the women's suffrage movement.

The groundwork for the suffrage movement was laid in 1848 in Seneca Falls, New York, now considered the birthplace of the women's movement. Here ELIZABETH CADY STANTON drafted the Declaration of Rights and Sentiments, which demanded VOTING RIGHTS, property rights, educational opportunities, and economic EQUITY for women.

Rather than face the difficult task of obtaining approval of an amendment to the U.S. Constitution from an all-male Congress preoccupied with the question of SLAVERY, the suffragists decided to focus their attention on the separate states and seek state constitutional amendments. The state-by-state effort began in 1867 in Kansas with a REFERENDUM to enfranchise women. The referendum was defeated, but that same year the western territories of Wyoming and Utah provided the first victories for the suffragists.

The movement then suffered a series of setbacks beginning in January 1878 when the voting rights amendment was first introduced in Congress. The full Senate did not consider the amendment until 1887 and voted to defeat the bill. The suffragists continued their state-by-state strategy and won a referendum ballot in Colorado in 1893 and Idaho in 1896.

The suffragists mounted a final and decisive drive in the second decade of the 1900s with victories in Washington in 1910 and California in 1911. The following year Arizona, Kansas, and Oregon gave women the right to vote, and in 1913 Illinois also passed measures supporting suffrage as did Montana and Nevada in 1914. Women in eleven states voted in the 1916 presidential election. By this time the United States was also involved in WORLD WAR I, which brought national attention to the suffrage movement as well as to the important role women played in the war effort. During the war,

Suffragists march in a 1912 rally in New York City. In 1920, after decades of struggle for the right to vote, the Nineteenth Amendment's ratification granted female suffrage.

LIBRARY OF CONGRESS

an unprecedented number of women joined the depleted industrial and public service workforce. Women became an active and visible population of the labor sector that benefited the national economy. By the end of 1918 four more states—Michigan, Oklahoma, New York, and South Dakota—had approved women's suffrage.

With the requisite two-thirds majority, the U.S. House of Representatives introduced the amendment in January 1918. The vote was initially postponed, and the amendment was later defeated in October 1918 and again in February 1919. On June 4, 1919, almost 17 months after its introduction by the House of Representatives, the amendment was finally passed by the Senate. Having already considered and debated the voting rights issue for several years, the states ratified the amendment quickly. In August 1920 Tennessee became the thirty-sixth and last state necessary to ratify the enactment. With ratification complete, the Nineteenth Amendment was added to the U.S. Constitution on August 18, 1920.

FURTHER READINGS

Brown, Jennifer K. 1993. "The Nineteenth Amendment and Women's Equality." *Yale Law Journal* 102 (June).

Clift, Eleanor. 2003. *Founding Sisters and the Nineteenth Amendment.* Hoboken, N.J.: John Wiley & Sons.

Hillyard, Carrie. 1996. "The History of Suffrage and Equal Rights Provisions in State Constitutions." *BYU Journal of Public Law* 10 (winter).

Lind, Joellen. 1994. "Dominance and Democracy: The Legacy of Woman Suffrage for the Voting Right." *UCLA Women's Law Journal* 5 (fall).

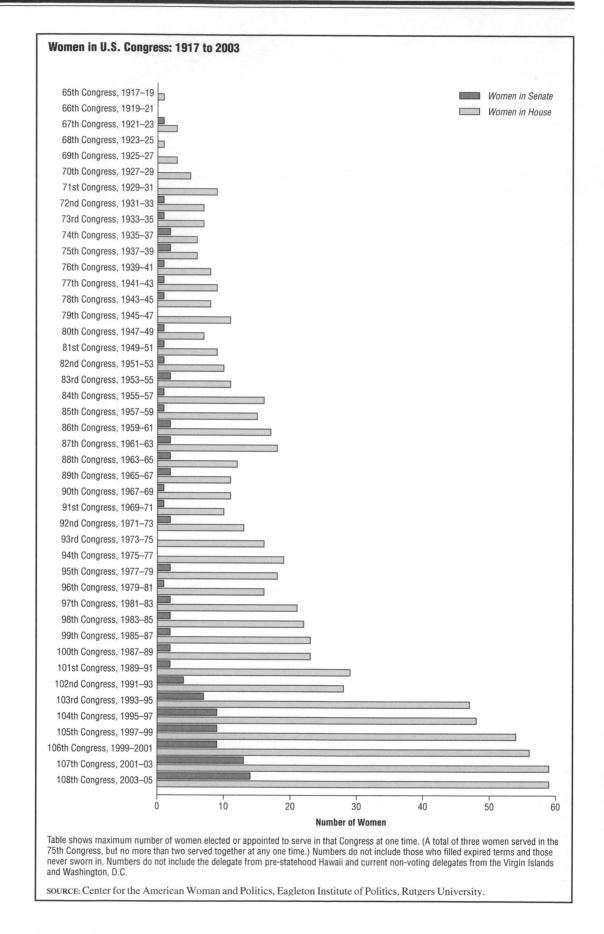

Women in U.S. Congress: 1917 to 2003

Women in Senate
Women in House

65th Congress, 1917–19
66th Congress, 1919–21
67th Congress, 1921–23
68th Congress, 1923–25
69th Congress, 1925–27
70th Congress, 1927–29
71st Congress, 1929–31
72nd Congress, 1931–33
73rd Congress, 1933–35
74th Congress, 1935–37
75th Congress, 1937–39
76th Congress, 1939–41
77th Congress, 1941–43
78th Congress, 1943–45
79th Congress, 1945–47
80th Congress, 1947–49
81st Congress, 1949–51
82nd Congress, 1951–53
83rd Congress, 1953–55
84th Congress, 1955–57
85th Congress, 1957–59
86th Congress, 1959–61
87th Congress, 1961–63
88th Congress, 1963–65
89th Congress, 1965–67
90th Congress, 1967–69
91st Congress, 1969–71
92nd Congress, 1971–73
93rd Congress, 1973–75
94th Congress, 1975–77
95th Congress, 1977–79
96th Congress, 1979–81
97th Congress, 1981–83
98th Congress, 1983–85
99th Congress, 1985–87
100th Congress, 1987–89
101st Congress, 1989–91
102nd Congress, 1991–93
103rd Congress, 1993–95
104th Congress, 1995–97
105th Congress, 1997–99
106th Congress, 1999–2001
107th Congress, 2001–03
108th Congress, 2003–05

0   10   20   30   40   50   60
Number of Women

Table shows maximum number of women elected or appointed to serve in that Congress at one time. (A total of three women served in the 75th Congress, but no more than two served together at any one time.) Numbers do not include those who filled expired terms and those never sworn in. Numbers do not include the delegate from pre-statehood Hawaii and current non-voting delegates from the Virgin Islands and Washington, D.C.

SOURCE: Center for the American Woman and Politics, Eagleton Institute of Politics, Rutgers University.

CROSS-REFERENCES

Anthony, Susan Brownell; Equal Rights Amendment; Women's Rights.

NINETY-DAY LETTER

The name given to a written notice sent to a taxpayer by the INTERNAL REVENUE SERVICE *regarding a deficiency in the payment of tax (26 U.S.C.A. § 6212 et seq.).*

The ninety-day letter, also known as the statutory notice of deficiency, suspends the running of the STATUTE OF LIMITATIONS regarding tax assessment for ninety days. During the ninety days following the mailing of a ninety-day letter, the taxpayer may consent to the assessment and pay the tax but later seek a refund in U.S. district court. If the taxpayer disputes the assessment or refuses to pay the additional amount, he or she may challenge the deficiency by filing a petition with the U.S. Tax Court. The ninety-day letter, sent by certified or registered mail, gives the taxpayer an opportunity to challenge an alleged deficiency before paying it. If the taxpayer neither pays the tax nor files a TAX COURT petition within the ninety-day period, the additional tax liability may be assessed promptly.

For taxpayers who reside outside the United States, the time period is extended to 150 days.

CROSS-REFERENCES

Taxation.

NINTH AMENDMENT

The Ninth Amendment to the U.S. Constitution reads:

> The enumeration in the Constitution, of certain rights, shall not be construed to deny or disparage others retained by the people.

The Ninth Amendment to the U.S. Constitution is somewhat of an enigma. It provides that the naming of certain rights in the Constitution does not take away from the people rights that are not named. Yet neither the language nor the history of the Ninth Amendment offers any hints as to the nature of the rights it was designed to protect.

Every year federal courts are asked to recognize new UNENUMERATED RIGHTS "retained by the people," and typically they turn to the Ninth Amendment. However, the federal judiciary does not base rulings exclusively on the Ninth Amendment; the courts usually cite the amendment as a secondary source of fundamental liberties. In particular, the Ninth Amendment has played a significant role in establishing a constitutional right to privacy.

Ratified in 1791, the Ninth Amendment is an outgrowth of a disagreement between the Federalists and the Anti-Federalists over the importance of attaching a BILL OF RIGHTS to the Constitution. When the Constitution was initially drafted by the Framers in 1787, it contained no Bill of Rights. The Anti-Federalists, who generally opposed ratification because they believed that the Constitution conferred too much power on the federal government, supported a Bill of Rights to serve as an additional constraint against despotism. The Federalists, on the other hand, supported ratification of the Constitution without a Bill of Rights because they believed that any enumeration of fundamental liberties was unnecessary and dangerous.

The Federalists contended that a Bill of Rights was unnecessary because in their view the federal government possessed only limited powers that were expressly delegated to it by the Constitution. They believed that all powers not constitutionally delegated to the federal government were inherently reserved to the people and the states. Nowhere in the Constitution, the Federalists pointed out, is the federal government given the power to trample on individual liberties. The Federalists feared that if the Constitution were to include a Bill of Rights that protected certain liberties from government encroachment, an inference would be drawn that the federal government could exercise an implied power to regulate such liberties.

ALEXANDER HAMILTON, one of the leading Federalists, articulated this concern in *The Federalist* No. 84. Why should a Bill of Rights, Hamilton asked, "declare that things shall not be done which there is no power to do?" For instance, Hamilton said it was unnecessary for a Bill of Rights to protect the FREEDOM OF THE PRESS when the federal government is not granted the power to regulate the press. A provision "against restraining the liberty of the press," Hamilton said, "afford[s] the clear implication that a power to prescribe proper regulations concerning it was intended to be vested in the national government."

The Federalists were also concerned that any constitutional enumeration of liberties might imply that other rights, not enumerated by the Constitution, would be surrendered to the government. A Bill of Rights, they feared, would quickly become the exclusive means by which the American people could secure their freedom and stave off tyranny. Federalist JAMES MADISON argued that any attempt to enumerate fundamental liberties would be incomplete and might imperil other freedoms not listed. A "positive declaration of some essential rights could not be obtained in the requisite latitude," Madison said. "If an enumeration be made of all our rights," he queried, "will it not be implied that everything omitted is given to the general government?"

Anti-Federalists and others who supported a Bill of Rights attempted to mollify the Federalists' concerns with three counterarguments. First, the Anti-Federalists underscored the fact that the Constitution guarantees certain liberties even without a Bill of Rights. For example, Article I of the Constitution prohibits Congress from suspending the writ of HABEAS CORPUS and from passing bills of attainder and EX POST FACTO LAWS. If these liberties could be enumerated without endangering other unenumerated liberties, Anti-Federalists reasoned, additional liberties, such as freedom of the press and religion, could be safeguarded in a Bill of Rights.

Second, while acknowledging that it would be impossible to enumerate every human liberty imaginable, supporters of a Bill of Rights maintained that this obstacle should not impede the Framers from establishing constitutional protection for certain essential liberties. THOMAS JEFFERSON, responding to Madison's claim that no Bill of Rights could ever be exhaustive, commented that "[h]alf a loaf is better than no bread. If we cannot secure all of our rights, let us secure what we can."

Third, Anti-Federalists argued that if there was a genuine risk that naming certain liberties would imperil others, then an additional constitutional amendment should be drafted to offer protection for all liberties not mentioned in the Bill of Rights. Such an amendment, the Anti-Federalists argued, would protect those liberties that might fall through the cracks of written constitutional provisions. This idea became the Ninth Amendment.

Unlike every other provision contained in the Bill of Rights, the Ninth Amendment had no predecessor in ENGLISH LAW. It stemmed solely from the genius of those who framed and ratified the Constitution. Ironically, Madison, who opposed a Bill of Rights in 1787, was the chief architect of the Ninth Amendment during the First Congress in 1789.

After reconsidering the arguments against a Bill of Rights, Madison said he was now convinced that such concerns could be overcome. It was still plausible, Madison believed, that the enumeration of particular rights might disparage other rights that were not enumerated. Yet Madison told Congress that he had attempted to guard against this danger by drafting the Ninth Amendment, which he submitted in the following form:

> The exceptions [to power] here or elsewhere in the constitution made in favor of particular rights, shall not be so construed as to diminish the just importance of other rights retained by the people, or as to enlarge the powers delegated by the constitution; but either as actual limitations on such powers, or as inserted merely for greater caution.

The House Select Committee, consisting of one representative from each state in the Union, reviewed and revised Madison's proposal until it gradually evolved into its present form. The debates in both houses of Congress add little to the original understanding of the Ninth Amendment. The Senate conducted its sessions in secret, and the House debates failed to offer a glimmer as to what unenumerated rights are protected by the Ninth Amendment, how such rights might be identified, or by what branch of government they should be enforced.

The Supreme Court did not attempt to answer these questions for more than 170 years. Until 1965 no Supreme Court decision made more than a passing reference to the Ninth Amendment. In 1958, Supreme Court Justice ROBERT H. JACKSON wrote that the rights protected by the Ninth Amendment "are still a mystery." Nevertheless, the dormant Ninth Amendment experienced a renaissance in GRISWOLD V. CONNECTICUT, 381 U.S. 479, 85 S. Ct. 1678, 14 L. Ed. 2d 510 (1965).

In *Griswold* the Supreme Court was asked to review the constitutionality of a Connecticut law that banned adult residents from using BIRTH CONTROL and prohibited anyone from assisting others to violate this law. In the majority opinion, Justice WILLIAM O. DOUGLAS, writing for the Court, rejected the notion that the judiciary is obligated to enforce only those rights that are expressly enumerated in the Constitution. On several occasions in the past, Douglas wrote, the Court has recognized rights that cannot be found in the written language of the Constitution.

Only briefly discussed in Douglas's majority opinion, the Ninth Amendment was the centerpiece of Justice ARTHUR GOLDBERG's concurring opinion. The language and history of the Ninth Amendment, Goldberg wrote, demonstrate that the Framers of the Constitution intended the judiciary to protect certain unwritten liberties with the same zeal that courts must protect those liberties expressly referenced in the Bill of Rights. The Ninth Amendment, Goldberg emphasized, reflects the Framers' original understanding that "other fundamental personal rights should not be denied protection simply because they are not specifically listed" in the Constitution.

Justices HUGO L. BLACK and POTTER STEWART criticized the Court for invoking the Ninth Amendment as a basis for its decision in *Griswold*. The Ninth Amendment, the dissenting justices said, does not explain what unenumerated rights are retained by the people or how these rights should be identified. Nor does the amendment authorize the Supreme Court, in contrast to the president or Congress, to enforce these rights. By reading the Ninth Amendment as creating a general right to privacy, Black and Stewart suggested, the unelected justices of the Supreme Court had substituted their own subjective notions of justice, liberty, and reasonableness for the wisdom and experience of the elected representatives in the Connecticut state legislature who were responsible for passing the birth control regulation.

The *Griswold* decision was the starting point of a continuing debate over the proper role of the Ninth Amendment in constitutional JURISPRUDENCE. One side of the debate reads the Ninth Amendment to mean that the Constitution protects not only those liberties written into the Bill of Rights but some additional liberties found outside the express language of any one provision. The other side sees no way to identify the unenumerated rights protected by the Ninth Amendment and no objective method by which to interpret and apply such rights. Under this view, courts that interpret and apply the Ninth Amendment do so in a manner that reflects the political and personal preferences of the presiding judge. Federal courts have attempted to reach a middle ground.

A number of federal courts have found that the Ninth Amendment is a rule of judicial construction, or a guideline for interpretation, and not an independent source of constitutional rights (*Mann v. Meachem*, 929 F. Supp. 622 [N.D.N.Y. 1996]). These courts view the Ninth Amendment as an invitation to liberally interpret the express provisions of the Constitution. However, federal courts will not recognize constitutional rights claimed to derive solely from the Ninth Amendment (*United States v. Vital Health Products*, 786 F. Supp. 761 [E.D. Wis. 1992]). By itself, one court held, the Ninth Amendment does not enunciate any substantive rights. Instead the amendment serves to protect other fundamental liberties that are implicit, though not mentioned, in the Bill of Rights (*Rothner v. City of Chicago*, 725 F. Supp. 945 [N.D. Ill. 1989]).

After *Griswold*, federal courts were flooded with novel claims based on unenumerated rights. Almost without exception, these novel Ninth Amendment claims were rejected.

For example, the Ninth Circuit Court of Appeals found no Ninth Amendment right to resist the draft (*United States v. Uhl*, 436 F.2d 773 [1970]). The Sixth Circuit Court ruled that there is no Ninth Amendment right to possess an unregistered submachine gun (*United States v. Warin*, 530 F.2d 103 [1976]). The Fourth Circuit Court held that the Ninth Amendment does not guarantee the right to produce, distribute, or experiment with mind-altering drugs such as marijuana (*United States v. Fry*, 787 F.2d 903 [1986]). The Eighth Circuit Court denied a claim asserting that the Ninth Amendment guaranteed Americans the right to a radiation-free environment (*Concerned Citizens of Nebraska v. U.S. Nuclear Regulatory Commission*, 970 F.2d 421 [1992]).

This series of cases has led some scholars to conclude that the Ninth Amendment may be returning to a constitutional hibernation. Yet the Ninth Amendment retains some vitality. In ROE V. WADE, the federal District Court for the Northern District of Texas ruled that a state law prohibiting ABORTION in all instances except to save the life of the mother violated the right to privacy guaranteed by the Ninth Amendment (314 F. Supp. 1217 [1970]).

On appeal the Supreme Court affirmed the district court's ruling, stating that the right to privacy, "whether it be founded in the Fourteenth Amendment's concept of personal liberty and restrictions upon state action, as we feel it is, or, as the District Court determined, in the

Ninth Amendment's reservation of rights to the people, is broad enough to encompass a woman's decision whether or not to terminate her pregnancy" (*Roe v. Wade*, 410 U.S. 113, 93 S. Ct. 705, 35 L. Ed. 2d 147 [1973]). Federal courts continue to rely on the Ninth Amendment in support of a woman's constitutional right to choose abortion under certain circumstances.

FURTHER READINGS

Abramson, Paul R., Steven D. Pinkerton, and Mark Huppin. 2003. *Sexual Rights in America: The Ninth Amendment and the Pursuit of Happiness*. New York.: New York Univ. Press.

DeRosa, Marshall L. 1996. *The Ninth Amendment and the Politics of Creative Jurisprudence: Disparaging the Fundamental Right of Popular Control*. New Brunswick, N.J.: Transaction.

Hardaway, Robert M. 2003. *No Price Too High: Victimless Crimes and the Ninth Amendment*. Westport, Conn.: Praeger.

Levy, Leonard. 1988. *Original Intent and the Framers' Constitution*. New York: Macmillan.

Yoo, John Choon. 1993. "Our Declaratory Ninth Amendment." *Emory Law Journal* 42.

CROSS-REFERENCES

Constitution of the United States; *Federalist Papers*; Penumbra.

NISI PRIUS

[Latin, Unless before.]

A court of *nisi prius* is a court that tries QUESTIONS OF FACT before one judge and, in some cases, a jury. In the United States, the term ordinarily applies to the trial level court where the case is heard by a jury, as opposed to a higher court that entertains appeals where no jury is present.

❖ NIXON, RICHARD MILHOUS

Richard Milhous Nixon was the 37th president of the United States. Though he made several major breakthroughs in his presidency, his involvement with the WATERGATE affair proved his undoing. In 1974 he became the only president ever to resign from office. Late in life Nixon's advice as a political analyst and foreign affairs expert was sought by both parties.

Nixon was born January 9, 1913, in Yorba Linda, California, the second of five sons of Francis A. Nixon and Hannah Milhous Nixon. His father had grown up on a farm in Ohio and arrived in California in 1907. He worked as a trolley car motorman in Whittier, where he met

Hannah Milhous. They were married in 1908. In 1922 they bought the grocery store and gas station where Nixon grew up. Nixon was a disciplined student who worked hard and received superior grades. He enjoyed playing football and participating in music, acting, and debating. A devout Quaker during his youth, he attended church four times a week.

When Nixon was 12, his younger brother Arthur died of tubercular encephalitis. His older brother, Harold, died when Nixon was 20, after a ten-year battle with tuberculosis. Harold's death was particularly traumatic for the family, as it had poured much of its limited resources into his treatment.

After graduating from high school, Nixon wanted to attend an Ivy League college but instead entered Whittier College, a small Quaker school close to home and within his family's financial means. He graduated second in his class and won a scholarship to Duke University Law School. At Duke, he was elected president of the Duke Bar Association and graduated third in his class.

In 1937, Nixon was admitted to the California bar and joined the firm of Wingert and Bewley in Whittier. He participated in civic groups; taught Sunday school; and acted in a community theater troupe, where he met Thelma Catherine Ryan, who was known as Patricia or Pat. They were married June 21, 1940, and had two children, Patricia ("Tricia") Nixon Cox and Julie Nixon Eisenhower. The Nixons would celebrate 53 years of marriage before Pat's death in 1993.

In 1941, Nixon took a job as an attorney with the Office of Price Administration in Washington, D.C. Seven months later, he applied for and received a Navy commission. He served as an operations officer with the South Pacific Combat Air Transport Command during WORLD WAR II.

Shortly after his return from the service, Nixon ran for Congress against incumbent California Democratic representative Jerry Voorhis. Nixon's campaign literature portrayed him as a returning veteran who had defended his country in the mud and jungles of the Solomon Islands while his opponent never left Washington, D.C. It also implied that Voorhis was endorsed by a Communist-supported POLITICAL ACTION COMMITTEE. At a time when fear of Communist subversion was widespread, Nixon's strategy worked. He came from behind in a race no one expected him to win to defeat Voorhis with 57 percent of the votes.

Nixon quickly made his mark in Washington, D.C. He became a vocal member of the House Committee on Un-American Activities, which investigated U.S. citizens suspected of having ties with or sympathies for the Communist party. One such case brought Nixon into the national spotlight. In 1948, ALGER HISS, a former STATE DEPARTMENT official, was investigated for allegedly passing secret information to the Communist government in the former Soviet Union. Nixon's determined pursuit of the case led to Hiss's indictment and eventual conviction for perjury.

In 1950 Nixon ran for the U.S. Senate against Democratic Representative Helen Gahagan Douglas. In an effort to discredit Douglas, he circulated a campaign flyer indicating that she had voted 354 times with Representative Vito Marcantonio of New York, a member of the Communist Workers party. The flyer, printed on pink paper, was known as the pink sheet, and Nixon often referred to Douglas as the pink lady, a link to the color red associated with COMMUNISM. Nixon defeated Douglas by a secure margin of 680,000 votes, raising speculation that his strident campaign may have been unnecessary.

In 1952 Republicans chose World War II hero General DWIGHT D. EISENHOWER as their nominee for president. Eisenhower chose Nixon as his running mate. The campaign encountered a crisis almost immediately. In September 1952, several newspapers disclosed that Nixon had received financial support from a secret fund raised by wealthy California business owners. This offense was viewed as shocking, and many people called for Nixon to withdraw from

Richard M. Nixon.
LIBRARY OF CONGRESS

the ticket. Instead, he took the offensive and pleaded his case on national television, delivering what came to be known as the "Checkers Speech." Nixon maintained his innocence, disclosed his financial situation to show he was in debt, and pointed out that his wife did not have a mink coat but rather wore "a respectable Republican cloth coat." He went on to say that a supporter in Texas had given the family a gift, a dog named Checkers, and that "the kids love the dog, and . . . we're going to keep it." The public's response was overwhelmingly positive and Nixon remained on the Republican ticket. Nixon had discovered the enormous power of television and had utilized it to his advantage, reaching a large audience without the need to endure press scrutiny.

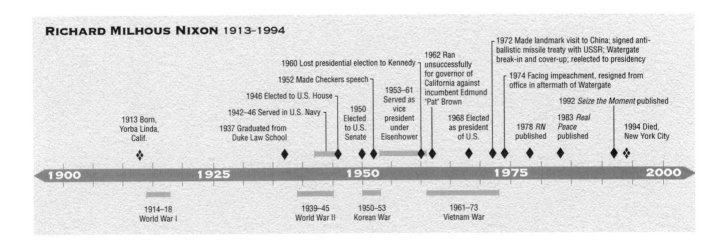

RICHARD MILHOUS NIXON 1913–1994

1913 Born, Yorba Linda, Calif.

1937 Graduated from Duke Law School

1942–46 Served in U.S. Navy

1946 Elected to U.S. House

1950 Elected to U.S. Senate

1952 Made Checkers speech

1953–61 Served as vice president under Eisenhower

1960 Lost presidential election to Kennedy

1962 Ran unsuccessfully for governor of California against incumbent Edmund "Pat" Brown

1968 Elected as president of U.S.

1972 Made landmark visit to China; signed anti-ballistic missile treaty with USSR; Watergate break-in and cover-up; reelected to presidency

1974 Facing impeachment, resigned from office in aftermath of Watergate

1978 *RN* published

1983 *Real Peace* published

1992 *Seize the Moment* published

1994 Died, New York City

1900   1925   1950   1975   2000

1914–18 World War I

1939–45 World War II

1950–53 Korean War

1961–73 Vietnam War

Eisenhower and Nixon received 55.1 percent of the popular vote in the 1952 election. Nixon served two terms as an unusually active vice president, honing his foreign policy skills during trips to 56 countries. Among the most famous of these journeys was a 1959 visit to Moscow, where he engaged in the celebrated Kitchen Debate with Soviet leader Nikita Khrushchev. The two men informally debated the merits of capitalism versus Communism while they toured the kitchen of a model home at a U.S. fair. Nixon's willingness to confront critics and his ability to turn adversity to his advantage earned him praise and acclaim.

In 1960, delegates at the Republican convention in Chicago nominated Nixon for president on the first ballot. He faced another young, energetic, popular contender, Democratic senator JOHN F. KENNEDY of Massachusetts. In the first of four televised debates with Kennedy, Nixon, who had been ill and was exhausted from campaigning, appeared haggard, strained, and tense. His appearance cost him many votes even though he had a keen command of the facts and debated well—indeed, those who listened to the debates on radio rather than watching them on television felt that Nixon had outdone Kennedy. Nixon lost the election, suffering his first political defeat, by a mere 119,000 votes. In spite of allegations of voting irregularities, particularly in Chicago, Nixon decided not to demand a recount and instead gracefully conceded to Kennedy.

After losing the 1960 election, Nixon ran for governor of California against Edmund "Pat" Brown in 1962 but was unable to unseat the incumbent. He moved to New York to practice law and almost immediately began preparing his comeback. In January 1968, he announced his candidacy for the presidency and was nominated on the Republicans' first ballot, defeating Governor Nelson A. Rockefeller of New York, and Governor RONALD REAGAN of California.

The DEMOCRATIC PARTY was in a shambles in 1968. President LYNDON B. JOHNSON withdrew as a candidate because of growing domestic unrest and opposition to the VIETNAM WAR. Senator ROBERT F. KENNEDY was assassinated in June 1968 while campaigning for the Democratic nomination. The Democrats nominated HUBERT H. HUMPHREY, Johnson's vice president. Nixon defeated Humphrey by a narrow margin. During his first term, Nixon appointed a broad-based cabinet that included both conservatives

and liberals. In his inaugural speech, he said that he hoped to "bridge the generation gap" and bring the country back together after years of unrest over Vietnam and RACIAL DISCRIMINATION. While he continued to pursue foreign policy goals, he also achieved much on the domestic front. He responded to strong public demand for expanded government services, and proposed a family assistance program that, had it not been voted down by Congress, would have been the most far-reaching WELFARE reform in modern history. He supported health and safety protection on the job and housing allowances for disadvantaged people. Nixon's administration built more subsidized housing units than any administration before or since. He expanded the Food Stamp Program and began the federal revenue-sharing program for local governments. Another lasting legacy was the creation of the ENVIRONMENTAL PROTECTION AGENCY.

Nixon also reshaped the Supreme Court. Under Chief Justice EARL WARREN, who had been appointed by President Eisenhower, the Court had taken what many felt was an ideologically liberal turn. During his presidency, Nixon appointed four members to the court: WARREN E. BURGER, as chief justice; and HARRY A. BLACKMUN, LEWIS F. POWELL JR., and WILLIAM H. REHNQUIST, as associate justices. The Burger Court began a retreat from liberalism and judicial activism that continued through the 1980s and 1990s.

Perhaps Nixon's most noteworthy triumphs were in foreign policy. In 1972 Nixon and his chief foreign affairs adviser, HENRY KISSINGER, traveled to Communist China to begin the process of reestablishing diplomatic relations with the Beijing government. The visit marked a major shift in U.S. policy toward China. The two governments shared a history of animosity, and the United States had long recognized the Nationalist Chinese government of Chiang Kai-shek, based on the island of Taiwan, as the official government of China. After Nixon's visit, the door was opened to diplomatic and trade dealings. Formal diplomatic relations with Communist China were established in 1978.

Nixon also opened negotiations with the Communist government in the former Soviet Union. He initiated the process known as détente by holding three summit meetings with Soviet leader Leonid Brezhnev. His efforts culminated in a breakthrough agreement in 1972 limiting the use of antiballistic missiles.

"THERE IS ONE THING SOLID AND FUNDAMENTAL IN POLITICS—THE LAW OF CHANGE. WHAT'S UP TODAY IS DOWN TOMORROW."
—RICHARD M. NIXON

One major goal that eluded Nixon in foreign policy was a quick end to the Vietnam War. After promising "peace with honor" during his campaign in 1968, he saw the war continue through his first term.

Though the war would end in January 1973, an event in June of 1972 marked the beginning of Nixon's downfall. At that time, during Nixon's campaign for reelection, a group of men working for the Committee to Reelect the President broke into the Democratic party headquarters in the Watergate office complex in Washington, D.C. It was a crime that would be traced back to the president.

In November, Nixon won a sweeping victory over his Democratic challenger, Senator George S. McGovern, of South Dakota, receiving 60.7 percent of the vote and carrying every state except Massachusetts. The following March, testimony before the Senate select committee investigating the incident implicated the White House. In televised hearings John W. Dean III, Nixon's White House counsel, told the Senate committee that Nixon had been involved from the start.

Further testimony revealed that Nixon had secretly recorded all conversations that took place in the Oval Office of the White House. Congress and prosecutors began efforts to obtain the tapes. In October 1973, his reputation in jeopardy, Nixon carried out what came to be called the Saturday Night Massacre. Angered by Watergate special prosecutor ARCHIBALD COX, Nixon ordered Attorney General ELLIOT L. RICHARDSON to dismiss Cox. Richardson refused and resigned. Deputy Attorney General William D. Ruckelshaus also refused to carry out the task and was dismissed. Finally, Solicitor General ROBERT H. BORK, appointed acting attorney general, dismissed Cox.

Calls for Nixon's resignation mounted, and IMPEACHMENT resolutions were referred to the House Judiciary Committee. On March 1, 1974, a federal GRAND JURY indicted seven former Nixon aides in the continuing cover-up of Watergate. Nixon was named as an unindicted coconspirator.

Nixon responded to pressure from both those who wanted him to prove himself innocent and those who believed him guilty, by announcing in April 1974 that he would release to the House Judiciary Committee edited transcripts of conversations regarding Watergate culled from his library of tape recordings. Though the committee responded that it would need the tapes themselves, Nixon refused to supply them. The edited transcripts alone were tremendously damaging. The transcripts implicated the Nixon White House not only in burglaries and cover-ups, but also illegal wiretaps, corruption of government agencies, domestic ESPIONAGE, unfair campaign tactics, and abuse of campaign funds. Eventually, 19 Nixon aides and associates served prison terms for their roles in these illegal activities.

By late July 1974, the House Judiciary Committee, in televised hearings, was deliberating ARTICLES OF IMPEACHMENT against Nixon. The articles charged him with OBSTRUCTION OF JUSTICE, abuse of power, and defiance of congressional subpoenas. It became clear that the full House would impeach him, and he would probably face conviction by the Senate. In early August, in response to a Supreme Court ruling (UNITED STATES V. NIXON, 418 U.S. 683, 94 S. Ct. 3090, 41 L. Ed. 2d 1039 [1974]), Nixon released the contested tape recordings that showed conclusively that he had been involved in the effort to halt the Federal Bureau of Investigation's probe of Watergate.

On August 7, 1974, facing certain impeachment, Nixon met with his family and aides and informed Secretary of State Kissinger of his decision to resign. He made this announcement to the nation in a television broadcast the evening of August 8. The following day, with his family around him, he bade an emotional farewell to his staff, boarded *Air Force One* with his wife, and flew home to San Clemente, California. Vice President GERALD R. FORD was sworn in to serve the remainder of Nixon's term. On September 8, President Ford granted Nixon an unconditional pardon for all federal crimes he "committed or may have committed or taken part in" while in office, thus ending the crisis that had gripped the nation for more than two years.

After his resignation Nixon published eight books and numerous newspaper and magazine articles. He traveled again to China, where he was warmly received, and in 1994, shortly before his death, he returned to Russia. Nixon came to be considered an elder statesman and political analyst. As an expert in foreign policy his advice and counsel were sought by Senator and presidential candidate BOB DOLE and President BILL CLINTON.

Nixon died April 22, 1994. All five living presidents at the time—Clinton, GEORGE H.W. BUSH, Reagan, JIMMY CARTER, and Ford—and their wives attended Nixon's funeral. Clinton delivered a eulogy in which he said:

> He suffered defeats that would have ended most political careers, yet he won stunning victories that many of the world's most popular leaders have failed to attain.

FURTHER READINGS

Ambrose, Stephen E. 1989. *Nixon: The Triumph of a Politician, 1962–1972.* New York: Simon & Schuster.

———. 1987. *Nixon: The Education of a Politician, 1913–1962.* New York: Simon & Schuster.

Brodie, Fawn M. 1981. *Richard M. Nixon: The Shaping of His Character.* New York: Norton.

Kutler, Stanley I., ed. 1998. *Abuse of Power: The New Nixon Tapes.* New York: Simon & Schuster.

Mankiewicz, Frank. 1973. *Perfectly Clear: Nixon from Whittier to Watergate.* New York: Quadrangle Books.

Morgan, Iwan. 2002. *Nixon.* New York: Oxford Univ. Press.

Nixon, Richard M. 1990. *In the Arena: A Memoir of Victory, Defeat and Renewal.* New York: Simon & Schuster.

———. 1978. *R.N.: The Memoirs of Richard Nixon.* New York: Grosset & Dunlap.

"Twenty-Five Years After Watergate" (special edition). 2000. *Hastings Law Journal* 51 (April).

White, Theodore H. 1975. *Breach of Faith: The Fall of Richard Nixon.* Atheneum Publications.

Wicker, Tom. 1991. *One of Us: Richard Nixon and the American Dream.* New York: Random House.

Wills, Garry. 1969. *Nixon Agonistes: The Crisis of the Self-Made Man.* Boston: Houghton Mifflin.

CROSS-REFERENCES

Cold War; Communism; Ervin, Samuel James, Jr.; Executive Privilege; Independent Counsel; Jaworski, Leon; Mitchell, John Newton; *New York Times Co. v. United States*; Watergate.

NIXON, UNITED STATES V.

In *United States v. Nixon,* 418 U.S. 683, 94 S. Ct. 3090, 41 L. Ed. 2d 1039 (1974), the U.S. Supreme Court recognized the doctrine of EXECUTIVE PRIVILEGE but held that it could not prevent the disclosure of materials needed for a criminal prosecution. The case arose during the WATERGATE political scandal, which involved President RICHARD M. NIXON and numerous members of his administration. The Court had to consider whether Nixon was required to turn over secret White House tape recordings to government prosecutors. Nixon claimed that the doctrine of executive privilege allowed him to refuse to release the tapes, while prosecutors argued that they had a right to obtain evidence of possible crimes, even if that evidence was held by the president of the United States.

The Watergate scandal began during the presidential campaign of 1972, in which Nixon defeated his Democratic opponent, Senator George McGovern of South Dakota, by a wide margin. Several months before the election, on June 17, a group of burglars broke into the DEMOCRATIC PARTY campaign headquarters in the Watergate building complex in Washington, D.C. Aggressive investigative reporting by the *Washington Post* uncovered connections to officials in the Nixon administration. Though the administration denied any wrongdoing, it soon became clear that members of the administration had tried to cover up the BURGLARY and connections to it that might include the president.

Under congressional and public pressure, Nixon appointed a special prosecutor. When it was revealed that the president had secretly taped conversations in the Oval Office in the White House, the prosecutor, ARCHIBALD COX, filed a subpoena to secure tapes that he believed were relevant to the criminal investigation. When Cox refused to withdraw his request, Nixon had him fired. The resulting public outrage forced Nixon to appoint LEON JAWORSKI as a new special prosecutor.

In March 1974 a federal GRAND JURY indicted seven Nixon associates for conspiracy to obstruct justice and for other offenses related to the Watergate burglary. Nixon himself was named as an unindicted co-conspirator. Upon Jaworski's motion the U.S. district court issued a new subpoena to the president, requiring him to produce certain tapes and documents pertaining to precisely identified meetings between the president and others. Although Nixon released edited transcripts of some of the subpoenaed conversations, his attorney moved to quash, or void, the subpoena on the grounds of executive privilege. When the district court denied the motion, the president appealed, and the case was quickly brought to the U.S. Supreme Court.

Nixon refused to release the tapes, contending that the doctrine of executive privilege gave him the right to withhold documents from Congress and the courts. Executive privilege, though not mentioned in the U.S. Constitution, was first asserted by GEORGE WASHINGTON. Presidents have argued that the privilege is inherent in executive power and is necessary to maintain the secrecy of information related to national security and to protect the confidentiality of their deliberations. Executive privilege did not become a major point of contention until the Nixon presidency, however. Nixon routinely used it during his first term to thwart congressional inquiries.

The Supreme Court, in a unanimous decision (Justice WILLIAM H. REHNQUIST recused himself because he had served in the Nixon administration), recognized for the first time the general legitimacy of executive privilege. Nevertheless, Chief Justice WARREN E. BURGER, writing for the Court, rejected Nixon's claim of "an absolute, unqualified Presidential privilege of IMMUNITY from judicial process under all circumstances." Burger found that [a]bsent a claim of need to protect military, diplomatic, or sensitive national security secrets," the need for protecting the confidentiality of presidential communications must give way to a legitimate request by the courts for information vital to a criminal prosecution. Burger noted that the judge would review the subpoenaed tapes in private to determine what portions should be released to the prosecutors. This confidential review would prevent sensitive but irrelevant information from being disclosed.

Nixon obeyed the order and turned the tapes over to the district court. When relevant portions were released, they revealed that the president had been intimately involved with the attempt to cover up White House involvement in the Watergate burglary. Less than three weeks after the Court announced its decision, Nixon resigned the presidency, thereby avoiding IMPEACHMENT by Congress.

FURTHER READINGS

Jaworski, Leon. 1976. *The Right and the Power: The Prosecution of Watergate.* New York: Reader's Digest.

Johnsen, Dawn. 1999. "Executive Privilege Since *United States v. Nixon*: Issues of Motivation and Accommodation." *Minnesota Law Review* 83 (May).

Rozell, Mark J. 1999. "Executive Privilege and the Modern Presidents: In Nixon's Shadow." *Minnesota Law Review* 83 (May).

Woodward, Bob. 1999. *Shadow: Five Presidents and the Legacy of Watergate.* New York: Simon & Schuster.

CROSS-REFERENCES

Nixon, Richard Milhous; Watergate.

NLRB V. JONES & LAUGHLIN STEEL CORP.

From the 1870s through the mid-1930s the U.S. Supreme Court was generally hostile to federal legislation that sought to regulate business through the use of the Constitution's COMMERCE CLAUSE. A conservative judiciary believed that the free market should govern economic activities; consequently laws that attempted to regulate labor relations were overturned. The Great Depression of the 1930s led to the presidential election in 1932 of FRANKLIN D. ROOSEVELT, who advocated an aggressive role for the federal government in national economic affairs. Congress consistently turned Roosevelt's legislative agenda into law yet the Supreme Court ruled these new laws unconstitutional. However, in the landmark case of *NLRB v. Jones & Laughlin Steel Corp.,* 301 U.S. 1, 57 S. Ct. 615, 81 L. Ed. 893 (1937), the Court reversed course, paving the way for NEW DEAL legislation and a new judicial attitude toward the Commerce Clause.

For generations LABOR UNIONS had confronted a business community that was hostile to the concept of COLLECTIVE BARGAINING. Therefore, the passage of the National Labor Relations Act (NLRA or WAGNER ACT) of 1935 (29 U.S.C.A. § 151 et seq.) was a dramatic recognition of workers' rights. The law gave workers the right to organize unions and to require employers to negotiate with a certified union. An elaborate administrative process was also established, headed by the National Labor Relations Board (NLRB). The NLRB was create to review complaints about alleged violations of the law and issue administrative sanctions against employers for retaliatory discharges based on union membership or organization activities. Employers vowed to test the constitutionality of the NLRA and the actions of the NLRB.

In July 1935, 13 employees of the Jones and Laughlin Steel Corporation plant in Aliquippa, Pennsylvania, were discharged for minor infractions of company rules. Most of these workers had been actively involved in a union. The union filed with the NLRB a charge of UNFAIR LABOR PRACTICES against the steel company, claiming that the discharges were because of union membership. At a subsequent NLRB hearing, Jones & Laughlin argued that the NLRA was unconstitutional because it regulated labor relations and not interstate commerce. Therefore, Congress had no authority to regulate labor relations. The NLRB rejected the argument and found that the company was the fourth largest steel producer in the United States and was clearly involved in interstate commerce. It ordered the workers reinstated and directed Jones & Laughlin to cease and desist from these labor practices. Jones & Laughlin appealed, confident that the Supreme Court would overturn what was viewed as the most radical piece of New Deal law.

In a stunning reversal of precedent the Court upheld the constitutionality of the NLRA on a 5–4 vote. Previous decisions striking down New Deal legislation had also come on 5–4 votes, with Chief Justice CHARLES EVANS HUGHES joining four conservative justices to constitute a majority. In this case Hughes joined the four liberal justices and wrote the majority opinion. The tenor of Hughes' opinion was significant, for he abandoned Court precedent that had considered labor relations outside the stream of interstate commerce. The previous year Hughes had embraced this idea, but in the present case he looked at the world differently. He concluded that DUE PROCESS and liberty of contract concerns were irrelevant.

The Court's decision made clear that the federal government had the constitutional authority to regulate labor relations. Hughes reasoned that labor strife, including strikes, affected interstate commerce. He stressed that the Commerce Clause was broad enough to permit Congress to extend its regulations to both interstate commerce and to any activity that affected commerce, directly or indirectly. What was important was the "effect upon commerce, not the source of the injury."

The Court concluded that the NLRA went no further than to "safeguard the right of employees to self-organization and to select representatives of their own choosing for collective bargaining." This was "a fundamental right." This declaration reversed over 100 years of judicial thinking about labor unions and endorsed the authority of Congress to protect this right.

This decision was a bitter defeat for the four conservatives justices: GEORGE SUTHERLAND, PIERCE BUTLER, WILLIS VAN DEVANTER, and JAMES MCREYNOLDS. In their dissents they argued that the NRLA violated the liberty of contract between an individual employee and an employer. Moreover, they held fast to the "stream of commerce" line of precedent. They could not see how the discharge of a few employees in a city in Pennsylvania had any connection to the sale and distribution of steel through the channels of interstate commerce.

Jones changed the face of labor relations by requiring employers to treat unions and union workers fairly. It also signaled an end to the Supreme Court's striking down New Deal laws that sought to reshape the national economy. From *Jones* onward the Court permitted the federal government to take a dominant role in matters of commerce. The balance of power between the federal government and state governments shifted dramatically in the years following this decision.

This decision also empowered Congress to apply the Commerce Clause to federal civil right legislation. The CIVIL RIGHTS ACT OF 1964 contains provisions banning segregated public accommodations that are a part of interstate commerce. Congress used the Commerce Clause as its authority because the Fourteenth Amendment's due process and EQUAL PROTECTION rights only apply to state and local government actions. Therefore, if the state does not mandate segregated facilities, the private discriminatory actions would be exempt from the FOURTEENTH AMENDMENT. Therefore, Congress claimed that segregated public accommodations affected interstate commerce. The Supreme Court, in *Heart of Atlanta Motel, Inc. v. United States*, 379 U.S. 241, 85 S. Ct. 348, 13 L. Ed. 2d 258 (1964), applied the *Jones* reasoning. It noted that 75 percent of the Heart of Atlanta Motel's clientele came from out of state and that it was strategically located near several interstate highways. Therefore, the business clearly affected interstate commerce. The Court upheld the constitutionality of this landmark legislation.

FURTHER READINGS

Hardin, Patrick, ed. 2002. *The Developing Labor Law: The Board, the Courts, and the National Labor Relations Act.* 4th ed. Washington, D.C.: Bureau of National Affairs.

NO BILL

A term that the foreman of the GRAND JURY writes across the face of a bill of indictment (a document drawn up by a prosecutor that states formal criminal charges against a designated individual) to indicate that the criminal charges alleged therein against a suspect have not been sufficiently supported by the evidence presented before it to warrant his or her criminal prosecution.

When the grand jury agrees that the evidence is sufficient to establish the commission of a crime, it returns an indictment endorsed by the grand jury foreman with the phrase *true bill* to indicate that the information presented before it is sufficient to justify the trial of the suspect.

NO CONTEST

The English translation of a nolo contendere *plea used in criminal cases. Generally the terms* nolo contendere *and* no contest *are used interchangeably in the legal community. The operation of a no contest plea is similar to a plea of guilty. A defendant who enters a no contest plea concedes the charges alleged without disputing or admitting guilt and without offering a defense. No contest has a different meaning in the context of a will.*

The modern no contest plea originated during the reign of Henry IV in England in the early 1400s. It was considered a prisoner's implied confession. In cases where a death sentence was not a possibility, a prisoner was allowed simply to ask the court for mercy rather than contest the issue of guilt or innocence. Today the no contest plea is defined by statute and is available in almost every state. Such a plea is considered a privilege and not an automatic right of a defendant. Consequently, a no contest plea is accepted only with the consent of the court, and a judge is vested with discretion to accept or reject the plea. A plea of no contest usually is not allowed in death penalty cases.

The court must address several procedural concerns before accepting a no contest plea. If it appears from the facts presented that the defendant did not commit the offense charged, the trial court will refuse a no contest plea. Generally, a defendant must also tender a no contest plea knowingly and voluntarily. A plea is not deemed knowing and voluntary unless the defendant has a full understanding of the charges alleged and the legal ramifications of PLEADING no contest. To ensure that the plea is freely tendered, the court will also inquire whether the defendant has received any threats or promises. The adherence to these standards varies among courts and jurisdictions. Some courts operate under the assumption that a no contest plea should be accepted in the absence of some reason to the contrary, whereas others require the defendant to strictly observe every legal requirement before they will accept the plea.

A plea of no contest is advantageous for defendants where the effects of a plea of guilty are too harsh. For example, a defendant might choose to enter a no contest plea to avoid the expense and publicity of a trial. Another procedural advantage of a no contest plea is that it cannot be used against the accused in any civil suit for the same act. For example, if a motorist pleads no contest to a criminal assault charge against a hitchhiker, the hitchhiker cannot introduce evidence of that plea in a related civil proceeding for assault to impeach the motorist's credibility.

One disadvantage of a no contest plea is that it carries the same legal effect as a conviction for sentencing purposes. Though a defendant may hope for leniency during sentencing for saving the court the time and costs of a trial or because of a bargain worked out with the prosecutors, the full range of penalties remain available to the court for the given crime. Thus, a defendant risks receiving the same punishment without the opportunity to offer a defense or a chance for an acquittal from a jury.

A second meaning of no contest relates to wills and the intentions of the testator. A no contest provision in a will provides that the gift or devise is given on the condition that no legal action is taken to challenge the will. If a legal challenge to the will is pursued, the no contest provision provides that the person bringing the action forfeits the gift or devise. The purpose of no contest clauses is to carry out the express wishes of the testator and to discourage litigation. Nonetheless, many courts refuse to enforce no contest clauses if the challenge is brought in GOOD FAITH and on PROBABLE CAUSE.

NO FAULT

A kind of automobile insurance that provides that each driver must collect the allowable amount of money from his or her own insurance carrier subsequent to an accident regardless of who was at fault.

No-fault insurance is required by statute in a number of states.

The term *no fault* is also used colloquially in reference to a type of DIVORCE in which a marriage can be dissolved on the basis of irretrievable breakdown or irreconcilable differences, without a requirement that either party prove that the spouse was guilty of any misconduct causing the end of the marriage.

CROSS-REFERENCES

Automobiles.

NO FAULT DIVORCE

See DIVORCE.

NO-LOAD FUND

A type of MUTUAL FUND *that does not impose extra charges for administrative and selling expenses incurred in offering its shares for sale to the public.*

NOLLE PROSEQUI

[Latin, Will not prosecute.]

The term *nolle prosequi* is used in reference to a formal entry upon the record made by a plaintiff in a civil lawsuit or a prosecutor in a criminal action in which that individual declares that he or she wishes to discontinue the action as to certain defendants, certain issues, or altogether. A *nolle prosequi* is commonly known as *nol pros.*

NOLO CONTENDERE

[Latin, I will not contest it.] *A plea in a criminal case by which the defendant answers the charges made in the indictment by declining to dispute or admit the fact of his or her guilt.*

The defendant who pleads *nolo contendere* submits for ajudgment fixing a fine or sentence the same as if he or she had pleaded guilty. The difference is that a plea of *nolo contendere* cannot later be used to prove wrongdoing in a civil suit for monetary damages, but a plea of guilty can. *Nolo contendere* is especially popular in antitrust actions, such as price-fixing cases, where it is very likely that civil actions for treble damages will be started after the defendant has been successfully prosecuted.

A plea of *nolo contendere* may be entered only with the permission of the court, and the court should accept it only after weighing its effect on the parties, the public, and the administration of justice.

NOMINAL

Trifling, token, or slight; not real or substantial; in name only.

Nominal capital, for example, refers to extremely small or negligible funds, the use of which in a particular business is incidental.

NOMINAL DAMAGES

Minimal money damages awarded to an individual in an action where the person has not suffered any substantial injury or loss for which he or she must be compensated.

This kind of damages reflects a legal recognition that a plaintiff's rights have been violated through a defendant's breach of duty or wrongful conduct. The amount awarded is ordinarily a trifling sum, such as a dollar, which varies according to the circumstances of each case. In certain jurisdictions, the amount of the award might include the costs of the lawsuit.

In general, nominal damages may be recovered by a plaintiff who is successful in establishing that he or she has suffered a loss or injury as a result of the defendant's wrongful conduct but is unable to adequately set forth proof of the nature and extent of the injury.

NON

[Latin, Not.] *A common prefix used to indicate negation.*

For example, the term *non sequitur* means "it does not follow."

NON OBSTANTE VEREDICTO

See JUDGMENT NOTWITHSTANDING THE VERDICT.

NON PROSEQUITUR

[Latin, He does not pursue, or follow up.] *The name of a judgment rendered by a court against a plaintiff because he or she fails to take any necessary steps, in legal proceedings, within the period prescribed for such proceedings by the practice of court.*

When a judgment of *non prosequitur* is entered against the plaintiff, he or she has failed to properly pursue the lawsuit and cannot subsequently obtain a judgment against the defendant. A failure of such nature would result in a dismissal of the action or in a default judgment in favor of the defendant.

NON SUI JURIS

[Latin, Not his own master.] *A term applied to an individual who lacks the legal capacity to act on his or her own behalf, such as an infant or an insane person.*

NON VULT CONTENDERE

[Latin, He does not wish to contest it.] *A type of plea that can be entered by a defendant who is unwilling to admit guilt but is willing to submit to the court for sentencing.*

The term, sometimes abbreviated *non vult,* is a variation of nolo contendere, which has the same meaning.

NONAGE

Infancy or minority; lack of requisite legal age.

Nonage entails various contractual disabilities and is a ground for ANNULMENT in some jurisdictions.

CROSS-REFERENCES

Infants.

NONCOMPETE AGREEMENT

A contract limiting a party from competing with a business after termination of employment or completion of a business sale.

Found in some business contracts, noncompete agreements are designed to protect a business owner's investment by restricting potential competition. Generally, businesses pursue these agreements in two instances: when hiring new employees, or when purchasing an established business. The noncompete agreement is a form of RESTRICTIVE COVENANT, a clause that adds limitations to the employment or sale contract. These agreements protect the business by restricting the other party from performing similar work for a specific period of time within a certain geographical area. First used in the nineteenth century, and common today in certain professions, noncompete agreements sometimes have an uncertain legal status. Courts do not always uphold them. Generally, courts evaluate such clauses for their reasonableness to determine whether they constitute an unfair restraint on trade.

The rationale behind noncompete agreements is an employer's self-interest. Typically, companies invest heavily in the training of their employees. Similarly, they have an interest in protecting their customer base, trade secrets, and other information vital to their success. The noncompete agreement is a form of protection against losses. The company does not wish to invest in an employee only to see the employee take the skills acquired, or the company's customers, to another employer. Thus, when hiring a new employee, the company may make her sign a noncompete agreement as part of a condition of employment. Likewise, the prospective purchaser of an established business may only buy it if the current owner is willing to sign a noncompete agreement.

In practice, such agreements are very specific in several respects. Usually the agreement will define a length of time, geographic radius in miles, and type of activity in which the employee promises to refrain from working after leaving her or his job. This is often the case in businesses that depend on an established group of customers. A hair salon, for example, may require its stylists to agree not to compete against it in neighboring hair salons. Noncompete agreements are also well established in fields where an individual is associated with a product or service. High-profile positions in the media typically require them. A television anchorwoman, for example, will typically be contractually bound not to work for a competing news channel in the same market for a period of time following the termination of her contract.

In legal challenges courts use a standard of reasonableness in deciding whether to uphold a noncompete agreement. Most states use a three-part test: the agreement must be reasonable in terms of length of time, size of geographical territory included, and the business's necessity for the agreement. Covenants restricting the sellers of businesses typically receive a lower level of scrutiny, whereas restrictions on the behavior of former employees are closely scrutinized.

Courts are primarily concerned with preventing unfair restraints on trade. In a free market, most businesses cannot reasonably assert a need to restrict competition. Many states will evaluate each separate part of an agreement using the so-called blue pencil doctrine of severability, under which certain parts of the agreement can be upheld as enforceable and others can be found unenforceable. A few states, however, throw out an entire agreement if any part of it is found to be an unfair restraint on trade.

FURTHER READINGS

Jordan, Thomas E. 1990. "The Application of Contract Law to Georgia Noncompete Agreements: Have We Been Overlooking Something Obvious?" *Mercer Law Review* 41 (winter).

CROSS-REFERENCES

Restraint of Trade.

NONCONFORMING USE

Continuing use of real property, permitted by ZONING *ordinances, in a manner in which other similar plots of land in the same area cannot ordinarily be used.*

Most municipal governments have enacted zoning ordinances that regulate the development of real estate within the municipality. The municipality is divided into zoning districts that permit a particular use of property: residence, business, or industry. Within these three main types of zoning districts, population density and building height may also be restricted. Zoning attempts to conserve the value of property and to encourage the most appropriate use of land throughout a particular locality.

When zoning is established, however, the ordinance cannot eliminate structures already in existence. Thus, if a district is zoned residential, the corner grocery store and neighborhood service station become nonconforming use sites. These businesses may remain even though they do not fit the predominant classification of real property in the zoning district.

As long as the property having nonconforming use status does not change, its status is protected. Problems arise, however, when change occurs. In general, substantial alterations in the nature of the business, new equipment that is not a replacement but a subterfuge to expand the use of the property, or a new structure amount to illegal expansion or extension. These types of actions will result in the loss of the nonconforming use status and the closing of the business. For example, if the corner grocery builds an addition to house a restaurant, that would be a significant change. If, however, the grocery updates its refrigeration equipment, that would not be an illegal change.

If a nonconforming use structure is destroyed or partially destroyed by fire or similar occurrences, zoning ordinances generally provide that if it is destroyed beyond a certain percentage, it cannot be rebuilt. Usually the owner loses the right to rebuild if 50 percent or more of the structure is damaged.

If a business stops operating at the nonconforming use site, zoning ordinances generally classify this as a discontinuance and revoke the nonconforming use status. The owner of the business must intend to abandon the use. Discontinuance due to repairs, acts of war or nature, government controls, foreclosure, condemnation, or injunctions are not regarded as manifesting intent to abandon the nonconforming use status if the situation is beyond the business owner's control.

Another tool to end nonconforming use situations is amortization, where the nonconforming use of a structure must cease within a zoning district at the end of the structure's estimated useful economic life. This device often is used in connection with billboards and junkyards.

Though municipalities may seek to end nonconforming use status through these various approaches, landowners usually retain this status until it becomes economically undesirable.

CROSS-REFERENCES

Land-Use Control.

NONFEASANCE

The intentional failure to perform a required duty or obligation.

Nonfeasance is a term used in TORT LAW to describe inaction that allows or results in harm to a person or to property. An act of nonfeasance can result in liability if (1) the actor owed a duty of care toward the injured person, (2) the actor failed to act on that duty, and (3) the failure to act resulted in injury.

Originally the failure to take affirmative steps to prevent harm did not create liability, and this rule was absolute. Over the years courts have recognized a number of situations in which a person who does not create a dangerous situation must nevertheless act to prevent harm.

Generally a person will not be held liable for a failure to act unless he or she had a preexisting relationship with the injured person. For example, if a bystander sees a stranger drowning and does not attempt a rescue, he cannot be liable for nonfeasance because he had no preexisting relationship with the drowning person. The bystander would not be liable for the drowning even if a rescue would have posed no risk to him.

However, if the victim is drowning in a public pool and the bystander is a lifeguard employed by the city, and if the lifeguard does not act to help, she may be held liable for the drowning because the lifeguard's employment places her in a relationship with swimmers in the pool. Because of this relationship, the lifeguard owes a duty to take affirmative steps to prevent harm to the swimmers.

Courts have found a preexisting relationship and a duty to act in various relationships, such as the relationship between HUSBAND AND WIFE, innkeeper and guest, employer and employee, jailer and prisoner, carrier and passenger, PARENT AND CHILD, school and pupil, and host and guest. A person who renders aid or protection to a stranger also may be found liable if the rescuer does not act reasonably and leaves the stranger in a more dangerous position, even if the rescuer had nothing to do with the initial cause of the stranger's dilemma.

Courts have found a duty to act if a person does something innocuous that later poses a threat and then fails to act to prevent harm. For example, assume that Johnny loans a powerful circular saw to Bobby. If Johnny later remembers that the bolt securing the blade is loose and that the blade will dislodge in a dangerous manner when the saw is used, Johnny must try to warn Bobby. If Bobby is injured because Johnny failed to act, Johnny can be held liable for nonfeasance.

In theory nonfeasance is distinct from misfeasance and malfeasance. Malfeasance is any act that is illegal or wrongful. Misfeasance is an act that is legal but improperly performed. Nonfeasance, by contrast, is a failure to act that results in harm.

In practice the distinctions between the three terms are nebulous and difficult to apply. Courts in various jurisdictions have crafted different rules relating to the terms. The most difficult issue that faces courts is whether to imply a duty to act and find liability for the failure to act.

Originally courts used the term nonfeasance to describe a failure to act that did not give rise to liability for injuries. The meaning of the term reversed direction over time, and most courts now use it to describe inaction that creates liability.

FURTHER READINGS

Kionka, Edward J. 1999. *Torts in a Nutshell.* 3d ed. St. Paul, Minn.: West Group.

Rowe, Jean Elting, and Theodore Silver. 1995. "The Jurisprudence of Action and Inaction in the Law of Tort: Solving the Puzzle of Nonfeasance and Misfeasance from the Fifteenth Through the Twentieth Centuries." *Duquesne Law Review* 33 (summer).

CROSS-REFERENCES

Good Samaritan Doctrine.

NONPROFIT

A corporation or an association that conducts business for the benefit of the general public without shareholders and without a profit motive.

Nonprofits are also called not-for-profit corporations. Nonprofit corporations are created according to state law. Like for-profit corporations, nonprofit corporations must file a statement of corporate purpose with the SECRETARY OF STATE and pay a fee, create articles of incorporation, con-

duct regular meetings, and fulfill other obligations to achieve and maintain corporate status.

Nonprofit corporations differ from profit-driven corporations in several respects. The most basic difference is that nonprofit corporations cannot operate for profit. That is, they cannot distribute corporate income to shareholders. The funds acquired by nonprofit corporations must stay within the corporate accounts to pay for reasonable salaries, expenses, and the activities of the corporation. If the income of a corporation inures to the personal benefit of any individual, the corporation is considered to be profit driven. Salaries are not considered personal benefits because they are necessary for the operation of the corporation. An excessive salary, however, may cause a corporation to lose its nonprofit status.

Nonprofit corporations are exempt from the income taxes that affect other corporations but only if they conduct business exclusively for the benefit of the general public. State laws on

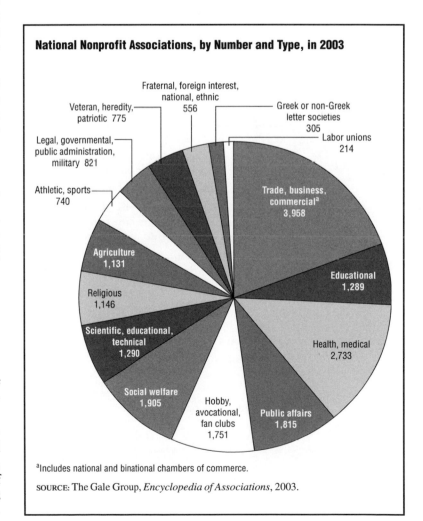

National Nonprofit Associations, by Number and Type, in 2003

Fraternal, foreign interest, national, ethnic 556
Veteran, heredity, patriotic 775
Greek or non-Greek letter societies 305
Legal, governmental, public administration, military 821
Labor unions 214
Athletic, sports 740
Trade, business, commercial[a] 3,958
Agriculture 1,131
Educational 1,289
Religious 1,146
Scientific, educational, technical 1,290
Health, medical 2,733
Social welfare 1,905
Hobby, avocational, fan clubs 1,751
Public affairs 1,815

[a]Includes national and binational chambers of commerce.

SOURCE: The Gale Group, *Encyclopedia of Associations*, 2003.

corporations vary from state to state, but generally states give tax breaks and exemptions to nonprofit corporations that are organized and operated exclusively for either a religious, charitable, scientific, public safety, literary, or educational purpose, or for the purpose of fostering international sports or preventing cruelty to children or animals. Nonprofit organizations may charge money for their services, and contributions to tax-exempt nonprofit organizations are tax deductible. The INTERNAL REVENUE SERVICE must approve the tax-exempt status of all nonprofit organizations except churches.

A vast number of organizations qualify for nonprofit status under the various definitions. Nonprofit organizations include churches, soup kitchens, charities, political associations, business leagues, fraternities, sororities, sports leagues, COLLEGES AND UNIVERSITIES, hospitals, museums, television stations, symphonies, and public interest law firms.

A nonprofit corporation with a public purpose is just one organization that qualifies for tax-exempt status. Under Section 501 of the INTERNAL REVENUE CODE (26 U.S.C.A. § 501), more than two dozen different categories of income-producing but not-for-profit organizations are exempt from federal income taxes. These other tax-exempt organizations include credit unions, civic leagues, recreational clubs, fraternal orders and societies, labor, agricultural, and horticultural organizations, small insurance companies, and organizations of past or present members of the armed forces of the United States.

The number of nonprofit corporations in the United States continued to increase into the twenty-first century. Although nonprofit corporations cannot produce dividends for investors, they provide income for the employees, and they foster work that benefits the public.

The activities of nonprofit corporations are regulated more strictly than the activities of other corporations. Nonprofit corporations cannot contribute to political campaigns, and they cannot engage in a substantial amount of legislative LOBBYING.

FURTHER READINGS

Barrett, David W. 1996. "A Call for More Lenient Director Liability Standards for Small, Charitable Nonprofit Corporations." *Indiana Law Journal* 71 (fall).

Hammack, David C., ed. 1998. *Making the Nonprofit Sector in the United States.* Bloomington: Indiana Univ. Press.

Ott, J. Steven, ed. 2001. *Understanding Nonprofit Organizations: Governance, Leadership, and Management.* Boulder, Colo.: Westview Press.

NONSUIT

A broad term for any of several ways to terminate a legal action without an actual determination of the controversy on the merits.

For instance, a *judgment of nonsuit* may be granted against a plaintiff who either fails to pursue, or abandons, the action.

NONSUPPORT

The failure of one individual to provide financial maintenance for another individual in spite of a legal obligation to do so.

Nonsupport of a spouse or child is a crime in some states and a ground for DIVORCE in certain jurisdictions.

CROSS-REFERENCES

Child Support.

❖ NORRIS, GEORGE WILLIAM

George William Norris was born July 11, 1861, in Sandusky County, Ohio. He graduated from Indiana Normal College in 1881 and pursued a career in law and politics.

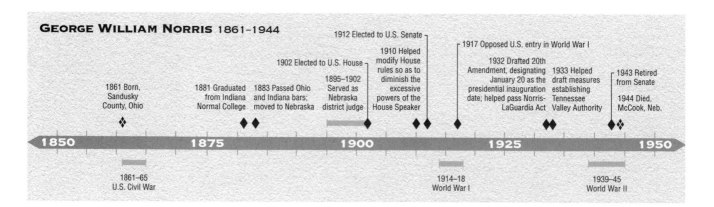

GEORGE WILLIAM NORRIS 1861–1944

1861 Born, Sandusky County, Ohio

1881 Graduated from Indiana Normal College

1883 Passed Ohio and Indiana bars; moved to Nebraska

1895–1902 Served as Nebraska district judge

1902 Elected to U.S. House

1910 Helped modify House rules so as to diminish the excessive powers of the House Speaker

1912 Elected to U.S. Senate

1917 Opposed U.S. entry in World War I

1932 Drafted 20th Amendment, designating January 20 as the presidential inauguration date; helped pass Norris-LaGuardia Act

1933 Helped draft measures establishing Tennessee Valley Authority

1943 Retired from Senate

1944 Died, McCook, Neb.

1850   1875   1900   1925   1950

1861–65 U.S. Civil War

1914–18 World War I

1939–45 World War II

George W. Norris. LIBRARY OF CONGRESS

After admission to the Ohio and Indiana bars in 1883, Norris established a law practice in Nebraska, where he also served as prosecuting attorney. He presided as a Nebraska district court judge from 1895 to 1902.

In 1903, Norris was elected to the U.S. House of Representatives. In 1910, he was instrumental in modifying the House rules so as to diminish the excessive powers of House Speaker Joseph Gurney Cannon.

In 1913, Norris was elected to the Senate, where he would serve for the next 30 years. He opposed the entry of the United States into WORLD WAR I but generally supported the policies of President FRANKLIN DELANO ROO- SEVELT. During Roosevelt's administrations, Norris was involved in several important activi- ties. In 1932, he drafted the TWENTIETH AMEND- MENT to the Constitution, which designated January 20 as the date of a presidential inaugu- ration instead of the traditional March 4, thus eliminating the need for a "lame duck" congres- sional session. During that same year, he was instrumental in the passage of the NORRIS- LAGUARDIA ACT (29 U.S.C.A. § 101 et seq.), which restricted the use of injunctions in labor disagreements. He also helped to draft measures for the establishment of the TENNESSEE VALLEY

AUTHORITY in 1933 and advocated programs for farm relief.

Norris died September 2, 1944, in McCook, Nebraska.

FURTHER READINGS

Norris, George William. 1992. *Fighting Liberal: The Autobi- ography of George W. Norris.* Reprint. Lincoln: Univ. of Nebraska Press.

NORRIS-LAGUARDIA ACT

The Norris-LaGuardia Act (29 U.S.C.A. § 101 et seq.) is one of the initial federal LABOR LAWS in favor of organized labor. It was enacted in 1932 to provide that contracts that limit an employee's right to join a LABOR UNION are unlawful. Such contracts are commonly known as YELLOW DOG CONTRACTS. Initially the law was known as the anti-injunction act since its numerous restrictions had the effect of stopping any federal court from issuing an INJUNCTION to end a labor dispute. In one part of the act, for example, there is a provision that an injunction prohibiting a strike cannot be issued unless the local police are either unwilling or unable to prevent damage or violence.

CROSS-REFERENCES

Labor Law.

NORTH AMERICAN FREE TRADE AGREEMENT

The North American Free Trade Agreement (NAFTA) was made between the United States, Canada, and Mexico, and took effect January 1, 1994. Its purpose is to increase the efficiency and fairness of trade among the three nations.

At the heart of NAFTA is a simple goal: the elimination of tariffs—the taxes each nation imposes on the others' imports—and other bureaucratic and legal barriers to trade. In addi- tion to its central terms, the massive, highly detailed agreement also includes so-called side agreements intended to ensure that each nation enforces its own labor and environmental laws. The bulk of its regulations are to be phased in over the course of 15 years.

The impetus for NAFTA developed in the 1980s. Its roots lie in the United States-Canada Free Trade Agreement of 1988—implemented by the United States-Canada Free Trade Agreement Implementation Act (19 U.S.C.A. § 2112 note [Supp. 1993])—which, by the mid-1990s, had already eliminated most trade barriers between the United States and Canada. With the world gradually becoming divided into large regional trading blocs where goods and services move freely, as in the European Union, NAFTA's supporters saw the inclusion of Mexico as necessary for North America to compete internationally.

In the United States, debate over NAFTA threatened to derail it. Proponents saw economic benefits for all three nations in the agreement. But opponents concentrated their attack on the implications for the relationship between the United States and Mexico. They feared several potential outcomes if NAFTA were signed: the loss of U.S. jobs, damage to the environment as a result of economic growth in Mexico, and the likelihood that U.S. safety regulations would be challenged as barriers to free trade.

In 1993, a coalition of consumer and environmental groups brought suit in an attempt to block congressional consideration of the agreement. In *Public Citizen v. United States Trade Representative*, 5 F.3d 549 (D.C. Cir. 1993), the coalition argued that the administration of President BILL CLINTON had failed to comply with the NATIONAL ENVIRONMENTAL POLICY ACT (42 U.S.C.A. §§ 4321 et seq. [1977]), which requires all federal agencies to submit environmental impact statements for all legislation or actions that affect the environment. The suit failed when a federal appellate court ruled that it had no authority to review the president's actions.

In response to anti-NAFTA criticisms, the White House negotiated three side agreements that were signed on September 14, 1993. The side agreements attempted to ensure that the three countries comply with their own labor and

environmental laws; established fines and limited trade sanctions for violations; and called for consultations by the members if increases in imports from one country appeared to be having a devastating effect on an industry in one of the other countries. Two months later NAFTA won congressional approval. The House of Representatives narrowly passed the implementing legislation (North American Free Trade Implementation Act [19 U.S.C.A. §§ 3314 et seq., Pub. L. No. 103-182, 107 Stat. 2057]), and the Senate also passed it.

NAFTA specifies a timetable for its changes. When the agreement went into effect on January 1, 1994, the United States eliminated all tariffs on 60 percent of imports from Mexico that previously were subject to tariffs. On January 1, 2003, more U.S. tariffs on Mexico's imports were removed, and 92 percent of previously taxed Mexican goods were able to enter the United States without tariffs. Finally, on January 1, 2008, all remaining tariffs on the three countries' goods will be eliminated. Other barriers were removed beginning January 1, 2000. For instance, U.S. banks, which had traditionally been shut out of Mexico, became free to take over as much as 15 percent of the Mexican financial market.

Investor Protection Provisions Under NAFTA

One of the more controversial provisions in NAFTA (Chapter 11) involves the "investor-to-state" dispute resolution process. This provision provides a vehicle and a forum for corporations and other companies to sue governments directly for what is called "regulatory expropriation," which is similar to EMINENT DOMAIN under domestic law. A company may allege regulatory EXPROPRIATION in such instances as the actual taking of property by a country through condemnation, or constructive taking by way of laws or regulations that negatively affect the commercial value of a property. In order for a company to bring suit under this provision, it need only show that it is an "investor party."

In *Metalclad Corp. v. Mexico*, a special NAFTA dispute resolutions panel awarded U.S. corporation Metalclad $16.7 million in damages under this provision. In response, Mexico filed an appeal. The decision was then reviewed by a neutral Canadian court, the Supreme Court of the Province of British Columbia, which upheld the decision, but slightly reduced the damages to

President Bill Clinton signs a NAFTA side agreement on September 14, 1993. NAFTA won congressional approval two months later.
AP/WIDE WORLD PHOTOS

$15 million. Both parties withdrew their appeals in 2001.

Metalclad, a U.S. waste-disposal company, requested the creation of the special NAFTA tribunal in 1997, after a local Mexican government condemned property that Metalclad owned. The property in question was a closed toxic-waste dumping site, which Metalclad had purchased, and which the company intended to clean up and reopen. After it purchased the site, Metalclad successfully secured permits for the $20 million project from Mexican federal authorities, including federal environmental agencies, but it had not coordinated with local authorities. Local and state authorities refused to issue permits to Metalclad, claiming that the site was part of a 600,000-acre protected environmental reserve.

Metalclad complained to NAFTA officials, charging that the Mexican government's actions constituted expropriation. Mexico countered that Metalclad had started construction without waiting for all levels of approval. In particular, what angered Mexican authorities was that Metalclad had bypassed local jurisdictional forums and gone directly to NAFTA, claiming $90 million in damages and lost profits. The Canadian court that reviewed the appeal found that the original NAFTA panel, meeting behind closed doors in Washington, had interpreted the NAFTA Chapter 11 investor protection clause too broadly. It disagreed with the panel's decision that federal, state, and local governments in Mexico had issued a series of contradictory declarations to Metalclad, which violated NAFTA's guarantee of clear and transparent rules to protect investors.

By 2001, at least nine companies had invoked NAFTA's investor protection clause to file multimillion-dollar damage claims against the three member countries of NAFTA. Many of them alleged trade-restrictive practices involving environmental regulations. Canada's Methanex Corporation filed a claim against the state of California, charging that the state's ban on the gasoline additive MTBE resulted in company losses of more than $1 billion. Conversely, the U.S.-based Ethyl Corporation was reimbursed $13 million in damages for Canada's restrictions on the importation of the gasoline additive MMT. Another U.S. company, S. D. Myers, sought $20 million in damages against Canada for its ban on importing PCB chemicals.

FURTHER READINGS

Hufbauer, Gary Clyde, et al. 2000. *NAFTA and the Environment: Seven Years Later.* Washington, D.C.: Institute for International Economics.

NAFTA Handbook. 2002. Buffalo, N.Y.: W. S. Hein.

CROSS-REFERENCES

Canada and the United States; Mexico and the United States.

NORTH ATLANTIC TREATY ORGANIZATION

The North Atlantic Treaty Organization (NATO) is a collective security group that was established by the North Atlantic Treaty (34 U.N.T.S. 243) in 1949 to block the threat of military aggression in Europe by the Soviet Union. NATO united Western Europe and North America in a commitment of mutual security and collective SELF-DEFENSE. Its 19 members (as of early 2004)—Belgium, Canada, the Czech Republic, Denmark, France, Germany, Greece, Hungary, Iceland, Italy, Luxembourg, the Netherlands, Norway, Portugal, Spain, Turkey, the United Kingdom, and the United States— have used NATO as a framework for cooperation in military, political, economic, and social matters.

NATO's military forces are organized into three main commands: the Atlantic Command, the Channel Command, and the Allied Command Europe. During peacetime, the three commands plan the defense of their areas and oversee and exercise the forces of member nations. The supreme Allied commander in Europe directs these units. Every supreme Allied commander through 1997 has been a U.S. general.

NATO established the North Atlantic Council, a nonmilitary policy group, in the 1950s. It is composed of permanent delegates from all member nations and is headed by a secretary-general. It is responsible for general policy, budget issues, and administrative actions. The Military Committee, consisting of the chiefs of staff of the member nations' armed forces, meets twice a year to define military policies and offer advice to the council.

The North Atlantic Treaty calls for the peaceful resolution of disputes, but article 5 pledges the use of the member nations' forces for collective self-defense. During the 1950s Western Europe was concerned about Soviet aggression. Though U.S. troops had been stationed in Europe since the end of WORLD WAR II,

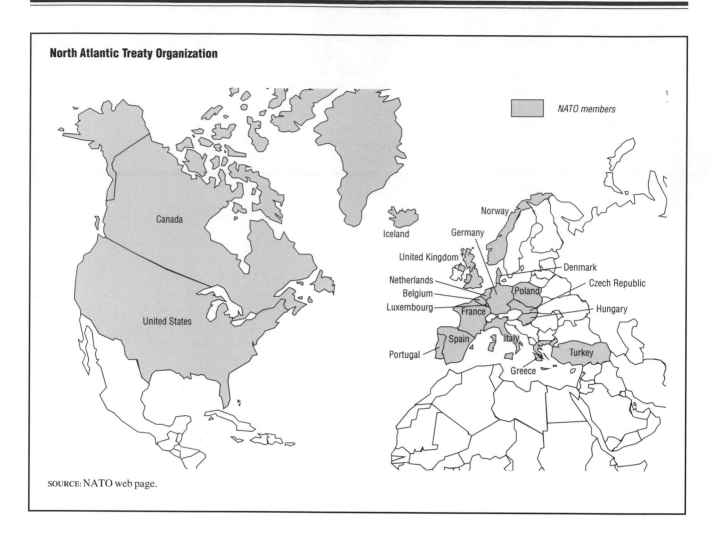

North Atlantic Treaty Organization

NATO members

Canada

United States

Iceland

Norway

Germany

United Kingdom

Netherlands

Belgium

Luxembourg

France

Poland

Denmark

Czech Republic

Hungary

Spain

Italy

Portugal

Turkey

Greece

SOURCE: NATO web page.

the United States and European nations did not have the resources to match the Soviet Army soldier for soldier. Instead the United States stated that it would use NUCLEAR WEAPONS against Soviet aggression in Europe.

In the 1960s the alliance was tested. President Charles de Gaulle of France complained about U.S. domination and control of NATO. In 1966 France expelled NATO troops from its soil and removed its troops from NATO command, but it remained a member of the organization. This action led to the relocation of NATO headquarters from Paris to Brussels.

With the collapse of COMMUNISM in Eastern Europe and in the Soviet Union and with the reunification of Germany, NATO underwent a reassessment period. As of 2003, 100,000 U.S. troops remain stationed in Europe, with another 10,000 troops stationed in Bosnia and Kosovo. In fact, the U.S. maintains the most powerful military force in Europe. Despite this situation, questions persist about the need for

NATO in a post-Cold-War world, with critics calling for Europe to shoulder more of its own defense burden.

Despite the criticism, few U.S. leaders have expressed the desire to dismantle NATO. Instead, leaders appear to be seeking a new mission for the organization. Some have suggested that the United States retain a foothold in Europe to insure political stability. Others urge using NATO as a tool to defend western interests outside Europe. Then, too, since September 11, 2001, NATO has taken on an additional role in the "War on Terrorism." As part of the expanded membership and roles envisioned for NATO, the group has opened its membership to former Communist bloc countries of Eastern Europe. Russian leaders have objected to this idea, seeing it as an attempt to end a Russian sphere of influence that has existed for 50 years. In addition, nearly a year after U.S. coalition troops ousted the Taliban, 5,500 NATO troops were sent to Afghanistan to take over peace-keeping duties.

This was the first time that NATO has mobilized a military force outside Europe.

This proposed expansion was met with hostility by Russia. In 1997, Russia entered into an agreement with NATO in which Russia itself accepted a small role in the alliance. This arrangement was an attempt to further thaw relations between Russia and the West. It also helped facilitate former Soviet bloc nations in joining the Western alliance. NATO formally expanded in 1999, when Poland, Hungary, and the Czech Republic joined. That expansion was approved only after long, contentious debate in the U.S. Senate and elsewhere.

In 2002, NATO entered into another new security agreement with Russia that further eased the entry of additional former Warsaw Pact countries into NATO. Under the new arrangement, Russia was given more authority in the new body than in the 1997 informal arrangement set up to nudge Moscow closer to the West. Even so, Russia's future involvement was expected to remain limited to certain areas, including crisis management, peacekeeping, and such military areas as air defense, search-and-rescue operations, and joint exercises.

On March 26, 2003, at NATO Headquarters, a special meeting of the North Atlantic Council was held for the signing of the Protocols of Accession. This ceremony marked the official invitation for joining NATO that was extended to seven countries: Bulgaria, Estonia, Latvia, Lithuania, Romania, Slovakia, and Slovenia. The seven countries were invited to join the Alliance at the NATO Summit in Prague in November 2002. The Protocols of Accession are amendments to the North Atlantic Treaty. When signed and ratified by the 19 NATO member countries, the new agreement will permit the invited countries to become parties to the treaty and members of NATO. From December 2002 to March 2003, a series of meetings were held between NATO and the individual invitees to discuss and formally confirm their interest, willingness, and ability to meet the political, legal, and military commitments of NATO membership.

FURTHER READINGS

Assenova, Margarita. 2003. *The Debate on NATO's Evolution.* Washington, D.C.: CSIS Press.

Duignan, Peter. 2000. *NATO: Its Past, Present, and Future.* Stanford, Calif.: Hoover Institution Press.

North Atlantic Treaty Organization. Available online at <www.nato.int> (accessed August 1, 2003).

Schmidt, Gustav, ed. 2001. *A History of NATO: The First Fifty Years.* New York: Palgrave.

CROSS-REFERENCES

Cold War; Communism.

NORTH PACIFIC FISHERIES CONVENTION, 1952

In the 1952 International Convention for the High Seas Fisheries of the North Pacific Ocean, Canada, Japan, and the United States joined together to establish cooperative measures for the conservation of the fishery stock of the North Pacific. The tripartite negotiations resulted in the creation of the International North Pacific Fisheries Commission, which, in addition to its duty to gather and compile information, is responsible for recommending changes in any conservation measures already in place. In limited situations, conservation measures may entail abstention from harvesting some stocks of fish.

CROSS-REFERENCES

Fish and Fishing.

NORTHWEST ATLANTIC FISHERIES CONVENTION, 1949

The Northwest Atlantic Fisheries Convention was held in Washington, D.C., in 1949. Its purpose was to conserve the fishery resources of the North Atlantic. The convention established the International Commission for Northwest Atlantic Fisheries.

CROSS-REFERENCES

Fish and Fishing.

NORTHWEST ORDINANCE

The Northwest Ordinance, officially known as the Ordinance of 1787, created the Northwest Territory, organized its governing structure, and established the procedures by which territories were admitted as states to the Union. It was derived from a proposal by THOMAS JEFFERSON concerning the formation of states from the territory acquired as a result of the Revolutionary War. The territory stretched from the Ohio River to the Mississippi River to the area around the Great Lakes and encompassed what is today Ohio, Indiana, Illinois, Michigan, Wisconsin, and part of Minnesota. The reaction to Jefferson's proposal was mixed, and it was only when the Ohio Company of Associates expressed interest in purchasing the land that Congress took action.

The ordinance, passed by Congress in July 1787, was significant in providing a framework for the admission of territories into the Union as states. A government composed of a governor, a secretary, and three judges appointed by Congress was established in the region north of the Ohio River. When the population of the territory reached 5,000, the inhabitants were authorized to elect a legislature and to be represented in the House of Representatives by a nonvoting member. When a designated area of the territory had 60,000 residents, that area could seek to become a state by complying with the requirements of the ordinance. Congress required that the territory be divided into at least three but not more than five states. Five states were eventually carved out of the territory.

Aside from the provisions concerning statehood, the Northwest Ordinance had two distinct prohibitions. There was to be no SLAVERY within the boundaries of the territory, and no law could be enacted that would impair a contract.

The Northwest Ordinance was important because it provided the foundation for the creation of later territories within the Union and established the process by which territories became states.

FURTHER READINGS

Williams, Frederick D., ed. 1989. *The Northwest Ordinance: Essays on Its Formulation, Provisions, and Legacy.* East Lansing: Michigan State Univ. Press.

Onuf, Peter S. 1987. *Statehood and Union: A History of the Northwest Ordinance.* Bloomington: Indiana Univ. Press.

CROSS-REFERENCES

Territories of the United States.

❖ NORTON, ELEANOR HOLMES

Eleanor Holmes Norton is a politician, lawyer, educator, and CIVIL RIGHTS activist. As the District of Columbia's delegate to the U.S. Congress, she expanded the district's power over its own affairs.

Norton, the eldest of three daughters, was born to Coleman Holmes and Vela Holmes on June 13, 1937, in Washington, D.C. Her father was a government employee in the District of Columbia, and her mother was a schoolteacher. Norton grew up in the segregated Washington, D.C., of the 1940s and 1950s and was a member of the last segregated class at Dunbar High School. Norton attended Antioch College, where she participated in many civil rights protests, and she graduated from Yale Law School.

In 1965, Norton became an attorney with the AMERICAN CIVIL LIBERTIES UNION (ACLU), seeking to defend the freedoms of speech, press, and assembly. The clients she represented were not always those she had imagined. Among them were former Alabama governor GEORGE WALLACE, an avowed segregationist, who had been denied a permit to speak at New York City's Shea Stadium, and a group of white supremacists who had been barred from holding a rally. The white supremacists' suit eventually went to the U.S. Supreme Court, where Norton argued it and won (*Carroll v. President of Princess Anne*, 393 U.S. 175, 89 S. Ct. 347, 21 L. Ed. 2d 325 [1968]).

In 1970, Norton became head of the New York City Commission on Human Rights. In 1977, President JIMMY CARTER appointed her to run the federal EQUAL EMPLOYMENT OPPORTUNITY COMMISSION (EEOC), which was facing a backlog of nearly 100,000 unsettled AFFIRMATIVE ACTION and discrimination complaints. At the EEOC, Norton initiated a system known as "rapid charge processing," which provided for informal settlement procedures. By late 1980, the backlog had dropped to 32,000 complaints. The National Association for the Advancement of Colored People (NAACP) criticized the agency's emphasis on settling individual complaints rather than attacking broad patterns of discrimination. But Norton argued that only by wiping out the backlog could the EEOC get to these broader issues. By the time she left the agency, it was taking on more sweeping investigations, antidiscrimination guidelines for employers were in place, and the Carter administration was enforcing workplace laws such as the EQUAL PAY ACT OF 1963 (29 U.S.C.A. 206) and the Age Discrimination in Employment Act of 1967 (29 U.S.C.A. 621).

Following Carter's defeat in 1980, Norton moved on to the Urban Institute. In 1982, she joined the law faculty at Georgetown University Law Center, where she wrote widely on civil rights and education issues. In 1990, Norton was elected the nonvoting D.C. delegate in the U.S. House of Representatives. During her first term, she helped the district government to obtain $300 million in new federal aid and a guarantee of steady increases in future aid. She secured seats on three House committees that greatly affect the district's economy, and she was the only freshman legislator to be invited on a congressional fact-finding mission to the Middle East following the Persian Gulf War.

Norton also sought to increase the power of the D.C. delegate position. The district's delegate to Congress is prohibited by the U.S. Constitution from becoming a full member of the House of Representatives, and had been allowed to vote only in legislative committees. Norton argued that because she could vote in other committees, she should also be allowed to vote in the committee of the whole, where most of the business of the full House is conducted. In February 1993, the House granted Norton and the representatives of four U.S. territories—Puerto Rico, Guam, the U.S. Virgin Islands, and American Samoa—a limited vote in the committee of the whole. The voting limitations included a provision that any time the delegates provided a margin of victory for legislation, a second vote would be held, from which the delegates would be excluded. Despite these restrictions, House Republicans filed suit in federal district court, asking that the delegates' right to vote be taken away. In March 1993, U.S. district judge Harold Greene rejected the challenge (*Michel v. Anderson*, 817 F. Supp. 126 [D.D.C.]). The Republicans then appealed the decision to the U.S. Court of Appeals for the District of Columbia Circuit, which upheld the lower court (14 F. 3d 623 [D.C. Cir. 1994]). Norton and the four territorial representatives retained their

Eleanor H. Norton.
JACQUES M. CHENET/CORBIS

voting privileges until January 1995, when a new House took them away.

Norton's efforts on behalf of the District of Columbia extended outside the House of Representatives. Traditionally, the senior senator from each state, if a member of the president's party, recommends to the president candidates for federal judgeships and U.S. attorney positions. Because the district has no senators, the president alone has made these appointments for it.

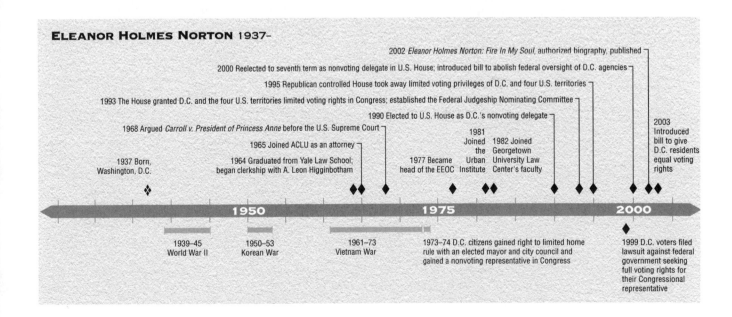

ELEANOR HOLMES NORTON 1937–

2002 *Eleanor Holmes Norton: Fire In My Soul*, authorized biography, published

2000 Reelected to seventh term as nonvoting delegate in U.S. House; introduced bill to abolish federal oversight of D.C. agencies

1995 Republican controlled House took away limited voting privileges of D.C. and four U.S. territories

1993 The House granted D.C. and the four U.S. territories limited voting rights in Congress; established the Federal Judgeship Nominating Committee

1990 Elected to U.S. House as D.C.'s nonvoting delegate

1968 Argued *Carroll v. President of Princess Anne* before the U.S. Supreme Court

1965 Joined ACLU as an attorney

1964 Graduated from Yale Law School; began clerkship with A. Leon Higginbotham

1981 Joined the Urban Institute

1982 Joined Georgetown University Law Center's faculty

1977 Became head of the EEOC

2003 Introduced bill to give D.C. residents equal voting rights

1937 Born, Washington, D.C.

1950

1975

2000

1939–45 World War II

1950–53 Korean War

1961–73 Vietnam War

1973–74 D.C. citizens gained right to limited home rule with an elected mayor and city council and gained a nonvoting representative in Congress

1999 D.C. voters filed lawsuit against federal government seeking full voting rights for their Congressional representative

In 1993, Norton convinced President BILL CLINTON to give her the advisory powers reserved for senators and to allow her to nominate candidates for a U.S. attorney position and five federal judgeships, becoming the first district congressional delegate to do so. Norton established the Federal Judicial Nominating Commission, composed of members from the district, to forward recommendations to her. All five of the judges Norton ultimately recommended to the president had been active in D.C. legal circles, and four of them lived in the district.

Norton also continued her predecessors' efforts to obtain statehood for the district. After a three-year effort to bring the issue to the House floor, the measure failed by a vote of 277–153. But Norton said that she would continue her efforts and that she would put new emphasis on gaining support for legislation that would expand the district's limited home rule. Norton also worked for increased federal contributions to the city's PENSION system, for an end to congressional review of the city's budget, and for the right of D.C. residents to choose local judges.

In 2003, Norton was serving her seventh term as the Congresswoman for the District of Columbia. She was a member of subcommittees on the House Committee on Government Reform and the House Transportation and Infrastructure Committee, where she has a full vote. She has served as Democratic chair of the Women's Caucus and has served in the Democratic House leadership group. She continues to fight for civil rights and human rights and to advocate strongly for full congressional voting representation for District of Columbia citizens.

Norton has served on numerous boards including the Rockefeller Foundation and the Board of Governors of the D.C. Bar Association. She has received more than 50 honorary degrees.

FURTHER READINGS

"Eleanor Holmes Norton." House of Representatives Website. Available online at <www.norton.house.gov> (accessed April 21, 2003).

Lester, Joan Steinau. 2003. *Fire In My Soul.* New York: Atria Books.

CROSS-REFERENCES

District of Columbia.

NOTARY PUBLIC

A public official whose main powers include administering oaths and attesting to signatures, *both important and effective ways to minimize* FRAUD *in legal documents.*

The origin of notaries public can be traced to ancient Rome, where a notarius was held in high regard as legal counsel. During that era only the few people who knew how to write were qualified to serve as a notarius. A notarius wrote legal documents, including contracts and wills, and retained them for safekeeping. A small fee was charged for those services, a tradition that continued to modern times.

As colonists settled in the New World, most transactions that required an oath or signature attestation were handled in the courts. During that period the few notaries who existed were appointed or elected in a manner similar to the election or appointment of judges. However, as trade with Europe began, the demand for notaries increased because of the large number of bills of exchange that needed to be witnessed. The authority to appoint notaries was transferred to the states, where the SECRETARY OF STATE (or another nonjudicial office) usually acted as the appointer.

In 1983 the Commission on Uniform State Laws passed the Uniform Law on Notarial Acts (14 U.L.A. 125), which covered nearly all aspects of the office of notary public, from the definition of duties to appointment policies. As of the early 2000s, most states use this model law as a basis for their own notary public statutes. These laws vary from state to state, and the amount of power that a state gives to notaries can depend on its history. For example, Louisiana was a French possession and used a civil code rather than a COMMON LAW. It gives its notaries broad powers—almost equal to those of a JUSTICE OF THE PEACE. In Louisiana notaries' powers include making "inventories, appraisements, and partitions; . . . all contracts and instruments of writing; [and holding] family meetings and meetings of creditors . . ." (La. Rev. Stat. Ann. § 35:2 [1996]).

California also gives notaries additional powers, allowing them to "demand acceptance and payment of foreign and inland bills of exchange, or promissory notes, to protest them for nonacceptance and nonpayment" (Cal. Gov't. Code § 8205 [West 1997]).

In some cases the notary responsible for a transaction has an invalid commission because of a technicality. If the notary already witnessed and completed the transaction before becoming aware of the problem, the transaction is still considered valid.

"ON BEHALF OF THE TAXPAYING CITIZENS I REPRESENT, I DEEPLY REGRET THE WITHDRAWAL OF THE VOTE I WON ON THE HOUSE FLOOR JUST TWO YEARS AGO."
—ELEANOR NORTON

Notaries public have two main duties that remain consistent from state to state. Perhaps the most important duty of a notary public is attesting to signatures on documents. This duty is important because it aids in minimizing fraud; signature attestation must be done with the notary and the signatory in a face-to-face setting.

The process of notarizing a signature is simple. The person who wants his or her signature notarized must present sufficient evidence to prove his or her identity and then sign the necessary document with the notary as a witness to the signing. The notary completes the process by stamping or sealing, dating, and signing the document. This face-to-face procedure helps ensure the authenticity of the signature.

A notary public may also administer oaths in depositions or other situations. Even though this type of oath may not take place in court, the witness can still be held accountable and be punished for perjury.

In Ohio a notary can also hold an affiant in CONTEMPT if he or she is a reluctant witness. In the U.S. Supreme Court case of *Bevan v. Krieger,* 289 U.S. 459, 53 S. Ct. 661, 77 L. Ed. 1316 (1933), a notary public held a witness in contempt because he refused to comply with the requirements of the subpoena he was served. The court ruled that the notary was acting within his powers when he held the witness in contempt.

To become a notary, a candidate must complete several steps. A candidate must fill out an application and submit it to the appropriate government agency, usually the respective state's department of the secretary of state or the U.S. DEPARTMENT OF STATE. As part of the application procedure, the candidate must also take an oath of office and submit a bond. The purpose of the bond is to offer a small amount of monetary insurance in case the notary is sued. On average, notarial bonds are less than $5,000. If a notary is sued for more money than the amount of the bond, the notary is still personally liable for the difference between the bond and the sum awarded to the plaintiff.

Once an application is approved and the notary is commissioned, the notary must register in the county in which he or she resides and pay a registration fee. The commission itself has a time limit, which can range from two to ten years, with an average limit of four years. To renew the commission, the notary must repeat the application process.

Most states require that a notary be at least 18 years old and be able to read and write English. However, the latter requirement may change in the future because of the increasing number of transactions that take place in languages other than English. Some states require potential notaries to pass an exam as part of the application process. Others may require a notary to keep a detailed journal of the transactions he or she officiates.

Until 1984 many states required that a notary be a U.S. citizen or a resident of the state in which he or she would serve as a notary, or both. However, in *Bernal v. Fainter,* 467 U.S. 216, 104 S. Ct. 2312, 81 L. Ed. 2d 175 (1984), the U.S. Supreme Court ruled that requiring a notary to be a U.S. citizen was unconstitutional under the Fourteenth Amendment's EQUAL PROTECTION CLAUSE. Therefore, even though the plaintiff in the case was actually a Mexican native and longtime resident alien, it was unconstitutional to deny him a notarial commission simply because he was not a U.S. citizen. Despite this ruling many states have kept the U.S. citizenship requirement in their statutes.

Another challenge to the procedure for becoming a notary occurred in the case of *Torasco v. Watkins,* 367 U.S. 488, 81 S. Ct. 1680, 6 L. Ed. 2d 982 (1961). In this case, an atheist objected to Maryland's notary public oath, which required him to acknowledge a belief in God. When his notary commission was denied, he sued. The case went to the U.S. Supreme Court, which ruled that, under both the Maryland Constitution and the U.S. Constitution, it was "repugnant" for an oath to require a belief in God.

Notaries can only be held liable for actions they take while performing the notary function. For example, although notaries are responsible for attesting to the validity of a signature, they are not responsible for the validity of the document. It is not considered MALPRACTICE for a notary to attest to a signature on a document that he or she knows is invalid.

A notary must "act as a reasonably prudent notary would act in the same situation." In an action against a notary, the BURDEN OF PROOF is on the plaintiff to show that the notary acted negligently. If the plaintiff meets this burden, the notary can be held personally liable for damages to all parties involved, including third parties.

FURTHER READINGS

Anderson, John C., and Michael L. Closen. 1999. "A Proposed Code of Ethics for Employers and Customers of Notaries: A Companion to the Notary Public Code of Professional Responsibility." *John Marshall Law Review* 32 (summer).

Closen, Michael L., and G. Grant Dixon III. 1992. "Notaries Public from the Time of the Roman Empire to the U.S. Today and Tomorrow." *North Dakota Law Review* 68.

Kussmaul, Wes. 2001. *The Future Needs You: The Notary Public in the Digital Age.* Waltham, Mass.: PKI Press.

Rothman, Raymond C. 1987. *Notary Public: Practices and Glossary.* Chatsworth, Calif.: National Notary Association.

Van Alstyne, Peter J. 1998. *Notary Law, Procedures & Ethics: A Complete Reference on Notarial Laws and Procedures in America.* Salt Lake City, Utah: Notary Law Institute.

CROSS-REFERENCES

Fraud; Signature.

NOTE

To take notice of. A COMMERCIAL PAPER *that contains an express and absolute promise by the maker to pay to a specific individual, to order, or to bearer a definite sum of money on demand or at a specifically designated time.*

NOTES OF DECISIONS

Annotations; concise summaries and references to the printed decisions of cases that are designed to explain particular RULES OF LAW *or applicable sections of statutes.*

NOTICE

Information; knowledge of certain facts or of a particular state of affairs. The formal receipt of papers that provide specific information.

There are various types of notice, each of which has different results. In general, notice deals with information that a party knows or should have known. In this context notice is an essential element of DUE PROCESS. Notice can also refer to commonly known facts that a court or ADMINISTRATIVE AGENCY may take into evidence.

Actual notice is information given to the party directly. The two kinds of actual notice are express notice and implied notice. An individual is deemed to have been given express notice when he or she actually hears it or reads it. Implied notice is deduced or inferred from the circumstances rather than from direct or explicit words. Courts will treat such information as though actual notice had been given.

Constructive notice is information that a court deems that an individual should have known. According to a RULE OF LAW that applies in such cases, the court will presume that a person knows the information because she could have been informed if proper diligence had been exercised. Constructive notice can be based on a legal relationship as well. For example, in the law governing partnerships, each partner is deemed to have knowledge of all the partnership business. If one partner engages in dishonest transactions, the other partners are presumed to know, regardless of whether they had actual knowledge of the transaction. The term *legal notice* is sometimes used interchangeably with constructive notice.

In certain cases involving the purchase of real property, an individual is charged with inquiry notice. When an individual wishes to purchase land, he ordinarily has the duty under the recording acts to check the title to the property to determine that the land is not subject to any encumbrances, which are claims, liens, mortgages, leases, EASEMENTS or right of ways, or unpaid taxes that have been lodged against the real property. In some situations, however, the individual must make a reasonable investigation outside of the records, such as in cases involving recorded but defective documents. This type of notice is known as inquiry notice.

Some states have notice recording statutes that govern the RECORDING OF LAND TITLES. Whereas inquiry notice deals with looking closely at documents that have been recorded, notice recording statutes state that an unrecorded conveyance of property is invalid against the title bought by a subsequent bona fide purchaser for value and without notice. This means that if John purchases a piece of land on a contract for deed from Tom and does not record the contract for deed, and if Tom resells the land to Jill, who has no notice of the prior sale, then Jill as a bona fide purchaser will prevail, and John's conveyance will be invalid.

The concept of notice is critical to the integrity of legal proceedings. Due process requires that legal action cannot be taken against anyone unless the requirements of notice and an opportunity to be heard are observed.

Legal proceedings are initiated by providing notice to the individual affected. If an individual is accused of a crime, he has a right to be notified of the charges. In addition, formal papers must be prepared to give the accused notice of the charges.

*A sample notice of
motion or objection*

Notice of Motion

Form 20A. Notice of Motion or Objection

[Caption as in Form 16A.]

NOTICE OF [MOTION TO   ] [OBJECTION TO   ]

_____ has filed papers with the court to [relief sought in motion or objection].

Your rights may be affected. You should read these papers carefully and discuss them with your attorney, if you have one in this bankruptcy case. (If you do not have an attorney, you may wish to consult one.)

If you do not want the court to [relief sought in motion or objection], or if you want the court to consider your views on the [motion] [objection], then on or before _____ , you or your attorney must:

(date)

[File with the court a written request for a hearing {or, if the court requires a written response, an answer, explaining your position} at:

_____
{address of the bankruptcy clerk's office}

If you mail your {request}{response} to the court for filing, you must mail it early enough so the court will receive it on or before the date stated above.

You must also mail a copy to:

_____
{movant's attorney's name and address}

_____
{names and addresses of others to be served}]

[Attend the hearing scheduled to be held on _____ , _____ , at
(date)   (year)

_____ a.m./p.m. in Courtroom _____ , United States Bankruptcy Court,

_____ .]
{address}

[Other steps required to oppose a motion or objection under local rule or court order.]

If you or your attorney do not take these steps, the court may decide that you do not oppose the relief sought in the motion or objection and may enter an order granting that relief.

Date: _____   Signature: _____

Name: _____

Address: _____

_____

Form B20A (Official Form 20A)
(9/97)

An individual who is being sued in a civil action must be provided with notice of the nature of the suit. State statutes prescribe the method of providing this type of notice. Courts are usually strict in requiring compliance with these laws, and ordinarily a plaintiff must put this information into a complaint that must be served upon the defendant in some legally adequate manner. The plaintiff may personally serve the complaint to the defendant. When that is not practical, the papers may be served through the mail. In some cases a court may allow, or require, service by posting or attaching the papers to the defendant's last known address or to a public place where the defendant is likely to see them. Typically, however, notice is given by publication of the papers in a local newspaper. When the defendant is not personally served, or is formally served in another state, the method of service is called substituted service.

Notice is also critical when suing a state or local government. Many states and municipalities have notice of claim provisions in their statutes and ordinances that state that, before a lawsuit is started, a notice of claim must be filed within a reasonable time, usually three to six months after the injury occurs. The notice must contain the date of injury, how it occurred, and other facts that establish that the prospective plaintiff has a viable CAUSE OF ACTION against the government. Failure to file a notice of claim within the prescribed time period prevents a plaintiff from filing a lawsuit unless exceptions to this requirement are provided by statute or ordinance.

Notice is also an important requirement in ending legal relationships. For example, a notice to quit is a written notification given either by the tenant to the landlord, or vice versa, indicating that either the tenant intends to surrender possession of the premises on a certain day or that the landlord intends to regain possession of the premises on a certain day. Many kinds of contracts require that similar notice be given to either renew or end the contractual relationship.

Notice may also refer to commonly known facts that a court or administrative agency may take into evidence during a trial or hearing. JUDICIAL NOTICE is a doctrine of evidence that allows a court to recognize and accept the existence of a commonly known fact without the need to establish its existence by the admission of evidence. Courts take judicial notice of historical events, federal, state, and international laws, business customs, and other facts that are not subject to reasonable dispute.

Administrative proceedings use the term *official notice* to describe a doctrine similar to judicial notice. A presiding administrative officer recognizes as evidence, without proof, certain kinds of facts that are not subject to reasonable dispute. Administrative agencies, unlike courts, have an explicit legislative function as well as an adjudicative function: they make rules. In rule making, agencies have wider discretion in taking official notice of law and policy, labeled *legislative facts*.

CROSS-REFERENCES

Due Process of Law; Legislative Facts; Personal Service; Recording of Land Titles; Registration of Land Titles; Service of Process; Title Search.

NOVATION

The substitution of a new contract for an old one. The new agreement extinguishes the rights and obligations that were in effect under the old agreement.

A novation ordinarily arises when a new individual assumes an obligation to pay that was incurred by the original party to the contract. It is distinguishable from the situation that occurs when another individual makes a guarantee that a debtor will pay what he or she owes to a creditor. In the case of a novation, the original debtor is totally released from the obligation, which is transferred to someone else. The nature of the transaction is dependent upon the agreement between the parties.

A novation also takes place when the original parties continue their obligation to one another, but a new agreement is substituted for the old one.

NUCLEAR NONPROLIFERATION TREATY

The Nuclear Nonproliferation Treaty (NPT), formally called the Treaty on the Nonproliferation of Nuclear Weapons, is the cornerstone of the international effort to halt the proliferation, or spread, of NUCLEAR WEAPONS (*State Department, United States Treaties and Other International Agreements,* Vol. 21, part 1 [1970], pp. 483–494). The NPT was first signed in 1968 by three nuclear powers —the United States, the Soviet Union, and the United Kingdom—and by nearly 100 states without nuclear weapons. It

A sample novation

Novation

NOVATION AGREEMENT

Agreement made _____ (date) between and among the following parties:

1. Seller: _____ (name), of _____ (address), _____ (city), _____ (county), _____ (state), referred to here as seller.

2. Buyer: _____ (name), of _____ (address), _____ (city), _____ (county), _____ (state), referred to here as buyer.

3. Party in Substitution: _____ (name), of _____ (address), _____ (city), _____ (county), _____ (state), referred to here as party in substitution.

SECTION ONE:

CONTRACT SUBJECT TO THIS AGREEMENT

This novation agreement is entered into with reference to a contract of sale entered into between seller and buyer, dated _____ _____, involving the sale of the following goods: _____ _____ .

A copy of the contract of sale, marked Exhibit _____, is attached to this agreement.

SECTION TWO:

NOVATION AGREEMENT

It is agreed by all parties in this novation agreement that party in substitution shall be substituted for _____ (buyer or seller) in the above-referenced contract of sale. Party in substitution shall acquire all the rights and become obligated to perform all the duties of

_____ (buyer or seller) that are here fully assigned and delegated to party in substitution, who undertakes full performance of

the above-referenced contract of sale in the place of _____ (buyer or seller) and makes a separate promise to faithfully and fully so perform.

SECTION THREE:

RELEASE OF BUYER OR SELLER FROM LIABILITIES

In consideration of this novation, _____ (buyer or seller) shall be relieved of any and all further obligations to perform under the above-referenced contract of sale and shall be fully relieved of further liability to any other party to this novation agreement arising out of the above-referenced contract of sale.

In witness whereof, the parties have executed this agreement at _____ (designate place of execution) the day and year first above written.

_____
Signature

_____
Signature

came into force in 1970, and by the mid 1990s it had been signed by 168 countries.

The NPT distinguishes between nuclear-weapon states and non-nuclear-weapon states. It identifies five nuclear-weapon states: China, France, the Soviet Union, the United Kingdom, and the United States.

Article II forbids non-nuclear-weapon states that are parties to the treaty to manufacture or otherwise acquire nuclear weapons or nuclear explosive devices. Article III concerns controls and inspections that are intended to prevent the diversion of nuclear energy from peaceful uses to nuclear weapons or explosive devices. These safeguards are applied only to non-nuclear-weapon states and only to peaceful nuclear activities. The treaty contains no provisions for verification of the efforts by nuclear-weapon states to prevent the proliferation of nuclear weapons.

Under the provisions of Article IV, all parties to the treaty, including non-nuclear-weapon states, may conduct nuclear research and development for peaceful purposes. In return for agreeing not to develop nuclear weapons, non-nuclear-weapon states receive two promises from nuclear-weapon states: the latter will help them to develop nuclear technology for peaceful purposes (Art. IV), and the latter will "pursue negotiations in GOOD FAITH on effective measures relating to cessation of the nuclear arms race at an early date and to nuclear disarmament" (Art. VI) (as quoted in U.S. Arms Control and Disarmament Agency 1982, 93).

Since 1975, NPT signatory countries have held a review conference every five years to discuss treaty compliance and enforcement.

North Korea has caused international concerns since 1993, with its attempts to develop a nuclear arsenal. In 1993, North Korea announced that it would withdraw from the NPT, only to rescind its withdrawal shortly thereafter. In 1994, North Korea and the United States entered into an agreement whereby the United States agreed to provide power supplies and other necessities in exchange for North Korea's promise not to pursue the development of nuclear weapons. However, in October 2002, North Korea announced that it would resume its program to develop these weapons. On January 10, 2003, it announced again that it would withdraw from the treaty, effective the following day. Although the NPT requires that nations adhere to a three-month waiting period to withdraw from the treaty, North Korea claimed that it had already done so, for it originally had announced its withdrawal in 1993. North Korea's attempts to develop nuclear weapons have brought crisis to that region, and South Korea and Japan have sought U.S. assistance to resolve the crisis through diplomacy.

FURTHER READINGS

Dekker, Guido den. 2001. *The Law of Arms Control: International Supervision and Enforcement.* Norwell, Mass.: Kluwer Law International.

Kegley, Charles W., Jr., and Eugene R. Wittkopf. 1993. *World Politics.* 4th ed. New York: St. Martin's Press.

Mandelbaum, Michael. 1995. "Lessons of the Next Nuclear War." *Foreign Affairs* (March–April).

Sheehan, Michael. 1988. *Arms Control: Theory and Practice.* Cambridge, Mass.: Blackwell.

U.S. Arms Control and Disarmament Agency. 1982. *Arms Control and Disarmament Agreements: Texts and Histories of Negotiations.*

CROSS-REFERENCES

Arms Control and Disarmament.

NUCLEAR POWER

A form of energy produced by an atomic reaction, capable of producing an alternative source of electrical power to that supplied by coal, gas, or oil.

The dropping of the atom bomb on Hiroshima, Japan, by the United States in 1945 initiated the atomic age. Nuclear energy immediately became a military weapon of terrifying magnitude. For the physicists who worked on the atom bomb, the promise of nuclear energy was not solely military. They envisioned nuclear power as a safe, clean, cheap, and abundant source of energy that would end society's dependence on fossil fuels. At the end of WORLD WAR II, leaders called for the peaceful use of nuclear energy.

Congress passed the Atomic Energy Act of 1946 (42 U.S.C.A. §§ 2011 et seq.), which shifted nuclear development from military to civilian government control. Very little development of commercial nuclear power occurred from 1946 to 1954 because the 1946 law maintained a federal government MONOPOLY over the control, use, and ownership of nuclear reactors and fuels.

Congress amended the Atomic Energy Act in 1954 (68 Stat. 919) to encourage the private commercial development of nuclear power. The act ended the federal government's monopoly over nonmilitary uses of nuclear energy and allowed private ownership of reactors under licensing procedures established by the Atomic

Energy Commission (AEC). Private power companies did not rush to build nuclear power plants because they feared the financial consequences of a nuclear accident. Congress responded by passing the Price-Anderson Act of 1957 (42 U.S.C.A. § 2210), which limited the liability of the nuclear power industry and assured compensation for the public. With the passage of the Price-Anderson Act, power companies began to build nuclear plants.

At first, nuclear power was attractive largely because the demand for electricity grew at a steady rate in the 1960s and coal-burning facilities were becoming an environmentally unacceptable alternative. The high price of oil during the mid-1970s continued to make nuclear power economically desirable and helped keep nuclear energy a prominent part of national energy plans. By the 1990s, approximately 110 nuclear plants were operating in the United States, supplying 20 percent of the nation's electricity.

A nuclear reactor produces energy through a chain reaction that splits a uranium nucleus, releasing energy in the form of heat. Fast breeder reactors, which use plutonium as fuel, generate more energy than they expend. Plutonium is not a natural element. It must be recycled from the excess uranium produced from a chain reaction. The radioactivity of plutonium is higher and its life is longer than that of any other element. Because of these characteristics, the public became concerned about the safety of its development and use.

Until 1969, the AEC did not have a formal process for evaluating the environmental impact of building nuclear power plants. In that year Congress passed the NATIONAL ENVIRONMENTAL POLICY ACT OF 1969 (42 U.S.C.A. §§ 4321–4370), which required environmental impact statements for all major federal activities. In the 1970s, the temper of nuclear regulation changed. People were no longer complacent about nuclear power safety or convinced by environmental claims made by industry and government.

This lack of public trust centered on the role of the AEC as both a promoter of nuclear technology and a regulator of the nuclear power industry. In 1974, realizing the cross purposes of promotion and safety, Congress passed the Energy Reorganization Act (42 U.S.C.A. §§ 5801–5879), which created two agencies with different missions. The NUCLEAR REGULATORY COMMISSION (NRC) is an independent agency

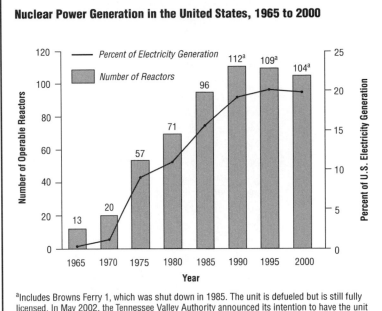

Nuclear Power Generation in the United States, 1965 to 2000

*Includes Browns Ferry 1, which was shut down in 1985. The unit is defueled but is still fully licensed. In May 2002, the Tennessee Valley Authority announced its intention to have the unit resume operation in 2007.

SOURCE: U.S. Energy Information Administration, *Annual Energy Review*.

responsible for safety and licensing. The Energy Research and Development Administration (ERDA), later absorbed into the ENERGY DEPARTMENT, is responsible for promotion and development of nuclear power. This alignment did not completely remove fundamental regulatory conflict for the NRC, because the agency is responsible both for licensing plants and for safety oversight. If the NRC is too vigorous in exercising its safety role, the resulting compliance costs act as a disincentive to invest in nuclear plants.

A nuclear facility cannot be built without a construction permit issued by the NRC. An environmental impact statement that assesses the effect the facility will have on the environment must also be filed with the ENVIRONMENTAL PROTECTION AGENCY (EPA). Once built, a nuclear plant must operate pursuant to a license from the NRC. A license requires that the facility use the lowest levels of radiation necessary to reasonably and efficiently maintain operations. The NRC also issues licenses for the use of nuclear materials, for transportation of nuclear materials, and for the export and import of nuclear materials, facilities, and components.

Nuclear power regulation is highly centralized in the federal government when nuclear safety and radiological hazards are at issue. States may address the financial capability of power companies to dispose of waste and may define state TORT liability for injuries suffered at nuclear facilities.

Public confidence in the nuclear power industry suffered a major blow in 1979 when an accident occurred at the Three Mile Island Nuclear Station near Harrisburg, Pennsylvania. No one was hurt during the accident although radioactive gases escaped through the plant's ventilating system. The accident did reveal, however, the nuclear power industry's lack of emergency preparedness. Following the incident, the NRC increased safety inspections, stepped up enforcement, required the retrofitting of systems to enhance safety, and developed emergency preparedness rules. These regulations delayed the opening of new nuclear plants during the early 1980s.

In 1986, however, the safety of nuclear power again was challenged when a nuclear reactor exploded at Chernobyl in the Ukraine. Radiation 50 times higher than that at Three Mile Island exposed people nearest the reactor, and a cloud of radioactive fallout spread to Western Europe, causing the deaths of more than 30 people. People the world over questioned the logic of using such a volatile energy source.

Nuclear power also became less attractive to energy companies in the 1980s. The problem of disposing of nuclear waste became the focal point for the industry. Congress passed the Nuclear Waste Policy Act of 1982 (42 U.S.C.A. §§ 10101-10226), which directed the Department of Energy to formally begin planning the disposal of nuclear wastes and imposed most of the costs of disposal on the industry. The escalating costs of waste disposal helped bring construction of new nuclear facilities to a stop.

The problem of what to do with nuclear waste has proved difficult to solve. Nuclear material is contained in fuel rods. When spent fuel rods and other waste products fill the storage capacity at utility plants, the plants must either expand their storage capacity or find permanent off-site storage. Developing permanent nuclear waste sites is imperative because nuclear waste continues to accumulate. In addition, more than one hundred of the nuclear power facilities must be permanently shut down between 2010 and 2025 because their equipment and infrastructure will no longer be safe. This will entail removing most radioactive elements within each plant's nuclear reactor and then razing the entire plant.

The federal government has encountered political controversy and public opposition in its attempt to identify potential permanent nuclear waste sites. Since 1986 it has been unsuccessful in finding an acceptable site. Yucca Mountain, Nevada, has been earmarked as a nuclear waste repository, against the objections of citizens of Nevada and other advocacy groups. In January 2002, Secretary of Energy Spencer Abraham sent a letter to Nevada Governor Kenny C. Guinn notifying Guinn that Abraham had recommended to President GEORGE W. BUSH the development of the Yucca Mountain site. Guinn responded that the decision was premature and that further testing was necessary. When Bush approved the development of the site, Guinn vetoed, thus sending the issue to Congress.

The House and Senate both passed resolutions in 2002 with significant majorities approving the development of the Yucca Mountain site. The Energy Department must apply for a license from the NRC in order to construct the site; the application is not expected to be filed until 2004. The state of Nevada filed lawsuits against Abraham, President Bush, the DOE, the NRC, and the Environmental Protection Agency, seeking to block the future development of this site.

The commercial prospects for nuclear energy have faded. The decommissioning of nuclear plants in the early twenty-first century will be a huge undertaking. The cost, per plant, will be more than one billion dollars. Utility customers will pay for the costs in higher utility rates, but power companies will have to devote significant amounts of time, energy, and money to complete the process.

FURTHER READINGS

"Nevada Yucca Mountain Lawsuits." Yucca Mountain: Eureka County Nuclear Waste Page. Available online at <www.yuccamountain.org/court/lawsuits.htm> (accessed August 9, 2003).

CROSS-REFERENCES

Energy Department; Environmental Law; Public Utilities; Solid Wastes, Hazardous Substances, and Toxic Pollutants.

NUCLEAR REGULATORY COMMISSION

The Nuclear Regulatory Commission (NRC) is an independent regulatory agency that oversees the civilian use of NUCLEAR POWER in the

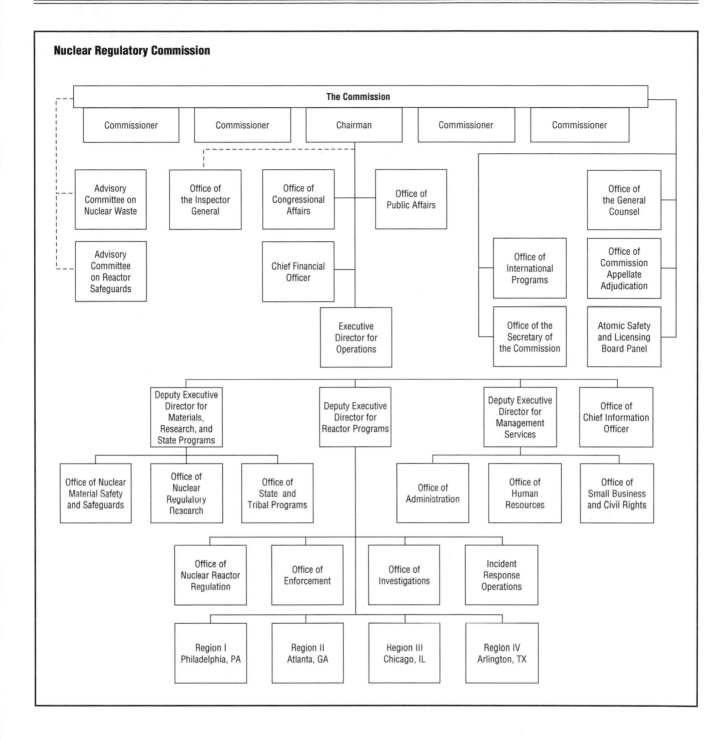

Nuclear Regulatory Commission

The Commission

Commissioner | Commissioner | Chairman | Commissioner | Commissioner

Advisory Committee on Nuclear Waste

Advisory Committee on Reactor Safeguards

Office of the Inspector General

Office of Congressional Affairs

Chief Financial Officer

Office of Public Affairs

Executive Director for Operations

Office of the General Counsel

Office of International Programs

Office of the Secretary of the Commission

Office of Commission Appellate Adjudication

Atomic Safety and Licensing Board Panel

Deputy Executive Director for Materials, Research, and State Programs

Deputy Executive Director for Reactor Programs

Deputy Executive Director for Management Services

Office of Chief Information Officer

Office of Nuclear Material Safety and Safeguards

Office of Nuclear Regulatory Research

Office of State and Tribal Programs

Office of Administration

Office of Human Resources

Office of Small Business and Civil Rights

Office of Nuclear Reactor Regulation

Office of Enforcement

Office of Investigations

Incident Response Operations

Region I Philadelphia, PA

Region II Atlanta, GA

Region III Chicago, IL

Region IV Arlington, TX

United States. It licenses and regulates the uses of nuclear energy to protect public health and safety, and the environment. The NRC's prime responsibility is to ensure that the more than 100 commercial nuclear power plants in the United States conform to its regulations. It also regulates the use of nuclear materials in the diagnosis and treatment of cancer, in sterilizing instruments, in smoke detectors, and in gauges used to detect explosives in luggage at airports.

The NRC was established under the provisions of the Energy Reorganization Act of 1974 (42 U.S.C.A. §5801) and EXECUTIVE ORDER No. 11,834 of January 15, 1975 (40 Fed. Reg. 2971). These actions dissolved the Atomic Energy Commission (AEC) and transferred the AEC's licensing and regulatory functions to the NRC. The AEC, which had both regulated and promoted nuclear power, fell out of favor because of these conflicting roles. Congress believed that the NRC, which has only a regulatory function, would better protect public health and safety, because it has no direct interest in the promotion of nuclear energy. The 1974 act also created the Energy Research and Development Administration (ERDA) to handle the promotion of nuclear energy. This agency became part of the ENERGY DEPARTMENT in 1977.

NRC headquarters are located in Rockville, Maryland. There are also four regional offices. The NRC is composed of five members, all of whom are appointed by the president. One member is designated as chairman and spokesperson. Policies and decisions of the commission are carried out by the Executive Director for Operations, who also oversees the various NRC offices, including the Office of Nuclear Reactor Regulation, the Office of Nuclear Material Safety and Safeguards, the Office of Nuclear Regulatory Research, the Office of Investigations, and the Office of Enforcement.

NRC fulfills its responsibilities through a system of licensing and regulation. The Office of Nuclear Reactor Regulation licenses the construction and operation of nuclear reactors and other nuclear facilities. It regulates site selection, design, construction, operation maintenance, and the decommissioning of facilities.

The Office of Nuclear Material Safety and Safeguards licenses and regulates the processing, handling, and transportation of nuclear materials. This office ensures the safe disposal of nuclear waste and is responsible for reviewing and assessing the safeguards against potential threats, thefts, and sabotage for all licensed facilities.

The Office of Nuclear Regulatory Research performs research to confirm reactor safety and to confirm the implementation of established safeguards and environmental protection policies. This office develops regulations, criteria, guides, standards, and codes that govern health, safety, the environment, and safeguards that pertain to all aspects of nuclear facilities.

Policies and procedures for investigating nuclear power licensees and contractors are developed by the NRC's Office of Investigations. The Office of Enforcement ensures that NRC requirements are enforced. The office has the power to give violation notices, enforce fines, and order license modification, suspension, or revocation.

In 1979, the credibility of the NRC, and the nuclear power industry in general, was questioned after an accident took place at the Three Mile Island nuclear power plant near Harrisburg, Pennsylvania. Almost half of the reactor's core melted, and radioactive steam escaped, but no major injuries were reported. NRC responded by reexamining safety requirements and imposing new regulations to correct deficiencies. It also required each nuclear plant to create a plan for evacuating the population within a ten-mile radius of the plant in the event of a reactor accident. Plant owners must work with state and local police, fire, and civil defense authorities to devise an emergency plan that is then tested and evaluated by the NRC and the FEDERAL EMERGENCY MANAGEMENT AGENCY.

Another issue of concern to the public and to the nuclear power industry is the problem of radioactive waste. The NRC has pressed Congress for a solution to this problem. As nuclear power plants age they accumulate spent nuclear fuel rods. On-site temporary storage at these facilities turned into long-term storage, which raised safety concerns with the NRC as early as the 1970s. The Nuclear Waste Policy Act of 1982 (42 U.S.C.A. §§ 10101-10226), authorized a study of possible storage sites. In 1987, Congress amended the act, directing that Yucca Mountain, Nevada, be studied as the only permanent storage site for nuclear waste. Yucca Mountain is located 90 miles northwest of Las Vegas. The law gave the state of Nevada VETO authority over approving the site, subject to a congressional override. The NRC and the Energy Department endorsed the Yucca Mountain site as geologically sound and capable of safely storing the waste for the thousands of years it will remain radioactive. However, political controversy in Congress and Nevada stalled a decision.

The nuclear power industry lobbied the Bush administration for approval of Yucca Mountain and, in 2002, the Energy Department and President GEORGE W. BUSH formally endorsed the storage site plan. The state of Nevada formally vetoed the site; Congress had 90 days to overrule the decision. In July 2002, Congress overturned the decision and authorized the spending of $69 billion to prepare Yucca Mountain to receive thousands of tons of nuclear waste currently at power plant sites around the United States.

The fear of TERRORISM played a part in the Yucca Mountain decision, as Congress expressed alarm that a terrorist might be able to steal or obtain spent radioactive material stored at power plant sites. Following the SEPTEMBER

11TH ATTACKS in 2001, the NRC launched a review of nuclear power plants to determine if there were security risks. The commission concluded that the heavy concrete construction of nuclear facilities made it highly unlikely that a Three Mile Island episode could occur if a terrorist flew a hijacked plane into a facility. However, during heightened terrorist alert periods the NATIONAL GUARD and local law enforcement agents now routinely patrol nuclear plants.

FURTHER READINGS

"History of the Civilian Radioactive Waste Management Program." Office of Civilian Radioactive Waste Management. Available online at <www.ocrwm.doe.gov> (accessed August 11, 2003).

"Nevada Yucca Mountain Lawsuits." Yucca Mountain: Eureka County Nuclear Waste Page. Available online at <www.yuccamountain.org/court/lawsuits.htm> (accessed August 9, 2003).

Nuclear Regulatory Commission. Available online at <www.nrc.gov> (accessed August 12, 2003).

U.S. Government Manual Website. Available online at <www.gpoaccess.gov/gmanual> (accessed November 10, 2003).

CROSS-REFERENCES

Environmental Law; Public Utilities; Solid Wastes, Hazardous Substances, and Toxic Pollutants.

NUCLEAR WEAPONS

Weapons of mass destruction that are powered by nuclear reaction. Types of nuclear weapons include atom bombs, hydrogen bombs, fission bombs, and fusion bombs.

The actions of countries in times of war are governed by INTERNATIONAL LAW that constantly changes with advancements in weapons technology. There is not, however, an international law that specifically addresses the use of nuclear weapons. The Geneva Conventions, in 1949, outlined rules to protect populations during armed conflict. They require distinguishing between civilians and soldiers, and prohibit indiscriminate methods of attack that are not directed at a specific military target. The conventions also prohibit weapons that cause unnecessary injury and those that cause long-term and severe environmental damage. Specific types of weapons are not mentioned. Many believe that given the extremely destructive power of nuclear weapons, they should be specifically prohibited. These critics contend that the use of nuclear weapons clearly violates international humanitarian law regarding armed conflict.

To clarify this issue, the United Nations General Assembly asked the INTERNATIONAL COURT OF JUSTICE (ICJ) for an ADVISORY OPINION regarding the legality of the threat or use of nuclear weapons. The opinion of the ICJ, handed down on July 8, 1996, is the most authoritative statement regarding the legality of nuclear weapons under international law. The ICJ concluded unanimously that the threat or use of such weapons should be consistent with existing international laws. The ICJ did not declare such weapons specifically illegal, but did state that the threat or use of nuclear weapons would generally be contrary to the rules of international law applicable in armed conflict, leaving the issue of SELF-DEFENSE open.

Advocates of nuclear disarmament contend that based on this ruling of the ICJ, the threat or use of nuclear weapons violates U.S. as well as international law. Article VI of the United States Constitution states, "all treaties made, or which shall be made, under the authority of the United States, shall be the supreme law of the land." The reasoning is that since the threat or use of nuclear weapons violates international treaties that the United States has signed and ratified (e.g., the GENEVA CONVENTION), then the threat or use of these weapons should be illegal.

Since the ICJ opinion was delivered in 1996, direct actions by the public in support of nuclear disarmament have increased. Some courts have recognized the legality of such actions. In October 1999, a Scottish judge dismissed a case against three women who had caused damage at a base, which was part of a Trident nuclear submarine defense program. The judge cited the ICJ opinion and claimed that the women were justified in their actions because they were attempting to thwart the use of illegal weapons. In June 1999, a jury in the state of Washington found four activists not guilty of blocking traffic into a Trident nuclear submarine base. The court relied on international law, including the ICJ opinion.

The one international treaty that attempts to safeguard against the threat of nuclear weapons is the NUCLEAR NON-PROLIFERATION TREATY (NPT). Under the treaty, the possession of nuclear weapons is prohibited by all states, except for the Nuclear Weapon States (NWS). The treaty defines an NWS as one that had manufactured and exploded a nuclear weapon or other nuclear explosive device prior to January 1, 1967, which limits membership to the

United States, the former Soviet Union (and its successor state, Russia), the United Kingdom, France, and China. Those few states possessing nuclear weapons are under obligation, as set forth in Article VI of the NPT, to "pursue negotiations in GOOD FAITH on effective measures relating to cessation of the nuclear arms race at an early date and to nuclear disarmament."

While the Nuclear Weapon States pledged to negotiate nuclear disarmament, the Non-Nuclear Weapon States (NNWS) pledged not to acquire nuclear weapons. As an incentive, the NNWS were promised assistance with research, production, and use of nuclear energy for peaceful purposes "without discrimination." Each NNWS also agreed to accept safeguards under the auspices of the INTERNATIONAL ATOMIC ENERGY AGENCY. These safeguards do not apply to the NWS.

The NPT was signed in 1968, and entered into force in 1970. Its initial duration was 25 years. In 1995, it was extended indefinitely, with a review conference to be held every five years. Nearly every country in the world, 188 total, is a party to the NPT, with three notable exceptions: India, Israel, and Pakistan. Each of these countries possesses nuclear weapons. Under the ICJ opinion, however, the obligation to negotiate elimination of nuclear arsenals applies to those states as well as the NWS.

Nuclear waste storage has also become an issue. High level radioactive waste is generally material from the core of a nuclear reactor or nuclear weapon. This waste includes uranium, plutonium, and other highly radioactive elements made during fission. Most of these elements have extremely long half-lives (some longer than 100,000 years), which means it will be a long time before the waste will settle to safe levels of radioactivity.

In 1982, Congress enacted legislation in the hopes of solving the problem of nuclear waste disposal in the United States. The Nuclear Waste Policy Act (42 U.S.C.A. §§ 10101-10226) made the U.S. ENERGY DEPARTMENT responsible for finding a site and building and operating an underground disposal facility called a geologic repository. The recommendation to use a geologic repository dates back to 1957 when the National Academy of Sciences recommended that the best means of protecting the environment and public health and safety would be to dispose of the waste in rock deep underground.

Based on Energy Department findings, three sites were designated as possible repositories: Hanford, Washington; Deaf Smith County, Texas; and Yucca Mountain, Nevada. In 1987, Congress amended the Nuclear Waste Policy Act and directed the Energy Department to study only Yucca Mountain. Yucca Mountain is located in a remote desert approximately ninety miles northwest of Las Vegas, Nevada. On July 23, 2002, President GEORGE W. BUSH signed House Joint Resolution 87, allowing the Energy Department to take the next steps in establishing a repository. The state of Nevada and the city of Las Vegas filed a number of suits against the Energy Department and various other federal entities. These suits challenge such things as the lack of compliance with the Nuclear Waste Policy Act and faulty design of the proposed facility.

FURTHER READINGS

Burroughs, John. 1997. *The Legality of Threat or Use of Nuclear Weapons: A Guide to the Historic Opinion of the International Court of Justice.* Piscataway, N.J.: Transaction.

Evan, William M., and Ved P. Nanda, eds. 1995. *Nuclear Proliferation and the Legality of Nuclear Weapons.* Lanham, Md.: University Press of America.

Moxley, Charles J. 2000. *Nuclear Weapons and International Law in the Post Cold War World.* Lanham, Md.: Austin & Winfield.

"Nevada Yucca Mountain Lawsuits." Yucca Mountain: Eureka County Nuclear Waste Page. Available online at <www.yuccamountain.org/court/lawsuits.htm> (accessed August 9, 2003).

CROSS-REFERENCES

Energy Department; Nuclear Power; Nuclear Regulatory Commission.

NUDUM PACTUM

See NAKED CONTRACT.

NUGATORY

Invalid; lacking legal force. A statute is nugatory if it has been declared unconstitutional.

NUISANCE

A legal action to redress harm arising from the use of one's property.

The two types of nuisance are private nuisance and public nuisance. A private nuisance is a civil wrong; it is the unreasonable, unwarranted, or unlawful use of one's property in a manner that substantially interferes with the enjoyment or use of another individual's property, without an actual TRESPASS or physical invasion to the land. A public nuisance is a criminal wrong; it is an act or omission that obstructs, damages, or inconveniences the rights of the community.

Public Nuisance

The term *public nuisance* covers a wide variety of minor crimes that threaten the health, morals, safety, comfort, convenience, or welfare of a community. Violators may be punished by a criminal sentence, a fine, or both. A defendant may also be required to remove a nuisance or to pay the costs of removal. For example, a manufacturer who has polluted a stream might be fined and might also be ordered to pay the cost of cleanup. Public nuisances may interfere with public health, such as in the keeping of diseased animals or a malarial pond. Public safety nuisances include shooting fireworks in the streets, storing explosives, practicing medicine without a license, or harboring a vicious dog. Houses of prostitution, illegal liquor establishments, GAMING houses, and unlicensed prizefights are examples of nuisances that interfere with public morals. Obstructing a highway or creating a condition to make travel unsafe or highly disagreeable are examples of nuisances threatening the public convenience.

A public nuisance interferes with the public as a class, not merely one person or a group of citizens. No civil remedy exists for a private citizen harmed by a public nuisance, even if his or her harm was greater than the harm suffered by others; a criminal prosecution is the exclusive remedy. However, if the individual suffers harm that is different from that suffered by the general public, the individual may maintain a TORT ACTION for damages. For example, if dynamiting has thrown a large boulder onto a public highway, those who use the highway cannot maintain a nuisance action for the inconvenience. However, a motorist who is injured from colliding with the boulder may bring a tort action for personal injuries.

Some nuisances can be both public and private in certain circumstances where the public nuisance substantially interferes with the use of an individual's adjoining land. For example, POLLUTION of a river might constitute both a public and a private nuisance. This is known as a mixed nuisance.

Private Nuisance

A private nuisance is an interference with a person's enjoyment and use of his land. The law recognizes that landowners, or those in rightful possession of land, have the right to the unimpaired condition of the property and to reasonable comfort and convenience in its occupation.

Examples of private nuisances abound. Nuisances that interfere with the physical condition of the land include vibration or blasting that damages a house; destruction of crops; raising of a water table; or the pollution of soil, a stream, or an underground water supply. Examples of nuisances interfering with the comfort, convenience, or health of an occupant are foul odors, noxious gases, smoke, dust, loud noises, excessive light, or high temperatures. Moreover, a nuisance may also disturb an occupant's mental tranquility, such as a neighbor who keeps a vicious dog, even though an injury is only threatened and has not actually occurred.

An attractive nuisance is a danger likely to lure children onto a person's land. For example, an individual who has a pool on his property has a legal obligation to take reasonable precautions, such as erecting a fence, to prevent foreseeable injury to children.

Trespass is sometimes confused with nuisance, but the two are distinct. A trespass action protects against an invasion of one's right to exclusive possession of land. If a landowner drops a tree across her neighbor's boundary line she has committed a trespass; if her dog barks all night keeping the neighbor awake, she may be liable for nuisance.

Legal Responsibility

A private nuisance is a tort, that is, a civil wrong. To determine accountability for an alleged nuisance, a court will examine three factors: the defendant's fault, whether there has been a substantial interference with the plaintiff's interest, and the reasonableness of the defendant's conduct.

Fault Fault means that the defendant intentionally, negligently, or recklessly interfered with the plaintiff's use and enjoyment of the land or that the defendant continued her conduct after learning of actual harm or substantial risk of future harm to the plaintiff's interest. For example, a defendant who continues to spray chemicals into the air after learning that they are blowing onto the plaintiff's land is deemed to be intending that result. Where it is alleged that a defendant has violated a statute, proving the elements of the statute will establish fault.

Substantial Interference The law is not intended to remedy trifles or redress petty annoyances. To establish liability under a nuisance theory, interference with the plaintiff's interest must be substantial. Determining substantial interference in cases where the physical condition of the property is affected will often be fairly straightforward. More challenging are those cases predicated on personal inconvenience, discomfort, or annoyance. To determine whether an interference is substantial, courts apply the standard of an ordinary member of the community with normal sensitivity and temperament. A plaintiff cannot, by putting his or her land to an unusually sensitive use, make a nuisance out of the defendant's conduct that would otherwise be relatively harmless.

Reasonableness of Defendant's Conduct If the interference with the plaintiff's interest is substantial, a determination must then be made that it is unreasonable for the plaintiff to bear it or to bear it without compensation. This is a BALANCING process weighing the respective interests of both parties. The law recognizes that the activities of others must be accommodated to a certain extent, particularly in matters of industry, commerce, or trade. The nature and gravity of the harm is balanced against the burden of preventing the harm and the usefulness of the conduct.

The following are factors to be considered:
- Extent and duration of the disturbance;
- Nature of the harm;
- Social value of the plaintiff's use of his or her property or other interest;
- Burden to the plaintiff in preventing the harm;
- Value of the defendant's conduct, in general and to the particular community;
- Motivation of the defendant;
- Feasibility of the defendant's mitigating or preventing the harm;
- Locality and suitability of the uses of the land by both parties.

ZONING boards use these factors to enact restrictions of property uses in specific locations. In this way, zoning laws work to prohibit public nuisances and to maintain the quality of a neighborhood.

Defenses

In an attempt to escape liability, a defendant may argue that legislation (such as zoning laws or licenses) authorizes a particular activity. Legislative authority will not excuse a defendant from liability if the conduct is unreasonable.

A defendant may not escape liability by arguing that others are also contributing to the harm; damages will be apportioned according to a defendant's share of the blame. Moreover, a defendant is liable even where his or her actions without the actions of others would not have constituted a nuisance.

Defendants sometimes argue that a plaintiff "came to a nuisance" by moving onto land next to an already operating source of interference. A new owner is entitled to the reasonable use and enjoyment of his or her land the same as anyone else, but the argument may be considered in determining the reasonableness of the defendant's conduct. It may also have an impact in determining damages because the purchase price may have reflected the existence of the nuisance.

Remedies

Redress for nuisance is commonly monetary damages. An INJUNCTION or abatement may also be proper under certain circumstances. An injunction orders a defendant to stop, remove, restrain, or restrict a nuisance or abandon plans for a threatened nuisance. In public nuisance cases, a fine or sentence may be imposed, in addition to abatement or injunctive relief.

Injunction is a drastic remedy, used only when damage or the threat of damage is irreparable and not satisfactorily compensable only by monetary damages. The court examines the economic hardships to the parties and the interest of the public in allowing the continuation of the enterprise.

A SELF-HELP remedy, abatement by the plaintiff, is available under limited circumstances. This privilege must be exercised within a reasonable time after learning of the nuisance and usually requires notice to the defendant and the defendant's failure to act. Reasonable force may be used to employ the abatement, and a plaintiff may be liable for unreasonable or unnecessary damages. For example, dead tree limbs extending dangerously over a neighbor's house may be removed by the neighbor in danger, after notifying the offending landowner of the nuisance. In cases where an immediate danger to health, property, or life exists, no notification is necessary.

FURTHER READINGS

Cleary, Joseph W. 2002. "Municipalities Versus Gun Manufacturers: Why Public Nuisance Claims Just Do Not Work." *University of Baltimore Law Review* 31 (spring).

Dodson, Robert D. 2002. "Rethinking Private Nuisance Law: Recognizing Esthetic Nuisances in the New Millennium." *South Carolina Environmental Law Journal* 10 (summer).

Fischel, William A. 1985. *The Economics of Zoning Laws: A Property Rights Approach to American Land Use Controls.* Baltimore, Md.: Johns Hopkins Univ. Press.

Paul, Ellen Frankel, and Howard Dickman, eds. 1990. *Liberty, Property, and the Future of Constitutional Development.* Albany: State Univ. of New York Press.

Scott, Michael S. 2001. *Loud Car Stereos.* Washington, D.C.: U.S. Dept. of Justice, Office of Community Oriented Policing Services.

Wade, John W., et al. 1994. *Prosser, Wade, and Schwartz's Cases and Materials on Torts.* 9th ed. Westbury, N.Y.: Foundation Press.

CROSS-REFERENCES

Land-Use Control; Tort Law.

NULL

Of no legal validity, force, or effect; nothing. As used in the phrase null and void, *refers to something that binds no one or is incapable of giving rise to any rights or duties under any circumstances.*

NUNC PRO TUNC

[Latin, Now for then.] *When courts take some action* nunc pro tunc, *that action has retroactive legal effect, as though it had been performed at a particular, earlier date.*

The most common use of *nunc pro tunc* is to correct past clerical errors, or omissions made by the court, that may hinder the efficient operation of the legal system. For example, if the written record of a trial court's judgment failed to correctly recite the judgment as the court rendered it, the court has the inherent power to change the record at a later date to reflect what happened at trial. The decision, as corrected, would be given legal force from the time of the initial decision so that neither party is prejudiced, or harmed, by the error. The purpose of *nunc pro tunc* is to correct errors or omissions to achieve the results intended by the court at the earlier time.

NUNCUPATIVE WILL

The oral expression of a person's wishes as to the disposition of his or her property to be performed or to take effect after the person's death, dictated by the person in his or her final illness before a sufficient number of witnesses and afterward reduced to writing. Such wills are invalid in certain states and in others are valid only under certain circumstances.

NUREMBERG TRIALS

The Nuremberg trials were a series of trials held between 1945 and 1949 in which the Allies prosecuted German military leaders, political officials, industrialists, and financiers for crimes they had committed during WORLD WAR II.

The first trial took place in Nuremberg, Germany, and involved twenty-four top-ranking survivors of the National Socialist German Workers' Party (Nazi Party). The subsequent trials were held throughout Germany and involved approximately two hundred additional defendants, including Nazi physicians who performed vile experiments on human subjects, concentration camp commandants who ordered the extermination of their prisoners, and judges who upheld Nazi practices.

World War II began in 1939 when Germany invaded Poland. Over the next few years, the European Axis powers (Germany, Italy, Albania, Bulgaria, Hungary, and Romania) successfully invaded and occupied France, Belgium, Luxembourg, Denmark, Norway, Greece, Yugoslavia, Czechoslovakia, Finland, and the Netherlands. But when ADOLF HITLER's troops invaded the Soviet Union, the Nazi war machine stalled. By the end of the war, the Axis powers were battered and beleaguered, and in 1945 they unconditionally surrendered to the United States, the Soviet Union, Great Britain, and France (the four Allied powers).

Although the surrender of the Axis powers brought the war to its formal conclusion, the Third Reich had left an indelible imprint on the world. During Germany's attempted conquest and occupation of Europe and Asia, the Nazis slaughtered, tortured, starved, and tormented over six million Jews and countless others—including Catholics, prisoners of war, dissenters, intelligentsia, nobility, and other innocent civilians. As part of their systematic effort to extinguish persons they deemed subversive, dangerous, or impure, the Nazis constructed concentration camps around Europe where they murdered their victims in gas chambers and incinerated their bodies in crematories. Persons who escaped this fate were deported to Nazi labor camps where they were compelled upon threat of death to work for the Third Reich.

The Allies had been discussing the idea of punishing war criminals since 1943 when U.S. president FRANKLIN D. ROOSEVELT, British prime minister Winston Churchill, and Soviet premier JOSEPH STALIN signed the Moscow Declaration promising to hold the Axis powers, particularly Germany, Italy, and Japan, responsible for any atrocities they committed during World War II. In 1944 Roosevelt and Churchill briefly entertained the idea of summarily executing the highest-ranking members of the Third Reich without a trial or legal proceeding of any kind.

However, by June of 1945, when delegations from the four Allied powers gathered in London at the International Conference of Military Trials, the U.S. representatives firmly believed that the Nazi leaders could not be executed without first being afforded the opportunity to defend themselves in a judicial proceeding. Principles of justice, fairness, and DUE PROCESS, delegates from the United States argued, required no less. U.S. leaders also feared that the Allies would be perceived as hypocritical for denying the vanquished powers the same basic legal rights that were denied to those persons summarily executed by Germany, Italy, and Japan during the war.

On August 8, 1945, the four Allied powers signed a convention called the Agreement for the Prosecution and Punishment of the Major War Criminals of the European Axis Powers, which set forth the parameters by which the accused would be tried. Under this convention, which is sometimes referred to as the London Agreement or Nuremberg Charter, the Allies would conduct the trials of leaders of the European Axis powers in Nuremberg, and would subsequently prosecute lower-ranking officials and less important figures in the four occupied zones of Germany. American military tribunals in the South Pacific, under the command of General Douglas MacArthur, tried accused Japanese war criminals.

The London Agreement also established the International Military Tribunal (IMT), which was a panel of eight judges, two named by each of the four Allied powers. One judge from each country actively presided at trial, and the other four sat on the panel as alternates. The four Allied powers also selected the prosecutors, who agreed to pursue a conviction against the defendants on behalf of the newly formed UNITED NATIONS.

Under the Nuremberg Charter, each defendant accused of a war crime was afforded the right to be represented by an attorney of his choice. The accused war criminals were presumed innocent by the tribunal and could not be convicted until their guilt was proven BEYOND A REASONABLE DOUBT. In addition, the defendants were guaranteed the right to challenge incriminating evidence, cross-examine adverse witnesses, and introduce exculpatory evidence of their own.

The court appointed interpreters to translate the proceedings into four languages: French, German, Russian, and English. Written evidence submitted by the prosecution was translated into the native language of each defendant. When considering the admissibility of particular documents or testimony, the IMT was not bound by technical RULES OF EVIDENCE common to Anglo-American systems of justice. The tribunal retained discretion to evaluate HEARSAY and other forms of evidence that are normally considered unreliable in the United States and Great Britain.

The IMT made all of its decisions by a majority vote of the four judges. On issues that divided the judges equally, the president of the court, Lord Justice Geoffrey Lawrence from Great Britain, was endowed with the deciding vote. In all other situations, a vote cast by Lawrence carried no greater weight than a vote cast by Soviet judge Ion Nikitchenko, French judge Henri Donnedieu de Vabres, American judge FRANCIS BIDDLE, or any of the alternates. The IMT's decisions, including any rulings, judgments, or sentences, were final and could not be appealed.

Neither the defense nor the prosecution was permitted to challenge the legal, political, or military authority of the court. The IMT said that its jurisdiction stemmed from the London Agreement that was promulgated by the Allies pursuant to their inherent legislative powers over the conquered nations, which had unconditionally surrendered. According to the tribunal, each Ally possessed the unqualified right to legislate over the territory that it occupied. By establishing the IMT, the court said, the Allies "had done together what any one of them might have done singly."

The IMT was given authority to hear four counts of criminal complaints: conspiracy, crimes against peace, WAR CRIMES, and crimes against humanity. Count I encompassed conspiracies to commit crimes against peace, whereas count II covered persons who committed such crimes in their individual capacities. Crimes against peace included the planning, preparation, initiation, and waging of aggressive war in violation of international treaties, agreements, or assurances. Crimes against peace differed from other war crimes, the tribunal said, in that they represented the "accumulated evil" of the Axis powers.

Count III consisted of war crimes committed in violation of the laws and customs of war as accepted and practiced around the world. This count aimed to punish those individuals who were responsible for issuing or executing orders that resulted in the plundering of public and private property, the wanton destruction of European cities and villages, the murder of captured Allied soldiers, and the CONSCRIPTION of civilians in occupied territories for deportation to German labor camps.

Count IV consisted of crimes against humanity, including murder, extermination, enslavement, and other inhumane acts committed against civilian populations, as well as every form of political, racial, and religious persecution carried out in furtherance of a crime punishable by the IMT. This count aimed to punish the most notorious crimes committed by the Nazi regime, such as GENOCIDE and torture. Early in the trial, however, the IMT ruled that the court did not have authority to try the defendants for crimes they committed before 1939 when World War II began.

Many of the prospective Nazi defendants were dead or could not be found after the war. Adolf Hitler, the totalitarian dictator of Germany who was the emotional and intellectual catalyst behind most of the war crimes committed by the Nuremberg defendants, Heinrich Himmler, head of the SS (*Schutzstaffel*, or Blackshirts, the Nazi organization in charge of the concentration camps and the Gestapo, the German secret police), and Paul Joseph Goebbels, the Nazi minister of propaganda, had all killed themselves during the final days of the war. BENITO MUSSOLINI, totalitarian dictator of Italy, was shot and hung by his own people in Milan in April 1945. Other German officials such as Karl Adolf Eichmann, a lieutenant colonel in the SS who was the architect of Hitler's "final solution" to exterminate the Jewish population in Europe and Asia, and Dr. Josef Mengele, a physician who performed barbaric experiments on prisoners at the concentration camp in Auschwitz, Poland, eluded the Allies by fleeing Germany after the war.

Not all of the Nazi leadership was able to escape justice. Twenty-four Nazi officials were indicted under the Nuremberg Charter for war crimes. The tribunal convicted eighteen of the defendants and acquitted three defendants (Dr. Hjalmar H. G. Schacht, president of the German Central Bank, Hans Fritzsche, propaganda minister for German radio, and Franz von Papen, vice chancellor of Germany). One defendant (Dr. Robert Ley, leader of the Nazi Labor Front) committed suicide before the proceedings began; one defendant (Gustav Krupp von Bohlen und Halbach, a German military industrialist) was deemed mentally and physically incompetent to stand trial; and one defendant (Martin Bormann, Hitler's secretary and head of the Nazi Party Chancellery) was tried and convicted in absentia because his whereabouts were unknown.

The trial began on November 20, 1945, and concluded on October 1, 1946. Thirty-three witnesses testified for the prosecution. Eighty witnesses testified for the defense, including nineteen of the defendants. An additional 140 witnesses provided evidence for the defense through written interrogatories. The prosecution introduced written evidence of its own, including original military, diplomatic, and government files of the Nazi regime that fell into the hands of the Allies after the collapse of the Third Reich.

ROBERT H. JACKSON, an associate justice of the U.S. Supreme Court, led the prosecution team. President HARRY S. TRUMAN had asked Jackson to assemble a staff of U.S. attorneys to investigate alleged war crimes and present evidence against the defendants. Jackson was joined on the prosecution team by Roman Rudenko, François de Menthon, and Sir Hartley Shawcross, the chief prosecutors for Russia, France, and Great Britain, respectively. Each of the four powers employed a number of assistant prosecutors as well.

Jackson commenced the trial with an OPENING STATEMENT that is considered one of the most eloquent in the annals of JURISPRUDENCE. "The wrongs which we seek to condemn and punish," Jackson said, "have been so calculated, so malignant, and so devastating that civilization cannot tolerate their being ignored because it cannot survive their being repeated. . . . That four great nations, flushed with victory and stung with injury, stay the hand of vengeance and voluntarily submit their captive enemies to judgment of the law is one of the most significant tributes that power has ever paid to reason."

Hermann Goering was the most powerful surviving member of the German government to be tried at Nuremberg. Goering had been elected president of the Reichstag (the German parliament) in 1932. After Hitler was named chancellor of Germany in 1933, Goering was appointed minister of interior for Prussia where he created the Gestapo and established the first concentration camps. In 1935 Goering became chief of the Luftwaffe (the German air force), and two years later he was made commissioner of the Four Year Plan, an economic program designed to make Germany self-sufficient in preparation for the ensuing Nazi blitzkrieg. After Germany's invasion of Finland in 1939, Goering was elevated to Reich marshall, the highest military rank in Germany, and designated as Hitler's successor in the event of Hitler's death.

The IMT convicted the Reich marshall on all four counts and sentenced him to death. The prosecution demonstrated that Goering had helped plan and direct the invasions of Poland and Austria. Other evidence indicated that Goering had ordered the Luftwaffe to destroy a business district in Rotterdam, Netherlands, even though the city had already surrendered. Goering was also implicated in the extermination of Polish intelligentsia, nobility, and clergy, the execution of British prisoners of war, the deportation of foreign laborers to Germany, the theft of art from French museums, and the suppression of domestic political opposition. Additionally, Goering admitted on cross-examination that he was responsible for promulgating laws that had facilitated the persecution of Jews throughout Europe.

Rudolph Hess was another influential Nazi official prosecuted at Nuremberg. Hess was a longtime friend of Hitler. In 1923 the two joined forces in an unsuccessful attempt to incite a Nazi revolution in a Munich tavern. Although Hitler was arrested and convicted of TREASON for his role in the so-called beer hall putsch, German interest in the Nazi movement grew after the publication of *Mein Kampf*, a manifesto Hitler dictated to Hess while serving his prison term. *Mein Kampf* planted the seeds of Aryan supremacy, German nationalism, anti-Semitism, and totalitarian government, seeds that Hess later cultivated in his capacity as deputy führer to the Third Reich.

During the Nuremberg trial, the prosecution offered evidence that Hess had signed orders authorizing the persecution of European Jews and the ransacking of churches. Documents signed by Hess and meetings he attended reflected his support for Hitler's plan to invade Czechoslovakia, Poland, France, Belgium, Luxembourg, and the Netherlands. Hess originally asserted a defense of amnesia to these charges, claiming that he had forgotten the entire period of his life in which he had acted as deputy führer. However, Hess withdrew this defense upon realizing that he would not stand trial with the other defendants if he were diagnosed as incompetent. Hess was convicted of counts I and II and sentenced to life imprisonment.

Joachim von Ribbentrop, Germany's foreign minister during World War II, was convicted on all four counts and sentenced to death. When he took the witness stand, the prosecution asked him if he considered Germany's invasions of Poland, Denmark, Norway, Greece, France, and the Soviet Union "acts of aggression." In each case Ribbentrop answered in the negative, arguing that such invasions were more properly described as acts of war. Confronted with evidence that he had urged the German regent of Hungary to exterminate the Jews in that country, Ribbentrop responded only by saying that he did not use those words exactly.

Dr. Ernst Kaltenbrunner was the head of the Reich Central Security Office, the Nazi organization in charge of the Gestapo and the SD (*Sicherheitsdienst*, Security Service, the German intelligence agency) and was second in command to Himmler at the SS. Kaltenbrunner faced a mountain of evidence demonstrating that he visited a number of concentration camps and had personally witnessed prisoners being gassed and incinerated. One letter signed by Kaltenbrunner authorized the execution of Allied prisoners of war, and another letter authorized the conscription and deportation of foreign laborers. Laborers who were too weak to contribute, Kaltenbrunner wrote, should be exe-

Twenty of the 24 defendants at the Nuremberg Trials listen to the hearings. Eighteen of the Nazi officials indicted by the International Military Tribunal were convicted; three were acquitted.

USHMM PHOTO
ARCHIVES

cutcd, rcgardlcss of thcir agc or gcndcr. Kaltenbrunner received a death sentence after being convicted under counts III and IV.

Alfrcd Roscnbcrg was thc Nazi ministcr for the occupied Eastern European territories. Rosenberg told Axis troops that the accepted rules of land warfare could be disregarded in areas under his control. He ordered the SEGRE-GATION of Jews into ghettos where his subordinates murdered them. His signature was found at the bottom of a directive approving the deportation of forty-five thousand youths to German labor camps. Cross-examined about his role in the unlawful confiscation of Jewish property, Rosenberg claimed that all such property was seized to protect it from Allied bombing raids. Rosenberg was found guilty on all four counts and sentenced to death by hanging.

Hans Frank, the governor-general of Poland during German occupation, was sentenced to hang after being convicted on counts III and IV. Frank described his administration's policy by stating that Poland was "treated like a colony" in which the Polish people became "the slaves of the Greater German World Empire." The tribunal found that this policy entailed the destruction of Poland as a national entity, the evisceration of all political opposition, and the ruthless exploitation of human resources to promote Hitler's reign of terror. While on the witness stand, Frank confessed to participating in the Nazis' systematic attempt to annihilate the Jewish race.

Wilhelm Frick, the German minister of interior, was found guilty on counts I, II, and III and sentenced to be hanged. Frick had signed decrees sanctioning the execution of Jews and other persons held in "protective custody" at the concentration camps and had given Himmler a blank check to take any "security measures" necessary to ensure the German foothold in the occupied territories. The tribunal also determined that Frick exercised supreme authority over Bohemia and Moravia and was responsible for implementing Hitler's policies of enslavement, deportation, torture, and extermination in these territories.

Wilhelm Keitel, field marshall for the High Command of the armed forces, was sentenced to die after being found guilty on every count. On direct examination Keitel admitted that there were "a large number of orders" bearing his signature that "contained deviations from existing international law." He also conceded that a number of atrocities had been committed under his command during Germany's invasion of the Soviet Union. As a defense to these charges, Keitel asserted that he had been following the orders of his superiors when committing these crimes. Yet some witnesses testifying on behalf of the defense tended to undermine this assertion.

Alfred Jodl, chief of the operations staff for the armed forces, also received the death sentence after being convicted on every count. During the early stages of World War II, Jodl had been asked to review an order drafted by Hitler authorizing German troops to execute all Soviet military commissars captured during the Nazi invasion of Russia. Aware that this order was a violation of the customs, practices, and laws governing the treatment of prisoners during times of war, Jodl made no attempt to dissuade Hitler from issuing it. Jodl was also found responsible for distributing an order that authorized the execution of Allied commandos caught by the Axis powers and for mobilizing the German army against its European foes.

Julius Streicher, an anti-Semitic propagandist, was found guilty of count IV and sentenced to death. Author, editor, and publisher of *Der Stuermer*, a privately owned Jew-baiting newspaper, Streicher held no meaningful government position with the Axis powers during World War II. Yet the tribunal determined that circulation of Streicher's racist newspaper had fueled the Nazis' maniacal hatred of Jews and fomented an atmosphere in which genocide was acceptable and desirable. The prosecution introduced an article Streicher had published during 1942 in which he described Jewish procreation as a curse of God that could only be lifted through a process of political and ethnic emasculation.

Albert Speer, Nazi minister of armaments, received a prison term of twenty years after being convicted on counts III and IV. Speer had fascinated Hitler long before the war with his architectural prowess, designing buildings that were both immense and imposing. After the war began, however, Speer's primary obligation was to supply the German armed forces with military supplies, equipment, and weapons. Thus, Speer became a lynchpin in the Nazi military empire. In an effort to maintain this empire, the prosecution demonstrated, Speer had repeatedly cajoled Hitler to procure foreign labor to work in his weapons factories.

Dr. Arthur Seyss-Inquart, an Austrian who was appointed by Hitler to govern Austria and the Netherlands during German occupation, was found guilty on counts II, III, and IV and sentenced to death for his confessed mistreatment of racial minorities in those territories, including the deportation of more than 250,000 Jews to Germany. Seyss-Inquart also assisted Hitler's takeover of Austria, Poland, and Czechoslovakia.

Baron Konstantin von Neurath, Reich protector of Czechoslovakia, was convicted on all four counts and sentenced to fifteen years in prison for participating in the Nazi militarization campaign. Hoping to immunize the Nazi regime from its obligations under INTERNATIONAL LAW, Neurath had advocated Germany's withdrawal from the LEAGUE OF NATIONS and denounced the Versailles Treaty that had formally concluded WORLD WAR I. Neurath was also implicated in various brutalities committed against the Czechoslovakian civilian population.

Baldur von Schirach, governor of occupied Vienna and leader of the Hitler Youth, was convicted on count IV and sentenced to a twenty-year prison term. The IMT determined that Schirach had provided the visceral foundations for the militarization of Germany's youngest Nazis through psychological and educational indoctrination and had conspired with Hitler to deport Viennese Jews to Poland where most of them met their death. Fritz Sauckel, the plenipotentiary general for the allocation of labor, was convicted on counts III and IV and sentenced to death for his central role in the Nazi forced labor program that enslaved more than eleven million Europeans.

Erich Raeder served as Germany's naval commander and chief until 1943 when he resigned due to a disagreement with Hitler, and he was succeeded by Karl Doenitz. Both Raeder and Doenitz were indicted under counts I, II, and III for war crimes committed on the high seas, and both were convicted based in part on evidence that they had authorized German submarines to fire on Allied commercial ships without warning in contravention of international law. Doenitz was sentenced to a ten-year prison term, and Raeder received a life sentence. Walther Funk, Nazi minister of economics, also received a life sentence for financing Germany's aggressive warfare and for exploiting foreign laborers in German industry.

The IMT declared four Nazi organizations to be criminal: the SS, the SD, the Gestapo, and the Nazi Party. A team of Allied attorneys, including American Telford Taylor, subsequently prosecuted individual members of these organizations. Three Nazi organizations were acquitted: the SA (*Sturmabteilung*, the paramilitary organization also known as the Brownshirts or Stormtroopers), and the general staff and High Command of the German armed forces.

The Nuremberg trials made three important contributions to international law. First, they established a precedent that all persons, regardless of their station or occupation in life, can be held individually accountable for their behavior during times of war. Defendants cannot insulate themselves from personal responsibility by blaming the country, government, or military branch for which they committed the particular war crime.

Second, the Nuremberg trials established that individuals cannot shield themselves from liability for war crimes by asserting that they were simply following orders issued by a superior in the chain of command. Subordinates in the military or government are now bound by their obligations under international law, obligations that transcend their duty to obey an order issued by a superior. Orders to initiate aggressive (as opposed to defensive) warfare, to violate recognized rules and customs of warfare, or to persecute civilians and prisoners are considered illegal under the Nuremberg principles.

Third, the Nuremberg trials clearly established three discrete substantive war crimes that are punishable under international law: crimes against peace, crimes against humanity, and crimes in violation of transnational obligations embodied in treaties and other agreements. Before the Nuremberg trials, these crimes were not well defined, and persons who committed such crimes had never been punished by a multinational tribunal. For these reasons the Nuremberg convictions have sometimes been criticized as EX POST FACTO justice.

The Nuremberg trials have also been criticized as "victor's justice." Historians have observed that the Allied nations that tried and convicted the leading Nazis at Nuremberg did not come to the table with clean hands. The Soviet Union had participated in Germany's invasion and occupation of Poland and had been implicated in the massacre of more than a thousand Poles in the Katyn forest. Bombing raids conducted by the United States and Great Britain during World War II left thousands of civilians dead in cities like Dresden, Germany, and Nagasaki and Hiroshima, Japan. President Roosevelt had implemented a relocation program for more than 100,000 Americans of Japanese descent that confined them to concentration camps around the United States.

The Nuremberg trials were not typical partisan trials, though. The defendants were afforded the RIGHT TO COUNSEL, plus a full panoply of evidentiary and procedural protections. The Nuremberg verdicts demonstrate that these protections were taken seriously by the tribunal. The IMT completely exonerated three defendants of war crimes and acquitted most of the remaining defendants of at least some charges. Thus, the Nuremberg trials, while not perfect, changed the face of international law, both procedurally and substantively.

FURTHER READINGS

Conot, Robert. 1983. *Justice at Nuremberg.* New York: Carrol & Graf.

Davidson, Eugene. 1997. *The Trial of the Germans.* Columbia: Univ. of Missouri Press.

Gilbert, G. M. 1995. *Nuremberg Diary.* New York: Da Capo Press.

Green, L.C. 1995. "Command Responsibility in International Humanitarian Law." *Transnational Law and Contemporary Problems* 5.

Lippman, Matthew. 1991. "Nuremberg: Forty-five Years Later." *Connecticut Journal of International Law* 7.

Persico, Joseph. 1994. *Nuremberg: Infamy on Trial.* New York: Penguin Books.

Taylor, Telford. 1992. *The Anatomy of the Nuremberg Trials.* New York: Little, Brown.

CROSS-REFERENCES

Tokyo Trial.

OATH

Any type of attestation by which an individual signifies that he or she is bound in conscience to perform a particular act truthfully and faithfully; a solemn declaration of truth or obligation.

An individual's appeal to God to witness the truth of what he or she is saying or a pledge to do something enforced by the individual's responsibility to answer to God.

Similarly an affirmation is a solemn and formal declaration that a statement is true; however, an affirmation includes no reference to God so it can be made by someone who does not believe in God or by an individual who has conscientious objections against swearing to God. Provisions in state statutes or constitutions ordinarily allow affirmations to be made as alternatives to oaths.

In order for an oath to be legally effective, it must be administered by a public official. The law creating each public office and describing the duties of the official ordinarily indicates who is authorized to administer the oath of office. A spoken oath is generally sufficient; however, a written and signed oath can be required by law.

The most famous oath prescribed by law in the United States is the oath repeated by the president-elect upon taking the office of the presidency.

President George W. Bush takes the oath of office from Chief Justice William Rehnquist on January 20, 2001. AFP/CORBIS

upon a cause, "by the way," that is, incidentally or collaterally, and not directly upon the question before the court or upon a point not necessarily involved in the determination of the cause, or introduced by way of illustration, or analogy or argument. Such are not binding as precedent.

CROSS-REFERENCES

Court Opinion.

OBITER DICTUM

[Latin, By the way.] *Words of an opinion entirely unnecessary for the decision of the case. A remark made or opinion expressed by a judge in a decision*

OBJECT

As a verb, to take exception to something; to declare or express the belief that something is improper or illegal.

As a noun, the thing sought to be accomplished or attained; aim; purpose; intention.

One might, for example, object to the admission of particular evidence at a trial.

The object of a civil suit, for example, might be to be compensated in the form of damages for an injury incurred.

OBJECTION

A formal attestation or declaration of disapproval concerning a specific point of law or procedure during the course of a trial; a statement indicating disagreement with a judge's ruling.

Some laws provide that an appeal to a higher tribunal can be based only upon errors objected to during the course of a trial conducted in a lower court. An error that initially slips by without any objection by the party's counsel cannot subsequently be set forth as a reason for the appeals court to overturn the original decision in a particular case. The making of objections in open court during the course of a proceeding is important so that on appeal, the appellate court can evaluate the record of the lower court action.

The FEDERAL RULES OF EVIDENCE, the Federal Rules of Civil Procedure, and the Federal Rules of Criminal Procedure govern the making of objections in federal actions. Comparable state provisions apply to state proceedings.

CROSS-REFERENCES

Civil Procedure; Evidence.

OBJECTIVE THEORY OF CONTRACT

A principle in U.S. law that the existence of a contract is determined by the legal significance of the external acts of a party to a purported agreement, rather than by the actual intent of the parties.

Some disagreement exists as to whether the COMMON LAW governing contracts required judges to determine the subjective intent of the parties in order to recognize the existence of a contract, or whether judges were required to view the external acts of the parties and then determine, in an objective manner, whether a contract had been formed. Some scholars maintain that the common law had long employed an objective test for recognizing a contract. Other scholars and writers claim that the widespread use of the objective theory of contracts in the courts was a much more recent phenomenon, perhaps developed during the late nineteenth century.

Whatever the specific origin of objective theory may be, it is clear that by the late nineteenth century American law had generally adopted it. Since then the theory has been heatedly debated among legal experts, and contracts scholars often take firm stances as either "objectivists" or "subjectivists." Within each of these theories are variations regarding the application of either a subjective or an objective view of contracts.

Legal historians note that many of the top judges and legal scholars of the late 1800s and early 1900s adhered to the objective theory of contract. Among these judges and scholars were CHRISTOPHER COLUMBUS LANGDELL, OLIVER WENDELL HOLMES, and SAMUEL WILLISTON. Judge LEARNED HAND of New York summarized the objective theory of contracts in a famous quote from a 1911 case (*Hotchkiss v. National City Bank*, 200 F. 287 [S.D.N.Y. 1911]):

> A contract has, strictly speaking, nothing to do with the personal, or individual, intent of the parties. A contract is an obligation attached by the mere force of law to certain acts of the parties, usually words, which ordinarily accompany and represent a known intent. If, however, it were proved by twenty bishops that either party when he used the words intended something else than the usual meaning which the law imposes on them, he would still be held, unless there were mutual mistake or something else of the sort.

The sharp dichotomy between the objective and subjective theories of contract should not suggest that an ordinary, everyday agreement would commonly be considered a binding contract under one theory but not under the other. If two parties enter into an agreement, subjectively intend to be bound by the agreement, and make external acts showing their intent to be bound by the agreement, then a court applying either the subjective theory or the objective theory of contract law would reach the same conclusion—that the parties had entered into a binding contract.

The major differences in the two theories arise when one party claims that he or she did not intend to enter into the agreement. For example, party A owns an automobile valued at $20,000. His neighbor, party B, asks party A for the amount of money which party A would be willing to sell the car. Party A, who has no intention of selling the car, and who knows that party B cannot afford to pay $20,000, says "I'd sell it to you for $1,000." Party B replies, "OK, it's a deal." Party A states that his offer was not serious, and that he never intended to sell the car for that amount of money. Nevertheless, a court could find that parties A and B had entered into a binding agreement—selling the car for $1,000— if a reasonable person in party B's position would have believed that party A intended to enter into such an agreement. However, if party A were to tell party B that he would sell the car for $5, then a court may be more likely to find that a reasonable person would not have believed that party A intended to be bound. Under a subjective theory of contract, party A could dispute the formation of a contract by introducing evidence that he did not actually intend to be bound by his statement (of either the $1,000 or the $5 sales price).

Although the objective theory of contracts applies in virtually all jurisdictions in the United States, some aspects of subjectivity are nevertheless present in American law. For instance, many of the grounds by which a party or parties may avoid a contract, such as mistake or duress, are based upon the subjective beliefs or intentions of the parties. Likewise, if the two parties specifically indicate that they agree *not* to be bound by an agreement, then a court will not recognize the agreement as enforceable. The court would similarly refuse to find the existence of a contract if one party did not intend to be bound and the other party knew or should have known that the first party did not intend to enter into a binding agreement.

FURTHER READINGS

Farnsworth, E. Allan. 1999. *Contracts.* New York: Aspen Law & Business.

Perillo, Joseph M. 2000. "The Origins of the Objective Theory of Contract Formation and Interpretation." *Fordham Law Review* 69 (November).

OBLIGATION

A generic term for any type of legal duty or liability.

In its original sense, the term *obligation* was very technical in nature and applied to the responsibility to pay money owed on certain written documents that were executed under seal. Currently obligation is used in reference to anything that an individual is required to do because of a promise, vow, oath, contract, or law. It refers to a legal or moral duty that an individual can be forced to perform or penalized for neglecting to perform.

An *absolute obligation* is one for which no legal alternative exists since it is an unconditional duty.

A *contractual obligation* arises as a result of an enforceable promise, agreement, or contract.

An *express obligation* is spelled out in direct and actual terms, and an *implied obligation* is inferred indirectly from the surrounding circumstances or from the actions of the individuals involved.

A *joint obligation* is one that binds two or more people to fulfill whatever is required, and a *several obligation* requires each of two or more individuals to fulfill the obligation in its entirety by himself or herself.

A *moral obligation* is binding upon the conscience and is fair but is not necessarily enforceable in law.

A *primary obligation* is one that must be performed since it is the main purpose of the contract that contains it, whereas a *secondary obligation* is only incidental to another principal duty or arises only in the event that the main obligation cannot be fulfilled.

A *penal obligation* is a penalty, such as the obligation to pay extra money if the terms or conditions of an agreement cannot be satisfied.

OBLIGEE

The individual to whom a particular duty or obligation is owed.

The obligation might be to pay a debt or involve the performance or nonperformance of a particular act.

The term *obligee* is often used synonymously with creditor.

OBLIGOR

The individual who owes another person a certain debt or duty.

The term *obligor* is often used interchangeably with debtor.

OBLITERATION

A destruction; an eradication of written words.

Obliteration is a method of revoking a WILL or a clause therein. Lines drawn through the signatures of witnesses to a will constitute an obliteration of the will even if the names are still decipherable.

OBSCENE

Offensive to recognized standards of decency.

The term *obscene* is applied to written, verbal, or visual works or conduct that treat sex in an objectionable or lewd or lascivious manner. Although the FIRST AMENDMENT guarantees freedom of expression, such constitutional protection is not extended to obscene works. To determine whether a work is obscene, the trier of fact applies the three-pronged guidelines established by the U.S. Supreme Court in MILLER V. CALIFORNIA, 413 U.S. 15, 93 S. Ct. 2607, 37 L. Ed. 2d 419 (1973):

> (a) whether the "average person, applying contemporary community standards" would find that the work depicting or describing sexual conduct when taken as a whole, appeals to the prurient interest. . ., (b) whether the work depicts or describes, in a patently offensive way, sexual conduct specifically defined by the applicable state law; and (c) whether the work, taken as a whole, lacks serious literary, artistic, political, or scientific value.

CROSS-REFERENCES

Freedom of Speech; Pornography.

OBSCENITY

The character or quality of being obscene; an act, utterance, or item tending to corrupt the public morals by its indecency or lewdness.

Obscenity is a legal term that applies to anything offensive to morals and is often equated with the term PORNOGRAPHY. Pornography, however, is a more limited term, which refers to the erotic content of books, magazines, films, and recordings. Obscenity includes pornography, but may also include nude dancing, sexually oriented commercial telephone messages, and scatological comedy routines. U.S. courts have had a difficult time determining what is obscene. This problem has serious implications, because if an act or an item is deemed obscene, it is not protected by the FIRST AMENDMENT.

Until the mid-nineteenth century and the Victorian era in Great Britain and the United States, sexually explicit material was not subject to statutory prohibition. The federal COMSTOCK LAW OF 1873 criminalized the transmission and receipt of "obscene," "lewd," or "lascivious" publications through the U.S. mail. U.S. courts looked to the English case of *Regina v. Hicklin,* 3 L.R.-Q.B. 360 (1868), for a legal definition of obscenity. The *Hicklin* test was "whether the tendency of the matter charged as obscenity is to deprave and corrupt those whose minds are open to such immoral influences, and into whose hands a publication of this sort may fall."

This test permitted judges to look at objectionable words or passages without regard for the work as a whole and without respect to any artistic, literary, or scientific value the work might have. In 1930, Massachusetts courts declared both Theodore Dreiser's novel *An American Tragedy* and D.H. Lawrence's novel *Lady Chatterly's Lover* obscene. An important break from *Hicklin* came in a lawsuit over the U.S. publication of James Joyce's novel *Ulysses.* Both at the trial and appellate levels, the federal courts held that the book was not obscene (*United States v. One Book Called "Ulysses,"* 5 F. Supp. 182 [S.D.N.Y. 1933], aff'd 72 F.2d 705 [2d Cir. 1934]). The courts rejected the *Hicklin* test and suggested a standard based on the effect on the average reader of the dominant theme of the work as a whole.

In 1957, the U.S. Supreme Court retired the *Hicklin* test in ROTH V. UNITED STATES, 354 U.S. 476, 77 S. Ct. 1304, 1 L. Ed. 2d 1498. Justice WILLIAM J. BRENNAN JR. stated that obscenity is "utterly without redeeming social importance" and therefore was not protected by the First Amendment. He announced, as a new test, "whether to the average person, applying contemporary community standards, the dominant theme of the material taken as a whole appeals to a prurient [lewd or lustful] interest." The new test was applicable to every level of government in the United States.

The *Roth* test proved difficult to use because every term in it eluded a conclusive definition. The Supreme Court justices could not fully agree what constituted "prurient interest" or what "redeeming social importance" meant. Justice POTTER STEWART expressed this difficulty at defining obscenity when he remarked, "I know it when I see it" (*Jacobellis v. Ohio,* 378 U.S. 184, 84 S. Ct. 1676, 12 L. Ed. 2d 793 [1964]).

The Supreme Court added requirements to the definition of obscenity in a 1966 case involving the bawdy English novel *Fanny Hill.* In *Memoir v. Massachusetts,* 383 U.S. 413, 86 S. Ct. 975, 16 L. Ed. 2d 1, the Court concluded that to establish obscenity, the material must, aside from appealing to the prurient interest, be "utterly without redeeming social value," and "patently offensive because it affronts contemporary community standards relating to the description of sexual matters." The requirement that the material be "utterly" without value made prosecution difficult. Defendants presented expert witnesses, such as well-known authors, critics, or scholars, who attested to the literary and artistic value of sexually charged books and films.

The Supreme Court did make conclusive rulings on two other areas of obscenity in the 1960s. In *Ginzburg v. United States*, 383 U.S. 463, 86 S. Ct. 942, 16 L. Ed. 2d 31 (1966), the Court held that "pandering" of material by mailed advertisements, designed to appeal to a prurient interest, could be prosecuted under the federal obscenity statute. Even if the material in publisher Ralph Ginzburg's *Eros* magazine was not obscene, the Court was willing to allow the government to punish Ginzburg for appealing to his prospective subscribers' prurient interest. In *Stanley v. Georgia*, 394 U.S. 557, 89 S. Ct. 1243, 22 L. Ed. 2d 542 (1969), the Court held that the First and Fourteenth Amendments prohibited making the private possession of obscene material a crime.

The failure of the WARREN COURT to achieve consensus over the *Roth* test kept the definition of obscenity in limbo. Then, in 1973, aided by conservative justices LEWIS F. POWELL JR. and WILLIAM H. REHNQUIST, Chief Justice WARREN EARL BURGER restated the constitutional definition of obscenity in MILLER V. CALIFORNIA, 413 U.S. 15, 93 S. Ct. 2607, 37 L. Ed. 2d 419. Burger explicitly rejected the "utterly without redeeming social value" standard:

> The basic guidelines for the trier of fact must be (a) whether the "average person, applying contemporary community standards" would find that the work, taken as a whole, appeals to the prurient interest . . ., (b) whether the work depicts or describes, in a patently offensive way, sexual conduct specifically defined by the applicable state law, and (c) whether the work, taken as a whole, lacks serious literary, artistic, political, or scientific value.

Burger noted that the new test was intended to address "'hard core' sexual conduct," which included "patently offensive representations or descriptions of ultimate sexual acts, normal or perverted, actual or simulated . . . masturbation, excretory functions, and lewd exhibitions of genitals."

In 1987, the Supreme Court modified the "contemporary community standards" criteria. In *Pope v. Illinois*, 481 U.S. 497, 107 S. Ct. 1918, 95 L. Ed. 2d 439, the Court stated that the "proper inquiry is not whether an ordinary member of any given community would find serious literary, artistic, political, and scientific value in allegedly obscene material, but whether a reasonable person would find such value in the material, taken as a whole." It is unclear whether the "reasonable person" standard represents a liberalization of the obscenity test.

In 1989, the Supreme Court unanimously held that the First Amendment's guarantee of free speech protected indecent, sexually explicit telephone messages (*Sable Communications of California, Inc. v. Federal Communications Commission*, 492 U.S. 115, 109 S. Ct. 2829, 106 L. Ed. 2d 93). The Court ruled that a federal law that attempted to ban "Dial-a-Porn" commercial phone services over interstate telephone lines (Pub. L. No. 100-297, 102 Stat. 424) to shield minors from obscenity was unconstitutional because it applied to indecent as well as obscene speech. The Court indicated, however, that obscene calls could be prohibited.

Congressional attempts to prevent the INTERNET from being used to distribute obscene materials have been blocked by Supreme Court decisions. The Communications Decency Act of 1996 (CDA), codified at 47 U.S.C.A. § 223(b), as amended, 47 U.S.C.A. § 223(b), was designed to outlaw obscene and indecent sexual material in cyberspace. One section made it a federal crime to use TELECOMMUNICATIONS to transmit "any comment, request, suggestion, proposal, image, or other communication which is obscene or indecent, knowing that the recipient of the communication is under 18 years of age, regardless of whether the maker of such communication placed the call or initiated the communication."

The AMERICAN CIVIL LIBERTIES UNION (ACLU) and 20 other plaintiffs immediately filed a lawsuit challenging the constitutionality of the CDA's provisions, especially the part of the CDA that dealt with indecent material. In *Reno v. American Civil Liberties Union*, 521 U.S. 844, 117 S .Ct. 2329, 138 L. Ed. 2d 874 (1997), the Supreme Court recognized the "legitimacy and importance of the congressional goal of protecting children from harmful materials," but ruled that the CDA abridged FREEDOM OF SPEECH and therefore was unconstitutional. The Court was most troubled by the CDA's "many ambiguities." The concern, in particular, was that the act's undefined terms *indecent* and *patently offensive* would provoke uncertainty as to how the two standards relate to each other

and just what they mean. The vagueness of this content-based regulation, along with its criminal penalties, led the Court to conclude that the CDA would have a "chilling effect" on free speech.

In addition, the CDA did not deal with key parts of the *Miller* test. One element from *Miller,* which was missing from the CDA, requires that the proscribed material must be "specifically defined by the applicable state law." This, in the Court's view, would have reduced the vagueness of the term "patently offensive." Another important element of the *Miller* test is the requirement that the material, "taken as a whole, lacks serious literary, artistic, political, or scientific value." The Court found that this "societal value" requirement allowed appellate courts "to impose some limitations and regularity on the definition by setting, as a MATTER OF LAW, a national floor for socially redeeming value." The failure of the CDA to include this element meant that the law posed a serious threat to censor speech that was outside the statute's scope.

Congress sought to address these deficiencies, in 1998, when it passed the Child Online Protection Act (COPA). COPA attempted to limit restrictions on pornographic material to communications made for commercial purposes. Although Congress incorporated the *Miller* test in hopes that the law would pass constitutional muster, the ACLU and a group of on-line website operators challenged the constitutionality of COPA, arguing that it was overbroad. In addition, the plaintiffs contended that the use of the

community standards test would give any community in the United States the ability to file civil and criminal lawsuits under COPA. The Supreme Court, in *Ashcroft v. American Civil Liberties Union,* 535 U.S. 564, 122 S. Ct. 1700, 152 L. Ed. 2d 771 (2002), issued what many legal commentators considered to be a murky decision that suggested the law might be overbroad. It referred the case back to the district court for a full hearing on the merits of the case.

Obscenity challenges are not restricted to pornographic content. In *City of Erie v. Pap's A. M.,* 529 U.S. 277, 120 S. Ct. 1382, 146 L .Ed. 2d 265 (2000), the Supreme Court moved from cyberspace to real estate when it held that a city could prevent the location of a nude dancing club using its ZONING law powers. The Court ruled that the zoning ordinance did not violate the First Amendment because the government sought to prevent the means of the expression and not the expression itself.

In 1994, Erie, Pennsylvania, enacted an ordinance that made it a crime to knowingly or intentionally appear in public in a "state of nudity." The Court held that nude dancing is "expressive conduct" that "falls only within the outer ambit" of First Amendment protection. It based its analysis on the framework for content-neutral restrictions on SYMBOLIC SPEECH set forth in the draft registration card case, *United States v. O'Brien,* 391 U.S. 367, 88 S. Ct.1673, 20 L. Ed. 2d 672 (1968). The first factor of the *O'Brien* test is whether the government regulation is within the constitutional power of the government to enact. The Court concluded that Erie had the power to protect public health and safety. The second factor is whether the regulation furthers an important or substantial government interest. The city based its ban on public nudity as a way of combating the harmful secondary effects associated with nude dancing. The preamble to the ordinance stated that Erie City Council had, for over 100 years, expressed "its findings that certain lewd, immoral activities carried on in public places for profit are highly detrimental to the public health, safety and welfare, and lead to the debasement of both women and men, promote violence, public intoxication, prostitution and other serious criminal activity." The Supreme Court found this an important government interest. The ordinance also satisfied *O'Brien's* third factor, that the government interest is unrelated to the suppression of free expression.

Assessing whether an activity or object is obscene based on community standards is problematic, especially when community values change over time. For example, in the case of the "cussin' canoeist," a Michigan man was convicted, in 1999, for violating an 1897 state law making it illegal to use obscenities and profanities while in public. He had been cited for loudly swearing while in a canoe on a public stream. However, the Michigan court of appeals reversed his conviction in 2002. The court struck down the nineteenth-century statute, ruling that the law unquestionably "operates to inhibit the exercise of First Amendment Rights" (*Michigan v. Boomer*, 250 Mich. App. 534, 655 N.W.2d 255 [Mich.App.2002]).

Another sticking point in obscenity prosecutions involves the often overbroad interpretation of what is obscene. In recent years, state appellate courts have struck down laws that made it criminally obscene for a parent to photograph his or her own child playing in a bathtub or running nude on a beach.

FURTHER READINGS

Harrison, Maureen, and Steve Gilbert, eds. 2000. *Obscenity and Pornography Decisions of the United States Supreme Court.* Carlsbad, Calif.: Excellent Books.

Hixson, Richard F. 1996. *Pornography and the Justices: The Supreme Court and the Intractable Obscenity Problem.* Carbondale: Southern Illinois Univ. Press.

Mackey, Thomas C. 2002. *Pornography on Trial: A Reference Handbook.* Santa Barbara, Calif.: ABC-CLIO.

CROSS-REFERENCES

Censorship; Dworkin, Andrea; Federal Communications Commission; Freedom of Speech; MacKinnon, Catharine Alice; Mass Communications Law; Movie Rating; Theaters and Shows; X Rating.

OBSTRUCTION OF JUSTICE

A criminal offense that involves interference, through words or actions, with the proper operations of a court or officers of the court.

The integrity of the judicial system depends on the participants' acting honestly and without fear of reprisals. Threatening a judge, trying to bribe a witness, or encouraging the destruction of evidence are examples of obstruction of justice. Federal and state laws make it a crime to obstruct justice.

Obstruction of justice in the federal courts is governed by a series of criminal statutes (18 U.S.C.A. §§ 1501–1517), which aim to protect the integrity of federal judicial proceedings as well as agency and congressional proceedings. Section 1503 is the primary vehicle for punishing those who obstruct or who endeavor to obstruct federal judicial proceedings.

Section 1503 proscribes obstructions of justice aimed at judicial officers, grand and petit jurors, and witnesses. The law makes it a crime to threaten, intimidate, or retaliate against these participants in a criminal or civil proceeding. In addition, section 1503 makes it illegal to attempt the BRIBERY of an official to alter the outcome of a judicial proceeding.

Besides these specific prohibitions, section 1503 contains the Omnibus Clause, which states that a person who "corruptly or by threats of force, or by threatening letter or communication, influences, obstructs, or impedes, or endeavors to influence, obstruct, or impede, the due administration of justice" is guilty of the crime of obstruction of justice. This clause offers broad protection to the "due administration of justice." Federal courts have read this clause expansively to proscribe any conduct that interferes with the judicial process.

To obtain a conviction under section 1503, the government must prove that there was a pending federal judicial proceeding, the defendant knew of the proceeding, and the defendant had corrupt intent to interfere with or attempted to interfere with the proceeding.

Two types of cases arise under the Omnibus Clause: the concealment, alteration, or destruction of documents; and the encouraging or rendering of false testimony. Actual obstruction is not needed as an element of proof to sustain a conviction. The defendant's endeavor to obstruct justice is sufficient. "Endeavor" has been defined by the courts as an effort to accomplish the purpose the statute was enacted to prevent. The courts have consistently held that "endeavor" constitutes a lesser threshold of purposeful activity than a criminal "attempt."

Federal obstruction of justice statutes have been used to prosecute government officials who have sought to prevent the disclosure of damaging information. The WATERGATE scandal of the 1970s involving President RICHARD M. NIXON is a classic example of this type of obstruction. A number of Nixon's top aides were convicted of obstruction of justice, including former attorney general JOHN N. MITCHELL. A federal GRAND JURY named Nixon himself as an unindicted coconspirator for the efforts to prevent disclosure of White House involvement in the 1972 BURGLARY of Democratic National Committee headquarters at the Watergate building complex in Washington, D.C.

FURTHER READINGS

Roush, Corey, and Rishi Varma. 1996. "Obstruction of Justice." *American Criminal Law Review* 33 (spring).

OCCUPANCY

Gaining or having physical possession of real property subject to, or in the absence of, legal right or title.

In a fire insurance policy, for example, the term *occupancy* is used in reference to the purpose to which the land or building is devoted or adopted, as indicated in the policy.

OCCUPATION

See MILITARY OCCUPATION.

OCCUPATIONAL DISEASE

A disease resulting from exposure during employment to conditions or substances that are detrimental to health (such as black lung disease contracted by miners).

An individual suffering from an occupational disease can seek compensation for his or her condition under WORKERS' COMPENSATION statutes or such federal legislation as the Black Lung Benefits Act of 1972, 30 U.S.C.A. § 901 et seq. Worker's compensation statutes typically require that the worker contract the disease during the course of employment; that the disease be peculiar to the worker's job by virtue of how it is caused and manifested or how job conditions result in a particular hazard, unlike employment in general; and that there be a substantially greater risk of contracting the disease or condition on the job in a different, more serious manner, than in general public experiences.

OCCUPATIONAL SAFETY AND HEALTH ACT OF 1970

Under the Occupational Safety and Health Act, 29 U.S.C.A. § 651 et seq., a business that negligently jeopardizes the lives or health of its workers commits a federal misdemeanor.

The Occupational Safety and Health Act of 1970 created the LABOR DEPARTMENT's Occupational Safety and Health Administration (OSHA) to serve as the federal government's workplace-safety watchdog, and the Occupational Safety and Health Review Commission (OSHRC) to rule on cases, forwarded to it by the Labor Department, of disagreements over the results of OSHA safety and health inspections.

The act authorizes civil fines up to $10,000 for instances where employers "willfully" expose workers to "serious" harm or death. Any act of criminal negligence can result in imprisonment of up to six months.

The Labor Department's assistant secretary for occupational safety and health has responsibility for overseeing OSHA. OSHA has its headquarters in Washington, D.C., and maintains ten regional offices. It develops and promulgates occupational safety and health standards and it issues regulations that enforce these standards. The essence of OSHA is its inspection responsibility. OSHA inspectors conduct investigations and inspections to determine the status of compliance with safety and health standards and regulations. If an inspector visits a work site and finds that the employer is not in compliance with OSHA regulations, the inspector issues a citation and proposes penalties.

From its inception, OSHA has been a controversial agency. Businesses have complained that OSHA regulations are often too bureaucratic, rigid, and hard to understand, making compliance difficult. Organized labor, on the other hand, has charged that OSHA is not diligent enough in enforcing the regulations.

During the administration of President RONALD REAGAN, the number of OSHA inspectors was reduced by 25 percent, making it even more difficult to investigate allegations of injuries. In addition, President Reagan, by EXECUTIVE ORDER No. 12,291 in 1981, permitted OSHA to certify that a company was in compliance with safety and health standards by reviewing paperwork submitted by the company.

OSHA standards and regulations touch every facet of workplace health and safety. The regulations establish maximum levels of exposure to lead, asbestos, chemicals, and other toxic substances, and they specify the proper safety gear for workers. For example, construction workers who work on scaffolding or on structural steel must wear a safety harness.

During the late 1990s, questions arose about whether OSHA regulations applied to commuters and work-at-home employees. In a response to an inquiry about these questions in November 1999, OSHA stated that employers who allow employees to work at home were indeed responsible for any injuries that occurred in the employee's home. This interpretation would mean that employers would have to inspect each employee's home and, if necessary, make necessary corrections to the home design, including cooling, heating, and ventilation systems. Although OSHA claimed that the letter did not represent official policy, several businesses and members of Congress heavily criticized the letter.

OSHA withdrew the responses to the letter in January 2000. According to statements by OSHA spokespersons, the regulations do not apply to most white-collar commuters who work at home. However, regulations do apply to employees who conduct hazardous manufacturing from their homes.

OSHA's letter regarding the regulation of home offices did not end with the agency's withdrawal of its response. In 2001, President GEORGE W. BUSH introduced a series of proposals, named the "New Freedom Initiatives," designed to enhance the opportunities for DISABLED PERSONS under the Americans with Disabilities Act. Among the proposals was a call to prevent OSHA from regulating home offices, including a specific reference to the 1999 OSHA letter.

OSHA works to improve health and safety through education and training programs. It also provides assistance to state occupational and health programs to maintain consistent national standards. Among its numerous initiatives, OSHA has sought to reduce ergonomic hazards in the workplace that cause pain and discomfort for millions of workers in the U.S. For example, in 2003, OSHA announced that it would work with the U.S. POSTAL SERVICE to reduce ergonomic injuries among employees of the service.

Employers have the right to dispute any alleged job-safety or health violation found during an OSHA inspection, the penalties OSHA has proposed, or the time given by OSHA to correct any hazardous situation. Employees and union representatives may file a case challenging the propriety of the time that OSHA has allowed for correction of any violation.

These cases are heard by OSHRC, an independent, QUASI-JUDICIAL agency. A case arises when a citation is issued against the employer as a result of an OSHA inspection and the employer contests the citation within 15 working days.

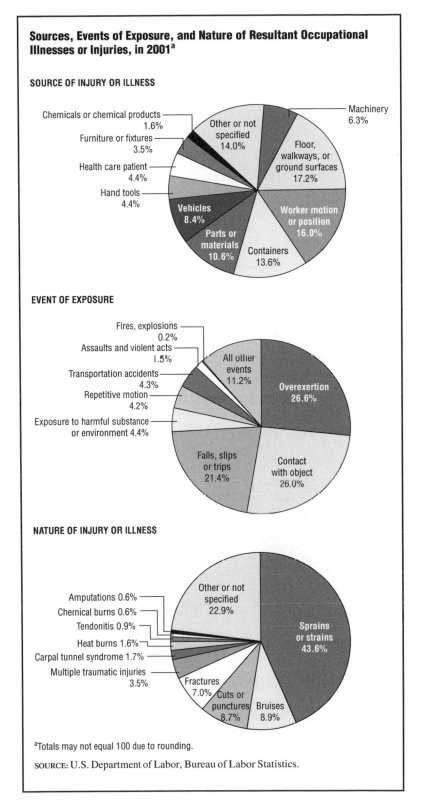

Sources, Events of Exposure, and Nature of Resultant Occupational Illnesses or Injuries, in 2001[a]

SOURCE OF INJURY OR ILLNESS

Chemicals or chemical products 1.6%
Furniture or fixtures 3.5%
Health care patient 4.4%
Hand tools 4.4%
Vehicles 8.4%
Parts or materials 10.6%
Containers 13.6%
Worker motion or position 16.0%
Floor, walkways, or ground surfaces 17.2%
Machinery 6.3%
Other or not specified 14.0%

EVENT OF EXPOSURE

Fires, explosions 0.2%
Assaults and violent acts 1.5%
Transportation accidents 4.3%
Repetitive motion 4.2%
Exposure to harmful substance or environment 4.4%
Falls, slips or trips 21.4%
Contact with object 26.0%
Overexertion 26.6%
All other events 11.2%

NATURE OF INJURY OR ILLNESS

Amputations 0.6%
Chemical burns 0.6%
Tendonitis 0.9%
Heat burns 1.6%
Carpal tunnel syndrome 1.7%
Multiple traumatic injuries 3.5%
Fractures 7.0%
Cuts or punctures 8.7%
Bruises 8.9%
Sprains or strains 43.6%
Other or not specified 22.9%

[a]Totals may not equal 100 due to rounding.

SOURCE: U.S. Department of Labor, Bureau of Labor Statistics.

All cases that require a hearing are assigned to an administrative law judge (ALJ), who decides the case. The government has the BURDEN OF PROOF. A substantial number of the decisions of the ALJs become final orders of the commission. However, each decision is subject to discretionary review by the three members of the commission upon the direction of any one of the three, if done within 30 days of the filing of the decision. A party who is dissatisfied with an ALJ decision does not have a right of appeal to the commission but must convince at least one commissioner to exercise discretion and to agree to have the commission hear the appeal. When discretionary review is taken, the commission issues its own decision. Once a case is decided, any person who has been adversely affected may file an appeal with a U.S. court of appeals.

The principal office of the commission is located in Washington, D.C. There are also three regional offices where commission judges are stationed.

FURTHER READINGS

U.S. Government Manual Website. Available online at <www.gpoaccess.gov/gmanual> (accessed November 10, 2003).

OSHA Website. Available online at <www.osha.gov> (accessed November 10, 2003).

CROSS-REFERENCES

Administrative Law and Procedure; Employment Law; Labor Law; Workers' Compensation.

❖ O'CONNOR, SANDRA DAY

Sandra Day O'Connor was appointed to the U.S. Supreme Court in 1981, becoming the first female justice on the high court. O'Connor has established herself as a moderate conservative who prefers narrow, limited holdings.

Sandra Day was born on March 26, 1930, in El Paso, Texas. She grew up in a remote part of southeastern Arizona, where her parents owned a 160,000-acre ranch. She spent her winters in El Paso, where she lived with her grandmother while attending school. In 1950, she graduated from Stanford University with a bachelor's degree in economics. She then attended Stanford Law School, where she graduated third in her class in 1952. WILLIAM H. REHNQUIST, who later would become her colleague on the U.S. Supreme Court, ranked first in the same law school class.

After law school, Day married John O'Connor, an attorney. She had hoped to join a law firm in Los Angeles or San Francisco, but none was willing to hire a woman attorney, although one did offer her a position as legal secretary. Instead,

O'Connor spent a year as a deputy county attorney in San Mateo, California. In 1953, she accompanied her husband, a member of the U.S. Army's Judge Advocate General's Corps, to West Germany. During the three years the couple spent in Germany, O'Connor worked as a civilian attorney for the Quartermaster Corps.

On their return from Germany in 1957, O'Connor and her husband settled in Phoenix, Arizona where she entered private practice. She soon became active in state and local government, serving as a member of the Maricopa County Board of Adjustments and Appeals (1960–1963) and the Governor's Committee on Marriage and the Family (1965). From 1965 to 1969, she served as assistant attorney general for Arizona.

In 1969, O'Connor was appointed to fill a vacancy in the Arizona Senate. She won election to a full term in 1970 and was reelected in 1972. After her re-election, her colleagues elected her to be majority leader, making her the first woman in the country to hold such a position.

During her years in the Arizona Senate, O'Connor voted in favor of the EQUAL RIGHTS AMENDMENT to the U.S. Constitution and supported the restoration of the death penalty and limitations on government spending. She also played an active role in REPUBLICAN PARTY politics, serving as state co-chair of the committee supporting the re-election of President RICHARD M. NIXON in 1972.

O'Connor's career shifted in 1974 with her election to the Maricopa County Superior Court. She became a respected trial judge and was appointed by Democratic Governor Bruce Babbitt to the Arizona Court of Appeals in 1979. In 1981, President RONALD REAGAN appointed her to the U.S. Supreme Court to replace justice POTTER STEWART.

O'Connor's decisions on the Court have revealed her to be a pragmatic conservative. She has written many concurring opinions that attempt to limit the majority's holding, suggesting ways that the Court could have decided an issue on narrower grounds. She has joined her conservative brethren in limiting the rights of defendants in CRIMINAL PROCEDURE cases and restricting federal intervention into areas that are reserved to the states. She has been an influential voice in reviewing challenges to AFFIRMATIVE ACTION programs. In her majority opinion in City of Richmond v. J.A. Croson Co., 488 U.S.

"THE PURPOSE OF STRICT SCRUTINY IS TO 'SMOKE OUT' ILLEGITIMATE USES OF RACE BY ASSURING THAT THE LEGISLATIVE BODY IS PURSUING A GOAL IMPORTANT ENOUGH TO WARRANT USE OF A HIGHLY SUSPECT TOOL."
—SANDRA DAY O'CONNOR

469, 109 S. Ct. 706, 102 L. Ed. 2d 854 (1989), O'Connor struck down a set-aside program for minority contractors. She concluded that these types of affirmative action programs can only be justified to remedy prior government discrimination instead of past societal discrimination. In *Adarand Constructors v. Pena*, 515 U.S. 200, 115 S. Ct. 2097, 132 L. Ed. 2d 158 (1995), O'Connor's opinion extended the holding of *Croson* by requiring that racial classifications by federal, state, and local governmental units must be subjected to the STRICT SCRUTINY of the courts. Although the decision clarified the standard by which affirmative action programs should be reviewed, lower federal and state courts have since struggled with this standard in their review of various types of programs.

O'Connor's position on ABORTION has been consistent. O'Connor has refused to join opinions written by some of her conservative colleagues arguing for the overruling of ROE V. WADE, 410 U.S. 113, 93 S. Ct. 705, 35 L. Ed. 2d 147, the 1973 decision that defined the right to choose abortion as a fundamental constitutional right. In *Planned Parenthood of Southeastern Pennsylvania v. Casey*, 505 U.S. 833, 112 S. Ct. 2791, 120 L. Ed. 2d 674 (1992), she joined Justices ANTHONY M. KENNEDY and DAVID H. SOUTER in an opinion that defended the reasoning of *Roe* and the line of cases that followed it. She has supported the rights of states to regulate abortion as long as the regulations are not too burdensome.

O'Connor has been the subject of several books about her life on and off the bench. In 2002, she published memoirs of her childhood, *Lazy B: Growing Up on a Cattle Ranch in the American Southwest*, which she co-wrote with her brother, H. Alan Day. Around the same time, her health began to suffer, and because she has been the swing vote on so many controversial issues during her tenure on the Court, several observers have speculated about

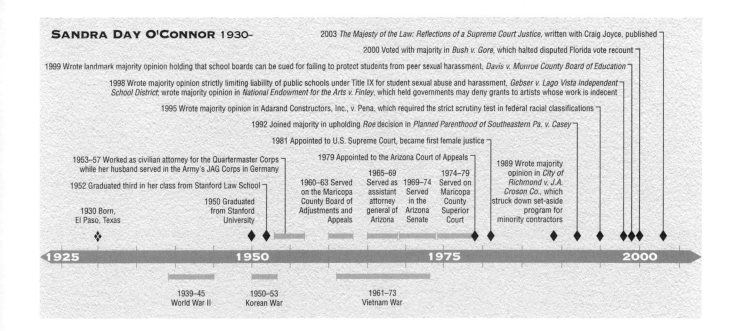

SANDRA DAY O'CONNOR 1930–

2003 *The Majesty of the Law: Reflections of a Supreme Court Justice*, written with Craig Joyce, published

2000 Voted with majority in *Bush v. Gore*, which halted disputed Florida vote recount

1999 Wrote landmark majority opinion holding that school boards can be sued for failing to protect students from peer sexual harassment, *Davis v. Monroe County Board of Education*

1998 Wrote majority opinion strictly limiting liability of public schools under Title IX for student sexual abuse and harassment, *Gebser v. Lago Vista Independent School District*; wrote majority opinion in *National Endowment for the Arts v. Finley*, which held governments may deny grants to artists whose work is indecent

1995 Wrote majority opinion in Adarand Constructors, Inc., v. Pena, which required the strict scrutiny test in federal racial classifications

1992 Joined majority in upholding *Roe* decision in *Planned Parenthood of Southeastern Pa. v. Casey*

1981 Appointed to U.S. Supreme Court, became first female justice

1979 Appointed to the Arizona Court of Appeals

1953–57 Worked as civilian attorney for the Quartermaster Corps while her husband served in the Army's JAG Corps in Germany

1952 Graduated third in her class from Stanford Law School

1960–63 Served on the Maricopa County Board of Adjustments and Appeals

1965–69 Served as assistant attorney general of Arizona

1969–74 Served in the Arizona Senate

1974–79 Served on Maricopa County Superior Court

1989 Wrote majority opinion in *City of Richmond v. J.A. Croson Co.*, which struck down set-aside program for minority contractors

1950 Graduated from Stanford University

1930 Born, El Paso, Texas

◄ 1925   1950   1975   2000 ►

1939–45 World War II

1950–53 Korean War

1961–73 Vietnam War

the direction it would take if she were to step down.

FURTHER READINGS

O'Connor, Sandra Day, and H. Alan Day. 2002. *Lazy B.* New York: Random House.

O'Connor, Sandra Day, with Craig Joyce. 2003. *The Majesty of the Law: Reflections of a Supreme Court Justice.* New York: Random House

❖ O'CONOR, CHARLES

Charles O'Conor achieved prominence as a New York attorney and as counsel for the prosecution in the trial of the notorious Tweed Ring.

O'Conor was born January 22, 1804, in New York City. After his ADMISSION TO THE BAR in 1824, O'Conor practiced law in New York for twenty years, specializing in corporation law. He attended the New York Constitutional Convention in 1846 and served as U.S. district attorney from 1853 to 1854.

In 1871 O'Conor began a four-year term as special deputy attorney general for New York State. During his tenure he acted as counsel for the prosecution in the trial of William M. ("Boss") Tweed and his followers, who controlled a corrupt political machine in New York City. The trial resulted in the disbandment of the Tweed Ring.

The year 1872 was a presidential election year and O'Conor was nominated for the presidency by a faction of the DEMOCRATIC PARTY known as the Straight-Out Democrats. After his unsuccessful presidential campaign, O'Conor served, in 1877, as counsel during the investigation of the controversial Rutherford B. Hayes-Samuel Tilden election results.

O'Conor died May 12, 1884, in Nantucket, Massachusetts.

Charles O'Conor. LIBRARY OF CONGRESS

OF COUNSEL

A term commonly applied in the PRACTICE OF LAW *to an attorney who has been employed to aid in the preparation and management of a particular case but who is not the principal attorney in the action.*

Of counsel is also sometimes used in reference to an attorney who is associated with a law firm, but is neither a partner nor an associate.

OF COURSE

Any action or step that an individual might take during judicial proceedings without being required to ask the judge's permission or that will

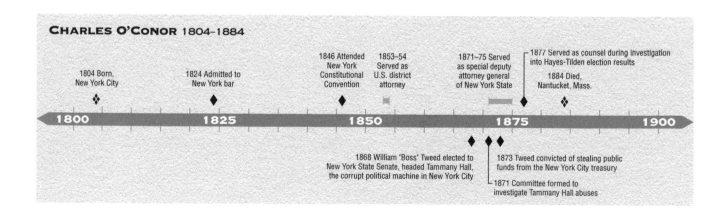

CHARLES O'CONOR 1804–1884

1804 Born, New York City

1824 Admitted to New York bar

1846 Attended New York Constitutional Convention

1853–54 Served as U.S. district attorney

1871–75 Served as special deputy attorney general of New York State

1877 Served as counsel during investigation into Hayes-Tilden election results

1884 Died, Nantucket, Mass.

1800   1825   1850   1875   1900

1868 William "Boss" Tweed elected to New York State Senate, headed Tammany Hall, the corrupt political machine in New York City

1873 Tweed convicted of stealing public funds from the New York City treasury

1871 Committee formed to investigate Tammany Hall abuses

receive the judge's automatic approval if the individual does ask permission; that which is a matter of right.

OF RECORD

Entered on the appropriate official documents maintained by a governmental body and that are usually available for inspection by the public.

A mortgage is of record when it is entered in the appropriate records of the clerk in the area where the mortgaged property is located. When it is recorded, notice is thereby provided to anyone interested in purchasing the land that it is subject to certain encumbrances.

An *attorney of record* is the lawyer whose name is contained in the records of the court as the principal lawyer handling an action.

CROSS-REFERENCES

Recording of Land Titles.

OFFENSE

A breach of law; a crime.

An offense may consist of a felony or a misdemeanor. The term is used to indicate a violation of public rights as opposed to private ones. For example, murder is an offense whereas LIBEL is not.

OFFER

A promise that, according to its terms, is contingent upon a particular act, forbearance, or promise given in exchange for the original promise or the performance thereof; a demonstration of the willingness of a party to enter into a bargain, made in such a way that another individual is justified in understanding that his or her assent to the bargain is invited and that such assent will conclude the bargain.

The making of an offer is the first of three steps in the traditional process of forming a valid contract: an offer, an acceptance of the offer, and an exchange of consideration. (Consideration is the act of doing something or promising to do something that a person is not legally required to do, or the forbearance or the promise to forbear from doing something that he or she has the legal right to do.)

An offer is a communication that gives the listener the power to conclude a contract. The question of whether a party in fact made an offer is a common question in a contract case.

The general rule is that it must be reasonable under the circumstances for the recipient to believe that the communication is an offer. The more definite the communication, the more likely it is to constitute an offer. If an offer spells out such terms as quantity, quality, price, and time and place of delivery, a court may find that an offer was made. For example, if a merchant says to a customer, "I will sell you a dozen high-grade widgets for $100 each to be delivered to your shop on December 31," a court would likely find such a communication sufficiently definite to constitute an offer. On the other hand, a statement such as "I am thinking of selling some widgets" would probably not be labeled an offer.

The question of whether a communication constitutes an offer can be significant. An offer may bind the offerer to the terms of the offer if the recipient of the offer responds by accepting the offer and giving the offerer a partial payment. If the offerer accepts the payment, a deal has been struck, and the offerer is legally obligated to follow through on the agreement. If the offerer fails to fulfill the terms of the offer, the offeree may seek a remedy in court.

There are many notable caveats to the general rules on offers. Generally, a simple price quote is not an offer. Advertisements are considered invitations for offers, not actual offers. However, an advertisement promising to pay an award may constitute an offer because only one person, or very few persons, will have the opportunity to accept the offer.

An oral offer cannot be enforced against the offerer for agreements concerning real estate, contracts for the sale of goods priced at $500 or more, and transactions that cannot be completed within one year. Such agreements must be in writing to be enforceable. These restrictions on oral offers are derived from the STATUTE OF FRAUDS, 29 Car. II, ch. 3, a law passed by the British Parliament in 1677 and designed in part to prevent false claims that an offer was tendered.

If a person rejects an offer, it is considered terminated. Likewise, if the recipient of an offer changes its terms, the original offer is terminated and a new offer is created. This new offer is called a counteroffer, and the original offerer may accept it.

In offers between merchants, a counteroffer may constitute acceptance of the original offer. Courts often hold that a contract is created when the facts show that two merchants agreed to make a sale but the recipient of the offer added terms to the agreement. In many such cases, a contract will be created as to the original offer, and the additional terms may be enforced. For example, assume that a wholesaler writes to a retailer, "Will sell 750 Grade A Fancy Pears immediately. Also have Grade A Fancy Cherries." If the retailer writes back, "Will take 750 Grade A Fancy Pears and 10 bushels of Grade A Fancy Cherries," a court may find that a contract had been created for the sale of pears and cherries.

Courts find offer and acceptance more readily in communications between merchants because merchants are more sophisticated than non-merchants in the practice of making agreements. Nevertheless, a counteroffer between merchants that adds new terms will not be enforced if the offer expressly limited acceptance to the terms of the offer, if the additional terms materially alter the intent of the parties, or if notification of rejection of the counteroffer was given to the recipient of the offer by the original offerer.

If an offer indicates that it will terminate within a certain period of time, it cannot be accepted after the time has expired. The passage of a reasonable length of time may automatically terminate an offer. The determination of a reasonable length of time depends on the circumstances surrounding the offer. For example, if a wholesaler contacts a retailer offering to sell perishable produce, the retailer cannot wait six weeks and then accept the offer. Even if an item is nonperishable, an unusually lengthy response time may terminate an offer. For example, if the usual practice in the lumber business is a response time of less than two weeks, the offerer may refuse to honor the offer if the recipient of the offer does not respond within that time period.

Some offers may be made irrevocable. An irrevocable offer is one that cannot be revoked by the offerer and terminates only upon the passage of time or rejection by the recipient. There are three types of irrevocable offers: (1) where the recipient of the offer pays the offerer for the promise to keep the offer open; (2) where the recipient of the offer partly or fully performs his or her obligations under the offer; and (3) firm offers under section 2-205 of the UNIFORM COMMERCIAL CODE. A firm offer is an assurance by a merchant to buy or sell goods. The assurance must be in writing. No consideration is necessary to support the promise that the offer will remain open. A firm offer created under section 2-205 remains open no more than ninety days.

OFFERING

See PUBLIC OFFERING.

OFFICE AUDIT

A thorough examination and verification of the tax returns and financial records of an individual or firm by the INTERNAL REVENUE SERVICE *in the office of the agent who is conducting the review.*

OFFICE OF MANAGEMENT AND BUDGET

The Office of Management and Budget (OMB), formerly the Bureau of the Budget, is an agency of the federal government that evaluates, formulates, and coordinates management procedures and program objectives within and among departments and agencies of the EXECUTIVE BRANCH. It also controls the administration of the FEDERAL BUDGET, while routinely providing the president of the United States with recommendations regarding budget proposals and relevant legislative enactments. The Bureau of the Budget was first established in the Executive Office of the President pursuant to REORGANIZATION PLAN No. 1 of 1939 (5 U.S.C.A. app.), effective July 1, 1939. Its functions were reorganized and the office renamed OMB by EXECUTIVE ORDER No. 11,541 of July 1, 1970. Since the reorganization, the OMB has played a central role in analyzing the federal budget and making recommendations for changes in the budget. Its director, who is appointed by the president, is a key advisor on fiscal policy. The director often appears before congressional committees to explain budgetary proposals.

The OMB assists the president in developing and maintaining effective government by reviewing the organizational structure and management procedures of the executive branch to ensure that the intended results are achieved. It works to develop efficient coordinating mechanisms to implement government activities and to expand interagency cooperation.

The OMB assists the president and executive departments and agencies in preparing the budget and in formulating the government's fiscal program. It also publishes the president's proposed *Budget of the U.S. Government* every year. Once Congress approves a budget, the OMB supervises and controls the administration of it. In addition, it advises the president on proposed legislation and recommends to the president whether to sign or VETO legislative enactments.

The office also assists in developing regulatory reform proposals and programs for paperwork reduction, especially reporting burdens of the public. The OMB helps in considering, clearing, and, where necessary, preparing proposed executive orders and proclamations that will have an impact on the federal budget.

The OMB has assumed an oversight role in determining the effectiveness of federal programs. It plans and develops information systems that provide the president with program performance data, and it plans, conducts, and promotes evaluation efforts that assist the president in assessing program objectives, performance, and efficiency.

The office also keeps the president informed of the progress of government agency activities with respect to work proposed, initiated, and completed. It coordinates work among the agencies of the executive branch to eliminate overlap and duplication of effort and to ensure that the funds appropriated by Congress are expended in the most economical manner.

Finally, OMB works to improve the economy, efficiency, and effectiveness of the procurement processes by directing procurement policies, regulations, procedures, and forms for the executive branch.

OMB is comprised of divisions that are organized by agency or program area and also by function. Resource Management Offices develop and support the president's Budget and Management proposals. The Budget Review Division provides technical support for budget-related negotiations and decisions. The Legislative Reference Division coordinates the position of the administration regarding budget-related legislation. Statutory offices include the Office of Federal Financial Management, the Office of Federal Procurement Policy, and the Office of Information and Regulatory Affairs.

FURTHER READINGS

Office of Management and Budget. Available online at <www.whitehouse.gov/omb> (accessed August 1, 2003).

CROSS-REFERENCES

Executive Branch.

OFFICE OF NATIONAL DRUG CONTROL POLICY

The Office of National Drug Control Policy (ONDCP) was established by the National Narcotics Leadership Act of 1988 (21 U.S.C.A. § 1501 et seq.) and began operations in January 1989.

ONDCP develops and coordinates the policies and objectives of the federal government's program for reducing the use of illicit drugs. ONDCP seeks ways to combat the manufacture and distribution of illegal drugs, drug-related crime and violence, and drug-related health consequences. The director of ONDCP is charged with producing the National Drug Control Strategy, which directs the U.S. anti-drug efforts and establishes a program, a budget, and guidelines for cooperation among federal, state, and local entities.

By law, the director also evaluates, coordinates, and oversees both the international and domestic anti-drug efforts of the EXECUTIVE BRANCH agencies and ensures that such efforts sustain and complement state and local anti-drug activities. The director is commonly referred to as the "drug czar" because he or she advises the president regarding changes in the organization, management, budgeting, and personnel of federal agencies that could affect the U.S. anti-drug efforts. The director is a member of the NATIONAL SECURITY COUNCIL and the Cabinet Council on Counternarcotics.

ONDCP drug-control priorities include treatment, prevention, domestic law enforcement, and interdiction and international initiatives. It presumes that chronic, hard-core drug use is a disease and that anyone suffering from the disease needs treatment. ONDCP seeks to create a balance between sanctions for drug-related criminal activity and treatment of an addictive disease.

In the area of prevention, ONDCP seeks to reverse the upward trend in drug use and find ways to empower communities to address their drug problems. It develops and implements initiatives that attempt to prevent illicit drug use by young people and other high-risk populations.

ONDCP also emphasizes the need for strong, effective law enforcement efforts, including strong sanctions against drug offenders. Key priorities for domestic law enforcement are the disruption and dismantling of drug trafficking organizations, including seizure of their assets, and the investigation, arrest, prosecution, and imprisonment of drug traffickers. It seeks to attack drug trafficking organizations at every level, from the drug kingpin to the street-corner dealer, through a careful coordination of federal, state, and local law enforcement efforts.

In the international sphere, ONDCP views interdiction as an important component of national drug policy. It cooperates with other nations in building their law enforcement institutions, attacking drug production facilities, interdicting drug shipments in both source and transit countries, and dismantling drug trafficking organizations.

The director of ONDCP is supported by a number of organizational units. The Office of Demand Reduction undertakes and oversees activities to reduce the demand for drugs, including drug education, drug prevention, drug treatment, and related efforts for the rehabilitation of persons addicted to drugs. This office also conducts research on drug use and periodically convenes expert panels to assess state-of-the-art approaches to reducing the demand for drugs.

The Office of Supply Reduction seeks to reduce the availability, production, and distribution of illicit drugs in the United States and abroad. The Office of State and Local Affairs coordinates agency relationships and outreach efforts to state and local government agencies. The Counter-Drug Technology Assessment Center is the central counter-drug enforcement research and development organization of the federal government. It works to identify the scientific and technological needs of federal, state, and local law enforcement agencies.

The election of President GEORGE W. BUSH in 2000 boosted efforts of conservatives who supported governmental funding for "faith-based" drug treatment programs. In 2003, the director of the ONDCP announced President Bush's plan for a three-year, $600 million voucher plan that would give such programs access to federal funds.

Also, in March 2003, John P. Walters, the director of the ONDCP, and Tom Ridge, Secretary of the HOMELAND SECURITY DEPARTMENT, jointly announced the appointment of Roger Mackin as counter-narcotics officer/U.S. interdiction coordinator. One of Mackin's responsibilities was to ensure that all Homeland Security Department counter-drug policies and efforts were aligned with the president's National Drug Control Strategy.

In April 2003, Walters testified before a House Appropriations Committee that ONDCP efforts had been a significant factor in the recent downturn in youth drug use. Among the ONDCP accomplishments were its media campaign that uses a Web site, ads, and other means of disseminating information about drugs and the organization's Technology Transfer Program that has brought updated technology and training to more than 20 percent of the nation's state and local police departments and sheriffs' offices.

At the same time, a 2003 report from the ONDCP stated that in 1992, the overall cost of drug abuse to the U.S. population was approximately $102 billion; the projected cost for the 2000 fiscal year (FY) was estimated to be $160.7 billion. In the same report, ONDCP restructured its budget to reflect new methods for reporting drug abuse. The requested drug control budget for FY 2004 was $11.7 billion.

FURTHER READINGS

Office of National Drug Control Policy Website. Available at <www.whitehousedrugpolicy.gov> (accessed August 1, 2003).

U.S. Government Manual Website. Available online at <www.gpoaccess.gov/gmanual> (accessed November 10, 2003).

CROSS-REFERENCES

Drugs and Narcotics; Executive Branch.

OFFICE OF THRIFT SUPERVISION

The Office of Thrift Supervision (OTS) was established as a bureau of the TREASURY DEPARTMENT in August 1989 as part of a major REORGANIZATION PLAN of the thrift regulatory structure mandated by the Financial Institutions Reform, Recovery, and Enforcement Act of 1989 (FIRREA) (12 U.S.C.A. § 1462a). The reorganization resulted from the savings and loan crisis of the 1980s, when a newly deregulated thrift industry invested in high-risk real estate ventures, many of which collapsed. This situation led to enormous financial losses and the call for more federal regulation and oversight.

The OTS is authorized to charter federal thrift institutions and to serve as the primary regulator of the 1,700 federal- and state-chartered thrifts that belong to the Savings Association Insurance Fund. Its purpose is to maintain the safety, soundness, and viability of the thrift industry by adopting regulations that seek to prevent unreasonable lending risks, examining and supervising thrift institutions, and enforcing compliance with federal laws and regulations. In addition to overseeing thrift institutions, the OTS also oversees companies that own thrifts and controls the acquisition of thrifts by such holding companies.

The OTS is organized into five main divisions. The Washington Operations Office develops national policy guidelines to clarify and implement statutes and regulations and establishes programs to implement new policies and laws. This division monitors the condition of the thrift industry and attempts to identify emerging supervisory problem areas.

The Regional Operations division examines and supervises thrift institutions through five regional offices located in Jersey City, Atlanta, Chicago, Dallas, and San Francisco. These offices also promote housing and other financial services in areas with the greatest need. The regional offices oversee the training and development of federal thrift regulators through accredited programs.

The Chief Counsel division provides a full range of legal services to the OTS, including drafting regulations, representing the agency in court, and taking enforcement actions against savings institutions that violate laws or regulations.

The staff of the Congressional Affairs division interacts with members of Congress, congressional staff, and committee members to accomplish the legislative objectives of the OTS. This division provides information to Congress about the office's supervisory, regulatory, and enforcement activities.

The Public Affairs division disseminates information, including policies, regulations, and key developments within the office. It also maintains an archive of business records and documented actions of the OTS and its predecessor, the Federal Home Loan Bank Board.

The OTS uses no tax money to fund its regulation. Its expenses are met through fees and assessments on the thrift institutions it regulates. The OTS is headed by a director appointed by the president and confirmed by the Senate to serve a five-year term.

Since 1999 the OTS has filed annual performance reports, and in 2000 it prepared a strategic report for 2000-2005. Since the late 1990s it has expanded its Web site, offering consumers information on the stability of the thrift institutions it regulates. In addition since 2001 it has prepared regulations in "plain English" to reduce confusion.

FURTHER READINGS

Office of Thrift Supervision. Available online at <www.ots.treas.gov> (accessed August 1, 2003).

U.S. Government Manual Website. Available online at <www.gpoaccess.gov/gmanual> (accessed November 10, 2003).

CROSS-REFERENCES

Savings and Loan Association; Treasury Department.

OFFICER

An individual with the responsibility of performing the duties and functions of an office, that is a duty or charge, a position of trust, or a right to exercise a public or private employment.

A *public officer* is ordinarily defined as an individual who has been elected or appointed to exercise the functions of an office for the benefit of the public. *Executive officers,* such as the president or state governors, are public officers charged with the duty to ascertain that the law is enforced and obeyed. A *legislative officer,* such as a member of Congress, has the duty of making the laws. A public officer whose duties include administering justice, adjudicating controversies, and interpreting the laws is called a *judicial officer.* A *de jure officer* is one who is legally appointed and qualified to exercise the office. A *de facto officer* is an individual who appears to be legally qualified and appointed to an office but is not due to some legal technicality, such as failure to file a financial disclosure statement within the time prescribed by statute.

A public office must be created either by statute or by constitutional provision. Public officers are distinguishable from employees in that they are required to take an oath of office and are appointed or elected to specified terms of office. The eligibility, duties, and compensation of public officers are defined by statute.

Removal from office occurs when an officer is dismissed from his or her position by a superior officer acting according to law. Sufficient cause must exist to justify the removal. When an individual is wrongfully removed from office, he or she may seek reinstatement.

A *military officer* is one who has been commissioned as such in the ARMED SERVICES.

An officer of a corporation is someone, such as the president, vice-president, treasurer, or secretary, whose main duties are to oversee the efficient operation of the business.

CROSS-REFERENCES

Officers of the Court.

OFFICERS OF THE COURT

An all-inclusive term for any type of court employee including judges, clerks, sheriffs, marshals, bailiffs, and constables.

An attorney is also regarded as being an officer of the court and must therefore comply with court rules.

OFFICIAL GAZETTE

A compilation published weekly by the PATENT AND TRADEMARK OFFICE *listing all the* PATENTS *and* TRADEMARKS *issued and registered, thereby providing notice to all interested parties.*

OFFSET

A contrary claim or demand that may cancel or reduce a given claim; a counterclaim. A kind of bookkeeping entry that counters the effect of a previous entry.

OKLAHOMA CITY BOMBING

See TERRORISM "The Oklahoma City Bombing" (Sidebar); VENUE "Venue and the Oklahoma City Bombing Case" (Sidebar).

OLD-AGE, SURVIVORS, AND DISABILITY INSURANCE

The federal Old-Age, Survivors, and Disability Insurance (OASDI) system was developed pursuant to the federal Social Security Act of 1935 (42 U.S.C.A. § 301 et seq. [1935]) to provide government benefits to eligible retirees, disabled individuals, and surviving spouses and their dependents.

OASDI benefits are monthly payments made to retired people, families whose wage earner has died, and workers who are unemployed because of sickness or accident. Workers qualify for such protection by having been employed for the mandatory minimum amount of time and by having made contributions to SOCIAL SECURITY. There is no financial need requirement. Once a worker qualifies for protection, his or her

family is also entitled to protection. The OASDI program is geared toward helping families as a matter of social policy.

The OASDI program is funded by payroll taxes levied on employees, their employers, and the self-employed. The rate of the contributions is based upon the employee's taxable income, up to a maximum taxable amount, with the employer contributing an equal amount. The self-employed person contributes twice the amount levied on an employee. In 1996 a tax rate of 6.2 percent was levied on earned income up to a maximum of $62,887 to fund OASDI.

Old-Age Benefits

Old-age benefits were the cornerstone of the original SOCIAL SECURITY ACT, which was passed in 1935. More than 25 million Americans receive old-age benefits each month, and those payments amount to almost $20 billion a year. Because of the increasing median age of the adult population, these figures are constantly increasing.

To be eligible for Social Security old-age benefits, a person must have worked a minimum number of calendar quarters, which increases with the worker's age. Forty quarters is the maximum requirement. Once a person earns credit for the required number of calendar quarters, she or he is insured. Workers born before 1950 can retire at age 65 with full benefits based on their average income during working years. For those workers born between 1950 and 1960, the retirement age has increased to age 66. Workers born in 1960 or later will be awarded full benefits for retirement at age 67. A person may retire at age 62 and receive less than full benefits. A worker's spouse who has not contributed to Social Security receives, at age 65, 50 percent of the amount paid to the worker.

Survivors' Benefits

Survivors' benefits are payments made to family members when a worker dies. The payments are intended to help ease the financial strain caused by the loss of the worker's income. Survivors can receive benefits if the deceased worker was employed and contributed to Social Security long enough to be considered insured.

When a wage earner dies, his or her spouse and unmarried minor children are entitled to receive benefits. In addition to monthly checks, the worker's surviving spouse, or if there is none, another eligible person, may receive a lump-sum payment of $255.

Disability Benefits

A person who becomes unable to work and expects to be disabled for at least twelve months or who will probably die from the condition can receive Social Security payments before reaching retirement age. A worker is eligible for disability benefits if she or he has worked enough years under Social Security before the onset of disabilities.

A disability is any physical or mental condition that prevents the worker from doing substantial work. Examples of disabilities that meet the Social Security criteria include brain damage, heart disease, kidney failure, severe arthritis, and serious mental illness.

The SOCIAL SECURITY ADMINISTRATION (SSA) determines whether a person's disability is serious enough to justify the awarding of benefits. The SSA determines whether the impairment is so severe that it significantly affects "basic work activity." If the answer is yes, the worker's medical data are compared with a set of guidelines known as the Listing of Impairments. If the claimant is found to suffer from a condition contained in this list, payment of the benefits will be approved. If the condition is less severe, SSA determines whether the impairment prevents the person from doing his or her former work. If not, the application will be denied. If so, a determination is made as to whether the impairment will prevent the applicant from doing other work present in the economy.

At this point SSA uses a series of guidelines that attempt to combine consideration of the applicant's residual functional capacity with the factors of age, education, and experience. The guidelines classify work into three types: sedentary work, light work, and medium work. If the SSA determines that an applicant can perform one of these types of work, it will deny benefits. A claimant may appeal this decision and ask for a hearing in which to present further evidence, including personal testimony. If the recommendation of the ADMINISTRATIVE LAW judge conducting the hearing is adverse, the claimant may appeal to the Social Security Administration's Appeals Council. If the claimant loses the appeal, she or he may file civil action in federal district court seeking review of the agency's adverse determination.

Three types of benefits are available to persons who meet the OASDI disability eligibility requirements: monthly cash payments, voca-

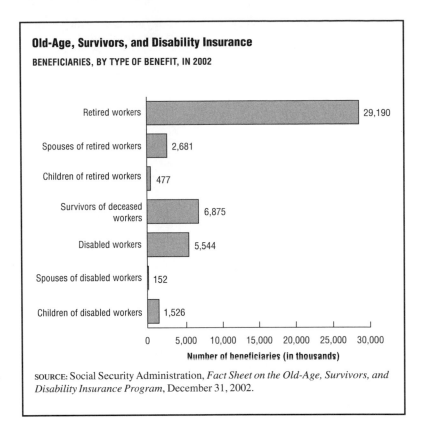

Old-Age, Survivors, and Disability Insurance

BENEFICIARIES, BY TYPE OF BENEFIT, IN 2002

Retired workers — 29,190
Spouses of retired workers — 2,681
Children of retired workers — 477
Survivors of deceased workers — 6,875
Disabled workers — 5,544
Spouses of disabled workers — 152
Children of disabled workers — 1,526

Number of beneficiaries (in thousands)

SOURCE: Social Security Administration, *Fact Sheet on the Old-Age, Survivors, and Disability Insurance Program*, December 31, 2002.

tional rehabilitation, and medical insurance. Cash payments begin, provided proper application has been made, with the sixth month of disability. The amount of the monthly payment depends on the amount of earnings on which the employee has paid Social Security taxes and the number of eligible dependents. The maximum for a family usually equals roughly the amount to which the disabled employee is entitled as an individual plus allowances for two dependents.

Vocational rehabilitation services are provided through a joint federal-state program. Persons receiving cash payments for disability may continue to receive them for a limited time after they begin to work or near the end of a program of vocational rehabilitation. This period is referred to as the "trial work period" and may last as long as nine months.

Medical services are available through the MEDICARE program in which a recipient of OASDI disability benefits begins to participate twenty-five months after the onset of disability.

FURTHER READINGS

Matheny, Ken. 2003. "Social Security Disability and the Older Worker: A Proposal for Reform." *Georgetown Journal on Poverty Law & Policy* 10 (winter).

Nickles, Don. 1999. "Retiring in America: Why the United States Needs a New Kind of Social Security for the New Millennium." *Harvard Journal on Legislation* 36 (winter).

Social Security Advisory Board. 2001. *Social Security Disability: The Basics.* Mechanicsburg: Pennsylvania Bar Institute.

Social Security and SSI Disability. 1999. New York: Practising Law Institute.

CROSS-REFERENCES

Disability Discrimination; Elder Law; Health Insurance; Senior Citizens.

OLMSTEAD V. UNITED STATES

Olmstead v. United States, 277 U.S. 438, 48 S. Ct. 564, 72 L. Ed. 944 (1928), was the first case dealing with the issue of whether messages passing over telephone wires are within the constitutional protection against unreasonable SEARCHES AND SEIZURES.

In *Olmstead,* several individuals were convicted of a conspiracy to violate the National Prohibition Act (41 Stat. 305) by illegally possessing, transporting, and importing intoxicating liquors, maintaining nuisances, and selling intoxicating liquors. The information leading to the discovery of the conspiracy was, for the most part, obtained through the interception of messages on the telephones of the conspirators by four federal PROHIBITION officers. Wires were placed along the ordinary telephone wires from the homes of four of the defendants and along the wires that led to their main office of operation. The insertion of the wires was made without any TRESPASS having been committed on any of the defendants' property since it was done in the basement of the large office building and in the streets near the residences.

The Supreme Court held that messages passing over telephone wires were not within the protection against unreasonable searches and seizures. The eavesdropper had to have physically trespassed in order for evidence procured by WIRETAPPING to be regarded as having been obtained unconstitutionally. The Court reasoned that, since there was no entry of the homes or offices of the defendants, there was no physical trespass. In addition, in spite of the fact that the evidence leading to the conviction was obtained in violation of a state statute that made it a misdemeanor to intercept telegraphic or telephonic messages, the Court indicated that the statute did not declare that evidence obtained in such manner would be inadmissible, and it was not inadmissible under COMMON LAW.

Subsequently the *Olmstead* case was overruled, the physical trespass doctrine abandoned, and the holding in *Olmstead* is no longer the law. Under current law, in order for ELECTRONIC SURVEILLANCE to be constitutionally permissible, it must be done pursuant to the prior authorization by a court.

❖ OLNEY, RICHARD

In the late nineteenth century, the Massachusetts-born attorney Richard Olney exerted a powerful influence over domestic and international affairs. From 1893 to 1895, Olney served as U.S. attorney general under President GROVER CLEVELAND and, from 1895 to 1897, as SECRETARY OF STATE. A nationalist with a forceful personality who took a broad view of federal power, Olney is remembered for two important actions during his public career that had long-lasting implications for U.S. law. First, as attorney general, he used the office in 1894 to break a strike by railway workers that hampered the delivery of mail nationwide. The outcome affected the rights of workers for more than a quarter of a century, thrust Olney into the national spotlight, and earned him the enmity of LABOR UNIONS. Second, after becoming secretary of state, he resolved a conflict between Venezuela and England that shaped U.S. foreign policy well into the twentieth century.

Born in Oxford, Massachusetts, on September 15, 1835, Olney was educated at Brown University and Harvard Law School. Admitted to the Boston bar in 1859, he established a successful law practice and earned recognition for his work with railroads. A brief political career followed with his election to the Massachusetts state legislature, where he served one term between 1873 and 1874. In 1893 he was appointed U.S. attorney general at the start of the second and deeply troubled administration of President Cleveland. The president became mired in public controversies, and his new attorney general would be at the heart of one of the worst.

When Olney assumed his duties in the DEPARTMENT OF JUSTICE, the nation was suffering from an economic depression. The Pullman Company, a Chicago-based railroad, cut its workers' pay to near-starvation wages but went on paying dividends to its shareholders. In 1894 the company's laborers staged a strike that spread nationwide under the auspices of the nascent American Railway Union: everywhere, railroad workers refused to handle Pullman train cars. Tensions escalated when railroad owners began firing the workers, and violence was threatened. The General Managers Association, a trade organization representing railroads, appealed to the Cleveland administration for federal intervention.

Because the strike had prevented the delivery of U.S. mails, Cleveland and Olney had to intervene. Olney had little sympathy for the workers. His first idea was to use the U.S. Army to crush them. Instead he sent 5000 special deputies to restore order. When riots followed, Olney arrested and prosecuted union leaders on grounds of conspiracy, and he won a sweeping federal court INJUNCTION to prevent workers from interfering with the railroads' operation. Appealing to the U.S. Supreme Court in 1895, union president EUGENE V. DEBS lost his case, and the strike was broken (*In re Debs*, 158 U.S. 564, 15 S. Ct. 900, 39 L. Ed. 1092). The Court's sanction of the injunction was a great boon to U.S. corporations, which thereafter sought court injunctions to break strikes until the practice was restrained during the 1930s. Nonetheless, Olney and Cleveland paid a high political price in the polls for their widely unpopular actions.

In 1895, toward the end of the Cleveland administration, the president appointed Olney secretary of state. At once Olney faced a foreign policy crisis: the conflict between Venezuela and Great Britain over the Venezuela-British Guiana boundary. As much a believer in U.S. supremacy as he was in federal power at home, Olney ordered Britain to enter ARBITRATION with Venezuela. His order relied on a broad reading of the MONROE DOCTRINE. As the basis of U.S. foreign policy in the nineteenth century, the Monroe Doctrine essentially preserved U.S.

Richard Olney.
ARCHIVE PHOTOS, INC.

independence in the Western Hemisphere. Although the doctrine prohibited foreign intervention in Latin American nations, Olney believed it permitted U.S. intervention to stop European interference with Latin American affairs. Britain ultimately resolved its conflict with Venezuela through arbitration in 1899. But the broader impact of Olney's views came later. His interpretation came to be known as the Olney Corollary to the Monroe Doctrine and was influential in the foreign policy of President THEODORE ROOSEVELT.

Olney left office in 1897 at the end of the unpopular Cleveland administration. Returning to private practice, he was touted as a possible presidential candidate in 1904, but he did not run. He died in Boston on April 8, 1917.

> "TODAY THE UNITED STATES IS PRACTICALLY SOVEREIGN ON THIS CONTINENT AND ITS FIAT IS LAW UPON THE SUBJECTS TO WHICH IT CONFINES ITS INTERPOSITION."
> —RICHARD OLNEY

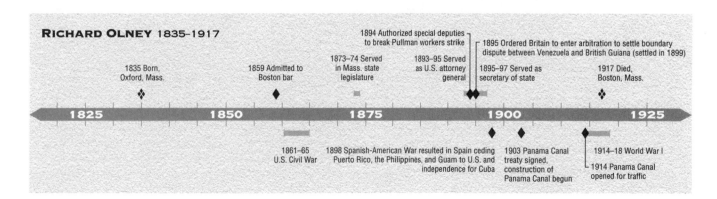

RICHARD OLNEY 1835–1917

1835 Born, Oxford, Mass.

1859 Admitted to Boston bar

1873–74 Served in Mass. state legislature

1893–95 Served as U.S. attorney general

1894 Authorized special deputies to break Pullman workers strike

1895 Ordered Britain to enter arbitration to settle boundary dispute between Venezuela and British Guiana (settled in 1899)

1895–97 Served as secretary of state

1917 Died, Boston, Mass.

1825　1850　1875　1900　1925

1861–65 U.S. Civil War

1898 Spanish-American War resulted in Spain ceding Puerto Rico, the Philippines, and Guam to U.S. and independence for Cuba

1903 Panama Canal treaty signed, construction of Panama Canal begun

1914–18 World War I

1914 Panama Canal opened for traffic

FURTHER READINGS

Brodsky, Alyn. 2000. *Grover Cleveland: A Study in Character.* New York: St. Martin's.

Eggert, Gerald G. 1974. *Richard Olney: Evolution of a Statesman.* University Park: Pennsylvania State Univ. Press.

James, Henry. 1971. *Richard Olney and His Public Service.* New York: Da Capo Press.

Jeffers, H. Paul. 2000. *An Honest President: The Life and Presidencies of Grover Cleveland.* New York: Morrow/Avon.

CROSS-REFERENCES

Cleveland, Stephen Grover; Debs, Eugene Victor; Labor Union; Monroe Doctrine.

OMBUDSPERSON

A public official who acts as an impartial intermediary between the public and government or bureaucracy, or an employee of an organization who mediates disputes between employees and management.

The Swedish legislature first created the position of ombudsperson in the early 1800s; the literal translation of *ombudsperson* is "an investigator of citizen complaints." This official was considered to be a person of "known legal ability and outstanding integrity" and was chosen by the Swedish parliament to serve a four-year term.

In modern times, an ombudsperson addresses concerns (such as administrative abuse or maladministration) that citizens or groups have about organizations or bureaucracies. In these situations, the ombudsperson acts as an impartial mediator between the two parties, providing a less threatening type of dispute resolution. For the ombudsperson to help reduce friction between citizens and the government, he or she must be viewed as trustworthy and neutral; the process will not work if one party believes that the ombudsperson is taking the side of the other party. Ombudspersons are bound by the oath of the Ombudsman's Association, which requires neutrality and confidentiality, requirements that are necessary to create trust between the persons involved in a dispute and the ombudsperson.

The power of the ombudsperson lies in his or her ability to investigate complaints of wrongdoing and then notify the public or the relevant government agencies, or both, of the findings. However, an ombudsperson cannot change or make laws, enforce any recommendations, or change administrative actions or decisions.

At the government level, the ombudsperson is appointed by the legislature of the state or county in which he or she serves. The ombudsperson typically has some law training, although a law degree is not required, and the ombusperson must be free of any political loyalties because the job requires neutrality. The goal of the ombudsperson is to assist the communication between the public and the government and help create solutions to problems that arise between the two parties, rather than punishing the wrongdoer. These solutions are aimed at reducing the possibility of similar problems in the future.

Friction between the public and government often can be attributed to the way laws or legislative policies are enforced. In these cases, the ombudsperson can try to reduce the friction by finding a more satisfactory method of carrying out the law. For example, even though police officers may legally enter a workplace to arrest an employee on charges of a crime, this practice can embarrass the employee and threaten her job, even if charges are later dropped. In this situation the ombudsperson would most likely confer with the police department to see if arrests for nonfelonies could be made safely outside the workplace.

The ombudsperson's role in U.S. government is not clearly defined; not all states use an ombudsperson within their governmental agencies. Compared with ombudspersons in other countries, an ombudsperson in the United States has a larger role in the mediation and negotiation of settlements. Government branches such as social and child WELFARE agencies, prisons, law enforcement agencies, and consumer bureaus often have ombudspersons within their ranks.

Although ombudspersons generally work in government agencies, county governments, and city governments, companies also may employ an ombudsperson as a confidential, neutral contact with whom employees can discuss their concerns. In the mid-1990s more than 200 private corporations employed an ombudsperson. A corporate ombudsperson serves as the point of contact for dispute resolution in a corporation. The corporate ombudsperson, who is typically a senior official within the company, helps employees work through a variety of work-related conflicts, such as dissatisfaction with salary, unethical behavior such as theft or FRAUD, terminations, discrimination, and SEXUAL HARASSMENT. In recent years issues such as government contract compliance and WHISTLE-BLOWING have also been handled by corporate ombudspersons.

The corporate ombudsperson's position arose from corporations' desire to increase the job satisfaction of their employees, improve the communication between employees and management, and avoid litigation. As of 1992, there were more than 1000 corporate ombudspersons practicing. On average, a corporate ombudsperson will handle 200 to 300 cases per year and deal with 2 to 8 percent of the corporate workforce.

A corporate ombudsperson works with employees and management by reviewing management decisions and intervening in employee-employee and employee-management disputes. Generally, the methods the corporate ombudsperson may use include responsive listening, investigation, mediation, direct resolution, and upward feedback to management. The ombudsperson allows an employee to voice her concerns and advises or counsels the employee on the best way to deal with the situation. If necessary, as is often the case in allegations of sexual harassment, for example, the ombudsperson can investigate the situation further.

Because of the variety of situations a corporate ombudsperson deals with and because corporate cultures vary from one company to another, there is no standard job description or authority level for corporate ombudspersons.

Other organizations that employ ombudspersons are hospitals, school districts, and universities. In the mid-1990s more than 100 COLLEGES AND UNIVERSITIES employed an ombudsperson, and more than 4000 hospitals offered ombudsperson services for patients. Many small businesses also have an office that handles client or citizen complaints and functions as an ombudsperson's office.

Ombudsperson confidentiality is important to the success of the office. If either party in a dispute believes that her concerns are not heard in confidence, communication with the ombudsperson will decline and the possibility of resolving a problem will also decline. Generally, communication with an ombudsperson is confidential. However, an ombudsperson is not required to maintain confidentiality regarding criminal behavior or conduct that threatens employee safety or company assets.

The question of whether an ombudsperson's communications with a party to a dispute are privileged (whether they may be protected from disclosure in court) is determined by courts on a case-by-case basis. Several cases have recognized an ombudsperson's privilege, including *Shabazz v. Scurr,* 662 F. Supp. 90 (S.D. Iowa 1987), which involved communications to a prison ombudsperson, and *Kientzy v. McDonnell Douglas Corp.,* 133 F.R.D. 570 (E.D. Mo. 1991), which involved a corporate ombudsperson.

FURTHER READINGS

Green, Mark T., and Laurel W. Eisner. 1998. "The Public Advocate for New York City: An Analysis of the Country's Only Elected Ombudsman." *New York Law School Law Review* 42 (summer-fall).

Gregory, Roy, and Philip Giddings, eds. 2000. *Righting Wrongs: The Ombudsman in Six Continents.* Washington, D.C.: IOS Press.

Hidén, Mikael. 1973. *The Ombudsman in Finland: The First Fifty Years.* Trans. by Aaron Bell. Berkeley, Calif.: Institute of Governmental Studies.

Rowat, Donald C., ed. 1965. *The Ombudsman: Citizen's Defender.* London: George Allen and Unwin.

Thompson, Brenda V. 1992. "Corporate Ombudsmen and Privileged Communications: Should Employee Communications to Corporate Ombudsmen Be Entitled to Privilege?" *University of Cincinnati Law Review* 61 (fall).

Wibbenmeyer, Kevin L. 1991. "Privileged Communication Extended to the Corporate Ombudsman-Employee Relationship via Federal Rule of Evidence 501." *Journal of Dispute Resolution* (fall).

Zagoria, Sam. 1988. *The Ombudsman: How Good Governments Handle Citizens' Grievances.* Cabin John, Md.: Seven Locks.

CROSS-REFERENCES

Administrative Law and Procedure; Alternative Dispute Resolution.

OMNIBUS

[Latin, For all; containing two or more independent matters.] *A term frequently used in reference to a legislative bill comprised of two or more general subjects that is designed to compel the executive to approve provisions that he or she would otherwise reject but that he or she signs into law to prevent the defeat of the entire bill.*

Laws governing the FEDERAL BUDGET are typically omnibus bills; for example, the Omnibus Consolidated Rescissions and Appropriations Act of 1996 (110 Stat. 1321).

ON DEMAND

Payable immediately on request.

A note that is payable on demand is one that is to be paid the moment payment is requested by the individual who has legal possession thereof.

CROSS-REFERENCES

Commercial Paper.

ON OR ABOUT

Near; approximately; without significant variance from an agreed date.

The phrase *on or about* is used to avoid being bound to a more precise statement than is required by law. For example, when an individual seeks to purchase a home, the date when the transaction is closed and the legal title and possession are transferred from seller to buyer is ordinarily scheduled on or about a particular date. The phrase is used to indicate that the parties recognize the fact that, although the exact date might not be convenient for both of them, the transaction should be completed as close to that date as is practicable.

ON POINT

Directly applicable or dispositive of the matter under consideration.

A statute or case is "on point" if it has direct application to the facts of a case currently before a tribunal for determination.

ONE PERSON, ONE VOTE

The principle that all citizens, regardless of where they reside in a state, are entitled to equal legislative representation.

This principle was enunciated by the Supreme Court in REYNOLDS V. SIMS, 377 U.S. 533, 84 S. Ct. 1362, 12 L. Ed. 2d 506 (1964). The Court ruled that a state's APPORTIONMENT plan for seats in both houses of a bicameral state legislature must allocate seats on a population basis so that the voting power of each voter be as equal as possible to that of any other voter.

CROSS-REFERENCES

Baker v. Carr.

❖ O'NEILL, THOMAS PHILLIP, JR.

In many ways, Democrat Tip O'Neill epitomized the cigar-smoking, deal-making American politician of a bygone era. A tough, gregarious leader, O'Neill was the formidable Speaker of the U.S. House of Representatives from 1977 to 1986. He was a die-hard liberal whose commit-

ment to America's poor and working class remained undiminished throughout his 35 years in Washington, D.C. When O'Neill died of cardiac arrest at age 81 on January 5, 1994, President BILL CLINTON eulogized him as one of the nation's most prominent and loyal champions of American workers and as a man who genuinely loved politics and people.

Thomas Phillip "Tip" O'Neill Jr. was born December 9, 1912, in a working-class section of Cambridge, Massachusetts. His Irish Catholic father, Thomas O'Neill Sr., was a bricklayer and member of the Cambridge City Council. His mother, Rose Tolan O'Neill, died when O'Neill was just one year old.

At an early age, O'Neill developed a passion for politics. When he was 15 years old, he spent hours working on Democrat Alfred E. Smith's unsuccessful presidential campaign against HERBERT HOOVER. During his senior year at Boston College, O'Neill ran for public office for the first time. He entered the race for the Cambridge City Council and lost by a mere 150 votes.

This early defeat taught the young candidate a valuable lesson about politics. Taking his local support for granted, O'Neill had failed to campaign in his own North Cambridge neighborhood. The voters from his district resented his neglect and did not back him as strongly as expected. O'Neill never repeated this tactical error. After the city council loss, O'Neill's father reportedly observed, "All politics is local." For years, O'Neill quoted his father's maxim and applied it to his work.

In 1936, the year he graduated from college, O'Neill enjoyed his first victory at the polls. Using the political leverage of jobs and favors, he won a seat in the Massachusetts House of Representatives, from the North Cambridge district. O'Neill served in the state legislature for 16 years. In 1952, he launched into national politics and was elected to the U.S. House of Representatives, beginning a congressional career that included an appointment as majority whip in 1971 and election as majority leader in 1972. He reached the pinnacle of legislative power in 1976 when he rose to the House speakership.

Outgoing and outspoken, O'Neill was known for his partisanship and for his skillful use of power. He embodied the liberal politics of the DEMOCRATIC PARTY during the late twentieth century. His support of federal social programs was unbending. As the political right grew in power, O'Neill fought conservative proposals such as a balanced budget because they threatened the education, housing, and WELFARE programs he cherished.

As Speaker of the House, O'Neill led Congress during the administrations of Presidents JIMMY CARTER, a Democrat, and RONALD REAGAN, a Republican. O'Neill did not respect Reagan's intellectual capabilities or his conservative policies. After clashing repeatedly with Reagan during his two terms in the White House, O'Neill called his fellow Irishman the least knowledgeable president he had ever worked with in 35 years in the nation's capitol. The two were polar opposites on nearly every political issue, particularly the government's role in American life.

O'Neill's legislative legacy includes a code of ethics for House members and a drive to impeach President RICHARD M. NIXON. O'Neill also was among the first Democrats to speak out against the VIETNAM WAR during the 1960s. He once told an interviewer that the only vote in his congressional career that he regretted was his affirmative vote on the GULF OF TONKIN RESOLUTION in 1964. (The resolution increased American troop involvement in Southeast Asia.) Partisan to a fault, O'Neill had voted for the measure because he felt duty bound to support the Democratic president, LYNDON B. JOHNSON.

While in office, O'Neill shared a bachelor apartment in Washington, D.C. with Representative Edward Boland of Massachusetts. His wife, Mildred ("Millie"), and their five children stayed in the home district. According to Capitol Hill legend, the refrigerator in the men's apartment was stocked mostly with diet soft drinks, beer, and cigars.

Thomas "Tip" O'Neill. UPI/CORBIS-BETTMANN

O'Neill did not survive more than a quarter century in Washington, D.C., without some tarnish to his reputation. In 1978, he was criticized for accepting favors from Tongsun Park, an influence-peddling rice merchant from South Korea. An ethics committee investigation concluded that O'Neill had shown bad judgment in allowing Park to throw parties for him. The committee cleared O'Neill of any illegalities.

O'Neill retired from Congress in 1987. He subsequently spent most of his time in Washington, D.C., or at Cape Cod with his wife. O'Neill wrote a best-selling book about his experiences in Washington, entitled *Man of the House,* and

"YOU CAN TEACH AN OLD DOG NEW TRICKS—IF THE OLD DOG WANTS TO LEARN."
—THOMAS "TIP" O'NEILL

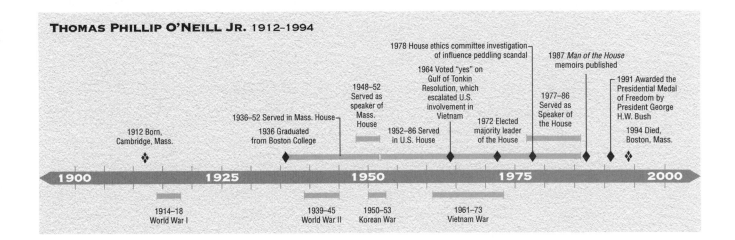

THOMAS PHILLIP O'NEILL JR. 1912–1994

1912 Born, Cambridge, Mass.

1936–52 Served in Mass. House
1936 Graduated from Boston College

1948–52 Served as speaker of Mass. House
1952–86 Served in U.S. House

1964 Voted "yes" on Gulf of Tonkin Resolution, which escalated U.S. involvement in Vietnam

1972 Elected majority leader of the House

1978 House ethics committee investigation of influence peddling scandal

1977–86 Served as Speaker of the House

1987 *Man of the House* memoirs published

1991 Awarded the Presidential Medal of Freedom by President George H.W. Bush

1994 Died, Boston, Mass.

1900   1925   1950   1975   2000

1914–18 World War I

1939–45 World War II

1950–53 Korean War

1961–73 Vietnam War

starred in popular commercials for credit cards. He died January 5, 1994, in Boston, Massachusetts.

O'Neill was a throwback to an earlier era of backroom politics on Capitol Hill. The colorful Massachusetts congressman was a master at pressuring representatives to pass or block key legislation. O'Neill enjoyed a national reputation but remained loyal to the constituents back home. He is remembered as an unapologetic liberal, proud of his role in assisting the poor, the unemployed, and the least privileged Americans. He was one of the last and most highly regarded of the old-style American politicians.

FURTHER READINGS

Farrell, John Aloysius. 2001. *Tip O'Neill and the Democratic Century.* Boston: Little, Brown.

ONUS PROBANDI

[Latin, The burden of proof.] *In the strict sense, a term used to indicate that if no evidence is set forth by the party who has the* BURDEN OF PROOF *to establish the existence of facts in support of an issue, then the issue must be found against that party.*

OPEN

To make accessible, visible, or available; to submit to review, examination, or inquiry through the elimination of restrictions or impediments.

To *open a judgment* means to render it capable of reexamination by removing or relaxing the bar of its finality. A judgment is ordinarily opened at the insistence of a party who is able to show good cause as to why the execution of the judgment would be inequitable.

To *open a court* is to formally announce, ordinarily through the bailiff, that the session has commenced and that the business before the tribunal will proceed.

The term *open* is also used as an adjective in reference to that which is patent, visible, apparent, or notorious, such as a defect in a product, or conduct such as lewdness.

OPEN ACCOUNT

An unpaid or unsettled account; an account with a balance that has not been ascertained, that is kept open in anticipation of future transactions. A type of credit extended by a seller to a buyer that permits the buyer to make purchases without a note or security and is based on an evaluation of the buyer's credit. A contractual obligation that may be modified by subsequent agreement of the parties, either by expressed consent or by consent implied from the conduct of the parties, provided the agreement changing the contractual obligation is based upon independent consideration.

OPEN BID

An offer to perform a contract, generally of a construction nature, in which the bidder reserves the right to reduce his or her bid to compete with a lower bid.

OPEN COURT

Common law requires a trial in open court; "open court" means a court to which the public has a right to be admitted. This term may mean either a court that has been formally convened and declared open for the transaction of its proper judicial business or a court that is freely open to spectators.

OPEN-END CONTRACT

An agreement that allows a buyer to make purchases over a period of time without a change in the price or terms by the seller.

OPEN-END CREDIT

A type of revolving account that permits an individual to pay, on a monthly basis, only a portion of the total amount due.

This type of CONSUMER CREDIT is frequently used in conjunction with bank and department store credit cards.

OPEN-END MORTGAGE

A mortgage that allows the borrowing of additional sums, often on the condition that a stated ratio of collateral value to the debt be maintained. A mortgage that provides for future advances on the mortgage and which so increases the amount of the mortgage.

OPEN LISTING

A type of real estate listing contract whereby any agent who has a right to participate in the open listing is entitled to a commission if he or she produces the sale.

OPEN SHOP

A business in which union and nonunion workers are employed. A business in which union member-

ship is not a condition of securing or maintaining employment.

The term *open shop* is frequently used to imply that the operator of this type of shop is, in effect, exercising discrimination against trade unions and hampering their advancement through the employment of nonunion employees.

CROSS-REFERENCES

Labor Union.

OPENING STATEMENT

An introductory statement made by the attorneys for each side at the start of a trial. The opening statement, although not mandatory, is seldom waived because it offers a valuable opportunity to provide an overview of the case to the jury and to explain the anticipated proof that will be presented during the course of the trial.

The primary purpose of an opening statement is to apprise the trier of fact, whether jury or court, of the issues in question and to summarize the evidence that the party intends to offer during the trial. The Supreme Court has characterized an opening statement as "ordinarily intended to do no more than to inform the jury in a general way of the nature of the action and defense so that they may better be prepared to understand the evidence" (*Best v. District of Columbia*, 291 U.S. 411, 54 S. Ct. 487, 78 L. Ed. 882 [1934]).

Most practitioners and legal scholars agree that an effective opening statement is vital to the trial process. The importance of an opening statement has been established by studies that showed that 80 percent of jurors' ultimate conclusions with respect to the verdict corresponded with their tentative opinion after opening statements. This is because an effective opening statement establishes the facts of the case and sets forth a legal theory and explanation for why the attorney's client should prevail.

An opening statement may be either a matter of right or a privilege depending on applicable state and local laws. A party may waive its option of presenting an opening statement because opening statements are not mandatory.

If a party chooses to give an opening statement, the party with the BURDEN OF PROOF will usually present its opening statement first. In a civil case, this means that the plaintiff's attorney presents an opening statement first. In a criminal case, the burden of proof rests on the prose-

cution. Therefore, the prosecution will be first to present an opening statement.

The defense may present its opening statement after the plaintiff or prosecution has given its opening statement. The defense also has the option of reserving the opening statement until after the plaintiff has presented its case. Courts have discretion to direct a different order of presentation of opening statements if it finds good reasons for such change in order.

Opening statements allow attorneys for each side to introduce themselves and to introduce the parties involved in the lawsuit. Additionally, attorneys will usually outline the important facts of the case during the opening statement to assist the jury in understanding the evidence that will be presented during the trial. An opening statement generally contains a brief explanation of the applicable law and a request for verdict. In a request for verdict, the attorney explains the verdict sought and explains the facts that will support the verdict. A well-planned opening statement serves as a road map of the trial.

Opening statements are often informal and narrative in form. The attorney tells the client's story and explains to the jury what the evidence will show. An opening statement, however, does not constitute evidence, and the jury cannot rely on it in reaching a verdict. The opening statement should be brief and general rather than long and detailed.

An attorney is limited in what he or she can say during an opening statement. An attorney may not discuss inadmissible evidence. This is especially true where the evidence was ruled inadmissible in a pretrial motion hearing. The attorney must reasonably believe that the matters stated will be supported by the evidence. In addition, statements that are purely argumentative are not proper during opening statements. An attorney may not assert personal opinions, comment about the evidence, or comment about the credibility of a witness during an opening statement.

Objections by opposing counsel during an opening statement are appropriate where the attorney presenting the opening statement engages in improper conduct. If the attorney fails to object to the inappropriate conduct, the objection is deemed waived, and the attorney cannot complain of such misconduct later in the trial.

A court usually has the discretion to employ one of several remedies for misconduct during an opening statement. The most common remedy for misconduct during an opening statement is jury admonition, where the judge simply instructs the jury to disregard the improper statement. Where misconduct is more serious, however, the following remedies may be available: (1) counsel may be cited for misconduct or CONTEMPT; (2) a mistrial may be declared; (3) a new trial may be ordered; (4) an appeal may be taken based on the misconduct.

An attorney can make damaging statements during the opening statement that legally bind the client. Such statements, known as "admissions," are not limited to the opening statement but can occur throughout the litigation process. Attorneys must use caution during the opening statement to avoid making damaging admissions.

The court may decide the case after the opening statement and before the jury ever has the opportunity to hear the evidence. A court can properly take the case from the jury where it is clear from the opening statement that the plaintiff cannot succeed on the merits or that the defendant has no valid defense. This is usually accomplished by an attorney bringing a motion for a directed verdict. Taking the case from the jury is an extreme measure and exercised with great caution. Courts favor allowing a case to be tried on its merits and rarely grant a directed verdict after the opening statement.

A strong opening statement will have a lasting impact on the trier of fact. It is often the jury's first introduction to the parties, the issues, and the trial procedure. The opening statement begins the process of persuasion, the ultimate goal of which is a favorable verdict.

FURTHER READINGS

Association of Trial Lawyers of America. 2001. "Opening Statement: Laying a Foundation." *Trial* 37 (February).

Clarke, Mercer Clarke. 2002. "Opening Statement from the Defense Perspective." *Trial Advocate Quarterly* 21 (spring).

Holmes, Grace W., and Mary I. Hiniker, eds. 1987. *Trial Techniques: Opening Statements and Closing Arguments.* Ann Arbor, Mich.: Institute of Continuing Legal Education.

OPERATION OF LAW

The manner in which an individual acquires certain rights or liabilities through no act or cooperation of his or her own, but merely by the application of the established legal rules to the particular transaction.

For example, when an individual dies intestate, the laws of DESCENT AND DISTRIBUTION provide for the inheritance of the estate by the heir. The property of the decedent is said to be transferred by operation of law.

OPINION

See COURT OPINION.

OPINION EVIDENCE

Evidence of what the witness thinks, believes, or infers in regard to facts in dispute, as distinguished from personal knowledge of the facts themselves. The RULES OF EVIDENCE ordinarily do not permit witnesses to testify as to opinions or conclusions.

When this type of evidence is expressed by an expert witness, it may be used only if scientific, technical, or specialized knowledge will aid the trier of fact in understanding the evidence or determining a fact in issue. In the event that the witness is not testifying as an expert, the witness's testimony is restricted to opinions or inferences that are rationally based upon his or her perception and are helpful to a clear understanding of the testimony or the determination of a fact in issue.

OPPRESSION

The offense, committed by a public official, of wrongfully inflicting injury, such as bodily harm or imprisonment, upon another individual under color of office.

Oppression, which is a misdemeanor, is committed through any act of cruelty, severity, unlawful exaction, or excessive use of authority.

OPTION

A privilege, for which a person has paid money, that grants that person the right to purchase or sell certain commodities or certain specified SECURITIES at any time within an agreed period for a fixed price.

A right, which operates as a continuing offer, given in exchange for consideration—something of value—to purchase or lease property at an agreed price and terms within a specified time.

An option is a type of contract that is used in the stock and commodity markets, in the leasing and sale of real estate, and in other areas where one party wants to acquire the legal right to buy something from or sell something to another party within a fixed period of time.

In the stock and commodity markets, options come in two primary forms, known as "calls" and "puts." A call gives the holder of the option the choice of buying or not buying stock or a commodities futures contract at a fixed price for a fixed period of time. A put gives the holder the option of selling or not selling stock or a commodities futures contract at a fixed price for a fixed period of time. Because an option only has value for a fixed period of time, its value decreases with the passage of time. Because of this feature, it is considered a "wasting" asset.

There are four parts to an option: the underlying security, the type of option (put or call), the strike price, and the expiration date. Take, for example, an "International Widget July 100 call." International Widget stock is the underlying security, July is the expiration month of the option, $100 is the strike price (sometimes referred to as the exercise price), and the option is a call, giving the holder of the call the right, not the obligation, to buy one hundred shares of International Widget at a price of $100. The holder of the call cannot buy the one hundred shares until the exercise date.

In the case of a commodity option, the right to purchase or sell pertains to an underlying physical commodity, such as a specific quantity of silver, or to a commodity futures contract. The period during which an option can be exercised is specified in the contract.

Stock option plans are used in business to reward employees. A stock option is a contract between the company and the employee giving the employee the right to purchase shares of company stock between certain dates at a price that is often fixed by the company or determinable by formula at the time the option is granted. For example, International Widget may issue an option to a key employee, which will allow the employee to purchase one hundred shares of stock at the fair market value at the grant date. The employee has five years in which to exercise that option. If the price increases above the grant-date fair market value, the employee will presumably exercise the option and realize an economic gain based on the spread between the fair market value at the grant date and the fair market value at the exercise date. If the price decreases after the option is granted, the employee will forgo exercising the option and thereby have no loss in economic value.

Options have a role in business outside the stock and commodity markets. In the law of contract, the option is a continuing offer to purchase or lease property. The offer is irrevocable for the stated period of time. Like most other contracts, the option contract is not terminated by the subsequent death or insanity of either party.

Options usually assume one of two forms. The seller can state to the purchaser, "If you pay me $500 today, I promise to sell Whiteacre to you for $50,000 on the condition that you pay the $50,000 within sixty days." If the purchaser pays the $500, a unilateral contract—an agreement in which there is a promise on only one side and a possibility of a performance by the other side—is created, and the offer is irrevocable. The seller of Whiteacre is obligated to perform if the purchaser pays the $50,000 within sixty days.

The second form of option contract is created when the seller states to the purchaser, "I offer to sell you Whiteacre for $50,000. This offer will remain open for sixty days if you pay $500 for this privilege." If the purchaser pays the $500, there is a collateral contract—an agreement made prior to, or simultaneous with, another agreement not to revoke the offer—and the seller is obligated not to revoke.

Acceptance of an option contract is operative when received by the offeror, rather than when sent. An option contract is interpreted strictly in favor of its creator and must be unequivocal and in accordance with the terms of the option. It is frequently said that "time is of the essence" in an option contract, but this means only that the option cannot be exercised after the offer has lapsed.

An offer can be accepted only by the person or persons for whom it is intended. Therefore, no assignment—a transfer to another of any property—of an offer can be made. The prohibition is based on the concept that everyone has the privilege of choosing with whom to contract. Once an offer has ripened into a contract, however, the rights thereby created are usually assignable. For example, if Jane offers an option to Jack to purchase Whiteacre, Jack cannot accept the option and then assign it to Joe. Once Jack and Jane enter into a contract for the sale of Whiteacre, Jack can assign his contract rights to Joe.

ORAL CONTRACT

An agreement between parties that is either partly in writing and partly dependent on spoken words or that is entirely dependent on spoken words.

An oral contract is enforceable unless its subject matter comes within the statute of frauds, an ENGLISH LAW adopted in the United States, that requires certain contracts to be in writing. For example, a contract to sell real property, to be enforceable, must be in writing to comply with the statute. An oral contract to sell PERSONAL PROPERTY for an amount less than that set in the statute does not fall within its limits and, therefore, is enforceable without being reduced to a writing. The UNIFORM COMMERCIAL CODE governs the enforceability of oral contracts in sales transactions involving merchants.

ORDEAL

One of the most ancient forms of trial in England that required the accused person to submit to a dangerous or painful test on the theory that God would intervene and disclose his or her guilt or innocence.

Trials by ordeal were a pagan custom that took on added ritual when Christianity was introduced into England. There were various ordeals, and at different times certain ordeals were reserved for people of higher rank, whereas others were used for common people. All were based on the belief that supernatural forces would rescue the innocent from perils to which they were exposed and would allow the guilty to be physically harmed.

The *ordeal of water* was performed by casting the suspect into a pond or river. If the suspect floated to the surface without any action of swimming, she was deemed guilty. If the suspect sank, she was pulled out and pronounced innocent. The *hot water ordeal* required the accused to plunge his bare arm up to the elbow into boiling water without injury. In the *ordeal of the cursed morsel,* the suspect swallowed a piece of dry bread with a feather in it. If the suspect did not choke, he was found innocent. The *ordeal of the red-hot iron* required the accused to carry a heated poker weighing one, two, or three pounds over a certain distance. After that, the suspect's hand was bound, and in three days the bandages were removed. If the wound had not become infected, the suspect was pronounced innocent. A variation of this ordeal required the accused person to walk barefoot and blindfolded over nine red-hot plowshares placed at uneven distances. The ordeals of the red-hot iron and the plowshares were also called the *fire ordeals* and were often reserved for nobility.

Evidence from very early cases indicates that there were more acquittals than convictions by ordeal, but the severity of the methods may have encouraged cheating. It is impossible to tell exactly how compelling the psychological stresses of the ordeal were, but all were administered amidst the ritual of the church at the high moment of the mass. In time church leaders came to disapprove of the participation of clergymen in a somewhat pagan tradition, and in 1215 priests were forbidden to take part in trials by ordeal. In remote places, the practice continued for a time as priests disobeyed the order, but eventually trial by ordeal was eliminated. This made the CRIMINAL LAW of England unenforceable because the chief means of determining guilt or innocence had been abolished.

The people were reluctant to accept a system that permitted a judge to determine the facts in a criminal case. That would be replacing the voice of God with that of a mortal man. For a while, the law enforcers imprisoned persons with a general reputation for wrongdoing, banished those guilty of moderately serious crimes, and required pledges of security to ensure the peacefulness of persons accused of small crimes. When these measures proved unsatisfactory, judges began calling upon groups of people in the community to make decisions. As many as forty-eight neighbors might be asked whether the accused was guilty or innocent. Their opinions were based on what they knew or could find out about the case and not on the presentation of evidence or testimony. This procedure was a forerunner of the modern jury.

ORDER

Direction of a court or judge normally made or entered in writing, and not included in a judgment, which determines some point or directs some step in the proceedings.

The decision of a court or judge is made in the form of an order. A court may issue an order after a motion of a party requesting the order, or the court itself may issue an order on its own discretion. For example, courts routinely issue scheduling orders, which set the timetable and procedure for managing a civil lawsuit. More substantive orders, however, typically are made following a motion by one of the parties.

A motion is an application for an order. The granting or denying of a motion is a matter of judicial discretion. When a motion is granted, the moving party (the party who requests the motion) is ordinarily limited to the relief requested in the application. Although no particular form is required, a court order granting a motion should be sufficiently explicit to enable the parties to do whatever is directed. Though a court is not obligated to issue an opinion, in most cases a party is entitled to have the reasons for the decision of the court stated in the order. The order must be consistent with the relief requested in the motion, and it should set forth any conditions on which relief is awarded.

In trial courts the attorney for a party who obtains a favorable ruling usually has the responsibility of writing a proposed order. A copy of the proposed order is furnished to the other party so that he or she can propose amendments to it. It is then presented to the court for settlement and approval. Courts are free, however, to modify proposed orders or to write their own order. Appellate courts routinely write their own orders.

To take effect, an order must be entered, filed, or incorporated into the minutes of the court. An entry or filing must be made with the court administrator within the prescribed time limits.

Aside from scheduling orders and other orders that deal with the administration of a case, there are several general categories of orders. An INTERLOCUTORY order is an order that does not decide the case but settles some intervening matters relating to it or affords some temporary relief. For example, in a DIVORCE case, a judge will issue an interlocutory order that sets the terms for temporary CHILD SUPPORT and VISITATION RIGHTS while the case is pending.

A RESTRAINING ORDER may be issued upon the filing of an application for an INJUNCTION forbidding the defendant to do the threatened act until the court has a hearing on the application. These types of orders are also called temporary restraining orders (TROs), because they are meant to be effective until the court decides whether to order an injunction. For example, if a neighborhood association seeks to prevent a land developer from cutting down a stand of trees, the association would seek an injunction to prevent the cutting and a TRO to forbid the developer from removing the trees before the court holds a hearing. If the association did not request a TRO, the developer could legally cut down the trees and effectively render the injunction request moot.

A final order is one that terminates the action itself or finally decides some matter litigated by the parties. In a civil lawsuit, the plaintiff may make many allegations and legal claims, some of which the court may dispose of during the litigation by the issuance of an order. When the court is ready to completely dispose of the case, it enters a final order. As part of the final order, the court directs that judgment be entered, which authorizes the court administrator to close the case in that court.

ORDER OF THE COIF

An unincorporated national scholastic honor society in law. Its purpose is to foster excellence in legal scholarship and to recognize those who have attained high grades in law school or who have distinguished themselves in the teaching of law. There are more than sixty chapters located in law schools throughout the country.

The honor society is named after the English Order of the Coif, the most ancient and one of the most honored institutions of the COMMON LAW. The coif was a close-fitting cap of white linen that covered the ears and was tied with strings under the chin, like a baby's bonnet. It originated in the twelfth century as a head covering for men and became part of the ecclesiastic and legal headgear, lasting until the sixteenth century. For a long period of time, English judges were selected only from the order.

The Order of the Coif honor society was formed in 1912 as a national organization. The national constitution sets requirements for election to membership and criteria for the creation of chapters at law schools. The order is a federated organization with authority in local matters vested in each chapter. Each chapter has its officers, and the national organization has an executive committee composed of three officers and three other members. Officers are elected every three years.

Law students who are graduating seniors are eligible for election to the Order of the Coif if they have completed 75 percent of their law studies in graded courses and their grade record ranks them in the top 10 percent of all graduating seniors of the chapter's school. A chapter may also elect members of the law school faculty if the chapter believes professors have exhibited qualities of scholarship consistent with the objectives of the order.

A chapter may each year elect to honorary membership one member of the legal profession who is recognized for his or her scholarship. Every three years the national executive committee may elect up to five honorary members who have attained national distinction for their contributions to the legal system.

In addition, every three years the Order of the Coif recognizes legal scholarship by conferring one or more awards on the author or authors of published legal works. The national executive committee also is empowered to establish other awards for the purpose of recognizing preeminent legal scholarship and leadership among law students, law professors, judges, and practitioners.

ORDINANCE

A law, statute, or regulation enacted by a MUNICIPAL CORPORATION.

An ordinance is a law passed by a municipal government. A municipality, such as a city, town, village, or borough, is a political subdivision of a state within which a municipal corporation has been established to provide local government to a population in a defined area.

Ordinances constitute the subject matter of municipal law. The power of municipal governments to enact ordinances is derived from the state constitution or statutes or through the legislative grant of a municipal charter. The charter in large part dictates how much power elected officials have to regulate actions within the municipality. Municipalities that have been granted "home rule" charters by the legislature have the most authority to act. If, however, a municipality enacts an ordinance that exceeds its charter or is in conflict with state or federal law, the ordinance can be challenged in court and ruled void.

Many ordinances deal with maintaining public safety, health, morals, and GENERAL WELFARE. For example, a municipality may enact housing ordinances that set minimum standards of habitability. Other ordinances deal with fire and safety regulations that residential, commercial, and industrial property owners must fol-

low. Many municipalities have enacted noise ordinances, which prohibit prescribed levels of noise after certain hours of the evening.

Ordinances may also deal with public streets and sidewalks. They typically include regulations regarding parking, snow removal, and littering. Restrictions on pets, including "pooper scooper" and leash laws, are also governed by municipal ordinances.

One of the most significant areas of municipal law is ZONING. Zoning ordinances constitute a master plan for land use within the municipality. A municipality is typically divided into residential, commercial, and industrial zoning districts. Zoning attempts to conserve the value of property and to encourage the most appropriate use of land throughout a particular locality.

In the past, many U.S. municipalities enacted a variety of ordinances regulating public morals and behavior. Many, such as ordinances that prohibited spitting on a public sidewalk, have been repealed or are rarely enforced.

ORGAN DONATION LAW

Dramatic developments in organ and tissue transplantation have allowed persons with life-threatening illnesses a chance to live. The successful transplantation of kidneys, livers, hearts, lungs, eyes, and skin has been enhanced by better surgical techniques and new drugs, such as cyclosporin, that prevent the body from rejecting a transplanted organ. Success, however, has led to an undersupply of organs for the estimated 30,000 patients each year who need a transplant. Laws have been enacted at the state and local level that attempt to provide a better system of organ donation and distribution and to encourage individuals to volunteer to be organ donors.

The Uniform Anatomical Gift Act that was drafted in 1968 was the first effort at providing a national organ and tissue donation policy. The act created a uniform legal procedure for persons who wish to donate organs and for hospitals and medical institutions that want to accept them. Under this model act, which has been adopted in some form by all 50 states, a person of sound mind, who is at least 18 years of age, may donate all or part of his or her own body. There are several ways for a donor to record the wish to make a donation. The donor may include the donation in a will. If part of a will, the provision becomes effective immediately upon death, unlike other provisions of the will, which need to go through probate before they become effective. In practical terms, however, a will may be ineffective. Time is of the essence in organ donation, and if the will is not read for several days, it may be too late to make an effective donation.

The uniform act provides for a more common form of recording a person's intention to make an organ donation: a donor card that may be carried in a wallet. States also allow this donor information to be imprinted on a driver's license. When a person applies for a driver's license, she or he has the option of including a desire to donate organs. Despite the simplicity of this option, it has not generated the quantity of donors that proponents of the procedure expected.

A written donation must be signed by the donor and witnessed by at least two other people. A donation can be made orally, but it too must be witnessed by at least two other people. A dying patient can communicate his or her wish to donate organs to an attending physician, who can act as one of the witnesses. However, the attending physician cannot be the doctor who removes or transplants the organ.

A person can revoke in writing or orally her or his intent to make an organ or tissue donation. If a dying person is unable to communicate and has not expressed an intent to donate, a family member or guardian can make a gift of all or part of the person's body, within certain limitations. In general, even if a person has expressed the intent to donate, physicians still ask permission of a family member or guardian.

The uniform act forbids the sale of body parts. The recipient cannot pay for the donated organ but must pay for the cost of transportation and transplant. Organs and tissue can only be received by hospitals, surgeons, physicians, educational institutions involved in medical or dental research, a storage facility for these institutions, or any specified individual who needs the organ personally for therapy or transplantation.

A 1986 federal law (42 U.S.C.A. § 1320b–8) requires all hospitals participating in MEDICARE or MEDICAID to implement a "required request" policy. Hospitals are required to discuss with potential donors and their families "the option of organ and tissue donation and their option to decline."

The 1984 National Organ Transplant Act (42 U.S.C.A. §§ 273 et seq.) initiated a national HEALTHCARE policy regarding ORGAN TRANSPLANTATION. The act provided funds to help establish "qualified organ procurement organizations," banned the interstate sale of organs, and created a task force to study organ transplantation policy issues. The 1986 task force report was an exhaustive examination of the medical, legal, social, and economic implications of organ procurement and transplantation. The 1986 required "request law" came from one of the task force's recommendations.

Despite these legal and medical mechanisms that seek to encourage organ donation, demand has continued to exceed supply. In 1996 it was estimated that eight people died every day waiting for a transplant that never came because of the donor shortage. In response, Congress enacted the Organ Donor Insert Card Act in 1996 (Pub. L. No. 104-91, 110 Stat. 1936). The act directed the secretary of the treasury to enclose with each tax refund check in 1997 an organ donor card. It was estimated that these

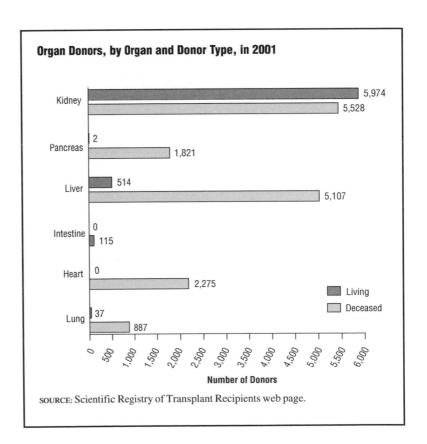

Organ Donors, by Organ and Donor Type, in 2001

Organ	Living	Deceased
Kidney	5,974	5,528
Pancreas	2	1,821
Liver	514	5,107
Intestine	0	115
Heart	0	2,275
Lung	37	887

Number of Donors

SOURCE: Scientific Registry of Transplant Recipients web page.

SHOULD DYING BABIES BE ORGAN DONORS?

As many as half of the approximately 1,500 children waiting for organ transplants each year die before donors can be found. The shortage of donors has led to calls for permitting the organs of children born with the birth defect anencephaly to be donated before the children die. The issue has proved controversial, as doctors and medical ethicists debate the legality and morality of allowing the harvesting of organs from a person who is not legally dead.

Anencephaly is a birth defect that prevents the skull and brain from fully developing. While the heart and other internal organs of anencephalic INFANTS often develop normally, most of the brain is missing. The anencephalic infant possesses a brain stem, which can keep breathing and heartbeat going temporarily. But because the cerebral cortex is missing, the infant has no thought or sensory functions and will never be conscious. Most of these infants die within hours or days of birth. Because of these bleak prospects, most of each year's 2,500 anencephalic pregnancies are aborted.

Some parents have forgone ABORTION but have sought to have their child's organs donated. Because the brain stem gradually fails after birth, an infant's heartbeat and breathing gradually slow until the infant dies of heart failure or stops breathing. The vital organs deteriorate, however, leaving them useless as transplants. The only way the organs can be used is if they are removed while the infant is still alive. This requirement cannot be met under current law because organ donation is premised on the dead donor rule: donors must be declared brain dead before their organs can be removed. An anencephalic infant exists in a gray area between life and death, but because the brain stem functions, he cannot be declared brain dead. Therefore, the harvesting of organs of anencephalic infants would require stretching the definition of death.

Some physicians, medical ethicists, and parents of anencephalic infants believe that such a redefinition should occur and that organ retrieval from an anencephalic infant at birth should be permitted. They argue that an anencephalic infant's profound abnormality makes it permissible to make an exception to the dead donor rule. It is a unique abnormality: the infant never experiences consciousness.

Proponents contend that, because these infants are never conscious, they do not meet the most minimal criteria for becoming a person. In 1995 the American Medical Association's (AMA) Council on Ethical and Judicial Affairs supported the idea of organ retrieval from anencephalic infants at birth on the basis that the infants' lack of consciousness meant that they could not suffer harm.

cards would reach 70 million U.S. families and would result in increased donations.

The location of a potential donee of a transplant has had a significant effect on whether the donee receives an organ. In 1998, for instance, a patient awaiting a kidney transplant could expect to be on a waiting list for only 107 days in Oregon, but as long as 1,680 days in New York. A severely ill patient in one state could die while waiting, even though a patient in another state could receive a transplant before he or she was even sick enough to be hospitalized.

Because of this disparity, the HEALTH AND HUMAN SERVICES DEPARTMENT (HHS) in 1998 issued the Organ Procurement and Transplantation Network, which changed the distribution and allocation of organs by broadening transplant areas. The old system of distribution and allocation allowed organs to be distributed locally first. This policy was based on the belief that local distribution gave states and local medical institutions an incentive to promote organ donation. If the organs were to be distributed regionally or nationally, states and hospitals might conclude that successful promotion of organ donations turned the state into a supplier for other states that were not as successful in encouraging donations.

The new regulations angered a number of states and hospitals. The state of Wisconsin, the University of Wisconsin Hospitals, and Froedert Memorial Lutheran Hospital filed a lawsuit in federal district court, claiming that the regulations would severely reduce the number of organs available to their patients. The plaintiffs alleged that the HHS lacked legislative authority to broaden the regional organ sharing networks. In addition, the plaintiffs claimed that the regulations would injure the hospitals financially because they would have to pay a larger amount of the transplantation network's operating costs. However, in an unpublished decision, a federal district court in Wisconsin dismissed the case because the plaintiffs lacked standing to file the lawsuit.

Proponents point out that it has been the parents of anencephalic infants who have sought to donate the babies' organs. As long as the harvesting of organs is done at the request of the parents and with their consent, the interests of the parents are not harmed. For these parents the desire to have some good come from the tragedy of giving birth to an anencephalic infant is the driving force in making their decision.

Finally, proponents note the shortage of organs for transplantation in children. Because of this shortage, many children die who might otherwise live a normal life if given a transplant. Some experts believe that using organs from anencephalic infants could mean up to an additional three hundred transplants a year. Faced with this prospect, proponents contend that society's interests are advanced by making a narrow exception to the dead donor rule.

Opponents are horrified at the idea of removing organs from a living infant. They contend that the dead donor rule is an important boundary in medical science. Crossing this line in the case of anencephalic infants, they contend, will cause a "slippery slope" effect. Physicians might ask to harvest organs from coma victims or from children with other severe, but nonfatal brain defects. Opponents argue that blurring the definition of brain death will have detrimental consequences to society greater than the benefit of obtaining organs from several hundred infants each year.

Critics further argue that anencephalic infants are human beings who deserve the protection of the law. They point out that, to be an organ donor, a person's entire brain must be declared dead. This means that the brain stem completely ceases to function and to produce electrical impulses and that the person has no reflexes or responses. Anencephalic infants do not meet all these criteria. They are not brain dead because the brain stem functions, they support their respiration independently, and they have responses and reflexes. These critics note that, only six months after its support of harvesting organs from anencephalic infants at birth, the AMA's Council on Ethical and Judicial Affairs reversed its decision, citing questions as to whether anencephalic infants are truly unconscious and whether they feel pain.

Though most of the critics ground their objections in ethical, moral, and religious concerns about the sanctity of human life, others have more pragmatic arguments. These critics argue that the debate itself over harvesting organs from anencephalic infants at birth harms the effort to recruit the general public as organ donors. The public may become fearful that the medical community is seeking ways to change the definition of death. The few hundred organs a year that could be gained through a change in law, these critics contend, is not worth the loss of thousands of potential donors.

Critics respect the desire of parents who wish to do something good through organ donation. Yet they contend that making parents feel better does not rank higher than society's interest in preserving human life. Unless a state passes a law that makes an exception to the dead donor rule, the use of anencephalic infants as organ sources immediately upon birth will not occur.

FURTHER READINGS

"Health Law." 1996. Law and Leading Attorneys Website. Available online at <www.lawlead.com> (accessed November 21, 2003).

MacLean, Pamela A. 2002. "Family Has Right to Bodies of Dead Children, Panel Decides." *Los Angeles Daily Journal* (April 17).

Shartle, Bryan. 2001. "Proposed Legislation for Safety Regulating the Increasing Number of Living Organ and Tissue Donations by Minors." *Louisiana Law Review* 61 (winter).

University of California, Irvine College of Medicine Website. Available online at <www.com.uci.edu> (accessed November 21, 2003).

CROSS-REFERENCES

Abortion; Death and Dying; Fetal Rights; Fetal Tissue Research; Health Care Law; Patients' Rights; Physicians and Surgeons.

ORGAN TRANSPLANTATION

The transfer of organs such as the kidneys, heart, or liver from one body to another.

The transplantation of human organs has become a common medical procedure. Typical organs transplanted are the kidneys, heart, liver, pancreas, cornea, skin, bones, and lungs. The organ most frequently transplanted is the cornea, followed by the kidney.

The first human organ transplants were performed in the early 1960s, when it became possible to use special tissue-matching techniques and immunosuppressive drugs that reduced the chance that a transplanted organ would be rejected by the host body. By the early 1980s, the new immunosuppressive drug cyclosporine led to great advances in the success rate of organ transplants.

Organ Shortages

As organ transplants became increasingly successful, the most significant problem related to them was the shortage of available organs. A large gap separated the high demand for organs and their scarce supply. Experts estimated that

ORGAN PROCUREMENT: IS IT BETTER TO GIVE OR TO SELL?

In the early days of organ transplant surgery, during the 1960s and 1970s, the practice was seen as experimental and risky. Patients' bodies often rejected a transplant, and the survival rate in many cases was deemed too low to be acceptable. However, with the development of new surgical procedures and the wide use of new immunosuppressive drugs such as cyclosporine in the 1980s, organ transplantation became a common medical technique available to more and more people. In the 1980s, over 400,000 transplants were performed in the United States. The age range of heart transplant recipients has expanded from forty-five to over sixty at the upper limit, and to infancy at the lower limit.

Results such as these have caused such a demand for organ transplants that there are far more potential organ recipients than available organs. Those who are deemed medically suitable to receive organs are put on long waiting lists, and it is often months or years before they get the organs they need; many others are deemed medically unsuitable and are not even put on waiting lists. Some have criticized the term *medically unsuitable* as an **ARBITRARY** and uncertain medical judgment used simply to prevent raising the hopes of those who are unlikely to get a timely transplant.

What should be done about this dire shortage of organs available for transplantation? Three different organ pro-

curement systems have been proposed as a means of alleviating the situation: an organ market, a presumed consent program, and a required request program. All three proposals have their advocates and detractors.

Organ Market Although the sale of human organs was made illegal by the 1985 National Organ Transplantation Act (42 U.S.C.A. § 274(e)), an organ market remains a widely discussed alternative to the generally accepted approach of encouraged voluntarism. Its supporters claim that the system of encouraged voluntarism, which supplies organs free of cost through altruistic donation, has created a rapidly worsening organ shortage.

Typically, advocates of the market system are quick to note that they do not support a market in organs from living donors, nor do they envision donors and recipients haggling in hospital rooms. Instead, they focus on paying potential donors a fixed amount for signing a contract that authorizes the future removal of one or more of their organs at death. This may, for example, occur in the form of a uniform cash payment or tax credit to all individuals who agree to sign a donor form on the back of their driver's license application. This type of arrangement is called a forward market because payment for the organ occurs well before the organ is removed. The amount paid for such donor contracts could be adjusted up or down depending on the demand for organs.

Some of those who call for an organ market take the economist's perspective and claim that it is the best alternative because it would maximize social welfare. The benefits of such a system would include an increase in the supply of organs, and thus the saving of many more lives and the improved health of many more patients. More patients who have to undergo the expensive and time-consuming procedure of kidney dialysis, for example, would be able to instead receive a transplant. Moreover, firms and individuals engaged in the procurement business would have a direct financial incentive to increase public awareness of the facts surrounding organ donation and transplantation.

Advocates claim that a market would also produce a number of indirect benefits. Medical professionals would be able to choose from a greater number of available organs from the dead—termed cadaveric organs—and obtain higher-quality organs that more precisely match the tissue type of the recipient. With more closely matched organs would come less need to rely on living donors, thus avoiding the pain, loss of pay, and risks associated with donor surgery. Moreover, more organs would mean more transplant operations, and with increased frequency, the cost of those operations would fall as hospitals and their staffs become more proficient at conducting and managing them. Organ market supporters also argue that an undersupply of organs leads to a black market, and that this market will only

by the late 1980s, three people were on transplant waiting lists for every available organ. Given the grossly inadequate supply of organs, many vexing ethical, legal, and political issues surrounded the question of what is the best way to harvest or procure organs.

A number of laws sought to address the problem of organ procurement. The Uniform

Anatomical Gift Act (8A U.L.A. 15-16 [1983]), drafted in 1968 and adopted in all 50 states, allows any competent adult to state in writing, including by signing a donor card or checking off an item on a driver's license application, whether he wishes to allow or forbid the use of her or his organs after death. The act also permits next of kin to authorize donation. Such a

become greater with time. Finally, an increase in the harvesting of cadaveric organs would eventually lead to greater social acceptance of the practice as part of the death process.

Critics see an organ market as not expanding the number of choices available but diminishing them, thereby undermining the ethical goal of individual autonomy and free choice. Even if sales were restricted to organs from those who are dead, they claim, the potential conflicts of interest on the part of physicians, patients, and families would erode the capability of individuals to make decisions about their own bodies. Critics also point out that if the sale of organs from living subjects were permitted, poor people would have economic incentives to sell their body parts, and as a result their own health could suffer.

Detractors of the market approach also claim that it would not increase the supply of organs and that the price of organs would be so high that few people would consent to give away their valuable organs. Some also claim that an organ market would result in lower-quality organs because poorer people, who are generally less healthy, would be more likely to sell organs for profit. Moreover, if organs had to be purchased, poor people would not be able to afford transplants. Market advocates counter that the total costs of organ transplantation would likely fall under a market system, making it more, not less, accessible to poor people.

Presumed Consent Program

The presumed consent system of organ procurement is currently used in many European countries. It means that medical professionals are presumed to have a deceased individual's and surviving family members' consent to remove needed organs, unless those individuals have earlier made known their objections to organ removal. Supporters of this system argue that it increases the supply of organs, makes the decision to remove organs much easier, and further removes the physician and hospital from liability.

Critics of the presumed consent system find fault with it for economic, legal, and ethical reasons. Looking at the program in terms of economics, they claim that it does not actually increase the number of organs harvested because it does not impose financial incentives for organ requests. As a result, medical staff still exhibit a reluctance to remove organs and that leads to a continuation of the organ shortage. Critics also claim that a presumed consent system is expensive to create and maintain. It requires the creation of large, centralized registries listing individuals' decisions regarding their own body, and these must be updated continuously. Mistakes inevitably occur, causing unwanted organ removal and expensive lawsuits.

Other critics of the presumed consent system find it legally suspect and charge that if it is implemented in the United States it will violate the DUE PROCESS CLAUSE of the Constitution.

Those who find fault with the ethical premise of presumed consent argue that it removes the moral dignity surrounding donation by making it mandatory. It also detracts from the goal of free choice and autonomous behavior by precluding the individual from making no decision or from leaving the decision to others.

Required Request Program

A required request program is a more moderate approach to the problem of organ donation. It seeks to reform the existing system of encouraged voluntarism by requiring that family members or guardians be given the opportunity to make an organ donation when a death has occurred. Such a program would require hospitals to have a specially trained person to approach families and inquire about organ donation at the time death is pronounced. The request would be noted in writing on the death certificate to ensure that medical providers comply with the policy. The required request system would allow for exceptions in cases where a request would not be in the best interests of family members or guardians, with such exceptions also duly noted on the death certificate. Such a system, its advocates claim, would increase freedom of choice by informing individuals of their options.

Proponents of this system point to statistics that indicate that in the U.S. public, the level of altruism regarding organ donation is quite high. In some hospitals, for example, over 60 percent of the families who were asked to donate the organs of loved ones agreed to do so. The problem with the current system, they maintain, is that donor cards do not adequately tap this altruistic sentiment. They also note that a required request system would ensure that donor cards or written directives are honored. With time, such requests would become a routine part of the death process in medical facilities, making them less surprising and less intrusive to family privacy at the time of death.

Critics of the required request system say that it would not do enough to change an already flawed organ procurement system. Moreover, they argue that approaching families in the hours following the death of a loved one imposes too much psychological distress.

program, termed encouraged voluntarism, relied on the free and autonomous choice of the individual or surviving family as the basis for organ donation.

Organ donation was also aided by brain-death statutes. These made it possible to declare as dead those who have lost whole-brain function but whose bodies are kept alive through artificial means. Such brain-dead persons become potential organ donors. In fact, most organs are obtained from accident victims who are injured in this way.

The combination of encouraged voluntarism and brain-death statutes did not produced adequate numbers of organs. For example, a 1984 study estimated that of the

20,000 people each year who die of accidents or strokes and are medically suitable organ donors, only 3,000 served as donors. Experts estimated that only 3 percent of those who serve as organ donors are actually carrying a donor card at the time they are pronounced dead.

A number of different problems contributed to this shortage of donated organs. Most people were fearful or uncomfortable with thoughts of death—particularly their own—and consequently did not contemplate organ donation. Others pointed out that some states had not yet enacted statutes that recognize brain death as the definition of death. Also, a general distrust of large, impersonal medical institutions kept many people from committing to organ donation. Many people were afraid that if they carried an organ donor card, they would not receive adequate medical treatment in an emergency. Moreover, medical professionals were generally not required to present the option of organ donation to critically ill or injured patients and their families. As a result, even if a person had a donor card, it might go unnoticed.

When the system of encouraged voluntarism established by the Uniform Anatomical Gift Act failed to increase the number of available organs adequately, some individuals advocated establishing a legal market in organs. Some versions of an organ market would allow living individuals to sell one of their kidneys at a market price. More commonly, organ market advocates pro-

posed the sale of organs taken only from those who have died—that is, cadaveric organs—usually through "forward contracts" signed when the patient was living. However, the sale of organs was barred by state and federal legislation, particularly the National Organ Transplant Act (42 U.S.C.A. § 274(e) [1985]), which stated, "It shall be unlawful for any person to knowingly acquire, receive or otherwise transfer any human organ for valuable consideration for use in human transplantation if the transfer affects interstate commerce." Rather than creating an organ market, Congress afterward sought to establish laws that established "required request" protocols. These protocols would require major hospitals to ask a patient's relatives if the wished to donate the patient's organs (Omnibus Reconciliation Act of 1986, Pub. L. No. 99-509, 100 Stat. 1874, 2009).

Some states went a step further, passing "presumed consent" laws that allowed for the removal of organs unless the next of kin objected or it was known that the potential donor objected to such a procedure while alive. Some of these laws allowed only the removal of corneas under such conditions; others applied only to unclaimed dead bodies. The huge demand for organs was expected to lead to the wider passage of presumed consent laws and the creation of market incentives for organ donation.

Controversial Issues

Organ transplants generate increasingly vexing legal and ethical questions as medical technology becomes more complex. Three controversial issues surrounding the subject are conception for organ donation, donor consent, and transplants from terminally disabled INFANTS.

In some instances, a child is conceived expressly for the purpose of using her organs for transplantation in another person, usually a blood relative. In 1990, for example, a California couple gave birth to a child they had conceived solely in hopes that the baby's bone marrow cells would save the life of their teenage daughter, who was dying of cancer. Although the legality of such conceptions was not challenged, the practice raised ethical questions relating to who may give informed consent for the donor child and whether such a practice may be considered CHILD ABUSE.

The problem of donor consent arose in lawsuits seeking to compel persons to donate

Organ Transplant Registration Waiting List, in 2001

Organ	Registrations
Kidney	51,144
Pancreas alone	403
Pancreas after kidney	686
Kidney-Pancreas	2,503
Liver	18,505
Intestine	180
Heart	4,096
Lung	3,802
Heart-Lung	209

SOURCE: Scientific Registry of Transplant Recipients web page.

organs to relatives. For example, in 1990, an Illinois family with a son who had leukemia brought a lawsuit seeking to compel the boy's half sister and half brother to submit to preliminary medical tests that would have established their suitability to serve as bone marrow donors. A judge, noting the objections of the mother of the half siblings, ruled that such tests would be an invasion of the potential donors' right of privacy. The Illinois Supreme Court later upheld this ruling (*Curran v. Bosze,* No. 70501 [Ill. filed Dec. 20, 1990]). In its opinion, the court outlined three critical factors in determining the best interests of the donating child: (1) the consenting parent must know the inherent risks and benefits of the procedure, (2) the primary caretaker of the child must be able to provide emotional support, and (3) there must be an existing, close relationship between the donor and the recipient.

The issue of organ donations made by terminally disabled infants came to national attention in 1992 when a Florida couple sought to have the organs of their anencephalic baby, Theresa Ann Campo Pearson, donated for use by other newborns. Anencephaly is a rare and always fatal gestational disorder in which the brain develops a stem, or lower brain, but not a cortex, or upper brain. Though the rest of the anencephalic infant's body is healthy, the disorder causes the child to die soon after birth. Theresa Ann's mother and father sought to have her declared brain dead, but a judge stated that under Florida statutes, a declaration of brain death may be made only if activity in all parts of the brain has ceased (Fla. Stat. ch. 382.009 [1992]). The judge noted that Theresa Ann had lower-brain activity. She died ten days after birth, without having donated her organs.

Critics of this decision argued that because anencephaly is always fatal, the organs of children with this disorder should be used to save other children. Supporters note that if an exception were made for anencephaly, other severely DISABLED PERSONS might be inappropriately targeted as a source for organs. Others argue that the life of one child, no matter how brief or unsatisfactory, cannot be taken to save another.

FURTHER READINGS

Blair, Roger D., and David L. Kaserman. 1991. "The Economics and Ethics of Alternative Cadaveric Organ Procurement Policies." *Yale Journal on Regulation* 8 (summer).

Bryan, Jenny, and John Clare. 2001. *Organ Farm: Pig to Human Transplants.* London: Carlton.

Caplan, Arthur L. 1992. *If I Were a Rich Man Could I Buy a Pancreas? and Other Essays on the Ethics of Health Care.* Bloomington: Indiana Univ. Press.

Gerritsen, Tess. 1996. *Harvest.* New York: Simon & Schuster.

Green, Reg. 2000. *The Nicholas Effect: A Boy's Gift to the World.* Cambridge, Mass.: O'Reilly & Associates.

Harris, Curtis E., and Stephen P. Alcorn. 2001. "To Solve a Deadly Shortage: Economic Incentives for Human Organ Donation." *Issues in Law & Medicine* 16 (spring).

Kaserman, David L., and A.H. Barnett. 2002. *The U.S. Organ Procurement System: A Prescription for Reform.* Washington, D.C.: AEI Press.

Koch, Tom. 2002. *Scarce Goods: Justice, Fairness, and Organ Transplantation.* Westport, Conn.: Praeger.

Kristof, Nicholas D. 2002. "Psst! Wanna Sell a Kidney?" *Chicago Daily Law Bulletin* (November 12).

Naylor, Chad D. 1989. "The Role of the Family in Cadaveric Organ Procurement." *Indiana Law Journal* 65 (winter).

Sylvia, Claire, and William Novak. 1997. *A Change of Heart.* New York: Little, Brown.

CROSS-REFERENCES

Death and Dying; Fetal Rights.

ORGANIC LAW

The fundamental law or constitution of a particular state or nation, either written or unwritten, that defines and establishes the manner in which its government will be organized.

ORGANIZATION

A generic term for any type of group or association of individuals who are joined together either formally or legally.

The term *organization* includes a corporation, government, partnership, and any type of civil or political association of people.

ORGANIZED CRIME

Criminal activity carried out by an organized enterprise.

Modern organized crime is generally understood to have begun in Italy in the late nineteenth century. The secretive Sicilian group La Cosa Nostra, along with other Sicilian mafia, were more powerful than the Italian government in the early twentieth century. In 1924 Benito Mussolini's fascist government rose to power, and Mussolini orchestrated a crackdown on the Italian mafia. Those mafiosi who were not jailed or killed were forced to flee the country. Many came to the United States, where they flourished in the art of bootlegging and other criminal activity. Since the 1920s organized crime has crossed ethnic lines and is associated with no particular ethnic group.

Congress and many states maintain laws that severely punish crime committed by criminal enterprises. On the federal level, Congress passed the Organized Crime Control Act in 1970. The declared purpose of the act is to eradicate organized crime by expanding evidence-gathering techniques for law enforcement, specifying more acts as being crimes, authorizing enhanced penalties, and providing for the FORFEITURE of property owned by criminal enterprises.

The Racketeer Influenced and Corrupt Organizations Act (RICO) (18 U.S.C.A. § 1961 et seq.) is the centerpiece of the Organized Crime Control Act. RICO is a group of statutes that define and set punishments for organized crime. The act's provisions apply to any enterprise that engages in RACKETEERING activity. Racketeering is the act of engaging in a pattern of criminal offenses. The list of offenses that constitute racketeering when committed more than once by an enterprise is lengthy. It includes EXTORTION, FRAUD, MONEY LAUNDERING, federal drug offenses, murder, KIDNAPPING, gambling, ARSON, ROBBERY, BRIBERY, dealing in obscene matter, counterfeiting, EMBEZZLEMENT, OBSTRUCTION OF JUSTICE, obstruction of law enforcement, tampering with witnesses, filing of a false statement to obtain a passport, passport forgery and false use or misuse of a passport, peonage, SLAVERY, unlawful receipt of WELFARE funds, interstate transport of stolen property, sexual exploitation of children, trafficking in counterfeit labels for audio and visual works, criminal infringement of copyrights, trafficking in contraband cigarettes, white slavery, violation of payment and loan restrictions to LABOR UNIONS, and harboring, aiding, assisting, or transporting illegal ALIENS. RICO also includes forfeiture provisions that allow the government to take the property of parties found guilty of violations of the act.

Modern organized criminal enterprises make money by specializing in a variety of crimes, including extortion, blackmail, gambling, loan-sharking, political corruption, and the manufacture and sale of illicit narcotics. Extortion, a time-tested endeavor of organized crime, is the acquisition of property through the use of threats or force. For instance, a criminal enterprise located in a certain neighborhood of a city may visit shopkeepers and demand a spe-cific amount of so-called protection money. If a shopkeeper does not pay the money, the criminal organization may strike at him, his property, or his family.

Blackmail is similar to extortion. It is committed when a person obtains money or value by accusing the victim of a crime, threatening the victim with harm or destruction of the victim's property, or threatening to reveal disgraceful facts about the victim.

Gambling and loan-sharking are other traditional activities of organized criminal enterprises. Where gambling is illegal, some organized crime groups act as the locus for gambling activity. In states where some gambling is legal and some gambling is illegal, organized crime groups offer illegal GAMING. Loan-sharking is the provision of loans at illegally high interest rates accompanied by the illegal use of force to collect on past due payments. In organized crime circles, such loans usually are made to persons who cannot obtain credit at legitimate financial institutions and who can serve the criminal enterprise in some way in the event they are unable to repay the loan. Loan-sharking provides organized criminal enterprises with money and helps enlarge the enterprise by bringing into the fold persons who owe a debt to the enterprise.

Political corruption has diminished as a focus of organized crime. In the first half of the twentieth century, some organized crime groups blackmailed or paid money to politicians in return for favorable legislation and favorable treatment from city hall. This sort of activity has decreased over the years as public scrutiny of political activity has increased.

The most recent major venture in organized crime is the manufacture and sale of illicit narcotics. This practice was prefigured in the activities of organized crime from 1919 to 1933. During this period alcohol was illegal under the EIGHTEENTH AMENDMENT to the U.S. Constitution, and the manufacture and sale of liquor was a favorite activity of organized crime groups. The manufacture and sale of illegal liquors, or bootlegging, was extremely profitable, and it gave organized crime a foothold in American life. Many organized criminal enterprises subsequently imitated bootlegging by selling other illegal drugs.

Violence often accompanies organized crime. Many crime syndicates use murder, torture, assault, and TERRORISM to keep themselves powerful and profitable. The constant threat of violence keeps victims and witnesses silent. Without them, prosecutors find it difficult to press charges against organized criminals.

The modern notion of organized crime in the United States has expanded beyond the prototypical paradigm of family operations. Organized crime in the early 2000s refers to any group of persons in a continuing operation of criminal activity, including street GANGS. To combat the violence and other illegal activity of street gangs, federal and state legislatures have passed laws pertaining specifically to street gangs. Many states provide extra punishment for persons in street gangs who are convicted of certain crimes.

On the federal level, a street gang is defined as an ongoing group, club, organization, or association of five or more persons formed for the purpose of committing a violent crime or drug offense, with members who have engaged in a continuing series of violent crimes or drug law violations that affect interstate or foreign commerce (18 U.S.C.A. § 521). Any person in a street gang convicted for committing or conspiring to commit a violent federal crime or certain federal drug offenses receives an extra ten years in prison beyond the prison sentence for the actual crime.

Despite stringent punishments, organized crime is difficult to eradicate. It tends to occur in large cities where anonymity is relatively easy to maintain. The size and hereditary makeup of many enterprises make them capable of surviving the arrest and imprisonment of numerous members. Many organized crime participants are careful, efficient, and professional criminals, making them difficult to apprehend.

Another reason organized crime is so durable is that the participants are extremely dedicated. The group looks after its own and there are serious consequences of betrayal. Members of organized crime groups often take an oath of allegiance. For example, members of La Cosa Nostra stated, "I enter alive into this organization and leave it dead."

FURTHER READINGS

Abadinsky, Howard. 2003. *Organized Crime.* 7th ed. Belmont, Calif.: Wadsworth/Thomson Learning.

Bonanno, Bill. 2000. *Bound by Honor: A Mafioso's Story.* New York: St. Martin's.

Goodwin, Brian. 2002. "Civil Versus Criminal RICO and the 'Eradication' of La Cosa Nostra." *New England Journal on Criminal & Civil Confinement* 28 (summer).

Jankiewicz, Sara. 1995. "Comment: Glasnost and the Growth of Global Organized Crime." *Houston Journal of International Law* 18 (fall).

Lyman, Michael D., and Gary W. Potter. 2004. *Organized Crime.* 3d ed. Upper Saddle River, N.J.: Pearson Prentice Hall.

CROSS-REFERENCES

Capone, Alphonse; Drugs and Narcotics; Eighteenth Amendment.

ORGANIZED CRIME CONTROL ACT OF 1970

See RACKETEERING.

ORIGINAL INTENT

The theory of interpretation by which judges attempt to ascertain the meaning of a particular provision of a state or federal constitution by determining how the provision was understood at the time it was drafted and ratified.

Sometimes called original understanding, originalism, or intentionalism, the theory of original intent is applied by judges when they are asked to exercise the power of JUDICIAL REVIEW during a legal proceeding. (The power of judicial review is the power of state and federal courts to review and invalidate laws that have been passed by the legislative and executive branches of government but violate a constitutional principle.)

Not every judge adheres to the theory of original intent, and many adherents fail to apply it in a uniform and faithful manner. Judges who do attempt to apply this judicial philosophy generally agree that only through its application may courts be bound by the law and not their own views of what is desirable. They also generally agree that courts must apply original intent in order to preserve the representative democracy created by the federal Constitution.

Originalists observe that the democracy created by the U.S. Constitution is marked by three essential features: a SEPARATION OF POWERS, FEDERALISM, and a BILL OF RIGHTS. The Constitution separates the powers of the federal government into three branches, which help foster what is known as a system of checks and balances. Article I of the Constitution delegates lawmaking power to the legislative branch, which comprises the two houses of Congress. This lawmaking power authorizes members of Congress to pass legislation that reflects the values of their voting constituency, usually consisting of a plurality or majority of the adults residing in the representative's home state. If a representative makes policy that is inconsistent with the values of the representative's constituents, the representative will likely be voted out of office at the next election and replaced by someone who is more sensitive to popular will. Under this system, Congress remains perpetually accountable to the U.S. people, who, originalists point out, are the ultimate source of authority from which the Constitution derives its legitimacy.

The EXECUTIVE BRANCH is also held accountable to the U.S. public at the voting booth. Every four years, U.S. citizens are given the opportunity to determine who will be president of their country. They generally vote for someone who is perceived to represent their economic, societal, and personal interests on a variety of issues, including taxes, the WELFARE system, and the right to live and die free from governmental restraint.

Article II empowers the president to sign the congressional acts that he approves and VETO the rest, enabling the executive branch to influence national policy, if not make it. The president may also influence national policy by promulgating executive decrees (which are orders issued by the executive branch without congressional approval) that are intended to implement a constitutional provision, federal law, or treaty. In addition, Article II charges the president with the responsibility of enforcing legislation that has been passed by Congress and signed into law.

Article III of the Constitution delegates federal judicial power to the U.S. Supreme Court and to other "inferior" federal courts that Congress may establish. Unlike the president and members of Congress, federal judges are largely unaccountable to the U.S. electorate. Once appointed to the bench by the president and confirmed by the Senate, a federal judge holds office for life, unless she or he retires or is removed for "treason, BRIBERY, or other high crimes and misdemeanors" (U.S. Const. art. II, § 4).

Although Article III does not confer the power of judicial review, in MARBURY V. MADISON, 5 U.S. (1 Cranch) 137, 2 L. Ed. 60 (1803), the Supreme Court ruled that it is "emphatically the duty" of the federal "judicial department to say what the law is" by "resolving the operation" of congressional legislation that conflicts with

the paramount law of the U.S. Constitution. *Marbury* thus emphasized the traditional role of courts as oracles of the law; however, it provided little guidance on how courts should interpret and apply the particular provisions of the Constitution.

Originalists attempt to provide this guidance. They argue that the interpretation of most written documents, legal or otherwise, involves a form of "communication" in which "the writer seeks to communicate with the reader," Constitutional interpretation is no different, originalists say, because it involves the attempt of judges, as readers, to understand the meaning of a constitutional provision as conveyed by the Framers and ratifiers who authored it. Originalists believe that judges who fail to employ this method of interpretation transform courts into naked power organs.

Originalists contend that judges who deviate from the original understanding of a constitutional provision are forced to replace that understanding with their own subjective sympathies, social preferences, and notions of reasonableness. When judges substitute their own value choices for those actually written in the Constitution, federal courts become super-legislatures that make decisions based on the personal will of judges and not the law of the land (*Day-Brite Lighting v. Missouri,* 342 U.S. 421, 72 S. Ct. 405, 96 L. Ed. 469 [1952]).

Originalists assert that judges who legislate from the bench violate the separation of powers by making law rather than interpreting and applying it. These judges also violate the principles of federalism, the second essential feature of U.S. constitutional democracy identified by originalists. Under these principles, courts must strike an appropriate balance between the sovereignties of state and federal governments, not allowing the smaller state governments to be wholly consumed by the ubiquitous federal government. Originalists contend that this balance impermissibly tips in favor of the federal government when federal courts invent new constitutional rights that state governments are then required to enforce.

Such rights have protected areas concerning homosexual behavior, ABORTION, CAPITAL PUNISHMENT and individual privacy. Justice CLARENCE THOMAS, an exponent of originalism, observed that "[t]he federal Constitution" is not meant to "address all ills in our society" (*Hudson v. McMillian,* 503 U.S. 1, 112 S. Ct. 995, 117 L.

Ed. 2d 156 [1992] [Thomas, J., dissenting]). Nor is the Constitution meant, Thomas said, "to prohibit everything that is intensely undesirable" (*Bennis v. Michigan,* 516 U.S.442, 116 S. Ct. 994, 134 L. Ed. 2d 68 [1996] [Thomas, J., concurring]). Originalists claim that the Constitution must protect only the areas of life that are expressly referred to or fairly implied by the explicit language of its text. In other words, where the Constitution stops speaking, the state governments may begin.

Respect for principles of federalism, then, is intimately connected with the third essential feature of U.S. Constitutional democracy identified by originalists, the Bill of Rights. The Bill of Rights protects certain freedoms from the popular will no matter how democratically the majority attempts to trample them. In all other areas, originalists assert, state and federal majorities are entitled to rule for no better reason than that they are majorities. Originalists explain that majority tyranny occurs if legislation invades areas properly left to individual freedom, and minority tyranny occurs if the majority is prevented from ruling where its power is legitimate.

Originalists argue that the judiciary facilitates minority tyranny by improperly interpreting the Bill of Rights to guarantee liberties not contemplated by the language and intent of the Framers. To avoid this pitfall, originalists believe, judges must safeguard only the liberties that can be clearly derived from the Constitution. Originalists cite a series of cases in which the Supreme Court recognized a right to privacy as the antithesis of proper constitutional interpretation.

In GRISWOLD V. CONNECTICUT, 381 U.S. 479, 85 S. Ct. 1678, 14 L. Ed. 2d 510 (1965), the Court struck down a state law forbidding married adults to use contraceptives, because it violated their right to privacy guaranteed by the First, Third, Fourth, Fifth, Ninth, and Fourteenth Amendments. Although a majority of the Court recognized privacy interests that may be inferred from these several constitutional amendments, Justice POTTER STEWART noted in a dissenting opinion that "no such general right of privacy" can be found in the express language of "the Bill of Rights" or "any other part of the Constitution." Originalists argue that courts cannot apply a general right to privacy in a politically neutral manner without protecting all sorts of illegal activities that are conducted in private, such as spousal abuse, price-fixing, and prostitution.

FURTHER READINGS

Bork, Robert H. 1990. *The Tempting of America: The Political Seduction of the Law.* New York: Free Press.

———. 1971. "Neutral Principles and Some First Amendment Problems." *Indiana Law Journal* 47.

Dworkin, Ronald. 1994. *Life's Dominion: An Argument about Abortion, Euthanasia, and Individual Freedom.* New York: Knopf.

———. 1990. Review of *Bork's Jurisprudence,* by Robert H. Bork. *University of Chicago Law Review* 57.

———. 1977. *Taking Rights Seriously.* Cambridge, Mass.: Harvard Univ. Press.

Graglia, Lino. 1992. "Interpreting the Constitution: Posner on Bork." *Stanford Law Review* 44.

Hand, Learned. 1958. *The Bill of Rights.* Cambridge, Mass.: Harvard Univ. Press.

Howard, Robert M., and Jeffrey A. Segal. 2002. "An Original Look at Originalism." *Law & Society Review* 36.

Levy, Leonard W. 2000. *Original Intent and the Framers' Constitution.* Chicago: Ivan R. Dee.

Pankratz, Jeffrey. 1992. "Neutral Principles and the Right to Neutral Access to the Courts." *Indiana Law Journal* 67.

Posner, Richard A. 1990. "Bork and Beethoven." *Stanford Law Review* 42.

Scalia, Antonin. 1989. "Originalism: The Lesser Evil." *University of Cincinnati Law Review* 57.

Scheef, Robert W. 2001. "'Public Citizens' and the Constitution: Bridging the Gap Between Popular Sovereignty and Original Intent." *Fordham Law Review* 69.

Wechsler, Herbert. 1959. "Toward Neutral Principles of Constitutional Law." *Harvard Law Review* 73.

CROSS-REFERENCES

Bork, Robert Heron; Constitution of the United States; Jurisprudence; Penumbra; Scalia, Antonin.

ORIGINAL JURISDICTION

The authority of a tribunal to entertain a lawsuit, try it, and set forth a judgment on the law and facts.

Original jurisdiction is distinguishable from appellate jurisdiction, which is the power of a court to hear and enter judgment upon a case brought for review. For example, the U.S. Supreme Court's caseload consists almost entirely appellate cases from the circuit courts of appeal. When two or more states are locked in a dispute, however, the Supreme Court has original jurisdiction to gather and hear evidence much like a trial court. The Court appoints a SPECIAL MASTER to hear the evidence and prepare factual findings. It then hears oral arguments and issues a decision as it does in appellate jurisdiction cases. Because it is the highest court in the United States, the Supreme Court's decision in original jurisdiction cases is final, with no right of appeal. An example of such a case is *New Jersey v. New York*, 523 U.S. 767, 118 S. Ct. 1726, 140 L. Ed. 2d 993 (1998), in which the Supreme Court took evidence and determined which state had claim to Ellis Island.

ORIGINAL WRIT

A document formerly used to commence a lawsuit in English courts.

Historically, the writ needed to start a personal action was a mandatory letter from the king, issued by the Chancery and sealed with the Great Seal. It was directed to the sheriff of the county where the wrong was supposed to have been committed and required the sheriff to command that the defendant either satisfy the plaintiff's claim or answer the charges that had been made. This form of writ has been replaced by the summons, which commences civil actions today, but the summons is still sometimes called an original writ.

ORIGINATION FEE

A charge imposed by a lending institution or a bank for the service of processing a loan.

For example, a bank might charge an individual who has applied for a student loan an origination fee of one percent for processing the application and granting the loan.

ORPHAN'S COURT

The designation of tribunals in a number of New England states that have probate or surrogate jurisdiction.

Such a court ordinarily has the power to handle such matters as the establishment of wills, the administration and distribution of decedents' estates, the supervision of the guardianship of INFANTS, and the control of their property.

OSTENSIBLE

Apparent; visible; exhibited.

Ostensible authority is power that a principal, either by design or through the absence of ordinary care, permits others to believe his or her agent possesses.

❖ OTIS, JAMES, JR.

James Otis Jr. was a Massachusetts lawyer who became a leading colonial political activist in the 1760s. His constitutional challenge to British governance of the colonies in the WRITS OF ASSISTANCE CASE in 1761 was one of the most important legal events leading to the American Revolution. A brilliant speaker and writer, Otis faded from the revolutionary scene as he struggled with alcoholism and mental illness.

Otis was born on February 5, 1725, in West Barnstable, Massachusetts. His father, James Otis Sr., was a prominent merchant and political figure in the colony. Otis graduated from Harvard College in 1743 and was admitted to the bar in 1748. He moved his law practice from Plymouth, Massachusetts, to Boston in 1750 and was appointed advocate general of the Boston vice-admiralty court in 1756. He served until 1761, when the furor over writs of assistance pushed Otis into becoming an opponent of the colonial government he served.

A writ of assistance was a general SEARCH WARRANT that allowed customs officers to command the assistance of any local public official in making entry and seizing contraband goods. Goods seized by use of the writ were brought before the vice-admiralty court, which determined if the goods had been imported lawfully. SMUGGLING had bedeviled the colonial government for many years, but the need for tax revenue during the course of the French and Indian War led to a crackdown. The use of the writ made revenue collection easier, but it upset the merchant community of Boston.

Otis resigned his position on the vice-admiralty court and agreed to represent the merchants in challenging the legality of the writs of assistance. At trial Otis argued that the writs were a form of tyranny. He coined the phrase "A man's home is his castle" to describe the sanctity and privacy that a citizen deserved from his or her government.

More important, he argued that the writs were unconstitutional under British law. Though England did not have a written constitution, Otis referred to the accumulation of practices and attitudes throughout English history that set limits on the power of government. In his view there were traditional limits beyond which the Parliament or the king could not legitimately go. The writs exceeded these bounds and were therefore null and void. Though he lost

James Otis Jr. LIBRARY OF CONGRESS

the *Writs of Assistance* case, his theory caught the public's attention. It provided justification for an increasing number of protests against taxation without representation. The case also elevated Otis as a radical colonial leader.

In May 1761 he was elected to the General Court of Massachusetts. This body, which served as the provincial legislature, gave Otis a platform to expound his radical political views. In 1762 he published *A Vindication of the Conduct of the House of Representatives of the Province of Massachusetts Bay.* In the pamphlet he defended the legislature's refusal to pay for ships that England had sent to protect the colony from pirates. He wrote numerous papers

to the other colonies and to the government in England arguing for political freedom. His ideas became a part of the address that the STAMP ACT Congress of 1765 sent to the House of Commons protesting taxation of the colonies.

As the colonies moved closer to breaking away from England, Otis's influence faded, the result of alcoholism and mental illness. In 1769 he was struck in the head by a customs officer who disliked Otis's views. This injury left him mentally incapacitated and unable to continue in public life. For the remainder of his life, Otis had few lucid moments. He died on May 23, 1783, in Andover, Massachusetts, after being struck by lightning.

FURTHER READINGS

Purcell, Jeffrey W. 1999. "James Otis: 'Flame of Fire' Revolutionary Opposing the Writs of Assistance and Loyal British Subject?" *Massachusetts Legal History* 5 (annual): 147–78.

CROSS-REFERENCES

Writs of Assistance Case.

❖ OTTO, WILLIAM TOD

William Tod Otto served as the reporter of decisions for the U.S. Supreme Court from 1875 to 1883. A distinguished lawyer, judge, and government administrator before his appointment as reporter, Otto is also noted for successfully arguing before the Supreme Court the case of *Murdock v. City of Memphis,* 87 U.S. (20 Wall.) 590, 22 L. Ed. 429 (1875), which resolved issues concerning the jurisdiction of the Court.

Otto was born on January 19, 1816, in Philadelphia, Pennsylvania. He earned a bachelor's degree in 1833 and a master's degree in 1836 from the University of Pennsylvania. Otto

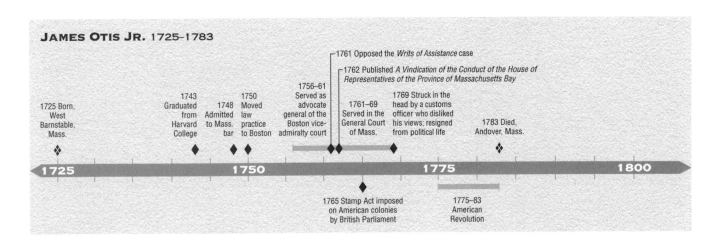

JAMES OTIS JR. 1725–1783

1725 Born, West Barnstable, Mass.

1743 Graduated from Harvard College

1748 Admitted to Mass. bar

1750 Moved law practice to Boston

1756–61 Served as advocate general of the Boston vice-admiralty court

1761 Opposed the *Writs of Assistance* case

1762 Published *A Vindication of the Conduct of the House of Representatives of the Province of Massachusetts Bay*

1761–69 Served in the General Court of Mass.

1769 Struck in the head by a customs officer who disliked his views; resigned from political life

1783 Died, Andover, Mass.

1725   1750   1775   1800

1765 Stamp Act imposed on American colonies by British Parliament

1775–83 American Revolution

William Tod Otto.
U.S. SUPREME COURT

claims against Spain from U.S. citizens living in its colony of Cuba.

In 1875 Otto argued *Murdock v. Memphis*, 20 Wall. 590 (1875), before the Supreme Court. The case concerned congressional changes to section 25 of the JUDICIARY ACT OF 1789, which granted appellate authority to the Supreme Court over federal question cases from the state courts (those cases involving federal constitutional or statutory issues) but excluded questions of state law from review by the Court. This meant that state courts had the final and unreviewable authority over the interpretation of the state constitution and laws. However, in the 1867 reenactment of section 25, Congress omitted the provision containing this exclusion. *Murdock* raised the question of whether the U.S. Supreme Court could now review questions of state law. The Court agreed with Otto, concluding that Congress's failure to clearly state its intent to radically change the scope of federal jurisdiction prevented the Court from inferring intent.

Shortly after the *Murdock* decision, Otto was appointed reporter of decisions, succeeding JOHN WILLIAM WALLACE. He was the first reporter to issue Supreme Court reports without his name appearing on the spine of each volume. Previous reporters had acted as their own publishers and distributors; thus they were entitled to use their names in marketing the volumes of court decisions. In 1874, however, Congress appropriated money for publishing the Court's opinions under government auspices. Otto, though hardly anonymous, assembled the reports for publication by the government.

Between 1875 and 1883, Otto edited 17 volumes (91–107 *United States Reports*). He left the

studied law in Philadelphia and then moved to Brownstown, Indiana, to open a private practice. In 1844 he was elected a judge of Indiana's Second Circuit court, a position he held until his defeat in the election of 1852. From 1847 to 1852, Otto also taught law at Indiana University.

Despite his election defeat, Otto remained interested in public office. Although he lost an election in 1858 for Indiana attorney general, he had the good fortune of supporting ABRAHAM LINCOLN for president at the 1860 Republican convention. President Lincoln named Otto assistant secretary of the interior in 1863. In this post Otto administered Indian affairs. He left the department in 1871 to serve as arbitrator for

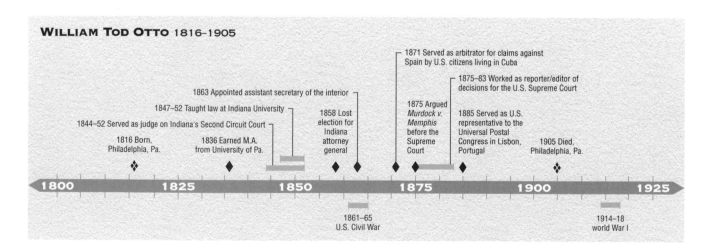

WILLIAM TOD OTTO 1816–1905

1871 Served as arbitrator for claims against Spain by U.S. citizens living in Cuba

1875–83 Worked as reporter/editor of decisions for the U.S. Supreme Court

1863 Appointed assistant secretary of the interior

1875 Argued *Murdock v. Memphis* before the Supreme Court

1847–52 Taught law at Indiana University

1858 Lost election for Indiana attorney general

1885 Served as U.S. representative to the Universal Postal Congress in Lisbon, Portugal

1844–52 Served as judge on Indiana's Second Circuit Court

1816 Born, Philadelphia, Pa.

1836 Earned M.A. from University of Pa.

1905 Died, Philadelphia, Pa.

1800   1825   1850   1875   1900   1925

1861–65 U.S. Civil War

1914–18 World War I

position to resume a private law practice and served as U.S. representative to the Universal Postal Congress in Lisbon, Portugal, in 1885.

Otto died on November 7, 1905, in Philadelphia.

OUT-OF-COURT SETTLEMENT

An agreement reached between the parties in a pending lawsuit that resolves the dispute to their mutual satisfaction and occurs without judicial intervention, supervision, or approval.

An out-of-court settlement provides that the parties relinquish their rights to pursue judicial remedies.

OUTLAWRY

A declaration under old ENGLISH LAW by which a person found in CONTEMPT on a civil or criminal process was considered an outlaw—that is, someone who is beyond the protection or assistance of the law.

During the Anglo-Saxon period of English history, a person who committed certain crimes lost whatever protection he or she had under the law, forfeited whatever property he or she owned, and could be killed by anyone. If the crime committed was TREASON or a felony, a declaration of outlawry was tantamount to a conviction and attainder. Outlawry for a misdemeanor did not, however, amount to a conviction for the offense. The Norman Conquest led to significant changes in the law governing outlawry, eventually leading to its abolition.

OUTPUT CONTRACT

In the law of sales, an agreement in which one party assents to sell his or her total production to another party, who agrees to purchase it.

This type of contract does not entail an illusory promise, a purported agreement that actually means nothing because it leaves to one party the choice of performance or nonperformance, even if the quantity of goods that are the subject of the contract is indefinite. It is also known as an *entire output contract,* and it is subject to the UNIFORM COMMERCIAL CODE, a body of law adopted by the states that governs commercial transactions.

CROSS-REFERENCES

Requirements Contract.

OUTSTANDING WARRANT

An order that has not yet been carried out; an order for which the action commanded has not been taken.

When the action ordered has been done, the warrant is said to have been executed.

OVERBREADTH DOCTRINE

A principle of JUDICIAL REVIEW that holds that a law is invalid if it punishes constitutionally protected speech or conduct along with speech or conduct that the government may limit to further a compelling government interest.

Legislatures sometimes pass laws that infringe on the FIRST AMENDMENT freedoms of religion, speech, press, and peaceable assembly. When a legislature passes such a law, a person with a sufficient interest affected by the legislation may challenge its constitutionality by bringing suit against the federal, state, or local sovereignty that passed it. One common argument in First Amendment challenges is that the statute is overbroad.

Under the overbreadth doctrine, a statute that affects First Amendment rights is unconstitutional if it prohibits more protected speech or activity than is necessary to achieve a compelling government interest. The excessive intrusion on First Amendment rights, beyond what the government had a compelling interest to restrict, renders the law unconstitutional.

If a statute is overbroad, the court may be able to save the statute by striking only the section that is overbroad. If the court cannot sever the statute and save the constitutional provisions, it may invalidate the entire statute.

The case of *Brockett v. Spokane Arcades, Inc.,* 472 U.S. 491, 105 S. Ct. 2794, 86 L. Ed. 2d 394 (1985), illustrates how the overbreadth doctrine works. At issue in *Brockett* was an OBSCENITY statute passed by the state of Washington. The statute declared to be a moral NUISANCE any place where lewd films were shown as a regular course of business and any place where lewd publications constituted a principal part of the stock in trade. Lewd matter was defined as being obscene matter, or any matter that appeals to the prurient interest. Under the statute the term *prurient* was defined as tending to incite lasciviousness or lust.

The Supreme Court in *Brockett* ruled that the Washington statute was overbroad because it prohibited lust-inciting materials. According to the Court, because lust is a normal sexual appetite, materials that include an appeal to lust enjoy First Amendment protection. Therefore, a statute that prohibits any material arousing lust is constitutionally overbroad.

The remedy in the *Brockett* case was not complete invalidation of the moral nuisance law. The Court directed that the reference to lust be excised from the statute and stated that the rest of the statute was valid. The statute, though originally overbroad, was still valid because it contained a severability clause and was still effective after its overbroad portion was struck.

CROSS-REFERENCES

Compelling State Interest; Freedom of Speech; Freedom of the Press.

OVERDRAFT

A check that is drawn on an account containing less money than the amount stated on the check.

The term *overdraft* is also used in reference to the condition that exists when VOUCHERS or purchase orders are drawn in amounts exceeding the amount that has been appropriated or budgeted.

CROSS-REFERENCES

Commercial Paper.

OVERHEAD

A sum total of the administrative or executive costs that relate to the management, conduct, or supervision of a business that are not attributable to any one particular product or department.

Expenses such as rent, taxes, insurance, lighting, heating, and other miscellaneous office expenses all fall under the category of overhead.

OVERREACHING

Exploiting a situation through FRAUD *or* UNCONSCIONABLE *conduct.*

OVERRIDE

An arrangement whereby commissions are made by sales managers based upon the sales made by their subordinate sales representatives. A term found in an agreement between a real estate agent and a property owner whereby the agent keeps the right to receive a commission for the sale of the property for a reasonable time after the agreement expires if the sale is made to a purchaser with whom the agent negotiated prior to the expiration of the agreement.

OVERRULE

The refusal by a judge to sustain an objection set forth by an attorney during a trial, such as an objection to a particular question posed to a witness. To make void, annul, supersede, or reject through a subsequent decision or action.

A judicial decision is overruled when a later decision, made by the same tribunal or a higher court in the same system, hands down a decision concerning the identical QUESTION OF LAW, which is in direct opposition to the earlier decision. The earlier decision is thereby overruled and deprived of its authority as precedent.

OVERT

Public; open; manifest.

The term *overt* is used in CRIMINAL LAW in reference to conduct that moves more directly toward the commission of an offense than do acts of planning and preparation that may ultimately lead to such conduct.

OVERT ACT

An open, manifest act from which criminality may be implied. An outward act done in pursuance and manifestation of an intent or design.

An overt act is essential to establish an attempt to commit a crime. It is also a key element in the crime of TREASON and has become a component of federal and some state criminal conspiracy laws. It also plays a role in the right of SELF-DEFENSE.

An attempt to commit a crime is an offense when an accused makes a substantial but unsuccessful effort to commit a crime. The elements of attempt include an intent to commit a crime, an apparent ability to complete the crime, and an overt act. An overt act is an act that is performed to execute the criminal intention and will naturally achieve that result unless prevented by some external cause. The act must directly move toward commission of the crime and must be more than acts of planning or preparation.

Defining when an act is more than preparatory has proved difficult. Several tests have been used to determine when an overt act has been committed. The "unequivocal" test states that a defendant's act, standing alone, is unequivocally consistent only with her or his intent to commit the allegedly attempted crime. This test has been criticized as too lenient on criminals because no act is truly unequivocal. A person who shoots someone several times can argue that she was only trying to injure the victim and that it was her skilled shooting and not luck that prevented the victim's death.

Some jurisdictions favor the "substantial act" test. They permit an attempt conviction when a defendant with the requisite criminal intent performs a substantial act towards the commission of the crime. Under this test, for example, a prospective burglar can be convicted of attempted BURGLARY if apprehended in an alley with burglary tools, even though he had not determined which building he was going to burglarize.

The "probable desistence" test asks whether the defendant had gone so far down the road of crime that it is unlikely that she or he would have voluntarily desisted from completing the crime. One way of measuring this probability is to look at the past criminal record of an accused. Thus, an accused with a previous record may be convicted under this test, because her past propensity makes it unlikely that she would have stopped taking the acts leading to the crime.

The need for an overt act also is required in federal and some state criminal conspiracy prosecutions. A conspiracy is a voluntary agreement by two or more persons to commit an unlawful act or to use unlawful means to accomplish an act that is not in itself unlawful. Under federal law the overt act must be an independent act that comes after the agreement or conspiracy and is performed to effect the objective of the conspiracy. The overt act itself need not be a criminal act, because its sole function is to demonstrate that the conspiracy is operative. If, for example, two persons conspire to rob a bank and rent a getaway car, the rental is an overt act that in itself is perfectly legal. Some states, however, still adhere to the common-law rule that an overt act is not required to prove a conspiracy.

An overt act that justifies the exercise of the right of self-defense is one that causes a reasonable person to perceive a present intention to cause his or her death or great bodily harm.

The federal crime of treason contains an overt act requirement. Article III, Section 3, Clause 1, of the U.S. Constitution provides, "No Person shall be convicted of Treason unless on the Testimony of two Witnesses to the same overt Act." In such a case, an overt act means a step taken to execute a treasonable purpose, as distinguished from mere words or a treasonable sentiment, purpose, or design not resulting in action. It is an act in furtherance of the crime.

CROSS-REFERENCES

Criminal Law.

OWNER

The person recognized by the law as having the ultimate control over, and right to use, property as long as the law permits and no agreement or COVENANT *limits his or her rights.*

OYER AND TERMINER

[French, To hear and decide.] *The designation "court of oyer and terminer" is frequently used as the actual title, or a portion of the title, of a state court that has criminal jurisdiction over felonious offenses.*

OYEZ

[French, Hear ye.] *A word used in some courts by the public crier to indicate that a proclamation is about to be made and to command attention to it.*

PACIFIC RAILROAD ACT

The Pacific Railroad Act, passed by Congress in 1862 (12 Stat. 489), authorized the construction of the first transcontinental railway line connecting the east and west coasts. The need for a transcontinental railway to facilitate transportation of persons and products across the United States became increasingly clear in the 1850s due to the acquisition of California and the resolution of the Oregon boundary dispute. In 1862, before the secession of the South from the Union, the REPUBLICAN PARTY in Congress was instrumental in enacting legislation that authorized the Union Pacific Railway and the Central Pacific Railroad to construct such a railway. The Union Pacific Railway was to begin construction at Omaha, Nebraska, with the objective of connecting with the Central Pacific Railroad, which was to begin construction at the same time at Sacramento, California. The law provided that after each railroad laid forty miles of track, it was to receive 6,400 acres of public lands and government loans ranging from $16,000 to $48,000 per mile of track completed.

Congress passed additional legislation in 1864 to provide more land and money to complete the project. The two lines finally met at Promontory Point, Utah, in 1869, thereby providing a fast means of access from the Missouri River and the Pacific Ocean by rail.

The Union Pacific Railway and the Central Pacific Railroad were merged into the Union Pacific Railroad in 1900 by Edward Harriman.

CROSS-REFERENCES

Railroad.

PACIFISM

A belief or policy in opposition to war or violence as a means of settling disputes. Pacifists maintain that unswerving nonviolence can bestow upon people a power greater than that achieved through the use of violent aggression.

Over the years, pacifism has acquired different meanings. As a consequence, it is practiced in a variety of ways. For example, pacifists may make an individual vow of nonviolence. They may also organize and actively pursue nonviolence and peace between nations. They may even assert that some form of support for selective violence is sometimes necessary to achieve worldwide peace.

History

The earliest form of recorded pacifism appear in the teachings of Siddhartha Gautama, who became known as the Buddha. The Buddha, or the Enlightened One, left his family at a young age and spent his life searching for a release from the human condition. Before dying in northeast India between 500 and 350 B.C., the Buddha taught the paths to elevated existence and inspired a new religion. Buddhism eventually spread from India to central and Southeast Asia, China, Korea, Japan, and the United States.

The teachings of Jesus Christ continued the attachment of nonviolence to organized reli-

Though better known for challenging injustices in British-ruled India, Gandhi also spent many years working for the rights of Indian residents of South Africa. AP/WIDE WORLD PHOTOS

gion. Christ taught, in part, that an appropriate response to violence is to "turn the other cheek" and offer no resistance.

As civilization expanded and distinct states were formed, Christianity was carried to developing areas. It became popularized as the official religion of entire states, the leaders of which sought to retain both Christianity and a stronghold on power. In the third century, the nonresistance aspect of Christianity was reconsidered, and certain passages in the Gospel were interpreted to mean that resistance is an acceptable reaction to evil forces.

Saint Augustine solidified Christianity's break with pure pacifism in the fifth century with a warmly received religious treatise. In *The City of God,* he maintained, in part, that peace could be realized only through the acceptance of Christianity and that the Church was to be defended.

More than a millennium passed before the next great pacifist movement was seen. In the fifteenth century, Martin Luther led the Protestant Reformation, which inspired religious creativity. Europeans who were disenchanted with Catholicism broke away from the Church in Rome, experimented with observations and practices, and founded their own religions. The most pacific of these was Anabaptism. Anabaptists practiced nonviolence and actively supported those suffering from violence.

In the seventeenth century, still more pacific religious groups were established, such as the Mennonites, the Brethren, and the Religious Society of Friends. Of these, the Friends have gathered the largest following in the United States.

Religious Society of Friends

In 1652, George Fox founded the Religious Society of Friends in England. Initially, Friends were known as Children of the Light, Publishers of Truth, or Friends of Truth. They held fast to the belief that there exists in all persons a light, which can be understood as the presence of God. With this reverence for other people, nonviolence came naturally. And, since God exists in all people, violence can be avoided by finding and revealing the Light in others.

Friends were also called Quakers, perhaps from the trembling some experience as they find the Inner Light during meetings. The nickname was originally coined by antagonists and intended as derisive, but many Friends began to use it in their own speech. *Quaker* soon lost its derogative connotation, and it remains the most recognized name for Friends.

A Friend's commitment to pacifism often came with no small dose of activism. Friends interrupted church services and refused to take oaths in seventeenth-century England, arguing that if one always tells the truth, one need not promise to do so. Friends ignored social niceties, refusing, for example, to remove their hat in the presence of royalty. Friends also used the informal *thee* and *thy* in place of the more respectful *you* and *your*. Within four years of the creation of the Society, Friends in England were being imprisoned by the thousands, and they began to seek refuge in the New World.

Ann Austin and Mary Fisher were the first Friends to reach colonial America from England. After their arrival in 1656, Austin and Fisher were imprisoned and deported. Friends who came after them suffered a similar fate.

Many of those who stayed moved to Rhode Island, which Roger Williams founded on religious freedom principles.

In 1681, Charles II gave to William Penn, a longtime Friend, the charter to colonial land in America as repayment for a debt owed to Penn's father. In 1682, Penn founded Pennsylvania as a "holy experiment," and many English and European Friends found permanent sanctuary there.

Friends continued their activism in colonial America by obstructing the business of SLAVERY. Many Friends published their opposition to slavery and assisted fugitive slaves. Friends also addressed other social issues, such as the treatment of mentally ill persons and the rights of women. With the onset of the Civil War, many Friends reconsidered their absolute refusal to participate in war and helped the Union forces and slaves. In World Wars I and II, many Friends took an active part in medical and relief work.

Mohandas K. Gandhi

Mohandas K. Gandhi was the first great modern pacifist. Born October 2, 1869, in Porbandar, India, Gandhi led a high-profile life dedicated to political and social reform through nonviolence.

During the 1900s, Gandhi experimented with various means of resolving conflict. Passive resistance, according to Gandhi, had to be supplemented by an active effort to understand and respect adversaries. In an atmosphere of respect, people could find peaceful, creative solutions. This active campaign for equality is called satyagraha, or "grasping for the truth."

Gandhi led a well-orchestrated political campaign for Indians in South Africa through the early 1900s. The movement reached its pinnacle in November 1913, when Gandhi led Indian miners on the Great March into Transvaal. The march was a profound show of determination, and the South African government opened negotiations with Gandhi shortly thereafter.

By promoting a variety of nonviolent activities designed to dramatize and call attention to social injustice, Gandhi won new rights for laborers, members of minorities, and poor people in South Africa and India. In many cases, however, Gandhi was working against centuries of hatred, and success was never absolute.

Martin Luther King Jr. and the Civil Rights Movement

Gandhi's campaigns became the inspiration and model for the U.S. CIVIL RIGHTS and polit-

Martin Luther King Jr. at the August 1963 March on Washington. Gandhi's campaigns became the inspiration and models used by King and other civil rights leaders during the 1950s and 1960s.
AP/WIDE WORLD PHOTOS

ical movements in the 1950s and 1960s. Among those inspired was MARTIN LUTHER KING JR. King was born in Atlanta on January 15, 1929, the son of a Baptist preacher. His Baptist upbringing was supplemented by the study of theology at Crozer Theological Seminary in Chester, Pennsylvania, where he was introduced to the nonviolent teachings of Gandhi.

In 1955, King became involved with the first great pacifist movement in the United States, the African American CIVIL RIGHTS MOVEMENT. He eventually spearheaded that movement. On December 1, ROSA PARKS, a black Montgomery resident, refused to surrender her seat on a bus to a white man. Her subsequent arrest for violating SEGREGATION laws sparked a boycott of the Montgomery transit system led by King and the black activists of the Montgomery Improvement Association. The boycott lasted over one year, until the Montgomery city government abolished segregation on buses. King's leadership had helped effect political change without the use of violence, and he resolved to build on the success.

In the late 1950s, King organized the SOUTHERN CHRISTIAN LEADERSHIP CONFERENCE (SCLC). The SCLC operated as a network for civil rights work and a platform from which to address the nation and the world. Armed only with fortitude, the moral rightness of a cause, and an exceptional gift for public speaking, King was able to garner widespread support for a

During an early 1970s anti-war rally in New York City, members of the Religious Society of Friends (aka Quakers) read the names of people killed in the Vietnam War. HULTON-DEUTSCH COLLECTION/CORBIS

series of popular campaigns that led to the end of official discrimination and segregation in the southern United States.

The influence of Gandhi on King was apparent. At the core of King's philosophy was nonviolence, but this pacifism was buttressed by action. Like Gandhi, King directed much of his energy toward the organization of nonviolent campaigns designed to call attention to social injustice. The campaigns did not always win the hearts and minds of other U.S. citizens. Occasionally, King and fellow civil rights activists suffered from the violence of their opponents.

Conscientious Objector Status

When the United States becomes involved in war, military service may become mandatory, and the status of CONSCIENTIOUS OBJECTOR (CO) is sought by pacifists to avoid military service. To qualify as a CO, one need only show "a sincere and meaningful" objection to all war (*Reiser v. Stone,* 791 F. Supp. 1072 [E.D. Pa. 1992] [quoting *Shaffer v. Schlesinger,* 531 F.2d 124 (3d Cir. 1976)]). This objection need not be grounded in religion. It is legitimate if it results from an "intensely personal" conviction that some might find "incomprehensible; or "incorrect" (*Reiser* [quoting *United States v. Seeger,* 380 U.S. 163, 85 S. Ct. 850, 13 L. Ed. 2d 733 (1965)]).

In *Reiser,* Dr. Lynda Dianne Reiser sought discharge from military service on the grounds of a conscientious objection to war. Reiser had entered the Army in 1983 in the Reserve Officers' Training Corps (ROTC) program at Wash-

ington and Jefferson College. After graduating in 1986, she sought and received a deferment of military service in order to attend Temple University Medical School. Upon graduation from medical school in 1990, Reiser sought and received another deferment in order to perform a one-year medical internship. In August 1990, Reiser informed the Army that she was a conscientious objector and that she would refuse the four years of military service required of her in return for the ROTC scholarship.

Although Reiser had possessed moral convictions approaching pacifism before entering the ROTC program, she had envisioned a career in medicine and expected her participation in military service to be minimal. In 1985, serious misgivings over military service began to take hold in Reiser. By 1989, her opposition to military service was firm. After treating a 16-year-old shooting victim, Reiser experienced nightmares and attempted to avoid all contact with violence. In April 1990, her beliefs crystallized into complete opposition to violence, war, and military service. Four months later, she applied for CO status.

The Department of the Army Conscientious Objector Review Board (DACORB) denied Reiser's application in September 1990. Despite supporting testimony from Army chaplain Colonel Ronald Miller and Army investigator Lieutenant Colonel Charles Nester, DACORB concluded that Reiser's belief in pacifism was not sincerely held.

Reiser appealed the DACORB decision to the U.S. District Court for the Eastern District of Pennsylvania. After reciting the chronology of the case and the legal standards for CO status, the court conducted a complete review of the record. This included an in-depth examination of Reiser's evolution to pacifism.

In addition to possessing a predisposition to nonviolence, Reiser had undergone a pacific metamorphosis that had not been disproved. Reiser had been deeply affected by the Kurt Vonnegut novel *Slaughterhouse Five* (1969) and had had her growing pacifism affirmed by roommates. She had also experienced a strengthening of her nonviolent convictions as a result of her medical training.

DACORB had ruled that Reiser had failed to prove that she would have "no rest or inner peace" if she were not discharged. This standard had been rejected by the court in an earlier case, which held that conscientious objectors need only show sincerity in their opposition to war (*Masser v. Connolly,* 514 F. Supp. 734, 740 [E.D. Pa. 1981]). According to the *Reiser* court, the "no rest or inner peace" standard was valid, but nothing in the record supported the DACORB conclusion that Reiser would lose no sleep over forced military service.

Because the timing of a CO application alone cannot be used to deny CO status, DACORB took pains to deemphasize the timing of Reiser's application. However, Reiser's application came less than one year before she was scheduled to begin military service, and DACORB was unable to let the issue go untouched. The timing of the application, admitted DACORB, called Reiser's sincerity into question.

DACORB use of application timing did call Reiser's sincerity into question. What DACORB failed to do, according to the court, was answer the question of Reiser's sincerity. Without additional support for its skepticism, DACORB use of application timing as a basis for rejecting CO status for Reiser carried no weight. The court ultimately reversed the DACORB decision and relieved Reiser of her obligation to work four years for the U.S. Army.

FURTHER READINGS

Beck, Sanderson. 2003. *Guides to Peace and Justice: Great Peacemakers, Philosophers of Peace, and World Peace Advocates.* Ojai, Calif.: World Peace Communications.

Burkholder, J. R., and John Bender. 1982. *Children of Peace.* Elgin, Ill.: Brethren.

Churchill, Ward, with Mike Ryan. 1998. *Pacifism as Pathology: Reflections on the Role of Armed Struggle in North America.* Winnipeg, Man.: Arbeiter Ring.

Kellett, Christine Hunter. 1984. "Draft Registration and the Conscientious Objector: A Proposal to Accommodate Constitutional Values." *Columbia Human Rights Law Review* 15.

Randle, Michael, ed. 2002. *Challenge to Nonviolence.* Bradford, U.K.: Univ. of Bradford, Dept. of Peace Studies.

Todd, Jack. 2001. *Desertion: In the Time of Vietnam.* Boston: Houghton Mifflin.

Wallis, Jim, ed. 1982. *Waging Peace: A Handbook for the Struggle to Abolish Nuclear Weapons.* New York: Harper and Row.

CROSS-REFERENCES

Civil Rights Movement; Conscientious Objector; Gandhi, Mohandas Karamchand; King, Martin Luther, Jr.

PACKING

The process of exercising unlawful, improper, or deceitful means to obtain a jury composed of individuals who are favorably disposed to the verdict sought.

PACT

A bargain, compact, or agreement. An agreement between two or more nations or states that is similar to, but less complex than, a treaty.

PACT OF PARIS

See KELLOGG-BRIAND PACT.

PACTA SUNT SERVANDA

[Latin, Promises must be kept.] *An expression signifying that the agreements and stipulations of the parties to a contract must be observed.*

PACTUM

[Latin, Pact.] *A compact, bargain, or agreement.*

❖ PAGE, ALAN CEDRIC

Alan Cedric Page, former Minnesota Vikings football star, has served as an associate justice of the Minnesota Supreme Court since 1993. Page gained athletic fame as one of the four "Purple People Eaters" for the Vikings' defense who were essential to the team's ten division titles and four Super Bowl appearances during the 1960s and 1970s. While still employed full-time as a professional football player, Page attended the University of Minnesota Law School full-time and graduated in 1978. He is the first and only African-American supreme court justice in the state of Minnesota.

One of four children of Georgianna Umbles and Howard Felix Page, Alan Page was born on August 7, 1945, in Canton, Ohio, the home of the Pro Football Hall of Fame. His mother, a country club attendant, and his father, a bar manager, always emphasized the importance of learning. They instilled strong values in him, and Page looked up to his parents as role models.

Page was an outstanding athlete in high school, but even at a young age, his aspirations went beyond the gridiron and into the courtroom. Page admired U.S. Supreme Court Justice THURGOOD MARSHALL and was a fan of the *Perry Mason* television show. He told *Parade Magazine* in 1990 that he viewed sports not as a goal, but as a means to achieve an education. "Even when I was playing professionally," he said, "I never viewed myself as a football player. There's far more to life than being an athlete."

Page graduated from the University of Notre Dame in 1967 with a B.A. in political science. At

"AT THE VERY BEST, ATHLETIC ACHIEVEMENT MIGHT OPEN A DOOR THAT DISCRIMINATION ONCE HELD SHUT. BUT THE DOORS SLAM QUICKLY ON THE UNPREPARED AND THE UNDER-EDUCATED."
—ALAN PAGE

Notre Dame, he was an All-American defensive end and played on the school's 1966 national championship team. Chosen in 1967 by the Vikings as their first-round draft choice, Page went on to earn the Most Valuable Player award in the National Football League in 1971. In the NFL, he played the position of defensive tackle. He logged fifteen seasons with the Vikings and Chicago Bears, starting in each of the 236 games he played during his career before retiring in 1981. He was elected to the Pro Football Hall of Fame in 1988 and to the College Football Hall of Fame in 1993.

After graduating from law school in 1978, he joined the law firm of Lindquist and Vennum in Minneapolis, where he specialized in labor and employment litigation from 1979 to 1984, overlapping with his final years in the NFL. He served as assistant attorney general for the state of Minnesota from 1987 to 1993.

Page established the Page Education Foundation in 1988 to increase the participation of minority youth in post-secondary education and work-readiness activities. Scholarship recipients tutor kindergarten through eighth-grade students for eight to ten hours each month during the school year while attending post-secondary school, thus creating a pyramid influencing younger students of color as mentors and role models.

Page regularly speaks to minority students about the importance of education. He also encourages adults to influence children to look at the values and good examples of hard work that decent Americans provide every day for "creating and sustaining hope for the future." He noted, "These are not the heroes who offer hope with promises of winning the lottery, becoming a rap star, or pulling down backboards and endorsement contracts in the NBA. These are simply men and women who get up every morning and do the things that citizens do."

Page was appointed to the Minnesota Supreme Court in 1993. In his 1998 re-election campaign, an opponent charged that Page's foundation activities violated canons regarding the judicial appearance of impartiality. The ethics complaint showed that donations to the scholarship fund had soared in recent years and that some of the contributors included companies and law firms with cases pending before the Minnesota Supreme Court. Page said that he refused to help raise funds and that he intentionally avoided any knowledge of his contributors. The complaint also charged that awarding scholarships only to minorities violated the judicial canon prohibiting any expressions of bias or prejudice. In February 1999, the Minnesota Board of Judicial Standards cleared Page of any ethics violations in the matter.

Page was in the news in 2000 when he was ticketed for driving with expired automobile license tabs, which is a sticker affixed to the license plate each year as proof that the owner has paid the annual license fee. He demanded a trial on the $57 fine, although the fine would have been reduced to $28 if he had agreed to pay. In court, Page's attorney offered documentation that his client had mailed a check for the tabs weeks before he received the ticket. The Minneapolis City Attorney's office argued that Page had an obligation to stay off the road until he received his tabs. However, the court ruled in Page's favor, finding that Page should not have been penalized for the state's delay.

Page has received a number of honors, both for his playing days and for his activities after retirement from the NFL. He was a recipient of the Dick Enberg Award and became a member of the Academic All-American Hall of Fame. He

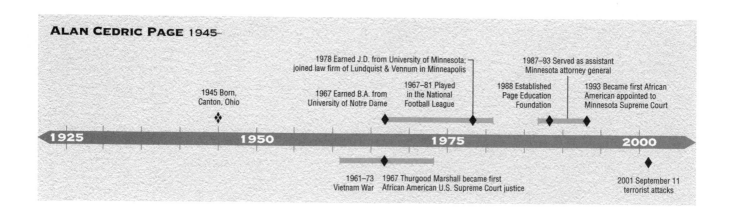

ALAN CEDRIC PAGE 1945–

1945 Born, Canton, Ohio

1967 Earned B.A. from University of Notre Dame

1978 Earned J.D. from University of Minnesota; joined law firm of Lundquist & Vennum in Minneapolis

1967–81 Played in the National Football League

1988 Established Page Education Foundation

1987–93 Served as assistant Minnesota attorney general

1993 Became first African American appointed to Minnesota Supreme Court

1925   1950   1975   2000

1961–73 Vietnam War

1967 Thurgood Marshall became first African American U.S. Supreme Court justice

2001 September 11 terrorist attacks

was named by the *Star Tribune* of Minneapolis and St. Paul as one of the 100 most influential Minnesotans in the twentieth century. He also has received honorary doctor of laws degrees from Notre Dame, St. John's University, Westfield State College, and Luther College.

While playing for the Vikings, Page married Diane Sims. They have four children.

FURTHER READINGS

Page, Alan. 1993. "A Message You May Not Hear In Law School" (lecture). *Ohio Northern University Law Review* 20 (fall-winter).

Starr, Cynthia, et al. 1994. "Home Court Advantage." *ABA Journal* 80 (February).

Robert Treat Paine.

❖ PAINE, ROBERT TREAT

Robert Treat Paine was born March 11, 1731, in Boston, Massachusetts. He graduated from Harvard University in 1749 and was admitted to the Massachusetts bar in 1757. After a brief career in the ministry, he became an eminent lawyer, politician, and judge.

Paine first won fame as an associate prosecuting attorney in the BOSTON MASSACRE trial. The Boston Massacre, which occurred in 1770, was a violent response to the passing of the TOWNSHEND ACTS by Great Britain. These acts decreed that CUSTOMS DUTIES would be imposed on the importation of tea, lead, glass, paints, and paper. When British troops were sent to Boston to enforce payment of the duties, the colonists harassed them to such an extent that they fired into a crowd, killing five men.

Subsequently Paine served two terms as a member of the Massachusetts Provincial Assembly, from 1773 to 1775 and from 1777 to 1778, acting as speaker during 1777 and 1778. During the next four years, he was an active member of

two congresses: the Provincial Congress, in 1774 and 1775, and the CONTINENTAL CONGRESS, from 1774 to 1778. In 1776 he signed the Declaration of Independence.

Paine continued to be active in Massachusetts government after the American Revolution. In 1777 he became the first attorney general of Massachusetts and held that office until 1790. From 1778 to 1780, he was involved in the enactment of the Massachusetts constitution and was instrumental in the establishment of the American Academy of Arts and Sciences in 1780.

In 1790, Paine became a justice of the Massachusetts Supreme Court, where he remained until 1804.

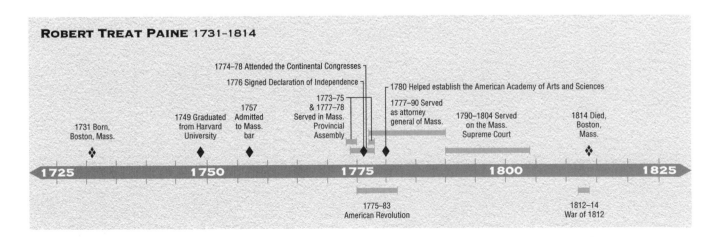

ROBERT TREAT PAINE 1731–1814

1774–78 Attended the Continental Congresses
1776 Signed Declaration of Independence
1780 Helped establish the American Academy of Arts and Sciences
1773–75 & 1777–78 Served in Mass. Provincial Assembly
1777–90 Served as attorney general of Mass.
1757 Admitted to Mass. bar
1749 Graduated from Harvard University
1790–1804 Served on the Mass. Supreme Court
1731 Born, Boston, Mass.
1814 Died, Boston, Mass.

1725   1750   1775   1800   1825

1775–83 American Revolution
1812–14 War of 1812

Paine died May 11, 1814, in Boston, Massachusetts.

CROSS-REFERENCES

Boston Massacre Soldiers; Massachusetts Constitution of 1780.

❖ PAINE, THOMAS

Social agitator Thomas Paine was an influential political writer whose support of revolution and republican government emboldened the American colonists to declare independence from England. In 1776, the corset-maker-turned-pamphleteer published the first of a sixteen-part series entitled *The American Crisis*. Paine's tract contained the stirring words "These are the times that try men's souls." Paine wrote the famous pamphlet to lift the spirits of the beleaguered Continental Army.

The effect of Paine's political writing was felt not only in America but also in England and France. After the American Revolution, Paine returned to his native Europe, where he supported the French Revolution. His political opinions ignited a storm in England and landed him in jail in France. During his lifetime, Paine's political views made him both tremendously popular and almost universally despised. In particular, his later writings about organized religion and deism offended many Americans. Shunned and penniless at the end of his life, Paine has only recently found his rightful place in history.

Paine was born into a poor English family on January 29, 1737, in Thetford, Norfolk, England. To help support his Quaker father and Anglican mother, Paine quit school at age thirteen and began training in corset making, his father's trade. Unhappy in his vocation, Paine left home and enlisted as a seaman in the Seven Years' War. Afterward, he traveled to London, where he became interested in science and mechanics. Paine held a variety of jobs, including customs official, preacher, and schoolteacher. At the urging of BENJAMIN FRANKLIN, while Franklin served as a colonial official in England, Paine immigrated to America. Arriving in Philadelphia in 1774, Paine became the managing editor of *Pennsylvania Magazine*.

In January 1776, Paine published his first important pamphlet, *Common Sense*. A phenomenal success, the publication sold more than five hundred thousand copies. Paine urged the American colonies not only to protest English taxation but to go further and declare independence. He also recommended calling a constitutional convention to establish a new government. Paine's tract was extremely influential in convincing the colonists to cut their ties with England; embrace the Revolution; and embark upon a new, republican form of government.

Paine served in the Continental Army and experienced firsthand the miserable conditions of war. To boost the soldiers' morale after a retreat, he wrote the influential series *The American Crisis*. Under orders from General Washington, Paine's pamphlet was read aloud to encourage the troops. *The American Crisis* has been given credit for inspiring the American victory in the Battle of Trenton.

Paine was elected to the CONTINENTAL CONGRESS in 1777, as secretary of the Committee of Foreign Affairs. He resigned under pressure in 1779 after publishing confidential information about treaty negotiations with France.

After the United States' victory over England, Paine devoted his time to perfecting his

"SOCIETY IN EVERY STATE IS A BLESSING, BUT GOVERNMENT, EVEN IN ITS BEST STATE, IS BUT A NECESSARY EVIL; IN ITS WORST STATE AN INTOLERABLE ONE."
—THOMAS PAINE

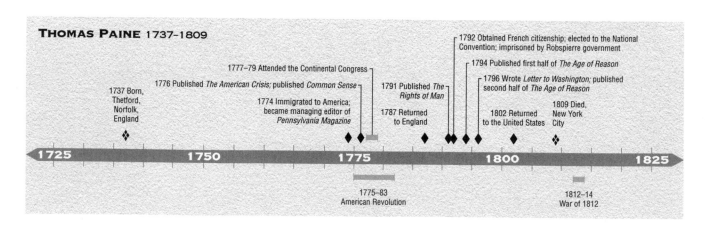

THOMAS PAINE 1737–1809

1737 Born, Thetford, Norfolk, England

1774 Immigrated to America; became managing editor of *Pennsylvania Magazine*

1776 Published *The American Crisis*; published *Common Sense*

1777–79 Attended the Continental Congress

1787 Returned to England

1791 Published *The Rights of Man*

1792 Obtained French citizenship; elected to the National Convention; imprisoned by Robspierre government

1794 Published first half of *The Age of Reason*

1796 Wrote *Letter to Washington*; published second half of *The Age of Reason*

1802 Returned to the United States

1809 Died, New York City

1725   1750   1775   1800   1825

1775–83 American Revolution

1812–14 War of 1812

inventions. In 1787, he returned to Europe to gather financial support and interest in his ideas for an iron bridge. While in England, Paine became caught up in the debate over the French Revolution. In 1791, he published the first part of *The Rights of Man*. It was a response to Edmund Burke's *Reflections on the Revolution in France* (1790), a vigorous denunciation of the events in France. Paine's *The Rights of Man* supported the revolution and upheld the dignity and rights of the common person. Controversial for its time, *The Rights of Man* sold two hundred thousand copies in England but Paine was forced out of that country under an indictment for TREASON.

Paine moved to France. After obtaining French citizenship, he was elected to the National Convention in 1792. Because Paine protested the execution of Louis XVI, he was arrested and imprisoned by the radical Robespierre government. Barely avoiding the guillotine, he spent ten months in a Luxembourg prison before his release was won by JAMES MONROE, U.S. ambassador to France. Paine wrote *Letter to Washington* in 1796, a critical look at the U.S. president's inability to quickly obtain Paine's freedom.

While in prison, Paine published in 1794 the first half of his most controversial work, *The Age of Reason*. The second half was printed in 1796, after his release. In *The Age of Reason*, Paine criticized organized religion and explained his own deist beliefs. Deism is a religious and philosophical belief that accepts the concept of God but views reason as the key to moral truths. Deism was confused by many of Paine's readers with atheism, the rejection of a belief in God. Because people mistook *The Age of Reason* for an atheist tract, Paine came under attack for his unorthodox religious views.

When Paine arrived in the United States in 1802, he was rejected by many of his former associates. His reputation was damaged by his misinterpreted deist beliefs and by his public criticism of the American hero GEORGE WASHINGTON.

Paine died June 8, 1809, in New York City, misunderstood and impoverished, with his role in the Revolutionary War downplayed by his detractors. He was buried on his farm in New Rochelle, New York. In 1819, political journalist William Cobbett made arrangements to have Paine reburied in England in a place of honor.

Thomas Paine.
PHOTOGRAPH OF PAINTING BY ROMNEY. NATIONAL ARCHIVES AND RECORDS ADMINISTRATION

Somehow, en route to England, Paine's remains were lost. They were never retrieved.

Paine's reputation as a political philosopher has been largely restored. He is remembered favorably for his rousing call to arms during the American Revolution and for his defense of republicanism and the rights of common people.

FURTHER READINGS

Aldridge, Alfred Owen. 1959. *Man of Reason: The Life of Thomas Paine.* Philadelphia: Lippincott.

Ayer, A.J. 1988. *Thomas Paine.* New York: Atheneum.

Keane, John. 2003. *Tom Paine: A Political Life.* New York: Grove Press.

PAIRING-OFF

In the practice of legislative bodies, a system by which two members, who belong to opposing political parties or are on opposite sides with respect to a certain question, mutually agree that they will both be absent from voting, either for a specified period or when a vote is to be taken on the particular question.

As a result of pairing-off, a vote is neutralized on each side of the question, and the comparative division of the legislature remains the same as if both members were present. The practice is said to have originated in the English House of Commons during the time of Oliver Cromwell.

PAIS

[French, The country; the neighborhood.] *A trial* per pais *denotes a trial by the country; that is, trial by jury.*

An ESTOPPEL in pais means that a party is prevented by his or her own conduct from obtaining the enforcement of a right which would operate to the detriment of another who justifiably relied on such conduct. This type of estoppel differs from an estoppel by deed or by record which, as a result of the language set out in a document, bars the enforcement of a claim against a party who acted in reliance upon those written terms.

PALIMONY

See ALIMONY; COHABITATION.

PALM OFF

To misrepresent inferior goods of one producer as superior goods made by a reputable, well-regarded competitor in order to gain commercial advantage and promote sales.

The doctrine of palming off is applied to the particular facts of a case in which the defendant is accused of engaging in UNFAIR COMPETITION against the plaintiff.

❖ PALMER, ALEXANDER MITCHELL

Alexander Mitchell Palmer served as U.S. attorney general from 1919 to 1921. Palmer, who also served as a congressman and federal judge, became a controversial figure for rounding up thousands of ALIENS in 1920 that he considered to be politically subversive. These "Palmer raids" violated basic civil liberties and ultimately discredited Palmer.

"FULLY 90
PERCENT OF THE
COMMUNIST AND
ANARCHIST
AGITATION IS
TRACEABLE TO
ALIENS."
—A. MITCHELL
PALMER

A. Mitchell Palmer. LIBRARY OF CONGRESS

Palmer was born May 4, 1872, in Moosehood, Pennsylvania. He graduated from Swarthmore College in 1891 and then studied law at Swarthmore, Lafayette College, and George Washington University. Though he did not earn a law degree, he passed the Pennsylvania bar exam and was admitted to the bar in 1893. He entered a small law firm in Stroudsberg, Pennsylvania, and practiced there until 1901. He then became a solo practitioner.

During the 1890s, Palmer became active in DEMOCRATIC PARTY politics. He was elected to the U.S. House of Representatives in 1908 where he served until 1915. In 1912 he played a key role in securing the Democratic presidential nomi-

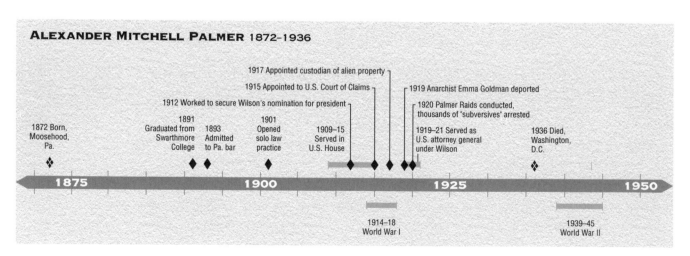

ALEXANDER MITCHELL PALMER 1872–1936

1917 Appointed custodian of alien property

1915 Appointed to U.S. Court of Claims

1919 Anarchist Emma Goldman deported

1912 Worked to secure Wilson's nomination for president

1920 Palmer Raids conducted, thousands of "subversives" arrested

1872 Born, Moosehood, Pa.

1891 Graduated from Swarthmore College

1893 Admitted to Pa. bar

1901 Opened solo law practice

1909–15 Served in U.S. House

1919–21 Served as U.S. attorney general under Wilson

1936 Died, Washington, D.C.

1875   1900   1925   1950

1914–18 World War I

1939–45 World War II

nation for New Jersey governor WOODROW WIL-SON. Following Wilson's victory that fall, Wilson asked Palmer to join his cabinet as secretary of war. Palmer's pacifist Quaker beliefs, however, precluded him from accepting the office.

In 1914 he ran for the U.S. Senate but lost. In April 1915 Wilson appointed him a judge of the United States Court of Claims. It was a brief appointment. He resigned in September and returned to his law practice. He continued his political career, however, serving as a member of the Democratic National Committee during Wilson's eight-year term.

In 1917, after the United States entered WORLD WAR I, Wilson appointed Palmer custodian of alien property. Palmer's duties included seizing and selling properties belonging to aliens, primarily Germans, and his methods often met with disapproval.

In March 1919 Wilson appointed Palmer U.S. attorney general. Though World War I was over, the Bolshevik Revolution in Russia caused political hysteria in western Europe and the United States. The Communist movement advocated world revolution, and U.S. leaders suspected that left-wing radicals, who were primarily aliens, were plotting to overthrow the government.

Palmer used the ESPIONAGE ACT OF 1917 and the SEDITION Act of 1918 to begin a crusade against this perceived threat. He deported the anarchist EMMA GOLDMAN and many other radicals, but these actions were a prelude to his unprecedented dragnets. On January 2, 1920, at Palmer's direction, federal agents in thirty-three cities rounded up six thousand persons suspected of subversive activities. Agents entered and searched homes without warrants, held persons without specific charges for long periods of time, and denied them legal counsel. Hundreds of aliens were deported. Palmer's actions were part of an anti-Communist "Red Scare" that ignored civil liberties in the pursuit of rooting out allegedly subversive activities. He steadfastly defended the raids in the face of widespread protests.

Palmer sought to succeed Wilson as president but lost the Democratic Party nomination in 1920. After leaving the office of attorney general in March 1921, Palmer resumed his private law practice and remained active in Democratic Party politics, campaigning for presidential candidate Alfred E. Smith in 1928 and FRANKLIN D. ROOSEVELT in 1932.

Palmer died May 11, 1936, in Washington, D.C.

FURTHER READINGS

Coben, Stanley. 1972. *A. Mitchell Palmer: Politician.* New York: Da Capo Press.

PALPABLE

Easily perceptible, plain, obvious, readily visible, noticeable, patent, distinct, manifest.

The term *palpable* usually refers to some type of egregious wrong, such as a governmental error or abuse of power.

PALSGRAF V. LONG ISLAND RAILROAD COMPANY

Palsgraf v. Long Island Railroad Company, 248 N.Y. 339, 162 N.E. 99, decided by the New York Court of Appeals in 1928, established the principle in TORT LAW that one who is negligent is liable only for the harm or the injury that is foreseeable and not for every injury that follows from his or her NEGLIGENCE.

The unique facts of the case created a need for a new application of the generally accepted theory that negligence is the absence of care, according to the circumstances. Mrs. Palsgraf was standing on a railroad platform when she was injured by falling scales. The scales toppled as the result of a shock of an explosion caused by an accident that occurred at the other end of the platform, "many feet away" from Palsgraf.

The accident involved a passenger with a package who was running to catch a departing train. As the passenger jumped to board the train, two railroad employees, one on the train and the other on the platform, reached for and pushed (respectively) him so he would not fall off it. The employees' help caused the passenger to drop the package. The package wrapped in newspaper contained fireworks that exploded upon hitting the tracks. The resulting explosion caused the scales to fall, striking Palsgraf. She sued the railroad for the conduct of its employees that led the passenger to drop his package of fireworks.

Both the trial court and the intermediate appellate court awarded judgment to the plaintiff, Palsgraf. The Court of Appeals decision, written by BENJAMIN CARDOZO, reversed the judgment. Cardozo stated that negligence is wrongful "because the eye of vigilance perceives the risk of danger ... The risk reasonably to be perceived defines the duty to be obeyed, and risk imports relation; it is to another or others within the range of apprehension." Given this principle, Cardozo reasoned that "Here, by concession, there was nothing in the situation to suggest to the most cautious mind that the parcel wrapped in newspaper would spread wreckage throughout the station."

The dissenting opinion offered that "Every one owes to the world at large the duty of refraining from those acts that may unreasonably threaten the safety of others . . . Unreasonable risk being taken, its consequences are not confined to those who might probably be hurt." It viewed the concept of proximate cause as "practical politics," not based on logic. Although it must be ". . . something without which the event would not happen," proximate cause means "that, because of convenience, of public policy, of a rough sense of justice, the law arbitrarily declines to trace a series of events beyond a certain point." The foreseeable or natural results of a negligent act affect a determination of whether the act is a proximate cause of the injuries. The dissenters, therefore, reasoned "given such an explosion as here, it needed no great foresight to predict that the natural result would be to injure one on the platform at no greater distance from its scene than was the plaintiff."

Manz, William H. 2003. "Palsgraf: Cardozo's Urban Legend?" *Dickinson Law Review* 107 (spring).

Weinrib, Ernest J. 2001. "The Passing of Palsgraf." *Vanderbilt Law Review* 54 (April).

PANDER

To pimp; to cater to the gratification of the lust of another. To entice or procure a person, by promises, threats, FRAUD, *or deception to enter any place in which prostitution is practiced for the purpose of prostitution.*

Pandering is established when the evidence shows that the accused succeeded in inducing a victim to become an inmate of a house of prostitution. One who solicits for a prostitute is a panderer.

The *pandering of obscenity* refers to the business of purveying, by some form of advertising, pictorial or graphic material that appeals to the prurient interest of customers or potential customers.

CROSS-REFERENCES

Obscene.

PANEL

A list of jurors to serve in a particular court or for the trial of a designated action. A group of judges of a lesser number than the entire court convened to decide a case, such as when a nine-member appellate court divides into three, three-member groups, and each group hears and decides cases. A plan in reference to prepaid legal services.

The term *open-panel legal services* refers to a plan in which legal services are paid for in advance, usually by insurance, but in which members can select their own lawyers. Under a closed panel, all legal services are rendered by a group of attorneys previously chosen by the insurer, the union, or another entity.

PAPER

A document that is filed or introduced in evidence in a lawsuit, as in the phrases papers in the case *and* papers on appeal.

Any written or printed statement, including letters, memoranda, legal or business documents, and books of account, in the context of the FOURTH AMENDMENT *to the U.S. Constitution, which protects the people from unreasonable* SEARCHES AND SEIZURES *with respect to their "papers" as well as their persons and houses.*

In the context of accommodation paper and COMMERCIAL PAPER, *a written or printed evidence of debt.*

PAR

In COMMERCIAL LAW, *equal; equality.*

The term *par* refers to an equality that exists between the nominal or face value of a document—such as a bill of exchange or a share of stock—and its actual selling value. When the values are equal, the share is said to be *at par*; if it can be sold for more than its face value, it is *above par*; if it is sold for less than its nominal value, it is *below par*.

PARALEGAL

See LEGAL ASSISTANT.

PARALLEL CITATION

A reference to the same case or statute published in two or more sources.

For example, BROWN V. BOARD OF EDUCATION OF TOPEKA, KANSAS, a landmark decision by the Supreme Court in 1954, can be located in

347 U.S. 483, 74 S. Ct. 686, and 98 L. Ed. 873. These references are parallel citations to reporters in which Supreme Court decisions are published.

PARAMOUNT TITLE

In the law of real property, ownership that is superior to the ownership with which it is compared, in the sense that the former is the source or the origin of the latter.

The term *paramount title* is, however, frequently used to signify a title that is merely better or stronger than another or will prevail over it. This usage is rarely correct, unless the superiority consists of the seniority of the title referred to as *paramount*.

PARCENER

A joint heir. Collectively the joint heirs are called coparceners.

PARDON

The action of an executive official of the government that mitigates or sets aside the punishment for a crime.

The granting of a pardon to a person who has committed a crime or who has been convicted of a crime is an act of clemency, which forgives the wrongdoer and restores the person's CIVIL RIGHTS. At the federal level, the president has the power to grant a pardon, and at the state level the governor or a pardon board made up of high-ranking state officials may grant it.

The power to grant a pardon derives from the English system in which the king had, as one of his royal prerogatives, the right to forgive virtually all forms of crimes against the crown. The Framers of the U.S. Constitution, in Article II, Section 2, Clause 1, provided that the president "shall have Power to grant Reprieves and Pardons for Offences against the United States, except in Cases of Impeachment." Throughout U.S. history the courts have interpreted this clause to give the president virtually unlimited power to issue pardons to individuals or groups and to impose conditions on the forgiveness.

The first major court case involving the pardon power, *Ex parte Garland*, 71 U.S. (4 Wall.) 333, 18 L. Ed. 366 (1866), established both the scope of the pardon power and the legal effect on a person who was pardoned. President ANDREW JOHNSON pardoned Arkansas attorney and Confederate sympathizer Alexander Hamil-

ton Garland, who had not been tried, for any offenses he might have committed during the Civil War. Garland sought to practice in federal court, but federal law required that he swear an oath that he never aided the Confederacy. Garland argued that the pardon absolved him of the need to take the oath. The Supreme Court agreed with Garland. It held that the scope of the pardon power "is unlimited, with the exception stated [impeachment]. It extends to every offence known to the law, and may be exercised at any time after its commission, either before legal proceedings are taken, or during their pendency, or after conviction and judgment."

The power to pardon applies only to offenses against the laws of the jurisdiction of which the pardoning official is the chief executive. Thus the president may only pardon for violations of federal law, and governors may only pardon for violations of the laws of their states.

A president or governor may grant a full (unconditional) pardon or a conditional pardon. The granting of an unconditional pardon fully restores an individual's civil rights forfeited upon conviction of a crime and restores the person's innocence as though he or she had never committed a crime. This means that a recipient of a pardon may regain the right to vote and to hold various positions of public trust.

A conditional pardon imposes a condition on the offender before it becomes effective. Typically this means the commutation of a sentence. For example, the president has the power under the Pardon Clause to commute a death sentence on the condition that the accused serve the rest of his or her life in prison without eligibility for PAROLE, even though a life sentence imposed directly by a court would otherwise be subject to parole. In upholding this type of conditional pardon, the Supreme Court in *Schick v. Reed*, 419 U.S. 256, 95 S. Ct. 379, 42 L. Ed. 2d 430 (1974), reasoned that "considerations of public policy and humanitarian impulses support an interpretation of that [pardon] power so as to permit the attachment of any condition which does not otherwise offend the Constitution."

Unless the pardon expressly states that it is issued because of a determination that the recipient was innocent, a pardon does not imply innocence. It is merely a forgiveness of the offense. It is generally assumed that acceptance of a pardon is an implicit ACKNOWLEDGMENT of guilt, for one cannot be pardoned unless one has committed an offense.

The Constitution allows two other pardon powers besides the power of commutation. It expressly speaks about the president's power to grant "reprieves." A reprieve differs from a pardon in that it establishes a temporary delay in the enforcement of the sentence imposed by the court, without changing the sentence or forgiving the crime. A reprieve might be issued for the execution of a prisoner to give the prisoner time to prove his or her innocence. A related power is the power to grant "amnesty," which is also implicit in the pardon power. AMNESTY is applied to whole classes or communities, instead of individuals. The power to issue an amnesty and the effect of an amnesty are the same as those for a pardon.

The most widely publicized pardons have involved political figures. President GERALD R. FORD's September 1974 pardon of former president RICHARD M. NIXON for all offenses that he had committed, or in which he had taken part, relieved Nixon from facing criminal prosecution for his role in the WATERGATE scandal. President Ford justified the pardon as a way to restore domestic tranquility to a nation that had spent two years in political turmoil.

In 1977, President JIMMY CARTER granted an amnesty to all persons who had unlawfully evaded the military draft during the VIETNAM WAR. Carter, too, justified his amnesty as a way to end a divisive period in U.S. history. In December 1992, President GEORGE H.W. BUSH pardoned six officials of the RONALD REAGAN administration who were implicated in the IRAN-CONTRA AFFAIR. Bush granted the pardons shortly before leaving office. He based the pardons on his belief that the officials had been prosecuted over policy differences rather than for criminal acts.

In January 2001, a day before leaving office, President BILL CLINTON issued pardons to several individuals, including financier Marc Rich and his associate Pincus Green. Rich and Green had fled to Switzerland in 1983 to avoid prosecution on FRAUD charges in the United States. Soon after the pardon was announced, it was revealed that Rich's ex-wife, Denise, had made a gift of $450,000 to the Clinton Library Founda-

On September 8, 1974, President Gerald Ford pardoned Richard Nixon, thereby allowing the former president to avoid possible criminal prosecution for his role in the Watergate scandal. AP/WIDE WORLD PHOTOS

tion and a $109,000 donation to the Senate campaign of HILLARY RODHAM CLINTON. The donations apparently were made during the period when she and several of Marc Rich's business associates were LOBBYING for the pardons. The news caused an uproar among Republicans and Democrats alike. Many of Clinton's strongest supporters said that even if there was no wrongdoing, the timing was at best a sign of extremely poor judgment. The revelations led to federal investigations. In March 2001, the House and Senate introduced legislation that would require stringent contributor disclosure for anyone seeking either a pardon or a commutation, as well as stricter disclosure rules for anyone donating to a presidential library (previously not subject to campaign disclosure laws).

FURTHER READINGS

"House Focuses on Clinton Staff in Pardon Probe." February 15, 2001. CNN.com: Inside Politics. Available online at <www.cnn.com/2001/ALLPOLITICS/02/15/pardon .hearing.02> (accessed August 14, 2003).

Isikoff, Michael. 2002. "Scandal Still Going." *Newsweek* (September 16).

Moore, Kathleen Dean. 1989. *Pardons: Justice, Mercy, and the Public Interest.* New York: Oxford Univ. Press.

CROSS-REFERENCES

Board of Pardons.

PARENS PATRIAE

[Latin, Parent of the country.] *A doctrine that grants the inherent power and authority of the state to protect persons who are legally unable to act on their own behalf.*

The *parens patriae* doctrine has its roots in English COMMON LAW. In feudal times various obligations and powers, collectively referred to as the "royal prerogative," were reserved to the king. The king exercised these functions in his role of father of the country.

In the United States, the *parens patriae* doctrine has had its greatest application in the treatment of children, mentally ill persons, and other individuals who are legally incompetent to manage their affairs. The state is the supreme guardian of all children within its jurisdiction, and state courts have the inherent power to intervene to protect the best interests of children whose welfare is jeopardized by controversies between parents. This inherent power is generally supplemented by legislative acts that define the scope of child protection in a state.

The state, acting as *parens patriae,* can make decisions regarding mental health treatment on behalf of one who is mentally incompetent to make the decision on his or her own behalf, but the extent of the state's intrusion is limited to reasonable and necessary treatment.

The doctrine of *parens patriae* has been expanded in the United States to permit the attorney general of a state to commence litigation for the benefit of state residents for federal antitrust violations (15 U.S.C.A. § 15c). This authority is intended to further the public trust, safeguard the general and economic welfare of a state's residents, protect residents from illegal practices, and assure that the benefits of federal law are not denied to the general population.

States may also invoke *parens patriae* to protect interests such as the health, comfort, and welfare of the people, interstate WATER RIGHTS, and the general economy of the state. For a state to have standing to sue under the doctrine, it must be more than a nominal party without a real interest of its own and must articulate an interest apart from the interests of particular private parties.

CROSS-REFERENCES

Antitrust Law; Child Abuse; Children's Rights; Infants.

PARENT AND CHILD

The legal relationship between a father or mother and his or her offspring.

The relationship between parent and child is of fundamental importance to U.S. society, because it preserves the safety and provides for the nurture of dependent individuals. For this reason, the parent-child relationship is given special legal consideration. Increasingly, local, state, and federal governments have become more involved in the relationship, especially when a child is abused or neglected. In addition, parental roles have shifted over time, and the law has moved with these changes. Legal rights that were once the sole province of the father are now shared with the mother, and, in general, the law seeks to treat parents equally.

The term *child* is used in the limited sense to indicate an individual below the age of majority. The more precise word for such an individual is *minor, juvenile,* or *infant.* The age of majority, which transforms a child legally into an adult, has traditionally been the age of 21 years. Many states, however, have reduced the age of majority to 18 years.

CHILDREN'S RIGHTS V. PARENTS' RIGHTS: YOU DON'T OWN ME . . . DO YOU?

In 1874, a badly beaten girl known only as Mary Ellen became the first legally recognized victim of **CHILD ABUSE** in the United States. Before 1874, society offered little protection for minors. Children were considered the property of their parents, and neither the government nor private individuals intervened when they were injured, overworked, or neglected. Mary Ellen was rescued from unfit parents only after the American Society for the Prevention of Cruelty to Animals (ASPCA) stepped in on her behalf. ASPCA advocates pointed out that if Mary Ellen were a horse or a dog, her mistreatment would be prohibited by statute. A judge agreed that the young girl deserved at least the same protection as an animal.

The status of U.S. children has improved dramatically since Mary Ellen's ordeal. At the turn of the twentieth century, a nationwide child protection movement helped eliminate the long hours, poor wages, and punishing conditions faced by child workers. **CHILD LABOR LAWS** paved the way for later reforms regarding compulsory educa-tion, foster care, protective services, **HEALTH CARE**, and criminal justice for juveniles.

Just how far these reforms should go is the subject of debate. A mild uproar over children's rights arose during the 1992 U.S. presidential race between incumbent **GEORGE H. W. BUSH** (R) and challenger **BILL CLINTON** (D). Scholarly articles written in the early 1970s by Clin-ton's wife, **HILLARY RODHAM CLINTON**, were at the heart of the controversy. A former lawyer for the Children's Defense Fund, Clinton ques-tioned the traditional legal pre-sumption of **INCOMPETENCY** for children. She believed that children were capable of mak-ing many of their own decisions; thus she proposed the elimination of minority status for children and suggested a new presumption of legal competence. Clin-ton also favored granting children the same substantive and procedural rights enjoyed by adults. Further, because chil-dren's interests are not always the same as their parents', Clinton felt that minors should be allowed to hire their own lawyers.

During the presidential campaign, Clinton's views were attacked by political opponents who claimed she encouraged children to sue their parents. Her critics predicted that Clinton's ideas would lead children to "divorce" their parents over trivial matters such as curfews, home-work, allowances, and household chores.

However, Clinton's views were actu-ally much less extreme than those of so-called child liberationists who believe that children should be allowed to vote, choose their residence, refuse to attend school, enter into contracts, and take part in activities currently reserved for adults. More radical child advocates maintain that children are just as rational as adults and that the nation's commitment to jus-tice requires equal treatment of all peo-ple, regardless of age.

Critics of children's rights believe conferring too many rights on children would erode parental authority and the traditional family. Many conservatives believe that children lack the wisdom to make important decisions and require the guidance of responsible adults. They approve of a paternalistic approach to children's welfare rather than one that empowers young people. Critics also

Parent-Child Relationship

In its most restricted use, the term *parent* refers only to a mother or father who is related to the child by blood. This definition holds whether the child is legitimate (the natural par-ents are married to each other) or illegitimate (the parents are not married to each other). As of 2003, as a result of statutes, adoptive parents have the same rights and responsibilities as nat-ural parents. Other persons standing in the place of natural parents, such as stepparents, are not, however, given such extensive rights and respon-sibilities. Although in some instances foster par-ents and foster care agencies have the legal responsibility to nurture a minor, they are not entitled to the full status of parent.

A child is the issue or offspring of his par-ents. A posthumous child is one conceived prior to, and born after, the death of his father. Such a child has the same inheritance rights as a child born while his father is alive. A child is not enti-tled to full legal rights unless the child is born alive. The law does not ordinarily consider a fetus to be a child.

Various rights and responsibilities that reflect the social goals of nurturing and protect-ing dependent individuals are attached to the status of parent and child. The public policy in favor of promoting the protection and care of minors gives rise to the legal presumption that the parent-child relationship exists when it is acknowledged by a parent or when a parent

resent the legal system's intrusion into parents' domain, arguing that parents are entitled to the final word in their children's upbringing. Conservatives fear that if children have ready access to attorneys, a rash of frivolous or retaliatory lawsuits will erupt, destroying many fragile families in need of help. So strong is this fear that the United States is one of only two countries (Somalia is the other) that have not ratified the United Nations Convention on the Rights of the Child. Among other concerns some critics have raised against children's rights are that children could be allowed legally to join GANGS or have ABORTIONS. Some critics have gone so far as to claim that ratification of the United Nations treaty would take control of children away from parents and hand it to the United Nations (even though the U.S. Constitution does not allow any treaty to override its precepts). Some groups, such as the Children's Rights Council (CRC), believe that children have the "right" to be raised in a two-parent household. One CRC goal is to keep marriages together, but, in the case of DIVORCE, it seeks to encourage parents to share custody equitably.

Three well-publicized cases illustrate the philosophical divide over children's and parents' rights.

Kingsley v. Kingsley In 1992, an eleven-year-old Florida boy went to court to terminate the rights of his biological parents. Gregory Kingsley retained attorney Jerri Blair to represent him in a proceeding to sever all ties with his natural parents, Rachel and Ralph Kingsley. Kingsley also petitioned for his own ADOPTION by his foster parents, Lizabeth and George Russ. Rachel Kingsley opposed her son's actions; her estranged husband did not.

Kingsley persuaded circuit court judge Thomas Kirk that he had been abandoned by his mother. Most of Kingsley's chaotic, impoverished life had been spent in and out of foster care. His unstable early environment was contrasted with the loving and more affluent home now offered by the Russ family. Kirk determined that Kingsley, a minor, had the capacity to bring the action and ordered both the termination of parental rights and the adoption.

Rachel's attorney, Jane Carey, complained that a child's wish had been declared more important than the preservation of the family. Carey worried that the termination of Rachel's rights sent a message to poor parents that they could never measure up to wealthier families. It also drove a symbolic wedge between U.S. children and their parents. To Gregory's supporters, however, the ruling was an important victory on behalf of neglected, mistreated children.

On appeal, Florida's Fifth District Court of Appeals determined that, as a minor, Kingsley could not initiate a proceeding to terminate his parents' rights (*Kingsley v. Kingsley*, 623 So. 2d 780 [1993]). Only a GUARDIAN AD LITEM, or friend of the court, could do so. Nonetheless, the appeals court upheld the termination of Rachel's parental rights because clear and convincing evidence demonstrated her ABANDONMENT of Kingsley and because Kingsley's foster parents had properly initiated the proceeding by filing separate termination petitions. The court also found that there was no legitimate reason to order Kingsley's adoption at the same time as Rachel's termination of rights. In fact, the simultaneous adoption order was in error because the termination order was subject to appeal.

Although Kingsley's initial triumph was diluted by the appeals court ruling, it challenged traditional notions of parental "ownership" of children.

Mays-Twigg Case Kimberly Mays of Florida was nine years old when she received shocking news: she had been switched at birth with another baby and raised by parents to whom she was not related. Mays was born in a rural Florida hospital in 1978. She was taken home by Robert Mays and his wife, Barbara Mays,

(continued)

resides with and raises the child. The relationship continues in the absence of unusual circumstances that mandate intervention by the state. Proper legal procedures must be followed when the state intervenes. Parents or children cannot alter or destroy the relationship either by themselves or merely by agreement.

Ordinarily a parent has the right to the custody and supervision of her child. In addition, a parent has the duty to care for and nurture her offspring. The child has the right to receive this care and nurture and the obligation to yield to reasonable parental guidance and supervision. The state has a duty to preserve family stability by ensuring proper care of children. The right of the family to privacy limits state regulation of the parent-child relationship to some extent, but modern laws dealing with CHILD ABUSE and neglect give the state greater powers to intervene.

A parent's duties extend beyond providing daily necessities and financial support. A court may reasonably expect that a parent will provide for the child's education, medical care, and social and religious training, as well as exhibit love and affection for the child. A parent must also discipline the child when necessary.

Constitutional Considerations

Statutes governing the parent-child relationship are primarily state laws. These laws must conform to the requirements of the U.S. Consti-

CHILDREN'S RIGHTS V. PARENTS' RIGHTS: YOU DON'T OWN ME . . . DO YOU?
(CONTINUED)

who later died of cancer. The only other Caucasian infant in the hospital at the time was a girl who was taken home and raised by Ernest and Regina Twigg. The switch was discovered after a blood test determined that the Twiggs' daughter, whom they had named Arlena, was not genetically related to them. A review of hospital records and further blood tests established that Mays was actually the Twiggs' biological daughter. After Arlena died of a heart defect in 1988, the Twiggs sought custody of Mays, and, failing that, attempted to win VISITATION RIGHTS. Mays requested an end to any contact with the Twiggs, saying visits with them were upsetting.

In August 1993, state circuit judge Stephen Dakan ruled that Mays was not required to meet with her biological parents because forced visitation was detrimental to her. Dakan reasoned that if a 15-year-old minor had the right to an abortion, Mays surely had the right to refuse contact with people who essentially were strangers.

Although Mays was allowed to sever ties with the Twiggs, she later chose to renew them. In a strange twist of events,

Mays moved in with the Twiggs in March 1994 because of personal conflicts with Robert Mays. She soon moved out of the Twiggs' home; by age 17, she was married and, by 19, she was a mother. Later, during a brief estrangement from her husband, she almost lost custody of her son.

Although the Mays-Twigg case suggests a weakening in the rights of biological parents, the DeBoer case indicates the opposite.

DeBoer Case Jessica DeBoer was raised from birth by Jan and Roberta DeBoer, a Michigan couple trying to adopt her. Cara Clausen, DeBoer's unmarried biological mother, terminated her parental rights shortly after DeBoer was born. Dan Schmidt, DeBoer's biological father, did not sign away his parental rights because, initially, Clausen named another man as the child's father. Clausen and Schmidt eventually married and decided to reclaim DeBoer. After much legal maneuvering, the Michigan Supreme Court ordered DeBoer, who was now age two, returned to her biological parents in Iowa, saying they had the greater legal claim to her (*DeBoers v. DeBoers*, 442 Mich. 648, 502 N.W.2d 649 [1993]).

Despite EXPERT TESTIMONY that it was not in DeBoer's best interests to be separated from the only home and parents she knew, the court ordered the girl turned over to the Schmidts. The DeBoers reluctantly complied with the order after exhausting every avenue of appeal.

Child rights advocates point to this case as an example of how children are still considered the property of their natural parents. At the same time, support groups for birth parents applaud the decision. They believe that Jessica DeBoer—who was renamed Anna Schmidt—belongs with Cara and Dan Schmidt because Dan never relinquished his parental rights and because blood ties have a special social and legal significance.

FURTHER READINGS

Alaimo, Kathleen, et al. 2002. *Children as Equals: Exploring the Rights of the Child.* New York: Univ. Press of America.

Archard, David. 2003. *Children, Family, and the State.* Aldershot, UK: Ashgate.

CROSS-REFERENCES

Child Abuse; Child Care; Child Custody.

tution and the constitution of the particular state. The U.S. Supreme Court has held that many provisions of the Constitution protect the parent-child relationship, as well as the rights of both parent and child.

The issue of the right to conceive or the right to give birth to a child is governed by Supreme Court decisions involving the right to privacy. With GRISWOLD V. STATE OF CONNECTICUT, 381 U.S. 479, 85 S. Ct. 1678, 14 L. Ed. 2d 510 (1965), the Court held that married people have the right to be educated about BIRTH CONTROL methods and to have access to contraceptive devices. The right was extended to unmarried people in *Eisenstadt v. Baird*, 405 U.S. 438, 92 S. Ct. 1029, 31 L. Ed. 2d 349 (1972). In ROE V. WADE, 410 U.S. 113, 93 S. Ct. 705, 35 L. Ed. 2d 147

(1973), the Court ruled that a woman has a right to have an ABORTION. Because an established legal principle states that a fetus is not a child, the state cannot interfere arbitrarily with the woman's decision to have an abortion by favoring the welfare of the fetus over her welfare.

Authority of Parents

Parents are entitled to the custody of their children. They are free to make all decisions relating to the welfare of their child as they see fit, short of violating laws that protect children from abuse and neglect. Courts will not interfere with reasonable directives set forth by parents to discipline their children.

Modern statutes and courts have reconsidered the father's traditional primary role and now give equal powers, rights, and duties to both parents. In the case of DIVORCE or separation, all rights of decision and control over the child go to the parent awarded custody, except when joint custody is awarded. In the case of the death of one parent, the other parent assumes custody.

The parent has the obligation to furnish a home for the child. A parent has the right to use CORPORAL PUNISHMENT, but it must not be so excessive as to constitute child abuse.

A parent's power over his child includes the authority and obligation to oversee medical treatment. A parent will most likely be held guilty of criminal neglect if he disregards the health requirements of his child. In cases where essential medical treatment is not procured for a child, juvenile authorities will start proceedings to provide care for the child and disciplinary action for the parent.

A controversial issue arises when a child is ill and the parents refuse health treatment for religious reasons. In an emergency that would jeopardize the child's life, a court may override the parental consent requirement and authorize treatment. A much greater obstacle exists when the parents, on religious grounds, refuse to provide their child with medical care that is important but not life threatening.

Parents are allowed broad discretion in making decisions regarding their child's education. This freedom, however, is not absolute and is tempered by compulsory state school attendance laws and the right of the state to require that the child be educated. However, most states now allow home schooling, with education provided by a parent.

A parent who fails to carry out obligations or abuses parental rights is guilty of a crime. A parent who fails to make certain that her child regularly goes to school can be held criminally liable for violating compulsory attendance laws. A number of states have criminal nonsupport and ABANDONMENT statutes that make it unlawful for a parent to neglect to provide for her child. Where essential support has been provided by an outside source, such as an agency or an individual, this source can initiate a lawsuit to recoup the expenses of services and supplies. A person who has custody or guardianship of a child can initiate a lawsuit to request that the noncustodial parent pay a suitable amount of money on a regular basis to support the child.

Custody

Parents usually have a legal right to custody of their own offspring. The Supreme Court has established that the right to CHILD CUSTODY by a parent is constitutionally protected. The general presumption of the courts is that a child's welfare is protected best when the natural ties of mother and father are preserved. In the absence of clear evidence that a child is in danger, the state must not interfere with the judgment of the parents.

When the two parents do not live together, the question arises as to where the child will reside. In some cases, one parent will agree to relinquish custody to the other parent without giving up any other parental privileges. Although the custodial parent supervises the child's daily care, the noncustodial parent ordinarily has the right to be told about significant occurrences in the child's life. In addition, the noncustodial parent is usually entitled to visit the child at regular intervals. The noncustodial parent may seek a change in custody arrangements if circumstances so mandate.

If separated or divorced parents cannot agree on custody arrangements, the court will intervene. The court considers the circumstances of each case in light of a parent's ability to support and care for the child. In all custodial decisions, the best interests of the child are of paramount importance.

A battle for custody of a child does not always involve the parents. Custody is frequently sought by other relatives, including grandparents, uncles, aunts, or others, such as stepparents or foster parents.

In the event that a child is illegitimate, the unwed mother has a primary custody right that traditionally could not be defeated by the father. However, the Supreme Court has recognized the unwed father's interest in his child and the potential ability to obtain custody or VISITATION RIGHTS (*Lehr v. Robertson*, 463 U.S. 248, 103 S. Ct. 2985, 77 L. Ed. 614 [1983]).

In many families, grandparents play an important role in the upbringing of children. When the parents of a child separate and divorce, many of these grandparents continue to play an active role in the children's lives. Every state has enacted legislation that allows a court to grant visitation rights to grandparents if the grandparents meet certain criteria. Such criteria often require that the visitation is in the best interests of the child, that one of the parents is deceased, and that the grandparent has cared for the child for a significant period of time prior to filing the petition.

In *Troxel v. Granville*, 530 U.S. 57, 120 S. Ct. 2054, 147 L. Ed. 2d 49 (2000), the U.S. Supreme Court held that a grandparent visitation statute in the state of Washington, which allowed a court to grant visitation rights to any person at any time if it was in the best interests of the child, was unconstitutional. Noting that this broad statute placed a substantial burden on the traditional parent-child relationship, Justice SANDRA DAY O'CONNOR held that the statute denied parents SUBSTANTIVE DUE PROCESS. However, the Court did not hold that all grandparent visitation statutes are unconstitutional, leaving this determination to the state courts. State legislatures have since struggled to draft grandparent visitation and custody statutes that remain constitutional under this decision.

Support

Generally a parent is responsible for support of a minor child. This responsibility encompasses the essentials of food, clothing, and shelter, as well as education and medical care. A parent who is unable to provide such support is excused. However, that parent must demonstrate an earnest effort to become employed so that he can fulfill his financial responsibility.

At COMMON LAW, the child's father had the primary duty to support the child. The law now recognizes that both parents have an equal responsibility for the support of a child.

Parents are not entitled to use money that belongs to the child (for example, an inheritance) for the child's support. Although a parent is allowed to petition the court to release a certain amount of money for the child's expenses, courts are generally unwilling to honor such requests unless warranted by the circumstances. It is, for example, proper to release funds to support a child whose only other means of support would be through public welfare.

State and federal governments have become more active in requiring parents to support their children. If parents live apart, whether by reason of divorce or separation, or if they have remained unmarried, various remedies are available to enforce court-issued CHILD SUPPORT orders. State statutes generally provide criminal misdemeanor penalties for a default on support obligations, but courts typically use the CONTEMPT power as an enforcement vehicle. Civil contempt

is imposed to encourage payment by jailing for an indeterminate time a parent who is able to pay. The parent is free to leave jail as soon as the parent makes the payment. Criminal contempt is imposed as punishment for default, the sentence being for a specific period.

States have also set up child support collection systems that use stronger enforcement methods to ensure compliance. If a parent fails to pay court-ordered child support, his tax refunds and wages can be garnished, and his driver's license can be revoked.

The federal government has sought to ensure that child support is paid. The Child Support Recovery Act of 1992 (18 U.S.C.A. § 338) makes willful failure to support a child in another state a federal crime. Prosecution is available for unpaid support exceeding $5,000 or for obligations unpaid longer than one year. Penalties range from imprisonment to fines. First offenses are misdemeanors; repeat offenses are felonies. In addition, federal courts may make the payment of child support a condition of PROBATION.

State governments have also sought to ensure that parents who are recipients of child support payments receive these payments. The Texas attorney general, for example, oversees a child support division, which is responsible for ensuring that child support payments are received and distributed properly. The division determines what is required on a case-by-case basis, but generally noncustodial parents must submit child support payments directly to the division, which then distributes this money to the custodial parent. If the noncustodial parent fails to make the child support payments, the division may locate the parent and take a number of remedial actions, including suspension of state licenses. Other states employ similar systems.

The general rule is that no one is obligated to support a child to whom the person is not related. A number of states, however, currently require a stepfather to support his wife's children if he lives with them. A child whose natural father does not contribute to her support might be allowed to receive welfare benefits unless she is adopted by the stepfather.

A parent's support obligation does not end merely because the parent is not living with the child. Upon divorce or legal separation, child support agreements arrange for the child's continued support. An identified father must aid in the support of his illegitimate child, even if they have never lived together.

The duty of a parent to support a minor child sometimes continues even when the child becomes a parent, such as the case of a 16-year-old girl who has an illegitimate child but continues to live with her parents. The unwed father, however, would have primary responsibility for support of his child provided he acknowledged the child as his or the court orders him to provide support following an action to establish his PATERNITY.

The common-law rule is that a parent has no obligation to support an adult child. Similarly, an adult child has no duty to support parents or grandparents. Some states, however, have altered this rule by enacting statutes that impose financial responsibilities upon people for their poverty-stricken relatives. Certain laws require parents to provide support for a child who is incapable of earning a living because of a mental or physical disability regardless of whether the child has reached the age of majority. Similarly, other statutes require children to support parents who would otherwise be dependent on public welfare.

Child's Earnings and Services

At common law, a father had the right to the earnings of a child. State statutes have modified this principle to give either a primary right to a child's earnings to the custodial parent or an equal right to both parents. The right to a child's wages stems from the parental duty of support and, therefore, can be destroyed if a parent neglects or deserts the child. States, however, also have enacted laws that place a child's earnings in trust until the child reaches the age of majority. These laws were originally passed in the 1930s to protect child actors and entertainers who earned large sums of money. Before these laws were passed, some of the parents of these children had squandered their children's incomes.

The issue of the services of a child, which range from performing simple household tasks to working in the family business, ordinarily arises when a child has been injured. A parent may sue the individual who caused the child harm and claim damages for both medical costs and loss of the child's services.

Wrongful Death and Wrongful Life Actions

A child is entitled to start a WRONGFUL DEATH action against anyone who causes the death of his parent. Parents may also sue for the wrongful death of children, although at times their economic value to the family is arguable. Parents may recover, however, for the loss of companionship or for their mental pain and suffering upon the loss of the child.

Some state laws prevent parents from recovering for the death of an adult child who is either financially independent or married. Ordinarily the parent who brings suit for wrongful death must be a legal parent, whether natural or adoptive. A parent who has neglected or failed to support a child generally cannot sue for wrongful death.

WRONGFUL LIFE cases arise when parents object to the birth of an unwanted or unplanned child. Cases have involved faulty sterilization, failure to diagnose a pregnancy, or, in the case of a pharmacist, dispensing the wrong birth control pills. In a majority of states, the courts refuse to entertain such suits, partly on grounds of public policy and partly on the theory that the benefit of having and keeping the child outweighs any damage. Other courts have allowed recovery, some holding that the probable enjoyment the child will bring must be offset by the cost of having and raising the child. Compensation for the cost of pregnancy and the pain and suffering of pregnancy and childbirth has been upheld.

Emancipation

Emancipation is a legal occurrence by which a child acquires the freedom attached to adulthood earlier than at the statutory age. There are no set procedures by which emancipation may be accomplished. Generally, enlistment in the armed forces, marriage, or becoming self-supporting will effect emancipation. Typically, the inquiry takes place after the fact, and if the child is found to be independent of the parents, emancipation has probably occurred, and the court will be more likely to recognize this emancipation.

An agreement may be made between the parents and the child whereby the child leaves the parents' home and establishes an independent life. Once this happens, the parents relinquish the right to custody and supervision of the child. Another important meaning of emancipation is that it ends the parental obligation of support.

Another important legal consideration relates to the effect of commercial dealings of persons who, but for emancipation, would have been minors. Once a nearly absolute defense, modern law has significantly restricted the effect of minority as a legal defense to contractual obligations to third parties. Thus, an emancipated 16-year-old girl who signs a contract to buy a car cannot avoid the terms of the contract by later PLEADING that she was underage and could not legally bind herself.

The issue of emancipation has declined in importance because most states have made 18 years the age of majority. The most serious questions concerning emancipation involved the age spread from 18 to 21 years.

Responsibility of Parents for Injuries

At common law, parents were not responsible for TORTS their children committed against third parties. When they had neglected their duty of supervision, parents could be held liable for their own NEGLIGENCE. This largely remains true, although many state statutes now hold parents vicariously liable for torts committed by their children, for a limited amount.

Another exception to parental IMMUNITY from liability for their child's torts is the "family purpose doctrine," which allows third parties to recover from parents when they were injured by children driving the family car. This doctrine is based on the idea that the child is acting as the parent's agent or authorized representative.

To promote family unity, a number of states have refused to permit lawsuits between parents and children for harm caused by negligence. Some states have rejected this doctrine, however, particularly in the event of automobile accidents. In such cases, it was perceived as unjust to allow strangers to obtain insurance benefits when family members were precluded from doing so. A majority of states, however, still regard a parent as immune from legal actions for exercising parental authority and also for injuries stemming from negligent supervision.

In Loco Parentis

Persons may act IN LOCO PARENTIS, "in place of the natural parents," in relation to the child in certain situations. Ordinarily, no one is responsible for a child's control or support unless that person is the parent, whether natural or adoptive, or has otherwise agreed to take care of the child. The question of whether a person acting in place of the parent has these responsibilities is contingent upon whether the person intended to undertake them. A college, for example, may act in loco parentis when it houses its students in college-supervised dormitories and imposes rules and regulations on student behavior.

FURTHER READINGS

Pardeck, John T. 2002. *Children's Rights: Policy and Practice.* New York: Haworth Social Work Practice Press.

Postman, Neil. 1982. *The Disappearance of Childhood.* New York: Delacorte.

Purdy, Laura M. 1992. *In Their Best Interest?* Ithaca, N.Y.: Cornell Univ. Press.

Richards, Janet Leach. 1999. "Children's Rights v. Parents' Rights: A Proposed Solution to the Custodial Relocation Conundrum." *New Mexico Law Review* 29 (spring).

Walker, Nancy E., Catherine M. Brooks, and Lawrence S. Wrightsman. 1999. *Children's Rights in the United States: In Search of a National Policy.* Thousand Oaks, Calif.: Sage Publications.

CROSS-REFERENCES

Adoption; Child Care; Child Labor Laws; Children's Defense Fund; Children's Rights; Descent and Distribution; Family Car Doctrine; Family Law; Fetal Rights; Fetal Tissue Research; Garnishment; *Gault, In re*; Guardian ad Litem; Guardian and Ward; Health Care Law; Illegitimacy; Infancy; Infants; Juvenile Law; Organ Donation Law "Should Dying Babies Be Organ Donors?" (In Focus); Paternity; Schools and School Districts.

PARENT COMPANY

An enterprise, which is also known as a parent corporation, that owns more than 50 percent of the voting shares of its subsidiary.

PARI CAUSA

[Latin, With equal right.] *Upon an equal footing; having the same rights or claims.*

PARI DELICTO

[Latin, In equal fault.] *The doctrine, also known as* in pari delicto, *that provides that courts will not enforce an invalid contract and that no party can recover in an action where it is necessary to prove the existence of an illegal contract in order to make his or her case.*

PARI MATERIA

[Latin, Of the same matter; on the same subject.] *The phrase used in connection with two laws relating to the same subject matter that must be analyzed with each other.*

For example, the federal gift tax provisions supplement the federal estate tax provisions.

The two are *in pari materia* and must be read together because the gift tax provisions were enacted to prevent the avoidance of estate taxes.

CROSS-REFERENCES

Estate and Gift Taxes.

PARI PASSU

[Latin, By an equal progress; equably; ratably; without preference.] *Used especially to describe creditors who, in marshalling assets, are entitled to receive out of the same fund without any precedence over each other.*

PARITY

Equality in amount or value. Equivalence of prices of farm products to the prices existing at some former date (the base period) or to the general cost of living; equivalence of prices of goods or services in two different markets. The relationship between two currencies such that they are exchangeable for each other at the par or official rate of exchange.

❖ PARKS, ROSA LOUISE MCCAULEY

Rosa Louise McCauley Parks sparked a year-long boycott of buses in Montgomery, Alabama, by the city's black community, when she refused to give up her seat to a white passenger on a segregated bus. Her arrest and trial on charges of violating SEGREGATION laws led to the U.S. Supreme Court's decision that segregation on the city's buses was unconstitutional, the rise of the MARTIN LUTHER KING JR. as a civil rights leader, and the emergence of the CIVIL RIGHTS MOVEMENT as a national cause.

Parks was born February 4, 1913, in Tuskegee, Alabama. She attended a one-room school in Pine Level, Alabama. There, one teacher taught 50 to 60 students, who were separated into rows by age. The students were responsible for cutting wood to heat the school, and occasionally a parent would deliver a load of wood to the school by wagon. Whereas the black community had to heat and even build its own schools, a new brick school for white children was constructed near Parks's home, paid for with public funds, including taxes paid by both blacks and whites, and heated at public expense. Black children's families helped them to plow and plant in the spring, and to harvest in the fall, so the children attended school only five months during the year; white children attended school for nine months.

Because Pine Level offered no schooling to black children beyond the sixth grade, Parks's mother sent her to Montgomery to live with relatives and to continue her education. But she was forced to drop out of high school during her junior year to care for her dying grandmother and, later, her ailing mother. She finally earned her high-school diploma in 1933 at the age of 20, a year after she had married Raymond Parks.

Her husband was the first activist whom Parks had met. He was a long-time member of the National Association for the Advancement of Colored People (NAACP). When he met Parks, he was working to raise money for the legal

"PEOPLE ALWAYS SAY THAT I DIDN'T GIVE UP MY SEAT BECAUSE I WAS TIRED, BUT THAT ISN'T TRUE. I WAS NOT TIRED PHYSICALLY. . .THE ONLY TIRED I WAS, WAS TIRED OF GIVING UP."
—ROSA PARKS

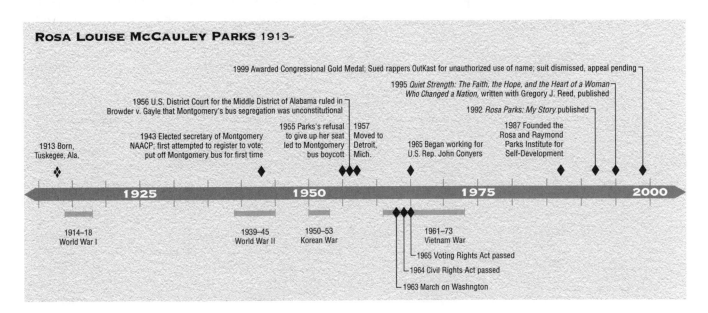

ROSA LOUISE MCCAULEY PARKS 1913–

1999 Awarded Congressional Gold Medal; Sued rappers OutKast for unauthorized use of name; suit dismissed, appeal pending

1995 *Quiet Strength: The Faith, the Hope, and the Heart of a Woman Who Changed a Nation,* written with Gregory J. Reed, published

1956 U.S. District Court for the Middle District of Alabama ruled in Browder v. Gayle that Montgomery's bus segregation was unconstitutional

1992 *Rosa Parks: My Story* published

1987 Founded the Rosa and Raymond Parks Institute for Self-Development

1955 Parks's refusal to give up her seat led to Montgomery bus boycott

1957 Moved to Detroit, Mich.

1943 Elected secretary of Montgomery NAACP; first attempted to register to vote; put off Montgomery bus for first time

1965 Began working for U.S. Rep. John Conyers

1913 Born, Tuskegee, Ala.

1925　　　　　1950　　　　　1975　　　　　2000

1914–18 World War I

1939–45 World War II

1950–53 Korean War

1961–73 Vietnam War

1965 Voting Rights Act passed

1964 Civil Rights Act passed

1963 March on Washngton

Rosa Parks. AP/WIDE
WORLD PHOTOS

defense of nine young black men, known as the Scottsboro Boys, who had been arrested for raping a white woman. Although the charges were unsubstantiated, all of the men were found guilty and all but one were scheduled to die in the electric chair in 1931. The NAACP and other national organizations were able to file an appeal on the men's behalf with the U.S. Supreme Court, which ordered a new trial. All of the defendants were eventually exonerated.

After the Scottsboro defendants were saved from execution, Parks and her husband became involved in voter registration. Parks first attempted to register to vote in 1943. Like most other black citizens, she was forced to take a literacy test. Although she believed that she had passed the test, she was denied twice. Then, before she could complete her registration, she had to pay an accumulated poll tax of $1.50 a year. Blacks and whites were subject to the poll tax. However, whites were allowed to register upon turning 21 and could simply pay the tax once per year from then on. On the other hand, blacks might not be able to register until they were much older, and they were then forced to pay the tax retroactively to the age of 21. Parks's tax totaled $16.50, a considerable amount of money at that time.

While Parks was making her second attempt to register to vote in 1943, she was put off of a

Montgomery city bus for the first time. Blacks had to follow certain rules when riding the bus, including stepping in the front door to pay their fare, then stepping off and going around to the back door to board the bus. They were required to sit at the back of the bus, even when the front section that was reserved for whites was empty. On this occasion, Parks boarded the bus in the front and made her way through the bus to the back. When the driver insisted that she leave the bus and re-enter through the back door, she refused. The driver then grabbed her coat sleeve and told her to get off his bus.

By that time, Parks was a member of the NAACP, one of only two women who were active in the local organization. At the 1943 meeting of the Montgomery branch, she was elected secretary. The Montgomery NAACP had begun to consider filing a lawsuit against the city over bus segregation, but it wanted a plaintiff who had a strong case.

On the evening of December 1, 1955, Parks left work and boarded the bus home. After she had paid her fare, she realized that the bus driver was the same one who had put her off of his bus 12 years earlier and whom she had since gone out of her way to avoid. Parks took a vacant seat in the front of the black section of the bus, near three other black passengers. As the bus began to fill up, a white man was left standing, and the bus driver demanded that Parks and the other blacks relinquish their seats. The other three people moved back, but Parks refused. The bus driver called the police, who arrested Parks and took her to the city jail. She was soon released on bail, and a trial date was set for the following week. Later that evening, Parks agreed to become the plaintiff whom the NAACP had been seeking to test the constitutionality of segregation on the buses.

That evening, leaders of the Montgomery Women's Political Caucus began calling for a bus boycott by the black community for December 5, to coincide with Parks's hearing. The 18 black-owned cab companies in the city agreed to stop at all of the bus stops on Monday and to charge only ten cents, the same as the bus fare.

When Monday came, the Montgomery city buses were nearly empty of black riders, marking the black community's first united protest against segregation. At her court hearing that day, Parks pleaded not guilty. The court ruled that she had violated the state segregation laws, and she was fined and given a suspended sentence and fined.

Earlier that day, several ministers in the city, including the Reverend Ralph D. Abernathy, decided to form a new organization, the Montgomery Improvement Association (MIA), to lead the boycott. The ministers felt that the NAACP did not have a large enough membership in Alabama to assume a leadership role, and they wanted to have a local group at the forefront so that no one could claim that outside agitators were running the demonstration. The group elected King as its president. King was then pastor of the Dexter Avenue Baptist Church. The group thought that he was the best candidate because he was so new to the city and to civil rights work that he had not yet made any strong friends or strong enemies.

The bus boycott lasted more than a year. Many black people lost their jobs because of their support of the boycott. Parks's husband resigned from his job as a barber at the Maxwell Field Air Force Base when the white shop owner ordered that there was to be no discussion of Parks or the protest in his shop. The city police tried to disrupt the protest by harassing groups of blacks who were waiting at city bus stops for the black-owned cabs and by threatening to arrest cabdrivers if they did not charge their regular fare.

Once the police actually began arresting the cabdrivers, the community developed a sophisticated, private transportation system consisting of 20 cars and 14 station wagons. Thirty-two pickup and transfer sites were established, and service was scheduled from 5:30 A.M. to 12:30 A.M. Through this system, several people were transported to and from work every day. Although white supporters of the boycott received threatening letters and telephone calls, many white women who were unwilling to go without household help transported their black housekeepers and cooks every day. Blacks were also subjected to violence. King's home and those of other boycott leaders were bombed. Drivers of the black car-pool were arrested for minor traffic violations, and insurance on the cars in the pool was canceled until King located a black insurance agent in Atlanta who arranged for Lloyd's of London to write a policy for some of the cars.

While the boycott continued, the fight over segregation began in the courts. In February 1956, after the appeal of Parks's conviction was dismissed on a technicality, lawyers filed suit in U.S. district court on behalf of five women, including Parks, who had been mistreated on the buses. The suit claimed that bus segregation was unconstitutional.

At the same time, white lawyers discovered an old state law that prohibited boycotts, and a GRAND JURY issued 89 indictments against King, other ministers and leaders of the MIA, and other citizens, including Parks. King was the first to be tried. He was found guilty and was sentenced to pay a $500 fine or to serve a year of hard labor. His conviction was successfully appealed, however, and no one else was brought to trial in connection with those boycotts.

In June 1956, a three-judge panel of a U.S. district court in Alabama ruled that Montgomery's bus segregation was unconstitutional (*Browder v. Gayle*, 142 F. Supp. 707 [M.D. Ala. 1956]). The city appealed the decision to the U.S. Supreme Court. On November 13, the high court upheld the district court (352 U.S. 903, 77 S. Ct. 145, 1 L. Ed. 2d 114). The boycotters decided to continue their demonstration until the order was official. On December 20, the Court's written decision arrived. On the following day, the black community ended the bus boycott.

In the beginning, INTEGRATION of the buses did not go smoothly. Snipers fired at buses, and the city imposed curfews that prevented buses from operating after 5:00 P.M., which kept people who worked until 5:00 from riding the buses home.

Because of the boycott, Parks and her husband received hate mail and threatening telephone calls. In 1957, they decided to move to Detroit, where Parks's younger brother, Sylvester, lived. Parks was spending a great deal of time traveling around the country speaking about the bus boycott and the civil rights movement. She often attended meetings of a new organization formed by King and other ministers, the SOUTHERN CHRISTIAN LEADERSHIP CONFERENCE. She also attended the 1963 March on Washington that was organized to push for civil rights legislation. By that time, black people all over the South were protesting segregation and were organizing boycotts.

In 1964, President LYNDON B. JOHNSON signed the CIVIL RIGHTS ACT, 42 U.S.C.A. § 1971, 1975a to 1975d, 2000a to 2000h-6, guaranteeing blacks the right to vote and to use public accommodations. But segregation was still pervasive in the South. In March 1965, King called for a mass march in Alabama, from Selma to Montgomery, to protest the treatment of civil rights demonstrators in Selma. Parks was invited to join the march for the final eight miles to the capital in Montgomery.

In 1965, Parks went to work for U.S. Representative John Conyers, whom she had supported in his campaign for the congressional seat from the First District in Michigan. Parks remained as Conyers's receptionist and office assistant until her retirement in 1988.

For a long time, Parks wanted to start an organization to help young people. In 1987, she founded the Rosa and Raymond Parks Institute for Self-Development, to offer classes in communications skills, health, economics, and political awareness.

Time magazine named Parks one of the 100 most influential people of the twentieth century, as a heroine and an icon. In 1996, President BILL CLINTON awarded Parks the Presidential Medal of Freedom, the highest civilian honor in the United States. In 1999, Congress awarded to her the Congressional Gold Medal of Honor, the highest award conferred by the U.S. government. "It is not an exaggeration to say that American history has moved through and with Rosa Parks.... This modest woman transformed an act designed to perpetuate the harsh rule of Jim Crow into the spark that ignited a determined and righteous crusade," said Spencer Abraham (R-Mich.), one of the sponsors of the award.

FURTHER READINGS

Celsi, Teresa. 1991. *Rosa Parks and the Montgomery Bus Boycott*. Brookfield, Conn.: Millbrook Press.

Parks, Rosa, with Jim Haskins. 1992. *Rosa Parks: My Story* New York: Dial.

Robinson, Jo Ann Gibson. 1987. *The Montgomery Bus Boycott and the Women Who Started It*. Knoxville, Tenn.: Univ. of Tennessee Press.

"Time 100: Heroes and Icons—Rosa Parks." 1999. Available online at <www.time.com/time/time100/heroes/profile/parks01.html> (accessed January 26, 2004).

CROSS-REFERENCES

Pacifism; *Powell v. Alabama*; Voting.

PARLIAMENTARY LAW

The general body of enacted rules and recognized usages governing the procedure of legislative assemblies and other deliberative sessions such as meetings of stockholders and directors of corporations, town meetings, and board meetings. Roberts Rules of Order are an example of such rules.

PARODY

A form of speech protected by the FIRST AMENDMENT *as a "distorted imitation" of an original work for the purpose of commenting on it.*

The use of parody as a means to express political and social views has a long history in the United States. Every president of the United States, including GEORGE WASHINGTON, has been the subject of satire and parody, often in the form of political cartoons. The cartoons, caricatures, and other forms of parody and satire typically distort and overly emphasize certain aspects of the subject's physical characteristics, such as ABRAHAM LINCOLN's lanky posture, FRANKLIN D. ROOSEVELT's jutting jaw and cigarette holder, RONALD REAGAN's long face and slick, black hair, and BILL CLINTON's large nose and red cheeks. Although often comical, political cartoons and other forms of satire and parody have often immortalized the individuals portrayed.

Parody and satire can be used for purposes beyond lighthearted comic intent. Many political cartoons, for example, have influenced the course of national debate. For instance, Thomas Nast, the famous nineteenth-century political cartoonist, published a series of post–Civil War cartoons in *Harper's Weekly* characterizing the activities of William M. "Boss" Tweed and other corrupt politicians in New York City's TAMMANY HALL political machine. More recently, countless political cartoonists drew caricatures of Clinton with Monica Lewinsky, the White House intern with whom Clinton had an affair. Clinton's dishonesty regarding the affair eventually led to his IMPEACHMENT by the House of Representatives in 1998.

Some forms of parody and satire are difficult to distinguish from truthful publications. Moreover, many forms of parody and satire can be particularly offensive to the subject of the parody. As a result, publication of various types of parody often involves litigation over libel, slander, and other types of DEFAMATION.

In 1988, the U.S. Supreme Court reviewed the most famous case involving the use of parody in *Hustler Magazine, Inc. v. Falwell*, 485 U.S. 46, 108 S. Ct. 816, 99 L. Ed. 2d 41 (1988). In 1983, the adult magazine *Hustler* published a parody of an advertisement for Campari Liqueur, which featured Jerry Falwell, a nationally recognized evangelist who is well known for his conservative commentary on political and social issues. The original advertisements contained interviews with celebrities discussing the "first time" they had consumed Campari. *Hustler*'s parody used a layout similar to the original advertisement, but included a fictitious interview with Falwell where he stated that his "first time" occurred with his mother in an outhouse.

Falwell brought suit, alleging libel and intentional infliction of emotional distress. The trial court found in favor of *Hustler* and its publisher, Larry Flynt, on the libel claim because the court found that no reasonable person would have believed the advertisement to be true. However, the court found *Hustler* and Flynt liable for intentional infliction for emotional distress. The Fourth Circuit Court of Appeals affirmed the district court's ruling.

The Supreme Court, per Justice WILLIAM REHNQUIST, reversed the Fourth Circuit. The Court has held in a line of cases regarding defamation that the First Amendment requires a plaintiff who is a public official or a public figure to demonstrate "actual malice," meaning it must be proven that the person being accused showed a reckless disregard as to whether a statement was true or false. These cases generally apply to claims of LIBEL AND SLANDER brought by public officials or public figures.

After reviewing a brief history of the use of parody in the United States, the Court found that the actual malice standard applies to cases involving intentional infliction of emotional distress as well. Since Falwell was unquestionably a public figure under the Court's analysis, he had to prove actual malice on the part of *Hustler*. The Court also rejected a claim by Falwell that this particular form of parody was so outrageous that it should not be the subject of First Amendment protection. This case establishes that the First Amendment protects forms of parody and satire involving public figures or public officials against a variety of claims, including libel, slander, and intentional infliction of emotional distress.

Parody also involves the application of other laws. Because many parodies mimic or copy other publications, the parodies may implicate COPYRIGHT and other INTELLECTUAL PROPERTY laws. In *Campbell v. Acuff-Rose Music, Inc.*, 510 U.S. 569, 114 S. Ct. 1164, 127 L. Ed. 2d 500 (1994), the Court reviewed whether a parody of Roy Orbison's song, "Oh, Pretty Woman," by the rap group 2 Live Crew violated the Copyright Act of 1976. The court of appeals held that the parody did not constitute fair use under copyright law, primarily due to its commercial character. The Supreme Court disagreed, holding that the commercial character of the song did not create a presumption that the parody violated fair use.

FURTHER READINGS

Beck, Joseph M. 2003. "Copyright and the First Amendment after *The Wind Done Gone*." *Vanderbilt Journal of Entertainment Law and Practice* 5 (spring).

Post, Robert C. 1990. "The Constitutional Concept of Public Discourse: Outrageous Opinion, Democratic Deliberation, and *Hustler Magazine v. Falwell*." *Harvard Law Review* 103 (January).

PAROL EVIDENCE

Parol refers to verbal expressions or words. Verbal evidence, such as the testimony of a witness at trial.

In the context of contracts, deeds, wills, or other writings, parol evidence refers to extraneous evidence such as an oral agreement (a parol contract), or even a written agreement, that is not included in the relevant written document. The parol evidence rule is a principle that preserves the integrity of written documents or agreements by prohibiting the parties from attempting to alter the meaning of the written document through the use of prior and contemporaneous oral or written declarations that are not referenced in the document.

Terms of a contract are commonly proposed, discussed, and negotiated before they are included in the final contract. When the parties to the negotiations do put their agreement in writing and acknowledge that the statement is the complete and exclusive declaration of their agreement, they have integrated the contract. The parol evidence rule applies to integrated contracts and provides that when parties put their agreement in writing, all prior and contemporaneous oral or written agreements merge in the writing. Courts do not permit integrated contracts to be modified, altered, amended, or changed in any way by prior or contemporaneous agreements that contradict the terms of the written agreement.

The parol evidence rule applies to written contracts to safeguard the terms of the contract. The courts assume by the parol evidence rule that contracts contain the terms and provisions that the parties specifically intended and lack those provisions that the parties did not want.

The parol evidence rule does not apply to written integrated contracts in some instances. For example, clerical or typographical errors found in the written agreement may be changed because the incorrect term does not represent the true agreement between the parties. Courts will also not apply the parol evidence rule to prohibit contradictory evidence that shows that the contract was entered into under duress, mistake, FRAUD, or UNDUE INFLUENCE. Finally, the parol evidence rule will not prevent evidence that shows the existence of a separate agreement between the parties.

The law of sales also involves numerous written and oral contracts to which the parol evidence rule may be applied. However, in sales the court may look to contemporaneous or prior agreements not to contradict a written agreement but to explain or supplement it. The court may examine such evidence based on the parties' course of dealing, usage of trade, course of conduct, or evidence of consistent additional terms. Parties' course of dealing refers to a situation where two parties have a history of working together and entering into numerous contracts with each other, and the court can look to that history to clarify or interpret their written expressions. Usage of trade refers to circumstances in which the parties are participants in a particular trade or industry that has established ways of doing business. The courts can examine those established and accepted methods within the industry to help explain a written agreement. Parties' course of conduct refers to the actions of the parties in carrying out the particular contract, such as if a party accepts without objection the continued performance of the other party. It is also permissible for a court to consider supplemental consistent evidence that would generally not be included in the written agreement as long as it does not contradict the terms of the original agreement.

FURTHER READINGS

Mann, Richard A., and Barry S. Roberts. 2004. *Essentials of Business Law and the Legal Environment.* 8th ed. Columbus, Oh.: Thomson/South-Western West.

CROSS-REFERENCES

Integrated Agreement; Oral Contract; Sales Law.

PAROLE

The conditional release of a person convicted of a crime prior to the expiration of that person's term of imprisonment, subject to both the supervision of the correctional authorities during the remainder of the term and a resumption of the imprisonment upon violation of the conditions imposed.

Parole is the early supervised release of a prison inmate. It is usually regulated by statutes, and these provisions vary from state to state. Parole boards created by statute possess the authority to release prisoners from incarceration. Parolees have no constitutional right to representation in parole hearings and parole revocation hearings, but many states provide representation to impoverished inmates and parolees in such hearings.

Parole was first used in the United States in New York in 1876. By the turn of the century, parole was prevalent in the states. In 1910 Congress established the U.S. Parole Commission and gave it the responsibility of evaluating and setting the release dates for federal prisoners.

Parole is used for several reasons. It is less expensive to supervise a parolee than to incarcerate a prisoner. A person on parole has an opportunity to contribute to society. At the same time, society still receives some protection because the parolee is supervised and can be revoked for the most minor of transgressions. Parole is also a method of rehabilitation, because it gives convicts supervision and guidance during their reentry into society.

Although parole laws vary from state to state, there are some common practices. In many states, the governor is charged with appointing a parole board. The duties of the board are to study the case histories of persons eligible for parole, deliberate on the record, conduct hearings, grant parole, craft the conditions for parole, issue warrants for persons charged with violation of parole, conduct revocation hearings, and grant final discharge to parolees.

States may charge parolees a small monthly fee to offset the costs of supervision. For example, in Kentucky, a person on parole for a felony must pay $10 per month while under active supervision, but no more than a total of $2,500; for a misdemeanor parole, the fee is not less than $10 per month and no more than $500 in all. Failure to pay these fees, without a good reason for the failure, may result in revocation of the parole, but revocation may not be based on failure to pay a fee unless the board first has held a hearing on the matter.

For lesser offenses, the determination of eligibility for parole is often left to the parole board. Parole will be ordered only if it serves the best interests of society. Parole is not considered to be a method of reducing sentences or awarding a pardon.

For more serious offenses, most states limit the discretion of the parole board. Parole statutes in these states generally identify a specified period of imprisonment that must be served before a prisoner is eligible for parole. The time periods are often a percentage of the prison sentence, and they can vary according to the crime for which the prospective parolee was convicted. In Arkansas, for example, persons convicted of first-degree murder, KIDNAPPING, aggravated ROBBERY, rape, and causing a catastrophe are not eligible for parole until they have served 70 percent of their prison sentence (Ark. Code Ann. § 16-93-611). For lesser felonies, persons must serve at least one-third of their sentence before becoming eligible for parole (Ark. Code Ann. § 16-93-608).

Parole has come under increasing attack since the 1970s. A powerful "truth in sentencing" movement has been successful in many states. Truth in sentencing is a catchphrase used to describe the notion that convicted criminals should serve the entire prison sentence handed down by the court. Many states have abolished parole entirely. In Virginia, for example, a felon who was committed after January 1, 1995, is ineligible for parole (Va. Code Ann. § 53.1-165.1). A felon may have prison time reduced from his sentence for good behavior, but in any case, the felon must serve at least 85 percent of the prison sentence.

At least 27 states and the District of Columbia now require violent offenders to serve 85 percent of their prison sentence before obtaining early release. Some of these states, like Virginia, have abolished parole entirely; others still allow parole for offenders as long as they have served the required time of their sentence. An additional 13 states, like Arkansas, require violent offenders to serve a substantial portion of their minimum sentence before being eligible for release. Fourteen states have abolished parole board release for all offenders, with at least six other states abolishing parole board release for certain violent or felony offenders.

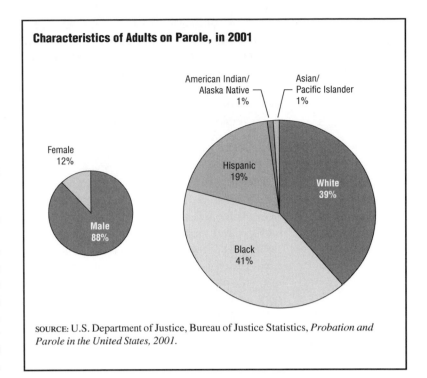

Characteristics of Adults on Parole, in 2001

Female 12%

Male 88%

American Indian/ Alaska Native 1%

Asian/ Pacific Islander 1%

Hispanic 19%

White 39%

Black 41%

SOURCE: U.S. Department of Justice, Bureau of Justice Statistics, *Probation and Parole in the United States, 2001.*

On the federal level, Congress abolished parole in the Comprehensive Crime Control Act of 1984 (Pub. L. No. 98-473 § 218(a)(5), 98 Stat. 1837, 2027 [repealing 18 U.S.C.A. § 4201 et seq.]). Federal prisoners may, however, earn a maximum of 54 days good time credit per year against their sentence (18 U.S.C.A. § 3624(b)).

The issue of victim's rights has also become important when dealing with parole. Most states now have laws requiring the victim or victim's families to be notified of a parole hearing. According to the National Center for the Victims of Crime (NCVC), as of 2000, 46 states and the District of Columbia required the victim or victim's families to be given a notice of a parole application or hearing at their request. Many states have gone further and required that a victim or their family be notified of their right to attend a parole hearing, the right to submit a victim impact statement, and the earliest estimated parole eligibility date.

Most states also allow victims the opportunity to comment on the offender's request for parole. The NCVC overview says that as of 2000, 46 states allow victims to submit impact testimony in person, 42 states permit written victim impact statements to be submitted, six states authorize the submission of audiotaped statements, seven states permit victims to submit videotaped statements, three states allow victims to be heard via teleconferencing, and eight states authorize the victim's counsel or representative to present a statement on the victim's behalf. Under certain circumstances, parolees may also be required to pay restitution as a condition of their parole.

Several important Supreme Court decisions were handed down at the end of the 1990s and beginning of the twenty-first century concerning parole. In 1998, in *Spencer v. Kemna*, 523 U.S. 1, 118 S. Ct. 978, 140 L. Ed. 2d 43 (1998), the Supreme Court ruled against a man who filed a petition for HABEAS CORPUS after his sentence had expired challenging allegedly unconstitutional parole revocation procedures. The Court agreed with the district court that the completion of his sentence made his habeas corpus petition moot. But the Court held that a presumption that criminal convictions have collateral consequences, which the Court had previously said could be considered in habeas challenge to propriety of conviction even after habeas petitioner was released from prison, could not be extended to revocations of parole, in order to satisfy the injury-in-fact requirement of the habeas corpus petition of the Constitution.

In the 2000 decision, *United States v. Johnson*, 529 U.S. 53, 120 S. Ct. 1114, 146 L. Ed. 2d 236 (2000), the Court ruled unanimously that a period of supervised release cannot commence until the prisoner is actually released from incarceration. The case involved a defendant whose convictions were vacated and his prison sentence reduced to a term less than that already served. The defendant moved for reduction of his supervised release term by the amount of extra time served on the vacated convictions. But the Court ruled that when a statute provides that a supervised release term does not commence until an individual is released from imprisonment, the word "released" means freed from confinement.

In another 2000 ruling, *Garner v. Jones*, 529 U.S. 244, 120 S. Ct. 1362, 146 L .Ed. 2d 236 (2000), the Court determined that retroactive application of Georgia's amended parole rule, changing the frequency of required parole reconsideration hearings for inmates serving life sentences from every three years to every eight years, did not necessarily violate the EX POST FACTO Clause of the Constitution. In its 6–3 decision, the Court emphasized that the States must have "due flexibility" in designing their parole procedures. There was no showing that the change in the law lengthened the inmate's time of actual imprisonment, the Court noted, and board had discretion to act in accordance with its assessment of each inmate's likelihood of release between reconsideration dates.

FURTHER READINGS

Bamonte, Thomas J. 1993. "The Viability of *Morrissey v. Brewer* and the Due Process Rights of Parolees and Other Conditional Releasees." *Southern Illinois University Law Journal* 18.

"Forum: Parole and Sentencing Reform in Virginia." 1995. *Virginia Journal of Social Policy and the Law* 2.

National Center for the Victims of Crime. 2000. "Victim's Rights at Parole: A Statutory Overview Summary." Available online at <www.ncvc.org/policy/issues/parole> (accessed August 5, 2003).

Zechman, Joseph A. 1988. "Constitutional Law—Due Process in Federal Parole Rescission Hearings—*Green v. McCall*, 822 F.2d 284 (2d Cir. 1987)." *Temple Law Review* 61.

CROSS-REFERENCES

Probation; Sentencing.

❖ PARSONS, THEOPHILUS

Theophilus Parsons served as chief justice of the Massachusetts Supreme Judicial Court from 1806 to 1813. A man of wide interests and learning, he is recognized for a series of decisions that defined legal principles that have shaped the American business corporation.

Parsons was born February 24, 1750, in Byfield, Massachusetts. He graduated from Harvard University in 1769 and was admitted to the Massachusetts bar in 1774. He established a successful legal practice in the area of Massachusetts that later became Portland, Maine. He gained prominence for his outspoken opinions at the ESSEX JUNTO, a 1778 gathering of merchants and lawyers from New England, the majority of whom resided in Essex County, Massachusetts. This group endorsed a state constitution that gave the state government broad authority.

Parsons strongly supported ratification of the U.S. Constitution. As a delegate to the 1788 Massachusetts Constitutional Convention that ratified the document, Parsons attempted to calm the fears of those delegates who worried about a strong federal government.

From 1787 to 1791, he served in the Massachusetts legislature. He maintained a lucrative COMMERCIAL LAW practice and became recognized as a distinguished lawyer. John Quincy Adams, future president of the United States and a member of the prominent Boston Adams family, read the law under Parson's tutelage during this period.

In 1805 Parsons again entered the state legislature, but his tenure was brief. In 1806 he was appointed chief justice of the Massachusetts Supreme Judicial Court, the state's highest court. His commercial law background proved valuable on the court because he decided cases involving shipping and insurance. More importantly, Parsons had the experience and confidence to decide cases involving business corporations at a time when very little COMMON LAW was available to guide him.

Much of what became common law in U.S. corporate law was first developed while Parsons served as chief justice. In 1799 Massachusetts became the first state to enact a set of laws governing business corporations. During this period corporations had to obtain their charters from the legislature. The legislature was liberally granting these charters, and soon the courts were filled with legal issues concerning this new type of private business entity.

The Massachusetts Supreme Judicial Court, under the influence of Parsons, assumed an activist role in defining the rights and responsibilities of corporations. In a series of decisions between 1806 and 1810, the court announced several basic principles. It recognized that a corporation was a private arrangement, closer to a contract than to a municipal government corporation. The court held that a corporation has a duty to be fair to its shareholders and that the shareholders have limited liability for the debts and obligations of the corporation. The court

Theophilus Parsons.
SOCIAL LAW LIBRARY, BOSTON, MASSACHUSETTS. SOURCE UNKNOWN

also ruled that a corporation could be sued in TORT. All of these decisions became part of U.S. corporate law in the nineteenth century.

Parsons was a Renaissance man. He studied mathematics and theoretical astronomy and was the author of many scientific studies. He died October 13, 1813, in Boston, Massachusetts.

FURTHER READINGS

Osgood, Russell K., ed. 1992. *The History of the Law in Massachusetts: The Supreme Judicial Court 1692–1992.* Boston: Supreme Judicial Court Historical Society.

CROSS-REFERENCES

Massachusetts Constitution of 1780.

PARTICULAR AVERAGE LOSS

In maritime law, damage sustained by a ship, cargo, or freight that is not recompensed by contri-

"THE LOVE OF PRECEDENT AND STABILITY . . . GIVES TO JUDICIAL DECISIONS AN AUTHORITY ALMOST LIKE THAT OF LAW ITSELF."
—THEOPHILUS PARSONS

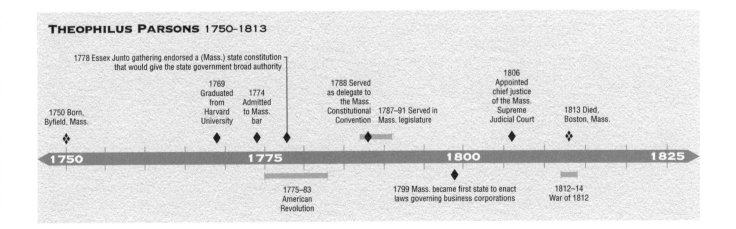

THEOPHILUS PARSONS 1750–1813

1778 Essex Junto gathering endorsed a (Mass.) state constitution that would give the state government broad authority

1769 Graduated from Harvard University

1774 Admitted to Mass. bar

1788 Served as delegate to the Mass. Constitutional Convention

1787–91 Served in Mass. legislature

1806 Appointed chief justice of the Mass. Supreme Judicial Court

1750 Born, Byfield, Mass.

1813 Died, Boston, Mass.

1750 1775 1800 1825

1775–83 American Revolution

1799 Mass. became first state to enact laws governing business corporations

1812–14 War of 1812

bution from all interests in the venture but must be borne by the owner of the damaged property.

Particular average loss is the opposite of general average loss, which denotes contribution by the various interests engaged in a maritime undertaking to recoup the loss of one of them for the voluntary sacrifice of a portion of the ship or cargo in order to save the remaining property and the lives of those on board, or for extraordinary expenses necessarily incurred for the common benefit and safety of all.

CROSS-REFERENCES

Admiralty and Maritime Law.

PARTICULARS

The details of a claim, or the separate items of an account.

When these are detailed in an orderly form for the purpose of informing a defendant, the statement is called a bill of particulars.

PARTIES

The persons who are directly involved or interested in any act, affair, contract, transaction, or legal proceeding; opposing litigants.

Persons who enter into a contract or other transactions are considered parties to the agreement. When a dispute results in litigation, the litigants are called parties to the lawsuit. U.S. law has developed principles that govern the rights and duties of parties. In addition, principles such as the standing doctrine determine whether a person is a rightful party to a lawsuit. Also, additional parties may be added to legal proceedings once litigation has begun.

Parties in Lawsuits

In court proceedings, the parties have common designations. In a civil lawsuit, the person who files the lawsuit is called the plaintiff, and the person being sued is called the defendant. In criminal proceedings, one party is the government, called the state, commonwealth, or the people of the United States, and the other party is the defendant. If a case is appealed, the person who files the appeal is called the appellant, and the other side is called either the respondent or the appellee. Numerous variations on these basic designations exist, depending on the court and its jurisdiction. Assigning party designations allows the legal system and its observers to quickly determine the basic status of each party to a lawsuit.

Parties as Adversaries

The U.S. legal system is based on the adversarial process, which requires parties to a legal proceeding to contend against each other. From this contest of competing interests, the issues are presented to the court and fully argued. In the end, one of the parties will obtain a favorable result.

For the adversary process to fulfill its mission of producing justice, it is vital that the issues at stake be argued by persons who have a genuine interest in them. Under the old rules of COMMON-LAW PLEADING, which used to regulate who could bring a lawsuit, only a person who actually held title to disputed property could be a party in a lawsuit concerning the property. This technicality sometimes prevented a person who had the most to gain or lose on the issue from becoming a party and presenting his or her case. This rule has now been replaced by laws requiring every action to be prosecuted by the real party in interest. This is most important when one person is managing an asset for the benefit of another. For example, administrators of a deceased person's estate can sue to protect the estate's interests without having to join the beneficiaries of the estate as parties. This modern rule sharpens the issues so that the decision in a case puts a controversy to rest for all the parties involved.

The U.S. Supreme Court has developed the standing doctrine to determine whether the litigants in a federal civil proceeding are the appropriate parties to raise the legal questions in the case. The Court has developed an elaborate body of principles defining the nature and contours of standing. In general, to have standing a party must have a personal stake in the outcome of the case. A plaintiff must have suffered some direct and substantial injury or be likely to suffer such an injury if a particular wrong is not redressed. A defendant must be the party responsible for perpetrating the alleged legal wrong.

A person has standing to challenge a law or policy on constitutional grounds if he can show that the enforcement of the law or implementation of the policy infringes on an individual constitutional right. On the other hand, in most cases a taxpayer does not have standing to challenge policies or programs he is forced to financially support.

Legal Entities that Can Be Parties

Only an actual legal entity may initiate a lawsuit. A natural person is a legal entity, for example, and any number of people can be parties on either side of a lawsuit. A corporation is endowed by its charter with existence as a separate legal entity. A business partnership is usually not considered a legal entity, but generally it can sue or be sued in the partnership name or in the names of the individual partners.

Many states permit lawsuits under a common name. This arrangement allows a business to be sued in the commonly used business name if it is clear who the owner or owners are. A lawsuit against Family Dry Cleaners, for example, may entitle the plaintiff to collect a judgment out of the value of the business property. The plaintiff will not be able to touch property that belongs to the owner or owners personally, however, unless they have also been named defendants in the action.

When a group of persons wishes to start a lawsuit, the group has several options. If, for example, a group of residential property owners wants to contest the construction of a toxic waste disposal site in its community, it can file a lawsuit listing each property owner as a plaintiff. The group could also select an association name that the court accepts (Citizens Against Toxic Waste) to represent those individuals. A more expensive alternative would be to incorporate the group and file the suit under the corporation's name.

The CLASS ACTION provides another option for bringing parties into a large-scale civil lawsuit. In a class action lawsuit, thousands and even millions of persons can be parties. To obtain a class action designation, the plaintiffs must convince the court that many persons possess similar interests in the subject matter of the lawsuit and that the plaintiffs can act on the group's behalf without specifically identifying every individual member of the group as a party to the litigation. The class action lawsuit can be an economical method of resolving civil claims that involve large numbers of persons with common interests, especially when the amount of each individual claim is too small to warrant independent legal actions by the claimants.

The Capacity to Sue or Be Sued

A person must have the requisite legal capacity to be a party to a lawsuit. Some people are considered non sui juris: they do not possess full civil and social rights under the law. A child is *non sui juris* because the law seeks to protect the child from his or her improvidence until the child reaches the age of majority. A child who

has not reached the age of majority has a legal disability. Others who suffer a similar legal disability include mentally ill persons, mentally retarded persons, and persons who are judged mentally incompetent because of illness, age, or infirmity. Legal disability does not mean, however, that persons in these categories are removed from civil actions. The claims or defenses of a person who is *non sui juris* usually can be asserted by a legal representative, such as a parent, guardian, trustee, or executor.

Prisoners also have limited rights as parties to civil actions. They can appeal their convictions and bring HABEAS CORPUS petitions to challenge the validity of their incarceration. They can file prisoners' rights cases for a violation of their federally protected CIVIL RIGHTS. Some states permit prisoners to defend themselves in an action that threatens them with FORFEITURE of their property, but most states will not permit prisoners to start a civil lawsuit against any other party during the period of incarceration. Convicted felons or prisoners given life sentences may suffer what is called civil death, a total loss of rights, including the right to be a party in a lawsuit.

Joinder of Additional Parties

Usually a plaintiff decides when, where, and whom she or he wants to sue. In some cases a plaintiff may wish to join, or add, other parties after the start of the lawsuit. Proper parties and necessary or indispensable parties may be added while the action is pending.

A proper party is anyone who may be a party in the lawsuit. The JOINDER, or addition, of a proper party in a pending lawsuit is entirely permissible. The court may allow the joinder of an additional party, but the lawsuit does not have to be dismissed if it does not. In some states anyone who has an interest in the subject of the controversy is a proper party in the lawsuit. Some courts encourage joinder of everyone who could be affected by the decision.

Under modern rules of procedure in many states and the federal courts, joinder is not encouraged to the point where a lawsuit becomes unwieldy or cluttered with unrelated parties and claims. Generally, joinder is approved where the claims of the persons sought to be joined arose out of the same transaction or event as the claims of the existing parties, so that all the claims may be settled by answering the same QUESTIONS OF LAW or fact.

The decision to join additional parties is within the discretion of the court. Courts are careful not to exclude parties with an interest in a lawsuit because a failure to join those parties might lead to a series of lawsuits with inconsistent verdicts. That could ultimately leave a deserving plaintiff without a remedy or force a defendant to pay a certain claim more than once.

Whether a person is potentially necessary or indispensable to an action depends on the character and extent of that person's interest in the subject of the lawsuit. It is fair and equitable to require any person who has an interest that can be affected by the lawsuit to be joined as a party. A person whose interest may be affected by the outcome of the case is considered necessary, and such a person should be joined if possible. A person whose interest is sure to be affected by the outcome of the lawsuit is considered an indispensable party, and the case cannot proceed without this person. The case must be dismissed, for example, if a person cannot be joined because he or she is beyond the jurisdiction of the court. In deciding whether a person should be a party to a lawsuit, the courts carefully weigh the consequences of proceeding without the person and seek a remedy that will give relief to those who are actual parties without doing great harm to a necessary or indispensable party who is missing.

Federal courts abandoned this analysis and terminology relating to necessary and indispensable parties in 1966. The Federal Rules of Civil Procedure focus on factors affecting the overall balance of fairness to the parties and potential parties involved rather than on categories of parties. Once a federal court determines that someone absent from the proceedings has an interest that can be affected by the case, the court must order that person to be joined as a party if it is practical to do so. If not, the court must weigh the competing interests of the plaintiff who would like to keep the case in federal court, the defendant who might be exposed to multiple lawsuits on the same issue, and the absent person whose rights may be lost if he or she does not become a party. The court must also consider how best to avoid wasting judicial time and resources and whether the case before it is the most efficient way to resolve the controversy.

Impleader

A defendant who feels that the plaintiff in a lawsuit should have sued someone else on the claim can bring that other person into the case. The procedure for doing this is called IMPLEADER, and the additional party is called a third-party defendant. The original defendant who impleads a third-party defendant is called a third-party plaintiff, but he or she continues to be a defendant in relation to the plaintiff.

For example, a restaurant patron who becomes ill after eating a ham dinner can sue the restaurant. The patron is the plaintiff, and the restaurant is the defendant. The restaurant may want to implead the meat-packing company that furnished the ham, if it believes that the meat was tainted before it was delivered to the restaurant. The restaurant cannot avoid being a defendant, but it can cover itself by impleading the meat packer and making that company a third-party defendant. If a jury finds that the ham was bad and that the patron is entitled to $10,000 damages, then the restaurant has an opportunity to show that its employees were not careless in preparing or serving the meat and that the restaurant should not be liable for the damages.

The decision to allow impleading of a third party is within the discretion of the court. The court also decides whether the third-party defendant may file claims against any of the other parties or whether the other parties may make additional claims against the third-party defendant. Permitting all parties to put forward all their claims in one action promotes efficient use of the courts, but a court will not permit additional parties or claims to complicate proceedings, delay resolution of the main controversy, or confuse a jury.

Intervention

A person can volunteer to become a party in a lawsuit by a procedure called intervention. A person might wish to intervene in a lawsuit if he or she has an interest that will be affected by the outcome of the case and the person believes that this interest will not be adequately protected by the other parties.

A court decides whether to permit an intervening party by BALANCING the interests of the person seeking to intervene with the additional burden imposed on the existing parties if the person is allowed to enter the lawsuit. The court considers whether the intervenor is raising the same issues already present in the case or whether the intervenor is seeking to inject new controversies into the case. The intervenor must demonstrate some practical effect of the outcome of the case on his or her rights or property. If a person is not allowed to intervene, the person is not bound by the judgment given in the case.

An intervenor must make the request to intervene in a motion to the court. Timing is important. If the case has already progressed beyond the preliminary stages, the court is likely to find that the intervenor's intrusion would prejudice the rights of the existing parties, which would be grounds for the court to deny the motion.

FURTHER READINGS

Cohen, Alan G., et al, eds. 1992. *The Living Law: A Guide to Modern Legal Research.* Rochester, N.Y.: Lawyers Cooperative.

Kraut, Jayson, et al. 1983. *American Jurisprudence.* Rochester, N.Y.: Lawyers Cooperative.

CROSS-REFERENCES

Adversary System.

PARTITION

Any division of real property or PERSONAL PROPERTY *between co-owners, resulting in individual ownership of the interests of each.*

The co-ownership of real and personal property can have many benefits to the parties. But when there is discord and the owners cannot agree on the use, improvement, or disposition of the property, all states have laws that permit the remedy of partition.

Most cases of partition involve real property. Persons can own property as tenants in common or joint tenants. As common owners of the property, they have equal rights in the use and enjoyment of the property. Partition statutes allow those who own property in common to sever their interests and take their individual share of the property.

Partition may be either voluntary or compulsory. Voluntary partition is when the cotenants (owners) divide the property themselves, usually by exchanging individual deeds. Each co-owner owns a part of the property and ceases to have an undivided interest in the whole. The parties can also provide for the sale of the property and divide the proceeds among themselves.

When the co-owners cannot agree on the value of the property and their rightful shares, they may select a disinterested third person, such as an arbitrator or an appraiser, to divide the property and to allot the shares. A voluntary partition by all the co-owners is legally effective unless there is a contractual challenge to its recognition. These challenges include allegations of FRAUD or unconscionability, or the allegation that the parties are seeking to defraud a third party by agreeing to the partition.

When the co-owners cannot agree to a voluntary partition, a lawsuit to compel partition can be filed to sever property interests. Unless there are exceptional circumstances, a tenant in common or a joint tenant has the absolute right to seek a compulsory partition. Partition must be made even if every other owner objects to it. The motives of the party seeking partition are irrelevant, and the court that hears the lawsuit has no discretion to deny partition. Its main function is to determine the method of executing the partition. Commonly the court will order the property sold and the proceeds divided, instead of ordering a physical partition of the property. If the title to the property is put into issue, most states permit the court to resolve this issue as well as the partition.

Both real and personal property can be subject to compulsory partition. Real property that can be subject to partition includes a building, a story of a building, the land on which a building rests, or the surface of land where there is an oil or gas lease.

Similarly, personal property can be subjected to compulsory partition. The fact that the property is owned in unequal shares does not affect the partition. The right has been enforced with respect to a cashier's check payable jointly to those who share a TENANCY IN COMMON, promissory notes, shares of stock in a corporation, and stocks of merchandise.

FURTHER READINGS

Thomas, David A., ed. 1998. *Thompson on Real Property.* Charlottesville, Va.: LEXIS.

CROSS-REFERENCES

Joint Tenancy.

PARTNERSHIP

An association of two or more persons engaged in a business enterprise in which the profits and losses are shared proportionally. The legal definition of a partnership is generally stated as "an association of two or more persons to carry on as co-owners a business for profit" (Revised Uniform Partnership Act § 101 [1994]).

Early English mercantile courts recognized a business form known as the *societas*. The *societas* provided for an accounting between its business partners, an agency relationship between partners in which individual partners could legally bind the partnership, and individual partner liability for the partnership's debts and obligations. As the regular English courts gradually recognized the *societas,* the business form eventually developed into the common-law partnership. England enacted its Partnership Act in 1890, and legal experts in the United States drafted a Uniform Partnership Act (UPA) in 1914. Every state has adopted some form of the UPA as its partnership statute; some states, however, have made revisions to the UPA or have adopted the Revised Uniform Partnership Act (RUPA), which legal scholars issued in 1994.

The authors of the initial UPA debated whether in theory a partnership should be treated as an aggregate of individual partners or as a corporate-like entity separate from its partners. The UPA generally opted for the aggregate theory in which individual partners ("an association") comprised the partnership. Under an aggregate theory, partners are co-owners of the business; the partnership is not a distinct legal entity. This led to the creation of a new property interest known as a "tenancy in partnership," a legal construct by which each partner co-owned partnership property. An aggregate approach nevertheless led to confusion as to whether a partnership could be sued or whether it could sue on its own behalf. Some courts took a technical approach to the aggregate theory and did not allow a partnership to sue on its own behalf. In addition, some courts would not allow a suit to go forward against a partnership unless the claimant named each partner in the complaint or added each partner as an "indispensable party."

The RUPA generally adopted the entity approach, which treats the partnership as a separate legal entity that may own property and sue on its own behalf. The RUPA nevertheless treats the partnership in some instances as an aggregate of co-owners; for example, it retains the joint liability of partners for partnership obligations. As a practical matter, therefore, the present-day partnership has both aggregate and entity attributes. The partnership, for instance, is considered an association of co-owners for tax purposes, and each co-owner is taxed on his or her proportional share of the partnership profits.

Formation

The formation of a partnership requires a voluntary "association" of persons who "co-own" the business and intend to conduct the business for profit. Persons can form a partnership by written or oral agreement, and a partnership agreement often governs the partners' relations to each other and to the partnership. The term *person* generally includes individuals, corporations, and other partnerships and business associations. Accordingly, some partnerships may contain individuals as well as large corporations. Family members may also form and operate a partnership, but courts generally look closely at the structure of a family business before recognizing it as a partnership for the benefit of the firm's creditors.

Certain conduct may lead to the creation of an implied partnership. Generally, if a person receives a portion of the profits from a business enterprise, the receipt of the profits is evidence of a partnership. If, however, a person receives a share of profits as repayment of a debt, wages, rent, or an ANNUITY, such transactions are considered "protected relationships" and do not lead to a legal inference that a partnership exists.

Relationship of Partners to Each Other

Each partner has a right to share in the profits of the partnership. Unless the partnership agreement states otherwise, partners share profits equally. Moreover, partners must contribute equally to partnership losses unless a partnership agreement provides for another arrangement. In some jurisdictions a partner is entitled to the return of her or his capital contributions. In jurisdictions that have adopted the RUPA, however, the partner is not entitled to such a return.

In addition to sharing in the profits, each partner also has a right to participate equally in the management of the partnership. In many partnerships a majority vote resolves disputes relating to management of the partnership. Nevertheless, some decisions, such as admitting a new partner or expelling a partner, require the partners' unanimous consent.

Each partner owes a fiduciary duty to the partnership and to copartners. This duty requires that a partner deal with copartners in GOOD FAITH, and it also requires a partner to

A sample partnership agreement

Partnership Agreement

This PARTNERSHIP AGREEMENT is made on the _____ day of _____ , 20 _____ between
_____ , whose address is
_____ and
_____ , whose address is
_____ .

NAME AND BUSINESS.

The parties hereby form a partnership under the name of _____ to conduct the business of
_____ .

The principal office of the business shall be at _____
_____ .

TERM.

The partnership shall begin on the _____ day of _____ , 20_____ , and shall continue until terminated as herein provided.

CAPITAL.

The capital of the partnership shall be contributed in cash by the partners as follows:

A separate capital account shall be maintained for each partner. Neither partner shall withdraw any part of his capital account. Upon the demand of either partner, the capital accounts of the partners shall be maintained at all times in the proportions in which the partners share in the profits and losses of the partnership.

PROFIT AND LOSS.

The net profits of the partnership shall be divided equally between the partners and the net losses shall be borne equally by them. A separate income account shall be maintained for each partner. Partnership profits and losses shall be charged or credited to the separate income account of each partner. If a partner has no credit balance in his income account, losses shall be charged to his capital account.

SALARIES AND DRAWINGS.

Neither partner shall receive any salary for services rendered to the partnership. Each partner may, from time to time, withdraw the credit balance in his income account.

INTEREST.

No interest shall be paid on the initial contributions to the capital of the partnership or on any subsequent contributions of capital.

MANAGEMENT DUTIES AND RESTRICTIONS.

The partners shall have equal rights in the management of the partnership business, and each partner shall devote his entire time to the conduct of the business. Without the consent of the other partner neither partner shall on behalf of the partnership borrow or lend money, or make, deliver, or accept any commercial paper, or execute any mortgage, security agreement, bond, or lease, or purchase or contract to purchase, or sell or contract to sell any property for or of the partnership other than the type of property bought and sold in the regular course of its business.

BANKING.

All funds of the partnership shall be deposited in its name in such checking account or accounts as shall be designated by the partners. All withdrawals therefrom are to be made upon checks signed by either partner.

BOOKS.

The partnership books shall be maintained at the principal office of the partnership, and each partner shall at all times have access thereto.

The books shall be kept on a fiscal year basis, commencing on the _____ day of _____
and ending on the _____ day of _____ , and shall be closed and balanced at the end of each fiscal year. An audit shall be made as of the closing date.

VOLUNTARY TERMINATION.

The partnership may be dissolved at any time by agreement of the partners, in which event the partners shall proceed with reasonable promptness to liquidate the business of the partnership. The partnership name shall be sold with the other assets of the business. The assets of the partnership business shall be used and distributed in the following order:

    (a) to pay or provide for the payment of all partnership liabilities and liquidating expenses and obligations;

    (b) to equalize the income accounts of the partners;

[continued]

Partnership Agreement

    (c) to discharge the balance of the income accounts of the partners;

    (d) to equalize the capital accounts of the partners; and

    (e) to discharge the balance of the capital accounts of the partners.

DEATH.

Upon the death of either partner, the surviving partner shall have the right either to purchase the interest of the decedent in the partnership or to terminate and liquidate the partnership business. If the surviving partner elects to purchase the decedent's interest, he shall serve notice in writing of such election, within three months after the death of the decedent, upon the executor or administrator of the decedent, or, if at the time of such election no legal representative has been appointed, upon any one of the known legal heirs of the decedent at the last-known address of such heir.

If the surviving partner elects to purchase the interest of the decedent in the partnership, the purchase price shall be equal to the decedent's capital account as at the date of his death plus the decedent's income account as at the end of the prior fiscal year, increased by his share of partnership profits or decreased by his share of partnership losses for the period from the beginning of the fiscal year in which his death occurred until the end of the calendar month in which his death occurred, and decreased by withdrawals charged to his income account during such period. No allowance shall be made for goodwill, trade name, patents, or other intangible assets, except as those assets have been reflected on the partnership books immediately prior to the decedent's death; but the survivor shall nevertheless be entitled to use the trade name of the partnership.

Except as herein otherwise stated, the procedure as to liquidation and distribution of the assets of the partnership business shall be the same as stated in the section regarding VOLUNTARY TERMINATION.

ARBITRATION.

Any controversy or claim arising out of or relating to this Agreement, or the breach hereof, shall be settled by arbitration in accordance with the rules, then obtaining, of the American Arbitration Association, and judgment upon the award rendered may be entered in any court having jurisdiction thereof.

In witness whereof the parties have signed this Agreement.

Executed this _____ day of _____ , 20_____.

_____
Signature

_____
Signature

Warning:

These forms are provided AS IS. They may not be any good. Even if they are good in one jurisdiction, they may not work in another. And the facts of your situation may make these forms inappropriate for you. They are for informational purposes only, and you should consult an attorney before using them.

account to copartners for any benefit that he or she receives while engaged in partnership business. If a partner generates profits for the partnership, for example, that partner must hold the profits as a trustee for the partnership. Each partner also has a duty of loyalty to the partnership. Unless copartners consent, a partner's duty of loyalty restricts the partner from using partnership property for personal benefit and restricts the partner from competing with the partnership, engaging in self-dealing, or usurping partnership opportunities.

Relationship of Partners to Third Persons

A partner is an agent of the partnership. When a partner has the apparent or actual authority and acts on behalf of the business, the partner binds the partnership and each of the partners for the resulting obligations. Similarly, a partner's admission concerning the partnership's affairs is considered an admission of the partnership. A partner may only bind the partnership, however, if the partner has the authority to do so and undertakes transactions while conducting the usual partnership business. If a third person, however, knows that the partner is not authorized to act on behalf of the partnership, the partnership is generally not liable for the partner's unauthorized acts. Moreover, a partnership is not responsible for a partner's wrongful acts or omissions committed after the dissolution of the partnership or after the dissociation of the partner. A partner who is new to the partnership is not liable for the obligations of the partnership that occurred prior to the partner's admission.

Liability

Generally, each partner is jointly liable with the partnership for the obligations of the partnership. In many states each partner is jointly and severally liable for the wrongful acts or omissions of a copartner. Although a partner may be sued individually for all the damages associated with a wrongful act, partnership agreements generally provide for indemnification of the partner for the portion of damages in excess of her or his own proportional share.

Some states that have adopted the RUPA provide that a partner is jointly and severally liable for the debts and obligations of the partnership. Nevertheless, before a partnership's creditor can levy a judgment against an individual partner, certain conditions must be met, including the return of an unsatisfied writ of execution against the partnership. A partner may also agree that the creditor need not exhaust partnership assets before proceeding to collect against that partner. Finally, a court may allow a partnership creditor to proceed against an individual partner in an attempt to satisfy the partnership's obligations.

Partnership Property

A partner may contribute PERSONAL PROPERTY to the partnership, but the contributed property becomes partnership property unless some other arrangement has been negotiated. Similarly, if the partnership purchases property with partnership assets, such property is presumed to be partnership property and is held in the partnership's name. The partnership may convey or transfer the property but only in the name of the partnership. Without the consent of all the partners, individual partners may not sell or assign partnership property.

In some jurisdictions the partnership property is considered personal property that each partner owns as a "tenant in partnership," but other jurisdictions expressly state that the partnership may own property. The tenant in partnership concept, which is the approach contained in the UPA, is the result of adopting an aggregate approach to partnerships. Because the aggregate theory is that the partnership is not a separate entity, it was thought that the partnership could not own property but that the individual partners must actually own it. This approach has led to considerable confusion, and the RUPA has expressly stated that the partnership may own partnership property.

Partnership Interests

A partner's interest in a partnership is considered personal property that may be assigned to other persons. If assigned, however, the person receiving the assigned interest does not become a partner. Rather, the assignee only receives the economic rights of the partner, such as the right to receive partnership profits. In addition, an assignment of the partner's interest does not give the assignee any right to participate in the management of the partnership. Such a right is a separate interest and remains with the partner.

Partnership Books

Generally, a partnership maintains separate books of account, which typically include records of the partnership's financial transactions and each partner's capital contributions. The books must be kept at the partnership's principal place of business, and each partner must have access to the books and be allowed to inspect and copy them upon demand. If a partnership denies a partner access to the books, he or she usually has a right to obtain an INJUNCTION from a court to compel the partnership to allow him or her to inspect and copy the books.

Partnership Accounting

Under certain circumstances a partner has a right to demand an accounting of the partnership's affairs. The partnership agreement, if any, usually sets forth a partner's right to a predissolution accounting. State law also generally allows for an accounting if copartners exclude a partner from the partnership business or if copartners wrongfully possess partnership property. In a court action for an accounting, the partners must provide a report of the partnership business and detail any transactions dealing with partnership property. In addition, the partners who bring a court action for an accounting may examine whether any partners have breached their duties to copartners or the partnership.

Taxation

One of the primary reasons to form a partnership is to obtain its favorable tax treatment. Because partnerships are generally considered an association of co-owners, each of the partners is taxed on her or his proportional share of partnership profits. Such taxation is considered "pass-through" taxation in which only the indimvidual partners are taxed. Although a partnership is required to file annual tax returns, it is not taxed as a separate entity. Rather, the profits of the partnership "pass through" to the individual partners, who must then pay individual taxes on such income.

Dissolution

A dissolution of a partnership generally occurs when one of the partners ceases to be a partner in the firm. Dissolution is distinct from the termination of a partnership and the "winding up" of partnership business. Although the term *dissolution* implies termination, dissolution is actually the beginning of the process that ultimately terminates a partnership. It is, in essence, a change in the relationship between the partners. Accordingly, if a partner resigns or if a partnership expels a partner, the partnership is considered legally dissolved. Other causes of dissolution are the BANKRUPTCY or death of a partner, an agreement of all partners to dissolve, or an event that makes the partnership business illegal. For instance, if a partnership operates a gambling casino and gambling subsequently becomes illegal, the partnership will be considered legally dissolved. In addition, a partner may withdraw from the partnership and thereby cause a dissolution. If, however, the partner withdraws in violation of a partnership agreement, the partner may be liable for damages as a result of the untimely or unauthorized withdrawal.

After dissolution, the remaining partners may carry on the partnership business, but the partnership is legally a new and different partnership. A partnership agreement may provide for a partner to leave the partnership without dissolving the partnership but only if the departing partner's interests are bought by the continuing partnership. Nevertheless, unless the partnership agreement states otherwise, dissolu-tion begins the process whereby the partnership's business will ultimately be wound up and terminated.

Dissociation

Under the RUPA, events that would otherwise cause dissolution are instead classified as the dissociation of a partner. The causes of dissociation are generally the same as those of dissolution. Thus, dissociation occurs upon receipt of a notice from a partner to withdraw, by expulsion of a partner, or by bankruptcy-related events such as the bankruptcy of a partner. Dissociation does not immediately lead to the winding down of the partnership business. Instead, if the partnership carries on the business and does not dissolve, it must buy back the former partner's interest. If, however, the partnership is dissolved under the RUPA, then its affairs must be wound up and terminated.

Winding Up

Winding up refers to the procedure followed for distributing or liquidating any remaining partnership assets after dissolution. Winding up also provides a priority-based method for discharging the obligations of the partnership, such as making payments to non-partner creditors or to remaining partners. Only partners who have not wrongfully caused dissolution or have not wrongfully dissociated may participate in winding up the partnership's affairs.

State partnership statutes set the procedure to be used to wind up partnership business. In addition, the partnership agreement may alter the order of payment and the method of liquidating the assets of the partnership. Generally, however, the liquidators of a partnership pay non-partner creditors first, followed by partners who are also creditors of the partnership. If any assets remain after satisfying these obligations, then partners who have contributed capital to the partnership are entitled to their capital contributions. Any remaining assets are then divided among the remaining partners in accordance with their respective share of partnership profits.

Under the RUPA, creditors are paid first, including any partners who are also creditors. Any excess funds are then distributed according to the partnership's distribution of profits and losses. If profits or losses result from a liquidation, such profits and losses are charged to the partners' capital accounts. Accordingly, if a partner has a negative balance upon winding up the partnership, that partner must pay the amount necessary to bring his or her account to zero.

Limited Partnerships

A limited partnership is similar in many respects to a general partnership, with one essential difference. Unlike a general partnership, a limited partnership has one or more partners who cannot participate in the management and control of the partnership's business. A partner who has such limited participation is considered a "limited partner" and does not generally incur personal liability for the partnership's obligations. Generally, the extent of liability for a limited partner is the limited partner's capital contributions to the partnership. For this reason, limited partnerships are often used to provide capital to a partnership through the capital contributions of its limited partners. Limited partnerships are frequently used in real estate and entertainment-related transactions.

The limited partnership did not exist at COMMON LAW. Like a general partnership, however, a limited partnership may govern its affairs according to a limited partnership agreement. Such an agreement, however, will be subject to applicable state law. States have for the most part relied on the Uniform Limited Partnership Act in adopting their limited partnership legislation. The Uniform Limited Partnership Act was revised in 1976 and 1985. Accordingly, a few states have retained the old uniform act, and other states have relied on either revision to the uniform act or on both revisions to the uniform act.

A limited partnership must have one or more general partners who manage the business and who are personally liable for partnership debts. Although one partner may be both a limited and a general partner, at all times there must be at least two different partners in a limited partnership. A limited partner may lose protection against personal liability if she or he participates in the management and control of the partnership, contributes services to the partnership, acts as a general partner, or knowingly allows her or his name to be used in partnership business. However, "safe harbors" exist in which a limited partner will not be found to have participated in the "control" of the partnership business. Safe harbors include consulting with the general partner with respect to partnership business, being a contractor or employee of a general partner, or winding up the limited partnership. If a limited partner is engaged solely in one of the activities defined as a safe harbor, then he or she is not considered a general partner with the accompanying potential liability.

Except where a conflict exists, the law of general partnerships applies equally to limited partnerships. Unlike general partnerships, however, limited partnerships must file a certificate with the appropriate state authority to form and carry on as a limited partnership. Generally, a certificate of limited partnership includes the limited partnership's name, the character of the limited partnership's business, and the names and addresses of general partners and limited partners. In addition, and because the limited partnership has a set term of duration, the certificate must state the date on which the limited partnership will dissolve. The contents of the certificate, however, will vary from state to state, depending on which uniform limited partnership act the state has adopted.

FURTHER READINGS

Gow, Niel. 2000. *A Practical Treatise on the Law of Partnership.* Buffalo, N.Y.: W.S. Hein.

Gregory, William A. 2001. *The Law of Agency and Partnership.* 3d ed. St. Paul, Minn.: West Group.

Hamilton, Robert W., and Jonathan R. Macey. 2003. *Cases and Materials on Corporations, Including Partnerships and Limited Liability Companies.* 8th ed. St. Paul, Minn.: West Group.

Hynes, J. Dennis. 2001. *Agency, Partnership, and the LLC in a Nutshell.* 2d ed. St. Paul, Minn.: West Group.

Moye, John E., ed. 1999. *The Law of Business Organizations.* 5th ed. Albany, N.Y.: West Legal Studies.

Partnerships, LLCs, and LLPs: Uniform Acts, Taxation, Drafting, Securities, and Bankruptcy. 12th ed. Vol. 1. 1996. Philadelphia: American Law Institute–American Bar Association Committee on Continuing Professional Education.

CROSS-REFERENCES

Joint and Several Liability; Limited Liability Partnership.

PARTY

Any person involved in a transaction or proceeding. A group of voters organized for the purpose of influencing governmental policy, particularly through the nomination and election of candidates for public office.

Plaintiffs and defendants are PARTIES in lawsuits, for example. They have the right to make claims and defenses, offer proof, and examine and cross-examine witnesses at trials. They can pursue appeals after unsatisfactory judgments if they satisfy designated criteria.

In the United States, the Democrats and the Republicans make up the two major national political parties.

CROSS-REFERENCES

Democratic Party; Republican Party.

PARTY OF THE FIRST PART

A phrase used in a document to avoid repeating the name of the persons first mentioned in it.

PARTY WALL

A partition erected on a property boundary, partly on the land of one owner and partly on the land of another, to provide common support to the structures on both sides of the boundary.

Each person owns as much of a party wall as is situated on his or her land. The wall is subject to cross-easements—reciprocal rights of use over the property of another—in favor of each owner for the support of his or her building or for the maintenance of the wall. A party wall can also be owned by adjoining tenants pursuant to a TENANCY IN COMMON, or the wall can belong entirely to one of the adjoining owners, subject to an EASEMENT or a right in the other owner to have it maintained as a dividing wall between the two tenements.

Creation

A party wall is ordinarily created by a contract between the adjoining owners, by statute, or by prescription. ADJOINING LANDOWNERS can enter into a contract to build a party wall. The parties can agree that the wall is to be located on land owned entirely by one of them or that it is to stand partly, usually equally, on both parcels. Under a typical arrangement, one party builds the wall and the other contributes to its construction. The parties can also agree that an existing dividing wall is to become a party wall.

Statutes authorizing the construction of a party wall by one of two adjoining owners when the line between the properties is vacant embody the COMMON LAW and have been upheld as a constitutionally valid exercise of the POLICE POWER of a state. These statutes are subject to a STRICT CONSTRUCTION since they permit the taking and permanent occupation of a portion of land.

When a wall between adjoining buildings has been continuously and uninterruptedly used as a party wall by the respective owners for a period of time set forth by statute, a prescriptive right to use the wall arises.

A party wall can also be created when the owner of buildings that stand on adjoining lots and share a common wall, which forms a part of each building, conveys the lots to different persons. Each owner acquires title to one-half the wall and an easement for its support as a party wall in the other half. This rule applies even though the deeds are silent concerning the rights of the parties in the wall. The result is the same when one of the lots is retained by the original common owner.

Duration

A party wall that is constructed without any reference to a time limitation implies permanency. A wall built as a result of an agreement loses its character as a party wall when the parties rescind, or cancel, the agreement. Although the title to one-half of such a party wall, which is jointly owned by adjoining landowners, cannot be waived or abandoned, a party wall easement can be extinguished when the party entitled to it renounces his interest.

The easement of support of adjoining buildings by the party wall ends when the wall becomes unfit for its purpose or is so decayed as to need rebuilding from its foundation. When the buildings are accidentally destroyed, the easement ends, even though a portion of the wall, or the whole wall, remains standing.

Manner of Use

A party wall is for the mutual benefit and convenience of both owners. Each adjoining

Row houses in the Georgetown area of Washington, D.C., share a wall in common, or a party wall. Whether the wall is owned jointly or wholly by one tenant, each party is entitled by easement to enjoy full use of the wall—on his own side. ALAN SCHEIN PHOTOGRAPHY/CORBIS

owner has the right to its full use as a party wall in the improvement and enjoyment of his property. Neither owner can use the wall in a manner that impairs the other's easement or interferes with his or her property rights.

An adjoining owner is not entitled to extend the front wall or rear wall of his building beyond the center of the party wall. In addition, an adjoining owner cannot extend the beams of her building beyond the center of the wall. Neither party can attach window shutters, exhaust pipes, anchor rods, or other projections or fixtures over the adjoining premises, even if the projection does not actually damage, or interfere with, the rights of the adjoining owner. An easement does not give either owner a right to construct and maintain a roof or cornice that extends beyond the party wall and over the property of the adjoining owner.

By common usage, a party wall has come to mean a solid wall. Unless an agreement exists between the adjoining property owners to the contrary, neither has a right to maintain windows or other openings in the wall unless they are necessary for air and light.

A party wall can be used by the adjoining owners for the construction and maintenance of chimney flues and fireplaces. Both parties are entitled to use a flue built into the middle of the wall, although the lower part of it is located wholly in the other owner's half of the wall.

Neither owner of a party wall has a right to maintain a sign on the other side of the wall, but either has a right to do so on his or her own side.

Destruction and Rebuilding

Ordinarily neither of the adjoining owners has the right to destroy or remove a party wall, but if a fire or other casualty causes the wall to become useless to either owner, it can be removed.

In a number of states, even though a party wall is sufficient to support existing structures, an adjoining owner can replace it with a stronger wall to support a new structure requiring greater reinforcement. The owner must replace the wall within a reasonable time without damaging the property of the adjoining owner.

Either party can replace a party wall that is dangerous to life or property or insufficient for the support of existing buildings. Neither owner has any right to have a dangerous wall bolstered by allowing it to rest upon, or be sustained by, the timbers, walls, or parts of the other's building.

No obligation is imposed upon either owner to erect a new party wall to replace a wall that has been destroyed by some accidental cause, even if the foundation of the wall remains firm and sound. When the adjoining buildings are destroyed and the party wall remains standing, neither adjoining owner is obliged to reconstruct her building as it existed.

Addition, Alteration, and Repair

Unless restricted by a conveyance, transfer, or a party wall agreement, either owner can add to, alter, or repair the wall. In doing so, the owner must not damage the adjoining property or impair the easement to which the owner is entitled.

Either party, for example, may increase the height of the wall, provided the increase does not diminish its strength. Similarly either party may underpin the wall and sink the foundation deeper or increase the thickness of the wall by adding to it on his own land.

Contribution

In some jurisdictions, an adjoining landowner who uses a wall built partly on his or her land by the other adjoining landowner has no duty to contribute to the cost of construction of the wall. If there is no evidence of the conditions under which the wall was built, courts presume that each person owns as much of the wall as is situated on his property and has no obligation to contribute to the other's wall.

In some jurisdictions, liability might be imposed by statute. For example, a statute might authorize one of two adjoining landowners to build a wall partly on the adjoining land and require the other landowner to contribute, if and when she used the wall in the construction and support of an adjoining building; until payment would be made, the wall would be owned exclusively by the builder.

The obligation to contribute can, of course, be a provision in the contract between adjoining landowners, but the agreement need not be express. It can be implied from the conduct of the parties, although a contract cannot be implied from the mere assent by one owner to the construction of a wall standing equally on the land of both.

FURTHER READINGS

Jacobus, Charles J. 1986. *Real Estate Law.* Paramus, N.J.: Prentice Hall.

Kraut, Jayson, et al. 1983. *American Jurisprudence.* Rochester, N.Y.: Lawyers Cooperative.

CROSS-REFERENCES

Boundaries.

PASS

As a verb, to utter or pronounce, as when the court passes *sentence upon a prisoner. Also to proceed; to be rendered or given, as when judgment is said to* pass *for the plaintiff in a suit.*

In legislative parlance, a bill or resolution is said to pass *when it is agreed to or enacted by the house, or when the body has sanctioned its adoption by the requisite majority of votes; in the same circumstances, the body is said to* pass *the bill or motion.*

When an auditor appointed to examine any accounts certifies to their correctness, she is said to pass *them; i.e., they pass through the examination without being detained or sent back for inaccuracy or imperfection.*

The term also means to examine anything and then authoritatively determine the disputed questions that it involves. In this sense a jury is said to pass upon *the rights or issues in litigation before them.*

In the language of conveyancing, the term means to move from one person to another; i.e. to be transferred or conveyed from one owner to another.

To publish; utter; transfer; circulate; impose fraudulently. This is the meaning of the word when referring to the offense of passing *counterfeit money or a forged paper.*

As a noun, permission to pass; a license to go or come; a certificate, emanating from authority, wherein it is declared that a designated person is permitted to go beyond certain boundaries that, without such authority, he could not lawfully pass. Also a ticket issued by a railroad or other transportation company, authorizing a designated person to travel free on its lines, between certain points or for a limited time.

PASSIM

[Latin, Everywhere.] A term frequently used to indicate a general reference to a book or legal authority.

PASSPORT

A document that indicates permission granted by a sovereign to its citizen to travel to foreign countries and return and requests foreign governments to allow that citizen to pass freely and safely.

With respect to INTERNATIONAL LAW, *a passport is a license of safe conduct, issued during a war, that authorizes an individual to leave a warring nation or to remove his or her effects from that nation to another country; it also authorizes a person to travel from country to country without being subject to arrest or detention because of the war.*

In maritime law, a passport is a document issued to a neutral vessel by its own government during a war that is carried on the voyage as evidence of the nationality of the vessel and as protection against the vessels of the warring nations. This paper is also labeled a pass, sea-pass, sea-letter, *or* sea-brief. *It usually contains the captain's or master's name and residence; the name, property, description, tonnage, and destination of the ship; the nature and quantity of the cargo; and the government under which it sails.*

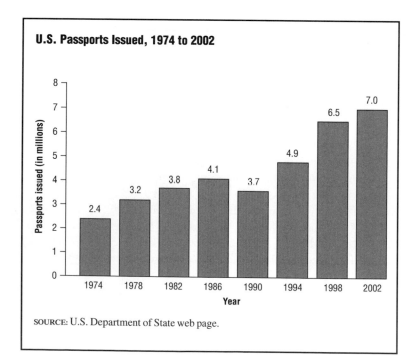

U.S. Passports Issued, 1974 to 2002

Year	Passports issued (in millions)
1974	2.4
1978	3.2
1982	3.8
1986	4.1
1990	3.7
1994	4.9
1998	6.5
2002	7.0

SOURCE: U.S. Department of State web page.

PAT. PEND.

An abbreviation displayed prominently on an invention for which an application for a patent has been made but has not yet been issued.

The term *Pat. Pend.* provides notice to all that the inventor has applied to the U.S. PATENT AND TRADEMARK OFFICE for the exclusive right to make, sell, and use his or her invention.

PATENT

Open; manifest; evident.

In the sale of PERSONAL PROPERTY, a *patent defect* is one that is clearly visible or that can be discovered by an inspection made by a person exercising ordinary care and prudence.

A patent defect in a legal description is one that cannot be corrected so that a new description must be used.

PATENT AND TRADEMARK OFFICE

The U.S. Patent and Trademark Office (PTO) is a federal agency that grants PATENTS and registers TRADEMARKS to qualified applicants. A division of the COMMERCE DEPARTMENT, the PTO was named the Patent Office when it was established by Congress in 1836. In 1975 it was renamed the Patent and Trademark Office to reflect its dual function. The PTO is now organized pursuant to 35 U.S.C.A. § 1 et seq.

Under the direction of the secretary of commerce, the PTO is run by the commissioner of patents and trademarks, a deputy commissioner, several assistant commissioners, and a support staff of more than 1,000 employees. The primary job of the commissioners is to review the merits of patent and trademark applications. Patents are typically issued upon a showing that a particular applicant has discovered or developed a new and useful process, machine, article of manufacture, chemical composition, or other invention. Trademark protection is typically afforded to applicants who are seeking to identify their commercial goods by means of a distinctive word, name, symbol, or other device.

Trademark applications must be submitted with a drawing of the proposed mark; patent applications must be accompanied by a detailed description of the invention. A filing fee is also required for both patent and trademark applications. Applications are reviewed at the PTO by persons of competent legal knowledge and scientific ability, though such persons need not be scientists or lawyers to qualify for the job. Because the application process often requires a significant amount of technical expertise and legal acumen, many applicants hire INTELLECTUAL PROPERTY attorneys to represent them. The commissioner of patents and trademarks maintains a roster of attorneys and other agents who are eligible to represent applicants in proceedings before the PTO. Each year the PTO receives hundreds of thousands of patent and trademark applications. However, only a fraction of the applications are approved. During the fiscal year of 2000 the PTO issued 176,087 patents and registered approximately 106,383 trademarks.

When the application process is completed, the PTO attaches its seal of authenticity to all patents and trademarks that have been approved. Additionally, the PTO publishes the *Official Gazette*, a weekly notice of all successful patent and trademark applications. Old editions of the *Gazette* dating back to 1872 are kept at a library in the PTO. The library contains more than 30 million documents, including ownership records for both U.S. and foreign patents and trademarks. The library is open to the public, and the PTO will furnish certified copies of patents, trademarks, and other library records to any interested person.

Patent applicants who are dissatisfied with a decision made by the PTO may appeal to the Board of Patent Appeals and Interferences. The board consists of the commissioner of patents and trademarks, the deputy commissioner, an assistant commissioner for patents, an assistant commissioner for trademarks, and individuals known as examiners-in-chief. Trademark applicants can appeal adverse decisions to the Trademark Trial and Appeal Board, which has a similar composition. Applicants who lose before either the Board of Patent Appeals and Interferences or the Trademark Trial and Appeal Board may appeal directly to the U.S. Court of Appeals for the Federal Circuit, which is vested with jurisdiction over most intellectual property matters.

In addition to examining the merits of patent and trademark applications, the PTO performs studies regarding the development of intellectual PROPERTY LAW at the domestic and international levels. These studies have allowed the PTO to establish a number of programs to recognize, identify, assess, and forecast technological trends and their utility to industry. The PTO has relied on these programs in its efforts to strengthen patent and trademark protection around the world.

The PTO, located in Arlington, Virginia, employs over 5,000 staff members to support its major functions of examining and issuing patents and examining and registering trademarks. Since 1991, the PTO has operated similarly to a private business, providing products and services in return for fees that pay for PTO

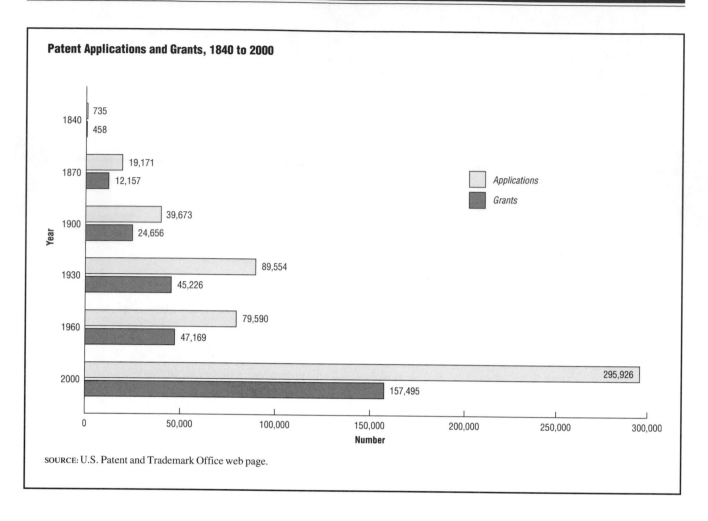

Patent Applications and Grants, 1840 to 2000

1840: 735 (Applications), 458 (Grants)
1870: 19,171 (Applications), 12,157 (Grants)
1900: 39,673 (Applications), 24,656 (Grants)
1930: 89,554 (Applications), 45,226 (Grants)
1960: 79,590 (Applications), 47,169 (Grants)
2000: 295,926 (Applications), 157,495 (Grants)

Year

Number

SOURCE: U.S. Patent and Trademark Office web page.

operations, although increased filings for patents and trademarks have caused fiscal strain. The PTO has responded by a variety of methods including electronic filing. The PTO features a user-friendly Web site that permits users to apply for a patent or file a trademark online as well as checking the status of patents and trademarks as they move through the application or filing process.

FURTHER READINGS

Patent and Trademark Office. Available online at <www.uspto.gov> (accessed August 1, 2003).

U.S. Government Manual Website. Available online at <www.gpoaccess.gov/gmanual> (accessed November 10, 2003).

CROSS-REFERENCES

Commerce Department; Intellectual Property; Jurisdiction.

PATENT WRIT

An open court order in earlier times; a writ that was not folded and sealed up as a close writ would be.

PATENTS

Rights, granted to inventors by the federal government, pursuant to its power under Article I, Section 8, Clause 8, of the U.S. Constitution, that permit them to exclude others from making, using, or selling an invention for a definite, or restricted, period of time.

The U.S. patent system is designed to encourage inventions that are useful to society by granting inventors the absolute right to exclude all others from using or profiting from their invention for a limited time, in exchange for disclosing the details of the invention to the public. Once a patent has expired, the public then has the right to make, use, or sell the invention.

Once a patent is granted, it is regarded as the PERSONAL PROPERTY of the inventor. An inventor's property rights in an invention itself are freely transferable and assignable. Often employees who invent something in the course and scope of their employment transfer and assign their property rights in the invention to their employer. In addition, a patent holder, or patentee, can grant a license to another to use the invention in exchange for payment or a royalty.

Inventors are not required to participate in the patent system, and they can elect instead to try to keep their invention a trade secret. However, if the inventor begins to sell his or her invention or allows the public to use it, others can study the invention and create impostor products. If this happens, the original inventor has no protection because he or she did not obtain a patent.

There are three types of patents: (1) design patents, (2) plant patents, and (3) utility patents. Design patents are granted to protect a unique appearance or design of an article of manufacture, whether it is surface ornamentation or the overall configuration of an object. Plant patents are granted for the invention and asexual reproduction of a new and distinct variety of plant, including mutants and hybrids. Utility patents are perhaps the most familiar, applying to machines, chemicals, and processes.

Governing Laws

Patent law in the United States is based upon statutes located in Title 35 of the U.S. Code, including the Patent Act of 1952. The rules of the PATENT AND TRADEMARK OFFICE, found in Title 37 of the CODE OF FEDERAL REGULATIONS, provide additional authority. In addition, the GENERAL AGREEMENT ON TARIFFS AND TRADE (GATT) has led to significant changes in U.S. patent law that are designed to bring some aspects of U.S. law into conformity with those of the country's trading partners. The GATT Implementation Act was signed into law in 1994, and those of its provisions that impact U.S. patent law began to take effect in 1995.

Patent Duration

One important change in U.S. patent law resulting from GATT is the duration of U.S. patents. Patents were originally given 14-year terms from the date of issue, until that was changed in 1861. From 1861 until the implementation of GATT, the term of a patent was 17 years from the date of issue. Under GATT, all patents issued after June 7, 1995, have a term of 20 years from the effective filing date. GATT contained a retroactive component which provided that all patents that had been issued, but not yet expired, as of June 7, 1995, would have a term that is the longer of 20 years from its effective filing date or 17 years from the date of issue. The effective filing date is the date on which the earliest U.S. application is filed under which priority is claimed. In the United States, patent rights begin when the patent is issued.

Upon expiration of the term, the invention becomes public property and is freely available for use, reproduction, or sale. Patents can be extended for up to five years under limited circumstances, including interference proceedings (proceedings to determine the priority of an invention), secrecy orders, and appellate review.

Patentable Inventions

The Patent Act provides a broad definition of what can be patented: any new or useful process, machine, manufacture, composition of matter, or any new and useful improvement thereof. Although these categories of patentable subject matter are broad, they are also exclusive, and any item that does not fall into one of them is not patentable.

As defined by the Patent Act, a process is a method of treating certain material to produce a specific physical change in the character or quality of that material. A machine is a device that uses energy to get work done. The term manufacture refers to a process whereby an article is made by the art or industry of people. A composition of matter is a compound produced from the combination of two or more specific ingredients that has properties different from, or in addition to, those separately possessed by each ingredient.

An improvement is any addition to, or alteration in, a known process, machine, manufacture, or composition that produces a useful result. The right to a patent of an improvement is restricted to the improvement itself and does not include the process, machine, or article improved.

Naturally occurring substances, such as a type of bacteria or an element, are not patentable. But a genetically engineered bacterium is patentable. The law of gravity and other laws of nature are not patentable. Other abstract principles, fundamental truths, calculation methods, mathematical algorithms, computer programs, and bookkeeping systems are not patentable. Ideas, mental theories, or plans of action alone, without concrete means to implement them, are not patentable, irrespective of how revolutionary and useful to humanity they might be.

Is the Human Genome Patentable?

Deoxyribonucleic acid (DNA) is often called the "blueprint of life." Between 1980 and the early 2000s efforts were made to patent the human genome, which contains the entire genetic code for the human species. These efforts have generated controversy, especially between members of the scientific and religious communities. In 1980 the U.S. Supreme Court contributed to the controversy by ruling that live, human-made microorganisms are patentable subject matter under the federal Patent Act. Applying the Supreme Court's ruling to the human species, the U.S. PATENT AND TRADEMARK OFFICE (USPTO) extended patent protection to isolated and purified strands of the human genome.

The U.S. Constitution gives Congress the power to "promote the Progress of Science and useful Arts, by securing for limited Times to Authors and Inventors the exclusive Right to their respective Writings and Discoveries." U.S.C.A. Const. Art. I Section 8, Clause 8. Pursuant to this authority, Congress enacted the Patent Act of 1952. July 19, 1952, c. 950, 66 Stat. 797. Section 101 of that act allows a patent to be obtained by anyone who "invents or discovers any new and useful process, machine, manufacture, or composition of matter, or any new and useful improvement thereof." 35 U.S.C.A. 101. Congress also created the USPTO to issue patents.

A patent is like a legally protected MONOPOLY over a specific INTELLECTUAL PROPERTY. Patents grant inventors the exclusive right to make, use, or sell their inventions for a period of 20 years. 35 U.S.C.A. 154. Patent holders can prevent anyone else from using their invention, even someone who innocently infringes on the patent holder's intellectual property rights by subsequently developing the same invention independently. Alternatively, patent holders can require that subsequent users pay licensing fees, ROYALTIES, and other forms of compensation for the right to make commercial use of an invention. In exchange for this broad, exclusive right over an invention, patent holders must disclose their invention to the public in terms that are sufficient to allow others in the same field to make use of it. 35 U.S.C.A. 112.

The patentability of inventions under U.S. law is determined by the Patent and Trademark Office (USPTO) in the DEPARTMENT OF COMMERCE. A patent

application is judged on four criteria. The invention must be "useful" in a practical sense (the inventor must identify some useful purpose for it), "novel" (i.e., not known or used before the filing), and "nonobvious" (i.e., not an improvement easily made by someone trained in the relevant area). The invention also must be described in sufficient detail as to enable one skilled in the field to use it for the stated purpose (sometimes called the "enablement" criterion). In general, raw products of nature are not patentable. DNA products usually become patentable when they have been isolated, purified, or modified to produce a unique form not found in nature. The USPTO has three years to issue a patent.

As of 2003 over 3 million genome-related patent applications have been filed. U.S. patent applications are confidential until a patent is issued. The human genome represents a biological map of the DNA in a body's cells. The human body is made up of roughly 1 trillion cells. Every cell contains 23 pairs of chromosomes, and each chromosome houses a single DNA molecule. The chief DNA task is to provide cells with instructions for building thousands of proteins that perform most of the body's essential chores. Proteins contain amino acids and enzymes that catalyze hormones, biochemical reactions, and major structural development, a process known as protein synthesis.

The legal controversy surrounding DNA patenting intensified during 1988 when Congress initiated the Human Genome Project (HGP), a 15-year, $3 billion dollar research project designed to map and sequence the entire human genome. The HGP goal is to develop diagnostic tests and treatments for more than 5,000 genetically-based diseases. A rough draft of the entire genome was completed in June 2000.

In 1995 a group of more than 200 Catholic priests, Protestant ministers, Jewish rabbis, and other religious leaders gathered in San Francisco at the annual Biotechnology Industry Organization conference to attack the laws that have allowed scientists to patent the DNA of various organisms. They argued that such laws violate the sanctity of life by unlocking divine secrets and enabling scientists to patent God's creations. Environmentalists, who assert that nature is devalued by laws enabling corporations to reduce a species and its molecules to ownership, have leveled a variation of this criticism. They raise questions about what will happen to society when its most basic notions about the distinctions between animate and inanimate objects are blurred, as human life becomes just another commodity to be bought and sold on the open market.

Some of the strongest criticism has come from the scientific community itself. Certain members of that community have argued that patenting human DNA sequences hampers the free flow of information necessary to most research projects. They contend that having to invest time in tracking down a patent holder, entering into licensing agreements, and paying royalties drives up costs, slows research, and provides disincentives for scientists to undertake research in the first place. They observe that two companies, Incyte Pharmaceuticals Inc. and Human Genome Sciences Inc., own more than half of the U.S. patents on human genetic structures, and thus can exact exorbitant fees from **HEALTHCARE** companies hoping to put their discoveries to use.

Proponents of DNA patenting point to the groundbreaking discoveries that have already been patented, including genetic links to breast cancer, colon cancer, multiple sclerosis, tuberculosis, diabetes, cystic fibrosis, Huntington's disease, and Alzheimer's disease. Proponents maintain that the speed at which these discoveries were made was dramatically increased by laws making them a commercially valuable, patentable invention.

FURTHER READINGS

Lyon, Jeff, and Peter Gorner. 1995. *Altered Fates: The Genetic Re-Engineering of Human Life.* New York: Norton.

Weissman, Gerald. 1995. *Democracy and DNA: American Dreams and Medical Progress.* New York: Wang and Hill.

Wilkie, Tim. 1993. *Perilous Knowledge: The Human Genome Project and Its Implications.* Los Angeles: Univ. of California Press.

CROSS-REFERENCES

Intellectual Property; Patent and Trademark Office.

However, the 2001 Supreme Court case *J.E.M. AG Supply, Inc. v. Pioneer Hi-Bred Intern., Inc.*, 534 U.S. 124, 122 S.Ct. 593, 151 L.Ed.2d 508 (2001), affirmed that newly developed plant breeds are patentable subject matter. In an opinion written by Justice CLARENCE THOMAS, the Court said that plants were patentable under the general utility patent statute. To obtain patent protection, a plant breeder must show that the plant it has developed is new, useful, and nonobvious, and must provide written description of plant and deposit of seed that is publicly accessible.

A process that uses a NATURAL LAW, fundamental principle, or mathematical equation can be patented. For example, in the 1981 decision of *Diamond v. Diehr*, 450 U.S. 175, 101 S. Ct. 1048, 67 L. Ed. 2d 155, the U.S. Supreme Court decided that an industrial process could be patented in spite of the fact that it depended upon a mathematical equation and involved the use of a computer program.

The *Diamond* ruling upheld a patent to two inventors for an improved process for molding rubber articles. A patent examiner had previously ruled against the inventors, finding that they sought patent protection for a computer program, which the Supreme Court had expressly said could not be patented. The process in question, which was patented, was developed to calculate with greater accuracy the amount of time required to obtain uniform curves in synthetic rubber molds.

As a further requirement for an invention to be patentable, it must meet three criteria: (1) novelty (it does not conflict with a prior pending patent application or a previously issued patent); (2) utility (virtually any amount of usefulness suffices); and (3) nonobviousness (the invention is not obvious to a person of ordinary skill in the art to which the invention pertains).

It is not always easy to determine what is an "ordinary level of skill" or what is "obvious" in deciding whether an invention meets the criterion of nonobviousness. The U.S. Supreme Court decision in *Graham v. John Deere Co.*, 383 U.S. 1, 86 S. Ct. 684, 15 L. Ed. 2d 545, 148 U.S.P.Q. 459 (1966), provides the analytical framework in which to decide whether an invention is nonobvious. Just because all the parts of an invention may be found in a prior art does not necessarily make the invention obvious.

Patents may be rejected for nonutility when their only use is a violation of public morals, such as a tool that can only be used to commit a crime.

Individuals Entitled to Patents

To be entitled to a patent, an inventor must be the first and original inventor. Joint inventors can obtain a patent for a joint invention, but none of them can obtain a valid patent as a sole inventor.

U.S. law requires that patent applications be filed in the name of and signed by the actual inventor or inventors. If one of the actual inventors is deceased, then the patent application may proceed in the names of the other inventors, but the application must still properly identify all inventors. If all of the inventors, or the sole inventor, are deceased, another person may file a patent application in their place, but only if the filing individual has a legal right to file (such as through descent of the inventors' personal property) and the inventors are still properly identified.

In the United States, the initial right to file for a patent rests with the actual inventor, even if that person is an employee who creates the invention in the course and scope of his or her employment using employer resources. However, it is a regular practice for employees engaged in research leading to patentable inventions to sign written contracts that specify that they will assign to their employer the exclusive rights under any patent obtained during the course of the employment. The employee may receive a certain percentage of the profits earned by the invention in exchange for the assignment of the patent.

Government employees, other than those employed in the Patent and Trademark Office, are entitled to obtain patents for their inventions or discoveries. During the period of employment and for one year thereafter, anyone who is employed in the Patent and Trademark Office is ineligible to acquire or take directly or indirectly, except by inheritance or BEQUEST, any rights in a patent that is issued or to be issued by the office.

Procedure for Obtaining a Patent

To obtain a valid patent, an inventor must make an application to the Patent and Trademark Office. Before making an application, inventors generally make a preliminary patentability search, a relatively low-cost search of all of the patents issued in the United States, to determine if it is feasible to proceed with an application. Often professional searchers perform these searches and give the results to a patent attorney who provides an opinion as to whether the invention is patentable. Although the preliminary search is not required by law, if it is performed, the inventor is required to provide all information obtained through that search to the Patent and Trademark Office if she ultimately files a patent application.

The application must include specifications and drawings of the proposed invention, an oath signed by the inventor, and the requisite fee. The Patent and Trademark Office keeps patent applications confidential until the patent is granted. The term *letters patent* refers to the document that contains the grant of a patent right.

Specification

A specification is a written description of the invention that includes the manner and process of creating, constructing, compounding, and using it. It should also state the practical limits of the operation of the invention. The description must be in complete, clear, concise, and precise terms to make the limits of the patent known, to protect the inventor, and to encourage the inventiveness of others by informing the public of what is still available for patent. Total disclosure of the invention is mandated to allow the public to freely use the invention once the patent has expired. No patent will be granted if the description purposely omits the complete truth about the invention in order to deceive the public.

The specification concludes with the claims, which explicitly describe both the structure of the invention and what it does. By regulation and time-honored tradition, the patent claims are written in the form of a continuous run-on sentence. The claims give the Patent and Trademark Office and the courts the opportunity to determine whether the subject matter is patentable or whether it has been anticipated by a previous invention. A claim can be either rejected by the Patent and Trademark Office or deemed invalid if it is vague, indefinite, or incomplete. The claim should cover only the actual invention. It can also be rejected if it is so broad as to include what is old and known information in addition to what is new. Each claim

An example of a patent

Patent

3,032,012
RETRACTABLE BALL POINT PEN
Charles K. Lovejoy, Atlanta, Ga., assignor to
Scripto, Inc., a corporation of Georgia
Filed July 19, 1960, Ser. No. 43,921
2 Claims. (Cl. 120–42.03)

This invention relates to writing instruments and more particularly to an improved ball point pen having a retractable writing unit wherein the extremity of the writing tip is inclined towards the central longitudinal axis of said pen barrel so as to afford a readily visible writing tip and achieve a near vertical writing angle formed between the axis of the inclined extremity of the writing tip and the writing surface when held by the writer in normal writing position.

In the past ball point pens have utilized angled writing tips, however, such angled tips were not frontally disposed of the central longitudinal axis of the pen barrel, frontally disposed being defined as that side of the writing instrument which the writer sees during writing when the pen is held in normal writing position. The advantage that is achieved by the present invention is that a readily visible writing tip is afforded which provides a near vertical writing angle formed between the axis of the inclined extremity of the writing tip and the writing surface when held by the writer in normal writing position. In addition, the present invention provides a writing instrument that is balanced, the reason for this being that the weight of the writing instrument is stably supported on the writing tip in an underslung fashion when in contact with the writing surface since the writing tip is above or frontally of the central longitudinal axis of the pen barrel which precludes any tendency to rotate in the writer's hand.

These and other features of the present invention are described in further detail below in connection with the accompanying drawings, in which:

FIG. 1 is a longitudinal cross section of the writing instrument according to the present invention showing the writing unit at projected position;

FIG. 2 is an enlarged longitudinal cross section of the forward portion of the pen shown in FIG. 1;

FIG. 3 is a transverse cross section taken along the line 3—3 in FIG. 2; and

FIG. 4 is a longitudinal cross section of the extremity of the writing tip.

Referring now in detail to the drawings, the writing instrument is generally designated by the reference numeral **10**, and has a retractable ball point writing unit **12** housed within forward barrel portion **14** and rear barrel portion **16** which are normally held together in releasable threaded engagement. The writing unit **12** is longitudinally slidable in inclined relation within the central bore **18** that is formed within forward barrel portion **14** and rear barrel portion **16** and which terminates at its forward end in an aperture **20**. The writing unit **12** is selectively projected or retracted by a projection and retraction mechanism **22** which can be of the type disclosed and claimed in U.S. Patent No. 2,930,354 and which may incorporate the further structural features that are disclosed and claimed in copending application Serial No. 739,545, filed June 3, 1958, now Patent Number 3,007,444. The details of this mechanism are clearly disclosed in the above mentioned issued patent and copending application and hence will not be discussed in detail here, but merely referred to generally by the reference numeral **22** which is recognized to include a latch L and a plunger P. The latch L in response to a depression of plunger P is adapted to engage longitudinally spaced latch shoulders disposed within rear barrel portion **16** for selectively positioning the writing unit at its projected or retracted position. The writing unit is normally urged toward retracted position by spring **24** which is positioned between shoulders **26** and **28** formed in the forward barrel portion **14** and on the writing unit **12**, respectively. Writing unit **12** has a forward metallic tube section **30** of reduced diameter which carries at its forward end writing tip **32**. The writing tip **32** is of general cylindrical shape having a conical extremity **34** formed about an axis **36** that is inclined to the axis **38** of the cylindrical portion of the writing tip **32**. The conical extremity **34** is also formed within the principal diameter that defines the cylindrical configuration of writing tip **32**. A ball **40** is rotatably housed within the angled, conical extremity **34**. The writing unit **12** is prevented from rotating within the central bore **18** by means of key **42**, which is attached to the forward metal tube portion **30**, being slidably disposed in slot **44** which is formed in forward barrel portion **14**. To illustrate the combined advantages of a readily visible writing tip having a near vertical writing angle, shown by reference numeral **46** and it can be readily seen in FIGS. 1 and 2 that the inclined writing extremity **34** is frontally disposed of the longitudinal axis **46** of the writing instrument. By this arrangement the writing extremity is clearly visible to the writer. The writing angle θ is shown as the angle formed between the axis **36** of the angled extremity **34** of writing tip **32** and the writing surface **48**. By referring to FIG. 2 it is readily seen that this angle approaches 90 degree when held in normal writing position.

The present invention has been described in detail above for purposes of illustrating only and is not intended to be limited by this description or otherwise except as defined in the appended claims.

I claim:

1. In a writing instrument having a barrel formed about a central longitudinal axis with a main central bore and an aperture formed in its forward end, a writing unit including a ball point writing tip at its forward end slidably disposed within said central bore for shifting between projected and retracted positions with respect to said forward barrel end, means normally biasing said writing unit toward retracted position and means for selectively positioning said writing unit at projected and retracted positions, the improvement of said ball point writing tip having a conical portion the axis of which is inclined toward the central longitudinal axis of said barrel, said conical portion terminating in a ball retaining lip which lies in a plane facing the longitudinal axis of said barrel and adapted for disposition through said forward barrel aperture so that said conical portion of the writing tip when projected is frontally disposed of and inclined toward said central longitudinal axis of said barrel to afford a visible writing tip having a near vertical writing angle when brought in contact with a writing surface and to provide a balanced writing instrument that precludes any tendency to rotate about said central longitudinal axis of said pen barrel when held by the writer in normal writing position.

2. In a writing instrument the improvement as defined in claim 1 and further characterized in that said writing unit is keyed against rotation within said barrel.

References Cited in the file of this patent
UNITED STATES PATENTS

2,449,939	Heyberger	Sept. 21, 1948
2,863,421	Rizzo	Dec. 9, 1958
3,000,352	Grube et al	Sept. 19, 1961

FOREIGN PATENTS

428,021	Italy	Feb. 12, 1947
1,167,185	France	July 7, 1958

must contain only one single and distinct invention, but more than one claim can be included in a single application. The inventor also must disclose in the specification what she considers to be the optimum way of practicing or using the invention.

Drawings

Drawings must be included in a patent application only when they are necessary for understanding the subject for which a patent is sought. If drawings are omitted, the commissioner of patents can require that they be submitted within two months from the time that the inventor receives notice. Drawings that are submitted after that time cannot be used with the application, and a patent can be denied due to the inadequacy of the specification.

The commissioner can require that the inventor provide a model of the invention. In addition, when the invention involves a composition of matter, the applicant might have to furnish a specimen of it for inspection or experimentation.

Oath and Fee

The application for a patent is accompanied by an oath that the inventor believes herself to be the first and original inventor. The patent laws of the United States do not discriminate on the basis of the citizenship of the inventor. An inventor from another country may apply for a patent on the same basis as a U.S. citizen.

An application for an original patent must be accompanied by a filing fee payable to the Patent and Trademark Office. Fees vary depending upon the type of application and the size of the entity applying for the patent. Small entities pay lower fees. When a patent is issued, the patentee must pay an additional fee. These fees also vary based on the size of the entity to whom the patent is issued. Additional fees are charged for maintaining a patent, which likewise vary with the size of the entity involved in the maintenance of the patent.

Patent and Trademark Office Proceedings

Upon receipt of an application for a patent, the commissioner must examine it to determine whether the applicant is entitled to a patent. The Patent and Trademark Office is not restricted to the use of technical evidence in reviewing applications but can act upon anything that establishes the facts with reasonable certainty.

A patent application can be rejected for substantial and reasonable grounds, such as when the alleged invention lacks usefulness or when the invention has been publicly used or sold previously. If the patent is rejected, the commissioner must notify the applicant of the rejection and the grounds for the rejection. An applicant can request a reexamination of the application and submit evidence to rebut the reasons for rejection. Failure to request a review is considered a waiver of the right to challenge the rejection.

A pending application may be amended until the Patent and Trademark Office ultimately decides the matter, either by issuing the patent or rejecting the patent application. New and enlarged claims can be added by amendment only when they are fairly within the scope of the original claim. An amendment that involves a material departure from the invention described in the original specification or enlarges the scope of the original application is invalid. When made within a reasonable time, amendments relate back to the original date of the application and are treated as if they were included in the original application. This is significant because time determines who will be entitled to the patent when two inventors claim essentially the same invention.

Loss or Denial of a Patent

An individual who has invented or discovered a process or object is entitled to a patent if the item or process falls within the specific categories of patentable matter and possesses the necessary attributes of invention, novelty, and utility.

Anticipation A patent will be denied in the event that anticipation occurs, which means that the complete invention was disclosed before the applicant's invention or discovery. This situation might arise when substantially similar elements that produce, or are capable of producing, the same results are found in previously invented machines that are known and commercially used. However, if the two similar inventions accomplish substantially different results or perform totally different functions, they are not deemed to be anticipated, and the second invention will be patentable even if it is essentially identical structurally to the first invention.

For a prior patent to anticipate a later invention, it must disclose the complete and operative invention in such full, clear, and exact terms as to enable a skilled individual involved in the art to practice the invention without the exercise of his or her own inventive skill. A process or instrument used for one purpose might anticipate an invention that uses essentially the same method for a new use if the latter is so comparable to the original invention that it would be apparent to a person experienced in the field. An invention is not anticipated if it has been produced previously due to an accident but is incapable of being repeated because the necessary knowledge to do so is lacking. If the results could be reproduced, however, the invention is considered anticipated.

Previous experimental efforts that are abandoned before the invention achieves actual results do not anticipate the invention. The invention is anticipated, however, if the experiment proves successful.

Statutory Bar Section 102(b) of 35 U.S.C.A. provides a statutory bar to some otherwise meritorious inventions. Under this rule, an inventor is not issued a patent if her invention was described in a book, catalog, magazine article, thesis, or trade publication in the United States or any other country before she invented it or more than a year before she filed the patent application. This statutory bar applies regardless of who made the invention discussed in the prior publication. Thus, if an inventor publishes a description of an invention or places the invention for sale or for public use, a statutory bar can result. Once an invention is placed for sale in the United States, the inventor has just one year in which to file a patent application or the right to patent that invention is forever lost. The clock begins when the invention is placed for sale, even if it is never actually sold. This rule is intended to guarantee that an inventor cannot expand the period of patent protection for the commercial exploitation of her MONOPOLY.

Abandonment and Forfeiture An inventor can lose the right to obtain a patent through ABANDONMENT. An invention is regarded as abandoned when it is subject to free and unrestricted public use.

A recognized exception to this general rule, called the "experimental use exception," occurs when an invention must be placed in the public use to determine its operability. However this exception is very narrow, and the inventor must be careful to document the invention to support a later claim of experimental use.

An inventor forfeits the right to a patent when she delays making a claim or hides the invention for an extensive period of time because such conduct unduly postpones the time that the public would be entitled to the subsequent free use of the invention. Delay in applying for a patent does not constitute abandonment if the inventor can demonstrate that she never intended to abandon the invention.

Priority When two or more inventors discover or invent the same thing, patent priority can deny a patent to one of the inventors. Patents are generally issued to the first inventor, as determined by certain guidelines. The Patent and Trademark Office commences an interference proceeding to determine the priority of invention between two or more inventors who are claiming substantially the same patentable invention and who each appear to be entitled to the patent but for the other's application. Such a proceeding examines the dates of conception and reduction to practice and also considers the diligence exercised by the individual who conceived of the invention first but did not reduce it to practice until after the other inventor had done so. The date of conception is the date when the idea, encompassing all the basic and necessary components of the invention, becomes so clearly defined in the mind of the inventor as to be capable of physical expression. Reduction to practice occurs when the way in which the invention works is readily demonstrable.

An inventor who is the first to conceive of an invention and reduce it to practice is entitled to a patent. When an inventor who first conceives of an invention exercises reasonable diligence in reducing it to practice, she will receive a patent, even if the inventor who was second to conceive of the idea was faster in reducing it to practice.

Another general rule is that an individual who actually reduces an invention to practice has priority over one who constructively reduces it to practice. Actual reduction takes place when the invention is put into practical form, whereas constructive reduction occurs when a patent application is filed with the Patent and Trademark Office.

Former U.S. patent law only allowed inventive activity that actually took place within the borders of the country to establish a date of invention. GATT has changed this restriction to allow foreign inventors to prove inventive activity that took place in another country to show a date of invention. Because the United States has a "first to invent" patent system, whereas most other countries have a "first to file" system, the United States had effectively discriminated against foreign inventors because it gave patents to the first inventor to actually make the invention in the United States. GATT addressed this issue that for many years was a disadvantage for U.S. trading partners.

Appeals

Applicants for a patent, or for the reissue of a patent, whose claims have twice been rejected can bring an appeal from the final decision of the primary examiner to the Patent Office Board of Appeals and Interferences. An applicant who is dissatisfied with the decision of the board of appeals can appeal to the U.S. Court of Appeals for the Federal Circuit or start a civil action against the commissioner in U.S. District Court for the District of Columbia within a specified period of time after the board issues its decision. The applicant is not permitted, however, to institute both a civil lawsuit and an appeal to the U.S. Court of Appeals for the Federal Circuit.

Reissue and Disclaimer

A reissued patent is the grant of a new patent that modifies the original invention by the addition of new elements. A reissued patent is essentially an amendment of the original patent effected to rectify some defect or insufficiency in it.

A disclaimer is the voluntary abandonment of some portion of a patent claim that would render it invalid for lack of novelty. It limits the claim to what is new and thereby saves the patentability of the item by circumventing the invalidity that would otherwise defeat the entire claim. An inventor who knows that a patent contains invalid claims should immediately file a disclaimer because the failure to do so could result in the rejection of the patent.

Assignment and Lease

An assignment is a transfer either of the entire patent, encompassing the exclusive right to make, use, and sell the invention, or a specified part thereof, in the United States. The assignment must be in writing and should be recorded in the Patent and Trademark Office. In the event that a patent is assigned but the assignment is not recorded, a later purchaser of the patent can use the purchased patent as if it had never been assigned.

An assignment is different from a license because a license merely provides the licensee with a temporary right to use the patent as agreed. A license need not be in writing. Whether a transfer is an assignment or a license is determined by reference to the contract between the parties. A patent license is personal to the licensee and cannot be transferred unless specifically indicated in the agreement. The licensor, the individual who issued the license to another, ordinarily requires the payment of a royalty for the use of the patent.

Marking Patented Items

A patentee or any authorized party who makes or sells any patented item must provide notice to the public that the article is patented by placing the word *patent* and the number given to the patent on the article. If the nature of the article prohibits such a designation, a label that contains the same information should be enclosed in, or marked on, its package. This marking requirement is not applicable to a patent for a process.

Inventors can mark their inventions with the words *patent pending* if they have a patent application on file and pending with the Patent and Trademark Office at the time the products are marked.

Federal law imposes a penalty for various forms of false marking, including marking an unpatented article with the word *patent,* or any term that implies that the article is patented, for the purpose of deceiving the public. If a patent holder fails to mark the patented product as required, he or she may not recover damages for any patent infringement that may take place as a result.

Infringement

Infringement is the unauthorized making, using, or selling for practical use or for profit an invention covered by a patent. Effective 1996, GATT also made the offer to sell a patented invention without the permission of the patentee a direct infringement violation.

Although no infringement can occur before a patent is issued, infringement can occur even if the infringer does not have any actual knowledge of the existence of a patent. A direct infringer is one who makes, uses, or sells the patented invention without permission from the patentee. An indirect infringer is one who actively encourages another to make, use, or sell a patented invention without permission. A contributory infringer is one who knowingly sells or supplies a part or component of the patented invention to another, unless the component is a staple article of commerce and is suitable for a substantial noninfringing use.

The definition of an infringement, provided in 35 U.S.C.A. § 271, has been greatly expanded in the late 1980s and 1990s. For example, it is an infringement to apply for federal FOOD AND DRUG ADMINISTRATION approval of a patented drug if the purpose is to obtain approval to manufacture, use, or sell the drug before its patent expires. It is also an infringement to provide a substantial portion of the components of a patented invention to someone outside of the United States so that the components can be assembled outside of the reaches of U.S. patent law. Similarly, it is an infringement to import into the United States a product made by a process covered by a U.S. patent although it was produced outside the United States.

Remedies

The Patent Act provides for several remedies in the event of an infringement, including injunctive relief, compensable damages, treble damages when appropriate to punish the infringer, payment of attorneys' fees in cases involving knowing infringement, and payment of the costs incurred in bringing the infringement claim in court.

The owner of a patent has a right of action for the unlawful invasion of patent rights by an infringement that has arisen within six years from the date when the lawsuit is initiated.

Injunction Courts frequently grant injunctions to protect property rights in patents. An INJUNCTION is a court decree that orders an infringer to stop illegally making, using, or selling the patented article. An injunction is only granted when an award of monetary damages will not adequately remedy the situation—for example, when an infringer plans to continue the unlawful acts. If an individual disobeys an injunction and continues to make use of an invention without permission, he will be guilty of CONTEMPT and subject to a fine or imprisonment or both.

Damages In an action for infringement of a patent, compensation for prior infringements can be awarded; however, compensation will be denied for use of the invention before the date the patent was issued. Where there is an infringement, the court will award the patentee actual damages adequate to compensate for the loss in an amount that is equal to a reasonable royalty for the infringing use, together with interest or costs set by the court. If the jury in a trial does not determine the amount of damages, the court will. In either case, the court, under the authority of statute, can increase the damages awarded by the jury up to three times the amount determined, called treble damages. Treble damages are punitive and awarded only in certain instances, such as when the infringer intentionally, in bad faith, infringed the patent.

The question of whether amendments to a patent can bar an infringement claim was ruled on by the Supreme Court in the 2002 case of *Festo Corp. v. Shoketsu Kinzoku Kogyo Kabushiki Co., Ltd.,* 535 U.S. 722, 122 S.Ct. 1831, 152 L.Ed.2d 944 (2002). In that case, the Court unanimously ruled that a patent amendment is not an absolute bar to a claim of infringement under the doctrine of equivalents. Justice ANTHONY KENNEDY, writing for the court, stated the patentee has the burden of proving that the amendment did not surrender the particular equivalent in question.

FURTHER READINGS

Battle, Carl W. 1997. *The Patent Guide: A Friendly Handbook for Protecting and Profiting from Patents.* New York: Allworth.

Mann, Richard A., and Barry S. Roberts. 2004. *Essentials of Business Law and the Legal Environment.* 8th ed. Columbus, Ohio.: Thomson/South-Western West.

Walterscheid, Edward C. 1996. "The Early Evolution of the U.S. Patent Law: Antecedents." *Journal of the Patent and Trademark Office Society* 78 (October).

Wilson, Lee. 1990. *Make It Legal: Copyright, Trademark, and Libel Law: Privacy and Publicity.* New York: Allworth.

CROSS-REFERENCES

Intellectual Property; License; Property Law; Royalty.

PATERNITY

The state or condition of a father; the relationship of a father.

English and U.S. COMMON LAW have recognized the importance of establishing the paternity of children. In the United States, a child born outside a legal marriage relationship will lose CHILD SUPPORT and inheritance rights if the fatherhood of the child is not legally established. The father may voluntarily acknowledge paternity in a legal document filed with a court

The Impossible Heir

In contemporary law the legal determination of paternity generally rests on the results of blood and genetic testing. However, there are times when it can be proved that it was impossible for a husband to be the father of his wife's child because the husband was absent during the period when conception occurred.

In an unusual reversal of modern law on paternity, the Alabama Supreme Court, in *Tierce v. Ellis,* 624 So. 2d 553 (1993), found that Dennis Tierce was the legitimate son of William Tierce, even though William was serving overseas in the armed forces during WORLD WAR II when Dennis was conceived.

William Tierce returned from the war to Alabama in December 1945 to discover that his wife Irene was six months pregnant. He immediately filed for DIVORCE on the ground of ADULTERY. The divorce was granted in February 1946. On April 4, 1946, Dennis Tierce was born. William Tierce was erroneously listed as the father on the birth certificate, but Tierce never knew of this mistake. He remarried and had five children, including his daughter, Sheila Ellis.

William Tierce died in 1972. When the executors of his estate filed a list of heirs in 1989, they listed Dennis as William's son. Sheila Ellis filed suit, challenging the paternity of Dennis and his status as an heir. The trial court ruled that it was impossible for Dennis to be the biological son of William.

The Alabama Supreme Court reversed, basing its decision on two grounds. First, under the Alabama Uniform Parentage Act (Ala. Code §§ 26-17-1 et seq. [1992 and Supp. 1994]), a husband is presumed to be the father of a child born within three hundred days of a divorce. Dennis was born sixty days after his parents' divorce. Second, the court invoked the COMMON LAW rule of repose, which requires a prompt disposition of a legal dispute. The court concluded that because William Tierce did not seek a paternity judgment during his divorce proceedings in 1946, his daughter could not now attempt to rebut the marital paternity presumption. Therefore, Dennis Tierce, the impossible heir, could claim a share of the estate of a person he never knew and to whom he was not related.

or may agree to have his name listed as the father on the child's birth certificate. If the man disputes fatherhood, the mother or the state government may initiate a legal proceeding, known as a paternity action, to adjudicate fatherhood.

The common law also established the "marital paternity presumption," which holds that a child born during a marriage is the offspring of the husband. Therefore, a child born as a result of the wife's adulterous affair is recognized as a legitimate child of the marriage. This rule recognized that ILLEGITIMACY brought social stigma as well as severe economic penalties to a child, including the inability to inherit from the husband of the child's mother. By establishing a presumption of paternity and therefore legitimacy, the rule promoted family stability and integrity.

This rule was developed at a time when no medical tests existed to prove paternity. In addition, a husband could not testify that he had no access to his wife at the time of conception. A husband could rebut the marital presumption only by proving his impotence or his absence from the country.

By the late nineteenth century, U.S. courts began to allow the defense of impossibility to rebut the marital presumption. The question of paternity became a fact that could be rebutted by clear and convincing evidence that procreation by the husband was impossible.

In 1973 the COMMISSIONERS ON UNIFORM LAWS proposed the Uniform Parentage Act (UPA), which sought to establish a consistent rule on adjudicating paternity disputes. The UPA, which has been adopted by 18 states, continued to use the marital paternity presumption. In addition, it presumes a mother's husband to be the natural father of a child if the child is born during the marriage or within 300 days after the marriage is terminated. The UPA does state, however, that a presumption of paternity may be rebutted by clear and convincing evidence.

Modern science has made the adjudication of paternity issues easier. Modern blood and genetic testing can accurately determine paternity. Human leukocyte antigen tissue typing can provide up to a 98 percent probability that a certain man is the father of a particular child. The use of DNA testing provides near-positive paternity identification. Many states that have adopted the UPA have created a presumption of paternity based solely on genetic testing. Some courts have questioned the need for the marital presumption at all because of the certainty produced by testing.

The evolving state of the martial presumption of paternity can be seen in the revised Uniform Parentage Act (UPA), published in 2000. While the new UPA retains all of the original presumptions related to marriage, it eliminates the clear and convincing evidence standard for rebutting an assumption of paternity. Instead it states that the presumption may be rebutted "only by admissible results of genetic testing excluding that man as the father of the child or identifying another man as the father of the child." The most recent UPA states: "The existence of modern genetic testing obviates this old approach to the problem of conflicting presumptions when a court is to determine paternity."

In determining a husband's paternity, the court may deny a request for genetic testing if it finds by clear and convincing evidence that the conduct of the mother or the presumed father means it would be unfair to allow that party to deny parentage and it would be wrong to end the father-child relationship. According to the new UPA, the alleged biological father of a child born to a married mother now has standing to bring an action to determine the existence or non-existence of the parent-child relationship. The new UPA also adopts a time limit to rebut the marital presumption to two years following the birth of the child if the presumed father lived in the same household as the child or treated the child as his own.

In addition to the changing provisions of the new UPA, genetic testing has also allowed most states to expand the categories of persons who can challenge the martial presumption and increase the chances that such challenges will be successful. With that, the marital presumption of paternity has become eroded. Twenty-two states now set a scientific standard for a conclusive presumption of non-paternity, while eight states establish a scientific standard for a conclusive presumption of paternity.

But despite the new emphasis on genetic testing, both the newly revised UPA and most state laws and courts put some emphasis on the best interests of the child. In states such as Arizona, Wisconsin, Kansas, Maryland, Montana and Minnesota, courts have said that the best interest of the child must be taken into account when determining paternity. In some cases, courts have upheld the right to refuse genetic tests if it is determined they are not in the best interest of the child; others have stated the best interests of the child must be taken into account after the genetic testing determines paternity.

FURTHER READINGS

Glennon, Theresa. 2000. "Somebody's Child: Evaluating the Erosion of the Marital Presumption of Paternity." *West Virginia Law Review* 102.

McDuff, Lawrence J. 1994. "The 'Inconceivable' Case of *Tierce v. Ellis.*" *Alabama Law Review* 46.

National Conference of Commissioners on Uniform State Laws. 2000. "Uniform Parentage Act." *Uniform Laws Annotated.* St. Paul, Minn.: West Group

CROSS-REFERENCES

DNA Evidence; Family Law; Paternity Suit.

PATERNITY SUIT

A civil action brought against an unwed father by an unmarried mother to obtain support for an illegitimate child and for payment of bills incident to the pregnancy and the birth.

A paternity suit, also known as an affiliation proceeding, is a criminal proceeding in certain states.

Generally the unwed mother initiates a paternity suit; in some jurisdictions, however, if the mother is a minor, proceedings must be initiated by a parent or guardian acting on her behalf.

CROSS-REFERENCES

Child Support; Illegitimacy; Parent and Child.

❖ PATERSON, WILLIAM

William Paterson was a distinguished public servant during the early years of the Republic of the United States, serving as governor of New Jersey, a Framer of the U.S. Constitution, a U.S. senator, and associate justice of the U.S. Supreme Court. In recognition of his service to New Jersey, the city of Paterson was named for him.

William Paterson.
LIBRARY OF CONGRESS

Paterson was born on December 24, 1745, in County Antrim, Ireland. He emigrated with his family to New Jersey in 1747 and graduated from the College of New Jersey (now Princeton University) in 1763. He was admitted to the New Jersey bar in 1768, establishing a law practice in New Bromley, New Jersey.

He entered government in 1775, serving in the New Jersey Provincial Congress. He became attorney general of New Jersey in 1776, holding the position for seven years. During this period he briefly served in the New Jersey Senate. He also participated in the New Jersey State Constitutional Convention in 1776.

Paterson played a key role in the U.S. Constitutional Convention, which was held in Philadelphia in 1787. As a delegate from New Jersey, Paterson sought to protect his and other small states from demands by larger states that representation be based on population. Paterson offered an alternative to the large-state proposition, or Virginia Plan. His New Jersey Plan went to the other extreme. He proposed that each state have one vote in Congress. Out of this conflict came the compromise that created two houses of Congress, with the House of Representatives based on population and the Senate on equal representation (two votes per state). The compromise also led to the creation of the Supreme Court in Article III of the U.S. Constitution. Paterson, who signed the Constitution, was a strong supporter of the document and campaigned for its adoption in New Jersey.

He was elected to the Senate in 1789 and was one of the authors of the JUDICIARY ACT OF 1789, which created the federal legal structure of Supreme Court, circuit court, and district court. The act created the office of attorney general and gave the Supreme Court the appellate jurisdiction to review state court decisions that involved the Constitution, federal laws, and treaties.

Paterson resigned in 1790 to run for governor of New Jersey. Easily elected, he left the governorship in 1793 when President GEORGE WASHINGTON appointed him an associate justice of the U.S. Supreme Court. His tenure on the Court revealed him to be a strong supporter of the federal government and an independent judiciary. His role as a Framer lent credibility to his conclusions as to what was the "original intent" of the drafters of the Constitution.

As a circuit judge (in that period Supreme Court justices also rode circuit), he conducted the TREASON trials of the participants in the

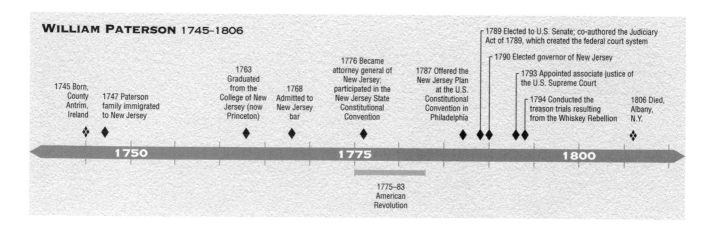

WILLIAM PATERSON 1745–1806

1745 Born, County Antrim, Ireland

1747 Paterson family immigrated to New Jersey

1763 Graduated from the College of New Jersey (now Princeton)

1768 Admitted to New Jersey bar

1776 Became attorney general of New Jersey; participated in the New Jersey State Constitutional Convention

1787 Offered the New Jersey Plan at the U.S. Constitutional Convention in Philadelphia

1789 Elected to U.S. Senate; co-authored the Judiciary Act of 1789, which created the federal court system

1790 Elected governor of New Jersey

1793 Appointed associate justice of the U.S. Supreme Court

1794 Conducted the treason trials resulting from the Whiskey Rebellion

1806 Died, Albany, N.Y.

1750   1775   1800

1775–83 American Revolution

WHISKEY REBELLION, a revolt in 1794 against the excise tax on whiskey imposed by Secretary of the Treasury ALEXANDER HAMILTON. He later presided over the trials of prominent Democratic-Republicans who were charged with SEDITION for criticizing President JOHN ADAMS.

Paterson died on September 9, 1806, in Albany, New York.

FURTHER READINGS

O'Connor, John E. 1979. *William Paterson, Lawyer and Statesman, 1745–1806.* New Brunswick, N.J.: Rutgers Univ. Press.

CROSS-REFERENCES

Constitution of the United States; "The New Jersey, or Paterson, Plan" (Appendix, Primary Document).

PATIENTS' RIGHTS

The legal interests of persons who submit to medical treatment.

For many years, common medical practice meant that physicians made decisions for their patients. This paternalistic view has gradually been supplanted by one promoting patient autonomy, whereby patients and doctors share the decision-making responsibility. Consequently doctor-patient relationships are very different now than they were just a few decades ago. However, conflicts still abound as the medical community and those it serves struggle to define their respective roles.

Consent

Consent, particularly informed consent, is the cornerstone of patients' rights. Consent is based on the inviolability of one's person. It means that doctors do not have the right to touch or treat a patient without that patient's approval because the patient is the one who must live with the consequences and deal with any discomfort caused by treatment. A doctor can be held liable for committing a BATTERY if the doctor touches the patient without first obtaining the patient's consent.

The shift in doctor-patient relationships seems inevitable in hindsight. In one early consent case, a doctor told a woman he would only be repairing some cervical and rectal tears; instead he performed a hysterectomy. In another case, a patient permitted her doctors to examine her under anesthesia but insisted that they not operate; the doctors removed a fibroid tumor during the procedure. In yet another case, a doctor assured a man that a proposed operation was simple and essentially without risk; the patient's left hand was paralyzed as a result of the surgery.

Consent must be voluntary, competent, and informed. Voluntary means that, when the patient gives consent, he or she is free from extreme duress and is not intoxicated or under the influence of medication and that the doctor has not coerced the patient into giving consent.

The law presumes that an adult is competent, but competency may be an issue in numerous instances. Competence is typically only challenged when a patient disagrees with a doctor's recommended treatment or refuses treatment altogether. If an individual understands the information presented regarding treatment, she or he is competent to consent to or refuse treatment.

Consent can be given verbally, in writing, or by one's actions. For example, a person has consented to a vaccination if she stands in line with others who are receiving vaccinations, observes the procedure, and then presents her arm to a HEALTHCARE provider. Consent is inferred in cases of emergency or unanticipated circumstances. For example, if unforeseen serious or life-threatening circumstances develop during surgery for which consent has been given, consent is inferred to allow doctors to take immediate further action to prevent serious injury or death. Consent is also inferred when an adult or child is found unconscious, or when an emergency otherwise necessitates immediate treatment to prevent serious harm or death.

Consent is not valid if the patient does not understand its meaning or if a patient has been misled. Children typically may not give consent; instead a parent or guardian must consent to medical treatment. Competency issues may arise with mentally ill individuals or those who have diminished mental capacity due to retardation or other problems. However, the fact that someone suffers from a mental illness or diminished mental capacity does not mean that the individual is incompetent. Depending on the type and severity of the disability, the patient may still have the ability to understand a proposed course of treatment. For example, in recent years most jurisdictions have recognized the right of hospitalized mental patients to refuse medication under certain circumstances. Numerous courts have ruled that a mental patient may have the right to refuse antipsychotic drugs, which can produce disturbing side effects.

If a patient is incompetent, technically only a legally appointed guardian can make treatment decisions. Commonly, however, physicians defer to family members on an informal basis, thereby avoiding a lengthy and expensive competency hearing. Consent by a family member demonstrates that the doctor consulted someone who knows the patient well and is likely to be concerned about the patient's well-being. This will probably be sufficient to dissuade a patient from suing for failure to obtain consent should the patient recover.

Legal, moral, and ethical questions arise in competency cases involving medical procedures not primarily for the patient's benefit. These cases typically arise in the context of organ donation from one sibling to another. Many of these cases are approved in the lower courts; the decisions frequently turn on an examination of the relationship between the donor and recipient. If the donor and recipient have a relationship that the donor is aware of, actively participates in, and benefits from, courts generally conclude that the benefits of continuing the relationship outweigh the risks and discomforts of the procedure. For example, one court granted permission for a kidney transplant from a developmentally disabled patient into his brother because the developmentally disabled boy was very dependent on the brother. In another case, a court approved a seven-year-old girl's donation of a kidney to her identical twin sister after experts and family testified to the close bond between the two. Conversely, a mother successfully fought to prevent testing of her three-and-a-half-year-old twins for a possible bone marrow transplant for a half brother because the children had only met the boy twice and were unaware that he was their brother.

Married or emancipated minors, including those in the ARMED SERVICES, are capable of giving their own consent. Emancipated means that the minor is self-supporting and lives independently of parents and parental control. In addition, under a theory known as the mature minor doctrine, certain minors may consent to treatment without first obtaining parental consent. If the minor is capable of understanding the nature, extent, and consequences of medical treatment, he or she may consent to medical care. Such situations typically involve older minors and treatments for the benefit of the minor (i.e., not ORGAN TRANSPLANT donors or blood donors) and usually involve relatively low-risk procedures. In recent years, however, some minors have sought the right to make life-or-death decisions. In 1989, a state court first recognized that a minor could make such a grave decision. A 17-year-old leukemia patient refused life-saving blood transfusions based on a deeply held, family-shared religious conviction. A psychologist testified that the girl had the maturity of a 22-year-old. Ironically, the young woman won her right to refuse treatment but was alive and healthy when the case was finally decided. She had been transfused before the slow judicial process needed to decide such a difficult question led to a ruling in her favor.

Some state statutes specifically provide that minors may give consent in certain highly charged situations, such as cases of venereal disease, pregnancy, and drug or alcohol abuse. A minor may also overrule parental consent in certain situations. In one case, a mother gave consent for an ABORTION for her 16-year-old unemancipated daughter, but the girl disagreed. A court upheld the daughter's right to withhold consent.

Courts often reach divergent outcomes when deciding whether to interfere with a parent's refusal to consent to a non-life-threatening procedure. One court refused to override a father's denial of consent for surgery to repair his son's harelip and cleft palate. But a different court permitted an operation on a boy suffering from a severe facial deformity even though his mother objected on religious grounds to the accompanying blood transfusion. In another case, a child was ordered to undergo medical treatments after the parents unsuccessfully treated the child's severe burns with herbal remedies.

Courts rarely hesitate to step in where a child's life is in danger. To deny a child a beneficial, life-sustaining treatment constitutes child neglect, and states have a duty to protect children from neglect. One case involved a mother who testified that she did not believe that her child was HIV positive, despite medical evidence to the contrary. The court ordered treatment, including AZT, for the child. Many other cases involve parents who want to treat a serious illness with nontraditional methods or whose religious beliefs forbid blood transfusions. Cases involving religious beliefs raise difficult questions under the First Amendment's Free Excise of Religion Clause, COMMON LAW, statutory rights of a parent in raising a child, and the state's traditional interest in protecting those unable to protect themselves.

When a child's life is in danger and parental consent is withheld, a hospital seeks a court-appointed guardian for the child. The guardian, often a hospital administrator, then consents to the treatment on behalf of the child. In an emergency case, a judge may make a decision over the telephone. In some cases, doctors may choose to act without judicial permission if time constraints do not allow enough time to reach a judge by telephone.

In 1982, a six-day-old infant with Down's syndrome died after a court approved a parental decision to withhold life-saving surgery. The child had a condition that made eating impossible. The baby was medicated but given no nourishment. The public furor over the *Baby Doe* case eventually helped spur the DEPARTMENT OF HEALTH AND HUMAN SERVICES to create regulations delineating when treatment may be withheld from a disabled infant. Treatment may be withheld if an infant is chronically and irreversibly comatose, if such treatment would merely prolong dying or would otherwise be futile in terms of survival of the infant, or if such treatment would be virtually futile in terms of survival and the treatment would be inhumane under these circumstances.

Although courts overrule parental refusal to allow treatment in many instances, far less common are cases where a court overrides an otherwise competent adult's denial of consent. The cases where courts have compelled treatment of an adult usually fall into two categories: when the patient was so physically weak that the court ruled that the patient could not reflect and make a choice to consent or refuse; or when the patient had minor children, even though the patient was fully competent to refuse consent. The possible civil or criminal liability of a hospital might also factor into a decision. A court typically will not order a terminally ill patient to undergo treatments to prolong life.

Informed Consent

Simply consenting to treatment is not enough. A patient must give *informed consent*. In essence, informed consent means that before a doctor can treat or touch a patient, the patient must be given some basic information about what the doctor proposes to do. Informed consent has been called the most important legal doctrine in patients' rights.

State laws and court decisions vary regarding informed consent, but the trend is clearly toward more disclosure rather than less. Informed consent is required not only in life-or-death situations but also in clinic and outpatient settings as well. A healthcare provider must first present information regarding risks, alternatives, and success rates. The information must be presented in language the patient can understand and typically should include the following:

- A description of the recommended treatment or procedure;
- A description of the risks and benefits—particularly exploring the risk of serious bodily disability or death;
- A description of alternative treatments and the risks and benefits of alternatives;
- The probable results if no treatment is undertaken;
- The probability of success and a definition of what the doctor means by success;
- Length and challenges of recuperation; and
- Any other information generally provided to patients in this situation by other qualified physicians.

Only material risks must be disclosed. A material risk is one that might cause a reasonable patient to decide not to undergo a recommended treatment. The magnitude of the risk also factors into the definition of a material risk. For example, one would expect that a one in 10,000 risk of death would always be disclosed, but not a one in 10,000 risk of a two-hour headache.

Plastic surgery and vasectomies illustrate two areas where the probability of success and the meaning of success should be explicitly delineated. For example, a man successfully sued his doctor after the doctor assured him that a vasectomy would be 100 percent effective as BIRTH CONTROL; the man's wife later became pregnant. Because the only purpose for having the procedure was complete sterilization, a careful explanation of probability of success was essential.

Occasionally, informed consent is not required. In an emergency situation where immediate treatment is needed to preserve a patient's health or life, a physician may be justified in failing to provide full and complete information to a patient. Moreover, where the risks are minor and well known to the average person, such as in drawing blood, a physician may dispense with full disclosure. In addition, some patients explicitly ask not to be informed of specific risks. In this situation, a doctor must only ascertain that the patient understands that there are unspecified risks of death and serious bodily disabilities; the doctor might ask the patient to sign a waiver of informed consent.

Finally, informed consent may be bypassed in rare cases in which a physician has objective evidence that informing a patient would render the patient unable to make a rational decision. Under these circumstances, a physician must disclose the information to another person designated by the patient.

Informed consent is rarely legally required to be in writing, but this does provide evidence that consent was in fact obtained. The more specific the consent, the less likely it will be construed against a doctor or a hospital in court. Conversely, blanket consent forms cover almost everything a doctor or hospital might do to a patient without mentioning anything specific and are easily construed against a doctor or hospital. However, blanket forms are frequently used upon admission to a hospital to provide proof of consent to noninvasive routine hospital procedures such as taking blood pressure. A consent form may not contain a clause waiving a patient's right to sue, unless state law provides for binding ARBITRATION upon mutual agreement. Moreover, consent can be predicated upon a certain surgeon doing a surgery. It can also be withdrawn at any time, subject to practical limitations.

Right to Treatment

In an emergency situation, a patient has a right to treatment, regardless of ability to pay. If a situation is likely to cause death, serious injury, or disability if not attended to promptly, it is an emergency. Cardiac arrest, heavy bleeding, profound shock, severe head injuries, and acute psychotic states are some examples of emergencies. Less obvious situations can also be emergencies: broken bones, fever, and cuts requiring stitches may also require immediate treatment.

Both public and private hospitals have a duty to administer medical care to a person experiencing an emergency. If a hospital has emergency facilities, it is legally required to provide appropriate treatment to a person experiencing an emergency. If the hospital is unable to provide emergency services, it must provide a referral for appropriate treatment. Hospitals cannot refuse to treat prospective patients on the basis of race, religion, or national origin, or refuse to treat someone with HIV or AIDS.

In 1986, Congress passed the Emergency Medical Treatment and Active Labor Act (EMTALA) (42 U.S.C.A. § 1395dd), which established criteria for emergency services and criteria for safe transfer of patients between hospitals. This statute was designed to prevent "patient dumping," that is, transferring undesirable patients to another facility. The law applies to all hospitals receiving federal funds, such as MEDICARE (almost all do). The law requires hospitals to provide a screening exam to determine if an emergency condition exists, provide stabilizing treatment to any emergency patient or to any woman in active labor before transfer, and continue treatment until a patient can be discharged or transferred without harm. It also delineates strict guidelines for the transfer of a patient who cannot be stabilized. A hospital that negligently or knowingly and willfully violates any of these provisions can be terminated or suspended from Medicare. The physician, the hospital, or both can also be penalized up to $50,000 for each knowing violation of the law.

One of the first cases brought under EMTALA involved a doctor who transferred a woman in active labor to a hospital 170 miles away. The woman delivered a healthy baby during the trip, but the doctor was fined $20,000 for the improper transfer of the woman. In addition to federal laws such as EMTALA, states may also impose by regulation or statute a duty on hospitals to administer emergency care.

There is no universal right to be admitted to a hospital in a nonemergency situation. In nonemergency cases, admission rights depend largely on the specific hospital, but basing admission on ability to pay is severely limited by statutes, regulations, and judicial decisions. For example, most hospitals obtained financial assistance from the federal government for construction; these hospitals are required to provide a reasonable volume of services to persons unable to pay. The amount of services to be provided is set by regulation, and the obligation continues for 20 years after construction is completed. Patients must be advised of the hospital's obligation under the law, or the hospital may be foreclosed from suing to collect on the bill. In addition, many states prohibit hospitals from denying admission based solely on inability to pay; some courts have made similar rulings against public hospitals based on hospital char-

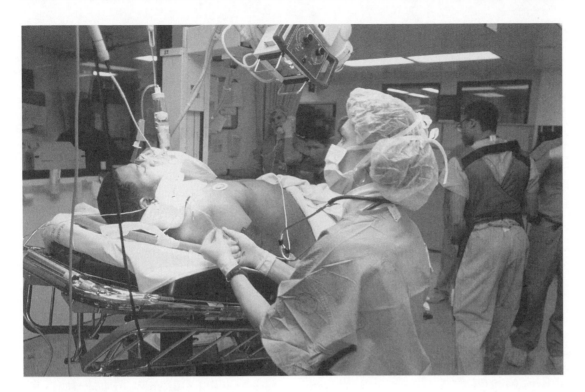

Under EMTALA hospitals are required to provide emergency treatment until a patient can be discharged or transferred without harm. The act was intended to curb the practice of "patient dumping."

ters and public policy reasons. Hospitals are also prohibited from requiring a deposit from a Medicare or MEDICAID patient.

Once a patient has been duly admitted to a hospital, she or he has a right to leave at any time, or the hospital could be liable for FALSE IMPRISONMENT. This is so even if the patient has not paid the bill or if the patient wants to leave against all medical advice. In rare cases, such as contagious disease cases, public health authorities may have state statutory or regulatory authority to quarantine a patient. In addition, state laws governing involuntary commitment of the mentally ill may be used to prevent a person of unsound mind from leaving the hospital if a qualified psychiatrist determines that the person is a danger to himself or herself or to the lives of others.

A doctor familiar with a patient's condition determines when a patient is ready for discharge and signs a written order to that effect. If the patient disagrees with a decision to discharge, she or he has the right to demand a consultation with a different physician before the order is carried out. The decision to discharge must be based solely on the patient's medical condition and not on nonpayment of medical bills.

In the mid-1990s, concern over maternity patients being discharged just a few hours after giving birth prompted legislation at both the state and federal levels. In September 1996, President BILL CLINTON signed a law ensuring a 48-hour hospital stay for a woman who gives birth vaginally and a 96-hour stay for a woman who has a caesarean section, unless the patient and the doctor agree to an earlier discharge. A number of state legislatures have passed similar laws as well.

With the rise of MANAGED CARE and Health Maintenance Organizations (HMOs), patients faced new issues involving the right to treatment. HMOs may deny authorization for expensive or experimental treatments, or for treatments provided outside the network of approved physicians. HMOs contend that they must control costs and make decisions that benefit the largest number of members. In response, state legislatures have enacted HMO regulations that seek to give patients a process for appealing the denial of benefits. The HMOs have opposed these measures and have vigorously defended their denial of benefits in court.

In *Moran v. Rush Prudential HMO, Inc.*, 536 U.S. 355, 122 S.Ct. 2151, 153 L.Ed.2d 375 (2002), the Supreme Court in a 5–4 decision upheld an Illinois law that required HMOs to provide independent review of disputes between the primary care physician and the HMO. The law mandated that the HMO must pay for services deemed medically necessary by the independent reviewer. Most importantly, the court ruled that the federal EMPLOYEE RETIREMENT INCOME SECURITY ACT (ERISA) did not PREEMPT the Illinois law. ERISA is an extremely complex and technical set of provisions that seek to protect employee benefit programs. The decision was significant because it empowered other states to enact similar laws that give patients more rights in obtaining treatment

Medical Experimentation

Medical progress and medical experimentation have always gone hand in hand, but patients' rights have sometimes been ignored in the process. Sometimes patients are completely unaware of the experimentation. Experimentation has also taken place in settings in which individuals may have extreme difficulty asserting their rights, such as in prisons, mental institutions, the military, and residences for the mentally disabled. Legitimate experimentation requires informed consent that may be withdrawn at any time.

Some of the more notorious and shameful instances of human experimentation in the United States in the twentieth century include a 1963 study in which terminally ill hospital patients were injected with live cancer cells to test their immune response; the TUSKEGEE SYPHILIS STUDY, begun before WORLD WAR II and continuing for 40 years, in which effective treatment was withheld from poor black males suffering from syphilis so that medical personnel could study the natural course of the disease; and a study where developmentally disabled children were deliberately infected with hepatitis to test potential vaccines.

Failure to obtain informed consent can arise even when consent has ostensibly been obtained. The California Supreme Court ruled in 1990 that a physician must disclose preexisting research and potential economic interests that may affect the doctor's medical judgment (*Moore v. Regents of the University of California*, 51 Cal. 3d 120, 793 P. 2d 479). The case involved excision of a patient's cells pursuant to surgery and other procedures to which the patient had consented. The surgery itself was not experimental; the experimentation took place after the surgery and other procedures. The cells were used in medical research that proved lucrative to the doctor and medical center.

Patients in teaching hospitals are frequently asked to participate in research. Participants do not surrender legal rights simply by agreeing to cooperate and validly obtained consent cannot protect a researcher from NEGLIGENCE.

In hospitals, human experimentation is typically monitored by an institutional review board (IRB). Federal regulation requires IRBs in all hospitals receiving federal funding. These boards review proposed research before patients are asked to participate and approve written consent forms. IRBs are meant to ensure that risks are minimized, the risks are reasonable in relation to anticipated benefits, the selection of subjects is equitable, and informed consent is obtained and properly documented. Federal regulations denominate specific items that must be covered when obtaining informed consent in experimental cases. IRB approval never obligates a patient to participate in research.

Advance Medical Directives

Every state has enacted advance medical directive legislation, but the laws vary widely. Advance medical directives are documents that are made at a time when a person has full decision-making capabilities and are used to direct medical care in the future when this capacity is lost. Many statutes are narrowly drawn and specify that they apply only to illnesses when death is imminent rather than illnesses requiring long-term life support, such as in end-stage lung, heart, or kidney failure; multiple sclerosis; paraplegia; and persistent vegetative state.

Patients sometimes use living wills to direct future medical care. Most commonly, living wills specify steps a patient does not want taken in cases of life-threatening or debilitating illness, but they may also be used to specify that a patient wants aggressive resuscitation measures used. Studies have shown that living wills often are not honored, despite the fact that federal law requires all hospitals, nursing homes, and other Medicare and Medicaid providers to ask patients on admission whether they have executed an advance directive. Some of the reasons living wills are not honored are medical personnel's fear of liability, the patient's failure to communicate his or her wishes, or misunderstanding or mismanagement by hospital personnel.

Another way individuals attempt to direct medical care is through a durable POWER OF ATTORNEY. A durable power of attorney, or proxy decision maker, is a written document wherein a person (the principal) designates another person to perform certain acts or make certain decisions on the principal's behalf. It is called durable because the power continues to be effective even after the principal becomes incompetent or it may only take effect after the principal becomes incompetent. As with a LIV-ING WILL, such a document has little power to compel a doctor to follow a patient's desires, but in the very least it serves as valuable evidence of a person's wishes if the matter is brought into court. A durable power of attorney may be used by itself or in conjunction with a living will.

When advance medical directives function as intended and are honored by physicians, they free family members from making extremely difficult decisions. They may also protect physicians. Standard medical care typically requires that a doctor provide maximum care. In essence, a living will can change the standard of care upon which a physician will be judged and may protect a physician from legal or professional repercussions for withholding or withdrawing care.

Right to Die

A number of cases have addressed the right to refuse life-sustaining medical treatment. Broadly speaking, under certain circumstances a person may have a right to refuse life-sustaining medical treatment or to have life-sustaining treatment withdrawn. On the one side in these cases is the patient's interest in autonomy, privacy, and bodily integrity. This side must be balanced against the state's traditional interests in the preservation of life, prevention of suicide, protection of dependents, and the protection of the integrity of the medical profession.

In IN RE QUINLAN, 355 A.2d 647 (1976), the New Jersey Supreme Court permitted withdrawal of life-support measures for a woman in a persistent vegetative state, although her condition was stable and her life expectancy stretched years into the future. Many of the emotional issues the country struggles with in the early 2000s were either a direct result of or were influenced by this case, including living wills and other advance medical directives, the right to refuse unwanted treatment, and physician-assisted suicide.

The first U.S. Supreme Court decision addressing the difficult question regarding the removal of life support was *Cruzan v. Director, Missouri Department of Health*, 497 U.S. 261, 110 S. Ct. 2841, 111 L. Ed. 2d 224 (1990). *Cruzan* involved a young woman rendered permanently comatose after a car accident. Her parents petitioned to have her feeding tube removed. The Supreme Court ruled that the evidence needed to be clear and convincing that the young woman had explicitly authorized the termination of treatment prior to becoming incompetent. The Court ruled that the evidence had not been clear and convincing, but upon remand to the state court the family presented new testimony that was deemed clear and convincing. The young woman died 12 days after her feeding tube was removed.

The Supreme Court decided two right-to-die cases in 1997, *Quill v. Vacco*, 521 U.S. 793, 117 S.Ct. 2293, 138 L.Ed.2d 834 (1997), and WASHINGTON V. GLUCKSBERG, 521 U.S. 702, 117 S.Ct. 2258, 138 L.Ed.2d 772 (1997). In *Glucksberg*, the appellate courts in New York and Washington had struck down laws banning physician-assisted suicide as violations of EQUAL PROTECTION and DUE PROCESS, respectively. The Supreme Court reversed both decisions, finding no constitutional right to assisted suicide, thus upholding states' power to ban the practice.

Though both cases were considered together, *Glucksberg* was the key right-to-die decision. Dr. Harold Glucksberg and three other physicians sought a DECLARATORY JUDGMENT that the state of Washington's law prohibiting assisted suicide was unconstitutional as applied to terminally ill, mentally competent adults. The Supreme Court voted unanimously to sustain the Washington law, though five of the nine justices filed concurring opinions in *Quill* and *Glucksberg*. Chief Justice WILLIAM REHNQUIST, writing for the Court, based much of his analysis on historical and legal traditions. The fact that most western democracies make it a crime to assist a suicide was backed up by over 700 years of Anglo-American common-law tradition that has punished or disapproved of suicide or assisting suicide. This "deeply rooted" opposition to assisted suicides had been reaffirmed by the Washington legislature in 1975 when the current prohibition had been enacted and again in 1979 when it passed a Natural Death Act. This law declared that the refusal or withdrawal of treatment did not constitute suicide, but it explicitly stated that the act did not authorize EUTHANASIA.

The doctors had argued that the law violated the SUBSTANTIVE DUE PROCESS component of the FOURTEENTH AMENDMENT. Unlike procedural due process which focuses on whether the right steps have been taken in a legal matter, substantive due process looks to fundamental rights that are implicit in the amendment. For the Court to recognize a fundamental liberty, the liberty must be deeply rooted in U.S. history and it must be carefully described. The Court rejected this argument because U.S. history has not recognized a "right to die" and therefore it is not a fundamental right. Employing the RATIONAL BASIS TEST of constitutional review, the Court concluded that the law was "rationally related to legitimate government interests" and thus passed constitutional muster.

Privacy and Confidentiality

Confidentiality between a doctor and patient means that a doctor has the express or implied duty not to disclose information received from the patient to anyone not directly involved with the patient's care. Confidentiality is important so that healthcare providers have knowledge of all facts, regardless of how personal or embarrassing, that might have a bearing on a patient's health. Patients must feel that it is safe to communicate such information freely. Although this theory drives doctor-patient confidentiality, the reality is that many people have routine and legitimate access to a patient's records. A hospital patient might have several doctors, nurses, and support personnel on every shift, and a patient might also see a therapist, nutritionist, or pharmacologist, to name a few.

The law requires some confidential information to be reported to authorities. For example, birth and death certificates must be filed; CHILD ABUSE cases must be reported; and infectious, contagious, or communicable diseases must be reported. In addition, confidential information may also be disclosed pursuant to a judicial proceeding or to notify a person to whom a patient may pose a danger.

In spite of the numerous exceptions to the contrary, patients legitimately demand and expect confidentiality in many areas of their treatment. Generally speaking, patients must be asked to consent before being photographed or having others unrelated to the case (including medical students) observe a medical procedure; they have the right to refuse to see anyone not connected to a hospital; they have the right to have a person of the patient's own sex present during a physical examination conducted by a member of the opposite sex; they have the right

to refuse to see persons connected with the hospital who are not directly involved in the patient's care and treatment (including social workers and chaplains); and they have the right to be protected from having details of their condition made public.

A patient owns the information contained in medical records, but the owner of the paper on which they are written is usually considered the actual owner of the records. The patient's legal interest in the records generally means that the patient has a right to see the records and is entitled to a complete copy of them. The patient's rights are subject to reasonable limitations such as requiring inspection and copying to be done on the doctor's premises during working hours.

Federal Patients' Bill of Rights

Dissatisfaction with an expanding corporate healthcare industry dominated by profit margins has spawned numerous reform ideas. One idea that has gained a foothold is a patients' federal BILL OF RIGHTS. In 1997, President Bill Clinton appointed an Advisory Commission on Consumer Protection and Quality in the Health Care Industry. The commission was directed to propose a "consumer bill of rights." The 34-member commission developed a bill of rights that identified eight key areas: information disclosure, choice of providers and plans, access to emergency service, participation in treatment decisions, respect and nondiscrimination, confidentiality of health information, complaints and appeals, and consumer responsibilities.

The proposed rights include: the right to receive accurate, easily understood information in order to make informed health care decisions; the right to a choice of healthcare providers that is sufficient to ensure access to appropriate high-quality health care; the right to access emergency healthcare services; the right and responsibility to fully participate in all decisions related to their health care; the right to considerate, respectful care from all members of the healthcare system at all times and under all circumstances; the right to communicate with healthcare providers in confidence and to have the confidentiality of their individually identifiable healthcare information protected; the right to a fair and efficient process for resolving differences with their health plans, healthcare providers, and the institutions that serve them; and the responsibility of consumers to do their part in protecting their health. This bill of rights has been debated in Congress and there are bipartisan areas of agreement, but, as of 2003, no final action has taken on enacting a set of rights into federal law.

FURTHER READINGS

Annas, George J. 2003. *The Rights of Patients.* 3d ed. Carbondale: Southern Illinois Univ. Press.

Barnes, James A. 2002. "Action Versus Inaction." *National Journal* (March 9).

"Dying Wishes Are Ignored by Hospitals, Doctors." 1996. *Trial* 32 (February).

Hoffmann, Diane E., Sheryl Itkin Zimmerman, and Catherine J. Tompkins. 1996. "The Dangers of Directives or the False Security of Forms." *Journal of Law, Medicine, and Ethics* 24 (spring).

"Living Wills." *West's Legal Forms (Elder Law).* 1994 and 1996 Supps. St. Paul, Minn.: West.

Oberman, Michelle. 1996. "Minor Rights and Wrongs." *Journal of Law, Medicine, and Ethics* 24 (summer).

Rodwin, Marc A. 1994. "Patient Accountability and Quality of Care: Lessons from Medical Consumerism and the Patients' Rights, Women's Health and Disability Rights Movements." *American Journal of Law and Medicine* 20 (spring-summer).

CROSS-REFERENCES

Acquired Immune Deficiency Syndrome; Competent; Death and Dying; Duress; Fetal Rights; Genetic Screening; Health Care Law; Health Insurance; Liability; Organ Transplantation; Physicians and Surgeons; Privacy; Privileged Communication.

PATRONAGE

The practice or custom observed by a political official of filling government positions with qualified employees of his or her own choosing.

When the candidate of a political party wins an election, the newly elected official has the right to appoint a certain numbers of persons to jobs in the government. This is the essence of the patronage system, also known as the spoils system ("To the victor go the spoils"): appointing persons to government positions on the basis of political support and work rather than on merit, as measured by objective criteria. Though the patronage system exists at all levels of U.S. government, the number of positions that are available through patronage has decreased dramatically since the 1880s.

The patronage system thrived in the U.S. federal government until 1883. In 1820 Congress limited federal administrators to four-year terms, leading to constant turnover. By the 1860s and the Civil War, patronage had led to widespread inefficiency and political corrup-

tion. Where patronage had once been confined to the cabinet, department heads, and foreign ambassadorships, by the 1860s low-level government positions were subject to patronage. The loss of a presidential election by a political party signaled wholesale turnover in the federal government. When President BENJAMIN HARRISON took office in 1889, 31,000 federal postmaster positions changed hands.

The assassination of President JAMES GARFIELD in 1881 by a disgruntled office seeker who did not receive a political appointment spurred Congress to pass the Civil Service Act, or Pendleton Act of 1883 (5 U.S.C.A. § 1101 et seq.). The act, which at the time only applied to 10 percent of the federal workforce, created a Civil Service Commission and advocated a merit system for the selection of government employees. By 1980, 90 percent of federal positions had become part of the civil service system. In addition, the passage in 1939 of the HATCH ACT (53 Stat. 1147) curtailed or restricted most partisan political activities of federal employees.

State and local governments have employed large patronage systems. Big-city political machines in places such as New York, Boston, and Chicago thrived in the late nineteenth century. A patronage system not only rewards political supporters for past support, it also encourages future support, because persons who have a patronage job try to retain it by campaigning for the party at the next election.

Large-scale patronage systems declined steadily during the twentieth century. During the Progressive Era (1900–1920), "good government" reformers overthrew political machines and installed civil service systems. Chicago, under Mayor Richard J. Daley, remained the last bastion of patronage, existing in its purest form until the late 1970s.

Patronage has its defenders. It is a way to maintain a strong political organization by offering campaign workers rewards. More importantly, patronage puts people into government who agree with the political agenda of the victor. Cooperation, loyalty, and trust flow from this arrangement. Finally, patronage guarantees some turnover, bringing new people and new ideas into the system.

Opponents have long agreed that patronage is acceptable at the highest levels of government. Presidents, governors, and mayors are entitled to select their cabinet and department heads. However, history indicates that patronage systems extending far down the organizational chain are susceptible to inefficiency and corruption.

Congress took another look at patronage issues in the Civil Service Reform Act of 1978 (92 Stat. 1121–1131, 5 U.S.C.A. 1201–1209). Concerned that federal bureaucrats were too independent and unresponsive to elected officials, the act replaced the Civil Service Commission with the Office of Personnel Management, under closer control of the president. The act also created the Senior Executive Service, which gives the president greater discretion in reassigning top officials to departments and agencies.

CROSS-REFERENCES

Bureaucracy; Civil Service; Tammany Hall.

❖ PAUL, ALICE STOKES

Alice Stokes Paul was a militant U.S. suffrage leader who is best remembered as the author in 1923 of the EQUAL RIGHTS AMENDMENT. Paul, who for decades played a major role in the National Woman's Party, also successfully lobbied for the inclusion of a ban against SEX DISCRIMINATION in title VII of the CIVIL RIGHTS ACT OF 1964 (42 U.S.C.A. § 2000e et seq.).

Paul was born on January 11, 1885, in Moorestown, New Jersey. She graduated from Swarthmore College in 1905 and then went to England to do graduate work. While in England, Paul became involved with the British suffragettes and received three jail sentences for participating in militant actions. She returned to the United States in 1910 and continued her graduate work at the University of Pennsylvania. She earned a Ph.D. in social work in 1912.

"IF THE WOMEN OF THE WORLD HAD NOT BEEN EXCLUDED FROM WORLD AFFAIRS, THINGS TODAY MIGHT HAVE BEEN DIFFERENT."
—ALICE PAUL

Alice Paul. BETTMANN/CORBIS

In 1913 Paul formed the Congressional Union for Woman Suffrage, which later became the National Woman's Party (NWP). She advocated a more militant position to publicize the need for an amendment to the U.S. Constitution. Paul organized marches, rallies, and protests outside the White House. As in England, she was jailed three times for organizing and participating in suffrage protests. While in jail she waged hunger strikes, resulting in her hospitalization where she was force-fed.

With the ratification of the NINETEENTH AMENDMENT to the Constitution in 1920, which

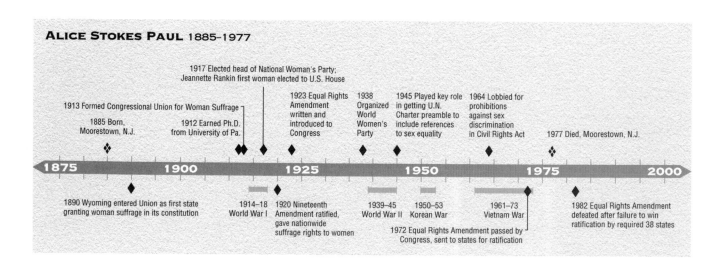

ALICE STOKES PAUL 1885–1977

1917 Elected head of National Woman's Party; Jeannette Rankin first woman elected to U.S. House

1913 Formed Congressional Union for Woman Suffrage

1885 Born, Moorestown, N.J.

1912 Earned Ph.D. from University of Pa.

1923 Equal Rights Amendment written and introduced to Congress

1938 Organized World Women's Party

1945 Played key role in getting U.N. Charter preamble to include references to sex equality

1964 Lobbied for prohibitions against sex discrimination in Civil Rights Act

1977 Died, Moorestown, N.J.

1875　1900　1925　1950　1975　2000

1890 Wyoming entered Union as first state granting woman suffrage in its constitution

1914–18 World War I

1920 Nineteenth Amendment ratified, gave nationwide suffrage rights to women

1939–45 World War II

1950–53 Korean War

1961–73 Vietnam War

1972 Equal Rights Amendment passed by Congress, sent to states for ratification

1982 Equal Rights Amendment defeated after failure to win ratification by required 38 states

gave women the vote, Paul shifted her focus to the legal inequality of women. In 1923 she wrote the equal rights amendment, which she called the Lucretia Mott amendment, in honor of the nineteenth-century feminist leader. The proposed amendment stated that "Equality of rights under the law shall not be denied or abridged by the United States or by any State on account of sex" and that "the Congress shall have the power to enforce, by appropriate legislation, the provisions of this article." Paul's proposed amendment was introduced to Congress in 1923, but it would not be approved until March 1972. However, the amendment failed to be ratified by the thirty-eight states required under the Constitution.

Paul continued to lead the NWP, and in 1938 she organized the World Party for Equal Rights for Women, known as the World Woman's Party. She played a key role in seeing that the preamble to the United Nations Charter included references to sex equality. During the debates over the 1964 Civil Rights Act, Paul and the NWP helped lobby for the inclusion of sex discrimination as illegal conduct.

Paul died on July 9, 1977, in Moorestown, New Jersey.

FURTHER READINGS

Butler, Amy E. 2002. *Two Paths to Equality: Alice Paul and Ethel M. Smith in the ERA Debate, 1921–1929.* Albany: State Univ. of New York Press.

Lunardini, Christine A. 1986. *From Equal Suffrage to Equal Rights: Alice Paul and the National Woman's Party, 1910–1928.* New York: New York Univ. Press.

PAUPER

An impoverished person who is supported at public expense; an indigent litigant who is permitted to sue or defend without paying costs; an impoverished criminal defendant who has a right to receive legal services without charge.

PAWN

To deliver PERSONAL PROPERTY *to another as a pledge or as security for a debt. A deposit of goods with a creditor as security for a sum of money borrowed.*

In common usage, pawn signifies a pledge of goods, as distinguished from a pledge of intangible personal property, such as a contract right. In a more limited sense, it denotes a deposit of personal property with a pawnbroker as security for a loan. A pawned article is retained until the loan is repaid within a certain time. If it is not repaid on time, the pawnbroker may sell the item.

PAWNBROKER

A person who engages in the business of lending money, usually in small sums, in exchange for PERSONAL PROPERTY *deposited with him or her that can be kept or sold if the borrower fails or refuses to repay the loan.*

PAXTON'S CASE

See WRITS OF ASSISTANCE CASE.

PAY EQUITY

See COMPARABLE WORTH.

PAYABLE

Justly due; legally enforceable.

A sum of money is said to be payable when a person is under an obligation to pay it. The term may therefore signify an obligation to pay at a future time, but when used without qualification, it ordinarily means that the debt is due to be paid immediately.

PAYEE

The person who is to receive the stated amount of money on a check, bill, or note.

PAYMENT

The fulfillment of a promise; the performance of an agreement. A delivery of money, or its equivalent in either specific property or services, by a debtor to a creditor.

P.C.

An abbreviation for professional corporation, which is a special corporation established by professionals, such as physicians, accountants, or, in some states, attorneys, who practice together.

In most jurisdictions, a professional corporation may be organized by professionals who render a personal service to the public that requires a license and that, before proper statutory organization, could not be performed by a corporation.

One of the main reasons professionals incorporate is to gain certain tax benefits. Incorporation neither changes PROFESSIONAL

RESPONSIBILITY nor protects those incorporating from liability for MALPRACTICE.

PEACE BOND

The posting of money in court, as required by a judge or magistrate, by a person who has threatened to commit a breach of the peace.

PEACE OFFICERS

Sheriffs, constables, marshals, city police officers, and other public officials whose duty it is to enforce and preserve the public order.

❖ PECKHAM, RUFUS WHEELER

Rufus Wheeler Peckham served as an associate justice of the U.S. Supreme Court from 1895 to 1909. A prominent New York attorney and judge, Peckham was a conservative judge who believed that state and federal government had limited authority to regulate business activity. He expressed this belief most clearly in LOCHNER V. NEW YORK, 198 U.S. 45, 25 S. Ct. 539, 49 L. Ed. 937 (1905), a case that is best remembered for the dissent of Justice OLIVER WENDELL HOLMES JR.

Peckham was born in Albany, New York, on November 8, 1838, into a family of prominent lawyers and judges. He attended private schools and studied abroad as a young man. He read the law in his father's Albany law office and was admitted to the New York bar in 1859, following the lead of his older brother, Wheeler Hazard Peckham. After almost ten years in private practice, he began his career in New York government in 1868 when he became district attorney of Albany County. He served until 1872.

An active participant in New York State DEMOCRATIC PARTY politics, Peckham and his

Rufus Wheeler Peckham. LIBRARY OF CONGRESS

brother Wheeler were aligned with the upstate wing of the party, which was often in conflict with the New York City faction that was dominated by the corrupt TAMMANY HALL regime. Wheeler Peckham was instrumental in the 1873 prosecution of the Tweed Ring, the Tammany machine run by William M. ("Boss") Tweed. His efforts would later hurt his legal career.

From 1880 to 1881, Rufus Peckham served as corporation counsel for the city of Albany. In 1883 he was elected to the New York Supreme Court (the state's trial court), and in 1886 he was appointed to the New York Court of Appeals (the state's highest court). In 1895 President

"THE GENERAL RIGHT TO MAKE A CONTRACT IN RELATION TO HIS BUSINESS IS PART OF THE LIBERTY OF THE INDIVIDUAL PROTECTED BY THE FOURTEENTH AMENDMENT . . . THE RIGHT TO PURCHASE OR TO SELL LABOR IS PART OF THE LIBERTY PROTECTED BY THIS AMENDMENT."
—RUFUS WHEELER PECKHAM

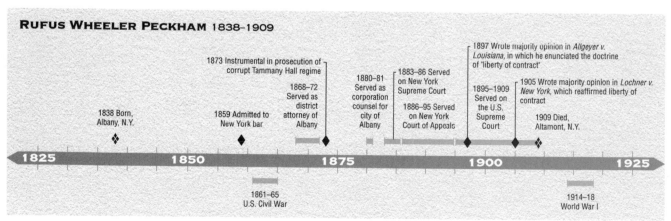

RUFUS WHEELER PECKHAM 1838–1909

1838 Born, Albany, N.Y.

1859 Admitted to New York bar

1868–72 Served as district attorney of Albany

1873 Instrumental in prosecution of corrupt Tammany Hall regime

1880–81 Served as corporation counsel for city of Albany

1883–86 Served on New York Supreme Court

1886–95 Served on New York Court of Appeals

1895–1909 Served on the U.S. Supreme Court

1897 Wrote majority opinion in *Allgeyer v. Louisiana*, in which he enunciated the doctrine of "liberty of contract"

1905 Wrote majority opinion in *Lochner v. New York*, which reaffirmed liberty of contract

1909 Died, Altamont, N.Y.

1825　　1850　　1875　　1900　　1925

1861–65 U.S. Civil War

1914–18 World War I

GROVER CLEVELAND nominated Peckham to the U.S. Supreme Court. This followed Cleveland's unsuccessful attempt to appoint Wheeler Peckham to the High Court in 1894. The appointment of Wheeler Peckham failed when New York Senators Edward Murphy Jr. and David Bennett Hill, both aligned with the New York City Democratic machine, blocked the nomination.

Rufus Peckham had little trouble winning confirmation. He joined a Supreme Court that was generally hostile to attempts by state and federal government to regulate business and the economy. Peckham fit right in. In *Allgeyer v. Louisiana*, 165 U.S. 578, 17 S. Ct. 427, 41 L. Ed. 832 (1897), he wrote the majority opinion that struck down a Louisiana insurance law as being a violation of the federal DUE PROCESS CLAUSE. He enunciated the doctrine of "liberty of contract" as a limit on state regulation of business. Government could not limit a person from entering "into all contracts which may be proper, necessary, and essential" to the conduct of a person's life.

Peckham reaffirmed liberty of contract in *Lochner*. In his majority opinion, Peckham held that a New York State law that limited bakers to no more than ten hours of work a day violated the "liberty of contract" guaranteed by the FOURTEENTH AMENDMENT, which provided that no state was to "deprive any person of life, liberty or property without due process of law." The state's power to regulate was restricted to matters of health, safety, and welfare. In Peckham's view the restriction of hours did not fit into any of these three areas and therefore the law unconstitutionally interfered with the right of bakers and bakery companies to negotiate work hours and work conditions. Justice Holmes, in his dissent, castigated Peckham and the majority for reading into the Constitution their particular economic theory and for not practicing judicial restraint.

Despite Peckham's opposition to government regulation, he did support ANTITRUST LAWS. This was consistent, in his view, with maintaining individual economic liberty. He articulated his support and helped restore some of the authority of federal antitrust efforts in *United States v. Trans-Missouri Freight Association*, 166 U.S. 290, 17 S. Ct. 540, 41 L. Ed. 1007 (1897), *United States v. Joint-Traffic Association*, 171 U.S. 505, 19 S. Ct. 25, 43 L. Ed. 259 (1898), and *Addyston Pipe & Steel Company v. United States*, 175 U.S. 211, 20 S. Ct. 96, 44 L. Ed. 136 (1899).

Peckham died on October 24, 1909, in Altamont, New York.

CROSS-REFERENCES

Labor Law.

PECULATION

The unlawful appropriation, by a depositary of public funds, of the government property entrusted to the care of the depository; the fraudulent diversion to an individual's personal use of money or goods entrusted to that person's care.

PECUNIARY

Monetary; relating to money; financial; consisting of money or that which can be valued in money.

PEDERASTY

The criminal offense of unnatural copulation between men.

The term *pederasty* is usually defined as anal intercourse of a man with a boy. Pederasty is a form of SODOMY.

PEDOPHILIA

See CHILD MOLESTATION.

PEERS

Equals; those who are an individual's equals in rank and station.

The traditional phrase *trial by a jury of his peers* means trial by a jury of citizens.

PEN REGISTER

A device that decodes or records electronic impulses, allowing outgoing numbers from a telephone to be identified.

The use of pen registers is governed by a 1986 federal statute, Pen Registers and Trap and Trace Devices (18 U.S.C.A. §§ 3121–3127). The statute also governs the use of trap devices, which are used to identify the originating number from which the wire or electronic communications were transmitted. Neither device enables the listening or recording of the actual communication.

In *Smith v. Maryland*, 442 U.S. 735, 99 S. Ct. 2577, 61 L. Ed. 2d 220 (1979), the U.S. Supreme Court upheld the constitutionality of the use of pen registers, declaring that the use of a pen register is not an invasion of privacy. In the *Smith* case, Patricia McDonough, the victim of a ROBBERY, began receiving threatening and obscene telephone calls from a man identifying himself as the robber. In one instance the man asked her to step out on her porch, and when she did, she identified the car that she had previously described to the police as belonging to the robber. The police traced the license plate number and learned that Smith was the registered owner. With this information the police asked the telephone company to install a pen register at its office to record the numbers dialed from Smith's telephone. The register revealed that a call was placed from Smith's residence to McDonough's telephone, and with this information, along with other evidence, the police obtained a warrant to search Smith's residence. During the search the police found Smith's telephone book open to the page where McDonough's name and address appeared. Smith was arrested, and McDonough identified him from a six-man lineup as the man who had robbed her.

Smith asserted that the installation of the pen register violated his constitutional rights and that "all fruits derived from the pen register" should be suppressed. The Court of Appeals of Maryland held that no constitutionally protected right of privacy existed in the numbers dialed into a telephone. Therefore, use of the pen register did not violate the FOURTH AMENDMENT, which guarantees the "right of the people to be secure in their persons, house, papers and effects, against unreasonable searches and seizures."

The Supreme Court held that in determining whether a government-initiated ELECTRONIC SURVEILLANCE constitutes a "search" within the meaning of the Fourth Amendment, it must determine "whether the person invoking the protection can claim a 'justifiable,' 'reasonable,' or a 'legitimate expectation' of privacy" (*Smith*). The Court examined the government activity that was being challenged and stated that Smith "could not claim that his property was invaded or that the police intruded into a constitutionally protected area" because the pen register was installed on the telephone company's property. The determination as to whether a "search" took place depended on whether Smith had a "legitimate expectation of privacy" regarding the numbers dialed into his telephone.

In its analysis the Court stated that it is doubtful that people expect privacy in the telephone numbers they dial. People realize that the numbers go through the telephone company once they are dialed, and they also realize that the telephone company keeps records for billing purposes of long-distance numbers dialed. Furthermore, most telephone books inform subscribers that the company has the capacity to "identify to the authorities the origin of unwelcome and troublesome calls." The Court held that Smith probably did not have an expectation of privacy in the telephone numbers he dialed but that even if he did, the expectation was not "legitimate." Therefore, the use of the pen register was not a "search" within the Fourth Amendment, and thus a SEARCH WARRANT was not required for its installation.

The dissent in *Smith*, as well as legal commentators, have expressed concern regarding the holding that there is no legitimate right of privacy in the numbers dialed into the telephone. They assert that there is a reasonable and legitimate expectation of privacy when the numbers are dialed from a person's residence. Justice POTTER STEWART, in his dissent, stated that using a telephone within a person's home is private conduct and that, without question, this conduct is entitled to Fourth and FOURTEENTH AMENDMENT protection.

Although *Smith* upheld the constitutionality of the installation of a pen register without a warrant, 18 U.S.C.A. § 3123 now requires a court order, based on a law enforcement officer's declaration that the information is relevant to an ongoing investigation, before a pen register may be installed.

Many states have enacted legislation similar to the federal statutes regulating the use of pen registers and trap and trace devices. At the state level, Caller ID and its use of Calling Party Identification has been challenged on several different theories with varying outcomes. Caller ID is a service provided by telephone companies that records each calling party's telephone number, enabling the receiving party to view the number before answering the telephone.

Proponents of Caller ID, primarily telephone companies, believe that it provides additional security to customers because it can detect and prevent obscene and harassing calls and may facilitate emergency response services. The telephone companies also state that customers are able to screen their calls with the service, thus enhancing their privacy.

Opponents of Caller ID argue that the service is an invasion of privacy because some callers may wish to remain anonymous, especially callers with unlisted telephone numbers or users of a confidential crisis hot line. Furthermore, opponents argue that Caller ID is a violation of state and federal trap or trace device statutes.

In determining the legality of Caller ID, states tend to follow either *Barasch v. Pennsylvania Public Utility Commission*, 133 Pa. Cmwlth. 285, 576 A.2d 79 (1990), affirmed 529 Pa. 523, 605 A.2d 1198 (1992), or *Southern Bell Telephone & Telegraph Co. v. Hamm*, 306 S.C. 70, 409 S.E.2d 775 (1991). In *Barasch* the court held that the use of Caller ID was a violation of Pennsylvania's constitutional right of privacy. The court reasoned that people do have a reasonable expectation that the numbers dialed into the telephone are as private as the content of the conversation. In addition, the court held that the Caller ID service violated the state's WIRETAPPING and Electronic Surveillance Control Act (18 Pa. Cons. Stat. Ann. §§ 5701–5781) (1978) governing the use of trap and trace devices. The statute provides that pen registers and trap and trace devices may not be installed without a court order unless one of the statutory exceptions exists. One of the exceptions provided in section 5771(b)(2) of the act is that if the user of the service consents to the installation of the pen register or trap and trace device, then a court order is not necessary. The Commonwealth Court's decision in *Barasch* held that because both the calling party and the recipient are users of the service, both must give their consent. The Pennsylvania Supreme Court upheld this part of the Commonwealth Court's holding.

Conversely, in *Hamm* the court held that Caller ID was not an invasion of privacy because an individual does not have a legitimate expectation of privacy in the numbers dialed into the telephone. Furthermore, although South Carolina has a similar exception to the general prohibition of trap and trace devices, the court held that "user of the service" meant only the subscriber and that therefore consent by the calling party is not necessary. The courts that follow the rationale of *Hamm* agree that unless indicated otherwise in the statutes, the purpose of trap or trace device statutes is to protect telephone users from unauthorized third-party or government intrusions and not merely to protect users from one another.

Many states have proposed or have already passed legislation authorizing the use of Caller ID. In addition, telephone companies offering Caller ID also offer per-call and per-line blocking to those individuals who wish to remain anonymous. In per-call blocking, a caller may block the transmission of his or her telephone number by dialing a specified code number before dialing. In per-line blocking, the number is blocked on every call unless the caller dials a specified code number to disable the block for a particular call.

FURTHER READINGS

Diffie, Whitfield, and Susan Landau. 1999. *Privacy on the Line: The Politics of Wiretapping and Encryption.* Cambridge, Mass.: MIT Press.

Haglund, Rich. 2003. "Applying Pen Register and Trap and Trace Devices to Internet Communications: As Technology Changes, Is Congress or the Supreme Court Best-Suited to Protect Fourth Amendment Expectations of Privacy?" *Vanderbilt Journal of Entertainment Law and Practice* 5.

Lee, Laurie Thomas. 1993. "U.S. Telecommunications Privacy Policy and Caller ID." *California Western Law Review* 30.

Mason, Geoffrey C. 1996. "Electronic Surveillance." *Georgetown Law Journal* 84.

Regan, Priscilla M. 1995. *Legislating Privacy Technology, Social Values, and Public Policy.* Chapel Hill: Univ. of North Carolina Press.

Schultz, Christian David Hammel. 2001. "Unrestricted Federal Agent: 'Carnivore' and the Need to Revise the Pen Register Statute." *Notre Dame Law Review* 76.

Zitter, Jay M. 1993. "Caller ID System, Allowing Telephone Call Recipient to Ascertain Number of Telephone from Which Call Originated, as Violation of Right to Privacy, Wiretapping Statute, or Similar Protections." *American Law Reports* 9.

CROSS-REFERENCES

Search and Seizure; Wiretapping.

PENAL

Punishable; inflicting a punishment.

PENALTY

A punitive measure that the law imposes for the performance of an act that is proscribed, or for the failure to perform a required act.

Penalty is a comprehensive term with many different meanings. It entails the concept of punishment—either corporal or pecuniary, civil or criminal—although its meaning is usually confined to pecuniary punishment. The law can impose a penalty, and a private contract can provide for its assessment. Pecuniary penalties are frequently negotiated in construction contracts, in the event that the project is not completed by the specified date.

PENDENT JURISDICTION

The discretionary power of a federal court to permit the assertion of a related state law claim, along with a federal claim between the same parties, properly before the court, provided that the federal claim and the state law claim derive from the same set of facts.

Generally, in the CIVIL LAW, claims based on federal law are heard in federal court, and claims based on state law are heard in state court. The principle of pendent jurisdiction creates an exception to this general rule by allowing a plaintiff who has filed a claim based on federal law in federal court to add a state law claim to the case. This may be done only if the state law claim arose out of the same transaction or occurrence, or nucleus of facts, that gave rise to the federal claim.

For example, assume that a plaintiff has filed suit in federal court alleging that the respondent has violated her CIVIL RIGHTS under the CIVIL RIGHTS ACT OF 1964 (42 U.S.C.A. § 2000a et seq.). Assume further that the claim arises from an incident in which the plaintiff was denied service at a public restaurant based on her perceived national origin. If the plaintiff was also physically harmed by the respondent in the incident, she may want to file claims for ASSAULT AND BATTERY. Assault and battery of a private party are state law claims; no federal laws exist under which the plaintiff could bring such claims. Pendent jurisdiction would give the fed-

eral court the authority to hear the assault and battery claims because they arose out of the same incident that gave rise to the federal civil rights claims.

Pendent jurisdiction is a rule of judicial convenience and efficiency. If federal courts could not hear state law claims, many plaintiffs would be forced to present two cases in two courts involving essentially the same matter. Such a rule would be unduly expensive for plaintiffs, would increase the number of cases in the court system, and could lead to seemingly inconsistent results from different courts concerning related matters.

CROSS-REFERENCES

Jurisdiction.

PENDENTE LITE

[Latin, Pending the litigation.] During the actual progress of a lawsuit.

PENDING

Begun, but not yet completed; during; before the conclusion of; prior to the completion of; unsettled; in the process of adjustment.

A lawsuit is said to be pending from its inception until the issuance of a final judgment by a court. The phrase *pending appeal* refers to the time before an appeal is taken, as well as to the period during which an appeal is in progress.

❖ PENDLETON, GEORGE HUNT

George Hunt Pendleton was a prominent nineteenth-century lawyer, congressman, senator, and ambassador who played the central role in passing the Civil Service Act, also known as the

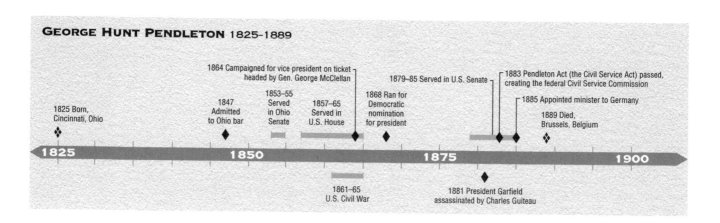

GEORGE HUNT PENDLETON 1825–1889

1825 Born, Cincinnati, Ohio

1847 Admitted to Ohio bar

1853–55 Served in Ohio Senate

1857–65 Served in U.S. House

1864 Campaigned for vice president on ticket headed by Gen. George McClellan

1868 Ran for Democratic nomination for president

1879–85 Served in U.S. Senate

1883 Pendleton Act (the Civil Service Act) passed, creating the federal Civil Service Commission

1885 Appointed minister to Germany

1889 Died, Brussels, Belgium

1825   1850   1875   1900

1861–65 U.S. Civil War

1881 President Garfield assassinated by Charles Guiteau

Pendleton Act of 1883 (5 U.S.C.A. § 1101 et seq.). The Pendleton Act established a federal civil service system that was based on merit rather than on political patronage.

Pendleton was born on July 29, 1825, in Cincinnati, Ohio. After his admission to the Ohio bar in 1847, he established a law practice in Cincinnati. He soon turned his attention toward politics. A lifelong member of the DEMOCRATIC PARTY, Pendleton was elected to the Ohio Senate in 1853, where he served for two years. In 1857 he was elected to the U.S. House of Representatives, where he served until 1865. During the Civil War, Pendleton gained national prominence for his opposition to President Abraham Lincoln's suspension of HABEAS CORPUS and other wartime measures that restricted civil liberties. In 1864 he was the Democratic vice-presidential candidate, campaigning for peace between the North and the South on a ticket headed by Union General George B. McClellan. Lincoln and Vice President ANDREW JOHNSON won reelection.

After the war Pendleton became the leader of the greenbacker movement, which sought to redeem Civil War bonds in paper currency (greenbacks) instead of gold. His advocacy of this cause cost him the 1868 Democratic presidential nomination, because East Coast Democrats disagreed with the scheme.

Pendleton did not reenter national politics until 1879, when he was elected to the U.S. Senate. By 1883 the federal government was plagued by inefficiency and corruption, most of which was attributed to the way federal employees were hired. Under the patronage system (also known as the "spoils system"), federal employees were hired and fired for political reasons. It was understood that presidents were entitled to reward political allies with cabinet posts, judgeships, and diplomatic posts, but the spoils system extended to routine and low-level government workers. This created employee turnover when a president left office and the opposition party came into power.

The 1881 assassination of President JAMES GARFIELD by a disappointed office seeker led to the passage of the Pendleton Act in 1883. The act, which created a federal Civil Service Commission that administered a merit-based, open selection process for hiring government employees, began the process of professionalizing the federal government. Politics and factors such as religion and nationality were to have no

George H. Pendleton.
LIBRARY OF CONGRESS

bearing on the hiring of civil servants. Although the act initially covered only about 10 percent of the jobs, subsequent legislation increased the percentage and it grew steadily.

Pendleton's efforts at patronage reform cost him his Senate seat. Democratic leaders who preferred political patronage prevented his return to the Senate for a second term in 1885. President GROVER CLEVELAND appointed Pendleton minister to Germany in that year. He served in this position until his death on November 24, 1889, in Brussels, Belgium.

FURTHER READINGS

Case, H. Manley. 1986. "Federal Employee Job Rights: The Pendleton Act of 1883 to the Civil Service Reform Act of 1978." *Howard Law Journal* 29 (spring).

PENITENTIARY

A prison or place of confinement where persons convicted of felonies serve their term of imprisonment.

CROSS-REFERENCES

Jail.

PENNSYLVANIA CONSTITUTION OF 1776

In 1776 Pennsylvania enacted its first state constitution in direct response to the Declaration of Independence and the instructions of the Second Continental Congress to the colonies to reject British rule. Dedicated to the idea of placing authority in the hands of the people, and specifying a broad range of rights, the constitution proved to be controversial. Over the next fourteen years, criticism of the document came both from within Pennsylvania and from across the new nation, and the state replaced the constitution in 1790.

With the signing of the Declaration of Independence, the American Revolution had begun. Congress issued two resolutions in May 1776 calling for the colonies to reject British rule and establish governments based on the authority of the people. Pennsylvania had refused to join the rebellion, and Congress hoped to win its support. Instead, revolutionaries in Pennsylvania quickly held public meetings and devoted themselves to electing representatives to a constitutional convention. The noted American statesman and philosopher BENJAMIN FRANKLIN was instrumental in organizing and leading the endeavor. The constitution was debated and revised for four months and was approved on September 28, 1776.

Although five other states also adopted constitutions during this time, the Pennsylvania document was unique. In outlook, the constitution bore the mark of the French philosopher JEAN-JACQUES ROUSSEAU, a critic of representative government who viewed it as a necessary evil. Thus, under the Pennsylvania Constitution, government would aspire to the democratic ideal of maximum participation by citizens while simultaneously ensuring fair, just, and LEGAL REPRESENTATION by politicians.

The constitution pursued this goal in several ways. It created a unicameral legislature— having only one body—a feature unique among American states. Legislators were to be "persons most noted for wisdom and virtue" and were required to swear that they would do nothing "injurious to the people." In an effort to rotate the largest number of people in and out of office, the rules mandated annual elections and limited terms to four out of every seven years. The framers had two goals: to make representatives more responsive to the people, and to allow bad politicians to be removed from office swiftly. To ensure participation by citizens, lawmaking itself was controlled. No bill could be enacted until it had been printed for general reading and, except in rare instances, until a year after its printing.

Strikingly, no provision was made for a state governor. Instead, the executive function fell to an elected twelve-member executive council. These members served staggered three-year terms, making them ineligible for reelection until four years after their terms ended. The framers believed that this approach not only served to train more citizens for political leadership, it also helped to thwart what they most detested: "an inconvenient aristocracy" of politicians. The council and the legislature elected a president and vice president. The president could not exercise any power—whether appointing judges or commanding the state's militia—without the consent of a majority of the council.

Just as the constitution placed restraints on lawmakers, so did it look skeptically at the judiciary. Pennsylvania judges were not given independence. The legislature could revoke judgeships, which lasted seven years, for "misbehavior" at any time. As an additional limitation on the judiciary, the constitution created a special body called the Council of Censors, which met every seven years to review the constitutionality of laws.

The rights granted by the Pennsylvania Constitution were among the most liberal in the United States at that time. The right to vote was based on a minimal property interest; it belonged to free men above the age of twenty-one who had resided in the state for one year and had paid public taxes, as well as to the sons of freeholders. The constitution defended the free exercise of religion, stating that no "man who acknowledges the being of a God, [may] be justly deprived or abridged of any civil right as a citizen" regardless of his "religious sentiments or peculiar mode of religious worship." Other significant liberties included the right to buy one's release from military service, not to be taxed without the consent of lawmakers, and to receive liberal DUE PROCESS in court.

Despite its idealism the Pennsylvania Constitution was neither a success at home nor outside the state. Critics complained about its heavy reliance on a revolving, and extremely powerful, legislature. Influential forces in the state, particularly those in business, attacked the uncertain conditions that it created for commerce. The Federalists, who believed in a strong federal government, detested its independence. Lawyers and judges decried the weakened judiciary. By 1790 the experiment had ended: the state replaced the constitution with one modeled on the U.S. Constitution's SEPARATION OF POWERS and its adherence to the idea of a republic.

FURTHER READINGS

Williams, Robert F. 1989. "The State Constitutions of the Founding Decade: Pennsylvania's Radical Constitution and Its Influences on American Constitutionalism." *Temple Law Review* 62 (summer).

Witte, Harry L. 1995. "Judicial Selection in the People's Democratic Republic of Pennsylvania: Here the People Rule?" *Temple Law Review* 68 (fall).

PENNY STOCKS

Inexpensive issues of stock, typically selling at less than $1 a share, in companies that often are newly formed or involved in highly speculative ventures.

Penny stocks are usually available for sale over-the-counter, that is, among brokers and customers themselves, as opposed to being listed on the American Stock Exchange or the New York Stock Exchange.

PENOLOGY

The science of prison administration and rehabilitation of criminals.

PENSION

A benefit, usually money, paid regularly to retired employees or their survivors by private businesses and federal, state, and local governments. Employers are not required to establish pension benefits but do so to attract qualified employees.

The first pension plan in the United States was created by the American Express Company in 1875. A few LABOR UNIONS and state and local governments began to offer pension plans shortly thereafter, and by 1935 governments in half the states and many businesses were offering pension plans. In 1997 about half of all U.S. workers had pension plans.

Employers establish pension plans by paying a certain amount of money into a pension fund. The money paid into this fund is not taxed to the employer, and it is not taxed to the employee until the employee retires and begins to collect pension benefits. The employer gives control of the pension fund to a trustee, who may invest the money in stocks and bonds and other financial endeavors to increase the fund. Some pension plans require the employee to make a small, periodic contribution to the fund.

The amount of pension that a pensioner receives depends on the type of pension plan. Pension plans generally can be divided into two categories: defined benefit plans and defined contribution plans. A defined benefit plan provides a set amount of benefits to a pensioner. Under a defined contribution plan, the employer places a certain amount of money in the employee's name into the pension fund and makes no promises concerning the level of pension benefits that the employee will receive upon retirement. Employers using defined contribution plans contribute an amount into the pension fund based on the employee's salary. As a result, higher-paid employees receive larger pensions than do lower-paid employees.

The same is true for defined benefit plans: employers tend to offer larger pensions to higher-paid employees. The difference between the two types of plans is that in a defined contribution plan, the employee assumes the risk of investment failure because the funds are not insured by the federal government. Under most defined benefit plans, the employer assumes the risk that pension funds will not be available. Employees assume little risk because most funds are insured by the federal government to a certain limit.

The most important issue to pensioners is the potential loss of their pension benefits. This issue is of less concern when the government is the employer because governments have access to additional funds. Such is not the case with private businesses. Before the 1970s employees did not always receive their promised pension benefits. An employee could lose his or her pension if the employer went out of business and employers could fire long-time employees just before their pensions vested to avoid paying pensions. Citing the profound effect that pension plans have on interstate commerce and the economic security of the country, Congress enacted the EMPLOYEE RETIREMENT INCOME SECURITY ACT of 1974 (ERISA) (29 U.S.C.A. § 1001 et seq.) to regulate pension plans created by private businesses other than religious organizations.

ERISA is a complex collection of federal statutes that take precedence over most state pension laws. The act encourages the creation of pension funds by making employer contributions to pension funds tax free. ERISA also is designed to ensure that pension funds promised to an employee will be available. It establishes rules for the vesting of pensions based on the employee's age and length of employment. Under the law an employer using a pension plan that is not funded by the employees may choose one of several methods for vesting of pensions.

An employer may allow all pension benefits to become nonforfeitable once the employee has completed five years of employment. In the alternative, an employee may be guaranteed a percentage of pension funds according to length of service, with the percentage increasing as the length of service increases. An employee with three years of service is guaranteed 20 percent of the derived benefit from the employer contributions to the pension plan. After four years the employee has a right to 40 percent of the benefits; after five years the percentage is 60; after six years the percentage is 80; and an employee who completes seven years of service becomes fully vested. An employee is always entitled to the amount of money she or he has contributed to a pension fund.

Under ERISA, the fiduciaries who control the pension funds must meet certain reporting requirements. The act restricts the kinds of investments that trustees can make using pension funds. It mandates that employers make annual contributions to pension funds, and it devises formulas for setting minimum contribution levels. These formulas are created in actuarial tables based on such factors as the turnover of the participants in the plan, the life expectancy of the participants, the amount of money in pensions promised to employees, and the success of the pension fund's investments. The act authorizes criminal penalties for violators of pension laws and provides CIVIL LAW remedies to victims of pension misuse or abuse.

An employer who is delinquent in making contributions to the pension fund may have to pay penalties. ERISA requires employers to report to pension holders significant facts regarding the pension fund, such as a summary describing in clear language how the plan works, what benefits it provides, and how such benefits can be received. The employer also must report annually to each employee the amount of benefits that have accrued and have vested, and the earliest date on which the employee's pension will vest as of the date of the report.

ERISA created the Pension Benefit Guaranty Corporation (PBGC) to ensure the payment of certain benefits of pension plans. PBGC is a government corporation within the U.S. DEPARTMENT OF LABOR that is governed by the secretaries of labor, commerce, and treasury, and funded by premiums collected from pension plans. If an employer is unable to meet pension obligations, the PBGC may make the payments for the employer. PBGC covers only defined benefit pension plans, with the exception of church-based pension plans. Religious organizations are excepted because courts and legislatures consider church-based pensions to be an ecclesiastical matter beyond the authority of the law.

An employee cannot lose pension benefits by retiring early. Under defined benefit plans, the employee may begin to receive pension benefits upon reaching the normal retirement age of 65 years. If an employee retires before reaching age 59.5 and begins drawing from his pension, his pension payments are taxed at a 10 percent annual rate in addition to any regular income taxes. This excise tax is levied because pension funds are designed to promote security after retirement.

The excise tax does not apply to a pension given to a surviving spouse when the employee dies before the pension is fully paid, even if the employee dies before reaching age 59.5. Employees who become disabled before age 59.5 do not have to pay the excise tax, nor do persons who specifically choose to receive the pension payments as an ANNUITY or periodically. In addition, the excise tax does not apply to pensions of employees over the age of 55 years who have separated from their employer, certain pensions paid for medical expenses, and pension payments made pursuant to certain divorce-related court orders.

ERISA does not regulate pension plans with 25 or fewer participants or plans that are solely for business partners or a sole proprietor. Employees of businesses not covered by ERISA may look to state statutes governing pensions that contain regulations and requirements similar to those in ERISA.

Congress refined the tax consequences of pensions in January 1996. Under the Pension Source Act (Pub. L. No. 104-95, amending title 4 of U.S.C.A. § 114), a state that imposes income taxes may not tax pension benefits earned in the state if the pensioner is living in a state that does not impose personal INCOME TAX.

Pensions are an attractive component of employee compensation packages. The money that the employer withholds during the working life of the employee is not taxed, and the money in a pension fund can be increased through investments. When the pensioned employee retires, she or he can ask for the entire pension in one lump sum or can take the pension as an annuity, which is a series of payments that lasts for a specified period of time. If the retiree lives long enough, she or he will receive more money than the employer originally withheld. If the pensioner dies before the pension is fully paid, her or his surviving spouse or another designated survivor may receive the remainder of the pension. A retiree who has worked at several companies may receive several pensions.

Individuals who are self-employed have their own pension options. A self-employed worker may establish a KEOGH PLAN, which is a type of retirement plan for self-employed workers that is comparable to a pension plan. Under a Keogh plan, the worker makes tax-free payments into a fund and receives larger payments upon retirement.

An INDIVIDUAL RETIREMENT ACCOUNT (IRA) is another way to provide for security in retirement. An IRA is a personal retirement account that workers may establish in addition to, or instead of, a pension. Employers may establish similar personal retirement accounts for their employees. These accounts are called 401K plans, after the section of the INTERNAL REVENUE CODE that authorizes them. Under a 401K plan, a worker deposits a portion of his or her gross earnings into the account to avoid income tax on that portion of the earnings. The earnings are subject to taxation when the retiring worker receives them. If the worker is in a lower tax bracket by retirement, he or she will end up paying less tax on the portion of the earnings in the IRA.

Pension benefits are distinct from other retirement benefits such as SOCIAL SECURITY and medical assistance. A pension may reduce slightly the amount of Social Security benefits that a government employee receives.

FURTHER READINGS

Abramson, Stephen. 2003. *Financial Professional's Guide to Qualified Retirement Plans: Planning, Implementation, Operation, and Compliance.* 2d ed. New York: Aspen.

Driggers, Martin S., Jr. 1996. "Minister's Pension Contract Is an 'Ecclesiastical Matter' Not Reviewable by the Court." *South Carolina Law Review* 48 (autumn).

Gregory, David. 1987. "The Scope of ERISA Preemption of State Law: A Study in Effective Federalism." *University of Pittsburgh Law Review* 48 (winter).

Lantry, Terry L. 1996. "Retirees' Pensions Insulated from State Income Tax." *Taxation for Lawyers* 25 (November–December).

Lewis, Barbara, and Dan Otto. 2002. "Sunset Cruise; Take Advantage of New Laws to Make Your Pensions More Valuable." *Los Angeles Daily Journal* (January 15).

Peterson, Pete. 1996. *Will America Grow Up Before It Grows Old?: How the Coming Social Security Crisis Threatens You, Your Family, and Your Country.* New York: David McKay.

Snyder, Michael B. 1999. *Qualified Plan Investments: Fiduciary Responsibilities and Strategies.* St. Paul, Minn.: West Group.

CROSS-REFERENCES

Social Security.

PENT ROAD

A street that is closed at its terminal points.

The term *pent*, which means penned or confined, is used to distinguish this type of road from an open highway that leads to other thoroughfares. Pent roads are frequently adjacent to the lands of persons who are constructing connecting arteries across their own property to secure needed outlets.

PENTAGON PAPERS

See NEW YORK TIMES CO. V. UNITED STATES.

PENUMBRA

The rights guaranteed by implication in a constitution or the implied powers of a rule.

The original and literal meaning of *penumbra* is "a space of partial illumination between the perfect shadow . . . on all sides and the full light" (*Merriam Webster's Collegiate Dictionary,* 10th ed., 1996). The term was created and introduced by astronomer Johannes Kepler in 1604 to describe the shadows that occur during eclipses. However, in legal terms penumbra is most often used as a metaphor describing a doctrine that refers to implied powers of the federal government. The doctrine is best known from the Supreme Court decision of GRISWOLD V. CONNECTICUT, 381 U.S. 479, 85 S. Ct. 1678, 14 L. Ed. 2d 510 (1965), where Justice WILLIAM O. DOUGLAS used it to describe the concept of an individual's constitutional right of privacy.

The history of the legal use of the penumbra metaphor can be traced to a federal decision written by Justice STEPHEN J. FIELD in the 1871 decision of *Montgomery v. Bevans,* 17 F.Cas. 628 (9th C.C.D. Cal.). (At the time, Field was performing circuit duty while a member of the Supreme Court.) Since the *Montgomery* decision, the penumbra metaphor has not been used often. In fact, more than half of its original uses can be attributed to just four judges: OLIVER

WENDELL HOLMES, JR., LEARNED HAND, BEN-JAMIN N. CARDOZO, and William O. Douglas.

In an 1873 article on the theory of TORTS, Justice Holmes used the term penumbra to describe the "gray area where logic and principle falter." In later decisions, Justice Holmes developed the penumbra doctrine as representing the "outer bounds of authority emanating from a law." Justice Holmes usually used the word in an attempt to describe the need to draw ARBITRARY lines when forming legislation. For instance, in the decision of *Danforth v. Groton Water Co.,* Holmes referred to constitutional rules as lacking mathematical exactness, stating that they, "[l]ike those of the COMMON LAW, end in a penumbra where the Legislature has a certain freedom in fixing the line, as has been recognized with regard to the police power" (178 Mass. 472, 476–77, 59 N.E. 1033, 1034 [1901]).

Judge Hand expanded the meaning of the word in opinions written between 1915 and 1950 by using it to indicate the vague borders of words or concepts. He used it to emphasize the difficulty in defining and interpreting statutes, contracts, TRADEMARKS, or ideas.

Justice Cardozo's use of the penumbra metaphor in opinions written between 1934 and 1941 was similar to Holmes's application, but Justice Douglas took a different approach. Rather than using it to highlight the difficulty of drawing lines or determining the meaning of words or concepts, he used the term when he wanted to refer to a peripheral area or an indistinct boundary of something specific.

Douglas's most famous use of penumbra is in the *Griswold* decision. In the *Griswold* case, appellants Estelle Griswold, executive director of the Planned Parenthood League of Connecticut, and Dr. C. Lee Buxton, a medical professor at Yale Medical School and director of the league's office in New Haven, were convicted for prescribing contraceptive devices and giving contraceptive advice to married persons in violation of a Connecticut statute. They challenged the constitutionality of the statute, which made it unlawful to use any drug or medicinal article for the purpose of preventing conception, on behalf of the married persons with whom they had a professional relationship. The Supreme Court held that the statute was unconstitutional

The concept of penumbra involves trying to divine the spirit of the law from its letter. In 1965, Estelle Griswold (left) of Planned Parenthood and Mrs. Ernest Jahncke of the Parenthood League react to the Supreme Court's use of this method to interpret a Connecticut statute forbidding the distribution of contraceptives to married couples as a violation of their privacy rights.
BETTMANN/CORBIS

because it was a violation of a person's right to privacy. In his opinion, Douglas stated that the specific guarantees of the BILL OF RIGHTS have penumbras "formed by emanations from those guarantees that help give them life and substance," and that the right to privacy exists within this area.

Since *Griswold,* the penumbra doctrine has primarily been used to represent implied powers that emanate from a specific rule, thus extending the meaning of the rule into its periphery or penumbra.

FURTHER READINGS

Greely, Henry T. 1989. "A Footnote to 'Penumbra' in *Griswold v. Connecticut.*" *Constitutional Commentary* 6.

Helscher, David. 1994. "*Griswold v. Connecticut* and the Unenumerated Right of Privacy." *Northern Illinois University Law Review* 15.

Henly, Burr. 1987. "'Penumbra': The Roots of a Legal Metaphor." *Hastings Constitutional Law Quarterly* 15.

McLaughlin, Gerald. 1999. "Creating a Clear and Unequivocal Standard for Letter of Credit Notices: The Penumbra of the UCP." *Journal of Banking and Finance Law and Practice* 10 (September): 263–64.

Worsham, Julia B.L. 1999. "Privacy Outside of the Penumbra: A Discussion of Hawaii's Right to Privacy." *The University of Hawaii Law Review* 21 (summer): 273–315.

CROSS-REFERENCES

Judicial Review; Jurisprudence.

PEONAGE

A condition of enforced servitude by which a person is restrained of his or her liberty and compelled to labor in payment of some debt or obligation.

CROSS-REFERENCES

Involuntary Servitude.

PEOPLE

The aggregate of the individuals who comprise a state or a nation.

In a more restricted sense, as generally used in CONSTITUTIONAL LAW, the entire body of those citizens of a state or a nation who are invested with political power for political purposes (the qualified voters).

PEOPLE FOR THE ETHICAL TREATMENT OF ANIMALS

People for the Ethical Treatment of Animals (PETA) is an international nonprofit organization that supports ANIMAL RIGHTS and has spawned a tremendous amount of conflict and controversy from its inception. The organization, which has been headquartered in Norfolk, Virginia, since 1996, was founded in 1980 by Ingrid Newkirk, who had worked at an animal shelter and then as a deputy sheriff in Montgomery County, Maryland, where she focused on animal-cruelty cases. She was also chief of Animal Disease Control for the Public Health Commission of the District of Columbia.

Newkirk became increasingly horrified at the inhumane treatment of animals that she encountered in her work, particularly in so-called "factory farms," which confine hundreds to thousands of animals (usually chickens, pigs, turkeys, or cows) in one facility, and in research laboratories. While other organizations are dedicated to seeing that animals are treated humanely, none is as radical in both outlook and strategies as PETA. Newkirk has been quoted as saying, "When it comes to feelings like hunger, pain, and thirst, a rat is a pig is a dog is a boy." The organization's philosophy is uncompromising: "animals are not ours to eat, wear, experiment on, or use for entertainment." The organization's goals to inform and educate the public and policy-makers about animal abuse and to stop such abuse wherever possible are carried out in a number of ways.

PETA is a grassroots organization run by hundreds of volunteers under the leadership of Newkirk, Dan Mathews, vice-president of campaigns, and Bruce Friedrich, director of vegan outreach. The vegan philosophy prohibits eating, wearing, or using any kind of animal products including milk, eggs, honey, and wool or leather products.

PETA has been called "the most successful radical organization in America." With over 750,000 members and supporters in the United States and around the world, the organization has an annual budget of approximately $14 million, almost all of which is raised by small contributions from individuals.

In addition to familiar protest tactics such as letter-writing campaigns and corporate boycotts, the organization makes prolific use of multiple Web sites that proselytize against numerous issues, including the fur trade (furis-murder.com), fishing (fishinghurts.com), zoos (wildlifepimps.com), tobacco companies that continue to do animal testing (smokinganimals.com), and fast food restaurants. PETA has been particularly successful in appealing to youth between the ages of 13 and 24 who are interested in the humane treatment of animals as well as vegetarianism and veganism. The organization's youth-oriented Web site peta2.com advertises PETA as the "largest and boldest animal rights organization in the world."

PETA supporters have staged hundreds of flamboyant activities in the United States and Europe in which they have sprayed red paint on fur coats while the coats were being worn, tossed containers of currency covered with fake blood on audiences at the International Fur Fair, dropped a dead raccoon on the plate of a *Vogue* magazine editor as she dined at a fashionable New York restaurant, sat naked in cages and crawled along streets wearing leg-hold traps on their feet.

In November 2002, PETA activists disrupted a Victoria's Secret lingerie show that was being watched on network television by 11 million viewers. Despite extremely high security, several women managed to leap onto the stage in front of Brazilian supermodel Gisele Bundchen with signs that read "Gisele: Fur Scum." Bundchen had been featured in a series of ads promoting a line of Blackglama brand mink furs. Although the PETA supporters were quickly arrested and jailed, the subsequent news stories and video clips of the incident were played throughout the world, eclipsing coverage of the show and gaining maximum publicity for PETA.

Like its other strategies, PETA advertising campaigns are designed to create maximum interest by both attracting and repelling political and public attention. Some of PETA ad campaigns featuring nude female celebrities under the slogan "I'd rather go naked than wear fur" have drawn the ire of both conservative and feminist groups. When PETA ran a series of ads lampooning the dairy industry's "Got Milk?" campaign with a "Got Beer?" ad that ran in numerous college newspapers, the organization was attacked by MOTHERS AGAINST DRUNK DRIVING (MADD) for making light of alcohol abuse by college students.

In February 2003, PETA launched what many considered its most inflammatory campaign to date, a traveling exhibit called "Holocaust on Your Plate," which compared human abuse and mistreatment of animals to the torture, cruelty, and death inflicted by the Nazis on concentration camp victims. Numerous writers and organizations including the ANTI-DEFAMATION LEAGUE denounced the PETA exhibit, but the organization succeeded once again in making the news.

Other organizations have sought IRS revocation of the PETA nonexempt status citing the violence of the rhetoric used by PETA leaders and activists and its support of the Animal Liberation Front, which has been labeled a "domestic terrorist" group and openly claims to use damage and destruction of property to save animals.

Even the organization's critics, however, agree that PETA has been instrumental in a number of victories ranging from closing laboratories where animals were mistreated to getting cosmetic corporations to stop animal testing and persuading car manufacturers not to use animals as auto crash test subjects. PETA also successfully applied pressure to various fast food corporations to add vegetarian options to their menus and to institute regulations for better treatment of poultry and livestock by their producers.

FURTHER READINGS

Guillermo, Kathy Snow. 1993. *Monkey Business: The Disturbing Case that Launched the Animal Rights Movement.* Washington, D.C.: National Press Books.

People for the Ethical Treatment of Animals. Available online at <www.peta.org> (accessed August 1, 2003).

Specter, Michael. 2003. "The Extremist: The Woman Behind the Most Successful Radical Group in America." *New Yorker* (April 14).

CROSS-REFERENCES

Animal Rights.

PER

[Latin, By, through, or by means of.]

PER CAPITA

[Latin, By the heads or polls.] A term used in the DESCENT AND DISTRIBUTION *of the estate of one who dies without a will. It means to share and share alike according to the number of individuals.*

In a per capita distribution, an equal share of an estate is given to each heir, all of whom stand in equal degree of relationship from a decedent. For example, a woman died intestate, that is, without a will. Her husband and three children predeceased her, and her only living heirs are her ten grandchildren. These grandchildren will take per capita. In other words, each grandchild will receive one-tenth of the estate.

Per capita differs from per stirpes, where persons do not inherit in their individual capacity but take as part of a group represented by a deceased ancestor closer in line to the decedent.

PER CURIAM

[Latin, By the court.] A phrase used to distinguish an opinion of the whole court from an opinion written by any one judge.

Sometimes *per curiam* signifies an opinion written by the chief justice or presiding judge; it can also refer to a brief oral announcement of the disposition of a case by the court that is unaccompanied by a written opinion.

PER QUOD

[Latin, Whereby.] With respect to a complaint in a civil action, a phrase that prefaces the recital of the consequences of certain acts as a ground of special harm to the plaintiff.

At COMMON LAW, this term acquired two meanings in the law of DEFAMATION: with respect to slander, it signified that proof of special damages was required; in regard to LIBEL, it meant that proof of extrinsic circumstances was required.

Words that are actionable *per quod* do not furnish a basis for a lawsuit upon their face but are only litigable because of extrinsic facts showing the circumstances under which they were uttered or the damages ensuing to the defamed party therefrom.

CROSS-REFERENCES

Extrinsic Evidence; Libel and Slander.

PER SE

[Latin, In itself.] Simply as such; in its own nature without reference to its relation.

In the law of DEFAMATION, slander *per se* refers to certain language that is actionable as slander in and of itself without proof of special damages, such as the situation in which a person is falsely accused of having committed a crime. Defamation per se is in contradistinction to defamation per quod, which requires proof of special damages.

CROSS-REFERENCES

Libel and Slander.

PER STIRPES

[Latin, By roots or stocks; by representation.] A term used to denote a method used in dividing the estate of a person. A person who takes per stirpes,

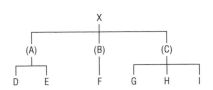

Per Stirpes vs. Per Capita

- Per Capita, D gets 1/6th; F gets 1/6; G gets 1/6th
- Per Stirpes, D gets 1/6th; F gets 1/3; G gets 1/9th

SOURCE: Professor Don R. Castleman, "Intestate Succession—Lineal Descendents," class notes for Decedents Estates and Trusts course, Wake Forest University School of Law.

sometimes called by right of representation, does not inherit in an individual capacity but as a member of a group.

In a per stirpes distribution, a group represents a deceased ancestor. The group takes the proportional share to which the deceased ancestor would have been entitled if still living.

For example, a man died intestate; his wife predeceased him. He had four children, three of whom are still living at the time of his death. The deceased child had three children, all still living. These three grandchildren will share equally in one-fourth of their grandfather's estate, the share the deceased parent would have taken if still alive. The three living children will also each receive one-fourth of the estate.

Per stirpes differs from per capita, in which an equal share is given to each of a number of persons who all stand in equal degree of relationship to the deceased.

CROSS-REFERENCES

Descent and Distribution.

PERCENTAGE LEASE

A rental agreement, usually with respect to a retail business property, whereby a portion of the gross sales or net sales of the tenant is used to determine the rent.

There is generally a provision in a percentage lease that calls for a minimum or base rental. It protects the lessor in the event of poor sales.

PEREMPTORY CHALLENGE

The right to challenge a juror without assigning, or being required to assign, a reason for the challenge.

During the selection of a jury, both parties to the proceeding may challenge prospective jurors for a lack of impartiality, known as a challenge for cause. A party may challenge an unlimited number of prospective jurors for cause. Parties also may exercise a limited number of peremptory challenges. These challenges permit a party to remove a prospective juror without giving a reason for the removal.

Peremptory challenges provide a more impartial and better qualified jury. Peremptory challenges allow an attorney to reject a potential juror for real or imagined partiality that would be difficult to demonstrate under the challenge for cause category. These challenges, however, have become more difficult to exercise because the U.S. Supreme Court has forbidden peremptory strikes based on race or gender.

Parties do not have a federal constitutional right to exercise peremptory challenges. Peremptory challenges are granted by statute or by case law. The number of challenges is usually determined by statute, but some jurisdictions allow the trial court to grant additional peremptory challenges. In federal court each side is entitled to three peremptory challenges. If more than two parties are involved in the proceeding, the court may either grant additional challenges or restrict the parties to the minimum number of challenges.

Peremptory challenges came under legal attack in the 1980s. Critics claimed that white prosecutors used their peremptory challenges to remove African Americans from the jury when the criminal defendant was also African American because the prosecutors thought that the potential jurors would be sympathetic to a member of their own race. This constituted RACIAL DISCRIMINATION and a violation of the Fourteenth Amendment's EQUAL PROTECTION CLAUSE.

The U.S. Supreme Court, in *Batson v. Kentucky,* 476 U.S. 79, 106 S. Ct. 1712, 90 L. Ed. 2d 69 (1986), prohibited prosecutors from excluding prospective jurors on the basis of race. Under the *Batson* test, a defendant may object to a prosecutor's peremptory challenge. The prosecutor then must "come forward with a neutral explanation for challenging black jurors." If the prosecutor cannot offer a neutral explanation, the court will not excuse the juror.

The Court extended this holding in criminal proceedings in two later cases. In *Powers v.*

Ohio, 499 U.S. 400, 111 S. Ct. 1364, 113 L. Ed. 2d 411 (1991), the Court broadened the *Batson* rule by stating that a defendant need not be of the same race as the excluded juror in order to successfully challenge the juror's exclusion. In *Georgia v. McCollum,* 505 U.S. 42, 112 S. Ct. 2348, 120 L. Ed. 2d 33 (1992), the Court held that the defense's exercise of peremptory challenges to strike African American jurors on the basis of their race was equally forbidden. Previously, the court had ruled in *Edmonson v. Leesville Concrete Co.,* 500 U.S. 614, 111 S. Ct. 2077, 114 L. Ed. 2d 660 (1991), that in civil trials a private party could not exclude prospective jurors on account of their race by using peremptory challenges. This series of decisions makes any racial exclusion in jury selection constitutionally suspect.

The Supreme Court has also forbidden peremptory challenges based on gender. In *J. E. B. v. Alabama,* 511 U.S. 127, 114 S. Ct. 1419, 128 L. Ed. 2d 89 (1994), the Court ruled that striking jurors on the basis of gender serves to perpetuate stereotypes that are prejudicial and based on historical discrimination. No overriding STATE INTEREST justified peremptory challenges on the basis of gender. Permitting gender-based strikes could also have undermined the *Batson* holding, because gender might be used as an excuse for racial discrimination.

In an extension of *Batson,* the Supreme Court of Connecticut ruled that the Equal Protection Clause barred the prosecutor from striking prospective jurors based on their religious affiliation. The court, in *State v. Hodge,* 726 A.2d 531 (Conn.1999), distinguished religious beliefs and religious affiliations. It held that litigants could strike prospective jurors whose religious beliefs would prevent them from performing their duties as jurors.

FURTHER READINGS

Beck, Cobrun R. 1998. "The Current State of the Peremptory Challenge." *William and Mary Law Review* 39 (February).

Fahey, William F. 1996. "Peremptory Challenges." *Federal Lawyer* 43 (October).

Hoffman, Morris B. 1997. "Peremptory Challenges Should Be Abolished: A Trial Judge's Perspective." *University of Chicago Law Review* 64 (summer).

Schwartz, Edward P., and Warren F. Schwartz. 1996. "The Challenge of Peremptory Challenges." *Journal of Law, Economics & Organization* 12 (October).

CROSS-REFERENCES

Case Law; Federal Courts; Jurisdiction; Jury; Trial.

PEREMPTORY RULING

An immediate and absolute decision by the court on some point of law that is rendered without consideration of alternatives.

PERFECT

Complete; finished; executed; enforceable; without defect; merchantable; marketable.

To perfect a title is to record or register it in the proper place so that one's ownership will be established against all others.

PERFORMANCE

The fulfillment or accomplishment of a promise, contract, or other obligation according to its terms.

Part performance entails the completion of some portion of what either party to a contract has agreed to do. With respect to the sale of goods, the payment—or receipt and acceptance of goods—makes an oral sales contract, otherwise unenforceable because of the STATUTE OF FRAUDS, enforceable in regard to goods for which payment has been made and accepted or which have been received and accepted.

SPECIFIC PERFORMANCE is an equitable doctrine that compels a party to execute the agreement according to its terms where monetary damages would be inadequate compensation for the breach of an agreement, as in the case of a sale of land. In regard to the sale of goods, a court orders specific performance only where the goods are unique or in other proper circumstances.

PERIL

The designated contingency, risk, or hazard against which an insured seeks to protect himself or herself when purchasing a policy of insurance.

Among the various types of perils for which insurance coverage is available are fire, theft, illness, and death.

PERJURY

A crime that occurs when an individual willfully makes a false statement during a judicial proceeding, after he or she has taken an oath to speak the truth.

The common-law crime of perjury is now governed by both state and federal laws. In addition, the MODEL PENAL CODE, which has been adopted in some form by many states and promulgated by the Commission on Uniform State Laws, also sets forth the following basic elements for the crime of perjury: (1) a false statement is made under oath or equivalent affirmation during a judicial proceeding; (2) the statement must be material or relevant to the proceeding; and (3) the witness must have the SPECIFIC INTENT to deceive.

The punishment for perjury in most states, and under federal law, is the imposition of a fine, imprisonment, or both. Federal law also imposes sentencing enhancements when the court determines that a defendant has falsely testified on her own behalf and is convicted. Under the Federal Sentencing Guidelines, the court is required to automatically increase the defendant's sentence.

Two federal statutes govern the crime of perjury in federal proceedings. Title 18 U.S.C.A. § 1621 codifies the COMMON LAW of perjury and consists of the elements listed above. In 1970, the scope of section 1621 was expanded by the enactment of 18 U.S.C.A. § 1623. Section 1623 changes the definition of intent from willfully offering false testimony to merely having knowledge that the testimony is false. In addition it adds to the definition of perjury to include the witness's use of information, including any book, paper, document, record, recording, or other material she knows contains a false material declaration, and includes proceedings that are ancillary to any court, such as affidavits and depositions, and GRAND JURY proceedings. Section 1623 also contains a retraction defense. If, during the proceeding in which the false statement was made, the person admits to the falsity of the statement before it is evident that the falsity has been or will be exposed, and as long as the falsity does not affect the proceeding substantially, prosecution will be barred under section 1623.

Commentators believe that the existence of these two federal statutes actually frustrates the goals of Congress to encourage truthful statements. The reasoning behind this concern is that when a retraction exists, prosecutors may charge a witness with perjury under section 1621 and when a retraction does not exist, the witness may be charged under section 1623.

Two variations of perjury are SUBORNATION OF PERJURY and false swearing; in many states these two variations are separate offenses. Subornation of perjury is a crime in which the defendant does not actually testify falsely but instead induces, persuades, instigates, or in some way procures another witness to commit perjury. False swearing is a false statement made under oath but not made during an official proceeding. Some states have created a separate offense for false swearing, while others have enacted perjury statutes to include this type of false statement. These crimes also may be punished by the imposition of a fine, imprisonment, or both.

FURTHER READINGS

Aycock, George W. III. 1993. "Nothing But the Truth: A Solution to the Current Inadequacies of the Federal Perjury Statutes." *Valparaiso Law Review* 28.

Curriden, Mark. 1995. "The Lies Have It." *ABA Journal* 81.

Feinstein, Ami L. 1993. "*United States v. Dunnigan* and Sentence Enhancements for Perjury: Constitutional Perhaps, but Unnecessary in Fact." *American Criminal Law Review* 31.

❖ PERKINS, FRANCES

At a time when few women achieved prominence in national politics, Frances Perkins distinguished herself as a public official, a respected labor and industry expert, and an adviser to the president of the United States. When Perkins was named secretary of labor by President FRANKLIN D. ROOSEVELT in 1933, she became the first woman in U.S. history to hold a cabinet post. Perkins used her position to help launch the sweeping social and economic reforms of the NEW DEAL.

Perkins was born April 10, 1880, in Boston, and raised in Worcester, Massachusetts. After graduating from Worcester Classical High School, Perkins attended Mount Holyoke College, where she studied physics and chemistry and was class president. As a senior at Mount Holyoke, Perkins was influenced by Jacob A. Riis's 1890 book *How the Other Half Lives* and by

a speech given by Florence Kelley, the general secretary of the National Consumers League. Perkins's growing awareness of the plight of underprivileged U.S. citizens would lead to her life's work as a labor activist. After graduating from Mount Holyoke in 1902, Perkins pursued further studies in economics and sociology at the University of Pennsylvania and Columbia University. She earned a master's degree from Columbia in 1910.

After graduate school, Perkins briefly taught biology and physics in a school in Lake Forest, Illinois. In her off-hours, she volunteered at Jane Addams's Hull House, in nearby Chicago, and at other settlement houses. There, Perkins witnessed the poverty and wretched working conditions endured by thousands of U.S. citizens. Determined to help improve the plight of workers, she returned to New York City to work as a lobbyist with her mentor, Kelley, at the New York Consumers League.

Perkins's task was formidable. Throughout the early twentieth century, U.S. businesses were unregulated: workers in sweatshops worked long hours for low pay in unsafe working conditions. There were no BUILDING CODES to ensure the employees' safety, no regular inspections of equipment and machinery, and no limit to the number of hours employees could work. Children routinely were employed in factories, mills, and mines under the most miserable conditions. Some women worked nineteen hours a day with their children by their side.

An industrial tragedy heightened Perkins's resolve to force changes in the workplace. On March 25, 1911, a fire broke out at the Triangle Shirtwaist Company, in New York City. Perkins happened to be in the neighborhood and watched as employees trapped on the top three floors of the burning ten-story building jumped

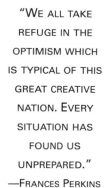

"WE ALL TAKE REFUGE IN THE OPTIMISM WHICH IS TYPICAL OF THIS GREAT CREATIVE NATION. EVERY SITUATION HAS FOUND US UNPREPARED."
—FRANCES PERKINS

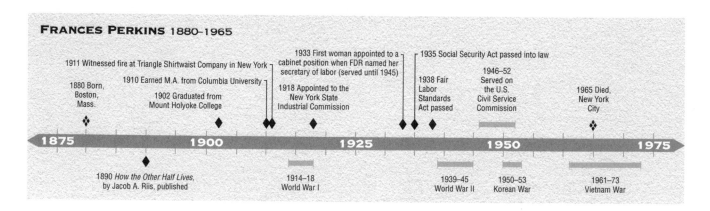

FRANCES PERKINS 1880–1965

1880 Born, Boston, Mass.

1890 *How the Other Half Lives,* by Jacob A. Riis, published

1902 Graduated from Mount Holyoke College

1910 Earned M.A. from Columbia University

1911 Witnessed fire at Triangle Shirtwaist Company in New York

1914–18 World War I

1918 Appointed to the New York State Industrial Commission

1933 First woman appointed to a cabinet position when FDR named her secretary of labor (served until 1945)

1935 Social Security Act passed into law

1938 Fair Labor Standards Act passed

1939–45 World War II

1946–52 Served on the U.S. Civil Service Commission

1950–53 Korean War

1961–73 Vietnam War

1965 Died, New York City

1875   1900   1925   1950   1975

from windows to their death. The door to the only stairway in the building had been locked by employers, to halt break-ins. One hundred workers perished inside the building, and forty-seven jumped or fell to their death. The owners of the company were later absolved of criminal negligence for the disaster and collected $64,925 in property damage insurance.

In the fire's aftermath, the New York State Factory Commission was created, with Perkins named as chief investigator. She also became a member of the Committee on Safety of the City of New York and lobbied hard for legislation to make the workplace safer. She toured the state with Alfred E. Smith and ROBERT F. WAGNER and documented the deplorable conditions faced by workers. An exhaustive investigation led to new laws to protect the labor force.

A major success for Perkins was the passage of a bill by the New York Legislature to limit the workweek to fifty-four hours for women and children. The bill was vigorously opposed by the employers of the four hundred thousand female factory workers throughout the state. While LOBBYING for the bill, Perkins became acquainted with Roosevelt, who was a New York state senator. Although Roosevelt's support of the fifty-four-hour bill was lukewarm, Perkins developed a professional relationship with him that grew stronger as Roosevelt's views on labor and government began to mirror her own.

In 1913 Perkins married Paul Caldwell Wilson and rejected prevailing social convention by retaining her maiden name for professional purposes. In 1918 she was appointed to the New York State Industrial Commission.

Perkins's work with Roosevelt in New York led to a position in the federal government. When Roosevelt was elected president in 1932, he asked Perkins to become secretary of labor. Although she argued that a female trade unionist should be nominated for the post, she eventually accepted the position. Perkins became the only cabinet member to serve during all four of Roosevelt's terms of office.

When Roosevelt took office, the country was in the midst of the Great Depression. About a third of the nation's workforce was unemployed. As labor secretary, Perkins helped shape the SOCIAL SECURITY ACT (42 U.S.C.A. § 301 et seq.), a key component of Roosevelt's New Deal. Passed by the U.S. Congress in 1935, the act allowed qualified workers in commerce and

Frances Perkins.
LIBRARY OF CONGRESS

industry to collect OLD-AGE, SURVIVORS, AND DISABILITY INSURANCE benefits. The new program required employers and employees to make contributions to a federal PENSION fund for aged and DISABLED PERSONS. In this way, workers and their families were financially protected in the event of unemployment, old age, or the death of a wage earner. Although critics likened the plan to SOCIALISM, SOCIAL SECURITY became a successful federal entitlement program.

Perkins also helped develop the FAIR LABOR STANDARDS ACT of 1938 (29 U.S.C.A. § 201 et seq.), which limited the number of hours employees could work for MINIMUM WAGE. The law also placed restrictions on child labor. It prohibited children under sixteen years of age from working in most jobs, and made hazardous occupations unavailable to workers under eighteen years of age. The Wage and Hour Division of the LABOR DEPARTMENT was also established by the act.

After Roosevelt's death in 1945, Perkins served briefly in the administration of President HARRY S. TRUMAN. She left Truman's cabinet to serve on the U.S. Civil Service Commission from 1946 to 1952. Perkins then taught courses at Cornell University's School of Industrial and Labor Relations. She died in New York City on May 14, 1965, at the age of eighty-five.

FURTHER READINGS

Pasachoff, Naomi. 1999. *Frances Perkins: Champion of the New Deal.* New York: Oxford Univ. Press.

Pirro, Jeanine Ferris. 1999. "Reforming the Urban Workplace: The Legacy of Frances Perkins." *Fordham Urban Law Journal* 26 (May).

Whitney, Sharon, and Tom Raynor. 1986. *Women in Politics.* New York: Franklin Watts.

CROSS-REFERENCES

Child Labor Laws; Labor Law.

PERMISSIVE COUNTERCLAIM

A claim by a defendant opposing the claim of the plaintiff and seeking some relief from the plaintiff for the defendant.

Once a plaintiff sues a defendant in a civil action, the defendant has the right to assert a legal claim of her own against the plaintiff. This is known as a counterclaim. A counterclaim makes assertions that the defendant *could have made* in a lawsuit if the plaintiff had not already begun an action. A counterclaim is distinct from a mere defense, which seeks only to defeat the plaintiff's lawsuit, in that it seeks a form of relief. There are two types of counterclaims: compulsory counterclaims and permissive counterclaims. Both are governed in federal court by rule 13 of the Federal Rules of CIVIL PROCEDURE. The rules in state courts are similar.

The compulsory counterclaim arises from the same transaction or occurrence that forms the basis of the plaintiff's suit. For example, a car accident between two drivers leads to a personal injury lawsuit, but the defendant asserts in a compulsory counterclaim that the plaintiff actually owes him damages for injuries. A compulsory counterclaim generally must be part of the initial answer to the plaintiff's action and cannot be made later in the suit or in a separate lawsuit.

By contrast, the permissive counterclaim arises from an event unrelated to the matter on which the plaintiff's suit is based. For example, John Smith breaks his leg while visiting the home of Jane Doe. Smith sues Doe, alleging that she negligently left her child's roller skate on her front porch. In a permissive counterclaim, Doe asserts that Smith owes her money. The court will rule separately on plaintiff Smith's and defendant Doe's respective claims; if both claims are permitted to proceed, *Smith v. Doe* will involve the two parties' respective allegations of NEGLIGENCE and a bad debt.

Counterclaims are usually valid only if it is possible to make the same claim by starting a lawsuit. Thus, in the example of Smith and Doe, Doe can only make her permissive counterclaim if the STATUTE OF LIMITATIONS on collection of the debt has not expired. Permissive counterclaims need not be made in the initial PLEADING; they can be made at a later time or even in another lawsuit. This flexibility may help the defendant's legal strategy: she can wait and sue in a different court, in order to have another judge hear the case or to avoid arguing the merits of separate claims before the same jury.

PERPETRATOR

A term commonly used by law enforcement officers to designate a person who actually commits a crime.

PERPETUATING TESTIMONY

The procedure permitted by federal and state discovery rules for preserving the attestation of a witness that might otherwise be lost prior to the trial in which it is intended to be used.

The usual method of perpetuating testimony is by taking a deposition. It is usually allowed when a witness is aged and infirm or is about to leave the state.

PERPETUATION OF EVIDENCE

The procedure employed to assure that proof will be available for possible use at a later trial.

The police, for example, can deposit a murder weapon with the court, prior to the day set for trial of the accused, for purposes of perpetuation of evidence.

PERPETUITIES

See RULE AGAINST PERPETUITIES.

PERQUISITES

Fringe benefits or other incidental profits or benefits accompanying an office or position.

The abbreviation *perks* is used in reference to extraordinary benefits afforded to business executives, such as country club memberships or the free use of automobiles.

PERSON

In general usage, a human being; by statute, however, the term can include firms, labor organiza-

tions, *partnerships, associations, corporations, legal representatives, trustees, trustees in* BANK-RUPTCY, *or receivers.*

A corporation is a "person" for purposes of the constitutional guarantees of EQUAL PROTECTION OF LAWS and DUE PROCESS OF LAW.

Foreign governments otherwise eligible to sue in United States courts are "persons" entitled to institute a suit for treble damages for alleged antitrust violations under the CLAYTON ACT (15 U.S.C.A. § 12 et seq.).

Illegitimate children are "persons" within the meaning of the Equal Protection Clause of the FOURTEENTH AMENDMENT to the U.S. Constitution.

The phrase *interested person* refers to heirs, devisees, children, spouses, creditors, beneficiaries, and any others having a property right in, or a claim against, a trust estate or the estate of a decedent, ward, or protected person. It also refers to personal representatives and to fiduciaries.

PERSONAL ACTIONS

Lawsuits initiated in order, among other things, to recover damages for some injury to a plaintiff's personal right or property, for breach of contract, for money owed on a debt, or for the recovery of a specific item of PERSONAL PROPERTY.

Under the old COMMON LAW, personal actions were one of the three categories of FORMS OF ACTION, the other two being real actions and mixed actions. The right to bring personal actions was an innovation in a day when the only useful property was land. There were few consumer goods and little money in ancient England. From the ACCESSION of the Norman kings in 1066, the royal right to supervise ownership and possession of land was seldom questioned. Only when the security of land ownership was seen to depend on the peace of individual persons were personal actions like debt, DETINUE, and TRESPASS permitted.

PERSONAL INJURY

Any violation of an individual's right, other than his or her rights in property.

The term *personal injury* is not confined to physical injuries, although NEGLIGENCE cases usually do involve bodily injuries.

CROSS-REFERENCES

Tort Law.

PERSONAL JURISDICTION

The power of a court to hear and determine a lawsuit involving a defendant by virtue of the defendant's having some contact with the place where the court is located.

Personal jurisdiction, also known as in personam (against the person) jurisdiction, gives a court the authority to make decisions binding on the persons involved in a civil case. Every state has personal jurisdiction over persons within its territory. Conversely, no state can exercise personal jurisdiction and authority over persons outside its territory unless the persons have manifested some contact with the state.

The authority of the court to issue orders to persons present within the territory comes from the sovereign power of the government. The court's authority allows it to reach all residents of a state, including those who are outside the state for a short period and out-of-state residents who enter the state even briefly.

Deciding whether an individual is within the personal jurisdiction of a court has not been difficult to determine. Difficulty has arisen when courts have had to decide whether corporations were subject to personal jurisdiction. Corporations have a legal existence and a legal identity but not a tangible existence. They are subject to lawsuits involving TORT and contract. As corporations became national economic entities, the courts of a state had difficulty finding personal jurisdiction if the corporation was not located within that state.

Courts established that a corporation is always subject to the jurisdiction of the courts in the state where it was incorporated. States also require corporations to file written consents to personal jurisdiction before they can conduct business within the state. Other states require that either the corporation designate an agent to accept legal process (the legal documents initiating a lawsuit) in the state or that the state attorney general be authorized to accept process for all out-of-state corporations doing business within the state.

In 1945 the U.S. Supreme Court modernized personal jurisdiction requirements when it announced the "minimum contacts" test in *International Shoe Co. v. Washington,* 326 U.S. 310, 66 S. Ct. 154, 90 L. Ed. 95. The Court held that courts could constitutionally exercise jurisdiction over a nonresident defendant if the defendant had sufficient contacts with the state such that forcing the person to litigate in that forum did not offend "traditional notions of fair play and substantial justice." Because of the ease of modern communication and transportation, it is usually not unfair to require a party to defend itself in a state in which it conducts business activity.

The threshold of minimum contacts varies. Where the action arises out of or is related to the defendant's contacts with the state, the quantity of contacts necessary to establish personal jurisdiction may be truly minimal. In such cases the nature and quality of the contact are the determining factors. In the case of a nonresident motorist who causes an injury in the forum state (the state of the court asserting jurisdiction), the interest of the state in providing a forum for its residents and regulating its highways, coupled with the defendant's having purposefully entered the state, permits the state to fairly assert personal jurisdiction.

A corporation or individual not physically present in a state may invoke personal jurisdiction by making a single contact with the state by telephone, mail, or facsimile transmission. In *Hanson v. Denckla,* 357 U.S. 235, 78 S. Ct. 1228, 2 L. Ed. 2d 1283 (1958), the Court ruled that even a single transaction can trigger personal jurisdiction when the defendant purposely avails itself of the privilege of conducting activities with the forum state and invokes the benefits and protection of state law.

States quickly took advantage of *International Shoe* by enacting "long-arm statutes." These statutes allow the state to reach out and obtain jurisdiction over anyone who is not present in the state but who transacts business within the state, commits a tort within the state, commits a tort outside the state that causes injury within the state, or owns, uses, or possesses real property within the state.

Personal jurisdiction in the federal courts is governed by rule 4 of the Federal Rules of Civil Procedure. Rule 4 directs each federal district court to follow the law on personal jurisdiction that is in force in the state courts where the federal court is located. Federal courts may use state LONG-ARM STATUTES to reach defendants beyond the territory of their normal authority. With cases that can only be brought in federal court, such as lawsuits involving federal SECURITIES and ANTITRUST LAWS, federal courts may exercise personal jurisdiction over a defendant no matter where the defendant is found.

When a person wishes to challenge personal jurisdiction, he or she must take care in appearing before the court in the forum state. If the defendant makes a general appearance, the court will take this to be an unqualified submission to the personal jurisdiction of the court. The defendant waives the right to raise any jurisdictional defects.

To prevent this from happening, a defendant must request a special appearance before the court. A special appearance is made for the limited purpose of challenging the sufficiency of the SERVICE OF PROCESS or the personal jurisdiction of the court. If any other issues are raised, the proceeding becomes a general appearance. The court must then determine whether it has jurisdiction over the defendant. If the defendant is found to be within the personal jurisdiction of the court, the issue may be appealed. Some states permit an immediate appeal, whereas others make the defendant raise the issue after the case has been heard on its merits in the trial court.

FURTHER READINGS

Cebik, Sarah R. 1998. "'A Riddle Wrapped in a Mystery Inside an Enigma': General Personal Jurisdiction and Notions of Sovereignty." *Annual Survey of American Law* 1998 (winter): 1–48.

Redish, Martin H. 1998. "Of New Wine and Old Bottles: Personal Jurisdiction, the Internet, and the Nature of Constitutional Evolution." *Jurimetrics Journal of Law, Science and Technology* 38 (summer): 575–610.

PERSONAL PROPERTY

Everything that is the subject of ownership that does not come under the denomination of real property; any right or interest that an individual has in movable things.

Personal property can be divided into two major categories: (1) corporeal personal property, including such items as animals, merchandise, and jewelry; and (2) incorporeal personal property, comprised of such rights as stocks, bonds, PATENTS, and copyrights.

Possession

Possession is a property interest under which an individual is able to exercise power over something to the exclusion of all others. It is a basic property right that entitles the possessor to (1) the right to continue peaceful possession against everyone except someone having a superior right; (2) the right to recover a chattel that has been wrongfully taken; and (3) the right to recover damages against wrongdoers.

Possession requires a degree of actual control over the object, coupled with the intent to possess and exclude others. The law recognizes two basic types of possession: actual and constructive.

Actual possession exists when an individual knowingly has direct physical control over an object at a given time. For example, an individual wearing a particular piece of valuable jewelry has actual possession of it. *Constructive possession* is the power and intent of an individual to control a particular item, even though it is not physically in that person's control. For example, an individual who has the key to a bank safe deposit box, which contains a valuable piece of jewelry that she owns, is said to be in constructive possession of the jewelry.

Possession of Animals

Animals ferae naturae, or wild animals, are those that cannot be completely domesticated. A degree of force or skill is necessary to maintain control over them. Gaining possession is a means of obtaining title to, or ownership of, wild animals.

Generally an owner of land has the right to capture or kill a wild animal on her property and upon doing so, the animal is regarded as belonging to that individual because she owns the soil. The traditional legal principle has been that one who tames a wild animal is regarded as its owner provided it appears to exhibit animus revertendi, or the intent to return to the owner's domicile. Conversely when a captured wild animal escapes and returns to its natural habitat without any apparent intent to return to the captor's domicile, the captor forfeits all personal property right and the animal may be captured by anyone.

Lost, Mislaid, and Abandoned Property

Personal property is considered to be *lost* if the owner has involuntarily parted with it and is ignorant of its location. *Mislaid property* is that which an owner intentionally places somewhere with the idea that he will eventually be able to find it again but subsequently forgets where it has been placed. *Abandoned property* is that to which the owner has intentionally relinquished all rights.

Lost or mislaid property continues to be owned by the person who lost or mislaid it. When one finds lost goods, the finder is entitled to possession against everyone with the exception of the true owner.

The finder of lost articles on land belonging to someone else is entitled to possession against everyone but the true owner, unless the finder is guilty of TRESPASS. The finder of misplaced goods has no right to their possession. The owner of the place where an article is mislaid has a right to the article against everyone but the true owner. Abandoned property can be possessed and owned by the first person who exercises dominion over it with an intent to claim it as his or her own. In any event, between the finder of a lost, mislaid, or abandoned article and the owner of the place where it is found, the law applies to whatever rule will most likely result in the return of the article to its rightful owner.

Ordinarily when articles are found by an employee during and within the scope of his employment, they are awarded to the employer rather than to the employee-finder.

Treasure trove is any gold or silver in coin, plate, or bullion that is hidden by an unknown owner in the earth or other private place for an extended period. The property is not considered treasure trove unless the identity of the owner cannot be ascertained. Under early COMMON LAW, the finder of a treasure trove took title to it against everyone but the true owner. This doctrine was altered in England by a statute granting title to the crown subject to the claims of the true owner. The U.S. law governing treasure trove has, for the most part, been merged into the law governing lost property. However, certain cases have held that the old treasure trove law has not been combined into the lost property statutes. In some instances, the early common law of England has been held to apply in the absence of a statute governing treasure trove. Regardless of which principles are applied, however, in the absence of contrary statutory provision, the title to treasure trove belongs to the finder against all others with the exception of the true owner. If there is a controversy as to ownership between the true owner and the state, the owner is entitled to treasure trove.

Confusion and Accession

Confusion and ACCESSION govern the acquisition of, or loss of title to, personal property by virtue of its being blended with, altered by, improved by, or commingled with the property of others. In confusion, the personal property of several different owners is commingled so that it cannot be separated and returned to its rightful owners, but the property retains its original characteristics. Any fungible (interchangeable) goods can be the subject of confusion.

In accession, the personal property of one owner is physically integrated with the property of another so that it becomes a constituent part of it, losing any separate identity. Accession can make the personal property of one owner become a substantially more valuable chattel as a result of the work of another person. This transformation occurs when the personal property becomes an entirely new chattel, such as when grapes are made into wine or timber is made into furniture.

Subject to the doctrine of accession, personal property can become real property through its transformation into a fixture. A fixture is a movable item that was originally personalty (personal property) but which has become attached to, and associated with, the land and is, therefore, considered a part of the real property.

Bailments

A BAILMENT is the rightful, temporary possession of goods by an individual other than the true owner. The individual who entrusts his property into the hands of another is called the bailor; the person who holds such property is the bailee. Ordinarily a bailment is effected for a designated purpose upon which the parties have agreed.

The word *bailment* is derived from the French term *bailler*, "to deliver." It is ordinarily regarded as a contractual relationship since the bailor and bailee—either expressly or implicitly—bind themselves to act according to specific terms. The bailee receives only control or possession of the property, and the bailor retains the ownership interests therein. While a bailment exists, the bailee has an interest in the property that is superior to all others, including the bailor, unless she violates some term of the agreement. When the purpose for which the property has been delivered has been accomplished, the property will be returned to the bailor or otherwise disposed of, according to his instructions.

A bailment differs from a sale, which is an intentional transfer of ownership of personal property in exchange for something of value, because a bailment involves only a transfer of possession or custody not of ownership. For example, a bailment is created when a person leaves his or her car and car keys at a parking garage. The parking garage receives a fee to hold the car in its custody.

Gifts

A gift is a voluntary transfer of personalty from one individual to another without compensation or consideration or the exchange of something of value. There are two main categories of gifts: inter vivos gifts, a voluntary, unconditional transfer of property between two living persons without consideration, and causa mortis, one that is made by a donor in anticipation of imminent death. The three requirements of a valid gift are delivery, donative intent, and acceptance.

Bona Fide Purchasers

A basic common-law principle is that an individual cannot pass a better title than she has, and a buyer can acquire no better title than that of the seller. A thief does not have title in stolen goods, so a person who purchases from the thief does not acquire title.

A bona fide purchaser is an individual who has bought property for value with no notice of any defects in the seller's title. If a seller indicates to a buyer that she has ownership or the authority to sell a particular item, the seller is prevented (estopped) from denying such representations if the buyer resells the property to a bona fide purchaser for value without notice of the true owner's rights. At common law, such an ESTOPPEL did not apply when an owner brought an item for services or repairs to a dealer in that type of goods and the dealer wrongfully sold the chattel. The bona fide purchaser, however, is now protected under such circumstances by the UNIFORM COMMERCIAL CODE (UCC).

A buyer who induces a sale through fraudulent representations acquires a VOIDABLE title from the seller. A voidable title is one which may be vacated by the seller, upon discovery of the buyer's FRAUD, at his option. The seller has the authority to transfer a good title to a bona fide purchaser for value without notice of the outstanding EQUITY. The voidable title rule is only applicable in situations where the owner is induced to part with title, not merely with possession, as a result of fraud or deception.

FURTHER READINGS

Burke, Barlow. 2003. *Personal Property in a Nutshell.* 3d ed. St. Paul, Minn.: West.

Huss, Rebecca J. 2002. "Valuing Man's and Woman's Best Friend: The Moral and Legal Status of Companion Animals." *Marquette Law Review* 86 (fall).

Jordan, Robert L., William D. Warren, and Steven D. Walt. 2000. *Secured Transactions in Personal Property.* 5th ed. New York: Foundation Press.

Miller, Kathleen. 1995. *Fair Share Divorce for Women.* Bellevue, Wash.: Miller Advisors.

Sykas, Abigail J. 2001. "Waste Not, Want Not: Can the Public Policy Doctrine Prohibit the Destruction of Property by Testamentary Direction?" *Vermont Law Review* 25 (summer).

CROSS-REFERENCES

Accession; Bailment; Chattel; Possession.

PERSONAL REPRESENTATIVE

A person who manages the financial affairs of another person who is unable to do so.

A personal representative is one kind of fiduciary—an individual whom another has trusted to manage her property and money. When a person dies, a personal representative generally is required to settle the decedent's financial affairs. In some instances, a living person may need a personal representative; for example, a minor might need a personal representative to make legal decisions for her. Personal representatives can be appointed by a court, nominated by will, or selected by the person involved. Their duties are performed under the supervision of probate courts, which are governed by state law.

When someone dies leaving property, a personal representative is required to administer the decedent's estate, which involves resolving any debts and handling the distribution of property. The jurisdiction, powers, and functions connected with administering the decedent's estate are usually entrusted to special tribunals, known as probate, surrogate, or ORPHANS' COURTS. These courts supervise the actions of the personal representative.

The choice of a personal representative depends on whether the decedent left a will, the legal document instructing how his estate is to be divided. If the will names a personal representative, that person is called an *executor* (male or female) or *executrix* (female). The court will accept the representative unless he does not meet statutory qualifications. These qualifications vary from state to state but largely concern such factors as age and conflict of interest. If there is no legally valid will, the decedent is said to have died intestate. In such cases, the court appoints a personal representative for the decedent's estate. The court-appointed representative is called an *administrator* (male or female) or *administratrix* (female).

In special instances, courts appoint one of three types of administrators. They are appointed when (1) an executor cannot or will not serve (*administrator cum testamento annexo*); (2) a prior executor or administrator has not completed the estate (*administrator de bonis non*); or (3) an interim administrator (special administrator), given restricted powers over the estate, is needed until a proper legal representative can be found.

Once approved by the court, personal representatives receive official sanction to fulfill their duties. Executors receive documents called letters testamentary—administrators receive letters of administration—authorizing the representative to handle the legal affairs of a decedent. Throughout the process of administering an estate, all personal representatives serve as officers of the court. They derive their authority from the court and thus serve at the court's pleasure. Their authority can be revoked on various grounds, ranging from neglect to incompetence. Primarily, they must act on behalf of all parties and all interests in the estate. They owe the beneficiaries an absolute duty of loyalty, or fiduciary duty, to administer the estate in their best interest.

In general, the personal representatives' duties are to settle and distribute the estate. This complicated task may require the assistance of an attorney or a trust company, so-called *coexecutors*. The personal representative's first task is to collect and preserve the assets of the estate. The personal representative also oversees the appraisal of the estate's assets, where necessary. The personal representative must also pay the estate's creditors, as well as any ESTATE AND GIFT TAXES due under federal law. Finally, the representative sees to the distribution of the remaining estate among the decedent's beneficiaries. If there are no beneficiaries, the state usually receives the property.

FURTHER READINGS

Graves, Herman S. 2000. "Estate Administrative Expenses And the Personal Representative." *Colorado Lawyer* 29 (September).

Krier, Kenneth D. 1991. "The Attorney as Personal Representative or Trustee." *Florida Bar Journal* 65 (Janurary).

Ross, Bruce S., and Henry T. Moore, Jr. 1986–1996. *California Practice Guide: Probate.* The Rutter Group.

PERSONAL SERVICE

The actual delivery of process to the individual to whom it is directed or to someone authorized to receive it on his or her behalf.

SERVICE OF PROCESS is the delivery of legal notice to a party in a case. Any party who is being sued is entitled to advance notice of the suit. Notice consists of a copy of the complaint and a summons to appear in court. If a party does not receive notice of a lawsuit, the court will dismiss the case.

Personal service of the complaint and summons is a form of actual notice. Actual notice occurs when the summons and complaint are delivered personally to the respondent. The two other basic forms of process service are substituted service and constructive service. Substituted service is personal delivery to the residence of the respondent or notice given to an agent of the respondent. Constructive service is notice delivered through publication in a newspaper.

If a party cannot be reached in person, substituted service may be made by mailing the summons and complaint by certified or first-class mail. If a party cannot be found, notice may be served by publication in a newspaper.

The U.S. Supreme Court has ruled that service of process should be reasonably calculated to apprise interested parties of the pendency of the action and afford them an opportunity to be heard. The reasonableness of the notice must be considered in light of all the circumstances. For example, if a party receiving notice lives in an apartment building with many children living in the building, one notice left on the front door of the apartment may not be sufficient because it is possible that the children may take the papers (*Greene v. Lindsey,* 456 U.S. 444, 102 S. Ct. 1874, 72 L. Ed. 2d 249 [1982]).

PERSONALTY

Goods; chattels; articles; movable property, whether animate or inanimate.

CROSS-REFERENCES

Personal Property.

PERSUASIVE AUTHORITY

Sources of law, such as related cases or legal encyclopedias, that the court consults in deciding a case, but which, unlike binding authority, the court need not apply in reaching its conclusion.

PETIT JURY

The ordinary panel of twelve persons called to issue a verdict in a civil action or a criminal prosecution.

Petit jury is used interchangeably with petty jury.

PETIT LARCENY

A form of larceny—the stealing of another's personal property—in which the value of the property taken is generally less than $50.

At COMMON LAW, the penalty for the offense was whipping or some other CORPORAL PUNISHMENT. Under modern-day statutes, it is usually a fine, imprisonment, or both.

PETITION

A written application from a person or persons to some governing body or public official asking that some authority be exercised to grant relief, favors, or privileges.

A formal application made to a court in writing that requests action on a certain matter.

The FIRST AMENDMENT to the U.S. Constitution guarantees to the people the right to petition the government for the redress of grievances. Petitions are also used to collect signatures to enable a candidate to get on a ballot or put an issue before the electorate. Petitions can serve as a way of pressuring elected officials to adhere to the position expressed by the petitioners.

The right to petition the government for correction of public grievances derives from the English MAGNA CHARTA of 1215 and the English BILL OF RIGHTS of 1689. One of the colonists' objections to British rule before the American Revolution was the king's refusal to act on their petitions of redress. The Founders attempted to address this concern with the First Amendment, which affirms the right of the people to petition their government. Almost all states adopted similar guarantees of petition in their own constitutions.

Between 1836 and 1840, abolitionists collected the signatures of two million people on petitions against SLAVERY and sent them to the U.S. House of Representatives. In the early twentieth century, states passed laws allowing initiative (the proposing of legislation by the people) and recall (an election to decide whether an elected official should be removed from office). Both processes start with the collection of a minimum number of signatures on a petition. Small political parties often use petitions to collect signatures to enable their candidates to be placed on the election ballot.

Petitions are also directed to courts of law and administrative agencies and boards. A petition may be made ex parte (without the presence of the opposing party) where there are no parties in opposition. For example, the executor of an estate may file a petition with the probate court requesting approval to sell property that belongs to the estate or trust.

In contested matters, however, the opposing party must be served with the petition and be given the opportunity to appear in court to argue the merits of the issues it contains. A prisoner may file a petition for a writ of HABEAS CORPUS, in which the prisoner requests a hearing to determine whether he or she is entitled to be released from custody because of unconstitutional or illegal actions by the government. The prisoner must serve the government office that prosecuted him or her with a copy of the petition. The writ of habeas corpus, like many other types of writs, is discretionary; the court is free to deny the petition.

PETITION IN BANKRUPTCY

A document filed in a specialized federal court to commence a proceeding to provide a means by which a debtor who is unwilling or financially unable to pay personal debts will satisfy the claims of his or her creditors as they come due.

There are two types of petitions in BANK-RUPTCY cases. A voluntary petition is filed by a debtor who wants to make arrangements for the payment of debts and be relieved of liability for them. An involuntary petition is filed by a statutorily prescribed number of creditors whose aggregate sum of claims exceed a specific amount.

A petition in bankruptcy lists the debtor's assets, liabilities, and debts so that a realistic arrangement for the payment of creditors can be devised.

PETITIONER

One who presents a formal, written application to a court, officer, or legislative body that requests action on a certain matter.

In March 1998, Aaron Wallace, president of the National Education Association, announces the collection of more than 400,000 signatures on a petition requesting increased spending on education in the state of Florida.
AP/WIDE WORLD PHOTOS

In legal proceedings initiated by a petition, the respondent is the person against whom relief is sought, or who opposes the petition. One who appeals from a judgment is a petitioner.

PETITORY ACTION

A legal proceeding by which the plaintiff seeks to establish and enforce his or her title to property, as distinguished from a possessory proceeding, where the plaintiff's right to possession is the issue. Such petitory actions must be based on a claim of legal title to the property, as opposed to a mere equitable interest in it.

In ADMIRALTY, suits to try title to property independent of questions concerning possession.

In the civil-law jurisdiction of Louisiana, a proceeding instituted by an alleged owner who does not have possession to determine ownership against one in possession.

CROSS-REFERENCES

Admiralty and Maritime Law.

PETTY OFFENSE

A minor crime, the maximum punishment for which is generally a fine or a short term in a prison or a house of correction.

In some states, a petty offense is a classification in addition to misdemeanor and felony.

Under federal law, a petty offense is any misdemeanor, the penalty for which does not exceed imprisonment for a period of six months, a fine of not more than $5,000, or both. Since a petty offense is one that is punishable by no more than a six-month sentence, the accused is not constitutionally entitled to a jury trial, which would be in order if the accused were charged with a serious offense.

PHARMACIST

See DRUGGIST.

PHILADELPHIA LAWYER

A colloquial term that was initially a compliment to the legal expertise and competence of an attorney due to the outstanding reputation of the Philadelphia bar during colonial times. More recently the term has become a disparaging label for an attorney who is skillful in the manipulation of the technicalities and intricacies of the law to the advantage of his or her client, although the spirit of the law might be violated.

For example, an attorney who uses repeated motions for postponement of an action or excessive discovery requests as dilatory tactics primarily for the advantages that inure to his or her client, as opposed to legitimate grounds for such actions, might be regarded as a Philadelphia lawyer.

PHOTO LINEUP

A presentation of photographs to a victim or witness of a crime.

A photo lineup, also known as a photo array and or photo display, is a procedure used by law enforcement personnel to discover or confirm the identity of a criminal suspect. Generally a police officer shows a set of photographs to a victim or witness and asks whether he or she recognizes one of the persons in the photographs as the perpetrator. A positive identification of a suspect can be used to place the suspect under arrest, and the act of identification may be used later as evidence in the prosecution of the defendant.

The Supreme Court has ruled that photo lineups should not be unduly suggestive (*Manson v. Brathwaite,* 432 U.S. 98, 97 S. Ct. 2243, 53 L. Ed. 2d 140 [1977]). That is, a photo lineup should not be conducted in such a way as to highlight the suspect and elicit an identification of the suspect. If a photo lineup is unduly suggestive, any affirmative identification of a suspect may be excluded from her or his subsequent prosecution.

Police officers typically avoid suggestive photo lineups because they are interested in apprehending the right person. Toward this end, they may ask a witness to look at more than one photo lineup containing the suspect to see if the witness can identify the suspect more than once. Each photo lineup may contain as many as six or more photographs of different persons. Furthermore, to be effective, a photo lineup should contain pictures of persons who look similar to the suspect. For example, if police suspect a Caucasian male and a witness remembers seeing a blond, light-skinned male, the photo lineup will not consist of five pictures of dark-haired, dark-skinned males and one picture of the suspect.

For public safety reasons, police officers do not always take the time to arrange a photo lineup to show witnesses. In some cases officers may use only one picture of a suspect. In case of violent crime, for example, police may need to act swiftly and locate a particular suspect. In *Manson,* the Supreme Court ruled that using one photograph for the purpose of identifying a person as a criminal suspect is not unduly suggestive.

The use of photographs in a criminal investigation is just one identification procedure used by police. Other procedures include show-ups and in-person lineups. A show-up is the exhibition of a particular criminal suspect to a victim or witness shortly after the crime occurred. An in-person lineup is the live presentation of several persons, including the suspect, to the witness.

Courts examine all the circumstances surrounding an identification. To determine whether any identification is unduly suggestive and therefore inadmissible at trial, courts analyze seven factors, including the opportunity the witness had to view the suspect, the degree of attention the witness paid to the suspect, the accuracy of the witness's description before viewing the suspect or the suspect's photograph, the witness's level of certainty in identifying the suspect, and the length of time that elapsed between the crime and the witness's viewing of the suspect.

A criminal defendant does not have the right to have an attorney present at a photographic lineup until after he or she is indicted or formally charged (*United States v. Ash,* 413 U.S. 300, 93 S. Ct. 2568, 37 L. Ed. 2d 619 [1973]). Nor does a criminal defendant have the right to a hearing, outside the presence of the jury, to make an attempt to block the presentation of photographic identifications (*Watkins v. Sowders,* 449 U.S. 341, 101 S. Ct. 654, 66 L. Ed. 2d 549 [1981]). However, a defendant does have the right to show to the judge and jury any photographic evidence used in the case, to challenge the witnesses on cross-examination, and to argue to the judge or jury that the photo identification procedure was unduly suggestive and that any identification from it should be disregarded (*United States v. Ash,* 413 U.S. 300, 93 S. Ct. 2568, 37 L. Ed. 2d 619 [1973]).

CROSS-REFERENCES

Criminal Law; Criminal Procedure; Due Process of Law; Right to Counsel.

PHYSICAL FACT

In the law of evidence, an event having a corporeal existence, as distinguished from a mere conception of the mind; one that is visible, audible, or tangible, such as the sound of footsteps or impressions made by human feet on the ground.

PHYSICIAN-ASSISTED SUICIDE

See EUTHANASIA "Euthanasia and Physician-Assisted Suicide" (In Focus).

PHYSICIAN-PATIENT PRIVILEGE

See PHYSICIANS AND SURGEONS; PRIVILEGED COMMUNICATION.

PHYSICIANS AND SURGEONS

Physicians and surgeons are medical practitioners who treat illness and injury by prescribing medication, performing diagnostic tests and evaluations, performing surgery, and providing other medical services and advice. Physicians and surgeons are highly trained and duly authorized by law to practice medicine.

The education and focus of chiropractors, dentists, and optometrists differ from those of physicians and surgeons. However, the laws relating to physicians and surgeons generally apply to these medical professionals as well. In addition, these HEALTHCARE providers are subject to laws regulating their specific area of practice. They are prohibited by law from practicing medicine or surgery.

A physician or surgeon does not have an unqualified right to practice medicine. The state legislature determines who is to be allowed this privilege and exercises its POLICE POWER to protect the public from deception, FRAUD, and incompetence. A legislature's authority to regulate the practice of medicine is, broadly speaking, only limited by the requirements that the rules are reasonable, bear some relation to the object to be attained, and do not violate any constitutional rights. Legislatures have the power to require a license or certificate to practice medicine within the state and to make practicing medicine without a license a criminal offense.

Statutes and regulations carefully regulate who may use the title "doctor." Use of the title or its abbreviation without an indication of the type of degree—D.O., M.D., etc.—is specifically forbidden in many states unless the person holds a physician's and surgeon's certificate.

State statutes delineate requirements for a license to practice medicine. To obtain a license, an applicant must demonstrate requisite education and knowledge. A college degree and graduation from an accredited medical school typically fulfills the education requirement, and passing a state-licensing exam demonstrates an applicant's skills. State law determines who may sit for an exam and typically limits the number of tries an applicant has to pass the exam. Specialists, such as cardiologists, ophthalmologists, pediatricians, and neurosurgeons, must usually pass further exams beyond the initial licensing exam.

Applicants typically must also meet certain physical health standards and establish that they are of good moral character. Generally speaking, good moral character means that a person is reliable, trustworthy, and not likely to deceive the public. An applicant who is refused a license because of a lack of good moral character is entitled to receive notice of the reasons and to have a hearing on the issues. State laws typically provide for JUDICIAL REVIEW of a denial, after all administrative appeals have been exhausted.

Under certain circumstances physicians licensed in another state may be permitted to waive examination. Commissioned medical officers in the ARMED SERVICES are typically exempt from a state's licensing statute when performing official medical services within the state.

State legislatures have routinely delegated the authority to supervise licensing, exam, and suspension and revocation procedures to a state board of medical examiners. A board's power is limited to the express powers given to it by statute and the implied powers necessary to carry out the express powers.

For action to be taken against a practitioner, a nexus must exist between the acts or omissions and the fitness or competency required to practice medicine. In other words, past isolated incidents unrelated to the profession are generally insufficient by themselves to form a basis for a disciplinary action.

Statutes commonly use words such as *unprofessional, dishonorable,* or *immoral conduct* when describing conduct warranting suspension or revocation. Other terms sometimes used are *gross immorality, willful or wanton misconduct, malpractice, gross violation of one's professional duties, gross misconduct in the practice of the profession,* or *grossly unprofessional conduct of a type likely to deceive or defraud.* These terms are not required to be defined with any particularity. Instead, every case is judged on its own particular facts. Some of the reasons that physicians or surgeons have had their licenses revoked or suspended are: failure to keep complete and accurate records of controlled substances, conviction of a crime (particularly one involving moral turpitude), drunkenness, ABANDONMENT of a patient, deliberate falsification of medical records, fraud in procuring a license, professional incompetence, assisting or aiding another in the unlicensed practice of medicine, and sexual imposition on a patient. A license revocation in one state may be the basis for revocation in another.

State boards are charged with the duty of investigating allegations of professional misconduct. Depending upon the licensing statute, a patient, the state or state licensing board, or any other person may instigate a complaint. During the investigative stage, before a determination has been made to institute formal revocation proceedings, no requirement exists that the physician be informed of the nature of the charges, know the name of the complainant, or participate in selecting any documents. However, a license to practice medicine cannot be revoked without DUE PROCESS OF LAW. Due process means that the physician must receive notice of the intended action and have an opportunity to be heard. The complainant has the burden to establish the facts in order to justify revocation.

Judicial review of a suspension or revocation is limited to a determination of whether the deciding board abused its discretion. A court will examine whether a sanction is so disproportionate to the offense that it is shocking to a reasonable person's sense of fairness in light of all the circumstances.

Generally speaking, a physician with a license to practice medicine has the unlimited authority to prescribe for and treat the ill and afflicted and may choose to employ any legitimate method of treatment. In some instances state law might permit a physician to practice optometry or dentistry, although the converse is never permitted.

A physician stands in a fiduciary relationship to her patients, meaning that the physician must always exercise the utmost GOOD FAITH and trust when dealing with patients. A confidential relationship exists between the parties: because a patient must feel free to disclose any information that might pertain to treatment and diagnosis, the physician has the professional obligation to keep information confidential absent a patient's consent. But a physician cannot attempt to shield his own incompetence by refusing to disclose information. Moreover, a physician may have a statutory duty to reveal information concerning a patient. Doctors are required to provide authorities with information regarding birth and death, CHILD ABUSE, and contagious or infectious diseases. A physician may also have a duty to disclose confidential information to third parties in other circumstances.

Physicians and their patients have a contractual relationship. A request for an appointment will not suffice to form a doctor-patient relationship, but a telephone call to initiate treatment might. The relationship continues until treatment is completed or upon agreement by the parties. The physician agrees to treat the patient but rarely promises a specific outcome or cure. If a doctor promises a specific outcome but fails to deliver it, the doctor may be liable for breach of contract. One example would be a surgeon who promises that cosmetic surgery will produce certain results.

A physician's conduct must always meet the standard of care set by the profession, or he may be liable for MALPRACTICE. Physicians and surgeons must possess and exercise the same level of skill and learning ordinarily possessed and exercised by other members of their profession under similar circumstances.

Although not absolute in every instance, some of the responsibilities a physician or surgeon has toward a patient include a duty to

- Fully inform a patient of her condition;
- Notify a patient of the results of a diagnosis or test;
- Inform the patient of the need for different treatment or refer the patient to a specialist or other qualified practitioner;
- Continue medical care until proper termination of the relationship;
- Give proper notice before withdrawal from treatment;
- Not abandon a patient, including making arrangements for treatment during absences;
- Treat nonpaying patients the same as those who pay;
- Use diligence in treatment in providing all necessary care;
- Obtain a patient's informed consent before performing a medical procedure;
- Instruct others as to the care and treatment of a patient;
- Warn others of exposure to communicable and infectious diseases.

A patient has a duty to cooperate with a physician and participate in treatment and diagnosis. For example, a patient does not have a general duty to volunteer unsolicited information but is required to disclose a complete and accurate medical history upon questioning by a physician. A patient also must return for further treatment when required. Failure to cooperate or participate in treatment may result in a limited recovery for a physician's malpractice or completely bar recovery, depending upon the circumstances of the case.

Malpractice occurs when a patient is injured by a physician's bad or unskillful practices. Malpractice is the failure to do something that a reasonably careful physician or surgeon would do, or doing something a reasonably careful physician would not do, under the same circumstances. In other words, malpractice is a deviation from an established standard of practice—a failure to exercise the required degree of skill, care, and diligence or follow accepted rules. It can be willful or due to lack of skill or neglect; it can be a single act or something occurring over the course of treatment.

Ordinarily, in the absence of a special agreement, a physician need not exercise extraordinary skill. Nor must a physician anticipate consequences resulting from peculiar characteristics and conditions of a patient, if the physician has no knowledge of them or would not be expected to reasonably discover them. Not every wrongful act by a physician amounts to malpractice. A physician is ordinarily not liable for injurious consequences if she exercises the required degree of skill and care. A want of skill or care must be the proximate cause or a substantial factor in the injury or death, but not necessarily the sole cause.

The standard of care was traditionally determined with reference to the geographic locality of the treatment, meaning the level of care exercised by other physicians or surgeons in good standing in the same general line of practice in the same or similar locality. The locality standard developed when there were significant differences in the opportunities for continuing medical education and vast differences in access to hospitals. However, the twenty-first century's increased ease in dissemination of information, coupled with more uniform methods of treatment, have significantly downgraded the importance of the locality rule. Many jurisdictions now view locality as only one factor to examine rather than a conclusive limit on the degree of skill required. Other authorities have completely abandoned the locality rule in favor of a national standard.

Specialists are held to the standard of care of other specialists in the same field under similar circumstances. This typically means that specialists, because of their advanced training and knowledge, are held to a higher standard than that required of general practitioners. Even though not certified as a specialist, those who hold themselves out to be specialists or perform procedures normally done by specialists will be held to a specialist's standard.

A physician must refer a patient or seek a consultation if he knows, or should know, that the treatment of a particular patient is beyond his skill. If a physician fails to make a referral or seek a consultation, he will be held to the standard of care applicable to the appropriate specialty that should have been consulted.

A physician or surgeon is bound to follow the methods that are generally approved and recognized by the profession but is not limited to the most generally accepted treatment meth-

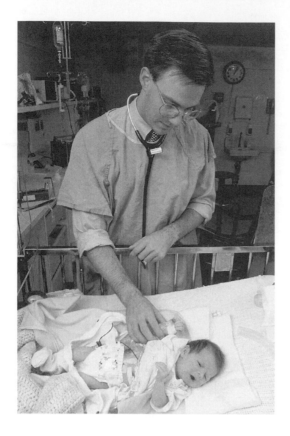

ods. Determining whether a treatment is a respected minority treatment can present a difficult task. Nevertheless, a practitioner who otherwise adheres to the applicable standard of care will typically not be held liable for an error in judgment in choosing from different accepted treatments or diagnostic methods. A physician's actions are viewed in terms of the state of medicine at the time of the claimed malpractice, rather than on subsequent medical discoveries or knowledge.

A physician has a non-delegable duty of care, which means that the physician is responsible for injury caused by assistants, employees, agents, or apprentices, when that injury is caused by a lack of proper skill or care. For example, a surgeon who retains control over the procedures used by an anesthesiologist may be liable for the negligent actions of the anesthesiologist. Generally, a physician will not be liable for a hospital's NEGLIGENCE or the negligence of others not within his control but may be liable where the negligence is discoverable by the physician in the ordinary course of treatment.

A physician may have an affirmative duty toward a third person who is not the physician's patient when there is a foreseeable risk of harm of the third person by the patient, of which the physician is aware or should be aware. For example, this duty may arise when a psychiatric patient threatens to harm a known victim or when a patient with a sexually transmitted disease refuses to notify his sexual partners of the illness. At least in the latter case, a physician's duty would generally be limited to those persons readily identified as being in danger. To prevail on such a claim, a third party must demonstrate that she was within the scope of a foreseeable risk of harm and that negligent treatment of the patient was the proximate cause of her injuries.

A minority of states recognize WRONGFUL LIFE claims. These are actions brought by or on behalf of a disabled child, alleging that the child was born due to a doctor's negligent failure to properly advise the parents, even though the doctor did not cause the disability. The first case to recognize a wrongful life claim took place in 1980 in California, when a doctor negligently failed to detect Tay-Sachs disease (*Curlender v. Bio-Science Laboratories,* 106 Cal. App. 3d 811, 165 Cal. Rptr. 477 [Cal. App. 1980]). The parents had specifically sought prenatal testing for the crippling disease. The severely disabled baby girl had a life expectancy of no more than four years. The court ruled that the serious nature of the harm, coupled with the fact that the disease went undetected because of a lack of due medical attention, sufficed to permit the action.

WRONGFUL BIRTH and wrongful life actions arise out of the same set of circumstances but are brought by different parties. In a wrongful life suit, the child (or someone acting on behalf of the child) is the plaintiff; in the wrongful birth case, the parents bring suit. Often the term *wrongful birth* encompasses two categories: wrongful conception or WRONGFUL PREGNANCY cases involve a woman who gave birth to an unwanted but healthy child; wrongful birth involves a child who was born with a handicap.

Wrongful pregnancy cases may arise when the defendant negligently performs a sterilization procedure or otherwise provides ineffective contraception; when a doctor negligently performs an ABORTION, resulting in the birth of a healthy child; or when a physician negligently fails to diagnose a pregnancy and the mother is thereby denied the choice of an abortion at a timely stage. A majority of states recognize a wrongful pregnancy CAUSE OF ACTION. Most, however, limit damages to the pain associated with the failed procedures. A few jurisdictions permit recovery of child-rearing expenses, but some of those states require that the award be offset by the parents' emotional benefits of raising a healthy child.

Wrongful life claims are permitted in some jurisdictions, but some courts have ruled that the cause of action does not exist in the absence of a statute giving rise to the claim. In addition, the cause of action has been specifically eliminated by statute in some jurisdictions.

In 1989 Congress created the National Practitioner Data Bank (NPDB) to mandate collection of information regarding incompetent practitioners. The NPDB began operation on September 1, 1990; its reporting requirements are not retroactive. The data bank collects information on all malpractice payments of more than one dollar made on behalf of physicians, dentists, and other licensed healthcare practitioners. The NPDB also collects information regarding disciplinary actions taken by state medical and dental boards. Additionally, it monitors professional review actions taken by hospitals and other entities adversely affecting a physician's clinical privileges for more than 30 days and a practitioner's voluntary surrender of clinical privileges during an investigation for incompetence or improper professional conduct. The NPDB also collects information on adverse actions by professional societies against its members.

Insurers, hospitals, medical societies, and boards of medicine must report to the NPDB; plaintiffs or their attorneys may not submit reports. Practitioners receive copies of the reports against them and have an opportunity to dispute the accuracy of the information.

The data bank has been criticized because the current regulations sometimes allow "corporate shielding" to protect practitioners from being reported. Because only individuals, not entities, must be reported, a practitioner would probably not be reported when a malpractice settlement was made on behalf of an incorporated group practice without naming a specific physician. Others criticize the data bank's one-dollar requirement, arguing that "nuisance" claims under a certain amount should not be reported or that different specialties should be given different monetary thresholds before reporting is mandated.

By regulation hospitals must query the NPDB when considering a physician for a med-

ical staff appointment or for clinical privileges. They must also query at least once every two years concerning any physician who is on its medical staff or has clinical privileges at the hospital. Boards of medical examiners, professional societies, other state licensing boards, or other healthcare entities that are entering an employment or affiliation arrangement with a physician may also request information at any time. In addition, a physician may query the NPDB concerning his own record at any time. Attorneys may have access in very limited circumstances where proof exists that a hospital failed to make a required query.

MEDICAL MALPRACTICE insurers are not allowed access to NPDB information. Access to information in the NPDB is available to entities that meet the eligibility requirements defined in the provisions of P.L. No. 99–660 and the NPDB regulations. In order to access information, entities must first register with the Data Bank. NPDB information is not available to the general public. However, the NPDB maintains an INTERNET site and makes available information in a form that does not identify any particular entity or practitioner.

FURTHER READINGS

Appleby, Kristyn S., and Joane Tarver. 1994. "Confidentiality of Medical Records." *Trial Diplomacy Journal* (September-October).

Borzo, Greg. 1996. "Liability Records Going On Line in Massachusetts." *American Medical News* (July 1).

Guglielmo, Wayne J. 1996. "Are Doctors Evading the Malpractice Data Bank?" *Medical Economics* (May 28).

Jackson, Anthony. 1995. "Action for Wrongful Life, Wrongful Pregnancy, and Wrongful Birth in the United States and England." *Loyola of Los Angeles International and Comparative Law Journal* (April).

Koop, C. Everett. 1991. *Koop: The Memoirs of America's Family Doctor.* New York: Random House.

National Practitioner Data Bank. Available online at <www.npdb-hipdb.com> (accessed August 22, 2003).

Snider, Howard C., Jr. 1989. *A Jury of My Peers: A Surgeon's Encounter with a Malpractice Crisis.* Greenwood, Fla.: Penkevill.

CROSS-REFERENCES

Health Care Law; Health Insurance; Malpractice; Managed Care; Medicaid; Medicare; Patients' Rights; Physician-Patient Privilege; Privileged Communication.

PICKETING

The presence at an employer's business of one or more employees and/or other persons who are publicizing a labor dispute, influencing employees or customers to withhold their work or business, respectively, or showing a union's desire to represent employees; picketing is usually accompanied by patrolling with signs.

CROSS-REFERENCES

Labor Law; Labor Union.

PIERCE THE CORPORATE VEIL

See CORPORATIONS "Piercing the Corporate Veil" (In Focus).

❖ PIERCE, FRANKLIN

Franklin Pierce served as the fourteenth president of the United States from 1853 to 1857. He was the youngest person to be elected president up to that time. A northern Democrat who sought to preserve southern SLAVERY, Pierce's administration proved a failure because he antagonized the growing abolitionist movement by signing the KANSAS-NEBRASKA ACT of 1854, which gave the two new territories the option of whether to permit slavery. Pierce was unable to win renomination for a second term.

Pierce was born on November 23, 1804, in Hillsboro, New Hampshire. His parents were Benjamin and Anna Kendrick Pierce. Pierce graduated from Bowdoin College in 1824 and returned home to take over his father's duties as postmaster, after his father entered politics. Pierce studied law with a local attorney and was admitted to the New Hampshire bar in 1827. In that same year his father was elected governor of New Hampshire, which proved helpful to Pierce's own nascent political ambitions.

Pierce was elected as a Democrat to the New Hampshire legislature in 1829 and in 1832 was elected to the U.S. House of Representatives. A strong supporter of President ANDREW JACKSON, Pierce also became associated with the cause of slavery. In 1835 he attacked the flood of abolitionist petitions addressed to the House, which contained the signatures of more than two million people. He joined southern Democrats in imposing a "gag rule" that prevented the House from receiving or debating these petitions.

In 1837 Pierce was elected to the U.S. Senate. He resigned in 1842 for personal reasons and returned to Concord, New Hampshire, to become the federal district attorney. Except for a brief tour of duty as an Army officer during the Mexican War (1846–48), Pierce remained out of the political arena until the DEMOCRATIC PARTY national convention in 1852. The three leading candidates for the presidential nomination, Lewis Cass, STEPHEN A. DOUGLAS, and JAMES BUCHANAN, failed to win the necessary votes after forty-eight ballots. The convention turned to Pierce on the forty-ninth ballot as a compromise candidate who, though virtually unknown nationally, enjoyed support from northern and southern Democrats. He easily defeated General Winfield Scott, the WHIG PARTY candidate, in November 1852.

Pierce took office in March 1853, at a time when the issue of slavery threatened to divide both the Democratic and Whig parties, as well as the nation itself. Pierce sought to ease tensions by appointing a cabinet that contained a mix of southern and northern officials. Still critical of abolitionism, he enraged the antislavery movement with his signing of the Kansas-Nebraska Act of 1854. The act repealed the MISSOURI

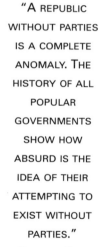

"A REPUBLIC WITHOUT PARTIES IS A COMPLETE ANOMALY. THE HISTORY OF ALL POPULAR GOVERNMENTS SHOW HOW ABSURD IS THE IDEA OF THEIR ATTEMPTING TO EXIST WITHOUT PARTIES."
—FRANKLIN PIERCE

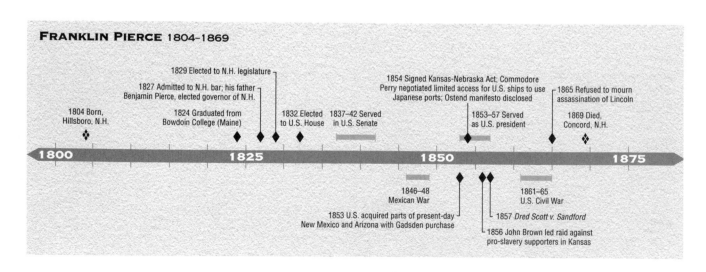

FRANKLIN PIERCE 1804–1869

1804 Born, Hillsboro, N.H.

1824 Graduated from Bowdoin College (Maine)

1827 Admitted to N.H. bar; his father Benjamin Pierce, elected governor of N.H.

1829 Elected to N.H. legislature

1832 Elected to U.S. House

1837–42 Served in U.S. Senate

1854 Signed Kansas-Nebraska Act; Commodore Perry negotiated limited access for U.S. ships to use Japanese ports; Ostend manifesto disclosed

1853–57 Served as U.S. president

1865 Refused to mourn assassination of Lincoln

1869 Died, Concord, N.H.

1800   1825   1850   1875

1846–48 Mexican War

1853 U.S. acquired parts of present-day New Mexico and Arizona with Gadsden purchase

1861–65 U.S. Civil War

1857 *Dred Scott v. Sandford*

1856 John Brown led raid against pro-slavery supporters in Kansas

COMPROMISE OF 1820, which restricted the boundaries of slavery to the same latitude as the southern boundary of Missouri—36° 30′ north latitude. The new territories of Kansas and Nebraska were organized according to the principle of popular sovereignty, which permitted voters to determine for themselves whether slavery would be a legalized institution at the time of the territories' admission as states.

Abolitionists saw the popular sovereignty principle as a means of extending slavery northward and westward. Pierce proved weak and indecisive as violence erupted in Kansas and Nebraska. On May 25, 1856, the militant abolitionist JOHN BROWN led a raid against supporters of slavery at Pottawatomie Creek, Kansas, killing five persons. Though appalled at the raid, Pierce said nothing and did little to address the growing violence between abolitionists and supporters of slavery that soon gave the territory the name "Bleeding Kansas." His support of slavery led to defections from the Democratic party and ultimately contributed to the establishment of the antislavery REPUBLICAN PARTY.

Pierce did achieve some success in foreign affairs. In 1854 Pierce received the report of Commodore Matthew C. Perry's expedition to Japan and the news that U.S. ships would have limited access to Japanese ports. His administration acquired a strip of land near the Mexican border for $10 million in the Gadsden Purchase of 1853, negotiated a fishing rights treaty with Canada in 1854, and in 1856 signed a treaty with Great Britain resolving disputes in Central America.

However, Pierce's popularity was damaged by his secret attempt to buy Cuba from Spain. The public disclosure of the October 1854 diplomatic statement called the Ostend Manifesto shocked Congress and the public. The manifesto discussed ways in which the United States might acquire or annex Cuba with or without the willingness of Spain to sell it. Pierce was forced to disclaim responsibility for the plan, but his integrity was placed in doubt.

Pierce was not renominated by the Democratic party in 1856, largely because of his difficulties with the Kansas-Nebraska Act and his ineffective leadership. The party turned to James Buchanan, who was elected but did little to resolve the political and sectional differences over slavery.

Pierce retired from public life in 1857 and returned to Concord, New Hampshire, to prac-

Franklin Pierce.
LIBRARY OF CONGRESS

tice law. He became a vocal critic of President ABRAHAM LINCOLN during the Civil War, however, attacking the EMANCIPATION PROCLAMATION of 1863. When, in April 1865, he failed to hang a flag in mourning for the assassinated Lincoln, a mob attacked his home.

Pierce died in Concord on October 8, 1869.

FURTHER READINGS

Gara, Larry. 1991. *The Presidency of Franklin Pierce.* Lawrence: Univ. Press of Kansas.

Nichols, Roy F. 1988. *Franklin Pierce: Young Hickory of the Granite Hills.* 2d ed. Norwalk, Conn.: Easton Press.

❖ PIERREPONT, EDWARDS

Edwards Pierrepont was a well-known lawyer, judge, and orator before serving as attorney general of the United States under President ULYSSES S. GRANT.

Pierrepont was born on March 4, 1817, in North Haven, Connecticut. When baptized, he was given the name Munson Edwards Pierpont. He legally discarded his given first name and changed the spelling of his family name. He graduated from Yale University in 1837 and Yale Law School in 1840 and then moved to Columbus, Ohio, to open his first law practice. By 1845 he had returned to the East Coast and entered a legal partnership in New York City. Over the next decade, he established a reputation of being a tough trial attorney and gifted courtroom orator.

In 1857 he was elected a judge of the Superior Court of the City of New York; he held the

"A PARDON IS . . . EVIDENCE . . . THAT GUILT HAS ONCE EXISTED, BUT, AT THE SAME TIME, THAT IT HAS BEEN ENTIRELY BLOTTED OUT, SO THAT IN THE EYE OF THE LAW THE OFFENDER IS AS INNOCENT AS IF HE NEVER COMMITTED THE OFFENSE."
—EDWARDS PIERREPONT

position until 1860 when he resigned to resume the PRACTICE OF LAW.

In the years before the U.S. CIVIL WAR, Pierrepont was said to have had his fingers on the pulse of the nation. He was often asked to speak at civic and political functions, and he privately advised ABRAHAM LINCOLN on issues of the day both before and after Lincoln was elected president. During the war Pierrepont represented the government against prisoners of state confined in U.S. military prisons and forts.

As a Lincoln confidant and supporter, Pierrepont was among those who organized the president's 1864 reelection effort. When the campaign was aborted by an assassin's bullet, the government appointed Pierrepont to handle the prosecution of John H. Surratt for his part in Lincoln's murder.

Pierrepont left Washington, D.C., and returned to New York after the war, but he remained in the public eye. As a private attorney, he continued to represent high-profile clients who included railroad barons and postwar industrialists. He also resumed his interest in politics at the state level. In April 1867 he was elected to participate in an effort to revise the state constitution, and he helped to organize local support for the 1868 presidential bid of General Ulysses S. Grant.

In recognition of his efforts, Pierrepont was appointed U.S. attorney for the southern district of New York in 1869, but he resigned just six months later to join the Committee of Seventy established in 1870 to force State Senator William Marcy ("Boss") Tweed from office. (After the Civil War, New York City government was dominated by TAMMANY HALL, a corrupt and abusive DEMOCRATIC PARTY patronage organization that operated under Tweed's direction.)

Pierrepont continued to support Grant when he ran for a second term in 1872. Following Grant's reelection, Pierrepont declined a diplomatic post in Russia because he was still involved in the efforts to clean up New York City government. But when Grant offered him a cabinet post in April 1875, Pierrepont was ready to accept.

He served as attorney general of the United States from May 1875 to May 1876. On the domestic front, Pierrepont did not depart significantly from the policies of his predecessor, GEORGE H. WILLIAMS; he maintained Williams's MORATORIUM on CIVIL RIGHTS prosecutions in the South and generally ignored the issues surrounding white violence against blacks. He was more interested in restoring the international economic influence and political clout that the United States had lost during the years following the war.

As attorney general, Pierrepont is most often remembered for his contributions to INTERNATIONAL LAW, including opinions that addressed issues of natural and acquired nationality and grounds for EXTRADITION (15 Op. Att'y Gen. 15 [1875]; 15 Op. Att'y Gen. 500 [1875]).

In May 1876 Pierrepont was named U.S. minister to Great Britain. Before Pierrepont's term of service, the English court rarely gave U.S. presidents and their representatives special treatment. When President Grant visited London in 1877, Pierrepont worked to ensure that Grant would be accorded the same honors and treatment as royal heads of state. Other governments soon followed Great Britain's example in acknowledging the United State's elected leaders.

During his years in London, Pierrepont devoted much of his time to studying England's financial system. When he returned to the

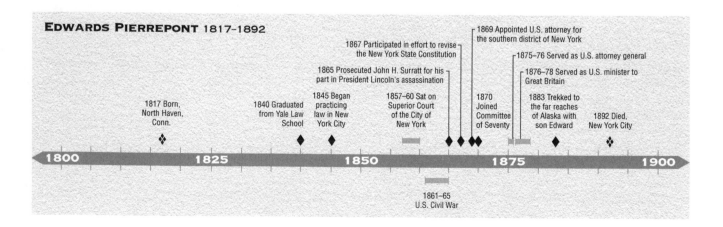

EDWARDS PIERREPONT 1817–1892

1817 Born, North Haven, Conn.

1840 Graduated from Yale Law School

1845 Began practicing law in New York City

1857–60 Sat on Superior Court of the City of New York

1865 Prosecuted John H. Surratt for his part in President Lincoln's assassination

1867 Participated in effort to revise the New York State Constitution

1869 Appointed U.S. attorney for the southern district of New York

1870 Joined Committee of Seventy

1875–76 Served as U.S. attorney general

1876–78 Served as U.S. minister to Great Britain

1883 Trekked to the far reaches of Alaska with son Edward

1892 Died, New York City

1861–65 U.S. Civil War

1800   1825   1850   1875   1900

United States in 1878, he published a number of pamphlets on the subject of U.S. and international financial systems, including a controversial 1887 flyer that advocated an international treaty to establish monetary policy, and recommended a common currency based on the value of silver, rather than the gold standard of the day.

In his later years, Pierrepont continued to practice law and edited many of his famous speeches for publication. He received many awards and citations during his long career, including honorary degrees from Yale University, Columbia College in Washington, D.C., and Oxford University in England.

In May 1883, at the age of sixty-six, Pierrepont accompanied his son, Edward Willoughby Pierrepont, to the far reaches of Alaska. Upon their return, father and son published a widely praised paper entitled "From Fifth Avenue to Alaska," for which the son was awarded a fellowship in the Royal Geographical Society of England. Although the rigors of the journey took a toll on the younger man, who died in 1884, the elder Pierrepont lived until 1892. He died March 6, 1892, in New York City.

PILOT

In maritime law, a person who assumes responsibility for a vessel at a particular place for the purpose of navigating it through a river or channel, or from or into a port.

The captain, or master, of a large ship has total command in the high seas. However, when a ship enters or leaves a port, or enters a river or channel, the captain turns over navigation to a local pilot. Because of safety and commercial concerns, state and federal maritime law governs the licensing and regulation of pilots.

A docking pilot directs the tugboats that pull a ship from the pier. Once the ship has cleared the pier and is under way in the harbor, the docking pilot leaves the ship and turns navigation over to a harbor pilot. Every ship that enters and leaves a port must have a harbor pilot aboard. Once the ship reaches open water, a small boat picks up the harbor pilot and returns the pilot to port. The captain then resumes full command of the ship.

The harbor pilot must have a thorough knowledge of every channel, sandbar, and other obstacle that could run the ship aground, strike another ship, or cause an accident that would endanger the ship, its crew, its cargo, and any passengers on board. The pilot must also be an experienced sailor who knows how to maneuver a ship through crowded harbors.

Either the state or federal government licenses pilots to ensure that vessels will be properly operated in state and U.S. waters. Federal law requires that federally registered pilots navigate ships on the Great Lakes, and state law regulates the need for pilots in bays, inlets, rivers, harbors, and ports. Where the waters are the boundary between two states, the owner of the ship can hire a pilot who has been licensed by either state to navigate the vessel to and from port.

State and federal laws impose qualifications for a pilot's license. A pilot must have the highest degree of skill as a sailor and may be tested on that knowledge. The individual may be required to submit written references from persons for whom he or she has served as an apprentice. In addition, the applicant must obtain a reference from a licensed pilot. The pilot may also be required to post a bond.

Once licensed, the pilot must act in a professional manner. A license can be revoked or suspended for adequate cause, such as when the pilot has operated the ship while intoxicated. The pilot has the right to appeal to a court an administrative body's decision to deny licensure or to impose discipline.

The legal rights and responsibilities of the harbor pilot's action in navigating vessels are well settled. The pilot has primary control of the navigation of the vessel, and the crew must obey any pilot order. The pilot is empowered to issue steering directions and to set the course and speed of the ship and the time, place, and manner of anchoring it. The captain is in command of the ship except for navigation purposes. The captain can properly assume command over the ship when the pilot is obviously incompetent or intoxicated.

The pilot must possess and exercise the ordinary skill and care of one who is an expert in a profession. A pilot can be held personally liable to the owners of the vessel and to other injured parties for damages resulting from NEGLIGENCE that causes a collision. The pilot will be responsible for damages if his or her handling of the ship was unreasonable, according to persons of nautical experience and good seamanship, at the time of the accident. The negligence of a pilot in the performance of duty is a maritime TORT within the jurisdiction of a court of ADMIRALTY, which deals only with maritime actions.

CROSS-REFERENCES

Admiralty and Maritime Law; Airlines.

PIMP

In feudal England, a type of tenure by which a tenant was permitted to use real property that belonged to a lord in exchange for the performance of some service, such as providing young women for the use and pleasure of the lord.

An individual who, for a fee, supplies another individual with a prostitute for sexual purposes. To pander, or cater to the sexual desires of others in exchange for money.

CROSS-REFERENCES

Prostitution.

PINKERTON AGENTS

The Pinkerton National Detective Agency was founded in 1850 in Chicago by ALLAN PINKERTON. It was one of the first private detective agencies in the United States, and its agents played an important role in law enforcement in the nineteenth and early twentieth century. Pinkerton agents were employed to capture bank robbers, counterfeiters, and forgers, but

Pinkerton Agents, hired as strikebreakers, surrendered to armed miners during the 1892 Homestead Strike in Pennsylvania. AP/WIDE WORLD PHOTOS

they also were used to infiltrate LABOR UNIONS and disrupt strikes.

Allan Pinkerton established offices throughout the country. A Pinkerton innovation was photographing criminals after arrest. The "mug shot" soon was adopted by police departments. By the 1870s the Pinkerton agency had the largest collection of mug shots in the world. Agents would clip out newspaper stories about a criminal and include this information in the criminal's file. When a crime was committed in town, the sheriff could send descriptions by witnesses to the agency, and the agents would provide a photograph and a detailed description of the suspect to law enforcement agencies in nearby communities.

In the late 1870s, coal mining operators in Pennsylvania hired Pinkerton agents to disrupt union organizing. Some agents infiltrated the Molly Maguires, a secret organization of Pennsylvania and West Virginia coal miners. After a long and highly publicized trial in which Pinkerton agents were witnesses, nineteen miners were hanged for crimes committed during the strike.

Pinkerton agents chased bandits across the United States after the Civil War, including the gang led by Jesse and Frank James. Robert Pinkerton, the son of Allan, led the group that followed and captured the Younger Brothers Gang in 1874. Pinkerton agents also pursued, unsuccessfully, Butch Cassidy (Robert Parker) and the Sundance Kid (Harry Longabough) as the pair robbed trains and banks in the southwestern United States in the late 1890s.

The Pinkerton agency remains in existence and has its headquarters in Encino, California. The agency provides investigative services, uniformed security officers, security systems, and other products and services associated with personal and business security.

FURTHER READINGS

Horan, James D. 1968. *The Pinkertons: The Detective Dynasty That Made History.* New York: Crown Publishers.

Morn, Allen. 1982. *"The Eye that Never Sleeps": A History of the Pinkerton National Detective Agency.* Bloomington: Indiana Univ. Press

❖ PINKERTON, ALLAN

Allan Pinkerton was a famous nineteenth-century detective and founder of the Pinkerton National Detective Agency. Pinkerton served as a spy during the U.S. CIVIL WAR and was renowned for preventing the assassination of

President-Elect ABRAHAM LINCOLN in 1861. He became a controversial figure when large companies hired his "Pinkerton men" to break LABOR UNION strikes through the use of intimidation and violence.

Pinkerton was born on August 25, 1819, in Glasgow, Scotland. His father was a police sergeant, but as a young man Pinkerton did not seek a police job. Instead he apprenticed as a cooper and learned to make barrels. In 1842, after he completed his apprenticeship, Pinkerton emigrated to the United States. He settled in Chicago and set up a cooper's shop.

In 1843 Pinkerton moved his business to Dundee, in Kane County, Illinois. In that year he discovered and captured a gang of counterfeiters. The event changed Pinkerton's life. He became involved with police work and was appointed deputy sheriff of Kane County in 1846. He soon shifted to a similar position in Cook County, with headquarters in Chicago.

In 1850 he resigned as a deputy and started the Pinkerton National Detective Agency. This private detective agency, which specialized in railroad theft cases, became the most famous organization of its kind. Pinkerton soon opened branches in several cities. In 1866 his agents recovered $700,000 stolen from the Adams Express Company and captured the thieves.

Pinkerton's public image was enhanced by his discovery in 1861 of a plot to assassinate Abraham Lincoln as the president-elect traveled by train from Springfield, Illinois, to Washington, D.C. With the outbreak of the Civil War, Pinkerton entered the Union army as a major.

Allan Pinkerton.
LIBRARY OF CONGRESS

He was commissioned by General George B. McClellan to create a SECRET SERVICE of the U.S. Army to investigate criminal activity, such as payroll thefts and murder. Pinkerton also headed an organization, under the name E. J. Allan, that worked to obtain military information in the Southern states.

Following the Civil War, Pinkerton returned to his detective agency. His agency soon became an integral part in the wars between labor and management that became common in the 1870s. States enacted laws that gave corporations the authority to create their own private police

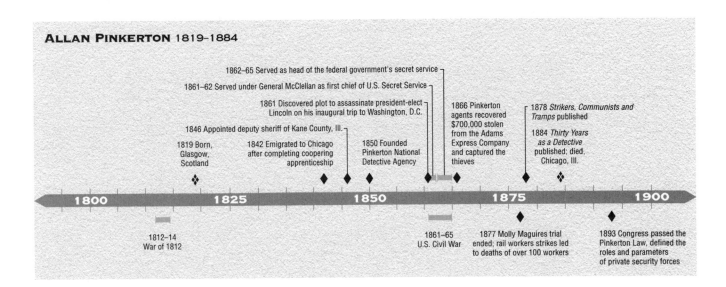

ALLAN PINKERTON 1819–1884

1862–65 Served as head of the federal government's secret service

1861–62 Served under General McClellan as first chief of U.S. Secret Service

1861 Discovered plot to assassinate president-elect Lincoln on his inaugural trip to Washington, D.C.

1846 Appointed deputy sheriff of Kane County, Ill.

1819 Born, Glasgow, Scotland

1842 Emigrated to Chicago after completing coopering apprenticeship

1850 Founded Pinkerton National Detective Agency

1866 Pinkerton agents recovered $700,000 stolen from the Adams Express Company and captured the thieves

1878 *Strikers, Communists and Tramps* published

1884 *Thirty Years as a Detective* published; died, Chicago, Ill.

| 1800 | 1825 | 1850 | 1875 | 1900 |

1812–14 War of 1812

1861–65 U.S. Civil War

1877 Molly Maguires trial ended; rail workers strikes led to deaths of over 100 workers

1893 Congress passed the Pinkerton Law, defined the roles and parameters of private security forces

forces or to contract with established police agencies. Pinkerton created groups of armed men known as Pinkerton men, who were contracted out for a daily fee to corporations with labor problems. Their menacing attitudes and use of violence were despised by labor unions and their supporters.

In 1877 the United States was beset by a number of railroad strikes. Pinkerton's agents were used as strikebreakers, and their harsh actions toward the labor unions were criticized. James McParlan, a Pinkerton agent, infiltrated the Molly Maguires, a secret organization of Pennsylvania and West Virginia coal miners. From 1872 to 1876, McParlan became part of the Molly Maguires, who were responsible for TERRORISM in the coal fields. He later testified in a series of trials that led to the conviction and hanging of ten men for murder.

Pinkerton, an unabashed self-promoter, wrote an account called *The Molly Maguires and the Detectives* (1877). In 1878 he wrote *Strikers, Communists and Tramps* in which he defended the use of his agents as strikebreakers, arguing that he was protecting workers by opposing unionism. He wrote about his role in foiling the Lincoln assassination in *The Spy of the Rebellion* (1883) and his autobiography *Thirty Years as a Detective* (1884).

Pinkerton died on July 1, 1884, in Chicago.

FURTHER READINGS

Mackay, James. 1997. *Allan Pinkerton: The First Private Eye.* New York: J. Wiley & Sons.

❖ PINKNEY, WILLIAM

William Pinkney was a lawyer, statesman, and diplomat before serving as attorney general of the United States under President JAMES MADISON.

Pinkney was born in Annapolis, Maryland, on March 17, 1764. Though his early education was sporadic during the Revolutionary war years, Pinkney was a diligent student. He originally studied medicine, but in 1783 he met Judge SAMUEL CHASE. Chase thought the young medical student would make a good lawyer and offered to tutor him. For the next three years, Pinkney read law in Chase's Baltimore office. He was admitted to the bar in 1786.

In 1787 Pinkney established a law practice in rural Harford County, Maryland. With encouragement from Chase, he also became active in local politics. In 1788 he was elected to the Maryland House of Delegates, the lower house of the legislative assembly. In the legislature, Pinkney established a reputation as an eloquent speaker and a skillful lawmaker.

By 1792 Pinkney had left his seat in the house of delegates to serve on Maryland's executive council, a body appointed to advise or assist the governor in the execution of official duties. Pinkney lived and practiced law in Annapolis during his term of council service, from 1792 to 1795.

In 1796 President GEORGE WASHINGTON appointed Pinkney to the tribunal responsible for enforcing the British Treaty of 1794 (or Jay's Treaty). This treaty, negotiated by Supreme Court Chief Justice JOHN JAY, established an international commission to arbitrate boundary disputes between the United States and Great Britain, and to settle charges of interference with merchant shipping and trade between the two countries.

Pinkney served on the commission for the next eight years. The experience made him an expert in the fields of ADMIRALTY and INTERNATIONAL LAW, but his long stay in England took a toll on his personal finances. Unlike other diplomats of his day, Pinkney was not a wealthy man. By 1804 he had decided it was time to capitalize on his acquired expertise. He returned to Maryland and established a legal practice in Baltimore. Before long, he was a familiar and respected figure in Maryland's seaports and courtrooms. In 1805 he served as attorney general of Maryland while continuing to build his private practice.

In 1806 Great Britain renewed its aggression against U.S. ships in international waters. President THOMAS JEFFERSON asked Pinkney to accompany Envoy (and future president) JAMES MONROE to England to negotiate an agreement on the shipping rights of neutrals. Though Pinkney was reluctant to leave a law practice that was just beginning to prosper, he agreed to go. It was not one of his better decisions. Monroe departed England in 1807, leaving Pinkney to serve as resident minister. Pinkney pleaded for a replacement, but Jefferson ignored him. It was four years before Pinkney was relieved of his duties by Jefferson's successor, President Madison.

When Pinkney returned to Baltimore in 1811, he found that his practice had once again been devastated by his absence. In need of income while rebuilding his client base, he ran for, and was elected to, the Maryland state senate. By December of 1811, Pinkney had resigned his seat to accept President Madison's appointment as attorney general of the United States.

In 1811, the attorney general's post was still a part-time position that allowed the officeholder to continue in private practice—and to pursue other interests and commitments. Shortly after taking office, Pinkney chose to demonstrate his support for the WAR OF 1812 by enlisting and serving with a rifle company. This absence, and others required by Pinkney's law practice, contributed to growing sentiment that the country needed a full-time attorney general who resided in Washington, D.C. When Congress instituted a residency requirement in 1814, Pinkney chose to resign rather than put his law practice in jeopardy for a third time. Madison, who had supported the residency requirement, was disappointed with Pinkney's decision.

Even though the residency debate became the defining issue of his term, Pinkney made other contributions while in office. He advised on international trade matters, and worked with Supreme Court Justice JOSEPH STORY to improve the federal criminal code.

Friends and neighbors in Pinkney's home district apparently failed to consider his stand on the residency issue when they drafted him as a candidate for the U.S. House of Representatives in 1815. Members of Congress were not required to live in Washington, D.C., but most of them did while Congress was in session. Pinkney was elected but refused to serve.

It was almost two years before Pinkney reentered the public arena. In 1817 he accepted a diplomatic post as minister to Russia and special

William Pinkney.
HULTON/ARCHIVE BY GETTY IMAGES

envoy to Naples. This time, he served only the designated term abroad.

In 1818 Pinkney returned to Baltimore and the PRACTICE OF LAW. For the next two years, he was actively involved in many of the cases heard before the U.S. Supreme Court—including two celebrated confrontations in which he bested lawyer and orator DANIEL WEBSTER (TRUSTEES OF DARTMOUTH COLLEGE V. WOODWARD, 17 U.S. (4 Wheat.) 518, 4 L. Ed. 629 [1819]; M'CULLOCH V. STATE OF MARYLAND, 17 U.S. (4 Wheat.) 316, 4 L. Ed. 579 [1819]).

He also made amends for his earlier refusal to serve the people of Maryland in Congress. In 1820 he was elected to the U.S. Senate. He took his seat but did not complete the term. He died in Washington, D.C., on February 25, 1822.

"THE FREE SPIRIT OF OUR CONSTITUTION AND OF OUR PEOPLE IS NO ASSURANCE AGAINST THE PROPENSION OF UNBRIDLED POWER TO ABUSE."
—WILLIAM PINKNEY

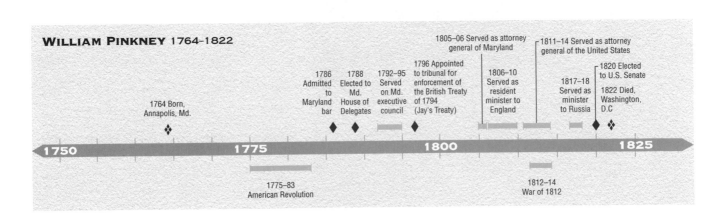

WILLIAM PINKNEY 1764–1822

1764 Born, Annapolis, Md.

1786 Admitted to Maryland bar

1788 Elected to Md. House of Delegates

1792–95 Served on Md. executive council

1796 Appointed to tribunal for enforcement of the British Treaty of 1794 (Jay's Treaty)

1805–06 Served as attorney general of Maryland

1806–10 Served as resident minister to England

1811–14 Served as attorney general of the United States

1817–18 Served as minister to Russia

1820 Elected to U.S. Senate

1822 Died, Washington, D.C

1750   1775   1800   1825

1775–83 American Revolution

1812–14 War of 1812

FURTHER READINGS

Baade, Hans W. 1991. "'Original Intent' in Historical Perspective: Some Critical Glosses." *Texas Law Review* 69 (April).

Forte, David F. 1996. "Marbury's Travail: Federalist Politics and William Marbury's Appointment as Justice of the Peace." *Catholic University Law Review* 45 (winter).

Hickey, Donald R. 1987. "The Monroe-Pinkney Treaty of 1806: A Reappraisal." *William and Mary Quarterly* 44.

Ireland, Robert M. 1986. *The Legal Career of William Pinkney, 1764–1822.* New York: Garland.

Jay, Stewart. 1985. "Origins of Federal Common Law: Part One." *University of Pennsylvania Law Review* 133 (June).

Rowe, Gary D. 1992. "The Sound of Silence: *United States v. Hudson & Goodwin,* the Jeffersonian Ascendancy, and the Abolition of Federal Common Law Crimes." *Yale Law Journal* 101 (January).

PIRACY

The act of violence or depredation on the high seas; also, the theft of INTELLECTUAL PROPERTY, *especially in electronic media.*

Piracy is a crime with ancient origins. As long as there have been ships at sea, pirates have sought to steal from them. Internationally, laws against piracy have ancient origins, too, but U.S. law developed chiefly in the eighteenth and nineteenth century. The power to criminalize piracy originated in the U.S. Constitution, which was followed by the first federal law in 1790 and crucial revisions over the next sixty years. Additionally, the United States and other nations cooperated to combat piracy in the twentieth century. This resulted in a unique shared view of jurisdiction: piracy on the high seas can be punished by any nation. In the late twentieth century, the term *piracy* grew to include COPYRIGHT violations of intellectual property such as music, films, and computer software.

The Constitution addresses piracy in Article 1, Section 8. It gives Congress "the Power ... To define and punish Piracies and Felonies committed on the high Seas, and Offenses against the Law of Nations." Generally, the definition of pirates meant rogue operators at sea—independent criminals who hijacked ships, stole their cargo, or committed violence against their crew. But standards in all areas under the law changed in response to judicial rulings and to historical incidents, forming by the mid-1800s what became the basis for contemporary law.

In 1790 Congress enacted the first substantive antipiracy law, a broad ban on murder and ROBBERY at sea that carried the death penalty. In 1818, however, the U.S. Supreme Court ruled that the law was limited to crimes involving U.S. citizens: U.S. jurisdiction did not cover foreigners whose piracy targeted other foreigners (*United States v. Palmer,* 16 U.S. [3 Wheat.] 610). A year later, in 1819, Congress responded by passing an antipiracy law to extend U.S. jurisdiction over pirates of all nationalities.

By the mid-nineteenth century, two other important changes occurred. Penalties for certain piracy crimes—revolt and mutiny—were reduced and were no longer punishable by death. Then the Mexican War of 1846–48 brought a radical extension of the definition of a pirate. The traditional definition of an independent criminal was broadened to include sailors acting on commissions from foreign nations, if and when their commissions violated U.S. treaties with their government. The Piracy Act of 1847, which established this broader definition, marked the last major change in U.S. piracy law.

Today, the primary source of antipiracy law is title 18, chapter 81, of the United States Code, although numerous other antipiracy provisions are scattered throughout the code. Additionally, international cooperation has shaped a unique form of jurisdictional agreement among nations. Significant in bringing about this cooperation was the GENEVA CONVENTION on the High Seas of April 29, 1958 and the 1982 United Nations Convention on the Law of the Sea. The primary effect of such agreements is to allow

In addition to its traditional nautical connotations, piracy has come to refer to copyright violations as well. Pirated material is displayed during this press conference held by members of various trade groups to discuss the issue of pirated goods from China. AP/WIDE WORLD PHOTOS

pirates to be apprehended on the high seas—meaning outside of territorial limits—by the authorities of any nation and punished under its own law. This standard is unique because nations are generally forbidden by INTERNATIONAL LAW from interfering with the vessels of another nation on the high seas. It arose because piracy itself has never vanished; in fact, since the 1970s, it has appeared to have undergone a resurgence.

Apart from its traditional definition, piracy also refers to copyright violations. Committed both in the United States and abroad, this form of piracy includes the unauthorized storage, reproduction, distribution, or sale of intellectual property—for example, music CDs, movie videocassettes, and even fashion designs. The term has been applied, in particular, to the piracy of computer software, which is highly susceptible to theft because of its ease of duplication. Estimates of the cost to copyright holders ranges in the billions of dollars annually. U.S. law protects copyright holders under the Copyright Act (17 U.S.C.S. § 109 [1993]), and a 1992 federal law makes software piracy a felony (Pub. L. No. 102-561, 106 Stat. 4233, codified at 18 U.S.C.A. § 2319 [1988 & 1992 Supp.]). Since the 1990s, a number of international treaties and conventions, as well as diplomatic initiatives, have sought to forge greater cooperation among nations to combat such piracy.

FURTHER READINGS

Menefee, Samuel Pyeatt. 1990/1991. "'Yo Heave Ho!': Updating America's Piracy Laws." *California Western International Law Journal* 21.

Short, Greg. 1994. "Combatting Software Piracy: Can Felony Penalties for Copyright Infringement Curtail the Copying of Computer Software?" *Santa Clara Computer and High Technology Law Journal* 10 (June).

CROSS-REFERENCES

Admiralty and Maritime Law; Computer Crime; Hijacking.

❖ PITNEY, MAHLON

Mahlon Pitney served as an associate justice of the U.S. Supreme Court from 1912 to 1922. A lawyer, legislator, and New Jersey Supreme Court judge before his appointment, Pitney was a judicial conservative who believed in "liberty of contract" and who generally opposed efforts to protect the right of workers to join unions.

Pitney was born on February 5, 1858, in Morristown, New Jersey. His father, Henry Pitney, was a lawyer and state supreme court judge. Pitney graduated from Princeton University in 1879 and then studied law with a lawyer instead of attending law school. He was admitted to the New Jersey bar in 1882. He practiced law in Dover, New Jersey, from 1882 to 1889. He returned to Morristown to assume control of his father's firm in 1889, when his father was appointed to the New Jersey Supreme Court.

Pitney began a brief political career in the 1890s. He was elected to the U.S. House of Representatives in 1895 as a Republican and served two terms. In 1899 he was elected to the New Jersey Senate, serving as president in 1901. He abandoned the political arena in 1901 when he was appointed to the New Jersey Supreme Court. He served as chancellor, the state's highest judicial post, from 1908 to 1912.

In 1912 President WILLIAM HOWARD TAFT appointed Pitney to the U.S. Supreme Court. During his ten years on the court, Pitney wrote many opinions that dealt with unions and business and their regulation by government. Pitney, an economic conservative, was generally hostile to government interference with employers and

> "THE CONSTITUTION . . . IMPOSES UPON THE STATES NO OBLIGATION TO CONFER UPON THOSE WITHIN THEIR JURISDICTION EITHER THE RIGHT OF FREE SPEECH OR THE RIGHT OF SILENCE."
> —MAHLON PITNEY

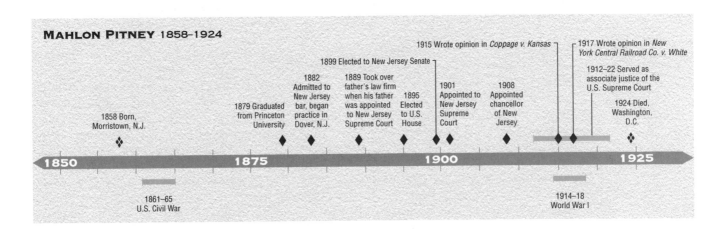

MAHLON PITNEY 1858–1924

- 1858 Born, Morristown, N.J.
- 1879 Graduated from Princeton University
- 1882 Admitted to New Jersey bar, began practice in Dover, N.J.
- 1889 Took over father's law firm when his father was appointed to New Jersey Supreme Court
- 1895 Elected to U.S. House
- 1899 Elected to New Jersey Senate
- 1901 Appointed to New Jersey Supreme Court
- 1908 Appointed chancellor of New Jersey
- 1915 Wrote opinion in *Coppage v. Kansas*
- 1917 Wrote opinion in *New York Central Railroad Co. v. White*
- 1912–22 Served as associate justice of the U.S. Supreme Court
- 1924 Died, Washington, D.C.

1850   1875   1900   1925

- 1861–65 U.S. Civil War
- 1914–18 World War I

Mahlon Pitney.
CORBIS

place and reduced the ability of individuals and small companies to compete. Most importantly, Pitney supported state WORKERS' COMPENSATION statutes, which had just been introduced as a way to protect workers hurt on the job. In *New York Central Railroad Co. v. White*, 243 U.S. 188, 37 S. Ct. 247, 61 L. Ed. 667 (1917), and in several subsequent cases, Pitney ruled that employers were liable for the injuries suffered by their workers during the course of employment. Workers' compensation statutes changed the legal landscape for employers and employees. States created administrative systems that quickly and fairly compensated employees for their injuries. Employers were no longer able to invoke common-law TORT rules to avoid liability. Without Pitney's leadership on this issue, the laws might not have survived judicial scrutiny.

Pitney suffered a stroke in August 1922 and resigned from the Court in December. He died on December 9, 1924, in Washington, D.C.

FURTHER READINGS

Belknap, Michal R. 1986. "Mr. Justice Pitney and Progressivism." *Seton Hall Law Review* 16 (spring).

P.J.

An abbreviation for presiding judge, the individual who directs, controls, or governs a particular tribunal as its chief officer.

PLAGIARISM

The act of appropriating the literary composition of another author, or excerpts, ideas, or passages therefrom, and passing the material off as one's own creation.

Plagiarism is theft of another person's writings or ideas. Generally, it occurs when someone steals expressions from another author's composition and makes them appear to be his own work. Plagiarism is not a legal term; however, it is often used in lawsuits. Courts recognize acts of plagiarism as violations of COPYRIGHT law, specifically as the theft of another person's INTELLECTUAL PROPERTY. Because copyright law allows a variety of creative works to be registered as the property of their owners, lawsuits alleging plagiarism can be based on the appropriation of any form of writing, music, and visual images.

Plagiarism can take a broad range of forms. At its simplest and most extreme, plagiarism involves putting one's own name on someone

employees. During the time Pitney was on the court, U.S. LABOR UNIONS were struggling to survive in a legal environment that favored employers. In *Coppage v. Kansas*, 236 U.S. 1, 35 S. Ct. 240, 59 L. Ed. 441 (1915), Pitney struck down a Kansas statute that prohibited an employer from using force or coercion to prevent employees from joining a union.

Pitney's hostility to unions and government regulation of business was based on his belief in individualism and unrestricted freedom in the marketplace. He subscribed to the liberty of contract theory that commanded widespread support on the Supreme Court. Pitney believed that liberty of contract was guaranteed by the FOURTEENTH AMENDMENT to the U.S. Constitution, which provided that no state was to "deprive any person of life, liberty or property without DUE PROCESS of law." Government regulation of work hours and working conditions was unconstitutional because regulation deprived employer and employee of the liberty to negotiate terms of employment. Likewise, unions hurt individualism by insisting on COLLECTIVE BARGAINING.

Pitney applied these beliefs to business as well. He supported antitrust statutes because monopolies, like unions, distorted the market-

else's work; this is commonly seen in schools when a student submits a paper that someone else has written. Schools, colleges, and universities usually have explicit guidelines for reviewing and punishing plagiarism by students and faculty members. In copyright lawsuits, however, allegations of plagiarism are more often based on partial theft. It is not necessary to exactly duplicate another's work in order to infringe a copyright: it is sufficient to take a substantial portion of the copyrighted material. Thus, for example, plagiarism can include copying language or ideas from another novelist, basing a new song in large part on another's musical composition, or copying another artist's drawing or photograph.

Courts and juries have a difficult time determining when unlawful copying has occurred. One thing the plaintiff must show is that the alleged plagiarist had access to the copyrighted work. Such evidence might include a showing that the plaintiff sent the work to the defendant in an attempt to sell it or that the work was publicly available and widely disseminated.

Once access is proven, the plaintiff must show that the alleged plagiarism is based on a substantial similarity between the two works. In *Abkco Music, Inc. v. Harrisongs Music, Ltd.*, 722 F.2d 988 (2d Cir 1983), the Second Circuit Court of Appeals found "unconscious" infringement by the musician George Harrison, whose song "My Sweet Lord" was, by his own admission, strikingly similar to the plaintiff's song, "He's So Fine." Establishing a substantial similarity can be quite difficult as it is essentially a subjective process.

Not every unauthorized taking of another's work constitutes plagiarism. Exceptions are made under copyright law for so-called fair use, as in the case of quoting a limited portion of a published work or mimicking it closely for purposes of PARODY and satire. Furthermore, similarity alone is not proof of plagiarism. Courts recognize that similar creative inspiration may occur simultaneously in two or more people. In Hollywood, for example, where well-established conventions govern filmmaking, this conventionality often leads to similar work. As early as 1942, in *O'Rourke v. RKO Radio Pictures*, 44 F. Supp. 480, the Massachusetts District Court ruled against a screenwriter who alleged that a movie studio had stolen parts of his unproduced screenplay *Girls' Reformatory* for its film *Condemned Women*. The court noted that the similar plot details in both stories—prison riots,

escapes, and love affairs between inmates and officials—might easily be coincidental.

Sometimes the question is one of proper attribution. In January 2002, two highly regarded historians, Stephen Ambrose and Doris Kearns Goodwin, were accused of plagiarism in *The Weekly Standard*. The magazine revealed that Ambrose (who died in October 2002) took passages from another author's work and used them in his 2001 book *The Wild Blue*, while Goodwin used passages from several authors in her 1987 book *The Fitzgeralds and the Kennedys*. Both authors apologized, acknowledging that they had erred and adding that their failure to provide proper attribution was completely inadvert. Goodwin went so far as to address her mistakes in an essay in *Time* magazine. They agreed to correct the problem in future editions of the books in question. While some of their colleagues accepted the explanation, others questioned whether authors of such talent and prominence were in fact being disingenuous considering that both had borrowed numerous passages, not just one or two.

The INTERNET has added a new layer to the question of plagiarism, particularly among high school and college students. In the mid-1990s a number of Web sites cropped up that offered term papers, thesis papers, and dissertations for sale. These "paper mills" make it easy for students to purchase papers instead of writing their own. (The fact that many of the papers being sold are poorly written and minimally researched is apparently of little concern.) A similarly egregious problem results from the wide array of legitimate reports many Web sites make available on the Internet for research purposes. Unscrupulous students with a computer can easily copy large blocks of these reports and paste them into their own papers. Anecdotal evidence suggests that while the ease of copying information has not led to a dramatic increase in plagiarism among honest students, those who have already cheated are likely to make frequent use of electronic resources to continue cheating. Students who use the "copy-and-paste" writing method are being thwarted by instructors who simply type questionable phrases into search engines; if the passage exists in another paper, the search engine will probably find it.

FURTHER READINGS

Keyt, Aaron. 1988. "An Improved Framework for Music Plagiarism Litigation." *California Law Review* 76 (March).

Lewis, Mark. 2002. "Doris Kearns Goodwin and the Credibility Gap." *Forbes* (February 27) .

Mayfield, Kendra. 2001. "Cheating's Never Been Easier." *Wired* (September 4).

CROSS-REFERENCES

Copyright; Literary Property; Music Publishing; Publishing Law.

PLAIN-ERROR RULE

The principle that an appeals court can reverse a judgment and order a new trial because of a serious mistake in the proceedings, even though no objection was made at the time the mistake occurred.

The issuance of inconsistent instructions to a jury that would result in a miscarriage of justice, for example, can furnish the basis for a new trial, even though no timely and proper objection to the instructions was made. Although a person is entitled to a fair trial, he or she is not entitled to a flawless one; the individual does not have the right to a new trial merely because a HARMLESS ERROR has been committed.

PLAIN-MEANING RULE

A principle used by courts in interpreting contracts that provides that the objective definitions of contractual terms are controlling, irrespective of whether the language comports with the actual intention of either party.

The plain meaning of the contract will be followed where the words used—whether written or oral—have a clear and unambiguous meaning. Words are given their ordinary meaning; technical terms are given their technical meaning; and local, cultural, or TRADE USAGE of terms are recognized as applicable. The circumstances surrounding the formation of the contract are also admissible to aid in the interpretation.

PLAIN VIEW DOCTRINE

In the context of searches and seizures, the principle that provides that objects perceptible by an officer who is rightfully in a position to observe them can be seized without a SEARCH WARRANT and are admissible as evidence.

The U.S. Supreme Court has developed and refined the plain view doctrine over time. In *Coolidge v. New Hampshire,* 403 U.S. 443, 91 S.Ct. 2022, 29 L.Ed.2d 564 (1971), the Court ruled that the seizure of two automobiles in plain view during the arrest of the defendant, along with later findings of gunpowder, did not violate the defendant's FOURTH AMENDMENT rights (protection against unreasonable SEARCH AND SEIZURE).

The Court also has drawn distinctions between *searches* and *seizures* in applying the plain view doctrine. In *Arizona v. Hicks,* 480 U.S. 321, 197 S.Ct. 1149, 94 L.Ed.2d 347 (1987), the Court held that no seizure occurred when a police officer called to the scene of a shooting incident recorded serial numbers of stereo equipment he observed in plain view, and which he believed had been stolen. Nevertheless, the officer's actions in moving the equipment to find the serial numbers constituted a search; the officer had a "reasonable suspicion" that the equipment had been stolen, but it was not supported by PROBABLE CAUSE.

PLAINTIFF

The party who sues in a civil action; a complainant; the prosecution—that is, a state or the United States representing the people—in a criminal case.

PLAINTIFF IN ERROR

The unsuccessful party in a lawsuit who commences proceedings for appellate review of the action because a mistake or "error" has been made resulting in a judgment against him or her; an appellant.

PLAT

A map of a town or a section of land that has been subdivided into lots showing the location and boundaries of individual parcels with the streets, alleys, EASEMENTS, and rights of use over the land of another.

A plat is usually drawn to scale.

PLEA

A formal response by the defendant to the affirmative assertions of the plaintiff in a civil case or to the charges of the prosecutor in a criminal case.

Under the old system of COMMON-LAW PLEADING, a plea was the defendant's first PLEADING in a case, the document in which he set out reasons why the plaintiff should not win on the claim made in his or her declaration. Rather than enter a plea, a defendant could file a demurrer, which was a pleading in which the defendant argued that the plaintiff had not made out a legally sufficient case. If the defendant did not demur, he responded to the plaintiff's declaration with a plea.

There were two kinds of pleas, *dilatory* and *peremptory*. A dilatory plea did not argue against the merits of the plaintiff's claim but challenged that individual's right to have the court hear the case. It was called dilatory not because it unfairly delayed the trial but simply because it postponed the time when, if ever, the court would reach the merits of the case. A plea in abatement was a dilatory plea.

A peremptory plea, also called a plea in bar, did reach the merits of the case. It set out certain facts that the defendant claimed would bar the granting of relief to the plaintiff.

The plea could be a traverse, a full denial of the plaintiff's version of the facts. In that situation, the issue was defined, and the case went to trial for a determination in favor of one party or the other.

The plea could be a confession and avoidance, by which the defendant conceded the truth of the plaintiff's allegations but asserted new facts by which she sought to avoid the legal effect of the plaintiff's claim. For example, the defendant could admit that she had made a bargain as claimed by the plaintiff and then add that she was a minor at the time that she entered into the agreement and therefore could not be bound by it. At that point, no issue would yet have been disputed by both parties, and the plaintiff would have to respond to the plea. The plaintiff had the same range of possible responses that the defendant had had when she selected the plea, but the plaintiff's responsive pleading was called a replication. If the plaintiff raised a new question, the defendant had to respond with a rejoinder. After that, the pleading process could bounce back and forth with a sur-rejoinder, a rebutter, and a surrebutter. Common-law pleading thus became so complex and hypertechnical that it has now been replaced by CODE PLEADING and pleading similar to that of the federal CIVIL PROCEDURE.

A defendant could also enter a plea in a case in EQUITY. This was a special kind of answer to a bill in equity, that showed one or more reasons why the suit should be dismissed, delayed, or barred entirely. Since the procedures for cases at law and in equity have been merged, the plea in equity has also been abolished.

A criminal defendant has some options in responding to charges made against him. The rules of CRIMINAL PROCEDURE in the federal courts and many state courts permit a defendant to enter a plea of guilty, not guilty, or nolo contendere, which means "I do not wish to contest it." If a defendant fails or refuses to enter any plea at all, the court will enter a plea of "not guilty" for that individual, and then the trial may begin.

PLEA BARGAINING

The process whereby a criminal defendant and prosecutor reach a mutually satisfactory disposition of a criminal case, subject to court approval.

Plea bargaining can conclude a criminal case without a trial. When it is successful, plea bargaining results in a plea agreement between the prosecutor and defendant. In this agreement, the defendant agrees to plead guilty without a trial, and, in return, the prosecutor agrees to dismiss certain charges or make favorable sentence recommendations to the court. Plea bargaining is expressly authorized in statutes and in court rules.

In federal court, for example, plea bargaining is authorized by subsection (e) of rule 11 of the Federal Rules of Criminal Procedure. Under rule 11(e), a prosecutor and defendant may enter into an agreement whereby the defendant pleads guilty and the prosecutor offers either to move for dismissal of a charge or charges, recommend to the court a particular sentence or agree not to oppose the defendant's request for a particular sentence, or agree that a specific sentence is the appropriate disposition of the case. A prosecutor can agree to take any or all of these actions in a plea agreement. Under rule 11(e), plea bargaining must take place before trial unless the parties show good cause for the delay.

Generally a judge will authorize a plea bargain if the defendant makes a knowing and voluntary waiver of his or her right to a trial, the defendant understands the charges, the defendant understands the maximum sentence he or she could receive after PLEADING guilty, and the defendant makes a voluntary confession, in court, to the alleged crime. Even if a defendant agrees to plead guilty, a judge may decline to accept the guilty plea and plea agreement if the charge or charges have no factual basis.

PLEA BARGAINING: A SHORTCUT TO JUSTICE

Plea bargaining is widely used in the criminal justice system, yet seldom praised. Plea agreements are troublesome because they are something less than a victory for all involved. Prosecutors are loath to offer admitted criminals lighter sentences than those authorized by law. Likewise, most criminal defendants are less than enthusiastic over the prospect of openly admitting criminal behavior without the benefit of a trial. Despite the reservations of the parties, plea agreements resolve roughly nine out of every ten criminal cases. The sheer numbers have caused many legal observers to question the propriety of rampant plea bargaining.

Some critics of plea bargaining argue that the process is unfair to criminal defendants. These critics claim that prosecutors possess too much discretion in choosing the charges that a criminal defendant may face. When a defendant is arrested, prosecutors have the authority to level any charge if they possess enough facts to support a reasonable belief that the defendant committed the offense. This standard is called **PROBABLE CAUSE**, and it is a lower standard than ability to prove a charge **BEYOND A REASONABLE DOUBT**, the standard that the prosecution must meet at trial. Thus, for leverage, a prosecutor may tack on similar, more serious charges without believing that the charges can be proved beyond a reasonable doubt at trial.

Because prosecutors are evaluated in large part on their conviction rates, they are forced to try to win at all costs. According to some critics, prosecutors use overcharging to coerce guilty pleas from defendants and deprive them of the procedural safeguards and the full investigation of the trial process.

For example, assume that a defendant is arrested for trespassing. Assume further that the **TRESPASS** was an honest mistake and that the defendant was, by happenstance, on the property of a former spouse. In addition to trespassing, the prosecutor may charge the defendant, on the facts, with **STALKING** and attempted **BURGLARY**. The prospect of facing a trial on three separate criminal charges may induce the defendant to plea bargain because the potential cumulative punishment for all three crimes is severe. Ultimately the defendant may plead guilty to, and forfeit the right to a trial on, the trespassing charge, the only charge that stands a chance of being proved beyond a reasonable doubt. Such a plea bargain, claim some critics, is an illusory bargain for criminal defendants.

The practice of overcharging is impermissible, and courts may dismiss superfluous charges. However, courts are reluctant to prevent the prosecution from presenting a case on a charge that is supported by probable cause. Prosecutors have discretion in plea bargaining, and they may withdraw offers after making them. A defendant is also free to reject a plea bargain. In many cases, where a plea bargain is withdrawn or rejected and the case goes to trial, the defendant, if found guilty, receives punishment more severe than that offered by the prosecution in the plea bargain. This has been called the

The judge does not participate in plea bargain discussions. Prosecutors have discretion whether to offer a plea bargain. However, a prosecutor may not base the determination of whether to negotiate on the basis of an unjustifiable standard such as race, religion, or some other **ARBITRARY** classification.

Plea bargaining can be advantageous for both prosecutors and defendants. Prosecutors may seek a plea bargain in certain cases to save valuable court time for high-priority cases. Prosecutors often are amenable to plea bargaining with a defendant who admits guilt and accepts responsibility for a crime: plea bargaining in this context is considered the defendant's reward for confessing. Prosecutors also accept plea bargains because they are evaluated in large part according to their conviction rates and all plea bargains result in a conviction because the defendant must plead guilty as part of the plea agreement.

Criminal defendants may also benefit from plea bargaining. Plea agreements provide quick relief from the anxiety of criminal prosecution because they shorten the prosecution process. Furthermore, plea agreements usually give defendants less punishment than they would receive if they were found guilty of all charges after a full trial. For example, assume that a defendant has been charged with one count of driving under the influence and one count of possession of a controlled substance with intent to sell. If the defendant goes to trial and is found guilty on both counts, he could receive a prison sentence of several years. However, if he agrees to plead guilty to the charge of possession with intent to sell, the prosecutor may drop the driving-under-the-influence charge. The net result would be a slightly shorter prison sentence than would result with inclusion of the other count. As part of the same deal, the prosecutor also may agree to reduce the remaining charge in

"trial penalty" and it is another source of criticism of the plea bargain.

A defendant who goes to trial and is found guilty of a serious felony receives, on the average, a prison sentence that is twice as long as the sentence offered in a plea bargain for the same offense. A defendant cannot be penalized for **PLEADING** not guilty and going to trial, but the U.S. Supreme Court has not held that it is impermissible to punish defendants with sentences that are longer than those offered in plea agreements. When overcharging and the trial penalty are combined in the regular practice of plea bargaining, defendants have little choice but to plead guilty, and virtually every criminal act may be disposed of without a trial. This, according to some critics, is a perversion of the criminal justice system.

Other critics focus on the benefits that plea bargaining gives to defendants. They argue that plea bargaining softens the deterrent effect of punishment because it gives criminal defendants the power to bargain for lesser punishments. These critics note that experienced criminals are more likely to receive favorable plea bargains because they are familiar with the criminal justice system. According to these critics, plea bargaining subverts the

proposition that a criminal should receive a punishment suited to the crime.

Critics of plea bargaining tend to be either scholars or crime victims. Scholars complain of prosecutorial coercion, and crime victims decry the lighter sentences that plea bargaining produces. Defenders of plea bargaining tend to be the players in the system. These are judges, prosecutors, criminal defendants, and criminal defense attorneys. The majority of these persons accept plea bargaining as a necessary tool in the administration of criminal justice. They point out that critics of plea bargaining have no solution to the lack of judicial resources. Without increased funding for more courts, judges, prosecutors, and court employees, plea bargaining is a necessity in most jurisdictions.

In response to the overcharging argument, supporters of plea bargaining note that the prosecutor's discretion in charging is a concept deeply ingrained in U.S. law, and for good reason. A prosecutor is not required to decide the case before trial. Instead the prosecutor is required to press charges based on the facts and to present evidence to support the charges. If there is no reasonable interpretation of the facts to support a certain charge, the charge will be dis-

missed. The judge or jury makes the final decision of whether the evidence warrants conviction on a certain offense. Defendants may receive harsher sentences upon conviction at trial, but in any case the sentence must be authorized by law. Thus, procedural safeguards effectively protect criminal defendants from the perils of overcharging.

Proponents of plea bargaining also contend that both defendants and society reap benefits. Defendants benefit because both the defendant and prosecutor help to fashion an appropriate punishment. Society benefits because it is spared the cost of lengthy trials while defendants admit to crimes and still receive punishment. Although the punishment pursuant to a plea agreement is generally less severe than that imposed upon conviction after a trial, the process nevertheless produces a deterrent effect on criminal behavior because prosecutors are able to obtain more convictions. Each conviction places a defendant under the supervision of the criminal justice system, and this decreases the defendant's freedom. Moreover, subsequent convictions after a guilty plea can be punished more harshly because defendants are punished in large part according to their criminal history.

exchange for something from the defendant. For example, the prosecutor may ask the defendant to testify against the supplier of the drugs or to build a case against the supplier by acting as an agent for the police. A reduced charge, such as from possession with intent to sell down to simple possession, would further decrease any possible prison sentence. Finally, the prosecutor may agree to recommend to the court that the defendant serve a shorter prison sentence than the maximum term allowable under the simple possession statute.

Courts have generally upheld bargains whereby one defendant agrees to testify against another defendant or to provide evidence that incriminates another suspect. Some criminal defendants have sought to challenge these arrangements when other defendants have testified against them. For example, in *United States v. Singleton*, 165 F.3d 1297 (10th Cir. 1999), prosecutors struck a deal with Napoleon Dou-

glas, a drug dealer, whereby the prosecutors agreed to reduce the charges against him if he agreed to testify against Sonya E. Singleton. A trial court convicted Singleton of conspiring to distribute drugs and of MONEY LAUNDERING. Singleton's attorney argued during the trial and later on appeal that the deal between the prosecutors and Douglas amounted to BRIBERY in violation of 18 U.S.C.A. § 201(c)(2) (2000). Although a panel of the United States Court of Appeals for the Tenth Circuit initially agreed with Singleton, the court sitting en banc overruled the panel and affirmed the conviction. According to the court, the federal bribery statute did not apply to the federal government with respect to plea bargains.

Defendants are not required to enter into plea negotiations or accept a plea agreement offer. Some defendants choose to decline a plea bargain if they believe that the risk of conviction is outweighed by the possibility of acquittal.

Other defendants may disregard the risks and make a principled choice to proceed to trial. Some of these defendants seek to use trial proceedings as a forum for expressing dissent, and others merely wish to exercise their constitutional right to a trial or to publicly declare their version of events.

Prosecutors, likewise, are not obliged to plea bargain. When the alleged crime is particularly heinous or the case is highly publicized or politically charged, a prosecutor may be reluctant to offer any deals to the defendant in deference to victims or public sentiment. For example, a prosecutor may not offer a bargain to a person accused of a brutal rape and murder because such acts are widely considered to deserve the maximum allowable punishment.

The political influence on plea bargaining is more nebulous. Because prosecutors are hired by federal, state, and local governments, they often have political ties. If a case involves a prominent member of a political party, a prosecutor may refuse to offer a plea bargain to avoid the appearance of favoritism.

When a court accepts a plea agreement, the guilty plea operates as a conviction, and the defendant cannot be retried on the same offense. However, if the defendant breaches a plea agreement, the prosecution may reprosecute the defendant. For example, assume that Defendant A, as part of the plea agreement, must testify against Defendant B. If Defendant A pleads guilty pursuant to this agreement but later refuses to testify against Defendant B, the prosecutor may seek a revocation of the plea agreement and guilty plea.

If the government breaches a plea agreement, the defendant may seek to withdraw the guilty plea, ask the court to enforce the agreement, or ask the court for a favorable modification in the sentence. The government breaches a plea agreement when it fails to deliver its part of the plea agreement. For example, if a prosecutor agrees to dismiss a certain charge but later reneges on this promise, the defendant may withdraw her guilty plea. An unenthusiastic sentence recommendation by a prosecutor is not a breach of a plea agreement (*United States v. Benchimol*, 471 U.S. 453, 105 S. Ct. 2013, 85 L. Ed. 2d 462 [1985]).

Some prosecutors demand that defendants waive certain constitutional rights in exchange for a plea bargain. One such right involves *Brady* evidence, which consists of exculpatory or IMPEACHMENT evidence that tends to prove the factual innocence of the defendant. Under the case of *Brady v. Maryland*, 373 U.S. 83, 83 S. Ct. 1194, 10 L. Ed. 2d 215 (1963), the U.S. Supreme Court requires prosecutors to inform defendants of such evidence. In 2001, the U.S. Court of Appeals for the Ninth Circuit held that it was unconstitutional for prosecutors to withhold a departure recommendation on grounds that the defendant refused to waive his or her right to *Brady* evidence (*United States v. Ruiz*, 241 F.3d 1157 [9th Cir. 2001]). A unanimous Supreme Court, however, disagreed, holding that the "Constitution does not require the government to disclose material evidence prior to entering a plea agreement with a criminal defendant" (*United States v. Ruiz*, 536 U.S. 622, 122 S. Ct. 2450, 153 L. Ed. 2d 586 [2002]).

When a prosecutor or defendant revokes a plea agreement, the statements made during the bargaining period are not admissible against the defendant in a subsequent trial. This rule is designed to foster free and open negotiations. There are, however, notable exceptions. The rule applies only to prosecutors: a defendant's statements to government agents are admissible. Furthermore, a prosecutor may use statements made by the defendant during plea negotiations at a subsequent trial to impeach the defendant's credibility after the defendant testifies.

Many jurisdictions maintain statutes that require victim notification of plea bargaining. In Indiana, for example, a prosecutor must notify the victim of a felony of negotiations with the defendant or the defendant's attorney concerning a recommendation that the prosecutor may make to the court. If an agreement is reached, the prosecutor must show the agreement to the victim, and the victim may give a statement to the court at the sentencing hearing (Ind. Code § 35-35-3-2 [1996]).

Plea bargaining was not favored in colonial America. In fact, courts actively discouraged defendants from pleading guilty. Courts gradually accepted guilty pleas in the nineteenth century. As populations increased and court procedural safeguards increased, courts became overcrowded, and trials became lengthier. This made trial in every case an impossibility. By the twentieth century, the vast majority of criminal cases were resolved with guilty pleas. In the early 2000s, plea bargaining is conducted in almost every criminal case, and roughly nine out of ten plea discussions yield plea agreements.

FURTHER READINGS

Gifford, Donald G. 1983. "Meaningful Reform of Plea Bargaining: The Control of Prosecutorial Discretion." *University of Illinois Law Review* 37.

Herman, Nicholas Herman. 1997. *Plea Bargaining.* Charlottesville, Va.: Lexis Law.

Hessick, F. Andrew, III, and Reshma M. Saujani. 2002. "Plea Bargaining and Convicting the Innocent: The Role of Prosecutor, the Defense Counsel, and the Judge." *BYU Journal of Public Law* 16.

Heumann, Milton. 2002. "Plea Bargaining: Process and Outcome." *Criminal Law Bulletin* 38.

Nasheri, Hedieh. 1998. *Betrayal of Due Process: A Comparative Assessment of Plea Bargaining in the United States and Canada.* Lanham, Md.: Univ. Press of America.

Odiaga, Ursula. 1989. "The Ethics of Judicial Discretion in Plea Bargaining." *Georgetown Journal of Legal Ethics* 2.

Scott, Robert E., and William J. Stuntz. 1992. "Plea Bargaining as Contract." *Yale Law Journal* 101.

Soni, Anjili, and Michael E. McCann. 1996. "Guilty Pleas." *Georgetown Law Journal* 84.

CROSS-REFERENCES

Beyond a Reasonable Doubt; Criminal Law; Criminal Procedure; District and Prosecuting Attorneys; Due Process of Law; Probable Cause.

PLEA IN ABATEMENT

In COMMON-LAW PLEADING, *a response by the defendant that does not dispute the plaintiff's claim but objects to its form or the time or place where it is asserted.*

A plea in abatement does not absolutely defeat the plaintiff's claim because, even if the plea is successful, the plaintiff may renew the lawsuit in a proper form, time, or place. For this reason, it is called a dilatory plea, because it has the effect of postponing the time when a court considers the actual merits of the case of each party.

The plea in abatement was abolished as a particular form of response by the defendant when common-law pleading was replaced by CODE PLEADING and later by pleading rules, such as the federal Rules of Civil Procedure. Sometimes the term is still loosely used for modern procedural devices that accomplish what the old plea in abatement used to do.

CROSS-REFERENCES

Civil Procedure.

PLEA IN BAR

An answer to a plaintiff's claim that absolutely and entirely defeats it.

A plea in bar sets forth matters that deny the plaintiff's right to maintain his or her lawsuit; for example, because the STATUTE OF LIMITATIONS has expired or because the claim necessarily overrides a constitutionally protected right of the defendant.

PLEADING

Asking a court to grant relief. The formal presentation of claims and defenses by parties to a lawsuit. The specific papers by which the allegations of parties to a lawsuit are presented in proper form; specifically the complaint of a plaintiff and the answer of a defendant plus any additional responses to those papers that are authorized by law.

Different systems of pleading have been organized generally to serve four functions: (1) to give notice of the claim or defense; (2) to reveal the facts of the case; (3) to formulate the issues that have to be resolved; and (4) to screen the flow of cases into a particular court. Different systems may rely on the pleadings to accomplish these purposes or may use the pleadings along with other procedural devices, such as discovery, PRETRIAL CONFERENCE among the parties, or SUMMARY JUDGMENT.

Originally in ancient England, the parties simply presented themselves to a tribunal and explained their dispute. This worked well enough in the local courts and in the feudal courts where a lord heard cases involving his tenants, but the great common-law courts of the king demanded more formality. From the end of the fourteenth to the middle of the sixteenth century, the royal courts began more and more to demand written pleadings that set out a party's position in a case. Predictably the shift resulted in more formality and more rigid technical requirements that were difficult to satisfy. Thus the course of COMMON-LAW PLEADING was perilous. A claim or defense that did not exactly fit the requirements of the common-law FORMS OF ACTION was thrown out with no opportunity to amend it and come back into court.

Some relief was offered by the courts of EQUITY, which were not bound by the same complex system of pleading. Beginning in the fourteenth century, the authority of such courts increased in proportion to the rigidity of the common-law pleading. Equity was the conscience of the judicial system and was charged with doing complete justice regardless of technicalities. Cases were tried before a single judge without a jury, and the judge could allow different claims and various parties all in one proceeding. Some pretrial discovery of the other party's evidence was permitted. The initial pleading by a petitioner in equity was the bill, but states that now have the same procedures for law and equity specify the complaint as the first pleading in all kinds of civil actions today.

Despite criticism, common-law pleading endured in England and in the United States for several centuries. Beginning in 1848, some states replaced it by law with a new system called CODE PLEADING. The statutes enacting code pleading abolished the old forms of action and set out a procedure that required the plaintiff simply to state in a complaint facts that warranted legal relief. A defendant was authorized to resist the plaintiff's demand by denying the truth of the facts in the complaint or by stating new facts that defeated them. The defendant's response is called an answer.

In 1938, federal courts began using a modern system of pleading set out in the federal Rules of Civil Procedure. This system has been so effective that many states have enacted substantially the same rules of pleading. A pleading by a plaintiff or defendant under these rules is intended simply to give the other party adequate notice of the claim or defense. This notice must give the adversary enough information so that she can determine the evidence that she wants to uncover during pretrial discovery and then adequately prepare for trial. Because of this underlying purpose, modern federal pleading is also called notice pleading. The other objectives of earlier kinds of pleading are accomplished by different procedural devices provided for in the Federal Rules of Civil Procedure.

CROSS-REFERENCES

Civil Procedure.

PLEBISCITE

See REFERENDUM.

PLEDGE

A BAILMENT or delivery of PERSONAL PROPERTY to a creditor as security for a debt or for the performance of an act.

Sometimes called *bailment*, pledges are a form of security to assure that a person will repay a debt or perform an act under contract. In a pledge one person temporarily gives possession of property to another party. Pledges are typically used in securing loans, pawning property for cash, and guaranteeing that contracted work will be done. Every pledge has three parts: two separate parties, a debt or obligation, and a contract of pledge. The law of pledges is quite old, but in contemporary U.S. law it is governed in most states by the provisions for SECURED TRANSACTIONS in article 9 of the UNIFORM COMMERCIAL CODE.

Pledges are different from sales. In a sale both possession and ownership of property are permanently transferred to the buyer. In a pledge only possession passes to a second party. The first party retains ownership of the property in question, while the second party takes possession of the property until the terms of the contract are satisfied. The second party must also have a lien—or legal claim—upon the property in question. If the terms are not met, the second party can sell the property to satisfy the debt. Any excess profit from the sale must be paid to the debtor, or first party. But if the sale does not meet the amount of the debt, legal action may be necessary.

A contract of pledge specifies what is owed, the property that shall be used as a pledge, and conditions for satisfying the debt or obligation. In a simple example, John asks to borrow $500 from Mary. Mary decides first that John will have to pledge his stereo as security that he will repay the debt by a specific time. In law John is called the *pledgor,* and Mary the *pledgee.* The stereo is referred to as *pledged property.* As in any common pledge contract, possession of the pledged property is transferred to the pledgee. At the same time, however, ownership (or title) of the pledged property remains with the pledgor. John gives the stereo to Mary, but he still legally owns it. If John repays the debt under the contractual agreement, Mary must return the stereo. But if he fails to pay, she can sell it to satisfy his debt.

Pledged property must be in the possession of a pledgee. This can be accomplished in one of two ways. The property can be in the pledgee's *actual* possession, meaning physical possession (for example, Mary keeps John's stereo at her house). Otherwise, it can be in the *constructive* possession of the pledgee, meaning that the pledgee has some control over the property, which typically occurs when actual possession is

Pledge of Shares of Stock

BE IT KNOWN, for value received, the undersigned _____ (Pledgor) of _____

hereby deposits, delivers to and pledges with _____ (Pledges) of_____
as collateral security to secure the payment of the following described debt owning Pledges:

The share of stock, described as _____ shares of stock of _____ (Corporation)
represented as Stock Certificates No(s).

It is further agreed:

1. Pledgee may assign or transfer said debt and the collateral pledged hereunder to any third party.

2. In the event a stock dividend or further issue of stock in the Corporation is issued to the Pledgor, the Pledgor shall pledge said shares as additional collateral for the debt.

3. That during the term of this pledge agreement, and so long as it is not in default, the Pledgor shall have full rights to vote said shares and be entitled to all dividends income, except that stock dividends shall also be pledged.

4. That during the pendency of this agreement, the Pledgor shall not issue any proxy or assignment of rights to the pledged shares.

5. The Pledgor warrants and represents it has good title to the shares being pledge, they are free from liens and encumbrances or prior pledge, and the Pledgor has full authority to transfer said shares as collateral security.

6. Upon default of payment of the debt, or breach of this pledge agreement, the Pledgee or holder shall have full rights to foreclose on the pledged shares and exercise its rights as a secured party pursuant to Article 9 of the Uniform Commercial Code; and said rights being cumulative with any other rights the Pledgee or holder may have against the Pledgor.

The Pledgor understands that upon foreclosure the pledged shares may be sold at public auction or public sale. The Pledgor shall be provided reasonable notice of any said intended sale and the Pledgor shall have full rights to redeem said shares at any time prior to said sale upon payment of the balance due hereunder, and accrued costs of collection. In the event the shares shall be sold for less than the amount then owing, the Pledgor shall be liable for any deficiency.

Upon payment of the obligation for which the shares are pledged, the shares shall be returned to the Pledgor and this pledge agreement shall be terminated.

This pledge agreement shall be binding upon and inure to the benefit of the parties, their successors, assigns and personal representatives.

Upon default the Pledgor shall pay all reasonable attorneys' fees and cost of collections.

Signed this _____ day of _____, 20____.

_____
Witness

_____
Pledgor

_____
Witness

_____
Pledgor

---

impossible. For example, a pledgee has constructive possession of the contents of a pledgor's safety deposit box at a bank when the pledgor gives the pledgee the only keys to the box.

In pledges both parties have certain rights and liabilities. The contract of pledge represents only one set of these: the terms under which the debt or obligation will be fulfilled and the pledged property returned. On the one hand, the pledgor's rights extend to the safekeeping and protection of his property while it is in possession of the pledgee. The property cannot be used without permission unless use is necessary for its preservation, such as exercising a live ani-

mal. Unauthorized use of the property is called conversion and may make the pledgee liable for damages; thus, Mary should not use John's stereo while in possession of it.

For the pledgee, on the other hand, there is more than the duty to care for the pledgor's property. The pledgee has the right to the possession and control of any income accruing during the period of the pledge, unless an agreement to the contrary exists. This income reduces the amount of the debt, and the pledgor must account for it to the pledgee. Additionally, the pledgee is entitled to be reimbursed for expenses incurred in retaining, caring for, and protecting the property. Finally, the pledgee need not remain a party to the contract of pledge indefinitely. She can sell or assign her interest under the contract of the pledge to a third party. However, the pledgee must notify the pledgor that the contract of pledge has been sold or reassigned; otherwise, she is guilty of conversion.

PLESSY V. FERGUSON

An 1896 decision by the Supreme Court, *Plessy v. Ferguson,* 163 U.S. 537, 16 S. Ct. 1138, 41 L. Ed. 256, upheld the constitutionality of an 1890 Louisiana statute requiring white and "colored" persons to be furnished "separate but equal" accommodations on railway passenger cars.

The plaintiff, Homer Adolph Plessy, who was seven-eights Caucasian and one-eighth African, paid for a first-class seat on a Louisiana railroad. He took a seat in the coach that was reserved for white passengers, but the conductor told him to leave the "white" car and go to the "colored" coach under threat of being expelled from the train and arrested. When Plessy refused, he was ejected from the train and imprisoned. He was prosecuted for violating the law, which he

asserted was unconstitutional and violated the THIRTEENTH AMENDMENT to the U.S. Constitution, which abolished SLAVERY, and the FOURTEENTH AMENDMENT to the Constitution, which prohibited certain restrictive legislative acts by the states.

The Supreme Court agreed to decide the constitutionality of the law. It reasoned that, although the Thirteenth Amendment intended to abolish slavery, it was insufficient to protect the "colored" people from certain harsh state laws that treated them unequally. The Fourteenth Amendment was enacted "to enforce the absolute equality of the two races before the law . . . (but) it could not have been intended to abolish distinctions based upon color or to enforce social as distinguished from political equality. . . ." The Court decided that the law establishing separate but equal public accommodations and facilities was a reasonable exercise of the POLICE POWER of a state to promote the public good. "If the two races are to meet upon terms of social equality, it must be the result of voluntary consent of the individuals."

Only Justice JOHN MARSHALL HARLAN dissented, on the ground that such a law "interferes with the personal freedom of citizens" under the

In Plessy v. Ferguson *(1896), the Supreme Court maintained that the Fourteenth Amendment was not intended to enforce social equality of races, a decision that stood for 58 years.*

CORBIS-BETTMANN

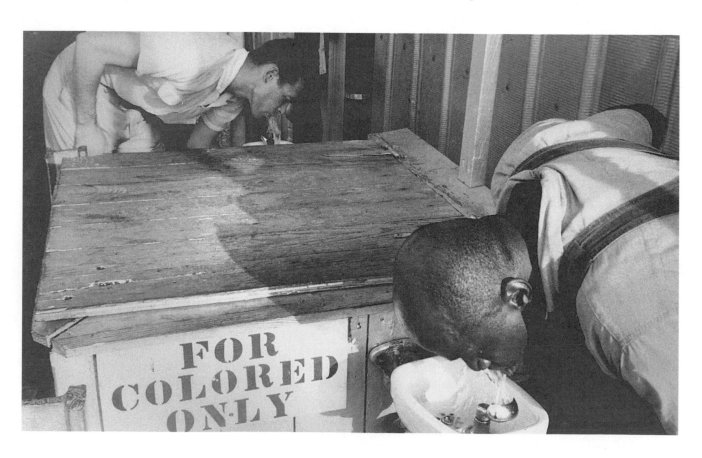

guise of legal equality. He maintained that the constitutional guarantees in this country were to be color-blind.

In 1954, the Supreme Court overruled this decision and recognized that separate but equal educational facilities were inherently unequal in BROWN V. BOARD OF EDUCATION OF TOPEKA, KANSAS, 347 U.S. 483, 74 S. Ct. 686, 98 L. Ed. 873 (1954). Subsequent Supreme Court decisions prohibited racial SEGREGATION in any public facilities and accommodations.

FURTHER READINGS

Anderson, Wayne. 2004. *Plessy v. Ferguson: Legalizing Segregation.* New York: Rosen.

Medley, Keith Weldon. 2003. *We as Freemen: Plessy v. Ferguson.* Gretna, La.: Pelican.

Postema, Gerald J., ed. 1997. *Racism and the Law: The Legacy and Lessons of Plessy.* Boston: Kluwer Academic.

Thomas, Brook, ed. 1997. *Plessy v. Ferguson: A Brief History with Documents.* Boston: Bedford.

CROSS-REFERENCES

Civil Rights; Civil Rights Movement; Integration; Jim Crow Laws; "Plessy v. Ferguson" (Appendix, Primary Document).

PLURALITY

The opinion of an appellate court in which more justices join than in any concurring opinion.

The excess of votes cast for one candidate over those votes cast for any other candidate.

Appellate panels are made up of three or more justices. In some cases the justices disagree over the outcome of the case to such an extent that a majority opinion cannot be achieved. (A majority opinion is one in which the number of justices who join is larger than the number of justices who do not.) To resolve such disagreements and reach a final decision, two or more justices publish opinions called concurring opinions, and the other justices decide which of these concurring opinions they will join. The concurring opinion in which more justices join than any other is called a plurality opinion. Plurality decisions can reflect a disagreement among the justices over a legal issue in a case or can reveal deeper ideological differences among the members of the court.

The term *plurality* is also used to describe the outcome of an election that involves more than two candidates. The candidate who receives the greatest number of votes is said to have received a plurality of the votes. In contrast, the term *majority* is used to describe the outcome of an election involving only two candidates; the winner is said to have received a majority of the votes.

A candidate who has a plurality of the votes can also have a majority of the votes, but only if she receives a number of votes greater than that cast for all the other candidates combined. Mathematically, a candidate with a plurality has a majority if she receives more than one-half of the total number of votes cast. If candidate John Doe has a plurality, he has earned more votes than any other candidate, but whether he has a majority depends on how many votes he won.

CROSS-REFERENCES

Court Opinion.

A.	Atlantic Reporter	ACT	American College Test
A. 2d	Atlantic Reporter, Second Series	Act'g Legal Adv.	Acting Legal Advisor
AA	Alcoholics Anonymous	ACUS	Administrative Conference of the United States
AAA	American Arbitration Association; Agricultural Adjustment Act of 1933	ACYF	Administration on Children, Youth, and Families
AALS	Association of American Law Schools	A.D. 2d	Appellate Division, Second Series, N.Y.
AAPRP	All African People's Revolutionary Party	ADA	Americans with Disabilities Act of 1990
AARP	American Association of Retired Persons	ADAMHA	Alcohol, Drug Abuse, and Mental Health Administration
AAS	American Anti-Slavery Society	ADC	Aid to Dependent Children
ABA	American Bar Association; Architectural Barriers Act of 1968; American Bankers Association	ADD	Administration on Developmental Disabilities
		ADEA	Age Discrimination in Employment Act of 1967
ABC	American Broadcasting Companies, Inc. (formerly American Broadcasting Corporation)	ADL	Anti-Defamation League
		ADR	Alternative dispute resolution
		AEC	Atomic Energy Commission
ABM	Antiballistic missile	AECB	Arms Export Control Board
ABM Treaty	Anti-Ballistic Missile Treaty of 1972	AEDPA	Antiterrorism and Effective Death Penalty Act
ABVP	Anti-Biased Violence Project	A.E.R.	All England Law Reports
A/C	Account	AFA	American Family Association; Alabama Freethought Association
A.C.	Appeal cases		
ACAA	Air Carrier Access Act		
ACCA	Armed Career Criminal Act of 1984	AFB	American Farm Bureau
		AFBF	American Farm Bureau Federation
ACF	Administration for Children and Families	AFDC	Aid to Families with Dependent Children
ACLU	American Civil Liberties Union	aff'd per cur.	Affirmed by the court
ACRS	Accelerated Cost Recovery System	AFIS	Automated fingerprint identification system
ACS	Agricultural Cooperative Service	AFL	American Federation of Labor

AFL-CIO	American Federation of Labor and Congress of Industrial Organizations	ANA	Administration for Native Americans
AFRes	Air Force Reserve	Ann. Dig.	Annual Digest of Public International Law Cases
AFSC	American Friends Service Committee	ANPA	American Newspaper Publishers Association
AFSCME	American Federation of State, County, and Municipal Employees	ANSCA	Alaska Native Claims Act
		ANZUS	Australia-New Zealand-United States Security Treaty Organization
AGRICOLA	Agricultural Online Access		
AIA	Association of Insurance Attorneys	AOA	Administration on Aging
		AOE	Arizonans for Official English
AIB	American Institute for Banking	AOL	America Online
AID	Artificial insemination using a third-party donor's sperm; Agency for International Development	AP	Associated Press
		APA	Administrative Procedure Act of 1946
		APHIS	Animal and Plant Health Inspection Service
AIDS	Acquired immune deficiency syndrome	App. Div.	Appellate Division Reports, N.Y. Supreme Court
AIH	Artificial insemination using the husband's sperm	Arb. Trib., U.S.-British	Arbitration Tribunal, Claim Convention of 1853, United States and Great Britain Convention of 1853
AIM	American Indian Movement		
AIPAC	American Israel Public Affairs Committee		
		Ardcor	American Roller Die Corporation
AIUSA	Amnesty International, U.S.A. Affiliate	ARPA	Advanced Research Projects Agency
AJS	American Judicature Society		
ALA	American Library Association	ARPANET	Advanced Research Projects Agency Network
Alcoa	Aluminum Company of America	ARS	Advanced Record System
		Art.	Article
ALEC	American Legislative Exchange Council	ARU	American Railway Union
		ASCME	American Federation of State, County, and Municipal Employees
ALF	Animal Liberation Front		
ALI	American Law Institute		
ALJ	Administrative law judge	ASCS	Agriculture Stabilization and Conservation Service
All E.R.	All England Law Reports		
ALO	Agency Liaison	ASM	Available Seatmile
A.L.R.	American Law Reports	ASPCA	American Society for the Prevention of Cruelty to Animals
ALY	*American Law Yearbook*		
AMA	American Medical Association		
		Asst. Att. Gen.	Assistant Attorney General
AMAA	Agricultural Marketing Agreement Act	AT&T	American Telephone and Telegraph
Am. Dec.	American Decisions	ATFD	Alcohol, Tobacco and Firearms Division
amdt.	Amendment		
Amer. St. Papers, For. Rels.	American State Papers, Legislative and Executive Documents of the Congress of the U.S., Class I, Foreign Relations, 1832–1859	ATLA	Association of Trial Lawyers of America
		ATO	Alpha Tau Omega
		ATTD	Alcohol and Tobacco Tax Division
		ATU	Alcohol Tax Unit
AMS	Agricultural Marketing Service	AUAM	American Union against Militarism
AMVETS	American Veterans (of World War II)	AUM	Animal Unit Month
		AZT	Azidothymidine

BAC	Blood alcohol concentration	CAA	Clean Air Act
BALSA	Black-American Law Student Association	CAB	Civil Aeronautics Board; Corporation for American Banking
BATF	Bureau of Alcohol, Tobacco and Firearms	CAFE	Corporate average fuel economy
BBS	Bulletin Board System	Cal. 2d	California Reports, Second Series
BCCI	Bank of Credit and Commerce International	Cal. 3d	California Reports, Third Series
BEA	Bureau of Economic Analysis		
Bell's Cr. C.	Bell's English Crown Cases	CALR	Computer-assisted legal research
Bevans	United States Treaties, etc. *Treaties and Other International Agreements of the United States of America, 1776–1949* (compiled under the direction of Charles I. Bevans, 1968–76)	Cal. Rptr.	California Reporter
		CAP	Common Agricultural Policy
		CARA	Classification and Ratings Administration
		CATV	Community antenna television
BFOQ	Bona fide occupational qualification	CBO	Congressional Budget Office
BI	Bureau of Investigation	CBS	Columbia Broadcasting System
BIA	Bureau of Indian Affairs; Board of Immigration Appeals	CBOEC	Chicago Board of Election Commissioners
BID	Business improvement district	CCC	Commodity Credit Corporation
		CCDBG	Child Care and Development Block Grant of 1990
BJS	Bureau of Justice Statistics		
Black.	Black's United States Supreme Court Reports	C.C.D. Pa.	Circuit Court Decisions, Pennsylvania
Blatchf.	Blatchford's United States Circuit Court Reports	C.C.D. Va.	Circuit Court Decisions, Virginia
BLM	Bureau of Land Management	CCEA	Cabinet Council on Economic Affairs
BLS	Bureau of Labor Statistics	CCP	Chinese Communist Party
BMD	Ballistic missile defense	CCR	Center for Constitutional Rights
BNA	Bureau of National Affairs		
BOCA	Building Officials and Code Administrators International	C.C.R.I.	Circuit Court, Rhode Island
		CD	Certificate of deposit; compact disc
BOP	Bureau of Prisons	CDA	Communications Decency Act
BPP	Black Panther Party for Self-defense	CDBG	Community Development Block Grant Program
Brit. and For.	British and Foreign State Papers	CDC	Centers for Disease Control and Prevention; Community Development Corporation
BSA	Boy Scouts of America		
BTP	Beta Theta Pi		
Burr.	James Burrows, *Report of Cases Argued and Determined in the Court of King's Bench during the Time of Lord Mansfield* (1766–1780)	CDF	Children's Defense Fund
		CDL	Citizens for Decency through Law
		CD-ROM	Compact disc read-only memory
BVA	Board of Veterans Appeals	CDS	Community Dispute Services
c.	Chapter	CDW	Collision damage waiver
C³I	Command, Control, Communications, and Intelligence	CENTO	Central Treaty Organization
		CEO	Chief executive officer
		CEQ	Council on Environmental Quality
C.A.	Court of Appeals		

CERCLA	Comprehensive Environmental Response, Compensation, and Liability Act of 1980	CLASP	Center for Law and Social Policy
cert.	*Certiorari*	CLE	Center for Law and Education; Continuing Legal Education
CETA	Comprehensive Employment and Training Act	CLEO	Council on Legal Education Opportunity; Chief Law Enforcement Officer
C & F	Cost and freight		
CFC	Chlorofluorocarbon	CLP	Communist Labor Party of America
CFE Treaty	Conventional Forces in Europe Treaty of 1990	CLS	Christian Legal Society; critical legal studies (movement); Critical Legal Studies (membership organization)
C.F. & I.	Cost, freight, and insurance		
C.F.R	Code of Federal Regulations		
CFNP	Community Food and Nutrition Program		
CFTA	Canadian Free Trade Agreement	C.M.A.	Court of Military Appeals
CFTC	Commodity Futures Trading Commission	CMEA	Council for Mutual Economic Assistance
Ch.	Chancery Division, English Law Reports	CMHS	Center for Mental Health Services
CHAMPVA	Civilian Health and Medical Program at the Veterans Administration	C.M.R.	Court of Military Review
		CNN	Cable News Network
		CNO	Chief of Naval Operations
CHEP	Cuban/Haitian Entrant Program	CNOL	Consolidated net operating loss
CHINS	Children in need of supervision	CNR	Chicago and Northwestern Railway
CHIPS	Child in need of protective services	CO	Conscientious Objector
		C.O.D.	Cash on delivery
Ch.N.Y.	Chancery Reports, New York	COGP	Commission on Government Procurement
Chr. Rob.	Christopher Robinson, *Reports of Cases Argued and Determined in the High Court of Admiralty* (1801–1808)	COINTELPRO	Counterintelligence Program
		Coke Rep.	Coke's English King's Bench Reports
		COLA	Cost-of-living adjustment
CIA	Central Intelligence Agency	COMCEN	Federal Communications Center
CID	Commercial Item Descriptions		
C.I.F.	Cost, insurance, and freight	Comp.	Compilation
CINCNORAD	Commander in Chief, North American Air Defense Command	Conn.	Connecticut Reports
		CONTU	National Commission on New Technological Uses of Copyrighted Works
C.I.O.	Congress of Industrial Organizations	Conv.	Convention
CIPE	Center for International Private Enterprise	COPA	Child Online Protection Act (1998)
C.J.	Chief justice	COPS	Community Oriented Policing Services
CJIS	Criminal Justice Information Services	Corbin	Arthur L. Corbin, *Corbin on Contracts: A Comprehensive Treatise on the Rules of Contract Law* (1950)
C.J.S.	Corpus Juris Secundum		
Claims Arb. under Spec. Conv., Nielsen's Rept.	Frederick Kenelm Nielsen, *American and British Claims Arbitration under the Special Agreement Concluded between the United States and Great Britain, August 18, 1910* (1926)	CORE	Congress on Racial Equality
		Cox's Crim. Cases	Cox's Criminal Cases (England)
		COYOTE	Call Off Your Old Tired Ethics

CPA	Certified public accountant	DACORB	Department of the Army Conscientious Objector Review Board
CPB	Corporation for Public Broadcasting, the		
CPI	Consumer Price Index	Dall.	Dallas's Pennsylvania and United States Reports
CPPA	Child Pornography Prevention Act	DAR	Daughters of the American Revolution
CPSC	Consumer Product Safety Commission	DARPA	Defense Advanced Research Projects Agency
Cranch	Cranch's United States Supreme Court Reports	DAVA	Defense Audiovisual Agency
CRF	Constitutional Rights Foundation	D.C.	United States District Court; District of Columbia
CRR	Center for Constitutional Rights	D.C. Del.	United States District Court, Delaware
CRS	Congressional Research Service; Community Relations Service	D.C. Mass.	United States District Court, Massachusetts
		D.C. Md.	United States District Court, Maryland
CRT	Critical race theory	D.C.N.D.Cal.	United States District Court, Northern District, California
CSA	Community Services Administration		
CSAP	Center for Substance Abuse Prevention	D.C.N.Y.	United States District Court, New York
CSAT	Center for Substance Abuse Treatment	D.C.Pa.	United States District Court, Pennsylvania
CSC	Civil Service Commission	DCS	Deputy Chiefs of Staff
CSCE	Conference on Security and Cooperation in Europe	DCZ	District of the Canal Zone
		DDT	Dichlorodiphenyltricloro-ethane
CSG	Council of State Governments	DEA	Drug Enforcement Administration
CSO	Community Service Organization	Decl. Lond.	Declaration of London, February 26, 1909
CSP	Center for the Study of the Presidency	Dev. & B.	Devereux & Battle's North Carolina Reports
C-SPAN	Cable-Satellite Public Affairs Network	DFL	Minnesota Democratic-Farmer-Labor
CSRS	Cooperative State Research Service	DFTA	Department for the Aging
CSWPL	Center on Social Welfare Policy and Law	Dig. U.S. Practice in Intl. Law	Digest of U.S. Practice in International Law
CTA	*Cum testamento annexo* (with the will attached)	Dist. Ct.	D.C. United States District Court, District of Columbia
Ct. Ap. D.C.	Court of Appeals, District of Columbia		
Ct. App. No. Ireland	Court of Appeals, Northern Ireland	D.L.R.	Dominion Law Reports (Canada)
Ct. Cl.	Court of Claims, United States	DMCA	Digital Millennium Copyright Act
		DNA	Deoxyribonucleic acid
Ct. Crim. Apps.	Court of Criminal Appeals (England)	Dnase	Deoxyribonuclease
		DNC	Democratic National Committee
CTI	Consolidated taxable income		
Ct. of Sess., Scot.	Court of Sessions, Scotland	DOC	Department of Commerce
CU	Credit union	DOD	Department of Defense
CUNY	City University of New York	DODEA	Department of Defense Education Activity
Cush.	Cushing's Massachusetts Reports		
		Dodson	Dodson's Reports, English Admiralty Courts
CWA	Civil Works Administration; Clean Water Act		
		DOE	Department of Energy

DOER	Department of Employee Relations	ERA	Equal Rights Amendment
DOJ	Department of Justice	ERDC	Energy Research and Development Commission
DOL	Department of Labor	ERISA	Employee Retirement Income Security Act of 1974
DOMA	Defense of Marriage Act of 1996		
DOS	Disk operating system	ERS	Economic Research Service
DOT	Department of Transportation	ERTA	Economic Recovery Tax Act of 1981
DPT	Diphtheria, pertussis, and tetanus	ESA	Endangered Species Act of 1973
DRI	Defense Research Institute		
DSAA	Defense Security Assistance Agency	ESF	Emergency support function; Economic Support Fund
DUI	Driving under the influence; driving under intoxication	ESRD	End-Stage Renal Disease Program
DVD	Digital versatile disc	ETA	Employment and Training Administration
DWI	Driving while intoxicated	ETS	Environmental tobacco smoke
EAHCA	Education for All Handicapped Children Act of 1975	et seq.	*Et sequentes* or *et sequentia* ("and the following")
EBT	Examination before trial	EU	European Union
E.coli	Escherichia coli	Euratom	European Atomic Energy Community
ECPA	Electronic Communications Privacy Act of 1986		
ECSC	Treaty of the European Coal and Steel Community	Eur. Ct. H.R.	European Court of Human Rights
EDA	Economic Development Administration	Ex.	English Exchequer Reports, Welsby, Hurlstone & Gordon
EDF	Environmental Defense Fund	Exch.	Exchequer Reports (Welsby, Hurlstone & Gordon)
E.D.N.Y.	Eastern District, New York	Ex Com	Executive Committee of the National Security Council
EDP	Electronic data processing		
E.D. Pa.	Eastern-District, Pennsylvania	Eximbank	Export-Import Bank of the United States
EDSC	Eastern District, South Carolina	F.	Federal Reporter
EDT	Eastern daylight time	F. 2d	Federal Reporter, Second Series
E.D. Va.	Eastern District, Virginia	FAA	Federal Aviation Administration; Federal Arbitration Act
EEC	European Economic Community; European Economic Community Treaty	FAAA	Federal Alcohol Administration Act
EEOC	Equal Employment Opportunity Commission	FACE	Freedom of Access to Clinic Entrances Act of 1994
EFF	Electronic Frontier Foundation	FACT	Feminist Anti-Censorship Task Force
EFT	Electronic funds transfer	FAIRA	Federal Agriculture Improvement and Reform Act of 1996
Eliz.	Queen Elizabeth (Great Britain)		
Em. App.	Temporary Emergency Court of Appeals	FAMLA	Family and Medical Leave Act of 1993
ENE	Early neutral evaluation	Fannie Mae	Federal National Mortgage Association
Eng. Rep.	English Reports		
EOP	Executive Office of the President	FAO	Food and Agriculture Organization of the United Nations
EPA	Environmental Protection Agency; Equal Pay Act of 1963	FAR	Federal Acquisition Regulations

FAS	Foreign Agricultural Service	FIP	Forestry Incentives Program
FBA	Federal Bar Association	FIRREA	Financial Institutions Reform, Recovery, and Enforcement Act of 1989
FBI	Federal Bureau of Investigation	FISA	Foreign Intelligence Surveillance Act of 1978
FCA	Farm Credit Administration		
F. Cas.	Federal Cases	FISC	Foreign Intelligence Surveillance Court of Review
FCC	Federal Communications Commission		
FCIA	Foreign Credit Insurance Association	FJC	Federal Judicial Center
		FLSA	Fair Labor Standards Act
FCIC	Federal Crop Insurance Corporation	FMC	Federal Maritime Commission
FCLAA	Federal Cigarette Labeling and Advertising Act	FMCS	Federal Mediation and Conciliation Service
FCRA	Fair Credit Reporting Act	FmHA	Farmers Home Administration
FCU	Federal credit unions		
FCUA	Federal Credit Union Act	FMLA	Family and Medical Leave Act of 1993
FCZ	Fishery Conservation Zone		
FDA	Food and Drug Administration	FNMA	Federal National Mortgage Association, "Fannie Mae"
FDIC	Federal Deposit Insurance Corporation	F.O.B.	Free on board
		FOIA	Freedom of Information Act
FDPC	Federal Data Processing Center	FOMC	Federal Open Market Committee
FEC	Federal Election Commission	FPA	Federal Power Act of 1935
FECA	Federal Election Campaign Act of 1971	FPC	Federal Power Commission
		FPMR	Federal Property Management Regulations
Fed. Cas.	Federal Cases		
FEHA	Fair Employment and Housing Act	FPRS	Federal Property Resources Service
FEHBA	Federal Employees Health Benefit Act	FR	Federal Register
		FRA	Federal Railroad Administration
FEMA	Federal Emergency Management Agency	FRB	Federal Reserve Board
FERC	Federal Energy Regulatory Commission	FRC	Federal Radio Commission
		F.R.D.	Federal Rules Decisions
FFB	Federal Financing Bank	FSA	Family Support Act
FFDC	Federal Food, Drug, and Cosmetics Act	FSB	Federal'naya Sluzhba Bezopasnosti (the Federal Security Service of Russia)
FGIS	Federal Grain Inspection Service		
		FSLIC	Federal Savings and Loan Insurance Corporation
FHA	Federal Housing Administration	FSQS	Food Safety and Quality Service
FHAA	Fair Housing Amendments Act of 1998	FSS	Federal Supply Service
FHWA	Federal Highway Administration	F. Supp.	Federal Supplement
		FTA	U.S.-Canada Free Trade Agreement of 1988
FIA	Federal Insurance Administration		
FIC	Federal Information Centers; Federation of Insurance Counsel	FTC	Federal Trade Commission
		FTCA	Federal Tort Claims Act
		FTS	Federal Telecommunications System
FICA	Federal Insurance Contributions Act	FTS2000	Federal Telecommunications System 2000
FIFRA	Federal Insecticide, Fungicide, and Rodenticide Act	FUCA	Federal Unemployment Compensation Act of 1988

FUTA	Federal Unemployment Tax Act	HBO	Home Box Office
FWPCA	Federal Water Pollution Control Act of 1948	HCFA	Health Care Financing Administration
FWS	Fish and Wildlife Service	H.Ct.	High Court
GAL	Guardian ad litem	HDS	Office of Human Development Services
GAO	General Accounting Office; Governmental Affairs Office	Hen. & M.	Hening & Munford's Virginia Reports
GAOR	General Assembly Official Records, United Nations	HEW	Department of Health, Education, and Welfare
GAAP	Generally accepted accounting principles	HFCA	Health Care Financing Administration
GA Res.	General Assembly Resolution (United Nations)	HGI	Handgun Control, Incorporated
GATT	General Agreement on Tariffs and Trade	HHS	Department of Health and Human Services
GCA	Gun Control Act	Hill	Hill's New York Reports
Gen. Cls. Comm.	General Claims Commission, United States and Panama; General Claims United States and Mexico	HIRE	Help through Industry Retraining and Employment
		HIV	Human immunodeficiency virus
Geo. II	King George II (Great Britain)	H.L.	House of Lords Cases (England)
Geo. III	King George III (Great Britain)	H. Lords	House of Lords (England)
GHB	Gamma-hydroxybutrate	HMO	Health Maintenance Organization
GI	Government Issue	HNIS	Human Nutrition Information Service
GID	General Intelligence Division		
GM	General Motors	Hong Kong L.R.	Hong Kong Law Reports
GNMA	Government National Mortgage Association, "Ginnie Mae"	How.	Howard's United States Supreme Court Reports
		How. St. Trials	Howell's English State Trials
GNP	Gross national product	HUAC	House Un-American Activities Committee
GOP	Grand Old Party (Republican Party)		
GOPAC	Grand Old Party Action Committee	HUD	Department of Housing and Urban Development
GPA	Office of Governmental and Public Affairs	Hudson, Internatl. Legis.	Manley Ottmer Hudson, ed., *International Legislation: A Collection of the Texts of Multipartite International Instruments of General Interest Beginning with the Covenant of the League of Nations* (1931)
GPO	Government Printing Office		
GRAS	Generally recognized as safe		
Gr. Br., Crim. Ct. App.	Great Britain, Court of Criminal Appeals		
GRNL	Gay Rights-National Lobby		
GSA	General Services Administration	Hudson, World Court Reps.	Manley Ottmer Hudson, ea., *World Court Reports* (1934–)
Hackworth	Green Haywood Hackworth, *Digest of International Law* (1940–1944)	Hun	Hun's New York Supreme Court Reports
Hay and Marriott	Great Britain. High Court of Admiralty, *Decisions in the High Court of Admiralty during the Time of Sir George Hay and of Sir James Marriott, Late Judges of That Court* (1801)	Hunt's Rept.	Bert L. Hunt, *Report of the American and Panamanian General Claims Arbitration* (1934)
		IAEA	International Atomic Energy Agency
		IALL	International Association of Law Libraries

IBA	International Bar Association	IRA	Individual retirement account; Irish Republican Army
IBM	International Business Machines	IRC	Internal Revenue Code
ICA	Interstate Commerce Act	IRCA	Immigration Reform and Control Act of 1986
ICBM	Intercontinental ballistic missile	IRS	Internal Revenue Service
ICC	Interstate Commerce Commission; International Criminal Court	ISO	Independent service organization
		ISP	Internet service provider
ICJ	International Court of Justice	ISSN	International Standard Serial Numbers
ICM	Institute for Court Management	ITA	International Trade Administration
IDEA	Individuals with Disabilities Education Act of 1975	ITI	Information Technology Integration
IDOP	International Dolphin Conservation Program	ITO	International Trade Organization
IEP	Individualized educational program	ITS	Information Technology Service
IFC	International Finance Corporation	ITT	International Telephone and Telegraph Corporation
IGRA	Indian Gaming Regulatory Act of 1988	ITU	International Telecommunication Union
IJA	Institute of Judicial Administration	IUD	Intrauterine device
IJC	International Joint Commission	IWC	International Whaling Commission
ILC	International Law Commission	IWW	Industrial Workers of the World
ILD	International Labor Defense	JAGC	Judge Advocate General's Corps
Ill. Dec.	Illinois Decisions		
ILO	International Labor Organization	JCS	Joint Chiefs of Staff
		JDL	Jewish Defense League
IMF	International Monetary Fund	JNOV	Judgment *non obstante veredicto* ("judgment nothing to recommend it" or "judgment notwithstanding the verdict")
INA	Immigration and Nationality Act		
IND	Investigational new drug		
INF Treaty	Intermediate-Range Nuclear Forces Treaty of 1987	JOBS	Jobs Opportunity and Basic Skills
INS	Immigration and Naturalization Service	John. Ch.	Johnson's New York Chancery Reports
INTELSAT	International Telecommunications Satellite Organization	Johns.	Johnson's Reports (New York)
Interpol	International Criminal Police Organization	JP	Justice of the peace
		K.B.	King's Bench Reports (England)
Int'l. Law Reps.	International Law Reports		
Intl. Legal Mats.	International Legal Materials	KFC	Kentucky Fried Chicken
IOC	International Olympic Committee	KGB	Komitet Gosudarstvennoi Bezopasnosti (the State Security Committee for countries in the former Soviet Union)
IPDC	International Program for the Development of Communication		
IPO	Intellectual Property Owners	KKK	Ku Klux Klan
IPP	Independent power producer	KMT	Kuomintang (Chinese, "national people's party")
IQ	Intelligence quotient		
I.R.	Irish Reports	LAD	Law Against Discrimination

LAPD	Los Angeles Police Department		II, 35 vols. [1876–1908]; Series III [1909–])
LC	Library of Congress	Mass.	Massachusetts Reports
LCHA	Longshoremen's and Harbor Workers Compensation Act of 1927	MCC	Metropolitan Correctional Center
LD50	Lethal dose 50	MCCA	Medicare Catastrophic Coverage Act of 1988
LDEF	Legal Defense and Education Fund (NOW)	MCH	Maternal and Child Health Bureau
LDF	Legal Defense Fund, Legal Defense and Educational Fund of the NAACP	MCRA	Medical Care Recovery Act of 1962
LEAA	Law Enforcement Assistance Administration	MDA	Medical Devices Amendments of 1976
L.Ed.	Lawyers' Edition Supreme Court Reports	Md. App.	Maryland, Appeal Cases
		M.D. Ga.	Middle District, Georgia
LI	Letter of interpretation	Mercy	Movement Ensuring the Right to Choose for Yourself
LLC	Limited Liability Company		
LLP	Limited Liability Partnership	Metc.	Metcalf's Massachusetts Reports
LMSA	Labor-Management Services Administration	MFDP	Mississippi Freedom Democratic party
LNTS	League of Nations Treaty Series	MGT	Management
Lofft's Rep.	Lofft's English King's Bench Reports	MHSS	Military Health Services System
L.R.	Law Reports (English)	Miller	David Hunter Miller, ea., *Treaties and Other International Acts of the United States of America* (1931–1948)
LSAC	Law School Admission Council		
LSAS	Law School Admission Service		
LSAT	Law School Aptitude Test	Minn.	Minnesota Reports
LSC	Legal Services Corporation; Legal Services for Children	MINS	Minors in need of supervision
		MIRV	Multiple independently targetable reentry vehicle
LSD	Lysergic acid diethylamide		
LSDAS	Law School Data Assembly Service	MIRVed ICBM	Multiple independently targetable reentry vehicled intercontinental ballistic missile
LTBT	Limited Test Ban Treaty		
LTC	Long Term Care		
MAD	Mutual assured destruction	Misc.	Miscellaneous Reports, New York
MADD	Mothers against Drunk Driving	Mixed Claims Comm., Report of Decs	Mixed Claims Commission, United States and Germany, Report of Decisions
MALDEF	Mexican American Legal Defense and Educational Fund		
Malloy	William M. Malloy, ed., *Treaties, Conventions International Acts, Protocols, and Agreements between the United States of America and Other Powers* (1910–1938)	M.J.	Military Justice Reporter
		MLAP	Migrant Legal Action Program
		MLB	Major League Baseball
		MLDP	Mississippi Loyalist Democratic Party
		MMI	Moslem Mosque, Incorporated
Martens	Georg Friedrich von Martens, ea., *Noveau recueil général de traités et autres actes relatifs aux rapports de droit international* (Series I, 20 vols. [1843–1875]; Series	MMPA	Marine Mammal Protection Act of 1972
		Mo.	Missouri Reports
		MOD	Masters of Deception
		Mod.	Modern Reports, English King's Bench, etc.

Moore, Dig. Intl. Law	John Bassett Moore, *A Digest of International Law*, 8 vols. (1906)	NARAL	National Abortion and Reproductive Rights Action League
Moore, Intl. Arbs.	John Bassett Moore, *History and Digest of the International Arbitrations to Which United States Has Been a Party*, 6 vols. (1898)	NARF	Native American Rights Fund
		NARS	National Archives and Record Service
		NASA	National Aeronautics and Space Administration
Morison	William Maxwell Morison, *The Scots Revised Report: Morison's Dictionary of Decisions* (1908–09)	NASD	National Association of Securities Dealers
		NATO	North Atlantic Treaty Organization
M.P.	Member of Parliament	NAVINFO	Navy Information Offices
MP3	MPEG Audio Layer 3	NAWSA	National American Woman's Suffrage Association
MPAA	Motion Picture Association of America	NBA	National Bar Association; National Basketball Association
MPAS	Michigan Protection and Advocacy Service		
MPEG	Motion Picture Experts Group	NBC	National Broadcasting Company
mpg	Miles per gallon	NBLSA	National Black Law Student Association
MPPDA	Motion Picture Producers and Distributors of America	NBS	National Bureau of Standards
MPRSA	Marine Protection, Research, and Sanctuaries Act of 1972	NCA	Noise Control Act; National Command Authorities
		NCAA	National Collegiate Athletic Association
M.R.	Master of the Rolls		
MS-DOS	Microsoft Disk Operating System	NCAC	National Coalition against Censorship
MSHA	Mine Safety and Health Administration	NCCB	National Consumer Cooperative Bank
MSPB	Merit Systems Protection Board	NCE	Northwest Community Exchange
MSSA	Military Selective Service Act	NCF	National Chamber Foundation
N/A	Not Available		
NAACP	National Association for the Advancement of Colored People	NCIP	National Crime Insurance Program
		NCJA	National Criminal Justice Association
NAAQS	National Ambient Air Quality Standards	NCLB	National Civil Liberties Bureau
NAB	National Association of Broadcasters	NCP	National contingency plan
NABSW	National Association of Black Social Workers	NCSC	National Center for State Courts
NACDL	National Association of Criminal Defense Lawyers	NCUA	National Credit Union Administration
NAFTA	North American Free Trade Agreement of 1993	NDA	New drug application
		N.D. Ill.	Northern District, Illinois
NAGHSR	National Association of Governors' Highway Safety Representatives	NDU	National Defense University
		N.D. Wash.	Northern District, Washington
NALA	National Association of Legal Assistants	N.E.	North Eastern Reporter
		N.E. 2d	North Eastern Reporter, Second Series
NAM	National Association of Manufacturers	NEA	National Endowment for the Arts; National Education Association
NAR	National Association of Realtors		

NEH	National Endowment for the Humanities	NORML	National Organization for the Reform of Marijuana Laws
NEPA	National Environmental Protection Act; National Endowment Policy Act	NOW	National Organization for Women
NET Act	No Electronic Theft Act	NOW LDEF	National Organization for Women Legal Defense and Education Fund
NFIB	National Federation of Independent Businesses		
NFIP	National Flood Insurance Program	NOW/PAC	National Organization for Women Political Action Committee
NFL	National Football League		
NFPA	National Federation of Paralegal Associations	NPDES	National Pollutant Discharge Elimination System
NGLTF	National Gay and Lesbian Task Force	NPL	National priorities list
		NPR	National Public Radio
NHL	National Hockey League	NPT	Nuclear Non-Proliferation Treaty of 1970
NHRA	Nursing Home Reform Act of 1987		
NHTSA	National Highway Traffic Safety Administration	NRA	National Rifle Association; National Recovery Act
Nielsen's Rept.	Frederick Kenelm Nielsen, *American and British Claims Arbitration under the Special Agreement Concluded between the United States and Great Britain, August 18, 1910* (1926)	NRC	Nuclear Regulatory Commission
		NRLC	National Right to Life Committee
		NRTA	National Retired Teachers Association
		NSA	National Security Agency
		NSC	National Security Council
		NSCLC	National Senior Citizens Law Center
NIEO	New International Economic Order	NSF	National Science Foundation
NIGC	National Indian Gaming Commission	NSFNET	National Science Foundation Network
NIH	National Institutes of Health	NSI	Network Solutions, Inc.
NIJ	National Institute of Justice	NTIA	National Telecommunications and Information Administration
NIRA	National Industrial Recovery Act of 1933; National Industrial Recovery Administration		
NIST	National Institute of Standards and Technology	NTID	National Technical Institute for the Deaf
N.J.	New Jersey Reports	NTIS	National Technical Information Service
N.J. Super.	New Jersey Superior Court Reports	NTS	Naval Telecommunications System
NLEA	Nutrition Labeling and Education Act of 1990	NTSB	National Transportation Safety Board
NLRA	National Labor Relations Act	NVRA	National Voter Registration Act
NLRB	National Labor Relations Board		
NMFS	National Marine Fisheries Service	N.W.	North Western Reporter
		N.W. 2d	North Western Reporter, Second Series
No.	Number	NWSA	National Woman Suffrage Association
NOAA	National Oceanic and Atmospheric Administration	N.Y.	New York Court of Appeals Reports
NOC	National Olympic Committee	N.Y. 2d	New York Court of Appeals Reports, Second Series
NOI	Nation of Islam	N.Y.S.	New York Supplement Reporter
NOL	Net operating loss		

N.Y.S. 2d	New York Supplement Reporter, Second Series	OPIC	Overseas Private Investment Corporation
NYSE	New York Stock Exchange	Ops. Atts. Gen.	Opinions of the Attorneys-General of the United States
NYSLA	New York State Liquor Authority	Ops. Comms.	Opinions of the Commissioners
N.Y. Sup.	New York Supreme Court Reports	OPSP	Office of Product Standards Policy
NYU	New York University	O.R.	Ontario Reports
OAAU	Organization of Afro American Unity	OR	Official Records
OAP	Office of Administrative Procedure	OSHA	Occupational Safety and Health Act
OAS	Organization of American States	OSHRC	Occupational Safety and Health Review Commission
OASDI	Old-age, Survivors, and Disability Insurance Benefits	OSM	Office of Surface Mining
OASHDS	Office of the Assistant Secretary for Human Development Services	OSS	Office of Strategic Services
		OST	Office of the Secretary
		OT	Office of Transportation
OCC	Office of Comptroller of the Currency	OTA	Office of Technology Assessment
OCED	Office of Comprehensive Employment Development	OTC	Over-the-counter
		OTS	Office of Thrift Supervisors
OCHAMPUS	Office of Civilian Health and Medical Program of the Uniformed Services	OUI	Operating under the influence
		OVCI	Offshore Voluntary Compliance Initiative
OCSE	Office of Child Support Enforcement	OWBPA	Older Workers Benefit Protection Act
OEA	Organización de los Estados Americanos	OWRT	Office of Water Research and Technology
OEM	Original Equipment Manufacturer	P.	Pacific Reporter
		P. 2d	Pacific Reporter, Second Series
OFCCP	Office of Federal Contract Compliance Programs	PAC	Political action committee
OFPP	Office of Federal Procurement Policy	Pa. Oyer and Terminer	Pennsylvania Oyer and Terminer Reports
OIC	Office of the Independent Counsel	PATCO	Professional Air Traffic Controllers Organization
OICD	Office of International Cooperation and Development	PBGC	Pension Benefit Guaranty Corporation
OIG	Office of the Inspector General	PBS	Public Broadcasting Service; Public Buildings Service
OJARS	Office of Justice Assistance, Research, and Statistics	P.C.	Privy Council (English Law Reports)
OMB	Office of Management and Budget	PC	Personal computer; politically correct
OMPC	Office of Management, Planning, and Communications	PCBs	Polychlorinated biphenyls
		PCIJ	Permanent Court of International Justice Series A-Judgments and Orders (1922–30)
ONP	Office of National Programs		Series B-Advisory Opinions (1922–30)
OPD	Office of Policy Development		Series A/B-Judgments, Orders, and Advisory Opinions (1931–40)
OPEC	Organization of Petroleum Exporting Countries		

PCIJ (cont'd.)	Series C-Pleadings, Oral Statements, and Documents relating to Judgments and Advisory Opinions (1923–42)	PNET	Peaceful Nuclear Explosions Treaty
		PONY	Prostitutes of New York
		POW-MIA	Prisoner of war-missing in action
	Series D-Acts and Documents concerning the Organization of the World Court (1922 –47)	Pratt	Frederic Thomas Pratt, *Law of Contraband of War, with a Selection of Cases from Papers of the Right Honourable Sir George Lee* (1856)
	Series E-Annual Reports (1925–45)		
PCP	Phencyclidine	PRIDE	Prostitution to Independence, Dignity, and Equality
P.D.	Probate Division, English Law Reports (1876–1890)	Proc.	Proceedings
PDA	Pregnancy Discrimination Act of 1978	PRP	Potentially responsible party
		PSRO	Professional Standards Review Organization
PD & R	Policy Development and Research	PTO	Patents and Trademark Office
Pepco	Potomac Electric Power Company	PURPA	Public Utilities Regulatory Policies Act
Perm. Ct. of Arb.	Permanent Court of Arbitration	PUSH	People United to Serve Humanity
PES	Post-Enumeration Survey		
Pet.	Peters' United States Supreme Court Reports	PUSH-Excel	PUSH for Excellence
		PWA	Public Works Administration
PETA	People for the Ethical Treatment of Animals	PWSA	Ports and Waterways Safety Act of 1972
PGA	Professional Golfers Association	Q.B.	Queen's Bench (England)
PGM	Program	QTIP	Qualified Terminable Interest Property
PHA	Public Housing Agency		
Phila. Ct. of Oyer and Terminer	Philadelphia Court of Oyer and Terminer	Ralston's Rept.	Jackson Harvey Ralston, ed., *Venezuelan Arbitrations of 1903* (1904)
PhRMA	Pharmaceutical Research and Manufacturers of America	RC	Regional Commissioner
PHS	Public Health Service	RCRA	Resource Conservation and Recovery Act
PIC	Private Industry Council		
PICJ	Permanent International Court of Justice	RCWP	Rural Clean Water Program
		RDA	Rural Development Administration
Pick.	Pickering's Massachusetts Reports	REA	Rural Electrification Administration
PIK	Payment in Kind		
PINS	Persons in need of supervision	Rec. des Decs. des Trib. Arb. Mixtes	G. Gidel, ed., *Recueil des décisions des tribunaux arbitraux mixtes, institués par les traités de paix* (1922–30)
PIRG	Public Interest Research Group		
P.L.	Public Laws		
PLAN	Pro-Life Action Network	Redmond	Vol. 3 of Charles I. Bevans, *Treaties and Other International Agreements of the United States of America, 1776–1949* (compiled by C. F. Redmond) (1969)
PLC	Plaintiffs' Legal Committee		
PLE	Product liability expenses		
PLI	Practicing Law Institute		
PLL	Product liability loss		
PLLP	Professional Limited Liability Partnership		
PLO	Palestine Liberation Organization	RESPA	Real Estate Settlement Procedure Act of 1974
PLRA	Prison Litigation Reform Act of 1995	RFC	Reconstruction Finance Corporation

RFRA	Religious Freedom Restoration Act of 1993	SCCC	South Central Correctional Center
RIAA	Recording Industry Association of America	SCLC	Southern Christian Leadership Conference
RICO	Racketeer Influenced and Corrupt Organizations	Scott's Repts.	James Brown Scott, ed., *The Hague Court Reports,* 2 vols. (1916–32)
RLUIPA	Religious Land Use and Institutionalized Persons Act	SCS	Soil Conservation Service; Social Conservative Service
RNC	Republican National Committee	SCSEP	Senior Community Service Employment Program
Roscoe	Edward Stanley Roscoe, ed., *Reports of Prize Cases Determined in the High Court Admiralty before the Lords Commissioners of Appeals in Prize Causes and before the judicial Committee of the Privy Council from 1745 to 1859* (1905)	S.Ct.	Supreme Court Reporter
		S.D. Cal.	Southern District, California
		S.D. Fla.	Southern District, Florida
		S.D. Ga.	Southern District, Georgia
		SDI	Strategic Defense Initiative
		S.D. Me.	Southern District, Maine
		S.D.N.Y.	Southern District, New York
		SDS	Students for a Democratic Society
ROTC	Reserve Officers' Training Corps	S.E.	South Eastern Reporter
RPP	Representative Payee Program	S.E. 2d	South Eastern Reporter, Second Series
R.S.	Revised Statutes	SEA	Science and Education Administration
RTC	Resolution Trust Corp.	SEATO	Southeast Asia Treaty Organization
RUDs	Reservations, understandings, and declarations	SEC	Securities and Exchange Commission
Ryan White CARE Act	Ryan White Comprehensive AIDS Research Emergency Act of 1990	Sec.	Section
		SEEK	Search for Elevation, Education and Knowledge
SAC	Strategic Air Command	SEOO	State Economic Opportunity Office
SACB	Subversive Activities Control Board	SEP	Simplified employee pension plan
SADD	Students against Drunk Driving	Ser.	Series
SAF	Student Activities Fund	Sess.	Session
SAIF	Savings Association Insurance Fund	SGLI	Servicemen's Group Life Insurance
SALT	Strategic Arms Limitation Talks	SIP	State implementation plan
SALT I	Strategic Arms Limitation Talks of 1969–72	SLA	Symbionese Liberation Army
SAMHSA	Substance Abuse and Mental Health Services Administration	SLAPPs	Strategic Lawsuits Against Public Participation
		SLBM	Submarine-launched ballistic missile
Sandf.	Sandford's New York Superior Court Reports	SNCC	Student Nonviolent Coordinating Committee
S and L	Savings and loan	So.	Southern Reporter
SARA	Superfund Amendment and Reauthorization Act	So. 2d	Southern Reporter, Second Series
SAT	Scholastic Aptitude Test	SPA	Software Publisher's Association
Sawy.	Sawyer's United States Circuit Court Reports	Spec. Sess.	Special Session
SBA	Small Business Administration	SPLC	Southern Poverty Law Center
		SRA	Sentencing Reform Act of 1984
SBI	Small Business Institute		

SS	*Schutzstaffel* (German, "Protection Echelon")	TVA	Tennessee Valley Authority
SSA	Social Security Administration	TWA	Trans World Airlines
SSI	Supplemental Security Income	UAW	United Auto Workers; United Automobile, Aerospace, and Agricultural Implements Workers of America
START I	Strategic Arms Reduction Treaty of 1991		
START II	Strategic Arms Reduction Treaty of 1993	U.C.C.	Uniform Commercial Code; Universal Copyright Convention
Stat.	United States Statutes at Large		
STS	Space Transportation Systems	U.C.C.C.	Uniform Consumer Credit Code
St. Tr.	State Trials, English	UCCJA	Uniform Child Custody Jurisdiction Act
STURAA	Surface Transportation and Uniform Relocation Assistance Act of 1987	UCMJ	Uniform Code of Military Justice
		UCPP	Urban Crime Prevention Program
Sup. Ct. of Justice, Mexico	Supreme Court of Justice, Mexico	UCS	United Counseling Service
Supp.	Supplement	UDC	United Daughters of the Confederacy
S.W.	South Western Reporter		
S.W. 2d	South Western Reporter, Second Series	UFW	United Farm Workers
		UHF	Ultrahigh frequency
SWAPO	South-West Africa People's Organization	UIFSA	Uniform Interstate Family Support Act
SWAT	Special Weapons and Tactics	UIS	Unemployment Insurance Service
SWP	Socialist Workers Party		
TDP	Trade and Development Program	UMDA	Uniform Marriage and Divorce Act
Tex. Sup.	Texas Supreme Court Reports	UMTA	Urban Mass Transportation Administration
THAAD	Theater High-Altitude Area Defense System	U.N.	United Nations
THC	Tetrahydrocannabinol	UNCITRAL	United Nations Commission on International Trade Law
TI	Tobacco Institute		
TIA	Trust Indenture Act of 1939	UNCTAD	United Nations Conference on Trade and Development
TIAS	Treaties and Other International Acts Series (United States)		
		UN Doc.	United Nations Documents
TNT	Trinitrotoluene	UNDP	United Nations Development Program
TOP	Targeted Outreach Program		
TPUS	Transportation and Public Utilities Service	UNEF	United Nations Emergency Force
TQM	Total Quality Management	UNESCO	United Nations Educational, Scientific, and Cultural Organization
Tripartite Claims Comm., Decs. and Ops.	Tripartite Claims Commission (United States, Austria, and Hungary), Decisions and Opinions		
		UNICEF	United Nations Children's Fund (formerly United Nations International Children's Emergency Fund)
TRI-TAC	Joint Tactical Communications		
TRO	Temporary restraining order		
TS	Treaty Series, United States	UNIDO	United Nations Industrial and Development Organization
TSCA	Toxic Substance Control Act		
TSDs	Transporters, storers, and disposers	Unif. L. Ann.	Uniform Laws Annotated
TSU	Texas Southern University	UN Repts. Intl. Arb. Awards	United Nations Reports of International Arbitral Awards
TTBT	Threshold Test Ban Treaty		
TV	Television		

UNTS	United Nations Treaty Series	VIN	Vehicle identification number
UPI	United Press International		
URESA	Uniform Reciprocal Enforcement of Support Act	VISTA	Volunteers in Service to America
		VJRA	Veterans Judicial Review Act of 1988
U.S.	United States Reports		
U.S.A.	United States of America	V.L.A.	Volunteer Lawyers for the Arts
USAF	United States Air Force		
USA PATRIOT Act	Uniting and Strengthening America by Providing Appropriate Tools Required to Intercept and Obstruct Terrorism Act	VMI	Virginia Military Institute
		VMLI	Veterans Mortgage Life Insurance
		VOCAL	Victims of Child Abuse Laws
		VRA	Voting Rights Act
U.S. App. D.C.	United States Court of Appeals for the District of Columbia	WAC	Women's Army Corps
		Wall.	Wallace's United States Supreme Court Reports
U.S.C.	United States Code; University of Southern California	Wash. 2d	Washington Reports, Second Series
U.S.C.A.	United States Code Annotated	WAVES	Women Accepted for Volunteer Service
U.S.C.C.A.N.	United States Code Congressional and Administrative News	WCTU	Women's Christian Temperance Union
		W.D. Wash.	Western District, Washington
USCMA	United States Court of Military Appeals	W.D. Wis.	Western District, Wisconsin
		WEAL	West's Encyclopedia of American Law, Women's Equity Action League
USDA	U.S. Department of Agriculture		
USES	United States Employment Service	Wend.	Wendell's New York Reports
		WFSE	Washington Federation of State Employees
USF	U.S. Forestry Service		
USFA	United States Fire Administration	Wheat.	Wheaton's United States Supreme Court Reports
USGA	United States Golf Association	Wheel. Cr. Cases	Wheeler's New York Criminal Cases
USICA	International Communication Agency, United States	WHISPER	Women Hurt in Systems of Prostitution Engaged in Revolt
USMS	U.S. Marshals Service	Whiteman	Marjorie Millace Whiteman, Digest of International Law, 15 vols. (1963–73)
USOC	U.S. Olympic Committee		
USSC	U.S. Sentencing Commission		
USSG	United States Sentencing Guidelines	WHO	World Health Organization
		WIC	Women, Infants, and Children program
U.S.S.R.	Union of Soviet Socialist Republics		
		Will. and Mar.	King William and Queen Mary (Great Britain)
UST	United States Treaties		
USTS	United States Travel Service	WIN	WESTLAW Is Natural; Whip Inflation Now; Work Incentive Program
v.	Versus		
VA	Veterans Administration		
VAR	Veterans Affairs and Rehabilitation Commission	WIPO	World Intellectual Property Organization
		WIU	Workers' Industrial Union
VAWA	Violence against Women Act	W.L.R.	Weekly Law Reports, England
VFW	Veterans of Foreign Wars		
VGLI	Veterans Group Life Insurance	WPA	Works Progress Administration
Vict.	Queen Victoria (Great Britain)	WPPDA	Welfare and Pension Plans Disclosure Act

WTO	World Trade Organization	YMCA	Young Men's Christian Association
WWI	World War I		
WWII	World War II	YWCA	Young Women's Christian Association
Yates Sel. Cas.	Yates's New York Select Cases